Less managing. More teaching. Greater learning.

INSTRUCTORS...

Would you like your **students** to show up for class **more prepared**?
(Let's face it, class is much more fun if everyone is engaged and prepared...)

Want an **easy way to assign** homework online and track student **progress**?
(Less time grading means more time teaching...)

Want an **instant view** of student or class performance relative to learning objectives? *(No more wondering if students understand...)*

Need to **collect data and generate reports** required for administration or accreditation? *(Say goodbye to manually tracking student learning outcomes...)*

Want to **record and post your lectures** for students to view online?

With **McGraw-Hill's** *Connect*® *Plus Business Statistics,*

INSTRUCTORS GET:

- Simple **assignment management,** allowing you to spend more time teaching.
- **Auto-graded** assignments, quizzes, and tests.
- **Detailed Visual Reporting** where student and section results can be viewed and analyzed.
- Sophisticated **online testing** capability.
- A **filtering and reporting** function that allows you to easily select Excel-based homework problems as well as assign and report on materials that are correlated to accreditation standards, learning outcomes, and Bloom's taxonomy.
- An easy-to-use **lecture capture** tool.
- The option to **upload course documents** for student access.

Want an online, **searchable version** of your textbook?

Wish your textbook could be **available online** while you're doing your assignments?

Connect® Plus Business Statistics eBook

If you choose to use *Connect® Plus Business Statistics*, you have an affordable and searchable online version of your book integrated with your other online tools.

Connect® Plus Business Statistics eBook offers features like:

- Topic search
- Direct links from assignments
- Adjustable text size
- Jump to page number
- Print by section
- Highlight
- Take notes
- Access instructor highlights/notes

Want to get more **value** from your textbook purchase?

Think learning business statistics should be a bit more **interesting**?

Check out the STUDENT RESOURCES section under the *Connect®* Library tab.

Here you'll find a wealth of resources designed to help you achieve your goals in the course. You'll find things like **quizzes, PowerPoints, and Internet activities** to help you study. Every student has different needs, so explore the STUDENT RESOURCES to find the materials best suited to you.

Bruce L. Bowerman
Miami University

Richard T. O'Connell
Miami University

Emily S. Murphree
Miami University

Business Statistics in Practice

SEVENTH EDITION

with major contributions by

Steven C. Huchendorf
University of Minnesota

Dawn C. Porter
University of Southern California

Patrick J. Schur
Miami University

The McGraw·Hill Companies

McGraw-Hill
Irwin

BUSINESS STATISTICS IN PRACTICE, SEVENTH EDITION

Published by McGraw-Hill/Irwin, a business unit of The McGraw-Hill Companies, Inc., 1221 Avenue of the Americas, New York, NY, 10020. Copyright © 2014 by The McGraw-Hill Companies, Inc. All rights reserved. Printed in the United States of America. Previous editions © 2011, 2009, and 2007. No part of this publication may be reproduced or distributed in any form or by any means, or stored in a database or retrieval system, without the prior written consent of The McGraw-Hill Companies, Inc., including, but not limited to, in any network or other electronic storage or transmission, or broadcast for distance learning.

Some ancillaries, including electronic and print components, may not be available to customers outside the United States.

This book is printed on acid-free paper.

1 2 3 4 5 6 7 8 9 0 RJE/RJE 1 0 9 8 7 6 5 4 3

ISBN   978-0-07-352149-7
MHID   0-07-352149-3

Senior Vice President, Products & Markets: *Kurt L. Strand*
Vice President, General Manager, Products & Markets: *Brent Gordon*
Vice President, Content Production & Technology Services: *Kimberly Meriwether David*
Managing Director: *Douglas Reiner*
Senior Brand Manager: *Thomas Hayward*
Executive Director of Development: *Ann Torbert*
Senior Development Editor: *Wanda J. Zeman*
Director of Digital Content: *Doug Ruby*
Senior Marketing Manager: *Heather A. Kazakoff*
Lead Project Manager: *Harvey Yep*
Senior Buyer: *Michael R. McCormick*
Lead Designer: *Matthew Baldwin*
Cover/Interior Designer: *Matthew Baldwin*
Cover Image: *© Bloomberg via Getty Images*
Content Licensing Specialist: *Joanne Mennemeier*
Photo Researcher: *PoYee Oster*
Lead Media Project Manager: *Daryl Horrocks*
Media Project Manager: *Joyce J. Chappetto*
Typeface: *10/12 Times New Roman*
Compositor: *MPS Limited*
Printer: *R. R. Donnelley*

All credits appearing on page or at the end of the book are considered to be an extension of the copyright page.

Library of Congress Cataloging-in-Publication Data

Bowerman, Bruce L.
    Business statistics in practice / Bruce L. Bowerman, Miami University; Richard T. O'Connell,
Miami University; Emily S. Murphree, Miami University.—Seventh edition.
        pages cm.—(The Mcgraw-Hill/Irwin series in operations and decision sciences)
    Includes index.
    ISBN-13: 978-0-07-352149-7 (alk. paper)
    ISBN-10: 0-07-352149-3 (alk. paper)
    1. Commercial statistics. 2. Statistics. I. O'Connell, Richard T. II. Murphree, Emily. III. Title.
HF1017.B654 2014
519.5024'65—dc23

2012044956

The Internet addresses listed in the text were accurate at the time of publication. The inclusion of a website does not indicate an endorsement by the authors or McGraw-Hill, and McGraw-Hill does not guarantee the accuracy of the information presented at these sites.

www.mhhe.com

About the Authors

Bruce L. Bowerman Bruce L. Bowerman is emeritus professor of decision sciences at Miami University in Oxford, Ohio. He received his Ph.D. degree in statistics from Iowa State University in 1974, and he has over 40 years of experience teaching basic statistics, regression analysis, time series forecasting, survey sampling, and design of experiments to both

undergraduate and graduate students. In 1987 Professor Bowerman received an Outstanding Teaching award from the Miami University senior class, and in 1992 he received an Effective Educator award from the Richard T. Farmer School of Business Administration. Together with Richard T. O'Connell, Professor Bowerman has written 19 textbooks. These include *Forecasting and Time Series: An Applied Approach; Forecasting, Time Series, and Regression: An Applied Approach* (also coauthored with Anne B. Koehler); and *Linear Statistical Models: An Applied Approach.* The first edition of *Forecasting and Time Series* earned an Outstanding Academic Book award from *Choice* magazine. Professor Bowerman has also published a number of articles in applied stochastic processes, time series forecasting, and statistical education. In his spare time, Professor Bowerman enjoys watching movies and sports, playing tennis, and designing houses.

Richard T. O'Connell Richard T. O'Connell is emeritus professor of decision sciences at Miami University in Oxford, Ohio. He has more than 35 years of experience teaching basic statistics, statistical quality control and process improvement, regression analysis, time series forecasting, and design of experiments to both undergraduate and graduate business students.

He also has extensive consulting experience and has taught workshops dealing with statistical process control and process improvement for a variety of companies in the Midwest. In 2000 Professor O'Connell received an Effective Educator award from the Richard T. Farmer School of Business Administration. Together with Bruce L. Bowerman, he has written 19 textbooks. These include *Forecasting and Time Series: An Applied Approach; Forecasting, Time Series, and Regression: An Applied Approach* (also coauthored with Anne B. Koehler); and *Linear Statistical Models: An Applied Approach.* Professor O'Connell has published a number of articles in the area of innovative statistical education. He is one of the first college instructors in the United States to integrate statistical process control and process improvement methodology into his basic business statistics course. He (with Professor Bowerman) has written several articles advocating this approach. He has also given presentations on this subject at meetings such as the Joint Statistical Meetings of the American Statistical Association and the Workshop on Total Quality Management: Developing Curricula and Research Agendas (sponsored by the Production and Operations Management Society). Professor O'Connell received an M.S. degree in decision sciences from Northwestern University in 1973, and he is currently a member of both the Decision Sciences Institute and the American Statistical Association. In his spare time, Professor O'Connell enjoys fishing, collecting 1950s and 1960s rock music, and following the Green Bay Packers and Purdue University sports.

Emily S. Murphree Emily S. Murphree is Associate Professor of Statistics in the Department of Mathematics and Statistics at Miami University in Oxford, Ohio. She received her Ph.D. degree in statistics from the University of North Carolina and does research in applied probability. Professor Murphree received Miami's College of Arts and Science Distin-

guished Educator Award in 1998. In 1996, she was named one of Oxford's Citizens of the Year for her work with Habitat for Humanity and for organizing annual Sonia Kovalevsky Mathematical Sciences Days for area high school girls. In 2012 she was recognized as "A Teacher Who Made a Difference" by the University of Kentucky.

In *Business Statistics in Practice, Seventh Edition,* we provide a modern, practical, and unique framework for teaching an introductory course in business statistics. As in previous editions, we employ real or realistic examples, continuing case studies, and a business improvement theme to teach the material. Moreover, we believe that this seventh edition features more concise and lucid explanations, an improved topic flow, and a judicious use of realistic and compelling examples. Overall, the seventh edition is 80 pages shorter than the sixth edition while covering all previous material as well as additional topics. Below we outline the attributes and new features we think make this book an effective learning tool.

- **Continuing case studies that tie together different statistical topics.** These continuing case studies span not only individual chapters but also groups of chapters. Students tell us that when new statistical topics are developed in the context of familiar cases, their "fear factor" is reduced. Of course, to keep the examples from becoming overtired, we introduce new case studies throughout the book.

- **Business improvement conclusions that explicitly show how statistical results lead to practical business decisions.** After appropriate analysis and interpretation, examples and case studies often result in a business improvement conclusion. To emphasize this theme of business improvement, icons **BI** are placed in the page margins to identify when statistical analysis has led to an important business conclusion. The text of each conclusion is also highlighted in yellow for additional clarity.

- **Examples exploited to motivate an intuitive approach to statistical ideas.** Most concepts and formulas, particularly those that introductory students find most challenging, are first approached by working through the ideas in accessible examples. Only after simple and clear analysis within these concrete examples are more general concepts and formulas discussed.

- **A shorter and more intuitive introduction to business statistics in Chapter 1.** Chapter 1 begins with an improved example introducing data and how data can be used to make a successful offer to purchase a house. Random sampling is introducing informally in the context of more tightly focused case studies. [The technical discussion about how to select random samples and other types of samples is in Chapter 7 (Sampling and Sampling Distributions), but the reader has the option of reading about sampling in Chapter 7 immediately after Chapter 1.] Chapter 1 also includes a new discussion of ethical guidelines for practitioners of statistics. Throughout the book, statistics is presented as a broad discipline requiring not simply analytical skills but also judgment and personal ethics.

- **A more streamlined discussion of the graphical and numerical methods of descriptive statistics.** Chapters 2 and 3 utilize several new examples, including an example leading off Chapter 2 that deals with college students' pizza brand preferences. In addition, the explanations of some of the more complicated topics have been simplified. For example, the discussion of percentiles, quartiles, and box plots has been shortened and clarified.

- **An improved, well-motivated discussion of probability and probability distributions in Chapters 4, 5, and 6.** In Chapter 4, methods for calculating probabilities are more clearly motivated in the context of two new examples. We use the Crystal Cable Case, which deals with studying cable television and Internet penetration rates, to illustrate many probabilistic concepts and calculations. Moreover, students' understanding of the important concepts of conditional probability and statistical independence is sharpened by a new real-world case involving gender discrimination at a pharmaceutical company. The probability distribution, mean, and standard deviation of a discrete random variable are all motivated and explained in a more succinct discussion in Chapter 5. An example illustrates how knowledge of a mean and standard deviation are enough to estimate potential investment returns. Chapter 5 also features an improved introduction to the binomial distribution where the previous careful discussion is supplemented by an illustrative tree diagram. Students can now see the origins of all the factors in the binomial formula more clearly. For those students studying the hypergeometric distribution and its relationship to the binomial distribution, a new example is used to show how more simply calculated binomial probabilities can approximate hypergeometric probabilities. Chapter 5 ends with an optional section where joint probabilities and covariances are explained in the context of portfolio diversification. In Chapter 6, continuous probabilities are developed by improved examples. The coffee temperature case introduces the key ideas and is eventually used to help study the normal distribution. Similarly, the elevator waiting time case is used to explore the continuous uniform distribution.

AUTHORS

- **A shorter and clearer discussion of sampling distributions and statistical inference in Chapters 7 through 11.** In Chapter 7, the discussion of sampling distributions is improved by using an example that deals with a small population and then seamlessly proceeding to a related large population example. We have completely rewritten and simplified the introduction to confidence intervals in Chapter 8. The logic and interpretation of a 95% confidence interval is taken up first in the car mileage case. Then we build upon this groundwork to provide students a new graphically based procedure for finding confidence intervals for any level of confidence. We also distinguish between the interpretation of a confidence interval and a tolerance interval. Chapter 8 concludes with an optional section about estimating parameters of finite populations when using either random or stratified random sampling. Hypothesis testing procedures (using both the critical value and p-value approaches) are summarized efficiently and visually in new summary boxes in Chapter 9. Students will find these summary boxes much more transparent than traditional summaries lacking visual prompts. These summary boxes are featured throughout the chapters covering inferences for one mean or one proportion (Chapter 9), inferences for two means or two proportions (Chapter 10), and inferences for one or two variances (the new Chapter 11), as well as in later chapters covering regression analysis.

- **Simpler and improved discussions about comparing means, proportions, and variances.** In Chapter 10 we mention the unrealistic "known variance" case only briefly and move swiftly to the more realistic "unknown variance" case. As previously indicated, inference for population variances has been moved to the new Chapter 11. In Chapter 12 (Experimental Design and Analysis of Variance) we have simplified and greatly shortened the discussion of F-tests and multiple comparisons for one-way ANOVA, the randomized block design, and the two-way ANOVA. Chapter 13 covers chi-square goodness-of-fit tests and tests of independence.

- **Streamlined and improved discussions of simple and multiple regression, time series forecasting, and statistical quality control.** As in the sixth edition, we use the Tasty Sub Shop Case to introduce the ideas of both simple and multiple regression analysis. This case has been popular with our readers. Regression is now presented in two rather than three chapters. The Durbin-Watson test and transformations of variables are introduced in the simple linear regression chapter (Chapter 14) because they arise naturally in the context of residual analysis. However, both of these topics can be skipped without loss of continuity. After discussing the basics of multiple regression, Chapter 15 has five innovative, advanced sections that can be covered in any order. These optional sections explain (1) using dummy variables, (2) using squared and interaction terms, (3) model building and the effects of multicollinearity, (4) residual analysis in multiple regression (including a short discussion of outlying and influential observations), and (5) logistic regression. The treatment of these topics has been noticeably shortened and improved. Although we include all the regression material found in prior editions of this book, we do so in approximately 40 fewer pages. In Chapter 16 (Time Series Forecasting and Index Numbers), explanations of basic techniques have been simplified and, for advanced readers, an optional new 7-page introduction to Box-Jenkins models has been added. Chapter 17, which deals with process improvement, has been streamlined by relying on a single case, the hole location case, to explain $\bar{X}$ and R charts as well as establishing process control, pattern analysis, and capability studies.

- **Increased emphasis on Excel and MINITAB throughout the text.** The main text features Excel and MINITAB outputs. The end of chapter appendices provide improved step-by-step instructions about how to perform statistical analyses using these software packages as well as MegaStat, an Excel add-in.

Bruce L. Bowerman
Richard T. O'Connell
Emily S. Murphree

Chapter Introductions

Each chapter begins with a list of the section topics that are covered in the chapter, along with chapter learning objectives and a preview of the case study analysis to be carried out in the chapter.

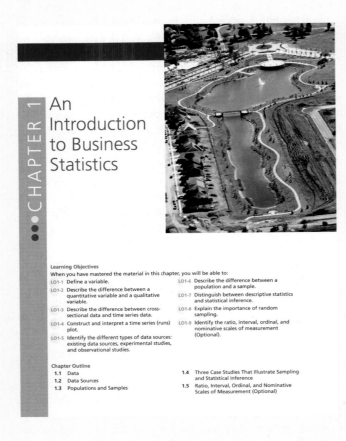

•••○ CHAPTER 1
An Introduction to Business Statistics

Learning Objectives

When you have mastered the material in this chapter, you will be able to:

LO1-1 Define a variable.

LO1-2 Describe the difference between a quantitative variable and a qualitative variable.

LO1-3 Describe the difference between cross-sectional data and time series data.

LO1-4 Construct and interpret a time series (runs) plot.

LO1-5 Identify the different types of data sources: existing data sources, experimental studies, and observational studies.

LO1-6 Describe the difference between a population and a sample.

LO1-7 Distinguish between descriptive statistics and statistical inference.

LO1-8 Explain the importance of random sampling.

LO1-9 Identify the ratio, interval, ordinal, and nominative scales of measurement (Optional).

Chapter Outline

1.1 Data

1.2 Data Sources

1.3 Populations and Samples

1.4 Three Case Studies That Illustrate Sampling and Statistical Inference

1.5 Ratio, Interval, Ordinal, and Nominative Scales of Measurement (Optional)

The subject of **statistics** involves the study of how to collect, analyze, and interpret data. **Data** are facts and figures from which conclusions can be drawn. Such conclusions are important to the decision making of many professions and organizations. For example, **economists** use conclusions drawn from the latest data on unemployment and inflation to help the government make policy decisions. **Financial planners** use recent trends in stock market prices and economic conditions to make investment decisions. **Accountants** use **sample data** concerning a company's *actual sales revenues* to assess whether the company's *claimed sales revenues* are valid. **Marketing professionals** help businesses decide which products to develop and market by using data that reveal consumer preferences. **Production supervisors** use manufacturing data to evaluate, control, and improve product quality. **Politicians** rely on data from public opinion polls to formulate legislation and to devise campaign strategies. **Physicians and hospitals** use data on the effectiveness of drugs and surgical procedures to provide patients with the best possible treatment.

In this chapter we begin to see how we collect and analyze data. As we proceed through the chapter, we introduce several case studies. These case studies (and others to be introduced later) are revisited throughout later chapters as we learn the statistical methods needed to analyze them. Briefly, we will begin to study three cases:

The Cell Phone Case. A bank estimates its cellular phone costs and decides whether to outsource management of its wireless resources by studying the calling patterns of its employees.

The Marketing Research Case. A bottling company investigates consumer reaction to a new bottle design for one of its popular soft drinks.

The Car Mileage Case. To determine if it qualifies for a federal tax credit based on fuel economy, an automaker studies the gas mileage of its new midsize model.

1.1 Data ●○○

Data sets, elements, and variables We have said that data are facts and figures from which conclusions can be drawn. Together, the data that are collected for a particular study are referred to as a **data set**. For example, Table 1.1 is a data set that gives information about the new homes sold in a Florida luxury home development over a recent three-month period. Potential buyers in this housing community could choose either the "Diamond" or the "Ruby" home model design and could have the home built on either a lake lot or a treed lot (with or water access).

In order to understand the data in Table 1.1, note that any data set provides information about some group of individual **elements**, which may be people, objects, events, or other entities. The information that a data set provides about its elements usually describes one or more characteristics of these elements.

Any characteristic of an element is called a **variable**.

For the data set in Table 1.1, each sold home is an element, and four variables are used to describe the homes. These variables are (1) the home model design, (2) the type of lot on which the home was built, (3) the list (asking) price, and (4) the (actual) selling price. Moreover, each home model design came with "everything included"—specifically, a complete, luxury interior package and a choice of one of three different architectural exteriors. Therefore, because there were no interior or exterior options to purchase, the (actual) selling price of a home depended solely on the home model design and whatever price reduction (based partially on the lot type) that the community developer (builder) was willing to give.

LO1-1 Define a variable.

TABLE 1.1 A Data Set Describing Five Home Sales ⓓ HomeSales

Home	Model Design	Lot Type	List Price	Selling Price
1	Diamond	Lake	$494,000	$494,000
2	Ruby	Treed	$447,000	$398,000
3	Diamond	Treed	$494,000	$440,000
4	Diamond	Treed	$494,000	$469,000
5	Ruby	Lake	$447,000	$447,000

Continuing Case Studies and Business Improvement Conclusions

The main chapter discussions feature real or realistic examples, continuing case studies, and a business improvement theme. The continuing case studies span individual chapters and groups of chapters and tie together different statistical topics. To emphasize the text's theme of business improvement, icons **BI** are placed in the page margins to identify when statistical analysis has led to an important business improvement conclusion. Each conclusion is also highlighted in yellow for additional clarity. For example, in Chapters 1 and 3 we consider **The Cell Phone Case**:

TABLE 1.4 A Sample of Cellular Usages (in minutes) for 100 Randomly Selected Employees ⓓ CellUse

75	485	37	547	753	93	897	694	797	477
654	578	504	670	490	225	509	247	597	173
496	553	0	198	507	157	672	296	774	479
0	822	705	814	20	513	546	801	721	273
879	433	420	521	648	41	528	359	367	948
511	704	535	585	341	530	216	512	491	0
542	562	49	505	461	496	241	624	885	259
571	338	503	529	737	444	372	555	290	830
719	120	468	730	853	18	479	144	24	513
482	683	212	418	399	376	323	173	669	611

EXAMPLE 3.5 The Cell Phone Case: Reducing Cellular Phone Costs Ⓒ

Suppose that a cellular management service tells the bank that if its cellular cost per minute for the random sample of 100 bank employees is over 18 cents per minute, the bank will benefit from automated cellular management of its calling plans. Last month's cellular usages for the 100 randomly selected employees are given in Table 1.4 (page 9), and a dot plot of these usages is given in the page margin. If we add together the usages, we find that the 100 employees used a total of 46,625 minutes. Furthermore, the total cellular cost incurred by the 100 employees is found to be $9,317 (this total includes base costs, overage costs, long distance, and roaming). This works out to an average of $9,317/46,625 = $.1998, or 19.98 cents per minute. Because this average cellular cost per minute exceeds 18 cents per minute, the bank will hire the cellular management service to manage its calling plans.

BI

TEXT'S FEATURES

Figures and Tables

Throughout the text, charts, graphs, tables, and Excel and MINITAB outputs are used to illustrate statistical concepts. For example:

- In Chapter 3 (**Descriptive Statistics: Numerical Methods**), the following figures are used to help explain the **Empirical Rule**. Moreover, in **The Car Mileage Case** an automaker uses the Empirical Rule to find estimates of the "typical," "lowest," and "highest" mileage that a new midsize car should be expected to get in combined city and highway driving. In actual practice, real automakers provide similar information broken down into separate estimates for city and highway driving—see the Buick LaCrosse new car sticker in Figure 3.14.

- In chapter 7 (**Sampling and Sampling Distributions**), the following figures (and others) are used to help explain the **sampling distribution of the sample mean** and the **Central Limit Theorem**. In addition, the figures describe different applications of random sampling in **The Car Mileage Case**, and thus this case is used as an integrative tool to help students understand sampling distributions.

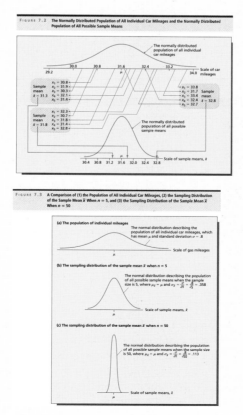

- In Chapter 8 (**Confidence Intervals**), the following figure (and others) are used to help explain the meaning of a **95 percent confidence interval** for the population mean. Furthermore, in **The Car Mileage Case** an automaker uses a confidence interval procedure specified by the Environmental Protection Agency to find the EPA estimate of a new midsize model's true mean mileage.

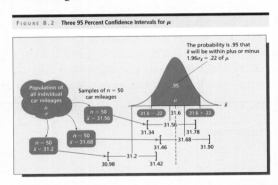

FIGURE 8.2   Three 95 Percent Confidence Intervals for μ

- In Chapter 9 (**Hypothesis Testing**), a five-step hypothesis testing procedure, **new graphical hypothesis testing summary boxes,** and many graphics are used to show how to carry out hypothesis tests.

The Five Steps of Hypothesis Testing

1. State the null hypothesis H_0 and the alternative hypothesis H_a.
2. Specify the level of significance α.
3. Select the test statistic.

Using a critical value rule:

4. Determine the critical value rule for deciding whether to reject H_0.
5. Collect the sample data, compute the value of the test statistic, and decide whether to reject H_0 by using the critical value rule. Interpret the statistical results.

Using a p-value:

4. Collect the sample data, compute the value of the test statistic, and compute the p-value.
5. Reject H_0 at level of significance α if the p-value is less than α. Interpret the statistical results.

FIGURE 9.5   Testing H_0: $\mu = 1.5$ versus H_a: $\mu < 1.5$ by Using a Critical Value and the p-Value

- In Chapters 14 and 15 (**Simple Linear and Multiple Regression**), a substantial number of data plots, Excel and MINITAB outputs, and other graphics are used to teach simple and multiple regression analysis. For example, in **The Tasty Sub Shop Case** a business entrepreneur uses data plotted in Figures 15.1 and 15.2 and the Excel and MINITAB outputs in Figure 15.4 to predict the yearly revenue of a Tasty Sub Shop restaurant on the basis of the population and business activity near a potential Sub Shop location. Using the **95 percent prediction interval** on the MINITAB output and projected restaurant operating costs, the entrepreneur decides whether to build a Tasty Sub Shop restaurant on the potential site.

TEXT'S FEATURES

FIGURE 15.1 Plot of y (Yearly Revenue) versus x_1 (Population Size)

FIGURE 15.2 Plot of y (Yearly Revenue) versus x_2 (Business Rating)

FIGURE 15.4 Excel and MINITAB Outputs of a Regression Analysis of the Tasty Sub Shop Revenue Data in Table 15.1 Using the Model $y = \beta_0 + \beta_1 x_1 + \beta_2 x_2 + \varepsilon$

(a) The Excel output

Regression Statistics

Multiple R	0.9905
R Square	0.9810 [8]
Adjusted R Square	0.9756 [9]
Standard Error	36.6856 [7]
Observations	10

ANOVA	df	SS	MS	F	Significance F
Regression	2	486355.7 [10]	243177.8	180.689 [13]	9.46E-07 [14]
Residual	7	9420.8 [11]	1345.835		
Total	9	495776.5 [12]			

	Coefficients	Standard Error [4]	t Stat [5]	P-value [6]	Lower 95% [19]	Upper 95% [19]
Intercept	125.289 [1]	40.9333	3.06	0.0183	28.4969	222.0807
population	14.1996 [2]	0.9100	15.60	1.07E-06	12.0478	16.3517
bus_rating	22.8107 [3]	5.7692	3.95	0.0055	9.1686	36.4527

(b) The MINITAB output

```
The regression equation is
revenue = 125 + 14.2 population + 22.8 bus_rating

Predictor      Coef      SE Coef[4]        T[5]        P[6]
Constant     125.29[1]      40.93          3.06       0.018
population   14.1996[2]      0.91          15.6       0.000
bus_rating   22.811[3]       5.769         3.95       0.006

S = 36.6856[7]           R-Sq = 98.10%[8]       R-Sq(adj) = 97.6%[9]

Analysis of Variance

Source          DF       SS          MS          F            P
Regression       2    486356[10]   243178      180.69[13]   0.000[14]
Residual Error   7      9421[11]     1346
Total            9    495777[12]

Predicted Values for New Observations
  New Obs     Fit[15]    SE Fit[16]      95% CI[17]            95% PI[18]
     1        956.6         15        (921.0, 992.2)      (862.8, 1050.4)

Values of Predictors for New Observations
  New Obs     population    bus_rating
     1           47.3
```

[1] b_0	[2] b_1	[3] b_2	[4] s_{b_j} = standard error of the estimate b_j	[5] t statistics	[6] p-values for t statistics	[7] s = standard error
[8] R^2	[9] Adjusted R^2	[10] Explained variation	[11] SSE = Unexplained variation	[12] Total variation	[13] F(model) statistic
[14] p-value for F(model)	[15] $\hat{y}$ = point prediction when $x_1 = 47.3$ and $x_2 = 7$		[16] $s_{\hat{y}}$ = standard error of the estimate $\hat{y}$	
[17] 95% confidence interval when $x_1 = 47.3$ and $x_2 = 7$	[18] 95% prediction interval when $x_1 = 47.3$ and $x_2 = 7$		[19] 95% confidence interval for β_j	

Exercises

Many of the exercises in the text require the analysis of real data. Data sets are identified by an icon in the text and are included on the Online Learning Center (OLC): www.mhhe.com/bowerman7e. Exercises in each section are broken into two parts—"Concepts" and "Methods and Applications"—and there are supplementary and Internet exercises at the end of each chapter.

2.8 Fifty randomly selected adults who follow professional sports were asked to name their favorite professional sports league. The results are as follows where MLB = Major League Baseball, MLS = Major League Soccer, NBA = National Basketball Association, NFL = National Football League, and NHL = National Hockey League. ⬤S ProfSports

NFL	NBA	NFL	MLB	MLB	NHL	NFL	NFL	MLS	MLB
MLB	NFL	MLB	NBA	NBA	NFL	NFL	NFL	NHL	NBA
NBA	NFL	NHL	NFL	MLS	NFL	MLB	NFL	MLB	NFL
NHL	MLB	NHL	NFL	NFL	NFL	MLB	NFL	NBA	NFL
MLS	NFL	MLB	NBA	NFL	NFL	MLB	NBA	NFL	NFL

a Find the frequency distribution, relative frequency distribution, and percent frequency distribution for these data.
b Construct a frequency bar chart for these data.
c Construct a pie chart for these data.
d Which professional sports league is most popular with these 50 adults? Which is least popular?

Chapter Ending Material and Excel/MINITAB/MegaStat® Tutorials

The end-of-chapter material includes a chapter summary, a glossary of terms, important formula references, and comprehensive appendices that show students how to use Excel, MINITAB, and MegaStat.

Chapter Summary

We began this chapter by presenting and comparing several measures of **central tendency.** We defined the **population mean** and we saw how to estimate the population mean by using a **sample mean.** We also defined the **median** and **mode,** and we compared the mean, median, and mode for symmetrical distributions and for distributions that are skewed to the right or left. We then studied measures of **variation** (or **spread**). We defined the **range, variance,** and **standard deviation,** and we saw how to estimate a population variance and standard deviation by using a sample. We learned that a good way to interpret the standard deviation when a population is (approximately) normally distributed is to use the **Empirical Rule,** and we studied **Chebyshev's Theorem,** which gives us intervals containing reasonably large fractions of

the population units no matter what the population's shape might be. We also saw that, when a data set is highly skewed, it is best to use **percentiles** and **quartiles** to measure variation, and we learned how to construct a **box-and-whiskers plot** by using quartiles.

After learning how to measure and depict central tendency and variability, we presented several optional topics. First, we discussed several numerical measures of the relationship between two variables. These included the **covariance,** the **correlation coefficient,** and the **least squares line.** We then introduced the concept of a **weighted mean** and also explained how to compute descriptive statistics for **grouped data.** Finally, we showed how to calculate the **geometric mean** and demonstrated its interpretation.

Constructing a scatter plot of sales volume versus advertising expenditure as in Figure 2.24 on page 67 (data file: SalesPlot.xlsx):

- Enter the advertising and sales data in Table 2.20 on page 67 into columns A and B—advertising expenditures in column A with label "Ad Exp" and sales values in column B with label "Sales Vol." **Note: The variable to be graphed on the horizontal axis must be in the first column** (that is, the left-most column) **and the variable to be graphed on the vertical axis must be in the second column** (that is, the rightmost column).
- Select the entire range of data to be graphed.
- Select Insert : Scatter : Scatter with only Markers
- The scatter plot will be displayed in a graphics window. Move the plot to a chart sheet and edit appropriately.

Glossary of Terms

box-and-whiskers display (box plot): A graphical portrayal of a data set that depicts both the central tendency and variability of the data. It is constructed using Q_1, M_d, and Q_3. (pages 123, 124)
central tendency: A term referring to the middle of a population or sample of measurements. (page 101)

outlier (in a box-and-whiskers display): A measurement less than the lower limit or greater than the upper limit. (page 124)
percentile: The value such that a specified percentage of the measurements in a population or sample fall at or below it. (page 120)
point estimate: A one-number estimate for the value of a population parameter. (page 101)

McGraw-Hill *Connect® Business Statistics* is an online assignment and assessment solution that connects students with the tools and resources they'll need to achieve success through faster learning, higher retention, and more efficient studying. It provides instructors with tools to quickly pick content and assignments according to the topics they want to emphasize.

Online Assignments. *Connect Business Statistics* helps students learn more efficiently by providing practice material and feedback when they are needed. *Connect* grades homework automatically and provides feedback on any questions that students may have missed.

Integration of Excel Data Sets. A convenient feature is the inclusion of an Excel data file link in many problems using data files in their calculation. The link allows students to easily launch into Excel, work the problem, and return to *Connect* to key in the answer.

Student Resource Library. The *Connect Business Statistics* Student Library is the place for students to access additional resources. The Student Library provides quick access to recorded lectures, practice materials, eBooks, data files, PowerPoint files, and more.

Simple Assignment Management and Smart Grading. When it comes to studying, time is precious. *Connect Business Statistics* helps students learn more efficiently by providing feedback and practice material when they need it, where they need it. When it comes to teaching, your time also is precious. The grading function enables you to:

- Have assignments scored automatically, giving students immediate feedback on their work and side-by-side comparisons with correct answers.

- Access and review each response; manually change grades or leave comments for students to review.

Student Reporting. *Connect Business Statistics* keeps instructors informed about how each student, section, and class is performing, allowing for more productive use of lecture and office hours. The progress-tracking function enables you to:

- View scored work immediately and track individual or group performance with assignment and grade reports.

- Access an instant view of student or class performance relative to learning objectives.

- Collect data and generate reports required by many accreditation organizations, such as AACSB.

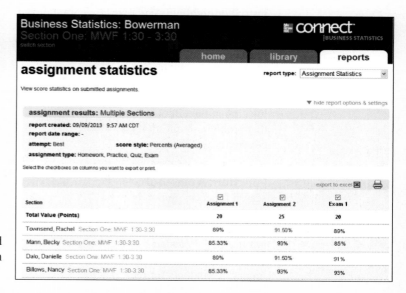

Instructor Library. The *Connect Business Statistics* Instructor Library is your repository for additional resources to improve student engagement in and out of class. You can select and use any asset that enhances your lecture. The *Connect Business Statistics* Instructor Library includes:

- eBook
- PowerPoint presentations
- Test Bank
- Instructor's Solutions Manual
- Digital Image Library

BUSINESS STATISTICS

Connect® Plus Business Statistics includes a seamless integration of an eBook and *Connect Business Statistics.* Benefits of the rich functionality integrated into the product are outlined below.

Integrated Media-Rich eBook. An integrated media-rich eBook allows students to access media in context with each chapter. Students can highlight, take notes, and access shared instructor highlights and notes to learn the course material.

Dynamic Links. Dynamic links provide a connection between the problems or questions you assign to your students and the location in the eBook where that problem or question is covered.

Powerful Search Function. A powerful search function pinpoints and connects key concepts in a snap. This state-of-the-art, thoroughly tested system supports you in preparing students for the world that awaits. For more information about *Connect,* go to www.mcgrawhillconnect.com or contact your local McGraw-Hill sales representative.

Connect Packaging Options

Connect with 2 Semester Access Card: 0077534735
Connect Plus with 2 Semester Access Card: 0077534751

Tegrity Campus: Lectures 24/7

Tegrity Campus is a service that makes class time available 24/7. With *Tegrity Campus,* you can automatically capture every lecture in a searchable format for students to review when they study and complete assignments. With a simple one-click start-and-stop process, you capture all computer screens and corresponding audio. Students can replay any part of any class with easy-to-use browser-based viewing on a PC or Mac.

Educators know that the more students can see, hear, and experience class resources, the better they learn. In fact, studies prove it. With *Tegrity Campus,* students quickly recall key moments by using *Tegrity Campus*'s unique search feature. This search helps students efficiently find what they need, when they need it, across an entire semester of class recordings. Help turn all your students' study time into learning moments immediately supported by your lecture. To learn more about *Tegrity,* watch a two-minute Flash demo at http://tegritycampus.mhhe.com.

WHAT SOFTWARE IS AVAILABLE

MegaStat® for Microsoft Excel® 2003, 2007, and 2010 (and Excel: Mac 2011)

CD ISBN: 0077496442. (Windows only)

Access Card ISBN: 0077426274. Note: Best option for both Windows and Mac users. MegaStat is a full-featured Excel add-in by J. B. Orris of Butler University that is available with this text. It performs statistical analyses within an Excel workbook. It does basic functions such as descriptive statistics, frequency distributions, and probability calculations, as well as hypothesis testing, ANOVA, and regression.

MegaStat output is carefully formatted. Ease-of-use features include AutoExpand for quick data selection and Auto Label detect. Since MegaStat is easy to use, students can focus on learning statistics without being distracted by the software. MegaStat is always available from Excel's main menu. Selecting a menu item pops up a dialog box. MegaStat works with all recent versions of Excel.

MINITAB® (ISBN: 007305237x)

Minitab® Student Version 14 is available to help students solve the business statistics exercises in the text. This software is available in the student version and can be packaged with any McGraw-Hill business statistics text.

McGraw-Hill Customer Care Information

At McGraw-Hill, we understand that getting the most from new technology can be challenging. That's why our services don't stop after you purchase our products. You can e-mail our Product Specialists 24 hours a day to get product-training online. Or you can search our knowledge bank of Frequently Asked Questions on our support website. For Customer Support, call **800-331-5094**, e-mail hmsupport@mcgraw-hill.com, or visit www.mhhe.com/support. One of our Technical Support Analysts will be able to assist you in a timely fashion.

Online Learning Center: www.mhhe.com/bowerman7e

The Online Learning Center (OLC) is the text website with online content for both students and instructors. It provides the instructor with a complete Instructor's Manual in Word format, the complete Test Bank in both Word files and computerized EZ Test format, Instructor PowerPoint slides, text art files, an introduction to ALEKS®, an introduction to McGraw-Hill *Connect Business Statistics*®, access to the eBook, and more.

All test bank questions are available in an EZ Test electronic format. Included are a number of multiple-choice, true/false, and short-answer questions and problems. The answers to all questions are given, along with a rating of the level of difficulty, Bloom's taxonomy question type, and AACSB knowledge category.

Online Course Management

McGraw-Hill Higher Education and Blackboard have teamed up. What does this mean for you?

- **Single sign-on.** Now you and your students can access McGraw-Hill's *Connect*® and *Create*® right from within your Blackboard course—all with one single sign-on.

- **Deep integration of content and tools.** You get a single sign-on with *Connect* and *Create*, and you also get integration of McGraw-Hill content and content engines right into Blackboard. Whether you're choosing a book for your course or building *Connect* assignments, all the tools you need are right where you want them—inside of Blackboard.

- **One grade book.** Keeping several grade books and manually synchronizing grades into Blackboard is no longer necessary. When a student completes an integrated *Connect* assignment, the grade for that assignment automatically (and instantly) feeds your Blackboard grade center.

- **A solution for everyone.** Whether your institution is already using Blackboard or you just want to try Blackboard on your own, we have a solution for you. McGraw-Hill and Blackboard can now offer you easy access to industry-leading technology and content, whether your campus hosts it or we do. Be sure to ask your local McGraw-Hill representative for details.

CourseSmart

CourseSmart is a convenient way to find and buy eTextbooks. CourseSmart has the largest selection of eTextbooks available anywhere, offering thousands of the most commonly adopted textbooks from a wide variety of higher education publishers. CourseSmart eTextbooks are available in one standard online reader with full text search, notes and highlighting, and e-mail tools for sharing notes between classmates. Visit www.CourseSmart.com for more information on ordering.

Online Learning Center: www.mhhe.com/bowerman7e

The Online Learning Center (OLC) provides students with the following content:

- Quizzes—self-grading to assess knowledge of the material
- Data sets—import into Excel for quick calculation and analysis
- PowerPoint—gives an overview of chapter content
- Appendixes—quick look-up when the text isn't available

Business Statistics Center (BSC): www.mhhe.com/bstat/

The BSC contains links to statistical publications and resources, software downloads, learning aids, statistical websites and databases, and McGraw-Hill/Irwin product websites and online courses.

ALEKS®

ALEKS is an assessment and learning program that provides individualized instruction in Business Statistics, Business Math, and Accounting. Available online in partnership with McGraw-Hill/Irwin, ALEKS interacts with students much like a skilled human tutor, with the ability to assess precisely a student's knowledge and provide instruction on the exact topics the student is most ready to learn. By providing topics to meet individual students' needs, allowing students to move between explanation and practice, correcting and analyzing errors, and defining terms, ALEKS helps students to master course content quickly and easily.

ALEKS also includes an Instructor Module with powerful, assignment-driven features and extensive content flexibility. ALEKS simplifies course management and allows instructors to spend less time with administrative tasks and more time directing student learning.

To learn more about ALEKS, visit www.aleks.com/highered/business. ALEKS is a registered trademark of ALEKS Corporation.

ACKNOWLEDGMENTS

We wish to thank many people who have helped to make this book a reality. We thank Drena Bowerman, who spent many hours cutting and taping and making trips to the copy shop, so that we could complete the manuscript on time. As indicated on the title page, we thank Professor Steven C. Huchendorf, University of Minnesota; Dawn C. Porter, University of Southern California; and Patrick J. Schur, Miami University, for major contributions to this book. We also thank Susan Cramer of Miami University for helpful advice on writing this book.

We also wish to thank the people at McGraw-Hill/Irwin for their dedication to this book. These people include executive editors Thomas Hayward and Steve Schuetz, who are extremely helpful resources to the authors; executive editor Dick Hercher, who persuaded us initially to publish with McGraw-Hill/Irwin and who continues to offer sound advice and support; senior developmental editor Wanda Zeman, who has shown great dedication to the improvement of this book; and lead project manager Harvey Yep, who has very capably and diligently guided this book through its production and who has been a tremendous help to the authors. We also thank our former executive editor, Scott Isenberg, for the tremendous help he has given us in developing all of our McGraw-Hill business statistics books.

Many reviewers have contributed to this book, and we are grateful to all of them. They include

Lawrence Acker, Harris-Stowe State University
Ajay K. Aggarwal, Millsaps College
Mohammad Ahmadi, University of Tennessee–Chattanooga
Sung K. Ahn, Washington State University
Imam Alam, University of Northern Iowa
Eugene Allevato, Woodbury University
Mostafa S. Aminzadeh, Towson University
Henry Ander, Arizona State University–Tempe
Randy J. Anderson, California State University–Fresno
Mohammad Bajwa, Northampton Community College
Ron Barnes, University of Houston–Downtown
John D. Barrett, University of North Alabama
Mary Jo Boehms, Jackson State Community College
Pamela A. Boger, Ohio University–Athens
David Booth, Kent State University
Dave Bregenzer, Utah State University
Philip E. Burian, Colorado Technical University–Sioux Falls
Giorgio Canarella, California State University–Los Angeles
Margaret Capen, East Carolina University
Priscilla Chaffe-Stengel, California State University–Fresno
Ali A. Choudhry, Florida International University
Richard Cleary, Bentley College
Bruce Cooil, Vanderbilt University
Sam Cousley, University of Mississippi
Teresa A Dalton, University of Denver
Nit Dasgupta, University of Wisconsin–Eau Claire
Linda Dawson, University of Washington–Tacoma
Jay Devore, California Polytechnic State University
Bernard Dickman, Hofstra University
Joan Donohue, University of South Carolina
Anne Drougas, Dominican University
Mark Eakin, University of Texas–Arlington
Hammou Elbarmi, Baruch College
Soheila Fardanesh, Towson University
Nicholas R. Farnum, California State University–Fullerton
James Flynn, Cleveland State University
Lillian Fok, University of New Orleans
Tom Fox, Cleveland State Community College

Charles A. Gates Jr., Olivet Nazarene University
Linda S. Ghent, Eastern Illinois University
Allen Gibson, Seton Hall University
Scott D. Gilbert, Southern Illinois University
Nicholas Gorgievski, Nichols College
TeWhan Hahn, University of Idaho
Clifford B. Hawley, West Virginia University
Rhonda L. Hensley, North Carolina A&T State University
Eric Howington, Valdosta State University
Zhimin Huang, Adelphi University
Steven C. Huchendorf, University of Minnesota
C. Thomas Innis, University of Cincinnati
Jeffrey Jarrett, University of Rhode Island
Craig Johnson, Brigham Young University
Valerie M. Jones, Tidewater Community College
Nancy K. Keith, Missouri State University
Thomas Kratzer, Malone University
Alan Kreger, University of Maryland
Michael Kulansky, University of Maryland
Risa Kumazawa, Georgia Southern University
David A. Larson, University of South Alabama
John Lawrence, California State University–Fullerton
Lee Lawton, University of St. Thomas
John D. Levendis, Loyola University–New Orleans
Barbara Libby, Walden University
Carel Ligeon, Auburn University–Montgomery
Kenneth Linna, Auburn University–Montgomery
David W. Little, High Point University
Donald MacRitchie, Framingham State College
Edward Markowski, Old Dominion University
Mamata Marme, Augustana College
Jerrold H. May, University of Pittsburgh
Brad McDonald, Northern Illinois University
Richard A. McGowan, Boston College
Christy McLendon, University of New Orleans
John M. Miller, Sam Houston State University
Robert Mogull, California State University–Sacramento
Jason Molitierno, Sacred Heart University

ACKNOWLEDGMENTS

Daniel Monchuck, University of Southern Mississippi
Tariq Mughal, University of Utah
Patricia Mullins, University of Wisconsin–Madison
Thomas Naugler, Johns Hopkins University
Robert Nauss, University of Missouri–St. Louis
Quinton J. Nottingham, Virginia Tech University
Barbara A. Osyk, University of Akron
Ceyhun Ozgur, Valparaiso University
Tom Page, Michigan State University
Linda M. Penas, University of California–Riverside
Cathy Poliak, University of Wisconsin–Milwaukee
Simcha Pollack, St. John's University
Michael D. Polomsky, Cleveland State University
Robert S. Pred, Temple University
Srikant Raghavan, Lawrence Technological University
Sunil Ramlall, University of St. Thomas
Steven Rein, California Polytechnic State University
Donna Retzlaff-Roberts, University of South Alabama
David Ronen, University of Missouri–St. Louis
Peter Royce, University of New Hampshire
Fatollah Salimian, Salisbury University
Yvonne Sandoval, Pima Community College
Sunil Sapra, California State University–Los Angeles
Patrick J. Schur, Miami University
William L. Seaver, University of Tennessee
Kevin Shanahan, University of Texas–Tyler
Arkudy Shemyakin, University of St. Thomas
Charlie Shi, Diablo Valley College

Joyce Shotick, Bradley University
Plamen Simeonov, University of Houston Downtown
Bob Smidt, California Polytechnic State University
Rafael Solis, California State University–Fresno
Toni M. Somers, Wayne State University
Ronald L. Spicer, Colorado Technical University–Sioux Falls
Mitchell Spiegel, Johns Hopkins University
Timothy Staley, Keller Graduate School of Management
David Stoffer, University of Pittsburgh
Cliff Stone, Ball State University
Durai Sundaramoorthi, Missouri Western State University
Courtney Sykes, Colorado State University
Bedassa Tadesse, University of Minnesota–Duluth
Stanley Taylor, California State University–Sacramento
Patrick Thompson, University of Florida
Doug T. Tran, California State University–Los Angeles
Bulent Uyar, University of Northern Iowa
Emmanuelle Vaast, Long Island University–Brooklyn
Ed Wallace, Malcolm X College
Bin Wang, Saint Edwards University
Allen Webster, Bradley University
Blake Whitten, University of Iowa
Susan Wolcott-Hanes, Binghamton University
Mustafa Yilmaz, Northeastern University
Gary Yoshimoto, Saint Cloud State University
William F. Younkin, Miami University
Xiaowei Zhu, University of Wisconsin–Milwaukee

We also wish to thank the error checkers, Lou Patille, Colorado Heights University, and Peter Royce, University of New Hampshire, who were very helpful. Most importantly, we wish to thank our families for their acceptance, unconditional love, and support.

Bruce Bowerman
Richard O'Connell
Emily Murphree

Chapter-by-Chapter Revisions for 7th Edition

Chapter 1
- Importance of data made clearer in initial example.
- Intuitive explanation of random sampling and introduction of 3 major case studies made more concise.
- New subsection on ethical statistical practice.
- Cable cost example updated.
- Data set for coffee temperature case expanded and ready for use in continuous probability distribution chapter.

Chapter 2
- Pizza preference data replace Jeep preference data in creating bar and pie charts and in business decision making.
- Seven new data sets added.
- Eighteen new exercises replace former exercises.

Chapter 3
- Section on percentages, quartiles, and box plots completely rewritten, simplified, and shortened.
- Ten new data sets used.
- Nineteen new exercises replace former exercises.

Chapter 4
- Main discussion in chapter rewritten and simplified.
- Cable penetration example (based on Time Warner Cable) replaces newspaper subscription example.
- Employment discrimination case (based on real pharmaceutical company) used in conditional probability section.
- Exercises updated in this and all subsequent chapters.

Chapter 5
- Introduction to discrete probability distributions rewritten, simplified, and shortened.
- Binominal distribution introduced using a tree diagram.
- Discussion of hypergeometric distribution improved and slightly expanded.
- Includes new optional section on joint distributions and covariance previously found in an appendix.

Chapter 6
- Introduction to continuous probability distributions improved and motivated by coffee temperature data.
- Uniform distribution section now begins with an example.
- Normal distribution motivated by tie-in to coffee temperature data.

Chapter 7
- A seamless development of the sampling distribution of the sample mean beginning with a small population example and proceeding through the Central Limit Theorem.
- Includes optional section deriving the mean and variance of the sample mean (previously found in an appendix).

Chapter 8
- Introduction to confidence intervals rewritten and simplified.
- Improved graphics help students construct confidence intervals.

- Optional section on parameters of finite populations shortened and simplified; short section on estimation in stratified sampling added.

Chapter 9
- Introduction to z tests streamlined and improved.
- Summary boxes feature innovative graphics to help students test hypotheses using critical values and p-values.

Chapter 10
- Comparison of two population means moves more quickly to the realistic unknown variance case.

Chapter 11
- New chapter covering the chi-square and F distributions and their applications to inferences about one or two population variances.

Chapter 12 (Chapter 11 in the Sixth Edition)
- Discussion of one-way, randomized block, and two-way ANOVA streamlined and simplified.
- Multiple comparisons shortened by emphasizing Tukey procedures.

Chapter 13 (Chapter 12 in the Sixth Edition)
- No significant changes.

Chapter 14 (Chapter 13 in the Sixth Edition)
- Discussion of simple linear regression model and least squares estimation streamlined.
- Durbin-Watson test and model transformations now included in this initial regression chapter.

Chapter 15
- This chapter combines the Sixth Edition's Chapter 14 and Chapter 15. It concludes with 5 innovative and flexible sections which can be covered in any order.

Chapter 16
- Time series regression simplified; new software output is used.
- Exponential smoothing coverage updated and shortened.
- New section on Box-Jenkins models is added.
- Index numbers examples updated.

Chapter 17
- X bar and R charts presented concisely using one example.

Chapter 18
- No significant changes.

Chapter 19
- No significant changes.

Brief Table of Contents

Table of Contents

DEDICATION

Bruce L. Bowerman
To my wife, children, sister, and other family members:
Drena
Michael, Jinda, Benjamin, and Lex
Asa and Nicole
Susan
Fiona, Radeesa, and Barney
Daphne, Chloe, and Edgar
Gwyneth and Tony
Bobby and Callie
Marmalade, Randy, and Penney
Clarence, Quincy, Teddy, Julius, Charlie, and Sally

Richard T. O'Connell
To my children and grandchild:
Christopher, Bradley, and Sam

Emily S. Murphree
To Kevin and the Math Ladies

Business Statistics in Practice

SEVENTH EDITION

CHAPTER 1

An Introduction to Business Statistics

Learning Objectives

When you have mastered the material in this chapter, you will be able to:

LO1-1 Define a variable.

LO1-2 Describe the difference between a quantitative variable and a qualitative variable.

LO1-3 Describe the difference between cross-sectional data and time series data.

LO1-4 Construct and interpret a time series (runs) plot.

LO1-5 Identify the different types of data sources: existing data sources, experimental studies, and observational studies.

LO1-6 Describe the difference between a population and a sample.

LO1-7 Distinguish between descriptive statistics and statistical inference.

LO1-8 Explain the importance of random sampling.

LO1-9 Identify the ratio, interval, ordinal, and nominative scales of measurement (Optional).

Chapter Outline

1.1 Data

1.2 Data Sources

1.3 Populations and Samples

1.4 Three Case Studies That Illustrate Sampling and Statistical Inference

1.5 Ratio, Interval, Ordinal, and Nominative Scales of Measurement (Optional)

The subject of **statistics** involves the study of how to collect, analyze, and interpret data. **Data** are facts and figures from which conclusions can be drawn. Such conclusions are important to the decision making of many professions and organizations. For example, **economists** use conclusions drawn from the latest data on unemployment and inflation to help the government make policy decisions. **Financial planners** use recent trends in stock market prices and economic conditions to make investment decisions. **Accountants** use **sample data** concerning a company's *actual sales revenues* to assess whether the company's *claimed sales revenues* are valid. **Marketing professionals** help businesses decide which products to develop and market by using data that reveal consumer preferences. **Production supervisors** use manufacturing data to evaluate, control, and improve product quality. **Politicians** rely on data from public opinion polls to formulate legislation and to devise campaign strategies. **Physicians and hospitals** use data on the effectiveness of drugs and surgical procedures to provide patients with the best possible treatment.

In this chapter we begin to see how we collect and analyze data. As we proceed through the chapter, we introduce several case studies. These case studies (and others to be introduced later) are revisited throughout later chapters as we learn the statistical methods needed to analyze them. Briefly, we will begin to study three cases:

The Cell Phone Case. A bank estimates its cellular phone costs and decides whether to outsource management of its wireless resources by studying the calling patterns of its employees.

The Marketing Research Case. A bottling company investigates consumer reaction to a new bottle design for one of its popular soft drinks.

The Car Mileage Case. To determine if it qualifies for a federal tax credit based on fuel economy, an automaker studies the gas mileage of its new midsize model.

1.1 Data ● ● ●

LO1-1 Define a variable.

Data sets, elements, and variables   We have said that data are facts and figures from which conclusions can be drawn. Together, the data that are collected for a particular study are referred to as a **data set.** For example, Table 1.1 is a data set that gives information about the new homes sold in a Florida luxury home development over a recent three-month period. Potential buyers in this housing community could choose either the "Diamond" or the "Ruby" home model design and could have the home built on either a lake lot or a treed lot (with no water access).

In order to understand the data in Table 1.1, note that any data set provides information about some group of individual **elements,** which may be people, objects, events, or other entities. The information that a data set provides about its elements usually describes one or more characteristics of these elements.

Any characteristic of an element is called a **variable.**

For the data set in Table 1.1, each sold home is an element, and four variables are used to describe the homes. These variables are (1) the home model design, (2) the type of lot on which the home was built, (3) the list (asking) price, and (4) the (actual) selling price. Moreover, each home model design came with "everything included"—specifically, a complete, luxury interior package and a choice of one of three different architectural exteriors. Therefore, because there were no interior or exterior options to purchase, the (actual) selling price of a home depended solely on the home model design and whatever price reduction (based partially on the lot type) that the community developer (builder) was willing to give.

TABLE 1.1   A Data Set Describing Five Home Sales   DS HomeSales

Home	Model Design	Lot Type	List Price	Selling Price
1	Diamond	Lake	$494,000	$494,000
2	Ruby	Treed	$447,000	$398,000
3	Diamond	Treed	$494,000	$440,000
4	Diamond	Treed	$494,000	$469,000
5	Ruby	Lake	$447,000	$447,000

The data in Table 1.1 are real (with some minor modifications to protect privacy) and were provided by a business executive—a friend of the authors—who recently received a promotion and needed to move to central Florida. While searching for a new home, the executive and his family visited the luxury home community and decided they wanted to purchase a Diamond model on a treed lot. The list price of this home was $494,000, but the developer offered to sell it for an "incentive" price of $469,000. Intuitively, the incentive price's $25,000 savings off list price seemed like a good deal. However, the executive resisted making an immediate decision. Instead, he decided to collect data on the selling prices of new homes recently sold in the community and use the data to assess whether the developer might be amenable to a lower offer. In order to collect "relevant data," the executive talked to local real estate professionals and learned that new homes sold in the community during the previous three months were a good indicator of current home value. Using real estate sales records, the executive also learned that five of the community's new homes had sold in the previous three months. The data given in Table 1.1 are the data that the executive collected about these five homes.

LO1-2 Describe the difference between a quantitative variable and a qualitative variable.

In order to understand the conclusions the business executive reached using the data in Table 1.1, we need to further discuss variables. For any variable describing an element in a data set, we carry out a **measurement** to assign a value of the variable to the element. For example, in the real estate example, real estate sales records gave the actual selling price of each home to the nearest dollar. In another example, a credit card company might measure the time it takes for a cardholder's bill to be paid to the nearest day. Or, in a third example, an automaker might measure the gasoline mileage obtained by a car in city driving to the nearest one-tenth of a mile per gallon by conducting a mileage test on a driving course prescribed by the Environmental Protection Agency (EPA). If the possible measurements of the values of a variable are numbers that represent quantities (that is, "how much" or "how many"), then the variable is said to be **quantitative.** For example, the actual selling price of a home, the payment time of a bill, and the gasoline mileage of a car are all quantitative. However, if we simply record into which of several categories an element falls, then the variable is said to be **qualitative** or **categorical.** Examples of categorical variables include (1) a person's gender, (2) the make of an automobile, (3) whether a person who purchases a product is satisfied with the product, and (4) the type of lot on which a home is built.[1]

Of the four variables in Table 1.1, two variables—list price and selling price—are quantitative, and two variables—model design and lot type—are qualitative. Furthermore, when the business executive examined Table 1.1, he noted that homes on lake lots had sold at their list price, but homes on treed lots had not. Because the executive and his family wished to purchase a Diamond model on a treed lot, the executive also noted that two Diamond models on treed lots had sold in the previous three months. One of these Diamond models had sold for the incentive price of $469,000, but the other had sold for a lower price of $440,000. Hoping to pay the lower price for his family's new home, the executive offered $440,000 for the Diamond model on the treed lot. Initially, the home builder turned down this offer, but two days later the builder called back and accepted the offer. The executive had used data to buy the new home for $54,000 less than the list price and $29,000 less than the incentive price!

LO1-3 Describe the difference between cross-sectional data and time series data.

LO1-4 Construct and interpret a time series (runs) plot.

Cross-sectional and time series data   Some statistical techniques are used to analyze *cross-sectional data,* while others are used to analyze *time series data.* **Cross-sectional data** are data collected at the same or approximately the same point in time. For example, suppose that a bank wishes to analyze last month's cell phone bills for its employees. Then, because the cell phone costs given by these bills are for different employees in the same month, the cell phone costs are cross-sectional data. **Time series data** are data collected over different time periods. For example, Table 1.2 presents the average basic cable television rate in the United States for each of the years 1999 to 2009. Figure 1.1 is a **time series plot**—also called a **runs plot**—of these data. Here we plot each television rate on the vertical scale versus its corresponding time index on the horizontal scale. For instance, the first cable rate ($28.92) is plotted versus 1999, the second cable rate ($30.37) is plotted versus 2000, and so forth. Examining the time series plot, we see that the cable rates increased substantially from 1999 to 2009. Finally, because the five homes in Table 1.1 were sold over a three-month period that represented a relatively stable real estate market, we can consider the data in Table 1.1 to essentially be cross-sectional data.

---

[1]Optional Section 1.5 discusses two types of quantitative variables (ratio and interval) and two types of qualitative variables (ordinal and nominative).

TABLE 1.2	The Average Basic Cable Rates in the U.S. from 1999 to 2009 DS BasicCable

Year	Average Basic Cable Rate
1999	$ 28.92
2000	30.37
2001	32.87
2002	34.71
2003	36.59
2004	38.14
2005	39.63
2006	41.17
2007	42.72
2008	44.28
2009	46.13

Source: U.S. Energy Information Administration, http://www.eia.gov/

FIGURE 1.1 Time Series Plot of the Average Basic Cable Rates in the U.S. from 1999 to 2009 DS BasicCable

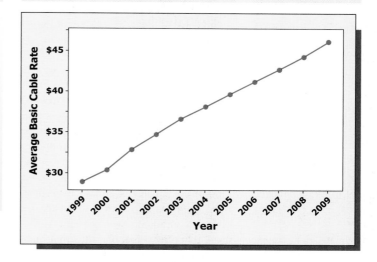

1.2 Data Sources ● ● ●

Data can be obtained from *existing sources* or from **experimental and observational studies.**

Existing sources   Sometimes we can use data *already gathered* by public or private sources. The Internet is an obvious place to search for electronic versions of government publications, company reports, and business journals, but there is also a wealth of information available in the reference section of a good library or in county courthouse records.

If a business needs information about incomes in the Northeastern states, a natural source is the US Census Bureau's website at http://www.census.gov. By following various links posted on the homepage, you can find income and demographic data for specific regions of the country. Other useful websites for economic and financial data are listed in Table 1.3. All of these are trustworthy sources.

LO1-5 Identify the different types of data sources: existing data sources, experimental studies, and observational studies.

TABLE 1.3	Examples of Public Economic and Financial Data Sites	
Title	**Website**	**Data Type**
Global Financial Data	https://www.globalfinancialdata.com/index.html	Annual data on stock markets, inflation rates, interest rates, exchange rates, etc.
National Bureau of Economic Research Macrohistory Database	http://www.nber.org/databases/macrohistory/contents/index.html	Historic data on production, construction, employment, money, prices, asset market transactions, foreign trade, and government activity
Federal Reserve Economic Data	http://research.stlouisfed.org/fred2/	Historical U.S. economic and financial data, including daily U.S. interest rates, monetary and business indicators, exchange rate, balance of payments, and regional economic data
Bureau of Labor Statistics	http://stats.bls.gov/	Data concerning employment, inflation, consumer spending, productivity, safety, labor demographics, and the like.
WebEc Economics Data	http://netec.wustl.edu/WebEc/	One of the best complete economics data links including both international and domestic data categorized by area and country
Economic Statistics Briefing Room	http://clinton2.nara.gov/fsbr/esbr.htm	Links to the most current available values of federal economic indicators in 8 categories

Source: Prepared by Lan Ma and Jeffrey S. Simonoff. The authors provide no warranty as to the accuracy of the information provided.

However, given the ease with which anyone can post documents, pictures, weblogs, and videos on the World Wide Web, not all sites are equally reliable. If we were to use a search engine from Google, Netscape, Yahoo, Ask.com, or AltaVista (just to name a few) to find information about the price of a two-bedroom apartment in Manhattan, we would be inundated by millions of "hits." (In fact, a recent search on Google using the keywords "price 2 bedroom apartments Manhattan" yielded 1,040,000 sites.) Some of the sources will be more useful, exhaustive, and error-free than others. Fortunately, the search engines prioritize the lists and provide the most relevant and highly used sites first.

Obviously, performing such web searches costs next to nothing and takes relatively little time, but the tradeoff is that we are also limited in terms of the type of information we are able to find. Another option may be to use a private data source. Most companies keep employee records, for example, and retail establishments retain information about their customers, products, and advertising results. Manufacturing companies may collect information about their processes and defect propagation in order to monitor quality. If we have no affiliation with these companies, however, these data may be more difficult to obtain.

Another alternative would be to contact a data collection agency, which typically incurs some kind of cost. You can either buy subscriptions or purchase individual company financial reports from agencies like Dun & Bradstreet, Bloomberg, Dow Jones & Company, Travel Industry of America, Graduate Management Admission Council, and the Educational Testing Service. If you need to collect specific information, some companies, such as ACNielsen and Information Resources, Inc., can be hired to collect the information for a fee.

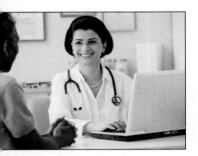

Experimental and observational studies   There are many instances when the data we need are not readily available from a public or private source. The data might not have been collected at all or they may have been collected in a statistically unsound manner. In cases like these, we need to collect the data ourselves. Suppose we work for a soft drink producer and want to assess consumer reactions to a new bottled water. Since the water has not been marketed yet, we may choose to conduct taste tests, focus groups, or some other market research. Projecting political election results also requires information that is not readily available. In this case, exit polls and telephone surveys are commonly used to obtain the information needed to predict voting trends. New drugs for fighting disease are tested by collecting data under carefully controlled and monitored experimental conditions. In many marketing, political, and medical situations of these sorts, companies hire outside consultants or statisticians to help them obtain appropriate data. Regardless of whether newly minted data are gathered in-house or by paid outsiders, this type of data collection requires much more time, effort, and expense than are needed when data can be found from public or private sources.

When initiating a study, we first define our variable of interest, or **response variable.** Other variables, typically called **factors,** that may be related to the response variable of interest will also be measured. When we are able to set or manipulate the values of these factors, we have an **experimental study.** For example, a pharmaceutical company might wish to determine the most appropriate daily dose of a cholesterol-lowering drug for patients having cholesterol levels over 240 mg/dL, a level associated with a high risk of coronary disease. (http://www.heart.org/HEARTORG/Conditions/Cholesterol/AboutCholesterol/What-Your-Cholesterol-Levels-Mean_UCM_305562_Article.jsp) The company can perform an experiment in which one sample of patients receives a placebo; a second sample receives some low dose; a third a higher dose; and so forth. This is an experiment because the company controls the amount of drug each group receives. The optimal daily dose can be determined by analyzing the patients' responses to the different dosage levels given.

When analysts are unable to control the factors of interest, the study is **observational.** In studies of diet and cholesterol, patients' diets are not under the analyst's control. Patients are often unwilling or unable to follow prescribed diets; doctors might simply ask patients what they eat and then look for associations between the factor *diet* and the response variable *cholesterol.*

Asking people what they eat is an example of performing a **survey.** In general, people in a survey are asked questions about their behaviors, opinions, beliefs, and other characteristics. For instance, shoppers at a mall might be asked to fill out a short questionnaire which seeks their opinions about a new bottled water. In other observational studies, we might simply observe the behavior of people. For example, we might observe the behavior of shoppers as they look at a store display, or we might observe the interactions between students and teachers.

Exercises for Sections 1.1 and 1.2

CONCEPTS

connect

1.1 Define what we mean by a *variable,* and explain the difference between a quantitative variable and a qualitative (categorical) variable.

1.2 Below we list several variables. Which of these variables are quantitative and which are qualitative? Explain.

  a The dollar amount on an accounts receivable invoice.
  b The net profit for a company in 2009.
  c The stock exchange on which a company's stock is traded.
  d The national debt of the United States in 2009.
  e The advertising medium (radio, television, or print) used to promote a product.

1.3 Discuss the difference between cross-sectional data and time series data. If we record the total number of cars sold in 2011 by each of 10 car salespeople, are the data cross-sectional or time series data? If we record the total number of cars sold by a particular car salesperson in each of the years 2007, 2008, 2009, 2010, and 2011, are the data cross-sectional or time series data?

1.4 Consider a medical study that is being performed to test the effect of smoking on lung cancer. Two groups of subjects are identified; one group has lung cancer and the other one doesn't. Both are asked to fill out a questionnaire containing questions about their age, sex, occupation, and number of cigarettes smoked per day. What is the response variable? Which are the factors? What type of study is this (experimental or observational)?

METHODS AND APPLICATIONS

1.5 Consider the five homes in Table 1.1 (page 3). What do you think you would have to pay for a Ruby model on a treed lot?

1.6 Consider the five homes in Table 1.1 (page 3). What do you think you would have to pay for a Diamond model on a lake lot? For a Ruby model on a lake lot?

1.7 The number of Bismark X-12 electronic calculators sold at Smith's Department Stores over the past 24 months have been: 197, 211, 203, 247, 239, 269, 308, 262, 258, 256, 261, 288, 296, 276, 305, 308, 356, 393, 363, 386, 443, 308, 358, and 384. Make a time series plot of these data. That is, plot 197 versus month 1, 211 versus month 2, and so forth. What does the time series plot tell you? **DS** CalcSale

1.3 Populations and Samples ● ● ●

We often collect data in order to study a population.

LO1-6 Describe the difference between a population and a sample.

A **population** is the set of all elements about which we wish to draw conclusions.

Examples of populations include (1) all of last year's graduates of Dartmouth College's Master of Business Administration program, (2) all current MasterCard cardholders, and (3) all Buick LaCrosses that have been or will be produced this year.

   We usually focus on studying one or more variables describing the population elements. If we carry out a measurement to assign a value of a variable to each and every population element, we have a *population of measurements* (sometimes called *observations*). If the population is small, it is reasonable to do this. For instance, if 150 students graduated last year from the Dartmouth College MBA program, it might be feasible to survey the graduates and to record all of their starting salaries. In general:

If we examine all of the population measurements, we say that we are conducting a **census** of the population.

   Often the population that we wish to study is very large, and it is too time-consuming or costly to conduct a census. In such a situation, we select and analyze a subset (or portion) of the population elements.

A **sample** is a subset of the elements of a population.

For example, suppose that 8,742 students graduated last year from a large state university. It would probably be too time-consuming to take a census of the population of all of their starting salaries. Therefore, we would select a sample of graduates, and we would obtain and record their starting salaries. When we measure a characteristic of the elements in a sample, we have a **sample of measurements.**

We often wish to describe a population or sample.

Descriptive statistics is the science of describing the important aspects of a set of measurements.

As an example, if we are studying a set of starting salaries, we might wish to describe (1) how large or small they tend to be, (2) what a typical salary might be, and (3) how much the salaries differ from each other.

When the population of interest is small and we can conduct a census of the population, we will be able to directly describe the important aspects of the population measurements. However, if the population is large and we need to select a sample from it, then we use what we call **statistical inference.**

Statistical inference is the science of using a sample of measurements to make generalizations about the important aspects of a population of measurements.

For instance, we might use a sample of starting salaries to **estimate** the important aspects of a population of starting salaries. In the next section, we begin to look at how statistical inference is carried out.

1.4 Three Case Studies That Illustrate Sampling and Statistical Inference ● ● ●

Random samples   When we select a sample from a population, we hope that the information contained in the sample reflects what is true about the population. One of the best ways to achieve this goal is to select a *random sample*. In Section 7.1 we will precisely define a random sample.[2] For now, it suffices to know that one intuitive way to select a random sample would begin by placing numbered slips of paper representing the population elements in a suitable container. We would thoroughly mix the slips of paper and (blindfolded) choose slips of paper from the container. The numbers on the chosen slips of paper would identify the randomly selected population elements that make up the random sample. In Section 7.1 we will discuss more practical methods for selecting a random sample. We will also see that, although in many situations it is not possible to select a sample that is exactly random, we can sometimes select a sample that is approximately random.

We now introduce three case studies that illustrate the need for a random (or approximately random) sample and the use of such a sample in making statistical inferences. After studying these cases, the reader has the option of studying Section 7.1 (see page 267) and learning practical ways to select random and approximately random samples.

EXAMPLE 1.1 The Cell Phone Case: Reducing Cellular Phone Costs

Part 1: The cost of company cell phone use   Rising cell phone costs have forced companies having large numbers of cellular users to hire services to manage their cellular and other wireless resources. These cellular management services use sophisticated software and mathematical models to choose cost-efficient cell phone plans for their clients. One such firm, mindWireless of Austin, Texas, specializes in automated wireless cost management. According to Kevin Whitehurst, co-founder of mindWireless, cell phone carriers count on *overage*—using more minutes than one's plan allows—and *underage*—using fewer minutes than those already paid for—to deliver almost half of their revenues.[3] As a result, a company's typical cost of cell phone use can be excessive—18 cents per minute or more. However, Mr. Whitehurst explains that by using mindWireless automated cost management to select calling plans, this cost can be reduced to 12 cents per minute or less.

In this case we consider a bank that wishes to decide whether to hire a cellular management service to choose its employees' calling plans. While the bank has over 10,000 employees on

---

[2]Actually, there are several different kinds of random samples. The type we will define is sometimes called a *simple random sample*. For brevity's sake, however, we will use the term *random sample*.

[3]The authors would like to thank Kevin Whitehurst for help in developing this case.

TABLE 1.4	A Sample of Cellular Usages (in minutes) for 100 Randomly Selected Employees
	DS CellUse

75	485	37	547	753	93	897	694	797	477
654	578	504	670	490	225	509	247	597	173
496	553	0	198	507	157	672	296	774	479
0	822	705	814	20	513	546	801	721	273
879	433	420	521	648	41	528	359	367	948
511	704	535	585	341	530	216	512	491	0
542	562	49	505	461	496	241	624	885	259
571	338	503	529	737	444	372	555	290	830
719	120	468	730	853	18	479	144	24	513
482	683	212	418	399	376	323	173	669	611

many different types of calling plans, a cellular management service suggests that by studying the calling patterns of cellular users on 500-minute-per-month plans, the bank can accurately assess whether its cell phone costs can be substantially reduced. The bank has 2,136 employees on a variety of 500-minute-per-month plans with different basic monthly rates, different overage charges, and different additional charges for long distance and roaming. It would be extremely time consuming to analyze in detail the cell phone bills of all 2,136 employees. Therefore, the bank will estimate its cellular costs for the 500-minute plans by analyzing last month's cell phone bills for a *random sample* of 100 employees on these plans.[4]

Part 2: A random sample   When the random sample of 100 employees is chosen, the number of cellular minutes used by each sampled employee during last month (the employee's *cellular usage*) is found and recorded. The 100 cellular-usage figures are given in Table 1.4. Looking at this table, we can see that there is substantial overage and underage—many employees used far more than 500 minutes, while many others failed to use all of the 500 minutes allowed by their plan. In Chapter 3 we will use these 100 usage figures to estimate the bank's cellular costs and decide whether the bank should hire a cellular management service.

EXAMPLE 1.2 The Marketing Research Case: Rating a Bottle Design

Part 1: Rating a bottle design   The design of a package or bottle can have an important effect on a company's bottom line. In this case a brand group wishes to research consumer reaction to a new bottle design for a popular soft drink. To do this, the brand group will show consumers the new bottle and ask them to rate the bottle image. For each consumer interviewed, a bottle image **composite score** will be found by adding the consumer's numerical responses to the five questions shown in Figure 1.2. It follows that the minimum possible bottle image composite

FIGURE 1.2	The Bottle Design Survey Instrument

Please circle the response that most accurately describes whether you agree or disagree with each statement about the bottle you have examined.

Statement	Strongly Disagree						Strongly Agree
The size of this bottle is convenient.	1	2	3	4	5	6	7
The contoured shape of this bottle is easy to handle.	1	2	3	4	5	6	7
The label on this bottle is easy to read.	1	2	3	4	5	6	7
This bottle is easy to open.	1	2	3	4	5	6	7
Based on its overall appeal, I like this bottle design.	1	2	3	4	5	6	7

[4]In Chapter 8 we will discuss how to plan the *sample size*—the number of elements (for example, 100) that should be included in a sample. Throughout this book we will take large enough samples to allow us to make reasonably accurate statistical inferences.

TABLE 1.5	A Sample of Bottle Design Ratings (Composite Scores for a Sample of 60 Shoppers) DS Design								
34	33	33	29	26	33	28	25	32	33
32	25	27	33	22	27	32	33	32	29
24	30	20	34	31	32	30	35	33	31
32	28	30	31	31	33	29	27	34	31
31	28	33	31	32	28	26	29	32	34
32	30	34	32	30	30	32	31	29	33

score is 5 (resulting from a response of 1 on all five questions) and the maximum possible bottle image composite score is 35 (resulting from a response of 7 on all five questions). Furthermore, experience has shown that the smallest acceptable bottle image composite score for a successful bottle design is 25.

Part 2: An approximately random sample   Because it is impossible to show the new bottle to "all consumers," the brand group will use the *mall intercept method* to select a sample of consumers. This method chooses a mall and a sampling time so that shoppers at the mall during the sampling time are a representative cross-section of all consumers. Then, shoppers are intercepted as they walk past a designated location in such a way that an approximately random sample of shoppers at the mall is selected. When the brand group uses this mall intercept method to interview a sample of 60 shoppers at a mall on a particular Saturday, the 60 bottle image composite scores in Table 1.5 are obtained. Because these scores vary from a minimum of 20 to a maximum of 35, we might infer that *most* consumers would rate the new bottle design between 20 and 35. Furthermore, 57 of the 60 composite scores are at least 25. Therefore, we might estimate that a proportion of 57/60 = .95 (that is, 95 percent) of all consumers would give the bottle design a composite score of at least 25. In future chapters we will further analyze the composite scores.

Processes   Sometimes we are interested in studying the population of all of the elements that will be or could potentially be produced by a *process*.

> A **process** is a sequence of operations that takes inputs (labor, materials, methods, machines, and so on) and turns them into outputs (products, services, and the like).

Processes produce output *over time*. For example, this year's Buick LaCrosse manufacturing process produces LaCrosses over time. Early in the model year, General Motors might wish to study the population of the city driving mileages of all Buick LaCrosses that will be produced during the model year. Or, even more hypothetically, General Motors might wish to study the population of the city driving mileages of all LaCrosses that could *potentially* be produced by this model year's manufacturing process. The first population is called a **finite population** because only a finite number of cars will be produced during the year. The second population is called an **infinite population** because the manufacturing process that produces this year's model could in theory always be used to build "one more car." That is, theoretically there is no limit to the number of cars that could be produced by this year's process. There are a multitude of other examples of finite or infinite hypothetical populations. For instance, we might study the population of all waiting times that will or could potentially be experienced by patients of a hospital emergency room. Or we might study the population of all the amounts of grape jelly that will be or could potentially be dispensed into 16-ounce jars by an automated filling machine. To study a population of potential process observations, we sample the process—often at equally spaced time points—over time.

EXAMPLE 1.3 The Car Mileage Case: Estimating Mileage

Part 1: Auto fuel economy   Personal budgets, national energy security, and the global environment are all affected by our gasoline consumption. Hybrid and electric cars are a vital part of a long-term strategy to reduce our nation's gasoline consumption. However, until use of these cars is

TABLE 1.6		A Sample of 50 Mileages			DS GasMiles
30.8	30.8	32.1	32.3	32.7	**Note: Time**
31.7	30.4	31.4	32.7	31.4	**order is given**
30.1	32.5	30.8	31.2	31.8	**by reading**
31.6	30.3	32.8	30.7	31.9	**down the**
32.1	31.3	31.9	31.7	33.0	**columns from**
33.3	32.1	31.4	31.4	31.5	**left to right.**
31.3	32.5	32.4	32.2	31.6	
31.0	31.8	31.0	31.5	30.6	
32.0	30.5	29.8	31.7	32.3	
32.4	30.5	31.1	30.7	31.4	

FIGURE 1.3   **A Time Series Plot of the 50 Mileages**

more widespread and affordable, the most effective way to conserve gasoline is to design gasoline powered cars that are more fuel efficient.[5] In the short term, "that will give you the biggest bang for your buck," says David Friedman, research director of the Union of Concerned Scientists' Clean Vehicle Program.[6]

In this case study we consider a tax credit offered by the federal government to automakers for improving the fuel economy of gasoline powered midsize cars. According to *The Fuel Economy Guide—2012 Model Year,* virtually every gasoline powered midsize car equipped with an automatic transmission has an EPA combined city and highway mileage estimate of 26 miles per gallon (mpg) or less.[7] Furthermore, the EPA has concluded that a 5 mpg increase in fuel economy is significant and feasible.[8] Therefore, suppose that the government has decided to offer the tax credit to any automaker selling a midsize model with an automatic transmission that achieves an EPA combined city and highway mileage estimate of at least 31 mpg.

Part 2: Sampling a process   Consider an automaker that has recently introduced a new midsize model with an automatic transmission and wishes to demonstrate that this new model qualifies for the tax credit. In order to study the population of all cars of this type that will or could potentially be produced, the automaker will choose a sample of 50 of these cars. The manufacturer's production operation runs 8 hour shifts, with 100 midsize cars produced on each shift. When the production process has been fine tuned and all start-up problems have been identified and corrected, the automaker will select one car at random from each of 50 consecutive production shifts. Once selected, each car is to be subjected to an EPA test that determines the EPA combined city and highway mileage of the car.

Suppose that when the 50 cars are selected and tested, the sample of 50 EPA combined mileages shown in Table 1.6 is obtained. A time series plot of the mileages is given in Figure 1.3. Examining this plot, we see that, although the mileages vary over time, they do not seem to vary in any unusual way. For example, the mileages do not tend to either decrease or increase (as did the basic cable rates in Figure 1.1) over time. This intuitively verifies that the midsize car manufacturing process is producing consistent car mileages over time, and thus we can regard the 50 mileages as an approximately random sample that can be used to make statistical inferences about the population of all possible midsize car mileages. Therefore, because the 50 mileages vary from a minimum of 29.8 mpg to a maximum of 33.3 mpg, we might conclude that most midsize cars produced by the manufacturing process will obtain between 29.8 mpg and 33.3 mpg. Moreover, because 38 out of the 50 mileages—or 76 percent of the mileages—are greater than or equal to the tax credit standard of 31 mpg, we have some evidence that the "typical car" produced by the process will meet or exceed the tax credit standard. We will further evaluate this evidence in later chapters.

[5, 6]Bryan Walsh, "Plugged In," *Time*, September 29, 2008 (see page 56).

[7]The "26 miles per gallon (mpg) or less" figure relates to midsize cars with an automatic transmission *and* at least a 4 cylinder, 2.4 liter engine (such cars are the most popular midsize models). Therefore, when we refer to a midsize car with an automatic transmission in future discussions, we are assuming that the midsize car also has at least a 4 cylinder, 2.4 liter engine.

[8]The authors wish to thank Jeff Alson of the EPA for this information.

Ethical guidelines for statistical practice   The American Statistical Association, the leading U.S. professional statistical association, has developed the report "Ethical Guidelines for Statistical Practice."[9] This report provides information that helps statistical practitioners to consistently use ethical statistical practices and that helps users of statistical information avoid being misled by unethical statistical practices. Unethical statistical practices can take a variety of forms, including:

- **Improper sampling**   Purposely selecting a biased sample—for example, using a nonrandom sampling procedure that overrepresents population elements supporting a desired conclusion or that underrepresents population elements not supporting the desired conclusion—is unethical. In addition, discarding already sampled population elements that do not support the desired conclusion is unethical. More will be said about proper and improper sampling in Chapter 7.

- **Misleading charts, graphs, and descriptive measures**   In Section 2.7, we will present an example of how misleading charts and graphs can distort the perception of changes in salaries over time. Using misleading charts or graphs to make the salary changes seem much larger or much smaller than they really are is unethical. In Section 3.1, we will present an example illustrating that many populations of individual or household incomes contain a small percentage of very high incomes. These very high incomes make the *population mean income* substantially larger than the *population median income*. In this situation we will see that the population median income is a better measure of the typical income in the population. Using the population mean income to give an inflated perception of the typical income in the population is unethical.

- **Inappropriate statistical analysis or inappropriate interpretation of statistical results**   The American Statistical Association report emphasizes that selecting many different samples and running many different tests can eventually (by random chance alone) produce a result that makes a desired conclusion seem to be true, when the conclusion really isn't true. Therefore, continuing to sample and run tests until a desired conclusion is obtained and not reporting previously obtained results that do not support the desired conclusion is unethical. Furthermore, we should always report our sampling procedure and sample size and give an estimate of the reliability of our statistical results. Estimating this reliability will be discussed in Chapter 7 and beyond.

The above examples are just an introduction to the important topic of unethical statistical practices. The American Statistical Association report contains 67 guidelines organized into eight areas involving general professionalism and ethical responsibilities. These include responsibilities to clients, to research team colleagues, to research subjects, and to other statisticians, as well as responsibilities in publications and testimony and responsibilities of those who employ statistical practitioners.

Exercises for Sections 1.3 and 1.4

CONCEPTS

connect

1.8   Define a *population*. Give an example of a population.

1.9   Explain the difference between a census and a sample.

1.10   Explain the term *descriptive statistics*. Explain the term *statistical inference*.

1.11   Define a process.

METHODS AND APPLICATIONS

1.12   THE VIDEO GAME SATISFACTION RATING CASE   DS VideoGame

A company that produces and markets video game systems wishes to assess its customers' level of satisfaction with a relatively new model, the XYZ-Box. In the six months since the introduction of the model, the company has received 73,219 warranty registrations from purchasers. The company

---
[9]American Statistical Association, "Ethical Guidelines for Statistical Practice," 1999.

will select a random sample of 65 of these registrations and will conduct telephone interviews with the purchasers. Specifically, each purchaser will be asked to state his or her level of agreement with each of the seven statements listed on the survey instrument given in Figure 1.4. Here, the level of agreement for each statement is measured on a 7-point Likert scale. Purchaser satisfaction will be measured by adding the purchaser's responses to the seven statements. It follows that for each consumer the minimum composite score possible is 7 and the maximum is 49. Furthermore, experience has shown that a purchaser of a video game system is "very satisfied" if his or her composite score is at least 42. Suppose that when the 65 customers are interviewed, their composite scores are as given in Table 1.7. Using the data, estimate limits between which most of the 73,219 composite scores would fall. Also, estimate the proportion of the 73,219 composite scores that would be at least 42.

1.13   THE BANK CUSTOMER WAITING TIME CASE   ⒹⓈ WaitTime

A bank manager has developed a new system to reduce the time customers spend waiting to be served by tellers during peak business hours. Typical waiting times during peak business hours under the current system are roughly 9 to 10 minutes. The bank manager hopes that the new system will lower typical waiting times to less than six minutes and wishes to evaluate the new system. When the new system is operating consistently over time, the bank manager decides to select a sample of 100 customers that need teller service during peak business hours. Specifically, for each of 100 peak business hours, the first customer that starts waiting for teller service at or after a randomly selected time during the hour will be chosen. In Exercise 7.5 (see page 271) we will discuss how to obtain a randomly selected time during an hour. When each customer is chosen, the number of minutes the customer spends waiting for teller service is recorded. The 100 waiting times that are observed are given in Table 1.8. Using the data, estimate limits between which the waiting times of most of the customers arriving during peak business hours would be. Also, estimate the proportion of waiting times of customers arriving during peak business hours that are less than six minutes.

FIGURE 1.4   The Video Game Satisfaction Survey Instrument

Statement	Strongly Disagree						Strongly Agree
The game console of the XYZ-Box is well designed.	1	2	3	4	5	6	7
The game controller of the XYZ-Box is easy to handle.	1	2	3	4	5	6	7
The XYZ-Box has high quality graphics capabilities.	1	2	3	4	5	6	7
The XYZ-Box has high quality audio capabilities.	1	2	3	4	5	6	7
The XYZ-Box serves as a complete entertainment center.	1	2	3	4	5	6	7
There is a large selection of XYZ-Box games to choose from.	1	2	3	4	5	6	7
I am totally satisfied with my XYZ-Box game system.	1	2	3	4	5	6	7

TABLE 1.7   Composite Scores for the Video Game Satisfaction Rating Case   ⒹⓈ VideoGame

39	44	46	44	44
45	42	45	44	42
38	46	45	45	47
42	40	46	44	43
42	47	43	46	45
41	44	47	48	
38	43	43	44	
42	45	41	41	
46	45	40	45	
44	40	43	44	
40	46	44	44	
39	41	41	44	
40	43	38	46	
42	39	43	39	
45	43	36	41	

TABLE 1.8   Waiting Times (in Minutes) for the Bank Customer Waiting Time Case   ⒹⓈ WaitTime

1.6	6.2	3.2	5.6	7.9	6.1	7.2
6.6	5.4	6.5	4.4	1.1	3.8	7.3
5.6	4.9	2.3	4.5	7.2	10.7	4.1
5.1	5.4	8.7	6.7	2.9	7.5	6.7
3.9	.8	4.7	8.1	9.1	7.0	3.5
4.6	2.5	3.6	4.3	7.7	5.3	6.3
6.5	8.3	2.7	2.2	4.0	4.5	4.3
6.4	6.1	3.7	5.8	1.4	4.5	3.8
8.6	6.3	.4	8.6	7.8	1.8	5.1
4.2	6.8	10.2	2.0	5.2	3.7	5.5
5.8	9.8	2.8	8.0	8.4	4.0	
3.4	2.9	11.6	9.5	6.3	5.7	
9.3	10.9	4.3	1.3	4.4	2.4	
7.4	4.7	3.1	4.8	5.2	9.2	
1.8	3.9	5.8	9.9	7.4	5.0	

TABLE 1.9
Trash Bag Breaking Strengths
DS TrashBag

48.5	50.7
52.3	48.2
53.5	51.5
50.5	49.0
50.3	51.7
49.6	53.2
51.0	51.1
48.3	52.6
50.6	51.2
50.2	49.5
52.5	49.4
47.5	51.9
50.9	52.0
49.8	48.8
50.0	46.8
50.8	51.3
53.0	49.3
50.9	54.0
49.9	49.2
50.1	51.4

Time Series Plot of Strength

LO1-9 Identify the ratio, interval, ordinal, and nominative scales of measurement (Optional).

1.14   THE TRASH BAG CASE[10]   DS TrashBag

A company that produces and markets trash bags has developed an improved 30-gallon bag. The new bag is produced using a specially formulated plastic that is both stronger and more biodegradable than previously used plastics, and the company wishes to evaluate the strength of this bag. The *breaking strength* of a trash bag is considered to be the amount (in pounds) of a representative trash mix that when loaded into a bag suspended in the air will cause the bag to sustain significant damage (such as ripping or tearing). The company has decided to select a sample of 40 of the new trash bags. For each of 40 consecutive hours, the first trash bag produced at or after a randomly selected time during the hour is chosen. The bag is then subjected to a *breaking strength test*. The 40 breaking strengths obtained are given in Table 1.9. Estimate limits between which the breaking strengths of most trash bags would fall. Assume that the trash bag manufacturing process is operating consistently over time.

1.5 Ratio, Interval, Ordinal, and Nominative Scales of Measurement (Optional) ● ● ●

In Section 1.1 we said that a variable is **quantitative** if its possible values are *numbers that represent quantities* (that is, "how much" or "how many"). In general, a quantitative variable is measured on a scale having a *fixed unit of measurement* between its possible values. For example, if we measure employees' salaries to the nearest dollar, then one dollar is the fixed unit of measurement between different employees' salaries. There are two types of quantitative variables: **ratio** and **interval.** A **ratio variable** is a quantitative variable measured on a scale such that ratios of its values are meaningful and there is an inherently defined zero value. Variables such as salary, height, weight, time, and distance are ratio variables. For example, a distance of zero miles is "no distance at all," and a town that is 30 miles away is "twice as far" as a town that is 15 miles away.

An **interval variable** is a quantitative variable where ratios of its values are not meaningful and there is not an inherently defined zero value. Temperature (on the Fahrenheit scale) is an interval variable. For example, zero degrees Fahrenheit does not represent "no heat at all," just that it is very cold. Thus, there is no inherently defined zero value. Furthermore, ratios of temperatures are not meaningful. For example, it makes no sense to say that 60° is twice as warm as 30°. In practice, there are very few interval variables other than temperature. Almost all quantitative variables are ratio variables.

In Section 1.1 we also said that if we simply record into which of several categories a population (or sample) unit falls, then the variable is **qualitative** (or **categorical**). There are two types of qualitative variables: **ordinal** and **nominative.** An **ordinal variable** is a qualitative variable for which there is a meaningful *ordering,* or *ranking,* of the categories. The measurements of an ordinal variable may be nonnumerical or numerical. For example, a student may be asked to rate the teaching effectiveness of a college professor as excellent, good, average, poor, or unsatisfactory. Here, one category is higher than the next one; that is, "excellent" is a higher rating than "good," "good" is a higher rating than "average," and so on. Therefore, teaching effectiveness is an ordinal variable having nonnumerical measurements. On the other hand, if (as is often done) we substitute the numbers 4, 3, 2, 1, and 0 for the ratings excellent through unsatisfactory, then teaching effectiveness is an ordinal variable having numerical measurements.

In practice, both numbers and associated words are often presented to respondents asked to rate a person or item. When numbers are used, statisticians debate whether the ordinal variable is "somewhat quantitative." For example, statisticians who claim that teaching effectiveness rated as 4, 3, 2, 1, or 0 is *not* somewhat quantitative argue that the difference between 4 (excellent) and 3 (good) may not be the same as the difference between 3 (good) and 2 (average). Other statisticians argue that as soon as respondents (students) see equally spaced numbers (even though the numbers are described by words), their responses are affected enough to make the variable (teaching effectiveness) somewhat quantitative. Generally speaking, the specific words associated with the numbers probably substantially affect whether an ordinal variable may be

---

[10]This case is based on conversations by the authors with several employees working for a leading producer of trash bags. For purposes of confidentiality, we have withheld the company's name.

considered somewhat quantitative. It is important to note, however, that in practice numerical ordinal ratings are often analyzed as though they are quantitative. Specifically, various arithmetic operations (as discussed in Chapters 2 through 14) are often performed on numerical ordinal ratings. For example, a professor's teaching effectiveness average and a student's grade point average are calculated.

To conclude this section, we consider the second type of qualitative variable. A **nominative variable** is a qualitative variable for which there is no meaningful ordering, or ranking, of the categories. A person's gender, the color of a car, and an employee's state of residence are nominative variables.

Exercises for Section 1.5

CONCEPTS

1.15 Discuss the difference between a ratio variable and an interval variable.

1.16 Discuss the difference between an ordinal variable and a nominative variable.

connect

METHODS AND APPLICATIONS

1.17 Classify each of the following qualitative variables as ordinal or nominative. Explain your answers.

Qualitative Variable	Categories
Statistics course letter grade	A B C D F
Door choice on *Let's Make A Deal*	Door #1 Door #2
Television show classifications	TV-G TV-PG TV-14 TV-MA
Personal computer ownership	Yes No
Restaurant rating	***** **** *** ** *
Income tax filing status	Married filing jointly Married filing separately Single Head of household Qualifying widow(er)

1.18 Classify each of the following qualitative variables as ordinal or nominative. Explain your answers.

Qualitative Variable	Categories
Personal computer operating system	DOS Windows XP Windows Vista Windows 7
Motion picture classifications	G PG PG-13 R NC-17 X
Level of education	Elementary Middle school High school College Graduate school
Rankings of the top 10 college football teams	1 2 3 4 5 6 7 8 9 10
Exchange on which a stock is traded	AMEX NYSE NASDAQ Other
Zip code	45056 90015 etc.

Chapter Summary

We began this chapter by discussing **data.** We learned that the data that are collected for a particular study are referred to as a **data set,** and we learned that **elements** are the entities described by a data set. In order to determine what information we need about a group of elements, we define important **variables,** or characteristics, describing the elements. **Quantitative variables** are variables that use numbers to measure quantities (that is, "how much" or "how many") and **qualitative, or categorical, variables** simply record into which of several categories an element falls.

We next discussed the difference between cross-sectional data and time series data. **Cross-sectional data** are data collected at the same or approximately the same point in time. **Time series data** are data collected over different time periods. There are various **sources of data.** Specifically, we can obtain data from **existing sources** or from **experimental or observational studies** done in-house or by paid outsiders.

We often collect data to study a **population,** which is the set of all elements about which we wish to draw conclusions. We saw that, since many populations are too large to examine in their entirety, we frequently study a population by selecting a **sample,** which is a subset of the population elements. Next we learned that, if the information contained in a sample is to accurately represent the population, then the sample should be **randomly selected** from the population.

We concluded this chapter with optional Section 1.5, which considered different types of quantitative and qualitative variables. We learned that there are two types of **quantitative variables—ratio variables,** which are measured on a scale such that ratios of its values are meaningful and there is an inherently defined zero value, and **interval variables,** for which ratios are not meaningful and there is no inherently defined zero value. We also saw that there are two types of **qualitative variables—ordinal variables,** for which there is a meaningful ordering of the categories, and **nominative variables,** for which there is no meaningful ordering of the categories.

Glossary of Terms

categorical (qualitative) variable: A variable having values that indicate into which of several categories a population element belongs. (pages 4, 14)

census: An examination of all the elements in a population. (page 7)

cross-sectional data: Data collected at the same or approximately the same point in time. (page 4)

data: Facts and figures from which conclusions can be drawn. (page 3)

data set: Facts and figures, taken together, that are collected for a statistical study. (page 3)

descriptive statistics: The science of describing the important aspects of a set of measurements. (page 8)

element: A person, object, or other entity about which we wish to draw a conclusion. (page 3)

experimental study: A statistical study in which the analyst is able to set or manipulate the values of the factors. (page 6)

factor: A variable that may be related to the response variable. (page 6)

finite population: A population that contains a finite number of elements. (page 10)

infinite population: A population that is defined so that there is no limit to the number of elements that could potentially belong to the population. (page 10)

interval variable: A quantitative variable such that ratios of its values are not meaningful and for which there is not an inherently defined zero value. (page 14)

measurement: The process of assigning a value of a variable to an element in a population or sample. (page 4)

nominative variable: A qualitative variable for which there is no meaningful ordering, or ranking, of the categories. (page 15)

observational study: A statistical study in which the analyst is not able to control the values of the factors. (page 6)

ordinal variable: A qualitative variable for which there is a meaningful ordering or ranking of the categories. (page 14)

population: The set of all elements about which we wish to draw conclusions. (page 7)

process: A sequence of operations that takes inputs and turns them into outputs. (page 10)

qualitative (categorical) variable: A variable having values that indicate into which of several categories a population element belongs. (pages 4, 14)

quantitative variable: A variable having values that are numbers representing quantities. (pages 4, 14)

ratio variable: A quantitative variable such that ratios of its values are meaningful and for which there is an inherently defined zero value. (page 14)

response variable: A variable of interest that we wish to study. (page 6)

sample: A subset of the elements in a population. (page 7)

statistical inference: The science of using a sample of measurements to make generalizations about the important aspects of a population. (page 8)

survey: An instrument employed to collect data. (page 6)

time series data: Data collected over different time periods. (page 4)

time series plot (runs plot): A plot of time series data versus time. (page 4)

variable: A characteristic of a population or sample element. (page 3)

Supplementary Exercises

1.19   THE COFFEE TEMPERATURE CASE ⓭ Coffee

According to the website of the American Association for Justice[11] Stella Liebeck of Albuquerque, New Mexico, was severely burned by McDonald's coffee in February 1992. Liebeck, who received third-degree burns over 6 percent of her body, was awarded \$160,000 in compensatory damages and \$480,000 in punitive damages. A postverdict investigation revealed that the coffee temperature at the local Albuquerque McDonald's had dropped from about 185°F before the trial to about 158° after the trial.

This case concerns coffee temperatures at a fast-food restaurant. Because of the possibility of future litigation and to possibly improve the coffee's taste, the restaurant wishes to study the temperature of the coffee it serves. To do this, the restaurant personnel measure the temperature of the coffee being dispensed (in degrees Fahrenheit) at a randomly selected time during each of the 24 half-hour periods from 8 A.M. to 7:30 P.M. on a given day. This is then repeated on a second day, giving the 48 coffee temperatures in Table 1.10. Make a time series plot of the coffee temperatures, and assuming process consistency, estimate limits between which most of the coffee temperatures at the restaurant would fall.

1.20   In the article "Accelerating Improvement" published in *Quality Progress,* Gaudard, Coates, and Freeman describe a restaurant that caters to business travelers and has a self-service breakfast buffet. Interested in customer satisfaction, the manager conducts a survey over a three-week period and finds that the main customer complaint is having to wait too long to be seated. On each day from September 11 to October 1, a problem-solving team records the percentage of patrons who must wait more than one minute to be seated. A time series plot of the daily percentages is shown in Figure 1.5.[12] What does the time series plot tell us about how to improve the waiting time situation?

[11]American Association for Justice, June 16, 2006.

[12]The source of Figure 1.5 is M. Gaudard, R. Coates, and L. Freeman, "Accelerating Improvement," *Quality Progress,* October 1991, pp. 81–88. © 1991 American Society for Quality Control. Used with permission.

TABLE 1.10	The Coffee Temperatures for Exercise 1.19 ⊙ Coffee		
154°F	156	158	166
165	151	160	158
148	161	153	173
157	157	161	162
160	154	160	155
157	159	158	150
152	155	169	165
149	153	163	154
171	173	146	160
168	164	167	162
165	161	162	159
164	151	159	166

Note: **Time order is given by reading down the columns from left to right.**

FIGURE 1.5 **Runs Plot of Daily Percentages of Customers Waiting More Than One Minute to Be Seated (for Exercise 1.20)**

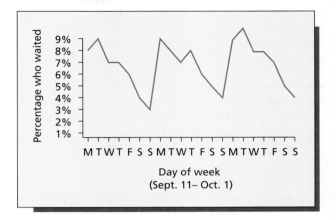

1.21 Internet Exercise

The website maintained by the U.S. Census Bureau provides a multitude of social, economic, and government data. In particular, this website houses selected data from the most recent *Statistical Abstract of the United States* (http://www.census.gov/compendia/statab/). Among these selected features are "Frequently Requested Tables" that can be accessed simply by clicking on the label. Go to the U.S. Census Bureau website and open the "Frequently requested tables" from the *Statistical Abstract*. Find the table of "Consumer Price Indexes by Major Groups." Construct runs plots of (1) the price index for all items over time (years), (2) the price index for food over time, (3) the price index for fuel oil over time, and (4) the price index for electricity over time. For each runs plot, describe apparent trends in the price index.

Excel, MegaStat, and MINITAB for Statistics

In this book we use three types of software to carry out statistical analysis—Excel 2010, MegaStat, and MINITAB 16. **Excel** is, of course, a general purpose electronic spreadsheet program and analytical tool. The analysis Tool-Pak in Excel includes many procedures for performing various kinds of basic statistical analyses. **MegaStat** is an add-in package that is specifically designed for performing statistical analysis in the Excel spreadsheet environment. **MINITAB** is a computer package designed expressly for conducting statistical analysis. It is widely used at many colleges and universities and in a large number of business organizations. The principal advantage of Excel is that, because of its broad acceptance among students and professionals as a multipurpose analytical tool, it is both well-known and widely available. The advantages of a special-purpose statistical software package like MINITAB are that it provides a far wider range of statistical procedures and it offers the experienced analyst a range of options to better control the analysis. The advantages of MegaStat include (1) its ability to perform a number of statistical calculations that are not automatically done by the procedures in the Excel ToolPak and (2) features that make it easier to use than Excel for a wide variety of statistical analyses. In addition, the output obtained by using MegaStat is automatically placed in a standard Excel spreadsheet and can be edited by using any of the features in Excel. MegaStat can be copied from the book's website. Excel, MegaStat, and MINITAB, through built-in functions, programming languages, and macros, offer almost limitless power. Here, we will limit our attention to procedures that are easily accessible via menus without resort to any special programming or advanced features.

Commonly used features of Excel 2010, MegaStat, and MINITAB 16 are presented in this chapter along with an initial application—the construction of a time series plot of the gas mileages in Table 1.6. You will find that the limited instructions included here, along with the built-in help features of all three software packages, will serve as a starting point from which you can discover a variety of other procedures and options. Much more detailed descriptions of MINITAB 16 can be found in other sources, in particular in the manual *Meet MINITAB 16 for Windows.* This manual is available in print and as a pdf file, viewable using Adobe Acrobat Reader, on the MINITAB Inc. website— go to http://www.minitab.com/uploadedFiles/Shared_Resources/Documents/MeetMinitab/EN16_MeetMinitab.pdf. Similarly, there are a number of alternative reference materials for Microsoft Excel 2010. Of course, an understanding of the related statistical concepts is essential to the effective use of any statistical software package.

Appendix 1.1 ■ Getting Started with Excel

Because Excel 2010 may be new to some readers, and because the Excel 2010 window looks somewhat different from previous versions of Excel, we will begin by describing some characteristics of the Excel 2010 window. Versions of Excel prior to 2007 employed many drop-down menus. This meant that many features were "hidden" from the user, which resulted in a steep learning curve for beginners. In Excel 2007 and 2010, Microsoft tried to reduce the number of features that are hidden in drop-down menus. Therefore, Excel 2010 displays all of the applicable commands needed for a particular type of task at the top of the Excel window. These commands are represented by a tab-and-group arrangement called the **ribbon**—see the right side of the illustration of an Excel 2010 window below. The commands displayed in the ribbon are regulated by a series of **tabs** located near the top of the ribbon. For example, in the illustration below, the **Home tab** is selected. If we selected a different tab, say, for example, the **Page Layout tab,** the commands displayed by the ribbon would be different.

We now briefly describe some basic features of the Excel 2010 window:

1 **File button:** By clicking on this button, the user obtains a menu of often used commands—for example, Open, Save, Print, and so forth. This menu also provides access to a large number of Excel options settings.

2 **Tabs:** Clicking on a tab results in a ribbon display of features, commands, and options related to a particular type of task. For example, when the *Home tab* is selected (as in the figure below), the features, commands, and options displayed by the ribbon are all related to making entries into the Excel worksheet. As another example, if the *Formulas tab* is selected, all of the features, commands, and options displayed in the ribbon relate to using formulas in the Excel worksheet.

3 **Quick access toolbar:** This toolbar displays buttons that provide shortcuts to often used commands. Initially, this toolbar displays Save, Undo, and Redo buttons. The user can customize this toolbar by adding shortcut buttons for other commands (such as, New, Open, Quick Print, and so forth). This can be done by clicking on the arrow button directly to the right of the Quick Access toolbar and by making selections from the "Customize" drop-down menu that appears.

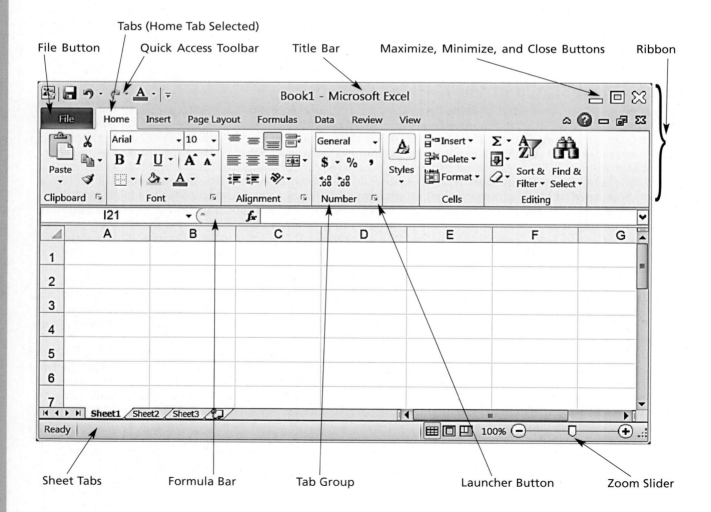

4   **Title bar:** This bar shows the name of the currently active workbook and contains the Quick Access Toolbar as well as the Maximize, Minimize, and Close buttons.

5   **Ribbon:** A grouping of toolbars, tabs, commands, and features related to performing a particular kind of task—for example, making entries into the Excel spreadsheet. The particular features displayed in the ribbon are controlled by selecting a *Tab.* If the user is working in the spreadsheet workspace and wishes to reduce the number of features displayed by the ribbon, this can be done by right-clicking on the ribbon and by selecting "Minimize the Ribbon." We will often Minimize the Ribbon in the Excel appendices of this book in order to focus attention on operations being performed and results being displayed in the Excel spreadsheet.

6   **Sheet tabs:** These tabs show the name of each sheet in the Excel workbook. When the user clicks a sheet tab, the selected sheet becomes active and is displayed in the Excel spreadsheet. The name of a sheet can be changed by double-clicking on the appropriate sheet tab and by entering the new name.

7   **Formula bar:** When a worksheet cell is selected, the formula bar displays the current content of the cell. If the cell content is defined by a formula, the defining formula is displayed in the formula bar.

8   **Tab group:** This is a labeled grouping of commands and features related to performing a particular type of task.

9   **Launcher button:** Some of the tab groups have a launcher button—for example, the Clipboard, Font, Alignment, and Number tab groups each have such a button. Clicking on the launcher button opens a dialog box or task pane related to performing operations in the tab group.

10   **Zoom slider:** By moving this slider right or left, the cells in the Excel spreadsheet can be enlarged or reduced in size.

We now take a look at some features of Excel that are common to many analyses. When the instructions call for a sequence of selections, the sequence will be presented in the following form:

Select Home : Format : Row Height

This notation indicates that we first select the Home tab on the ribbon, then we select Format from the Cells Group on the ribbon, and finally we select Row Height from the Format drop-down menu.

For many of the statistical and graphical procedures in Excel, it is necessary to provide a range of cells to specify the location of data in the spreadsheet. Generally, the range may be specified either by typing the cell locations directly into a dialog box or by dragging the selected range with the mouse. Although for the experienced user, it is usually easier to use the mouse to select a range, the instructions that follow will, for precision and clarity, specify ranges by typing in cell locations. The selected range may include column or variable labels—labels at the tops of columns that serve to identify variables. When the selected range includes such labels, it is important to select the "Labels check box" in the analysis dialog box.

Starting Excel   Procedures for starting Excel may vary from one installation to the next. If you are using a public computing laboratory, you may wish to consult local documentation. For typical Excel installations, you will generally be able to start Excel with a sequence of selections from the Microsoft Windows start menu something like the following:

Start : All Programs : Microsoft Office :
Microsoft Excel 2010

You can also start Excel with a previously saved Excel spreadsheet (like GasMiles.xlsx or one of the other data files that can be downloaded from this book's website) by double-clicking on the spreadsheet file's icon in Windows Explorer.

After starting Excel, the display will generally show a blank Excel workbook.

Help resources Like most Windows programs, Excel includes on-line help via a Help Menu that includes search capability as well as a table of contents. To display the Help Menu, click on the "Question Mark" button in the upper-right corner of the ribbon.

Entering data (entering the gas mileages in Table 1.6 on page 11) from the keyboard (data file: GasMiles.xlsx):

- In a new Excel workbook, click on cell A1 in Sheet1 and type a label—that is, a variable name—say, Mileage, for the gasoline mileages.

- Beginning in cell A2 (directly under the column label Mileage) type the mileages from Table 1.6 on page 11 down the column, pressing the Enter key following each entry.

Saving data (saving the gasoline mileage data):

- To begin, click on the **File** button and select **Save As**.

- In the "Save As" dialog box, select the destination drive and folder. Here we have selected a file folder called New Data Files in Rick's System folder on the local C drive.

- Enter the desired file name in the "File name" window. In this case we have chosen the name GasMiles.

- Select Excel Workbook in the "Save as type" window.

- Click the **Save** button in the "Save As" dialog box.

Retrieving an Excel spreadsheet containing the gasoline mileages in Table 1.6 on page 11 (data file: GasMiles.xlsx):

- Select **File : Open**

  That is, click on the File button and then select Open.

- In the Open dialog box, select the desired source drive, folder, and file. Here we have selected the GasMiles file in a folder named New Data Files in Rick's System folder on the local C drive. When you select the desired file by clicking on it, the file name will be shown in the "File name" window.

- Click the Open button in the Open dialog box.

Creating a time series (runs) plot similar to Figure 1.3 on page 11 (data file: GasMiles.xlsx):

- Enter the gasoline mileage data into column A of the worksheet with label Mileage in cell A1.

- Click on any cell in the column of mileages, or select the range of the data to be charted by dragging with the mouse. Selecting the range of the data is good practice because—if this is not done—Excel will sometimes try to construct a chart using all of the data in your worksheet. The result of such a chart is often nonsensical. Here, of course, we only have one column of data—so there would be no problem. But, in general, it is a good idea to select the data before constructing a graph.

- Select **Insert : Line : 2-D Line : Line with Markers**

  Here select the Insert tab and then select Line from the Charts group. When Line is selected, a gallery of line charts will be displayed. From the gallery, select the desired chart—in this case a 2-D Line chart with markers. The proper chart can be selected by looking at the sample pictures. As an alternative, if the cursor is hovered over a picture, a descriptive "tool tip" of the chart type will be displayed. In this case, the "Line with Markers" tool tip was obtained by hovering the cursor over the highlighted picture.

- When you click on the "2-D Line with Markers" icon, the chart will appear in a graphics window and the Chart Tools ribbon will be displayed.

- To prepare the chart for editing, it is best to move the chart to a new worksheet—called a "chart sheet." To do this, click on the **Design tab** and select **Move Chart.**

- In the Move Chart dialog box, select the "New sheet" option, enter a name for the new sheet— here, "Runs Plot"—into the "New sheet" window, and click OK.

- The Chart Tools ribbon will be displayed and the chart will be placed in a chart sheet in a larger format that is more convenient for editing.

- In order to edit the chart, select the **Layout** tab from the Chart Tools ribbon. By making selections from the ribbon, many chart attributes can be edited. For instance, when you click on Axes as shown, various options for formatting the horizontal and vertical axes can be selected.

- A chart can also be edited by right-clicking on the portion of the chart that we wish to revise. For instance, in the screen shown, we have right-clicked on one of the plotted data points. When this is done, we obtain a menu as shown. If we select "Format Data Series," we obtain a dialog box that provides many options for editing the data series (the plotted points and their connecting lines). For example, if (as shown) we select

Line Color : Solid Line

and then click on the Color arrow button, we obtain a drop-down menu that allows us to select a desired color for the connecting lines between the plotted points. We can edit other portions of the chart in the same way.

- Here we show an edited runs plot. This revised chart was constructed from the original runs plot created by Excel using various options like those illustrated above. This chart can be copied directly from the worksheet (simply right-click on the graph and select Copy from the pop-up menu) and can then be pasted into a word-processing document.

The chart can be printed from this worksheet as follows:

- Select **File : Print**
  That is, click on the File button and then select Print.
- Select the desired printer in the Printer Name window and then click Print.

There are many print options available in Excel —for printing a selected range, selected sheets, or an entire workbook—making it possible to build and print fairly sophisticated reports directly from Excel.

Printing a spreadsheet with an embedded graph:

- Click outside the graph to print both the worksheet contents (here the mileage data) and the graph. Click on the graph to print only the graph.

- Select **File : Print**

  That is, click on the File button and then select Print.

- Select the desired printer in the Printer Name window and click OK in the Print dialog box.

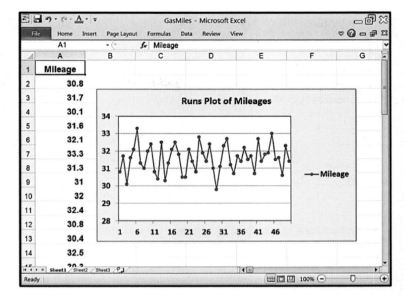

Including Excel output in reports   You can easily copy Excel results—selected spreadsheet ranges and graphs—to the Windows clipboard. Then paste them into an open word processing document. Once copied to a word-processing document, Excel results can be documented, edited, resized, and rearranged as desired into a cohesive record of your analysis. The cut and paste process is quite similar to the MINITAB examples at the end of Appendix 1.3.

Calculated Results   As we proceed through this book, you will see that Excel often expresses calculated results that are fractions in **scientific notation**. For example, Excel might express the results of a calculation as 7.77 E-6. To get the decimal point equivalent, the "E-6" says we must move the decimal point 6 places to the left. This would give us the fraction .00000777.

Appendix 1.2 ■ Getting Started with MegaStat

MegaStat, which was developed by Professor J. B. Orris of Butler University, is an Excel add-in that performs statistical analyses within an Excel workbook. Instructions for installing MegaStat can be found on this book's website.

- After installation, you can access MegaStat by clicking on the Add-Ins tab (on the ribbon) and by then selecting MegaStat from the Add-Ins group of Menu Commands. When you select MegaStat, the MegaStat menu appears as shown in the screen. Most of the menu options display sub-menus. If a menu item is followed by an ellipsis (...), clicking it will display a dialog box for that option.

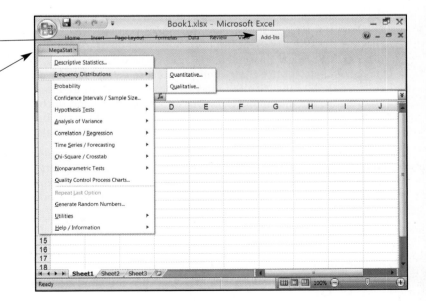

- A dialog box allows you to specify the data to be used and other inputs and options. A typical dialog box is shown in the screen to the right.

- After you have selected the needed data and options, you click OK. The dialog box then disappears and MegaStat performs the analysis.

Descriptive statistics

	Input range
Select Defaults	Select/Clear All
☑ Mean	☐ Sum, sum of squares, SSX
☑ Sample variance and standard deviation	☐ Standard error of the mean
☑ Minimum, maximum, range	☐ Population variance and standard deviation
☐ Median, quartiles, mode, outliers	☐ Confidence interval 95%
☐ Boxplot	☐ Empirical rule
☐ DotPlot (Max dots: auto ◄ ►)	☐ Tolerance interval 99.73% (±3s)
☐ Stem and Leaf Plot (☐ Split stem)	☐ Skewness, kurtosis, CV
☐ Runs Plot	☐ Suggested interval width for frequency distribution
☐ Normal Curve Plot	☐ Normal curve goodness of fit

OK   Clear   Cancel   Help

Before we look at specific dialog boxes, we will describe some features that are common to all of the options. Mega-Stat use is intuitive and very much like other Excel operations; however, there are some features unique to MegaStat.

Data selection   Most MegaStat dialog boxes have fields where you select input ranges that contain the data to be used. Such a field is shown in the dialog box illustrated above—it is the long horizontal window with the label "Input range" to its right. Input ranges can be selected using four methods:

1   Pointing and dragging with the mouse. Simply select the desired data by pointing to the data, by left-clicking on the first data item, and dragging the cursor to select the rest of the data as illustrated below.

Because the dialog box "pops-up" on the screen, it may block some of your data. You can move a dialog box around on the screen by placing the mouse pointer over the title bar (colored area at the top), and by then clicking and holding the left mouse button while dragging the dialog box to a new location. You can even drag it partially off the screen.

You will also notice that when you start selecting data by dragging the mouse pointer, the dialog box will collapse to a smaller size to help you see the underlying data. It will automatically return to full size when you release the mouse button. You can also collapse and uncollapse the dialog box manually by clicking the collapse (-) button at the right end of the field. Clicking the button again will uncollapse the dialog box. (Never use the X button to try to collapse or uncollapse a dialog box.)

2   Using MegaStat's AutoExpand feature. Pointing and dragging to select data can be tedious if you have a lot of data. When you drag the mouse down it is easy to overshoot the selection and then you have to drag the mouse back until you get the area correctly selected. AutoExpand allows rapid data selection without having to drag through the entire column of data. Here's how it works:

- Make sure the input box has the focus (that is, click in it to make the input box active). An input box has the focus when the insertion pointer is blinking in it.

- Click in one cell of the column you want. If more than one column is being selected, drag the mouse across the columns.

- Right-click over the input field or left-click the label "Input Range" to the right of the input box. The data range will expand to include all of the rows in the region where you selected one row.

This procedure is illustrated below. In the left screen, we have left-clicked on one cell in the column of data labeled Mileage. In the right screen, we see the result after we right-click over the input field or left-click on the label "Input range." Notice that the entire column of data has been selected in the right screen. This can be seen by examining the input field or by looking at the column of data.

With a little practice you will find this is a very efficient way to select data. The only time you cannot use it is when you want to use a partial column of data. You should also be aware that the autoexpand stops when it finds a blank cell; thus any summations or other calculations at the bottom of a column would be selected.

Note: When using the above methods of data selection you may select variables in an alternating sequence by holding the CTRL key while making multiple selections.

3 **Typing the name of a named range.** If you have previously identified a range of cells using Excel's name box, you may use that name to specify a data range in a MegaStat dialog box. This method can be very useful if you are using the same data for several different statistical procedures.

4 **Typing a range address.** You may type any valid Excel range address, for example, $A$1:$A$101, into the input field. This is the most cumbersome way to specify data ranges, but it certainly works.

Data labels   For most procedures, the first cell in each input range can be a label. If the first cell in a range is text, it is considered a label; if the first cell is a numeric value, it is considered data. If you want to use numbers as variable labels, you must enter the numbers as text by preceding them with a single quote mark—for instance, '2. Even though Excel stores times and dates as numbers, MegaStat will recognize them as labels if they are formatted as time/date values. If data labels are not part of the input range, the program automatically uses the cell immediately above the data range as a label if it contains a text value. If an option can consider the entire first row (or column) of an input range as labels, any numeric value in the row will cause the entire row to be treated as data. Finally, if the program detects sequential integers (1,2,3...) in a location where you might want labels, it will display a warning message. Otherwise, the rule is: **text cells are labels, numeric cells are data.**

Output   When you click OK on a MegaStat dialog box, it performs some statistical analysis and needs a place to put its output. It looks for a worksheet named Output. If it finds one, it goes to the end of it and appends its output; if it doesn't find an Output worksheet, it creates one. MegaStat will never make any changes to the user's worksheets; it only sends output to its Output sheet.

MegaStat makes a good attempt at formatting the output, but **it is important to remember that the Output sheet is just a standard Excel worksheet and can be modified in any way by the user.** You can adjust column widths and change any formatting that you think needs improvement. You can insert, delete, and modify cells. You can copy all or part of the output to another worksheet or to another application such as a word processor.

When the program generates output, it adjusts column widths for the current output. If you have previous output from a different option already in the Output sheet, the column widths for the previous output may be altered. You can attempt to fix this by manually adjusting the column widths. Alternatively, you can make it a practice to always start a new output sheet. The **Utilities menu** has options for **deleting the Output sheet, for making a copy of it, and for starting a new one.**

An example   We now give an example of using MegaStat to carry out statistical analysis. When the instructions call for a sequence of selections, the sequence will be presented in the following form:

Add-Ins : MegaStat : Probability : Counting Rules

This notation says that **Add-Ins** is the first selection (from the ribbon), **MegaStat** is the second selection from the Add-Ins group of Menu Commands; next **Probability** is selected from the MegaStat drop-down menu; and finally **Counting Rules** is selected from the Probability submenu.

Creating a time series (runs) plot of gasoline mileages similar to Figure 1.3 on page 11 (data file: GasMiles.xlsx):

- Enter the mileage data in Table 1.6 on page 11 into column A with the label Mileage in cell A1 and with the 50 mileages in cells A2 through A51.

- Select **Add-Ins : MegaStat : Descriptive Statistics**

- In the Descriptive Statistics dialog box, enter the range $A$1:$A$51 into the Input range box. The easiest way to do this is to use the MegaStat AutoExpand feature. Simply select one cell in column A (say, cell A4, for instance) by clicking on the cell. Then, either right-click in the Input range box or left-click on the label "Input range" to the right of the Input range box.

- Place a checkmark in the Runs Plot checkbox.

- Click OK in the Descriptive Statistics dialog box.

MegaStat places the resulting analysis (in this case the runs plot) in an output worksheet. This is a standard Excel worksheet, which can be edited using any of the usual Excel features. For instance, by right-clicking on various portions of the runs plot graphic, the plot can be edited in many ways. Here we have right-clicked on the plot area. By selecting **Format Plot Area,** we are able to edit the graphic in a variety of ways.

In the Format Plot Area dialog box, we can add color to the runs plot and edit the plot in many other ways.

Alternatively, we can edit the runs plot by selecting

Chart Tools : Layout

By making selections from the Labels, Axes, and Background groups, the plot can be edited in a variety of ways. For example, in the screen shown we have selected the Plot Area button in the Background group. This gives us many options for editing the plot area of the graphic.

Appendix 1.3 ■ Getting Started with MINITAB

We begin with a look at some features of MINITAB that are common to most analyses. When the instructions call for a sequence of selections from a series of menus, the sequence will be presented in the following form:

Stat : Basic Statistics : Descriptive Statistics

This notation indicates that Stat is the first selection from the Minitab menu bar, next Basic Statistics is selected from the Stat pull-down menu, and finally Descriptive Statistics is selected from the Basic Statistics pull-down menu.

Starting MINITAB   Procedures for starting MINITAB may vary from one installation to the next. If you are using a public computing laboratory, you may have to consult local documentation. For typical MINITAB installations, you will generally be able to start MINITAB with a sequence of selections from the Microsoft Windows Start menu something like the following:

- Select **Start : Programs : Minitab : Minitab 15 Statistical Software English**

You can also start MINITAB with a previously saved MINITAB worksheet (like GasMiles.MTW or one of the many other data files that can be downloaded from this book's website) by double-clicking on the worksheet's icon in the Windows Explorer.

After you start MINITAB, the display is partitioned into two working windows. These windows serve the following functions:

- The "Session window" is the area where MINITAB commands and basic output are displayed.
- The "Data window" is an Excel-like worksheet where data can be entered and edited.

Help resources   Like most Windows programs, MINITAB includes online help via a Help Menu. The Help feature includes standard Contents and Search entries as well as Tutorials that introduce MINITAB concepts and walk through some typical MINITAB sessions. Also included is a StatGuide that provides guidance for interpreting statistical tables and graphs in a practical, easy-to-understand way.

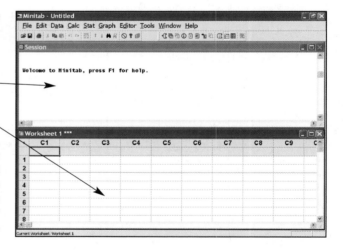

Entering data (entering the gasoline mileage data in Table 1.6 on page 11) from the keyboard:

- In the Data window, click on the cell directly below C1 and type a name for the variable—say, Mpg—and press the Enter key.
- Starting in row 1 under column C1, type the values for the variable (gasoline mileages from Table 1.6 on page 11) down the column, pressing the Enter key after each number is typed.

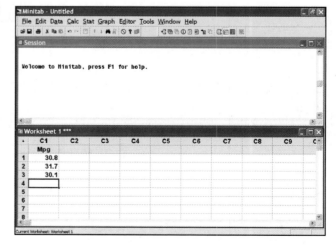

Saving data (saving the gasoline mileage data):

- Select **File : Save Current Worksheet As**

- In the "Save Worksheet As" dialog box, use the "Save in" drop-down menu to select the destination drive and folder. (Here we have selected a folder named Data Files on the Local C drive.)

- Enter the desired file name in the File name box. Here we have chosen the name GasMiles. MINITAB will automatically add the extension .MTW.

- Click the Save button in the "Save Worksheet As" dialog box.

Retrieving a MINITAB worksheet containing the gasoline mileage data in Table 1.6 (data file: GasMiles .MTW):

- Select **File : Open Worksheet**

- In the Open Worksheet dialog box, use the "Look in" drop-down menu to select the source drive and folder. (Here we have selected a folder named Data Files on the Local C drive.)

- Enter the desired file name in the File name box. (Here we have chosen the MINITAB worksheet GasMiles.MTW.)

- Click the Open button in the Open Worksheet dialog box.

- MINITAB may display a dialog box with the message, "A copy of the content of this file will be added to the current project." If so, click OK.

Creating a time series (or runs) plot similar to Figure 1.3 on page 11 (data file: GasMiles.MTW):

- Select **Graph : Time Series Plot**

- In the Time Series Plots dialog box, select Simple, which produces a time series plot of data that is stored in a single column, and click OK.

- In the "Time Series Plot—Simple" dialog box, enter the name of the variable, Mpg, into the Series window. Do this either (1) by typing its name, or (2) by double-clicking on its name in the list of variables on the left side of the dialog box. Here, this list consists of the single variable Mpg in column C1.

- Click OK in the "Time Series Plot—Simple" dialog box.

- **The time series plot** will appear in a graphics window.

- **The graph can be edited** by right-clicking on the portion you wish to edit. For instance, here we have right-clicked on the data region.
- Selecting "Edit Data Region" from the pop-up window gives a dialog box that allows you to edit this region. The x and y scales, x and y axis labels, title, plot symbols, connecting lines, data region, figure region, and so forth can all be edited by right-clicking on that particular portion of the graph.

- For instance, after right-clicking on the data region and then selecting "Edit Data Region" from the pop-up menu, the Edit Data Region dialog box allows us to edit various attributes of this region. As shown, selecting Custom and clicking on the Background Color arrow allows us to change the background color of the data region.

Printing a high-resolution graph similar to Figure 1.3 on page 11 (data file: GasMiles.MTW):

- Click in the graphics window to select it as the active window.

- Select **File : Print Graph** to print the graph.

- Select the appropriate printer and click OK in the Print dialog box.

Saving the high-resolution graph:

- Click on the graph to make the graphics window the active window.

- Select **File : Save Graph As**

- In the "Save Graph As" dialog box, use the "Save in" drop-down menu to select the destination drive and folder (here we have selected the DVD/CD-RW drive).

- Enter the desired file name in the File name box (here we have chosen the name MileagePlot). MINITAB will automatically add the file extension .MGF.

- Click the Save button in the "Save Graph As" dialog box.

Printing data from the Session window (shown) or Data window (data file: GasMiles.MTW):
To print selected output from the Session window:

- Use the mouse to select the desired output or text (selected output will be reverse-highlighted in black).

- Select **File : Print Session Window**

- In the Print dialog box, the Print range will be the "Selection" option. To print the entire session window, select the Print range to be "All."

- Select the desired printer from the Printer Name drop-down menu.

- Click OK in Print dialog box.

To print the contents of the Data window (that is, to print the MINITAB worksheet):

- Click in the Data window to select it as active.
- Select **File : Print Worksheet**
- Make selections as desired in the Data Window Print Options dialog box, add a title in the Title window if desired, and click OK.
- Select the desired printer from the Printer Name drop-down menu and click OK in the Print dialog box.

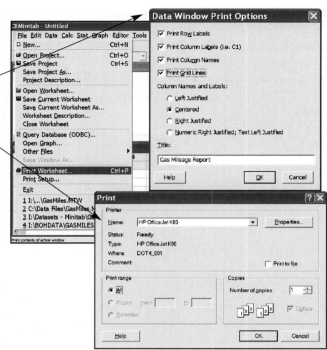

Including MINITAB output in reports   The immediately preceding examples show how to print various types of output directly from MINITAB. Printing is a useful way to capture a quick hard-copy record of an analysis result. However, you may prefer at times to collect selected analysis results and arrange them with related narrative documentation in a report that can be saved and printed as a unit. This is easily accomplished by copying selected MINITAB results to the Windows clipboard and by pasting them into your favorite word processor. Once copied to a word processor document, MINITAB results can be documented, edited, resized, and rearranged as desired into a cohesive record of your analysis. The following sequence of screens illustrates the process of copying MINITAB output into a Microsoft Word document.

Copying session window output to a word processing document:

- Be sure to have a word processing document open to receive the results.
- Use the scroll bar on the right side of the Session window to locate the results you wish to copy and drag the mouse to select the desired output (selected output will be reverse-highlighted in black).
- Copy the selected output to the Windows clipboard by clicking the Copy icon on the MINITAB toolbar or by right-clicking on the selected text and then selecting Copy from the pop-up menu.
- Switch to your word processing document by clicking the Microsoft Word button on the Windows task bar.
- Click in your word processing document to position the cursor at the desired insertion point.
- Click the Paste button on the word processing power bar or right-click at the insertion point and select Paste from the pop-up menu.
- Return to your MINITAB session by clicking the MINITAB button on the Windows task bar.

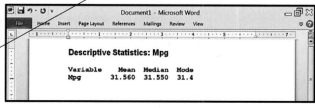

Copying high-resolution graphics output to a word processing document:

- Be sure to have a word processing document open to receive the results.
- Copy the selected contents of the high-resolution graphics window to the Windows clipboard by right-clicking in the graphics window and by then clicking Copy Graph on the pop-up menu.
- Switch to your word processing document by clicking the Microsoft Word button on the Windows task bar.
- Click in your word processing document to position the cursor at the desired insertion point.
- Click the Paste button on the word processor power bar or right-click at the insertion point and select Paste from the pop-up menu.
- Return to your MINITAB session by clicking the MINITAB button on the Windows task bar.

Results　Here is how the copied results might appear in Microsoft Word. These results can be edited, resized, repositioned, and combined with your own additional documentation to create a cohesive record of your analysis.

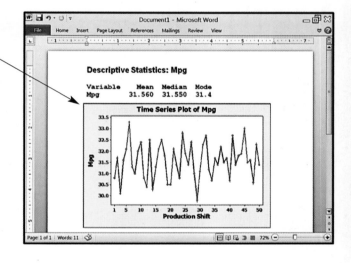

CHAPTER 2

Descriptive Statistics: Tabular and Graphical Methods

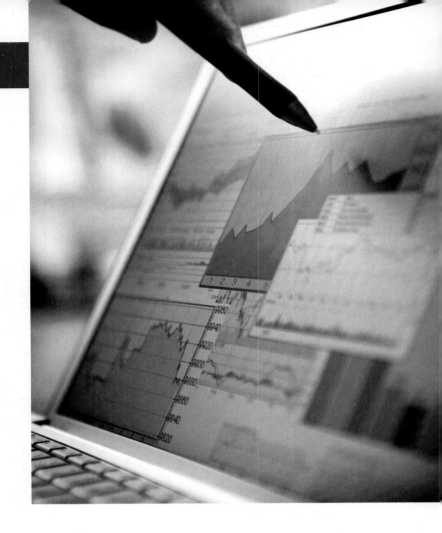

Learning Objectives

When you have mastered the material in this chapter, you will be able to:

LO2-1 Summarize qualitative data by using frequency distributions, bar charts, and pie charts.

LO2-2 Construct and interpret Pareto charts (Optional).

LO2-3 Summarize quantitative data by using frequency distributions, histograms, frequency polygons, and ogives.

LO2-4 Construct and interpret dot plots.

LO2-5 Construct and interpret stem-and-leaf displays.

LO2-6 Examine the relationships between variables by using contingency tables (Optional).

LO2-7 Examine the relationships between variables by using scatter plots (Optional).

LO2-8 Recognize misleading graphs and charts (Optional).

Chapter Outline

2.1 Graphically Summarizing Qualitative Data

2.2 Graphically Summarizing Quantitative Data

2.3 Dot Plots

2.4 Stem-and-Leaf Displays

2.5 Contingency Tables (Optional)

2.6 Scatter Plots (Optional)

2.7 Misleading Graphs and Charts (Optional)

n Chapter 1 we saw that although we can sometimes take a census of an entire population, we often must randomly select a sample from a population. When we have taken a census or a sample, we typically wish to describe the observed data set. In particular, we describe a sample in order to make inferences about the sampled population.

In this chapter we begin to study **descriptive statistics,** which is the science of describing the important characteristics of a data set. The techniques of descriptive statistics include **tabular and graphical methods,** which are discussed in this chapter, and **numerical methods,** which are

discussed in Chapter 3. We will see that, in practice, the methods of this chapter and the methods of Chapter 3 are used together to describe data. We will also see that the methods used to describe quantitative data differ somewhat from the methods used to describe qualitative data. Finally, we will see that there are methods—both graphical and numerical—for studying the relationships between variables.

We will illustrate the methods of this chapter by describing the cell phone usages, bottle design ratings, and car mileages introduced in the cases of Chapter 1. In addition, we introduce two new cases:

The e-billing Case: A management consulting firm assesses how effectively a new electronic billing system reduces bill payment times.

The Brokerage Firm Case: A financial broker examines whether customer satisfaction depends upon the type of investment product purchased.

2.1 Graphically Summarizing Qualitative Data ● ● ●

Frequency distributions   When data are qualitative, we use names to identify the different categories (or classes). Often we summarize qualitative data by using a frequency distribution.

> A **frequency distribution** is a table that summarizes the number (or **frequency**) of items in each of several nonoverlapping classes.

LO2-1 Summarize qualitative data by using frequency distributions, bar charts, and pie charts.

EXAMPLE 2.1 Describing Pizza Preferences

A business entrepreneur plans to open a pizza restaurant in a college town. There are currently six pizza restaurants in town: four chain restaurants—Domino's Pizza, Little Caesars Pizza, Papa John's Pizza, and Pizza Hut—and two local establishments—Bruno's Pizza and Will's Uptown Pizza. Before developing a basic pizza recipe (crust ingredients, sauce ingredients, and so forth), the entrepreneur wishes to study the pizza preferences of the college students in town. In order to do this, the entrepreneur selects a random sample of 50 students enrolled in the local college and asks each sampled student to name his or her favorite among the six pizza places in town. The survey results are given in Table 2.1.

Part 1: Studying pizza preferences by using a frequency distribution   Unfortunately, the raw data in Table 2.1 do not reveal much useful information about the pattern of pizza preferences. In order to summarize the data in a more useful way, we can construct a frequency distribution. To do this we simply count the number of times each of the six pizza restaurants appears in Table 2.1. We find that Bruno's appears 8 times, Domino's appears 2 times, Little Caesars appears 9 times, Papa John's appears 19 times, Pizza Hut appears 4 times, and Will's Uptown Pizza appears 8 times. The frequency distribution for the pizza preferences is given in Table 2.2—a list of each of the six restaurants along with their corresponding counts (or **frequencies**). The frequency distribution shows us how the preferences are distributed among the six restaurants. The purpose of the frequency distribution is to make the data easier to understand. Certainly, looking at the frequency distribution in Table 2.2 is more informative than looking at the raw data in Table 2.1. We see that Papa John's is the most popular restaurant, and that Papa John's is roughly twice as popular as each of the next three runners up—Bruno's, Little Caesars, and Will's. Finally, Pizza Hut and Domino's are the least preferred restaurants.

TABLE 2.1	Pizza Preferences of 50 College Students	DS PizzaPref		
Little Caesars	Papa John's	Bruno's	Papa John's	Domino's
Papa John's	Will's Uptown	Papa John's	Pizza Hut	Little Caesars
Pizza Hut	Little Caesars	Will's Uptown	Little Caesars	Bruno's
Papa John's	Bruno's	Papa John's	Will's Uptown	Papa John's
Bruno's	Papa John's	Little Caesars	Papa John's	Little Caesars
Papa John's	Little Caesars	Bruno's	Will's Uptown	Papa John's
Will's Uptown	Papa John's	Will's Uptown	Bruno's	Papa John's
Papa John's	Domino's	Papa John's	Pizza Hut	Will's Uptown
Will's Uptown	Bruno's	Pizza Hut	Papa John's	Papa John's
Little Caesars	Papa John's	Little Caesars	Papa John's	Bruno's

TABLE 2.2	A Frequency Distribution of Pizza Preferences DS PizzaFreq
Restaurant	**Frequency**
Bruno's	8
Domino's	2
Little Caesars	9
Papa John's	19
Pizza Hut	4
Will's Uptown	8
	50

TABLE 2.3	Relative Frequency and Percent Frequency Distributions for the Pizza Preference Data DS PizzaPercents	
Restaurant	**Relative Frequency**	**Percent Frequency**
Bruno's	8/50 = .16	16%
Domino's	.04	4%
Little Caesars	.18	18%
Papa John's	.38	38%
Pizza Hut	.08	8%
Will's Uptown	.16	16%
	1.0	100%

When we wish to summarize the proportion (or fraction) of items in each class, we employ the **relative frequency** for each class. If the data set consists of n observations, we define the relative frequency of a class as follows:

$$\textbf{Relative frequency} \text{ of a class} = \frac{\text{frequency of the class}}{n}$$

This quantity is simply the fraction of items in the class. Further, we can obtain the **percent frequency** of a class by multiplying the relative frequency by 100.

Table 2.3 gives a relative frequency distribution and a percent frequency distribution of the pizza preference data. A **relative frequency distribution** is a table that lists the relative frequency for each class, and a **percent frequency distribution** lists the percent frequency for each class. Looking at Table 2.3, we see that the relative frequency for Bruno's pizza is 8/50 = .16 and that (from the percent frequency distribution) 16% of the sampled students preferred Bruno's pizza. Similarly, the relative frequency for Papa John's pizza is 19/50 = .38 and 38% of the sampled students preferred Papa John's pizza. Finally, the sum of the relative frequencies in the relative frequency distribution equals 1.0, and the sum of the percent frequencies in the percent frequency distribution equals 100%. These facts are true for all relative frequency and percent frequency distributions.

Part 2: Studying pizza preferences by using bar charts and pie charts   A **bar chart** is a graphic that depicts a frequency, relative frequency, or percent frequency distribution. For example, Figure 2.1 gives an Excel bar chart of the pizza preference data. On the horizontal axis we have placed a label for each class (restaurant), while the vertical axis measures frequencies. To construct the bar chart, Excel draws a bar (of fixed width) corresponding to each class label. Each bar is drawn so that its height equals the frequency corresponding to its label. Because the height of each bar is a frequency, we refer to Figure 2.1 as a **frequency bar chart.** Notice that

FIGURE 2.1   Excel Bar Chart of the Pizza Preference Data

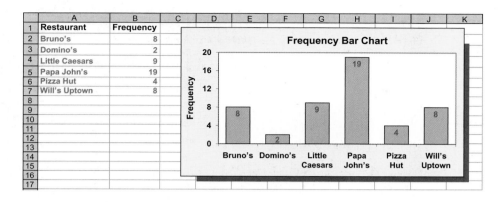

FIGURE 2.2   MINITAB Percent Bar Chart of the Pizza Preference Data

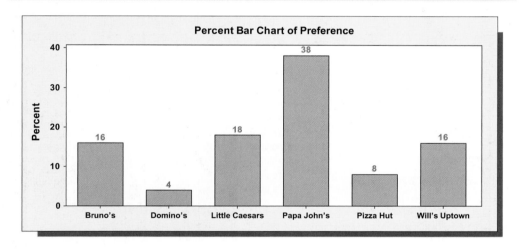

there are gaps between the bars. When data are qualitative, the bars should always be separated by gaps in order to indicate that each class is separate from the others. The bar chart in Figure 2.1 clearly illustrates that, for example, Papa John's pizza is preferred by more sampled students than any other restaurant and Domino's pizza is least preferred by the sampled students.

If desired, the bar heights can represent relative frequencies or percent frequencies. For instance, Figure 2.2 is a MINITAB **percent bar chart** for the pizza preference data. Here the heights of the bars are the percentages given in the percent frequency distribution of Table 2.3. Lastly, the bars in Figures 2.1 and 2.2 have been positioned vertically. Because of this, these bar charts are called **vertical bar charts.** However, sometimes bar charts are constructed with horizontal bars and are called **horizontal bar charts.**

A **pie chart** is another graphic that can be used to depict a frequency distribution. When constructing a pie chart, we first draw a circle to represent the entire data set. We then divide the circle into sectors or "pie slices" based on the relative frequencies of the classes. For example, remembering that a circle consists of 360 degrees, Bruno's Pizza (which has relative frequency .16) is assigned a pie slice that consists of .16(360) = 57.6 degrees. Similarly, Papa John's Pizza (with relative frequency .38) is assigned a pie slice having .38(360) = 136.8 degrees. The resulting pie chart (constructed using Excel) is shown in Figure 2.3. Here we have labeled the pie slices using the percent frequencies. The pie slices can also be labeled using frequencies or relative frequencies.

FIGURE 2.3   **Excel Pie Chart of the Pizza Preference Data**

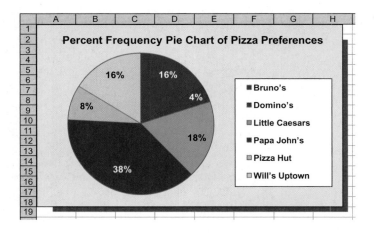

FIGURE 2.4   **Excel Frequency Table and Pareto Chart of Labeling Defects**   DS Labels

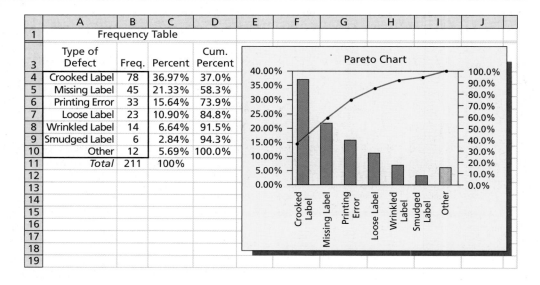

LO2-2 Construct and interpret Pareto charts (Optional).

The Pareto chart (Optional)   **Pareto charts** are used to help identify important quality problems and opportunities for process improvement. By using these charts we can prioritize problem-solving activities. The Pareto chart is named for Vilfredo Pareto (1848–1923), an Italian economist. Pareto suggested that, in many economies, most of the wealth is held by a small minority of the population. It has been found that the **"Pareto principle"** often applies to defects. That is, only a few defect types account for most of a product's quality problems.

   To illustrate the use of Pareto charts, suppose that a jelly producer wishes to evaluate the labels being placed on 16-ounce jars of grape jelly. Every day for two weeks, all defective labels found on inspection are classified by type of defect. If a label has more than one defect, the type of defect that is most noticeable is recorded. The Excel output in Figure 2.4 presents the frequencies and percentages of the types of defects observed over the two-week period.

   In general, the first step in setting up a **Pareto chart** summarizing data concerning types of defects (or categories) is to construct a frequency table like the one in Figure 2.4. Defects or categories should be listed at the left of the table in *decreasing order by frequencies*—the defect with the highest frequency will be at the top of the table, the defect with the second-highest frequency below the first, and so forth. If an "other" category is employed, it should be placed at the bottom of the table. The "other" category should not make up 50 percent or more of the total of the frequencies, and the frequency for the "other" category should not exceed the frequency for the defect at the top of the table. If the frequency for the "other" category is too high, data should be collected so that the "other" category can be broken down into new categories. Once the frequency and the percentage for each category are determined, a cumulative percentage for each category is computed. As illustrated in Figure 2.4, the cumulative percentage for a particular category is the sum of the percentages corresponding to the particular category and the categories that are above that category in the table.

A Pareto chart is simply a bar chart having the different kinds of defects or problems listed on the horizontal scale. The heights of the bars on the vertical scale typically represent the frequency of occurrence (or the percentage of occurrence) for each defect or problem. The bars are arranged in decreasing height from left to right. Thus, the most frequent defect will be at the far left, the next most frequent defect to its right, and so forth. If an "other" category is employed, its bar is placed at the far right. The Pareto chart for the labeling defects data is given in Figure 2.4. Here the heights of the bars represent the percentages of occurrences for the different labeling defects, and the vertical scale on the far left corresponds to these percentages. The chart graphically illustrates that crooked labels, missing labels, and printing errors are the most frequent labeling defects.

As is also illustrated in Figure 2.4, a Pareto chart is sometimes augmented by plotting a **cumulative percentage point** for each bar in the Pareto chart. The vertical coordinate of this cumulative percentage point equals the cumulative percentage in the frequency table corresponding to the bar. The cumulative percentage points corresponding to the different bars are connected by line segments, and a vertical scale corresponding to the cumulative percentages is placed on the far right. Examining the cumulative percentage points in Figure 2.4, we see that crooked and missing labels make up 58.3 percent of the labeling defects and that crooked labels, missing labels, and printing errors make up 73.9 percent of the labeling defects.

Technical note   The Pareto chart in Figure 2.4 illustrates using an "other" category which combines defect types having low frequencies into a single class. In general, when we employ a frequency distribution, a bar chart, or a pie chart and we encounter classes having small class frequencies, it is common practice to combine the classes into a single "other" category. Classes having frequencies of 5 percent or less are usually handled this way.

Exercises for Section 2.1

CONCEPTS

2.1   Explain the purpose behind constructing a frequency or relative frequency distribution.

2.2   Explain how to compute the relative frequency and percent frequency for each class if you are given a frequency distribution.

2.3   Find an example of a pie chart or bar chart in a newspaper or magazine. Copy it, and hand it in with a written analysis of the information conveyed by the chart.

connect

METHODS AND APPLICATIONS

2.4   A multiple choice question on an exam has four possible responses—(a), (b), (c), and (d). When 250 students take the exam, 100 give response (a), 25 give response (b), 75 give response (c), and 50 give response (d).
  a   Write out the frequency distribution, relative frequency distribution, and percent frequency distribution for these responses.
  b   Construct a bar chart for these data using frequencies.

2.5   Consider constructing a pie chart for the exam question responses in Exercise 2.4.
  a   How many degrees (out of 360) would be assigned to the "pie slice" for the response (a)?
  b   How many degrees would be assigned to the "pie slice" for response (b)?
  c   Construct the pie chart for the exam question responses.

Product	Relative Frequency
W	.15
X	—
Y	.36
Z	.28

2.6 Consider the partial relative frequency distribution of consumer preferences for four products—W, X, Y, and Z—that is shown in the page margin.
  a Find the relative frequency for product X.
  b If 500 consumers were surveyed, give the frequency distribution for these data.
  c Construct a percent frequency bar chart for these data.
  d If we wish to depict these data using a pie chart, find how many degrees (out of 360) should be assigned to each of products W, X, Y, and Z. Then construct the pie chart.

2.7 Below we give the overall dining experience ratings (Outstanding, Very Good, Good, Average, or Poor) of 30 randomly selected patrons at a restaurant on a Saturday evening.   **DS** RestRating

Outstanding	Good	Very Good	Very Good	Outstanding	Good
Outstanding	Outstanding	Outstanding	Very Good	Very Good	Average
Very Good	Outstanding	Outstanding	Outstanding	Outstanding	Very Good
Outstanding	Good	Very Good	Outstanding	Very Good	Outstanding
Good	Very Good	Outstanding	Very Good	Good	Outstanding

  a Find the frequency distribution and relative frequency distribution for these data.
  b Construct a percentage bar chart for these data.
  c Construct a percentage pie chart for these data.

2.8 Fifty randomly selected adults who follow professional sports were asked to name their favorite professional sports league. The results are as follows where MLB = Major League Baseball, MLS = Major League Soccer, NBA = National Basketball Association, NFL = National Football League, and NHL = National Hockey League.   **DS** ProfSports

NFL	NBA	NFL	MLB	MLB	NHL	NFL	NFL	MLS	MLB
MLB	NFL	MLB	NBA	NBA	NFL	NFL	NFL	NHL	NBA
NBA	NFL	NHL	NFL	MLS	NFL	MLB	NFL	MLB	NFL
NHL	MLB	NHL	NFL	NFL	NFL	MLB	NFL	NBA	NFL
MLS	NFL	MLB	NBA	NFL	NFL	MLB	NBA	NFL	NFL

  a Find the frequency distribution, relative frequency distribution, and percent frequency distribution for these data.
  b Construct a frequency bar chart for these data.
  c Construct a pie chart for these data.
  d Which professional sports league is most popular with these 50 adults? Which is least popular?

2.9 The National Automobile Dealers Association (NADA) publishes *AutoExec* magazine, which annually reports on new vehicle sales and market shares by manufacturer. As given on the *AutoExec* magazine website in May 2006, new vehicle market shares in the United States for 2005 were as follows[1]: Chrysler/Dodge/Jeep 13.6%, Ford 18.3%, GM 26.3%, Japanese (Toyota/Honda/Nissan) 28.3%, other imports 13.5%. Construct a percent frequency bar chart and a percentage pie chart for the 2005 auto market shares.   **DS** AutoShares05

2.10 Figure 2.5 gives a percentage pie chart of new vehicle market shares in the U.S. for 2010 as given by GoodCarBadCar.net. Use this pie chart and your results from Exercise 2.9 to write an analysis explaining how new vehicle market shares in the United States have changed from 2005 to 2010.   **DS** AutoShares10

2.11 On January 11, 2005, the Gallup Organization released the results of a poll investigating how many Americans have private health insurance. The results showed that among Americans making less than $30,000 per year, 33% had private insurance, 50% were covered by Medicare/Medicaid, and 17% had no health insurance, while among Americans making $75,000 or more per year, 87% had private insurance, 9% were covered by Medicare/Medicaid, and 4% had no health insurance.[2] Use bar and pie charts to compare health coverage of the two income groups.

2.12 In an article in *Quality Progress,* Barbara A. Cleary reports on improvements made in a software supplier's responses to customer calls. In this article, the author states:

> In an effort to improve its response time for these important customer-support calls, an inbound telephone inquiry team was formed at PQ Systems, Inc., a software and training organization in Dayton, Ohio. The team found that 88 percent of the customers' calls were already being answered immediately by the technical support group, but those who had to be called back had to wait an average of 56.6 minutes. No customer complaints had been registered, but the team believed that this response rate could be improved.

[1]Source: www.autoexecmag.com, May 15, 2006.
[2]Source: http://gallup.com/poll/content/default.aspx?ci=14581.

FIGURE 2.5   **A Pie Chart of U.S. Automobile Sales in 2010 as given by GoodCarBadCar.net (for Exercise 2.10)**
Ⓓ AutoShares10

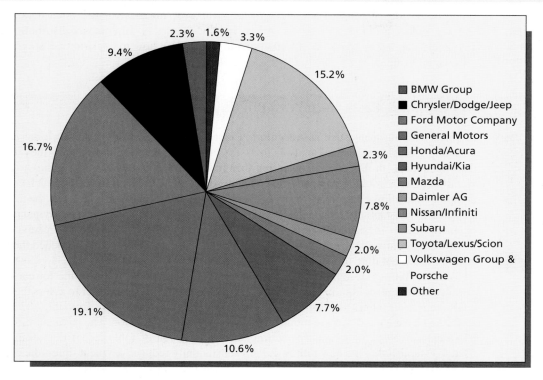

Source: http://www.goodcarbadcar.net/2011/01/new-vehicle-market-share-by-brand-in_05.html (accessed 5/29/12).

FIGURE 2.6   **A Pareto Chart for Incomplete Customer Calls (for Exercise 2.12)**

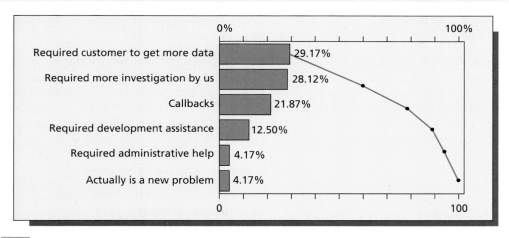

Source: B. A. Cleary, "Company Cares about Customers' Calls," *Quality Progress* (November 1993), pp. 60–73. Copyright © 1993 American Society for Quality Control. Used with permission.

As part of its improvement process, the company studied the disposition of complete and incomplete calls to its technical support analysts. A call is considered complete if the customer's problem has been resolved; otherwise the call is incomplete. Figure 2.6 shows a Pareto chart analysis for the incomplete customer calls.

   a   What percentage of incomplete calls required "more investigation" by the analyst or "administrative help"?

   b   What percentage of incomplete calls actually presented a "new problem"?

   c   In light of your answers to *a* and *b*, can you make a suggestion?

2.2 Graphically Summarizing Quantitative Data ● ● ●

LO2-3 Summarize
        quantitative
data by using
frequency distribu-
tions, histograms,
frequency polygons,
and ogives.

Frequency distributions and histograms   We often need to summarize and describe the shape of the distribution of a population or sample of **measurements**. Such data are often summarized by grouping the measurements into the classes of a frequency distribution and by displaying the data in the form of a **histogram.** We explain how to construct a histogram in the following example.

EXAMPLE 2.2 The e-billing Case: Reducing Bill Payment Times[3]

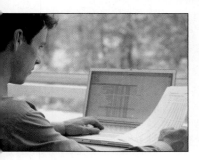

Major consulting firms such as Accenture, Ernst & Young Consulting, and Deloitte & Touche Consulting employ statistical analysis to assess the effectiveness of the systems they design for their customers. In this case a consulting firm has developed an electronic billing system for a Hamilton, Ohio, trucking company. The system sends invoices electronically to each customer's computer and allows customers to easily check and correct errors. It is hoped that the new billing system will substantially reduce the amount of time it takes customers to make payments. Typical payment times—measured from the date on an invoice to the date payment is received—using the trucking company's old billing system had been 39 days or more. This exceeded the industry standard payment time of 30 days.

The new billing system does not automatically compute the payment time for each invoice because there is no continuing need for this information. Therefore, in order to assess the system's effectiveness, the consulting firm selects a random sample of 65 invoices from the 7,823 invoices processed during the first three months of the new system's operation. The payment times for the 65 sample invoices are manually determined and are given in Table 2.4. If this sample can be used to establish that the new billing system substantially reduces payment times, the consulting firm plans to market the system to other trucking firms.

Looking at the payment times in Table 2.4, we can see that the shortest payment time is 10 days and that the longest payment time is 29 days. Beyond that, it is pretty difficult to interpret the data in any meaningful way. To better understand the sample of 65 payment times, the consulting firm will form a frequency distribution of the data and will graph the distribution by constructing a histogram. Similar to the frequency distributions for qualitative data we studied in Section 2.1, the frequency distribution will divide the payment times into classes and will tell us how many of the payment times are in each class.

Step 1: Find the number of classes   One rule for finding an appropriate number of classes says that the number of classes should be the smallest whole number K that makes the quantity 2^K greater than the number of measurements in the data set. For the payment time data we have 65 measurements. Because $2^6 = 64$ is less than 65 and $2^7 = 128$ is greater than 65, we should use $K = 7$ classes. Table 2.5 gives the appropriate number of classes (determined by the 2^K rule) to use for data sets of various sizes.

Step 2: Find the class length   We find the length of each class by computing

$$\text{approximate class length} = \frac{\text{largest measurement} - \text{smallest measurement}}{\text{number of classes}}$$

TABLE 2.4	A Sample of Payment Times (in Days) for 65 Randomly Selected Invoices DS PayTime									
22	29	16	15	18	17	12	13	17	16	15
19	17	10	21	15	14	17	18	12	20	14
16	15	16	20	22	14	25	19	23	15	19
18	23	22	16	16	19	13	18	24	24	26
13	18	17	15	24	15	17	14	18	17	21
16	21	25	19	20	27	16	17	16	21	

[3]This case is based on a real problem encountered by a company that employs one of our former students. For purposes of confidentiality, we have withheld the company's name.

TABLE 2.5	Recommended Number of Classes for Data Sets of *n* Measurements*
Number of Classes	**Size, *n*, of the Data Set**
2	$1 \leq n < 4$
3	$4 \leq n < 8$
4	$8 \leq n < 16$
5	$16 \leq n < 32$
6	$32 \leq n < 64$
7	$64 \leq n < 128$
8	$128 \leq n < 256$
9	$256 \leq n < 528$
10	$528 \leq n < 1056$

*For completeness sake we have included all values of $n \geq 1$ in this table. However, we do not recommend constructing a histogram with fewer than 16 measurements.

TABLE 2.6	Seven Nonoverlapping Classes for a Frequency Distribution of the 65 Payment Times
Class 1	10 days and less than 13 days
Class 2	13 days and less than 16 days
Class 3	16 days and less than 19 days
Class 4	19 days and less than 22 days
Class 5	22 days and less than 25 days
Class 6	25 days and less than 28 days
Class 7	28 days and less than 31 days

Because the largest and smallest payment times in Table 2.4 are 29 days and 10 days, the approximate class length is $(29 - 10)/7 = 2.7143$. To obtain an easier to read final class length, we round this value. Commonly, the approximate class length is rounded up to the precision of the data measurements (that is, increased to the next number that has the same number of decimal places as the data measurements). For instance, because the payment times are measured to the nearest day, we round 2.7143 days up to 3 days.

Step 3: Form nonoverlapping classes of equal width

We can form the classes of the frequency distribution by defining the **boundaries** of the classes. To find the first class boundary, we find the smallest payment time in Table 2.4, which is 10 days. This value is the lower boundary of the first class. Adding the class length of 3 to this lower boundary, we obtain $10 + 3 = 13$, which is the upper boundary of the first class and the lower boundary of the second class. Similarly, the upper boundary of the second class and the lower boundary of the third class equals $13 + 3 = 16$. Continuing in this fashion, the lower boundaries of the remaining classes are 19, 22, 25, and 28. Adding the class length 3 to the lower boundary of the last class gives us the upper boundary of the last class, 31. These boundaries define seven nonoverlapping classes for the frequency distribution. We summarize these classes in Table 2.6. For instance, the first class—10 days and less than 13 days—includes the payment times 10, 11, and 12 days; the second class—13 days and less than 16 days—includes the payment times 13, 14, and 15 days; and so forth. Notice that the largest *observed* payment time—29 days—is contained in the last class. In cases where the largest measurement is not contained in the last class, we simply add another class. Generally speaking, the guidelines we have given for forming classes are not inflexible rules. Rather, they are intended to help us find reasonable classes. Finally, the method we have used for forming classes results in classes of equal length. Generally, forming classes of equal length will make it easier to appropriately interpret the frequency distribution.

Step 4: Tally and count the number of measurements in each class

Having formed the classes, we now count the number of measurements that fall into each class. To do this, it is convenient to tally the measurements. We simply list the classes, examine the payment times in Table 2.4 one at a time, and record a tally mark corresponding to a particular class each time we encounter a measurement that falls in that class. For example, because the first four payment times in Table 2.4 are 22, 19, 16, and 18, the first four tally marks are shown below. Here, for brevity, we express the class "10 days and less than 13 days" as "$10 < 13$" and use similar notation for the other classes.

Class	First 4 Tally Marks	All 65 Tally Marks	Frequency
$10 < 13$		*III*	3
$13 < 16$		*7HL 7HL IIII*	14
$16 < 19$	*II*	*7HL 7HL 7HL 7HL III*	23
$19 < 22$	*I*	*7HL 7HL II*	12
$22 < 25$	*I*	*7HL III*	8
$25 < 28$		*IIII*	4
$28 < 31$		*I*	1

TABLE 2.7	Frequency Distributions of the 65 Payment Times		
Class	Frequency	Relative Frequency	Percent Frequency
10 < 13	3	3/65 = .0462	4.62%
13 < 16	14	14/65 = .2154	21.54
16 < 19	23	.3538	35.38
19 < 22	12	.1846	18.46
22 < 25	8	.1231	12.31
25 < 28	4	.0615	6.15
28 < 31	1	.0154	1.54

FIGURE 2.7 A Frequency Histogram of the 65 Payment Times

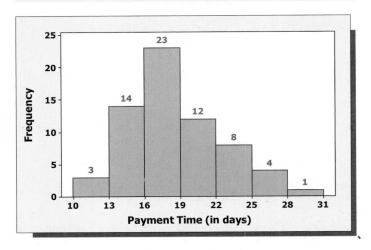

After examining all 65 payment times, we have recorded 65 tally marks—see the bottom of page 43. We find the **frequency** for each class by counting the number of tally marks recorded for the class. For instance, counting the number of tally marks for the class "13 < 16", we obtain the frequency 14 for this class. The frequencies for all seven classes are summarized in Table 2.7. This summary is the **frequency distribution** for the 65 payment times. Table 2.7 also gives the *relative frequency* and the *percent frequency* for each of the seven classes. The **relative frequency** of a class is the proportion (fraction) of the total number of measurements that are in the class. For example, there are 14 payment times in the second class, so its relative frequency is $14/65 = .2154$. This says that the proportion of the 65 payment times that are in the second class is .2154, or, equivalently, that $100(.2154)\% = 21.54\%$ of the payment times are in the second class. A list of all of the classes—along with each class relative frequency—is called a **relative frequency distribution.** A list of all of the classes—along with each class percent frequency—is called a **percent frequency distribution.**

Step 5: Graph the histogram We can graphically portray the distribution of payment times by drawing a **histogram.** The histogram can be constructed using the frequency, relative frequency, or percent frequency distribution. To set up the histogram, we draw rectangles that correspond to the classes. The base of the rectangle corresponding to a class represents the payment times in the class. The height of the rectangle can represent the class frequency, relative frequency, or percent frequency.

We have drawn a **frequency histogram** of the 65 payment times in Figure 2.7. The first (leftmost) rectangle, or "bar," of the histogram represents the payment times 10, 11, and 12. Looking at Figure 2.7, we see that the base of this rectangle is drawn from the lower boundary (10) of the first class in the frequency distribution of payment times to the lower boundary (13) of the second class. The height of this rectangle tells us that the frequency of the first class is 3. The second histogram rectangle represents payment times 13, 14, and 15. Its base is drawn from the lower boundary (13) of the second class to the lower boundary (16) of the third class, and its height tells us that the frequency of the second class is 14. The other histogram bars are constructed similarly. Notice that there are no gaps between the adjacent rectangles in the histogram. Here, although the payment times have been recorded to the nearest whole day, the fact that the histogram bars touch each other emphasizes that a payment time could (in theory) be any number on the horizontal axis. In general, histograms are drawn so that adjacent bars touch each other.

Looking at the frequency distribution in Table 2.7 and the frequency histogram in Figure 2.7, we can describe the payment times:

1 None of the payment times exceeds the industry standard of 30 days. (Actually, all of the payment times are less than 30—remember the largest payment time is 29 days.)

2 The payment times are concentrated between 13 and 24 days (57 of the 65, or $(57/65) \times 100 = 87.69\%$, of the payment times are in this range).

3 More payment times are in the class "16 < 19" than are in any other class (23 payment times are in this class).

FIGURE 2.8   A Percent Frequency Histogram of the 65 Payment Times

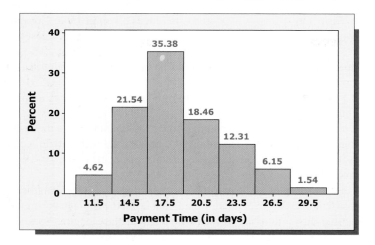

Notice that the frequency distribution and histogram allow us to make some helpful conclusions about the payment times, whereas looking at the raw data (the payment times in Table 2.4 on page 42) did not.

A **relative frequency histogram** and a **percent frequency histogram** of the payment times would both be drawn like Figure 2.7 except that the heights of the rectangles would represent, respectively, the relative frequencies and the percent frequencies in Table 2.7. For example, Figure 2.8 gives a percent frequency histogram of the payment times. This histogram also illustrates that we sometimes label the classes on the horizontal axis using the **class midpoints.** Each class midpoint is exactly halfway between the boundaries of its class. For instance, the midpoint of the first class, 11.5, is halfway between the class boundaries 10 and 13. The midpoint of the second class, 14.5, is halfway between the class boundaries 13 and 16. The other class midpoints are found similarly. The percent frequency distribution of Figure 2.8 tells us that 21.54% of the payment times are in the second class (which has midpoint 14.5 and represents the payment times 13, 14, and 15).

In the following box we summarize the steps needed to set up a frequency distribution and histogram:

Constructing Frequency Distributions and Histograms

1   Find the number of classes. Generally, the number of classes K should equal the smallest whole number that makes the quantity 2^K greater than the total number of measurements n (see Table 2.5 on page 43).

2   Compute the approximate **class length:**

$$\frac{\text{largest measurement } - \text{ smallest measurement}}{K}$$

Often the final class length is obtained by rounding this value up to the same level of precision as the data.

3   Form nonoverlapping classes of equal length. Form the classes by finding the **class boundaries.** The lower boundary of the first class is the smallest measurement in the data set. Add the class length to this boundary to obtain the next boundary. Successive boundaries are found by repeatedly adding the class length until the upper boundary of the last (Kth) class is found.

4   Tally and count the number of measurements in each class. The **frequency** for each class is the count of the number of measurements in the class. The **relative frequency** for each class is the fraction of measurements in the class. The **percent frequency** for each class is its relative frequency multiplied by 100%.

5   Graph the histogram. To draw a **frequency histogram,** plot each frequency as the height of a rectangle positioned over its corresponding class. Use the class boundaries to separate adjacent rectangles. A **relative frequency histogram** and a **percent histogram** are graphed in the same way except that the heights of the rectangles are, respectively, the relative frequencies and the percent frequencies.

The procedure in the above box is not the only way to construct a histogram. Often, histograms are constructed more informally. For instance, it is not necessary to set the lower boundary of the first (leftmost) class equal to the smallest measurement in the data. As an example, suppose that we wish to form a histogram of the 50 gas mileages given in Table 1.6 (page 11). Examining the mileages, we see that the smallest mileage is 29.8 mpg and that the largest mileage is 33.3 mpg. Therefore, it would be convenient to begin the first (leftmost) class at 29.5 mpg and end the last (rightmost) class at 33.5 mpg. Further, it would be reasonable to use classes that are .5 mpg in length. We would then use 8 classes: 29.5 < 30, 30 < 30.5, 30.5 < 31, 31 < 31.5, 31.5 < 32, 32 < 32.5, 32.5 < 33, and 33 < 33.5. A histogram of the gas mileages employing these classes is shown in Figure 2.9.

Sometimes it is desirable to let the nature of the problem determine the histogram classes. For example, to construct a histogram describing the ages of the residents in a city, it might be reasonable to use classes having 10-year lengths (that is, under 10 years, 10–19 years, 20–29 years, 30–39 years, and so on).

Notice that in our examples we have used classes having equal class lengths. In general, it is best to use equal class lengths whenever the raw data (that is, all the actual measurements) are available. However, sometimes histograms are formed with unequal class lengths—particularly when we are using published data as a source. Economic data and data in the social sciences are often published in the form of frequency distributions having unequal class lengths. Dealing with this kind of data is discussed in Exercise 2.81. Also discussed in this exercise is how to deal with **open-ended** classes. For example, if we are constructing a histogram describing the yearly incomes of U.S. households, an open-ended class could be households earning over $500,000 per year.

As an alternative to constructing a frequency distribution and histogram by hand, we can use software packages such as Excel and MINITAB. Each of these packages will automatically define histogram classes for the user. However, these automatically defined classes will not necessarily be the same as those that would be obtained using the manual method we have previously described. Furthermore, the packages define classes by using different methods. (Descriptions of how the classes are defined can often be found in help menus.) For example, Figure 2.10 gives a MINITAB frequency histogram of the payment times in Table 2.4. Here, MINITAB has defined 11 classes and has labeled five of the classes on the horizontal axis using midpoints (12, 16, 20, 24, 28). It is easy to see that the midpoints of the unlabeled classes are 10, 14, 18, 22, 26, and 30. Moreover, the boundaries of the first class are 9 and 11, the boundaries of the second class are 11 and 13, and so forth. MINITAB counts frequencies as we have previously described. For instance, one payment time is at least 9 and less than 11, two payment times are at least 11 and less than 13, seven payment times are at least 13 and less than 15, and so forth.

| FIGURE 2.9 | A Percent Frequency Histogram of the Gas Mileages: The Gas Mileage Distribution Is Symmetrical and Mound Shaped |

| FIGURE 2.10 | A MINITAB Frequency Histogram of the Payment Times with Automatic Classes: The Payment Time Distribution Is Skewed to the Right |

FIGURE 2.11 An Excel Frequency Histogram of the Bottle Design Ratings: The Distribution of Ratings Is Skewed to the Left

Figure 2.11 gives an Excel frequency distribution and histogram of the bottle design ratings in Table 1.5. Excel labels histogram classes using their upper class boundaries. For example, the first class has an upper class boundary equal to the smallest rating of 20 and contains only this smallest rating. The boundaries of the second class are 20 and 22, the boundaries of the third class are 22 and 24, and so forth. The last class corresponds to ratings more than 36. Excel's method for counting frequencies differs from that of MINITAB (and, therefore, also differs from the way we counted frequencies by hand in Example 2.2). Excel assigns a frequency to a particular class by counting the number of measurements that are greater than the lower boundary of the class and less than or equal to the upper boundary of the class. For example, one bottle design rating is greater than 20 and less than or equal to (that is, at most) 22. Similarly, 15 bottle design ratings are greater than 32 and at most 34.

In Figure 2.10 we have used MINITAB to automatically form histogram classes. It is also possible to force software packages to form histogram classes that are defined by the user. We explain how to do this in the appendices at the end of this chapter. Because Excel does not always automatically define acceptable classes, the classes in Figure 2.11 are a modification of Excel's automatic classes. We also explain this modification in the appendices at the end of this chapter.

Some common distribution shapes We often graph a frequency distribution in the form of a histogram in order to visualize the *shape* of the distribution. If we look at the histogram of payment times in Figure 2.10, we see that the right tail of the histogram is longer than the left tail. When a histogram has this general shape, we say that the distribution is **skewed to the right.** Here the long right tail tells us that a few of the payment times are somewhat longer than the rest. If we look at the histogram of bottle design ratings in Figure 2.11, we see that the left tail of the histogram is much longer than the right tail. When a histogram has this general shape, we say that the distribution is **skewed to the left.** Here the long tail to the left tells us that, while most of the bottle design ratings are concentrated above 25 or so, a few of the ratings are lower than the rest. Finally, looking at the histogram of gas mileages in Figure 2.9, we see that the right and left tails of the histogram appear to be mirror images of each other. When a histogram has this general shape, we say that the distribution is **symmetrical.** Moreover, the distribution of gas mileages appears to be piled up in the middle or **mound shaped.**

Mound-shaped, symmetrical distributions as well as distributions that are skewed to the right or left are commonly found in practice. For example, distributions of scores on standardized tests such as the SAT and ACT tend to be mound shaped and symmetrical, whereas distributions of scores on tests in college statistics courses might be skewed to the left—a few students don't study and get scores much lower than the rest. On the other hand, economic data such as income data are often skewed to the right—a few people have incomes much higher than most others.

Many other distribution shapes are possible. For example, some distributions have two or more peaks—we will give an example of this distribution shape later in this section. It is often very useful to know the shape of a distribution. For example, knowing that the distribution of bottle design ratings is skewed to the left suggests that a few consumers may have noticed a problem with design that others didn't see. Further investigation into why these consumers gave the design low ratings might allow the company to improve the design.

Frequency polygons   Another graphical display that can be used to depict a frequency distribution is a **frequency polygon.** To construct this graphic, we plot a point above each class midpoint at a height equal to the frequency of the class—the height can also be the class relative frequency or class percent frequency if so desired. Then we connect the points with line segments. As we will demonstrate in the following example, this kind of graphic can be particularly useful when we wish to compare two or more distributions.

EXAMPLE 2.3 Comparing Two Grade Distributions

Table 2.8 lists (in increasing order) the scores earned on the first exam by the 40 students in a business statistics course taught by one of the authors several semesters ago. Figure 2.12 gives a percent frequency polygon for these exam scores. Because exam scores are often reported by using 10-point grade ranges (for instance, 80 to 90 percent), we have defined the following classes: $30 < 40$, $40 < 50$, $50 < 60$, $60 < 70$, $70 < 80$, $80 < 90$, and $90 < 100$. This is an example of letting the situation determine the classes of a frequency distribution, which is common practice when the situation naturally defines classes. The points that form the polygon have been plotted corresponding to the midpoints of the classes (35, 45, 55, 65, 75, 85, 95). Each point is plotted at a height that equals the percentage of exam scores in its class. For instance, because 10 of the 40 scores are at least 90 and less than 100, the plot point corresponding to the class midpoint 95 is plotted at a height of 25 percent.

Looking at Figure 2.12, we see that there is a concentration of scores in the 85 to 95 range and another concentration of scores around 65. In addition, the distribution of scores is somewhat skewed to the left—a few students had scores (in the 30s and 40s) that were quite a bit lower than the rest.

This is an example of a distribution having two peaks. When a distribution has multiple peaks, finding the reason for the different peaks often provides useful information. The reason for the two-peaked distribution of exam scores was that some students were not attending class regularly. Students who received scores in the 60s and below admitted that they were cutting class, whereas students who received higher scores were attending class on a regular basis.

After identifying the reason for the concentration of lower scores, the instructor established an attendance policy that forced students to attend every class—any student who missed a class was

T A B L E 2 . 8	Exam Scores for the First Exam Given in a Statistics Class ⑤ FirstExam			
32	63	69	85	91
45	64	69	86	92
50	64	72	87	92
56	65	76	87	93
58	66	78	88	93
60	67	81	89	94
61	67	83	90	96
61	68	83	90	98

F I G U R E   2 . 1 2   A Percent Frequency Polygon of the Exam Scores

TABLE 2.9	Exam Scores for the Second Statistics Exam—after a New Attendance Policy ⑤ SecondExam			
55	74	80	87	93
62	74	82	88	94
63	74	83	89	94
66	75	84	90	95
67	76	85	91	97
67	77	86	91	99
71	77	86	92	
73	78	87	93	

FIGURE 2.13   Percent Frequency Polygons of the Scores on the First Two Exams in a Statistics Course

to be dropped from the course. Table 2.9 presents the scores on the second exam—after the new attendance policy. Figure 2.13 presents (and allows us to compare) the percent frequency polygons for both exams. We see that the polygon for the second exam is single peaked—the attendance policy[4] eliminated the concentration of scores in the 60s, although the scores are still somewhat skewed to the left.

Cumulative distributions and ogives   Another way to summarize a distribution is to construct a **cumulative distribution.** To do this, we use the same number of classes, the same class lengths, and the same class boundaries that we have used for the frequency distribution of a data set. However, in order to construct a **cumulative frequency distribution,** we record for each class *the number of measurements that are less than the upper boundary of the class.* To illustrate this idea, Table 2.10 gives the cumulative frequency distribution of the payment time distribution summarized in Table 2.7 (page 44). Columns (1) and (2) in this table give the frequency distribution of the payment times. Column (3) gives the **cumulative frequency** for each class. To see how these values are obtained, the cumulative frequency for the class 10 < 13 is the number of payment times less than 13. This is obviously the frequency for the class 10 < 13, which is 3. The cumulative frequency for the class 13 < 16 is the number of payment times less than 16, which is obtained by adding the frequencies for the first two classes—that is, 3 + 14 = 17. The cumulative frequency for the class 16 < 19 is the number of payment times less than 19— that is, 3 + 14 + 23 = 40. We see that, in general, a cumulative frequency is obtained by summing the frequencies of all classes representing values less than the upper boundary of the class.

TABLE 2.10	A Frequency Distribution, Cumulative Frequency Distribution, Cumulative Relative Frequency Distribution, and Cumulative Percent Frequency Distribution for the Payment Time Data			
(1) Class	**(2)** Frequency	**(3)** Cumulative Frequency	**(4)** Cumulative Relative Frequency	**(5)** Cumulative Percent Frequency
10 < 13	3	3	3/65 = .0462	4.62%
13 < 16	14	17	17/65 = .2615	26.15
16 < 19	23	40	.6154	61.54
19 < 22	12	52	.8000	80.00
22 < 25	8	60	.9231	92.31
25 < 28	4	64	.9846	98.46
28 < 31	1	65	1.0000	100.00

[4]Other explanations are possible. For instance, all of the students who did poorly on the first exam might have studied harder for the second exam. However, the instructor's 30 years of teaching experience suggest that attendance was the critical factor.

FIGURE 2.14　A Percent Frequency Ogive of the Payment Times

Column (4) gives the **cumulative relative frequency** for each class, which is obtained by summing the relative frequencies of all classes representing values less than the upper boundary of the class. Or, more simply, this value can be found by dividing the cumulative frequency for the class by the total number of measurements in the data set. For instance, the cumulative relative frequency for the class 19 < 22 is 52/65 = .8. Column (5) gives the **cumulative percent frequency** for each class, which is obtained by summing the percent frequencies of all classes representing values less than the upper boundary of the class. More simply, this value can be found by multiplying the cumulative relative frequency of a class by 100. For instance, the cumulative percent frequency for the class 19 < 22 is .8 (100) = 80 percent.

As an example of interpreting Table 2.10, 60 of the 65 payment times are 24 days or less, or, equivalently, 92.31 percent of the payment times (or a fraction of .9231 of the payment times) are 24 days or less. Also, notice that the last entry in the cumulative frequency distribution is the total number of measurements (here, 65 payment times). In addition, the last entry in the cumulative relative frequency distribution is 1.0 and the last entry in the cumulative percent frequency distribution is 100%. In general, for any data set, these last entries will be, respectively, the total number of measurements, 1.0, and 100%.

An **ogive** (pronounced "oh-jive") is a graph of a cumulative distribution. To construct a frequency ogive, we plot a point above each upper class boundary at a height equal to the cumulative frequency of the class. We then connect the plotted points with line segments. A similar graph can be drawn using the cumulative relative frequencies or the cumulative percent frequencies. As an example, Figure 2.14 gives a percent frequency ogive of the payment times. Looking at this figure, we see that, for instance, a little more than 25 percent (actually, 26.15 percent according to Table 2.10) of the payment times are less than 16 days, while 80 percent of the payment times are less than 22 days. Also notice that we have completed the ogive by plotting an additional point at the lower boundary of the first (leftmost) class at a height equal to zero. This depicts the fact that none of the payment times is less than 10 days. Finally, the ogive graphically shows that all (100 percent) of the payment times are less than 31 days.

Exercises for Section 2.2

CONCEPTS

connect

2.13 Explain:
   a Why we construct a frequency distribution and a histogram for a data set.
   b The difference between a frequency histogram and a frequency polygon.
   c The difference between a frequency polygon and a frequency ogive.

2.14 Explain how to find:
   a The frequency for a class.
   b The relative frequency for a class.
   c The percent frequency for a class.

2.15 Explain what each of the following distribution shapes looks like. Then draw a picture that illustrates each shape.
  a Symmetrical and mound shaped
  b Double peaked
  c Skewed to the right
  d Skewed to the left

METHODS AND APPLICATIONS

2.16 Consider the following data: ⑤ HistoData

36	39	36	35	36	20	19
46	40	42	34	41	36	42
40	38	33	37	22	33	28
38	38	34	37	17	25	38

  a Find the number of classes needed to construct a histogram.
  b Find the class length.
  c Define nonoverlapping classes for a frequency distribution.
  d Tally the number of values in each class and develop a frequency distribution.
  e Draw a histogram for these data.
  f Develop a percent frequency distribution.

2.17 Consider the frequency distribution of exam scores given below.

Class	Frequency
90 < 100	12
80 < 90	17
70 < 80	14
60 < 70	5
50 < 60	2

  a Develop a relative frequency distribution and a percent frequency distribution.
  b Develop a cumulative frequency distribution and a cumulative percent frequency distribution.
  c Draw a frequency polygon.
  d Draw a frequency ogive.

THE MARKETING RESEARCH CASE ⑤ Design

Recall that 60 randomly selected shoppers have rated a new bottle design for a popular soft drink. The data are given below.

34	33	33	29	26	33	28	25	32	33
32	25	27	33	22	27	32	33	32	29
24	30	20	34	31	32	30	35	33	31
32	28	30	31	31	33	29	27	34	31
31	28	33	31	32	28	26	29	32	34
32	30	34	32	30	30	32	31	29	33

Use these data to work exercises 2.18 and 2.19.

2.18 **a** Find the number of classes that should be used to construct a frequency distribution and histogram for the bottle design ratings.
  b If we round up to the nearest whole rating point, show that we should employ a class length equal to 3.
  c Define the nonoverlapping classes for a frequency distribution.
  d Tally the number of ratings in each class and develop a frequency distribution.
  e Draw the frequency histogram for the ratings data, and describe the distribution shape. ⑤ Design

2.19 **a** Construct a relative frequency distribution and a percent frequency distribution for the bottle design ratings.
  b Construct a cumulative frequency distribution and a cumulative percent frequency distribution.
  c Draw a frequency ogive for the bottle design ratings. ⑤ Design

2.20 Table 2.11 gives the 25 most powerful celebrities and their annual pay as ranked by the editors of *Forbes* magazine and as listed on the Forbes.com website on June 14, 2011. ⑤ PowerCeleb
  a Develop a frequency distribution for the celebrity pay data and draw a histogram.
  b Develop a cumulative frequency distribution and a cumulative percent frequency distribution for the celebrity pay data.
  c Draw a percent frequency ogive for the celebrity pay data.

TABLE 2.11   The 25 Most Powerful Celebrities as Rated by *Forbes* Magazine   DS PowerCeleb

Power Ranking	Celebrity Name	Pay ($mil)	Power Ranking	Celebrity Name	Pay ($mil)
1	Lady Gaga	90	14	Kobe Bryant	53
2	Oprah Winfrey	290	15	Leonardo Dicaprio	77
3	Justin Bieber	53	16	Black Eyed Peas	61
4	U2	195	17	Donald Trump	60
5	Elton John	100	18	Dr. Phil McGraw	80
6	Tiger Woods	75	19	Tyler Perry	130
7	Taylor Swift	45	20	Paul McCartney	67
8	Bon Jovi	125	21	Jennifer Aniston	28
9	Simon Cowell	90	22	Steven Spielberg	107
10	LeBron James	48	23	Rush Limbaugh	64
11	Angelina Jolie	30	24	Ryan Seacrest	61
12	Katy Perry	44	25	Roger Federer	47
13	Johnny Depp	50			

Source: http://www.forbes.com/wealth/celebrities (accessed June 14, 2011).

FIGURE 2.15   Excel Frequency Histogram of the 65 Satisfaction Ratings (for Exercise 2.21)

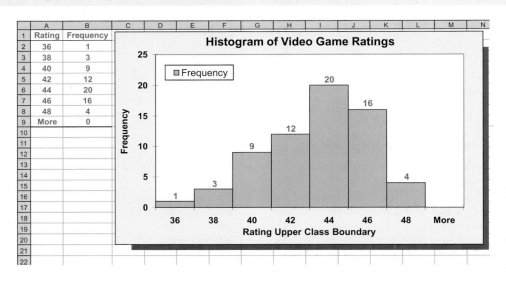

2.21   THE VIDEO GAME SATISFACTION RATING CASE   DS VideoGame

Recall that Table 1.7 (page 13) presents the satisfaction ratings for the XYZ-Box video game system that have been given by 65 randomly selected purchasers. Figure 2.15 gives the Excel output of a histogram of these satisfaction ratings.

a   Describe where the satisfaction ratings seem to be concentrated.
b   Describe and interpret the shape of the distribution of ratings.
c   Write out the eight classes used to construct this histogram.
d   Construct a cumulative frequency distribution of the satisfaction ratings using the histogram classes.

2.22   THE BANK CUSTOMER WAITING TIME CASE   DS WaitTime

Recall that Table 1.8 (page 13) presents the waiting times for teller service during peak business hours of 100 randomly selected bank customers. Figure 2.16 gives the MINITAB output of a histogram of these waiting times that has been constructed using automatic classes.

a   Describe where the waiting times seem to be concentrated.
b   Describe and interpret the shape of the distribution of waiting times.
c   What is the class length that has been automatically defined by MINITAB?
d   Write out the automatically defined classes and construct a cumulative percent frequency distribution of the waiting times using these classes.

FIGURE 2.16   **MINITAB Frequency Histogram of the 100 Waiting Times Using Automatic Classes (for Exercise 2.22)**

FIGURE 2.17   **Percent Frequency Histogram of the 40 Breaking Strengths (for Exercise 2.23)**

2.23 THE TRASH BAG CASE   DS TrashBag

Recall that Table 1.9 (page 14) presents the breaking strengths of 40 trash bags selected during a 40-hour pilot production run. Figure 2.17 gives a percent frequency histogram of these breaking strengths.

  a Describe where the breaking strengths seem to be concentrated.

  b Describe and interpret the shape of the distribution of breaking strengths.

  c What is the class length?

  d Write out the classes and construct a percent frequency ogive for the breaking strengths using these classes.

2.24 Table 2.12 gives the franchise value and 2010 revenues for each of the 30 teams in Major League Baseball as reported by *Forbes* magazine and as listed on the Forbes.com website on June 14, 2011.   DS MLBTeams

  a Develop a frequency distribution and a frequency histogram for the 30 team values. Then describe the distribution of team values.

  b Develop a percent frequency distribution and a percent frequency histogram for the 30 team revenues. Then describe the distribution of team revenues.

  c Draw a percent frequency polygon for the 30 team values.

2.25 Table 2.13 gives America's top 40 best small companies of 2010 as rated on the Forbes.com website on June 14, 2011.   DS SmallComp

  a Develop a frequency distribution and a frequency histogram for the sales values. Describe the distribution of these sales values.

  b Develop a percent frequency histogram for the sales growth values and then describe this distribution.

TABLE 2.12   Major League Baseball Team Valuations and Revenues as Given on the Forbes.com Website on June 14, 2011 (for Exercise 2.24)   DS MLBTeams

Rank	Team	Value ($mil)	Revenue ($mil)	Rank	Team	Value ($mil)	Revenue ($mil)
1	New York Yankees	1,700	427	16	Washington Nationals	417	194
2	Boston Red Sox	912	272	17	Colorado Rockies	414	188
3	Los Angeles Dodgers	800	246	18	Baltimore Orioles	411	175
4	Chicago Cubs	773	258	19	San Diego Padres	406	159
5	New York Mets	747	233	20	Arizona Diamondbacks	396	180
6	Philadelphia Phillies	609	239	21	Detroit Tigers	385	192
7	San Francisco Giants	563	230	22	Milwaukee Brewers	376	179
8	Texas Rangers	561	206	23	Cincinnati Reds	375	179
9	Los Angeles Angels	554	222	24	Florida Marlins	360	143
10	Chicago White Sox	526	210	25	Cleveland Indians	353	168
11	St Louis Cardinals	518	207	26	Kansas City Royals	351	160
12	Minnesota Twins	490	213	27	Toronto Blue Jays	337	168
13	Atlanta Braves	482	201	28	Tampa Bay Rays	331	166
14	Houston Astros	474	197	29	Oakland Athletics	307	161
15	Seattle Mariners	449	204	30	Pittsburgh Pirates	304	160

Source: http://www.forbes.com/lists/2011/33/baseball-valuations-11_land.html (accessed June 14, 2011).

TABLE 2.13   America's Top 40 Best Small Companies of 2010 as Rated by *Forbes* Magazine (for Exercise 2.25)   DS SmallComp

Rank	Company	Sales ($mil)	Sales Growth (%)	Rank	Company	Sales ($mil)	Sales Growth (%)
1	Medifast	218	41	21	TransDigm Group	802	22
2	InterDigital	359	17	22	Quality Systems	308	27
3	American Public Education	174	49	23	Continental Resources	906	15
4	Deckers Outdoor	869	33	24	Balchem	235	31
5	WebMD Health	480	28	25	HMS Holdings In	261	39
6	NutriSystem	534	63	26	Interactive Intelligence	143	21
7	National Presto Industries	491	27	27	VSE	960	42
8	Industrial Services of America	285	3	28	Under Armour	926	34
9	True Religion Apparel	335	54	29	F5 Networks	803	31
10	Transcend Services	84	33	30	InnerWorkings	439	64
11	Rackspace Hosting	698	51	31	Akamai Technologies	930	35
12	UFP Technologies	115	8	32	Lumber Liquidators	598	26
13	GeoResources	98	86	33	Allegiant Travel	604	47
14	Strayer Education	579	22	34	Steven Madden	570	7
15	Tempur Pedic International	986	4	35	KMG Chemicals	195	35
16	iRobot	373	27	36	Sapient	766	23
17	Dolby Laboratories	859	21	37	Concur Technologies	280	37
18	Hittite Microwave	200	24	38	Syntel	469	19
19	Capella Education	385	23	39	Atwood Oceanics	621	33
20	LoopNet	75	37	40	FactSet Research Systems	641	21

Source: http://www.forbes.com/lists/2010/23/best-small-companies-10_land.html (accessed June 14, 2011).

LO2-4 Construct and interpret dot plots.

2.3 Dot Plots ● ● ●

A very simple graph that can be used to summarize a data set is called a **dot plot.** To make a dot plot we draw a horizontal axis that spans the range of the measurements in the data set. We then place dots above the horizontal axis to represent the measurements. As an example, Figure 2.18(a) shows a dot plot of the exam scores in Table 2.8. Remember, these are the scores for the first exam given before implementing a strict attendance policy. The horizontal axis spans exam

FIGURE 2.18   Comparing Exam Scores Using Dot Plots

(a) Dot Plot of Scores on Exam 1: Before Attendance Policy

(b) Dot Plot of Scores on Exam 2: After Attendance Policy

scores from 30 to 100. Each dot above the axis represents an exam score. For instance, the two dots above the score of 90 tell us that two students received a 90 on the exam. The dot plot shows us that there are two concentrations of scores—those in the 80s and 90s and those in the 60s. Figure 2.18(b) gives a dot plot of the scores on the second exam (which was given after imposing the attendance policy). As did the percent frequency polygon for Exam 2 in Figure 2.13, this second dot plot shows that the attendance policy eliminated the concentration of scores in the 60s.

Dot plots are useful for detecting **outliers,** which are unusually large or small observations that are well separated from the remaining observations. For example, the dot plot for exam 1 indicates that the score 32 seems unusually low. How we handle an outlier depends on its cause. If the outlier results from a measurement error or an error in recording or processing the data, it should be corrected. If such an outlier cannot be corrected, it should be discarded. If an outlier is not the result of an error in measuring or recording the data, its cause may reveal important information. For example, the outlying exam score of 32 convinced the author that the student needed a tutor. After working with a tutor, the student showed considerable improvement on Exam 2. A more precise way to detect outliers is presented in Section 3.3.

Exercises for Section 2.3

CONCEPTS

2.26   When we construct a dot plot, what does the horizontal axis represent? What does each dot represent?

2.27   If a data set consists of 1,000 measurements, would you summarize the data set using a histogram or a dot plot? Explain.

METHODS AND APPLICATIONS

2.28   The following data consist of the number of students who were absent in a professor's statistics class each day during the last month.   DS AbsenceData

2	0	3	1	2	5	8	0	1	4
1	10	6	2	2	0	3	6	0	1

Construct a dot plot of these data, and then describe the distribution of absences.

2.29   The following are the revenue growth rates for 30 fast-growing companies.   DS RevGrowth30

93%	43%	91%	49%	70%	44%	71%	70%	52%	59%
33%	40%	60%	35%	51%	48%	39%	61%	25%	87%
87%	46%	38%	30%	33%	43%	29%	38%	60%	32%

Develop a dot plot for these data and describe the distribution of revenue growth rates.

2.30   The yearly home run totals for Babe Ruth during his career as a New York Yankee are as follows (the totals are arranged in increasing order): 22, 25, 34, 35, 41, 41, 46, 46, 46, 47, 49, 54, 54, 59, 60. Construct a dot plot for these data and then describe the distribution of home run totals.
   🔵 RuthsHomers

LO2-5 Construct and interpret stem-and-leaf displays.

2.4 Stem-and-Leaf Displays ● ● ●

Another simple graph that can be used to quickly summarize a data set is called a **stem-and-leaf display.** This kind of graph places the measurements in order from smallest to largest, and allows the analyst to simultaneously see all of the measurements in the data set and see the shape of the data set's distribution.

EXAMPLE 2.4 The Car Mileage Case: Estimating Mileage

Table 2.14 presents the sample of 50 gas mileages for the new midsize model previously introduced in Chapter 1. To develop a stem-and-leaf display, we note that the sample mileages range from 29.8 to 33.3 and we place the leading digits of these mileages—the whole numbers 29, 30, 31, 32, and 33—in a column on the left side of a vertical line as follows.

```
29 |
30 |
31 |
32 |
33 |
```

This vertical arrangement of leading digits forms the **stem** of the display. Next, we pass through the mileages in Table 2.14 one at a time and place each last digit (the tenths place) to the right of the vertical line in the row corresponding to its leading digits. For instance, the first three mileages—30.8, 31.7, and 30.1—are arranged as follows:

```
29 |
30 | 8 1
31 | 7
32 |
33 |
```

We form the **leaves** of the display by continuing this procedure as we pass through all 50 mileages. After recording the last digit for each of the mileages, we sort the digits in each row from smallest to largest and obtain the stem-and-leaf display that follows:

```
29 | 8
30 | 1 3 4 5 5 6 7 7 8 8 8
31 | 0 0 1 2 3 3 4 4 4 4 4 5 5 6 6 7 7 7 8 8 9 9
32 | 0 1 1 1 2 3 3 4 4 5 5 7 7 8
33 | 0 3
```

As we have said, the numbers to the left of the vertical line form the stem of the display. Each number to the right of the vertical line is a leaf. Each combination of a stem value and a leaf value

TABLE 2.14   A Sample of 50 Mileages for a New Midsize Model   🔵 GasMiles

30.8	30.8	32.1	32.3	32.7
31.7	30.4	31.4	32.7	31.4
30.1	32.5	30.8	31.2	31.8
31.6	30.3	32.8	30.7	31.9
32.1	31.3	31.9	31.7	33.0
33.3	32.1	31.4	31.4	31.5
31.3	32.5	32.4	32.2	31.6
31.0	31.8	31.0	31.5	30.6
32.0	30.5	29.8	31.7	32.3
32.4	30.5	31.1	30.7	31.4

represents a measurement in the data set. For instance, the first row in the display

$$29 \mid 8$$

tells us that the first two digits are 29 and that the last (tenth place) digit is 8—that is, this combination represents the mileage 29.8 mpg. Similarly, the last row

$$33 \mid 0\ 3$$

represents the mileages 33.0 mpg and 33.3 mpg.

   The entire stem-and-leaf display portrays the overall distribution of the sample mileages. It groups the mileages into classes, and it graphically illustrates how many mileages are in each class, as well as how the mileages are distributed within each class. The first class corresponds to the stem 29 and consists of the mileages from 29.0 to 29.9. There is one mileage—29.8—in this class. The second class corresponds to the stem 30 and consists of the mileages from 30.0 to 30.9. There are 11 mileages in this class. Similarly, the third, fourth, and fifth classes correspond to the stems 31, 32, and 33 and contain, respectively, 22 mileages, 14 mileages, and 2 mileages. Moreover, the stem-and-leaf display shows that the distribution of mileages is quite symmetrical. To see this, imagine turning the stem-and-leaf display on its side so that the vertical line becomes a horizontal number line. We see that the display now resembles a symmetrically shaped histogram. However, *the stem-and-leaf display is advantageous because it allows us to actually see the measurements in the data set* in addition to the distribution's shape.

   When constructing a stem-and-leaf display, there are no rules that dictate the number of stem values (rows) that should be used. If we feel that the display has collapsed the mileages too closely together, we can stretch the display by assigning each set of leading digits to two or more rows. This is called *splitting the stems*. For example, in the following stem-and-leaf display of the mileages the first (uppermost) stem value of 30 is used to represent mileages between 30.0 and 30.4. The second stem value of 30 is used to represent mileages between 30.5 and 30.9.

```
29 | 8
30 | 1 3 4
30 | 5 5 6 7 7 8 8 8
31 | 0 0 1 2 3 3 4 4 4 4 4
31 | 5 5 6 6 7 7 7 8 8 9 9
32 | 0 1 1 1 2 3 3 4 4
32 | 5 5 7 7 8
33 | 0 3
```

Notice that, in this particular case, splitting the stems produces a display that seems to more clearly reveal the symmetrical shape of the distribution of mileages.

   Most statistical software packages can be used to construct stem-and-leaf displays. Figure 2.19 gives a MINITAB stem-and-leaf display of the 50 sample mileages. This output has been obtained by splitting the stems—MINITAB produced this display automatically. MINITAB also provides

FIGURE 2.19   MINITAB Stem-and-Leaf Display of the 50 Mileages

```
Stem-and-Leaf Display: Mpg
Stem-and-leaf of Mpg N = 50
Leaf unit = 0.10

   1     29   8
   4     30   134
  12     30   55677888
  23     31   00123344444
 (11)    31   55667778899
  16     32   011123344
   7     32   55778
   2     33   03
```

an additional column of numbers (on the left) that provides information about how many mileages are in the various rows. For example, if we look at the MINITAB output, the 11 (in parentheses) tells us that there are 11 mileages between 31.5 mpg and 31.9 mpg. The 12 (no parentheses) tells us that a total of 12 mileages are at or below 30.9 mpg, while the 7 tells us that a total of 7 mileages are at or above 32.5 mpg.

It is possible to construct a stem-and-leaf display from measurements containing any number of digits. To see how this can be done, consider the following data which consists of the number of DVD players sold by an electronics manufacturer for each of the last 12 months.

| 13,502 | 15,932 | 14,739 | 15,249 | 14,312 | 17,111 | DS DVDPlayers |
| 19,010 | 16,121 | 16,708 | 17,886 | 15,665 | 16,475 | |

To construct a stem-and-leaf display, we will use only the first three digits of each sales value and we will define leaf values consisting of one digit. The stem will consist of the values 13, 14, 15, 16, 17, 18, and 19 (which represent thousands of units sold). Each leaf will represent the remaining three digits rounded to the nearest 100 units sold. For example, 13,502 will be represented by placing the leaf value 5 in the row corresponding to 13. To express the fact that the leaf 5 represents 500, we say that the **leaf unit** is 100. Using this procedure, we obtain the following stem-and-leaf display:

$$\text{Leaf unit} = 100$$

```
13 | 5
14 | 3 7
15 | 2 7 9
16 | 1 5 7
17 | 1 9
18 |
19 | 0
```

The standard practice of always using a single digit for each leaf allows us to construct a stem-and-leaf display for measurements having any number of digits as long as we appropriately define a leaf unit. However, it is not possible to recover the original measurements from such a display. If we do not have the original measurements, the best we can do is to approximate them by multiplying the digits in the display by the leaf unit. For instance, the measurements in the row corresponding to the stem value 17 can be approximated to be $171 \times (100) = 17,100$ and $179 \times (100) = 17,900$. In general, leaf units can be any power of 10 such as 0.1, 1, 10, 100, 1000, and so on. If no leaf unit is given for a stem-and-leaf display, we assume its value is 1.0.

We summarize how to set up a stem-and-leaf display in the following box:

Constructing a Stem-and-Leaf Display

1 Decide what units will be used for the stems and the leaves. Each leaf must be a single digit and the stem values will consist of appropriate leading digits. As a general rule, there should be between 5 and 20 stem values.

2 Place the stem values in a column to the left of a vertical line with the smallest value at the top of the column and the largest value at the bottom of the column.

3 To the right of the vertical line, enter the leaf for each measurement into the row corresponding to the proper stem value. Each leaf should be a single digit—these can be rounded values that were originally more than one digit if we are using an appropriately defined leaf unit.

4 Rearrange the leaves so that they are in increasing order from left to right.

If we wish to compare two distributions, it is convenient to construct a **back-to-back stem-and-leaf display.** Figure 2.20 presents a back-to-back stem-and-leaf display for the previously discussed exam scores. The left side of the display summarizes the scores for the first exam. Remember, this exam was given before implementing a strict attendance policy. The right side of the display summarizes the scores for the second exam (which was given after imposing the attendance policy). Looking at the left side of the display, we see that for the first exam there are two concentrations of scores—those in the 80s and 90s and those in the 60s. The right side of the

---

FIGURE 2.20   **A Back-to-Back Stem-and-Leaf Display of the Exam Scores**

```
           Exam 1            Exam 2
                2   | 3 |
                    | 3 |
                    | 4 |
                5   | 4 |
                0   | 5 |
               86   | 5 | 5
           443110   | 6 | 2 3
          9987765   | 6 | 6 7 7
                2   | 7 | 1 3 4 4 4
               86   | 7 | 5 6 7 7 8
              331   | 8 | 0 2 3 4
           987765   | 8 | 5 6 6 7 7 8 9
         43322100   | 9 | 0 1 1 2 3 3 4 4
               86   | 9 | 5 7 9
```

display shows that the attendance policy eliminated the concentration of scores in the 60s and illustrates that the scores on exam 2 are almost single peaked and somewhat skewed to the left.

     Stem-and-leaf displays are useful for detecting **outliers,** which are unusually large or small observations that are well separated from the remaining observations. For example, the stem-and-leaf display for exam 1 indicates that the score 32 seems unusually low. How we handle an outlier depends on its cause. If the outlier results from a measurement error or an error in recording or processing the data, it should be corrected. If such an outlier cannot be corrected, it should be discarded. If an outlier is not the result of an error in measuring or recording the data, its cause may reveal important information. For example, the outlying exam score of 32 convinced the author that the student needed a tutor. After working with a tutor, the student showed considerable improvement on Exam 2. A more precise way to detect outliers is presented in Section 3.3.

Exercises for Section 2.4

CONCEPTS

2.31   Explain the difference between a histogram and a stem-and-leaf display.

2.32   What are the advantages of using a stem-and-leaf display?

2.33   If a data set consists of 1,000 measurements, would you summarize the data set by using a stem-and-leaf display or a histogram? Explain.

METHODS AND APPLICATIONS

2.34   The following data consist of the revenue growth rates (in percent) for a group of 20 firms. Construct a stem-and-leaf display for these data.   DS RevGrowth20

36	59	42	65	91	32	56	28	49	51
30	55	33	63	70	44	42	83	53	43

2.35   The following data consist of the profit margins (in percent) for a group of 20 firms. Construct a stem-and-leaf display for these data.   DS ProfitMar20

25.2	16.1	22.2	15.2	14.1	15.2	14.4	15.9	10.4	14.0
16.4	13.9	10.4	13.8	14.9	16.1	15.8	13.2	16.8	12.6

2.36   The following data consist of the sales figures (in millions of dollars) for a group of 20 firms. Construct a stem-and-leaf display for these data. Use a leaf unit equal to 100.   DS Sales20

6835	1973	2820	5358	1233	3291	2707	3291	2675	3707
3517	1449	2384	1376	1725	6047	7903	4616	1541	4189

2.37   **THE e-BILLING CASE AND THE MARKETING RESEARCH CASE**

Figure 2.21 gives stem-and-leaf displays of the payment times in Table 2.4 on page 42 and of the bottle design ratings in Table 1.5 on page 10. Describe the shapes of the two displays.   DS Paytime   DS Design

FIGURE 2.21   **Stem-and-Leaf Displays of the Payment Times and Bottle Design Ratings (for Exercise 2.37)**

Payment Times

10	0
11	
12	00
13	000
14	0000
15	0000000
16	000000000
17	00000000
18	000000
19	00000
20	000
21	0000
22	000
23	00
24	000
25	00
26	0
27	0
28	
29	0

Ratings

20	0
21	
22	0
23	
24	0
25	00
26	00
27	000
28	0000
29	00000
30	000000
31	00000000
32	00000000000
33	0000000000
34	00000
35	0

FIGURE 2.22   **Stem-and-Leaf Display of the 40 Breaking Strengths (for Exercise 2.38)**

Stem-and-leaf plot for strength
Stem unit = 1   Leaf unit = 0.1

Frequency	Stem	Leaf
1	46	8
0	47	
1	47	5
2	48	2 3
2	48	5 8
4	49	0 2 3 4
4	49	5 6 8 9
4	50	0 1 2 3
6	50	5 6 7 8 9 9
5	51	0 1 2 3 4
3	51	5 7 9
2	52	0 3
2	52	5 6
2	53	0 2
1	53	5
1	54	0
40		

2.38   THE TRASH BAG CASE   DS TrashBag

Figure 2.22 gives a stem-and-leaf display of the sample of 40 breaking strengths in the trash bag case.
a Use the stem-and-leaf display to describe the distribution of breaking strengths.
b Write out the 10 smallest breaking strengths as they would be expressed in the original data.

2.39   Babe Ruth's record of 60 home runs in a single year was broken by Roger Maris, who hit 61 home runs in 1961. The yearly home run totals for Ruth in his career as a New York Yankee are (arranged in increasing order) 22, 25, 34, 35, 41, 41, 46, 46, 46, 47, 49, 54, 54, 59, and 60. The yearly home run totals for Maris over his career in the American League are (arranged in increasing order) 8, 13, 14, 16, 23, 26, 28, 33, 39, and 61. Compare Ruth's and Maris's home run totals by constructing a back-to-back stem-and-leaf display. What would you conclude about Maris's record-breaking year?   DS HomeRuns

2.40   THE BANK CUSTOMER WAITING TIME CASE   DS WaitTime

Table 2.15 reproduces the 100 waiting times for teller service that were originally given in Table 1.8 (page 13).
a Construct a stem-and-leaf display of the waiting times.
b Describe the distribution of the waiting times.

2.41   THE VIDEO GAME SATISFACTION RATING CASE   DS VideoGame

Recall that 65 purchasers have participated in a survey and have rated the XYZ-Box video game system. The composite ratings that have been obtained are as follows:

39	38	40	40	40	46	43	38	44	44	44
45	42	42	47	46	45	41	43	46	44	42
38	46	45	44	41	45	40	36	48	44	47
42	44	44	43	43	46	43	44	44	46	43
42	40	42	45	39	43	44	44	41	39	45
41	39	46	45	43	47	41	45	45	41	

a Construct a stem-and-leaf display for the 65 composite ratings. Hint: Each whole number rating can be written with an "implied tenth place" of zero. For instance, 39 can be written as 39.0. Use the implied zeros as the leaf values and the whole numbers 36, 37, 38, 39, etc. as the stem values.
b Describe the distribution of composite ratings.
c If we consider a purchaser to be "very satisfied" if his or her composite score is at least 42, can we say that almost all purchasers of the XYZ-Box video game system are "very satisfied"?

TABLE 2.15   Waiting Times (in Minutes) for the Bank Customer Waiting Time Case (for Exercise 2.40)   ⚪S WaitTime

1.6	6.2	3.2	5.6	7.9	6.1	7.2
6.6	5.4	6.5	4.4	1.1	3.8	7.3
5.6	4.9	2.3	4.5	7.2	10.7	4.1
5.1	5.4	8.7	6.7	2.9	7.5	6.7
3.9	.8	4.7	8.1	9.1	7.0	3.5
4.6	2.5	3.6	4.3	7.7	5.3	6.3
6.5	8.3	2.7	2.2	4.0	4.5	4.3
6.4	6.1	3.7	5.8	1.4	4.5	3.8
8.6	6.3	.4	8.6	7.8	1.8	5.1
4.2	6.8	10.2	2.0	5.2	3.7	5.5
5.8	9.8	2.8	8.0	8.4	4.0	
3.4	2.9	11.6	9.5	6.3	5.7	
9.3	10.9	4.3	1.3	4.4	2.4	
7.4	4.7	3.1	4.8	5.2	9.2	
1.8	3.9	5.8	9.9	7.4	5.0	

2.5 Contingency Tables (Optional) ⚪ ⚫ ⚫

Previous sections in this chapter have presented methods for summarizing data for a single variable. Often, however, we wish to use statistics to study possible relationships between several variables. In this section we present a simple way to study the relationship between two variables. Crosstabulation is a process that classifies data on two dimensions. This process results in a table that is called a **contingency table**. Such a table consists of rows and columns—the rows classify the data according to one dimension and the columns classify the data according to a second dimension. Together, the rows and columns represent all possibilities (or *contingencies*).

LO2-6 Examine the relationships between variables by using contingency tables (Optional).

EXAMPLE 2.5 The Brokerage Firm Case: Studying Client Satisfaction

An investment broker sells several kinds of investment products—a stock fund, a bond fund, and a tax-deferred annuity. The broker wishes to study whether client satisfaction with its products and services depends on the type of investment product purchased. To do this, 100 of the broker's clients are randomly selected from the population of clients who have purchased shares in exactly one of the funds. The broker records the fund type purchased by each client and has one of its investment counselors personally contact the client. When contacted, the client is asked to rate his or her level of satisfaction with the purchased fund as high, medium, or low. The resulting data are given in Table 2.16.

Looking at the raw data in Table 2.16, it is difficult to see whether the level of client satisfaction varies depending on the fund type. We can look at the data in an organized way by constructing a contingency table. A cross-tabulation of fund type versus level of client satisfaction is shown in Table 2.17. The classification categories for the two variables are defined along the left and top margins of the table. The three row labels—bond fund, stock fund, and tax deferred annuity—define the three fund categories and are given in the left table margin. The three column labels—high, medium, and low—define the three levels of client satisfaction and are given along the top table margin. Each row and column combination, that is, each fund type and level of satisfaction combination, defines what we call a "cell" in the table. Because each of the randomly selected clients has invested in exactly one fund type and has reported exactly one level of satisfaction, each client can be placed in a particular cell in the contingency table. For example, because client number 1 in Table 2.16 has invested in the bond fund and reports a high level of client satisfaction, client number 1 can be placed in the upper left cell of the table (the cell defined by the Bond Fund row and High Satisfaction column).

We fill in the cells in the table by moving through the 100 randomly selected clients and by tabulating the number of clients who can be placed in each cell. For instance, moving through the 100 clients results in placing 15 clients in the "bond fund—high" cell, 12 clients in the

TABLE 2.16   Results of a Customer Satisfaction Survey Given to 100 Randomly Selected Clients Who Invest in One of Three Fund Types—a Bond Fund, a Stock Fund, or a Tax-Deferred Annuity   DS Invest

Client	Fund Type	Level of Satisfaction	Client	Fund Type	Level of Satisfaction	Client	Fund Type	Level of Satisfaction
1	BOND	HIGH	35	STOCK	HIGH	69	BOND	MED
2	STOCK	HIGH	36	BOND	MED	70	TAXDEF	MED
3	TAXDEF	MED	37	TAXDEF	MED	71	TAXDEF	MED
4	TAXDEF	MED	38	TAXDEF	LOW	72	BOND	HIGH
5	STOCK	LOW	39	STOCK	HIGH	73	TAXDEF	MED
6	STOCK	HIGH	40	TAXDEF	MED	74	TAXDEF	LOW
7	STOCK	HIGH	41	BOND	HIGH	75	STOCK	HIGH
8	BOND	MED	42	BOND	HIGH	76	BOND	HIGH
9	TAXDEF	LOW	43	BOND	LOW	77	TAXDEF	LOW
10	TAXDEF	LOW	44	TAXDEF	LOW	78	BOND	MED
11	STOCK	MED	45	STOCK	HIGH	79	STOCK	HIGH
12	BOND	LOW	46	BOND	HIGH	80	STOCK	HIGH
13	STOCK	HIGH	47	BOND	MED	81	BOND	MED
14	TAXDEF	MED	48	STOCK	HIGH	82	TAXDEF	MED
15	TAXDEF	MED	49	TAXDEF	MED	83	BOND	HIGH
16	TAXDEF	LOW	50	TAXDEF	MED	84	STOCK	MED
17	STOCK	HIGH	51	STOCK	HIGH	85	STOCK	HIGH
18	BOND	HIGH	52	TAXDEF	MED	86	BOND	MED
19	BOND	MED	53	STOCK	HIGH	87	TAXDEF	MED
20	TAXDEF	MED	54	TAXDEF	MED	88	TAXDEF	LOW
21	TAXDEF	MED	55	STOCK	LOW	89	STOCK	HIGH
22	BOND	HIGH	56	BOND	HIGH	90	TAXDEF	MED
23	TAXDEF	MED	57	STOCK	HIGH	91	BOND	HIGH
24	TAXDEF	LOW	58	BOND	MED	92	TAXDEF	HIGH
25	STOCK	HIGH	59	TAXDEF	LOW	93	TAXDEF	LOW
26	BOND	HIGH	60	TAXDEF	LOW	94	TAXDEF	LOW
27	TAXDEF	LOW	61	STOCK	MED	95	STOCK	HIGH
28	BOND	MED	62	BOND	LOW	96	BOND	HIGH
29	STOCK	HIGH	63	STOCK	HIGH	97	BOND	MED
30	STOCK	HIGH	64	TAXDEF	MED	98	STOCK	HIGH
31	BOND	MED	65	TAXDEF	MED	99	TAXDEF	MED
32	TAXDEF	MED	66	TAXDEF	LOW	100	TAXDEF	MED
33	BOND	HIGH	67	STOCK	HIGH			
34	STOCK	MED	68	BOND	HIGH			

TABLE 2.17   A Contingency Table of Fund Type versus Level of Client Satisfaction

Fund Type	Level of Satisfaction			Total
	High	Medium	Low	
Bond Fund	15	12	3	30
Stock Fund	24	4	2	30
Tax Deferred Annuity	1	24	15	40
Total	40	40	20	100

"bond fund—medium" cell, and so forth. The counts in the cells are called the **cell frequencies.** In Table 2.17 these frequencies tell us that 15 clients invested in the bond fund and reported a high level of satisfaction, 4 clients invested in the stock fund and reported a medium level of satisfaction, and so forth.

The far right column in the table (labeled Total) is obtained by summing the cell frequencies across the rows. For instance, these totals tell us that 15 + 12 + 3 = 30 clients invested in the bond fund, 24 + 4 + 2 = 30 clients invested in the stock fund, and 1 + 24 + 15 = 40 clients invested in the tax deferred annuity. These **row totals** provide a frequency distribution for the different fund types. By dividing the row totals by the total of 100 clients surveyed, we can obtain relative frequencies; and by multiplying each relative frequency by 100, we can obtain percent frequencies. That is, we can obtain the frequency, relative frequency, and percent frequency distributions for fund type as follows:

Fund Type	Frequency	Relative Frequency	Percent Frequency
Bond fund	30	30/100 = .30	.30 (100) = 30%
Stock fund	30	30/100 = .30	.30 (100) = 30%
Tax deferred annuity	40	40/100 = .40	.40 (100) = 40%
	100		

We see that 30 percent of the clients invested in the bond fund, 30 percent invested in the stock fund, and 40 percent invested in the tax deferred annuity.

The bottom row in the table (labeled Total) is obtained by summing the cell frequencies down the columns. For instance, these totals tell us that $15 + 24 + 1 = 40$ clients reported a high level of satisfaction, $12 + 4 + 24 = 40$ clients reported a medium level of satisfaction, and $3 + 2 + 15 = 20$ clients reported a low level of satisfaction. These **column totals** provide a frequency distribution for the different satisfaction levels (see below). By dividing the column totals by the total of 100 clients surveyed, we can obtain relative frequencies, and by multiplying each relative frequency by 100, we can obtain percent frequencies. That is, we can obtain the frequency, relative frequency, and percent frequency distributions for level of satisfaction as follows:

Level of Satisfaction	Frequency	Relative Frequency	Percent Frequency
High	40	40/100 = .40	.40 (100) = 40%
Medium	40	40/100 = .40	.40 (100) = 40%
Low	20	20/100 = .20	.20 (100) = 20%
	100		

We see that 40 percent of all clients reported high satisfaction, 40 percent reported medium satisfaction, and 20 percent reported low satisfaction.

We have seen that the totals in the margins of the contingency table give us frequency distributions that provide information about each of the variables *fund type* and *level of client satisfaction.* However, the main purpose of constructing the table is to investigate possible relationships *between* these variables. Looking at Table 2.17, we see that clients who have invested in the stock fund seem to be highly satisfied and that those who have invested in the bond fund seem to have a high to medium level of satisfaction. However, clients who have invested in the tax deferred annuity seem to be less satisfied.

One good way to investigate relationships such as these is to compute **row percentages** and **column percentages.** We compute row percentages by dividing each cell's frequency by its corresponding row total and by expressing the resulting fraction as a percentage. For instance, the row percentage for the upper left-hand cell (bond fund and high level of satisfaction) in Table 2.17 is $(15/30) \times 100\% = 50\%$. Similarly, column percentages are computed by dividing each cell's frequency by its corresponding column total and by expressing the resulting fraction as a percentage. For example, the column percentage for the upper left-hand cell in Table 2.17 is $(15/40) \times 100\% = 37.5\%$. Table 2.18 summarizes all of the row percentages for the different fund types in Table 2.17. We see that each row in Table 2.18 gives a percentage frequency distribution of level of client satisfaction given a particular fund type.

For example, the first row in Table 2.18 gives a percent frequency distribution of client satisfaction for investors who have purchased shares in the bond fund. We see that 50 percent of

TABLE 2.18   **Row Percentages for Each Fund Type**

	Level of Satisfaction			
Fund Type	**High**	**Medium**	**Low**	**Total**
Bond Fund	50%	40%	10%	100%
Stock Fund	80%	13.33%	6.67%	100%
Tax Deferred	2.5%	60%	37.5%	100%

FIGURE 2.23   **Bar Charts Illustrating Percent Frequency Distributions of Client Satisfaction as Given by the Row Percentages for the Three Fund Types in Table 2.18**

bond fund investors report high satisfaction, while 40 percent of these investors report medium satisfaction, and only 10 percent report low satisfaction. The other rows in Table 2.18 provide percent frequency distributions of client satisfaction for stock fund and annuity purchasers.

All three percent frequency distributions of client satisfaction—for the bond fund, the stock fund, and the tax deferred annuity—are illustrated using bar charts in Figure 2.23. In this figure, the bar heights for each chart are the respective row percentages in Table 2.18. For example, these distributions tell us that 80 percent of stock fund investors report high satisfaction, while 97.5 percent of tax deferred annuity purchasers report medium or low satisfaction. Looking at the entire table of row percentages (or the bar charts in Figure 2.23), we might conclude that stock fund investors are highly satisfied, that bond fund investors are quite satisfied (but, somewhat less so than stock fund investors), and that tax-deferred-annuity purchasers are less satisfied than either stock fund or bond fund investors. In general, row percentages and column percentages help us to quantify relationships such as these.

In the investment example, we have cross-tabulated two qualitative variables. We can also cross-tabulate a quantitative variable versus a qualitative variable or two quantitative variables against each other. If we are cross-tabulating a quantitative variable, we often define categories by using appropriate ranges. For example, if we wished to cross-tabulate level of education (grade school, high school, college, graduate school) versus income, we might define income classes $0–$50,000, $50,001–$100,000, $100,001–$150,000, and above $150,000.

Exercises for Section 2.5

CONCEPTS

connect

2.42 Explain the purpose behind constructing a contingency table.

2.43 A contingency table consists of several "cells". Explain how we fill the cells in the table.

2.44 Explain how to compute (1) the row percentages for a contingency table, and (2) the column percentages. What information is provided by the row percentages in a particular row of the table? What information is provided by the column percentages in a particular column of the table?

METHODS AND APPLICATIONS

Exercises 2.45 through 2.47 are based on the following situation:

The marketing department at the Rola-Cola Bottling Company is investigating the attitudes and preferences of consumers toward Rola-Cola and a competing soft drink, Koka-Cola. Forty randomly selected shoppers are given a "blind taste-test" and are asked to give their cola preferences. The results are given in Table 2.19—each shopper's preference, Rola-Cola or Koka-Cola, is revealed to the shopper only after he or she has tasted both brands without knowing which cola is which. In addition, each survey participant is asked to answer three more questions: (1) Have you previously purchased Rola-Cola: Yes

TABLE 2.19 Rola-Cola Bottling Company Survey Results ⬭ ColaSurvey

Shopper	Cola Preference	Previously Purchased?	Sweetness Preference	Monthly Cola Consumption	Shopper	Cola Preference	Previously Purchased?	Sweetness Preference	Monthly Cola Consumption
1	Koka	No	Very Sweet	4	21	Koka	No	Very Sweet	4
2	Rola	Yes	Sweet	8	22	Rola	Yes	Not So Sweet	9
3	Koka	No	Not So Sweet	2	23	Rola	Yes	Not So Sweet	3
4	Rola	Yes	Sweet	10	24	Koka	No	Not So Sweet	2
5	Rola	No	Very Sweet	7	25	Koka	No	Sweet	5
6	Rola	Yes	Not So Sweet	6	26	Rola	Yes	Very Sweet	7
7	Koka	No	Very Sweet	4	27	Koka	No	Very Sweet	7
8	Rola	No	Very Sweet	3	28	Rola	Yes	Sweet	8
9	Koka	No	Sweet	3	29	Rola	Yes	Not So Sweet	6
10	Rola	No	Very Sweet	5	30	Koka	No	Not So Sweet	3
11	Rola	Yes	Sweet	7	31	Koka	Yes	Sweet	10
12	Rola	Yes	Not So Sweet	13	32	Rola	Yes	Very Sweet	8
13	Rola	Yes	Very Sweet	6	33	Koka	Yes	Sweet	4
14	Koka	No	Very Sweet	2	34	Rola	No	Sweet	5
15	Koka	No	Not So Sweet	7	35	Rola	Yes	Not So Sweet	3
16	Rola	Yes	Sweet	9	36	Koka	No	Very Sweet	11
17	Koka	No	Not So Sweet	1	37	Rola	Yes	Not So Sweet	9
18	Rola	Yes	Very Sweet	5	38	Rola	No	Very Sweet	6
19	Rola	No	Sweet	4	39	Koka	No	Not So Sweet	2
20	Rola	No	Sweet	12	40	Rola	Yes	Sweet	5

or No? (2) What is your sweetness preference for cola drinks: very sweet, sweet, or not so sweet? (3) How many 12-packs of cola drinks does your family consume in a typical month? These responses are also given in Table 2.19.

2.45 Construct a contingency table using cola preference (Rola or Koka) as the row variable and Rola-Cola purchase history (Yes or No) as the column variable. Based on the table, answer the following.

a How many shoppers who preferred Rola-Cola in the blind taste test had previously purchased Rola-Cola?

b How many shoppers who preferred Koka-Cola in the blind taste test had not previously purchased Rola-Cola?

c What kind of relationship, if any, seems to exist between cola preference and Rola-Cola purchase history?

2.46 Construct a contingency table using cola preference (Rola or Koka) as the row variable and sweetness preference (very sweet, sweet, or not so sweet) as the column variable. Based on the table, answer the following:

a How many shoppers who preferred Rola-Cola in the blind taste test said that they preferred a cola drink to be either very sweet or sweet?

b How many shoppers who preferred Koka-Cola in the blind taste test said that they preferred a cola drink to be not so sweet?

c What kind of relationship, if any, seems to exist between cola preference and sweetness preference?

2.47 Construct a contingency table using cola preference (Rola or Koka) as the row variable and the number of 12-packs consumed in a typical month (categories 0 through 5, 6 through 10, and more than 10) as the column variable. Based on the table, answer the following:

a How many shoppers who preferred Rola-Cola in the blind taste test purchase 10 or fewer 12-packs of cola drinks in a typical month?

b How many shoppers who preferred Koka-Cola in the blind taste test purchase 6 or more 12-packs of cola drinks in a typical month?

c What kind of relationship, if any, seems to exist between cola preference and cola consumption in a typical month?

2.48 A marketing research firm wishes to study the relationship between wine consumption and whether a person likes to watch professional tennis on television. One hundred randomly selected people are asked whether they drink wine and whether they watch tennis. The following results are obtained: DS WineCons

	Watch Tennis	Do Not Watch Tennis	Total
Drink Wine	16	24	40
Do Not Drink Wine	4	56	60
Total	20	80	100

a   What percentage of those surveyed both watch tennis and drink wine? What percentage of those surveyed do neither?
b   Using the survey data, construct a table of row percentages.
c   Using the survey data, construct a table of column percentages.
d   What kind of relationship, if any, seems to exist between whether or not a person watches tennis and whether or not a person drinks wine?
e   Illustrate your conclusion of part (d) by plotting bar charts of appropriate column percentages for people who watch tennis and for people who do not watch tennis.

2.49   In a survey of 1,000 randomly selected U.S. citizens aged 21 years or older, 721 believed that the amount of violent television programming had increased over the past 10 years, 454 believed that the overall quality of television programming had gotten worse over the past 10 years, and 362 believed both.

a   Use this information to fill in the contingency table below.

	TV Violence Increased	TV Violence Not Increased	Total
TV Quality Worse			
TV Quality Not Worse			
Total			

b   Using the completed contingency table, construct a table of row percentages.
c   Using the completed contingency table, construct a table of column percentages.
d   What kind of relationship, if any, seems to exist between whether a person believed that TV violence had increased over the past ten years and whether a person believed that the overall quality of TV programming had gotten worse over the past ten years?
e   Illustrate your answer to part (d) by constructing bar charts of appropriate row percentages.

In Exercises 2.50 and 2.51 we consider the results of a Gallup Lifestyle Poll about restaurant tipping habits as reported by the Gallup News Service on January 8, 2007. The poll asked Americans to recommend the percentage of a restaurant bill that should be left as a tip. As reported on galluppoll.com, Americans gave an overall (average) recommendation of 16.2 percent.

2.50   As part of its study, Gallup investigated a possible relationship between tipping attitudes and income. Using the poll results, the following row percentages can be obtained for three income ranges—less than \$30,000; \$30,000 through \$74,999; and \$75,000 or more.   DS RowPercents

	Appropriate Tip Percent*				
Income	Less than 15%	15%	16–19%	20% or more	Total
Less than \$30,000	28.41%	42.04%	1.14%	28.41%	100%
\$30,000 through \$74,999	15.31%	42.86%	6.12%	35.71%	100%
\$75,000 or more	8.16%	32.66%	9.18%	50.00%	100%

*Among those surveyed having an opinion.

a   Construct a percentage bar chart of recommended tip percentage for each of the three income ranges.
b   Using the bar charts, describe the relationship between recommended tip percentage and income level.

2.51   Gallup also asked survey participants if they have ever eaten at a restaurant and left no tip at all because of poor service. Almost half (46 percent) of those surveyed said they have done so. Because it seems that whether or not a person has left a restaurant without tipping might be related to a person's generosity in terms of recommended tip percentage, the survey investigated this possible relationship. Using the poll results, the column percentages at the top of page 67 can be obtained for each of the categories "Yes, have left without tipping" and "No, have not left without tipping."   DS ColPercents

	Tip less than 15%	Tip 15% through 19%	Tip 20% or more
Yes, have left without tipping	64%	50%	35%
No, have not left without tipping	36%	50%	65%
Total	100%	100%	100%

a Construct a percentage bar chart of the categories "Yes, have left without tipping" and "No, have not left without tipping" for each of the tip categories "less than 15%," "15% through 19%," and "20% or more."

b Using the bar charts, describe the relationship between whether or not a person has left without tipping and tipping generosity.

2.6 Scatter Plots (Optional) ● ● ●

LO2-7 Examine the relationships between variables by using scatter plots (Optional).

We often study relationships between variables by using graphical methods. A simple graph that can be used to study the relationship between two variables is called a **scatter plot.** As an example, suppose that a marketing manager wishes to investigate the relationship between the sales volume (in thousands of units) of a product and the amount spent (in units of $10,000) on advertising the product. To do this, the marketing manager randomly selects 10 sales regions having equal sales potential. The manager assigns a different level of advertising expenditure for January 2011 to each sales region as shown in Table 2.20. At the end of the month, the sales volume for each region is recorded as also shown in Table 2.20.

A scatter plot of these data is given in Figure 2.24. To construct this plot, we place the variable advertising expenditure (denoted x) on the horizontal axis and we place the variable sales volume (denoted y) on the vertical axis. For the first sales region, advertising expenditure equals 5 and sales volume equals 89. We plot the point with coordinates $x = 5$ and $y = 89$ on the scatter plot to represent this sales region. Points for the other sales regions are plotted similarly. The scatter plot shows that there is a positive relationship between advertising expenditure and sales volume—that is, higher values of sales volume are associated with higher levels of advertising expenditure.

We have drawn a straight line through the plotted points of the scatter plot to represent the relationship between advertising expenditure and sales volume. We often do this when the relationship between two variables appears to be a **straight line,** or **linear.** Of course, the relationship between x and y in Figure 2.24 is not perfectly linear—not all of the points in the scatter plot are exactly on the line. Nevertheless, because the relationship between x and y appears to be approximately linear, it seems reasonable to represent the general relationship between these variables using a straight line. In future chapters we will explain ways to quantify such a relationship—that is, describe such a relationship numerically. We will show that we can statistically express the strength of a linear relationship and that we can calculate the equation of the line that best fits the points of a scatter plot.

TABLE 2.20	Values of Advertising Expenditure (in $10,000s) and Sales Volume (in 1000s) for Ten Sales Regions ⑤ SalesPlot	
Sales Region	Advertising Expenditure, x	Sales Volume, y
1	5	89
2	6	87
3	7	98
4	8	110
5	9	103
6	10	114
7	11	116
8	12	110
9	13	126
10	14	130

FIGURE 2.24   A Scatter Plot of Sales Volume versus Advertising Expenditure

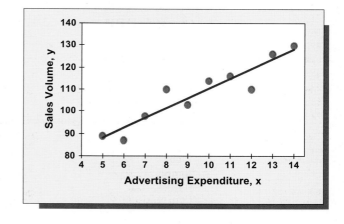

FIGURE 2.25 A Positive Linear Relationship	FIGURE 2.26 Little or No Linear Relationship	FIGURE 2.27 A Negative Linear Relationship
		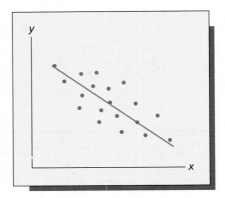

A scatter plot can reveal various kinds of relationships. For instance, Figures 2.25, 2.26, and 2.27 show several possible relationships between two variables x and y. Figure 2.25 shows a relationship similar to that of our advertising expenditure–sales volume example—here y has a tendency to increase as x increases. Figure 2.26 illustrates a situation in which x and y do not appear to have any linear relationship. Figure 2.27 illustrates a negative linear relationship—here y has a tendency to decrease as x increases. Finally, not all relationships are linear. In Chapter 15 we will consider how to represent and quantify curved relationships.

To conclude this section, recall from Chapter 1 that a **time series plot** (also called a **runs plot**) is a plot of individual process measurements versus time. This implies that a time series plot is a scatter plot, where values of a process variable are plotted on the vertical axis versus corresponding values of time on the horizontal axis.

Exercises for Section 2.6

CONCEPTS

2.52 Explain the purpose for constructing a scatter plot of y versus x.

2.53 Draw a scatter plot of y versus x in which y increases in a linear fashion as x increases.

2.54 Draw a scatter plot of y versus x in which y decreases in a linear fashion as x increases.

2.55 Draw a scatter plot of y versus x in which there is little or no linear relationship between y and x.

2.56 Discuss the relationship between a scatter plot and a time series plot.

METHODS AND APPLICATIONS

2.57 **THE REAL ESTATE SALES PRICE CASE**   DS RealEst

A real estate agency collects data concerning $y =$ the sales price of a house (in thousands of dollars), and $x =$ the home size (in hundreds of square feet). The data are given in Table 2.21. Construct a scatter plot of y versus x and interpret what the plot says.

2.58 **THE NATURAL GAS CONSUMPTION CASE**   DS GasCon1

Table 2.22 gives the average hourly outdoor temperature (x) in a city during a week and the city's natural gas consumption (y) during the week for each of the previous eight weeks (the temperature readings are expressed in degrees Fahrenheit and the natural gas consumptions are expressed in millions of cubic feet of natural gas). The MINITAB output in Figure 2.28 gives a scatter plot of y versus x. Discuss the nature of the relationship between y and x.

TABLE 2.21

Real Estate Sales Price Data

DS RealEst

Sales Price (y)	Home Size (x)
180	23
98.1	11
173.1	20
136.5	17
141	15
165.9	21
193.5	24
127.8	13
163.5	19
172.5	25

Source: Reprinted with permission from *The Real Estate Appraiser and Analyst,* Spring 1986. Copyright 1986 by the Appraisal Institute, Chicago, Illinois.

TABLE 2.22	The Natural Gas Consumption Data DS GasCon1							
Week	1	2	3	4	5	6	7	8
Temperature, x	28.0	28.0	32.5	39.0	45.9	57.8	58.1	62.5
Natural Gas Consumption, y	12.4	11.7	12.4	10.8	9.4	9.5	8.0	7.5

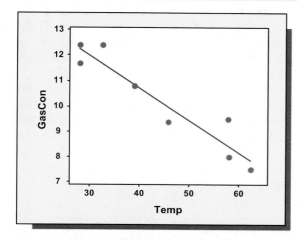

FIGURE 2.28 MINITAB Scatter Plot of the Natural Gas Consumption Data (for Exercise 2.58)

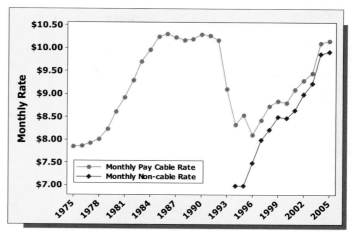

FIGURE 2.29 Time Series Plots for Exercise 2.59 **DS** PayTVRates

FIGURE 2.30 A Scatter Plot of Units Sold versus Shelf Space (for Exercise 2.60)

Source: W. R. Dillon, T. J. Madden, and N. H. Firtle, *Essentials of Marketing Research* (Burr Ridge, IL: Richard D. Irwin, Inc., 1993), p. 452. Copyright © 1993. Reprinted by permission of McGraw-Hill Companies, Inc.

FIGURE 2.31 Excel Output of the Mean Restaurant Ratings and a Scatter Plot of Mean Preference versus Mean Taste (for Exercise 2.61) **DS** FastFood

	A	B	C	D	E	F
1	Restaurant	Meantaste	Meanconv	Meanfam	Meanprice	Meanpref
2	Borden Burger	3.5659	2.7005	2.5282	2.9372	4.2552
3	Hardee's	3.329	3.3483	2.7345	2.7513	4.0911
4	Burger King	2.4231	2.7377	2.3368	3.0761	3.0052
5	McDonald's	2.0895	1.938	1.4619	2.4884	2.2429
6	Wendy's	1.9661	2.892	2.3376	4.0814	2.5351
7	White Castle	3.8061	3.7242	2.6515	1.708	4.7812

Source: The Ohio State University.

2.59 Figure 2.29 gives a time series plot of the average U.S. monthly pay cable TV rate (for premium services) for each year from 1975 to 2005. Figure 2.29 also gives a time series plot of the average monthly non-cable (mostly satellite) TV rate (for premium services) for each year from 1994 to 2005.[5] Satellite TV became a serious competitor to cable TV in the early 1990s. Does it appear that the emergence of satellite TV had an influence on cable TV rates? What happened after satellite TV became more established in the marketplace? **DS** PayTVRates

2.60 Figure 2.30 gives a scatter plot of the number of units sold, *y*, of 20 varieties of a canned soup versus the amount of shelf space, *x*, allocated to each variety. Do you think that sales are affected by the amount of allocated shelf space, or vice versa?

2.61 THE FAST-FOOD RESTAURANT RATING CASE **DS** FastFood

Figure 2.31 presents the ratings given by 406 randomly selected individuals of six fast food restaurants on the basis of taste, convenience, familiarity, and price. The data were collected by researchers at The Ohio State University in the early 1990s. Here, 1 is the best rating and 6 the worst. In addition, each individual ranked the restaurants from 1 through 6 on the basis of overall preference. Interpret the Excel scatter plot, and construct and interpret other relevant scatter plots.

---

[5]The time series data for this exercise are on the website for this book.

2.7 Misleading Graphs and Charts (Optional) ● ● ●

The statistical analyst's goal should be to present the most accurate and truthful portrayal of a data set that is possible. Such a presentation allows managers using the analysis to make informed decisions. However, it is possible to construct statistical summaries that are misleading. Although we do not advocate using misleading statistics, you should be aware of some of the ways statistical graphs and charts can be manipulated in order to distort the truth. By knowing what to look for, you can avoid being misled by a (we hope) small number of unscrupulous practitioners.

As an example, suppose that the nurses at a large hospital will soon vote on a proposal to join a union. Both the union organizers and the hospital administration plan to distribute recent salary statistics to the entire nursing staff. Suppose that the mean nurses' salary at the hospital and the mean nurses' salary increase at the hospital (expressed as a percentage) for each of the last four years are as follows:

Year	Mean Salary	Mean Salary Increase (Percent)
1	$60,000	3.0%
2	61,600	4.0
3	63,500	4.5
4	66,100	6.0

The hospital administration does not want the nurses to unionize and, therefore, hopes to convince the nurses that substantial progress has been made to increase salaries without a union. On the other hand, the union organizers wish to portray the salary increases as minimal so that the nurses will feel the need to unionize.

Figure 2.32 gives two bar charts of the mean nurses' salaries at the hospital for each of the last four years. Notice that in Figure 2.32(a) the administration has started the vertical scale of the bar chart at a salary of $58,000 by using a *scale break* (⌇). Alternatively, the chart could be set up without the scale break by simply starting the vertical scale at $58,000. Starting the vertical scale at a value far above zero makes the salary increases look more dramatic. Notice that when the union organizers present the bar chart in Figure 2.32(b), which has a vertical scale starting at zero, the salary increases look far less impressive.

Figure 2.33 presents two bar charts of the mean nurses' salary increases (in percentages) at the hospital for each of the last four years. In Figure 2.33(a), the administration has made the widths of the bars representing the percentage increases proportional to their heights. This makes the upward movement in the mean salary increases look more dramatic because the observer's eye tends to compare the areas of the bars, while the improvements in the mean salary increases are really only proportional to the heights of the bars. When the union organizers present the bar chart of Figure 2.33(b), the improvements in the mean salary increases look less impressive because each bar has the same width.

FIGURE 2.32   **Two Bar Charts of the Mean Nurses' Salaries at a Large Hospital for the Last Four Years**

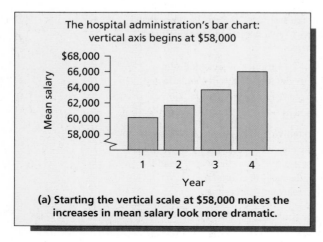

(a) Starting the vertical scale at $58,000 makes the increases in mean salary look more dramatic.

(b) When the vertical scale starts at zero, the increases in mean salary look less impressive.

FIGURE 2.33   **Two Bar Charts of the Mean Nurses' Salary Increases at a Large Hospital for the Last Four Years.**

(a) Making the width of the bars proportional to the heights of the bars makes the improvements in the mean salary look more dramatic.

(b) The improvements in the mean salary increases look less impressive when the widths of the bars are the same.

FIGURE 2.34   **Two Time Series Plots of the Mean Nurses' Salary Increases at a Large Hospital for the Last Four Years**

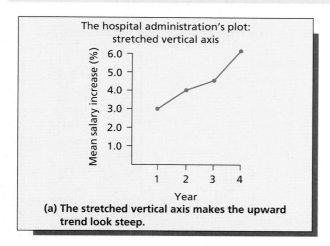

(a) The stretched vertical axis makes the upward trend look steep.

(b) The compressed vertical axis makes the upward trend look very gradual.

    Figure 2.34 gives two time series plots of the mean nurses' salary increases at the hospital for the last four years. In Figure 2.34(a) the administration has stretched the vertical axis of the graph. That is, the vertical axis is set up so that the distances between the percentages are large. This makes the upward trend of the mean salary increases appear to be steep. In Figure 2.34(b) the union organizers have compressed the vertical axis (that is, the distances between the percentages are small). This makes the upward trend of the mean salary increases appear to be gradual. As we will see in the exercises, stretching and compressing the horizontal axis in a time series plot can also greatly affect the impression given by the plot.

    It is also possible to create totally different interpretations of the same statistical summary by simply using different labeling or captions. For example, consider the bar chart of mean nurses' salary increases in Figure 2.33(b). To create a favorable interpretation, the hospital administration might use the caption "Salary Increase Is Higher for the Fourth Year in a Row." On the other hand, the union organizers might create a negative impression by using the caption "Salary Increase Fails to Reach 10% for Fourth Straight Year."

    In summary, we do not approve of using statistics to mislead and distort reality. Statistics should be used to present the most truthful and informative summary of the data that is possible. However, it is important to carefully study any statistical summary so that you will not be misled. Look for manipulations such as stretched or compressed axes on graphs, axes that do not begin at zero, and bar charts with bars of varying widths. Also, carefully think about assumptions, and make your own conclusions about the meaning of any statistical summary rather than relying on captions written by others. Doing these things will help you to see the truth and to make well-informed decisions.

Exercises for Section 2.7

CONCEPTS

2.62 When we construct a bar chart or graph, what is the effect of starting the vertical axis at a value that is far above zero? Explain.

2.63 Find an example of a misleading use of statistics in a newspaper, magazine, corporate annual report, or other source. Then explain why your example is misleading.

METHODS AND APPLICATIONS

2.64 Figure 2.35 gives two more time series plots of the previously discussed mean nurses' salary increases. In Figure 2.35(a) the hospital administration has compressed the horizontal axis. In Figure 2.35(b) the union organizers have stretched the horizontal axis. Discuss the different impressions given by the two time series plots.

2.65 In the article "How to Display Data Badly" in the May 1984 issue of *The American Statistician*, Howard Wainer presents a *stacked bar chart* of the number of public and private elementary schools (1929–1970). This bar chart is given in Figure 2.36. Wainer also gives a line graph of the number of private elementary schools (1930–1970). This graph is shown in Figure 2.37.

FIGURE 2.35 **Two Time Series Plots of the Mean Nurses' Salary Increases at a Large Hospital for the Last Four Years (for Exercise 2.64)**

(a) The administration's plot: compressed horizontal axis

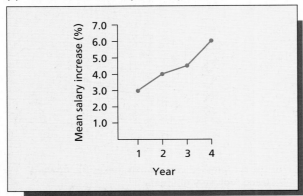

(b) The union organizer's plot: stretched horizontal axis

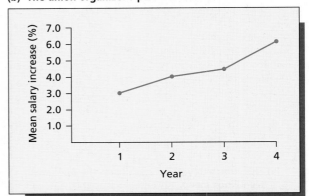

FIGURE 2.36 **Wainer's Stacked Bar Chart (for Exercise 2.65)**

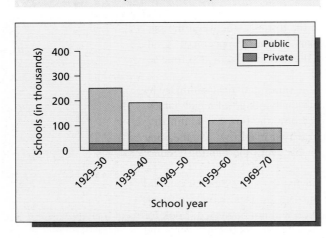

FIGURE 2.37 **Wainer's Line Graph (for Exercise 2.65)**

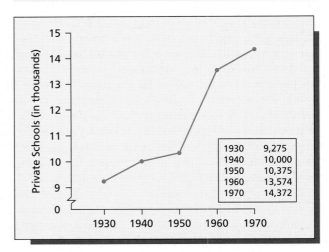

1930	9,275
1940	10,000
1950	10,375
1960	13,574
1970	14,372

a Looking at the bar chart of Figure 2.36, does there appear to be an increasing trend in the number of private elementary schools from 1930 to 1970?

b Looking at the line graph of Figure 2.37, does there appear to be an increasing trend in the number of private elementary schools from 1930 to 1970?

c Which portrayal of the data do you think is more appropriate? Explain why.

d Is either portrayal of the data entirely appropriate? Explain.

Chapter Summary

We began this chapter by explaining how to summarize qualitative data. We learned that we often summarize this type of data in a table that is called a **frequency distribution.** Such a table gives the **frequency, relative frequency,** or **percent frequency** of items that are contained in each of several nonoverlapping classes or categories. We also learned that we can summarize qualitative data in graphical form by using **bar charts** and **pie charts** and that qualitative quality data are often summarized using a special bar chart called a **Pareto chart.** We continued in Section 2.2 by discussing how to graphically portray quantitative data. In particular, we explained how to summarize such data by using frequency distributions and histograms. We saw that a **histogram** can be constructed using frequencies, relative frequencies, or percentages, and that we often construct histograms using statistical software such as MINITAB or the analysis toolpak in Excel. We used histograms to describe the shape of a distribution and we saw that distributions are sometimes **mound shaped and symmetrical,** but that a distribution can also be **skewed (to the right** or **to the left**). We also learned that a frequency distribution can be graphed by using a **frequency polygon** and that a graph of a **cumulative frequency distribution** is called an **ogive.** In Sections 2.3 and 2.4 we showed how to summarize relatively small data sets by using **dot plots** and **stem-and-leaf displays.** These graphics allow us to see all of the measurements in a data set and to (simultaneously) see the shape of the data set's distribution. Next, we learned about how to describe the relationship between two variables. First, in optional Section 2.5 we explained how to construct and interpret a **contingency table,** which classifies data on two dimensions using a table that consists of rows and columns. Then, in optional Section 2.6 we showed how to construct a **scatter plot.** Here, we plot numerical values of one variable on a horizontal axis versus numerical values of another variable on a vertical axis. We saw that we often use such a plot to look at possible straight-line relationships between the variables. Finally, in optional Section 2.7 we learned about misleading graphs and charts. In particular, we pointed out several graphical tricks to watch for. By careful analysis of a graph or chart, one can avoid being misled.

Glossary of Terms

bar chart: A graphical display of data in categories made up of vertical or horizontal bars. Each bar gives the frequency, relative frequency, or percentage frequency of items in its corresponding category. (page 36)

class midpoint: The point in a class that is halfway between the lower and upper class boundaries. (page 45)

contingency table: A table consisting of rows and columns that is used to classify data on two dimensions. (page 61)

cumulative frequency distribution: A table that summarizes the number of measurements that are less than the upper class boundary of each class. (page 49)

cumulative percent frequency distribution: A table that summarizes the percentage of measurements that are less than the upper class boundary of each class. (page 50)

cumulative relative frequency distribution: A table that summarizes the fraction of measurements that are less than the upper class boundary of each class. (page 50)

dot plot: A graphical portrayal of a data set that shows the data set's distribution by plotting individual measurements above a horizontal axis. (page 54)

frequency distribution: A table that summarizes the number of items (or measurements) in each of several nonoverlapping classes. (pages 35, 44)

frequency polygon: A graphical display in which we plot points representing each class frequency (or relative frequency or percent frequency) above their corresponding class midpoints and connect the points with line segments. (page 48)

histogram: A graphical display of a frequency distribution, relative frequency distribution, or percentage frequency distribution. It divides measurements into classes and graphs the frequency, relative frequency, or percentage frequency for each class. (pages 42, 44)

ogive: A graph of a cumulative distribution (frequencies, relative frequencies, or percent frequencies may be used). (page 50)

outlier: An unusually large or small observation that is well separated from the remaining observations. (pages 55, 59)

Pareto chart: A bar chart of the frequencies or percentages for various types of defects. These are used to identify opportunities for improvement. (page 38)

percent frequency distribution: A table that summarizes the percentage of items (or measurements) in each of several nonoverlapping classes. (pages 36, 44)

pie chart: A graphical display of data in categories made up of "pie slices." Each pie slice represents the frequency, relative frequency, or percentage frequency of items in its corresponding category. (page 37)

relative frequency distribution: A table that summarizes the fraction of items (or measurements) in each of several nonoverlapping classes. (pages 36, 44)

scatter plot: A graph that is used to study the possible relationship between two variables y and x. The observed values of y are plotted on the vertical axis versus corresponding observed values of x on the horizontal axis. (page 67)

skewed to the left: A distribution shape having a long tail to the left. (page 47)

skewed to the right: A distribution shape having a long tail to the right. (page 47)

stem-and-leaf display: A graphical portrayal of a data set that shows the data set's distribution by using stems consisting of leading digits and leaves consisting of trailing digits. (page 56)

symmetrical distribution: A distribution shape having right and left sides that are "mirror images" of each other. (page 47)

Important Formulas and Graphics

Frequency distribution: pages 35, 44, 45

Relative frequency: pages 36, 45

Percent frequency: pages 36, 45

Bar chart: pages 36, 37

Pie chart: page 37

Pareto chart: page 38

Histogram: page 45

Frequency polygon: page 48

Cumulative distribution: page 49

Ogive: page 50

Dot plot: page 54

Stem-and-leaf display: page 58

Contingency table: page 61

Scatter plot: page 67

Time series plot: page 68

Supplementary Exercises

connect

2.66 At the end of 2011 Chrysler Motors was trying to decide whether or not to discontinue production of a Jeep model introduced in 2002—the Jeep Liberty. Although Liberty sales had generally declined since 2007 with the cancellation of one Jeep model and the introduction of three new Jeep models, Liberty sales had continued to be good (and the Liberty name had retained a positive image) at some Jeep dealerships. Suppose that the owner of one such dealership in Cincinnati, Ohio, wished to present Chrysler with evidence that Liberty sales were still an important part of total sales at his dealership. To do this, the owner decided to compare his dealership's Liberty sales in 2011 with those in 2006. Recently summarized sales data show that in 2011 the owner's dealership sold 30 Jeep Compasses, 50 Jeep Grand Cherokees, 45 Jeep Libertys, 40 Jeep Patriots, 28 Jeep Wranglers, and 35 Jeep Wrangler Unlimiteds. Such summarized sales data were not available for 2006, but raw sales data were found. Denoting the four Jeep models sold in 2006 (Commander, Grand Cherokee, Liberty, and Wrangler) as C, G, L, and W, these raw sales data are shown in Table 2.23. Construct percent bar charts of (1) Jeep sales in 2011 and (2) Jeep sales in 2006. Compare the charts and write a short report supporting the owner's position that in 2011 Liberty sales were still an important part of sales at his dealership. DS JeepSales

| TABLE 2.23 | 2006 Sales at a Greater Cincinnati Jeep Dealership DS JeepSales |

W	L	L	W	G	C	C	L	C	L	G	W	C	L	L	C	C	G	L	L	W	C	G	G	C	L
L	L	G	L	C	C	G	C	C	G	C	L	W	W	G	G	W	G	C	W	W	G	L	L	L	G
G	L	G	C	C	C	C	C	G	G	L	G	G	L	L	L	C	C	G	C	L	G	G	G	L	
L	G	L	L	G	L	C	W	G	L	G	L	G	G	G	C	G	W	G	L	L	L	L	C	C	L
G	L	C	L	C	L	L	L	C	G	L	C	L	W	L	W	G	W	C	W	C	W	C	L	C	
C	G	C	C	C	C	C	C	G	C	C	W	G	C	G	L	L	C	L	L	G	G	G	L		
L	L	C	G	L	C	C	L	L	G	G	L	L	L	C	G	L	C	L	W	L	L	C	G	C	
G	G	G	L	C	L	L	G	L	C	C	L	G	W	W	W	C	C	C	G	G	L	G	C	G	
C	L	L	G	G	L	W	W	L	C	C	C	G	W	C	C	W	L	G	W	L	L	L	G	G	
G	W	L	L	C	G	C	C	W	C	L	L	L	L	G	G	W	L	L	C	L	G	G	W	G	G

Exercises 2.67 through 2.74 are based on the data in Table 2.24. This table gives the results of the J.D. Power initial quality study of 2010 automobiles. Each model is rated on overall mechanical quality and overall design quality on a scale from "among the best" to "the rest"—see the scoring legend at the bottom of the table. DS JDPower

TABLE 2.24　Results of the J. D. Power Initial Quality Study of 2010 Automobiles　JDPower

Company	Country of Origin	Overall Quality Mechanical	Overall Quality Design	Company	Country of Origin	Overall Quality Mechanical	Overall Quality Design
Acura	Japan	●●●●	●●●●	Lexus	Japan	●●●●●	●●●
Audi	Germany	●●●	●●●	Lincoln	United States	●●●	●●●
BMW	Germany	●●●	●●●	Mazda	Japan	●●●	●●●
Buick	United States	●●●	●●	Mercedes-Benz	Germany	●●●●●	●●●
Cadillac	United States	●●●	●●●	Mercury	United States	●●●	●●●
Chevrolet	United States	●●●	●●●	MINI	Great Britain	●●●	●●
Chrysler	United States	●●●	●●●	Mitsubishi	Japan	●●	●●●
Dodge	United States	●●●	●●	Nissan	Japan	●●●	●●●
Ford	United States	●●●	●●●●	Porsche	Germany	●●●●	●●●●●
GMC	United States	●●●	●●	Ram	United States	●●●	●●●●
Honda	Japan	●●●	●●●●	Scion	Japan	●●●	●●●
Hyundai	Korea	●●●	●●●●	Subaru	Japan	●●●	●●●
Infiniti	Japan	●●●	●●●●	Suzuki	Japan	●●●	●●●
Jaguar	Great Britain	●●	●●●	Toyota	Japan	●●●	●●●
Jeep	United States	●●	●●●	Volkswagen	Germany	●●	●●●
Kia	Korea	●●	●●●	Volvo	Sweden	●●●	●●●
Land Rover	Great Britain	●●	●●●				

Scoring Legend

●●●●● Among the best　　●●● About average
●●●● Better than most　　●● The rest

Source: http://www.jdpower.com/autos/quality-ratings-by-brand/

2.67 Develop a frequency distribution of the overall mechanical quality ratings. Describe the distribution.　**DS** JDPower

2.68 Develop a relative frequency distribution of the overall design quality ratings. Describe the distribution.　**DS** JDPower

2.69 Construct a percentage bar chart of the overall mechanical quality ratings for each of the following: automobiles of United States origin; automobiles of Pacific Rim origin (Japan/Korea); and automobiles of European origin (Germany/Great Britain/Sweden). Compare the three distributions in a written report.　**DS** JDPower

2.70 Construct a percentage pie chart of the overall design quality ratings for each of the following: automobiles of United States origin; automobiles of Pacific Rim origin (Japan/Korea); and automobiles of European origin (Germany/Great Britain/Sweden). Compare the three distributions in a written report.　**DS** JDPower

2.71 Construct a contingency table of automobile origin versus overall mechanical quality rating. Set up rows corresponding to the United States, the Pacific Rim (Japan/Korea), and Europe (Germany/Great Britain/Sweden), and set up columns corresponding to the ratings "among the best" through "the rest." Describe any apparent relationship between origin and overall mechanical quality rating.　**DS** JDPower

2.72 Develop a table of row percentages for the contingency table you set up in Exercise 2.71. Using these row percentages, construct a percentage frequency distribution of overall mechanical quality rating for each of the United States, the Pacific Rim, and Europe. Illustrate these three frequency distributions using percent bar charts and compare the distributions in a written report.　**DS** JDPower

2.73 Construct a contingency table of automobile origin versus overall design quality rating. Set up rows corresponding to the United States, the Pacific Rim (Japan/Korea), and Europe (Germany/Great Britain/Sweden), and set up columns corresponding to the ratings "among the best" through "the rest." Describe any apparent relationship between origin and overall design quality.　**DS** JDPower

2.74 Develop a table of row percentages for the contingency table you set up in Exercise 2.73. Using these row percentages, construct a percentage frequency distribution of overall design quality rating for each of the United States, the Pacific Rim, and Europe. Illustrate these three frequency distributions using percentage pie charts and compare the distributions in a written report.　**DS** JDPower

THE CIGARETTE ADVERTISEMENT CASE ⮞ ModelAge

In an article in the *Journal of Marketing,* Mazis, Ringold, Perry, and Denman discuss the perceived ages of models in cigarette advertisements.[6] To quote the authors:

> Most relevant to our study is the Cigarette Advertiser's Code, initiated by the tobacco industry in 1964. The code contains nine advertising principles related to young people, including the following provision (*Advertising Age* 1964): "Natural persons depicted as smokers in cigarette advertising shall be at least 25 years of age and shall not be dressed or otherwise made to appear to be less than 25 years of age."

Tobacco industry representatives have steadfastly maintained that code provisions are still being observed. A 1988 Tobacco Institute publication, "Three Decades of Initiatives by a Responsible Cigarette Industry," refers to the industry code as prohibiting advertising and promotion "directed at young people" and as "requiring that models in advertising must be, and must appear to be, at least 25 years old." John R. Nelson, Vice President of Corporate Affairs for Philip Morris, wrote, "We employ only adult models in our advertising who not only are but *look* over 25." However, industry critics have charged that current cigarette advertising campaigns use unusually young-looking models, thereby violating the voluntary industry code.

Suppose that a sample of 50 people is randomly selected at a shopping mall. Each person in the sample is shown a typical cigarette advertisement and is asked to estimate the age of the model in the ad. The 50 perceived age estimates so obtained are given below. Use these data to do Exercises 2.75 through 2.78.

26	30	23	27	27	32	28	19	25	29
31	28	24	26	29	27	28	17	28	21
30	28	25	31	22	29	18	27	29	23
28	26	24	30	27	25	26	28	20	24
29	32	27	17	30	27	21	29	26	28

2.75 Consider constructing a frequency distribution and histogram for the perceived age estimates. ⮞ ModelAge
   a Develop a frequency distribution, a relative frequency distribution, and a percent frequency distribution for the perceived age estimates using eight classes each of length 2. Note that, while the procedure presented in Section 2.2 would tell us to use six classes, in this case we get a more informative frequency distribution by using eight classes.
   b Draw a frequency histogram for the perceived age estimates.
   c Describe the shape of the distribution of perceived age estimates.

2.76 Construct a frequency polygon of the perceived age estimates. Use the classes of Exercise 2.75. ⮞ ModelAge

2.77 Construct a dot plot of the perceived age estimates and describe the shape of the distribution. What percentage of the perceived ages are below the industry's code provision of 25 years old? Do you think that this percentage is too high? ⮞ ModelAge

2.78 Using the frequency distribution you developed in Exercise 2.75, develop: ⮞ ModelAge
   a A cumulative frequency distribution.
   b A cumulative relative frequency distribution.
   c A cumulative percent frequency distribution.
   d A frequency ogive of the perceived age estimates.
   e How many perceived age estimates are 28 or less?
   f What percentage of perceived age estimates are 22 or less?

2.79 Table 2.25 presents data concerning the largest U.S. charities as rated on the Forbes.com website on June 14, 2011.
   a Construct a percent frequency histogram of each of (1) the charities' private support figures, (2) the charities' total revenues, and (3) the charities' fundraising efficiencies.
   b Describe the shape of each histogram. ⮞ Charities

2.80 The price/earnings ratio of a firm is a multiplier applied to a firm's earnings per share (EPS) to determine the value of the firm's common stock. For instance, if a firm's earnings per share is $5,

---

[6]Source: M. B. Mazis, D. J. Ringold, E. S. Perry, and D. W. Denman, "Perceived Age and Attractiveness of Models in Cigarette Advertisements," *Journal of Marketing* 56 (January 1992), pp. 22–37.

TABLE 2.25 Data Concerning the Largest U.S. Charities as Rated by *Forbes* Magazine DS Charities

Name	Private Support ($mil)	Total Revenue ($mil)	Fundraising Efficiency (%)	Name	Private Support ($mil)	Total Revenue ($mil)	Fundraising Efficiency (%)
Academy for Educational Development	51	414	100	Billy Graham Evangelistic Association	85	96	94
Aeras Global TB Vaccine Foundation	63	71	100	Boston Symphony Orchestra	52	100	85
Alzheimer's Association	189	206	80	Boy Scouts of America	375	1.13	87
American Cancer Society	898	897	75	Boys & Girls Clubs of America	625	1.47	88
American Civil Liberties Foundation	62	73	88	Brookings Institute	57	75	95
American Diabetes Association	156	205	70	Brother's Brother Foundation	267	269	100
American Enterprise Institute	59	51	98	Campus Crusade for Christ	473	509	92
American Heart Association	440	464	75	Cape Cod Healthcare	57	603	95
American Jewish Joint Distribution Committee	245	244	99	CARE USA	384	692	94
American Kidney Foundation	173	172	98	Carter Center	153	114	95
American Museum of Natural History	63	135	91	Catholic Charities USA	939	4.27	93
American National Red Cross	661	2.95	81	Catholic Medical Mission Board	279	280	99
American Nicaraguan Foundation	193	197	100	Catholic Relief Services	220	777	90
American SPCA	91	139	78	ChildFund International	216	211	90
AmeriCares Foundation	1.19	1.19	99	Children International	146	146	88
Anti-Defamation League of B'nai B'rith	49	66	84	Children's Hospital Boston	89	1.37	76
Art Institute of Chicago	77	180	89	Children's Hospital Los Angeles	95	547	86
Arthritis Foundation	84	117	85	Children's Hospital Philadelphia	52	1.87	73
Asia Foundation	51	143	99	Children's Memorial Hospital	68	624	75
Big Brothers Big Sisters of America	214	295	83	Children's Network International	62	62	100

Source: http://www.forbes.com/lists/2010/14/charity-10_land.html (accessed June 14, 2011).

and if its price/earnings ratio (or P/E ratio) is 10, then the market value of each share of common stock is ($5)(10) = $50. To quote Stanley B. Block and Geoffrey A. Hirt in their book *Foundations of Financial Management*:[7]

> The P/E ratio indicates expectations about the future of a company. Firms expected to provide returns greater than those for the market in general with equal or less risk often have P/E ratios higher than the market P/E ratio.

In the figure below we give a dot plot of the P/E ratios for 30 fast-growing companies. Describe the distribution of the P/E ratios.

2.81 In this exercise we consider how to deal with class lengths that are unequal (and with open-ended classes) when setting up histograms. Often data are published in this form and we wish to

ⒹⓈ ISO 9000

Annual Savings	Number of Companies
0 to $10K	162
$10K to 25K	62
$25K to 50K	53
$50K to 100K	60
$100K to 150K	24
$150K to 200K	19
$200K to 250K	22
$250K to 500K	21
(>$500K)	37

Note: (K = 1000)

construct a histogram. An example is provided by data concerning the benefits of ISO 9000 registration published by CEEM Information Services. According to CEEM:[8]

> ISO 9000 is a series of international standards for quality assurance management systems. It establishes the organizational structure and processes for assuring that the production of goods or services meet a consistent and agreed-upon level of quality for a company's customers.

CEEM presents the results of a Quality Systems Update/Deloitte & Touche survey of ISO 9000–registered companies conducted in July 1993. Included in the results is a summary of the total annual savings associated with ISO 9000 implementation for surveyed companies. The findings (in the form of a frequency distribution of ISO 9000 savings) are given on the page margin. Notice that the classes in this distribution have unequal lengths and that there is an open-ended class (>$500K).

To construct a histogram for these data, we select one of the classes as a base. It is often convenient to choose the shortest class as the base (although it is not necessary to do so). Using this choice, the 0 to $10K class is the base. This means that we will draw a rectangle over the 0 to $10K class having a height equal to 162 (the frequency given for this class in the published data). Because the other classes are longer than the base, the heights of the rectangles above these classes will be adjusted. To do this we employ a rule that says that the area of a rectangle positioned over a particular class should represent the relative proportion of measurements in the class. Therefore, we proceed as follows. The length of the $10K to 25K class differs from the base class by a factor of $(25 - 10)/(10 - 0) = 3/2$, and, therefore, we make the height of the rectangle over the $10K to 25K class equal to $(2/3)(62) = 41.333$. Similarly, the length of the $25K to 50K class differs from the length of the base class by a factor of $(50 - 25)/(10 - 0) = 5/2$, and, therefore, we make the height of the rectangle over the $25K to 50K class equal to $(2/5)(53) = 21.2$.

a Use the procedure just outlined to find the heights of the rectangles drawn over all the other classes (with the exception of the open-ended class, >$500K).

b Draw the appropriate rectangles over the classes (except for >$500K). Note that the $250K to 500K class is a lot longer than the others. There is nothing wrong with this as long as we adjust its rectangle's height.

c We complete the histogram by placing a star (∗) to the right of $500K on the scale of measurements and by noting "37" next to the ∗ to indicate 37 companies saved more than $500K. Complete the histogram by doing this.

2.82 A basketball player practices free throws by taking 25 shots each day, and he records the number of shots missed each day in order to track his progress. The numbers of shots missed on days 1 through 30 are, respectively, 17, 15, 16, 18, 14, 15, 13, 12, 10, 11, 11, 10, 9, 10, 9, 9, 9, 10, 8, 10, 6, 8, 9, 8, 7, 9, 8, 7, 5, 8.   ⒹⓈ FreeThrw

a Construct a stem-and-leaf display and a time series plot of the numbers of missed shots.

b Do you think that the stem-and-leaf display is representative of the numbers of shots that the player will miss on future days? Why or why not?

2.83 Figure 2.38 was used in various Chevrolet magazine advertisements in 1997 to compare the overall resale values of Chevrolet, Dodge, and Ford trucks in the years from 1990 to 1997. What is somewhat misleading about this graph?

2.84 In the Fall 1993 issue of *VALIC Investment Digest,* the Variable Annuity Life Insurance Company used pie charts to illustrate an investment strategy called **rebalancing.** This strategy involves reviewing an investment portfolio annually to return the asset mix (stocks, bonds, Treasury bills, and so on) to a preselected allocation mix. VALIC describes rebalancing as follows (refer to the pie charts in Figure 2.39):

Rebalancing—A Strategy to Keep Your Allocation on Track

> Once you've established your ideal asset allocation mix, many experts recommend that you review your portfolio at least once a year to make sure your portfolio remains consistent with your preselected asset allocation mix. This practice is referred to as *rebalancing.*
>
> For example, let's assume a moderate asset allocation mix of 50 percent equities funds, 40 percent bond funds, and 10 percent cash-equivalent funds. The chart [see Figure 2.39] based on data provided by Ibbotson, a major investment and consulting firm, illustrates how rebalancing works. Using the Standard & Poor's 500 Index, the Salomon Brothers Long-Term High-Grade Corporate Bond Index, and the U.S. 30-day Treasury bill average as a cash-equivalent rate, our hypothetical portfolio balance on 12/31/90 is $10,000. One year later the account had grown to $12,380. By the end of 1991, the allocation had changed to 52.7%/38.7%/8.5%. The third pie chart illustrates how the account was once again rebalanced to return to a 50%/40%/10% asset allocation mix.

FIGURE 2.38

A Graph Comparing the Resale Values of Chevy, Dodge, and Ford Trucks

Source: Reprinted courtesy of General Motors Corporation.

[8]Source: CEEM Information Services, Fairfax, Virginia. *Is ISO 9000 for You?*

FIGURE 2.39   Using Pie Charts to Illustrate Portfolio Rebalancing (for Exercise 2.84)

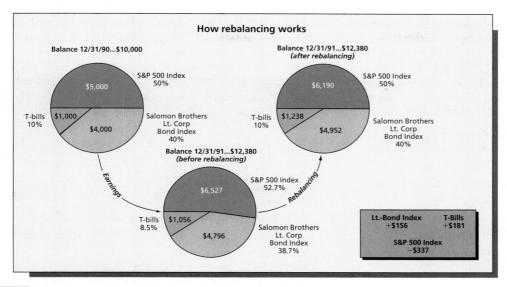

Source: The Variable Annuity Life Insurance Company, *VALIC* 6, no. 4 (Fall 1993).

Rebalancing has the potential for more than merely helping diversify your portfolio. By continually returning to your original asset allocation, it is possible to avoid exposure to more risk than you previously decided you were willing to assume.

a Suppose you control a $100,000 portfolio and have decided to maintain an asset allocation mix of 60 percent stock funds, 30 percent bond funds, and 10 percent government securities. Draw a pie chart illustrating your portfolio (like the ones in Figure 2.39).

b Over the next year your stock funds earn a return of 30 percent, your bond funds earn a return of 15 percent, and your government securities earn a return of 6 percent. Calculate the end-of-year values of your stock funds, bond funds, and government securities. After calculating the end-of-year value of your entire portfolio, determine the asset allocation mix (percent stock funds, percent bond funds, and percent government securities) of your portfolio before rebalancing. Finally, draw an end-of-year pie chart of your portfolio before rebalancing.

c Rebalance your portfolio. That is, determine how much of the portfolio's end-of-year value must be invested in stock funds, bond funds, and government securities in order to restore your original asset allocation mix of 60 percent stock funds, 30 percent bond funds, and 10 percent government securities. Draw a pie chart of your portfolio after rebalancing.

2.85   Internet Exercise

The Gallup Organization provides market research and consulting services around the world. Gallup publishes the Gallup Poll, a widely recognized barometer of American and international opinion. The Gallup website provides access to many recent Gallup studies. Although a subscription is needed to access the entire site, many articles about recent Gallup Poll results can be accessed free of charge. To find poll results, go to the Gallup home page (http://www.gallup.com/) and click on the Gallup Poll icon or type the web address http://www.galluppoll.com/ directly into your web browser. The poll results are presented using a variety of statistical summaries and graphics that we have learned about in this chapter.

a Go to the Gallup Organization website and access several of the articles presenting recent poll results.

Find and print examples of some of the statistical summaries and graphics that we studied in this chapter. Then write a summary describing which statistical methods and graphics seem to be used most frequently by Gallup when presenting poll results.

b Read the results of a Gallup poll that you find to be of particular interest and summarize (in your own words) its most important conclusions. Cite the statistical evidence in the article that you believe most clearly backs up each conclusion.

c By searching the web, or by searching other sources (such as newspapers and magazines), find an example of a misleading statistical summary or graphic. Print or copy the misleading example and write a paragraph describing why you think the summary or graphic is misleading.

Appendix 2.1 ■ Tabular and Graphical Methods Using Excel

The instructions in this section begin by describing the entry of data into an Excel spreadsheet. Alternatively, the data may be downloaded from this book's website. The appropriate data file name is given at the top of each instruction block. Please refer to Appendix 1.1 for further information about entering data, saving data, and printing results in Excel.

Construct a frequency distribution and frequency bar chart of pizza preferences as in Table 2.2 and Figure 2.1 on pages 36 and 37 (data file: PizzaPref.xlsx):

- Enter the pizza preference data in Table 2.1 on page 36 into column A with label Preference in cell A1.

We obtain the frequency distribution and bar chart by forming what is called a **PivotTable**. This is done as follows:

- Select **Insert : PivotTable : PivotChart**

  Note: Be sure to click on the arrow below PivotTable in order to obtain the PivotChart selection.

- In the Create PivotTable with PivotChart dialog box, click "Select a table or range."

- Enter the range of the data to be analyzed into the Table/Range window. Here we have entered the range of the pizza preference data A1:A51—that is, the entries in rows 1 through 51 in column A. The easiest way to do this is to click in the Table/Range window and to then use the mouse to drag the cursor from cell A1 through cell A51.

- Select "New Worksheet" to have the PivotTable and PivotChart output displayed in a new worksheet.

- Click OK in the Create PivotTable with PivotChart dialog box.

- In the **PivotTable Field List task pane,** place a checkmark in the checkbox to the left of the column label "Preference"—when you do this, the label "Preference" will also be placed in the Axis Fields area.

- Also drag the label "Preference" and drop it into the Σ Values area. When this is done, the label will automatically change to "Count of Preference" and the PivotTable will be displayed in the new worksheet.

  The PivotChart (bar chart) will also be displayed in a graphics window in the new worksheet.

  Note: You may need to close the PivotTable Field List task pane in order to see the bar chart.

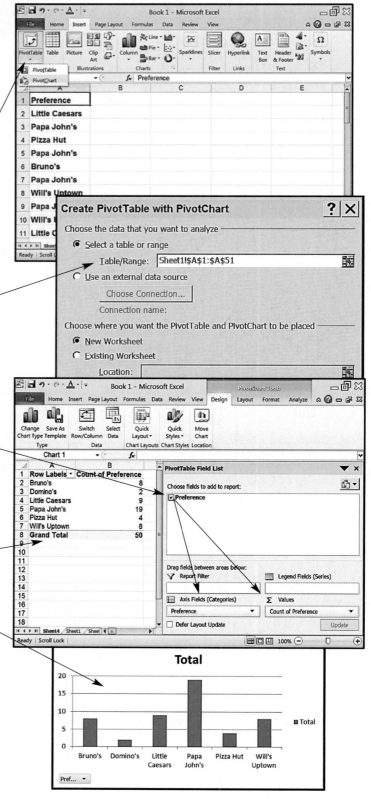

- As demonstrated in Appendix 1.1, move the bar chart to a new worksheet before editing.

- In the new worksheet, the chart can be edited by selecting the **Layout** tab. By clicking on the Labels, Axes, Background, Analysis, and Properties groups, many of the chart characteristics can be edited, data labels (the numbers above the bars that give the bar heights) can be inserted, and so forth. Alternatively, the chart can be edited by right-clicking on various portions of the chart and by using the pop-up menus that are displayed.

- To calculate relative frequencies and percent frequencies of the pizza preferences as in Table 2.3 on page 36, enter the cell formula =B2/B$8 into cell C2 and copy this cell formula down through all of the rows in the PivotTable (that is, through cell C8) to obtain a relative frequency for each row and the total relative frequency of 1.00. Copy the cells containing the relative frequencies into cells D2 through D8, select them, right-click on them, and format the cells to represent percentages to the decimal place accuracy you desire.

Construct a frequency bar chart of pizza preferences from a frequency distribution (data file: PizzaFreq.xlsx):

- Enter the frequency distribution of pizza preferences in Table 2.2 on page 36 as shown in the screen with the various restaurant identifiers in column A (with label Restaurant) and with the corresponding frequencies in column B (with label Frequency).

- Select the entire data set using the mouse.

- Select **Insert : PivotTable : PivotChart**

- In the Create PivotTable with PivotChart dialog box, click "Select a table or range."

- Enter the entire range of the data into the Table/Range window. Here we have entered the range of the frequency distribution—that is, A1 : B8. Again, the easiest way to do this is to click in the Table/Range window and then to select the range of the data with the mouse.

- Select "New Worksheet" to have the PivotTable and PivotChart output displayed in a new worksheet and click OK in the Create PivotTable with PivotChart dialog box.

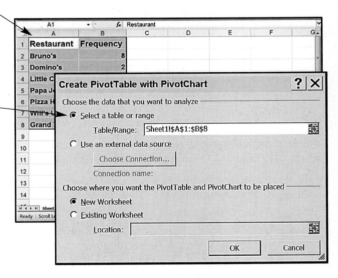

- Place checkmarks in the checkboxes to the left of the fieldnames Restaurant and Frequency. When this is done, the fieldname Restaurant will be placed in the Axis Fields area, "Sum of Frequency" will be placed in the Σ Values area, the Pivot Table will be placed in the new worksheet, and the Pivot Chart (bar chart) will be constructed. You may need to close the PivotTable Field List pane to see the chart. The chart can be moved to a new sheet and edited as previously described.

- **A bar chart can also be constructed without using a pivot table.** To do this, select the entire frequency distribution with the mouse. Then, select Insert: Bar: **All Chart Types**. In the Insert Chart dialog box, select Column from the chart type list on the right, select Clustered Column from the gallery of charts on the right, and click OK.

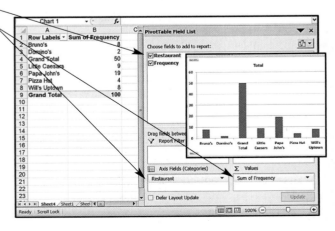

- This method can also be used to construct bar charts of relative frequency and percent frequency distributions. Simply enter the relative or percent distribution into the worksheet, select the entire distribution with the mouse and make the same selections as in the preceeding bullet.

Construct a percentage pie chart of pizza preferences as in Figure 2.3 on page 38 (data file: PizzaPercents.xlsx):

- Enter the percent frequency distribution of pizza preferences in Table 2.3 on page 36 as shown in the screen with the various restaurant identifiers in column A (with label Restaurant) and with the corresponding percent frequencies in column B (with label Percent Freq).
- Select the entire data set using the mouse.
- Select **Insert : Pie : 2-Pie : Pie**
- The pie chart is edited in the same way a bar chart is edited—see the instructions above related to editing bar charts.

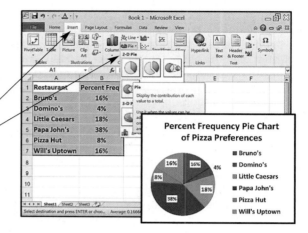

Constructing frequency distributions and histograms using Excel's Analysis ToolPak: The Analysis ToolPak is an Excel add-in that is used for a variety of statistical analyses—including construction of frequency distributions and histograms from raw (that is, un-summarized) data. The ToolPak is available when Microsoft Office or Excel is installed. However, in order to use it, the ToolPak must first be loaded. To see if the Analysis ToolPak has been loaded on your computer, click the **Microsoft File Button,** click **Options,** and finally click **Add-Ins.** If the ToolPak has been loaded on your machine, it will appear in the list of **Active Application Add-ins.** If Analysis ToolPak does not appear in this list, select **Excel Add-ins** in the **Manage** box and click **Go.** In the **Add-ins** box, place a checkmark in the **Analysis ToolPak** checkbox, and then click **OK.** Note that, if the Analysis ToolPak is not listed in the Add-Ins available box, click **Browse** to attempt to find it. If you get prompted that the Analysis ToolPak is not currently installed on your computer, click **Yes** to install it. In some cases, you might need to use your original MS Office or Excel CD/DVD to install and load the Analysis ToolPak by going through the setup process.

Constructing a frequency histogram of the bottle design ratings as in Figure 2.11 on page 47 (data file: Design.xlsx):

- Enter the 60 bottle design ratings in Table 1.5 on page 10 into Column A with label Rating in cell A1.
- Select **Data : Data Analysis**
- In the Data Analysis dialog box, select Histogram in the Analysis Tools window and click OK.
- In the Histogram dialog box, click in the Input Range window and select the range of the data A1:A61 into the Input Range window by dragging the mouse from cell A1 through cell A61.
- Place a checkmark in the Labels checkbox.
- Under "Output options," select "New Worksheet Ply."
- Enter a name for the new worksheet in the New Worksheet Ply window—here Histogram 1.
- Place a checkmark in the Chart Output checkbox.
- Click OK in the Histogram dialog box.
- Notice that we are leaving the Bin Range window blank. This will cause Excel to define automatic classes for the frequency distribution and histogram. However, because Excel's automatic classes are often not appropriate, we will revise these automatic classes as follows.

- The frequency distribution will be displayed in the new worksheet and the histogram will be displayed in a graphics window.

Notice that Excel defines what it calls bins when constructing the histogram. The bins define the automatic classes for the histogram. The bins that are automatically defined by Excel are often cumbersome—the bins in this example are certainly inconvenient for display purposes! Although one might be tempted to simply round the bin values, we have found that the rounded bin values can produce an unacceptable histogram with unequal class lengths (whether this happens depends on the particular bin values in a given situation).

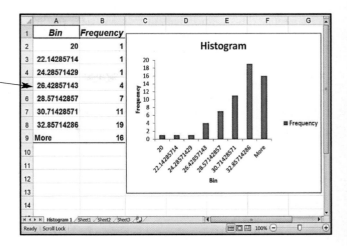

To obtain more acceptable results, **we suggest that new bin values be defined that are roughly based on the automatic bin values.** We can do this as follows. First, we note that the smallest bin value is 20 and that this bin value is expressed using the same decimal place accuracy as the original data (recall that the bottle design ratings are all whole numbers). Remembering that Excel obtains a cell frequency by counting the number of measurements that are less than or equal to the upper class boundary and greater than the lower class boundary, the first class contains bottle design ratings less than or equal to 20. Based on the authors' experience, the first automatic bin value given by Excel is expressed to the same decimal place accuracy as the data being analyzed. However, if the smallest bin value were to be expressed using more decimal places than the original data, then **we suggest rounding it down to the decimal place accuracy of the original data being analyzed.** Frankly, the authors are not sure that this would ever need to be done—it was not necessary in any of the examples we have tried. Next, find the class length of the Excel automatic classes and round it to a convenient value. For the bottle design ratings, using the first and second bin values in the screen, the class length is 22.14285714 − 20 which equals 2.14285714. To obtain more convenient classes, we will round this value to 2. Starting at the first automatic bin value of 20, we now construct classes having length equal to 2. This gives us new bin values of 20, 22, 24, 26, and so on. We suggest continuing to define new bin values until a class containing the largest measurement in the data is found. Here, the largest bottle design rating is 35 (see Table 1.5 on page 10). Therefore, the last bin value is 36, which says that the last class will contain ratings greater than 34 and less than or equal to 36—that is, the ratings 35 and 36.

We suggest constructing classes in this way unless one or more measurements are unusually large compared to the rest of the data—we might call these unusually large measurements **outliers.** We will discuss outliers more thoroughly in Chapter 3 (and in later chapters). For now, if we (subjectively) believe that one or more outliers exist, we suggest placing these measurements in the "more" class and placing a histogram bar over this class having the same class length as the other bars. In such a situation, we must recognize that the Excel histogram will not be technically correct because **the area of the bar (or rectangle) above the "more" class will not necessarily equal the relative proportion of measurements in the class.** Nevertheless—given the way Excel constructs histogram classes—the approach we suggest seems reasonable. In the bottle design situation, the largest rating of 35 is not unusually large and, therefore, the "more" class will not contain any measurements.

To construct the revised histogram:

- Open a new worksheet, copy the bottle design ratings into column A and enter the new bin values into column B (with label Bin) as shown.

- Select **Data : Data Analysis : Histogram**

- Click OK in the Data Analysis dialog box.

- In the Histogram dialog box, select the range of the ratings data A1:A61 into the Input Range window.

- Click in the Bin Range window and enter the range of the bin values B1:B10.

- Place a checkmark in the Labels checkbox.

- Under "Output options," select "New Worksheet Ply" and enter a name for the new worksheet— here Histogram 2.

- Place a checkmark in the Chart Output checkbox.

- Click OK in the Histogram dialog box.

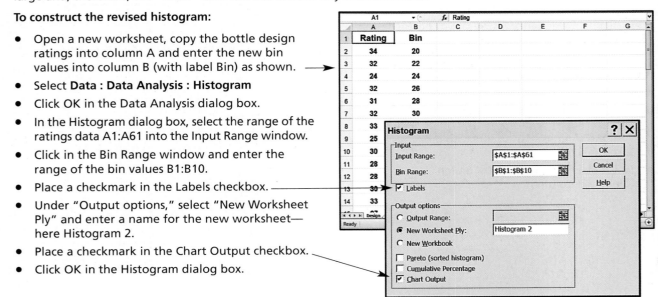

- The revised frequency distribution will be displayed in the new worksheet and the histogram will be displayed in a graphics window.

- Click in the graphics window and (as demonstrated in Appendix 1.1) move the histogram to a new worksheet for editing.

- The histogram will be displayed in the new chart sheet in a much larger format that makes it easier to carry out editing.

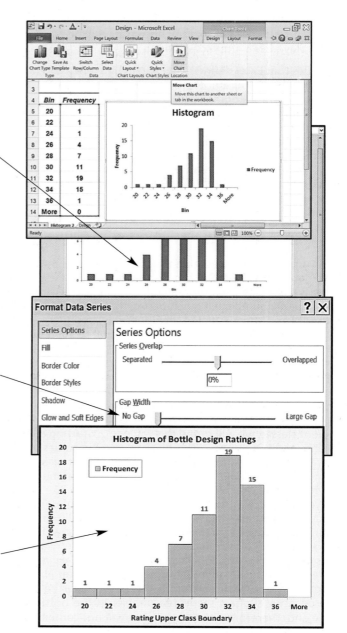

To remove the gaps between the histogram bars:

- Right click on one of the histogram bars and select Format Data Series from the pop-up window.

- Set the gap width to zero by moving the gap width slider to "No Gap" and click "Close" in the Format Data Series dialog box.

- By selecting the Chart Tools Layout tab, the histogram can be edited in many ways. This can also be done by right clicking on various portions of the histogram and by making desired pop-up menu selections.

- To obtain **data labels** (the numbers on the tops of the bars that indicate the bar heights), right click on one of the histogram bars and select "Add data labels" from the pop-up menu.

After final editing, the histogram might look like the one illustrated in Figure 2.11 on page 47.

Constructing a frequency histogram of bottle design ratings from summarized data:

- Enter the **midpoints** of the frequency distribution classes into column A with label Midpoint and enter the class frequencies into column B with label Frequency.

- Use the mouse to select the cell range that contains the frequencies (here, cells B2 through B10).

- Select **Insert : Column : 2-D Column (Clustered Column)**

- Right-click on the chart that is displayed and click on Select Data in the pop-up menu.

- In the Select Data Source dialog box, click on the Edit button in the "Horizontal (Category) Axis Labels" window.

- In the Axis Labels dialog box, use the mouse to enter the cell range that contains the midpoints (here, A2:A10) into the "Axis label range" window.

- Click OK in the Axis Labels dialog box.

- Click OK in the Select Data Source dialog box.

- Move the chart that appears to a chart sheet, remove the gaps between the bars as previously shown, and edit the chart as desired.

Relative frequency or percent frequency histograms would be constructed in the same way with the class midpoints in column A of the Excel spreadsheet and with the relative or percent frequencies in column B.

We now show how to construct a **frequency polygon from summarized data.**

Note that, if the data are **not summarized,** first use the Histogram option in the Analysis ToolPak to develop a summarized frequency distribution.

- Enter the class midpoints and class frequencies as shown previously for summarized data.

- Use the mouse to select the cell range that contains the frequencies.

- Select **Insert : Line : Line with markers**

- Right-click on the chart that is displayed and click on Select Data in the pop-up menu.

- In the Select Data Source dialog box, click on the Edit button in the "Horizontal (Category) Axis Labels" window.

- In the Axis Labels dialog box, use the mouse to enter the cell range that contains the midpoints into the "Axis label range" window.

- Click OK in the Axis Labels dialog box.

- Click OK in the Select Data Source dialog box.

- Move the chart that appears to a chart sheet, and edit the chart as desired.

To construct a percent frequency ogive for the bottle design rating distribution (data file: Design.xlsx):

Follow the instructions for constructing a histogram by using the Analysis ToolPak with changes as follows:

- In the Histogram dialog box, place a checkmark in the Cumulative Percentage checkbox.

- After moving the histogram to a chart sheet, right-click on any histogram bar.

- Select "Format Data Series" from the pop-up menu.

- In the "Format Data Series" dialog box, (1) select Fill from the list of "Series Options" and select "No fill" from the list of Fill options; (2) select Border Color from the list of "Series Options" and select "No line" from the list of Border Color options; (3) Click Close.

- Click on the chart to remove the histogram bars.

Construct a contingency table of fund type versus level of client satisfaction as in Table 2.17 on page 62 (data file: Invest.xlsx):

- Enter the customer satisfaction data in Table 2.16 on page 62—fund types in column A with label "Fund Type" and satisfaction ratings in column B with label "Satisfaction Rating."

- Select **Insert : PivotTable : PivotTable**

- In the Create PivotTable dialog box, click "Select a table or range."

- By dragging with the mouse, enter the range of the data to be analyzed into the Table/Range window. Here we have entered the range of the client satisfaction data A1:B101.

- Select the New Worksheet option to place the PivotTable in a new worksheet.

- Click OK in the Create PivotTable dialog box.

- In the PivotTable Field List task pane, drag the label "Fund Type" and drop it into the Row Labels area.

- Also drag the label "Fund Type" and drop it into the Σ Values area. When this is done, the label will automatically change to "Count of Fund Type."

- Drag the label "Satisfaction Rating" into the Column Labels area.

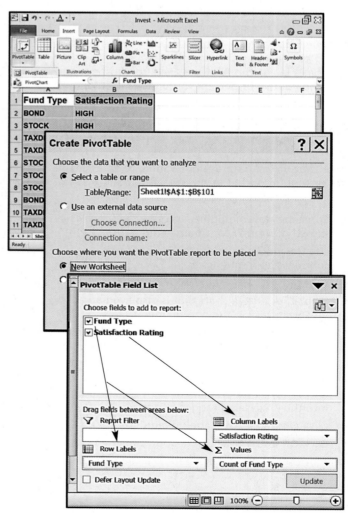

- The PivotTable will be created and placed in a new worksheet.

- Now right-click inside the PivotTable and select PivotTable Options from the pop-up menu.

- In the PivotTable Options dialog box, select the Totals & Filters tab and make sure that a checkmark has been placed in each of the "Show grand totals for rows" and the "Show grand totals for columns" checkboxes.

- Select the Layout & Format tab, place a check-mark in the "For empty cells show" checkbox and enter 0 (the number zero) into its corresponding window. (For the customer satisfaction data, none of the cell frequencies equal zero, but, in general, this setting should be made to prevent empty cells from being left blank in the contingency table.)

- To change the order of the column labels from the default alphabetical ordering (High, Low, Medium) to the more logical ordering of High, Medium, Low, right-click on LOW, select Move from the pop-up menu, and select "Move LOW to End."

- The contingency table is now complete.

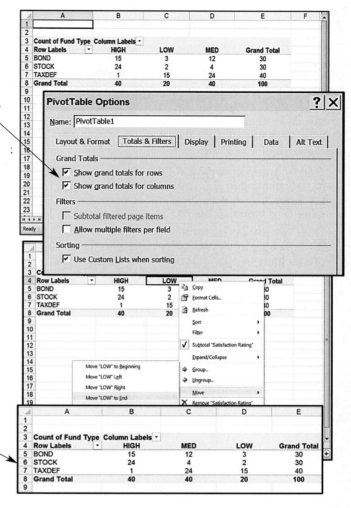

Constructing a scatter plot of sales volume versus advertising expenditure as in Figure 2.24 on page 67 (data file: SalesPlot.xlsx):

- Enter the advertising and sales data in Table 2.20 on page 67 into columns A and B—advertising expenditures in column A with label "Ad Exp" and sales values in column B with label "Sales Vol." **Note: The variable to be graphed on the horizontal axis must be in the first column** (that is, the left-most column) and **the variable to be graphed on the vertical axis must be in the second column** (that is, the rightmost column).

- Select the entire range of data to be graphed.

- Select **Insert : Scatter : Scatter with only Markers**

- The scatter plot will be displayed in a graphics window. Move the plot to a chart sheet and edit appropriately.

Appendix 2.2 ■ Tabular and Graphical Methods Using MegaStat

The instructions in this section begin by describing the entry of data into an Excel worksheet. Alternatively, the data may be downloaded from this book's website. The appropriate data file name is given at the top of each instruction block. Please refer to Appendix 1.1 for further information about entering data, saving data, and printing results in Excel. Please refer to Appendix 1.2 for more information about MegaStat basics.

Construct a frequency distribution and bar chart of Jeep sales in Table 2.23 on page 74 (data file: JeepSales.xlsx):

- Enter the Jeep sales data in Table 2.23 on page 74 (C = Commander; G = Grand Cherokee; L = Liberty; W = Wrangler) into column A with label Jeep Model in cell A1.

- Enter the categories for the qualitative variable (C, G, L, W) into the worksheet. Here we have placed them in cells B2 through B5—the location is arbitrary.

- Select **Add-Ins : MegaStat : Frequency Distributions : Qualitative**

- In the "Frequency Distributions—Qualitative" dialog box, use the AutoExpand feature to enter the range A1:A252 of the Jeep sales data into the Input Range window.

- Enter the cell range B2:B5 of the categories (C, G, L, W) into the "specification range" window.

- Place a checkmark in the "histogram" checkbox to obtain a bar chart.

- Click OK in the "Frequency Distributions—Qualitative" dialog box.

- The frequency distribution and bar chart will be placed in a new output sheet.

- The output can be edited in the output sheet. Alternatively, the bar chart can be moved to a chart sheet (see Appendix 1.1) for more convenient editing.

Construct a frequency distribution and percent frequency histogram of the gas mileages as in Figure 2.9 on page 46 (data file: GasMiles.xlsx):

- Enter the gasoline mileage data in Table 1.6 on page 11 into column A with the label Mpg in cell A1 and with the 50 gas mileages in cells A2 to A51.

- Select **Add-Ins : MegaStat : Frequency Distributions : Quantitative**

- In the "Frequency Distributions—Quantitative" dialog box, use the AutoExpand feature to enter the range A1:A51 of the gas mileages into the Input Range window.

- To obtain **automatic classes** for the histogram, leave the "interval width" and "lower boundary of first interval" windows blank.

- Place a checkmark in the Histogram checkbox.

- Click OK in the "Frequency Distributions—Quantitative" dialog box.

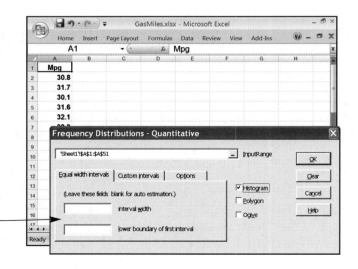

- The frequency distribution and histogram will be placed in a new output worksheet.

- The chart can be edited in the Output worksheet or you can move the chart to a chart sheet for editing.

- To obtain **data labels** (the numbers on the tops of the bars that indicate the bar heights), right click on one of the histogram bars and select "Add data labels" from the pop-up menu.

To construct a frequency polygon and a percent frequency ogive, simply place checkmarks in the Polygon and Ogive checkboxes in the "Frequency Distributions—Quantitative" dialog box.

Construct a percent frequency histogram of the bottle design ratings similar to Figure 2.11 on page 47 with **user specified classes** (data file: Design.xlsx):

- Enter the 60 bottle design ratings in Table 1.5 on page 10 into Column A with label Rating in cell A1.

- Select **Add-Ins : MegaStat : Frequency Distributions : Quantitative**

- In the "Frequency Distributions—Quantitative" dialog box, use the AutoExpand feature to enter the input range A1:A61 of the bottle design ratings into the Input Range window.

- Enter the class width (in this case equal to 2) into the "interval width" window.

- Enter the lower boundary of the first—that is, leftmost—class (or interval) of the histogram (in this case equal to 20) into the "lower boundary of first interval" window.

- Make sure that the Histogram checkbox is checked.

- Click OK in the "Frequency Distributions—Quantitative" dialog box.

- We obtain a histogram with class boundaries 20, 22, 24, 26, 28, 30, 32, 34, and 36. Note that the appearance of this histogram is not exactly the same as that of the Excel histogram in Figure 2.11 on page 47 because MegaStat and Excel count frequencies differently. While MegaStat counts frequencies as we have described in Example 2.2, recall that Excel counts the number of measurements that are greater than the lower boundary of a class and less than or equal to the upper boundary of the class.

- The histogram can be moved to a chart sheet for editing purposes.

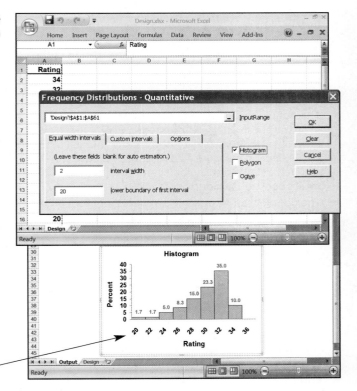

Construct a dot plot (as in Figure 2.18 on page 55) **and a stem-and-leaf display** (as in Figure 2.20 on page 59) of the scores on the first statistics exam as discussed in Example 2.3 on page 48 (data file: FirstExam.xlsx):

- Enter the 40 scores for exam 1 in Table 2.8 on page 48 into column A with label "Exam 1" in cell A1.

- Select **Add-Ins : MegaStat : Descriptive Statistics.**

- In the "Descriptive Statistics" dialog box, use the AutoExpand feature to enter the range A1:A41 of the exam scores into the "Input range" window.

- Place a checkmark in the DotPlot checkbox to obtain a dot plot.

- Place a checkmark in the "Stem and Leaf Plot" checkbox to obtain a stem-and-leaf display.

- Place a checkmark in the "Split Stem" checkbox. (In general, whether or not this should be done depends on how you want the output to appear. You may wish to construct two plots—one with the Split Stem option and one without—and then choose the output you like best.) In the exam score situation, the Split Stem option is needed to obtain a display that looks like the one in Figure 2.20.

- Click OK in the "Descriptive Statistics" dialog box.

- The dot plot and stem-and-leaf display will be placed in an output sheet. Here, the stem-and-leaf display we have obtained for exam 1 is the "mirror image" of the display shown in Figure 2.20 (because we have constructed a single display for exam 1, while Figure 2.20 shows back-to-back displays for both exams 1 and 2).

- The dot plot can be moved to a chart sheet for editing.

Construct a contingency table of fund type versus level of client satisfaction as in Table 2.17 on page 62 (data file: Invest.xlsx):

- Enter the customer satisfaction data in Table 2.16 on page 62—fund types in column A with label FundType and satisfaction ratings in column B with label SRating.

- Enter the three labels (BOND; STOCK; TAXDEF) for the qualitative variable FundType into cells C2, C3, and C4 as shown in the screen.

- Enter the three labels (HIGH; MED; LOW) for the qualitative variable SRating into cells C6, C7, and C8 as shown in the screen.

- Select **Add-Ins : MegaStat : Chi-Square/CrossTab : Crosstabulation**

- In the Crosstabulation dialog box, use the AutoExpand feature to enter the range A1:A101 of the row variable FundType into the "Row variable Data range" window.

- Enter the range C2:C4 of the labels of the qualitative variable FundType into the "Row variable Specification range window."

- Use the AutoExpand feature to enter the range B1:B101 of the column variable SRating into the "Column variable Data range" window.

- Enter the range C6:C8 of the labels of the qualitative variable SRating into the "Column variable Specification range window."

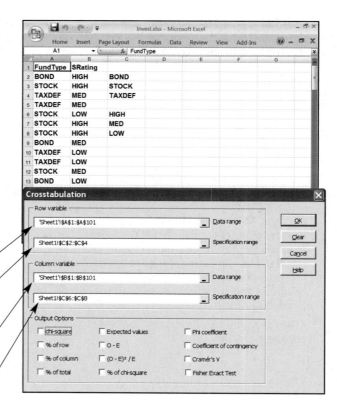

- Uncheck the "chi-square" checkbox.
- Click OK in the Crosstabulation dialog box.
- The contingency table will be displayed in an Output worksheet.
- **Row percentages and column percentages** can be obtained by simply placing checkmarks in the "% of row" and "% of column" checkboxes.

Construct a scatter plot of sales volume versus advertising expenditure as in Figure 2.24 on page 67 (data file: SalesPlot.xlsx):

- Enter the advertising and sales data in Table 2.20 on page 67 into columns A and B—advertising expenditures in column A with label "Ad Exp" and sales values in column B with label "Sales Vol."
- Select **Add-Ins : MegaStat : Correlation/Regression : Scatterplot**
- In the Scatterplot dialog box, use the AutoExpand feature to enter the range A1:A11 of the advertising expenditures into the "horizontal axis" window.
- Use the AutoExpand feature to enter the range B1:B11 of the sales volumes into the "vertical axis" window.
- Uncheck the "Plot linear regression line" checkbox.
- Under Display options, select Markers.
- Click OK in the Scatterplot dialog box.
- The scatterplot is displayed in an Output worksheet and can be moved to a chart sheet for editing.

Appendix 2.3 ■ Tabular and Graphical Methods Using MINITAB

The instructions in this section begin by describing the entry of data into the MINITAB data window. Alternatively, the data may be downloaded from this book's website. The appropriate data file name is given at the top of each instruction block. Please refer to Appendix 1.3 for further information about entering data, saving data, and printing results when using MINITAB.

Construct a frequency distribution of pizza preferences as in Table 2.2 on page 36 (data file: PizzaPref .MTW):

- Enter the pizza preference data in Table 2.1 on page 36 into column C1 with label (variable name) Pizza Preference.

- Select **Stat : Tables : Tally Individual Variables**

- In the Tally Individual Variables dialog box, enter the variable name 'Pizza Preference' into the Variables window. Because this variable name consists of more than one word, we must enclose the name in single quotes—this defines both the words Pizza and Preference to be parts of the same variable name.

- Place a checkmark in the Display "Counts" checkbox to obtain frequencies.

  We would check "Percents" to obtain percent frequencies, "Cumulative counts" to obtain cumulative frequencies, and "Cumulative percents" to obtain cumulative percent frequencies.

- Click OK in the Tally Individual Variables dialog box.

- The frequency distribution is displayed in the Session window.

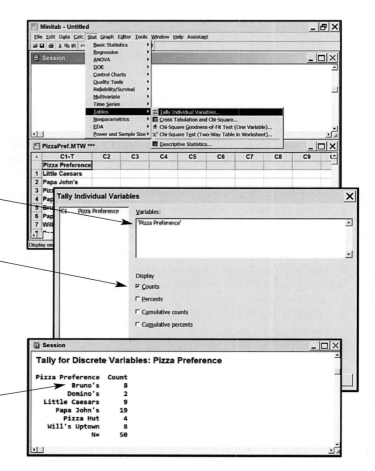

Construct a bar chart of the pizza preference distribution from the raw preference data similar to the bar chart in Figure 2.1 on page 37 (data file: PizzaPref.MTW):

- Enter the pizza preference data in Table 2.1 on page 36 into column C1 with label (variable name) Pizza Preference.

- Select **Graph : Bar Chart**

- In the Bar Charts dialog box, select "Counts of unique values" from the "Bars represent" pull-down menu.

- Select "Simple" from the gallery of bar chart types (this is the default selection, which is indicated by the reverse highlighting in black).

- Click OK in the Bar Charts dialog box.

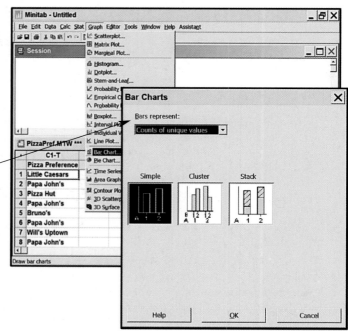

- In the "Bar Chart—Counts of unique values, Simple" dialog box, enter the variable name 'Pizza Preference' into the "Categorical variables" window. Be sure to remember the single quotes around the name Pizza Preference.

- To obtain **data labels** (numbers at the tops of the bars that indicate the heights of the bars—in this case, the frequencies), click on the Labels... button.

- In the "Bar Chart—Labels" dialog box, click on the Data Labels tab and select "Use y-value labels". This will produce data labels that are equal to the category frequencies.

- Click OK in the "Bar Chart—Labels" dialog box.

- Click OK in the "Bar Chart—Counts of unique values, Simple" dialog box.

- The bar chart will be displayed in a graphics window. The chart may be edited by right-clicking on various portions of the chart and by using the pop-up menus that appear—see Appendix 1.3 for more details.

- Here we have obtained a frequency bar chart. **To obtain a percent frequency bar chart** (as in Figure 2.2 on page 37) click on the Chart Options... button and select "Show Y as Percent" in the "Bar Chart—Options" dialog box.

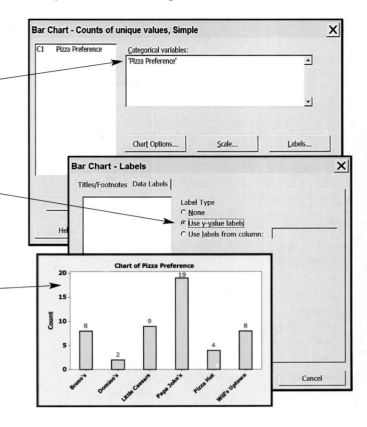

Construct a bar chart from the tabular frequency distribution of pizza preferences in Table 2.2 on page 36 (data file: PizzaFreq.MTW):

- Enter the tabular distribution of pizza preferences from Table 2.2 as shown in the screen with the pizza restaurants in column C1 (with the variable name Restaurant) and with the associated frequencies in column C2 (with variable name Frequency).

- Select **Graph : Bar Chart**

- In the Bar Charts dialog box, select "Values from a table" in the "Bars represent" pull-down menu.

- Select "One column of values—Simple" from the gallery of bar chart types.

- Click OK in the Bar Charts dialog box.

- In the "Bar Chart—Values from a table, One column of values, Simple" dialog box, enter the variable name Frequency into the "Graph variables" window and then enter the variable name Restaurant into the "Categorical variable" window.

- Click on the Labels... button and select "Use y-value labels" as shown previously.

- Click OK in the "Bar Chart—Labels" dialog box.

- Click OK in the "Bar Chart—Values from a table, One column of values, Simple" dialog box.

- The bar chart will be displayed in a graphics window.

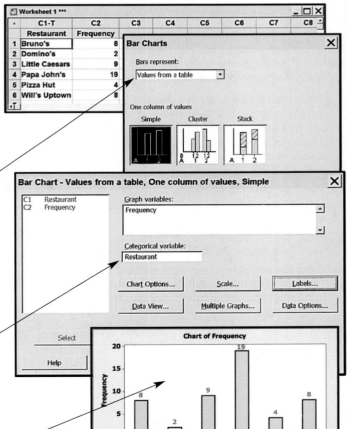

Construct a pie chart of pizza preference percentages similar to that shown in Figure 2.3 on page 38.

- Enter the pizza preference data in Table 2.1 on page 36 into column C1 with label (variable name) Pizza Preference.

- Select **Graph : Pie Chart**

- In the Pie Chart dialog box, select "Chart counts of unique values."

- Enter the variable name 'Pizza Preference' into the "Categorical variables" window. Be sure to remember the single quotes around the name Pizza Preference.

- In the Pie Chart dialog box, click on the Labels... button.

- In the "Pie Chart—Labels" dialog box, click on the Slice Labels tab.

- Place checkmarks in the Category name, Percent, and "Draw a line from label to slice" checkboxes.

    To obtain a frequency pie chart, select Frequency rather than Percent in this dialog box. Or, both Percent and Frequency can be selected.

- Click OK in the "Pie Chart—Labels" dialog box.

- Click OK in the Pie Chart dialog box.

- The pie chart will appear in a graphics window.

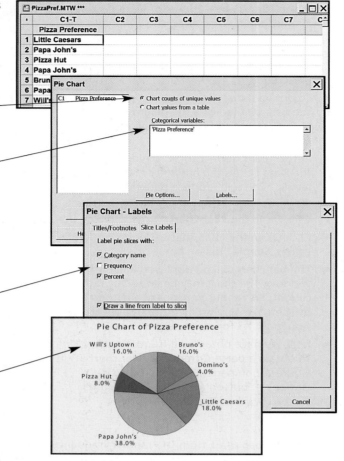

Construct a pie chart from the tabular frequency distribution of pizza preferences in Table 2.3 on page 36 (data file: PizzaPercents.MTW):

- Enter the pizza preference percent frequency distribution from Table 2.3 as shown in the screen with the pizza restaurants in column C1 (with variable name Restaurant) and with the associated percent frequencies in column C2 (with variable name Percent Freq).

- Select **Graph : Pie Chart**

- In the Pie Chart dialog box, select "Chart values from a table."

- Enter the variable name Restaurant into the "Categorical variable" window.

- Enter the variable name 'Percent Freq' into the "Summary variables" window. Be sure to remember the single quotes around the name Percent Freq.

- Continue by following the previously given directions for adding data labels and for generating the pie chart.

Construct a frequency histogram of the payment times in Figure 2.10 on page 46 (data file: PayTime .MTW):

- Enter the payment time data from Table 2.4 on page 42 into column C1 with variable name PayTime.
- Select **Graph : Histogram**
- In the Histograms dialog box, select Simple from the gallery of histogram types and click OK.
- In the "Histogram—Simple" dialog box, enter the variable name PayTime into the Graph Variables window and click on the Scale button.

- In the "Histogram—Scale" dialog box, click on the "Y- Scale Type" tab and select **Frequency** to obtain a frequency histogram. We would select **Percent** to request a percent frequency histogram. Then click OK in the "Histogram—Scale" dialog box.
- **Data labels** are requested in the same way as we have demonstrated for bar charts. Click on the Labels... button in the "Histogram—Simple" dialog box. In the "Histogram—Labels" dialog box, click on the Data Labels tab and select "Use y-value labels." Then click OK in the "Histogram—Labels" dialog box.

- To create the histogram, click OK in the "Histogram—Simple" dialog box.
- The histogram will appear in a graphics window and can be edited as described in Appendix 1.3.
- The histogram can be selected for printing or can be copied and pasted into a word processing document. (See Appendix 1.3.)

- Notice that MINITAB **automatically** defines classes for the histogram bars, and automatically provides labeled tick marks (here 12, 16, 20, 24 and 28) on the *x*-scale of the histogram. These automatic classes are not the same as those we formed in Example 2.2, summarized in Table 2.7, and illustrated in Figure 2.7 on page 44. However, we can edit the automatically constructed histogram to produce the histogram classes of Figure 2.7. This is sometimes called **"binning."**

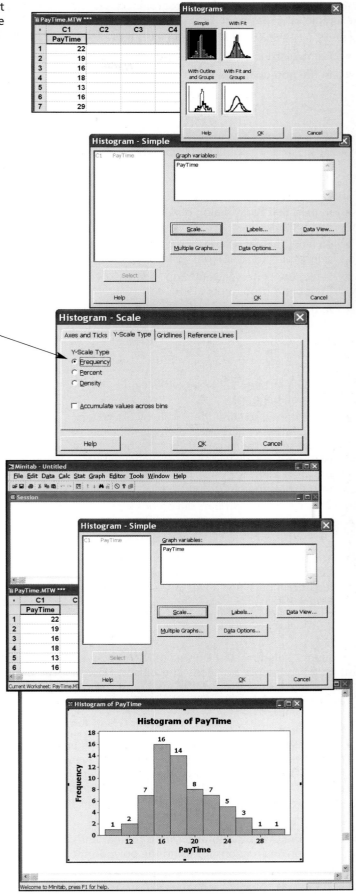

To obtain user specified histogram classes—for example, the payment time histogram classes of Figure 2.7 on page 44 (data file: PayTime.MTW):

- Right-click inside any of the histogram bars.
- In the pop-up menu, select "Edit bars."

- In the "Edit Bars" dialog box, select the Binning tab.
- To label the x-scale by using class boundaries, select the "Interval Type" to be Cutpoint.
- Select the "Interval Definition" to be Midpoint/Cutpoint positions.
- In the Midpoint/Cutpoint positions window, enter the class boundaries (or cutpoints)

  10   13   16   19   22   25   28   31

  as given in Table 2.7 or shown in Figure 2.7 (both on page 44).
- If we wished to label the x-scale by using class midpoints as in Figure 2.8 on page 45, we would select the "Interval Type" to be Midpoint and we would enter the midpoints of Figure 2.8 (11.5, 14.5, 17.5, and so forth) into the Midpoint/Cutpoint positions window.
- Click OK in the Edit Bars dialog box.

- The histogram in the graphics window will be edited to produce the class boundaries, histogram bars, and x-axis labels shown in Figure 2.7.

Frequency Polygons and Ogives: MINITAB does not have automatic procedures for constructing frequency polygons and ogives. However, these graphics can be constructed quite easily by using the MINITAB Graph Annotation Tools. To access these tools and have them placed on the MINITAB toolbar, select

Tools : Toolbars : Graph Annotation Tools

- **To construct a frequency polygon,** follow the preceding instructions for constructing a histogram. In addition, however, click on the Data View button, select the Data Display tab, place a checkmark in the Symbols checkbox (also uncheck the Bars checkbox). This will result in plotted points above the histogram classes—rather than bars. Now select the polygon tool

from the Graph Annotation Tools toolbar and draw connecting lines to form the polygon. Instructions for using the polygon tool can be found in the MINITAB help resources listed under "To create a polygon."

- **To construct an ogive,** follow the above instructions for constructing a frequency polygon. In addition, however, click on the Scale button, select the "Y-Scale Type" tab, and place a checkmark in the "Accumulate values across bins" checkbox. This will result in a plot of cumulative frequencies—rather than histogram bars. Now select the polyline tool

from the Graph Annotation Tools toolbar and draw connecting lines to form the ogive. Instructions for using the polyline tool can be found in the MINITAB help resources listed under "To create a polyline."

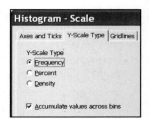

Construct a dot plot of the exam scores as in Figure 2.18(a) on page 55 (data file: FirstExam.MTW):

- Enter the scores for exam 1 in Table 2.8 on page 48 into column C1 with variable name 'Score on Exam 1'.
- Select **Graph : Dot Plot**
- In the Dotplots dialog box, select "One Y Simple" from the gallery of dot plots.
- Click OK in the Dotplots dialog box.
- In the "Dotplot—One Y, Simple" dialog box, enter the variable name 'Score on Exam 1' into the "Graph variables" window. Be sure to include the single quotes.
- Click OK in the "Dotplot—One Y, Simple" dialog box.
- The dotplot will be displayed in a graphics window.
- To change the x-axis labels (or, **ticks**), right-click on any one of the existing labels (say, the 45, for instance) and select "Edit X Scale..." from the popup menu.
- In the Edit Scale dialog box, select the Scale tab and select "Position of Ticks" as the "Major Tick Positions" setting.
- Enter the desired ticks (30 40 50 60 70 80 90 100) into the "Position of ticks" window and click OK in the Edit Scale dialog box.
- The x-axis labels (ticks) will be changed and the new dot plot will be displayed in the graphics window.

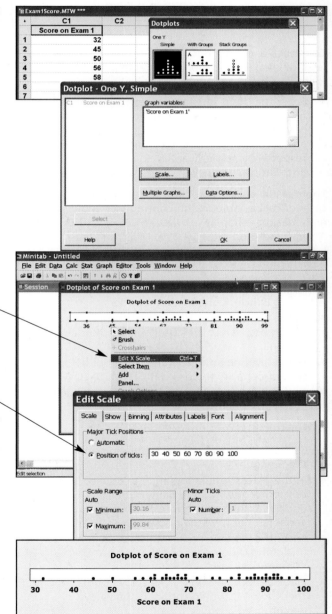

Construct a stem-and-leaf display of the gasoline mileages as in Figure 2.19 on page 57 (data file: GasMiles.MTW):

- Enter the mileage data from Table 2.14 on page 56 into column C1 with variable name Mpg.
- Select **Graph : Stem-and-Leaf**
- In the Stem-and-Leaf dialog box, enter the variable name Mpg into the "Graph Variables" window.
- Click OK in the Stem-and-Leaf dialog box.
- The stem-and-leaf display appears in the Session window and can be selected for printing or copied and pasted into a word processing document. (See Appendix 1.3.)

Construct a contingency table of fund type versus level of client satisfaction as in Table 2.17 on page 62 (data file: Invest.MTW):

- Enter the client satisfaction data from Table 2.16 on page 62 with client number in column C1 having variable name Client, and with fund type and satisfaction rating in columns C2 and C3, respectively, having variable names 'Fund Type' and 'Satisfaction Level'.

The default ordering for the different levels of each categorical variable in the contingency table will be alphabetical—that is, BOND, STOCK, TAXDEF for 'Fund Type' and HIGH, LOW, MED for 'Satisfaction Level'. **To change the ordering to HIGH, MED, LOW** for 'Satisfaction Level':

- Click on any cell in column C3 (Satisfaction Level).
- Select **Editor : Column : Value order**
- In the "Value Order for C3 (Satisfaction Level)" dialog box, select the "User-specified order" option.
- In the "Define an order (one value per line)" window, specify the order HIGH, MED, LOW.
- Click OK in the "Value Order for C3 (Satisfaction Level)" dialog box.

To construct the contingency table:

- Select **Stat : Tables : Cross Tabulation and Chi-Square**
- In the "Cross Tabulation and Chi-Square" dialog box, enter the variable name 'Fund Type' (including the single quotes) into the "Categorical variables: For rows" window.
- Enter the variable name 'Satisfaction Level' (including the single quotes) into the "Categorical variables: For columns" window.
- Place a checkmark in the "Display Counts" checkbox. We would check "Display Row percents" to produce a table of row percentages and we would check "Display Column percents" to produce a table of column percentages.
- Click OK in the "Cross Tabulation and Chi-Square" dialog box to obtain results in the Session window.

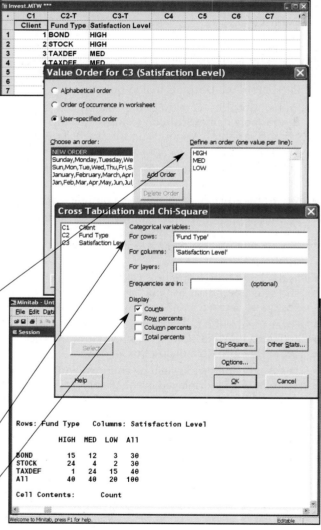

Construct a scatter plot of sales volume versus advertising expenditure as in Figure 2.24 on page 67 (data file: SalesPlot.MWT).

- Enter the sales and advertising data in Table 2.20 (on page 67)—sales region in column C1 (with variable name 'Sales Region'), advertising expenditure in column C2 (with variable name 'Adv Exp'), and sales volume in column C3 (with variable name 'Sales Vol').

- Select **Graph : Scatterplot**

- In the Scatterplots dialog box, select "With Regression" from the gallery of scatterplots in order to produce a scatterplot with a "best line" fitted to the data (see Chapter 14 for discussion of this "best line"). Select "Simple" if a fitted line is not desired.

- Click OK in the Scatterplots dialog box.

- In the "Scatterplot—With Regression" dialog box, enter the variable name 'Sales Vol' (including the single quotes) into row 1 of the "Y variables" window and enter the variable name 'Adv Exp' (including the single quotes) into row 1 of the "X variables" window.

- Click OK in the "Scatterplot—With Regression" dialog box.

- The scatterplot and fitted line will be displayed in a graphics window.

- Additional plots can be obtained by placing appropriate variable names in other rows in the "Y variables" and "X variables" windows.

CHAPTER 3

Descriptive Statistics: Numerical Methods

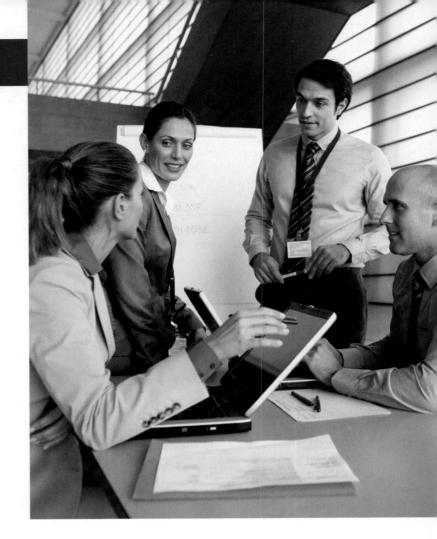

Learning Objectives

When you have mastered the material in this chapter, you will be able to:

LO3-1 Compute and interpret the mean, median, and mode.

LO3-2 Compute and interpret the range, variance, and standard deviation.

LO3-3 Use the Empirical Rule and Chebyshev's Theorem to describe variation.

LO3-4 Compute and interpret percentiles, quartiles, and box-and-whiskers displays.

LO3-5 Compute and interpret covariance, correlation, and the least squares line (Optional).

LO3-6 Compute and interpret weighted means and the mean and standard deviation of grouped data (Optional).

LO3-7 Compute and interpret the geometric mean (Optional).

Chapter Outline

3.1 Describing Central Tendency

3.2 Measures of Variation

3.3 Percentiles, Quartiles, and Box-and-Whiskers Displays

3.4 Covariance, Correlation, and the Least Squares Line (Optional)

3.5 Weighted Means and Grouped Data (Optional)

3.6 The Geometric Mean (Optional)

n this chapter we study numerical methods for describing the important aspects of a set of measurements. If the measurements are values of a quantitative variable, we often describe (1) what a typical measurement might be and (2) how the measurements vary, or differ, from each other. For example, in the car mileage case we might estimate (1) a typical EPA gas mileage for the new midsize model and (2) how the EPA mileages vary from car to car. Or, in the marketing research case, we might estimate (1) a typical bottle design rating and (2) how the bottle design ratings vary from consumer to consumer.

Taken together, the graphical displays of Chapter 2 and the numerical methods of this chapter give us a basic understanding of the important aspects of a set of measurements. We will illustrate this by continuing to analyze the car mileages, payment times, bottle design ratings, and cell phone usages introduced in Chapters 1 and 2.

3.1 Describing Central Tendency ● ● ●

LO3-1 Compute and interpret the mean, median, and mode.

The mean, median, and mode   In addition to describing the shape of the distribution of a sample or population of measurements, we also describe the data set's **central tendency.** A measure of central tendency represents the *center* or *middle* of the data. Sometimes we think of a measure of central tendency as a *typical value.* However, as we will see, not all measures of central tendency are necessarily typical values.

One important measure of central tendency for a population of measurements is the **population mean.** We define it as follows:

The **population mean,** which is denoted μ and pronounced *mew,* is the average of the population measurements.

More precisely, the population mean is calculated by adding all the population measurements and then dividing the resulting sum by the number of population measurements. For instance, suppose that Chris is a college junior majoring in business. This semester Chris is taking five classes and the numbers of students enrolled in the classes (that is, the class sizes) are as follows:

Class	Class Size	DS ClassSizes
Business Law	60	
Finance	41	
International Studies	15	
Management	30	
Marketing	34	

The mean μ of this population of class sizes is

$$\mu = \frac{60 + 41 + 15 + 30 + 34}{5} = \frac{180}{5} = 36$$

Because this population of five class sizes is small, it is possible to compute the population mean. Often, however, a population is very large and we cannot obtain a measurement for each population element. Therefore, we cannot compute the population mean. In such a case, we must estimate the population mean by using a sample of measurements.

In order to understand how to estimate a population mean, we must realize that the population mean is a **population parameter.**

A **population parameter** is a number calculated using the population measurements that describes some aspect of the population. That is, a population parameter is a descriptive measure of the population.

There are many population parameters, and we discuss several of them in this chapter. The simplest way to estimate a population parameter is to make a **point estimate,** which is a one-number estimate of the value of the population parameter. Although a point estimate is a guess of a population parameter's value, it should not be a *blind guess.* Rather, it should be an educated guess based on sample data. One sensible way to find a point estimate of a population parameter is to use a **sample statistic.**

> A **sample statistic** is a number calculated using the sample measurements that describes some aspect of the sample. That is, a sample statistic is a descriptive measure of the sample.

The sample statistic that we use to estimate the population mean is the **sample mean,** which is denoted as $\bar{x}$ (pronounced *x bar*) and is the average of the sample measurements.

In order to write a formula for the sample mean, we employ the letter n to represent the number of sample measurements, and we refer to n as the **sample size.** Furthermore, we denote the sample measurements as $x_1, x_2, \ldots, x_n$. Here x_1 is the first sample measurement, x_2 is the second sample measurement, and so forth. We denote the last sample measurement as x_n. Moreover, when we write formulas we often use *summation notation* for convenience. For instance, we write the sum of the sample measurements

$$x_1 + x_2 + \cdots + x_n$$

as $\sum_{i=1}^{n} x_i$. Here the symbol Σ simply tells us to add the terms that follow the symbol. The term x_i is a generic (or representative) observation in our data set, and the $i = 1$ and the n indicate where to start and stop summing. Thus

$$\sum_{i=1}^{n} x_i = x_1 + x_2 + \cdots + x_n$$

We define the sample mean as follows:

The **sample mean** $\bar{x}$ is defined to be

$$\bar{x} = \frac{\sum_{i=1}^{n} x_i}{n} = \frac{x_1 + x_2 + \cdots + x_n}{n}$$

and is the **point estimate of the population mean** μ.

EXAMPLE 3.1 The Car Mileage Case: Estimating Mileage

In order to offer its tax credit, the federal government has decided to define the "typical" EPA combined city and highway mileage for a car model as the mean μ of the population of EPA combined mileages that would be obtained by all cars of this type. Here, using the mean to represent a typical value is probably reasonable. We know that some individual cars will get mileages that are lower than the mean and some will get mileages that are above it. However, because there will be many thousands of these cars on the road, the mean mileage obtained by these cars is probably a reasonable way to represent the model's overall fuel economy. Therefore, the government will offer its tax credit to any automaker selling a midsize model equipped with an automatic transmission that achieves a mean EPA combined mileage of at least 31 mpg.

To demonstrate that its new midsize model qualifies for the tax credit, the automaker in this case study wishes to use the sample of 50 mileages in Table 3.1 to estimate μ, the model's mean mileage. Before calculating the mean of the entire sample of 50 mileages, we will illustrate the formulas involved by calculating the mean of the first five of these mileages. Table 3.1 tells us that $x_1 = 30.8, x_2 = 31.7, x_3 = 30.1, x_4 = 31.6$, and $x_5 = 32.1$, so the sum of the first five mileages is

$$\sum_{i=1}^{5} x_i = x_1 + x_2 + x_3 + x_4 + x_5$$
$$= 30.8 + 31.7 + 30.1 + 31.6 + 32.1 = 156.3$$

Therefore, the mean of the first five mileages is

$$\bar{x} = \frac{\sum_{i=1}^{5} x_i}{5} = \frac{156.3}{5} = 31.26$$

TABLE 3.1	A Sample of 50 Mileages	DS GasMiles		
30.8	30.8	32.1	32.3	32.7
31.7	30.4	31.4	32.7	31.4
30.1	32.5	30.8	31.2	31.8
31.6	30.3	32.8	30.7	31.9
32.1	31.3	31.9	31.7	33.0
33.3	32.1	31.4	31.4	31.5
31.3	32.5	32.4	32.2	31.6
31.0	31.8	31.0	31.5	30.6
32.0	30.5	29.8	31.7	32.3
32.4	30.5	31.1	30.7	31.4

Of course, intuitively, we are likely to obtain a more accurate point estimate of the population mean by using all of the available sample information. The sum of all 50 mileages can be verified to be

$$\sum_{i=1}^{50} x_i = x_1 + x_2 + \cdots + x_{50} = 30.8 + 31.7 + \cdots + 31.4 = 1578$$

Therefore, the mean of the sample of 50 mileages is

$$\bar{x} = \frac{\sum_{i=1}^{50} x_i}{50} = \frac{1578}{50} = 31.56$$

This point estimate says we estimate that the mean mileage that would be obtained by all of the new midsize cars that will or could potentially be produced this year is 31.56 mpg. Unless we are extremely lucky, however, there will be **sampling error.** That is, the point estimate $\bar{x} = 31.56$ mpg, which is the average of the sample of fifty randomly selected mileages, will probably not exactly equal the population mean μ, which is the average mileage that would be obtained by all cars. Therefore, although $\bar{x} = 31.56$ provides some evidence that μ is at least 31 and thus that the automaker should get the tax credit, it does not provide definitive evidence. In later chapters, we discuss how to assess the *reliability* of the sample mean and how to use a measure of reliability to decide whether sample information provides definitive evidence.

Another descriptive measure of the central tendency of a population or a sample of measurements is the **median.** Intuitively, the median divides a population or sample into two roughly equal parts. We calculate the median, which is denoted M_d, as follows:

Consider a population or a sample of measurements, and arrange the measurements in increasing order. The **median,** M_d, is found as follows:

1 If the number of measurements is odd, the median is the middlemost measurement in the ordering.

2 If the number of measurements is even, the median is the average of the two middlemost measurements in the ordering.

For example, recall that Chris's five classes have sizes 60, 41, 15, 30, and 34. To find the median of the population of class sizes, we arrange the class sizes in increasing order as follows:

15   30   (34)   41   60

Because the number of class sizes is odd, the median of the population of class sizes is the middlemost class size in the ordering. Therefore, the median is 34 students (it is circled).

As another example, suppose that in the middle of the semester Chris decides to take an additional class—a sprint class in individual exercise. If the individual exercise class has 30 students, then the sizes of Chris's six classes are (arranged in increasing order):

15   30   (30)   (34)   41   60

Because the number of classes is even, the median of the population of class sizes is the average of the two middlemost class sizes, which are circled. Therefore, the median is $(30 + 34)/2 = 32$ students. Note that, although two of Chris's classes have the same size, 30 students, each observation is listed separately (that is, 30 is listed twice) when we arrange the observations in increasing order.

As a third example, if we arrange the sample of 50 mileages in Table 3.1 in increasing order, we find that the two middlemost mileages—the 25th and 26th mileages—are 31.5 and 31.6. It follows that the median of the sample is 31.55. Therefore, we estimate that the median mileage that would be obtained by all of the new midsize cars that will or could potentially be produced this year is 31.55 mpg. The Excel output in Figure 3.1 shows this median mileage, as well as the previously calculated mean mileage of 31.56 mpg. Other quantities given on the output will be discussed later in this chapter.

A third measure of the central tendency of a population or sample is the **mode,** which is denoted M_o.

> The **mode,** M_o, of a population or sample of measurements is the measurement that occurs most frequently.

For example, the mode of Chris's six class sizes is 30. This is because more classes (two) have a size of 30 than any other size. Sometimes the highest frequency occurs at more than one measurement. When this happens, two or more modes exist. When exactly two modes exist, we say the data are *bimodal.* When more than two modes exist, we say the data are *multimodal.* If data are presented in classes (such as in a frequency or percent histogram), the class having the highest frequency or percent is called the *modal class.* For example, Figure 3.2 shows a histogram of the car mileages that has two modal classes—the class from 31.0 mpg to 31.5 mpg and the class from 31.5 mpg to 32.0 mpg. Because the mileage 31.5 is in the middle of the modal classes, we might estimate that the population mode for the new midsize model is 31.5 mpg. Or, alternatively, because the Excel output in Figure 3.1 tells us that the mode of the sample of 50 mileages is 31.4 mpg (it can be verified that this mileage occurs five times in Table 3.1), we might estimate that the population mode is 31.4 mpg. Obviously, these two estimates are somewhat contradictory. In general, it can be difficult to define a reliable method for estimating the population mode. Therefore, although it can be informative to report the modal class or classes in a frequency or percent histogram, the mean or median is used more often than the mode when we wish to describe a data set's central tendency by using a single number. Finally, the mode is a useful descriptor of qualitative data. For example, we have seen in Chapter 2 that the most preferred pizza restaurant in the college town was Papa John's, which was preferred by 38 percent of the college students.

Comparing the mean, median, and mode   Often we construct a histogram for a sample to make inferences about the shape of the sampled population. When we do this, it can be useful to "smooth out" the histogram and use the resulting *relative frequency curve* to describe the shape

FIGURE 3.1	Excel Output of Statistics Describing the 50 Mileages

Mileage

Mean	31.56
Standard Error	0.1128
Median	31.55
Mode	31.4
Standard Deviation	0.7977
Sample Variance	0.6363
Kurtosis	−0.5112
Skewness	−0.0342
Range	3.5
Minimum	29.8
Maximum	33.3
Sum	1578
Count	50

FIGURE 3.2	A Percent Histogram Describing the 50 Mileages

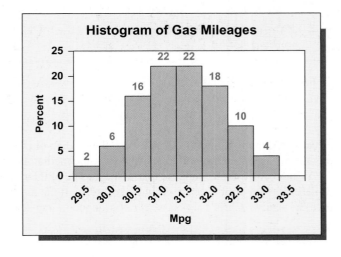

FIGURE 3.3 **Typical Relationships among the Mean μ, the Median M_d, and the Mode M_o**

(a) A symmetrical curve   (b) A curve skewed to the right   (c) A curve skewed to the left

of the population. Relative frequency curves can have many shapes. Three common shapes are illustrated in Figure 3.3. Part (a) of this figure depicts a population described by a symmetrical relative frequency curve. For such a population, the mean (μ), median (M_d), and mode (M_o) are all equal. Note that in this case all three of these quantities are located under the highest point of the curve. It follows that when the frequency distribution of a sample of measurements is approximately symmetrical, then the sample mean, median, and mode will be nearly the same. For instance, consider the sample of 50 mileages in Table 3.1. Because the histogram of these mileages in Figure 3.2 is approximately symmetrical, the mean—31.56—and the median—31.55—of the mileages are approximately equal to each other.

Figure 3.3(b) depicts a population that is skewed to the right. Here the population mean is larger than the population median, and the population median is larger than the population mode (the mode is located under the highest point of the relative frequency curve). In this case the population mean *averages in* the large values in the upper tail of the distribution. Thus the population mean is more affected by these large values than is the population median. To understand this, we consider the following example.

EXAMPLE 3.2 Household Incomes

An economist wishes to study the distribution of household incomes in a Midwestern city. To do this, the economist randomly selects a sample of $n = 12$ households from the city and determines last year's income for each household.[1] The resulting sample of 12 household incomes—arranged in increasing order—is as follows (the incomes are expressed in dollars):

     7,524   11,070   18,211   26,817   36,551   ⟨41,286⟩

     ⟨49,312⟩   57,283   72,814   90,416   135,540   190,250

 Incomes

Because the number of incomes is even, the median of the incomes is the average of the two middlemost incomes, which are enclosed in ovals. Therefore, the median is $(41{,}286 + 49{,}312)/2 =$ \$45,299. The mean of the incomes is the sum of the incomes, 737,074, divided by 12, or \$61,423 (rounded to the nearest dollar). Here, the mean has been affected by averaging in the large incomes \$135,540 and \$190,250 and thus is larger than the median. The median is said to be resistant to these large incomes because the value of the median is affected only by the position of these large incomes in the ordered list of incomes, not by the exact sizes of the incomes. For example, if the largest income were smaller—say \$150,000—the median would remain the same but the mean would decrease. If the largest income were larger—say \$300,000—the median would also remain the same but the mean would increase. Therefore, the median is resistant to large values but the mean is not. Similarly, the median is resistant to values that are much smaller than most of the measurements. In general, we say that **the median is resistant to extreme values.**

Figure 3.3(c) depicts a population that is skewed to the left. Here the population mean is smaller than the population median, and the population median is smaller than the population mode. In this case the population mean *averages in* the small values in the lower tail of the distribution, and the

---

[1]Note that, realistically, an economist would sample many more than 12 incomes from a city. We have made the sample size in this case small so that we can simply illustrate various ideas throughout this chapter.

mean is more affected by these small values than is the median. For instance, in a survey several years ago of 20 Decision Sciences graduates at Miami University, 18 of the graduates had obtained employment in business consulting that paid a mean salary of about $43,000. One of the graduates had become a Christian missionary and listed his salary as $8,500, and another graduate was working for his hometown bank and listed his salary as $10,500. The two lower salaries decreased the overall mean salary to about $39,650, which was below the median salary of about $43,000.

When a population is skewed to the right or left with a very long tail, the population mean can be substantially affected by the extreme population values in the tail of the distribution. In such a case, the population median might be better than the population mean as a measure of central tendency. For example, the yearly incomes of all people in the United States are skewed to the right with a very long tail. Furthermore, the very large incomes in this tail cause the mean yearly income to be inflated above the typical income earned by most Americans. Because of this, the median income is more representative of a typical U.S. income.

When a population is symmetrical or not highly skewed, then the population mean and the population median are either equal or roughly equal, and both provide a good measure of the population central tendency. In this situation, we usually make inferences about the population mean because much of statistical theory is based on the mean rather than the median.

EXAMPLE 3.3 The Marketing Research Case: Rating A Bottle Design

The Excel output in Figure 3.4 tells us that the mean and the median of the sample of 60 bottle design ratings are 30.35 and 31, respectively. Because the histogram of the bottle design ratings in Figure 3.5 is not highly skewed to the left, the sample mean is not much less than the sample median. Therefore, using the mean as our measure of central tendency, we estimate that the mean rating of the new bottle design that would be given by all consumers is 30.35. This is considerably higher than the minimum standard of 25 for a successful bottle design.

EXAMPLE 3.4 The e-billing Case: Reducing Bill Payment Times

The MINITAB output in Figure 3.6 gives a histogram of the 65 payment times, and the MINITAB output in Figure 3.7 tells us that the mean and the median of the payment times are 18.108 days and 17 days, respectively. Because the histogram is not highly skewed to the right, the sample mean is not much greater than the sample median. Therefore, using the mean as our measure of central tendency, we estimate that the mean payment time of all bills using the new billing system is 18.108 days. This is substantially less than the typical payment time of 39 days that had been experienced using the old billing system.

| FIGURE 3.4 | **Excel Output of Statistics Describing the 60 Bottle Design Ratings** |

| FIGURE 3.5 | **Excel Frequency Histogram of the 60 Bottle Design Ratings** |

STATISTICS	
Mean	30.35
Standard Error	0.401146
Median	31
Mode	32
Standard Deviation	3.107263
Sample Variance	9.655085
Kurtosis	1.423397
Skewness	−1.17688
Range	15
Minimum	20
Maximum	35
Sum	1821
Count	60

FIGURE 3.6 **MINITAB Frequency Histogram of the 65 Payment Times**

FIGURE 3.7 **MINITAB Output of Statistics Describing the 65 Payment Times**

Variable	Count	Mean	StDev	Variance		
PayTime	65	18.108	3.961	15.691		

Variable	Minimum	Q1	Median	Q3	Maximum	Range
PayTime	10.000	15.000	17.000	21.000	29.000	19.000

EXAMPLE 3.5 The Cell Phone Case: Reducing Cellular Phone Costs

Suppose that a cellular management service tells the bank that if its cellular cost per minute for the random sample of 100 bank employees is over 18 cents per minute, the bank will benefit from automated cellular management of its calling plans. Last month's cellular usages for the 100 randomly selected employees are given in Table 1.4 (page 9), and a dot plot of these usages is given in the page margin. If we add together the usages, we find that the 100 employees used a total of 46,625 minutes. Furthermore, the total cellular cost incurred by the 100 employees is found to be $9,317 (this total includes base costs, overage costs, long distance, and roaming). This works out to an average of $9,317/46,625 = $.1998, or 19.98 cents per minute. Because this average cellular cost per minute exceeds 18 cents per minute, the bank will hire the cellular management service to manage its calling plans.

To conclude this section, note that the mean and the median convey useful information about a population having a relative frequency curve with a sufficiently regular shape. For instance, the mean and median would be useful in describing the mound-shaped, or single-peaked, distributions in Figure 3.3. However, these measures of central tendency do not adequately describe a double-peaked distribution. For example, the mean and the median of the exam scores in the double-peaked distribution of Figure 2.12 (page 48) are 75.225 and 77. Looking at the distribution, neither the mean nor the median represents a *typical* exam score. This is because the exam scores really have *no central value*. In this case the most important message conveyed by the double-peaked distribution is that the exam scores fall into two distinct groups.

Exercises for Section 3.1

CONCEPTS

3.1 Explain the difference between each of the following:
  a A population parameter and its point estimate.
  b A population mean and a corresponding sample mean.

3.2 Explain how the population mean, median, and mode compare when the population's relative frequency curve is
a Symmetrical.
b Skewed with a tail to the left.
c Skewed with a tail to the right.

METHODS AND APPLICATIONS

3.3 Calculate the mean, median, and mode of each of the following populations of numbers:
a 9, 8, 10, 10, 12, 6, 11, 10, 12, 8
b 110, 120, 70, 90, 90, 100, 80, 130, 140

3.4 Calculate the mean, median, and mode for each of the following populations of numbers:
a 17, 23, 19, 20, 25, 18, 22, 15, 21, 20
b 505, 497, 501, 500, 507, 510, 501

3.5 **THE VIDEO GAME SATISFACTION RATING CASE** ⓄⓈ VideoGame

Recall that Table 1.7 (page 13) presents the satisfaction ratings for the XYZ-Box game system that have been given by 65 randomly selected purchasers. Figures 3.8 and 3.11(a) give the MINITAB and Excel outputs of statistics describing the 65 satisfaction ratings.
a Find the sample mean on the outputs. Does the sample mean provide some evidence that the mean of the population of all possible customer satisfaction ratings for the XYZ-Box is at least 42? (Recall that a "very satisfied" customer gives a rating that is at least 42.) Explain your answer.
b Find the sample median on the outputs. How do the mean and median compare? What does the histogram in Figure 2.15 (page 52) tell you about why they compare this way?

3.6 **THE BANK CUSTOMER WAITING TIME CASE** ⓄⓈ WaitTime

Recall that Table 1.8 (page 13) presents the waiting times for teller service during peak business hours of 100 randomly selected bank customers. Figures 3.9 and 3.11(b) give the MINITAB and Excel outputs of statistics describing the 100 waiting times.
a Find the sample mean on the outputs. Does the sample mean provide some evidence that the mean of the population of all possible customer waiting times during peak business hours is less than six minutes (as is desired by the bank manager)? Explain your answer.
b Find the sample median on the outputs. How do the mean and median compare? What does the histogram in Figure 2.16 (page 53) tell you about why they compare this way?

3.7 **THE TRASH BAG CASE** ⓄⓈ TrashBag

Consider the trash bag problem. Suppose that an independent laboratory has tested 30-gallon trash bags and has found that none of the 30-gallon bags currently on the market has a mean breaking strength of 50 pounds or more. On the basis of these results, the producer of the new, improved trash bag feels sure that its 30-gallon bag will be the strongest such bag on the market if the new trash bag's mean breaking strength can be shown to be at least 50 pounds. Recall that Table 1.9 (page 14) presents the breaking strengths of 40 trash bags of the new type that were selected during

---

FIGURE 3.8   **MINITAB Output of Statistics Describing the 65 Satisfaction Ratings (for Exercise 3.5)**

Variable	Count	Mean	StDev	Variance		
Ratings	65	42.954	2.642	6.982		

Variable	Minimum	Q1	Median	Q3	Maximum	Range
Ratings	36.000	41.000	43.000	45.000	48.000	12.000

FIGURE 3.9   **MINITAB Output of Statistics Describing the 100 Waiting Times (for Exercise 3.6)**

Variable	Count	Mean	StDev	Variance		
WaitTime	100	5.460	2.475	6.128		

Variable	Minimum	Q1	Median	Q3	Maximum	Range
WaitTime	0.400	3.800	5.250	7.200	11.600	11.200

FIGURE 3.10   **MINITAB Output of Statistics Describing the 40 Breaking Strengths (for Exercise 3.7)**

```
Variable      Count    Mean    StDev    Variance
Strength         40   50.575   1.644     2.702

Variable     Minimum      Q1   Median      Q3   Maximum   Range
Strength      46.800   49.425   50.650   51.650    54.000   7.200
```

FIGURE 3.11   **Excel Outputs of Statistics Describing Two Data Sets**

(a) Satisfaction rating statistics

Ratings	
Mean	42.9538
Standard Error	0.3277
Median	43
Mode	44
Standard Deviation	2.6424
Sample Variance	6.9822
Kurtosis	−0.3922
Skewness	−0.4466
Range	12
Minimum	36
Maximum	48
Sum	2792
Count	65

(b) Waiting time statistics

WaitTime	
Mean	5.46
Standard Error	0.2475
Median	5.25
Mode	5.8
Standard Deviation	2.4755
Sample Variance	6.1279
Kurtosis	−0.4050
Skewness	0.2504
Range	11.2
Minimum	0.4
Maximum	11.6
Sum	546
Count	100

FIGURE 3.12   **Excel Output of Breaking Strength Statistics**

Strength	
Mean	50.575
Standard Error	0.2599
Median	50.65
Mode	50.9
Standard Deviation	1.6438
Sample Variance	2.7019
Kurtosis	−0.2151
Skewness	−0.0549
Range	7.2
Minimum	46.8
Maximum	54
Sum	2023
Count	40

---

a 40-hour pilot production run. Figures 3.10 and 3.12 give the MINITAB and Excel outputs of statistics describing the 40 breaking strengths.

a Find the sample mean on the outputs. Does the sample mean provide some evidence that the mean of the population of all possible trash bag breaking strengths is at least 50 pounds? Explain your answer.

b Find the sample median on the outputs. How do the mean and median compare? What does the histogram in Figure 2.17 (page 53) tell you about why they compare this way?

3.8   Lauren is a college sophomore majoring in business. This semester Lauren is taking courses in accounting, economics, management information systems, public speaking, and statistics. The sizes of these classes are, respectively, 350, 45, 35, 25, and 40. Find the mean and the median of the class sizes. What is a better measure of Lauren's "typical class size"—the mean or the median?

In the National Basketball Association (NBA) lockout of 2011, the owners of NBA teams wished to change the existing collective bargaining agreement with the NBA Players Association. The owners wanted a "hard salary cap" restricting the size of team payrolls. This would allow "smaller market teams" having less revenue to be (1) financially profitable and (2) competitive (in terms of wins and losses) with the "larger market teams." The NBA owners also wanted the players to agree to take less than the 57 percent share of team revenues that they had been receiving. The players opposed these changes. Table 3.2 gives, for each NBA team, the team's 2009–2010 revenue, player expenses (including benefits and bonuses), and operating income as given on the Forbes.com website on October 26, 2011. Here, the operating income of a team is basically the team's profit (that is, the team's revenue minus the team's expenses—including player expenses, arena expenses, etc.—but not including some interest, depreciation, and tax expenses). Use the data in Table 3.2 to do Exercises 3.9 through 3.15.

3.9   Construct a histogram and a stem-and-leaf display of the teams' revenues.

3.10   Compute the mean team revenue and the median team revenue, and explain the difference between the values of these statistics.

3.11   Construct a histogram and a stem-and-leaf display of the teams' player expenses.

TABLE 3.2   National Basketball Association Team Revenues, Player Expenses, and Operating Incomes as Given on the Forbes.com Website on October 26, 2011 Ⓞ NBAIncome

Rank	Team	Revenue ($mil)	Player Expenses ($mil)	Operating Income ($mil)	Rank	Team	Revenue ($mil)	Player Expenses ($mil)	Operating Income ($mil)
1	New York Knicks	226	86	64.0	16	Utah Jazz	121	76	−3.9
2	Los Angeles Lakers	214	91	33.4	17	Philadelphia 76ers	110	69	−1.2
3	Chicago Bulls	169	74	51.3	18	Oklahoma City Thunder	118	62	22.6
4	Boston Celtics	151	88	4.2	19	Washington Wizards	107	73	−5.2
5	Houston Rockets	153	67	35.9	20	Denver Nuggets	113	79	−11.7
6	Dallas Mavericks	146	81	−7.8	21	New Jersey Nets	89	64	−10.2
7	Miami Heat	124	78	−5.9	22	Los Angeles Clippers	102	62	11.0
8	Phoenix Suns	147	69	20.4	23	Atlanta Hawks	105	70	−7.3
9	San Antonio Spurs	135	84	−4.7	24	Sacramento Kings	103	72	−9.8
10	Toronto Raptors	138	72	25.3	25	Charlotte Bobcats	98	73	−20.0
11	Orlando Magic	108	86	−23.1	26	New Orleans Hornets	100	74	−5.9
12	Golden State Warriors	119	70	14.3	27	Indiana Pacers	95	71	−16.9
13	Detroit Pistons	147	64	31.8	28	Memphis Grizzlies	92	59	−2.6
14	Portland Trail Blazers	127	64	10.7	29	Minnesota Timberwolves	95	67	−6.7
15	Cleveland Cavaliers	161	90	2.6	30	Milwaukee Bucks	92	69	−2.0

Source: http://www.forbes.com/lists/2011/32/basketball-valuations-11.

3.12 Compute the mean team player expense and the median team player expense and explain the difference between the values of these statistics.

3.13 Construct a histogram and a stem-and-leaf display of the teams' operating incomes.

3.14 Compute the mean team operating income and the median team operating income, and explain the difference between the values of these statistics.

3.15 The mean team operating income is the operating income each NBA team would receive if the NBA owners divided the total of their operating incomes equally among the 30 NBA teams. (Of course, some of the owners might object to dividing their operating incomes equally among the teams).

   a How would the players use the mean team operating income to justify their position opposing a hard salary cap?

   b Use Table 3.2 to find the number of NBA teams that made money (that is, had a positive operating income) and the number of teams that lost money (had a negative operating income).

   c How would the owners use the results of part (b) and the median team operating income to justify their desire for a hard salary cap?

LO3-2 Compute and interpret the range, variance, and standard deviation.

3.2 Measures of Variation ● ● ●

Range, variance, and standard deviation   In addition to estimating a population's central tendency, it is important to estimate the **variation** of the population's individual values. For example, Figure 3.13 shows two histograms. Each portrays the distribution of 20 repair times (in days) for personal computers at a major service center. Because the mean (and median and mode) of each distribution equals four days, the measures of central tendency do not indicate any difference between the American and National Service Centers. However, the repair times for the American Service Center are clustered quite closely together, whereas the repair times for the National Service Center are spread farther apart (the repair time might be as little as one day, but could also be as long as seven days). Therefore, we need measures of variation to express how the two distributions differ.

One way to measure the variation of a set of measurements is to calculate the *range*.

Consider a population or a sample of measurements. The **range** of the measurements is the largest measurement minus the smallest measurement.

In Figure 3.13, the smallest and largest repair times for the American Service Center are three days and five days; therefore, the range is $5 - 3 = 2$ days. On the other hand, the range for the

F I G U R E   3 . 1 3   **Repair Times for Personal Computers at Two Service Centers**

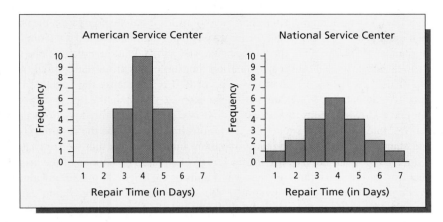

National Service Center is $7 - 1 = 6$ days. The National Service Center's larger range indicates that this service center's repair times exhibit more variation.

In general, the range is not the best measure of a data set's variation. One reason is that it is based on only the smallest and largest measurements in the data set and therefore may reflect an extreme measurement that is not entirely representative of the data set's variation. For example, in the marketing research case, the smallest and largest ratings in the sample of 60 bottle design ratings are 20 and 35. However, to simply estimate that most bottle design ratings are between 20 and 35 misses the fact that 57, or 95 percent, of the 60 ratings are at least as large as the minimum rating of 25 for a successful bottle design. In general, to fully describe a population's variation, it is useful to estimate intervals that contain *different percentages* (for example, 70 percent, 95 percent, or almost 100 percent) of the individual population values. To estimate such intervals, we use the **population variance** and the **population standard deviation.**

The Population Variance and Standard Deviation

The **population variance** σ^2 (pronounced *sigma squared*) is the average of the squared deviations of the individual population measurements from the population mean μ.

   The **population standard deviation** σ (pronounced *sigma*) is the positive square root of the population variance.

For example, consider again the population of Chris's class sizes this semester. These class sizes are 60, 41, 15, 30, and 34. To calculate the variance and standard deviation of these class sizes, we first calculate the population mean to be

$$\mu = \frac{60 + 41 + 15 + 30 + 34}{5} = \frac{180}{5} = 36$$

Next, we calculate the deviations of the individual population measurements from the population mean $\mu = 36$ as follows:

$(60 - 36) = 24 \quad (41 - 36) = 5 \quad (15 - 36) = -21 \quad (30 - 36) = -6 \quad (34 - 36) = -2$

Then we compute the sum of the squares of these deviations:

$$(24)^2 + (5)^2 + (-21)^2 + (-6)^2 + (-2)^2 = 576 + 25 + 441 + 36 + 4 = 1082$$

Finally, we calculate the population variance σ^2, the average of the squared deviations, by dividing the sum of the squared deviations, 1,082, by the number of squared deviations, 5. That is, σ^2 equals $1,082/5 = 216.4$. Furthermore, this implies that the population standard deviation σ (the positive square root of σ^2) is $\sqrt{216.4} = 14.71$.

   To see that the variance and standard deviation measure the variation, or spread, of the individual population measurements, suppose that the measurements are spread far apart. Then, many measurements will be far from the mean μ, many of the squared deviations from the mean will be large, and the sum of squared deviations will be large. It follows that the average of the squared deviations—the population variance—will be relatively large. On the other hand, if the population measurements are clustered close together, many measurements will be close to μ, many of the squared deviations from the mean will be small, and the average of the squared deviations—the population variance—will be small. Therefore, the more spread out the population measurements, the larger is the population variance, and the larger is the population standard deviation.

To further understand the population variance and standard deviation, note that one reason we square the deviations of the individual population measurements from the population mean is that the sum of the raw deviations themselves is zero. This is because the negative deviations cancel the positive deviations. For example, in the class size situation, the raw deviations are 24, 5, −21, −6, and −2, which sum to zero. Of course, we could make the deviations positive by finding their absolute values. We square the deviations instead because the resulting population variance and standard deviation have many important interpretations that we study throughout this book. Since the population variance is an average of squared deviations of the original population values, the variance is expressed in squared units of the original population values. On the other hand, the population standard deviation—the square root of the population variance—is expressed in the same units as the original population values. For example, the previously discussed class sizes are expressed in numbers of students. Therefore, the variance of these class sizes is $\sigma^2 = 216.4$ (students)^2, whereas the standard deviation is $\sigma = 14.71$ students. Since the population standard deviation is expressed in the same units as the population values, it is more often used to make practical interpretations about the variation of these values.

When a population is too large to measure all the population units, we estimate the population variance and the population standard deviation by the **sample variance** and the **sample standard deviation.** We calculate the sample variance by dividing the sum of the squared deviations of the sample measurements from the sample mean by $n - 1$, the sample size minus one. Although we might intuitively think that we should divide by n rather than $n - 1$, it can be shown that dividing by n tends to produce an estimate of the population variance that is too small. On the other hand, dividing by $n - 1$ tends to produce a larger estimate that we will show in Chapter 7 is more appropriate. Therefore, we obtain:

The Sample Variance and the Sample Standard Deviation

The **sample variance** s^2 (pronounced *s squared*) is defined to be

$$s^2 = \frac{\sum_{i=1}^{n} (x_i - \bar{x})^2}{n - 1} = \frac{(x_1 - \bar{x})^2 + (x_2 - \bar{x})^2 + \cdots + (x_n - \bar{x})^2}{n - 1}$$

and is the **point estimate of the population variance** σ^2.

The **sample standard deviation** $s = \sqrt{s^2}$ is the positive square root of the sample variance and is the **point estimate of the population standard deviation** σ.

EXAMPLE 3.6 The Car Mileage Case: Estimating Mileage

To illustrate the calculation of the sample variance and standard deviation, we begin by considering the first five mileages in Table 3.1 (page 103): $x_1 = 30.8$, $x_2 = 31.7$, $x_3 = 30.1$, $x_4 = 31.6$, and $x_5 = 32.1$. Because the mean of these five mileages is $\bar{x} = 31.26$, it follows that

$$\sum_{i=1}^{5} (x_i - \bar{x})^2 = (x_1 - \bar{x})^2 + (x_2 - \bar{x})^2 + (x_3 - \bar{x})^2 + (x_4 - \bar{x})^2 + (x_5 - \bar{x})^2$$

$$= (30.8 - 31.26)^2 + (31.7 - 31.26)^2 + (30.1 - 31.26)^2$$
$$+ (31.6 - 31.26)^2 + (32.1 - 31.26)^2$$

$$= (-.46)^2 + (.44)^2 + (-1.16)^2 + (.34)^2 + (.84)^2$$

$$= 2.572$$

Therefore, the variance and the standard deviation of the sample of the first five mileages are

$$s^2 = \frac{2.572}{5 - 1} = .643 \qquad \text{and} \qquad s = \sqrt{.643} = .8019$$

Of course, intuitively, we are likely to obtain more accurate point estimates of the population variance and standard deviation by using all the available sample information. Recall that the mean of all 50 mileages is $\bar{x} = 31.56$. Using this sample mean, it can be verified that

$$\sum_{i=1}^{50}(x_i - \bar{x})^2 = (x_1 - \bar{x})^2 + (x_2 - \bar{x})^2 + \cdots + (x_{50} - \bar{x})^2$$

$$= (30.8 - 31.56)^2 + (31.7 - 31.56)^2 + \cdots + (31.4 - 31.56)^2$$

$$= (-.76)^2 + (.14)^2 + \cdots + (-.16)^2$$

$$= 31.18$$

Therefore, the variance and the standard deviation of the sample of 50 mileages are

$$s^2 = \frac{31.18}{50 - 1} = .6363 \quad \text{and} \quad s = \sqrt{.6363} = .7977.$$

Notice that the Excel output in Figure 3.1 (page 104) gives these quantities. Here $s^2 = .6363$ and $s = .7977$ are the point estimates of the variance, σ^2, and the standard deviation, σ, of the population of the mileages of all the cars that will be or could potentially be produced. Furthermore, the sample standard deviation is expressed in the same units (that is, miles per gallon) as the sample values. Therefore $s = .7977$ mpg.

Before explaining how we can use s^2 and s in a practical way, we present a formula that makes it easier to compute s^2. This formula is useful when we are using a handheld calculator that is not equipped with a statistics mode to compute s^2.

The **sample variance** can be calculated using the *computational formula*

$$s^2 = \frac{1}{n-1}\left[\sum_{i=1}^{n}x_i^2 - \frac{\left(\sum_{i=1}^{n}x_i\right)^2}{n}\right]$$

EXAMPLE 3.7 The e-billing Case: Reducing Bill Payment Times

Consider the sample of 65 payment times in Table 2.4 (page 42). Using these data, it can be verified that

$$\sum_{i=1}^{65}x_i = x_1 + x_2 + \cdots + x_{65} = 22 + 19 + \cdots + 21 = 1{,}177 \quad \text{and}$$

$$\sum_{i=1}^{65}x_i^2 = x_1^2 + x_2^2 + \cdots + x_{65}^2 = (22)^2 + (19)^2 + \cdots + (21)^2 = 22{,}317$$

Therefore,

$$s^2 = \frac{1}{(65 - 1)}\left[22{,}317 - \frac{(1{,}177)^2}{65}\right] = \frac{1{,}004.2464}{64} = 15.69135$$

and $s = \sqrt{s^2} = \sqrt{15.69135} = 3.9612$ days. Note that the MINITAB output in Figure 3.7 on page 107 gives these results in slightly rounded form.

A practical interpretation of the standard deviation: The Empirical Rule One type of relative frequency curve describing a population is the **normal curve,** which is discussed in Chapter 6. The normal curve is a symmetrical, bell-shaped curve and is illustrated in Figure 3.14(a). If a population is described by a normal curve, we say that the population is **normally distributed,** and the following result can be shown to hold.

LO3-3 Use the Empirical Rule and Chebyshev's Theorem to describe variation.

FIGURE 3.14   The Empirical Rule and Tolerance Intervals for a Normally Distributed Population

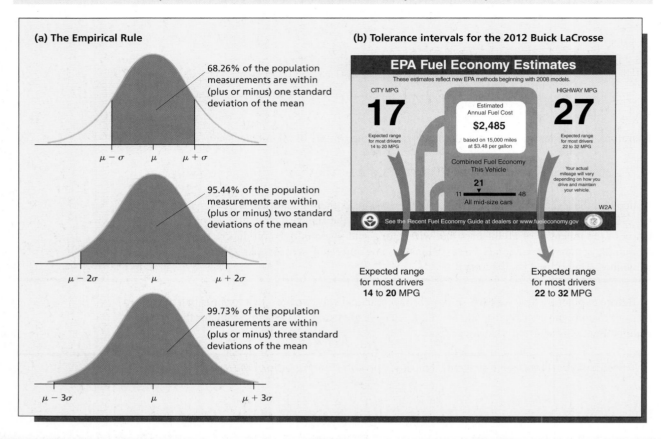

The Empirical Rule for a Normally Distributed Population

I f a population has **mean** μ and **standard deviation** σ and is **described by a normal curve**, then, as illustrated in Figure 3.14(a),

1 68.26 percent of the population measurements are within (plus or minus) one standard deviation of the mean and thus lie in the interval $[\mu - \sigma, \mu + \sigma] = [\mu \pm \sigma]$

2 95.44 percent of the population measurements are within (plus or minus) two standard devi-

ations of the mean and thus lie in the interval $[\mu - 2\sigma, \mu + 2\sigma] = [\mu \pm 2\sigma]$

3 99.73 percent of the population measurements are within (plus or minus) three standard deviations of the mean and thus lie in the interval $[\mu - 3\sigma, \mu + 3\sigma] = [\mu \pm 3\sigma]$

In general, an interval that contains a specified percentage of the individual measurements in a population is called a **tolerance interval.** It follows that the one, two, and three standard deviation intervals around μ given in (1), (2), and (3) are tolerance intervals containing, respectively, 68.26 percent, 95.44 percent, and 99.73 percent of the measurements in a normally distributed population. Often we interpret the *three-sigma interval* $[\mu \pm 3\sigma]$ to be a tolerance interval that contains *almost all* of the measurements in a normally distributed population. Of course, we usually do not know the true values of μ and σ. Therefore, we must estimate the tolerance intervals by replacing μ and σ in these intervals by the mean $\bar{x}$ and standard deviation s of a sample that has been randomly selected from the normally distributed population.

EXAMPLE 3.8 The Car Mileage Case: Estimating Mileage

Again consider the sample of 50 mileages. We have seen that $\bar{x} = 31.56$ and $s = .7977$ for this sample are the point estimates of the mean μ and the standard deviation σ of the population of all mileages. Furthermore, the histogram of the 50 mileages in Figure 3.15 suggests that the

FIGURE 3.15   Estimated Tolerance Intervals in the Car Mileage Case

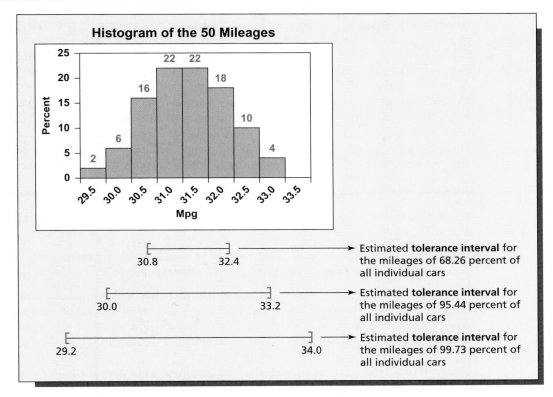

population of all mileages is normally distributed. To illustrate the Empirical Rule more simply, we will round $\bar{x}$ to 31.6 and s to .8. It follows that, using the interval

1   $[\bar{x} \pm s] = [31.6 \pm .8] = [31.6 - .8, 31.6 + .8] = [30.8, 32.4]$, we estimate that 68.26 percent of all individual cars will obtain mileages between 30.8 mpg and 32.4 mpg.

2   $[\bar{x} \pm 2s] = [31.6 \pm 2(.8)] = [31.6 \pm 1.6] = [30.0, 33.2]$, we estimate that 95.44 percent of all individual cars will obtain mileages between 30.0 mpg and 33.2 mpg.

3   $[\bar{x} \pm 3s] = [31.6 \pm 3(.8)] = [31.6 \pm 2.4] = [29.2, 34.0]$, we estimate that 99.73 percent of all individual cars will obtain mileages between 29.2 mpg and 34.0 mpg.

Figure 3.15 depicts these estimated tolerance intervals, which are shown below the histogram. Because the difference between the upper and lower limits of each estimated tolerance interval is fairly small, we might conclude that the variability of the individual car mileages around the estimated mean mileage of 31.6 mpg is fairly small. Furthermore, the interval $[\bar{x} \pm 3s] = [29.2, 34.0]$ implies that almost any individual car that a customer might purchase this year will obtain a mileage between 29.2 mpg and 34.0 mpg.

Before continuing, recall that we have rounded $\bar{x}$ and s to one decimal point accuracy in order to simplify our initial example of the Empirical Rule. If, instead, we calculate the Empirical Rule intervals by using $\bar{x} = 31.56$ and $s = .7977$ and then round the interval endpoints to one decimal place accuracy at the end of the calculations, we obtain the same intervals as obtained above. In general, however, rounding intermediate calculated results can lead to inaccurate final results. Because of this, throughout this book we will avoid greatly rounding intermediate results.

We next note that if we actually count the number of the 50 mileages in Table 3.1 that are contained in each of the intervals $[\bar{x} \pm s] = [30.8, 32.4]$, $[\bar{x} \pm 2s] = [30.0, 33.2]$, and $[\bar{x} \pm 3s] = [29.2, 34.0]$, we find that these intervals contain, respectively, 34, 48, and 50 of the 50 mileages. The corresponding sample percentages—68 percent, 96 percent, and 100 percent—are close to the theoretical percentages—68.26 percent, 95.44 percent, and 99.73 percent—that apply to a normally distributed population. This is further evidence that the population of all mileages is (approximately) normally distributed and thus that the Empirical Rule holds for this population.

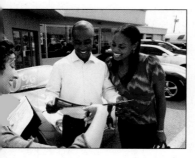

To conclude this example, we note that the automaker has studied the combined city and highway mileages of the new model because the federal tax credit is based on these combined mileages. When reporting fuel economy estimates for a particular car model to the public, however, the EPA realizes that the proportions of city and highway driving vary from purchaser to purchaser. Therefore, the EPA reports both a combined mileage estimate and separate city and highway mileage estimates to the public. Figure 3.14(b) presents a window sticker that summarizes these estimates for the 2012 Buick LaCrosse equipped with a six-cylinder engine and an automatic transmission. The city mpg of 17 and the highway mpg of 27 given at the top of the sticker are point estimates of, respectively, the mean city mileage and the mean highway mileage that would be obtained by all such 2012 LaCrosses. The expected city range of 14 to 20 mpg says that most LaCrosses will get between 14 mpg and 20 mpg in city driving. The expected highway range of 22 to 32 mpg says that most LaCrosses will get between 22 mpg and 32 mpg in highway driving. The combined city and highway mileage estimate for the LaCrosse is 21 mpg.

Skewness and the Empirical Rule   The Empirical Rule holds for normally distributed populations. In addition:

> The Empirical Rule also approximately holds for populations having **mound-shaped (single-peaked) distributions that are not very skewed to the right or left.**

In some situations, the skewness of a mound-shaped distribution can make it tricky to know whether to use the Empirical Rule. This will be investigated in the end-of-section exercises. When a distribution seems to be too skewed for the Empirical Rule to hold, it is probably best to describe the distribution's variation by using **percentiles,** which are discussed in the next section.

Chebyshev's Theorem   If we fear that the Empirical Rule does not hold for a particular population, we can consider using **Chebyshev's Theorem** to find an interval that contains a specified percentage of the individual measurements in the population. Although Chebyshev's Theorem technically applies to any population, we will see that it is not as practically useful as we might hope.

Chebyshev's Theorem

Consider any population that has mean μ and standard deviation σ. Then, for any value of k greater than 1, at least $100(1 - 1/k^2)\%$ of the population measurements lie in the interval $[\mu \pm k\sigma]$.

For example, if we choose k equal to 2, then at least $100(1 - 1/2^2)\% = 100(3/4)\% = 75\%$ of the population measurements lie in the interval $[\mu \pm 2\sigma]$. As another example, if we choose k equal to 3, then at least $100(1 - 1/3^2)\% = 100(8/9)\% = 88.89\%$ of the population measurements lie in the interval $[\mu \pm 3\sigma]$. As yet a third example, suppose that we wish to find an interval containing at least 99.73 percent of all population measurements. Here we would set $100(1 - 1/k^2)\%$ equal to 99.73%, which implies that $(1 - 1/k^2) = .9973$. If we solve for k, we find that $k = 19.25$. This says that at least 99.73 percent of all population measurements lie in the interval $[\mu \pm 19.25\sigma]$. Unless σ is extremely small, this interval will be so long that it will tell us very little about where the population measurements lie. We conclude that Chebyshev's Theorem can help us find an interval that contains a reasonably high percentage (such as 75 percent or 88.89 percent) of all population measurements. However, unless σ is extremely small, Chebyshev's Theorem will not provide a useful interval that contains almost all (say, 99.73 percent) of the population measurements.

Although Chebyshev's Theorem technically applies to any population, it is only of practical use when analyzing a **non-mound-shaped** (for example, a double-peaked) **population that is not *very* skewed to the right or left.** Why is this? First, **we would not use Chebyshev's Theorem to describe a mound-shaped population that is not very skewed because we can use the Empirical Rule** to do this. In fact, the Empirical Rule is better for such a population because it gives us a shorter interval that will contain a given percentage of measurements. For example, if the Empirical Rule can be used to describe a population, the interval $[\mu \pm 3\sigma]$ will contain

99.73 percent of all measurements. On the other hand, if we use Chebyshev's Theorem, the interval $[\mu \pm 19.25\sigma]$ is needed. As another example, the Empirical Rule tells us that 95.44 percent of all measurements lie in the interval $[\mu \pm 2\sigma]$, whereas Chebyshev's Theorem tells us only that at least 75 percent of all measurements lie in this interval.

It is also not appropriate to use Chebyshev's Theorem—or any other result making use of the population standard deviation σ—to describe a population that is very skewed. This is because, if a population is very skewed, the measurements in the long tail to the left or right will inflate σ. This implies that tolerance intervals calculated using σ will be too long to be useful. In this case, it is best to measure variation by using **percentiles,** which are discussed in the next section.

z-scores We can determine the relative location of any value in a population or sample by using the mean and standard deviation to compute the value's z-score. For any value x in a population or sample, the **z-score** corresponding to x is defined as follows:

---

z-score:

$$z = \frac{x - \text{mean}}{\text{standard deviation}}$$

The z-score, which is also called the *standardized value,* is the number of standard deviations that x is from the mean. A positive z-score says that x is above (greater than) the mean, while a negative z-score says that x is below (less than) the mean. For instance, a z-score equal to 2.3 says that x is 2.3 standard deviations above the mean. Similarly, a z-score equal to -1.68 says that x is 1.68 standard deviations below the mean. A z-score equal to zero says that x equals the mean.

A z-score indicates the relative location of a value within a population or sample. For example, below we calculate the z-scores for each of the profit margins for five competing companies in a particular industry. For these five companies, the mean profit margin is 10% and the standard deviation is 3.406%.

Company	Profit margin, x	x − mean	z-score
1	8%	8 − 10 = −2	−2/3.406 = −.59
2	10	10 − 10 = 0	0/3.406 = 0
3	15	15 − 10 = 5	5/3.406 = 1.47
4	12	12 − 10 = 2	2/3.406 = .59
5	5	5 − 10 = −5	−5/3.406 = −1.47

These z-scores tell us that the profit margin for Company 3 is the farthest above the mean. More specifically, this profit margin is 1.47 standard deviations above the mean. The profit margin for Company 5 is the farthest below the mean—it is 1.47 standard deviations below the mean. Because the z-score for the Company 2 equals zero, its profit margin equals the mean.

Values in two different populations or samples having the same z-score are the same number of standard deviations from their respective means and, therefore, have the same relative locations. For example, suppose that the mean score on the midterm exam for students in Section A of a statistics course is 65 and the standard deviation of the scores is 10. Meanwhile, the mean score on the same exam for students in Section B is 80 and the standard deviation is 5. A student in Section A who scores an 85 and a student in Section B who scores a 90 have the same relative locations within their respective sections because their z-scores, $(85 - 65)/10 = 2$ and $(90 - 80)/5 = 2$, are equal.

The coefficient of variation Sometimes we need to measure the size of the standard deviation of a population or sample relative to the size of the population or sample mean. The **coefficient of variation,** which makes this comparison, is defined for a population or sample as follows:

$$\text{coefficient of variation} = \frac{\text{standard deviation}}{\text{mean}} \times 100$$

The coefficient of variation compares populations or samples having different means and different standard deviations. For example, suppose that the mean yearly return for a particular stock fund, which we call Stock Fund 1, is 10.39 percent with a standard deviation of 16.18 percent, while the mean yearly return for another stock fund, which we call Stock Fund 2, is 7.7 percent with a standard deviation of 13.82 percent. It follows that the coefficient of variation for Stock Fund 1 is $(16.18/10.39) \times 100 = 155.73$, and that the coefficient of variation for Stock Fund 2 is $(13.82/7.7) \times 100 = 179.48$. This tells us that, for Stock Fund 1, the standard deviation is 155.73 percent of the value of its mean yearly return. For Stock Fund 2, the standard deviation is 179.48 percent of the value of its mean yearly return.

In the context of situations like the stock fund comparison, the coefficient of variation is often used as a measure of *risk* because it measures the variation of the returns (the standard deviation) relative to the size of the mean return. For instance, although Stock Fund 2 has a smaller standard deviation than does Stock Fund 1 (13.82 percent compared to 16.18 percent), Stock Fund 2 has a higher coefficient of variation than does Stock Fund 1 (179.48 versus 155.73). This says that, *relative to the mean return,* the variation in returns for Stock Fund 2 is higher. That is, we would conclude that investing in Stock Fund 2 is riskier than investing in Stock Fund 1.

Exercises for Section 3.2

connect

CONCEPTS

3.16 Define the range, variance, and standard deviation for a population.

3.17 Discuss how the variance and the standard deviation measure variation.

3.18 The Empirical Rule for a normally distributed population and Chebyshev's Theorem have the same basic purpose. In your own words, explain what this purpose is.

METHODS AND APPLICATIONS

3.19 Consider the following population of five numbers: 5, 8, 10, 12, 15. Calculate the range, variance, and standard deviation of this population.

3.20 Table 3.3 gives data concerning the 10 most valuable Nascar team valuations and their revenues as given on the Forbes.com website on June 14, 2011. Calculate the population range, variance, and standard deviation of the 10 valuations and of the 10 revenues.   **DS** Nascar

3.21 Consider Exercise 3.20.   **DS** Nascar
  a Compute and interpret the z-score for each Nascar team valuation.
  b Compute and interpret the z-score for each Nascar team revenue.

3.22 In order to control costs, a company wishes to study the amount of money its sales force spends entertaining clients. The following is a random sample of six entertainment expenses (dinner costs for four people) from expense reports submitted by members of the sales force.   **DS** DinnerCost

$157 $132 $109 $145 $125 $139

  a Calculate $\bar{x}$, s^2, and s for the expense data. In addition, show that the two different formulas for calculating s^2 give the same result.
  b Assuming that the distribution of entertainment expenses is approximately normally distributed, calculate estimates of tolerance intervals containing 68.26 percent, 95.44 percent, and 99.73 percent of all entertainment expenses by the sales force.
  c If a member of the sales force submits an entertainment expense (dinner cost for four) of $190, should this expense be considered unusually high (and possibly worthy of investigation by the company)? Explain your answer.
  d Compute and interpret the z-score for each of the six entertainment expenses.

3.23 **THE TRASH BAG CASE**   **DS** TrashBag

The mean and the standard deviation of the sample of 40 trash bag breaking strengths are $\bar{x} = 50.575$ and $s = 1.6438$.
  a What does the histogram in Figure 2.17 (page 53) say about whether the Empirical Rule should be used to describe the trash bag breaking strengths?

TABLE 3.3 Top 10 Highest Nascar Team Valuations and Revenues as Given on the Forbes.com Website on June 14, 2011.

Rank	Team	Value ($mil)	Revenue ($mil)
1	Hendrick Motorsports	350	177
2	Roush Fenway	224	140
3	Richard Childress	158	90
4	Joe Gibbs Racing	152	93
5	Penske Racing	100	78
6	Stewart-Haas Racing	95	68
7	Michael Waltrip Racing	90	58
8	Earnhardt Ganassi Racing	76	59
9	Richard Petty Motorsports	60	80
10	Red Bull Racing	58	48

Source: http://www.forbes.com/2011/02/23/nascar-highest-paid-drivers-business-sports-nascar-11_land.htm1 (accessed 6/14/2011).

b Use the Empirical Rule to calculate estimates of tolerance intervals containing 68.26 percent, 95.44 percent, and 99.73 percent of all possible trash bag breaking strengths.

c Does the estimate of a tolerance interval containing 99.73 percent of all breaking strengths provide evidence that almost any bag a customer might purchase will have a breaking strength that exceeds 45 pounds? Explain your answer.

d How do the percentages of the 40 breaking strengths in Table 1.9 (page 14) that actually fall into the intervals $[\bar{x} \pm s]$, $[\bar{x} \pm 2s]$, and $[\bar{x} \pm 3s]$ compare to those given by the Empirical Rule? Do these comparisons indicate that the statistical inferences you made in parts *b* and *c* are reasonably valid?

3.24 THE BANK CUSTOMER WAITING TIME CASE DS WaitTime

The mean and the standard deviation of the sample of 100 bank customer waiting times are $\bar{x} = 5.46$ and $s = 2.475$.

a What does the histogram in Figure 2.16 (page 53) say about whether the Empirical Rule should be used to describe the bank customer waiting times?

b Use the Empirical Rule to calculate estimates of tolerance intervals containing 68.26 percent, 95.44 percent, and 99.73 percent of all possible bank customer waiting times.

c Does the estimate of a tolerance interval containing 68.26 percent of all waiting times provide evidence that at least two-thirds of all customers will have to wait less than eight minutes for service? Explain your answer.

d How do the percentages of the 100 waiting times in Table 1.8 (page 13) that actually fall into the intervals $[\bar{x} \pm s]$, $[\bar{x} \pm 2s]$, and $[\bar{x} \pm 3s]$ compare to those given by the Empirical Rule? Do these comparisons indicate that the statistical inferences you made in parts *b* and *c* are reasonably valid?

3.25 THE VIDEO GAME SATISFACTION RATING CASE DS VideoGame

The mean and the standard deviation of the sample of 65 customer satisfaction ratings are $\bar{x} = 42.95$ and $s = 2.6424$.

a What does the histogram in Figure 2.15 (page 52) say about whether the Empirical Rule should be used to describe the satisfaction ratings?

b Use the Empirical Rule to calculate estimates of tolerance intervals containing 68.26 percent, 95.44 percent, and 99.73 percent of all possible satisfaction ratings.

c Does the estimate of a tolerance interval containing 99.73 percent of all satisfaction ratings provide evidence that 99.73 percent of all customers will give a satisfaction rating for the XYZ-Box game system that is at least 35 (the minimal rating of a "satisfied" customer)? Explain your answer.

d How do the percentages of the 65 customer satisfaction ratings in Table 1.7 (page 13) that actually fall into the intervals $[\bar{x} \pm s]$, $[\bar{x} \pm 2s]$, and $[\bar{x} \pm 3s]$ compare to those given by the Empirical Rule? Do these comparisons indicate that the statistical inferences you made in parts *b* and *c* are reasonably valid?

TABLE 3.4   ATM Transaction Times (in Seconds) for 63 Withdrawals   **DS** ATMTime

Transaction	Time	Transaction	Time	Transaction	Time
1	32	22	34	43	37
2	32	23	32	44	32
3	41	24	34	45	33
4	51	25	35	46	33
5	42	26	33	47	40
6	39	27	42	48	35
7	33	28	46	49	33
8	43	29	52	50	39
9	35	30	36	51	34
10	33	31	37	52	34
11	33	32	32	53	33
12	32	33	39	54	38
13	42	34	36	55	41
14	34	35	41	56	34
15	37	36	32	57	35
16	37	37	33	58	35
17	33	38	34	59	37
18	35	39	38	60	39
19	40	40	32	61	44
20	36	41	35	62	40
21	32	42	33	63	39

3.26 Consider the 63 automatic teller machine (ATM) transaction times given in Table 3.4 above.
   a Construct a histogram (or a stem-and-leaf display) for the 63 ATM transaction times. Describe the shape of the distribution of transaction times.   **DS** ATMTime
   b When we compute the sample mean and sample standard deviation for the transaction times, we find that $\bar{x} = 36.56$ and $s = 4.475$. Compute each of the intervals $[\bar{x} \pm s]$, $[\bar{x} \pm 2s]$, and $[\bar{x} \pm 3s]$. Then count the number of transaction times that actually fall into each interval and find the percentage of transaction times that actually fall into each interval.
   c How do the percentages of transaction times that fall into the intervals $[\bar{x} \pm s]$, $[\bar{x} \pm 2s]$, and $[\bar{x} \pm 3s]$ compare to those given by the Empirical Rule? How do the percentages of transaction times that fall into the intervals $[\bar{x} \pm 2s]$ and $[\bar{x} \pm 3s]$ compare to those given by Chebyshev's Theorem?
   d Explain why the Empirical Rule does not describe the transaction times extremely well.

3.27 Consider three stock funds, which we will call Stock Funds 1, 2, and 3. Suppose that Stock Fund 1 has a mean yearly return of 10.93 percent with a standard deviation of 41.96 percent, Stock Fund 2 has a mean yearly return of 13 percent with a standard deviation of 9.36 percent, and Stock Fund 3 has a mean yearly return of 34.45 percent with a standard deviation of 41.16 percent.
   a For each fund, find an interval in which you would expect 95.44 percent of all yearly returns to fall. Assume returns are normally distributed.
   b Using the intervals you computed in part *a*, compare the three funds with respect to average yearly returns and with respect to variability of returns.
   c Calculate the coefficient of variation for each fund, and use your results to compare the funds with respect to risk. Which fund is riskier?

LO3-4 Compute and interpret percentiles, quartiles, and box-and-whiskers displays.

3.3 Percentiles, Quartiles, and Box-and-Whiskers Displays ● ● ●

Percentiles, quartiles, and five-number displays   In this section we consider **percentiles** and their applications. We begin by defining the ***p*th percentile.**

For a set of measurements arranged in increasing order, the ***p*th percentile** is a value such that p percent of the measurements fall at or below the value, and $(100 - p)$ percent of the measurements fall at or above the value.

There are various procedures for calculating percentiles. **One procedure for calculating the pth percentile for a set of n measurements uses the following three steps:**

Step 1: Arrange the measurements in increasing order.

Step 2: Calculate the index

$$i = \left(\frac{p}{100}\right)n$$

Step 3:   **(a)** If i is not an integer, round up to obtain the next integer greater than i. This integer denotes the position of the pth percentile in the ordered arrangement.

          (b) If i is an integer, the pth percentile is the average of the measurements in positions i and $i + 1$ in the ordered arrangement.

To illustrate the calculation and interpretation of percentiles, recall in the household income situation that an economist has randomly selected a sample of $n = 12$ households from a Midwestern city and has determined last year's income for each household. In order to assess the variation of the population of household incomes in the city, we will calculate various percentiles for the sample of incomes. Specifically, we will calculate the 10th, 25th, 50th, 75th, and 90th percentiles of these incomes. The first step is to arrange the incomes in increasing order as follows:

7,524   11,070   18,211   26,817   36,551   41,286

49,312   57,283   72,814   90,416   135,540   190,250

To find the 10th percentile, we calculate (in step 2) the index

$$i = \left(\frac{p}{100}\right)n = \left(\frac{10}{100}\right)12 = 1.2$$

Because $i = 1.2$ is not an integer, step 3(a) says to round $i = 1.2$ up to 2. It follows that the 10th percentile is the income in position 2 in the ordered arrangement—that is, 11,070. To find the 25th percentile, we calculate the index

$$i = \left(\frac{p}{100}\right)n = \left(\frac{25}{100}\right)12 = 3$$

Because $i = 3$ is an integer, step 3(b) says that the 25th percentile is the average of the incomes in positions 3 and 4 in the ordered arrangement—that is, $(18,211 + 26,817)/2 = 22,514$. To find the 50th percentile, we calculate the index

$$i = \left(\frac{p}{100}\right)n = \left(\frac{50}{100}\right)12 = 6$$

Because $i = 6$ is an integer, step 3(b) says that the 50th percentile is the average of the incomes in positions 6 and 7 in the ordered arrangement—that is, $(41,286 + 49,312)/2 = 45,299$. To find the 75th percentile, we calculate the index

$$i = \left(\frac{p}{100}\right)n = \left(\frac{75}{100}\right)12 = 9$$

Because $i = 9$ is an integer, step 3(b) says that the 75th percentile is the average of the incomes in positions 9 and 10 in the ordered arrangement—that is, $(72,814 + 90,416)/2 = 81,615$. To find the 90th percentile, we calculate the index

$$i = \left(\frac{p}{100}\right)n = \left(\frac{90}{100}\right)12 = 10.8$$

Because $i = 10.8$ is not an integer, step 3(a) says to round $i = 10.8$ up to 11. It follows that the 90th percentile is the income in position 11 in the ordered arrangement—that is, 135,540.

One appealing way to describe the variation of a set of measurements is to divide the data into four parts, each containing approximately 25 percent of the measurements. This can be done by defining the *first, second,* and *third quartiles* as follows:

The **first quartile,** denoted Q_1, is the **25th percentile.**
The **second quartile** (or **median**), denoted M_d, is the **50th percentile.**
The **third quartile,** denoted Q_3, is the **75th percentile.**

Note that the second quartile is simply another name for the median. Furthermore, the procedure we have described here that is used to find the 50th percentile (second quartile) will always give the same result as the previously described procedure (see Section 3.1) for finding the median. To illustrate how the quartiles divide a set of measurements into four parts, consider the following display of the sampled incomes, which shows the first quartile (the 25th percentile), $Q_1 = 22{,}514$, the median (the 50th percentile), $M_d = 45{,}299$, and the third quartile (the 75th percentile), $Q_3 = 81{,}615$:

| 7,524 | 11,070 | 18,211 | | 26,817 | 36,551 | 41,286 | |

$$Q_1 = 22{,}514 \qquad\qquad\qquad\qquad M_d = 45{,}299$$

| | 49,312 | 57,283 | 72,814 | | 90,416 | 135,540 | 190,250 |

$$Q_3 = 81{,}615$$

Using the quartiles, we estimate that for the household incomes in the Midwestern city: (1) 25 percent of the incomes are less than or equal to \$22,514, (2) 25 percent of the incomes are between \$22,514 and \$45,299, (3) 25 percent of the incomes are between \$45,299 and \$81,615, and (4) 25 percent of the incomes are greater than or equal to \$81,615. In addition, to assess some of the lowest and highest incomes, the 10th percentile estimates that 10 percent of the incomes are less than or equal to \$11,070, and the 90th percentile estimates that 10 percent of the incomes are greater than or equal to \$135,540.

Household Income Five-Number Summary

We sometimes describe a set of measurements by using a **five-number summary.** The summary consists of (1) the smallest measurement; (2) the first quartile, Q_1; (3) the median, M_d; (4) the third quartile, Q_3; and (5) the largest measurement. It is easy to graphically depict a five-number summary. For example, we have seen that for the 12 household incomes, the smallest income is \$7,524, $Q_1 = \$22{,}514$, $M_d = \$45{,}299$, $Q_3 = \$81{,}615$, and the largest income is \$190,250. It follows that a graphical depiction of this five-number summary is as shown in the page margin. Notice that we have drawn a vertical line extending from the smallest income to the largest income. In addition, a rectangle is drawn that extends from Q_1 to Q_3, and a horizontal line is drawn to indicate the location of the median. The summary divides the incomes into four parts, with the middle 50 percent of the incomes depicted by the rectangle. The summary indicates that the largest 25 percent of the incomes is much more spread out than the smallest 25 percent of the incomes and that the second-largest 25 percent of the incomes is more spread out than the second-smallest 25 percent of the incomes. Overall, the summary indicates that the incomes are fairly highly skewed toward the larger incomes.

In general, unless percentiles correspond to very high or very low percentages, they are resistant (like the median) to extreme values. For example, the 75th percentile of the household incomes would remain \$81,615 even if the largest income (\$190,250) were, instead, \$7,000,000. On the other hand, the standard deviation in this situation would increase. In general, if a population is highly skewed to the right or left, the standard deviation is so large that using it to describe variation does not provide much useful information. For example, the standard deviation of the 12 household incomes is inflated by the large incomes \$135,540 and \$190,250 and can be calculated to be \$54,567. Because the mean of the 12 incomes is \$61,423, Chebyshev's Theorem says that we estimate that at least 75 percent of all household incomes in the city are in the interval $[\bar{x} \pm 2s] = [61{,}423 \pm 2(54{,}567)] = [-47{,}711, 170{,}557]$; that is, are \$170,557 or less. This is much less informative than using the 75th percentile, which estimates that 75 percent of all household incomes are less than or equal to \$81,615. In general, if a population is highly skewed to the right or left, it can be best to describe the variation of the population by using various percentiles. This is what we did when we estimated the variation of the household incomes in the city by using the 10th, 25th, 50th, 75th, and 90th percentiles of the 12 sampled incomes and when we depicted this variation by using the five-number summary. Using other percentiles can also be informative. For example, the Bureau of the Census sometimes assesses the variation of all household incomes in the United States by using the 20th, 40th, 60th, and 80th percentiles of these incomes.

We next define the **interquartile range,** denoted IQR, to be the difference between the third quartile Q_3 and the first quartile Q_1. That is, $IQR = Q_3 - Q_1$. This quantity can be interpreted as the length of the interval that contains the *middle 50 percent* of the measurements. For instance, the interquartile range of the 12 household incomes is $Q_3 - Q_1 = 81{,}615 - 22{,}514 = 59{,}101$.

This says that we estimate that the middle 50 percent of all household incomes fall within a range that is $59,101 long.

The procedure we have presented for calculating the first and third quartiles is not the only procedure for computing these quantities. In fact, several procedures exist, and, for example, different statistical computer packages use several somewhat different methods for computing the quartiles. These different procedures sometimes obtain different results, but the overall objective is always to divide the data into four equal parts.

Box-and-whiskers displays (box plots)   A more sophisticated modification of the graphical five-number summary is called a **box-and-whiskers display** (sometimes called a **box plot**). Such a display is constructed by using Q_1, M_d, Q_3, and the interquartile range. As an example, suppose that 20 randomly selected customers give the following satisfaction ratings (on a scale of 1 to 10) for a DVD recorder:

1   3   5   5   7   8   8   8   8   8   8   9   9   9   9   9   10   10   10   10

DS DVDSat

The MINITAB output in Figure 3.16 says that for these ratings $Q_1 = 7.25$, $M_d = 8$, $Q_3 = 9$, and $IQR = Q_3 - Q_1 = 9 - 7.25 = 1.75$. To construct a box-and-whiskers display, we first draw a box that extends from Q_1 to Q_3. As shown in Figure 3.17, for the satisfaction ratings data this box extends from $Q_1 = 7.25$ to $Q_3 = 9$. The box contains the middle 50 percent of the data set. Next a vertical line is drawn through the box at the value of the median M_d. This line divides the data set into two roughly equal parts. We next define what we call the **lower** and **upper limits.** The **lower limit** is located $1.5 \times IQR$ below Q_1 and the **upper limit** is located $1.5 \times IQR$ above Q_3. For the satisfaction ratings data, these limits are

$$Q_1 - 1.5(IQR) = 7.25 - 1.5(1.75) = 4.625 \quad \text{and} \quad Q_3 + 1.5(IQR) = 9 + 1.5(1.75) = 11.625$$

The lower and upper limits help us to draw the plot's **whiskers:** dashed lines extending below Q_1 and above Q_3 (as in Figure 3.17). One whisker is drawn from Q_1 to the smallest measurement between the lower and upper limits. For the satisfaction ratings data, this whisker extends from $Q_1 = 7.25$ down to 5, because 5 is the smallest rating between the lower and upper limits 4.625 and 11.625.

FIGURE 3.16   **MINITAB Output of Statistics Describing the 20 Satisfaction Ratings**

Variable	Count	Mean	StDev	Range	
Rating	20	7.700	2.430	9.000	

Variable	Minimum	Q1	Median	Q3	Maximum
Rating	1.000	7.250	8.000	9.000	10.000

FIGURE 3.17   **Constructing a Box Plot of the Satisfaction Ratings**

FIGURE 3.18   MINITAB Output of a Box Plot of the Satisfaction Ratings

The other whisker is drawn from Q_3 to the largest measurement between the lower and upper limits. For the satisfaction ratings data, this whisker extends from $Q_3 = 9$ up to 10, because 10 is the largest rating between the lower and upper limits 4.625 and 11.625. The lower and upper limits are also used to identify *outliers*. An **outlier** is a measurement that is separated from (that is, different from) most of the other measurements in the data set. A measurement that is less than the lower limit or greater than the upper limit is considered to be an outlier. We indicate the location of an outlier by plotting this measurement with the symbol *. For the satisfaction rating data, the ratings 1 and 3 are outliers because they are less than the lower limit 4.625. Figure 3.18 gives the MINITAB output of a box-and-whiskers plot of the satisficating ratings.

We now summarize how to construct a box-and-whiskers plot.

Constructing a Box-and-Whiskers Display (Box Plot)

1 Draw a **box** that extends from the first quartile Q_1 to the third quartile Q_3. Also draw a vertical line through the box located at the median M_d.

2 Determine the values of the **lower** and **upper limits**. The **lower limit** is located $1.5 \times IQR$ below Q_1 and the **upper limit** is located $1.5 \times IQR$ above Q_3. That is, the lower and upper limits are

$$Q_1 - 1.5(IQR) \quad \text{and} \quad Q_3 + 1.5(IQR)$$

3 Draw **whiskers** as dashed lines that extend below Q_1 and above Q_3. Draw one whisker from Q_1 to the *smallest* measurement that is between the lower and upper limits. Draw the other whisker from Q_3 to the *largest* measurement that is between the lower and upper limits.

4 A measurement that is less than the lower limit or greater than the upper limit is an **outlier**. Plot each outlier using the symbol *.

When interpreting a box-and-whiskers display, keep several points in mind. First, the box (between Q_1 and Q_3) contains the middle 50 percent of the data. Second, the median (which is inside the box) divides the data into two roughly equal parts. Third, if one of the whiskers is longer than the other, the data set is probably skewed in the direction of the longer whisker. Last, observations designated as outliers should be investigated. Understanding the root causes behind the outlying observations will often provide useful information. For instance, understanding why two of the satisfaction ratings in the box plot of Figure 3.18 are substantially lower than the great majority of the ratings may suggest actions that can improve the DVD recorder manufacturer's product and/or service. Outliers can also be caused by inaccurate measuring, reporting, or plotting of the data. Such possibilities should be investigated, and incorrect data should be adjusted or eliminated.

Graphical five-number summaries and box-and-whiskers displays are perhaps best used to compare different sets of measurements. We demonstrate this use of such displays in the following example.

EXAMPLE 3.9 The Standard and Poor's 500 Case

Figure 3.19 shows box plots of the percentage returns of stocks on the Standard and Poor's 500 (S&P 500) for different time horizons of investment. Figure 3.19(a) compares a 1-year time horizon with a 3-year time horizon. We see that there is a 25 percent chance of a negative return (loss)

(a) 1-year versus 3-year   **(b) 5-year versus 10-year**   **(c) 10-year versus 20-year**

Data from Global Financial Data
Source: http//junkcharts.typepad.com/junk_charts/boxplot/.

for the 3-year horizon and a 25 percent chance of earning more than 50 percent on the principal during the three years. Figures 3.19(b) and (c) compare a 5-year time horizon with a 10-year time horizon and a 10-year time horizon with a 20-year time horizon. We see that there is still a positive chance of a loss for the 10-year horizon, but the median return for the 10-year horizon almost doubles the principal (a 100 percent return, which is about 8 percent per year compounded). With a 20-year horizon, there is virtually no chance of a loss, and there were two positive outlying returns of over 1000 percent (about 13 percent per year compounded).

Exercises for Section 3.3

CONCEPTS

connect

3.28 Explain each of the following in your own words: a percentile; the first quartile, Q_1; the third quartile, Q_3; and the interquartile range, *IQR*.

3.29 Discuss how a box-and-whiskers display is used to identify outliers.

METHODS AND APPLICATIONS

3.30 Recall from page 123 that 20 randomly selected customers give the following satisfaction ratings (on a scale of 1 to 10) for a DVD recorder: 1, 3, 5, 5, 7, 8, 8, 8, 8, 8, 8, 9, 9, 9, 9, 9, 10, 10, 10, 10.
  DS DVDSat

    a Using the technique discussed on page 121, find the first quartile, median, and third quartile for these data.

    b Do you obtain the same values for the first quartile and the third quartile that are shown on the MINITAB output in Figure 3.16 on page 123?

    c Using your results, construct a graphical display of a five-number summary and a box-and-whiskers display.

3.31 Thirteen internists in the Midwest are randomly selected, and each internist is asked to report last year's income. The incomes obtained (in thousands of dollars) are 152, 144, 162, 154, 146, 241, 127, 141, 171, 177, 138, 132, 192. Find: DS DrSalary

    a The 90th percentile.

    b The median.

    c The first quartile.

    d The third quartile.

    e The 10th percentile.

    f The interquartile range.

    g Develop a graphical display of a five-number summary and a box-and-whiskers display.

FIGURE 3.20   **MINITAB Output of Statistics Describing the 65 Payment Times**

Variable	Count	Mean	StDev	Variance
PayTime	65	18.108	3.961	15.691

Variable	Minimum	Q1	Median	Q3	Maximum	Range
PayTime	10.000	15.000	17.000	21.000	29.000	19.000

3.32   Construct a box-and-whiskers display of the following 12 household incomes (see page 122):

7,524	11,070	18,211	26,817	36,551	41,286	Incomes
49,312	57,283	72,814	90,416	135,540	190,250

3.33   Consider the following cases:
   a   THE e-BILLING CASE   DS PayTime
       Figure 3.20 gives the MINITAB output of statistics describing the 65 payment times in
       Table 2.4 on page 42. Construct a graphical display of a five-number summary and a box-and-
       whiskers display of the payment times.
   b   THE MARKETING RESEARCH CASE   DS Design
       Consider the 60 bottle design ratings in Table 1.5 on page 10. The smallest rating is 20,
       $Q_1 = 29$, $M_d = 31$, $Q_3 = 33$, and the largest rating is 35. Construct a graphical display of this
       five-number summary and a box-and-whiskers display of the bottle design ratings.
   c   Discuss the difference between the skewness of the 65 payment times and the skewness of the
       60 bottle design ratings.

3.34   Figure 3.21 gives graphical displays of five-number summaries of a large company's employee
       salaries for different salary grades, with a comparison of salaries for males and females and a
       comparison of actual salaries to the prescribed salary ranges for the salary grades.
   a   What inequities between males and females are apparent? Explain.
   b   How closely are the prescribed salary ranges being observed? Justify your answer.

FIGURE 3.21   **Employee Salaries by Salary Grade and Gender**

3.35 On its website, the *Statesman Journal* newspaper (Salem, Oregon, 2005) reports mortgage loan interest rates for 30-year and 15-year fixed-rate mortgage loans for a number of Willamette Valley lending institutions. Of interest is whether there is any systematic difference between 30-year rates and 15-year rates (expressed as annual percentage rate or APR). The table below displays the 30-year rate and the 15-year rate for each of nine lending institutions. To the right of the table are given side-by-side MINITAB box-and-whiskers plots of the 30-year rates and the 15-year rates. Interpret the plots by comparing the central tendencies and variabilities of the 15- and 30-year rates.   **DS** Mortgage

Lending Institution	30-Year	15-Year
Blue Ribbon Home Mortgage	5.375	4.750
Coast To Coast Mortgage Lending	5.250	4.750
Community Mortgage Services Inc.	5.000	4.500
Liberty Mortgage	5.375	4.875
Jim Morrison's MBI	5.250	4.875
Professional Valley Mortgage	5.250	5.000
Mortgage First	5.750	5.250
Professional Mortgage Corporation	5.500	5.125
Resident Lending Group Inc.	5.625	5.250

Source: http://online.statesmanjournal.com/mortrates.cfm

3.4 Covariance, Correlation, and the Least Squares Line (Optional) ● ● ●

LO3-5 Compute and interpret covariance, correlation, and the least squares line (Optional).

In Section 2.6 we discussed how to use a scatter plot to explore the relationship between two variables x and y. To construct a scatter plot, a sample of n pairs of values of x and y—(x_1, y_1), $(x_2, y_2), \ldots, (x_n, y_n)$—is collected. Then, each value of y is plotted against the corresponding value of x. If the plot points seem to fluctuate around a straight line, we say that there is a **linear relationship** between x and y. For example, suppose that 10 sales regions of equal sales potential for a company were randomly selected. The advertising expenditures (in units of $10,000) in these 10 sales regions were purposely set in July of last year at the values given in the second column of Figure 3.22(a) on the next page. The sales volumes (in units of $10,000) were then recorded for the 10 sales regions and are given in the third column of Figure 3.22(a). A scatter plot of sales volume, y, versus advertising expenditure, x, is given in Figure 3.22(b) and shows a linear relationship between x and y.

A measure of the **strength of the linear relationship** between x and y is the **covariance**. The **sample covariance** is calculated by using the sample of n pairs of observed values of x and y.

The **sample covariance** is denoted as s_{xy} and is defined as follows:

$$s_{xy} = \frac{\sum_{i=1}^{n} (x_i - \bar{x})(y_i - \bar{y})}{n - 1}$$

To use this formula, we first find the mean $\bar{x}$ of the n observed values of x and the mean $\bar{y}$ of the n observed values of y. For each observed (x_i, y_i) combination, we then multiply the deviation of x_i from $\bar{x}$ by the deviation of y_i from $\bar{y}$ to form the product $(x_i - \bar{x})(y_i - \bar{y})$. Finally, we add together the n products $(x_1 - \bar{x})(y_1 - \bar{y})$, $(x_2 - \bar{x})(y_2 - \bar{y}), \ldots, (x_n - \bar{x})(y_n - \bar{y})$ and divide the resulting sum by $n - 1$. For example, the mean of the 10 advertising expenditures in Figure 3.22(a) is $\bar{x} = 9.5$, and the mean of the 10 sales volumes in Figure 3.22(a) is $\bar{y} = 108.3$. It follows that the numerator of s_{xy} is the sum of the values of $(x_i - \bar{x})(y_i - \bar{y}) = (x_i - 9.5)(y_i - 108.3)$.

FIGURE 3.22   The Sales Volume Data, and a Scatter Plot

(a) The sales volume data   Ⓓ SalesPlot

Sales Region	Advertising Expenditure, x	Sales Volume, y
1	5	89
2	6	87
3	7	98
4	8	110
5	9	103
6	10	114
7	11	116
8	12	110
9	13	126
10	14	130

(b) A scatter plot of sales volume versus advertising expenditure

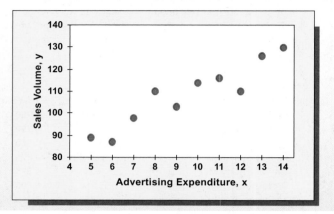

TABLE 3.5   The Calculation of the Numerator of s_{xy}

	x_i	y_i	$(x_i - 9.5)$	$(y_i - 108.3)$	$(x_i - 9.5)(y_i - 108.3)$
	5	89	−4.5	−19.3	86.85
	6	87	−3.5	−21.3	74.55
	7	98	−2.5	−10.3	25.75
	8	110	−1.5	1.7	−2.55
	9	103	−0.5	−5.3	2.65
	10	114	0.5	5.7	2.85
	11	116	1.5	7.7	11.55
	12	110	2.5	1.7	4.25
	13	126	3.5	17.7	61.95
	14	130	4.5	21.7	97.65
Totals	95	1083	0	0	365.50

Table 3.5 shows that this sum equals 365.50, which implies that the sample covariance is

$$s_{xy} = \frac{\sum (x_i - \bar{x})(y_i - \bar{y})}{n - 1} = \frac{365.50}{9} = 40.61111$$

To interpret the covariance, consider Figure 3.23(a). This figure shows the scatter plot of Figure 3.22(b) with a vertical blue line drawn at $\bar{x} = 9.5$ and a horizontal red line drawn at $\bar{y} = 108.3$. The lines divide the scatter plot into four quadrants. Points in quadrant I correspond to x_i greater than $\bar{x}$ and y_i greater than $\bar{y}$ and thus give a value of $(x_i - \bar{x})(y_i - \bar{y})$ greater than 0. Points in quadrant III correspond to x_i less than $\bar{x}$ and y_i less than $\bar{y}$ and thus also give a value of $(x_i - \bar{x})(y_i - \bar{y})$ greater than 0. It follows that if s_{xy} is positive, the points having the greatest influence on $\Sigma(x_i - \bar{x})(y_i - \bar{y})$ and thus on s_{xy} must be in quadrants I and III. Therefore, a positive value of s_{xy} (as in the sales volume example) indicates a positive linear relationship between x and y. That is, as x increases, y increases.

If we further consider Figure 3.23(a), we see that points in quadrant II correspond to x_i less than $\bar{x}$ and y_i greater than $\bar{y}$ and thus give a value of $(x_i - \bar{x})(y_i - \bar{y})$ less than 0. Points in quadrant IV correspond to x_i greater than $\bar{x}$ and y_i less than $\bar{y}$ and thus also give a value of $(x_i - \bar{x})(y_i - \bar{y})$ less than 0. It follows that if s_{xy} is negative, the points having the greatest influence on $\Sigma(x_i - \bar{x})(y_i - \bar{y})$ and thus on s_{xy} must be in quadrants II and IV. Therefore, a negative value of s_{xy} indicates a negative linear relationship between x and y. That is, as x increases, y decreases, as shown in Figure 3.23(b). For example, a negative linear relationship might exist between average hourly outdoor temperature (x) in a city during a week and the city's natural gas consumption (y) during the week. That is, as the average hourly outdoor temperature increases, the city's natural gas consumption would decrease. Finally,

FIGURE 3.23   **Interpretation of the Sample Covariance**

(a) Partitioning the scatter plot of sales volume versus advertising expenditure: s_{xy} positive

(b) s_{xy} negative

(c) s_{xy} near zero

note that if s_{xy} is near zero, the (x_i, y_i) points would be fairly evenly distributed across all four quadrants. This would indicate little or no linear relationship between x and y, as shown in Figure 3.23(c).

From the previous discussion, it might seem that a large positive value for the covariance indicates that x and y have a strong positive linear relationship and a very negative value for the covariance indicates that x and y have a strong negative linear relationship. However, one problem with using the covariance as a measure of the strength of the linear relationship between x and y is that the value of the covariance depends on the units in which x and y are measured. A measure of the strength of the linear relationship between x and y that does not depend on the units in which x and y are measured is the **correlation coefficient.**

The sample correlation coefficient is denoted as r and is defined as follows:

$$r = \frac{s_{xy}}{s_x s_y}$$

Here, s_{xy} is the previously defined sample covariance, s_x is the sample standard deviation of the sample of x values, and s_y is the sample standard deviation of the sample of y values.

For the sales volume data:

$$s_x = \sqrt{\frac{\sum_{i=1}^{10}(x_i - \bar{x})^2}{9}} = 3.02765 \quad \text{and} \quad s_y = \sqrt{\frac{\sum_{i=1}^{10}(y_i - \bar{y})^2}{9}} = 14.30656$$

Therefore, the sample correlation coefficient is

$$r = \frac{s_{xy}}{s_x s_y} = \frac{40.61111}{(3.02765)(14.30656)} = .93757$$

It can be shown that the sample correlation coefficient r is always between -1 and 1. A value of r near 0 implies little linear relationship between x and y. A value of r close to 1 says that x and y have a strong tendency to move together in a straight-line fashion with a positive slope and, therefore, that x and y are highly related and **positively correlated.** A value of r close to -1 says that x and y have a strong tendency to move together in a straight-line fashion with a negative slope and, therefore, that x and y are highly related and **negatively correlated.** Note that if $r = 1$, the (x, y) points fall exactly on a positively sloped straight line, and, if $r = -1$, the (x, y) points fall exactly on a negatively sloped straight line. For example, since $r = .93757$ in the sales volume example, we conclude that advertising expenditure (x) and sales volume (y) have a strong tendency to move together in a straight-line fashion with a positive slope. That is, x and y have a strong positive linear relationship.

We next note that the sample covariance s_{xy} is the point estimate of the **population covariance,** which we denote as σ_{xy}, and the sample correlation coefficient r is the point estimate of the **population correlation coefficient,** which we denote as ρ. To define σ_{xy} and ρ, let μ_x and σ_x denote the mean and the standard deviation of the population of all possible x values, and let μ_y and σ_y denote the mean and the standard deviation of the population of all possible y values. Then, σ_{xy} is the average of all possible values of $(x - \mu_x)(y - \mu_y)$, and ρ equals $\sigma_{xy}/(\sigma_x\sigma_y)$. Similar to r, ρ is always between -1 and 1.

After establishing that a strong positive or a strong negative linear relationship exists between two variables x and y, we might wish to predict y on the basis of x. This can be done by drawing a straight line through a scatter plot of the observed data. Unfortunately, however, if different people *visually* drew lines through the scatter plot, their lines would probably differ from each other. What we need is the "best line" that can be drawn through the scatter plot. Although there are various definitions of what this best line is, one of the most useful best lines is the *least squares line.* The least squares line will be discussed in detail in Chapter 14. For now, we will say that, intuitively, the **least squares line** is the line that minimizes the sum of the squared vertical distances between the points on the scatter plot and the line.

It can be shown that the **slope b_1** (defined as rise/run) of the least squares line is given by the equation

$$b_1 = \frac{s_{xy}}{s_x^2}$$

In addition, the **y-intercept b_0** of the least squares line (where the line intersects the y-axis when x equals 0) is given by the equation

$$b_0 = \bar{y} - b_1\bar{x}$$

For example, recall that for the sales volume data in Figure 3.22(a), $s_{xy} = 40.61111$, $s_x = 3.02765$, $\bar{x} = 9.5$, and $\bar{y} = 108.3$. It follows that the slope of the least squares line for these data is

$$b_1 = \frac{s_{xy}}{s_x^2} = \frac{40.61111}{(3.02765)^2} = 4.4303$$

The y-intercept of the least squares line is

$$b_0 = \bar{y} - b_1\bar{x} = 108.3 - 4.4303(9.5) = 66.2122$$

Furthermore, we can write the equation of the least squares line as

$$\hat{y} = b_0 + b_1x$$
$$= 66.2122 + 4.4303x$$

Here, since we will use the line to predict y on the basis of x, we call $\hat{y}$ **the predicted value of y** when the advertising expenditure is x. For example, suppose that we will spend $100,000 on advertising in a sales region in July of a future year. Because an advertising expenditure of $100,000 corresponds to an x of 10, a prediction of sales volume in July of the future year is (see Figure 3.24):

$$\hat{y} = 66.2122 + 4.4303(10)$$
$$= 110.5152 \text{ (that is, \$1,105,152)}$$

Is this prediction likely to be accurate? If the least squares line developed from last July's data applies to the future July, then, because the sample correlation coefficient $r = .93757$ is fairly close to 1, we might hope that the prediction will be reasonably accurate. However, we will see in

FIGURE 3.24   **The Least Squares Line for the Sales Volume Data**

Chapter 14 that a sample correlation coefficient near 1 does not necessarily mean that the least squares line will predict accurately. We will also study (in Chapter 14) better ways to assess the potential accuracy of a prediction.

Exercises for Section 3.4

CONCEPTS

connect™

3.36 Discuss what the covariance and the correlation coefficient say about the linear relationship between two variables x and y.

3.37 Discuss how the least squares line is used to predict y on the basis of x.

METHODS AND APPLICATIONS

3.38 **THE NATURAL GAS CONSUMPTION CASE**   ⑤ GasCon1

Below we give the average hourly outdoor temperature (x) in a city during a week and the city's natural gas consumption (y) during the week for each of eight weeks (the temperature readings are expressed in degrees Fahrenheit and the natural gas consumptions are expressed in millions of cubic feet of natural gas—denoted MMcf). The output to the right of the data is obtained when MINITAB is used to fit a least squares line to the natural gas consumption data.

Week	Average Hourly Temperature, x (°F)	Weekly Natural Gas Consumption, y (MMcf)
1	28.0	12.4
2	28.0	11.7
3	32.5	12.4
4	39.0	10.8
5	45.9	9.4
6	57.8	9.5
7	58.1	8.0
8	62.5	7.5

⑤ GasCon1

It can be shown that for the gas consumption data:

$$\bar{x} = 43.98 \qquad \bar{y} = 10.2125 \qquad \sum_{i=1}^{8}(x_i - \bar{x})^2 = 1404.355$$

$$\sum_{i=1}^{8}(y_i - \bar{y})^2 = 25.549 \qquad \sum_{i=1}^{8}(x_i - \bar{x})(y_i - \bar{y}) = -179.6475$$

a Calculate s_{xy}, s_x, s_y, and r.

b Using the formulas on page 130, calculate the values $b_1 = -.1279$ and $b_0 = 15.84$ on the MINITAB output.

c Find a prediction of the natural gas consumption during a week when the average hourly temperature is 40° Fahrenheit.

3.39 **THE SERVICE TIME CASE** ⊙ SrvcTime

Accu-Copiers, Inc., sells and services the Accu-500 copying machine. As part of its standard service contract, the company agrees to perform routine service on this copier. To obtain information about the time it takes to perform routine service, Accu-Copiers has collected data for 11 service calls. The data are given on the left below, and the Excel output of a least squares line fit to these data is given on the right below.

Service Call	Number of Copiers Serviced, x	Number of Minutes Required, y
1	4	109
2	2	58
3	5	138
4	7	189
5	1	37
6	3	82
7	4	103
8	5	134
9	2	68
10	4	112
11	6	154

⊙ SrvcTime

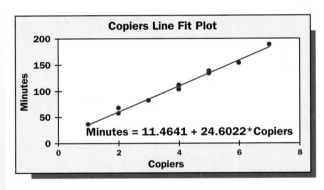

a The sample correlation coefficient r can be calculated to equal .9952 for the service time data. What does this value of r say about the relationship between x and y?

b Predict the service time for a future service call on which five copiers will be serviced.

LO3-6 Compute and interpret weighted means and the mean and standard deviation of grouped data (Optional).

3.5 Weighted Means and Grouped Data (Optional) ⊙ ● ●

Weighted means   In Section 3.1 we studied the mean, which is an important measure of central tendency. In order to calculate a mean, we sum the population (or sample) measurements, and then divide this sum by the number of measurements in the population (or sample). When we do this, each measurement counts equally. That is, each measurement is given the same importance or weight.

Sometimes it makes sense to give different measurements unequal weights. In such a case, a measurement's weight reflects its importance, and the mean calculated using the unequal weights is called a **weighted mean.**

We calculate a weighted mean by multiplying each measurement by its weight, summing the resulting products, and dividing the resulting sum by the sum of the weights:

Weighted Mean

The weighted mean equals

$$\frac{\sum w_i x_i}{\sum w_i}$$

where
x_i = the value of the ith measurement
w_i = the weight applied to the ith measurement

Such a quantity can be computed for a population of measurements or for a sample of measurements.

In order to illustrate the need for a weighted mean and the required calculations, suppose that an investor obtained the following percentage returns on different amounts invested in four stock funds:

Stock Fund	Amount Invested	Percentage Return
1	$50,000	9.2%
2	$10,000	12.8%
3	$10,000	−3.3%
4	$30,000	6.1%

DS StockRtn

If we wish to compute a mean percentage return for the total of $100,000 invested, we should use a weighted mean. This is because each of the four percentage returns applies to a different amount invested. For example, the return 9.2 percent applies to $50,000 invested and thus should count more heavily than the return 6.1 percent, which applies to $30,000 invested.

The percentage return measurements are $x_1 = 9.2$ percent, $x_2 = 12.8$ percent, $x_3 = -3.3$ percent, and $x_4 = 6.1$ percent, and the weights applied to these measurements are $w_1 = \$50,000$, $w_2 = \$10,000$, $w_3 = \$10,000$, and $w_4 = \$30,000$. That is, we are weighting the percentage returns by the amounts invested. The weighted mean is computed as follows:

$$\mu = \frac{50,000(9.2) + 10,000(12.8) + 10,000(-3.3) + 30,000(6.1)}{50,000 + 10,000 + 10,000 + 30,000}$$

$$= \frac{738,000}{100,000} = 7.38\%$$

In this case the unweighted mean of the four percentage returns is 6.2 percent. Therefore, the unweighted mean understates the percentage return for the total of $100,000 invested.

The weights chosen for calculating a weighted mean will vary depending on the situation. For example, in order to compute the grade point average of a student, we would weight the grades A(4), B(3), C(2), D(1), and F(0) by the number of hours of A, the number of hours of B, the number of hours of C, and so forth. Or, in order to compute a mean profit margin for a company consisting of several divisions, the profit margins for the different divisions might be weighted by the sales volumes of the divisions. Again, the idea is to choose weights that represent the relative importance of the measurements in the population or sample.

Descriptive statistics for grouped data   We usually calculate measures of central tendency and variability using the individual measurements in a population or sample. However, sometimes the only data available are in the form of a frequency distribution or a histogram. For example, newspapers and magazines often summarize data using frequency distributions and histograms without giving the individual measurements in a data set. Data summarized in frequency distribution or histogram form are often called **grouped data.** In this section we show how to compute descriptive statistics for such data.

Suppose we are given a frequency distribution summarizing a sample of 65 customer satisfaction ratings for a consumer product.

Satisfaction Rating	Frequency
36–38	4
39–41	15
42–44	25
45–47	19
48–50	2

DS SatRatings

Because we do not know each of the 65 individual satisfaction ratings, we cannot compute an exact value for the mean satisfaction rating. However, we can calculate an approximation of this mean. In order to do this, we use the midpoint of each class to represent the measurements in the class. When we do this, we are really assuming that the average of the measurements in each class equals the class midpoint. Letting M_i denote the midpoint of class i, and letting f_i denote the frequency of class i, we compute the mean by calculating a weighted mean of the class midpoints using the class frequencies as the weights. The logic here is that if f_i measurements are included in class i, then the midpoint of class i should count f_i times in the weighted mean. In this case, the sum of the weights equals the sum of the class frequencies, which equals the sample size. Therefore, we obtain the following equation for the sample mean of grouped data:

Sample Mean for Grouped Data

$$\bar{x} = \frac{\sum f_i M_i}{\sum f_i} = \frac{\sum f_i M_i}{n}$$

where
$f_i =$ the frequency for class i
$M_i =$ the midpoint for class i
$n = \sum f_i =$ the sample size

Table 3.6 summarizes the calculation of the mean satisfaction rating for the previously given frequency distribution of satisfaction ratings. Note that in this table each midpoint is halfway between its corresponding class limits. For example, for the first class $M_1 = (36 + 38)/2 = 37$. We find that the sample mean satisfaction rating is 43.

We can also compute an approximation of the sample variance for grouped data. Recall that when we compute the sample variance using individual measurements, we compute the squared deviation from the sample mean $(x_i - \bar{x})^2$ for each individual measurement x_i and then sum the squared deviations. For grouped data, we do not know each of the x_i values. Because of this, we again let the class midpoint M_i represent each measurement in class i. It follows that we compute the squared deviation $(M_i - \bar{x})^2$ for each class and then sum these squares, weighting each squared deviation by its corresponding class frequency f_i. That is, we approximate $\sum (x_i - \bar{x})^2$ by using $\sum f_i(M_i - \bar{x})^2$. Finally, we obtain the sample variance for the grouped data by dividing this quantity by the sample size minus 1. We summarize this calculation in the following box:

Sample Variance for Grouped Data

$$s^2 = \frac{\sum f_i(M_i - \bar{x})^2}{n - 1}$$

where $\bar{x}$ is the sample mean for the grouped data.

Table 3.7 illustrates calculating the sample variance of the previously given frequency distribution of satisfaction ratings. We find that the sample variance is $s^2 = 8.15625$ and, therefore, that the sample standard deviation is $s = \sqrt{8.15625} = 2.8559$.

TABLE 3.6   Calculating the Sample Mean Satisfaction Rating

Satisfaction Rating	Frequency (f_i)	Class Midpoint (M_i)	$f_i M_i$
36–38	4	37	4(37) = 148
39–41	15	40	15(40) = 600
42–44	25	43	25(43) = 1,075
45–47	19	46	19(46) = 874
48–50	2	49	2(49) = 98
	$n = 65$		2,795

$$\bar{x} = \frac{\sum f_i M_i}{n} = \frac{2,795}{65} = 43$$

TABLE 3.7 Calculating the Sample Variance of the Satisfaction Ratings

Satisfaction Rating	Frequency f_i	Class Midpoint M_i	Deviation $(M_i - \bar{x})$	Squared Deviation $(M_i - \bar{x})^2$	$f_i(M_i - \bar{x})^2$
36–38	4	37	$37 - 43 = -6$	36	$4(36) = 144$
39–41	15	40	$40 - 43 = -3$	9	$15(9) = 135$
42–44	25	43	$43 - 43 = 0$	0	$25(0) = 0$
45–47	19	46	$46 - 43 = 3$	9	$19(9) = 171$
48–50	2	49	$49 - 43 = 6$	36	$2(36) = 72$
	65				$\sum f_i(M_i - \bar{x})^2 = 522$

$$s^2 = \text{sample variance} = \frac{\sum f_i(M_i - \bar{x})^2}{n-1} = \frac{522}{65 - 1} = 8.15625$$

Finally, although we have illustrated calculating the mean and variance for grouped data in the context of a sample, similar calculations can be done for a population of measurements. If we let N be the size of the population, the grouped data formulas for the population mean and variance are given in the following box:

Population Mean for Grouped Data

$$\mu = \frac{\sum f_i M_i}{N}$$

Population Variance for Grouped Data

$$\sigma^2 = \frac{\sum f_i(M_i - \mu)^2}{N}$$

Exercises for Section 3.5

CONCEPTS

3.40 Consider calculating a student's grade point average using a scale where 4.0 represents an A and 0.0 represents an F. Explain why the grade point average is a weighted mean. What are the x_i values? What are the weights?

3.41 When we perform grouped data calculations, we represent the measurements in a class by using the midpoint of the class. Explain the assumption that is being made when we do this.

3.42 When we compute the mean, variance, and standard deviation using grouped data, the results obtained are approximations of the population (or sample) mean, variance, and standard deviation. Explain why this is true.

METHODS AND APPLICATIONS

3.43 Sound City sells the TrueSound-XL, a top-of-the-line satellite car radio. Over the last 100 weeks, Sound City has sold no radios in three of the weeks, one radio in 20 of the weeks, two radios in 50 of the weeks, three radios in 20 of the weeks, four radios in 5 of the weeks, and five radios in 2 of the weeks. The following table summarizes this information. 📀 TrueSound

Number of Radios Sold	Number of Weeks Having the Sales Amount
0	3
1	20
2	50
3	20
4	5
5	2

Compute a weighted mean that measures the average number of radios sold per week over the 100 weeks.

3.44 The following table gives a summary of the grades received by a student for the first 64 semester hours of university coursework. The table gives the number of semester hours of A, B, C, D, and F earned by the student among the 64 hours.   ⑤ Grades

Grade	Number of Hours
A (that is, 4.00)	18
B (that is, 3.00)	36
C (that is, 2.00)	7
D (that is, 1.00)	3
F (that is, 0.00)	0

a By assigning the numerical values, 4.00, 3.00, 2.00, 1.00, and 0.00 to the grades A, B, C, D, and F (as shown), compute the student's grade point average for the first 64 semester hours of coursework.

b Why is this a weighted average?

3.45 The following frequency distribution summarizes the weights of 195 fish caught by anglers participating in a professional bass fishing tournament.   ⑤ BassWeights

Weight (Pounds)	Frequency
1–3	53
4–6	118
7–9	21
10–12	3

a Calculate the (approximate) sample mean for these data.

b Calculate the (approximate) sample variance for these data.

3.46 The following is a frequency distribution summarizing earnings per share (EPS) growth data for the 30 fastest-growing firms as given on *Fortune* magazine's website on March 16, 2005.   ⑤ EPSGrowth

EPS Growth (Percent)	Frequency
0–49	1
50–99	17
100–149	5
150–199	4
200–249	1
250–299	2

Source: http://www.fortune.com (accessed March 16, 2005).

Calculate the (approximate) population mean, variance, and standard deviation for these data.

3.47 The Data and Story Library website (a website devoted to applications of statistics) gives a histogram of the ages of a sample of 60 CEOs. We present the data in the form of a frequency distribution below.   ⑤ CEOAges

Age (Years)	Frequency
28–32	1
33–37	3
38–42	3
43–47	13
48–52	14
53–57	12
58–62	9
63–67	1
68–72	3
73–77	1

Source: http://lib.stat.cmu.edu/DASL/Stories/ceo.html (accessed April 15, 2005).

Calculate the (approximate) sample mean, variance, and standard deviation of these data.

3.6 The Geometric Mean (Optional) ⦿ ● ●

LO3-7 Compute and inter- pret the geometric mean (Optional).

In Section 3.1 we defined the mean to be the average of a set of population or sample measurements. This mean is sometimes referred to as the arithmetic mean. While very useful, the arithmetic mean is not a good measure of the rate of change exhibited by a variable over time. To see this, consider the rate at which the value of an investment changes—its rate of return. Suppose that an initial investment of $10,000 increases in value to $20,000 at the end of one year and then decreases in value to its original $10,000 value after two years. The rate of return for the first year, R_1, is

$$R_1 = \left(\frac{20,000 - 10,000}{10,000}\right) \times 100\% = 100\%$$

and the rate of return for the second year, R_2, is

$$R_2 = \left(\frac{10,000 - 20,000}{20,000}\right) \times 100\% = -50\%$$

Although the value of the investment at the beginning and end of the two-year period is the same, the arithmetic mean of the yearly rates of return is $(R_1 + R_2)/2 = (100\% + (-50\%))/2 = 25\%$. This arithmetic mean does not communicate the fact that the value of the investment is unchanged at the end of the two years.

To remedy this situation, we define the **geometric mean** of the returns to be **the constant return R_g, that yields the same wealth at the end of the investment period as do the actual returns.** In our example, this says that if we express R_g, R_1, and R_2 as decimal fractions (here $R_1 = 1$ and $R_2 = -.5$),

$$(1 + R_g)^2 \times 10,000 = (1 + R_1)(1 + R_2) \times 10,000$$

or

$$R_g = \sqrt{(1 + R_1)(1 + R_2)} - 1$$
$$= \sqrt{(1 + 1)(1 + (-.5))} - 1$$
$$= \sqrt{1} - 1 = 0$$

Therefore, the geometric mean R_g expresses the fact that the value of the investment is unchanged after two years.

In general, if $R_1, R_2, \ldots, R_n$ are returns (expressed in decimal form) over n time periods:

The **geometric mean** of the returns $R_1, R_2, \ldots, R_n$ is

$$R_g = \sqrt[n]{(1 + R_1)(1 + R_2) \cdots (1 + R_n)} - 1$$

and the ending value of an initial investment ℓ experiencing returns $R_1, R_2, \ldots, R_n$ is $\ell(1 + R_g)^n$.

As another example, suppose that in year 3 our investment's value increases to $25,000, which says that the rate of return for year 3 (expressed as a percentage) is

$$R_3 = \left(\frac{25,000 - 10,000}{10,000}\right) \times 100\%$$
$$= 150\%$$

Since (expressed as decimals) $R_1 = 1$, $R_2 = -.5$, and $R_3 = 1.5$, the geometric mean return at the end of year 3 is

$$R_g = \sqrt[3]{(1 + 1)(1 + (-.5))(1 + 1.5)} - 1$$
$$= 1.3572 - 1$$
$$= .3572$$

and the value of the investment after 3 years is

$$10,000 (1 + .3572)^3 = \$25,000$$

Exercises for Section 3.6

connect

CONCEPTS

3.48 In words, explain the interpretation of the geometric mean return for an investment.

3.49 If we know the initial value of an investment and its geometric mean return over a period of years, can we compute the ending value of the investment? If so, how?

METHODS AND APPLICATIONS

3.50 Suppose that a company's sales were $5,000,000 three years ago. Since that time sales have grown at annual rates of 10 percent, -10 percent, and 25 percent.
  a Find the geometric mean growth rate of sales over this three-year period.
  b Find the ending value of sales after this three-year period.

3.51 Suppose that a company's sales were $1,000,000 four years ago and are $4,000,000 at the end of the four years. Find the geometric mean growth rate of sales.

3.52 The following table gives the value of the Dow Jones Industrial Average (DJIA), NASDAQ, and the S&P 500 on the first day of trading for the years 2008 through 2010.   **DS** StockIndex

Year	DJIA	NASDAQ	S&P 500
2008	13,043.96	2,609.63	1,447.16
2009	9,034.69	1,632.21	931.80
2010	10,583.96	2,308.42	1,132.99

Source: http://www.davemanuel.com/where-did-the-djia-nasdaq-sp500-trade-on.php..

  a For each stock index, compute the rate of return from 2008 to 2009 and from 2009 to 2010.
  b Calculate the geometric rate of return for each stock index for the period from 2008 to 2010.
  c Suppose that an investment of $100,000 is made in 2008 and that the portfolio performs with returns equal to those of the DJIA. What is the investment worth in 2010?
  d Repeat part (c) for the NASDAQ and the S&P 500.

3.53 Refer to Exercise 3.52. The values of the DJIA on the first day of trading in 2005, 2006, and 2007 were 10,729.43, 10,847.41, and 12,474.52.
  a Calculate the geometric rate of return for the DJIA from 2005 to 2010.
  b If an investment of $100,000 is made in 2005 and the portfolio performs with returns equal to those of the DJIA, what is the investment worth in 2010?

Chapter Summary

We began this chapter by presenting and comparing several measures of **central tendency.** We defined the **population mean** and we saw how to estimate the population mean by using a **sample mean.** We also defined the **median** and **mode,** and we compared the mean, median, and mode for symmetrical distributions and for distributions that are skewed to the right or left. We then studied measures of **variation** (or *spread*). We defined the **range, variance,** and **standard deviation,** and we saw how to estimate a population variance and standard deviation by using a sample. We learned that a good way to interpret the standard deviation when a population is (approximately) normally distributed is to use the **Empirical Rule,** and we studied **Chebyshev's Theorem,** which gives us intervals containing reasonably large fractions of

the population units no matter what the population's shape might be. We also saw that, when a data set is highly skewed, it is best to use **percentiles** and **quartiles** to measure variation, and we learned how to construct a **box-and-whiskers plot** by using the quartiles.

After learning how to measure and depict central tendency and variability, we presented several optional topics. First, we discussed several numerical measures of the relationship between two variables. These included the **covariance,** the **correlation coefficient,** and the **least squares line.** We then introduced the concept of a **weighted mean** and also explained how to compute descriptive statistics for **grouped data.** Finally, we showed how to calculate the **geometric mean** and demonstrated its interpretation.

Glossary of Terms

box-and-whiskers display (box plot): A graphical portrayal of a data set that depicts both the central tendency and variability of the data. It is constructed using Q_1, M_d, and Q_3. (pages 123, 124)

central tendency: A term referring to the middle of a population or sample of measurements. (page 101)

Chebyshev's Theorem: A theorem that (for any population) allows us to find an interval that contains a specified percentage of the individual measurements in the population. (page 116)

coefficient of variation: A quantity that measures the variation of a population or sample relative to its mean. (page 117)

correlation coefficient: A numerical measure of the linear relationship between two variables that is between -1 and 1. (page 129)

covariance: A numerical measure of the linear relationship between two variables that depends upon the units in which the variables are measured. (page 127)

Empirical Rule: For a normally distributed population, this rule tells us that 68.26 percent, 95.44 percent, and 99.73 percent, respectively, of the population measurements are within one, two, and three standard deviations of the population mean. (page 114)

first quartile (denoted Q_1): A value below which approximately 25 percent of the measurements lie; the 25th percentile. (page 121)

geometric mean: The constant return (or rate of change) that yields the same wealth at the end of several time periods as do actual returns. (page 137)

grouped data: Data presented in the form of a frequency distribution or a histogram. (page 133)

interquartile range (denoted IQR): The difference between the third quartile and the first quartile (that is, $Q_3 - Q_1$). (page 122)

least squares line: The line that minimizes the sum of the squared vertical differences between points on a scatter plot and the line. (page 130)

lower and upper limits (in a box-and-whiskers display): Points located $1.5 \times IQR$ below Q_1 and $1.5 \times IQR$ above Q_3. (page 123)

measure of variation: A descriptive measure of the spread of the values in a population or sample. (page 110)

median (denoted M_d): A measure of central tendency that divides a population or sample into two roughly equal parts. (page 103)

mode (denoted M_o): The measurement in a sample or a population that occurs most frequently. (page 104)

mound-shaped: Description of a relative frequency curve that is "piled up in the middle." (page 116)

normal curve: A bell-shaped, symmetrical relative frequency curve. We will present the exact equation that gives this curve in Chapter 6. (page 113)

outlier (in a box-and-whiskers display): A measurement less than the lower limit or greater than the upper limit. (page 124)

percentile: The value such that a specified percentage of the measurements in a population or sample fall at or below it. (page 120)

point estimate: A one-number estimate for the value of a population parameter. (page 101)

population mean (denoted μ): The average of a population of measurements. (page 101)

population parameter: A descriptive measure of a population. It is calculated using the population measurements. (page 101)

population standard deviation (denoted σ): The positive square root of the population variance. It is a measure of the variation of the population measurements. (page 111)

population variance (denoted σ^2): The average of the squared deviations of the individual population measurements from the population mean. It is a measure of the variation of the population measurements. (page 111)

range: The difference between the largest and smallest measurements in a population or sample. It is a simple measure of variation. (page 110)

sample mean (denoted $\bar{x}$): The average of the measurements in a sample. It is the point estimate of the population mean. (page 102)

sample size (denoted n): The number of measurements in a sample. (page 102)

sample standard deviation (denoted s): The positive square root of the sample variance. It is the point estimate of the population standard deviation. (page 112)

sample statistic: A descriptive measure of a sample. It is calculated from the measurements in the sample. (page 102)

sample variance (denoted s^2): A measure of the variation of the sample measurements. It is the point estimate of the population variance. (page 112)

third quartile (denoted Q_3): A value below which approximately 75 percent of the measurements lie; the 75th percentile. (page 121)

tolerance interval: An interval of numbers that contains a specified percentage of the individual measurements in a population. (page 114)

weighted mean: A mean where different measurements are given different weights based on their importance. (page 132)

z-score (of a measurement): The number of standard deviations that a measurement is from the mean. This quantity indicates the relative location of a measurement within its distribution. (page 117)

Important Formulas

The population mean, μ: page 101

The sample mean, $\bar{x}$: page 102

The median: page 103

The mode: page 104

The population range: page 110

The population variance, σ^2: page 111

The population standard deviation, σ: page 111

The sample variance, s^2: pages 112 and 113

The sample standard deviation, s: page 112

Computational formula for s^2: page 113

The Empirical Rule: page 114

Chebyshev's Theorem: page 116

z-score: page 117

The coefficient of variation: page 117

Supplementary Exercises

connect

3.54   In the book *Modern Statistical Quality Control and Improvement,* Nicholas R. Farnum presents data concerning the elapsed times from the completion of medical lab tests until the results are recorded on patients' charts. Table 3.8 gives the times it took (in hours) to deliver and chart the results of 84 lab tests over one week. Use the techniques of this and the previous chapter to determine if there are some deliveries with excessively long waiting times. Which deliveries might be investigated in order to discover reasons behind unusually long delays?   ⑤ LabTest

3.55   Figure 3.25 gives five-number summaries comparing the base yearly salaries of employees in marketing and employees in research for a large company. Interpret these summaries.

3.56   THE INVESTMENT CASE   ⑤ InvestRet

The Fall 1995 issue of *Investment Digest,* a publication of The Variable Annuity Life Insurance Company of Houston, Texas, discusses the importance of portfolio diversification for long-term investors. The article states:

> While it is true that investment experts generally advise long-term investors to invest in variable investments, they also agree that the key to any sound investment portfolio is diversification. That is, investing in a variety of investments with differing levels of historical return and risk.
>
> Investment risk is often measured in terms of the volatility of an investment over time. When volatility, sometimes referred to as *standard deviation,* increases, so too does the level of return. Conversely, as risk (standard deviation) declines, so too do returns.

TABLE 3.8	Elapsed Time (in Hours) for Completing and Delivering Medical Lab Tests ⑤ LabTest		
6.1	8.7	1.1	4.0
2.1	3.9	2.2	5.0
2.1	7.1	4.3	8.8
3.5	1.2	3.2	1.3
1.3	9.3	4.2	7.3
5.7	6.5	4.4	16.2
1.3	1.3	3.0	2.7
15.7	4.9	2.0	5.2
3.9	13.9	1.8	2.2
8.4	5.2	11.9	3.0
24.0	24.5	24.8	24.0
1.7	4.4	2.5	16.2
17.8	2.9	4.0	6.7
5.3	8.3	2.8	5.2
17.5	1.1	3.0	8.3
1.2	1.1	4.5	4.4
5.0	2.6	12.7	5.7
4.7	5.1	2.6	1.6
3.4	8.1	2.4	16.7
4.8	1.7	1.9	12.1
9.1	5.6	13.0	6.4

Source: N. R. Farnum, *Modern Statistical Quality Control and Improvement,* p. 55. Reprinted by permission of Brooks/Cole, an imprint of the Wadsworth Group, a division of Thompson Learning. Fax 800-730-2215.

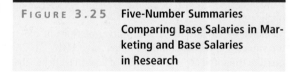

FIGURE 3.25   **Five-Number Summaries Comparing Base Salaries in Marketing and Base Salaries in Research**

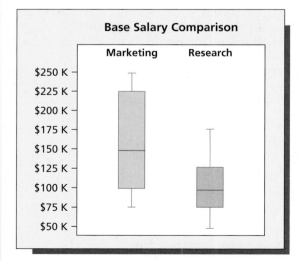

Source: http://nelsontouchconsulting.wordpress.com/2011/01/07/behold-the-box-plot/.

FIGURE 3.26   **The Risk/Return Trade-Off (for Exercise 3.56)**

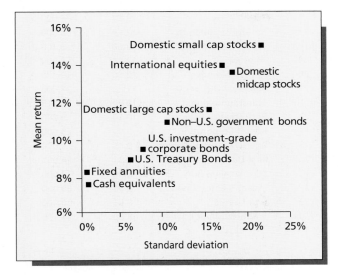

TABLE 3.9   **Mean Return and Standard Deviation for Nine Investment Classes** DS InvestRet

Investment Class	Mean Return	Standard Deviation
Fixed annuities	8.31%	.54%
Cash equivalents	7.73	.81
U.S. Treasury bonds	8.80	5.98
U.S. investment-grade corporate bonds	9.33	7.92
Non–U.S. government bonds	10.95	10.47
Domestic large cap stocks	11.71	15.30
International equities	14.02	17.16
Domestic midcap stocks	13.64	18.19
Domestic small cap stocks	14.93	21.82

Source: The Variable Annuity Life Insurance Company, *VALIC* 9 (1995), no. 3.

In order to explain the relationship between the return on an investment and its risk, *Investment Digest* presents a graph of mean return versus standard deviation (risk) for nine investment classes over the period from 1970 to 1994. This graph, which *Investment Digest* calls the "risk/return trade-off," is shown in Figure 3.26. The article says that this graph

> . . . illustrates the historical risk/return trade-off for a variety of investment classes over the 24-year period between 1970 and 1994.
>
> In the chart, cash equivalents and fixed annuities, for instance, had a standard deviation of 0.81% and 0.54% respectively, while posting returns of just over 7.73% and 8.31%. At the other end of the spectrum, domestic small-cap stocks were quite volatile—with a standard deviation of 21.82%—but compensated for that increased volatility with a return of 14.93%.
>
> The answer seems to lie in asset allocation. Investment experts know the importance of asset allocation. In a nutshell, asset allocation is a method of creating a diversified portfolio of investments that minimize historical risk and maximize potential returns to help you meet your retirement goals and needs.

Suppose that, by reading off the graph of Figure 3.26, we obtain the mean return and standard deviation combinations for the various investment classes as shown in Table 3.9.

Further suppose that future returns in each investment class will behave as they have from 1970 to 1994. That is, for each investment class, regard the mean return and standard deviation in Table 3.9 as the population mean and the population standard deviation of all possible future returns. Then do the following:

a Assuming that future returns for the various investment classes are mound-shaped, for each investment class compute intervals that will contain approximately 68.26 percent and 99.73 percent of all future returns.

b Making no assumptions about the population shapes of future returns, for each investment class compute intervals that will contain at least 75 percent and 88.89 percent of all future returns.

c Assuming that future returns are mound-shaped, find

    (1) An estimate of the maximum return that might be realized for each investment class.

    (2) An estimate of the minimum return (or maximum loss) that might be realized for each investment class.

d Assuming that future returns are mound-shaped, which two investment classes have the highest estimated maximum returns? What are the estimated minimum returns (maximum losses) for these investment classes?

e Assuming that future returns are mound-shaped, which two investment classes have the smallest estimated maximum returns? What are the estimated minimum returns for these investment classes?

TABLE 3.10   America's 30 Largest Private Companies of 2010 as Rated by *Forbes* Magazine   DS LargeComp

Rank	Company	Revenue ($bil)	Employees	Rank	Company	Revenue ($bil)	Employees
1	Cargill	109.84e	130,500	16	Toys "R" Us	13.57	68,000
2	Koch Industries	100.00e	70,000	17	Enterprise Holdings	12.60	68,000
3	Bechtel	30.80	49,000	18	Love's Travel Stops	12.60^2	6,700
4	HCA	30.05	190,000	19	Aramark	12.54e	255,000
5	Mars	28.00	65,000	20	Reyes Holdings	12.50	10,300
6	Chrysler	27.90e	41,200	21	Fidelity Investments	11.49	37,000
7	PricewaterhouseCoopers	26.57	161,718	22	TransMontaigne	10.23e	815
8	Publix Super Markets	24.32	142,000	23	Performance Food	10.10	9,800
9	Ernst & Young	21.26	141,000	24	Kiewit Corporation	9.99	25,900
10	C&S Wholesale Grocers	20.40e	16,600	25	Energy Future Holdings	9.55	9,030
11	US Foodservice	18.96	25,000	26	First Data	9.31	24,900
12	Pilot Flying J	17.00	23,000	27	SC Johnson & Son	8.96e	12,000
13	HE Butt Grocery	15.10e	75,000	28	Harrah's Entertainment	8.91	69,000
14	Cox Enterprises	14.70	66,000	29	Giant Eagle	8.61	36,000
15	Meijer	14.25e	72,200	30	Southern Wine & Spirits	8.60	11,100

e = Forbes estimate
2 = Company-provided estimate

Source: http://www.forbes.com/lists/2010/21/private-companies-10_land.html (accessed June 14, 2011).

3.57 Table 3.10 gives data concerning America's 30 largest private companies of 2010 as rated by *Forbes* magazine.

a Construct a box-and-whiskers display of the large company revenues.

b Construct a box-and-whiskers display of the large company numbers of employees.

c Interpret the displays of parts (a) and (b).   DS LargeComp

3.58 **THE FLORIDA POOL HOME CASE**   DS PoolHome

In Florida, real estate agents refer to homes having a swimming pool as *pool homes*. In this case, Sunshine Pools Inc. markets and installs pools throughout the state of Florida. The company wishes to estimate the percentage of a pool's cost that can be recouped by a buyer when he or she sells the home. For instance, if a homeowner buys a pool for which the current purchase price is $30,000 and then sells the home in the current real estate market for $20,000 more than the homeowner would get if the home did not have a pool, the homeowner has recouped $(20,000/30,000) \times 100\% = 66.67\%$ of the pool's cost. To make this estimate, the company randomly selects 80 homes from all of the homes sold in a Florida city (over the last six months) having a size between 2,000 and 3,500 square feet. For each sampled home, the following data are collected: selling price (in thousands of dollars); square footage; the number of bathrooms; a niceness rating (expressed as an integer from 1 to 7 and assigned by a real estate agent); and whether or not the home has a pool (1 = yes, 0 = no). The data are given in Table 3.11. Figure 3.27 gives descriptive statistics for the 43 homes having a pool and for the 37 homes that do not have a pool.

a Using Figure 3.27, compare the mean selling prices of the homes having a pool and the homes that do not have a pool.

b Using these data, and assuming that the average current purchase price of the pools in the sample is $32,500, estimate the percentage of a pool's cost that can be recouped when the home is sold.

c The comparison you made in part (a) could be misleading. Noting that different homes have different square footages, numbers of bathrooms, and niceness ratings, explain why.

TABLE 3.11   **The Florida Pool Home Data**   ⓓⓢ PoolHome

Home	Price ($1000s)	Size (Sq Feet)	Number of Bathrooms	Niceness Rating	Pool? yes=1; no=0	Home	Price ($1000s)	Size (Sq Feet)	Number of Bathrooms	Niceness Rating	Pool? yes=1; no=0
1	260.9	2666	2 1/2	7	0	41	285.6	2761	3	6	1
2	337.3	3418	3 1/2	6	1	42	216.1	2880	2 1/2	2	0
3	268.4	2945	2	5	1	43	261.3	3426	3	1	1
4	242.2	2942	2 1/2	3	1	44	236.4	2895	2 1/2	2	1
5	255.2	2798	3	3	1	45	267.5	2726	3	7	0
6	205.7	2210	2 1/2	2	0	46	220.2	2930	2 1/2	2	0
7	249.5	2209	2	7	0	47	300.1	3013	2 1/2	6	1
8	193.6	2465	2 1/2	1	0	48	260.0	2675	2	6	0
9	242.7	2955	2	4	1	49	277.5	2874	3 1/2	6	1
10	244.5	2722	2 1/2	5	0	50	274.9	2765	2 1/2	4	1
11	184.2	2590	2 1/2	1	0	51	259.8	3020	3 1/2	2	1
12	325.7	3138	3 1/2	7	1	52	235.0	2887	2 1/2	1	1
13	266.1	2713	2	7	0	53	191.4	2032	2	3	0
14	166.0	2284	2 1/2	2	0	54	228.5	2698	2 1/2	4	0
15	330.7	3140	3 1/2	6	1	55	266.6	2847	3	2	1
16	289.1	3205	2 1/2	3	1	56	233.0	2639	3	3	0
17	268.8	2721	2 1/2	6	1	57	343.4	3431	4	5	1
18	276.7	3245	2 1/2	2	1	58	334.0	3485	3 1/2	5	1
19	222.4	2464	3	3	1	59	289.7	2991	2 1/2	6	1
20	241.5	2993	2 1/2	1	0	60	228.4	2482	2 1/2	2	0
21	307.9	2647	3 1/2	6	1	61	233.4	2712	2 1/2	1	1
22	223.5	2670	2 1/2	4	0	62	275.7	3103	2 1/2	2	1
23	231.1	2895	2 1/2	3	0	63	290.8	3124	2 1/2	3	1
24	216.5	2643	2 1/2	3	0	64	230.8	2906	2 1/2	2	0
25	205.5	2915	2	1	0	65	310.1	3398	4	4	1
26	258.3	2800	3 1/2	2	1	66	247.9	3028	3	4	0
27	227.6	2557	2 1/2	3	1	67	249.9	2761	2	5	0
28	255.4	2805	2	3	1	68	220.5	2842	3	3	0
29	235.7	2878	2 1/2	4	0	69	226.2	2666	2 1/2	6	0
30	285.1	2795	3	7	1	70	313.7	2744	2 1/2	7	1
31	284.8	2748	2 1/2	7	1	71	210.1	2508	2 1/2	4	0
32	193.7	2256	2 1/2	2	0	72	244.9	2480	2 1/2	5	0
33	247.5	2659	2 1/2	2	1	73	235.8	2986	2 1/2	4	0
34	274.8	3241	3 1/2	4	1	74	263.2	2753	2 1/2	7	0
35	264.4	3166	3	3	1	75	280.2	2522	2 1/2	6	1
36	204.1	2466	2	4	0	76	290.8	2808	2 1/2	7	1
37	273.9	2945	2 1/2	5	1	77	235.4	2616	2 1/2	3	0
38	238.5	2727	3	1	1	78	190.3	2603	2 1/2	2	0
39	274.4	3141	4	4	1	79	234.4	2804	2 1/2	4	0
40	259.6	2552	2	7	1	80	238.7	2851	2 1/2	5	0

FIGURE 3.27   **Descriptive Statistics for Homes With and Without Pools (for Exercise 3.58)**

Descriptive Statistics (Homes with Pools)	Price	Descriptive Statistics (Homes without Pools)	Price
count	43	count	37
mean	276.056	mean	226.900
sample variance	937.821	sample variance	609.902
sample standard deviation	30.624	sample standard deviation	24.696
minimum	222.4	minimum	166
maximum	343.4	maximum	267.5
range	121	range	101.5

3.59   Internet Exercise

The Data and Story Library (DASL) houses a rich collection of data sets useful for teaching and learning statistics, from a variety of sources, contributed primarily by university faculty members. DASL can be reached through the BSC by clicking on the Data Bases button in the BSC home screen and by then clicking on the Data and Story Library link. The DASL can also be reached directly using the url http://lib.stat.cmu.edu/DASL/. The objective of this exercise is to retrieve a data set of chief executive officer salaries and to construct selected graphical and numerical statistical summaries of the data.

a   From the McGraw-Hill/Irwin Business Statistics Center Data Bases page, go to the DASL website and select "List all topics." From the Stories by Topic page, select Economics, then CEO Salaries to reach the CEO Salaries story. From the CEO Salaries story page, select the Datafile Name: CEO Salaries to reach the data set page. The data set includes the ages and salaries (save for a single missing observation) for a sample of 60 CEOs. Capture these observations and copy them into an Excel or MINITAB worksheet. This data capture can be accomplished in a number of ways. One simple approach is to use simple copy and paste procedures from the DASL data set to Excel or MINITAB (data sets CEOSal.xlsx, CEOSal.MTW).

b   Use your choice of statistical software to create graphical and numerical summaries of the CEO Salaries data and use these summaries to describe the data. In Excel, create a histogram of salaries and generate descriptive statistics. In MINITAB, create a histogram, stem-and-leaf display, box plot, and descriptive statistics. Offer your observations about typical salary level, the variation in salaries, and the shape of the distribution of CEO salaries.

Appendix 3.1 ■ Numerical Descriptive Statistics Using Excel

The instructions in this section begin by describing the entry of data into an Excel worksheet. Alternatively, the data may be downloaded from this book's website. The appropriate data file name is given at the top of each instruction block. Please refer to Appendix 1.1 for further information about entering data, saving data, and printing results when using Excel.

Numerical descriptive statistics for the bottle design ratings in Figure 3.4 on page 106 (data file: Design.xlsx):

- Enter the bottle design ratings data into column A with the label Rating in cell A1 and with the 60 design ratings from Table 1.5 on page 10 in cells A2 to A61.

- Select **Data : Data Analysis : Descriptive Statistics.**

- Click OK in the Data Analysis dialog box.

- In the Descriptive Statistics dialog box, enter the range for the data, A1:A61, into the "Input Range" box.

- Check the "Labels in First Row" checkbox.

- Click in the "Output Range" window and enter the desired cell location for the upper left corner of the output, say cell C1.

- Check the "Summary Statistics" checkbox.

- Click OK in the Descriptive Statistics dialog box.

- The descriptive statistics summary will appear in cells C1:D15. Drag the column C border to reveal complete labels for all statistics.

Least squares line, correlation, and covariance for the sales volume data in Figure 3.22(a) on page 128 (data file: SalesPlot.xlsx):

To compute the equation of the least squares line:

- Follow the directions in Appendix 2.1 for constructing a scatter plot of sales volume versus advertising expenditure.

- When the scatter plot is displayed in a graphics window, move the plot to a chart sheet.

- In the new chart sheet, right-click on any of the plotted points in the scatter plot (Excel refers to the plotted points as the **data series**) and select Add Trendline from the pop-up menu.

- In the Format Trendline dialog box, select Trendline Options.

- In the Trendline Options task pane, select Linear for the "Trend/Regression Type".

- Place a checkmark in the "Display Equation on chart" checkbox.

- Click the Close button in the Format Trendline dialog box.

- The Trendline equation will be displayed in the scatter plot and the chart can then be edited appropriately.

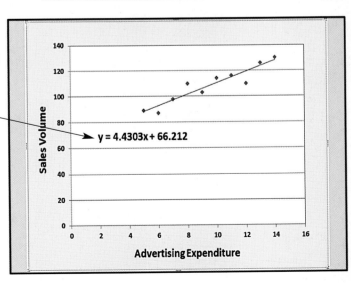

$y = 4.4303x + 66.212$

To compute the sample covariance between sales volume and advertising expenditure:

- Enter the advertising and sales data in Figure 3.22(a) on page 128 into columns A and B—advertising expenditures in column A with label "Ad Exp" and sales values in column B with label "Sales Vol".
- Select **Data : Data Analysis : Covariance**
- Click OK in the Data Analysis dialog box.
- In the Covariance dialog box, enter the range of the data, A1:B11 into the Input Range window.
- Select "Grouped By: Columns" if this is not already the selection.
- Place a checkmark in the "Labels in first row" checkbox.
- Under "Output options", select Output Range and enter the cell location for the upper left corner of the output, say A14, in the Output Range window.
- Click OK in the Covariance dialog box.

The Excel ToolPak Covariance routine calculates the population covariance. This quantity is the value in cell B16 (=36.55). To compute the sample covariance from this value, we will multiply by $n/(n-1)$ where n is the sample size. In this situation, the sample size equals 10. Therefore, we can compute the sample covariance as follows:

- Type the label "Sample Covariance" in cell E15.
- In cell E16 write the cell formula =(10/9)*B16 and type enter.
- The sample covariance (=40.6111111) is the result in cell E16.

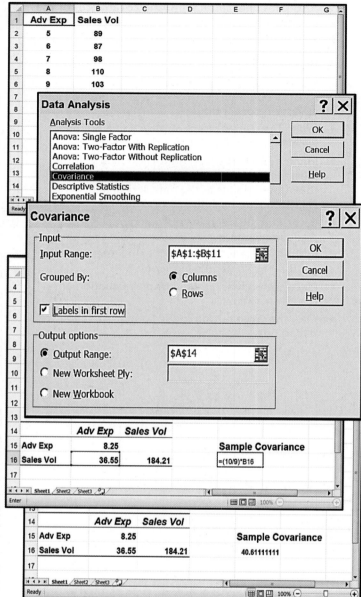

To compute the sample correlation coefficient between sales volume and advertising expenditure:

- Select **Data : Data Analysis : Correlation**
- In the correlation dialog box, enter the range of the data, A1:B11 into the Input Range window.
- Select "Grouped By: Columns" if this is not already the selection.
- Place a checkmark in the "Labels in first row" checkbox.
- Under output options, select "New Worksheet Ply" to have the output placed in a new worksheet and enter the name Output for the new worksheet.
- Click OK in the Correlation dialog box.
- The sample correlation coefficient (=0.93757) is displayed in the Output worksheet.

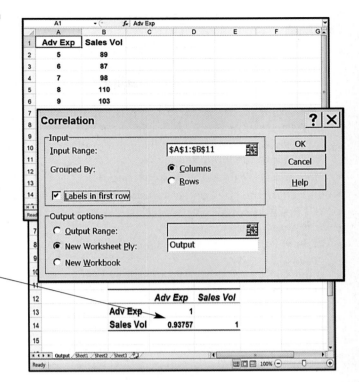

Appendix 3.2 ■ Numerical Descriptive Statistics Using MegaStat

The instructions in this section begin by describing the entry of data into an Excel worksheet. Alternatively, the data may be downloaded from this book's website. The appropriate data file name is given at the top of each instruction block. Please refer to Appendix 1.1 for further information about entering data, saving data, and printing results in Excel. Please refer to Appendix 1.2 for more information about using MegaStat.

To analyze the gas mileage data in Table 3.1 on page 103 (data file: GasMiles.xlsx):

- Enter the mileage data from Table 3.1 into column A with the label Mpg in cell A1 and with the 50 gas mileages in cells A2 through A51.

To compute descriptive statistics similar to those given in Figure 3.1 on page 104:

- Select **Add-Ins : MegaStat : Descriptive Statistics**
- In the "Descriptive Statistics" dialog box, use the AutoExpand feature to enter the range A1:A51 into the Input Range box.
- Place checkmarks in the checkboxes that correspond to the desired statistics. If tolerance intervals based on the Empirical Rule are desired, check the "Empirical Rule" checkbox.
- Click OK in the "Descriptive Statistics" dialog box.
- The output will be placed in an Output worksheet.

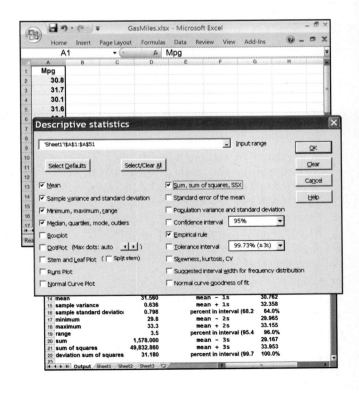

To construct a box plot of satisfaction ratings (data file: DVDSat.xlsx):

- Enter the satisfaction rating data on page 123 into column A with the label Ratings in cell A1 and with the 20 satisfaction ratings in cells A2 to A21.

- Select **Add-Ins : MegaStat : Descriptive Statistics**

- In the "Descriptive Statistics" dialog box, use the AutoExpand feature to enter the input range A1:A21 into the Input Range box.

- Place a checkmark in the Boxplot checkbox.

- Click OK in the "Descriptive Statistics" dialog box.

- The box plot output will be placed in an output worksheet.

- Move the box plot to a chart sheet and edit as desired.

- **Note:** MegaStat constructs box plots by using **inner** and **outer fences**. The **inner fences** are what we have called the lower and upper limits and are located $1.5 \times IQR$ below Q_1 and $1.5 \times IQR$ above Q_3. The **outer fences** are located $3 \times IQR$ below Q_1 and $3 \times IQR$ above Q_3. Measurements that are located between the inner and outer fences are called **mild outliers**, and measurements that are located outside of the outer fences are called **extreme outliers**.

Least squares line and correlation for the sales volume data in Figure 3.22(a) on page 128 (data file: SalesPlot.xlsx):

To compute the equation of the least squares line:

- Enter the advertising and sales data in Figure 3.22(a) on page 128 into columns A and B—advertising expenditures in column A with label "Ad Exp" and sales values in column B with label "Sales Vol".

- Select **Add-Ins : MegaStat : Correlation / Regression : Scatterplot**

- In the Scatterplot dialog box, use the AutoExpand feature to enter the range of the values of advertising expenditure (x), A1:A11, into the "horizontal axis" window.

- Enter the range of the values of sales volume (y), B1:B11, into the "vertical axis" window.

- Place a checkmark in the "Plot linear regression line" checkbox.

- Select Markers as the Display option.

- Click OK in the Scatterplot dialog box.

- The equation of the least squares line is displayed in the scatterplot.

- Move the scatterplot to a chart sheet and edit the plot as desired.

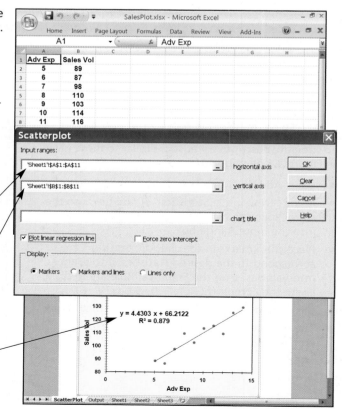

To compute the sample correlation coefficient between sales volume (*y*) and advertising expenditure (*x*):

- Select **Add-Ins : MegaStat : Correlation / Regression : Correlation Matrix**
- In the Correlation Matrix dialog box, use the mouse to select the range of the data A1:B11 into the Input window.
- Click OK in the Correlation Matrix dialog box.
- The sample correlation coefficient between advertising expenditure and sales volume is displayed in an output sheet.

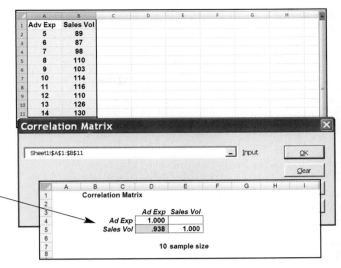

Appendix 3.3 ■ Numerical Descriptive Statistics Using MINITAB

The instructions in this section begin by describing the entry of data into the MINITAB data window. Alternatively, the data may be downloaded from this book's website. The appropriate data file name is given at the top of each instruction block. Please refer to Appendix 1.3 for further information about entering data, saving data, and printing results when using MINITAB.

Numerical descriptive statistics in Figure 3.7 on page 107 (data file: PayTime.MTW):

- Enter the payment time data from Table 2.4 (page 42) into column C1 with variable name PayTime.
- Select **Stat : Basic Statistics : Display Descriptive Statistics.**
- In the Display Descriptive Statistics dialog box, select the variable Paytime into the Variables window.
- In the Display Descriptive Statistics dialog box, click on the Statistics button.
- In the "Descriptive Statistics—Statistics" dialog box, enter checkmarks in the checkboxes corresponding to the desired descriptive statistics. Here we have checked the mean, standard deviation, variance, first quartile, median, third quartile, minimum, maximum, range, and N total checkboxes.
- Click OK in the "Descriptive Statistics—Statistics" dialog box.
- Click OK in the Display Descriptive Statistics dialog box.
- The requested descriptive statistics are displayed in the session window.

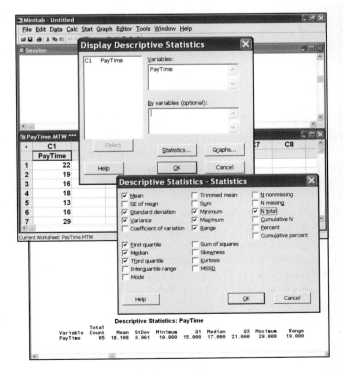

Box plot similar to Figure 3.18 on page 124 (data file DVDSat.MTW):

- Enter the satisfaction rating data from page 123 into column C1 with variable name Ratings.

- Select **Graph : Boxplot**

- In the Boxplots dialog box, select "One Y, Simple" and click OK.

- In the "Boxplot—One Y, Simple" dialog box, select Ratings into the "Graph variables" window.

- Click on the Scale button, select the Axes and Ticks tab, check "Transpose value and category scales" and click OK.

- Click OK in the "Boxplot—One Y, Simple" dialog box.

- The box plot is displayed in a graphics window.

- Note that the box plot produced by MINITAB is based on quartiles computed using methods somewhat different from those presented in Section 3.3 of this book. Consult the MINITAB help menu for a precise description of the box plot construction method used.

Least squares line, correlation, and covariance for the sales volume data in Section 3.4 (data file: SalesPlot.MTW):

To compute the equation of the least squares line:

- Enter the sales and advertising data in Figure 3.22(a) on page 128—advertising expenditure in column C1 with variable name 'Adv Exp', and sales volume in column C2 with variable name 'Sales Vol'.

- Select **Stat : Regression : Fitted Line Plot**

- In the Fitted Line Plot dialog box, enter the variable name 'Sales Vol' (including the single quotes) into the "Response (Y)" window.

- Enter the variable name 'Adv Exp' (including the single quotes) into the "Predictor (X)" window.

- Select Linear for the "Type of Regression Model."

- Click OK in the Fitted Line Plot dialog box.

- A scatter plot of sales volume versus advertising expenditure that includes the equation of the least squares line will be displayed in a graphics window.

To compute the sample correlation coefficient:

- Select **Stat : Basic Statistics : Correlation**

- In the Correlation dialog box, enter the variable names 'Adv Exp' and 'Sales Vol' (including the single quotes) into the Variables window.

- Remove the checkmark from the "Display p-values" checkbox—or keep this checked as desired (we will learn about *p*-values in later chapters).

- Click OK in the Correlation dialog box.

- The correlation coefficient will be displayed in the session window.

To compute the sample covariance:

- Select **Stat : Basic Statistics : Covariance**

- In the Covariance dialog box, enter the variable names 'Adv Exp' and 'Sales Vol' (including the single quotes) into the Variables window.

- Click OK in the Covariance dialog box.

- The covariance will be displayed in the session window.

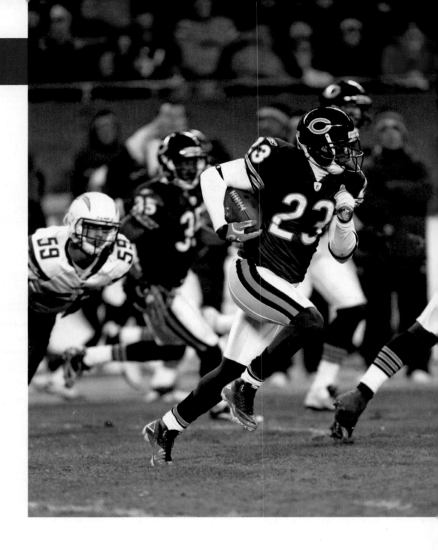

CHAPTER 4

Probability

Learning Objectives

After mastering the material in this chapter, you will be able to:

LO4-1 Define a probability and a sample space.

LO4-2 List the outcomes in a sample space and use the list to compute probabilities.

LO4-3 Use elementary probability rules to compute probabilities.

LO4-4 Compute conditional probabilities and assess independence.

LO4-5 Use Bayes' Theorem to update prior probabilities to posterior probabilities (Optional).

LO4-6 Use elementary counting rules to compute probabilities (Optional).

Chapter Outline

4.1 Probability and Sample Spaces

4.2 Probability and Events

4.3 Some Elementary Probability Rules

4.4 Conditional Probability and Independence

4.5 Bayes' Theorem (Optional)

4.6 Counting Rules (Optional)

4.1 Probability and Sample Spaces ● ● ●

LO4-1 Define a probability and a sample space.

An introduction to probability and sample spaces   We use the concept of **probability** to deal with uncertainty. Intuitively, the probability of an event is a number that measures the chance, or likelihood, that the event will occur. For instance, the probability that your favorite football team will win its next game measures the likelihood of a victory. The probability of an event is always a number between 0 and 1. The closer an event's probability is to 1, the higher is the likelihood that the event will occur; the closer the event's probability is to 0, the smaller is the likelihood that the event will occur. For example, if you believe that the probability that your favorite football team will win its next game is .95, then you are almost sure that your team will win. However, if you believe that the probability of victory is only .10, then you have very little confidence that your team will win.

When performing statistical studies, we sometimes collect data by **performing a controlled experiment.** For instance, we might purposely vary the operating conditions of a manufacturing process in order to study the effects of these changes on the process output. Alternatively, we sometimes obtain data by **observing uncontrolled events.** For example, we might observe the closing price of a share of General Motors' stock every day for 30 trading days. In order to simplify our terminology, we will use the word *experiment* to refer to either method of data collection. We now formally define an experiment and the *sample space* of an experiment.

An **experiment** is any process of observation that has an uncertain outcome. The **sample space** of an experiment is the set of all possible outcomes for the experiment. The possible outcomes are sometimes called **experimental outcomes** or **sample space outcomes.**

When specifying the sample space of an experiment, we must define the sample space outcomes so that on any single repetition of the experiment, one and only one sample space outcome will occur. For example, if we consider the experiment of tossing a coin and observing whether the upward face of the coin shows as a "head" or a "tail," then the sample space consists of the outcomes "head" and "tail." If we consider the experiment of rolling a die and observing the number of dots showing on the upward face of the die, then the sample space consists of the outcomes 1, 2, 3, 4, 5, and 6. If we consider the experiment of subjecting an automobile to a "pass-fail" tailpipe emissions test, then the sample space consists of the outcomes "pass" and "fail."

Assigning probabilities to sample space outcomes   We often wish to assign probabilities to sample space outcomes. This is usually done by using one of three methods: the *classical method,* the *relative frequency method,* or the *subjective method.* Regardless of the method used, **probabilities must be assigned to the experimental outcomes so that two conditions are met:**

1   The probability assigned to each sample space outcome must be between 0 and 1. That is, if E represents a sample space outcome and if $P(E)$ represents the probability of this outcome, then $0 \leq P(E) \leq 1$.

2   The probabilities of all of the sample space outcomes must sum to 1.

The **classical method** of assigning probabilities can be used when the sample space outcomes are equally likely. For example, consider the experiment of tossing a fair coin. Here, there are *two* equally likely sample space outcomes—head (H) and tail (T). Therefore, logic suggests that the probability of observing a head, denoted $P(H)$, is $1/2 = .5$, and that the probability of observing a tail, denoted $P(T)$, is also $1/2 = .5$. Notice that each probability is between 0 and 1. Furthermore, because H and T are all of the sample space outcomes, $P(H) + P(T) = 1$. In general, if there are N equally likely sample space outcomes, the probability assigned to each sample space outcome is $1/N$. To illustrate this, consider the experiment of rolling a fair die. It would seem reasonable to think that the six sample space outcomes 1, 2, 3, 4, 5, and 6 are equally likely, and thus each outcome is assigned a probability of $1/6$. If $P(1)$ denotes the probability that one dot appears on the upward face of the die, then $P(1) = 1/6$. Similarly, $P(2) = 1/6$, $P(3) = 1/6$, $P(4) = 1/6$, $P(5) = 1/6$, and $P(6) = 1/6$.

Before discussing the *relative frequency method* for assigning probabilities, we note that probability is often interpreted to be a **long run relative frequency.** To illustrate this, consider tossing a fair coin—a coin such that the probability of its upward face showing as a head is .5. If we get 6 heads in the first 10 tosses, then the relative frequency, or fraction, of heads is $6/10 = .6$. If we get 47 heads in the first 100 tosses, the relative frequency of heads is $47/100 = .47$. If we get 5,067 heads in the first 10,000 tosses, the relative frequency of heads is $5,067/10,000 = .5067$.[1] Note that the relative frequency of heads is approaching (that is, getting closer to) .5. The long run relative frequency interpretation of probability says that, if we tossed the coin an indefinitely large number of times (that is, a number of times *approaching infinity*), the relative frequency of heads obtained would approach .5. Of course, in actuality it is impossible to toss a coin (or perform any experiment) an indefinitely large number of times. Therefore, a relative frequency interpretation of probability is a mathematical idealization. To summarize, suppose that E is an experimental outcome that might occur when a particular experiment is performed. Then the probability that E will occur, $P(E)$, can be interpreted to be the number that would be approached by the relative frequency of E if we performed the experiment an indefinitely large number of times. It follows that we often think of a probability in terms of the percentage of the time the experimental outcome would occur in many repetitions of the experiment. For instance, when we say that the probability of obtaining a head when we toss a coin is .5, we are saying that, when we repeatedly toss the coin an indefinitely large number of times, we will obtain a head on 50 percent of the repetitions.

Sometimes it is either difficult or impossible to use the classical method to assign probabilities. Since we can often make a relative frequency interpretation of probability, we can estimate a probability by performing the experiment in which an outcome might occur many times. Then, we estimate the probability of the experimental outcome to be the proportion of the time that the outcome occurs during the many repetitions of the experiment. For example, to estimate the probability that a randomly selected consumer prefers Coca-Cola to all other soft drinks, we perform an experiment in which we ask a randomly selected consumer for his or her preference. There are two possible experimental outcomes: "prefers Coca-Cola" and "does not prefer Coca-Cola." However, we have no reason to believe that these experimental outcomes are equally likely, so we cannot use the classical method. We might perform the experiment, say, 1,000 times by surveying 1,000 randomly selected consumers. Then, if 140 of those surveyed said that they prefer Coca-Cola, we would estimate the probability that a randomly selected consumer prefers Coca-Cola to all other soft drinks to be $140/1,000 = .14$. This is an example of the **relative frequency method** of assigning probability.

If we cannot perform the experiment many times, we might estimate the probability by using our previous experience with similar situations, intuition, or special expertise that we may possess. For example, a company president might estimate the probability of success for a one-time business venture to be .7. Here, on the basis of knowledge of the success of previous similar ventures, the opinions of company personnel, and other pertinent information, the president believes that there is a 70 percent chance the venture will be successful.

---

[1] The South African mathematician John Kerrich actually obtained this result when he tossed a coin 10,000 times while imprisoned by the Germans during World War II.

When we use experience, intuitive judgement, or expertise to assess a probability, we call this the **subjective method** of assigning probability. Such a probability (called a **subjective probability**) may or may not have a relative frequency interpretation. For instance, when the company president estimates that the probability of a successful business venture is .7, this may mean that, if business conditions similar to those that are about to be encountered could be repeated many times, then the business venture would be successful in 70 percent of the repetitions. Or the president may not be thinking in relative frequency terms but rather may consider the venture a "one-shot" proposition. We will discuss some other subjective probabilities later. However, the interpretations of statistical inferences we will explain in later chapters are based on the relative frequency interpretation of probability. For this reason, we will concentrate on this interpretation.

4.2 Probability and Events ● ● ●

LO4-2 List the outcomes in a sample space and use the list to compute probabilities.

At the beginning of this chapter, we informally talked about events. We now give the formal definition of an event.

An **event** is a set of one or more sample space outcomes.

For example, if we consider the experiment of tossing a fair die, the event "at least five spots will show on the upward face of the die" consists of the sample space outcomes 5 and 6. That is, the event "at least five spots will show on the upward face of the die" will occur if and only if one of the sample space outcomes 5 or 6 occurs.

To find the probability that an event will occur, we can use the following result.

The **probability of an event** is the **sum of the probabilities of the sample space outcomes** that correspond to the event.

As an example, we have seen that if we consider the experiment of tossing a fair die, then the sample space outcomes 5 and 6 correspond to the occurrence of the event "at least five spots will show on the upward face of the die." Therefore, the probability of this event is

$$P(5) + P(6) = \frac{1}{6} + \frac{1}{6} = \frac{2}{6} = \frac{1}{3}$$

EXAMPLE 4.1 Boys and Girls

A newly married couple plans to have two children. Naturally, they are curious about whether their children will be boys or girls. Therefore, we consider the experiment of having two children. In order to find the sample space of this experiment, we let B denote that a child is a boy and G denote that a child is a girl. Then, it is useful to construct the tree diagram shown in Figure 4.1. This diagram pictures the experiment as a two-step process—having the first child, which could be either a boy or a girl (B or G), and then having the second child, which could also be either a boy or a girl (B or G). Each branch of the tree leads to a sample space outcome. These outcomes are listed at the right ends of the branches. We see that there are four sample space outcomes. Therefore, the sample space (that is, the set of all the sample space outcomes) is

$$BB \quad BG \quad GB \quad GG$$

In order to consider the probabilities of these outcomes, suppose that boys and girls are equally likely each time a child is born. Intuitively, this says that each of the sample space outcomes is equally likely. That is, this implies that

$$P(BB) = P(BG) = P(GB) = P(GG) = \frac{1}{4}$$

FIGURE 4.1 A Tree Diagram of the Genders of Two Children

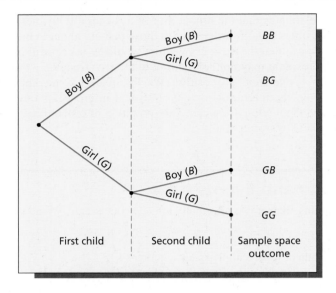

Therefore:

1 The probability that the couple will have two boys is

$$P(BB) = \frac{1}{4}$$

because two boys will be born if and only if the sample space outcome *BB* occurs.

2 The probability that the couple will have one boy and one girl is

$$P(BG) + P(GB) = \frac{1}{4} + \frac{1}{4} = \frac{1}{2}$$

because one boy and one girl will be born if and only if one of the sample space outcomes *BG* or *GB* occurs.

3 The probability that the couple will have two girls is

$$P(GG) = \frac{1}{4}$$

because two girls will be born if and only if the sample space outcome *GG* occurs.

4 The probability that the couple will have at least one girl is

$$P(BG) + P(GB) + P(GG) = \frac{1}{4} + \frac{1}{4} + \frac{1}{4} = \frac{3}{4}$$

because at least one girl will be born if and only if one of the sample space outcomes *BG*, *GB*, or *GG* occurs.

EXAMPLE 4.2 Pop Quizzes

A student takes a pop quiz that consists of three true–false questions. If we consider our experiment to be answering the three questions, each question can be answered correctly or incorrectly. We will let *C* denote answering a question correctly and *I* denote answering a

FIGURE 4.2   A Tree Diagram of Answering Three True–False Questions

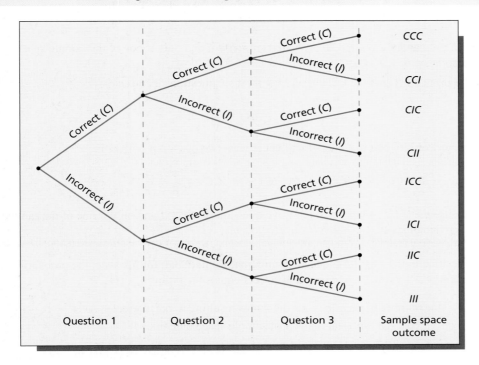

question incorrectly. Figure 4.2 depicts a tree diagram of the sample space outcomes for the experiment. The diagram portrays the experiment as a three-step process—answering the first question (correctly or incorrectly, that is, C or I), answering the second question, and answering the third question. The tree diagram has eight different branches, and the eight sample space outcomes are listed at the ends of the branches. We see that the sample space is

CCC	CCI	CIC	CII
ICC	ICI	IIC	III

Next, suppose that the student was totally unprepared for the quiz and had to blindly guess the answer to each question. That is, the student had a 50–50 chance (or .5 probability) of correctly answering each question. Intuitively, this would say that each of the eight sample space outcomes is equally likely to occur. That is,

$$P(CCC) = P(CCI) = \cdots = P(III) = \frac{1}{8}$$

Therefore:

1   The probability that the student will get all three questions correct is

$$P(CCC) = \frac{1}{8}$$

2   The probability that the student will get exactly two questions correct is

$$P(CCI) + P(CIC) + P(ICC) = \frac{1}{8} + \frac{1}{8} + \frac{1}{8} = \frac{3}{8}$$

because two questions will be answered correctly if and only if one of the sample space outcomes *CCI*, *CIC*, or *ICC* occurs.

3	The probability that the student will get exactly one question correct is

$$P(CII) + P(ICI) + P(IIC) = \frac{1}{8} + \frac{1}{8} + \frac{1}{8} = \frac{3}{8}$$

because one question will be answered correctly if and only if one of the sample space outcomes *CII*, *ICI*, or *IIC* occurs.

4	The probability that the student will get all three questions incorrect is

$$P(III) = \frac{1}{8}$$

5	The probability that the student will get at least two questions correct is

$$P(CCC) + P(CCI) + P(CIC) + P(ICC) = \frac{1}{8} + \frac{1}{8} + \frac{1}{8} + \frac{1}{8} = \frac{1}{2}$$

because the student will get at least two questions correct if and only if one of the sample space outcomes *CCC*, *CCI*, *CIC*, or *ICC* occurs.

Notice that in the true–false question situation, we find that, for instance, the probability that the student will get exactly one question correct equals the ratio

$$\frac{\text{the number of sample space outcomes resulting in one correct answer}}{\text{the total number of sample space outcomes}} = \frac{3}{8}$$

In general, when a sample space is finite we can use the following method for computing the probability of an event.

If all of the sample space outcomes are equally likely, then the probability that an event will occur is equal to the ratio

$$\frac{\text{the number of sample space outcomes that correspond to the event}}{\text{the total number of sample space outcomes}}$$

It is important to emphasize, however, that we can use this rule only when all of the sample space outcomes are equally likely (as they are in the true–false question situation). If the sample space outcomes are not equally likely, the rule may give an incorrect probability.

EXAMPLE 4.3 Choosing a CEO

A company is choosing a new chief executive officer (CEO). It has narrowed the list of candidates to four finalists (identified by last name only)—Adams, Chung, Hill, and Rankin. If we consider our experiment to be making a final choice of the company's CEO, then the experiment's sample space consists of the four possible outcomes:

$A \equiv$ Adams will be chosen as CEO.

$C \equiv$ Chung will be chosen as CEO.

$H \equiv$ Hill will be chosen as CEO.

$R \equiv$ Rankin will be chosen as CEO.

Next, suppose that industry analysts feel (subjectively) that the probabilities that Adams, Chung, Hill, and Rankin will be chosen as CEO are .1, .2, .5, and .2, respectively. That is, in probability notation

$$P(A) = .1 \qquad P(C) = .2 \qquad P(H) = .5 \qquad \text{and} \qquad P(R) = .2$$

Also, suppose only Adams and Hill are internal candidates (they already work for the company). Letting *INT* denote the event that "an internal candidate will be selected for the CEO position," then *INT* consists of the sample space outcomes *A* and *H* (that is, *INT* will occur if and only if either of the sample space outcomes *A* or *H* occurs). It follows that $P(INT) = P(A) + P(H) = .1 + .5 = .6$. This says that the probability that an internal candidate will be chosen to be CEO is .6.

Finally, it is important to understand that if we had ignored the fact that sample space outcomes are not equally likely, we might have tried to calculate *P(INT)* as follows:

$$P(INT) = \frac{\text{the number of internal candidates}}{\text{the total number of candidates}} = \frac{2}{4} = .5$$

This result would be incorrect. Because the sample space outcomes are not equally likely, we have seen that the correct value of *P(INT)* is .6, not .5.

EXAMPLE 4.4 The Crystal Cable Case: Market Penetration

Like all companies, cable companies send shareholders reports on their profits, dividends, and return on equity. They often supplement this information with some metrics unique to the cable business. To construct one such metric, a cable company can compare the number of households it actually serves to the number of households its current transmission lines could reach (without extending the lines). The number of households that the cable company's lines could reach is called its number of **cable passings,** while the ratio of the number of households the cable company actually serves to its number of cable passings is called the company's **cable penetration.** There are various types of cable penetrations—one for cable television, one for cable Internet, one for cable phone, and others. Moreover, a cable penetration is a probability, and interpreting it as such will help us to better understand various techniques to be discussed in the next section. For example, in a recent quarterly report, Crystal Cable reported that it had 12.4 million cable television customers and 27.4 million cable passings.[2] Consider randomly selecting one of Crystal's cable passings. That is, consider selecting one cable passing by giving each and every cable passing the same chance of being selected. Let *A* be the event that the randomly selected cable passing has Crystal's cable television service. Then, because the sample space of this experiment consists of 27.4 million equally likely sample space outcomes (cable passings), it follows that

$$P(A) = \frac{\text{the number of cable passings that have Crystal's cable television service}}{\text{the total number of cable passings}}$$

$$= \frac{12.4}{27.4}$$

$$= .45$$

This probability is Crystal's cable television penetration and says that the probability that a randomly selected cable passing has Crystal's cable television service is .45. That is, 45 percent of Crystal's cable passings have Crystal's cable television service.

To conclude this section, we note that in optional Section 4.6 we discuss several *counting rules* that can be used to count the number of sample space outcomes in an experiment. These rules are particularly useful when there are many sample space outcomes and thus these outcomes are difficult to list.

---

[2]Although these numbers are hypothetical, they are similar to results actually found in Time Warner Cable's quarterly reports. See www.TimeWarnerCable.com. Click on Investor Relations.

Exercises for Sections 4.1 and 4.2

CONCEPTS

connect™

4.1 Define the following terms: *experiment, event, probability, sample space.*

4.2 Explain the properties that must be satisfied by a probability.

METHODS AND APPLICATIONS

4.3 Two randomly selected grocery store patrons are each asked to take a blind taste test and to then state which of three diet colas (marked as *A*, *B*, or *C*) he or she prefers.
  a Draw a tree diagram depicting the sample space outcomes for the test results.
  b List the sample space outcomes that correspond to each of the following events:
    (1) Both patrons prefer diet cola *A*.
    (2) The two patrons prefer the same diet cola.
    (3) The two patrons prefer different diet colas.
    (4) Diet cola *A* is preferred by at least one of the two patrons.
    (5) Neither of the patrons prefers diet cola *C*.
  c Assuming that all sample space outcomes are equally likely, find the probability of each of the events given in part *b*.

4.4 Suppose that a couple will have three children. Letting *B* denote a boy and *G* denote a girl:
  a Draw a tree diagram depicting the sample space outcomes for this experiment.
  b List the sample space outcomes that correspond to each of the following events:
    (1) All three children will have the same gender.
    (2) Exactly two of the three children will be girls.
    (3) Exactly one of the three children will be a girl.
    (4) None of the three children will be a girl.
  c Assuming that all sample space outcomes are equally likely, find the probability of each of the events given in part *b*.

4.5 Four people will enter an automobile showroom, and each will either purchase a car (*P*) or not purchase a car (*N*).
  a Draw a tree diagram depicting the sample space of all possible purchase decisions that could potentially be made by the four people.
  b List the sample space outcomes that correspond to each of the following events:
    (1) Exactly three people will purchase a car.
    (2) Two or fewer people will purchase a car.
    (3) One or more people will purchase a car.
    (4) All four people will make the same purchase decision.
  c Assuming that all sample space outcomes are equally likely, find the probability of each of the events given in part *b*.

4.6 The U.S. Census Bureau compiles data on family income and summarizes its findings in *Current Population Reports*. The table below is a frequency distribution of the annual incomes for a random sample of U.S. families. Find an estimate of the probability that a randomly selected U.S. family has an income between $60,000 and $199,999.

Income	Frequency (in thousands)
Under $20,000	11,470
$20,000–$39,999	17,572
$40,000–$59,999	14,534
$60,000–$79,999	11,410
$80,000–$99,999	7,535
$100,000–$199,999	11,197
$200,000 and above	2,280
	75,998

4.7 Let *A*, *B*, *C*, *D*, and *E* be sample space outcomes forming a sample space. Suppose that $P(A) = .2$, $P(B) = .15$, $P(C) = .3$, and $P(D) = .2$. What is $P(E)$? Explain how you got your answer.

4.3 Some Elementary Probability Rules ● ● ●

We can often calculate probabilities by using formulas called **probability rules.** We will begin by presenting the simplest probability rule: the *rule of complements*. To start, we define the complement of an event:

Given an event A, the **complement of A** is the event consisting of all sample space outcomes that do not correspond to the occurrence of A. The complement of A is denoted $\overline{A}$. Furthermore, $P(\overline{A})$ denotes **the probability that A will not occur.**

Figure 4.3 is a **Venn diagram** depicting the complement $\overline{A}$ of an event A. In any probability situation, either an event A or its complement $\overline{A}$ must occur. Therefore, we have

$$P(A) + P(\overline{A}) = 1$$

This implies the following result:

F I G U R E 4.3

The Complement of an Event (the Shaded Region Is $\overline{A}$, the Complement of A)

The Rule of Complements

Consider an event A. Then, **the probability that A will not occur** is

$$P(\overline{A}) = 1 - P(A)$$

EXAMPLE 4.5 The Crystal Cable Case: Market Penetration

Recall from Example 4.4 that the probability that a randomly selected cable passing has Crystal's cable television service is .45. It follows that the probability of the complement of this event (that is, the probability that a randomly selected cable passing does not have Crystal's cable television service) is $1 - .45 = .55$.

We next define the *intersection* of two events. Consider performing an experiment a single time. Then:

Given two events A and B, the **intersection of A and B** is the event that occurs if both A and B simultaneously occur. The intersection is denoted by $A \cap B$. Furthermore, $P(A \cap B)$ denotes **the probability that *both* A *and* B *will simultaneously occur.***

EXAMPLE 4.6 The Crystal Cable Case: Market Penetration

Recall from Example 4.4 that Crystal Cable has 27.4 million cable passings. Consider randomly selecting one of these cable passings, and define the following events:

$A \equiv$ the randomly selected cable passing has Crystal's cable television service.

$\overline{A} \equiv$ the randomly selected cable passing does not have Crystal's cable television service.

$B \equiv$ the randomly selected cable passing has Crystal's cable Internet service.

$\overline{B} \equiv$ the randomly selected cable passing does not have Crystal's cable Internet service.

$A \cap B \equiv$ the randomly selected cable passing has both Crystal's cable television service and Crystal's cable Internet service.

$A \cap \overline{B} \equiv$ the randomly selected cable passing has Crystal's cable television service and does not have Crystal's cable Internet service.

TABLE 4.1 A Contingency Table Summarizing Crystal's Cable Television and Internet Penetration (Figures In Millions Of Cable Passings)

Events	Has Cable Internet Service, B	Does Not Have Cable Internet Service, $\overline{B}$	Total
Has Cable Television Service, A	6.5	5.9	12.4
Does Not Have Cable Television Service, $\overline{A}$	3.3	11.7	15.0
Total	9.8	17.6	27.4

$\overline{A} \cap B \equiv$ the randomly selected cable passing does not have Crystal's cable television service and does have Crystal's cable Internet service.

$\overline{A} \cap \overline{B} \equiv$ the randomly selected cable passing does not have Crystal's cable television service and does not have Crystal's cable Internet service.

Table 4.1 is a *contingency table* that summarizes Crystal's cable passings. Using this table, we can calculate the following probabilities, each of which describes some aspect of Crystal's cable penetrations:

1 Because 12.4 million out of 27.4 million cable passings have Crystal's cable television service, A, then

$$P(A) = \frac{12.4}{27.4} = .45$$

This says that 45 percent of Crystal's cable passings have Crystal's cable television service (as previously seen in Example 4.4).

2 Because 9.8 million out of 27.4 million cable passings have Crystal's cable Internet service, B, then

$$P(B) = \frac{9.8}{27.4} = .36$$

This says that 36 percent of Crystal's cable passings have Crystal's cable Internet service.

3 Because 6.5 million out of 27.4 million cable passings have Crystal's cable television service and Crystal's cable Internet service, $A \cap B$, then

$$P(A \cap B) = \frac{6.5}{27.4} = .24$$

This says that 24 percent of Crystal's cable passings have both of Crystal's cable services.

4 Because 5.9 million out of 27.4 million cable passings have Crystal's cable television service, but do not have Crystal's cable Internet service, $A \cap \overline{B}$, then

$$P(A \cap \overline{B}) = \frac{5.9}{27.4} = .22$$

This says that 22 percent of Crystal's cable passings have only Crystal's cable television service.

5   Because 3.3 million out of 27.4 million cable passings do not have Crystal's cable television service, but do have Crystal's cable Internet service, $\overline{A} \cap B$, then

$$P(\overline{A} \cap B) = \frac{3.3}{27.4} = .12$$

This says that 12 percent of Crystal's cable passings have only Crystal's cable Internet service.

6   Because 11.7 million out of 27.4 million cable passings do not have Crystal's cable television service and do not have Crystal's cable Internet service, $\overline{A} \cap \overline{B}$, then

$$P(\overline{A} \cap \overline{B}) = \frac{11.7}{27.4} = .43$$

This says that 43 percent of Crystal's cable passings have neither of Crystal's cable services.

We next consider the *union* of two events. Again consider performing an experiment a single time. Then:

Given two events A and B, the **union of A and B** is the event that occurs if A or B (or both) occur. The union is denoted $A \cup B$. Furthermore, $P(A \cup B)$ denotes **the probability that A or B (or both) will occur.**

EXAMPLE 4.7 The Crystal Cable Case: Market Penetration

Consider randomly selecting one of Crystal's 27.4 million cable passings, and define the event

$A \cup B \equiv$ the randomly selected cable passing has Crystal's cable television service or Crystal's cable Internet service (or both)—that is, has at least one of the two services.

Looking at Table 4.1, we see that the cable passings that have Crystal's cable television service or Crystal's cable Internet service are (1) the 5.9 million cable passings that have only Crystal's cable television service, $A \cap \overline{B}$, (2) the 3.3 million cable passings that have only Crystal's cable Internet service, $\overline{A} \cap B$, and (3) the 6.5 million cable passings that have both Crystal's cable television service and Crystal's cable Internet service, $A \cap B$. Therefore, because a total of 15.7 million cable passings have Crystal's cable television service or Crystal's cable Internet service (or both), it follows that

$$P(A \cup B) = \frac{15.7}{27.4} = .57$$

This says that the probability that the randomly selected cable passing has Crystal's cable television service or Crystal's cable Internet service (or both) is .57. That is, 57 percent of Crystal's cable passings have Crystal's cable television service or Crystal's cable Internet service (or both). Notice that $P(A \cup B) = .57$ does not equal

$$P(A) + P(B) = .45 + .36 = .81$$

Logically, the reason for this is that both $P(A) = .45$ and $P(B) = .36$ count the 24 percent of the cable passings that have both Crystal's cable television service and Crystal's cable Internet service. Therefore, the sum of $P(A)$ and $P(B)$ counts this 24 percent of the cable passings once too often. It follows that if we subtract $P(A \cap B) = .24$ from the sum of $P(A)$ and $P(B)$, then we will obtain $P(A \cup B)$. That is,

$$P(A \cup B) = P(A) + P(B) - P(A \cap B)$$
$$= .45 + .36 - .24 = .57$$

Noting that Figure 4.4 shows **Venn diagrams** depicting the events A, B, $A \cap B$, and $A \cup B$, we have the following general result:

The Addition Rule

Let A and B be events. Then, **the probability that *A or B (or both) will occur*** is

$$P(A \cup B) = P(A) + P(B) - P(A \cap B)$$

The reasoning behind this result has been illustrated at the end of Example 4.7. Similarly, the Venn diagrams in Figure 4.4 show that when we compute $P(A) + P(B)$, we are counting each of the sample space outcomes in $A \cap B$ twice. We correct for this by subtracting $P(A \cap B)$.

We next define the idea of *mutually exclusive events:*

Mutually Exclusive Events

Two events A and B are **mutually exclusive** if they have no sample space outcomes in common. In this case, the events A and B cannot occur simultaneously, and thus

$$P(A \cap B) = 0$$

Noting that Figure 4.5 is a Venn diagram depicting two mutually exclusive events, we consider the following example.

EXAMPLE 4.8 **Selecting Playing Cards**

Consider randomly selecting a card from a standard deck of 52 playing cards. We define the following events:

$J \equiv$ the randomly selected card is a jack.

$Q \equiv$ the randomly selected card is a queen.

$R \equiv$ the randomly selected card is a red card (that is, a diamond or a heart).

Because there is no card that is both a jack and a queen, the events J and Q are mutually exclusive. On the other hand, there are two cards that are both jacks and red cards—the jack of diamonds and the jack of hearts—so the events J and R are not mutually exclusive.

We have seen that for any two events A and B, the probability that A or B (or both) will occur is

$$P(A \cup B) = P(A) + P(B) - P(A \cap B)$$

Therefore, when calculating $P(A \cup B)$, we should always subtract $P(A \cap B)$ from the sum of $P(A)$ and $P(B)$. However, when A and B are mutually exclusive, $P(A \cap B)$ equals 0. Therefore, in this case—and only in this case—we have the following:

The Addition Rule for Two Mutually Exclusive Events

Let A and B be **mutually exclusive** events. Then, **the probability that *A or B will occur*** is

$$P(A \cup B) = P(A) + P(B)$$

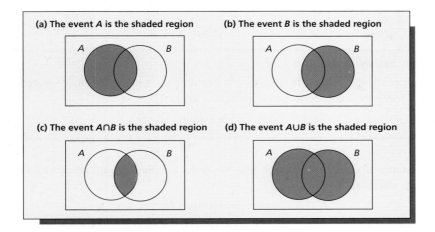

FIGURE 4.4   Venn Diagrams Depicting the Events *A*, *B*, *A* ∩ *B*, and *A* ∪ *B*

(a) The event *A* is the shaded region

(b) The event *B* is the shaded region

(c) The event *A*∩*B* is the shaded region

(d) The event *A*∪*B* is the shaded region

FIGURE 4.5
Two Mutually
Exclusive Events

EXAMPLE 4.9   Selecting Playing Cards

Again consider randomly selecting a card from a standard deck of 52 playing cards, and define the events

   $J \equiv$ the randomly selected card is a jack.

   $Q \equiv$ the randomly selected card is a queen.

   $R \equiv$ the randomly selected card is a red card (a diamond or a heart).

Because there are four jacks, four queens, and 26 red cards, we have $P(J) = \frac{4}{52}$, $P(Q) = \frac{4}{52}$, and $P(R) = \frac{26}{52}$. Furthermore, since there is no card that is both a jack and a queen, the events J and Q are mutually exclusive and thus $P(J \cap Q) = 0$. It follows that the probability that the randomly selected card is a jack or a queen is

$$P(J \cup Q) = P(J) + P(Q)$$
$$= \frac{4}{52} + \frac{4}{52} = \frac{8}{52} = \frac{2}{13}$$

Because there are two cards that are both jacks and red cards—the jack of diamonds and the jack of hearts—the events J and R are not mutually exclusive. Therefore, the probability that the randomly selected card is a jack or a red card is

$$P(J \cup R) = P(J) + P(R) - P(J \cap R)$$
$$= \frac{4}{52} + \frac{26}{52} - \frac{2}{52} = \frac{28}{52} = \frac{7}{13}$$

We now consider an arbitrary group of events—$A_1, A_2, \ldots, A_N$. We will denote the probability that A_1 or A_2 or $\cdots$ or A_N occurs (that is, the probability that at least one of the events occurs) as $P(A_1 \cup A_2 \cup \cdots \cup A_N)$. Although there is a formula for this probability, it is quite complicated and we will not present it in this book. However, sometimes we can use sample spaces to reason out such a probability. For instance, in the playing card situation of Example 4.9, there are four jacks, four queens, and 22 red cards that are not jacks or queens (the 26 red cards minus the two red jacks and the two red queens). Therefore, because there are a total of 30 cards corresponding to the event $J \cup Q \cup R$, it follows that

$$P(J \cup Q \cup R) = \frac{30}{52} = \frac{15}{26}$$

Because some cards are both jacks and red cards, and because some cards are both queens and red cards, we say that the events J, Q, and R are not mutually exclusive. When, however, a group of events is mutually exclusive, there is a simple formula for the probability that at least one of the events will occur:

The Addition Rule for N Mutually Exclusive Events

The events A_1, A_2, ..., A_N are mutually exclusive if no two of the events have any sample space outcomes in common. In this case, no two of the events can occur simultaneously, and

$$P(A_1 \cup A_2 \cup \cdots \cup A_N) = P(A_1) + P(A_2) + \cdots + P(A_N)$$

As an example of using this formula, again consider the playing card situation and the events J and Q. If we define the event

$$K \equiv \text{the randomly selected card is a king}$$

then the events J, Q, and K are mutually exclusive. Therefore,

$$P(J \cup Q \cup K) = P(J) + P(Q) + P(K)$$
$$= \frac{4}{52} + \frac{4}{52} + \frac{4}{52} = \frac{12}{52} = \frac{3}{13}$$

Exercises for Section 4.3

CONCEPTS

connect

4.8 Explain what it means for two events to be mutually exclusive; for N events.

4.9 If A and B are events, define (in words) $\overline{A}$, $A \cup B$, $A \cap B$, and $\overline{A} \cap \overline{B}$.

METHODS AND APPLICATIONS

4.10 Consider a standard deck of 52 playing cards, a randomly selected card from the deck, and the following events:

$$R = \text{red} \quad B = \text{black} \quad A = \text{ace} \quad N = \text{nine} \quad D = \text{diamond} \quad C = \text{club}$$

a Describe the sample space outcomes that correspond to each of these events.

b For each of the following pairs of events, indicate whether the events are mutually exclusive. In each case, if you think the events are mutually exclusive, explain why the events have no common sample space outcomes. If you think the events are not mutually exclusive, list the sample space outcomes that are common to both events.

(1) R and A (3) A and N (5) D and C
(2) R and C (4) N and C

4.11 The following contingency table summarizes the number of students at a college who have a Mastercard or a Visa credit card.

	Have Visa	Do Not Have Visa	Total
Have Mastercard	1,000	1,500	2,500
Do not have Mastercard	3,000	4,500	7,500
Total	4,000	6,000	10,000

a Find the probability that a randomly selected student
(1) Has a Mastercard.
(2) Has a VISA.
(3) Has both credit cards.

TABLE 4.2   **Results of a Concept Study for a New Wine Cooler** 📀 WineCooler

		Gender			Age Group	
Rating	Total	Male	Female	21–24	25–34	35–49
Extremely appealing (5)	151	68	83	48	66	37
(4)	91	51	40	36	36	19
(3)	36	21	15	9	12	15
(2)	13	7	6	4	6	3
Not at all appealing (1)	9	3	6	4	3	2

Source: W. R. Dillon, T. J. Madden, and N. H. Firtle, *Essentials of Marketing Research* (Burr Ridge, IL: Richard D. Irwin, Inc., 1993), p. 390.

    b Find the probability that a randomly selected student
      (1) Has a Mastercard or a VISA.
      (2) Has neither credit card.
      (3) Has exactly one of the two credit cards.

4.12 The card game of Euchre employs a deck that consists of all four of each of the aces, kings, queens, jacks, tens, and nines (one of each suit—clubs, diamonds, spades, and hearts). Find the probability that a randomly selected card from a Euchre deck is a jack (J), a spade (S), a jack or an ace (A), a jack or a spade. Are the events J and A mutually exclusive? J and S? Why or why not?

4.13 Each month a brokerage house studies various companies and rates each company's stock as being either "low risk" or "moderate to high risk." In a recent report, the brokerage house summarized its findings about 15 aerospace companies and 25 food retailers in the following table:

Company Type	Low Risk	Moderate to High Risk
Aerospace company	6	9
Food retailer	15	10

If we randomly select one of the total of 40 companies, find
    a The probability that the company is a food retailer.
    b The probability that the company's stock is "low risk."
    c The probability that the company's stock is "moderate to high risk."
    d The probability that the company is a food retailer and has a stock that is "low risk."
    e The probability that the company is a food retailer or has a stock that is "low risk."

4.14 In the book *Essentials of Marketing Research,* William R. Dillon, Thomas J. Madden, and Neil H. Firtle present the results of a concept study for a new wine cooler. Three hundred consumers between 21 and 49 years old were randomly selected. After sampling the new beverage, each was asked to rate the appeal of the phrase

    Not sweet like wine coolers, not filling like beer, and more refreshing than wine or mixed drinks

as it relates to the new wine cooler. The rating was made on a scale from 1 to 5, with 5 representing "extremely appealing" and with 1 representing "not at all appealing." The results obtained are given in Table 4.2. Estimate the probability that a randomly selected 21- to 49-year-old consumer
    a Would give the phrase a rating of 5.
    b Would give the phrase a rating of 3 or higher.
    c Is in the 21–24 age group; the 25–34 age group; the 35–49 age group.
    d Is a male who gives the phrase a rating of 4.
    e Is a 35- to 49-year-old who gives the phrase a rating of 1.

4.15 In Exercise 4.14 estimate the probability that a randomly selected 21- to 49-year-old consumer is a 25- to 49-year-old who gives the phrase a rating of 5.

4.4 Conditional Probability and Independence ● ● ●

Conditional probability In Table 4.3 we repeat Table 4.1 summarizing data concerning Crystal cable's 27.4 million cable passings. Suppose that we randomly select a cable passing and that the chosen cable passing reports that it has Crystal's cable Internet service. Given this new

LO4-4 Compute conditional probabilities and assess independence.

TABLE 4.3   A Contingency Table Summarizing Crystal's Cable Television and Internet Penetration (Figures In Millions Of Cable Passings)

Events	Has Cable Internet Service, B	Does Not Have Cable Internet Service, $\overline{B}$	Total
Has Cable Television Service, A	6.5	5.9	12.4
Does Not Have Cable Television Service, $\overline{A}$	3.3	11.7	15.0
Total	9.8	17.6	27.4

information, we wish to find the probability that the cable passing has Crystal's cable television service. This new probability is called a **conditional probability.**

> The **probability of the event A, given the condition that the event B *has occurred*,** is written as $P(A|B)$—pronounced "the probability of A given B." We often refer to such a probability as the **conditional probability of A given B.**

In order to find the conditional probability that a randomly selected cable passing has Crystal's cable television service, given that it has Crystal's cable Internet service, notice that if we know that the randomly selected cable passing has Crystal's cable Internet service, we know that we are considering one of Crystal's 9.8 million cable Internet customers (see Table 4.3). That is, we are now considering what we might call a **reduced sample space** of Crystal's 9.8 million cable Internet customers. Because 6.5 million of these 9.8 million cable Internet customers also have Crystal's cable television service, we have

$$P(A|B) = \frac{6.5}{9.8} = .66$$

This says that the probability that the randomly selected cable passing has Crystal's cable television service, given that it has Crystal's cable Internet service, is .66. That is, 66 percent of Crystal's cable Internet customers also have Crystal's cable television service.

Next, suppose that we randomly select another cable passing from Crystal's 27.4 million cable passings, and suppose that this newly chosen cable passing reports that it has Crystal's cable television service. We now wish to find the probability that this cable passing has Crystal's cable Internet service. We write this new probability as $P(B|A)$. If we know that the randomly selected cable passing has Crystal's cable television service, we know that we are considering a reduced sample space of Crystal's 12.4 million cable television customers (see Table 4.3). Because 6.5 million of these 12.4 million cable television customers also have Crystal's cable Internet service, we have

$$P(B|A) = \frac{6.5}{12.4} = .52$$

This says that the probability that the randomly selected cable passing has Crystal's cable Internet service, given that it has Crystal's cable television service, is .52. That is, 52 percent of Crystal's cable television customers also have Crystal's cable Internet service.

If we divide both the numerator and denominator of each of the conditional probabilities $P(A|B)$ and $P(B|A)$ by 27.4, we obtain

$$P(A|B) = \frac{6.5}{9.8} = \frac{6.5/27.4}{9.8/27.4} = \frac{P(A \cap B)}{P(B)}$$

$$P(B|A) = \frac{6.5}{12.4} = \frac{6.5/27.4}{12.4/27.4} = \frac{P(A \cap B)}{P(A)}$$

We express these conditional probabilities in terms of $P(A)$, $P(B)$, and $P(A \cap B)$ in order to obtain a more general formula for a conditional probability. We need a more general formula because, although we can use the reduced sample space approach we have demonstrated to find conditional probabilities when all of the sample space outcomes are equally likely, this approach may not give correct results when the sample space outcomes are *not* equally likely. We now give expressions for conditional probability that are valid for any sample space.

Conditional Probability

1 The **conditional probability of the event A given that the event B has occurred** is written $P(A \mid B)$ and is defined to be

$$P(A \mid B) = \frac{P(A \cap B)}{P(B)}$$

Here we assume that $P(B)$ is greater than 0.

2 The **conditional probability of the event B given that the event A has occurred** is written $P(B \mid A)$ and is defined to be

$$P(B \mid A) = \frac{P(A \cap B)}{P(A)}$$

Here we assume that $P(A)$ is greater than 0.

If we multiply both sides of the equation

$$P(A \mid B) = \frac{P(A \cap B)}{P(B)}$$

by $P(B)$, we obtain the equation

$$P(A \cap B) = P(B)P(A \mid B)$$

Similarly, if we multiply both sides of the equation

$$P(B \mid A) = \frac{P(A \cap B)}{P(A)}$$

by $P(A)$, we obtain the equation

$$P(A \cap B) = P(A)P(B \mid A)$$

In summary, we now have two equations that can be used to calculate $P(A \cap B)$. These equations are often referred to as the **general multiplication rule** for probabilities.

The General Multiplication Rule—Two Ways to Calculate $P(A \cap B)$

Given any two events A and B,

$$P(A \cap B) = P(A)P(B \mid A)$$
$$= P(B)P(A \mid B)$$

EXAMPLE 4.10 Gender Issues at a Pharmaceutical Company

At a large pharmaceutical company, 52 percent of the sales representatives are women, and 44 percent of the sales representatives having a management position are women. (There are various types of management positions in the sales division of the pharmaceutical company.) Given that 25 percent of the sales representatives have a management position, we wish to find

- The percentage of the sales representatives that have a management position and are women.
- The percentage of the female sales representatives that have a management position.
- The percentage of the sales representatives that have a management position and are men.
- The percentage of the male sales representatives that have a management position.

In order to find these percentages, consider randomly selecting one of the sales representatives. Then, let W denote the event that the randomly selected sales representative is a woman, and let M denote the event that the randomly selected sales representative is a man. Also, let MGT denote the event that the randomly selected sales representative has a management position. The information given at the beginning of this example says that 52 percent of the sales representatives are women and 44 percent of the sales representatives having a management position are women. This implies that $P(W) = .52$ and that $P(W \mid MGT) = .44$. The information given at the beginning of this example also says that 25 percent of the sales representatives have a management position. This implies that $P(MGT) = .25$. To find the percentage of the sales representatives that have a management position and are women, we find $P(MGT \cap W)$. The general multiplication rule tells us that

$$P(MGT \cap W) = P(MGT)P(W \mid MGT) = P(W)P(MGT \mid W)$$

Although we know that $P(W) = .52$, we do not know $P(MGT \mid W)$. Therefore, we cannot calculate $P(MGT \cap W)$ as $P(W)P(MGT \mid W)$. However, because we know that $P(MGT) = .25$ and $P(W \mid MGT) = .44$, we can calculate

$$P(MGT \cap W) = P(MGT)P(W \mid MGT) = (.25)(.44) = .11$$

This says that 11 percent of the sales representatives have a management position and are women. Moreover,

$$P(MGT \mid W) = \frac{P(MGT \cap W)}{P(W)} = \frac{.11}{.52} = .2115$$

This says that 21.15 percent of the female sales representatives have a management position.

To find the percentage of the sales representatives that have a management position and are men, we find $P(MGT \cap M)$. Because we know that 52 percent of the sales representatives are women, the rule of complements tells us that 48 percent of the sales representatives are men. That is, $P(M) = .48$. We also know that 44 percent of the sales representatives having a management position are women. It follows (by an extension of the rule of complements) that 56 percent of the sales representatives having a management position are men. That is, $P(M \mid MGT) = .56$. Using the fact that $P(MGT) = .25$, the general multiplication rule implies that

$$P(MGT \cap M) = P(MGT)P(M \mid MGT) = (.25)(.56) = .14$$

This says that 14 percent of the sales representatives have a management position and are men. Moreover,

$$P(MGT \mid M) = \frac{P(MGT \cap M)}{P(M)} = \frac{.14}{.48} = .2917$$

This says that 29.17 percent of the male sales representatives have a management position.

We have seen that $P(MGT) = .25$, while $P(MGT \mid W) = .2115$. Because $P(MGT \mid W)$ is less than $P(MGT)$, the probability that a randomly selected sales representative will have a management position is smaller if we know that the sales representative is a woman than it is if we have no knowledge of the sales representative's gender. Another way to see this is to recall that $P(MGT \mid M) = .2917$. Because $P(MGT \mid W) = .2115$ is less than $P(MGT \mid M) = .2917$, the probability that a randomly selected sales representative will have a management position is smaller if the sales representative is a woman than it is if the sales representative is a man.

Independence In Example 4.10 the probability of the event *MGT* is influenced by whether the event *W* occurs. In such a case, we say that the events *MGT* and *W* are **dependent.** If $P(MGT \mid W)$ were equal to $P(MGT)$, then the probability of the event *MGT* would not be influenced by whether *W* occurs. In this case we would say that the events *MGT* and *W* are **independent.** This leads to the following definition:

Independent Events

Two events *A* and *B* are **independent** if and only if

1 $P(A \mid B) = P(A)$ or, equivalently,

2 $P(B \mid A) = P(B)$

Here we assume that $P(A)$ and $P(B)$ are greater than 0.

EXAMPLE 4.11 Gender Issues at a Pharmaceutical Company

Recall that 52 percent of the pharmaceutical company's sales representatives are women. If 52 percent of the sales representatives having a management position were also women, then $P(W \mid MGT)$ would equal $P(W) = .52$. Moreover, recalling that $P(MGT) = .25$, it would follow that

$$P(MGT \mid W) = \frac{P(MGT \cap W)}{P(W)} = \frac{P(MGT)P(W \mid MGT)}{P(W)} = \frac{P(MGT)(.52)}{.52} = P(MGT)$$

That is, 25 percent of the female sales representatives—as well as 25 percent of all of the sales representatives—would have a management position. Of course, this independence is only hypothetical. The actual pharmaceutical company data led us to conclude that *MGT* and *W* are dependent. Specifically, because $P(MGT \mid W) = .2115$ is less than $P(MGT) = .25$ and $P(MGT \mid M) = .2917$, we conclude that women are less likely to have a management position at the pharmaceutical company. Looking at this another way, note that the ratio of $P(MGT \mid M) = .2917$ to $P(MGT \mid W) = .2115$ is $.2917/.2115 = 1.3792$. This says that **the probability that a randomly selected sales representative will have a management position is 37.92 percent higher if the sales representative is a man than it is if the sales representative is a woman.** Moreover, this conclusion describes the actual employment conditions that existed at Novartis Pharmaceutical Company from 2002 to 2007.[3] In the largest gender discrimination case ever to go to trial, Sanford, Wittels, and Heisler LLP used data implying the conclusion above—along with evidence of salary inequities and women being subjected to a hostile and sexist work environment—to successfully represent a class of 5,600 female sales representatives against Novartis. On May 19, 2010, a federal jury awarded $250 million to the class. The award was the largest ever in an employment discrimination case, and in November 2010 a final settlement agreement between Novartis and its female sales representatives was reached.

If the occurrences of the events *A* and *B* have nothing to do with each other, then we know that *A* and *B* are independent events. This implies that $P(A \mid B)$ equals $P(A)$ and that $P(B \mid A)$ equals $P(B)$. Recall that the general multiplication rule tells us that, for any two events *A* and *B*, we can say that $P(A \cap B) = P(A)P(B \mid A)$. Therefore, if $P(B \mid A)$ equals $P(B)$, it follows that $P(A \cap B) = P(A)P(B)$.

[3]Source: http://www.bononilawgroup.com/blog/2010/07/women-win-a-bias-suit-against-novartis.shtml

This equation is called the **multiplication rule for independent events.** To summarize:

The Multiplication Rule for Two Independent Events

If *A* and *B* are **independent events,** then

$$P(A \cap B) = P(A)P(B)$$

As a simple example, let *C* denote the event that your favorite college football team wins its first game next season, and let *P* denote the event that your favorite professional football team wins its first game next season. Suppose you believe that $P(C) = .6$ and $P(P) = .6$. Then, because the outcomes of a college football game and a professional football game would probably have nothing to do with each other, it is reasonable to assume that *C* and *P* are independent events. It follows that

$$P(C \cap P) = P(C)P(P) = (.6)(.6) = .36$$

This probability might seem surprisingly low. That is, because you believe that each of your teams has a 60 percent chance of winning, you might feel reasonably confident that both your college and professional teams will win their first game. Yet the chance of this happening is really only .36!

Next, consider a group of events $A_1, A_2, \ldots, A_N$. Intuitively, the events $A_1, A_2, \ldots, A_N$ are independent if the occurrences of these events have nothing to do with each other. Denoting the probability that all of these events will simultaneously occur as $P(A_1 \cap A_2 \cap \cdots \cap A_N)$, we have the following:

The Multiplication Rule for *N* Independent Events

If $A_1, A_2, \ldots, A_N$ are independent events, then

$$P(A_1 \cap A_2 \cap \cdots \cap A_N) = P(A_1)P(A_2) \cdots P(A_N)$$

EXAMPLE 4.12 An Application of the Independence Rule: Customer Service

This example is based on a real situation encountered by a major producer and marketer of consumer products. The company assessed the service it provides by surveying the attitudes of its customers regarding 10 different aspects of customer service—order filled correctly, billing amount on invoice correct, delivery made on time, and so forth. When the survey results were analyzed, the company was dismayed to learn that only 59 percent of the survey participants indicated that they were satisfied with all 10 aspects of the company's service. Upon investigation, each of the 10 departments responsible for the aspects of service considered in the study insisted that it satisfied its customers 95 percent of the time. That is, each department claimed that its error rate was only 5 percent. Company executives were confused and felt that there was a substantial discrepancy between the survey results and the claims of the departments providing the services. However, a company statistician pointed out that there was no discrepancy. To understand this, consider randomly selecting a customer from among the survey participants, and define 10 events (corresponding to the 10 aspects of service studied):

$A_1 \equiv$ the customer is satisfied that the order is filled correctly (aspect 1).

$A_2 \equiv$ the customer is satisfied that the billing amount on the invoice is correct (aspect 2).

$\vdots$

$A_{10} \equiv$ the customer is satisfied that the delivery is made on time (aspect 10).

Also, define the event

$S \equiv$ the customer is satisfied with all 10 aspects of customer service.

Because 10 different departments are responsible for the 10 aspects of service being studied, it is reasonable to assume that all 10 aspects of service are independent of each other. For instance, billing amounts would be independent of delivery times. Therefore, $A_1, A_2, \ldots, A_{10}$ are independent events, and

$$P(S) = P(A_1 \cap A_2 \cap \cdots \cap A_{10})$$
$$= P(A_1)P(A_2) \cdots P(A_{10})$$

If, as the departments claim, each department satisfies its customers 95 percent of the time, then the probability that the customer is satisfied with all 10 aspects is

$$P(S) = (.95)(.95) \cdots (.95) = (.95)^{10} = .5987$$

This result is almost identical to the 59 percent satisfaction rate reported by the survey participants.

If the company wants to increase the percentage of its customers who are satisfied with all 10 aspects of service, it must improve the quality of service provided by the 10 departments. For example, to satisfy 95 percent of its customers with all 10 aspects of service, the company must require each department to raise the fraction of the time it satisfies its customers to x, where x is such that $(x)^{10} = .95$. It follows that

$$x = (.95)^{\frac{1}{10}} = .9949$$

and that each department must satisfy its customers 99.49 percent of the time (rather than the current 95 percent of the time).

Exercises for Section 4.4

CONCEPTS

connect

4.16 Give an example of a conditional probability that would be of interest to you.

4.17 Explain what it means for two events to be independent.

METHODS AND APPLICATIONS

4.18 The following contingency table summarizes the number of students at a college who have a Mastercard and/or a Visa credit card.

	Have Visa	Do Not Have Visa	Total
Have Mastercard	1,000	1,500	2,500
Do Not Have Mastercard	3,000	4,500	7,500
Total	4,000	6,000	10,000

    a   Find the proportion of Mastercard holders who have VISA cards. Interpret and write this proportion as a conditional probability.

    b   Find the proportion of VISA cardholders who have Mastercards. Interpret and write this proportion as a conditional probability.

    c   Are the events *having a Mastercard* and *having a VISA* independent? Justify your answer.

4.19 Each month a brokerage house studies various companies and rates each company's stock as being either "low risk" or "moderate to high risk." In a recent report, the brokerage house summarized its findings about 15 aerospace companies and 25 food retailers in the following table:

Company Type	Low Risk	Moderate to High Risk
Aerospace company	6	9
Food retailer	15	10

If we randomly select one of the total of 40 companies, find

a   The probability that the company's stock is moderate to high risk given that the firm is an aerospace company.

b   The probability that the company's stock is moderate to high risk given that the firm is a food retailer.

c   Determine if the events *the firm is a food retailer* and *the firm's stock is low risk* are independent. Explain.

4.20   John and Jane are married. The probability that John watches a certain television show is .4. The probability that Jane watches the show is .5. The probability that John watches the show, given that Jane does, is .7.

a   Find the probability that both John and Jane watch the show.

b   Find the probability that Jane watches the show, given that John does.

c   Do John and Jane watch the show independently of each other? Justify your answer.

4.21   In Exercise 4.20, find the probability that either John or Jane watches the show.

4.22   In the July 29, 2001 issue of the *Journal News* (Hamilton, Ohio), Lynn Elber of the Associated Press reported that "while 40 percent of American families own a television set with a V-chip installed to block designated programs with sex and violence, only 17 percent of those parents use the device."[4]

a   Use the report's results to find an estimate of the probability that a randomly selected American family has used a V-chip to block programs containing sex and violence.

b   According to the report, more than 50 percent of parents have used the TV rating system (TV-14, etc.) to control their children's TV viewing. How does this compare to the percentage using the V-chip?

4.23   According to the Associated Press report (in Exercise 4.22), 47 percent of parents who have purchased TV sets after V-chips became standard equipment in January 2000 are aware that their sets have V-chips, and of those who are aware of the option, 36 percent have programmed their V-chips. Using these results, find an estimate of the probability that a randomly selected parent who has bought a TV set since January 2000 has programmed the V-chip.

4.24   Fifteen percent of the employees in a company have managerial positions, and 25 percent of the employees in the company have MBA degrees. Also, 60 percent of the managers have MBA degrees. Using the probability formulas,

a   Find the proportion of employees who are managers and have MBA degrees.

b   Find the proportion of MBAs who are managers.

c   Are the events *being a manager* and *having an MBA* independent? Justify your answer.

4.25   In Exercise 4.24, find the proportion of employees who either have MBAs or are managers.

4.26   Consider Exercise 4.14 (page 167). Using the results in Table 4.2 (page 167), estimate the probability that a randomly selected 21- to 49-year-old consumer would

a   Give the phrase a rating of 4 or 5 given that the consumer is male; give the phrase a rating of 4 or 5 given that the consumer is female. Based on these results, is the appeal of the phrase among males much different from the appeal of the phrase among females? Explain.

b   Give the phrase a rating of 4 or 5, given that the consumer is in the 21–24 age group; given that the consumer is in the 25–34 age group; given that the consumer is in the 35–49 age group. Based on these results, which age group finds the phrase most appealing? Least appealing?

4.27   In a survey of 100 insurance claims, 40 are fire claims (*FIRE*), 16 of which are fraudulent (*FRAUD*). Also, there are a total of 40 fraudulent claims.

a   Construct a contingency table summarizing the claims data. Use the pairs of events *FIRE* and $\overline{FIRE}$, *FRAUD* and $\overline{FRAUD}$.

b   What proportion of the fire claims are fraudulent?

c   Are the events *a claim is fraudulent* and *a claim is a fire claim* independent? Use your probability of part *b* to prove your answer.

4.28   Recall from Exercise 4.3 (page 160) that two randomly selected customers are each asked to take a blind taste test and then to state which of three diet colas (marked as *A*, *B*, or *C*) he or she prefers. Suppose that cola *A*'s distributor claims that 80 percent of all people prefer cola *A* and that only 10 percent prefer each of colas *B* and *C*.

a   Assuming that the distributor's claim is true and that the two taste test participants make independent cola preference decisions, find the probability of each sample space outcome.

b   Find the probability that neither taste test participant will prefer cola *A*.

c   If, when the taste test is carried out, neither participant prefers cola *A*, use the probability you computed in part *b* to decide whether the distributor's claim seems valid. Explain.

---

[4]Source: *Journal News* (Hamilton, Ohio), July 29, 2001, p. C5.

4.29 A sprinkler system inside an office building has two types of activation devices, $D1$ and $D2$, which operate independently. When there is a fire, if either device operates correctly, the sprinkler system is turned on. In case of fire, the probability that $D1$ operates correctly is .95, and the probability that $D2$ operates correctly is .92. Find the probability that

a Both $D1$ and $D2$ will operate correctly.

b The sprinkler system will come on.

c The sprinkler system will fail.

4.30 A product is assembled using 10 different components, each of which must meet specifications for five different quality characteristics. Suppose that there is a .9973 probability that each individual specification will be met. Assuming that all 50 specifications are met independently, find the probability that the product meets all 50 specifications.

4.31 In Exercise 4.30, suppose that we wish to have a 99.73 percent chance that all 50 specifications will be met. If each specification will have the same chance of being met, how large must we make the probability of meeting each individual specification?

4.32 GENDER ISSUES AT A DISCOUNT CHAIN

Suppose that 65 percent of a discount chain's employees are women and 33 percent of the discount chain's employees having a management position are women. If 25 percent of the discount chain's employees have a management position, what percentage of the discount chain's female employees have a management position?

4.33 In a murder trial in Los Angeles, the prosecution claims that the defendant was cut on the left middle finger at the murder scene, but the defendant claims the cut occurred in Chicago, the day after the murders had been committed. Because the defendant is a sports celebrity, many people noticed him before he reached Chicago. Twenty-two people saw him casually, one person on the plane to Chicago carefully studied his hands looking for a championship ring, and another person stood with him as he signed autographs and drove him from the airport to the hotel. None of these 24 people saw a cut on the defendant's finger. If in fact he was not cut at all, it would be extremely unlikely that he left blood at the murder scene.

a Because a person casually meeting the defendant would not be looking for a cut, assume that the probability is .9 that such a person would not have seen the cut, even if it was there. Furthermore, assume that the person who carefully looked at the defendant's hands had a .5 probability of not seeing the cut even if it was there and that the person who drove the defendant from the airport to the hotel had a .6 probability of not seeing the cut even if it was there. Given these assumptions, and also assuming that all 24 people looked at the defendant independently of each other, what is the probability that none of the 24 people would have seen the cut, even if it was there?

b What is the probability that at least one of the 24 people would have seen the cut if it was there?

c Given the result of part *b* and given the fact that none of the 24 people saw a cut, do you think the defendant had a cut on his hand before he reached Chicago?

d How might we estimate what the assumed probabilities in *a* would actually be? (Note: This would not be easy.)

4.5 Bayes' Theorem (Optional) ● ● ●

LO4-5 Use Bayes' Theorem to update prior probabilities to posterior probabilities (Optional).

Sometimes we have an initial or **prior probability** that an event will occur. Then, based on new information, we revise the prior probability to what is called a **posterior probability.** This revision can be done by using a theorem called **Bayes' theorem.**

EXAMPLE 4.13 Should HIV Testing Be Mandatory?

HIV (Human Immunodeficiency Virus) is the virus that causes AIDS. Although many have proposed mandatory testing for HIV, statisticians have frequently spoken against such proposals. In this example, we use Bayes' theorem to see why.

Let HIV represent the event that a randomly selected American has the HIV virus, and let $\overline{HIV}$ represent the event that a randomly selected American does not have this virus. Because it is estimated that .6 percent of the American population have the HIV virus, $P(HIV) = .006$ and $P(\overline{HIV}) = .994$. A diagnostic test is used to attempt to detect whether a person has HIV. According to historical data, 99.9 percent of people with HIV receive a positive (*POS*) result when this test is administered, while 1 percent of people who do not have HIV receive a positive result. That is, $P(POS \mid HIV) = .999$ and $P(POS \mid \overline{HIV}) = .01$. If we administer the test to a randomly selected American (who may or may not have HIV) and the person receives a positive test result, what is the probability that the person actually has HIV? This probability is

$$P(HIV \mid POS) = \frac{P(HIV \cap POS)}{P(POS)}$$

The idea behind Bayes' theorem is that we can find $P(HIV \mid POS)$ by thinking as follows. A person will receive a positive result (POS) if the person receives a positive result and actually has HIV—that is, $(HIV \cap POS)$—or if the person receives a positive result and actually does not have HIV—that is, $(\overline{HIV} \cap POS)$. Therefore,

$$P(POS) = P(HIV \cap POS) + P(\overline{HIV} \cap POS)$$

This implies that

$$
\begin{aligned}
P(HIV \mid POS) &= \frac{P(HIV \cap POS)}{P(POS)} \\[2mm]
&= \frac{P(HIV \cap POS)}{P(HIV \cap POS) + P(\overline{HIV} \cap POS)} \\[2mm]
&= \frac{P(HIV)P(POS \mid HIV)}{P(HIV)P(POS \mid HIV) + P(\overline{HIV})P(POS \mid \overline{HIV})} \\[2mm]
&= \frac{.006(.999)}{.006(.999) + (.994)(.01)} = .38
\end{aligned}
$$

This probability says that, if all Americans were given a test for HIV, only 38 percent of the people who get a positive result would actually have HIV. That is, 62 percent of Americans identified as having HIV would actually be free of the virus! The reason for this rather surprising result is that, because so few people actually have HIV, the majority of people who test positive are people who are free of HIV and, therefore, erroneously test positive. This is why statisticians have spoken against proposals for mandatory HIV testing.

In the preceding example, there were two *states of nature*—HIV and $\overline{HIV}$—and two outcomes of the diagnostic test—POS and $\overline{POS}$. In general, there might be any number of states of nature and any number of experimental outcomes. This leads to a general statement of Bayes' theorem.

Bayes' Theorem

Let $S_1, S_2, \ldots, S_k$ be k mutually exclusive states of nature, one of which must be true, and suppose that $P(S_1)$, $P(S_2), \ldots, P(S_k)$ are the prior probabilities of these states of nature. Also, let E be a particular outcome of an experiment designed to help determine which state of nature is really true. Then, the **posterior probability** of a particular state of nature, say S_i, given the experimental outcome E, is

$$P(S_i \mid E) = \frac{P(S_i \cap E)}{P(E)} = \frac{P(S_i)P(E \mid S_i)}{P(E)}$$

where

$$P(E) = P(S_1 \cap E) + P(S_2 \cap E) + \cdots + P(S_k \cap E)$$

$$= P(S_1)P(E \mid S_1) + P(S_2)P(E \mid S_2) + \cdots + P(S_k)P(E \mid S_k)$$

Specifically, if there are two mutually exclusive states of nature, S_1 and S_2, one of which must be true, then

$$P(S_i \mid E) = \frac{P(S_i)P(E \mid S_i)}{P(S_1)P(E \mid S_1) + P(S_2)P(E \mid S_2)}$$

We have illustrated Bayes' theorem when there are two states of nature in Example 4.13. In the next example, we consider three states of nature.

EXAMPLE 4.14 The Oil Drilling Case: Site Selection

An oil company is attempting to decide whether to drill for oil on a particular site. There are three possible states of nature:

1 No oil (state of nature S_1, which we will denote as *none*)

2 Some oil (state of nature S_2, which we will denote as *some*)

3 Much oil (state of nature S_3, which we will denote as *much*)

Based on experience and knowledge concerning the site's geological characteristics, the oil company feels that the prior probabilities of these states of nature are as follows:

$$P(S_1 \equiv none) = .7 \qquad P(S_2 \equiv some) = .2 \qquad P(S_3 \equiv much) = .1$$

In order to obtain more information about the potential drilling site, the oil company can perform a seismic experiment, which has three readings—low, medium, and high. Moreover, information exists concerning the accuracy of the seismic experiment. The company's historical records tell us that

1 Of 100 past sites that were drilled and produced no oil, 4 sites gave a high reading. Therefore,

$$P(high \mid none) = \frac{4}{100} = .04$$

2 Of 400 past sites that were drilled and produced some oil, 8 sites gave a high reading. Therefore,

$$P(high \mid some) = \frac{8}{400} = .02$$

3 Of 300 past sites that were drilled and produced much oil, 288 sites gave a high reading. Therefore,

$$P(high \mid much) = \frac{288}{300} = .96$$

Intuitively, these conditional probabilities tell us that sites that produce no oil or some oil seldom give a high reading, while sites that produce much oil often give a high reading.

Now, suppose that when the company performs the seismic experiment on the site in question, it obtains a high reading. The previously given conditional probabilities suggest that, given this new information, the company might feel that the likelihood of much oil is higher than its prior probability $P(much) = .1$, and that the likelihoods of some oil and no oil are lower than the prior probabilities $P(some) = .2$ and $P(none) = .7$. To be more specific, we wish to *revise the prior probabilities* of no, some, and much oil to what we call *posterior probabilities*. We can do this by using Bayes' theorem as follows.

If we wish to compute $P(none \mid high)$, we first calculate

$$P(high) = P(none \cap high) + P(some \cap high) + P(much \cap high)$$
$$= P(none)P(high \mid none) + P(some)P(high \mid some) + P(much)P(high \mid much)$$
$$= (.7)(.04) + (.2)(.02) + (.1)(.96) = .128$$

Then Bayes' theorem says that

$$P(none \mid high) = \frac{P(none \cap high)}{P(high)} = \frac{P(none)P(high \mid none)}{P(high)} = \frac{.7(.04)}{.128} = .21875$$

Similarly, we can compute $P(some \mid high)$ and $P(much \mid high)$ as follows.

$$P(some \mid high) = \frac{P(some \cap high)}{P(high)} = \frac{P(some)P(high \mid some)}{P(high)} = \frac{.2(.02)}{.128} = .03125$$

$$P(much \mid high) = \frac{P(much \cap high)}{P(high)} = \frac{P(much)P(high \mid much)}{P(high)} = \frac{.1(.96)}{.128} = .75$$

These revised probabilities tell us that, given that the seismic experiment gives a high reading, the revised probabilities of no, some, and much oil are .21875, .03125, and .75, respectively.

Because the posterior probability of much oil is .75, we might conclude that we should drill on the oil site. However, this decision should also be based on economic considerations. The science of **decision theory** provides various criteria for making such a decision. An introduction to decision theory can be found in Chapter 19.

In this section we have only introduced Bayes' theorem. There is an entire subject called **Bayesian statistics,** which uses Bayes' theorem to update prior belief about a probability or population parameter to posterior belief. The use of Bayesian statistics is controversial in the case where the prior belief is largely based on subjective considerations, because many statisticians do not believe that we should base decisions on subjective considerations. Realistically, however, we all do this in our daily lives. For example, how each of us viewed the evidence in the O. J. Simpson murder trial had a great deal to do with our prior beliefs about both O. J. Simpson and the police.

Exercises for Section 4.5

CONCEPTS

4.34   What is a prior probability? What is a posterior probability?

4.35   Explain the purpose behind using Bayes' theorem.

METHODS AND APPLICATIONS

4.36   Suppose that A_1, A_2, and B are events where A_1 and A_2 are mutually exclusive and

$$P(A_1) = .8 \qquad P(B \mid A_1) = .1$$
$$P(A_2) = .2 \qquad P(B \mid A_2) = .3$$

Use this information to find $P(A_1 \mid B)$ and $P(A_2 \mid B)$.

4.37   Suppose that A_1, A_2, A_3, and B are events where A_1, A_2, and A_3 are mutually exclusive and

$$P(A_1) = .2 \qquad P(A_2) = .5 \qquad P(A_3) = .3$$
$$P(B \mid A_1) = .02 \qquad P(B \mid A_2) = .05 \qquad P(B \mid A_3) = .04$$

Use this information to find $P(A_1 \mid B)$, $P(A_2 \mid B)$ and $P(A_3 \mid B)$.

4.38   Again consider the diagnostic test for HIV discussed in Example 4.13 (page 175) and recall that $P(POS \mid HIV) = .999$ and $P(POS \mid \overline{HIV}) = .01$, where POS denotes a positive test result. Assuming that the percentage of people who have HIV is 1 percent, recalculate the probability that a randomly selected person has HIV, given that his or her test result is positive.

4.39   A department store is considering a new credit policy to try to reduce the number of customers defaulting on payments. A suggestion is made to discontinue credit to any customer who has been one week or more late with his/her payment at least twice. Past records show 95 percent of defaults were late at least twice. Also, 3 percent of all customers default, and 30 percent of those who have not defaulted have had at least two late payments.
   a   Find the probability that a customer with at least two late payments will default.
   b   Based on part *a*, should the policy be adopted? Explain.

4.40   A company administers an "aptitude test for managers" to aid in selecting new management trainees. Prior experience suggests that 60 percent of all applicants for management trainee positions would be successful if they were hired. Furthermore, past experience with the aptitude test indicates that 85 percent of applicants who turn out to be successful managers pass the test and 90 percent of applicants who do not turn out to be successful managers fail the test.
   a   If an applicant passes the "aptitude test for managers," what is the probability that the applicant will succeed in a management position?
   b   Based on your answer to part *a*, do you think that the "aptitude test for managers" is a valuable way to screen applicants for management trainee positions? Explain.

4.41   **THE OIL DRILLING CASE**

Recall that the prior probabilities of no oil (*none*), some oil (*some*), and much oil (*much*) are:

$$P(\text{none}) = .7 \qquad P(\text{some}) = .2 \qquad P(\text{much}) = .1$$

Of 100 past sites that were drilled and produced no oil, 5 gave a medium reading. Of the 400 past sites that were drilled and produced some oil, 376 gave a medium reading. Of the 300 past sites that were drilled and produced much oil, 9 gave a medium reading. This implies that the conditional probabilities of a medium reading (medium) given no oil, some oil, and much oil are:

$$P(\text{medium} \mid \text{none}) = \frac{5}{100} = .05$$

$$P(\text{medium} \mid \text{some}) = \frac{376}{400} = .94$$

$$P(\text{medium} \mid \text{much}) = \frac{9}{300} = .03$$

Calculate the posterior probabilities of no, some, and much oil, given a medium reading.

4.42 THE OIL DRILLING CASE

Of 100 past sites that were drilled and produced no oil, 91 gave a low reading. Of the 400 past sites that were drilled and produced some oil, 16 gave a low reading. Of the 300 past sites that were drilled and produced much oil, 3 gave a low reading. Calculate the posterior probabilities of no, some, and much oil, given a low reading.

4.43 Three data entry specialists enter requisitions into a computer. Specialist 1 processes 30 percent of the requisitions, specialist 2 processes 45 percent, and specialist 3 processes 25 percent. The proportions of incorrectly entered requisitions by data entry specialists 1, 2, and 3 are .03, .05, and .02, respectively. Suppose that a random requisition is found to have been incorrectly entered. What is the probability that it was processed by data entry specialist 1? By data entry specialist 2? By data entry specialist 3?

4.44 A truth serum given to a suspect is known to be 90 percent reliable when the person is guilty and 99 percent reliable when the person is innocent. In other words, 10 percent of the guilty are judged innocent by the serum and 1 percent of the innocent are judged guilty. If the suspect was selected from a group of suspects of which only 5 percent are guilty of having committed a crime, and the serum indicates that the suspect is guilty of having committed a crime, what is the probability that the suspect is innocent?

4.6 Counting Rules (Optional) ● ● ●

LO4-6 Use elementary counting rules to compute probabilities (Optional).

Consider the situation in Example 4.2 (page 156) in which a student takes a pop quiz that consists of three true–false questions. If we consider our experiment to be answering the three questions, each question can be answered correctly or incorrectly. We will let C denote answering a question correctly and I denote answering a question incorrectly. Figure 4.6 depicts a tree diagram of the sample space outcomes for the experiment. The diagram portrays the experiment as a three-step process—answering the first question (correctly or incorrectly, that is, C or I), answering the second question (correctly or incorrectly, that is, C or I), and answering the third question (correctly or incorrectly, that is, C or I). The tree diagram has eight different branches, and the eight distinct sample space outcomes are listed at the ends of the branches.

In general, a rule that is helpful in determining the number of experimental outcomes in a multiple-step experiment is as follows:

A Counting Rule for Multiple-Step Experiments

If an experiment can be described as a sequence of k steps in which there are n_1 possible outcomes on the first step, n_2 possible outcomes on the second step, and so on, then the total number of experimental outcomes is given by $(n_1)(n_2) \cdots (n_k)$.

For example, the pop quiz example consists of three steps in which there are $n_1 = 2$ possible outcomes on the first step, $n_2 = 2$ possible outcomes on the second step, and $n_3 = 2$ possible outcomes on the third step. Therefore, the total number of experimental outcomes is $(n_1)(n_2)(n_3) = (2)(2)(2) = 8$, as is shown in Figure 4.6. Now suppose the student takes a pop quiz consisting of

FIGURE 4.6   **A Tree Diagram of Answering Three True–False Questions**

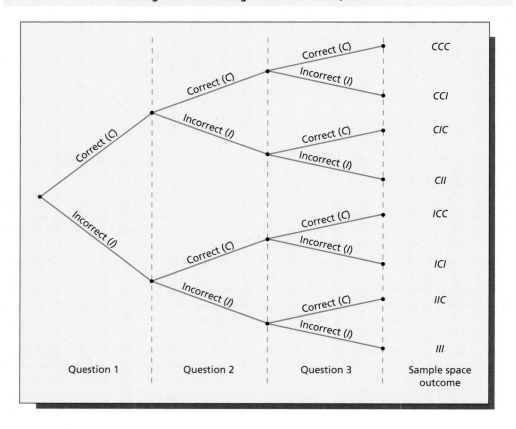

five true–false questions. Then, there are $(n_1)(n_2)(n_3)(n_4)(n_5) = (2)(2)(2)(2)(2) = 32$ experimental outcomes. If the student is totally unprepared for the quiz and has to blindly guess the answer to each question, the 32 experimental outcomes might be considered to be equally likely. Therefore, since only one of these outcomes corresponds to all five questions being answered correctly, the probability that the student will answer all five questions correctly is 1/32.

As another example, suppose a bank has three branches; each branch has two departments, and each department has four employees. One employee is to be randomly selected to go to a convention. Because there are $(n_1)(n_2)(n_3) = (3)(2)(4) = 24$ employees, the probability that a particular one will be randomly selected is 1/24.

Next, consider the population of last year's percentage returns for six high-risk stocks. This population consists of the percentage returns −36, −15, 3, 15, 33, and 54 (which we have arranged in increasing order). Now consider randomly selecting without replacement a sample of $n = 3$ stock returns from the population of six stock returns. Below we list the 20 distinct samples of $n = 3$ returns that can be obtained:

Sample	n = 3 Returns in Sample	Sample	n = 3 Returns in Sample
1	−36, −15, 3	11	−15, 3, 15
2	−36, −15, 15	12	−15, 3, 33
3	−36, −15, 33	13	−15, 3, 54
4	−36, −15, 54	14	−15, 15, 33
5	−36, 3, 15	15	−15, 15, 54
6	−36, 3, 33	16	−15, 33, 54
7	−36, 3, 54	17	3, 15, 33
8	−36, 15, 33	18	3, 15, 54
9	−36, 15, 54	19	3, 33, 54
10	−36, 33, 54	20	15, 33, 54

Because each sample is specified only with respect to which returns are contained in the sample, and therefore not with respect to the different orders in which the returns can be randomly selected, each sample is called a **combination of $n = 3$ stock returns selected from $N = 6$ stock returns.** In general, the following result can be proven:

A Counting Rule for Combinations

The number of combinations of n items that can be selected from N items is

$$\binom{N}{n} = \frac{N!}{n!\,(N - n)!}$$

where

$$N! = N(N - 1)(N - 2) \cdots 1$$
$$n! = n(n - 1)(n - 2) \cdots 1$$

Note: 0! is defined to be 1.

For example, the number of combinations of $n = 3$ stock returns that can be selected from the six previously discussed stock returns is

$$\binom{6}{3} = \frac{6!}{3!(6 - 3)!} = \frac{6!}{3!\,3!} = \frac{6 \cdot 5 \cdot 4\,(3 \cdot 2 \cdot 1)}{(3 \cdot 2 \cdot 1)\,(3 \cdot 2 \cdot 1)} = 20$$

The 20 combinations are listed on the previous page. As another example, the Ohio lottery system uses the random selection of 6 numbers from a group of 47 numbers to determine each week's lottery winner. There are

$$\binom{47}{6} = \frac{47!}{6!\,(47 - 6)!} = \frac{47 \cdot 46 \cdot 45 \cdot 44 \cdot 43 \cdot 42\,(41!)}{6 \cdot 5 \cdot 4 \cdot 3 \cdot 2 \cdot 1\,(41!)} = 10{,}737{,}573$$

combinations of 6 numbers that can be selected from 47 numbers. Therefore, if you buy a lottery ticket and pick six numbers, the probability that this ticket will win the lottery is 1/10,737,573.

Exercises for Section 4.6

CONCEPTS

4.45   Explain why counting rules are useful.

4.46   Explain when it is appropriate to use the counting rule for multiple-step experiments.

4.47   Explain when it is appropriate to use the counting rule for combinations.

connect™

METHODS AND APPLICATIONS

4.48   A credit union has two branches; each branch has two departments, and each department has four employees. How many total people does the credit union employ? If you work for the credit union, and one employee is randomly selected to go to a convention, what is the probability that you will be chosen?

4.49   Construct a tree diagram (like Figure 4.6) for the situation described in Exercise 4.48.

4.50   How many combinations of two high-risk stocks could you randomly select from eight high-risk stocks? If you did this, what is the probability that you would obtain the two highest-returning stocks?

4.51   A pop quiz consists of three true–false questions and three multiple choice questions. Each multiple choice question has five possible answers. If a student blindly guesses the answer to every question, what is the probability that the student will correctly answer all six questions?

4.52   A company employs eight people and plans to select a group of three of these employees to receive advanced training. How many ways can the group of three employees be selected?

4.53   The company of Exercise 4.52 employs Mr. Withrow, Mr. Church, Ms. David, Ms. Henry, Mr. Fielding, Mr. Smithson, Ms. Penny, and Mr. Butler. If the three employees who will receive advanced training are selected at random, what is the probability that Mr. Church, Ms. Henry, and Mr. Butler will be selected for advanced training?

Chapter Summary

In this chapter we studied **probability.** We began by defining an **event** to be an experimental outcome that may or may not occur and by defining the **probability of an event** to be a number that measures the likelihood that the event will occur. We learned that a probability is often interpreted as a **long-run relative frequency,** and we saw that probabilities can be found by examining **sample spaces** and by using **probability rules.** We learned several important probability rules—**addition rules, multiplication rules,** and **the rule of complements.** We

also studied a special kind of probability called a **conditional probability,** which is the probability that one event will occur given that another event occurs, and we used probabilities to define **independent events.** We concluded this chapter by studying two optional topics. The first of these was **Bayes' theorem,** which can be used to update a **prior** probability to a **posterior** probability based on receiving new information. Second, we studied **counting rules** that are helpful when we wish to count sample space outcomes.

Glossary of Terms

Bayes' theorem: A theorem (formula) that is used to compute posterior probabilities by revising prior probabilities. (page 176)

Bayesian statistics: An area of statistics that uses Bayes' Theorem to update prior belief about a probability or population parameter to posterior belief. (page 178)

complement (of an event): If A is an event, the complement of A is the event that A will not occur. (page 161)

conditional probability: The probability that one event will occur given that we know that another event occurs. (page 168)

decision theory: An approach that helps decision makers to make intelligent choices. (page 178)

dependent events: When the probability of one event is influenced by whether another event occurs, the events are said to be dependent. (page 171)

event: A set of one or more sample space outcomes. (page 155)

experiment: A process of observation that has an uncertain outcome. (page 153)

independent events: When the probability of one event is not influenced by whether another event occurs, the events are said to be independent. (page 171)

mutually exclusive events: Events that have no sample space outcomes in common, and, therefore, cannot occur simultaneously. (page 164)

prior probability: The initial probability that an event will occur. (page 175)

probability (of an event): A number that measures the chance, or likelihood, that an event will occur when an experiment is carried out. (pages 153, 155)

posterior probability: A revised probability obtained by updating a prior probability after receiving new information. (page 175)

sample space: The set of all possible experimental outcomes (sample space outcomes). (page 153)

sample space outcome: A distinct outcome of an experiment (that is, an element in the sample space). (page 153)

subjective probability: A probability assessment that is based on experience, intuitive judgment, or expertise. (page 155)

Important Formulas

Probabilities when all sample space outcomes are equally likely: page 158

The rule of complements: page 161

The addition rule for two events: page 164

The addition rule for two mutually exclusive events: page 164

The addition rule for N mutually exclusive events: page 166

Conditional probability: pages 168, 169

The general multiplication rule: page 169

Independence: page 171

The multiplication rule for two independent events: page 172

The multiplication rule for N independent events: page 172

Bayes' theorem: page 176

Counting rule for multiple-step experiments: page 179

Counting rule for combinations: page 181

Supplementary Exercises

connect

Exercises 4.54 through 4.57 are based on the following situation: An investor holds two stocks, each of which can rise (R), remain unchanged (U), or decline (D) on any particular day.

4.54 Construct a tree diagram showing all possible combined movements for both stocks on a particular day (for instance, RR, RD, and so on, where the first letter denotes the movement of the first stock, and the second letter denotes the movement of the second stock).

4.55 If all outcomes are equally likely, find the probability that both stocks rise; that both stocks decline; that exactly one stock declines.

4.56 Find the probabilities you found in Exercise 4.55 by assuming that for each stock $P(R) = .6, P(U) = .1$, and $P(D) = .3$, and assuming that the two stocks move independently.

4.57 Assume that for the first stock (on a particular day)

$$P(R) = .4, \ P(U) = .2, \ P(D) = .4$$

and that for the second stock (on a particular day)

$$P(R) = .8, \ P(U) = .1, \ P(D) = .1$$

Assuming that these stocks move independently, find the probability that both stocks decline; the probability that exactly one stock rises; the probability that exactly one stock is unchanged; the probability that both stocks rise.

The Bureau of Labor Statistics reports on a variety of employment statistics. "College Enrollment and Work Activity of 2004 High School Graduates" provides information on high school graduates by gender, by race, and by labor force participation as of October 2004.[5] (All numbers are in thousands.) The following two tables provide sample information on the "Labor force status of persons 16 to 24 years old by educational attainment and gender, October 2004." Using the information contained in the tables, do Exercises 4.58 through 4.62. **DS** LabForce

Women, Age 16 to 24	Civilian Labor Force Employed	Civilian Labor Force Unemployed	Not in Labor Force	Row Total	Men, Age 16 to 24	Civilian Labor Force Employed	Civilian Labor Force Unemployed	Not in Labor Force	Row Total
< High School	662	205	759	1,626	< High School	1,334	334	472	2,140
HS degree	2,050	334	881	3,265	HS degree	3,110	429	438	3,977
Some college	1,352	126	321	1,799	Some college	1,425	106	126	1,657
Bachelors degree or more	921	55	105	1,081	Bachelors degree or more	708	37	38	783
Column Total	4,985	720	2,066	7,771	Column Total	6,577	906	1,074	8,557

4.58 Find an estimate of the probability that a randomly selected female aged 16 to 24 is in the civilian labor force, if she has a high school degree. **DS** LabForce

4.59 Find an estimate of the probability that a randomly selected female aged 16 to 24 is in the civilian labor force, if she has a bachelors degree or more. **DS** LabForce

4.60 Find an estimate of the probability that a randomly selected female aged 16 to 24 is employed, if she is in the civilian labor force and has a high school degree. **DS** LabForce

4.61 Find an estimate of the probability that a randomly selected female aged 16 to 24 is employed, if she is in the civilian labor force and has a bachelor's degree or more. **DS** LabForce

4.62 Repeat Exercises 4.58 through 4.61 for a randomly selected male aged 16 to 24. In general, do the tables imply that labor force status and employment status depend upon educational attainment? Explain your answer. **DS** LabForce

Suppose that in a survey of 1,000 U.S. residents, 721 residents believed that the amount of violent television programming had increased over the past 10 years, 454 residents believed that the overall quality of television programming had decreased over the past 10 years, and 362 residents believed both. Use this information to do Exercises 4.63 through 4.69.

4.63 What proportion of the 1,000 U.S. residents believed that the amount of violent programming had increased over the past 10 years?

---

[5]Source: *College Enrollment and Work Activity of 2004 High School Graduates*, Table 2, "Labor force status of persons 16 to 24 years old by school enrollment, educational attainment, sex, race, and Hispanic or Latino ethnicity, October 2004," www.bls.gov.

4.64   What proportion of the 1,000 U.S. residents believed that the overall quality of programming had decreased over the past 10 years?

4.65   What proportion of the 1,000 U.S. residents believed that both the amount of violent programming had increased and the overall quality of programming had decreased over the past 10 years?

4.66   What proportion of the 1,000 U.S. residents believed that either the amount of violent programming had increased or the overall quality of programming had decreased over the past 10 years?

4.67   What proportion of the U.S. residents who believed that the amount of violent programming had increased believed that the overall quality of programming had decreased?

4.68   What proportion of the U.S. residents who believed that the overall quality of programming had decreased believed that the amount of violent programming had increased?

4.69   What sort of dependence seems to exist between whether U.S. residents believed that the amount of violent programming had increased and whether U.S. residents believed that the overall quality of programming had decreased? Explain your answer.

4.70   Enterprise Industries has been running a television advertisement for Fresh liquid laundry detergent. When a survey was conducted, .21 of the individuals surveyed had purchased Fresh, .41 of the individuals surveyed had recalled seeing the advertisement, and .13 of the individuals surveyed had purchased Fresh and recalled seeing the advertisement.
  a   What proportion of the individuals surveyed who recalled seeing the advertisement had purchased Fresh?
  b   Based on your answer to part *a*, does the advertisement seem to have been effective? Explain.

4.71   A company employs 400 salespeople. Of these, 83 received a bonus last year, 100 attended a special sales training program at the beginning of last year, and 42 both attended the special sales training program and received a bonus. (Note: the bonus was based totally on sales performance.)
  a   What proportion of the 400 salespeople received a bonus last year?
  b   What proportion of the 400 salespeople attended the special sales training program at the beginning of last year?
  c   What proportion of the 400 salespeople both attended the special sales training program and received a bonus?
  d   What proportion of the salespeople who attended the special sales training program received a bonus?
  e   Based on your answers to parts *a* and *d*, does the special sales training program seem to have been effective? Explain your answer.

4.72   On any given day, the probability that the Ohio River at Cincinnati is polluted by a carbon tetrachloride spill is .10. Each day, a test is conducted to determine whether the river is polluted by carbon tetrachloride. This test has proved correct 80 percent of the time. Suppose that on a particular day the test indicates carbon tetrachloride pollution. What is the probability that such pollution actually exists?

4.73   In the book *Making Hard Decisions: An Introduction to Decision Analysis,* Robert T. Clemen presents an example in which he discusses the 1982 John Hinckley trial. In describing the case, Clemen says:

   In 1982 John Hinckley was on trial, accused of having attempted to kill President Reagan. During Hinckley's trial, Dr. Daniel R. Weinberger told the court that when individuals diagnosed as schizophrenics were given computerized axial tomography (CAT) scans, the scans showed brain atrophy in 30% of the cases compared with only 2% of the scans done on normal people. Hinckley's defense attorney wanted to introduce as evidence Hinckley's CAT scan, which showed brain atrophy. The defense argued that the presence of atrophy strengthened the case that Hinckley suffered from mental illness.

  a   Approximately 1.5 percent of the people in the United States suffer from schizophrenia. If we consider the prior probability of schizophrenia to be .015, use the information given to find the probability that a person has schizophrenia given that a person's CAT scan shows brain atrophy.
  b   John Hinckley's CAT scan showed brain atrophy. Discuss whether your answer to part *a* helps or hurts the case that Hinckley suffered from mental illness.
  c   It can be argued that .015 is not a reasonable prior probability of schizophrenia. This is because .015 is the probability that a randomly selected U.S. citizen has schizophrenia. However, John Hinckley was not a randomly selected U.S. citizen. Rather, he was accused of attempting to assassinate the president. Therefore, it might be reasonable to assess a higher prior probability of schizophrenia. Suppose you are a juror who believes there is only a 10 percent chance that Hinckley suffers from schizophrenia. Using .10 as the prior probability of schizophrenia,

find the probability that a person has schizophrenia given that a person's CAT scan shows brain atrophy.

d If you are a juror with a prior probability of .10 that John Hinckley suffers from schizophrenia and given your answer to part *c*, does the fact that Hinckley's CAT scan showed brain atrophy help the case that Hinckley suffered from mental illness?

e If you are a juror with a prior probability of .25 that Hinckley suffers from schizophrenia, find the probability of schizophrenia given that Hinckley's CAT scan showed brain atrophy. In this situation, how strong is the case that Hinckley suffered from mental illness?

4.74 Below we give two contingency tables of data from reports submitted by airlines to the U.S. Department of Transportation. The data concern the numbers of on-time and delayed flights for Alaska Airlines and America West Airlines at five major airports. 📀 AirDelays

Alaska Airlines	On Time	Delayed	Total
Los Angeles	497	62	559
Phoenix	221	12	233
San Diego	212	20	232
San Francisco	503	102	605
Seattle	1,841	305	2,146
Total	3,274	501	3,775

America West	On Time	Delayed	Total
Los Angeles	694	117	811
Phoenix	4,840	415	5,255
San Diego	383	65	448
San Francisco	320	129	449
Seattle	201	61	262
Total	6,438	787	7,225

Source: A. Barnett, "How Numbers Can Trick You," *Technology Review,* October 1994, pp. 38–45. Copyright © 1994 MIT Technology Review. Reprinted by permission of the publisher via Copyright Clearance Center.

a What percentage of all Alaska Airlines flights were delayed? That is, use the data to estimate the probability that an Alaska Airlines flight will be delayed. Do the same for America West Airlines. Which airline does best overall?

b For Alaska Airlines, find the percentage of delayed flights at each airport. That is, use the data to estimate each of the probabilities $P(\text{delayed} \mid \text{Los Angeles})$, $P(\text{delayed} \mid \text{Phoenix})$, and so on. Then do the same for America West Airlines. Which airline does best at each individual airport?

c We find that America West Airlines does worse at every airport, yet America West does best overall. This seems impossible, but it is true! By looking carefully at the data, explain how this can happen. Hint: Consider the weather in Phoenix and Seattle. (This exercise is an example of what is called *Simpson's paradox.*)

4.75 Internet Exercise

What is the age, gender, and ethnic composition of U.S. college students? As background for its 1995 study of college students and their risk behaviors, the Centers for Disease Control and Prevention collected selected demographic data—age, gender, and ethnicity—about college students. A report on the 1995 National Health Risk Behavior Survey can be found at the CDC website by going directly to http://www.cdc.gov/mmwr/preview/mmwrhtml/00049859.htm. This report includes a large number of tables, the first of which summarizes the demographic information for the sample of $n = 4609$ college students. An excerpt from Table 1 is given on the right.

Using conditional probabilities, discuss (a) the dependence between age and gender and (b) the dependence between age and ethnicity for U.S. college students. 📀 CDCData

```
TABLE 1. Demographic Characteristics of
Undergraduate College Students Aged >=18
Years, by Age Group — United States, National
College Health Risk Behavior Survey, 1995
==============================================
                        Age Group (%)
                       ---------------------
Category      Total (%)  18-24 Years  >=25 Years
----------------------------------------------
Total           --         63.6         36.4

Sex
  Female        55.5       52.0         61.8
  Male          44.5       48.0         38.2
Race/ethnicity
  White*        72.8       70.9         76.1
  Black*        10.3       10.5          9.6
  Hispanic       7.1        6.9          7.4
  Other          9.9       11.7          6.9
```

CHAPTER 5

Discrete Random Variables

Learning Objectives

After mastering the material in this chapter, you will be able to:

LO5-1 Explain the difference between a discrete random variable and a continuous random variable.

LO5-2 Find a discrete probability distribution and compute its mean and standard deviation.

LO5-3 Use the binomial distribution to compute probabilities.

LO5-4 Use the Poisson distribution to compute probabilities (Optional).

LO5-5 Use the hypergeometric distribution to compute probabilities (Optional).

LO5-6 Compute and understand the covariance between two random variables (Optional).

Chapter Outline

e often use what we call **random variables** to describe the important aspects of the outcomes of experiments. In this chapter we introduce two important types of random variables—**discrete random variables** and **continuous random variables**—and learn how to find probabilities concerning discrete random variables. As one application, we will begin to see how to use probabilities concerning discrete random variables to make statistical inferences about populations.

5.1 Two Types of Random Variables ● ● ●

LO5-1 Explain the difference between a discrete random variable and a continuous random variable.

We begin with the definition of a random variable:

A **random variable** is a variable that assumes numerical values that are determined by the outcome of an experiment, where one and only one numerical value is assigned to each experimental outcome.

Before an experiment is carried out, its outcome is uncertain. It follows that, because a random variable assigns a number to each experimental outcome, a random variable can be thought of as *representing an uncertain numerical outcome*.

To illustrate the idea of a random variable, suppose that Sound City sells and installs car stereo systems. One of Sound City's most popular stereo systems is the TrueSound-XL, a top-of-the-line satellite car radio. Consider (the experiment of) selling the TrueSound-XL radio at the Sound City store during a particular week. If we let x denote the number of radios sold during the week, then x is a random variable. That is, looked at before the week, the number of radios x that will be sold is uncertain, and, therefore, x is a random variable.

Notice that x, the number of TrueSound-XL radios sold in a week, might be 0 or 1 or 2 or 3, and so forth. In general, when the possible values of a random variable can be counted or listed, we say that the random variable is a **discrete random variable.** That is, either a discrete random variable may assume a finite number of possible values or the possible values may take the form of a *countable* sequence or list such as 0, 1, 2, 3, 4, . . . (a *countably infinite* list).

Some other examples of discrete random variables are

1 The number, x, of the next three customers entering a store who will make a purchase. Here x could be 0, 1, 2, or 3.

2 The number, x, of four patients taking a new antibiotic who experience gastrointestinal distress as a side effect. Here x could be 0, 1, 2, 3, or 4.

3 The number, x, of television sets in a sample of 8 five-year-old television sets that have not needed a single repair. Here x could be any of the values 0, 1, 2, 3, 4, 5, 6, 7, or 8.

4 The number, x, of major fires in a large city in the next two months. Here x could be 0, 1, 2, 3, and so forth (there is no definite maximum number of fires).

5 The number, x, of dirt specks in a one-square-yard sheet of plastic wrap. Here x could be 0, 1, 2, 3, and so forth (there is no definite maximum number of dirt specks).

The values of the random variables described in examples 1, 2, and 3 are countable and finite. In contrast, the values of the random variables described in 4 and 5 are countable and infinite (or countably infinite lists). For example, in theory there is no limit to the number of major fires that could occur in a city in two months.

Not all random variables have values that are countable. When a random variable may assume any numerical value in one or more intervals on the real number line, then we say that the random variable is a **continuous random variable.**

EXAMPLE 5.1 The Car Mileage Case: A Continuous Random Variable C

Consider the car mileage situation that we have discussed in Chapters 1–3. The EPA combined city and highway mileage, x, of a randomly selected midsize car is a continuous random variable. This is because, although we have measured mileages to the nearest one-tenth of a mile per gallon, technically speaking, the potential mileages that might be obtained correspond (starting at, perhaps, 26 mpg) to an interval of numbers on the real line. We cannot count or list the numbers in such an interval because they are infinitesimally close together. That is, given any two numbers in an interval on the real line, there is always another number between them. To understand this, try listing the mileages starting with 26 mpg. Would the next mileage be 26.1 mpg? No, because we could obtain a mileage of 26.05 mpg. Would 26.05 mpg be the next mileage? No, because we could obtain a mileage of 26.025 mpg. We could continue this line of reasoning indefinitely. That is, whatever value we would try to list as the *next mileage,* there would always be another mileage between this *next mileage* and 26 mpg.

Some other examples of continuous random variables are

1 The temperature (in degrees Fahrenheit) of a cup of coffee served at a McDonald's restaurant.

2 The weight (in ounces) of strawberry preserves dispensed by an automatic filling machine into a 16-ounce jar.

3 The time (in minutes) that a customer in a store must wait to receive a credit card authorization.

4 The interest rate (in percent) charged for mortgage loans at a bank.

Exercises for Section 5.1

connect

CONCEPTS

5.1 Explain the concept of a random variable.

5.2 Explain how the values of a discrete random variable differ from the values of a continuous random variable.

5.3 Classify each of the following random variables as discrete or continuous:
a x = the number of girls born to a couple who will have three children.
b x = the number of defects found on an automobile at final inspection.
c x = the weight (in ounces) of the sandwich meat placed on a submarine sandwich.
d x = the number of incorrect lab procedures conducted at a hospital during a particular week.
e x = the number of customers served during a given day at a drive-through window.
f x = the time needed by a clerk to complete a task.
g x = the temperature of a pizza oven at a particular time.

LO5-2 Find a discrete probability distribution and compute its mean and standard deviation.

5.2 Discrete Probability Distributions ● ● ●

The value assumed by a discrete random variable depends on the outcome of an experiment. Because the outcome of the experiment will be uncertain, the value assumed by the random variable will also be uncertain. However, it is often useful to know the probabilities that are associated with the different values that the random variable can take on. That is, we often wish to know the random variable's **probability distribution.**

The **probability distribution** of a discrete random variable is a table, graph, or formula that gives the probability associated with each possible value that the random variable can assume.

We denote the probability distribution of the discrete random variable x as $p(x)$. As we will demonstrate in Section 5.3 (which discusses the *binomial distribution*), we can sometimes use the sample space of an experiment and probability rules to find the probability distribution of a random variable. In other situations we collect data that will allow us to estimate the probabilities in a probability distribution.

EXAMPLE 5.2 The Sound City Case: Selling TrueSound-XL Radios

Recall that Sound City sells the TrueSound-XL car radio, and define the random variable x to be the number of such radios sold in a particular week at Sound City. Also, suppose that Sound City has kept historical records of TrueSound-XL sales during the last 100 weeks. These records show

TABLE 5.1	An Estimate (Based on 100 Weeks of Historical Data) of the Probability Distribution of x, the Number of TrueSound-XL Radios Sold at Sound City in a Week

x, Number of Radios Sold	p(x), the Probability of x
0	$p(0) = P(x = 0) = 3/100 = .03$
1	$p(1) = P(x = 1) = 20/100 = .20$
2	$p(2) = P(x = 2) = 50/100 = .50$
3	$p(3) = P(x = 3) = 20/100 = .20$
4	$p(4) = P(x = 4) = 5/100 = .05$
5	$p(5) = P(x = 5) = 2/100 = .02$

FIGURE 5.1   A Graph of the Probability Distribution of x, the Number of TrueSound-XL Radios Sold at Sound City in a Week

3 weeks with no radios sold, 20 weeks with one radio sold, 50 weeks with two radios sold, 20 weeks with three radios sold, 5 weeks with four radios sold, and 2 weeks with five radios sold. Because the records show 3 of 100 weeks with no radios sold, we estimate that $p(0) = p(x = 0)$ is $3/100 = .03$. That is, we estimate that the probability of no radios being sold during a week is .03. Similarly, because the records show 20 of 100 weeks with one radio sold, we estimate that $p(1) = P(x = 1)$ is $20/100 = .20$. That is, we estimate that the probability of exactly one radio being sold during a week is .20. Continuing in this way for the other values of the random variable x, we can estimate $p(2) = P(x = 2)$, $p(3) = P(x = 3)$, $p(4) = P(x = 4)$, and $p(5) = P(x = 5)$. Table 5.1 gives the entire estimated probability distribution of the number of TrueSound-XL radios sold at Sound City during a week, and Figure 5.1 shows a graph of this distribution. Moreover, such a probability distribution helps us to more easily calculate probabilities about events related to a random variable. For example, the probability of at least two radios being sold at Sound City during a week [that is, $P(x \geq 2)$] is $p(2) + p(3) + p(4) + p(5) = .50 + .20 + .05 + .02 = .77$. This says that we estimate that in 77 percent of all weeks, at least two TrueSound-XL radios will be sold at Sound City.

Finally, note that using historical sales data to obtain the estimated probabilities in Table 5.1 is reasonable if the TrueSound-XL radio sales process is stable over time. This means that the number of radios sold weekly does not exhibit any long-term upward or downward trends and is not seasonal (that is, radio sales are not higher at one time of the year than at others).

In general, a discrete probability distribution $p(x)$ must satisfy two conditions:

Properties of a Discrete Probability Distribution $p(x)$

A **discrete probability distribution $p(x)$** must be such that

1 $p(x) \geq 0$ for each value of x

2 $\sum\limits_{\text{All }x} p(x) = 1$

The first of these conditions says that each probability in a probability distribution must be zero or positive. The second condition says that the probabilities in a probability distribution must sum to 1. Looking at the probability distribution illustrated in Table 5.1, we can see that these properties are satisfied.

Suppose that the experiment described by a random variable x is repeated an indefinitely large number of times. If the values of the random variable x observed on the repetitions are recorded, we would obtain the population of all possible observed values of the random variable x. This population has a mean, which we denote as μ_x and which we sometimes call the **expected value of x.** In order to calculate μ_x, we multiply each value of x by its probability $p(x)$ and then sum the resulting products over all possible values of x.

The Mean, or Expected Value, of a Discrete Random Variable

The **mean**, or **expected value**, of a discrete random variable x is

$$\mu_x = \sum_{\text{All } x} xp(x)$$

EXAMPLE 5.3 The Sound City Case: Selling TrueSound-XL Radios

Remember that Table 5.1 gives the probability distribution of x, the number of TrueSound-XL radios sold in a week at Sound City. Using this distribution, it follows that

$$\mu_x = \sum_{\text{All } x} xp(x)$$
$$= 0p(0) + 1p(1) + 2p(2) + 3p(3) + 4p(4) + 5p(5)$$
$$= 0(.03) + 1(.20) + 2(.50) + 3(.20) + 4(.05) + 5(.02)$$
$$= 2.1$$

To see that such a calculation gives the mean of all possible observed values of x, recall from Example 5.2 that the probability distribution in Table 5.1 was estimated from historical records of TrueSound-XL sales during the last 100 weeks. Also recall that these historical records tell us that during the last 100 weeks Sound City sold

1 Zero radios in 3 of the 100 weeks, for a total of $0(3) = 0$ radios
2 One radio in 20 of the 100 weeks, for a total of $1(20) = 20$ radios
3 Two radios in 50 of the 100 weeks, for a total of $2(50) = 100$ radios
4 Three radios in 20 of the 100 weeks, for a total of $3(20) = 60$ radios
5 Four radios in 5 of the 100 weeks, for a total of $4(5) = 20$ radios
6 Five radios in 2 of the 100 weeks, for a total of $5(2) = 10$ radios

In other words, Sound City sold a total of

$$0 + 20 + 100 + 60 + 20 + 10 = 210 \text{ radios}$$

in 100 weeks, or an average of $210/100 = 2.1$ radios per week. Now, the average

$$\frac{210}{100} = \frac{0 + 20 + 100 + 60 + 20 + 10}{100}$$

can be written as

$$\frac{0(3) + 1(20) + 2(50) + 3(20) + 4(5) + 5(2)}{100}$$

which can be rewritten as

$$0\left(\frac{3}{100}\right) + 1\left(\frac{20}{100}\right) + 2\left(\frac{50}{100}\right) + 3\left(\frac{20}{100}\right) + 4\left(\frac{5}{100}\right) + 5\left(\frac{2}{100}\right)$$
$$= 0(.03) + 1(.20) + 2(.50) + 3(.20) + 4(.05) + 5(.02)$$

which is $\mu_x = 2.1$. That is, if observed sales values occur with relative frequencies equal to those specified by the probability distribution in Table 5.1, then the average number of radios sold per week is equal to the expected value of x and is 2.1 radios.

Of course, if we observe radio sales for another 100 weeks, the relative frequencies of the observed sales values would not (unless we are very lucky) be exactly as specified by the estimated probabilities in Table 5.1. Rather, the observed relative frequencies would differ somewhat from the estimated probabilities in Table 5.1, and the average number of radios sold per week would not exactly equal $\mu_x = 2.1$ (although the average would likely be close). However, the point is this: If the probability distribution in Table 5.1 were the true probability distribution of weekly radio sales, and if we were to observe radio sales for an indefinitely large number of weeks, then we would observe sales values with relative frequencies that are exactly equal to those specified by the probabilities in Table 5.1. In this case, when we calculate the expected value of x to be $\mu_x = 2.1$, we are saying that *in the long run* (that is, over an indefinitely large number of weeks) Sound City would average selling 2.1 TrueSound-XL radios per week.

EXAMPLE 5.4 The Life Insurance Case: Setting a Policy Premium

An insurance company sells a $20,000 whole life insurance policy for an annual premium of $300. Actuarial tables show that a person who would be sold such a policy with this premium has a .001 probability of death during a year. Let x be a random variable representing the insurance company's profit made on one of these policies during a year. The probability distribution of x is

x, Profit	p(x), Probability of x
$300 (if the policyholder lives)	.999
$300 − $20,000 = −$19,700	.001
(a $19,700 loss if the policyholder dies)	

The expected value of x (expected profit per year) is

$$\mu_x = \$300(.999) + (-\$19,700)(.001)$$
$$= \$280$$

This says that if the insurance company sells a very large number of these policies, it will average a profit of $280 per policy per year. Because insurance companies actually do sell large numbers of policies, it is reasonable for these companies to make profitability decisions based on expected values.

Next, suppose that we wish to find the premium that the insurance company must charge for a $20,000 policy if the company wishes the average profit per policy per year to be greater than $0. If we let *prem* denote the premium the company will charge, then the probability distribution of the company's yearly profit x is

x, Profit	p(x), Probability of x
prem (if policyholder lives)	.999
prem − $20,000 (if policyholder dies)	.001

The expected value of x (expected profit per year) is

$$\mu_x = prem(.999) + (prem - 20,000)(.001)$$
$$= prem - 20$$

In order for this expected profit to be greater than zero, the premium must be greater than $20. If, as previously stated, the company charges $300 for such a policy, the $280 charged in excess of the needed $20 compensates the company for commissions paid to salespeople, administrative costs, dividends paid to investors, and other expenses.

In general, it is reasonable to base decisions on an expected value if we perform the experiment related to the decision (for example, if we sell the life insurance policy) many times. If we do not (for instance, if we perform the experiment only once), then it may not be a good idea to base decisions on the expected value. For example, it might not be wise for you—as an individual—to sell one person a $20,000 life insurance policy for a premium of $300. To see this, again consider the probability distribution of yearly profit:

x, Profit	p(x), Probability of x
$300 (if policyholder lives)	.999
$300 − $20,000 = −$19,700 (if policyholder dies)	.001

and recall that the expected profit per year is $280. However, because you are selling only one policy, you will not receive the $280. You will either gain $300 (with probability .999) or you will lose $19,700 (with probability .001). Although the decision is personal, and although the chance of losing $19,700 is very small, many people would not risk such a loss when the potential gain is only $300.

Just as the population of all possible observed values of a discrete random variable x has a mean μ_x, this population also has a variance σ_x^2 and a standard deviation σ_x. Recall that the variance of a population is the average of the squared deviations of the different population values from the population mean. To find σ_x^2, we calculate $(x - \mu_x)^2$ for each value of x, multiply $(x - \mu_x)^2$ by the probability $p(x)$, and sum the resulting products over all possible values of x.

The Variance and Standard Deviation of a Discrete Random Variable

The **variance** of a discrete random variable x is

$$\sigma_x^2 = \sum_{\text{All } x} (x - \mu_x)^2 p(x)$$

The **standard deviation** of x is the positive square root of the variance of x. That is,

$$\sigma_x = \sqrt{\sigma_x^2}$$

EXAMPLE 5.5 The Sound City Case: Selling TrueSound-XL Radios

Table 5.1 gives the probability distribution of x, the number of TrueSound-XL radios sold in a week at Sound City. Remembering that we have calculated μ_x (in Example 5.3) to be 2.1 radios, it follows that

$$\sigma_x^2 = \sum_{\text{All } x} (x - \mu_x)^2 p(x)$$

$$= (0 - 2.1)^2 p(0) + (1 - 2.1)^2 p(1) + (2 - 2.1)^2 p(2) + (3 - 2.1)^2 p(3)$$
$$+ (4 - 2.1)^2 p(4) + (5 - 2.1)^2 p(5)$$

$$= (4.41)(.03) + (1.21)(.20) + (.01)(.50) + (.81)(.20) + (3.61)(.05) + (8.41)(.02)$$

$$= .89$$

and that the standard deviation of x is $\sigma_x = \sqrt{.89} = .9434$ radios. To make one interpretation of a standard deviation of .9434 radios, suppose that Sound City sells another top-of-the-line satellite car radio called the ClearTone-400. If the ClearTone-400 also has mean weekly sales of 2.1 radios, and if the standard deviation of the ClearTone-400's weekly sales is 1.2254 radios, we would conclude that there is more variability in the weekly sales of the ClearTone-400 than in the weekly sales of the TrueSound-XL.

In Chapter 3 we considered the percentage of measurements in a population that are within (plus or minus) one, two, or three standard deviations of the mean of the population. Similarly, we can consider the probability that a random variable x will be within (plus or minus) one, two,

FIGURE 5.2   The Interval $[\mu_x \pm 2\sigma_x]$ for the Probability Distribution Describing
              TrueSound-XL Radio Sales (see Table 5.1)

or three standard deviations of the mean of the random variable. For example, consider the probability distribution in Table 5.1 of x, the number of TrueSound-XL radios sold in a week at Sound City. Also, recall that $\mu_x = 2.1$ and $\sigma_x = .9434$. If (for instance) we wish to find the probability that x will be within (plus or minus) two standard deviations of μ_x, then we need to find the probability that x will lie in the interval

$$[\mu_x \pm 2\sigma_x] = [2.1 \pm 2(.9434)]$$
$$= [.2132, \ 3.9868]$$

As illustrated in Figure 5.2, there are three values of x ($x = 1$, $x = 2$, and $x = 3$) that lie in the interval [.2132, 3.9868]. Therefore, the probability that x will lie in the interval [.2132, 3.9868] is the probability that x will equal 1 or 2 or 3, which is $p(1) + p(2) + p(3) = .20 + .50 + .20 = .90$. This says that in 90 percent of all weeks, the number of TrueSound-XL radios sold at Sound City will be within (plus or minus) two standard deviations of the mean weekly sales of the TrueSound-XL radio at Sound City.

In general, consider any random variable with mean μ_x and standard deviation σ_x. Then, Chebyshev's Theorem (see Chapter 3, page 116) tells us that, for any value of k that is greater than 1, the probability is at least $1 - 1/k^2$ that x will be within (plus or minus) k standard deviations of μ_x and thus will lie in the interval $[\mu_x \pm k\sigma_x]$. For example, setting k equal to 2, the probability is at least $1 - 1/2^2 = 1 - 1/4 = 3/4$ that x will lie in the interval $[\mu_x \pm 2\sigma_x]$. Setting k equal to 3, the probability is at least $1 - 1/3^2 = 1 - 1/9 = 8/9$ that x will lie in the interval $[\mu_x \pm 3\sigma_x]$. If (as in the Sound City situation) we have the probability distribution of x, we can calculate exact probabilities, and thus we do not need the approximate probabilities given by Chebyshev's Theorem. However, in some situations we know the values of μ_x and σ_x, but we do not have the probability distribution of x. In such situations the approximate Chebyshev's probabilities can be quite useful. For example, let x be a random variable representing the return on a particular investment, and suppose that an investment prospectus tells us that, based on historical data and current market trends, the investment return has a mean (or expected value) of $\mu_x = \$1,000$ and a standard deviation of $\sigma_x = \$100$. It then follows from Chebyshev's Theorem that the probability is at least 8/9 that the investment return will lie in the interval $[\mu_x \pm 3\sigma_x] = [1000 \pm 3(100)] = [700, 1300]$. That is, the probability is fairly high that the investment will have a minimum return of \$700 and a maximum return of \$1300.

In the next several sections, we will see that a probability distribution $p(x)$ is sometimes specified by using a formula. As a simple example of this, suppose that a random variable x is equally likely to assume any one of n possible values. In this case we say that x is described by the discrete **uniform distribution** and we specify $p(x)$ by using the formula $p(x) = 1/n$. For example, if we roll a fair die and x denotes the number of spots that show on the upward face of the die, then x is uniformly distributed and $p(x) = 1/6$ for $x = 1, 2, 3, 4, 5$, and 6. As another example, if historical sales records show that a Chevrolet dealership is equally likely to sell 0, 1, 2, or 3 Chevy Malibus in a given week, and if x denotes the number of Chevy Malibus that the dealership sells in a week, then x is uniformly distributed and $p(x) = 1/4$ for $x = 0, 1, 2$, and 3.

Exercises for Section 5.2

CONCEPTS

5.4 What is a discrete probability distribution? Explain in your own words.

5.5 What conditions must be satisfied by the probabilities in a discrete probability distribution? Explain what these conditions mean.

5.6 Describe how to compute the mean (or expected value) of a discrete random variable, and interpret what this quantity tells us about the observed values of the random variable.

5.7 Describe how to compute the standard deviation of a discrete random variable, and interpret what this quantity tells us about the observed values of the random variable.

METHODS AND APPLICATIONS

5.8 Recall from Example 5.5 that Sound City also sells the ClearTone-400 satellite car radio. For this radio, historical sales records over the last 100 weeks show 6 weeks with no radios sold, 30 weeks with one radio sold, 30 weeks with two radios sold, 20 weeks with three radios sold, 10 weeks with four radios sold, and 4 weeks with five radios sold. Estimate and write out the probability distribution of x, the number of ClearTone-400 radios sold at Sound City during a week.

5.9 Use the estimated probability distribution in Exercise 5.8 to calculate μ_x, σ_x^2, and σ_x.

5.10 Use your answers to Exercises 5.8 and 5.9 to calculate the probabilities that x will lie in the intervals $[\mu_x \pm \sigma_x]$, $[\mu_x \pm 2\sigma_x]$, and $[\mu_x \pm 3\sigma_x]$.

5.11 The following table summarizes investment outcomes and corresponding probabilities for a particular oil well:

x = the outcome in \$	$p(x)$
−\$40,000 (no oil)	.25
10,000 (some oil)	.7
70,000 (much oil)	.05

  a Graph $p(x)$; that is, graph the probability distribution of x.
  b Find the expected monetary outcome. Mark this value on your graph of part *a*. Then interpret this value.
  c Calculate the standard deviation of x.

5.12 In the book *Foundations of Financial Management* (7th ed.), Stanley B. Block and Geoffrey A. Hirt discuss risk measurement for investments. Block and Hirt present an investment with the possible outcomes and associated probabilities given in Table 5.2. The authors go on to say that the probabilities

  may be based on past experience, industry ratios and trends, interviews with company executives, and sophisticated simulation techniques. The probability values may be easy to determine for the introduction of a mechanical stamping process in which the manufacturer has 10 years of past data, but difficult to assess for a new product in a foreign market.   **DS** OutcomeDist

  a Use the probability distribution in Table 5.2 to calculate the expected value (mean) and the standard deviation of the investment outcomes. Interpret the expected value.

TABLE 5.2   **Probability Distribution of Outcomes for an Investment**   📀 OutcomeDist

Outcome	Probability of Outcome	Assumptions
$300	.2	Pessimistic
600	.6	Moderately successful
900	.2	Optimistic

Source: S. B. Block and G. A. Hirt, *Foundations of Financial Management,* 7th ed., p. 378. Copyright © 1994. Reprinted by permission of McGraw-Hill Companies, Inc.

b Block and Hirt interpret the standard deviation of the investment outcomes as follows: "Generally, the larger the standard deviation (or spread of outcomes), the greater is the risk." Explain why this makes sense. Use Chebyshev's Theorem to illustrate your point.

c Block and Hirt compare three investments having the following means and standard deviations of the investment outcomes:

Investment 1	Investment 2	Investment 3
$\mu = \$600$	$\mu = \$600$	$\mu = \$600$
$\sigma = \$20$	$\sigma = \$190$	$\sigma = \$300$

Which of these investments involves the most risk? The least risk? Explain why by using Chebyshev's Theorem to compute an interval for each investment that will contain at least 8/9 of the investment outcomes.

d Block and Hirt continue by comparing two more investments:

Investment A	Investment B
$\mu = \$6,000$	$\mu = \$600$
$\sigma = \$600$	$\sigma = \$190$

The authors explain that Investment A

> appears to have a high standard deviation, but not when related to the expected value of the distribution. A standard deviation of $600 on an investment with an expected value of $6,000 may indicate less risk than a standard deviation of $190 on an investment with an expected value of only $600.
>
> We can eliminate the size difficulty by developing a third measure, the **coefficient of variation** (V). This term calls for nothing more difficult than dividing the standard deviation of an investment by the expected value. Generally, the larger the coefficient of variation, the greater is the risk.

$$\text{Coefficient of variation } (V) = \frac{\sigma}{\mu}$$

Calculate the coefficient of variation for investments A and B. Which investment carries the greater risk?

e Calculate the coefficient of variation for investments 1, 2, and 3 in part c. Based on the coefficient of variation, which investment involves the most risk? The least risk? Do we obtain the same results as we did by comparing standard deviations (in part c)? Why?

5.13 An insurance company will insure a $50,000 diamond for its full value against theft at a premium of $400 per year. Suppose that the probability that the diamond will be stolen is .005, and let x denote the insurance company's profit.

a Set up the probability distribution of the random variable x.

b Calculate the insurance company's expected profit.

c Find the premium that the insurance company should charge if it wants its expected profit to be $1,000.

5.14 In the book *Foundations of Financial Management* (7th ed.), Stanley B. Block and Geoffrey A. Hirt discuss a semiconductor firm that is considering two choices: (1) expanding the production of semiconductors for sale to end users or (2) entering the highly competitive home computer market. The cost of both projects is $60 million, but the net present value of the cash flows from sales and the risks are different.

FIGURE 5.3　**A Tree Diagram of Two Project Choices**

	(1) Sales	(2) Probability	(3) Present Value of Cash Flow from Sales ($ millions)	(4) Initial Cost ($ millions)	(5) Net Present Value, NPV = (3) − (4) ($ millions)
Expand semiconductor capacity	High	.50	$100	$60	$40
	Moderate	.25	75	60	15
	Low	.25	40	60	(20)
A Start					
B					
Enter home computer market	High	.20	$200	$60	$140
	Moderate	.50	75	60	15
	Low	.30	25	60	(35)

Source: S. B. Block and G. A. Hirt, *Foundations of Financial Management,* 7th ed., p. 387. Copyright © 1994. Reprinted by permission of McGraw-Hill Companies, Inc.

Figure 5.3 gives a tree diagram of the project choices. The tree diagram gives a probability distribution of expected sales for each project. It also gives the present value of cash flows from sales and the net present value (NPV = present value of cash flow from sales minus initial cost) corresponding to each sales alternative. Note that figures in parentheses denote losses.

a　For each project choice, calculate the expected net present value.

b　For each project choice, calculate the variance and standard deviation of the net present value.

c　Calculate the coefficient of variation for each project choice. See Exercise 5.12*d* for a discussion of the coefficient of variation.

d　Which project has the higher expected net present value?

e　Which project carries the least risk? Explain.

f　In your opinion, which project should be undertaken? Justify your answer.

5.15　Five thousand raffle tickets are to be sold at $10 each to benefit a local community group. The prizes, the number of each prize to be given away, and the dollar value of winnings for each prize are as follows: ⒟Ⓢ Raffle

Prize	Number to Be Given Away	Dollar Value
Automobile	1	$20,000
Entertainment center	2	3,000 each
DVD recorder	5	400 each
Gift certificate	50	20 each

If you buy one ticket, calculate your expected winnings. (Form the probability distribution of x = your dollar winnings, and remember to subtract the cost of your ticket.)

5.16　A survey conducted by a song rating service finds that the percentages of listeners *familiar* with *Poker Face* by Lady Gaga who would give the song ratings of 5, 4, 3, 2, and 1 are, respectively, 43 percent, 21 percent, 22 percent, 7 percent, and 7 percent. Assign the numerical values 1, 2, 3, 4, and 5 to the (qualitative) ratings 1, 2, 3, 4, and 5 and find an estimate of the probability distribution of x = this song's rating by a randomly selected listener who is familiar with the song.

5.17　In Exercise 5.16,

a　Find the expected value of the estimated probability distribution.

b　Interpret the meaning of this expected value in terms of all possible *Poker Face* listeners.

5.3 The Binomial Distribution ● ● ●

In this section we discuss what is perhaps the most important discrete probability distribution—the binomial distribution. We begin with an example.

LO5-3 Use the binomial distribution to compute probabilities.

EXAMPLE 5.6 Purchases at a Discount Store

Suppose that historical sales records indicate that 40 percent of all customers who enter a discount department store make a purchase. What is the probability that two of the next three customers will make a purchase?

In order to find this probability, we first note that the experiment of observing three customers making a purchase decision has several distinguishing characteristics:

1   The experiment consists of three identical *trials;* each trial consists of a customer making a purchase decision.

2   Two outcomes are possible on each trial: the customer makes a purchase (which we call a *success* and denote as *S*), or the customer does not make a purchase (which we call a *failure* and denote as *F*).

3   Because 40 percent of all customers make a purchase, it is reasonable to assume that $P(S)$, the probability that a customer will make a purchase, is .4 and is constant for all customers. This implies that $P(F)$, the probability that a customer will not make a purchase, is .6 and is constant for all customers.

4   We assume that customers make independent purchase decisions. That is, we assume that the outcomes of the three trials are independent of each other.

Using the tree diagram in Figure 5.4, we can find the sample space of the experiment of three customers making a purchase decision. As shown in the tree diagram, the sample space of the

---

FIGURE 5.4   A Tree Diagram of Three Customers Making a Purchase Decision

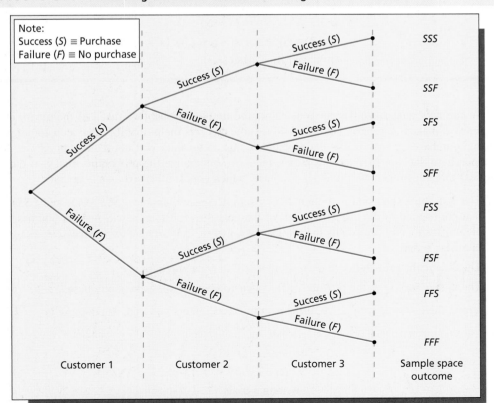

experiment consists of the following eight sample space outcomes:

SSS	*FSS*
SSF	*FSF*
SFS	*FFS*
SFF	*FFF*

Here the sample space outcome *SSS* represents the first customer making a purchase, the second customer making a purchase, and the third customer making a purchase. On the other hand, the sample space outcome *SFS* represents the first customer making a purchase, the second customer not making a purchase, and the third customer making a purchase. In addition, each sample space outcome corresponds to a specific number of customers (out of three customers) making a purchase. For example, the sample space outcome *SSS* corresponds to all three customers making a purchase. Each of the sample space outcomes *SSF*, *SFS*, and *FSS* corresponds to two out of three customers making a purchase. Each of the sample space outcomes *SFF*, *FSF*, and *FFS* corresponds to one out of three customers making a purchase. Finally, the sample space outcome *FFF* corresponds to none of the three customers making a purchase.

To find the probability that two out of the next three customers will make a purchase (the probability asked for at the beginning of this example), we consider the sample space outcomes *SSF*, *SFS*, and *FSS*. Because the trials (individual customer purchase decisions) are independent, we can multiply the probabilities associated with the different trial outcomes (each of which is *S* or *F*) to find the probability of a sequence of customer outcomes:

$$P(SSF) = P(S)P(S)P(F) = (.4)(.4)(.6) = (.4)^2(.6)$$
$$P(SFS) = P(S)P(F)P(S) = (.4)(.6)(.4) = (.4)^2(.6)$$
$$P(FSS) = P(F)P(S)P(S) = (.6)(.4)(.4) = (.4)^2(.6)$$

It follows that the probability that two out of the next three customers will make a purchase is

$$P(SSF) + P(SFS) + P(FSS)$$
$$= (.4)^2(.6) + (.4)^2(.6) + (.4)^2(.6)$$
$$= 3(.4)^2(.6) = .288$$

We can now generalize the previous result and find the probability that x of the next n customers will make a purchase. Here we will assume that p is the probability that a customer will make a purchase, $q = 1 - p$ is the probability that a customer will not make a purchase, and that purchase decisions (trials) are independent. To generalize the probability that two out of the next three customers will make a purchase, which equals $3(.4)^2(.6)$, we note that

1. The 3 in this expression is the number of sample space outcomes (*SSF*, *SFS*, and *FSS*) that correspond to the event "two out of the next three customers will make a purchase." Note that this number equals the number of ways we can arrange two successes among the three trials.

2. The .4 is p, the probability that a customer will make a purchase.

3. The .6 is $q = 1 - p$, the probability that a customer will not make a purchase.

Therefore, the probability that two of the next three customers will make a purchase is

$$\left(\begin{array}{c} \text{The number of ways} \\ \text{to arrange 2 successes} \\ \text{among 3 trials} \end{array} \right) p^2 q^1$$

Now, notice that, although each of the sample space outcomes *SSF*, *SFS*, and *FSS* represents a different arrangement of the two successes among the three trials, each of these sample space outcomes consists of two successes and one failure. For this reason, the probability of each of these sample space outcomes equals $(.4)^2(.6)^1 = p^2 q^1$. It follows that p is raised to a power that equals the number of successes (2) in the three trials, and q is raised to a power that equals the number of failures (1) in the three trials.

In general, each sample space outcome describing the occurrence of x successes (purchases) in n trials represents a different arrangement of x successes in n trials. However, each outcome consists of x successes and $n - x$ failures. Therefore, the probability of each sample space outcome is $p^x q^{n-x}$. It follows by analogy that the probability that x of the next n trials will be successes (purchases) is

$$\begin{pmatrix} \text{The number of ways} \\ \text{to arrange } x \text{ successes} \\ \text{among } n \text{ trials} \end{pmatrix} p^x q^{n-x}$$

We can use the expression we have just arrived at to compute the probability of x successes in the next n trials if we can find a way to calculate the number of ways to arrange x successes among n trials. It can be shown that:

The number of ways to arrange x *successes among* n *trials* equals

$$\frac{n!}{x! \, (n - x)!}$$

where $n!$ is pronounced "n factorial" and is calculated as $n! = n(n - 1)(n - 2) \cdots (1)$ and where (by definition) $0! = 1$.

For instance, using this formula, we can see that the number of ways to arrange $x = 2$ successes among $n = 3$ trials equals

$$\frac{n!}{x! \, (n - x)!} = \frac{3!}{2! \, (3 - 2)!} = \frac{3!}{2! \, 1!} = \frac{3 \cdot 2 \cdot 1}{2 \cdot 1 \cdot 1} = 3$$

Of course, we have previously seen that the three ways to arrange $x = 2$ successes among $n = 3$ trials are *SSF*, *SFS*, and *FSS*.

Using the preceding formula, we obtain the following general result:

The Binomial Distribution

A **binomial experiment** has the following characteristics:

1 The experiment consists of *n identical trials.*

2 Each trial results in a **success** or a **failure**.

3 The probability of a success on any trial is p and remains constant from trial to trial. This implies that the probability of failure, q, on any trial is $1 - p$ and remains constant from trial to trial.

4 The trials are **independent** (that is, the results of the trials have nothing to do with each other).

Furthermore, if we define the random variable

$x = $ the total number of successes in n trials of a binomial experiment

then we call x a **binomial random variable,** and the probability of obtaining x successes in n trials is

$$p(x) = \frac{n!}{x! \, (n - x)!} p^x q^{n-x}$$

Noting that we sometimes refer to the formula for $p(x)$ as the **binomial formula,** we illustrate the use of this formula in the following example.

EXAMPLE 5.7 Purchases at a Discount Store

Consider the discount department store situation discussed in Example 5.6. In order to find the probability that three of the next five customers will make purchases, we calculate

$$p(3) = \frac{5!}{3!\,(5-3)!}\,(.4)^3(.6)^{5-3} = \frac{5!}{3!\,2!}\,(.4)^3(.6)^2$$

$$= \frac{5\cdot4\cdot3\cdot2\cdot1}{(3\cdot2\cdot1)(2\cdot1)}\,(.4)^3(.6)^2$$

$$= 10(.064)(.36)$$

$$= .2304$$

Here we see that

1   $\frac{5!}{3!\,(5-3)!} = 10$ is the number of ways to arrange three successes among five trials. For instance, two ways to do this are described by the sample space outcomes *SSSFF* and *SFSSF.* There are eight other ways.

2   $(.4)^3(.6)^2$ is the probability of any sample space outcome consisting of three successes and two failures.

Thus far we have shown how to calculate binomial probabilities. We next give several examples that illustrate some practical applications of the binomial distribution. As we demonstrate in the first example, the term *success* does not necessarily refer to a *desirable* experimental outcome. Rather, it refers to an outcome that we wish to investigate.

EXAMPLE 5.8 The Phe-Mycin Case: Drug Side Effects

Antibiotics occasionally cause nausea as a side effect. A major drug company has developed a new antibiotic called Phe-Mycin. The company claims that, at most, 10 percent of all patients treated with Phe-Mycin would experience nausea as a side effect of taking the drug. Suppose that we randomly select $n = 4$ patients and treat them with Phe-Mycin. Each patient will either experience nausea (which we arbitrarily call a success) or will not experience nausea (a failure). We will assume that p, the true probability that a patient will experience nausea as a side effect, is .10, the maximum value of p claimed by the drug company. Furthermore, it is reasonable to assume that patients' reactions to the drug would be independent of each other. Let x denote the number of patients among the four who will experience nausea as a side effect. It follows that x is a binomial random variable, which can take on any of the potential values 0, 1, 2, 3, or 4. That is, anywhere between none of the patients and all four of the patients could potentially experience nausea as a side effect. Furthermore, we can calculate the probability associated with each possible value of x as shown in Table 5.3. For instance, the probability that none of the four randomly selected patients will experience nausea is

$$p(0) = P(x = 0) = \frac{4!}{0!\,(4-0)!}\,(.1)^0(.9)^{4-0}$$

$$= \frac{4!}{0!\,4!}\,(.1)^0(.9)^4$$

$$= \frac{4!}{(1)(4!)}\,(1)(.9)^4$$

$$= (.9)^4 = .6561$$

Because Table 5.3 lists each possible value of x and also gives the probability of each value, we say that this table gives the **binomial probability distribution of x.**

TABLE 5.3   **The Binomial Probability Distribution of x, the Number of Four Randomly Selected Patients Who Will Experience Nausea as a Side Effect of Being Treated with Phe-Mycin**

x (Number Who Experience Nausea)	$p(x) = \dfrac{n!}{x!\,(n-x)!}\,p^x(1-p)^{n-x}$
0	$p(0) = P(x = 0) = \dfrac{4!}{0!\,(4-0)!}\,(.1)^0(.9)^{4-0} = .6561$
1	$p(1) = P(x = 1) = \dfrac{4!}{1!\,(4-1)!}\,(.1)^1(.9)^{4-1} = .2916$
2	$p(2) = P(x = 2) = \dfrac{4!}{2!\,(4-2)!}\,(.1)^2(.9)^{4-2} = .0486$
3	$p(3) = P(x = 3) = \dfrac{4!}{3!\,(4-3)!}\,(.1)^3(.9)^{4-3} = .0036$
4	$p(4) = P(x = 4) = \dfrac{4!}{4!\,(4-4)!}\,(.1)^4(.9)^{4-4} = .0001$

FIGURE 5.5   **The Binomial Probability Distribution with $p = .10$ and $n = 4$**

(a) Excel output of the binomial distribution

Binomial distribution with n = 4 and p = 0.10

x	P(X = x)
0	0.6561
1	0.2916
2	0.0486
3	0.0036
4	0.0001

(b) A graph of the distribution

The binomial probabilities given in Table 5.3 need not be hand calculated. Excel and MINITAB can be used to calculate binomial probabilities. For instance, Figure 5.5(a) gives the Excel output of the binomial probability distribution listed in Table 5.3.[1] Figure 5.5(b) shows a graph of this distribution.

In order to interpret these binomial probabilities, consider administering the antibiotic Phe-Mycin to all possible samples of four randomly selected patients. Then, for example,

$$P(x = 0) = 0.6561$$

says that none of the four sampled patients would experience nausea in 65.61 percent of all possible samples. Furthermore, as another example,

$$P(x = 3) = 0.0036$$

says that three out of the four sampled patients would experience nausea in only .36 percent of all possible samples.

Another way to avoid hand calculating binomial probabilities is to use **binomial tables,** which have been constructed to give the probability of x successes in n trials. A table of binomial

[1]As we will see in this chapter's appendixes, we can use MINITAB to obtain output of the binomial distribution that is essentially identical to the output given by Excel.

TABLE 5.4   A Portion of a Binomial Probability Table

(a) A Table for $n = 4$ Trials

Values of p (.05 to .50)

↓	.05	.10	.15	.20	.25	.30	.35	.40	.45	.50	
0	.8145	.6561	.5220	.4096	.3164	.2401	.1785	.1296	.0915	.0625	4
1	.1715	.2916	.3685	.4096	.4219	.4116	.3845	.3456	.2995	.2500	3
Number of 2	.0135	.0486	.0975	.1536	.2109	.2646	.3105	.3456	.3675	.3750	2 Number of
Successes 3	.0005	.0036	.0115	.0256	.0469	.0756	.1115	.1536	.2005	.2500	1 Successes
4	.0000	.0001	.0005	.0016	.0039	.0081	.0150	.0256	.0410	.0625	0
	.95	.90	.85	.80	.75	.70	.65	.60	.55	.50	↑

Values of p (.50 to .95)

(b) A Table for $n = 8$ trials

Values of p (.05 to .50)

↓	.05	.10	.15	.20	.25	.30	.35	.40	.45	.50	
0	.6634	.4305	.2725	.1678	.1001	.0576	.0319	.0168	.0084	.0039	8
1	.2793	.3826	.3847	.3355	.2670	.1977	.1373	.0896	.0548	.0313	7
2	.0515	.1488	.2376	.2936	.3115	.2965	.2587	.2090	.1569	.1094	6
Number of 3	.0054	.0331	.0839	.1468	.2076	.2541	.2786	.2787	.2568	.2188	5 Number of
Successes 4	.0004	.0046	.0185	.0459	.0865	.1361	.1875	.2322	.2627	.2734	4 Successes
5	.0000	.0004	.0026	.0092	.0231	.0467	.0808	.1239	.1719	.2188	3
6	.0000	.0000	.0002	.0011	.0038	.0100	.0217	.0413	.0703	.1094	2
7	.0000	.0000	.0000	.0001	.0004	.0012	.0033	.0079	.0164	.0313	1
8	.0000	.0000	.0000	.0000	.0000	.0001	.0002	.0007	.0017	.0039	0
	.95	.90	.85	.80	.75	.70	.65	.60	.55	.50	↑

Values of p (.50 to .95)

probabilities is given in Table A.1 (page 783). A portion of this table is reproduced in Table 5.4(a) and (b). Part (a) of this table gives binomial probabilities corresponding to $n = 4$ trials. Values of p, the probability of success, are listed across the top of the table (ranging from $p = .05$ to $p = .50$ in steps of .05), and more values of p (ranging from $p = .50$ to $p = .95$ in steps of .05) are listed across the bottom of the table. When the value of p being considered is one of those across the top of the table, values of x (the number of successes in four trials) are listed down the left side of the table. For instance, to find the probabilities that we have computed in Table 5.3, we look in part (a) of Table 5.4 ($n = 4$) and read down the column labeled .10. Remembering that the values of x are on the left side of the table because $p = .10$ is on top of the table, we find the probabilities in Table 5.3 (they are shaded). For example, the probability that none of four patients will experience nausea is $p(0) = .6561$, the probability that one of the four patients will experience nausea is $p(1) = .2916$, and so forth. If the value of p is across the bottom of the table, then we read the values of x from the right side of the table. As an example, if p equals .70, then the probability of three successes in four trials is $p(3) = .4116$ (we have shaded this probability).

EXAMPLE 5.9 The Phe-Mycin Case: Drug Side Effects

Suppose that we wish to investigate whether p, the probability that a patient will experience nausea as a side effect of taking Phe-Mycin, is greater than .10, the maximum value of p claimed by the drug company. This assessment will be made by assuming, for the sake of argument, that p equals .10, and by using sample information to weigh the evidence against this assumption and in favor of the conclusion that p is greater than .10. Suppose that when a sample of $n = 4$ randomly selected patients is treated with Phe-Mycin, three of the four patients experience nausea. Because the fraction of patients in the sample that experience nausea is $3/4 = .75$, which is far greater than .10, we have some evidence contradicting the assumption that p equals .10. To evaluate the strength of this evidence, we calculate the probability that at least 3 out of 4 randomly selected patients would experience nausea as a side effect if, in fact, p equals .10. Using the binomial probabilities in Table 5.4(a), and realizing that the events $x = 3$ and $x = 4$ are mutually exclusive, we have

$$
\begin{aligned}
P(x \geq 3) &= P(x = 3 \text{ or } x = 4) \\
&= P(x = 3) + P(x = 4) \\
&= .0036 + .0001 \\
&= .0037
\end{aligned}
$$

This probability says that, if p equals .10, then in only .37 percent of all possible samples of four randomly selected patients would at least three of the four patients experience nausea as a side effect. This implies that, if we are to believe that p equals .10, then we must believe that we have observed a sample result that is so rare that it can be described as a 37 in 10,000 chance. Because observing such a result is very unlikely, we have very strong evidence that p does not equal .10 and is, in fact, greater than .10.

Next, suppose that we consider what our conclusion would have been if only one of the four randomly selected patients had experienced nausea. Because the sample fraction of patients who experienced nausea is $1/4 = .25$, which is greater than .10, we would have some evidence to contradict the assumption that p equals .10. To evaluate the strength of this evidence, we calculate the probability that at least one out of four randomly selected patients would experience nausea as a side effect of being treated with Phe-Mycin if, in fact, p equals .10. Using the binomial probabilities in Table 5.4(a), we have

$$
\begin{aligned}
P(x \geq 1) &= P(x = 1 \text{ or } x = 2 \text{ or } x = 3 \text{ or } x = 4) \\
&= P(x = 1) + P(x = 2) + P(x = 3) + P(x = 4) \\
&= .2916 + .0486 + .0036 + .0001 \\
&= .3439
\end{aligned}
$$

This probability says that, if p equals .10, then in 34.39 percent of all possible samples of four randomly selected patients, at least one of the four patients would experience nausea. Because it is not particularly difficult to believe that a 34.39 percent chance has occurred, we would not have much evidence against the claim that p equals .10.

Example 5.9 illustrates what is sometimes called the **rare event approach to making a statistical inference.** The idea of this approach is that if the probability of an observed sample result under a given assumption is *small,* then we have *strong evidence* that the assumption is false. Although there are no strict rules, many statisticians judge the probability of an observed sample result to be small if it is less than .05. The logic behind this will be explained more fully in Chapter 9.

EXAMPLE 5.10 The ColorSmart-5000 Case: TV Repairs

The manufacturer of the ColorSmart-5000 television set claims that 95 percent of its sets last at least five years without requiring a single repair. Suppose that we contact $n = 8$ randomly selected ColorSmart-5000 purchasers five years after they purchased their sets. Each purchaser's set will have needed no repairs (a success) or will have been repaired at least once (a failure). We will assume that p, the true probability that a purchaser's television set will require no repairs within five years, is .95, as claimed by the manufacturer. Furthermore, it is reasonable to believe that the repair records of the purchasers' sets are independent of each other. Let x denote the number of the $n = 8$ randomly selected sets that have lasted at least five years without a single repair. Then x is a binomial random variable that can take on any of the potential values 0, 1, 2, 3, 4, 5, 6, 7, or 8. The binomial distribution of x is listed in Table 5.5. Here we have obtained these probabilities from Table 5.4(b). To use Table 5.4(b), we look at the column corresponding to $p = .95$. Because $p = .95$ is listed at the bottom of the table, we read the values of x and their

TABLE 5.5   **The Binomial Distribution of x, the Number of Eight ColorSmart-5000 Television Sets That Have Lasted at Least Five Years Without Needing a Single Repair, When $p = .95$**

x, Number of Sets That Require No Repairs	$p(x) = \dfrac{8!}{x!\,(8-x)!}\,(.95)^x(.05)^{8-x}$
0	$p(0) = .0000$
1	$p(1) = .0000$
2	$p(2) = .0000$
3	$p(3) = .0000$
4	$p(4) = .0004$
5	$p(5) = .0054$
6	$p(6) = .0515$
7	$p(7) = .2793$
8	$p(8) = .6634$

FIGURE 5.6   **The Binomial Probability Distribution with $p = .95$ and $n = 8$**

(a) MINITAB output of the binomial distribution

```
Binomial with n = 8 and p = 0.95

   x        P ( X = x )
   3          0.0000
   4          0.0004
   5          0.0054
   6          0.0515
   7          0.2793
   8          0.6634
```

(b) A graph of the distribution

corresponding probabilities from bottom to top (we have shaded the probabilities). Notice that the values of x are listed on the right side of the table.

Figure 5.6(a) gives the MINITAB output of the binomial distribution with $p = .95$ and $n = 8$ (that is, the binomial distribution of Table 5.5). This binomial distribution is graphed in Figure 5.6(b). Now, suppose that when we actually contact eight randomly selected purchasers, we find that five out of the eight television sets owned by these purchasers have lasted at least five years without a single repair. Because the sample fraction, $5/8 = .625$, of television sets needing no repairs is less than .95, we have some evidence contradicting the manufacturer's claim that p equals .95. To evaluate the strength of this evidence, we will calculate the probability that five or fewer of the eight randomly selected televisions would last five years without a single repair if, in fact, p equals .95. Using the binomial probabilities in Table 5.5, we have

$$
\begin{aligned}
P(x \le 5) &= P(x = 5 \text{ or } x = 4 \text{ or } x = 3 \text{ or } x = 2 \text{ or } x = 1 \text{ or } x = 0) \\
&= P(x = 5) + P(x = 4) + P(x = 3) + P(x = 2) + P(x = 1) + P(x = 0) \\
&= .0054 + .0004 + .0000 + .0000 + .0000 + .0000 \\
&= .0058
\end{aligned}
$$

This probability says that, if p equals .95, then in only .58 percent of all possible samples of eight randomly selected ColorSmart-5000 televisions would five or fewer of the eight televisions last five years without a single repair. Therefore, if we are to believe that p equals .95, we must believe that a 58 in 10,000 chance has occurred. Because it is difficult to believe that such a small chance has occurred, we have strong evidence that p does not equal .95, and is, in fact, less than .95.

FIGURE 5.7   **Several Binomial Distributions**

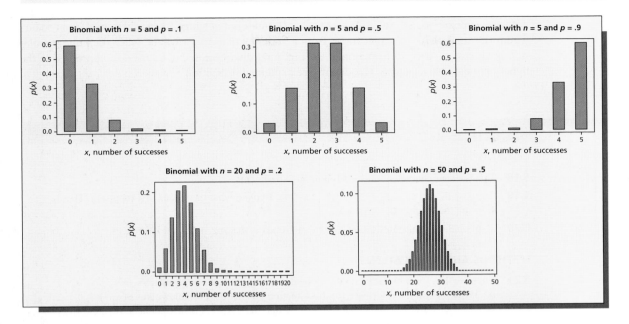

In Examples 5.8 and 5.10 we have illustrated binomial distributions with different values of n and p. The values of n and p are often called the **parameters** of the binomial distribution. Figure 5.7 shows several different binomial distributions. We see that, depending on the parameters, a binomial distribution can be skewed to the right, skewed to the left, or symmetrical.

We next consider calculating the mean, variance, and standard deviation of a binomial random variable. If we place the binomial probability formula into the expressions (given in Section 5.2) for the mean and variance of a discrete random variable, we can derive formulas that allow us to easily compute μ_x, σ_x^2, and σ_x for a binomial random variable. Omitting the details of the derivation, we have the following results:

The Mean, Variance, and Standard Deviation of a Binomial Random Variable

If x is a binomial random variable, then

$$\mu_x = np \qquad \sigma_x^2 = npq \qquad \sigma_x = \sqrt{npq}$$

where n is the number of trials, p is the probability of success on each trial, and $q = 1 - p$ is the probability of failure on each trial.

As a simple example, again consider the television manufacturer, and recall that x is the number of eight randomly selected ColorSmart-5000 televisions that last five years without a single repair. If the manufacturer's claim that p equals .95 is true (which implies that q equals $1 - p = 1 - .95 = .05$), it follows that

$$\mu_x = np = 8(.95) = 7.6$$
$$\sigma_x^2 = npq = 8(.95)(.05) = .38$$
$$\sigma_x = \sqrt{npq} = \sqrt{.38} = .6164$$

In order to interpret $\mu_x = 7.6$, suppose that we were to randomly select all possible samples of eight ColorSmart-5000 televisions and record the number of sets in each sample that last five years without a repair. If we averaged all of our results, we would find that the average number of sets per sample that last five years without a repair is equal to 7.6.

To conclude this section, note that in optional Section 5.5, we discuss the **hypergeometric distribution.** This distribution is related to the binomial distribution. The main difference between the two distributions is that in the case of the hypergeometric distribution, the trials are not independent and the probabilities of success and failure change from trial to trial. This occurs when we sample without replacement from a finite population. However, when the finite population is large compared to the sample, the binomial distribution can be used to approximate the hypergeometric distribution. The details are explained in Section 5.5.

Exercises for Section 5.3

CONCEPTS

connect

5.18 List the four characteristics of a binomial experiment.

5.19 Suppose that x is a binomial random variable. Explain what the values of x represent. That is, how are the values of x defined?

5.20 Explain the logic behind the rare event approach to making statistical inferences.

METHODS AND APPLICATIONS

5.21 Suppose that x is a binomial random variable with $n = 5$, $p = .3$, and $q = .7$.
  a Write the binomial formula for this situation and list the possible values of x.
  b For each value of x, calculate $p(x)$, and graph the binomial distribution.
  c Find $P(x = 3)$.
  d Find $P(x \le 3)$.
  e Find $P(x < 3)$.
  f Find $P(x \ge 4)$.
  g Find $P(x > 2)$.
  h Use the probabilities you computed in part b to calculate the mean, μ_x, the variance, σ_x^2, and the standard deviation, σ_x, of this binomial distribution. Show that the formulas for μ_x, σ_x^2, and σ_x given in this section give the same results.
  i Calculate the interval $[\mu_x \pm 2\sigma_x]$. Use the probabilities of part b to find the probability that x will be in this interval.

5.22 Thirty percent of all customers who enter a store will make a purchase. Suppose that six customers enter the store and that these customers make independent purchase decisions.
  a Let x = the number of the six customers who will make a purchase. Write the binomial formula for this situation.
  b Use the binomial formula to calculate
    (1) The probability that exactly five customers make a purchase.
    (2) The probability that at least three customers make a purchase.
    (3) The probability that two or fewer customers make a purchase.
    (4) The probability that at least one customer makes a purchase.

5.23 The customer service department for a wholesale electronics outlet claims that 90 percent of all customer complaints are resolved to the satisfaction of the customer. In order to test this claim, a random sample of 15 customers who have filed complaints is selected.
  a Let x = the number of sampled customers whose complaints were resolved to the customer's satisfaction. Assuming the claim is true, write the binomial formula for this situation.
  b Use the binomial tables (see Table A.1, page 783) to find each of the following if we assume that the claim is true:
    (1) $P(x \le 13)$.
    (2) $P(x > 10)$.
    (3) $P(x \ge 14)$.
    (4) $P(9 \le x \le 12)$.
    (5) $P(x \le 9)$.
  c Suppose that of the 15 customers selected, 9 have had their complaints resolved satisfactorily. Using part b, do you believe the claim of 90 percent satisfaction? Explain.

5.24 The United States Golf Association requires that the weight of a golf ball must not exceed 1.62 oz. The association periodically checks golf balls sold in the United States by sampling specific brands stocked by pro shops. Suppose that a manufacturer claims that no more than 1 percent of its brand of golf balls exceed 1.62 oz. in weight. Suppose that 24 of this manufacturer's golf balls are randomly selected, and let x denote the number of the 24 randomly selected golf balls that exceed 1.62 oz. Figure 5.8 gives part of an Excel output of the binomial distribution with $n = 24$, $p = .01$, and $q = .99$. (Note that, because $P(X = x) = .0000$ for values of x from 6 to 24, we omit these probabilities.) Use this output to:

a Find $P(x = 0)$, that is, find the probability that none of the randomly selected golf balls exceeds 1.62 oz. in weight.

b Find the probability that at least one of the randomly selected golf balls exceeds 1.62 oz. in weight.

c Find $P(x \leq 3)$.

d Find $P(x \geq 2)$.

e Suppose that 2 of the 24 randomly selected golf balls are found to exceed 1.62 oz. Using your result from part d, do you believe the claim that no more than 1 percent of this brand of golf balls exceed 1.62 oz. in weight?

5.25 An industry representative claims that 50 percent of all satellite dish owners subscribe to at least one premium movie channel. In an attempt to justify this claim, the representative will poll a randomly selected sample of dish owners.

a Suppose that the representative's claim is true, and suppose that a sample of four dish owners is randomly selected. Assuming independence, use an appropriate formula to compute:

    (1) The probability that none of the dish owners in the sample subscribes to at least one premium movie channel.

    (2) The probability that more than two dish owners in the sample subscribe to at least one premium movie channel.

b Suppose that the representative's claim is true, and suppose that a sample of 20 dish owners is randomly selected. Assuming independence, what is the probability that:

    (1) Nine or fewer dish owners in the sample subscribe to at least one premium movie channel?

    (2) More than 11 dish owners in the sample subscribe to at least one premium movie channel?

    (3) Fewer than five dish owners in the sample subscribe to at least one premium movie channel?

c Suppose that, when we survey 20 randomly selected dish owners, we find that 4 of the dish owners actually subscribe to at least one premium movie channel. Using a probability you found in this exercise as the basis for your answer, do you believe the industry representative's claim? Explain.

5.26 For each of the following, calculate μ_x, σ_x^2, and σ_x by using the formulas given in this section. Then (1) interpret the meaning of μ_x, and (2) find the probability that x falls in the interval $[\mu_x \pm 2\sigma_x]$.

a The situation of Exercise 5.22, where $x =$ the number of the six customers who will make a purchase.

b The situation of Exercise 5.23, where $x =$ the number of 15 sampled customers whose complaints were resolved to the customer's satisfaction.

c The situation of Exercise 5.24, where $x =$ the number of the 24 randomly selected golf balls that exceed 1.62 oz. in weight.

5.27 The January 1986 mission of the Space Shuttle *Challenger* was the 25th such shuttle mission. It was unsuccessful due to an explosion caused by an O-ring seal failure.

a According to NASA, the probability of such a failure in a single mission was $1/60,000$. Using this value of p and assuming all missions are independent, calculate the probability of no mission failures in 25 attempts. Then calculate the probability of at least one mission failure in 25 attempts.

b According to a study conducted for the Air Force, the probability of such a failure in a single mission was $1/35$. Recalculate the probability of no mission failures in 25 attempts and the probability of at least one mission failure in 25 attempts.

c Based on your answers to parts a and b, which value of p seems more likely to be true? Explain.

d How small must p be made in order to ensure that the probability of no mission failures in 25 attempts is .999?

FIGURE 5.8

Excel Output of the Binomial Distribution with $n = 24$, $p = .01$, and $q = .99$

Binomial distribution with n = 24 and p = 0.01

x	P (X = x)
0	0.7857
1	0.1905
2	0.0221
3	0.0016
4	0.0001
5	0.0000

5.4 The Poisson Distribution (Optional) ● ● ●

We now discuss a discrete random variable that describes the number of occurrences of an event over a specified interval of time or space. For instance, we might wish to describe (1) the number of customers who arrive at the checkout counters of a grocery store in one hour, or (2) the number of major fires in a city during the next two months, or (3) the number of dirt specks found in one square yard of plastic wrap.

LO5-4 Use the Poisson distribution to compute probabilities (Optional).

Such a random variable can often be described by a **Poisson distribution.** We describe this distribution and give two assumptions needed for its use in the following box:

The Poisson Distribution

Consider the number of times an event occurs over an interval of time or space, and assume that

1 The probability of the event's occurrence is the same for any two intervals of equal length, and

2 Whether the event occurs in any interval is independent of whether the event occurs in any other nonoverlapping interval.

Then, the probability that the event will occur x times in a *specified interval* is

$$p(x) = \frac{e^{-\mu}\mu^{x}}{x!}$$

Here μ is the mean (or expected) number of occurrences of the event in the *specified interval,* and $e = 2.71828\ldots$ is the base of Napierian logarithms.

In theory, there is no limit to how large x might be. That is, theoretically speaking, the event under consideration could occur an indefinitely large number of times during any specified interval. This says that a **Poisson random variable** might take on any of the values 0, 1, 2, 3, . . . and so forth. We will now look at an example.

EXAMPLE 5.11 The Air Safety Case: Traffic Control Errors

In an article in the August 15, 1998, edition of the *Journal News* (Hamilton, Ohio),[2] the Associated Press reported that the Cleveland Air Route Traffic Control Center, the busiest in the nation for guiding planes on cross-country routes, had experienced an unusually high number of errors since the end of July. An error occurs when controllers direct flights either within five miles of each other horizontally, or within 2,000 feet vertically at a height of 18,000 feet or more (the standard is 1,000 feet vertically at heights less than 18,000 feet). The controllers' union blamed the errors on a staff shortage, whereas the Federal Aviation Administration (FAA) claimed that the cause was improved error reporting and an unusual number of thunderstorms.

Suppose that an air traffic control center has been averaging 20.8 errors per year and that the center experiences 3 errors in a week. The FAA must decide whether this occurrence is unusual enough to warrant an investigation as to the causes of the (possible) increase in errors. To investigate this possibility, we will find the probability distribution of x, the number of errors in a week, when we assume that the center is still averaging 20.8 errors per year.

Arbitrarily choosing a time unit of one week, the average (or expected) number of errors per week is $20.8/52 = .4$. Therefore, we can use the Poisson formula (note that the Poisson assumptions are probably satisfied) to calculate the probability of no errors in a week to be

$$p(0) = P(x = 0) = \frac{e^{-\mu}\mu^{0}}{0!} = \frac{e^{-.4}(.4)^{0}}{1} = .6703$$

Similarly, the probability of three errors in a week is

$$p(3) = P(x = 3) = \frac{e^{-.4}(.4)^{3}}{3!} = \frac{e^{-.4}(.4)^{3}}{3 \cdot 2 \cdot 1} = .0072$$

As with the binomial distribution, tables have been constructed that give Poisson probabilities. A table of these probabilities is given in Table A.2 (page 787). A portion of this table is reproduced

---

[2]F. J. Frommer, "Errors on the Rise at Traffic Control Center in Ohio," *Journal News,* August 15, 1998.

TABLE 5.6   **A Portion of a Poisson Probability Table**

μ, **Mean Number of Occurrences**

x, Number of Occurrences	.1	.2	.3	.4	.5	.6	.7	.8	.9	1.0
0	.9048	.8187	.7408	.6703	.6065	.5488	.4966	.4493	.4066	.3679
1	.0905	.1637	.2222	.2681	.3033	.3293	.3476	.3595	.3659	.3679
2	.0045	.0164	.0333	.0536	.0758	.0988	.1217	.1438	.1647	.1839
3	.0002	.0011	.0033	.0072	.0126	.0198	.0284	.0383	.0494	.0613
4	.0000	.0001	.0003	.0007	.0016	.0030	.0050	.0077	.0111	.0153
5	.0000	.0000	.0000	.0001	.0002	.0004	.0007	.0012	.0020	.0031
6	.0000	.0000	.0000	.0000	.0000	.0000	.0001	.0002	.0003	.0005

μ, **Mean Number of Occurrences**

x, Number of Occurrences	1.1	1.2	1.3	1.4	1.5	1.6	1.7	1.8	1.9	2.0
0	.3329	.3012	.2725	.2466	.2231	.2019	.1827	.1653	.1496	.1353
1	.3662	.3614	.3543	.3452	.3347	.3230	.3106	.2975	.2842	.2707
2	.2014	.2169	.2303	.2417	.2510	.2584	.2640	.2678	.2700	.2707
3	.0738	.0867	.0998	.1128	.1255	.1378	.1496	.1607	.1710	.1804
4	.0203	.0260	.0324	.0395	.0471	.0551	.0636	.0723	.0812	.0902
5	.0045	.0062	.0084	.0111	.0141	.0176	.0216	.0260	.0309	.0361
6	.0008	.0012	.0018	.0026	.0035	.0047	.0061	.0078	.0098	.0120
7	.0001	.0002	.0003	.0005	.0008	.0011	.0015	.0020	.0027	.0034
8	.0000	.0000	.0001	.0001	.0001	.0002	.0003	.0005	.0006	.0009

Source: From Brooks/Cole © 1991.

TABLE 5.7   **The Poisson Distribution of x, the Number of Errors at an Air Traffic Control Center in a Week, When $\mu = .4$**

x, the Number of Errors in a Week	$p(x) = \dfrac{e^{-\mu}\mu^x}{x!}$
0	$p(0) = \dfrac{e^{-.4}(.4)^0}{0!} = .6703$
1	$p(1) = \dfrac{e^{-.4}(.4)^1}{1!} = .2681$
2	$p(2) = \dfrac{e^{-.4}(.4)^2}{2!} = .0536$
3	$p(3) = \dfrac{e^{-.4}(.4)^3}{3!} = .0072$
4	$p(4) = \dfrac{e^{-.4}(.4)^4}{4!} = .0007$
5	$p(5) = \dfrac{e^{-.4}(.4)^5}{5!} = .0001$
6	$p(6) = \dfrac{e^{-.4}(.4)^6}{6!} = .0000$

in Table 5.6. In this table, values of the mean number of occurrences, μ, are listed across the top of the table, and values of x (the number of occurrences) are listed down the left side of the table. In order to use the table in the traffic control situation, we look at the column in Table 5.6 corresponding to .4, and we find the probabilities of 0, 1, 2, 3, 4, 5, and 6 errors (we have shaded these probabilities). For instance, the probability of one error in a week is .2681. Also, note that the probability of any number of errors greater than 6 is so small that it is not listed in the table. Table 5.7 summarizes the Poisson distribution of x, the number of errors in a week. This table also shows how the probabilities associated with the different values of x are calculated.

FIGURE 5.9   The Poisson Probability Distribution with $\mu = .4$

(a) MINITAB output of the Poisson distribution

```
Poisson with mean = 0.4

    x           P( X = x )
    0            0.6703
    1            0.2681
    2            0.0536
    3            0.0072
    4            0.0007
    5            0.0001
    6            0.0000
```

(b) A graph of the distribution

Poisson probabilities can also be calculated by using MINITAB and Excel. For instance, Figure 5.9(a) gives the MINITAB output of the Poisson distribution presented in Table 5.7.[3] This Poisson distribution is graphed in Figure 5.9(b).

Next, recall that there have been three errors at the air traffic control center in the last week. This is considerably more errors than .4, the expected number of errors assuming the center is still averaging 20.8 errors per year. Therefore, we have some evidence to contradict this assumption. To evaluate the strength of this evidence, we calculate the probability that at least three errors will occur in a week if, in fact, μ equals .4. Using the Poisson probabilities in Figure 5.9(a), we obtain

$$P(x \geq 3) = p(3) + p(4) + p(5) + p(6) = .0072 + .0007 + .0001 + .0000 = .008$$

This probability says that, if the center is averaging 20.8 errors per year, then there would be three or more errors in a week in only .8 percent of all weeks. That is, if we are to believe that the control center is averaging 20.8 errors per year, then we must believe that an 8 in 1,000 chance has occurred. Because it is very difficult to believe that such a rare event has occurred, we have strong evidence that the average number of errors per week has increased. Therefore, an investigation by the FAA into the reasons for such an increase is probably justified.

EXAMPLE 5.12 Errors in Computer Code

In the book *Modern Statistical Quality Control and Improvement*, Nicholas R. Farnum (1994) presents an example dealing with the quality of computer software. In the example, Farnum measures software quality by monitoring the number of errors per 1,000 lines of computer code.

Suppose that the number of errors per 1,000 lines of computer code is described by a Poisson distribution with a mean of four errors per 1,000 lines of code. If we wish to find the probability of obtaining eight errors in 2,500 lines of computer code, we must adjust the mean of the Poisson distribution. To do this, we arbitrarily choose a *space unit* of one line of code, and we note that a mean of four errors per 1,000 lines of code is equivalent to 4/1,000 of an error per line of code. Therefore, the mean number of errors per 2,500 lines of code is (4/1,000)(2,500) = 10. It follows that

$$p(8) = \frac{e^{-\mu}\mu^8}{8!} = \frac{e^{-10}10^8}{8!} = .1126$$

---

[3]As we will show in the appendixes to this chapter, we can use Excel and MegaStat to obtain output of the Poisson distribution that is essentially identical to the output given by MINITAB.

FIGURE 5.10   **Several Poisson Distributions**

The mean, μ, is often called the *parameter* of the Poisson distribution. Figure 5.10 shows several Poisson distributions. We see that, depending on its parameter (mean), a Poisson distribution can be very skewed to the right or can be quite symmetrical.

Finally, if we place the Poisson probability formula into the general expressions (of Section 5.2) for μ_x, σ_x^2, and σ_x, we can derive formulas for calculating the mean, variance, and standard deviation of a Poisson distribution:

The Mean, Variance, and Standard Deviation of a Poisson Random Variable

Suppose that x is a **Poisson random variable.** If μ is the average number of occurrences of an event over the specified interval of time or space of interest, then

$$\mu_x = \mu \qquad \sigma_x^2 = \mu \qquad \sigma_x = \sqrt{\mu}$$

Here we see that both the mean and the variance of a Poisson random variable equal the average number of occurrences μ of the event of interest over the specified interval of time or space. For example, in the air traffic control situation, the Poisson distribution of x, the number of errors at the air traffic control center in a week, has a mean of $\mu_x = .4$ and a standard deviation of $\sigma_x = \sqrt{.4} = .6325$.

Exercises for Section 5.4

CONCEPTS

5.28   The values of a Poisson random variable are $x = 0, 1, 2, 3, \ldots$ Explain what these values represent.

5.29   Explain the assumptions that must be satisfied when a Poisson distribution adequately describes a random variable x.

connect™

METHODS AND APPLICATIONS

5.30   Suppose that x has a Poisson distribution with $\mu = 2$.
   a   Write the Poisson formula and describe the possible values of x.
   b   Starting with the smallest possible value of x, calculate $p(x)$ for each value of x until $p(x)$ becomes smaller than .001.
   c   Graph the Poisson distribution using your results of b.
   d   Find $P(x = 2)$.   **e**   Find $P(x \leq 4)$.   **f**   Find $P(x < 4)$.
   g   Find $P(x \geq 1)$ and $P(x > 2)$.   **h**   Find $P(1 \leq x \leq 4)$.
   i   Find $P(2 < x < 5)$.   **j**   Find $P(2 \leq x < 6)$.

5.31   Suppose that x has a Poisson distribution with $\mu = 2$.
   a   Use the formulas given in this section to compute the mean, μ_x, variance, σ_x^2, and standard deviation, σ_x.
   b   Calculate the intervals $[\mu_x \pm 2\sigma_x]$ and $[\mu_x \pm 3\sigma_x]$. Then use the probabilities you calculated in Exercise 5.30 to find the probability that x will be inside each of these intervals.

5.32   A bank manager wishes to provide prompt service for customers at the bank's drive-up window. The bank currently can serve up to 10 customers per 15-minute period without significant delay. The average arrival rate is 7 customers per 15-minute period. Let x denote the number of customers arriving per 15-minute period. Assuming x has a Poisson distribution:
   a   Find the probability that 10 customers will arrive in a particular 15-minute period.
   b   Find the probability that 10 or fewer customers will arrive in a particular 15-minute period.
   c   Find the probability that there will be a significant delay at the drive-up window. That is, find the probability that more than 10 customers will arrive during a particular 15-minute period.

5.33   A telephone company's goal is to have no more than five monthly line failures on any 100 miles of line. The company currently experiences an average of two monthly line failures per 50 miles of line. Let x denote the number of monthly line failures per 100 miles of line. Assuming x has a Poisson distribution:
   a   Find the probability that the company will meet its goal on a particular 100 miles of line.
   b   Find the probability that the company will not meet its goal on a particular 100 miles of line.
   c   Find the probability that the company will have no more than five monthly failures on a particular 200 miles of line.
   d   Find the probability that the company will have more than 12 monthly failures on a particular 150 miles of line.

5.34   A local law enforcement agency claims that the number of times that a patrol car passes through a particular neighborhood follows a Poisson process with a mean of three times per nightly shift. Let x denote the number of times that a patrol car passes through the neighborhood during a nightly shift.
   a   Calculate the probability that no patrol cars pass through the neighborhood during a nightly shift.
   b   Suppose that during a randomly selected night shift no patrol cars pass through the neighborhood. Based on your answer in part a, do you believe the agency's claim? Explain.
   c   Assuming that nightly shifts are independent and assuming that the agency's claim is correct, find the probability that exactly one patrol car will pass through the neighborhood on each of four consecutive nights.

5.35   When the number of trials, n, is large, binomial probability tables may not be available. Furthermore, if a computer is not available, hand calculations will be tedious. As an alternative, the Poisson distribution can be used to approximate the binomial distribution when n is large and p is small. Here the mean of the Poisson distribution is taken to be $\mu = np$. That is, when n is large and p is small, we can use the Poisson formula with $\mu = np$ to calculate binomial probabilities, and we will obtain results close to those we would obtain by using the binomial formula. A common rule is to use this approximation when $n/p \geq 500$.

     To illustrate this approximation, in the movie *Coma*, a young female intern at a Boston hospital was very upset when her friend, a young nurse, went into a coma during routine anesthesia at the hospital. Upon investigation, she found that 10 of the last 30,000 healthy patients at the hospital had gone into comas during routine anesthesias. When she confronted the hospital administrator with this fact and the fact that the national average was 6 out of 100,000 healthy patients going into comas during routine anesthesias, the administrator replied that 10 out of 30,000 was still quite small and thus not that unusual.
   a   Use the Poisson distribution to approximate the probability that 10 or more of 30,000 healthy patients would slip into comas during routine anesthesias, if in fact the true average at the hospital was 6 in 100,000. Hint: $\mu = np = 30,000(6/100,000) = 1.8$.
   b   Given the hospital's record and part a, what conclusion would you draw about the hospital's medical practices regarding anesthesia?
   (Note: It turned out that the hospital administrator was part of a conspiracy to sell body parts and was purposely putting healthy adults into comas during routine anesthesias. If the intern had taken a statistics course, she could have avoided a great deal of danger.)

5.36   Suppose that an automobile parts wholesaler claims that .5 percent of the car batteries in a shipment are defective. A random sample of 200 batteries is taken, and four are found to be defective.
   a   Use the Poisson approximation discussed in Exercise 5.35 to find the probability that four or more car batteries in a random sample of 200 such batteries would be found to be defective, if we assume that the wholesaler's claim is true.
   b   Based on your answer to part a, do you believe the claim? Explain.

5.5 The Hypergeometric Distribution (Optional) ◗ ● ●

The Hypergeometric Distribution

Suppose that a population consists of N items and that r of these items are *successes* and $(N - r)$ of these items are *failures*. If we randomly select n of the N items **without replacement**, it can be shown that the probability that x of the n randomly selected items will be successes is given by the **hypergeometric probability formula**

$$p(x) = \frac{\binom{r}{x}\binom{N - r}{n - x}}{\binom{N}{n}}$$

Here $\binom{r}{x}$ is the number of ways x successes can be selected from the total of r successes in the population, $\binom{N - r}{n - x}$ is the number of ways $n - x$ failures can be selected from the total of $N - r$ failures in the pupulation, and $\binom{N}{n}$ is the number of ways a sample of size n can be selected from a population of size N.

LO5-5 Use the hypergeometric distribution to compute probabilities (Optional).

To demonstrate the calculations, suppose that a population of $N = 6$ stocks consists of $r = 4$ stocks that are destined to give positive returns (that is, there are $r = 4$ *successes*) and $N - r = 6 - 4 = 2$ stocks that are destined to give negative returns (that is, there are $N - r = 2$ *failures*). Also suppose that we randomly select $n = 3$ of the six stocks in the population without replacement and that we define x to be the number of the three randomly selected stocks that will give a positive return. Then, for example, the probability that $x = 2$ is

$$p(x = 2) = \frac{\binom{r}{x}\binom{N - r}{n - x}}{\binom{N}{n}} = \frac{\binom{4}{2}\binom{2}{1}}{\binom{6}{3}} = \frac{\left(\frac{4!}{2!\,2!}\right)\left(\frac{2!}{1!\,1!}\right)}{\left(\frac{6!}{3!\,3!}\right)} = \frac{(6)(2)}{20} = .6$$

Similarly, the probability that $x = 3$ is

$$p(x = 3) = \frac{\binom{4}{3}\binom{2}{0}}{\binom{6}{3}} = \frac{\left(\frac{4!}{3!\,1!}\right)\left(\frac{2!}{0!\,2!}\right)}{\left(\frac{6!}{3!\,3!}\right)} = \frac{(4)(1)}{20} = .2$$

It follows that the probability that at least two of the three randomly selected stocks will give a positive return is $p(x = 2) + p(x = 3) = .6 + .2 = .8$.

If we place the hypergeometric probability formula into the general expressions (of Section 5.2) for μ_x and σ_x^2, we can derive formulas for the mean and variance of the hypergeometric distribution.

The Mean and Variance of a Hypergeometric Random Variable

Suppose that x is a hypergeometric random variable. Then

$$\mu_x = n\left(\frac{r}{N}\right) \qquad \text{and} \qquad \sigma_x^2 = n\left(\frac{r}{N}\right)\left(1 - \frac{r}{N}\right)\left(\frac{N - n}{N - 1}\right)$$

In the previous example, we have $N = 6$, $r = 4$, and $n = 3$. It follows that

$$\mu_x = n\left(\frac{r}{N}\right) = 3\left(\frac{4}{6}\right) = 2, \qquad \text{and}$$

$$\sigma_x^2 = n\left(\frac{r}{N}\right)\left(1 - \frac{r}{N}\right)\left(\frac{N - n}{N - 1}\right) = 3\left(\frac{4}{6}\right)\left(1 - \frac{4}{6}\right)\left(\frac{6 - 3}{6 - 1}\right) = .4$$

and that the standard deviation $\sigma_x = \sqrt{.4} = .6325$.

To conclude this section, note that, on the first random selection from the population of N items, the probability of a success is r/N. Because we are making selections *without replacement,* the probability of a success changes as we continue to make selections. However, **if the population size N is "much larger" than the sample size n (say, at least 20 times as large),** then making the selections will not substantially change the probability of a success. In this case, we can assume that the probability of a success stays essentially constant from selection to selection, and the different selections are essentially independent of each other. Therefore, **we can approximate the hypergeometric distribution by the binomial distribution.** That is, we can compute probabilities about the hypergeometric random variable x by using the easier binomial probability formula

$$p(x) = \frac{n!}{x!\,(n-x)!}\, p^x (1-p)^{n-x} = \frac{n!}{x!\,(n-x)!}\left(\frac{r}{N}\right)^x \left(1 - \frac{r}{N}\right)^{n-x}$$

where the binomial probability of success equals r/N.

EXAMPLE 5.13 Big Screen TV Repairs

Suppose that you own an electronics store and purchase (randomly select) 15 big screen TVs from a production run of 500. Of the 500 TVs, 450 are destined to last at least five years without needing a single repair. We will find the *exact* probability that at least 14 of the 15 big screen TVs will last at least five years without needing a single repair. If we let $x =$ the number of TVs that will last at least five years without needing a single repair, then x follows a hypergeometric distribution and $P(x \geq 14)$ is given by

$$P(x \geq 14) = P(x = 14) + P(x = 15) = p(14) + p(15).$$

Placing the values of $N = 500$, $r = 450$, $N - r = 50$, and $n = 15$ into the hypergeometric formula, and setting x equal to 14, we get

$$p(14) = \frac{\binom{450}{14}\binom{50}{1}}{\binom{500}{15}} = \frac{\left(\frac{450!}{14!\,436!}\right)\left(\frac{50!}{1!\,49!}\right)}{\frac{500!}{15!\,485!}}$$

Then, setting $x = 15$, we get

$$p(15) = \frac{\binom{450}{15}\binom{50}{0}}{\binom{500}{15}} = \frac{\left(\frac{450!}{15!\,435!}\right)\left(\frac{50!}{0!\,50!}\right)}{\frac{500!}{15!\,485!}}$$

A standard calculator may not be able to handle these calculations. Using a computer, we get $P(x \geq 14) = p(14) + p(15) = 0.5469$.

   As can be seen in this example, the calculation of hypergeometric probabilities can be difficult. However, because the population size $N = 500$ is at least 20 times the sample size $n = 15$, we can approximate this probability by using the binomial approximation to the hypergeometric distribution. Here, $p = 450/500 = 0.9$. Using this approximation, we get $P(x \geq 14) = p(14) + p(15)$, where

$$p(x) = \frac{15!}{x!\,(15-x)!}\,(0.9^x)(0.1^{15-x})$$

Using Table A.1 on page 783, where $n = 15$ and $p = .9$, we get $p(14) = .3432$ and $p(15) = .2059$. This gives us $P(x \geq 14) = .3432 + .2059 = .5491$. When we use the binomial approximation to find a hypergeometric probability, the calculations (either by formula or table) are much easier. Further, if used appropriately, the binomial approximation will give a result that is very close to the exact (hypergeometric) result. In this example, the results are the same to two decimal places.

Exercises for Section 5.5

CONCEPTS

5.37 In the context of the hypergeometric distribution, explain the meanings of N, r, and n.

5.38 When can a hypergeometric distribution be approximated by a binomial distribution? Explain carefully what this means.

METHODS AND APPLICATIONS

5.39 Suppose that x has a hypergeometric distribution with $N = 8$, $r = 5$, and $n = 4$. Find:

  a $P(x = 0)$ **e** $P(x = 4)$
  b $P(x = 1)$ **f** $P(x \geq 2)$
  c $P(x = 2)$ **g** $P(x < 3)$
  d $P(x = 3)$ **h** $P(x > 1)$

5.40 Suppose that x has a hypergeometric distribution with $N = 10$, $r = 4$, and $n = 3$.

  a Write out the probability distribution of x.
  b Find the mean μ_x, variance σ_x^2, and standard deviation σ_x of this distribution.

5.41 Among 12 metal parts produced in a machine shop, 3 are defective. If a random sample of three of these metal parts is selected, find:

  a The probability that this sample will contain at least two defectives.
  b The probability that this sample will contain at most one defective.

5.42 Suppose that you purchase (randomly select) 3 TV sets from a production run of 10 TV sets. Of the 10 TV sets, 9 are destined to last at least five years without needing a single repair. What is the probability that all three of your TV sets will last at least five years without needing a single repair?

5.43 Suppose that you own a car dealership and purchase (randomly select) 7 cars of a certain make from a production run of 200 cars. Of the 200 cars, 160 are destined to last at least five years without needing a major repair. Set up an expression using the hypergeometric distribution for the probability that at least 6 of your 7 cars will last at least five years without needing a major repair. Then, using the binomial tables (see Table A.1, page 783), approximate this probability by using the binomial distribution. What justifies the approximation? Hint: $p = r/N = 160/200 = .8$.

5.6 Joint Distributions and the Covariance (Optional) ● ● ●

Below we present (1) the probability distribution of x, the yearly proportional return for stock A, (2) the probability distribution of y, the yearly proportional return for stock B, and (3) the **joint probability distribution of (x, y),** the joint yearly proportional returns for stocks A and B [note that we have obtained the data below from Pfaffenberger and Patterson (1987)].

LO5-6 Compute and understand the covariance between two random variables (Optional).

x	$p(x)$	y	$p(y)$
−0.10	0.400	−0.15	0.300
0.05	0.125	−0.05	0.200
0.15	0.100	0.12	0.150
0.38	0.375	0.46	0.350
$\mu_x = .124$		$\mu_y = .124$	
$\sigma_x^2 = .0454$		$\sigma_y^2 = .0681$	
$\sigma_x = .2131$		$\sigma_y = .2610$	

Joint Distribution of (x, y)

Stock B Return, y	Stock A Return, x			
	−0.10	0.05	0.15	0.38
−0.15	0.025	0.025	0.025	0.225
−0.05	0.075	0.025	0.025	0.075
0.12	0.050	0.025	0.025	0.050
0.46	0.250	0.050	0.025	0.025

To explain the joint probability distribution, note that the probability of .250 enclosed in the rectangle is the probability that in a given year the return for stock A will be −.10 and the return for stock B will be .46. The probability of .225 enclosed in the oval is the probability that in a given year the return for stock A will be .38 and the return for stock B will be −.15. Intuitively, these two rather large probabilities say that (1) a negative return x for stock A tends to be associated with a highly positive return y for stock B, and (2) a highly positive return x for stock A tends to be associated with a negative return y for stock B. To further measure the association between x and y, we can calculate the *covariance* between x and y. To do this, we calculate $(x - \mu_x)(y - \mu_y) = (x - .124)(y - .124)$ for each combination of values of x and y. Then, we multiply each $(x - \mu_x)(y - \mu_y)$ value by the probability $p(x, y)$ of the (x, y) combination of values and add up the quantities that we obtain. The resulting number is the **covariance,** denoted σ_{xy}^2. For example, for the combination of values $x = -.10$ and $y = .46$, we calculate

$$(x - \mu_x)(y - \mu_y)\, p(x, y) = (-.10 - .124)(.46 - .124)(.250) = -.0188$$

Doing this for all combinations of (x, y) values and adding up the resulting quantities, we find that the covariance is $-.0318$. In general, a negative covariance says that as x increases, y tends to decrease in a linear fashion. A positive covariance says that as x increases, y tends to increase in a linear fashion.

In this situation, the covariance helps us to understand the importance of investment diversification. If we invest all of our money in stock A, we have seen that $\mu_x = .124$ and $\sigma_x = .2131$. If we invest all of our money in stock B, we have seen that $\mu_y = .124$ and $\sigma_y = .2610$. If we invest half of our money in stock A and half of our money in stock B, the return for the portfolio is $P = .5x + .5y$. To find the expected value of the portfolio return, we need to use a *property of expected values*. This property says if a and b are constants, and if x and y are random variables, then

$$\mu_{(ax + by)} = a\mu_x + b\mu_y$$

Therefore,

$$\mu_P = \mu_{(.5x + .5y)} = .5\mu_x + .5\mu_y = .5(.124) + .5(.124) = .124$$

To find the variance of the portfolio return, we must use a *property of variances*. In general, if x and y have a covariance σ_{xy}^2, and a and b are constants, then

$$\sigma_{(ax + by)}^2 = a^2\sigma_x^2 + b^2\sigma_y^2 + 2ab\sigma_{xy}^2$$

Therefore

$$\sigma_P^2 = \sigma_{(.5x + .5y)}^2 = (.5)^2\sigma_x^2 + (.5)^2\sigma_y^2 + 2(.5)(.5)\sigma_{xy}^2$$

$$= (.5)^2(.0454) + (.5)^2(.0681) + 2(.5)(.5)(-.0318) = .012475$$

and $\sigma_P = \sqrt{.012475} = .1117$. Note that, because $\mu_P = .124$ equals $\mu_x = .124$ and $\mu_y = .124$, the portfolio has the same expected return as either stock A or B. However, because $\sigma_P = .1117$ is less than $\sigma_x = .2131$ and $\sigma_y = .2610$, the portfolio is a less risky investment. In other words, diversification *can* reduce risk. Note, however, that the reason that σ_P is *less* than σ_x and σ_y is that $\sigma_{xy}^2 = -.0318$ *is negative*. Intuitively, this says that the two stocks tend to balance each other's returns. However, if the covariance between the returns of two stocks is positive, σ_P can be larger than σ_x and/or σ_y. The student will demonstrate this in Exercise 5.46.

Next, note that a measure of linear association between x and y that is unitless and always between -1 and 1 is the **correlation coefficient,** denoted ρ. We define ρ as follows:

The **correlation coefficient** between x and y is $\rho = \sigma_{xy}^2 / \sigma_x\sigma_y$

For the stock return example, ρ equals $(-.0318)/((.2131)(.2610)) = -.5717$.

To conclude this section, we summarize four properties of expected values and variances that we will use in optional Section 7.6 to derive some important facts about the sample mean:

Property 1: If a is a constant and x is a random variable, $\mu_{ax} = a\mu_x$.

Property 2: If $x_1, x_2, \ldots, x_n$ are random variables, $\mu_{(x_1 + x_2 + \cdots + x_n)} = \mu_{x_1} + \mu_{x_2} + \cdots + \mu_{x_n}$.

Property 3: If a is a constant and x is a random variable, $\sigma_{ax}^2 = a^2\sigma_x^2$.

Property 4: If $x_1, x_2, \ldots, x_n$ are statistically independent random variables (that is, if the value taken by any one of these independent variables is in no way associated with the value taken by any other of these random variables), then the covariance between any two of these random variables is zero and $\sigma_{(x_1 + x_2 + \cdots + x_n)}^2 = \sigma_{x_1}^2 + \sigma_{x_2}^2 + \cdots + \sigma_{x_n}^2$.

Exercises for Section 5.6

CONCEPTS

5.44 Explain the meaning of a negative covariance.

5.45 Explain the meaning of a positive covariance.

METHODS AND APPLICATIONS

5.46 Let x be the yearly proportional return for stock C, and let y be the yearly proportional return for stock D. If $\mu_x = .11$, $\mu_y = .09$, $\sigma_x = .17$, $\sigma_y = .17$, and $\sigma^2_{xy} = .0412$, find the mean and standard deviation of the portfolio return $P = .5x + .5y$. Discuss the risk of the portfolio.

5.47 Below we give a joint probability table for two utility bonds where the random variable x represents the percentage return for bond 1 and the random variable y represents the percentage return for bond 2.

			x			
y	8	9	10	11	12	$p(y)$
8	.03	.04	.03	.00	.00	.10
9	.04	.06	.06	.04	.00	.20
10	.02	.08	.20	.08	.02	.40
11	.00	.04	.06	.06	.04	.20
12	.00	.00	.03	.04	.03	.10
$p(x)$	.09	.22	.38	.22	.09	

Source: David K. Hildebrand and Lyman Ott, *Statistical Thinking for Managers,* 2nd edition (Boston, MA: Duxbury Press, 1987), p. 101.

In this table, probabilities associated with values of x are given in the row labeled $p(x)$ and probabilities associated with values of y are given in the column labeled $p(y)$. For example, $P(x = 9) = .22$ and $P(y = 11) = .20$. The entries inside the body of the table are joint probabilities—for instance, the probability that x equals 9 and y equals 10 is .08. Use the table to do the following:

a Calculate μ_x, σ_x, μ_y, σ_y, and σ^2_{xy}.

b Calculate the variance and standard deviation of a portfolio in which 50 percent of the money is used to buy bond 1 and 50 percent is used to buy bond 2. That is, find σ^2_P and σ_P, where $P = .5x + .5y$. Discuss the risk of the portfolio.

Chapter Summary

In this chapter we began our study of **random variables.** We learned that **a random variable represents an uncertain numerical outcome.** We also learned that a random variable whose values can be listed is called a **discrete random variable,** while the values of a **continuous random variable** correspond to one or more intervals on the real number line. We saw that a **probability distribution** of a discrete random variable is a table, graph, or formula that gives the probability associated with each of the random variable's possible values. We also discussed several descriptive measures of a discrete random variable—its **mean (or expected value),** its **variance,** and its **standard deviation.** We continued this chapter by studying two important, commonly used discrete probability distributions—the **binomial distribution** and the **Poisson distribution**—and we demonstrated how these distributions can be used to make statistical inferences. Finally, we studied a third important discrete probability distribution, the **hypergeometric distribution,** and we discussed **joint distributions** and the **covariance.**

Glossary of Terms

binomial distribution: The probability distribution that describes a binomial random variable. (page 199)

binomial experiment: An experiment that consists of n independent, identical trials, each of which results in either a success or a failure and is such that the probability of success on any trial is the same. (page 199)

binomial random variable: A random variable that is defined to be the total number of successes in n trials of a binomial experiment. (page 199)

binomial tables: Tables in which we can look up binomial probabilities. (pages 201, 202)

continuous random variable: A random variable whose values correspond to one or more intervals of numbers on the real number line. (page 187)

correlation coefficient: A unitless measure of the linear relationship between two random variables. (page 216)

covariance: A non-unitless measure of the linear relationship between two random variables. (page 216)

discrete random variable: A random variable whose values can be counted or listed. (page 187)

expected value (of a random variable): The mean of the population of all possible observed values of a random variable. That is, the long-run average value obtained if values of a random variable are observed a (theoretically) infinite number of times. (page 190)

hypergeometric distribution: The probability distribution that describes a hypergeometric random variable. (page 213)

hypergeometric random variable: A random variable that is defined to be the number of successes obtained in a random sample selected without replacement from a finite population of N elements that contains r successes and $N - r$ failures. (page 213)

joint probability distribution of (x, y): A probability distribution that assigns probabilities to all combinations of values of x and y. (page 215)

Poisson distribution: The probability distribution that describes a Poisson random variable. (page 208)

Poisson random variable: A discrete random variable that can often be used to describe the number of occurrences of an event over a specified interval of time or space. (page 208)

probability distribution (of a discrete random variable): A table, graph, or formula that gives the probability associated with each of the random variable's values. (page 188)

random variable: A variable that assumes numerical values that are determined by the outcome of an experiment. That is, a variable that represents an uncertain numerical outcome. (page 187)

standard deviation (of a random variable): The standard deviation of the population of all possible observed values of a random variable. It measures the spread of the population of all possible observed values of the random variable. (page 192)

variance (of a random variable): The variance of the population of all possible observed values of a random variable. It measures the spread of the population of all possible observed values of the random variable. (page 192)

Important Formulas

Properties of a discrete probability distribution: page 189

The mean (expected value) of a discrete random variable: page 190

Variance and standard deviation of a discrete random variable: page 192

Binomial probability formula: page 199

Mean, variance, and standard deviation of a binomial random variable: page 205

Poisson probability formula: page 208

Mean, variance, and standard deviation of a Poisson random variable: page 211

Hypergeometric probability formula: page 213

Mean and variance of a hypergeometric random variable: page 213

Correlation coefficient between x and y: page 216

Properties of expected values and variances: page 216

Supplementary Exercises

5.48   A rock concert promoter has scheduled an outdoor concert on July 4th. If it does not rain, the promoter will make $30,000. If it does rain, the promoter will lose $15,000 in guarantees made to the band and other expenses. The probability of rain on the 4th is .4.

   a   What is the promoter's expected profit? Is the expected profit a reasonable decision criterion? Explain.

   b   How much should an insurance company charge to insure the promoter's full losses? Explain your answer.

5.49   The demand (in number of copies per day) for a city newspaper, x, has historically been 50,000, 70,000, 90,000, 110,000, or 130,000 with the respective probabilities .1, .25, .4, .2, and .05.

   a   Graph the probability distribution of x.

   b   Find the expected demand. Interpret this value, and label it on the graph of part a.

   c   Using Chebyshev's Theorem, find the minimum percentage of all possible daily demand values that will fall in the interval $[\mu_x \pm 2\sigma_x]$.

   d   Calculate the interval $[\mu_x \pm 2\sigma_x]$. Illustrate this interval on the graph of part a. According to the probability distribution of demand x previously given, what percentage of all possible daily demand values fall in the interval $[\mu_x \pm 2\sigma_x]$?

5.50   United Medicine, Inc., claims that a drug, Viro, significantly relieves the symptoms of a certain viral infection for 80 percent of all patients. Suppose that this drug is given to eight randomly selected patients who have been diagnosed with the viral infection.

   a   Let x equal the number of the eight randomly selected patients whose symptoms are significantly relieved. What distribution describes the random variable x? Explain.

   b   Assuming that the company's claim is correct, find $P(x \le 3)$.

   c   Suppose that of the eight randomly selected patients, three have had their symptoms significantly relieved by Viro. Based on the probability in part b, would you believe the claim of United Medicine, Inc.? Explain.

5.51 A consumer advocate claims that 80 percent of cable television subscribers are not satisfied with their cable service. In an attempt to justify this claim, a randomly selected sample of cable subscribers will be polled on this issue.

   a Suppose that the advocate's claim is true, and suppose that a random sample of five cable subscribers is selected. Assuming independence, use an appropriate formula to compute the probability that four or more subscribers in the sample are not satisfied with their service.

   b Suppose that the advocate's claim is true, and suppose that a random sample of 25 cable subscribers is selected. Assuming independence, find:

     (1) The probability that 15 or fewer subscribers in the sample are not satisfied with their service.

     (2) The probability that more than 20 subscribers in the sample are not satisfied with their service.

     (3) The probability that between 20 and 24 (inclusive) subscribers in the sample are not satisfied with their service.

     (4) The probability that exactly 24 subscribers in the sample are not satisfied with their service.

   c Suppose that when we survey 25 randomly selected cable television subscribers, we find that 15 are actually not satisfied with their service. Using a probability you found in this exercise as the basis for your answer, do you believe the consumer advocate's claim? Explain.

5.52 A retail store has implemented procedures aimed at reducing the number of bad checks cashed by its cashiers. The store's goal is to cash no more than eight bad checks per week. The average number of bad checks cashed is three per week. Let x denote the number of bad checks cashed per week. Assuming that x has a Poisson distribution:

   a Find the probability that the store's cashiers will not cash any bad checks in a particular week.

   b Find the probability that the store will meet its goal during a particular week.

   c Find the probability that the store will not meet its goal during a particular week.

   d Find the probability that the store's cashiers will cash no more than 10 bad checks per two-week period.

   e Find the probability that the store's cashiers will cash no more than five bad checks per three-week period.

5.53 Suppose that the number of accidents occurring in an industrial plant is described by a Poisson process with an average of 1.5 accidents every three months. During the last three months, four accidents occurred.

   a Find the probability that no accidents will occur during the current three-month period.

   b Find the probability that fewer accidents will occur during the current three-month period than occurred during the last three-month period.

   c Find the probability that no more than 12 accidents will occur during a particular year.

   d Find the probability that no accidents will occur during a particular year.

5.54 A high-security government installation has installed four security systems to detect attempted break-ins. The four security systems operate independently of each other, and each has a .85 probability of detecting an attempted break-in. Assume an attempted break-in occurs. Use the binomial distribution to find the probability that at least one of the four security systems will detect it.

5.55 A new stain removal product claims to completely remove the stains on 90 percent of all stained garments. Assume that the product will be tested on 20 randomly selected stained garments, and let x denote the number of these garments from which the stains will be completely removed. Use the binomial distribution to find $P(x \leq 13)$ if the stain removal product's claim is correct. If x actually turns out to be 13, what do you think of the claim?

5.56 Consider Exercise 5.55, and find $P(x \leq 17)$ if the stain removal product's claim is correct. If x actually turns out to be 17, what do you think of the claim?

5.57 A state has averaged one small business failure per week over the past several years. Let x denote the number of small business failures in the next eight weeks. Use the Poisson distribution to find $P(x \geq 17)$ if the mean number of small business failures remains what it has been. If x actually turns out to be 17, what does this imply?

5.58 A candy company claims that its new chocolate almond bar averages 10 almonds per bar. Let x denote the number of almonds in the next bar that you buy. Use the Poisson distribution to find $P(x \leq 4)$ if the candy company's claim is correct. If x actually turns out to be 4, what do you think of the claim?

5.59 Consider Exercise 5.58, and find $P(x \leq 8)$ if the candy company's claim is true. If x actually turns out to be 8, what do you think of the claim?

Appendix 5.1 ■ Binomial, Poisson, and Hypergeometric Probabilities Using Excel

Binomial probabilities in Figure 5.5(a) on page 201:

- Enter the title, "Binomial with n = 4 and p = 0.10," in the cell location where you wish to place the binomial results. We have placed the title beginning in cell A2 (any other choice will do).

- In cell A3, enter the heading, x.

- Enter the values 0 through 4 in cells A4 through A8.

- In cell B3, enter the heading P(X = x).

- Click in cell B4 (this is where the first binomial probability will be placed). Click on the Insert Function button f_x on the Excel toolbar.

- In the Insert Function dialog box, select Statistical from the "Or select a category:" menu, select BINOM.DIST from the "Select a function:" menu, and click OK.

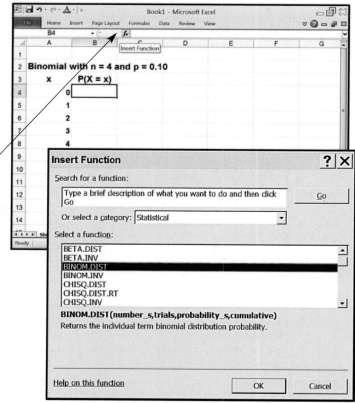

- In the BINOM.DIST Function Arguments dialog box, enter the cell location A4 (this cell contains the value for which the first binomial probability will be calculated) in the "Number_s" window.

- Enter the value 4 in the Trials window.

- Enter the value 0.10 in the "Probability_s" window.

- Enter the value 0 in the Cumulative window.

- Click OK in the BINOM.DIST Function Arguments dialog box.

- When you click OK, the calculated result (0.6561) will appear in cell B4. Double-click the drag handle (in the lower right corner) of cell B4 to automatically extend the cell formula to cells B5 through B8.

- The remaining probabilities will be placed in cells B5 through B8.

To obtain **hypergeometric probabilities:**

Enter data as above, click the Insert Function button, and then select HYPGEOM.DIST from the "Select a function" menu. In the Function Arguments dialog box:

- Enter the location of the initial number of successes in the Sample_s window.

- Enter the size of the sample in the Number_sample window.

- Enter the number of successes in the population in the Population_s window.

- Enter the size of the population in the Number_pop window.

Then click OK and proceed as above to compute the probabilities.

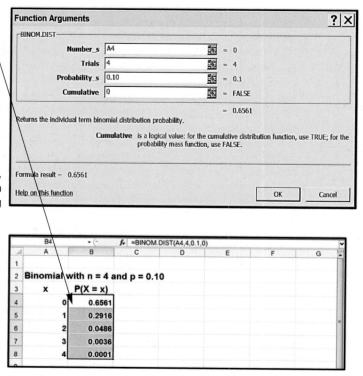

Poisson probabilities similar to Figure 5.9(a) on page 210:

- Enter the title "Poisson with mean = 0.40" in the cell location where you wish to place the Poisson results. Here we have placed the title beginning in cell A1 (any other choice will do).

- In cell A2, enter the heading, x.

- Enter the values 0 through 6 in cells A3 through A9.

- In cell B2, enter the heading, P(X = x).

- Click in cell B3 (this is where the first Poisson probability will be placed). Click on the Insert Function button f_x on the Excel toolbar.

- In the Insert Function dialog box, select Statistical from the "Or select a category" menu, select POISSON.DIST from the "Select a function:" menu, and click OK.

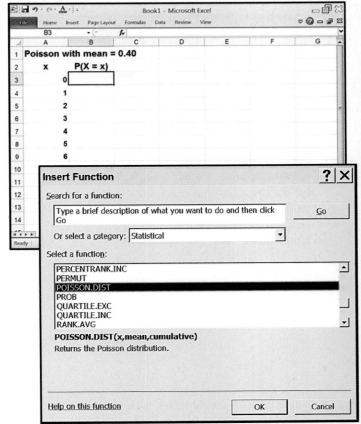

- In the POISSON.DIST Function Arguments dialog box, enter the cell location A3 (this cell contains the value for which the first Poisson probability will be calculated) in the "X" window.

- Enter the value 0.40 in the Mean window.

- Enter the value 0 in the Cumulative window.

- Click OK in the POISSON.DIST Function Arguments dialog box.

- The calculated result for the probability of 0 events will appear in cell B3.

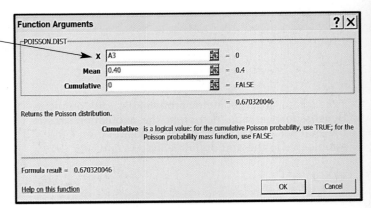

- Double-click the drag handle (in the lower right corner) of cell B3 to automatically extend the cell formula to cells B4 through B9.

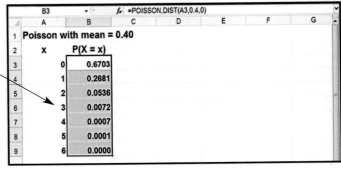

Appendix 5.2 ■ Binomial, Poisson, and Hypergeometric Probabilities Using MegaStat

Binomial probabilities similar to those in Figure 5.8 on page 207:

- Select **Add-Ins : MegaStat : Probability : Discrete Probability Distributions.**

- In the "Discrete Probability Distributions" dialog box, enter the number of trials (here equal to 24) and the probability of success *p* (here equal to .01) in the appropriate windows.

- Click the Display Graph checkbox if a plot of the distribution is desired.

- Click OK in the "Discrete Probability Distributions" dialog box.

The binomial output is placed in an output worksheet.

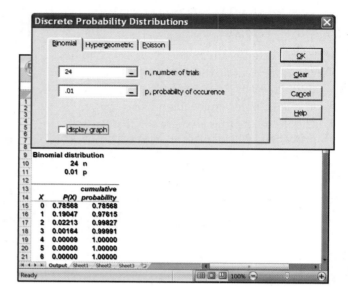

To calculate **Poisson probabilities,** click on the Poisson tab and enter the mean of the Poisson distribution. Then click OK.

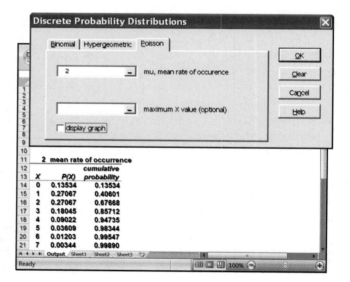

To calculate **Hypergeometric probabilities,** click on the Hypergeometric tab. Then enter the population size, the number of successes in the population, and the sample size in the appropriate windows and click OK.

Appendix 5.3 ■ Binomial, Poisson, and Hypergeometric Probabilities Using MINITAB

Binomial probabilities similar to Figure 5.5(a) on page 201:

- In the data window, enter the values 0 through 4 into column C1 and name the column x.
- Select **Calc : Probability Distributions : Binomial.**
- In the Binomial Distribution dialog box, select the Probability option by clicking.
- In the "Number of trials" window, enter 4 for the value of n.
- In the "Event Probability" window, enter 0.1 for the value of p.
- Select the "Input column" option and enter the variable name x into the "Input column" window.
- Click OK in the Binomial Distribution dialog box.
- The binomial probabilities will be displayed in the Session window.

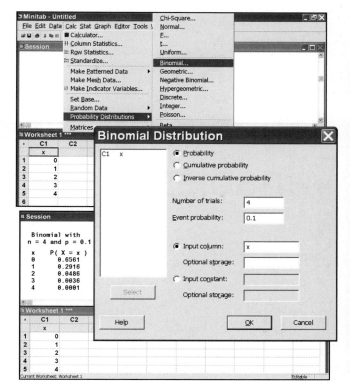

To compute **hypergeometric probabilities:**

- Enter data as above.
- Select **Calc : Probability Distributions : Hypergeometric.**
- In the Hypergeometric Distribution dialog box: Enter the "Population size," "Event count (number of successes) in population," "Sample Size," and enter x as the "Input column" option.
- Click OK to obtain the probabilities in the Session Window.

Poisson probabilities in Figure 5.9(a) on page 210:

- In the data window, enter the values 0 through 6 into column C1 and name the column x.
- Select **Calc : Probability Distributions : Poisson.**
- In the Poisson Distribution dialog box, select the Probability option by clicking it.
- In the Mean window, enter 0.4.
- Select the "Input column" option and enter the variable name x into the "Input column" window.
- Click OK in the Poisson Distribution dialog box.
- The Poisson probabilities will be displayed in the Session window.

CHAPTER 6

Continuous Random Variables

Learning Objectives

After mastering the material in this chapter, you will be able to:

LO6-1 Define a continuous probability distribution and explain how it is used.

LO6-2 Use the uniform distribution to compute probabilities.

LO6-3 Describe the properties of the normal distribution and use a cumulative normal table.

LO6-4 Use the normal distribution to compute probabilities.

LO6-5 Find population values that correspond to specified normal distribution probabilities.

LO6-6 Use the normal distribution to approximate binomial probabilities (Optional).

LO6-7 Use the exponential distribution to compute probabilities (Optional).

LO6-8 Use a normal probability plot to help decide whether data come from a normal distribution (Optional).

Chapter Outline

n Chapter 5 we defined discrete and continuous random variables. We also discussed discrete probability distributions, which are used to compute the probabilities of values of discrete random variables. In this chapter we discuss **continuous probability distributions.** These are used to find probabilities concerning continuous random variables. We begin by explaining the general idea behind a continuous probability distribution. Then we present three important continuous distributions—**the uniform, normal,** and **exponential distributions.** We also study when and how the normal distribution can be used to approximate the binomial distribution (which was discussed in Chapter 5).

We will illustrate the concepts in this chapter by using two cases:

The Car Mileage Case: A competitor claims that its midsize car gets better mileage than an automaker's new midsize model. The automaker uses sample information and a probability based on the normal distribution to provide strong evidence that the competitor's claim is false.

The Coffee Temperature Case: A fast-food restaurant uses the normal distribution to estimate the proportion of coffee it serves that has a temperature (in degrees Fahrenheit) inside the range 153° to 167°, the customer requirement for best-tasting coffee.

6.1 Continuous Probability Distributions ● ● ●

LO6-1 Define a continuous probability distribution and explain how it is used.

We have said in Section 5.1 that when a random variable may assume any numerical value in one or more intervals on the real number line, then the random variable is called a **continuous random variable.** For example, as discussed in Section 5.1, the EPA combined city and highway mileage of a randomly selected midsize car is a continuous random variable. Furthermore, the temperature (in degrees Fahrenheit) of a randomly selected cup of coffee at a fast-food restaurant is also a continuous random variable. We often wish to compute probabilities about the range of values that a continuous random variable x might attain. For example, suppose that marketing research done by a fast-food restaurant indicates that coffee tastes best if its temperature is between 153° F and 167° F. The restaurant might then wish to find the probability that x, the temperature of a randomly selected cup of coffee at the restaurant, will be between 153° and 167°. This probability would represent the proportion of coffee served by the restaurant that has a temperature between 153° and 167°. Moreover, one minus this probability would represent the proportion of coffee served by the restaurant that has a temperature outside the range 153° to 167°.

In general, to compute probabilities concerning a continuous random variable x, we assign probabilities to **intervals of values** by using what we call a **continuous probability distribution.** To understand this idea, suppose that $f(x)$ is a continuous function of the numbers on the real line, and consider the continuous curve that results when $f(x)$ is graphed. Such a curve is illustrated in the figure on the page margin. Then:

Continuous Probability Distributions

The curve $f(x)$ is the **continuous probability distribution** of the random variable x if the probability that x will be in a specified interval of numbers is the area under the curve $f(x)$ corresponding to the interval. Sometimes we refer to a continuous probability distribution as a **probability curve** or as a **probability density function.**

In this chapter we will study three continuous probability distributions—the *uniform, normal,* and *exponential* distributions. As an example of using a continuous probability distribution to describe a random variable, suppose that the fast-food restaurant will study the temperature of the coffee being dispensed at one of its locations. A temperature measurement is taken at a randomly selected time during each of the 24 half-hour periods from 8 A.M. to 7:30 P.M. on a given day. This is then repeated on a second day, giving the 48 coffee temperatures in Figure 6.1(a). Figure 6.1(b) shows a percent frequency histogram of the coffee temperatures. If we

FIGURE 6.1   The Coffee Temperature Data, Histogram, and Normal Curve

(a) The Coffee Temperature Data (Time Order Is Given By Reading Across And Then Down.)

154° F	165	148	157	160	157	152	149	171	168	165	164	156	151	161	157
154	159	155	153	173	164	161	151	158	160	153	161	160	158	169	163
146	167	162	159	166	158	173	162	155	150	165	154	160	162	159	166

(b) The Histogram

(c) The Normal Curve

were to smooth out the histogram with a continuous curve, we would get a curve similar to the symmetrical and bell-shaped curve in Figure 6.1(c). One continuous probability distribution that graphs as a symmetrical and bell-shaped curve is the *normal probability distribution* (or *normal curve*). Because the coffee temperature histogram looks like a normal curve, it is reasonable to conclude that x, the temperature of a randomly selected cup of coffee at the fast-food restaurant, is described by a normal probability distribution. It follows that the probability that x will be between 153° and 167° is the area under the coffee temperature normal curve between 153 and 167. In Section 6.3, where we discuss the normal curve in detail, we will find that this area is .7223. That is, in probability notation: $P(153 \leq x \leq 167) = .7223$ (see the blue area in Figure 6.1(c)). In conclusion, we estimate that 72.23 percent of the coffee served at the restaurant is within the range of temperatures that is best and 27.77 percent of the coffee served is not in this range. If management wishes a very high percentage of the coffee served to taste best, it must improve the coffee-making process by better controlling temperatures.

We now present some general properties of a continuous probability distribution. We know that any probability is 0 or positive, and we also know that the probability assigned to all possible values of x must be 1. It follows that, similar to the conditions required for a discrete probability distribution, a probability curve must satisfy the following:

Properties of a Continuous Probability Distribution

The **continuous probability distribution** (or **probability curve**) $f(x)$ of a random variable x must satisfy the following two conditions:

1 $f(x) \geq 0$ for any value of x.

2   The total area under the curve $f(x)$ is equal to 1.

We have seen that to calculate a probability concerning a continuous random variable, we must compute an appropriate area under the curve $f(x)$. Because there is no area under a continuous curve at a single point, or number, on the real line, the probability that a continuous random variable x will equal a single numerical value is always equal to 0. It follows that if $[a, b]$ denotes an arbitrary interval of numbers on the real line, then $P(x = a) = 0$ and $P(x = b) = 0$. Therefore, $P(a \leq x \leq b)$ equals $P(a < x < b)$ because each of the interval endpoints a and b has a probability that is equal to 0.

6.2 The Uniform Distribution ● ● ●

LO6-2 Use the uniform distribution to compute probabilities.

Suppose that over a period of several days the manager of a large hotel has recorded the waiting times of 1,000 people waiting for an elevator in the lobby at dinnertime (5:00 P.M. to 7:00 P.M.). The observed waiting times range from zero to four minutes. Furthermore, when the waiting times are arranged into a histogram, the bars making up the histogram have approximately equal heights, giving the histogram a rectangular appearance. This implies that the relative frequencies of all waiting times from zero to four minutes are about the same. Therefore, it is reasonable to use the continuous *uniform distribution* to describe the random variable x, the amount of time a randomly selected hotel patron spends waiting for an elevator. The equation describing the uniform distribution in this situation is

$$f(x) = \begin{cases} \dfrac{1}{4} & \text{for } 0 \leq x \leq 4 \\ 0 & \text{otherwise} \end{cases}$$

Noting that this equation is graphed in Figure 6.2(a), suppose that the hotel manager feels that an elevator waiting time of 2.5 minutes or more is unacceptably long. Therefore, to find the probability that a hotel patron will wait too long, the manager wishes to find the probability that a randomly selected patron will spend at least 2.5 minutes waiting for an elevator. This probability is the area under the curve $f(x)$ that corresponds to the interval [2.5, 4]. As shown in Figure 6.2(a), this probability is the area of a rectangle having a base equal to $4 - 2.5 = 1.5$ and a height equal to $1/4$. That is,

$$P(x \geq 2.5) = P(2.5 \leq x \leq 4) = \text{base} \times \text{height} = 1.5 \times \frac{1}{4} = .375$$

This says that 37.5 percent of all hotel patrons will spend at least 2.5 minutes waiting for an elevator at dinnertime. Based on this result, the hotel manager would probably decide that too many patrons are waiting too long for an elevator and that action should be taken to reduce elevator waiting times.

FIGURE 6.2   The Uniform Distribution

(a) A graph of the uniform distribution describing the elevator waiting times

(b) A graph of the general uniform distribution

In general, the equation that describes the uniform distribution is given in the following box and is graphed in Figure 6.2(b).

The Uniform Distribution

If c and d are numbers on the real line, the equation describing the **uniform distribution** is

$$f(x) = \begin{cases} \dfrac{1}{d-c} & \text{for } c \le x \le d \\ 0 & \text{otherwise} \end{cases}$$

Furthermore, the mean and the standard deviation of the population of all possible observed values of a random variable x that has a uniform distribution are

$$\mu_x = \frac{c+d}{2} \quad \text{and} \quad \sigma_x = \frac{d-c}{\sqrt{12}}$$

Notice that the total area under the uniform distribution is the area of a rectangle having a base equal to $(d-c)$ and a height equal to $1/(d-c)$. Therefore, the probability curve's total area is

$$\text{base} \times \text{height} = (d-c)\left(\frac{1}{d-c}\right) = 1$$

(remember that the total area under any continuous probability curve must equal 1). Furthermore, if a and b are numbers that are as illustrated in Figure 6.2(b), then the probability that x will be between a and b is the area of a rectangle with base $(b-a)$ and height $1/(d-c)$. That is,

$$P(a \le x \le b) = \text{base} \times \text{height} = (b-a)\left(\frac{1}{d-c}\right) = \frac{b-a}{d-c}$$

EXAMPLE 6.1 Elevator Waiting Times

In the introduction to this section we have said that the amount of time, x, that a randomly selected hotel patron spends waiting for the elevator at dinnertime is uniformly distributed between zero and four minutes. In this case, $c = 0$ and $d = 4$. Therefore,

$$f(x) = \begin{cases} \dfrac{1}{d-c} = \dfrac{1}{4-0} = \dfrac{1}{4} & \text{for } 0 \le x \le 4 \\ 0 & \text{otherwise} \end{cases}$$

Moreover, the mean waiting time for the elevator is

$$\mu_x = \frac{c+d}{2} = \frac{0+4}{2} = 2 \text{ (minutes)}$$

and the standard deviation of the waiting times is

$$\sigma_x = \frac{d-c}{\sqrt{12}} = \frac{4-0}{\sqrt{12}} = 1.1547 \text{ (minutes)}$$

Therefore, noting that $\mu_x - \sigma_x = 2 - 1.1547 = .8453$ and that $\mu_x + \sigma_x = 2 + 1.1547 = 3.1547$, the probability that the waiting time of a randomly selected patron will be within (plus or minus) one standard deviation of the mean waiting time is

$$P(.8453 \leq x \leq 3.1547) = (3.1547 - .8453) \times \frac{1}{4}$$

$$= .57735$$

Exercises for Sections 6.1 and 6.2

CONCEPTS

6.1 A discrete probability distribution assigns probabilities to individual values. To what are probabilities assigned by a continuous probability distribution?

6.2 How do we use the continuous probability distribution (or probability curve) of a random variable x to find probabilities? Explain.

6.3 What two properties must be satisfied by a continuous probability distribution (or probability curve)?

6.4 Is the height of a probability curve over a given point a probability? Explain.

6.5 When is it appropriate to use the uniform distribution to describe a random variable x?

METHODS AND APPLICATIONS

6.6 Suppose that the random variable x has a uniform distribution with $c = 2$ and $d = 8$.
   a Write the formula for the probability curve of x, and write an interval that gives the possible values of x.
   b Graph the probability curve of x.
   c Find $P(3 \leq x \leq 5)$.
   d Find $P(1.5 \leq x \leq 6.5)$.
   e Calculate the mean μ_x, variance σ_x^2, and standard deviation σ_x.
   f Calculate the interval $[\mu_x \pm 2\sigma_x]$. What is the probability that x will be in this interval?

6.7 Consider the figure given in the margin. Find the value h that makes the function $f(x)$ a valid continuous probability distribution.

6.8 Assume that the waiting time x for an elevator is uniformly distributed between zero and six minutes.
   a Write the formula for the probability curve of x.
   b Graph the probability curve of x.
   c Find $P(2 \leq x \leq 4)$.
   d Find $P(3 \leq x \leq 6)$.
   e Find $P(\{0 \leq x \leq 2\} \text{ or } \{5 \leq x \leq 6\})$.

6.9 Refer to Exercise 6.8.
   a Calculate the mean, μ_x, the variance, σ_x^2, and the standard deviation, σ_x.
   b Find the probability that the waiting time of a randomly selected patron will be within one standard deviation of the mean.

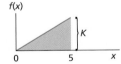

6.10 Consider the figure given in the margin. Find the value k that makes the function $f(x)$ a valid continuous probability distribution.

6.11 Suppose that an airline quotes a flight time of 2 hours, 10 minutes between two cities. Furthermore, suppose that historical flight records indicate that the actual flight time between the two cities, x, is uniformly distributed between 2 hours and 2 hours, 20 minutes. Letting the time unit be one minute,
   a Write the formula for the probability curve of x.
   b Graph the probability curve of x.
   c Find $P(125 \leq x \leq 135)$.
   d Find the probability that a randomly selected flight between the two cities will be at least five minutes late.

6.12 Refer to Exercise 6.11.
   a Calculate the mean flight time and the standard deviation of the flight time.
   b Find the probability that the flight time will be within one standard deviation of the mean.

6.13 Consider the figure given in the margin. Find the value c that makes the function $f(x)$ a valid continuous probability distribution.

connect™

6.14   A weather forecaster predicts that the May rainfall in a local area will be between three and six inches but has no idea where within the interval the amount will be. Let x be the amount of May rainfall in the local area, and assume that x is uniformly distributed over the interval three to six inches.

a   Write the formula for the probability curve of x and graph this probability curve.

b   What is the probability that May rainfall will be at least four inches? At least five inches?

6.15   Refer to Exercise 6.14 and find the probability that the observed May rainfall will fall within two standard deviations of the mean May rainfall.

LO6-3 Describe the properties of the normal distribution and use a cumulative normal table.

6.3 The Normal Probability Distribution ● ● ●

The normal curve   The bell-shaped appearance of the normal probability distribution is illustrated in Figure 6.3. The equation that defines this normal curve is given in the following box:

The Normal Probability Distribution

The **normal probability distribution** is defined by the equation

$$f(x) = \frac{1}{\sigma\sqrt{2\pi}}\, e^{-\frac{1}{2}\left(\frac{x-\mu}{\sigma}\right)^2} \quad \text{for all values of } x \text{ on the real line}$$

Here μ and σ are the mean and standard deviation of the population of all possible observed values of the random variable x under consideration. Furthermore, $\pi = 3.14159\ldots$, and $e = 2.71828\ldots$ is the base of Napierian logarithms.

Although this equation looks very intimidating, we will not use it to find areas (and thus probabilities) under the normal curve. Instead, we will use a *normal curve table*. What is important to know for now is that the normal probability distribution has several important properties:

1   There is an entire family of normal probability distributions; the specific shape of each normal distribution is determined by its mean μ and its standard deviation σ.

2   The highest point on the normal curve is located at the mean, which is also the median and the mode of the distribution.

3   The normal distribution is symmetrical: The curve's shape to the left of the mean is the mirror image of its shape to the right of the mean.

4   The tails of the normal curve extend to infinity in both directions and never touch the horizontal axis. However, the tails get close enough to the horizontal axis quickly enough to ensure that the total area under the normal curve equals 1.

5   Because the normal curve is symmetrical, the area under the normal curve to the right of the mean (μ) equals the area under the normal curve to the left of the mean, and each of these areas equals .5 (see Figure 6.3).

FIGURE 6.3

The Normal Probability Curve

The normal curve is symmetrical around μ, and the total area under the curve equals 1.

Intuitively, the mean μ positions the normal curve on the real line. This is illustrated in Figure 6.4(a). This figure shows two normal curves with different means μ_1 and μ_2 (where μ_1 is greater than μ_2) and with equal standard deviations. We see that the normal curve with mean μ_1 is centered farther to the right.

The variance σ^2 (and the standard deviation σ) measure the spread of the normal curve. This is illustrated in Figure 6.4(b), which shows two normal curves with the same mean and two different standard deviations σ_1 and σ_2. Because σ_1 is greater than σ_2, the normal curve with standard deviation σ_1 is more spread out (flatter) than the normal curve with standard deviation σ_2. In general, larger standard deviations result in normal curves that are flatter and more spread out, while smaller standard deviations result in normal curves that have higher peaks and are less spread out.

Suppose that a random variable x is described by a normal probability distribution (or is, as we say, **normally distributed**) with mean μ and standard deviation σ. If a and b are numbers on the

FIGURE 6.4 How the Mean μ and Standard Deviation σ Affect the Position and Shape of a Normal Probability Curve

(a) Two normal curves with different means and equal standard deviations. If μ_1 is greater than μ_2, the normal curve with mean μ_1 is centered farther to the right.

Normal curve with mean μ_2 and standard deviation σ

$\mu_1 > \mu_2$

Normal curve with mean μ_1 and standard deviation σ

μ_2 μ_1 x

(b) Two normal curves with the same mean and different standard deviations. If σ_1 is greater than σ_2, the normal curve with standard deviation σ_1 is flatter and more spread out.

Normal curve with mean μ and standard deviation σ_2

$\sigma_1 > \sigma_2$

Normal curve with mean μ and standard deviation σ_1

μ x

FIGURE 6.5 An Area under a Normal Curve Corresponding to the Interval [a, b]

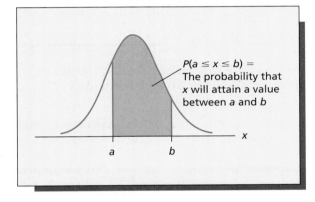

$P(a \leq x \leq b) =$ The probability that x will attain a value between a and b

a b x

FIGURE 6.6 Three Important Percentages Concerning a Normally Distributed Random Variable x with Mean μ and Standard Deviation σ

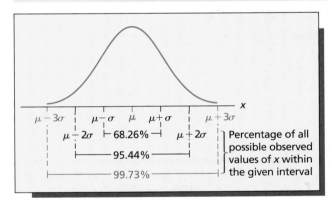

$\mu - 3\sigma$ $\mu - \sigma$ μ $\mu + \sigma$ $\mu + 3\sigma$ x

$\mu - 2\sigma$ $\vdash$ 68.26% $\dashv$ $\mu + 2\sigma$

95.44%

99.73%

Percentage of all possible observed values of x within the given interval

real line, we consider the probability that x will be between a and b. That is, we consider

$$P(a \leq x \leq b)$$

which equals the area under the normal curve with mean μ and standard deviation σ corresponding to the interval [a, b]. Such an area is depicted in Figure 6.5. We soon explain how to find such areas using a statistical table called a **normal table.** For now, we emphasize three important areas under a normal curve. These areas form the basis for the **Empirical Rule** for a normally distributed population. Specifically, if x is normally distributed with mean μ and standard deviation σ, it can be shown (using a normal table) that, as illustrated in Figure 6.6:

Three Important Areas under the Normal Curve

1 $P(\mu - \sigma \leq x \leq \mu + \sigma) = .6826$

This means that 68.26 percent of all possible observed values of x are within (plus or minus) one standard deviation of μ.

2 $P(\mu - 2\sigma \leq x \leq \mu + 2\sigma) = .9544$

This means that 95.44 percent of all possible observed values of x are within (plus or minus) two standard deviations of μ.

3 $P(\mu - 3\sigma \leq x \leq \mu + 3\sigma) = .9973$

This means that 99.73 percent of all possible observed values of x are within (plus or minus) three standard deviations of μ.

Finding normal curve areas   There is a unique normal curve for every combination of μ and σ. Because there are many (theoretically, an unlimited number of) such combinations, we would like to have one table of normal curve areas that applies to all normal curves. There is such a table, and we can use it by thinking in terms of how many standard deviations a value of interest is from the mean. Specifically, consider a random variable x that is normally distributed with mean μ and standard deviation σ. Then the random variable

$$z = \frac{x - \mu}{\sigma}$$

expresses the number of standard deviations that x is from the mean μ. To understand this idea, notice that if x equals μ (that is, x is zero standard deviations from μ), then $z = (\mu - \mu)/\sigma = 0$. However, if x is one standard deviation above the mean (that is, if x equals $\mu + \sigma$), then $x - \mu = \sigma$ and $z = \sigma/\sigma = 1$. Similarly, if x is two standard deviations below the mean (that is, if x equals $\mu - 2\sigma$), then $x - \mu = -2\sigma$ and $z = -2\sigma/\sigma = -2$. Figure 6.7 illustrates that for values of x of, respectively, $\mu - 3\sigma$, $\mu - 2\sigma$, $\mu - \sigma$, μ, $\mu + \sigma$, $\mu + 2\sigma$, and $\mu + 3\sigma$, the corresponding values of z are $-3, -2, -1, 0, 1, 2,$ and 3. This figure also illustrates the following general result:

The Standard Normal Distribution

If a random variable x (or, equivalently, the population of all possible observed values of x) is normally distributed with mean μ and standard deviation σ, then the random variable

$$z = \frac{x - \mu}{\sigma}$$

(or, equivalently, the population of all possible observed values of z) is normally distributed with mean 0 and standard deviation 1. A normal distribution (or curve) with mean 0 and standard deviation 1 is called a **standard normal distribution** (or **curve**).

Table A.3 (on pages 790 and 791) is a table of *cumulative* areas under the standard normal curve. This table is called a *cumulative normal table,* and it is reproduced as Table 6.1 (on pages 233 and 234). Specifically,

The **cumulative normal table** gives, for many different values of z, the area under the standard normal curve to the left of z.

FIGURE 6.7   **If x Is Normally Distributed with Mean μ and Standard Deviation σ, Then $z = \dfrac{x - \mu}{\sigma}$ Is Normally Distributed with Mean 0 and Standard Deviation 1**

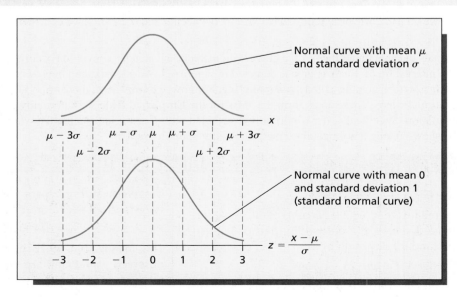

Two such areas are shown next to Table 6.1—one with a negative z value and one with a positive z value. The values of z in the cumulative normal table range from -3.99 to 3.99 in increments of .01. As can be seen from Table 6.1, values of z accurate to the nearest tenth are given in the far left column (headed z) of the table. Further graduations to the nearest hundredth $(.00, .01, .02, \ldots, .09)$ are given across the top of the table. The areas under the normal curve are given in the body of the table, accurate to four (or sometimes five) decimal places.

TABLE 6.1   **Cumulative Areas under the Standard Normal Curve**

z	0.00	0.01	0.02	0.03	0.04	0.05	0.06	0.07	0.08	0.09
−3.9	0.00005	0.00005	0.00004	0.00004	0.00004	0.00004	0.00004	0.00004	0.00003	0.00003
−3.8	0.00007	0.00007	0.00007	0.00006	0.00006	0.00006	0.00006	0.00005	0.00005	0.00005
−3.7	0.00011	0.00010	0.00010	0.00010	0.00009	0.00009	0.00008	0.00008	0.00008	0.00008
−3.6	0.00016	0.00015	0.00015	0.00014	0.00014	0.00013	0.00013	0.00012	0.00012	0.00011
−3.5	0.00023	0.00022	0.00022	0.00021	0.00020	0.00019	0.00019	0.00018	0.00017	0.00017
−3.4	0.00034	0.00032	0.00031	0.00030	0.00029	0.00028	0.00027	0.00026	0.00025	0.00024
−3.3	0.00048	0.00047	0.00045	0.00043	0.00042	0.00040	0.00039	0.00038	0.00036	0.00035
−3.2	0.00069	0.00066	0.00064	0.00062	0.00060	0.00058	0.00056	0.00054	0.00052	0.00050
−3.1	0.00097	0.00094	0.00090	0.00087	0.00084	0.00082	0.00079	0.00076	0.00074	0.00071
−3.0	0.00135	0.00131	0.00126	0.00122	0.00118	0.00114	0.00111	0.00107	0.00103	0.00100
−2.9	0.0019	0.0018	0.0018	0.0017	0.0016	0.0016	0.0015	0.0015	0.0014	0.0014
−2.8	0.0026	0.0025	0.0024	0.0023	0.0023	0.0022	0.0021	0.0021	0.0020	0.0019
−2.7	0.0035	0.0034	0.0033	0.0032	0.0031	0.0030	0.0029	0.0028	0.0027	0.0026
−2.6	0.0047	0.0045	0.0044	0.0043	0.0041	0.0040	0.0039	0.0038	0.0037	0.0036
−2.5	0.0062	0.0060	0.0059	0.0057	0.0055	0.0054	0.0052	0.0051	0.0049	0.0048
−2.4	0.0082	0.0080	0.0078	0.0075	0.0073	0.0071	0.0069	0.0068	0.0066	0.0064
−2.3	0.0107	0.0104	0.0102	0.0099	0.0096	0.0094	0.0091	0.0089	0.0087	0.0084
−2.2	0.0139	0.0136	0.0132	0.0129	0.0125	0.0122	0.0119	0.0116	0.0113	0.0110
−2.1	0.0179	0.0174	0.0170	0.0166	0.0162	0.0158	0.0154	0.0150	0.0146	0.0143
−2.0	0.0228	0.0222	0.0217	0.0212	0.0207	0.0202	0.0197	0.0192	0.0188	0.0183
−1.9	0.0287	0.0281	0.0274	0.0268	0.0262	0.0256	0.0250	0.0244	0.0239	0.0233
−1.8	0.0359	0.0351	0.0344	0.0336	0.0329	0.0322	0.0314	0.0307	0.0301	0.0294
−1.7	0.0446	0.0436	0.0427	0.0418	0.0409	0.0401	0.0392	0.0384	0.0375	0.0367
−1.6	0.0548	0.0537	0.0526	0.0516	0.0505	0.0495	0.0485	0.0475	0.0465	0.0455
−1.5	0.0668	0.0655	0.0643	0.0630	0.0618	0.0606	0.0594	0.0582	0.0571	0.0559
−1.4	0.0808	0.0793	0.0778	0.0764	0.0749	0.0735	0.0721	0.0708	0.0694	0.0681
−1.3	0.0968	0.0951	0.0934	0.0918	0.0901	0.0885	0.0869	0.0853	0.0838	0.0823
−1.2	0.1151	0.1131	0.1112	0.1093	0.1075	0.1056	0.1038	0.1020	0.1003	0.0985
−1.1	0.1357	0.1335	0.1314	0.1292	0.1271	0.1251	0.1230	0.1210	0.1190	0.1170
−1.0	0.1587	0.1562	0.1539	0.1515	0.1492	0.1469	0.1446	0.1423	0.1401	0.1379
−0.9	0.1841	0.1814	0.1788	0.1762	0.1736	0.1711	0.1685	0.1660	0.1635	0.1611
−0.8	0.2119	0.2090	0.2061	0.2033	0.2005	0.1977	0.1949	0.1922	0.1894	0.1867
−0.7	0.2420	0.2389	0.2358	0.2327	0.2296	0.2266	0.2236	0.2206	0.2177	0.2148
−0.6	0.2743	0.2709	0.2676	0.2643	0.2611	0.2578	0.2546	0.2514	0.2482	0.2451
−0.5	0.3085	0.3050	0.3015	0.2981	0.2946	0.2912	0.2877	0.2843	0.2810	0.2776
−0.4	0.3446	0.3409	0.3372	0.3336	0.3300	0.3264	0.3228	0.3192	0.3156	0.3121
−0.3	0.3821	0.3783	0.3745	0.3707	0.3669	0.3632	0.3594	0.3557	0.3520	0.3483
−0.2	0.4207	0.4168	0.4129	0.4090	0.4052	0.4013	0.3974	0.3936	0.3897	0.3859
−0.1	0.4602	0.4562	0.4522	0.4483	0.4443	0.4404	0.4364	0.4325	0.4286	0.4247
−0.0	0.5000	0.4960	0.4920	0.4880	0.4840	0.4801	0.4761	0.4721	0.4681	0.4641
0.0	0.5000	0.5040	0.5080	0.5120	0.5160	0.5199	0.5239	0.5279	0.5319	0.5359
0.1	0.5398	0.5438	0.5478	0.5517	0.5557	0.5596	0.5636	0.5675	0.5714	0.5753
0.2	0.5793	0.5832	0.5871	0.5910	0.5948	0.5987	0.6026	0.6064	0.6103	0.6141
0.3	0.6179	0.6217	0.6255	0.6293	0.6331	0.6368	0.6406	0.6443	0.6480	0.6517
0.4	0.6554	0.6591	0.6628	0.6664	0.6700	0.6736	0.6772	0.6808	0.6844	0.6879
0.5	0.6915	0.6950	0.6985	0.7019	0.7054	0.7088	0.7123	0.7157	0.7190	0.7224
0.6	0.7257	0.7291	0.7324	0.7357	0.7389	0.7422	0.7454	0.7486	0.7518	0.7549
0.7	0.7580	0.7611	0.7642	0.7673	0.7704	0.7734	0.7764	0.7794	0.7823	0.7852
0.8	0.7881	0.7910	0.7939	0.7967	0.7995	0.8023	0.8051	0.8078	0.8106	0.8133
0.9	0.8159	0.8186	0.8212	0.8238	0.8264	0.8289	0.8315	0.8340	0.8365	0.8389

(Table Continues)

$\frac{.02+.03}{2} = .0025$

| TABLE 6.1 | Cumulative Areas under the Standard Normal Curve (*Continued*) |

z	0.00	0.01	0.02	0.03	0.04	0.05	0.06	0.07	0.08	0.09
1.0	0.8413	0.8438	0.8461	0.8485	0.8508	0.8531	0.8554	0.8577	0.8599	0.8621
1.1	0.8643	0.8665	0.8686	0.8708	0.8729	0.8749	0.8770	0.8790	0.8810	0.8830
1.2	0.8849	0.8869	0.8888	0.8907	0.8925	0.8944	0.8962	0.8980	0.8997	0.9015
1.3	0.9032	0.9049	0.9066	0.9082	0.9099	0.9115	0.9131	0.9147	0.9162	0.9177
1.4	0.9192	0.9207	0.9222	0.9236	0.9251	0.9265	0.9279	0.9292	0.9306	0.9319
1.5	0.9332	0.9345	0.9357	0.9370	0.9382	0.9394	0.9406	0.9418	0.9429	0.9441
1.6	0.9452	0.9463	0.9474	0.9484	0.9495	0.9505	0.9515	0.9525	0.9535	0.9545
1.7	0.9554	0.9564	0.9573	0.9582	0.9591	0.9599	0.9608	0.9616	0.9625	0.9633
1.8	0.9641	0.9649	0.9656	0.9664	0.9671	0.9678	0.9686	0.9693	0.9699	0.9706
1.9	0.9713	0.9719	0.9726	0.9732	0.9738	0.9744	0.9750	0.9756	0.9761	0.9767
2.0	0.9772	0.9778	0.9783	0.9788	0.9793	0.9798	0.9803	0.9808	0.9812	0.9817
2.1	0.9821	0.9826	0.9830	0.9834	0.9838	0.9842	0.9846	0.9850	0.9854	0.9857
2.2	0.9861	0.9864	0.9868	0.9871	0.9875	0.9878	0.9881	0.9884	0.9887	0.9890
2.3	0.9893	0.9896	0.9898	0.9901	0.9904	0.9906	0.9909	0.9911	0.9913	0.9916
2.4	0.9918	0.9920	0.9922	0.9925	0.9927	0.9929	0.9931	0.9932	0.9934	0.9936
2.5	0.9938	0.9940	0.9941	0.9943	0.9945	0.9946	0.9948	0.9949	0.9951	0.9952
2.6	0.9953	0.9955	0.9956	0.9957	0.9959	0.9960	0.9961	0.9962	0.9963	0.9964
2.7	0.9965	0.9966	0.9967	0.9968	0.9969	0.9970	0.9971	0.9972	0.9973	0.9974
2.8	0.9974	0.9975	0.9976	0.9977	0.9977	0.9978	0.9979	0.9979	0.9980	0.9981
2.9	0.9981	0.9982	0.9982	0.9983	0.9984	0.9984	0.9985	0.9985	0.9986	0.9986
3.0	0.99865	0.99869	0.99874	0.99878	0.99882	0.99886	0.99889	0.99893	0.99897	0.99900
3.1	0.99903	0.99906	0.99910	0.99913	0.99916	0.99918	0.99921	0.99924	0.99926	0.99929
3.2	0.99931	0.99934	0.99936	0.99938	0.99940	0.99942	0.99944	0.99946	0.99948	0.99950
3.3	0.99952	0.99953	0.99955	0.99957	0.99958	0.99960	0.99961	0.99962	0.99964	0.99965
3.4	0.99966	0.99968	0.99969	0.99970	0.99971	0.99972	0.99973	0.99974	0.99975	0.99976
3.5	0.99977	0.99978	0.99978	0.99979	0.99980	0.99981	0.99981	0.99982	0.99983	0.99983
3.6	0.99984	0.99985	0.99985	0.99986	0.99986	0.99987	0.99987	0.99988	0.99988	0.99989
3.7	0.99989	0.99990	0.99990	0.99990	0.99991	0.99991	0.99992	0.99992	0.99992	0.99992
3.8	0.99993	0.99993	0.99993	0.99994	0.99994	0.99994	0.99994	0.99995	0.99995	0.99995
3.9	0.99995	0.99995	0.99996	0.99996	0.99996	0.99996	0.99996	0.99996	0.99997	0.99997

2.525 ⟶ (pointing to row 2.0)

As an example, suppose that we wish to find the area under the standard normal curve to the left of a z value of 2.00. This area is illustrated in Figure 6.8. To find this area, we start at the top of the leftmost column in Table 6.1 (previous page) and scan down the column past the negative z values. We then scan through the positive z values (which continue on the top of this page) until we find the z value 2.0—see the red arrow above. We now scan across the row in the table corresponding to the z value 2.0 until we find the column corresponding to the heading .00. The desired area (which we have shaded blue) is in the row corresponding to the z value 2.0 and in the column headed .00. This area, which equals .9772, is the probability that the random variable z will be less than or equal to 2.00. That is, we have found that $P(z \leq 2) = .9772$. Note that, because there is no area under the normal curve at a single value of z, there is no difference between $P(z \leq 2)$ and $P(z < 2)$. As another example, the area under the standard normal curve to the left of the z value 1.25 is found in the row corresponding to 1.2 and in the column corresponding to .05. We find that this area (also shaded blue) is .8944. That is, $P(z \leq 1.25) = .8944$ (see Figure 6.9).

We now show how to use the cumulative normal table to find several other kinds of normal curve areas. First, suppose that we wish to find the area under the standard normal curve to the right of a z value of 2—that is, we wish to find $P(z \geq 2)$. This area is illustrated in Figure 6.10 and is called a **right-hand tail area.** Because the total area under the normal curve equals 1, the area under the curve to the right of 2 equals 1 minus the area under the curve to the left of 2. Because Table 6.1 tells us that the area under the standard normal curve to the left of 2 is .9772, the area under the standard normal curve to the right of 2 is $1 - .9772 = .0228$. Said in an equivalent fashion, because $P(z \leq 2) = .9772$, it follows that $P(z \geq 2) = 1 - P(z \leq 2) = 1 - .9772 = .0228$.

FIGURE 6.8   Finding $P(z \leq 2)$

$P(z \leq 2)$
$= .9772$

FIGURE 6.9   Finding $P(z \leq 1.25)$

$P(z \leq 1.25)$
$= .8944$

FIGURE 6.10   Finding $P(z \geq 2)$

.9772

$P(z \geq 2)$
$= 1 - .9772$
$= .0228$

FIGURE 6.11   Finding $P(z \leq -2)$

$P(z \leq -2)$
$= .0228$

Next, suppose that we wish to find the area under the standard normal curve to the left of a z value of -2. That is, we wish to find $P(z \leq -2)$. This area is illustrated in Figure 6.11 and is called a **left-hand tail area.** The needed area is found in the row of the cumulative normal table corresponding to -2.0 (on page 233) and in the column headed by .00. We find that $P(z \leq -2) = .0228$. Notice that the area under the standard normal curve to the left of -2 is equal to the area under this curve to the right of 2. This is true because of the symmetry of the normal curve.

Figure 6.12 illustrates how to find the area under the standard normal curve to the right of -2. Because the total area under the normal curve equals 1, the area under the curve to the right of -2 equals 1 minus the area under the curve to the left of -2. Because Table 6.1 tells us that the area under the standard normal curve to the left of -2 is .0228, the area under the standard normal curve to the right of -2 is $1 - .0228 = .9772$. That is, because $P(z \leq -2) = .0228$, it follows that $P(z \geq -2) = 1 - P(z \leq -2) = 1 - .0228 = .9772$.

The smallest z value in Table 6.1 is -3.99, and the table tells us that the area under the standard normal curve to the left of -3.99 is .00003 (see Figure 6.13). Therefore, if we wish to find the area under the standard normal curve to the left of any z value less than -3.99, the most we can say (without using a computer) is that this area is less than .00003. Similarly, the area under

FIGURE 6.12   Finding $P(z \geq -2)$

.0228

$P(z \geq -2)$
$= 1 - .0228$
$= .9772$

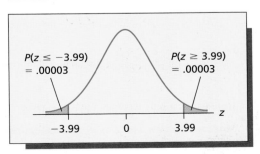

FIGURE 6.13   Finding $P(z \leq -3.99)$

$P(z \leq -3.99)$
$= .00003$

$P(z \geq 3.99)$
$= .00003$

FIGURE 6.14   **Calculating** $P(1 \leq z \leq 2)$

the standard normal curve to the right of any z value greater than 3.99 is also less than .00003 (see Figure 6.13).

Figure 6.14 illustrates how to find the area under the standard normal curve between 1 and 2. This area equals the area under the curve to the left of 2, which the normal table tells us is .9772, minus the area under the curve to the left of 1, which the normal table tells us is .8413. Therefore, $P(1 \leq z \leq 2) = .9772 - .8413 = .1359$.

To conclude our introduction to using the normal table, we will use this table to justify the Empirical Rule. Figure 6.15(a) illustrates the area under the standard normal curve between -1 and 1. This area equals the area under the curve to the left of 1, which the normal table tells us is .8413, minus the area under the curve to the left of -1, which the normal table tells us is .1587. Therefore, $P(-1 \leq z \leq 1) = .8413 - .1587 = .6826$. Now, suppose that a random variable x is normally distributed with mean μ and standard deviation σ, and remember that z is the number of standard deviations σ that x is from μ. It follows that when we say that $P(-1 \leq z \leq 1)$ equals .6826, we are saying that 68.26 percent of all possible observed values of x are between a point that is one standard deviation below μ (where z equals -1) and a point that is one standard deviation

FIGURE 6.15   **Some Areas under the Standard Normal Curve**

(a) $P(-1 \leq z \leq 1) = .8413 - .1587 = .6826$ (c) $P(-3 \leq z \leq 3) = .99865 - .00135 = .9973$

(b) $P(-2 \leq z \leq 2) = .9772 - .0228 = .9544$ (d) $P(-1.96 \leq z \leq 1.96) = .9750 - .0250 = .9500$

above μ (where z equals 1). That is, 68.26 percent of all possible observed values of x are within (plus or minus) one standard deviation of the mean μ.

Figure 6.15(b) illustrates the area under the standard normal curve between -2 and 2. This area equals the area under the curve to the left of 2, which the normal table tells us is .9772, minus the area under the curve to the left of -2, which the normal table tells us is .0228. Therefore, $P(-2 \le z \le 2) = .9772 - .0228 = .9544$. That is, 95.44 percent of all possible observed values of x are within (plus or minus) two standard deviations of the mean μ.

Figure 6.15(c) illustrates the area under the standard normal curve between -3 and 3. This area equals the area under the curve to the left of 3, which the normal table tells us is .99865, minus the area under the curve to the left of -3, which the normal table tells us is .00135. Therefore, $P(-3 \le z \le 3) = .99865 - .00135 = .9973$. That is, 99.73 percent of all possible observed values of x are within (plus or minus) three standard deviations of the mean μ.

Although the Empirical Rule gives the percentages of all possible values of a normally distributed random variable x that are within one, two, and three standard deviations of the mean μ, we can use the normal table to find the percentage of all possible values of x that are within any particular number of standard deviations of μ. For example, in later chapters we will need to know the percentage of all possible values of x that are within plus or minus 1.96 standard deviations of μ. Figure 6.15(d) illustrates the area under the standard normal curve between -1.96 and 1.96. This area equals the area under the curve to the left of 1.96, which the normal table tells us is .9750, minus the area under the curve to the left of -1.96, which the table tells us is .0250. Therefore, $P(-1.96 \le z \le 1.96) = .9750 - .0250 = .9500$. That is, 95 percent of all possible values of x are within plus or minus 1.96 standard deviations of the mean μ.

Some practical applications   We have seen how to use z values and the normal table to find areas under the standard normal curve. However, most practical problems are not stated in such terms. We now consider an example in which we must restate the problem in terms of the standard normal random variable z before using the normal table.

LO6-4 Use the normal distribution to compute probabilities.

EXAMPLE 6.2 The Car Mileage Case: Estimating Mileage

Recall from previous chapters that an automaker has recently introduced a new midsize model and that we have used the sample of 50 mileages to estimate that the population of mileages of all cars of this type is normally distributed with a mean mileage equal to 31.56 mpg and a standard deviation equal to .798 mpg. Suppose that a competing automaker produces a midsize model that is somewhat smaller and less powerful than the new midsize model. The competitor claims, however, that its midsize model gets better mileages. Specifically, the competitor claims that the mileages of all its midsize cars are normally distributed with a mean mileage μ equal to 33 mpg and a standard deviation σ equal to .7 mpg. In the next example we consider one way to investigate the validity of this claim. In this example we assume that the claim is true, and we calculate the probability that the mileage, x, of a randomly selected competing midsize car will be between 32 mpg and 35 mpg. That is, we wish to find $P(32 \le x \le 35)$. As illustrated in Figure 6.16 on the next page, this probability is the area between 32 and 35 under the normal curve having mean $\mu = 33$ and standard deviation $\sigma = .7$. In order to use the normal table, we must restate the problem in terms of the standard normal random variable z. The z value corresponding to 32 is

$$z = \frac{x - \mu}{\sigma} = \frac{32 - 33}{.7} = \frac{-1}{.7} = -1.43$$

which says that the mileage 32 is 1.43 standard deviations below the mean $\mu = 33$. The z value corresponding to 35 is

$$z = \frac{x - \mu}{\sigma} = \frac{35 - 33}{.7} = \frac{2}{.7} = 2.86$$

FIGURE 6.16   Finding $P(32 \leq x \leq 35)$ When $\mu = 33$ and $\sigma = .7$ by Using a Normal Table

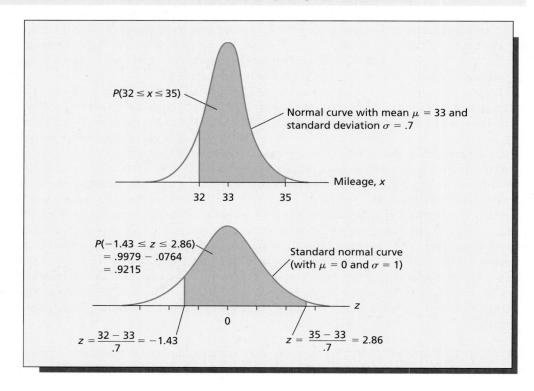

which says that the mileage 35 is 2.86 standard deviations above the mean $\mu = 33$. Looking at Figure 6.16, we see that the area between 32 and 35 under the normal curve having mean $\mu = 33$ and standard deviation $\sigma = .7$ equals the area between -1.43 and 2.86 under the standard normal curve. This equals the area under the standard normal curve to the left of 2.86, which the normal table tells us is .9979, minus the area under the standard normal curve to the left of -1.43, which the normal table tells us is .0764. We summarize this result as follows:

$$P(32 \leq x \leq 35) = P\left(\frac{32 - 33}{.7} \leq \frac{x - \mu}{\sigma} \leq \frac{35 - 33}{.7}\right)$$

$$= P(-1.43 \leq z \leq 2.86) = .9979 - .0764 = .9215$$

This probability says that, if the competing automaker's claim is valid, then 92.15 percent of all of its midsize cars will get mileages between 32 mpg and 35 mpg.

Example 6.2 illustrates the general procedure for finding a probability about a normally distributed random variable x. We summarize this procedure in the following box:

Finding Normal Probabilities

1 Formulate the problem in terms of the random variable x.

2 Calculate relevant z values and restate the problem in terms of the standard normal random variable

$$z = \frac{x - \mu}{\sigma}$$

3 Find the required area under the standard normal curve by using the normal table.

4 Note that it is always useful to draw a picture illustrating the needed area before using the normal table.

EXAMPLE 6.3 The Car Mileage Case: Estimating Mileage

Recall from Example 6.2 that the competing automaker claims that the population of mileages of all its midsize cars is normally distributed with mean $\mu = 33$ and standard deviation $\sigma = .7$. Suppose that an independent testing agency randomly selects one of these cars and finds that it gets a mileage of 31.2 mpg when tested as prescribed by the EPA. Because the sample mileage of 31.2 mpg is *less than* the claimed mean $\mu = 33$, we have some evidence that contradicts the competing automaker's claim. To evaluate the strength of this evidence, we will calculate the probability that the mileage, x, of a randomly selected midsize car would be *less than or equal to* 31.2 if, in fact, the competing automaker's claim is true. To calculate $P(x \leq 31.2)$ under the assumption that the claim is true, we find the area to the left of 31.2 under the normal curve with mean $\mu = 33$ and standard deviation $\sigma = .7$ (see Figure 6.17). In order to use the normal table, we must find the z value corresponding to 31.2. This z value is

$$z = \frac{x - \mu}{\sigma} = \frac{31.2 - 33}{.7} = -2.57$$

which says that the mileage 31.2 is 2.57 standard deviations below the mean mileage $\mu = 33$. Looking at Figure 6.17, we see that the area to the left of 31.2 under the normal curve having mean $\mu = 33$ and standard deviation $\sigma = .7$ equals the area to the left of -2.57 under the standard normal curve. The normal table tells us that the area under the standard normal curve to the left of -2.57 is .0051, as shown in Figure 6.17. It follows that we can summarize our calculations as follows:

$$P(x \leq 31.2) = P\left(\frac{x - \mu}{\sigma} \leq \frac{31.2 - 33}{.7}\right)$$

$$= P(z \leq -2.57) = .0051$$

This probability says that, if the competing automaker's claim is valid, then only 51 in 10,000 cars would obtain a mileage of less than or equal to 31.2 mpg. Because it is very difficult to believe that a 51 in 10,000 chance has occurred, we have very strong evidence against the competing automaker's claim. It is probably true that μ is less than 33 and/or σ is greater than .7 and/or the population of all mileages is not normally distributed.

FIGURE 6.17   Finding $P(x \leq 31.2)$ When $\mu = 33$ and $\sigma = .7$ by Using a Normal Table

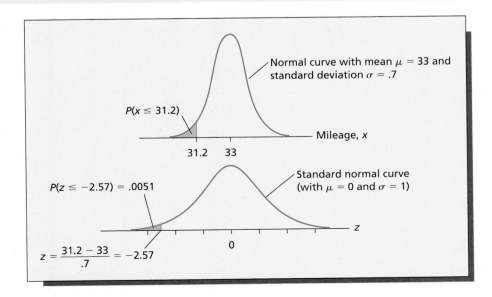

EXAMPLE 6.4 The Coffee Temperature Case: Meeting Customer Requirements

Recall that marketing research done by a fast-food restaurant indicates that coffee tastes best if its temperature is between 153°(F) and 167°(F). The restaurant has sampled the coffee it serves and observed the 48 temperature readings in Table 1.10 on page 17. The temperature readings have a mean $\bar{x} = 159.3958$ and a standard deviation $s = 6.4238$ and are described by a bell-shaped histogram. Using $\bar{x}$ and s as point estimates of the mean μ and the standard deviation σ of the population of all possible coffee temperatures, we wish to calculate the probability that x, the temperature of a randomly selected cup of coffee, is outside the customer requirements for best-testing coffee (that is, less than 153° or greater than 167°). In order to compute the probability $P(x < 153$ or $x > 167)$, we compute the z values

$$z = \frac{153 - 159.3958}{6.4238} = -1.00 \quad \text{and} \quad z = \frac{167 - 159.3958}{6.4238} = 1.18$$

Because the events $\{x < 153\}$ and $\{x > 167\}$ are mutually exclusive, we have

$$P(x < 153 \text{ or } x > 167) = P(x < 153) + P(x > 167)$$
$$= P(z < -1.00) + P(z > 1.18)$$
$$= .1587 + .1190 = .2777$$

This calculation is illustrated in Figure 6.18. The probability of .2777 implies that 27.77 percent of the coffee temperatures do not meet customer requirements and 72.23 percent of the coffee temperatures do meet these requirements. If management wishes a very high percentage of its coffee temperatures to meet customer requirements, the coffee-making process must be improved.

LO6-5 Find population values that correspond to specified normal distribution probabilities.

Finding a point on the horizontal axis under a normal curve   In order to use many of the formulas given in later chapters, we must be able to find the z value so that the tail area to the right of z under the standard normal curve is a particular value. For instance, we might need to find the z value so that the tail area to the right of z under the standard normal curve is .025. This z value is denoted $z_{.025}$, and we illustrate $z_{.025}$ in Figure 6.19(a). We refer to $z_{.025}$ as **the point on the horizontal axis under the standard normal curve that gives a right-hand tail area equal to .025.** It is easy to use the cumulative normal table to find such a point. For instance, in order to find $z_{.025}$, we note from Figure 6.19(b) that the area under the standard normal curve to the left of $z_{.025}$ equals .975. Remembering that areas under the standard normal curve to the left of z are

FIGURE 6.18   Finding $P(x < 153$ or $x > 167)$ in the Coffee Temperature Case

FIGURE 6.19   The Point $z_{.025} = 1.96$

(a) $z_{.025}$ is the point on the horizontal axis under the standard normal curve that gives a right-hand tail area equal to .025

(b) Finding $z_{.025}$

the four-digit (or five-digit) numbers given in the body of Table 6.1, we scan the body of the table and find the area .9750. We have shaded this area in Table 6.1 on page 234, and we note that the area .9750 is in the row corresponding to a z of 1.9 and in the column headed by .06. It follows that the z value corresponding to .9750 is 1.96. Because the z value 1.96 gives an area under the standard normal curve to its left that equals .975, it also gives a right-hand tail area equal to .025. Therefore, $z_{.025} = 1.96$.

In general, **we let z_α denote the point on the horizontal axis under the standard normal curve that gives a right-hand tail area equal to α.** With this definition in mind, we consider the following example.

EXAMPLE 6.5 The DVD Case: Managing Inventory

A large discount store sells 50 packs of HX-150 blank DVDs and receives a shipment every Monday. Historical sales records indicate that the weekly demand, x, for these 50 packs is normally distributed with a mean of $\mu = 100$ and a standard deviation of $\sigma = 10$. How many 50 packs should be stocked at the beginning of a week so that there is only a 5 percent chance that the store will run short during the week?

If we let st equal the number of 50 packs that will be stocked, then st must be chosen to allow only a .05 probability that weekly demand, x, will exceed st. That is, st must be chosen so that

$$P(x > st) = .05$$

Figure 6.20(a) on the next page shows that the number stocked, st, is located under the right-hand tail of the normal curve having mean $\mu = 100$ and standard deviation $\sigma = 10$. In order to find st, we need to determine how many standard deviations st must be above the mean in order to give a right-hand tail area that is equal to .05.

The z value corresponding to st is

$$z = \frac{st - \mu}{\sigma} = \frac{st - 100}{10}$$

and this z value is the number of standard deviations that st is from μ. This z value is illustrated in Figure 6.20(b), and it is the point on the horizontal axis under the standard normal curve that gives a right-hand tail area equal to .05. That is, the z value corresponding to st is $z_{.05}$. Since the area under the standard normal curve to the left of $z_{.05}$ is $1 - .05 = .95$—see Figure 6.20(b)—we look for .95 in the body of the normal table. In Table 6.1, we see that the areas closest to .95 are .9495, which has a corresponding z value of 1.64, and .9505, which has a corresponding z value of 1.65. Although it

FIGURE 6.20   **Finding the Number of 50 Packs of DVDs Stocked, *st*, so That $P(x > st) = .05$ When $\mu = 100$ and $\sigma = 10$**

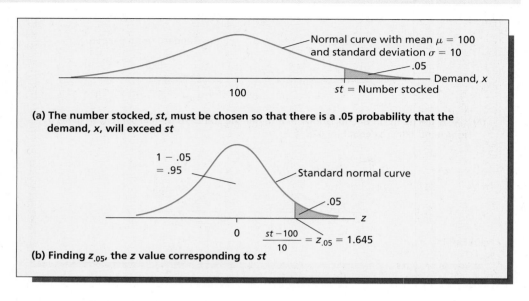

(a) The number stocked, *st*, must be chosen so that there is a .05 probability that the demand, *x*, will exceed *st*

(b) Finding $z_{.05}$, the *z* value corresponding to *st*

would probably be sufficient to use either of these *z* values, we will (because it is easy to do so) interpolate halfway between them and assume that $z_{.05}$ equals 1.645. To find *st*, we solve the equation

$$\frac{st - 100}{10} = 1.645$$

for *st*. Doing this yields

$$st - 100 = 1.645(10)$$

or

$$st = 100 + 1.645(10) = 116.45$$

This last equation says that *st* is 1.645 standard deviations ($\sigma = 10$) above the mean ($\mu = 100$). Rounding $st = 116.45$ up so that the store's chances of running short will be *no more* than 5 percent, the store should stock 117 of the 50 packs at the beginning of each week.

Sometimes we need to find the point on the horizontal axis under the standard normal curve that gives a particular **left-hand tail area** (say, for instance, an area of .025). Looking at Figure 6.21, it is easy to see that, if, for instance, we want a left-hand tail area of .025, the needed *z* value is $-z_{.025}$, where $z_{.025}$ gives a right-hand tail area equal to .025. To find $-z_{.025}$, we look for .025 in the body of the normal table and find that the *z* value corresponding to .025 is -1.96. Therefore, $-z_{.025} = -1.96$. In general, $-z_\alpha$ **is the point on the horizontal axis under the standard normal curve that gives a left-hand tail area equal to α.**

FIGURE 6.21   **The *z* Value $-z_{.025} = -1.96$ Gives a Left-Hand Tail Area of .025 under the Standard Normal Curve**

EXAMPLE 6.6 Setting A Guarantee Period

Extensive testing indicates that the lifetime of the Everlast automobile battery is normally distributed with a mean of $\mu = 60$ months and a standard deviation of $\sigma = 6$ months. The Everlast's manufacturer has decided to offer a free replacement battery to any purchaser whose Everlast battery does not last at least as long as the minimum lifetime specified in its guarantee. How can the manufacturer establish the guarantee period so that only 1 percent of the batteries will need to be replaced free of charge?

If the battery will be guaranteed to last l months, l must be chosen to allow only a .01 probability that the lifetime, x, of an Everlast battery will be less than l. That is, we must choose l so that

$$P(x < l) = .01$$

Figure 6.22(a) shows that the guarantee period, l, is located under the left-hand tail of the normal curve having mean $\mu = 60$ and standard deviation $\sigma = 6$. In order to find l, we need to determine how many standard deviations l must be below the mean in order to give a left-hand tail area that equals .01. The z value corresponding to l is

$$z = \frac{l - \mu}{\sigma} = \frac{l - 60}{6}$$

and this z value is the number of standard deviations that l is from μ. This z value is illustrated in Figure 6.22(b), and it is the point on the horizontal axis under the standard normal curve that gives a left-hand tail area equal to .01. That is, the z value corresponding to l is $-z_{.01}$. To find $-z_{.01}$, we look for .01 in the body of the normal table. Doing this, we see that the area closest to .01 is .0099, which has a corresponding z value of -2.33. Therefore, $-z_{.01}$ is (roughly) -2.33. To find l, we solve the equation

$$\frac{l - 60}{6} = -2.33$$

for l. Doing this yields

$$l - 60 = -2.33(6)$$

or

$$l = 60 - 2.33(6) = 46.02$$

Note that this last equation says that l is 2.33 standard deviations ($\sigma = 6$) below the mean ($\mu = 60$). Rounding $l = 46.02$ down so that *no more* than 1 percent of the batteries will need to be replaced free of charge, it seems reasonable to guarantee the Everlast battery to last 46 months.

BI

F I G U R E   6 . 2 2   **Finding the Guarantee Period, l, so That $P(x < l) = .01$ When $\mu = 60$ and $\sigma = 6$**

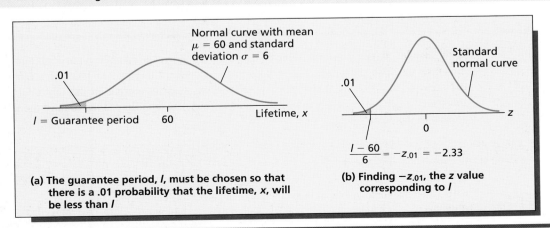

(a) The guarantee period, l, must be chosen so that there is a .01 probability that the lifetime, x, will be less than l

(b) Finding $-z_{.01}$, the z value corresponding to l

FIGURE 6.23   **Finding a Tolerance Interval [$\mu \pm k\sigma$] That Contains 99 Percent of the Measurements in a Normally Distributed Population**

Earlier in this section we saw that the intervals [$\mu \pm \sigma$], [$\mu \pm 2\sigma$], and [$\mu \pm 3\sigma$] are **tolerance intervals** containing, respectively, 68.26 percent, 95.44 percent, and 99.73 percent of the measurements in a normally distributed population having mean μ and standard deviation σ. In the following example we demonstrate how to use the normal table to find the value k so that the interval [$\mu \pm k\sigma$] contains any desired percentage of the measurements in a normally distributed population.

EXAMPLE 6.7 The Car Mileage Case: Estimating Mileage

Consider computing a tolerance interval [$\mu \pm k\sigma$] that contains 99 percent of the measurements in a normally distributed population having mean μ and standard deviation σ. As illustrated in Figure 6.23, we must find the value k so that the area under the normal curve having mean μ and standard deviation σ between ($\mu - k\sigma$) and ($\mu + k\sigma$) is .99. Because the total area under this normal curve is 1, the area under the normal curve that is not between ($\mu - k\sigma$) and ($\mu + k\sigma$) is $1 - .99 = .01$. This implies, as illustrated in Figure 6.23, that the area under the normal curve to the left of ($\mu - k\sigma$) is $.01/2 = .005$, and the area under the normal curve to the right of ($\mu + k\sigma$) is also $.01/2 = .005$. This further implies, as illustrated in Figure 6.23, that the area under the normal curve to the left of ($\mu + k\sigma$) is .995. Because the z value corresponding to a value of x tells us how many standard deviations x is from μ, the z value corresponding to ($\mu + k\sigma$) is obviously k. It follows that k is the point on the horizontal axis under the standard normal curve so that the area to the left of k is .995. Looking up .995 in the body of the normal table, we find that the values closest to .995 are .9949, which has a corresponding z value of 2.57, and .9951, which has a corresponding z value of 2.58. Although it would be sufficient to use either of these z values, we will interpolate halfway between them, and we will assume that k equals 2.575. It follows that the interval [$\mu \pm 2.575\sigma$] contains 99 percent of the measurements in a normally distributed population having mean μ and standard deviation σ. For example, recall that the histogram of the sample of 50 midsize car mileages in Figure 3.15 (page 115) suggests that the population of all midsize car mileages is normally distributed. Because the sample mean and the sample standard deviation are $\bar{x} = 31.56$ and $s = .7977$, we estimate that 99 percent of the new midsize cars will obtain mileages in the interval [$\bar{x} \pm 2.575s$] = [31.56 ± 2.575(.7977)] = [29.5, 33.6]—that is, will get mileages between 29.5 mpg and 33.6 mpg.

Whenever we use a normal table to find a z point corresponding to a particular normal curve area, we will use the *halfway interpolation* procedure illustrated in Examples 6.5 and 6.7 if the area we are looking for is exactly halfway between two areas in the table. Otherwise, as illustrated in Example 6.6, we will use the z value corresponding to the area in the table that is closest to the desired area.

Exercises for Section 6.3

CONCEPTS

connect

6.16   List five important properties of the normal probability curve.

6.17   Explain what the mean, μ, tells us about a normal curve, and explain what the standard deviation, σ, tells us about a normal curve.

6.18 If the random variable x is normally distributed, what percentage of all possible observed values of x will be
    a Within one standard deviation of the mean?
    b Within two standard deviations of the mean?
    c Within three standard deviations of the mean?

6.19 Explain how to compute the z value corresponding to a value of a normally distributed random variable. What does the z value tell us about the value of the random variable?

6.20 Explain how x relates to the mean μ if the z value corresponding to x
    a Equals zero.
    b Is positive.
    c Is negative.

6.21 Why do we compute z values when using the normal table? Explain.

METHODS AND APPLICATIONS

6.22 In each case, sketch the two specified normal curves on the same set of axes:
    a A normal curve with $\mu = 20$ and $\sigma = 3$, and a normal curve with $\mu = 20$ and $\sigma = 6$.
    b A normal curve with $\mu = 20$ and $\sigma = 3$, and a normal curve with $\mu = 30$ and $\sigma = 3$.
    c A normal curve with $\mu = 100$ and $\sigma = 10$, and a normal curve with $\mu = 200$ and $\sigma = 20$.

6.23 Let x be a normally distributed random variable having mean $\mu = 30$ and standard deviation $\sigma = 5$. Find the z value for each of the following observed values of x:
    a $x = 25$ **d** $x = 40$
    b $x = 15$ **e** $x = 50$
    c $x = 30$
    In each case, explain what the z value tells us about how the observed value of x compares to the mean, μ.

6.24 If the random variable z has a standard normal distribution, sketch and find each of the following probabilities:
    a $P(0 \leq z \leq 1.5)$ **d** $P(z \geq -1)$ **g** $P(-2.5 \leq z \leq .5)$
    b $P(z \geq 2)$ **e** $P(z \leq -3)$ **h** $P(1.5 \leq z \leq 2)$
    c $P(z \leq 1.5)$ **f** $P(-1 \leq z \leq 1)$ **i** $P(-2 \leq z \leq -.5)$

6.25 Suppose that the random variable z has a standard normal distribution. Sketch each of the following z points, and use the normal table to find each z point.
    a $z_{.01}$ **d** $-z_{.01}$
    b $z_{.05}$ **e** $-z_{.05}$
    c $z_{.02}$ **f** $-z_{.10}$

6.26 Suppose that the random variable x is normally distributed with mean $\mu = 1{,}000$ and standard deviation $\sigma = 100$. Sketch and find each of the following probabilities:
    a $P(1{,}000 \leq x \leq 1{,}200)$ **e** $P(x \leq 700)$
    b $P(x > 1{,}257)$ **f** $P(812 \leq x \leq 913)$
    c $P(x < 1{,}035)$ **g** $P(x > 891)$
    d $P(857 \leq x \leq 1{,}183)$ **h** $P(1{,}050 \leq x \leq 1{,}250)$

6.27 Suppose that the random variable x is normally distributed with mean $\mu = 500$ and standard deviation $\sigma = 100$. For each of the following, use the normal table to find the needed value k. In each case, draw a sketch.
    a $P(x \geq k) = .025$ **d** $P(x \leq k) = .015$ **g** $P(x \leq k) = .975$
    b $P(x \geq k) = .05$ **e** $P(x < k) = .985$ **h** $P(x \geq k) = .0228$
    c $P(x < k) = .025$ **f** $P(x > k) = .95$ **i** $P(x > k) = .9772$

6.28 Stanford–Binet IQ Test scores are normally distributed with a mean score of 100 and a standard deviation of 16.
    a Sketch the distribution of Stanford–Binet IQ test scores.
    b Write the equation that gives the z score corresponding to a Stanford–Binet IQ test score. Sketch the distribution of such z scores.
    c Find the probability that a randomly selected person has an IQ test score
        (1) Over 140.
        (2) Under 88.
        (3) Between 72 and 128.
        (4) Within 1.5 standard deviations of the mean.
    d Suppose you take the Stanford–Binet IQ Test and receive a score of 136. What percentage of people would receive a score higher than yours?

6.29 Weekly demand at a grocery store for a brand of breakfast cereal is normally distributed with a mean of 800 boxes and a standard deviation of 75 boxes.

    a What is the probability that weekly demand is

      (1) 959 boxes or less?

      (2) More than 1,004 boxes?

      (3) Less than 650 boxes or greater than 950 boxes?

    b The store orders cereal from a distributor weekly. How many boxes should the store order for a week to have only a 2.5 percent chance of running short of this brand of cereal during the week?

6.30 The lifetimes of a particular brand of DVD player are normally distributed with a mean of eight years and a standard deviation of six months. Find each of the following probabilities where x denotes the lifetime in years. In each case, sketch the probability.

    a $P(7 \leq x \leq 9)$ **e** $P(x \leq 7)$

    b $P(8.5 \leq x \leq 9.5)$ **f** $P(x \geq 7)$

    c $P(6.5 \leq x \leq 7.5)$ **g** $P(x \leq 10)$

    d $P(x \geq 8)$ **h** $P(x > 10)$

6.31 United Motors claims that one of its cars, the Starbird 300, gets city driving mileages that are normally distributed with a mean of 30 mpg and a standard deviation of 1 mpg. Let x denote the city driving mileage of a randomly selected Starbird 300.

    a Assuming that United Motors' claim is correct, find $P(x \leq 27)$.

    b If you purchase (randomly select) a Starbird 300 and your car gets 27 mpg in city driving, what do you think of United Motors' claim? Explain your answer.

6.32 An investment broker reports that the yearly returns on common stocks are approximately normally distributed with a mean return of 12.4 percent and a standard deviation of 20.6 percent. On the other hand, the firm reports that the yearly returns on tax-free municipal bonds are approximately normally distributed with a mean return of 5.2 percent and a standard deviation of 8.6 percent. Find the probability that a randomly selected

    a Common stock will give a positive yearly return.

    b Tax-free municipal bond will give a positive yearly return.

    c Common stock will give more than a 10 percent return.

    d Tax-free municipal bond will give more than a 10 percent return.

    e Common stock will give a loss of at least 10 percent.

    f Tax-free municipal bond will give a loss of at least 10 percent.

6.33 A filling process is supposed to fill jars with 16 ounces of grape jelly. Specifications state that each jar must contain between 15.95 ounces and 16.05 ounces. A jar is selected from the process every half hour until a sample of 100 jars is obtained. When the fills of the jars are measured, it is found that $\bar{x} = 16.0024$ and $s = .02454$. Using $\bar{x}$ and s as point estimates of μ and σ, estimate the probability that a randomly selected jar will have a fill, x, that is out of specification. Assume that the process is in control and that the population of all jar fills is normally distributed.

6.34 A tire company has developed a new type of steel-belted radial tire. Extensive testing indicates the population of mileages obtained by all tires of this new type is normally distributed with a mean of 40,000 miles and a standard deviation of 4,000 miles. The company wishes to offer a guarantee providing a discount on a new set of tires if the original tires purchased do not exceed the mileage stated in the guarantee. What should the guaranteed mileage be if the tire company desires that no more than 2 percent of the tires will fail to meet the guaranteed mileage?

6.35 Recall from Exercise 6.32 that yearly returns on common stocks are normally distributed with a mean of 12.4 percent and a standard deviation of 20.6 percent.

    a What percentage of yearly returns are at or below the 10th percentile of the distribution of yearly returns? What percentage are at or above the 10th percentile? Find the 10th percentile of the distribution of yearly returns.

    b Find the first quartile, Q_1, and the third quartile, Q_3, of the distribution of yearly returns.

6.36 Two students take a college entrance exam known to have a normal distribution of scores. The students receive raw scores of 63 and 93, which correspond to z scores (often called the standardized scores) of -1 and 1.5, respectively. Find the mean and standard deviation of the distribution of raw exam scores.

6.37 **THE TRASH BAG CASE**   📀 TrashBag

Suppose that a population of measurements is normally distributed with mean μ and standard deviation σ.

    a Write an expression (involving μ and σ) for a tolerance interval containing 98 percent of all the population measurements.

b Estimate a tolerance interval containing 98 percent of all the trash bag breaking strengths by using the fact that a random sample of 40 breaking strengths has a mean of $\bar{x} = 50.575$ and a standard deviation of $s = 1.6438$.

6.38 Consider the situation of Exercise 6.32.

   a Use the investment broker's report to estimate the maximum yearly return that might be obtained by investing in tax-free municipal bonds.

   b Find the probability that the yearly return obtained by investing in common stocks will be higher than the maximum yearly return that might be obtained by investing in tax-free municipal bonds.

6.39 In the book *Advanced Managerial Accounting*, Robert P. Magee discusses monitoring cost variances. A *cost variance* is the difference between a budgeted cost and an actual cost. Magee describes the following situation:

> Michael Bitner has responsibility for control of two manufacturing processes. Every week he receives a cost variance report for each of the two processes, broken down by labor costs, materials costs, and so on. One of the two processes, which we'll call process *A*, involves a stable, easily controlled production process with a little fluctuation in variances. Process *B* involves more random events: the equipment is more sensitive and prone to breakdown, the raw material prices fluctuate more, and so on.
>
> "It seems like I'm spending more of my time with process *B* than with process *A*," says Michael Bitner. "Yet I know that the probability of an inefficiency developing and the expected costs of inefficiencies are the same for the two processes. It's just the magnitude of random fluctuations that differs between the two, as you can see in the information below.
>
> "At present, I investigate variances if they exceed $2,500, regardless of whether it was process *A* or *B*. I suspect that such a policy is not the most efficient. I should probably set a higher limit for process *B*."

The means and standard deviations of the cost variances of processes *A* and *B*, when these processes are in control, are as follows:

	Process A	Process B
Mean cost variance (in control)	$ 0	$ 0
Standard deviation of cost variance (in control)	$5,000	$10,000

Furthermore, the means and standard deviations of the cost variances of processes *A* and *B*, when these processes are out of control, are as follows:

	Process A	Process B
Mean cost variance (out of control)	$7,500	$ 7,500
Standard deviation of cost variance (out of control)	$5,000	$10,000

   a Recall that the current policy is to investigate a cost variance if it exceeds $2,500 for either process. Assume that cost variances are normally distributed and that both Process *A* and Process *B* cost variances are in control. Find the probability that a cost variance for Process *A* will be investigated. Find the probability that a cost variance for Process *B* will be investigated. Which in-control process will be investigated more often?

   b Assume that cost variances are normally distributed and that both Process *A* and Process *B* cost variances are out of control. Find the probability that a cost variance for Process *A* will be investigated. Find the probability that a cost variance for Process *B* will be investigated. Which out-of-control process will be investigated more often?

   c If both Processes *A* and *B* are almost always in control, which process will be investigated more often?

   d Suppose that we wish to reduce the probability that Process *B* will be investigated (when it is in control) to .3085. What cost variance investigation policy should be used? That is, how large a cost variance should trigger an investigation? Using this new policy, what is the probability that an out-of-control cost variance for Process *B* will be investigated?

6.40 Suppose that yearly health care expenses for a family of four are normally distributed with a mean expense equal to $3,000 and a standard deviation of $500. An insurance company has decided to offer a health insurance premium reduction if a policyholder's health care expenses do not exceed a specified dollar amount. What dollar amount should be established if the insurance company wants families having the lowest 33 percent of yearly health care expenses to be eligible for the premium reduction?

6.41 Suppose that the 33rd percentile of a normal distribution is equal to 656 and that the 97.5th percentile of this normal distribution is 896. Find the mean μ and the standard deviation σ of the normal distribution. Hint: Sketch these percentiles.

6.4 Approximating the Binomial Distribution by Using the Normal Distribution (Optional) ● ● ●

Figure 6.24 illustrates several binomial distributions. In general, we can see that as n gets larger and as p gets closer to .5, the graph of a binomial distribution tends to have the symmetrical, bell-shaped appearance of a normal curve. It follows that, under conditions given in the following box, we can approximate the binomial distribution by using a normal distribution.

The Normal Approximation of the Binomial Distribution

Consider a binomial random variable x, where n is the number of trials performed and p is the probability of success on each trial. If n and p have values so that $np \geq 5$ and $n(1-p) \geq 5$, then x is approximately normally distributed with mean $\mu = np$ and standard deviation $\sigma = \sqrt{npq}$, where $q = 1 - p$.

This approximation is often useful because binomial tables for large values of n are often unavailable. The conditions $np \geq 5$ and $n(1-p) \geq 5$ must be met in order for the approximation to be appropriate. Note that if p is near 0 or near 1, then n must be larger for a good approximation, while if p is near .5, then n need not be as large.[1]

When we say that we can approximate the binomial distribution by using a normal distribution, we are saying that we can compute binomial probabilities by finding corresponding areas under a normal curve (rather than by using the binomial formula). We illustrate how to do this in the following example.

FIGURE 6.24   **Several Binomial Distributions**

_____
[1]As an alternative to the rule that both np and $n(1-p)$ must be at least 5, some statisticians suggest using the more conservative rule that both np and $n(1-p)$ must be at least 10.

FIGURE 6.25   Approximating the Binomial Probability $P(x = 23)$ by Using the Normal Curve When $\mu = np = 25$ and $\sigma = \sqrt{npq} = 3.5355$

EXAMPLE 6.8 The Continuity Correction

Consider the binomial random variable x with $n = 50$ trials and probability of success $p = .5$. This binomial distribution is one of those illustrated in Figure 6.24. Suppose we want to use the normal approximation to this binomial distribution to compute the probability of 23 successes in the 50 trials. That is, we wish to compute $P(x = 23)$. Because $np = (50)(.5) = 25$ is at least 5, and $n(1 - p) = 50(1 - .5) = 25$ is also at least 5, we can appropriately use the approximation. Moreover, we can approximate the binomial distribution of x by using a normal distribution with mean $\mu = np = 50(.5) = 25$ and standard deviation $\sigma = \sqrt{npq} = \sqrt{50(.5)(1 - .5)} = 3.5355$.

In order to compute the needed probability, we must make a **continuity correction.** This is because a discrete distribution (the binomial) is being approximated by a continuous distribution (the normal). Because there is no area under a normal curve at the single point $x = 23$, we must assign an area under the normal curve to the binomial outcome $x = 23$. It is logical to assign the area corresponding to the interval from 22.5 to 23.5 to the integer outcome $x = 23$. That is, the area under the normal curve corresponding to all values within .5 unit of the integer outcome $x = 23$ is assigned to the value $x = 23$. So we approximate the binomial probability $P(x = 23)$ by calculating the normal curve area $P(22.5 \leq x \leq 23.5)$. This area is illustrated in Figure 6.25. Calculating the z values

$$z = \frac{22.5 - 25}{3.5355} = -.71 \quad \text{and} \quad z = \frac{23.5 - 25}{3.5355} = -.42$$

we find that $P(22.5 \leq x \leq 23.5) = P(-.71 \leq z \leq -.42) = .3372 - .2389 = .0983$. Therefore, we estimate that the binomial probability $P(x = 23)$ is .0983.

Making the proper continuity correction can sometimes be tricky. A good way to approach this is to list the numbers of successes that are included in the event for which the binomial probability is being calculated. Then assign the appropriate area under the normal curve to each number of successes in the list. Putting these areas together gives the normal curve area that must be calculated. For example, again consider the binomial random variable x with $n = 50$ and $p = .5$. If we wish to find $P(27 \leq x \leq 29)$, then the event $27 \leq x \leq 29$ includes 27, 28, and 29 successes. Because we assign the areas under the normal curve corresponding to the intervals [26.5, 27.5], [27.5, 28.5], and [28.5, 29.5] to the values 27, 28, and 29, respectively, then the area to be found under the normal curve is $P(26.5 \leq x \leq 29.5)$. Table 6.2 on the next page gives several other examples.

TABLE 6.2   Several Examples of the Continuity Correction ($n = 50$)

Binomial Probability	Numbers of Successes Included in Event	Normal Curve Area (with Continuity Correction)
$P(25 < x \le 30)$	26, 27, 28, 29, 30	$P(25.5 \le x \le 30.5)$
$P(x \le 27)$	0, 1, 2, . . . , 26, 27	$P(x \le 27.5)$
$P(x > 30)$	31, 32, 33, . . . , 50	$P(x \ge 30.5)$
$P(27 < x < 31)$	28, 29, 30	$P(27.5 \le x \le 30.5)$

EXAMPLE 6.9 The Cheese Spread Case: Improving Profitability

A food processing company markets a soft cheese spread that is sold in a plastic container with an "easy pour" spout. Although this spout works extremely well and is popular with consumers, it is expensive to produce. Because of the spout's high cost, the company has developed a new, less expensive spout. While the new, cheaper spout may alienate some purchasers, a company study shows that its introduction will increase profits if fewer than 10 percent of the cheese spread's current purchasers are lost. That is, if we let p be the true proportion of all current purchasers who would stop buying the cheese spread if the new spout were used, profits will increase as long as p is less than .10.

Suppose that (after trying the new spout) 63 of 1,000 randomly selected purchasers say that they would stop buying the cheese spread if the new spout were used. To assess whether p is less than .10, we will assume for the sake of argument that p equals .10, and we will use the sample information to weigh the evidence against this assumption and in favor of the conclusion that p is less than .10. Let the random variable x represent the number of the 1,000 purchasers who say they would stop buying the cheese spread. Assuming that p equals .10, then x is a binomial random variable with $n = 1,000$ and $p = .10$. Because the sample result of 63 is less than $\mu = np = 1,000(.1) = 100$, the expected value of x when p equals .10, we have some evidence to contradict the assumption that p equals .10. To evaluate the strength of this evidence, we calculate the probability that *63 or fewer* of the 1,000 randomly selected purchasers would say that they would stop buying the cheese spread if the new spout were used if, in fact, p equals .10.

Because both $np = 1,000(.10) = 100$ and $n(1 - p) = 1,000(1 - .10) = 900$ are at least 5, we can use the normal approximation to the binomial distribution to compute the needed probability. The appropriate normal curve has mean $\mu = np = 1,000(.10) = 100$ and standard deviation $\sigma = \sqrt{npq} = \sqrt{1,000(.10)(1 - .10)} = 9.4868$. In order to make the continuity correction, we note that the discrete value $x = 63$ is assigned the area under the normal curve corresponding to the interval from 62.5 to 63.5. It follows that the binomial probability $P(x \le 63)$ is approximated by the normal probability $P(x \le 63.5)$. This is illustrated in Figure 6.26. Calculating the z value for 63.5 to be

$$z = \frac{63.5 - 100}{9.4868} = -3.85$$

FIGURE 6.26   Approximating the Binomial Probability $P(x \le 63)$ by Using the Normal Curve When $\mu = np = 100$ and $\sigma = \sqrt{npq} = 9.4868$

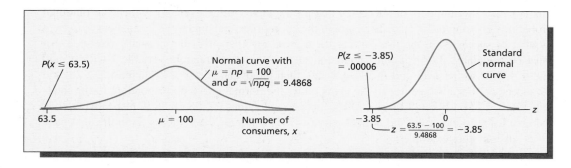

we find that

$$P(x \le 63.5) = P(z \le -3.85)$$

Using the normal table, we find that the area under the standard normal curve to the left of -3.85 is .00006. This says that, if p equals .10, then in only 6 in 100,000 of all possible random samples of 1,000 purchasers would 63 or fewer say they would stop buying the cheese spread if the new spout were used. Because it is very difficult to believe that such a small chance (a .00006 chance) has occurred, we have very strong evidence that p does not equal .10 and is, in fact, less than .10. Therefore, it seems that using the new spout will be profitable.

Exercises for Section 6.4

CONCEPTS

connect

6.42 Explain why it might be convenient to approximate binomial probabilities by using areas under an appropriate normal curve.

6.43 Under what condition may we use the normal approximation to the binomial distribution?

6.44 Explain how we make a continuity correction. Why is a continuity correction needed when we approximate a binomial distribution by a normal distribution?

METHODS AND APPLICATIONS

6.45 Suppose that x has a binomial distribution with $n = 200$ and $p = .4$.
  a Show that the normal approximation to the binomial can appropriately be used to calculate probabilities about x.
  b Make continuity corrections for each of the following, and then use the normal approximation to the binomial to find each probability:
   (1) $P(x = 80)$
   (2) $P(x \le 95)$
   (3) $P(x < 65)$
   (4) $P(x \ge 100)$
   (5) $P(x > 100)$

6.46 Repeat Exercise 6.45 with $n = 200$ and $p = .5$.

6.47 An advertising agency conducted an ad campaign aimed at making consumers in an Eastern state aware of a new product. Upon completion of the campaign, the agency claimed that 20 percent of consumers in the state had become aware of the product. The product's distributor surveyed 1,000 consumers in the state and found that 150 were aware of the product.
  a Assuming that the ad agency's claim is true:
   (1) Verify that we may use the normal approximation to the binomial.
   (2) Calculate the mean, μ, and the standard deviation, σ, we should use in the normal approximation.
   (3) Find the probability that 150 or fewer consumers in a random sample of 1,000 consumers would be aware of the product.
  b Should the distributor believe the ad agency's claim? Explain.

6.48 In order to gain additional information about respondents, some marketing researchers have used ultraviolet ink to precode questionnaires that promise confidentiality to respondents. Of 205 randomly selected marketing researchers who participated in an actual survey, 117 said that they disapprove of this practice. Suppose that, before the survey was taken, a marketing manager claimed that at least 65 percent of all marketing researchers would disapprove of the practice.
  a Assuming that the manager's claim is correct, calculate the probability that 117 or fewer of 205 randomly selected marketing researchers would disapprove of the practice. Use the normal approximation to the binomial.
  b Based on your result of part a, do you believe the marketing manager's claim? Explain.

6.49 When a store uses electronic article surveillance (EAS) to combat shoplifting, it places a small sensor on each item of merchandise. When an item is legitimately purchased, the sales clerk is supposed to remove the sensor to prevent an alarm from sounding as the customer exits the store. In an actual survey of 250 consumers, 40 said that if they were to set off an EAS alarm because store personnel (mistakenly) failed to deactivate merchandise leaving the store, they would never shop at that store again. A company marketing the alarm system claimed that no more than 5 percent of all consumers would say that they would never shop at that store again if they were subjected to a false alarm.

a Assuming that the company's claim is valid, use the normal approximation to the binomial to calculate the probability that at least 40 of the 250 randomly selected consumers would say that they would never shop at that store again if they were subjected to a false alarm.

b Do you believe the company's claim based on your answer to part *a*? Explain.

6.50 A department store will place a sale item in a special display for a one-day sale. Previous experience suggests that 20 percent of all customers who pass such a special display will purchase the item. If 2,000 customers will pass the display on the day of the sale, and if a one-item-per-customer limit is placed on the sale item, how many units of the sale item should the store stock in order to have at most a 1 percent chance of running short of the item on the day of the sale? Assume here that customers make independent purchase decisions.

LO6-7 Use the exponential distribution to compute probabilities (Optional).

6.5 The Exponential Distribution (Optional) ● ● ●

In Example 5.11 (pages 208–210), we considered an air traffic control center where controllers occasionally misdirect pilots onto flight paths dangerously close to those of other aircraft. We found that the number of these controller errors in a given time period has a Poisson distribution and that the control center is averaging 20.8 errors per year. However, rather than focusing on the number of errors occurring in a given time period, we could study the time elapsing between successive errors. If we let x denote the number of weeks elapsing between successive errors, then x is a continuous random variable that is described by what is called the *exponential distribution*. Moreover, because the control center is averaging 20.8 errors per year, the center is averaging a mean, denoted λ, of $20.8/52 = .4$ error per week and thus a mean of $52/20.8 = 2.5$ (that is, $1/\lambda = 1/.4 = 2.5$) weeks between successive errors.

In general, if the number of events occurring per unit of time or space (for example, the number of controller errors per week or the number of imperfections per square yard of cloth) has a Poisson distribution with mean λ, then the number of units, x, of time or space between successive events has an *exponential distribution* with mean $1/\lambda$. The equation of the probability curve describing the exponential distribution is given in the following formula box.

The Exponential Distribution

If x is described by an exponential distribution with mean $1/\lambda$, then the equation of the probability curve describing x is

$$f(x) = \begin{cases} \lambda e^{-\lambda x} & \text{for } x \geq 0 \\ 0 & \text{otherwise} \end{cases}$$

Using this probability curve, it can be shown that:

$$P(a \leq x \leq b) = e^{-\lambda a} - e^{-\lambda b}$$

In particular, because $e^0 = 1$ and $e^{-\infty} = 0$, this implies that

$$P(x \leq b) = 1 - e^{-\lambda b} \quad \text{and} \quad P(x \geq a) = e^{-\lambda a}$$

Furthermore, both the mean and the standard deviation of the population of all possible observed values of a random variable x that has an exponential distribution are equal to $1/\lambda$. That is, $\mu_x = \sigma_x = 1/\lambda$.

The graph of the equation describing the exponential distribution and the probability $P(a \leq x \leq b)$ where x is described by this exponential distribution are illustrated in Figure 6.27.

FIGURE 6.27   A Graph of the Exponential Distribution $f(x) = \lambda e^{-\lambda x}$

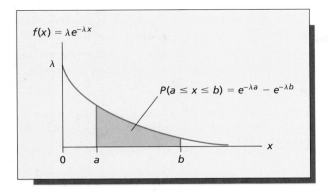

We illustrate the use of the exponential distribution in the following examples.

EXAMPLE 6.10 The Air Safety Case: Traffic Control Errors

We have seen in the air traffic control example that the control center is averaging $\lambda = .4$ error per week and $1/\lambda = 1/.4 = 2.5$ weeks between successive errors. Letting x denote the number of weeks elapsing between successive errors, the equation of the exponential distribution describing x is $f(x) = \lambda e^{-\lambda x} = .4e^{-.4x}$. For example, the probability that the time between successive errors will be between 1 and 2 weeks is

$$P(1 \leq x \leq 2) = e^{-\lambda a} - e^{-\lambda b} = e^{-\lambda(1)} - e^{-\lambda(2)}$$
$$= e^{-.4(1)} - e^{-.4(2)} = e^{-.4} - e^{-.8}$$
$$= .6703 - .4493 = .221$$

EXAMPLE 6.11 Emergency Room Arrivals

Suppose that the number of people who arrive at a hospital emergency room during a given time period has a Poisson distribution. It follows that the time, x, between successive arrivals of people to the emergency room has an exponential distribution. Furthermore, historical records indicate that the mean time between successive arrivals of people to the emergency room is seven minutes. Therefore, $\mu_x = 1/\lambda = 7$, which implies that $\lambda = 1/7 = .14286$. Noting that $\sigma_x = 1/\lambda = 7$, it follows that

$$\mu_x - \sigma_x = 7 - 7 = 0 \qquad \text{and} \qquad \mu_x + \sigma_x = 7 + 7 = 14$$

Therefore, the probability that the time between successive arrivals of people to the emergency room will be within (plus or minus) one standard deviation of the mean interarrival time is

$$P(0 \leq x \leq 14) = e^{-\lambda a} - e^{-\lambda b}$$
$$= e^{-(.14286)(0)} - e^{-(.14286)(14)}$$
$$= 1 - .1353$$
$$= .8647$$

To conclude this section we note that the exponential and related Poisson distributions are useful in analyzing waiting lines, or **queues**. In general, **queueing theory** attempts to determine the number of servers (for example, doctors in an emergency room) that strikes an optimal balance between the time customers wait for service and the cost of providing service. The reader is referred to any textbook on management science or operations research for a discussion of queueing theory.

Exercises for Section 6.5

CONCEPTS

connect

6.51 Give two examples of situations in which the exponential distribution might be used appropriately. In each case, define the random variable having an exponential distribution.

6.52 State the formula for the exponential probability curve. Define each symbol in the formula.

6.53 Explain the relationship between the Poisson and exponential distributions.

METHODS AND APPLICATIONS

6.54 Suppose that the random variable x has an exponential distribution with $\lambda = 2$.
   a Write the formula for the exponential probability curve of x. What are the possible values of x?
   b Sketch the probability curve.
   c Find $P(x \leq 1)$.
   d Find $P(.25 \leq x \leq 1)$.
   e Find $P(x \geq 2)$.
   f Calculate the mean, μ_x, the variance, σ_x^2, and the standard deviation, σ_x, of the exponential distribution of x.
   g Find the probability that x will be in the interval $[\mu_x \pm 2\sigma_x]$.

6.55 Repeat Exercise 6.54 with $\lambda = 3$.

6.56 Recall in Exercise 5.32 (page 212) that the number of customer arrivals at a bank's drive-up window in a 15-minute period is Poisson distributed with a mean of seven customer arrivals per 15-minute period. Define the random variable x to be the time (in minutes) between successive customer arrivals at the bank's drive-up window.
   a Write the formula for the exponential probability curve of x.
   b Sketch the probability curve of x.
   c Find the probability that the time between arrivals is:
      (1) Between one and two minutes.
      (2) Less than one minute.
      (3) More than three minutes.
      (4) Between $1/2$ and $3\frac{1}{2}$ minutes.
   d Calculate μ_x, σ_x^2, and σ_x.
   e Find the probability that the time between arrivals falls within one standard deviation of the mean; within two standard deviations of the mean.

6.57 The length of a particular telemarketing phone call, x, has an exponential distribution with mean equal to 1.5 minutes.
   a Write the formula for the exponential probability curve of x.
   b Sketch the probability curve of x.
   c Find the probability that the length of a randomly selected call will be:
      (1) No more than three minutes.
      (2) Between one and two minutes.
      (3) More than four minutes.
      (4) Less than 30 seconds.

6.58 The maintenance department in a factory claims that the number of breakdowns of a particular machine follows a Poisson distribution with a mean of two breakdowns every 500 hours. Let x denote the time (in hours) between successive breakdowns.
   a Find λ and μ_x.
   b Write the formula for the exponential probability curve of x.
   c Sketch the probability curve.
   d Assuming that the maintenance department's claim is true, find the probability that the time between successive breakdowns is at most five hours.
   e Assuming that the maintenance department's claim is true, find the probability that the time between successive breakdowns is between 100 and 300 hours.
   f Suppose that the machine breaks down five hours after its most recent breakdown. Based on your answer to part d, do you believe the maintenance department's claim? Explain.

6.59 Suppose that the number of accidents occurring in an industrial plant is described by a Poisson distribution with an average of one accident per month. Let x denote the time (in months) between successive accidents.
   a Find the probability that the time between successive accidents is:
      (1) More than two months.
      (2) Between one and two months.
      (3) Less than one week ($1/4$ of a month).

b   Suppose that an accident occurs less than one week after the plant's most recent accident. Would you consider this event unusual enough to warrant special investigation? Explain.

6.6 The Normal Probability Plot (Optional) ● ● ●

The **normal probability plot** is a graphic that is used to visually check whether sample data come from a normal distribution. In order to illustrate the construction and interpretation of a normal probability plot, consider the e-billing case and suppose that the trucking company operates in three regions of the country—the north, central, and south regions. In each region, 24 invoices are randomly selected and the payment time for each sampled invoice is found. The payment times obtained in each region are given in Table 6.3, along with MINITAB side-by-side box plots of the data. Examination of the data and box plots indicates that the payment times for the central region are skewed to the left, while the payment times for the south region are skewed to the right. The box plot of the payment times for the north region, along with the dot plot of these payment times in Figure 6.28, indicate that the payment times for the north region are approximately normally distributed.

We will begin by constructing a normal probability plot for the payment times from the north region. We first arrange the payment times in order from smallest to largest. The ordered payment times are shown in column (1) of Table 6.4 on the next page. Next, for each ordered payment time, we compute the quantity $i/(n + 1)$, where i denotes the observation's position in the ordered list of data and n denotes the sample size. For instance, for the first and second ordered payment times, we compute $1/(24 + 1) = 1/25 = .04$ and $2/(24 + 1) = 2/25 = .08$. Similarly, for the last (24th) ordered payment time, we compute $24/(24 + 1) = 24/25 = .96$. The positions ($i$ values) of all 24 payment times are given in column (2) of Table 6.4, and the corresponding values of $i/(n + 1)$ are given in column (3) of this table. We continue by computing what is called the **standardized normal quantile value** for each ordered payment time. This value (denoted O_i) is the z value that

LO6-8 Use a normal probability plot to help decide whether data come from a normal distribution (Optional).

TABLE 6.3   **Twenty-four Randomly Selected Payment Times for Each of Three Geographical Regions in the United States**   Ⓓ RegPayTime

North Region	Central Region	South Region
26	26	28
27	28	31
21	21	21
22	22	23
22	23	23
23	24	24
27	27	29
20	19	20
22	22	22
29	29	36
18	15	19
24	25	25
28	28	33
26	26	27
21	20	21
32	29	44
23	24	24
24	25	26
25	25	27
15	7	19
17	12	19
19	18	20
34	29	50
30	29	39

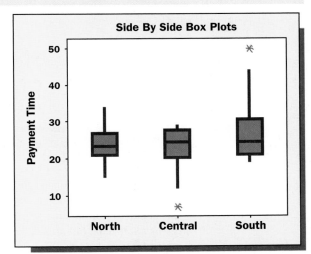

FIGURE 6.28   **Dot Plot of the Payment Times for the North Region**

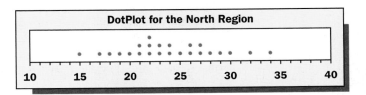

TABLE 6.4   Calculations for Normal Probability Plots in the e-billing Example

Ordered North Region Payment Times Column (1)	Observation Number (i) Column (2)	Area $i/(n+1)$ Column (3)	z value O_i Column (4)	Ordered Central Region Payment Times Column (5)	Ordered South Region Payment Times Column (6)
15	1	0.04	−1.75	7	19
17	2	0.08	−1.41	12	19
18	3	0.12	−1.18	15	19
19	4	0.16	−0.99	18	20
20	5	0.2	−0.84	19	20
21	6	0.24	−0.71	20	21
21	7	0.28	−0.58	21	21
22	8	0.32	−0.47	22	22
22	9	0.36	−0.36	22	23
22	10	0.4	−0.25	23	23
23	11	0.44	−0.15	24	24
23	12	0.48	−0.05	24	24
24	13	0.52	0.05	25	25
24	14	0.56	0.15	25	26
25	15	0.6	0.25	25	27
26	16	0.64	0.36	26	27
26	17	0.68	0.47	26	28
27	18	0.72	0.58	27	29
27	19	0.76	0.71	28	31
28	20	0.8	0.84	28	33
29	21	0.84	0.99	29	36
30	22	0.88	1.18	29	39
32	23	0.92	1.41	29	44
34	24	0.96	1.75	29	50

FIGURE 6.29   Calculating Standardized Normal Quantile Values

Tail area equals .04

$O_1 = -1.75$

(a) Calculating O_1

.08

$O_2 = -1.41$

(b) Calculating O_2

.96

$O_{24} = 1.75$

(c) Calculating O_{24}

gives an area of $i/(n+1)$ to its left under the standard normal curve. Figure 6.29 illustrates finding O_1, O_2, and O_{24}. For instance, O_1—the standardized normal quantile value corresponding to the first ordered residual—is the z value that gives an area of $1/(24+1) = .04$ to its left under the standard normal curve. As shown in Figure 6.29(a), the z value (to two decimal places) that gives a left-hand tail area closest to .04 is $O_1 = -1.75$. Similarly, O_2 is the z value that gives an area of $2/(24+1) = .08$ to its left under the standard normal curve. As shown in Figure 6.29(b), the z value (to two decimal places) that gives a left-hand tail area closest to .08 is $O_2 = -1.41$. As a final example, Figure 6.29(c) shows that O_{24}, the z value that gives an area of $24/(24+1) = .96$ to its left under the standard normal curve, is 1.75. The standardized normal quantile values corresponding to the 24 ordered payment times are given in column (4) of Table 6.4. Finally, we obtain the **normal probability plot** by plotting the 24 ordered payment times on the vertical axis versus the corresponding standardized normal quantile values (O_i values) on the horizontal axis. Figure 6.30 gives an Excel add-in (MegaStat) output of this normal probability plot.

In order to interpret the normal plot, notice that, although the areas in column (3) of Table 6.4 (that is, the $i/(n+1)$ values: .04, .08, .12, etc.) are equally spaced, the z values corresponding to

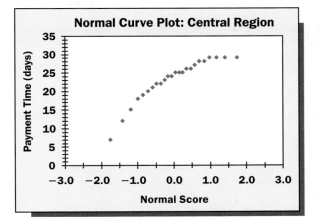

FIGURE 6.32 Excel Add-in (MegaStat) Normal Probability Plot for the South Region: Data Skewed to the Right

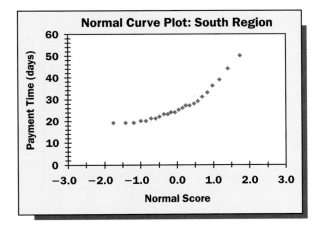

these areas are not equally spaced. Because of the mound-shaped nature of the standard normal curve, the negative z values get closer together as they get closer to the mean ($z = 0$) and the positive z values get farther apart as they get farther from the mean (more positive). If the distances between the payment times behave the same way as the distances between the z values—that is, if the distances between the payment times are proportional to the distances between the z values—then the normal probability plot will be a straight line. This would suggest that the payment times are normally distributed. Examining Figure 6.30, the normal probability plot for the payment times from the north region is approximately a straight line and, therefore, it is reasonable to assume that these payment times are approximately normally distributed.

Column (5) of Table 6.4 gives the ordered payment times for the central region, and Figure 6.31 plots these values versus the standardized normal quantile values in column (4). The resulting normal probability plot for the central region has a nonlinear appearance. The plot points rise more steeply at first and then continue to increase at a decreasing rate. This pattern indicates that the payment times for the central region are skewed to the left. Here the rapidly rising points at the beginning of the plot are due to the payment times being farther apart in the left tail of the distribution. Column (6) of Table 6.4 gives the ordered payment times for the south region, and Figure 6.32 gives the normal probability plot for this region. This plot also has a nonlinear appearance. The points rise slowly at first and then increase at an increasing rate. This pattern indicates that the payment times for the south region are skewed to the right. Here the rapidly rising points on the right side of the plot are due to the payment times being farther apart in the right tail of the distribution.

In the following box, we summarize how to construct and interpret a normal probability plot.

Normal Probability Plots

1 Order the values in the data from smallest to largest.

2 For each observation compute the area $i/(n + 1)$, where i denotes the position of the observation in the ordered listing and n is the number of observations.

3 Compute the standardized normal quantile value O_i for each observation. This is the z value

that gives an area of $i/(n + 1)$ to its left under the standard normal curve.

4 Plot the ordered data values versus the standardized normal quantile values.

5 If the resulting normal probability plot has a straight line appearance, it is reasonable to assume that the data come from a normal distribution.

Exercises for Section 6.6

CONCEPTS

6.60 Discuss how a normal probability plot is constructed.

6.61 If a normal probability plot has the appearance of a straight line, what should we conclude?

METHODS AND APPLICATIONS

6.62 Consider the sample of 12 incomes given in Example 3.2 (page 105).
    a Sort the income data from smallest to largest, and compute $i/(n + 1)$ for each observation.
    b Compute the standardized normal quantile value O_i for each observation.
    c Graph the normal probability plot for the salary data and interpret this plot. Does the plot indicate that the data are skewed? Explain.   Incomes

6.63 Consider the 20 DVD satisfaction ratings given on page 123. Construct a normal probability plot for these data and interpret the plot.   DVDSat

6.64 A normal probability plot can be constructed using MINITAB. Use the selections Stat : Basic Statistics : Normality test, and select the data to be analyzed. Although the MINITAB plot is slightly different from the plot outlined in this section, its interpretation is the same. Use MINITAB to construct a normal probability plot of the gas mileage data in Table 3.1 (page 103). Interpret the plot.   GasMiles

Chapter Summary

In this chapter we have discussed **continuous probability distributions.** We began by learning that **a continuous probability distribution is described by a continuous probability curve** and that in this context **probabilities are areas under the probability curve.** We next studied two important continuous probability distributions—**the uniform distribution** and **the normal distribution.** In particular, we concentrated on the normal distribution, which is the most important continuous probability distribution. We learned about the properties of the normal curve, and we saw how to use a **normal table** to find various areas under a

normal curve. We then demonstrated how we can use a normal curve probability to make a statistical inference. We continued with an optional section that explained how we can use a normal curve probability to approximate a binomial probability. Then we presented an optional section that discussed another important continuous probability distribution—**the exponential distribution,** and we saw how this distribution is related to the Poisson distribution. Finally, we concluded this chapter with an optional section that explained how to use a **normal probability plot** to decide whether data come from a normal distribution.

Glossary of Terms

continuous probability distribution (or **probability curve**): A curve that is defined so that the probability that a random variable will be in a specified interval of numbers is the area under the curve corresponding to the interval. (pages 225, 226)

cumulative normal table: A table in which we can look up areas under the standard normal curve. (pages 232–234)

exponential distribution: A probability distribution that describes the time or space between successive occurrences of an event when the number of times the event occurs over an interval of time or space is described by a Poisson distribution. (page 252)

normal probability distribution: The most important continuous probability distribution. Its probability curve is the *bell-shaped* normal curve. (page 230)

normal probability plot: A graphic used to visually check whether sample data come from a normal distribution. (page 255)

queueing theory: A methodology that attempts to determine the number of servers that strikes an optimal balance between the time customers wait for service and the cost of providing service. (page 253)

standard normal distribution (or curve): A normal distribution (or curve) having mean 0 and standard deviation 1. (page 232)

uniform distribution: A continuous probability distribution having a rectangular shape that says the probability is distributed evenly (or uniformly) over an interval of numbers. (page 228)

z_α **point:** The point on the horizontal axis under the standard normal curve that gives a right-hand tail area equal to α. (page 241)

$-z_\alpha$ **point:** The point on the horizontal axis under the standard normal curve that gives a left-hand tail area equal to α. (page 242)

z **value:** A value that tells us the number of standard deviations that a value x is from the mean of a normal curve. If the z value is positive, then x is above the mean. If the z value is negative, then x is below the mean. (page 232)

Important Formulas

The uniform probability curve: page 228

Mean and standard deviation of a uniform distribution: page 228

The normal probability curve: page 230

z values: page 232

Finding normal probabilities: page 238

Normal approximation to the binomial distribution: page 248

The exponential probability curve: page 252

Mean and standard deviation of an exponential distribution: page 252

Constructing a normal probability plot: page 258

Supplementary Exercises

connect

6.65 In a bottle-filling process, the amount of drink injected into 16 oz bottles is normally distributed with a mean of 16 oz and a standard deviation of .02 oz. Bottles containing less than 15.95 oz do not meet the bottler's quality standard. What percentage of filled bottles do not meet the standard?

6.66 In a murder trial in Los Angeles, a shoe expert stated that the range of heights of men with a size 12 shoe is 71 inches to 76 inches. Suppose the heights of all men wearing size 12 shoes are normally distributed with a mean of 73.5 inches and a standard deviation of 1 inch. What is the probability that a randomly selected man who wears a size 12 shoe:
  a Has a height outside the range 71 inches to 76 inches?
  b Is 74 inches or taller?
  c Is shorter than 70.5 inches?

6.67 In the movie *Forrest Gump,* the public school required an IQ of at least 80 for admittance.
  a If IQ test scores are normally distributed with mean 100 and standard deviation 16, what percentage of people would qualify for admittance to the school?
  b If the public school wishes 95 percent of all children to qualify for admittance, what minimum IQ test score should be required for admittance?

6.68 The amount of sales tax paid on a purchase is rounded to the nearest cent. Assume that the round-off error is uniformly distributed in the interval $-.5$ to .5 cent.
  a Write the formula for the probability curve describing the round-off error.
  b Graph the probability curve describing the round-off error.
  c What is the probability that the round-off error exceeds .3 cent or is less than $-.3$ cent?
  d What is the probability that the round-off error exceeds .1 cent or is less than $-.1$ cent?
  e Find the mean and the standard deviation of the round-off error.
  f Find the probability that the round-off error will be within one standard deviation of the mean.

6.69 A *consensus forecast* is the average of a large number of individual analysts' forecasts. Suppose the individual forecasts for a particular interest rate are normally distributed with a mean of 5.0 percent and a standard deviation of 1.2 percent. A single analyst is randomly selected. Find the probability that his/her forecast is:
  a At least 3.5 percent.
  b At most 6 percent.
  c Between 3.5 percent and 6 percent.

6.70 Recall from Exercise 6.69 that individual forecasts of a particular interest rate are normally distributed with a mean of 5 percent and a standard deviation of 1.2 percent.
  a What percentage of individual forecasts are at or below the 10th percentile of the distribution of forecasts? What percentage are at or above the 10th percentile? Find the 10th percentile of the distribution of individual forecasts.
  b Find the first quartile, Q_1, and the third quartile, Q_3, of the distribution of individual forecasts.

6.71 The scores on the entrance exam at a well-known, exclusive law school are normally distributed with a mean score of 200 and a standard deviation equal to 50. At what value should the lowest passing score be set if the school wishes only 2.5 percent of those taking the test to pass?

6.72 A machine is used to cut a metal automobile part to its desired length. The machine can be set so that the mean length of the part will be any value that is desired. The standard deviation of the lengths always runs at .02 inch. Where should the mean be set if we want only .4 percent of the parts cut by the machine to be shorter than 15 inches long?

6.73 A motel accepts 325 reservations for 300 rooms on July 1, expecting 10 percent no-shows on average from past records. Use the normal approximation to the binomial to find the probability that all guests who arrive on July 1 will receive a room.

6.74 Suppose a software company finds that the number of errors in its software per 1,000 lines of code is described by a Poisson distribution. Furthermore, it is found that there is an average of four errors per 1,000 lines of code. Letting x denote the number of lines of code between successive errors:
  a Find the probability that there will be at least 400 lines of code between successive errors in the company's software.
  b Find the probability that there will be no more than 100 lines of code between successive errors in the company's software.

6.75 **THE INVESTMENT CASE** ⒹⓈ InvestRet

  For each investment class in Table 3.9 (page 141), assume that future returns are normally distributed with the population mean and standard deviation given in Table 3.9. Based on this assumption:
  a For each investment class, find the probability of a return that is less than zero (that is, find the probability of a loss). Is your answer reasonable for all investment classes? Explain.
  b For each investment class, find the probability of a return that is:
  (1) Greater than 5 percent.
  (2) Greater than 10 percent.
  (3) Greater than 20 percent.
  (4) Greater than 50 percent.
  c For which investment classes is the probability of a return greater than 50 percent essentially zero? For which investment classes is the probability of such a return greater than 1 percent? Greater than 5 percent?
  d For which investment classes is the probability of a loss essentially zero? For which investment classes is the probability of a loss greater than 1 percent? Greater than 10 percent? Greater than 20 percent?

6.76 The daily water consumption for an Ohio community is normally distributed with a mean consumption of 800,000 gallons and a standard deviation of 80,000 gallons. The community water system will experience a noticeable drop in water pressure when the daily water consumption exceeds 984,000 gallons. What is the probability of experiencing such a drop in water pressure?

6.77 Suppose the times required for a cable company to fix cable problems in its customers' homes are uniformly distributed between 10 minutes and 25 minutes. What is the probability that a randomly selected cable repair visit will take at least 15 minutes?

6.78 Suppose the waiting time to get food after placing an order at a fast-food restaurant is exponentially distributed with a mean of 60 seconds. If a randomly selected customer orders food at the restaurant, what is the probability that the customer will wait at least:
  a 90 seconds?
  b Two minutes?

6.79 Net interest margin—often referred to as *spread*—is the difference between the rate banks pay on deposits and the rate they charge for loans. Suppose that the net interest margins for all U.S. banks are normally distributed with a mean of 4.15 percent and a standard deviation of .5 percent.
  a Find the probability that a randomly selected U.S. bank will have a net interest margin that exceeds 5.40 percent.
  b Find the probability that a randomly selected U.S. bank will have a net interest margin less than 4.40 percent.

c A bank wants its net interest margin to be less than the net interest margins of 95 percent of all U.S. banks. Where should the bank's net interest margin be set?

6.80 In an article in *Advertising Age,* Nancy Giges studies global spending patterns. Giges presents data concerning the percentage of adults in various countries who have purchased various consumer items (such as soft drinks, athletic footware, blue jeans, beer, and so on) in the past three months.

a Suppose we wish to justify the claim that fewer than 50 percent of adults in Germany have purchased blue jeans in the past three months. The survey reported by Giges found that 45 percent of the respondents in Germany had purchased blue jeans in the past three months.

   Assume that a random sample of 400 German adults was employed, and let p be the proportion of all German adults who have purchased blue jeans in the past three months. If, for the sake of argument, we assume that $p = .5$, use the normal approximation to the binomial distribution to calculate the probability that 45 percent or fewer of 400 randomly selected German adults would have purchased blue jeans in the past three months. Note: Because 45 percent of 400 is 180, you should calculate the probability that 180 or fewer of 400 randomly selected German adults would have purchased blue jeans in the past three months.

b Based on the probability you computed in part *a*, would you conclude that p is really less than .5? That is, would you conclude that fewer than 50 percent of adults in Germany have purchased blue jeans in the past three months? Explain.

6.81 Assume that the ages for first marriages are normally distributed with a mean of 26 years and a standard deviation of 4 years. What is the probability that a person getting married for the first time is in his or her twenties?

Appendix 6.1 ■ Normal Distribution Using Excel

Normal probability $P(X < 31.2)$ in Example 6.3 (page 239):

- Click in the cell where you wish to place the answer. Here we have clicked in cell A14. Then select the Insert Function button f_x from the Excel toolbar.
- In the Insert Function dialog box, select Statistical from the "Or select a category:" menu, select NORM.DIST from the "Select a function:" menu, and click OK.
- In the NORM.DIST Function Arguments dialog box, enter the value 31.2 in the X window.
- Enter the value 33 in the Mean window.
- Enter the value 0.7 in the Standard_dev window.
- Enter the value 1 in the Cumulative window.
- Click OK in the NORM.DIST Function Arguments dialog box.
- When you click OK in this dialog box, the answer will be placed in cell A14.

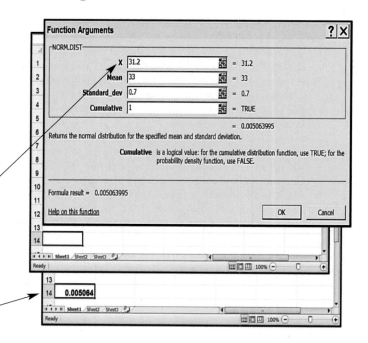

Normal probability $P(X < 153$ or $X > 167)$ in Example 6.4 (page 240):

- Enter the headings—x, P(X < x), P(X > x)–in the spreadsheet where you wish the results to be placed. Here we will enter these headings in cells A12, B12, and C12. The calculated results will be placed below the headings.
- In cells A13 and A14, enter the values 153 and 167.
- Click in cell B13 and select the Insert Function button f_x from the Excel toolbar.
- In the Insert Function dialog box, select Statistical from the "Or select a category:" menu, select NORM.DIST from the "Select a function:" menu, and click OK.
- In the NORM.DIST Function Arguments dialog box, enter the cell location A13 in the X window.
- Enter the value 159.3958 in the Mean window.
- Enter the value 6.4238 in the Standard_dev window.
- Enter the value 1 in the Cumulative window.
- Click OK in the NORM.DIST Function Arguments dialog box.
- When you click OK, the result for $P(X < 153)$ will be placed in cell B13. Double-click the drag-handle (in the lower right corner) of cell B13 to automatically extend the cell formula of B13 through cell B14.
- In cells C13 and C14, enter the formulas $=1-B13$ and $=1-B14$. The results for $P(X > 153)$ and $P(X > 167)$ will be placed in cells C13 and C14.
- In cell E14, enter the formula $= B13 + C14$.

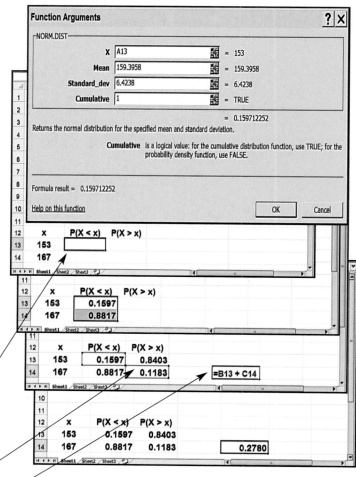

The desired probability is in cell E14, the sum of the lower tail probability for 153 and the upper tail probability for 167. This value differs slightly from the value in Example 6.4 because Excel carries out probability calculations to higher precision than can be achieved using normal probability tables.

Inverse normal probability *st* such that $P(X > st) =$ 0.05 in Example 6.5 (pages 241–242):

- Click in the cell where you wish the answer to be placed. Here we will click in cell A14. Select the Insert Function button f_x from the Excel toolbar.
- In the Insert Function dialog box, select Statistical from the "Or select a category:" menu, select NORM.INV from the "Select a function:" menu, and click OK.
- In the NORM.INV Function Arguments dialog box, enter the value 0.95 in the Probability window; that is,

    [$P(X < st) = 0.95$ when $P(X > st) = 0.05$.]

- Enter the value 100 in the Mean window.
- Enter the value 10 in the Standard_dev window.
- Click OK in the NORM.INV Function Arguments dialog box.
- When you click OK, the answer is placed in cell A14.

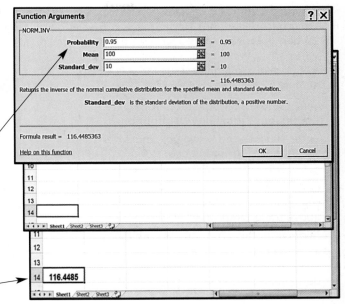

Appendix 6.2 ■ Normal Distribution Using MegaStat

Normal probability $P(X < 31.2)$ in Example 6.3 (page 239):

- Select **Add-ins : MegaStat : Probability : Continuous Probability Distributions**
- In the "Continuous Probability Distributions" dialog box, select the normal distribution tab.
- Enter the distribution mean (here equal to 33) and the distribution standard deviation (here equal to 0.7) in the appropriate boxes.
- Enter the value of *x* (here equal to 31.2) into the "Calculate p given x" window.
- Click OK in the "Continuous Probability Distributions" dialog box.
- The output includes **P(lower),** which is the area under the specified normal curve below the given value of *x*, and **P(upper),** which is the area under the specified normal curve above the given value of *x*. The value of *z* corresponding to the specified value of *x* is also included. In this case, $P(X < 31.2)$ equals $P(lower) = .0051$.
- (Optional) Click on the preview button to see the values of P(lower) and P(upper) before obtaining results in the Output worksheet.

Note that if a **standard normal distribution** is specified, 0 is entered in the mean box and 1 is entered in the standard deviation box—the "calculate P given X" box will read "Calculate P given z." In this case, when we enter a value of z in the "Calculate P given z" box, P(lower) and P(upper) are, respectively, the areas below and above the specified value of z under the standard normal curve.

Normal probability $P(X < 153$ or $X > 167)$ in Example 6.4 on page 240. Enter 159.3958 into the Mean box and enter 6.4238 into the Standard Deviation box. Find P(lower) corresponding to 153 and find P(upper) corresponding to 167. When these values are placed in the output worksheet, use a simple Excel cell formula to add them together.

Inverse normal probability *st* such that $P(X > st) = 0.05$ in Example 6.5 on pages 241–242:

- Select **Add-ins : MegaStat : Probability : Continuous Probability Distributions**

- Enter 100 into the Mean box and enter 10 into the Standard deviation box.

- Select the "Calculate x given P" option.

- Enter 0.05 into the P box. This is the area under the normal curve we want to have above *st* (that is, above the desired value of *x*).

- Click OK in the "Continuous Probability Distributions" dialog box.

- The output includes P(lower) and P(upper)—as defined above—as well as the desired value of *x* (in this case *x* equals 116.4485).

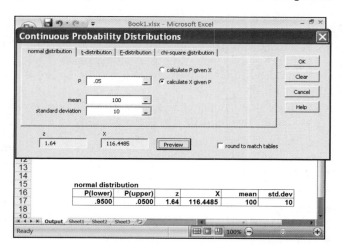

Appendix 6.3 ■ Normal Distribution Using MINITAB

Normal probability $P(X \leq 31.2)$ in Example 6.3 (page 239):

- Select **Calc : Probability Distributions : Normal.**

- In the Normal Distribution dialog box, select the Cumulative probability option.

- In the Mean window, enter 33.

- In the Standard deviation window, enter 0.7.

- Click on the "Input constant" option and enter 31.2 in the "Input constant" window.

- Click OK in Normal Distribution dialog box to see the desired probability in the Session window.

Normal probability $P(X < 153 \text{ or } X > 167)$ in Example 6.4 (page 240):

- In columns C1, C2, and C3, enter the variable names—x, P(X < x), and P(X > x).
- In column C1, enter the values 153 and 167.
- Select **Calc : Probability Distributions : Normal.**
- In the Normal Distribution dialog box, select the Cumulative probability option.
- In the Mean window, enter 159.3958.
- In the Standard deviation window, enter 6.4238.
- Click the "Input column" option, enter x in the "Input column" window, and enter 'P(X < x)' in the "Optional storage" window.
- Click OK in Normal Distribution dialog box.

- Select **Calc : Calculator.**
- In the Calculator dialog box, enter 'P(X > x)' in the "Store result in variable" window.
- Enter $1 - $ 'P(X < x)' in the Expression window.
- Click OK in the Calculator dialog box.

The desired probability is the sum of the lower tail probability for 153 and the upper tail probability for 167 or $0.159712 + 0.118255 = 0.277967$. This value differs slightly from the value in Example 6.4 because MINITAB carries out probability calculations to higher precision than can be achieved using normal probability tables.

Inverse normal probability to find the number of units stocked, st, such that $P(X > st) = 0.05$ in Example 6.5 (pages 241–242):

- Select **Calc : Probability Distributions : Normal.**
- In the Normal Distribution dialog box, select the Inverse cumulative probability option.
- In the Mean window, enter 100.
- In the Standard deviation window, enter 10.
- Click the "Input constant" option and enter 0.95 in the "Input constant" window. That is,

  $P(X \le st) = 0.95$ when $P(X > st) = 0.05$.

- Click OK in the Normal Distribution dialog box to see the desired value of st in the Session window.

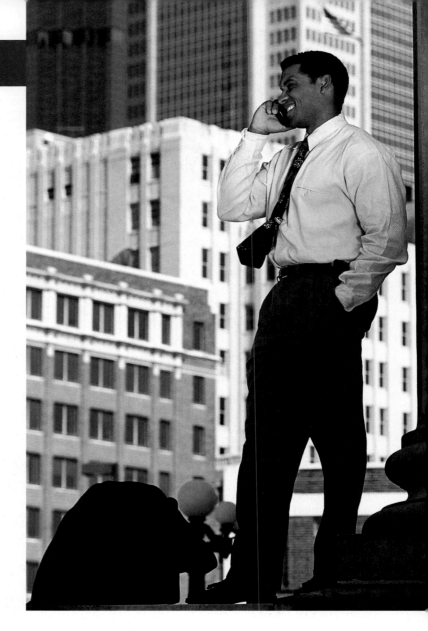

CHAPTER 7

Sampling and Sampling Distributions

Learning Objectives

After mastering the material in this chapter, you will be able to:

LO7-1 Explain the concept of random sampling and select a random sample.

LO7-2 Describe and use the sampling distribution of the sample mean.

LO7-3 Explain and use the Central Limit Theorem.

LO7-4 Describe and use the sampling distribution of the sample proportion.

LO7-5 Describe the basic ideas of stratified random, cluster, and systematic sampling (Optional).

LO7-6 Describe basic types of survey questions, survey procedures, and sources of error (Optional).

Chapter Outline

I n Chapter 1 we introduced random sampling. In this chapter we continue our discussion of random sampling by explaining what a random sample is and how to select a random sample. In addition, we discuss two probability distributions that are related to random sampling. To understand these distributions, note that if we select a random sample, then we use the sample mean as the point estimate of the population mean and the sample proportion as the point estimate of the population proportion. Two probability distributions that help us assess how accurate the sample mean and sample proportion are likely to be as point estimates are **the sampling distribution of the sample mean** and **the sampling distribution of the sample proportion**. After discussing random sampling in the first section of this chapter, we consider these sampling distributions in the next two sections. Moreover, using the car mileage case, the e-billing case, and the cheese spread case, we demonstrate how sampling distributions can be used to make statistical inferences.

The discussions of random sampling and of sampling distributions given in the first three sections of this chapter are necessary for understanding the rest of this book. The last three sections of this chapter consider advanced aspects of sampling and are optional. In the first optional section, we discuss three alternatives to random sampling—**stratified random sampling, cluster sampling,** and **systematic sampling.** In the second optional section, we discuss issues related to designing surveys and the errors that can occur in survey sampling. In the last optional section, we derive the mean and variance of the sample mean.

7.1 Random Sampling ● ● ●

LO7-1 Explain the concept of random sampling and select a random sample.

Selecting a random sample from a population is one of the best ways to ensure that the information contained in the sample reflects what is true about the population. To illustrate the idea of a random sample, consider the *cell phone case,* and recall that a bank has 2,136 employees on various 500-minute-per-month calling plans. In order to assess its cellular costs for these 500-minute plans, the bank will analyze in detail the cell phone bills for a random sample of 100 employees on these plans. One intuitive procedure for selecting a random sample of 100 employees from a population of 2,136 employees would begin by numbering the 2,136 employees from 1 to 2,136 and placing 2,136 identical slips of paper numbered from 1 to 2,136 in a suitable container. We would then thoroughly mix the slips of paper in the container and, blindfolded, choose one. The number on the chosen slip of paper would identify the first randomly selected employee. Next, still blindfolded, we would choose another slip of paper from the container. The number on the second slip would identify the second randomly selected employee. Continuing this process, we would select a total of 100 slips of paper from the container. The numbers on the 100 selected slips of paper would identify the 100 employees that make up the random sample.

In practice, numbering 2,136 (or any large number of) slips of paper would be very time consuming, and actual experience has shown that thoroughly mixing slips of paper (or the like) can be difficult. For these reasons, statisticians have developed more efficient and accurate methods for selecting a random sample. To discuss these methods, we let n, which we call the sample size, denote the number of elements in a sample. We then define a random sample of n elements—and explain how to select such a sample—as follows:[1]

1　If we select n elements from a population in such a way that every set of n elements in the population has the same chance of being selected, then the n elements we select are said to be a **random sample.**

2　In order to select a random sample of n elements from a population, we make n *random selections*—one at a time—from the population. On each **random selection,** we give every element remaining in the population for that selection the same chance of being chosen.

In making random selections from a population, we can sample *with or without replacement.* If we **sample with replacement,** we place the element chosen on any particular selection back into the population. Thus, we give this element a chance to be chosen on any succeeding selection. If we **sample without replacement,** we do not place the element chosen on a particular selection back into the population. Thus, we do not give this element a chance to be chosen on any succeeding selection. **It is best to sample without replacement.** Intuitively, this is because

---

[1]Actually, there are several different kinds of random samples. The type we will define is sometimes called a *simple random sample.* For brevity's sake, however, we will use the term *random sample.*

choosing the sample without replacement guarantees that all of the elements in the sample will be different, and thus we will have the fullest possible look at the population.

The first step in selecting a random sample is to obtain or make a numbered list of the population elements. Then, as illustrated in the following example, we can use a *random number table* or *computer-generated random numbers* to make random selections from the numbered list.

EXAMPLE 7.1 The Cell Phone Case: Reducing Cellular Phone Costs

In order to select a random sample of 100 employees from the population of 2,136 employees on 500-minute-per-month cell phone plans, the bank will make a numbered list of the 2,136 employees on 500-minute plans. The bank can then use a **random number table,** such as Table 7.1(a), to select the random sample. To see how this is done, note that any single-digit number in the table has been chosen in such a way that any of the single-digit numbers between 0 and 9 had the same chance of being chosen. For this reason, we say that any single-digit number in the table is a **random number** between 0 and 9. Similarly, any two-digit number in the table is a random number between 00 and 99, any three digit number in the table is a random number between 000 and 999, and so forth. Note that the table entries are segmented into groups of five to make the table easier to read. Because the total number of cell phone users on the 500-minute plans (2,136) is a four-digit number, we arbitrarily select any set of four digits in the table (we have circled these digits). This number, which is 0511, identifies the first randomly selected user. Then, moving in any direction from the 0511 (up, down, right, or left—it does not matter which), we select additional sets of four digits. These succeeding sets of digits identify additional randomly selected users. Here we arbitrarily move down from 0511 in the table. The first seven sets of four digits we obtain are

$$0511 \qquad 7156 \qquad 0285 \qquad 4461 \qquad 3990 \qquad 4919 \qquad 1915$$

(See Table 7.1(a)—these numbers are enclosed in a rectangle.) Because there are no users numbered 7156, 4461, 3990, or 4919 (remember only 2,136 users are on 500-minute plans), we ignore these numbers. This implies that the first three randomly selected users are those numbered 0511, 0285, and 1915. Continuing this procedure, we can obtain the entire random sample of 100 users. Notice that, because we are sampling without replacement, we should ignore any set of four digits previously selected from the random number table.

While using a random number table is one way to select a random sample, this approach has a disadvantage that is illustrated by the current situation. Specifically, since most four-digit random numbers are not between 0001 and 2136, obtaining 100 different, four-digit random numbers between 0001 and 2136 will require ignoring a large number of random numbers in the random number table, and we will in fact need to use a random number table that is larger than

TABLE 7.1   Random Numbers

(a) A portion of a random number table

33276	85590	79936	56865	05859	90106	78188
03427	90511	69445	18663	72695	52180	90322
92737	27156	33488	36320	17617	30015	74952
85689	20285	52267	67689	93394	01511	89868
08178	74461	13916	47564	81056	97735	90707
51259	63990	16308	60756	92144	49442	40719
60268	44919	19885	55322	44819	01188	55157
94904	01915	04146	18594	29852	71585	64951
58586	17752	14513	83149	98736	23495	35749
09998	19509	06691	76988	13602	51851	58104
14346	61666	30168	90229	04734	59193	32812
74103	15227	25306	76468	26384	58151	44592
24200	64161	38005	94342	28728	35806	22851
87308	07684	00256	45834	15398	46557	18510
07351	86679	92420	60952	61280	50001	94953

(b) MINITAB output of 100 different, four-digit random numbers between 1 and 2136

705	1131	169	1703	1709	609
1990	766	1286	1977	222	43
1007	1902	1209	2091	1742	1152
111	69	2049	1448	659	338
1732	1650	7	388	613	1477
838	272	1227	154	18	320
1053	1466	2087	265	2107	1992
582	1787	2098	1581	397	1099
757	1699	567	1255	1959	407
354	1567	1533	1097	1299	277
663	40	585	1486	1021	532
1629	182	372	1144	1569	1981
1332	1500	743	1262	1759	955
1832	378	728	1102	667	1885
514	1128	1046	116	1160	1333
831	2036	918	1535	660	
928	1257	1468	503	468	

Table 7.1(a). Although larger random number tables are readily available in books of mathematical and statistical tables, a good alternative is to use a computer software package, which can generate random numbers that are between whatever values we specify. For example, Table 7.1(b) gives the MINITAB output of 100 different, four-digit random numbers that are between 0001 and 2136 (note that the "leading 0's" are not included in these four-digit numbers). If used, the random numbers in Table 7.1(b) would identify the 100 employees that form the random sample. For example, the first three randomly selected employees would be employees 705, 1990, and 1007. When the number of cellular minutes used by each randomly selected employee is found and recorded, we obtain the sample of cellular usages that has been given in Table 1.4 (see page 9).

To conclude this example, note that computer software packages sometimes generate the same random number twice and thus are sampling with replacement. Because we wished to randomly select 100 employees without replacement, we had MINITAB generate more than 100 (actually, 110) random numbers. We then ignored the repeated random numbers to obtain the 100 different random numbers in Table 7.1(b).

Next, consider the *marketing research case,* and recall that we wish to select a sample of 60 shoppers at a large metropolitan shopping mall on a particular Saturday. Because it is not possible to list and number all of the shoppers who will be at the mall on this Saturday, we cannot select a random sample of these shoppers. However, we can select an *approximately* random sample of these shoppers. To see one way to do this, note that there are 6 ten-minute intervals during each hour, and thus there are 60 ten-minute intervals during the 10-hour period from 10 A.M. to 8 P.M.—the time when the shopping mall is open. Therefore, one way to select an approximately random sample is to choose a particular location at the mall that most shoppers will walk by and then randomly select—at the beginning of each ten-minute period—one of the first shoppers who walks by the location. Here, although we could randomly select one person from any reasonable number of shoppers who walk by, we will (arbitrarily) randomly select one of the first five shoppers who walk by. For example, starting in the upper left-hand corner of Table 7.1(a) and proceeding down the first column, note that the first three random numbers between 1 and 5 are 3, 5, and 1. This implies that (1) at 10 A.M. we would select the 3rd customer who walks by; (2) at 10:10 A.M. we would select the 5th shopper who walks by; (3) at 10:20 A.M. we would select the 1st customer who walks by, and so forth. Furthermore, assume that the composite score ratings of the new bottle design that would be given by all shoppers at the mall on the Saturday are representative of the composite score ratings that would be given by all possible consumers. It then follows that the composite score ratings given by the 60 sampled shoppers can be regarded as an approximately random sample that can be used to make statistical inferences about the population of all possible consumer composite score ratings.

As another example, consider the *car mileage case,* and recall that the automaker has decided to select a sample of 50 cars by randomly selecting one car from the 100 cars produced on each of 50 consecutive production shifts. If we number the 100 cars produced on a particular production shift from 00 to 99, we can randomly select a car from the shift by using a random number table or a computer software package to obtain a random number between 00 and 99. For example, starting in the upper left-hand corner of Table 7.1(a) and proceeding down the first column, we see that the first three random numbers between 00 and 99 are 33, 3, and 92. This implies that we would select car 33 from the first production shift, car 3 from the second production shift, car 92 from the third production shift, and so forth. Moreover, because a new group of 100 cars is produced on each production shift, repeated random numbers would not be discarded. For example, if the 15th and 29th random numbers are both 7, we would select the 7th car from the 15th production shift and the 7th car from the 29th production shift. When the 50 cars are selected and tested as prescribed by the EPA, the sample of 50 mileages that has been given in Table 1.6 (see page 11) is obtained. Furthermore, recall that we waited to randomly select the 50 cars from the 50 production shifts until the midsize car manufacturing process was operating consistently over time and recall that the time series plot in Figure 1.3 (page 11) intuitively verifies that the manufacturing process is producing consistent car mileages over time. It follows that we can regard the 50 mileages in Table 1.6 as an approximately random sample that can be used to make statistical inferences about the population of all possible midsize car mileages. (In Chapter 17 we will discuss more precisely how to assess whether a process is operating consistently over time.)

Random (or approximately random) sampling—as well as the more advanced kinds of sampling discussed in optional Section 7.4—are types of *probability sampling*. In general, **probability sampling** is sampling where we know the chance (or probability) that each element in the population will be included in the sample. If we employ probability sampling, the sample obtained can be used to make valid statistical inferences about the sampled population. However, if we do not employ probability sampling, we cannot make valid statistical inferences.

One type of sampling that is not probability sampling is **convenience sampling,** where we select elements because they are easy or convenient to sample. For example, if we select people to interview because they look "nice" or "pleasant," we are using convenience sampling. Another example of convenience sampling is the use of **voluntary response samples,** which are frequently employed by television and radio stations and newspaper columnists. In such samples, participants self-select—that is, whoever wishes to participate does so (usually expressing some opinion). These samples overrepresent people with strong (usually negative) opinions. For example, the advice columnist Ann Landers once asked her readers, "If you had it to do over again, would you have children?" Of the nearly 10,000 parents who *voluntarily* responded, 70 percent said that they would not. A probability sample taken a few months later found that 91 percent of parents would have children again.

Another type of sampling that is not probability sampling is **judgment sampling,** where a person who is extremely knowledgeable about the population under consideration selects population elements that he or she feels are most representative of the population. Because the quality of the sample depends upon the judgment of the person selecting the sample, it is dangerous to use the sample to make statistical inferences about the population.

To conclude this section, we consider a classic example where two types of sampling errors doomed a sample's ability to make valid statistical inferences. This example occurred prior to the presidential election of 1936, when the *Literary Digest* predicted that Alf Landon would defeat Franklin D. Roosevelt by a margin of 57 percent to 43 percent. Instead, Roosevelt won the election in a landslide. *Literary Digest*'s first error was to send out sample ballots (actually, 10 million ballots) to people who were mainly selected from the *Digest*'s subscription list and from telephone directories. In 1936 the country had not yet recovered from the Great Depression, and many unemployed and low-income people did not have phones or subscribe to the *Digest*. The *Digest*'s sampling procedure excluded these people, who overwhelmingly voted for Roosevelt. Second, only 2.3 million ballots were returned, resulting in the sample being a voluntary response survey. At the same time, George Gallup, founder of the Gallup Poll, was beginning to establish his survey business. He used a probability sample to correctly predict Roosevelt's victory. In optional Section 7.5 we discuss various issues related to designing surveys and more about the errors that can occur in survey samples. Optional Sections 7.4 and 7.5 can now be read at any time and in any order.

Exercises for Section 7.1

Companies:

1 Altria Group
2 PepsiCo
3 Coca-Cola
4 Archer Daniels
5 Anheuser-Bush
6 General Mills
7 Sara Lee
8 Coca-Cola Enterprises
9 Reynolds American
10 Kellogg
11 ConAgra Foods
12 HJ Heinz
13 Campbell Soup
14 Pepsi Bottling Group
15 Tyson Foods

CONCEPTS

7.1 Discuss how we select a random sample.

7.2 Explain why sampling without replacement is preferred to sampling with replacement.

METHODS AND APPLICATIONS

7.3 On the page margin, we list 15 companies that have historically performed well in the food, drink, and tobacco industries. Consider the random numbers given in the random number table of Table 7.1(a) on page 268. Starting in the upper left corner of Table 7.1(a) and moving down the two leftmost columns, we see that the first three two-digit numbers obtained are: 33, 03, and 92. Starting with these three random numbers, and moving down the two leftmost columns of Table 7.1(a) to find more two-digit random numbers, use Table 7.1(a) to randomly select five of these companies to be interviewed in detail about their business strategies. Hint: Note that we have numbered the companies from 1 to 15.

7.4 **THE VIDEO GAME SATISFACTION RATING CASE** VideoGame

A company that produces and markets video game systems wishes to assess its customers' level of satisfaction with a relatively new model, the XYZ-Box. In the six months since the introduction of the model, the company has received 73,219 warranty registrations from purchasers. The company will randomly select 65 of these registrations and will conduct telephone interviews with the purchasers. Assume that the warranty registrations are numbered from 1 to 73,219 in a computer.

Starting in the upper left corner of Table 7.1(a) and moving down the five leftmost columns, we see that the first three five-digit numbers obtained are: 33276, 03427, and 92737. Starting with these three random numbers and moving down the five leftmost columns of Table 7.1(a) to find more five-digit random numbers, use Table 7.1(a) to randomly select the numbers of the first 10 warranty registrations to be included in the sample of 65 registrations.

7.5   **THE BANK CUSTOMER WAITING TIME CASE**   WaitTime

Recall that when the bank manager's new teller system is operating consistently over time, the manager decides to record the waiting times of a sample of 100 customers that need teller service during peak business hours. For each of 100 peak business hours, the first customer that starts waiting for service at or after a randomly selected time during the hour will be chosen. Consider the peak business hours from 2:00 P.M. to 2:59 P.M., from 3:00 P.M. to 3:59 P.M., from 4:00 P.M. to 4:59 P.M., and from 5:00 P.M. to 5:59 P.M. on a particular day. Also, assume that a computer software system generates the following four random numbers between 00 and 59: 32, 00, 18, and 47. This implies that the randomly selected times during the first three peak business hours are 2:32 P.M., 3:00 P.M., and 4:18 P.M. What is the randomly selected time during the fourth peak business hour?

7.6   In an article entitled "Turned Off" in the June 2–4, 1995, issue of *USA Weekend,* Don Olmsted and Gigi Anders reported results of a survey where readers were invited to write in and express their opinions about sex and violence on television. The results showed that 96 percent of respondents were very or somewhat concerned about sex on TV, and 97 percent of respondents were very or somewhat concerned about violence on TV. Do you think that these results could be generalized to all television viewers in 1995? Why or why not?

7.2 The Sampling Distribution of the Sample Mean ● ● ●

LO7-2 Describe and use the sampling distribution of the sample mean.

Introductory ideas and basic properties   Suppose that we are about to randomly select a sample of *n* elements (for example, cars) from a population of elements. Also, suppose that for each sampled element we will measure the value of a characteristic of interest. (For example, we might measure the mileage of each sampled car.) Before we actually select the sample, there are many different samples of *n* elements and corresponding measurements that we might potentially obtain. Because different samples of measurements generally have different sample means, there are many different sample means that we might potentially obtain. It follows that, *before we draw the sample, the sample mean $\bar{x}$ is a random variable.*

The **sampling distribution of the sample mean** $\bar{x}$ is the probability distribution of the population of all possible sample means that could be obtained from all possible samples of the same size.

In order to illustrate the sampling distribution of the sample mean, we begin with an example that is based on the authors' conversations with University Chrysler/Jeep of Oxford, Ohio. In order to keep the example simple, we have used simplified car mileages to help explain the concepts.

EXAMPLE 7.2 The Car Mileage Case: Estimating Mean Mileage   Ⓒ

This is the first year that the automaker has offered its new midsize model for sale to the public. However, last year the automaker made six preproduction cars of this new model. Two of these six cars were randomly selected for testing, and the other four were sent to auto shows at which the new model was introduced to the news media and the public. As is standard industry practice, the automaker did not test the four auto show cars before or during the five months these auto shows were held because testing can potentially harm the appearance of the cars.

In order to obtain a preliminary estimate—to be reported at the auto shows—of the midsize model's combined city and highway driving mileage, the automaker subjected the two cars selected for testing to the EPA mileage test. When this was done, the cars obtained mileages of 30 mpg and 32 mpg. The mean of this sample of mileages is

$$\bar{x} = \frac{30 + 32}{2} = 31 \text{ mpg}$$

This sample mean is the point estimate of the mean mileage μ for the population of six preproduction cars and is the preliminary mileage estimate for the new midsize model that was reported at the auto shows.

TABLE 7.2   A Probability Distribution Describing the Population of Six Individual Car Mileages

Individual Car Mileage	29	30	31	32	33	34
Probability	1/6	1/6	1/6	1/6	1/6	1/6

FIGURE 7.1   A Comparison of Individual Car Mileages and Sample Means

(a) A graph of the probability distribution describing the population of six individual car mileages

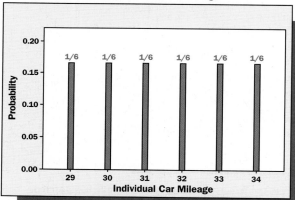

(b) A graph of the probability distribution describing the population of 15 sample means

TABLE 7.3   The Population of Sample Means

(a) The population of the 15 samples of $n = 2$ car mileages and corresponding sample means

Sample	Car Mileages	Sample Mean
1	29, 30	29.5
2	29, 31	30
3	29, 32	30.5
4	29, 33	31
5	29, 34	31.5
6	30, 31	30.5
7	30, 32	31
8	30, 33	31.5
9	30, 34	32
10	31, 32	31.5
11	31, 33	32
12	31, 34	32.5
13	32, 33	32.5
14	32, 34	33
15	33, 34	33.5

(b) A probability distribution describing the population of 15 sample means: the sampling distribution of the sample mean

Sample Mean	Frequency	Probability
29.5	1	1/15
30	1	1/15
30.5	2	2/15
31	2	2/15
31.5	3	3/15
32	2	2/15
32.5	2	2/15
33	1	1/15
33.5	1	1/15

When the auto shows were over, the automaker decided to further study the new midsize model by subjecting the four auto show cars to various tests. When the EPA mileage test was performed, the four cars obtained mileages of 29 mpg, 31 mpg, 33 mpg, and 34 mpg. Thus, the mileages obtained by the six preproduction cars were 29 mpg, 30 mpg, 31 mpg, 32 mpg, 33 mpg, and 34 mpg. The probability distribution of this population of six individual car mileages is given in Table 7.2 and graphed in Figure 7.1(a). The mean of the population of car mileages is

$$\mu = \frac{29 + 30 + 31 + 32 + 33 + 34}{6} = 31.5 \text{ mpg}$$

Note that the point estimate $\bar{x} = 31$ mpg that was reported at the auto shows is .5 mpg less than the true population mean μ of 31.5 mpg. Of course, different samples of two cars and corresponding mileages would have given different sample means. There are, in total, 15 samples of two mileages that could have been obtained by randomly selecting two cars from the population of six cars and subjecting the cars to the EPA mileage test. These samples correspond to the 15 combinations of two mileages that can be selected from the six mileages: 29, 30, 31, 32, 33, and 34. The samples are given, along with their means, in Table 7.3(a).

In order to find the probability distribution of the population of sample means, note that different sample means correspond to different numbers of samples. For example, because the sample mean of 31 mpg corresponds to 2 out of 15 samples—the sample (29, 33) and the sample (30, 32)—the probability of obtaining a sample mean of 31 mpg is 2/15. If we analyze all of the sample means in a similar fashion, we find that the probability distribution of the population of sample means is as given in Table 7.3(b). This distribution is the *sampling distribution of the sample mean*. A graph of this distribution is shown in Figure 7.1(b) and illustrates the accuracies of the different possible sample means as point estimates of the population mean. For example, whereas 3 out of 15 sample means exactly equal the population mean of 31.5 mpg, other sample means differ from the population mean by amounts varying from .5 mpg to 2 mpg.

As illustrated in Example 7.2, one of the purposes of the sampling distribution of the sample mean is to tell us how accurate the sample mean is likely to be as a point estimate of the population mean. Because the population of six individual car mileages in Example 7.2 is small, we were able (after the auto shows were over) to test all six cars, determine the values of the six car mileages, and calculate the population mean mileage. Often, however, the population of individual measurements under consideration is very large—either a large finite population or an infinite population. In this case, it would be impractical or impossible to determine the values of all of the population measurements and calculate the population mean. Instead, we randomly select a sample of individual measurements from the population and use the mean of this sample as the point estimate of the population mean. Moreover, although it would be impractical or impossible to list all of the many (perhaps trillions of) different possible sample means that could be obtained if the sampled population is very large, statisticians know various theoretical properties about the sampling distribution of these sample means. Some of these theoretical properties are intuitively illustrated by the sampling distribution of the 15 sample means in Example 7.2. Specifically, suppose that we will randomly select a sample of n individual measurements from a population of individual measurements having mean μ and standard deviation σ. Then, it can be shown that:

- **In many situations, the distribution of the population of all possible sample means looks, at least roughly, like a normal curve.** For example, consider Figure 7.1. This figure shows that, while the distribution of the population of six individual car mileages is a uniform distribution, the distribution of the population of 15 sample means has a somewhat bell-shaped appearance. Noting, however, that this rough bell-shaped appearance is not extremely close to the appearance of a normal curve, we wish to know when the distribution of all possible sample means is exactly or approximately normally distributed. Answers to this question will begin on the next page.

- **The mean, $\mu_{\bar{x}}$, of the population of all possible sample means is equal to μ, the mean of the population from which we will select the sample.** For example, the mean, $\mu_{\bar{x}}$, of the population of 15 sample means in Table 7.3(a) can be calculated by adding up the 15 sample means, which gives 472.5, and dividing by 15. That is, $\mu_{\bar{x}} = 472.5/15 = 31.5$, which is the same as μ, the mean of the population of six individual car mileages in Table 7.2. Furthermore, because $\mu_{\bar{x}}$ equals μ, we call the sample mean an **unbiased point estimate** of the population mean. This unbiasedness property says that, although most of the possible sample means that we might obtain are either above or below the population mean, there is no systematic tendency for the sample mean to overestimate or underestimate the population mean. That is, although we will randomly select only one sample, the unbiased sample mean is "correct on the average" in all possible samples.

- **The standard deviation, $\sigma_{\bar{x}}$, of the population of all posssible sample means is less than σ, the standard deviation of the population from which we will select the sample.** This is illustrated in Figure 7.1, which shows that the distribution of all possible sample means is less spread out than the distribution of all individual car mileages. Intuitively, we see that $\sigma_{\bar{x}}$ is smaller than σ because each possible sample mean is an average of n measurements (n equals 2 in Table 7.3). Thus, **each sample mean *averages out* high and low sample measurements and can be expected to be closer to the population mean μ than many of the individual population measurements would be.** It follows that the different possible sample means are more closely clustered around μ than are the individual population measurements.

FIGURE 7.2   **The Normally Distributed Population of All Individual Car Mileages and the Normally Distributed Population of All Possible Sample Means**

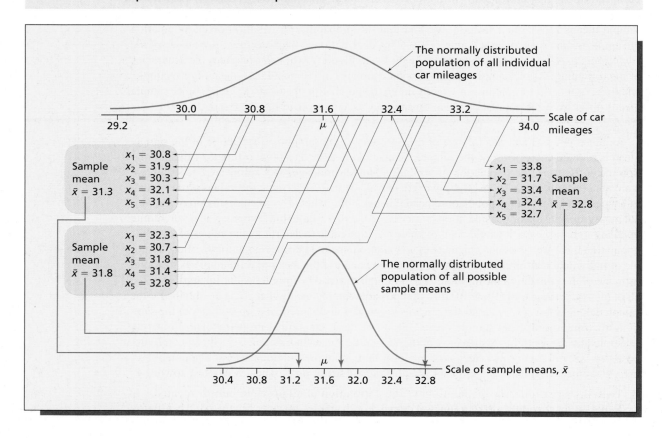

- **If the population from which we will select the sample is normally distributed, then for any sample size n the population of all possible sample means is normally distributed.** For example, consider the population of the mileages of all of the new midsize cars that could potentially be produced by this year's manufacturing process. As discussed in Chapter 1, we consider this population to be an infinite population because the automaker could always make "one more car." Moreover, assume that (as will be verified in a later example) this infinite population of all individual car mileages is normally distributed (see the top curve in Figure 7.2), and assume that the automaker will randomly select a sample of $n = 5$ cars, test them as prescribed by the EPA, and calculate the mean of the resulting sample mileages. It then follows that the population of all possible sample means that the automaker might obtain is normally distributed. This is illustrated in Figure 7.2 (see the bottom curve), which also depicts the unbiasedness of the sample mean $\bar{x}$ as a point estimate of the population mean μ. Specifically, note that the normally distributed population of all possible sample means is centered over μ, the mean of the normally distributed population of all individual car mileages. This says that, although most of the possible sample means that the automaker might obtain are either above or below the true population mean μ, the mean of all of the possible sample means that the automaker might obtain, $\mu_{\bar{x}}$, is equal to μ. To make Figure 7.2 easier to understand, we have assumed that the true value of the population mean mileage μ is 31.6 mpg. Of course, the true value of μ is really unknown. Our objective is to estimate μ, and to do this effectively, it is important to know more about $\sigma_{\bar{x}}$, the standard deviation of the population of all possible sample means. We will see that having a formula for $\sigma_{\bar{x}}$ will help us to choose a sample size n that is likely to make the sample mean $\bar{x}$ an accurate point estimate of the population mean μ. That is, although Figure 7.2 is based on selecting a sample of $n = 5$ car mileages, perhaps we should select a larger sample of, say, 50 or more car mileages. The following summary box gives a formula for $\sigma_{\bar{x}}$ and also summarizes other previously discussed facts about the probability distribution of the population of all possible sample means.

The Sampling Distribution of $\bar{x}$

Assume that the population from which we will randomly select a sample of n measurements has mean μ and standard deviation σ. Then, the population of all possible sample means

1 Has a normal distribution, if the sampled population has a normal distribution.

2 Has mean $\mu_{\bar{x}} = \mu$.

3 Has standard deviation $\sigma_{\bar{x}} = \dfrac{\sigma}{\sqrt{n}}$.

The formula for $\sigma_{\bar{x}}$ in (3) holds exactly if the sampled population is infinite. If the sampled population is finite, this formula holds approximately under conditions to be discussed at the end of this section.

Stated equivalently, the sampling distribution of $\bar{x}$ has mean $\mu_{\bar{x}} = \mu$, has standard deviation $\sigma_{\bar{x}} = \sigma/\sqrt{n}$ (if the sampled population is infinite), and is a normal distribution (if the sampled population has a normal distribution).[2]

The third result in the summary box says that, if the sampled population is infinite, then $\sigma_{\bar{x}} = \sigma/\sqrt{n}$. In words, $\sigma_{\bar{x}}$, the standard deviation of the population of all possible sample means, equals σ, the standard deviation of the sampled population, divided by the square root of the sample size n. It follows that, if the sample size n is greater than 1, then $\sigma_{\bar{x}} = \sigma/\sqrt{n}$ is smaller than σ. This is illustrated in Figure 7.2, where the sample size n is 5. Specifically, note that the normally distributed population of all possible sample means is less spread out than the normally distributed population of all individual car mileages. Furthermore, the formula $\sigma_{\bar{x}} = \sigma/\sqrt{n}$ says that $\sigma_{\bar{x}}$ decreases as n increases. That is, intuitively, when the sample size is larger, each possible sample averages more observations. Therefore, the resulting different possible sample means will differ from each other by less and thus will become more closely clustered around the population mean. It follows that, if we take a larger sample, we are more likely to obtain a sample mean that is near the population mean.

In order to better see how $\sigma_{\bar{x}} = \sigma/\sqrt{n}$ decreases as the sample size n increases, we will compute some values of $\sigma_{\bar{x}}$ in the context of the car mileage case. To do this, we will assume that, although we do not know the true value of the population mean μ, we do know the true value of the population standard deviation σ. Here, knowledge of σ might be based on theory or history related to the population under consideration. For example, because the automaker has been working to improve gas mileages, we cannot assume that we know the true value of the population mean mileage μ for the new midsize model. However, engineering data might indicate that the spread of individual car mileages for the automaker's midsize cars is the same from model to model and year to year. Therefore, if the mileages for previous models had a standard deviation equal to .8 mpg, it might be reasonable to assume that the standard deviation of the mileages for the new model will also equal .8 mpg. Such an assumption would, of course, be questionable, and in most real-world situations there would probably not be an actual basis for knowing σ. However, assuming that σ is known will help us to illustrate sampling distributions, and in later chapters we will see what to do when σ is unknown.

EXAMPLE 7.3 The Car Mileage Case: Estimating Mean Mileage

Part 1: Basic concepts   Consider the infinite population of the mileages of all of the new midsize cars that could potentially be produced by this year's manufacturing process. If we assume that this population is normally distributed with mean μ and standard deviation $\sigma = .8$ (see Figure 7.3(a)), and if the automaker will randomly select a sample of n cars and test them as prescribed by the EPA, it follows that the population of all possible sample means is normally distributed with mean $\mu_{\bar{x}} = \mu$ and standard deviation $\sigma_{\bar{x}} = \sigma/\sqrt{n} = .8/\sqrt{n}$. In order to show

---

[2]In optional Section 7.6 we derive the formulas $\mu_{\bar{x}} = \mu$ and $\sigma_{\bar{x}} = \sigma/\sqrt{n}$.

FIGURE 7.3   **A Comparison of (1) the Population of All Individual Car Mileages, (2) the Sampling Distribution of the Sample Mean $\bar{x}$ When $n = 5$, and (3) the Sampling Distribution of the Sample Mean $\bar{x}$ When $n = 50$**

that a larger sample is more likely to give a more accurate point estimate $\bar{x}$ of μ, compare taking a sample of size $n = 5$ with taking a sample of size $n = 50$. If $n = 5$, then

$$\sigma_{\bar{x}} = \frac{\sigma}{\sqrt{n}} = \frac{.8}{\sqrt{5}} = .358$$

and it follows (by the Empirical Rule) that 95.44 percent of all possible sample means are within plus or minus $2\sigma_{\bar{x}} = 2(.358) = .716$ mpg of the population mean μ. If $n = 50$, then

$$\sigma_{\bar{x}} = \frac{\sigma}{\sqrt{n}} = \frac{.8}{\sqrt{50}} = .113$$

and it follows that 95.44 percent of all possible sample means are within plus or minus $2\sigma_{\bar{x}} = 2(.113) = .226$ mpg of the population mean μ. Therefore, if $n = 50$, the different possible sample means that the automaker might obtain will be more closely clustered around μ than they will be if $n = 5$ (see Figures 7.3(b) and (c)). This implies that the larger sample of size $n = 50$ is more likely to give a sample mean $\bar{x}$ that is near μ.

FIGURE 7.4   **The Probability That $\bar{x} \geq 31.56$ When $\mu = 31$ in the Car Mileage Case**

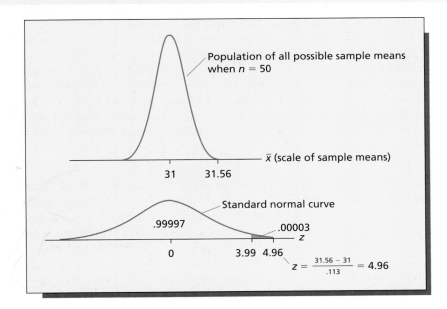

Part 2: Statistical inference   Recall from Chapter 3 that the automaker has randomly selected a sample of $n = 50$ mileages, which has mean $\bar{x} = 31.56$. We now ask the following question: If the population mean mileage μ exactly equals 31 mpg (the minimum standard for the tax credit), what is the probability of observing a sample mean mileage that is greater than or equal to 31.56 mpg? To find this probability, recall from Chapter 2 that a histogram of the 50 mileages indicates that the population of all individual mileages is normally distributed. Assuming that the population standard deviation σ is known to equal .8 mpg, it follows that the sampling distribution of the sample mean $\bar{x}$ is a normal distribution, with mean $\mu_{\bar{x}} = \mu$ and standard deviation $\sigma_{\bar{x}} = \sigma/\sqrt{n} = .8/\sqrt{50} = .113$. Therefore,

$$P(\bar{x} \geq 31.56 \quad \text{if} \quad \mu = 31) = P\left(z \geq \frac{31.56 - \mu_{\bar{x}}}{\sigma_{\bar{x}}}\right) = P\left(z \geq \frac{31.56 - 31}{.113}\right)$$

$$= P(z \geq 4.96)$$

To find $P(z \geq 4.96)$, notice that the largest z value given in Table A.3 (page 791) is 3.99, which gives a right-hand tail area of .00003. Therefore, because $P(z \geq 3.99) = .00003$, it follows that $P(z \geq 4.96)$ is less than .00003 (see Figure 7.4). The fact that this probability is less than .00003 says that, if μ equals 31, then fewer than 3 in 100,000 of all possible sample means are at least as large as the sample mean $\bar{x} = 31.56$ that we have actually observed. Therefore, if we are to believe that μ equals 31, then we must believe that we have observed a sample mean that can be described as a smaller than 3 in 100,000 chance. Because it is extremely difficult to believe that such a small chance would occur, we have extremely strong evidence that μ does not equal 31 and that μ is, in fact, larger than 31. This evidence would probably convince the federal government that the midsize model's mean mileage μ exceeds 31 mpg and thus that the midsize model deserves the tax credit.

To conclude this subsection, it is important to make two comments. First, the formula $\sigma_{\bar{x}} = \sigma/\sqrt{n}$ follows, in theory, from the formula for $\sigma_{\bar{x}}^2$, the variance of the population of all possible sample means. The formula for $\sigma_{\bar{x}}^2$ is $\sigma_{\bar{x}}^2 = \sigma^2/n$. Second, in addition to holding exactly if the sampled population is infinite, **the formula $\sigma_{\bar{x}} = \sigma/\sqrt{n}$ holds approximately if the sampled population is finite and much larger than (say, at least 20 times) the size of the sample.** For example, if we define the population of the mileages of all new midsize cars to be the population of the mileages of all cars that will actually be produced this year, then the population is finite. However, the population would be very large—certainly at least as large as 20 times any reasonable sample size. For example, if the automaker produces 100,000 new midsize cars this year, and if we randomly select a sample of $n = 50$ of these cars, then the population size of 100,000 is more than 20 times the sample size of 50 (which is 1,000). It follows that, even though the population is finite and thus the formula $\sigma_{\bar{x}} = \sigma/\sqrt{n}$ would not hold exactly, this formula would hold approximately. The exact formula for $\sigma_{\bar{x}}$ when the sampled population is finite is given in a technical note at the end of this section. It is important to use this exact formula if the sampled population is finite and less than 20 times the size of the sample. **However, with the exception of the populations considered in the technical note and in Section 8.5, we will assume that all of the remaining populations to be discussed in this book are either infinite or finite and at least 20 times the size of the sample. Therefore, it will be appropriate to use the formula $\sigma_{\bar{x}} = \sigma/\sqrt{n}$.**

LO7-3 Explain and use the Central Limit Theorem.

Sampling a nonnormally distributed population: The Central Limit Theorem   We now consider what can be said about the sampling distribution of $\bar{x}$ when the sampled population is not normally distributed. First, as previously stated, the fact that $\mu_{\bar{x}} = \mu$ is still true. Second, as also previously stated, the formula $\sigma_{\bar{x}} = \sigma/\sqrt{n}$ is exactly correct if the sampled population is infinite and is approximately correct if the sampled population is finite and much larger than (say, at least 20 times as large as) the sample size. Third, an extremely important result called the **Central Limit Theorem** tells us that, **if the sample size n is large, then the sampling distribution of $\bar{x}$ is approximately normal, even if the sampled population is not normally distributed.**

The Central Limit Theorem

If the sample size n is sufficiently large, then the population of all possible sample means is approximately normally distributed (with mean $\mu_{\bar{x}} = \mu$ and standard deviation $\sigma_{\bar{x}} = \sigma/\sqrt{n}$), no matter what probability distribution describes the sampled population. Furthermore, the larger the sample size n is, the more nearly normally distributed is the population of all possible sample means.

The Central Limit Theorem is illustrated in Figure 7.5 for several population shapes. Notice that as the sample size increases (from 2 to 6 to 30), the populations of all possible sample means become more nearly normally distributed. This figure also illustrates that, as the sample size increases, the spread of the distribution of all possible sample means decreases (remember that this spread is measured by $\sigma_{\bar{x}}$, which decreases as the sample size increases).

How large must the sample size be for the sampling distribution of $\bar{x}$ to be approximately normal? In general, the more skewed the probability distribution of the sampled population, the larger the sample size must be for the population of all possible sample means to be approximately normally distributed. For some sampled populations, particularly those described by symmetric distributions, the population of all possible sample means is approximately normally distributed for a fairly small sample size. In addition, studies indicate that, **if the sample size is at least 30, then for most sampled populations the population of all possible sample means is approximately normally distributed.** In this book, whenever the sample size n is at least 30, we will assume that the sampling distribution of $\bar{x}$ is approximately a normal distribution. Of course, if the sampled population is exactly normally distributed, the sampling distribution of $\bar{x}$ is exactly normal for any sample size.

We can see the shapes of sampling distributions such as those illustrated in Figure 7.5 by using computer simulation. Specifically, for a population having a particular probability distribution, we can have the computer draw a given number of samples of n observations, compute the mean of each sample, and arrange the sample means into a histogram. To illustrate this, consider the upper portion of Figure 7.6, which shows the exponential distribution describing the hospital emergency room interarrival times discussed in Example 6.11 (page 253). Figure 7.6(a) gives the results of a simulation in which MINITAB randomly selected 1,000 samples of $n = 5$ interarrival times from this exponential distribution, calculated the mean of each sample, and arranged the 1,000 sample means into a histogram. Figure 7.6(b) gives the results of a simulation in which

FIGURE 7.5   The Central Limit Theorem Says That the Larger the Sample Size Is, the More Nearly Normally Distributed Is the Population of All Possible Sample Means

(a) Several sampled populations

(b) Corresponding populations of all possible sample means for different sample sizes

FIGURE 7.6   Simulating the Sampling Distribution of the Sample Mean When Sampling from an Exponential Distribution

(a) A histogram of 1,000 sample means when $n = 5$

(b) A histogram of 1,000 sample means when $n = 30$

MINITAB randomly selected 1,000 samples of $n = 30$ interarrival times from the exponential distribution, calculated the mean of each sample, and arranged the 1,000 sample means into a histogram. Note that, whereas the histogram in Figure 7.6(a) is somewhat skewed to the right, the histogram in Figure 7.6(b) appears approximately bell-shaped. Therefore, we might conclude that when we randomly select a sample of n observations from an exponential distribution, the sampling distribution of the sample mean is somewhat skewed to the right when $n = 5$ and is approximately normal when $n = 30$.

EXAMPLE 7.4 The e-billing Case: Reducing Mean Bill Payment Time

Recall that a management consulting firm has installed a new computer-based electronic billing system in a Hamilton, Ohio, trucking company. Because of the previously discussed advantages of the new billing system, and because the trucking company's clients are receptive to using this system, the management consulting firm believes that the new system will reduce the mean bill payment time by more than 50 percent. The mean payment time using the old billing system was approximately equal to, but no less than, 39 days. Therefore, if μ denotes the new mean payment time, the consulting firm believes that μ will be less than 19.5 days. To assess whether μ is less than 19.5 days, the consulting firm has randomly selected a sample of $n = 65$ invoices processed using the new billing system and has determined the payment times for these invoices. The mean of the 65 payment times is $\bar{x} = 18.1077$ days, which is less than 19.5 days. Therefore, we ask the following question: If the population mean payment time is 19.5 days, what is the probability of observing a sample mean payment time that is less than or equal to 18.1077 days? To find this probability, recall from Chapter 2 that a histogram of the 65 payment times indicates that the population of all payment times is skewed with a tail to the right. However, the Central Limit Theorem tells us that, because the sample size $n = 65$ is large, the sampling distribution of $\bar{x}$ is approximately a normal distribution with mean $\mu_{\bar{x}} = \mu$ and standard deviation $\sigma_{\bar{x}} = \sigma/\sqrt{n}$. Moreover, whereas this is the first time that the consulting firm has implemented an electronic billing system for a trucking company, the firm has installed electronic billing systems for clients in other industries. Analysis of results from these installations shows that, although the population mean payment time μ varies from company to company, the population standard deviation σ of payment times is the same for different applications and equals 4.2 days. Assuming that σ also equals 4.2 days for the trucking company, it follows that $\sigma_{\bar{x}}$ equals $4.2/\sqrt{65} = .5209$ and that

$$P(\bar{x} \leq 18.1077 \text{ if } \mu = 19.5) = P\left(z \leq \frac{18.1077 - 19.5}{.5209}\right) = P(z \leq -2.67)$$

which is the area under the standard normal curve to the left of -2.67. The normal table tells us that this area equals .0038. This probability says that, if μ equals 19.5, then only .0038 of all possible sample means are at least as small as the sample mean $\bar{x} = 18.1077$ that we have actually observed. Therefore, if we are to believe that μ equals 19.5, we must believe that we have observed a sample mean that can be described as a 38 in 10,000 chance. It is very difficult to believe that such a small chance would occur, so we have very strong evidence that μ does not equal 19.5 and is, in fact, less than 19.5. We conclude that the new billing system has reduced the mean bill payment time by more than 50 percent.

Unbiasedness and minimum-variance estimates   Recall that a sample statistic is any descriptive measure of the sample measurements. For instance, the sample mean $\bar{x}$ is a statistic, and so are the sample median, the sample variance s^2, and the sample standard deviation s. Not only do different samples give different values of $\bar{x}$, different samples also give different values of the median, s^2, s, or any other statistic. It follows that, *before we draw the sample, any sample statistic is a random variable,* and

The **sampling distribution of a sample statistic** is the probability distribution of the population of all possible values of the sample statistic.

In general, we wish to estimate a population parameter by using a sample statistic that is what we call an *unbiased point estimate* of the parameter.

A sample statistic is an **unbiased point estimate** of a population parameter if the mean of the population of all possible values of the sample statistic equals the population parameter.

For example, we use the sample mean $\bar{x}$ as the point estimate of the population mean μ because $\bar{x}$ **is an unbiased point estimate of μ.** That is, $\mu_{\bar{x}} = \mu$. In words, the average of all the different possible sample means (that we could obtain from all the different possible samples) equals μ.

Although we want a sample statistic to be an unbiased point estimate of the population parameter of interest, we also want the statistic to have a small standard deviation (and variance). That is, we wish the different possible values of the sample statistic to be closely clustered around the population parameter. If this is the case, when we actually randomly select one sample and compute the sample statistic, its value is likely to be close to the value of the population parameter. Furthermore, some general results apply to estimating the mean μ of a normally distributed population. In this situation, it can be shown that both the sample mean and the sample median are unbiased point estimates of μ. In fact, there are many unbiased point estimates of μ. However, it can be shown that the variance of the population of all possible sample means is smaller than the variance of the population of all possible values of any other unbiased point estimate of μ. For this reason, **we call the sample mean a minimum-variance unbiased point estimate of μ.** When we use the sample mean as the point estimate of μ, we are more likely to obtain a point estimate close to μ than if we used any other unbiased sample statistic as the point estimate of μ. This is one reason why we use the sample mean as the point estimate of the population mean.

We next consider estimating the population variance σ^2. It can be shown that if the sampled population is infinite, then s^2 **is an unbiased point estimate of σ^2.** That is, the average of all the different possible sample variances that we could obtain (from all the different possible samples) is equal to σ^2. This is why we use a divisor equal to $n - 1$ rather than n when we estimate σ^2. It can be shown that, if we used n as the divisor when estimating σ^2, we would not obtain an unbiased point estimate of σ^2. When the population is finite, s^2 may be regarded as an approximately unbiased estimate of σ^2 as long as the population is fairly large (which is usually the case).

It would seem logical to think that, because s^2 is an unbiased point estimate of σ^2, s should be an unbiased point estimate of σ. This seems plausible, but it is not the case. There is no easy way to calculate an unbiased point estimate of σ. Because of this, the usual practice is to use s as the point estimate of σ (even though it is not an unbiased estimate).

This ends our discussion of the theory of point estimation. It suffices to say that in this book we estimate population parameters by using sample statistics that statisticians generally agree are best. Whenever possible, these sample statistics are unbiased point estimates and have small variances.

Technical Note: If we randomly select a sample of size n without replacement from a finite population of size N, then it can be shown that $\sigma_{\bar{x}} = (\sigma/\sqrt{n})\sqrt{(N - n)/(N - 1)}$, where the quantity $\sqrt{(N - n)/(N - 1)}$ is called the **finite population multiplier.** If the size of the sampled population is at least 20 times the size of the sample (that is, **if $N \geq 20n$), then the finite population multiplier is approximately equal to one, and $\sigma_{\bar{x}}$ approximately equals $\sigma/\sqrt{n}$.** However, if the population size N is smaller than 20 times the size of the sample, then the finite population multiplier is substantially less than one, and we must include this multiplier in the calculation of $\sigma_{\bar{x}}$. For instance, in Example 7.2, where the standard deviation σ of the population of $N = 6$ car mileages can be calculated to be 1.7078, and where $N = 6$ is only three times the sample size $n = 2$, it follows that

$$\sigma_{\bar{x}} = \frac{\sigma}{\sqrt{n}}\sqrt{\frac{N - n}{N - 1}} = \left(\frac{1.7078}{\sqrt{2}}\right)\sqrt{\frac{6 - 2}{6 - 1}} = 1.2076(.8944) = 1.08$$

We will see how this formula can be used to make statistical inferences in Section 8.5.

Exercises for Section 7.2

CONCEPTS

connect

7.7 Suppose that we will randomly select a sample of four measurements from a larger population of measurements. The sampling distribution of the sample mean $\bar{x}$ is the probability distribution of a population. In your own words, describe the elements in this population.

7.8 What does the Central Limit Theorem tell us about the sampling distribution of the sample mean?

METHODS AND APPLICATIONS

7.9 Suppose that we will take a random sample of size n from a population having mean μ and standard deviation σ. For each of the following situations, find the mean, variance, and standard deviation of the sampling distribution of the sample mean $\bar{x}$:

    a $\mu = 10$, $\sigma = 2$, $n = 25$ **c** $\mu = 3$, $\sigma = .1$, $n = 4$
    b $\mu = 500$, $\sigma = .5$, $n = 100$ **d** $\mu = 100$, $\sigma = 1$, $n = 1{,}600$

7.10 For each situation in Exercise 7.9, find an interval that contains (approximately or exactly) 99.73 percent of all the possible sample means. In which cases must we assume that the population is normally distributed? Why?

7.11 Suppose that we will randomly select a sample of 64 measurements from a population having a mean equal to 20 and a standard deviation equal to 4.

    a Describe the shape of the sampling distribution of the sample mean $\bar{x}$. Do we need to make any assumptions about the shape of the population? Why or why not?

    b Find the mean and the standard deviation of the sampling distribution of the sample mean $\bar{x}$.

    c Calculate the probability that we will obtain a sample mean greater than 21; that is, calculate $P(\bar{x} > 21)$. Hint: Find the z value corresponding to 21 by using $\mu_{\bar{x}}$ and $\sigma_{\bar{x}}$ because we wish to calculate a probability about $\bar{x}$. Then sketch the sampling distribution and the probability.

    d Calculate the probability that we will obtain a sample mean less than 19.385; that is, calculate $P(\bar{x} < 19.385)$.

THE GAME SHOW CASE

Exercises 7.12 through 7.16 are based on the following situation.

    Congratulations! You have just won the question-and-answer portion of a popular game show and will now be given an opportunity to select a grand prize. The game show host shows you a large revolving drum containing four identical white envelopes that have been thoroughly mixed in the drum. Each of the envelopes contains one of four checks made out for grand prizes of 20, 40, 60, and 80 thousand dollars. Usually, a contestant reaches into the drum, selects an envelope, and receives the grand prize in the envelope. Tonight, however, is a special night. You will be given the choice of either selecting one envelope or selecting two envelopes and receiving the average of the grand prizes in the two envelopes. If you select one envelope, the probability is 1/4 that you will receive any one of the individual grand prizes 20, 40, 60, and 80 thousand dollars. To see what could happen if you select two envelopes, do Exercises 7.12 through 7.16.

7.12 There are six combinations, or samples, of two grand prizes that can be randomly selected from the four grand prizes 20, 40, 60, and 80 thousand dollars. Four of these samples are (20, 40), (20, 60), (20, 80), and (40, 60). Find the other two samples.

7.13 Find the mean of each sample in Exercise 7.12.

7.14 Find the probability distribution of the population of six sample mean grand prizes.

7.15 If you select two envelopes, what is the probability that you will receive a sample mean grand prize of at least 50 thousand dollars?

7.16 Compare the probability distribution of the four individual grand prizes with the probability distribution of the six sample mean grand prizes. Would you select one or two envelopes? Why? Note: There is no one correct answer. It is a matter of opinion.

7.17 **THE BANK CUSTOMER WAITING TIME CASE**   WaitTime

    Recall that the bank manager wants to show that the new system reduces typical customer waiting times to less than six minutes. One way to do this is to demonstrate that the mean of the population of all customer waiting times is less than 6. Letting this mean be μ, in this exercise we wish to investigate whether the sample of 100 waiting times provides evidence to support the claim that μ is less than 6.

    For the sake of argument, we will begin by assuming that μ equals 6, and we will then attempt to use the sample to contradict this assumption in favor of the conclusion that μ is less than 6.

Recall that the mean of the sample of 100 waiting times is $\bar{x} = 5.46$ and assume that σ, the standard deviation of the population of all customer waiting times, is known to be 2.47.

a Consider the population of all possible sample means obtained from random samples of 100 waiting times. What is the shape of this population of sample means? That is, what is the shape of the sampling distribution of $\bar{x}$? Why is this true?

b Find the mean and standard deviation of the population of all possible sample means when we assume that μ equals 6.

c The sample mean that we have actually observed is $\bar{x} = 5.46$. Assuming that μ equals 6, find the probability of observing a sample mean that is less than or equal to $\bar{x} = 5.46$.

d If μ equals 6, what percentage of all possible sample means are less than or equal to 5.46? Because we have actually observed a sample mean of $\bar{x} = 5.46$, is it more reasonable to believe that (1) μ equals 6 and we have observed one of the sample means that is less than or equal to 5.46 when μ equals 6, or (2) that we have observed a sample mean less than or equal to 5.46 because μ is less than 6? Explain. What do you conclude about whether the new system has reduced the typical customer waiting time to less than six minutes?

7.18 THE VIDEO GAME SATISFACTION RATING CASE 🎮 VideoGame

Recall that a customer is considered to be very satisfied with his or her XYZ Box video game system if the customer's composite score on the survey instrument is at least 42. One way to show that customers are typically very satisfied is to show that the mean of the population of all satisfaction ratings is at least 42. Letting this mean be μ, in this exercise we wish to investigate whether the sample of 65 satisfaction ratings provides evidence to support the claim that μ exceeds 42 (and, therefore, is at least 42).

For the sake of argument, we begin by assuming that μ equals 42, and we then attempt to use the sample to contradict this assumption in favor of the conclusion that μ exceeds 42. Recall that the mean of the sample of 65 satisfaction ratings is $\bar{x} = 42.95$, and assume that σ, the standard deviation of the population of all satisfaction ratings, is known to be 2.64.

a Consider the sampling distribution of $\bar{x}$ for random samples of 65 customer satisfaction ratings. Use the properties of this sampling distribution to find the probability of observing a sample mean greater than or equal to 42.95 when we assume that μ equals 42.

b If μ equals 42, what percentage of all possible sample means are greater than or equal to 42.95? Because we have actually observed a sample mean of $\bar{x} = 42.95$, is it more reasonable to believe that (1) μ equals 42 and we have observed a sample mean that is greater than or equal to 42.95 when μ equals 42, or (2) that we have observed a sample mean that is greater than or equal to 42.95 because μ is greater than 42? Explain. What do you conclude about whether customers are typically very satisfied with the XYZ Box video game system?

7.19 In an article in the *Journal of Management,* Joseph Martocchio studied and estimated the costs of employee absences. Based on a sample of 176 blue-collar workers, Martocchio estimated that the mean amount of paid time lost during a three-month period was 1.4 days per employee with a standard deviation of 1.3 days. Martocchio also estimated that the mean amount of unpaid time lost during a three-month period was 1.0 day per employee with a standard deviation of 1.8 days. Suppose we randomly select a sample of 100 blue-collar workers. Based on Martocchio's estimates:

a What is the probability that the average amount of paid time lost during a three-month period for the 100 blue-collar workers will exceed 1.5 days? Assume σ equals 1.3 days.

b What is the probability that the average amount of unpaid time lost during a three-month period for the 100 blue-collar workers will exceed 1.5 days? Assume σ equals 1.8 days.

c Suppose we randomly select a sample of 100 blue-collar workers, and suppose the sample mean amount of unpaid time lost during a three-month period actually exceeds 1.5 days. Would it be reasonable to conclude that the mean amount of unpaid time lost has increased above the previously estimated 1.0 day? Explain. Assume σ still equals 1.8 days.

7.20 When a pizza restaurant's delivery process is operating effectively, pizzas are delivered in an average of 45 minutes with a standard deviation of 6 minutes. To monitor its delivery process, the restaurant randomly selects five pizzas each night and records their delivery times.

a For the sake of argument, assume that the population of all delivery times on a given evening is normally distributed with a mean of $\mu = 45$ minutes and a standard deviation of $\sigma = 6$ minutes. (That is, we assume that the delivery process is operating effectively.) Find the mean and the standard deviation of the population of all possible sample means, and calculate an interval containing 99.73 percent of all possible sample means.

b Suppose that the mean of the five sampled delivery times on a particular evening is $\bar{x} = 55$ minutes. Using the interval that you calculated in *a*, what would you conclude about whether the restaurant's delivery process is operating effectively? Why?

LO7-4 Describe and use the sampling distribution of the sample proportion.

7.3 The Sampling Distribution of the Sample Proportion ● ● ●

A food processing company markets a soft cheese spread that is sold in a plastic container with an "easy pour" spout. Although this spout works extremely well and is popular with consumers, it is expensive to produce. Because of the spout's high cost, the company has developed a new, less expensive spout. While the new, cheaper spout may alienate some purchasers, a company study shows that its introduction will increase profits if fewer than 10 percent of the cheese spread's current purchasers are lost. That is, if we let p be the true proportion of all current purchasers who would stop buying the cheese spread if the new spout were used, profits will increase as long as p is less than .10.

Suppose that (after trying the new spout) 63 of 1,000 randomly selected purchasers say that they would stop buying the cheese spread if the new spout were used. The point estimate of the population proportion p is the sample proportion $\hat{p} = 63/1,000 = .063$. This sample proportion says that we estimate that 6.3 percent of all current purchasers would stop buying the cheese spread if the new spout were used. Because $\hat{p}$ equals .063, we have some evidence that the population proportion p is less than .10. In order to determine the strength of this evidence, we need to consider the sampling distribution of $\hat{p}$. In general, assume that we will randomly select a sample of n elements from a population, and assume that a proportion p of all the elements in the population fall into a particular category (for instance, the category of consumers who would stop buying the cheese spread). Before we actually select the sample, there are many different samples of n elements that we might potentially obtain. The number of elements that fall into the category in question will vary from sample to sample, so the sample proportion of elements falling into the category will also vary from sample to sample. For example, if three possible random samples of 1,000 soft cheese spread purchasers had, respectively, 63, 58, and 65 purchasers say that they would stop buying the cheese spread if the new spout were used, then the sample proportions given by the three samples would be $\hat{p} = 63/1000 = .063$, $\hat{p} = 58/1000 = .058$, and $\hat{p} = 65/1000 = .065$. In general, before we randomly select the sample, there are many different possible sample proportions that we might obtain, and thus the sample proportion $\hat{p}$ is a random variable. In the following box we give the properties of the probability distribution of this random variable, which is called **the sampling distribution of the sample proportion $\hat{p}$.**

The Sampling Distribution of the Sample Proportion $\hat{p}$

The population of all possible sample proportions

1 Approximately has a normal distribution, if the sample size n is large.

2 Has mean $\mu_{\hat{p}} = p$.

3 Has standard deviation $\sigma_{\hat{p}} = \sqrt{\dfrac{p(1-p)}{n}}$.

Stated equivalently, the sampling distribution of $\hat{p}$ has mean $\mu_{\hat{p}} = p$, has standard deviation $\sigma_{\hat{p}} = \sqrt{p(1-p)/n}$, and is approximately a normal distribution (if the sample size n is large).

Property 1 in the box says that, if n is large, then the population of all possible sample proportions approximately has a normal distribution. Here, it can be shown that **n should be considered large if both np and $n(1 - p)$ are at least 5.**[3] Property 2, which says that $\mu_{\hat{p}} = p$, is valid for any sample size and tells us that $\hat{p}$ is an unbiased estimate of p. That is, although the sample proportion $\hat{p}$ that we calculate probably does not equal p, the average of all the different sample proportions that we could have calculated (from all the different possible samples) is equal to p. Property 3, which says that

$$\sigma_{\hat{p}} = \sqrt{\frac{p(1-p)}{n}}$$

---

[3]Some statisticians suggest using the more conservative rule that both np and $n(1 - p)$ must be at least 10.

is exactly correct if the sampled population is infinite and is approximately correct if the sampled population is finite and much larger than (say, at least 20 times as large as) the sample size. Property 3 tells us that the standard deviation of the population of all possible sample proportions decreases as the sample size increases. That is, the larger n is, the more closely clustered are all the different sample proportions around the true population proportion. Finally, note that the formula for $\sigma_{\hat{p}}$ follows, in theory, from the formula for $\sigma_{\hat{p}}^2$, the variance of the population of all possible sample proportions. The formula for $\sigma_{\hat{p}}^2$ is $\sigma_{\hat{p}}^2 = p(1 - p)/n$.

EXAMPLE 7.5 The Cheese Spread Case: Improving Profitability

In the cheese spread situation, the food processing company must decide whether p, the proportion of all current purchasers who would stop buying the cheese spread if the new spout were used, is less than .10. In order to do this, remember that when 1,000 purchasers of the cheese spread are randomly selected, 63 of these purchasers say they would stop buying the cheese spread if the new spout were used. Noting that the sample proportion $\hat{p} = .063$ is less than .10, we ask the following question. If the true population proportion is .10, what is the probability of observing a sample proportion that is less than or equal to .063?

If p equals .10, we can assume that the sampling distribution of $\hat{p}$ is approximately a normal distribution because both $np = 1{,}000(.10) = 100$ and $n(1 - p) = 1{,}000(1 - .10) = 900$ are at least 5. Furthermore, the mean and standard deviation of the sampling distribution of $\hat{p}$ are $\mu_{\hat{p}} = p = .10$ and

$$\sigma_{\hat{p}} = \sqrt{\frac{p(1 - p)}{n}} = \sqrt{\frac{(.10)(.90)}{1{,}000}} = .0094868$$

Therefore,

$$P(\hat{p} \leq .063 \text{ if } p = .10) = P\left(z \leq \frac{.063 - \mu_{\hat{p}}}{\sigma_{\hat{p}}}\right) = P\left(z \leq \frac{.063 - .10}{.0094868}\right)$$

$$= P(z \leq -3.90)$$

which is the area under the standard normal curve to the left of -3.90. The normal table tells us that this area equals .00005. This probability says that, if p equals .10, then only 5 in 100,000 of all possible sample proportions are at least as small as the sample proportion $\hat{p} = .063$ that we have actually observed. That is, if we are to believe that p equals .10, we must believe that we have observed a sample proportion that can be described as a 5 in 100,000 chance. It follows that we have extremely strong evidence that p does not equal .10 and is, in fact, less than .10. In other words, we have extremely strong evidence that fewer than 10 percent of current purchasers would stop buying the cheese spread if the new spout were used. It seems that introducing the new spout will be profitable.

Exercises for Section 7.3

CONCEPTS

7.21 What population is described by the sampling distribution of $\hat{p}$?

7.22 Suppose that we will randomly select a sample of n elements from a population and that we will compute the sample proportion $\hat{p}$ of these elements that fall into a category of interest. If we consider the sampling distribution of $\hat{p}$:

  a If the sample size n is large, the sampling distribution of $\hat{p}$ is approximately a normal distribution. What condition must be satisfied to guarantee that n is large enough to say that $\hat{p}$ is normally distributed?

  b Write formulas that express the central tendency and variability of the population of all possible sample proportions. Explain what each of these formulas means in your own words.

7.23 Describe the effect of increasing the sample size on the population of all possible sample proportions.

METHODS AND APPLICATIONS

7.24 In each of the following cases, determine whether the sample size n is large enough to say that the sampling distribution of $\hat{p}$ is a normal distribution.

    a $p = .4,\quad n = 100$ **d** $p = .8,\quad n = 400$

    b $p = .1,\quad n = 10$ **e** $p = .98,\quad n = 1{,}000$

    c $p = .1,\quad n = 50$ **f** $p = .99,\quad n = 400$

7.25 In each of the following cases, find the mean, variance, and standard deviation of the sampling distribution of the sample proportion $\hat{p}$.

    a $p = .5,\quad n = 250$ **c** $p = .8,\quad n = 400$

    b $p = .1,\quad n = 100$ **d** $p = .98,\quad n = 1{,}000$

7.26 For each situation in Exercise 7.25, find an interval that contains approximately 95.44 percent of all the possible sample proportions.

7.27 Suppose that we will randomly select a sample of $n = 100$ elements from a population and that we will compute the sample proportion $\hat{p}$ of these elements that fall into a category of interest. If the true population proportion p equals .9:

    a Describe the shape of the sampling distribution of $\hat{p}$. Why can we validly describe the shape?

    b Find the mean and the standard deviation of the sampling distribution of $\hat{p}$.

7.28 For the situation in Exercise 7.27, calculate the following probabilities. In each case sketch the sampling distribution and the probability.

    a $P(\hat{p} \geq .96)$

    b $P(.855 \leq \hat{p} \leq .945)$

    c $P(\hat{p} \leq .915)$

7.29 A past issue of *The Journal News* (Hamilton, Ohio) reported on a study conducted by the Kaiser Family Foundation regarding parents' use of television set V-chips for controlling their childrens' TV viewing. The study asked parents who own TVs equipped with V-chips whether they use the devices to block programs with objectionable content.

    a Suppose that we wish to use the study results to justify the claim that fewer than 20 percent of parents who own TV sets with V-chips use the devices. The study actually found that 17 percent of the parents polled used their V-chips. If the poll surveyed 1,000 parents, and if for the sake of argument we assume that 20 percent of parents who own V-chips actually use the devices (that is, $p = .2$), calculate the probability of observing a sample proportion of .17 or less. That is, calculate $P(\hat{p} \leq .17)$.

    b Based on the probability you computed in part a, would you conclude that fewer than 20 percent of parents who own TV sets equipped with V-chips actually use the devices? Explain.

7.30 On February 8, 2002, the Gallup Organization released the results of a poll concerning American attitudes toward the 19th Winter Olympic Games in Salt Lake City, Utah. The poll results were based on telephone interviews with a randomly selected national sample of 1,011 adults, 18 years and older, conducted February 4–6, 2002.

    a Suppose we wish to use the poll's results to justify the claim that more than 30 percent of Americans (18 years or older) say that figure skating is their favorite Winter Olympic event. The poll actually found that 32 percent of respondents reported that figure skating was their favorite event.[4] If, for the sake of argument, we assume that 30 percent of Americans (18 years or older) say figure skating is their favorite event (that is, $p = .3$), calculate the probability of observing a sample proportion of .32 or more; that is, calculate $P(\hat{p} \geq .32)$.

    b Based on the probability you computed in part a, would you conclude that more than 30 percent of Americans (18 years or older) say that figure skating is their favorite Winter Olympic event?

7.31 *Quality Progress*, February 2005, reports on improvements in customer satisfaction and loyalty made by Bank of America. A key measure of customer satisfaction is the response (on a scale from 1 to 10) to the question: "Considering all the business you do with Bank of America, what is your overall satisfaction with Bank of America?" Here, a response of 9 or 10 represents "customer delight."

    a Historically, the percentage of Bank of America customers expressing customer delight has been 48%. Suppose that we wish to use the results of a survey of 350 Bank of America customers to justify the claim that more than 48% of all current Bank of America customers would express customer delight. The survey finds that 189 of 350 randomly selected Bank of America customers express customer delight. If, for the sake of argument, we assume that the proportion of customer delight is $p = .48$, calculate the probability of observing a sample proportion greater than or equal to $189/350 = .54$. That is, calculate $P(\hat{p} \geq .54)$.

---

[4]Source: The Gallup Organization, www.gallup.com/poll/releases/, February 13, 2002.

b Based on the probability you computed in part *a*, would you conclude that more than 48 percent of current Bank of America customers express customer delight? Explain.

7.32 Again consider the survey of 350 Bank of America customers discussed in Exercise 7.31, and assume that 48% of Bank of America customers would currently express customer delight. That is, assume $p = .48$. Find:

　a The probability that the sample proportion obtained from the sample of 350 Bank of America customers would be within three percentage points of the population proportion. That is, find $P(.45 \leq \hat{p} \leq .51)$.

　b The probability that the sample proportion obtained from the sample of 350 Bank of America customers would be within six percentage points of the population proportion. That is, find $P(.42 \leq \hat{p} \leq .54)$.

7.33 Based on your results in Exercise 7.32, would it be reasonable to state that the survey's "margin of error" is ± 3 percentage points? ± 6 percentage points? Explain.

7.34 An article in *Fortune* magazine discussed "outsourcing." According to the article, outsourcing is "the assignment of critical, but noncore, business functions to outside specialists." This allows a company to immediately bring operations up to best-in-world standards while avoiding huge capital investments. The article included the results of a poll of business executives addressing the benefits of outsourcing.

　a Suppose we wish to use the poll's results to justify the claim that fewer than 20 percent of business executives feel that the benefits of outsourcing are either "less or much less than expected." The poll actually found that 15 percent of the respondents felt that the benefits of outsourcing were either "less or much less than expected." If 1,000 randomly selected business executives were polled, and if for the sake of argument, we assume that 20 percent of all business executives feel that the benefits of outsourcing are either less or much less than expected (that is, $p = .20$), calculate the probability of observing a sample proportion of .15 or less. That is, calculate $P(\hat{p} \leq .15)$.

　b Based on the probability you computed in part *a*, would you conclude that fewer than 20 percent of business executives feel that the benefits of outsourcing are either "less or much less than expected"? Explain.

7.35 *Fortune* magazine reported the results of a survey on executive training that was conducted by the Association of Executive Search Consultants. The survey showed that 75 percent of 300 polled CEOs believe that companies should have "fast-track training programs" for developing managerial talent.

　a Suppose we wish to use the results of this survey to justify the claim that more than 70 percent of CEOs believe that companies should have fast-track training programs. Assuming that the 300 surveyed CEOs were randomly selected, and assuming, for the sake of argument, that 70 percent of CEOs believe that companies should have fast-track training programs (that is, $p = .70$), calculate the probability of observing a sample proportion of .75 or more. That is, calculate $P(\hat{p} \geq .75)$.

　b Based on the probability you computed in part *a*, would you conclude that more than 70 percent of CEOs believe that companies should have fast-track training programs? Explain.

7.4 Stratified Random, Cluster, and Systematic Sampling (Optional) ● ● ●

LO7-5 Describe the basic ideas of stratified random, cluster, and systematic sampling (Optional).

Random sampling is not the only kind of sampling. Methods for obtaining a sample are called **sampling designs,** and the sample we take is sometimes called a **sample survey.** In this section we explain three sampling designs that are alternatives to random sampling—**stratified random sampling, cluster sampling,** and **systematic sampling.**

One common sampling design involves separately sampling important groups within a population. Then, the samples are combined to form the entire sample. This approach is the idea behind **stratified random sampling.**

In order to select a **stratified random sample,** we divide the population into nonoverlapping groups of similar elements (people, objects, etc.). These groups are called **strata.** Then a random sample is selected from each stratum, and these samples are combined to form the full sample.

It is wise to stratify when the population consists of two or more groups that differ with respect to the variable of interest. For instance, consumers could be divided into strata based on gender, age, ethnic group, or income.

As an example, suppose that a department store chain proposes to open a new store in a location that would serve customers who live in a geographical region that consists of (1) an industrial city, (2) a suburban community, and (3) a rural area. In order to assess the potential profitability of the proposed store, the chain wishes to study the incomes of all households in the region. In addition, the chain wishes to estimate the proportion and the total number of households whose members would be likely to shop at the store. The department store chain feels that the industrial city, the suburban community, and the rural area differ with respect to income and the store's potential desirability. Therefore, it uses these subpopulations as strata and takes a stratified random sample.

Taking a stratified sample can be advantageous because such a sample takes advantage of the fact that elements in the same stratum are similar to each other. It follows that a stratified sample can provide more accurate information than a random sample of the same size. As a simple example, if all of the elements in each stratum were exactly the same, then examining only one element in each stratum would allow us to describe the entire population. Furthermore, stratification can make a sample easier (or possible) to select. Recall that, in order to take a random sample, we must have a list, or **frame** of all of the population elements. Although a frame might not exist for the overall population, a frame might exist for each stratum. For example, suppose nearly all the households in the department store's geographical region have telephones. Although there might not be a telephone directory for the overall geographical region, there might be separate telephone directories for the industrial city, the suburb, and the rural area. For more discussion of stratified random sampling, see Section 8.5 and Mendenhall, Schaeffer, and Ott (1986).

Sometimes it is advantageous to select a sample in stages. This is a common practice when selecting a sample from a very large geographical region. In such a case, a frame often does not exist. For instance, there is no single list of all registered voters in the United States. There is also no single list of all households in the United States. In this kind of situation, we can use **multistage cluster sampling.** To illustrate this procedure, suppose we wish to take a sample of registered voters from all registered voters in the United States. We might proceed as follows:

Stage 1:   Randomly select a sample of counties from all of the counties in the United States.

Stage 2:   Randomly select a sample of townships from each county selected in Stage 1.

Stage 3:   Randomly select a sample of voting precincts from each township selected in Stage 2.

Stage 4:   Randomly select a sample of registered voters from each voting precinct selected in Stage 3.

We use the term *cluster sampling* to describe this type of sampling because at each stage we "cluster" the voters into subpopulations. For instance, in Stage 1 we cluster the voters into counties, and in Stage 2 we cluster the voters in each selected county into townships. Also, notice that the random sampling at each stage can be carried out because there are lists of (1) all counties in the United States, (2) all townships in each county, (3) all voting precincts in each township, and (4) all registered voters in each voting precinct.

As another example, consider sampling the households in the United States. We might use Stages 1 and 2 above to select counties and townships within the selected counties. Then, if there is a telephone directory of the households in each township, we can randomly sample households from each selected township by using its telephone directory. Because *most* households today have telephones, and telephone directories are readily available, most national polls are now conducted by telephone. Further, polling organizations have recognized that many households are giving up landline phones, and have developed ways to sample households that only have cell phones.

It is sometimes a good idea to combine stratification with multistage cluster sampling. For example, suppose a national polling organization wants to estimate the proportion of all registered voters who favor a particular presidential candidate. Because the presidential preferences of voters might tend to vary by geographical region, the polling organization might divide the United States into regions (say, Eastern, Midwestern, Southern, and Western regions). The polling organization might then use these regions as strata, and might take a multistage cluster sample from each stratum (region).

The analysis of data produced by multistage cluster sampling can be quite complicated. For a more detailed discussion of cluster sampling, see Mendenhall, Schaeffer, and Ott (1986).

In order to select a random sample, we must number the elements in a frame of all the population elements. Then we use a random number table (or a random number generator on a computer) to make the selections. However, numbering all the population elements can be quite time-consuming. Moreover, random sampling is used in the various stages of many complex sampling designs (requiring the numbering of numerous populations). Therefore, it is useful to have an alternative to random sampling. One such alternative is called **systematic sampling.** In order to systematically select a sample of n elements without replacement from a frame of N elements, we divide N by n and round the result down to the nearest whole number. Calling the rounded result ℓ, we then randomly select one element from the first ℓ elements in the frame— this is the first element in the systematic sample. The remaining elements in the sample are obtained by selecting every ℓth element following the first (randomly selected) element. For example, suppose we wish to sample a population of $N = 14,327$ allergists to investigate how often they have prescribed a particular drug during the last year. A medical society has a directory listing the 14,327 allergists, and we wish to draw a systematic sample of 500 allergists from this frame. Here we compute $14,327/500 = 28.654$, which is 28 when rounded down. Therefore, we number the first 28 allergists in the directory from 1 to 28, and we use a random number table to randomly select one of the first 28 allergists. Suppose we select allergist number 19. We interview allergist 19 and every 28th allergist in the frame thereafter, so we choose allergists 19, 47, 75, and so forth until we obtain our sample of 500 allergists. In this scheme, we must number the first 28 allergists, but we do not have to number the rest because we can "count off" every 28th allergist in the directory. Alternatively, we can measure the approximate amount of space in the directory that it takes to list 28 allergists. This measurement can then be used to select every 28th allergist.

Exercises for Section 7.4

CONCEPTS

connect

7.36 When is it appropriate to use stratified random sampling? What are strata, and how should strata be selected?

7.37 When is cluster sampling used? Why do we describe this type of sampling by using the term *cluster?*

7.38 Explain how to take a systematic sample of 100 companies from the 1,853 companies that are members of an industry trade association.

7.39 Explain how a stratified random sample is selected. Discuss how you might define the strata to survey student opinion on a proposal to charge all students a $100 fee for a new university-run bus system that will provide transportation between off-campus apartments and campus locations.

7.40 Marketing researchers often use city blocks as clusters in cluster sampling. Using this fact, explain how a market researcher might use multistage cluster sampling to select a sample of consumers from all cities having a population of more than 10,000 in a large state having many such cities.

7.5 More about Surveys and Errors in Survey Sampling (Optional) ● ● ●

We have seen in Section 1.2 that people in surveys are asked questions about their behaviors, opinions, beliefs, and other characteristics. In this section we discuss various issues related to designing surveys and the errors that can occur in survey sampling.

LO7-6 Describe basic types of survey questions, survey procedures, and sources of error (Optional).

Types of survey questions Survey instruments can use **dichotomous** ("yes or no"), **multiple-choice,** or **open-ended** questions. Each type of question has its benefits and drawbacks. Dichotomous questions are usually clearly stated, can be answered quickly, and yield data that are easily analyzed. However, the information gathered may be limited by this two-option format. If we limit voters to expressing support or disapproval for stem-cell research, we may not learn the nuanced reasoning that voters use in weighing the merits and moral issues involved. Similarly, in today's heterogeneous world, it would be unusual to use a dichotomous question to categorize a person's religious preferences. Asking whether respondents are Christian or non-Christian (or to use any other two categories like Jewish or non-Jewish; Muslim or non-Muslim) is certain to make some people feel their religion is being slighted. In addition, this is a crude way and unenlightening way to learn about religious preferences.

Multiple-choice questions can assume several different forms. Sometimes respondents are asked to choose a response from a list (for example, possible answers to the religion question could be Jewish; Christian; Muslim; Hindu; Agnostic; or Other). Other times, respondents are asked to choose an answer from a numerical range. We could ask the question:

"In your opinion, how important are SAT scores to a college student's success?"

Not important at all   1   2   3   4   5   Extremely important

These numerical responses are usually summarized and reported in terms of the average response, whose size tells us something about the perceived importance. The Zagat restaurant survey (www.zagat.com) asks diners to rate restaurants' food, décor, and service, each on a scale of 1 to 30 points, with a 30 representing an incredible level of satisfaction. Although the Zagat scale has an unusually wide range of possible ratings, the concept is the same as in the more common 5-point scale.

Open-ended questions typically provide the most honest and complete information because there are no suggested answers to divert or bias a person's response. This kind of question is often found on instructor evaluation forms distributed at the end of a college course. College students at Georgetown University are asked the open-ended question, "What comments would you give to the instructor?" The responses provide the instructor feedback that may be missing from the initial part of the teaching evaluation survey, which consists of numerical multiple-choice ratings of various aspects of the course. While these numerical ratings can be used to compare instructors and courses, there are no easy comparisons of the diverse responses instructors receive to the open-ended question. In fact, these responses are often seen only by the instructor and are useful, constructive tools for the teacher despite the fact they cannot be readily summarized.

Survey questionnaires must be carefully constructed so they do not inadvertently bias the results. Because survey design is such a difficult and sensitive process, it is not uncommon for a pilot survey to be taken before a lot of time, effort, and financing go into collecting a large amount of data. Pilot surveys are similar to the beta version of a new electronic product; they are tested out with a smaller group of people to work out the "kinks" before being used on a larger scale. Determination of the sample size for the final survey is an important process for many reasons. If the sample size is too large, resources may be wasted during the data collection. On the other hand, not collecting enough data for a meaningful analysis will obviously be detrimental to the study. Fortunately, there are several formulas that will help decide how large a sample should be, depending on the goal of the study and various other factors.

Types of surveys   There are several different survey types, and we will explore just a few of them. The **phone survey** is particularly well-known (and often despised). A phone survey is inexpensive and usually conducted by callers who have very little training. Because of this and the impersonal nature of the medium, the respondent may misunderstand some of the questions. A further drawback is that some people cannot be reached and that others may refuse to answer some or all of the questions. Phone surveys are thus particularly prone to have a low **response rate.**

The **response rate** is the proportion of all people whom we attempt to contact that actually respond to a survey. A low response rate can destroy the validity of a survey's results.

The popular television sitcom *Seinfeld* parodied the difficulties of collecting data through a phone survey. After receiving several calls from telemarketers, Jerry replied in exasperation:

"I'm sorry; I'm a little tied up now. Give me your home number and I'll call you back later. Oh! You don't like being called at home? Well, now you know how I feel."

Numerous complaints have been filed with the Federal Trade Commission (FTC) about the glut of marketing and survey telephone calls to private residences. The National Do Not Call Registry was created as the culmination of a comprehensive, three-year review of the Telemarketing Sales Rule (TSR) (www.ftc.gov/donotcall/). This legislation allows people to enroll their phone numbers on a website so as to prevent most marketers from calling them.

Self-administered surveys, or **mail surveys,** are also very inexpensive to conduct. However, these also have their drawbacks. Often, recipients will choose not to reply unless they receive some kind of financial incentive or other reward. Generally, after an initial mailing, the response rate will fall between 20 and 30 percent (www.pra.ca/resources/rates.pdf). Response rates can be raised with successive follow-up reminders, and after three contacts, they might reach between 65 and 75 percent. Unfortunately, the entire process can take significantly longer than a phone survey would.

Web-based surveys have become increasingly popular, but they suffer from the same problems as mail surveys. In addition, as with phone surveys, respondents may record their true reactions incorrectly because they have misunderstood some of the questions posed.

A personal interview provides more control over the survey process. People selected for interviews are more likely to respond because the questions are being asked by someone face-to-face. Questions are less likely to be misunderstood because the people conducting the interviews are typically trained employees who can clear up any confusion arising during the process. On the other hand, interviewers can potentially "lead" a respondent by body language which signals approval or disapproval of certain sorts of answers. They can also prompt certain replies by providing too much information. **Mall surveys** are examples of personal interviews. Interviewers approach shoppers as they pass by and ask them to answer the survey questions. Response rates around 50 percent are typical (http://en.wikipedia.org/wiki/Statistical_survey#Survey_methods). Personal interviews are more costly than mail or phone surveys. Obviously, the objective of the study will be important in deciding upon the survey type employed.

Errors occurring in surveys   In general, the goal of a survey is to obtain accurate information from a group, or sample, that is representative of the entire population of interest. We are trying to estimate some aspect (numerical descriptor) of the entire population from a subset of the population. This is not an easy task, and there are many pitfalls. First and foremost, the *target population* must be well defined and a *sample frame* must be chosen.

> The **target population** is the entire population of interest to us in a particular study.

Are we intending to estimate the average starting salary of students graduating from any college? Or from four year colleges? Or from business schools? Or from a particular business school?

> The **sample frame** is a list of sampling elements (people or things) from which the sample will be selected. It should closely agree with the target population.

Consider a study to estimate the average starting salary of students who have graduated from the business school at Miami University of Ohio over the last five years; the target population is obviously that particular group of graduates. A sample frame could be the Miami University Alumni Association's roster of business school graduates for the past five years. Although it will not be a perfect replication of the target population, it is a reasonable frame.

We now discuss two general classes of survey errors: **errors of non-observation** and **errors of observation.** From the sample frame, units are randomly chosen to be part of the sample. Simply by virtue of the fact that we are taking a sample instead of a census, we are susceptible to *sampling error.*

> **Sampling error** is the difference between a numerical descriptor of the population and the corresponding descriptor of the sample.

Sampling error occurs because our information is incomplete. We observe only the portion of the population included in the sample while the remainder is obscured. Suppose, for example, we wanted to know about the heights of 13-year-old boys. There is extreme variation in boys' heights at this age. Even if we could overcome the logistical problems of choosing a random sample of 20 boys, there is nothing to guarantee the sample will accurately reflect heights at this age. By sheer luck of the draw, our sample could include a higher proportion of tall boys than appears in the population. We would then overestimate average height at this age (to the chagrin of the shorter boys). Although samples tend to look more similar to their parent populations as the sample sizes increase, we should always keep in mind that sample characteristics and population characteristics are not the same.

If a sample frame is not identical to the target population, we will suffer from an *error of coverage.*

> **Undercoverage** occurs when some population elements are excluded from the process of selecting the sample.

Undercoverage was part of the problem dooming the *Literary Digest* Poll of 1936. Although millions of Americans were included in the poll, the large sample size could not rescue the poll results. The sample represented those who could afford phone service and magazine subscriptions in the lean Depression years, but in excluding everyone else, it failed to yield an honest picture of the entire American populace. Undercoverage often occurs when we do not have a complete, accurate list of all the population units. If we select our sample from an incomplete list, like a telephone directory or a list of all Internet subscribers in a region, we automatically eliminate those who cannot afford phone or Internet service. Even today, 7 to 8 percent of the people in the United States do not own telephones. Low-income people are often underrepresented in surveys. If underrepresented groups differ from the rest of the population with respect to the characteristic under study, the survey results will be biased.

Often, pollsters cannot find all the people they intend to survey, and sometimes people who are found will refuse to answer the questions posed. Both of these are examples of the **nonresponse** problem. Unfortunately, there may be an association between how difficult it is to find and elicit responses from people and the type of answers they give.

> **Nonresponse** occurs whenever some of the individuals who were supposed to be included in the sample are not.

For example, universities often conduct surveys to learn how graduates have fared in the workplace. The alumnus who has risen through the corporate ranks is more likely to have a current address on file with his alumni office and to be willing to share career information than a classmate who has foundered professionally. We should be politely skeptical about reports touting the average salaries of graduates of various university programs. In some surveys, 35 percent or more of the selected individuals cannot be contacted—even when several callbacks are made. In such cases, other participants are often substituted for those who cannot be contacted. If the substitutes and the originally selected participants differ with respect to the characteristic under study, the survey will be biased. Furthermore, people who will answer highly sensitive, personal, or embarrassing questions might be very different from those who will not.

As discussed in Section 1.2, the opinions of those who bother to complete a voluntary response survey may be dramatically different from those who do not. (Recall the Ann Landers question about having children.) The viewer voting on the popular television show *American Idol* is another illustration of **selection bias,** because only those who are interested in the outcome of the show will bother to phone in or text message their votes. The results of the voting are not representative of the performance ratings the country would give as a whole.

Errors of observation occur when data values are recorded incorrectly. Such errors can be caused by the data collector (the interviewer), the survey instrument, the respondent, or the data collection process. For instance, the manner in which a question is asked can influence the response. Or, the order in which questions appear on a questionnaire can influence the survey results. Or, the data collection method (telephone interview, questionnaire, personal interview, or direct observation) can influence the results. A **recording error** occurs when either the respondent or interviewer incorrectly marks an answer. Once data are collected from a survey, the results are often entered into a computer for statistical analysis. When transferring data from a survey form to a spreadsheet program like Excel, MINITAB, or MegaStat, there is potential for entering them incorrectly. Before the survey is administered, the questions need to be very carefully worded so that there is little chance of misinterpretation. A poorly framed question might yield results that lead to unwarranted decisions. Scaled questions are particularly susceptible to this type of error. Consider the question "How would you rate this course?" Without a proper explanation, the respondent may not know whether "1" or "5" is the best.

If the survey instrument contains highly sensitive questions and respondents feel compelled to answer, they may not tell the truth. This is especially true in personal interviews. We then have what is called **response bias.** A surprising number of people are reluctant to be candid about what they like to read or watch on television. People tend to over-report "good" activities like reading respected newspapers and underreport their "bad" activities like delighting in the *National Enquirer*'s stories of alien abductions and celebrity meltdowns. Imagine, then, the difficulty in getting honest answers about people's gambling habits, drug use, or sexual histories. Response bias can also occur when respondents are asked slanted questions whose wording influences the answer received. For example, consider the following question:

Which of the following best describes your views on gun control?

1   The government should take away our guns, leaving us defenseless against heavily armed criminals.
2   We have the right to keep and bear arms.

This question is biased toward eliciting a response against gun control.

Exercises for Section 7.5

CONCEPTS

7.41   Explain:
a   Three types of surveys and discuss their advantages and disadvantages.
b   Three types of survey questions and discuss their advantages and disadvantages.

7.42   Explain each of the following terms:
a   Undercoverage   **b**   Nonresponse   **c**   Response bias

7.43   A market research firm sends out a Web-based survey to assess the impact of advertisements placed on a search engine's results page. About 65% of the surveys were answered and sent back. What types of errors are possible in this scenario?

7.6 Derivation of the Mean and the Variance of the Sample Mean (Optional) ● ● ●

Before we randomly select the sample values $x_1, x_2, \ldots, x_n$ from a population having mean μ and variance σ^2, we note that, for $i = 1, 2, \ldots, n$, the ith sample value x_i is a random variable that can potentially be any of the values in the population. Moreover, it can be proven (and is intuitive) that

1   The mean (or expected value) of x_i, denoted μ_{x_i}, is μ, the mean of the population from which x_i will be randomly selected. That is, $\mu_{x_1} = \mu_{x_2} = \cdots = \mu_{x_n} = \mu$.

2   The variance of x_i, denoted $\sigma^2_{x_i}$, is σ^2, the variance of the population from which x_i will be randomly selected. That is, $\sigma^2_{x_1} = \sigma^2_{x_2} = \cdots = \sigma^2_{x_n} = \sigma^2$.

If we consider the sample mean $\bar{x} = \sum_{i=1}^{n} x_i/n$, then we can prove that $\mu_{\bar{x}} = \mu$ by using the following two properties of the mean discussed in Section 5.6:

Property 1: If a is a fixed number, $\mu_{ax} = a\mu_x$

Property 2: $\mu_{(x_1 + x_2 + \cdots + x_n)} = \mu_{x_1} + \mu_{x_2} + \cdots + \mu_{x_n}$

The proof that $\mu_{\bar{x}} = \mu$ is as follows:

$$\mu_{\bar{x}} = \mu\left(\sum_{i=1}^{n} x_i/n\right)$$

$$= \frac{1}{n}\mu\left(\sum_{i=1}^{n} x_i\right) \qquad \text{(see Property 1)}$$

$$= \frac{1}{n}\mu_{(x_1 + x_2 + \cdots + x_n)}$$

$$= \frac{1}{n}(\mu_{x_1} + \mu_{x_2} + \cdots + \mu_{x_n}) \qquad \text{(see Property 2)}$$

$$= \frac{1}{n}(\mu + \mu + \cdots + \mu) = \frac{n\mu}{n} = \mu$$

We can prove that $\sigma_{\bar{x}}^2 = \sigma^2/n$ by using the following two properties of the variance discussed in Section 5.6:

Property 3: If a is a fixed number, $\sigma_{ax}^2 = a^2\sigma_x^2$

Property 4: If $x_1, x_2, \cdots, x_n$ are statistically independent, $\sigma_{(x_1+x_2+\cdots+x_n)}^2 = \sigma_{x_1}^2 + \sigma_{x_2}^2 + \cdots + \sigma_{x_n}^2$

The proof that $\sigma_{\bar{x}}^2 = \sigma^2/n$ is as follows:

$$\sigma_{\bar{x}}^2 = \sigma^2\left(\sum_{i=1}^{n} x_i/n\right) = \left(\frac{1}{n}\right)^2 \sigma^2\left(\sum_{i=1}^{n} x_i\right) \qquad \text{(see Property 3)}$$

$$= \frac{1}{n^2}\,\sigma_{(x_1+x_2+\cdots+x_n)}^2$$

$$= \frac{1}{n^2}\,(\sigma_{x_1}^2 + \sigma_{x_2}^2 + \cdots + \sigma_{x_n}^2) \qquad \text{(see Property 4)}$$

$$= \frac{1}{n^2}\,(\sigma^2 + \sigma^2 + \cdots + \sigma^2) = \frac{n\sigma^2}{n^2} = \frac{\sigma^2}{n}$$

Note that we can use Property 4 if $x_1, x_2, \cdots, x_n$ are independent random variables. In general, $x_1, x_2, \cdots, x_n$ are independent if we are drawing these sample values from an infinite population. When we select a sample from an infinite population, a population value obtained on one selection can also be obtained on any other selection. This is because, since the population is infinite, there are an infinite number of repetitions of each population value. Therefore, because a value obtained on one selection is not precluded from being obtained on any other selection, the selections and thus $x_1, x_2, \cdots, x_n$ are statistically independent. Furthermore, this statistical independence approximately holds if the population size is much larger than (say, at least 20 times as large as) the sample size. Therefore, in this case $\sigma_{\bar{x}}^2 = \sigma^2/n$ is approximately correct.

Chapter Summary

We began this chapter by defining a random sample and by explaining how to use a **random number table** or **computer-generated random numbers** to select a **random sample.** We then discussed **sampling distributions.** A **sampling distribution** is the probability distribution that describes the population of all possible values of a sample statistic. In this chapter we studied the properties of two important sampling distributions—the sampling distribution of the sample mean, $\bar{x}$, and the sampling distribution of the sample proportion, $\hat{p}$.

Because different samples that can be randomly selected from a population give different sample means, there is a population of sample means corresponding to a particular sample size. The probability distribution describing the population of all possible sample means is called the **sampling distribution of the sample mean, $\bar{x}$.** We studied the properties of this sampling distribution when the sampled population is and is not normally distributed. We found that, when the sampled population has a normal distribution, then the sampling distribution of the sample mean is a normal distribution. Furthermore, the **Central Limit Theorem** tells us that, if the sampled population is not normally distributed, then the sampling distribution of the sample mean is approximately a normal distribution when the sample size is large (at least 30). We also saw that the mean of the sampling distribution of $\bar{x}$ always equals the mean of the sampled population, and we presented formulas for the variance and the standard deviation of this sampling distribution. Finally, we explained that the sample mean is a **minimum-variance unbiased point estimate** of the mean of a normally distributed population.

We also studied the properties of the **sampling distribution of the sample proportion $\hat{p}$.** We found that, if the sample size is large, then this sampling distribution is approximately a normal distribution, and we gave a rule for determining whether the sample size is large. We found that the mean of the sampling distribution of $\hat{p}$ is the population proportion p, and we gave formulas for the variance and the standard deviation of this sampling distribution.

Throughout our discussions of sampling distributions, we demonstrated that knowing the properties of sampling distributions can help us make statistical inferences about population parameters. In fact, we will see that the properties of various sampling distributions provide the foundation for most of the techniques to be discussed in future chapters.

We concluded this chapter with three optional sections. In the first optional section, we discussed some advanced sampling designs. Specifically, we introduced **stratified random sampling,** in which we divide a population into groups (**strata**) and then select a random sample from each group. We also introduced **multistage cluster sampling,** which involves selecting a sample in stages, and we explained how to select a **systematic sample.** In the second optional section, we discussed more about surveys, as well as some potential problems that can occur when conducting a sample survey—**undercoverage, nonresponse, response bias, and slanted questions.** In the last optional section, we derived the mean and the variance of the sampling distribution of the sample mean $\bar{x}$.

Glossary of Terms

Central Limit Theorem: A theorem telling us that when the sample size n is sufficiently large, then the population of all possible sample means is approximately normally distributed no matter what probability distribution describes the sampled population. (page 278)

cluster sampling (multistage cluster sampling): A sampling design in which we sequentially cluster population elements into subpopulations. (page 288)

convenience sampling: Sampling where we select elements because they are easy or convenient to sample. (page 270)

errors of non-observation: Sampling error related to population elements that are not observed. (page 291)

errors of observation: Sampling error that occurs when the data collected in a survey differs from the truth. (page 292)

judgment sampling: Sampling where an expert selects population elements that he/she feels are representative of the population. (page 270)

minimum-variance unbiased point estimate: An unbiased point estimate of a population parameter having a variance that is smaller than the variance of any other unbiased point estimate of the parameter. (page 281)

nonresponse: A situation in which population elements selected to participate in a survey do not respond to the survey instrument. (page 292)

probability sampling: Sampling where we know the chance (probability) that each population element will be included in the sample. (page 270)

random number table: A table containing random digits that is often used to select a random sample. (page 268)

random sample: A sample selected in such a way that every set of n elements in the population has the same chance of being selected. (page 267)

response bias: Bias in the results obtained when carrying out a statistical study that is related to how survey participants answer the survey questions. (page 292)

response rate: The proportion of all people whom we attempt to contact that actually respond to a survey. (page 290)

sample frame: A list of sampling elements from which a sample will be selected. It should closely agree with the target population. (page 291)

sampling distribution of a sample statistic: The probability distribution of the population of all possible values of the sample statistic. (page 280)

sampling distribution of the sample mean $\bar{x}$: The probability distribution of the population of all possible sample means obtained from samples of a particular size n. (page 271)

sampling distribution of the sample proportion $\hat{p}$: The probability distribution of the population of all possible sample proportions obtained from samples of a particular size n. (page 284)

sampling error: The difference between the value of a sample statistic and the population parameter; it occurs because not all of the elements in the population have been measured. (page 291)

sampling with replacement: A sampling procedure in which we place any element that has been chosen back into the population to give the element a chance to be chosen on succeeding selections. (page 267)

sampling without replacement: A sampling procedure in which we do not place previously selected elements back into the population and, therefore, do not give these elements a chance to be chosen on succeeding selections. (page 267)

selection bias: Bias in the results obtained when carrying out a statistical study that is related to how survey participants are selected. (page 292)

strata: The subpopulations in a stratified sampling design. (page 287)

stratified random sampling: A sampling design in which we divide a population into nonoverlapping subpopulations and then select a random sample from each subpopulation (stratum). (page 287)

systematic sample: A sample taken by moving systematically through the population. For instance, we might randomly select one of the first 200 population elements and then systematically sample every 200th population element thereafter. (page 289)

target population: The entire population of interest in a statistical study. (page 291)

unbiased point estimate: A sample statistic is an unbiased point estimate of a population parameter if the mean of the population of all possible values of the sample statistic equals the population parameter. (page 281)

undercoverage: A situation in sampling in which some groups of population elements are underrepresented. (page 292)

voluntary response sample: Sampling in which the sample participants self-select. (page 270)

Important Results and Formulas

The sampling distribution of the sample mean: pages 271 and 275
   when a population is normally distributed (page 275)
Central Limit Theorem (page 278)

The sampling distribution of the sample proportion: page 284

Supplementary Exercises

7.44   A company that sells and installs custom designed home theatre systems claims to have sold 977 such systems last year. In order to assess whether these claimed sales are valid, an accountant numbers the company's sales invoices from 1 to 977 and plans to select a random sample of 50 sales invoices. The accountant will then contact the purchasers listed on the 50 sampled sales invoices and determine whether the sales amounts on the invoices are correct. Starting in the upper left-hand corner of Table 7.1(a) (see page 268), determine which 50 of the 977 sales invoices should be included in the random sample. Note: There are many possible answers to this exercise.

7.45   THE TRASH BAG CASE   🖸 TrashBag

Recall that the trash bag manufacturer has concluded that its new 30-gallon bag will be the strongest such bag on the market if its mean breaking strength is at least 50 pounds. In order to provide statistical evidence that the mean breaking strength of the new bag is at least 50 pounds, the manufacturer randomly selects a sample of n bags and calculates the mean $\bar{x}$ of the breaking strengths of these bags. If the sample mean so obtained is at least 50 pounds, this provides some evidence that the mean breaking strength of all new bags is at least 50 pounds.

Suppose that (unknown to the manufacturer) the breaking strengths of the new 30-gallon bag are normally distributed with a mean of $\mu = 50.6$ pounds and a standard deviation of $\sigma = 1.62$ pounds.

a   Find an interval containing 95.44 percent of all possible sample means if the sample size employed is $n = 5$.

b   Find an interval containing 95.44 percent of all possible sample means if the sample size employed is $n = 40$.

c   If the trash bag manufacturer hopes to obtain a sample mean that is at least 50 pounds (so that it can provide evidence that the population mean breaking strength of the new bags is at least 50), which sample size ($n = 5$ or $n = 40$) would be best? Explain why.

7.46   THE STOCK RETURN CASE

The year 1987 featured extreme volatility on the stock market, including a loss of over 20 percent of the market's value on a single day. Figure 7.7(a) shows the percent frequency histogram of the percentage returns for the entire year 1987 for the population of all 1,815 stocks listed on the New York Stock Exchange. The mean and the standard deviation of the population of percentage returns are −3.5 percent and 26 percent, respectively. Consider drawing a random sample of $n = 5$ stocks from the population of 1,815 stocks and calculating the mean return, $\bar{x}$, of the sampled stocks. If we use a computer, we can generate all the different samples of five stocks that can be obtained (there are trillions of such samples) and calculate the corresponding sample mean returns. A percent frequency histogram describing the population of all possible sample mean returns is given in Figure 7.7(b). Comparing Figures 7.7(a) and (b), we see that, although the histogram of individual stock returns and the histogram of sample mean returns are both bell-shaped and centered over the same mean of −3.5 percent, the histogram of sample mean returns looks *less spread out* than the histogram of individual returns. A sample of 5 stocks is a portfolio of stocks, where the average return of the 5 stocks is the portfolio's return if we invest equal amounts of money in each of the 5 stocks. Because the sample mean returns are less spread out than the individual stock returns, we have illustrated that diversification reduces risk. Find the standard deviation of the population of all sample mean returns, and assuming that this population is normally distributed, find an interval that contains 95.44 percent of all sample mean returns.

FIGURE 7.7   The New York Stock Exchange in 1987: A Comparison of Individual Stock Returns and Sample Mean Returns

(a) The percent frequency histogram describing the population of individual stock returns

(b) The percent frequency histogram describing the population of all possible sample mean returns when $n = 5$

Source: Figure 7.7 is adapted with permission from John K. Ford, "A Method for Grading 1987 Stock Recommendations," *The American Association of Individual Investors Journal*, March 1988, pp. 16–17.

7.47 Suppose that we wish to assess whether more than 60 percent of all U.S. households in a particular income class bought life insurance last year. That is, we wish to assess whether p, the proportion of all U.S. households in the income class that bought life insurance last year, exceeds .60. Assume that an insurance survey is based on 1,000 randomly selected U.S. households in the income class and that 640 of these households bought life insurance last year.

    a Assuming that p equals .60 and the sample size is 1,000, what is the probability of observing a sample proportion that is at least .64?

    b Based on your answer in part a, do you think more than 60 percent of all U.S. households in the income class bought life insurance last year? Explain.

7.48 A computer supply house receives a large shipment of flash drives each week. Past experience has shown that the number of flaws (bad sectors) per flash drive is either 0, 1, 2, or 3 with probabilities .65, .2, .1, and .05, respectively.

    a Calculate the mean and standard deviation of the number of flaws per flash drive.

    b Suppose that we randomly select a sample of 100 flash drives. Describe the shape of the sampling distribution of the sample mean $\bar{x}$. Then compute the mean and the standard deviation of the sampling distribution of $\bar{x}$.

    c Sketch the sampling distribution of the sample mean $\bar{x}$ and compare it to the distribution describing the number of flaws on a single flash drive.

    d The supply house's managers are worried that the flash drives being received have an excessive number of flaws. Because of this, a random sample of 100 flash drives is drawn from each shipment and the shipment is rejected (sent back to the supplier) if the average number of flaws per flash drive for the 100 sample drives is greater than .75. Suppose that the mean number of flaws per flash drive for this week's entire shipment is actually .55. What is the probability that this shipment will be rejected and sent back to the supplier?

7.49 Each day a manufacturing plant receives a large shipment of drums of Chemical ZX-900. These drums are supposed to have a mean fill of 50 gallons, while the fills have a standard deviation known to be .6 gallon.

    a Suppose that the mean fill for the shipment is actually 50 gallons. If we draw a random sample of 100 drums from the shipment, what is the probability that the average fill for the 100 drums is between 49.88 gallons and 50.12 gallons?

    b The plant manager is worried that the drums of Chemical ZX-900 are underfilled. Because of this, she decides to draw a sample of 100 drums from each daily shipment and will reject the shipment (send it back to the supplier) if the average fill for the 100 drums is less than 49.85 gallons. Suppose that a shipment that actually has a mean fill of 50 gallons is received. What is the probability that this shipment will be rejected and sent back to the supplier?

Appendix 7.1 ■ Generating Random Numbers Using Excel

To create 100 random numbers between 1 and 2136 similar to those in Table 7.1(b) on page 268.

- Type the cell formula

    =RANDBETWEEN(1,2136)

    into cell A1 of the Excel worksheet and press the enter key. This will generate a random integer between 1 and 2136, which will be placed in cell A1.

- Using the mouse, copy the cell formula for cell A1 down through cell A100. This will generate 100 random numbers between 1 and 2136 in cells A1 through A100 (note that the random number in cell A1 will change when this is done—this is not a problem).

- The random numbers are generated with replacement. Repeated numbers would be skipped if the random numbers were being used to sample without replacement.

Appendix 7.2 ■ Generating Random Numbers Using MegaStat

To create 100 random numbers between 1 and 2136 similar to those in Table 7.1(b) on page 268:

- Select **Add-Ins : MegaStat : Generate Random Numbers...**

- In the Random Number Generation dialog box, enter 100 into the "Number of values to be generated" window.

- Click the right arrow button to select 0 Decimal Places.

- Select the Uniform tab, and enter 1 into the Minimum box and enter 2136 into the Maximum box.

- Click OK in the Random Number Generation dialog box.

The 100 random numbers will be placed in the Output Sheet. These numbers are generated with replacement. Repeated numbers would be skipped for random sampling without replacement.

Appendix 7.3 ■ Generating Random Numbers and Simulating Sampling Distributions Using MINITAB

To create 100 random numbers between 1 and 2136 similar to those in Table 7.1(b) on page 268:

- Select **Calc : Random Data : Integer**

- In the Integer Distribution dialog box, enter 100 into the "Number of rows of data to generate" window.

- Enter C1 into the "Store in column(s)" window.

- Enter 1 into the Minimum value box and enter 2136 into the Maximum value box.

- Click OK in the Integer Distribution dialog box.

The 100 random numbers will be placed in the Data Window in column C1. These numbers are generated with replacement. Repeated numbers would be skipped if the random numbers are being used to sample without replacement.

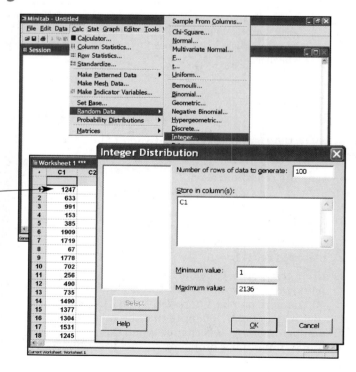

Histogram of sample means from an exponential distribution similar to Figure 7.6(a) on page 279:

In this example we construct a histogram of 1000 sample means from exponential samples of size 5.

- Select **Calc : Random Data : Exponential.**
- In the Exponential Distribution dialog box, enter 1000 into the "Number of rows of data to generate:" window.
- Enter C1-C5 in the "Store in column(s):" window to request 1000 values per column in columns C1 to C5.
- Be sure that 0.0 is the entry in the Threshold window.
- Enter 7 in the Scale window. This specifies the mean of the exponential distribution when the Threshold equals 0.
- Click OK in the Exponential Distribution dialog box. The 1000 exponential samples of size 5 will be generated in rows 1 through 1000.
- Select **Calc : Row Statistics.**
- In the Row Statistics dialog box, under "Statistic" select the Mean option.
- Enter C1-C5 in the "Input variables" window.
- Enter XBar5 in the "Store result in" window.

- Click OK in the Row Statistics dialog box to compute the means for the 1000 samples of size 5.

- Select **Stat : Basic Statistics : Display Descriptive Statistics.**
- In the Display Descriptive Statistics dialog box, enter XBar5 into the Variables window.
- Click on the Graphs... button.
- In the "Display Descriptive Statistics—Graphs" dialog box, check the "Histogram of data, with normal curve" checkbox.
- Click OK in the "Display Descriptive Statistics—Graphs" dialog box.
- Click OK in the Display Descriptive Statistics dialog box.

- The histogram will appear in a graphics window.

CHAPTER 8

Confidence Intervals

Learning Objectives

After mastering the material in this chapter, you will be able to:

LO8-1 Calculate and interpret a z-based confidence interval for a population mean when σ is known.

LO8-2 Describe the properties of the t distribution and use a t table.

LO8-3 Calculate and interpret a t-based confidence interval for a population mean when σ is unknown.

LO8-4 Determine the appropriate sample size when estimating a population mean.

LO8-5 Calculate and interpret a large sample confidence interval for a population proportion.

LO8-6 Determine the appropriate sample size when estimating a population proportion.

LO8-7 Find and interpret confidence intervals for parameters of finite populations (Optional).

Chapter Outline

8.1 z-Based Confidence Intervals for a Population Mean: σ Known

8.2 t-Based Confidence Intervals for a Population Mean: σ Unknown

8.3 Sample Size Determination

8.4 Confidence Intervals for a Population Proportion

8.5 Confidence Intervals for Parameters of Finite Populations (Optional)

e have seen that the sample mean is the point estimate of the population mean and the sample proportion is the point estimate of the population proportion. In general, although a point estimate is a reasonable one-number estimate of a population parameter (mean, proportion, or the like), the point estimate will not—unless we are extremely lucky—equal the true value of the population parameter.

In this chapter we study how to use a **confidence interval** to estimate a population parameter. A confidence interval for a population parameter is an interval, or range of numbers, constructed around the point estimate so that we are very sure, or confident, that the true value of the population parameter is inside the interval.

By computing such an interval, we estimate—with confidence—the possible values that a population parameter might equal. This, in turn, can help us to assess—with confidence—whether a particular business improvement has been made or is needed.

In order to illustrate confidence intervals, we revisit several cases introduced in earlier chapters and also introduce some new cases. For example:

In the **Car Mileage Case,** we use a confidence interval to provide strong evidence that the mean EPA combined city and highway mileage for the automaker's new midsize model meets the tax credit standard of 31 mpg.

In the **e-billing Case,** we use a confidence interval to more completely assess the reduction in mean payment time that was achieved by the new billing system.

In the **Cheese Spread Case,** we use a confidence interval to provide strong evidence that fewer than 10 percent of all current purchasers will stop buying the cheese spread if the new spout is used, and, therefore, that it is reasonable to use the new spout.

8.1 z-Based Confidence Intervals for a Population Mean: σ Known ● ● ●

LO8-1 Calculate and interpret a z-based confidence interval for a population mean when σ is known.

An introduction to confidence intervals for a population mean   In the *car mileage case*, we have seen that an automaker has introduced a new midsize model and wishes to estimate the mean EPA combined city and highway mileage, μ, that would be obtained by all cars of this type. In order to estimate μ, the automaker has conducted EPA mileage tests on a random sample of 50 of its new midsize cars and has obtained the sample of mileages in Table 1.6 (page 11). The mean of this sample of mileages, which is $\bar{x} = 31.56$ mpg, is the point estimate of μ. However, a sample mean will not—unless we are extremely lucky—equal the true value of a population mean. Therefore, the sample mean of 31.56 mpg does not, by itself, provide us with any confidence about the true value of the population mean μ. One way to estimate μ with confidence is to calculate a *confidence interval* for this mean.

A **confidence interval** for a population mean is an interval constructed around the sample mean so that we are reasonably sure, or confident, that this interval contains the population mean. Any confidence interval for a population mean is based on what is called a **confidence level.** This confidence level is a percentage (for example, 95 percent or 99 percent) that expresses how confident we are that the confidence interval contains the population mean. In order to explain the exact meaning of a confidence level, we will begin in the car mileage case by finding and interpreting a confidence interval for a population mean that is based on the most commonly used confidence level—the 95 percent level. Then we will generalize our discussion and show how to find and interpret a confidence interval that is based on any confidence level.

Before the automaker selected the sample of $n = 50$ new midsize cars and tested them as prescribed by the EPA, there were many samples of 50 cars and corresponding mileages that the automaker might have obtained. Because different samples generally have different sample means, we consider the probability distribution of the population of all possible sample means that would be obtained from all possible samples of $n = 50$ car mileages. In Chapter 7 we have seen that such a probability distribution is called the sampling distribution of the sample mean, and we have studied various properties of sampling distributions. Several of these properties tell us that, if the population of all individual midsize car mileages is normally distributed with mean μ and standard deviation σ,

FIGURE 8.1   The Sampling Distribution of the Sample Mean

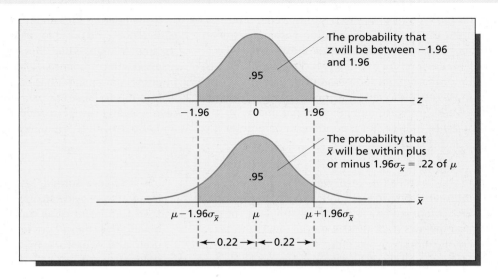

then for any sample size n the sampling distribution of the sample mean is a normal distribution with mean $\mu_{\bar{x}} = \mu$ and standard deviation $\sigma_{\bar{x}} = \sigma/\sqrt{n}$. Moreover, because the sample size n is 50, and because we can assume that the true value of the population standard deviation σ is 0.8 mpg (as discussed on page 275 of Chapter 7), it follows that

$$\sigma_{\bar{x}} = \frac{\sigma}{\sqrt{n}} = \frac{.8}{\sqrt{50}} = .113$$

This allows us to reason as follows:

1   In Chapter 6 (page 236) we have seen that the area under the standard normal curve between −1.96 and 1.96 is .95 (see Figure 8.1). This .95 area says that 95 percent of the values in any normally distributed population are within plus or minus 1.96 standard deviations of the mean of the population. Because the population of all possible sample means is normally distributed with mean μ and standard deviation $\sigma_{\bar{x}} = .113$, it follows that 95 percent of all possible sample means are within plus or minus $1.96\sigma_{\bar{x}} = 1.96(.113) = .22$ of the population mean μ. That is, **considered before we select the sample,** the probability is .95 that the sample mean $\bar{x}$ will be within plus or minus $1.96\sigma_{\bar{x}} = .22$ of the population mean μ (again, see Figure 8.1).

2   Saying

$$\bar{x} \text{ will be within plus or minus } .22 \text{ of } \mu$$

is the same as saying

$$\bar{x} \text{ will be such that the interval } [\bar{x} \pm .22] \text{ contains } \mu$$

To understand this, consider Figure 8.2. This figure illustrates three possible samples of 50 mileages and the means of these samples. Also, this figure assumes that (unknown to any human being) the true value of the population mean μ is 31.6. Then, as illustrated in Figure 8.2, because the sample mean $\bar{x} = 31.56$ is within .22 of $\mu = 31.6$, the interval $[31.56 \pm .22] = [31.34, 31.78]$ contains μ. Similarly, because the sample mean $\bar{x} = 31.68$ is within .22 of $\mu = 31.6$, the interval $[31.68 \pm .22] = [31.46, 31.90]$ contains μ. However, because the sample mean $\bar{x} = 31.2$ is not within .22 of $\mu = 31.6$, the interval $[31.2 \pm .22] = [30.98, 31.42]$ does not contain μ.

FIGURE 8.2   **Three 95 Percent Confidence Intervals for μ**

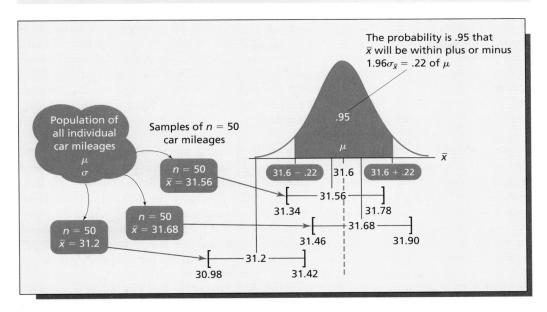

3   In statement 1 we showed that the probability is .95 that the sample mean $\bar{x}$ will be within plus or minus $1.96\sigma_{\bar{x}} = .22$ of the population mean μ. In statement 2 we showed that $\bar{x}$ being within plus or minus .22 of μ is the same as the interval $[\bar{x} \pm .22]$ containing μ. Combining these results, we see that the probability is .95 that the sample mean $\bar{x}$ will be such that the interval

$$[\bar{x} \pm 1.96\sigma_{\bar{x}}] = [\bar{x} \pm .22]$$

contains the population mean μ.

A 95 percent confidence interval for μ   Statement 3 says that, **before we randomly select the sample,** there is a .95 probability that we will obtain an interval $[\bar{x} \pm .22]$ that contains the population mean μ. In other words, 95 percent of all intervals that we might obtain contain μ, and 5 percent of these intervals do not contain μ. For this reason, we call the interval $[\bar{x} \pm .22]$ a **95 percent confidence interval for μ.** To better understand this interval, we must realize that, **when we actually select the sample,** we will observe one particular sample from the extremely large number of possible samples. Therefore, we will obtain one particular confidence interval from the extremely large number of possible confidence intervals. For example, recall that when the automaker randomly selected the sample of $n = 50$ cars and tested them as prescribed by the EPA, the automaker obtained the sample of 50 mileages given in Table 1.6. The mean of this sample is $\bar{x} = 31.56$ mpg, and a histogram constructed using this sample (see Figure 2.9 on page 46) indicates that the population of all individual car mileages is normally distributed. It follows that a 95 percent confidence interval for the population mean mileage μ of the new midsize model is

$$[\bar{x} \pm .22] = [31.56 \pm .22]$$

$$= [31.34, 31.78]$$

Because we do not know the true value of μ, we do not know for sure whether this interval contains μ. However, we are 95 percent confident that this interval contains μ. That is, we are 95 percent confident that μ is between 31.34 mpg and 31.78 mpg. What we mean by "95 percent confident" is that we hope that the confidence interval [31.34, 31.78] is one of the 95 percent of all confidence intervals that contain μ and not one of the 5 percent of all confidence intervals that do not contain μ. Here, we say that 95 percent is the **confidence level** associated with the confidence interval.

A practical application   To see a practical application of the automaker's confidence interval, recall that the federal government will give a tax credit to any automaker selling a midsize model equipped with an automatic transmission that has an EPA combined city and highway mileage estimate of at least 31 mpg. Furthermore, to ensure that it does not overestimate a car model's mileage, the EPA will obtain the model's mileage estimate by rounding down—to the nearest mile per gallon—the lower limit of a 95 percent confidence interval for the model's mean mileage μ. That is, the model's mileage estimate is an estimate of the smallest that μ might reasonably be. When we round down the lower limit of the automaker's 95 percent confidence interval for μ, [31.34, 31.78], we find that the new midsize model's mileage estimate is 31 mpg. Therefore, the automaker will receive the tax credit.[1]

BI

A general confidence interval procedure   We will next present a general procedure for finding a confidence interval for a population mean μ. To do this, we assume that the sampled population is normally distributed, or the sample size n is large. Under these conditions, the sampling distribution of the sample mean $\bar{x}$ is exactly (or approximately, by the Central Limit Theorem) a normal distribution with mean $\mu_{\bar{x}} = \mu$ and standard deviation $\sigma_{\bar{x}} = \sigma/\sqrt{n}$. In the previous subsection, we *started* with the normal points -1.96 and 1.96. Then we showed that, because the area under the standard normal curve between -1.96 and 1.96 is .95, the probability is .95 that the confidence interval $[\bar{x} \pm 1.96\sigma_{\bar{x}}]$ will contain the population mean. Usually, we do not start with two normal points, but rather we start by choosing the probability (for example, .95 or .99) that the confidence interval will contain the population mean. This probability is called the **confidence coefficient.** Next, we find the normal points that have a symmetrical area between them under the standard normal curve that is equal to the confidence coefficient. Then, using $\bar{x}$, $\sigma_{\bar{x}}$, and the normal points, we find the confidence interval that is based on the confidence coefficient. To illustrate this, we will start with a confidence coefficient of .95 and use the following three-step procedure to find the appropriate normal points and the corresponding 95 percent confidence interval for the population mean:

Step 1: As illustrated in Figure 8.3, place a symmetrical area of .95 under the standard normal curve and find the area in the normal curve tails beyond the .95 area. Because the entire area under the standard normal curve is 1, the area in both normal curve tails is $1 - .95 = .05$, and the area in each tail is .025.

Step 2: Find the normal point $z_{.025}$ that gives a right-hand tail area under the standard normal curve equal to .025, and find the normal point $-z_{.025}$ that gives a left-hand tail area under the curve equal to .025. As shown in Figure 8.3, the area under the standard normal curve between $-z_{.025}$ and $z_{.025}$ is .95, and the area under this curve to the left of $z_{.025}$ is .975. Looking up a cumulative area of .975 in Table A.3 (see page 790) or in Table 8.1 (which shows a portion of Table A.3), we find that $z_{.025} = 1.96$.

Step 3: Form the following 95 percent confidence interval for the population mean:

$$[\bar{x} \pm z_{.025}\sigma_{\bar{x}}] = \left[\bar{x} \pm 1.96\frac{\sigma}{\sqrt{n}} \right]$$

If all possible samples were used to calculate this interval, then 95 percent of the resulting intervals would contain the population mean. For example, recall in the car mileage case that $n = 50$, $\bar{x} = 31.56$, and $\sigma = .8$. Therefore, we can directly calculate the previously obtained 95 percent confidence interval for the midsize model's mean mileage μ as follows:

$$\left[\bar{x} \pm 1.96\frac{\sigma}{\sqrt{n}} \right] = \left[31.56 \pm 1.96\frac{.8}{\sqrt{50}} \right]$$
$$= [31.56 \pm .22]$$
$$= [31.34, 31.78]$$

---

[1] This example is based on the authors' conversations with the EPA. However, there are approaches for showing that μ is at least 31 mpg that differ from the approach that uses the confidence interval [31.34, 31.78]. Some of these other approaches are discussed in Chapter 9, but the EPA tells the authors that it would use the confidence interval approach described here.

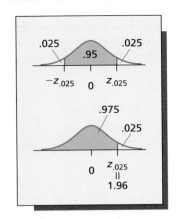

FIGURE 8.3   **The Point $z_{.025}$**

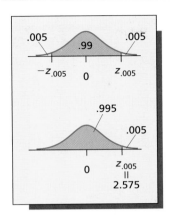

FIGURE 8.4   **The Point $z_{.005}$**

TABLE 8.1   **Cumulative Areas under the Standard Normal Curve**

z	0.00	0.01	0.02	0.03	0.04	0.05	0.06	0.07	0.08	0.09
1.5	0.9332	0.9345	0.9357	0.9370	0.9382	0.9394	0.9406	0.9418	0.9429	0.9441
1.6	0.9452	0.9463	0.9474	0.9484	0.9495	0.9505	0.9515	0.9525	0.9535	0.9545
1.7	0.9554	0.9564	0.9573	0.9582	0.9591	0.9599	0.9608	0.9616	0.9625	0.9633
1.8	0.9641	0.9649	0.9656	0.9664	0.9671	0.9678	0.9686	0.9693	0.9699	0.9706
1.9	0.9713	0.9719	0.9726	0.9732	0.9738	0.9744	0.9750	0.9756	0.9761	0.9767
2.0	0.9772	0.9778	0.9783	0.9788	0.9793	0.9798	0.9803	0.9808	0.9812	0.9817
2.1	0.9821	0.9826	0.9830	0.9834	0.9838	0.9842	0.9846	0.9850	0.9854	0.9857
2.2	0.9861	0.9864	0.9868	0.9871	0.9875	0.9878	0.9881	0.9884	0.9887	0.9890
2.3	0.9893	0.9896	0.9898	0.9901	0.9904	0.9906	0.9909	0.9911	0.9913	0.9916
2.4	0.9918	0.9920	0.9922	0.9925	0.9927	0.9929	0.9931	0.9932	0.9934	0.9936
2.5	0.9938	0.9940	0.9941	0.9943	0.9945	0.9946	0.9948	0.9949	0.9951	0.9952

We next start with a confidence coefficient of .99 and find the corresponding 99 percent confidence interval for the population mean:

Step 1: As illustrated in Figure 8.4, place a symmetrical area of .99 under the standard normal curve, and find the area in the normal curve tails beyond the .99 area. Because the entire area under the standard normal curve is 1, the area in both normal curve tails is $1 - .99 = .01$, and the area in each tail is .005.

Step 2: Find the normal point $z_{.005}$ that gives a right-hand tail area under the standard normal curve equal to .005, and find the normal point $-z_{.005}$ that gives a left-hand tail area under the curve equal to .005. As shown in Figure 8.4, the area under the standard normal curve between $-z_{.005}$ and $z_{.005}$ is .99, and the area under this curve to the left of $z_{.005}$ is .995. Looking up a cumulative area of .995 in Table A.3 (see page 790) or in Table 8.1, we find that $z_{.005} = 2.575$.

Step 3: Form the following 99 percent confidence interval for the population mean.

$$[\bar{x} \pm z_{.005}\sigma_{\bar{x}}] = \left[\bar{x} \pm 2.575\, \frac{\sigma}{\sqrt{n}} \right]$$

If all possible samples were used to calculate this interval, then 99 percent of the resulting intervals would contain the population mean. For example, in the car mileage case, a 99 percent confidence interval for the midsize model's mean mileage μ is:

$$\left[\bar{x} \pm 2.575\, \frac{\sigma}{\sqrt{n}} \right] = \left[31.56 \pm 2.575\, \frac{.8}{\sqrt{50}} \right]$$
$$= [31.56 \pm .29]$$
$$= [31.27, 31.85]$$

FIGURE 8.5   The Point $z_{\alpha/2}$

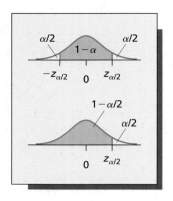

TABLE 8.2   The Normal Point $z_{\alpha/2}$ for Various Levels of Confidence

$100(1-\alpha)\%$	$1-\alpha$	α	$\alpha/2$	$1-\alpha/2$	$z_{\alpha/2}$
90%	.90	.10	.05	.95	$z_{.05} = 1.645$
95%	.95	.05	.025	.975	$z_{.025} = 1.96$
98%	.98	.02	.01	.99	$z_{.01} = 2.33$
99%	.99	.01	.005	.995	$z_{.005} = 2.575$

To compare the 95 percent confidence interval $[\bar{x} \pm 1.96(\sigma/\sqrt{n})]$ with the 99 percent confidence interval $[\bar{x} \pm 2.575(\sigma/\sqrt{n})]$, note that each of these confidence intervals can be expressed in the form $[\bar{x} \pm$ margin of error]. Here, for a given level of confidence, the **margin of error** expresses the furthest that the sample mean $\bar{x}$ might be from the population mean μ. Moreover, the margin of error $2.575(\sigma/\sqrt{n})$ used to compute the 99 percent interval is larger than the margin of error $1.96(\sigma/\sqrt{n})$ used to compute the 95 percent interval. Therefore, the 99 percent interval is the longer of these intervals. **In general, increasing the confidence level (1) has the advantage of making us more confident that μ is contained in the confidence interval, but (2) has the disadvantage of increasing the margin of error and thus providing a less precise estimate of the true value of μ.** Frequently, 95 percent confidence intervals are used to make conclusions. If conclusions based on stronger evidence are desired, 99 percent intervals are sometimes used. In the car mileage case, the fairly large sample size of $n = 50$ produces a 99 percent margin of error, $2.575(.8/\sqrt{50}) = .29$, that is not much larger than the 95 percent margin of error, $1.96(.8/\sqrt{50}) = .22$. Therefore, the 99 percent confidence interval for μ, $[31.56 \pm .29] = [31.27, 31.85]$, is not much longer than the 95 percent confidence interval for μ, $[31.56 \pm .22] = [31.34, 31.78]$.

In general, we let α denote the probability that a confidence interval for a population mean will *not* contain the population mean. This implies that $1 - \alpha$ is the probability that the confidence interval will contain the population mean. In order to find a confidence interval for a population mean that is based on a confidence coefficient of $1 - \alpha$ (that is, a **$100(1 - \alpha)$ percent confidence interval** for the population mean), we do the following:

Step 1: As illustrated in Figure 8.5, place a symmetrical area of $1 - \alpha$ under the standard normal curve, and find the area in the normal curve tails beyond the $1 - \alpha$ area. Because the entire area under the standard normal curve is 1, the combined areas in the normal curve tails are α, and the area in each tail is $\alpha/2$.

Step 2: Find the normal point $z_{\alpha/2}$ that gives a right-hand tail area under the standard normal curve equal to $\alpha/2$, and find the normal point $-z_{\alpha/2}$ that gives a left-hand tail area under this curve equal to $\alpha/2$. As shown in Figure 8.5, the area under the standard normal curve between $-z_{\alpha/2}$ and $z_{\alpha/2}$ is $(1-\alpha)$, and the area under this curve to the left of $z_{\alpha/2}$ is $1-\alpha/2$. **This implies that we can find $z_{\alpha/2}$ by looking up a cumulative area of $1-\alpha/2$ in Table A.3** (page 790).

Step 3: Form the following $100(1 - \alpha)$ percent confidence interval for the population mean.

$$[\bar{x} \pm z_{\alpha/2}\sigma_{\bar{x}}] = \left[\bar{x} \pm z_{\alpha/2}\frac{\sigma}{\sqrt{n}}\right]$$

If all possible samples were used to calculate this interval, then $100(1 - \alpha)$ percent of the resulting intervals would contain the population mean. Moreover, we call **$100(1 - \alpha)$ percent** the **confidence level** associated with the confidence interval.

The general formula that we just obtained for a $100(1 - \alpha)$ percent confidence interval for a population mean implies that we now have a formal way to find the normal point corresponding to a particular level of confidence. Specifically, we can set $100(1 - \alpha)$ percent equal to the particular level of confidence, solve for α, and use a cumulative normal table to find the normal point $z_{\alpha/2}$ corresponding to the cumulative area $1 - \alpha/2$. For example, suppose that we wish to find a 99 percent confidence interval for the population mean. Then, because $100(1 - \alpha)$ percent equals 99 percent, it follows that $1 - \alpha = .99$, $\alpha = .01$, $\alpha/2 = .005$, and $1 - \alpha/2 = .995$. Looking up .995 in a cumulative normal table, we find that $z_{\alpha/2} = z_{.005} = 2.575$. This normal point is the same normal point that we previously found using the three-step procedure and the normal curves illustrated in Figure 8.4. Table 8.2 summarizes finding the values of $z_{\alpha/2}$ for different values of the confidence level $100(1 - \alpha)$ percent.

The following box summarizes the formula used in calculating a $100(1 - \alpha)$ percent confidence interval for a population mean μ. This interval is based on the normal distribution and assumes that the true value of σ is known. If (as is usually the case) σ is not known, we can use a confidence interval for μ discussed in the next section.

A Confidence Interval for a Population Mean μ: σ Known

Suppose that the sampled population is normally distributed with mean μ and standard deviation σ. Then a $100(1 - \alpha)$ percent confidence interval for μ is

$$\left[\bar{x} \pm z_{\alpha/2} \frac{\sigma}{\sqrt{n}} \right] = \left[\bar{x} - z_{\alpha/2} \frac{\sigma}{\sqrt{n}}, \ \bar{x} + z_{\alpha/2} \frac{\sigma}{\sqrt{n}} \right]$$

Here, $z_{\alpha/2}$ is the normal point that gives a right-hand tail area under the standard normal curve of $\alpha/2$. The normal point $z_{\alpha/2}$ can be found by looking up a cumulative area of $1 - \alpha/2$ in Table A.3 (page 790). This confidence interval is also approximately valid for non-normal populations if the sample size is large (at least 30).

EXAMPLE 8.1 The e-billing Case: Reducing Mean Bill Payment Time

Recall that a management consulting firm has installed a new computer-based electronic billing system in a Hamilton, Ohio, trucking company. The population mean payment time using the trucking company's old billing system was approximately equal to, but no less than, 39 days. In order to assess whether the population mean payment time, μ, using the new billing system is substantially less than 39 days, the consulting firm will use the sample of $n = 65$ payment times in Table 2.4 to find a 99 percent confidence interval for μ. The mean of the 65 payment times is $\bar{x} = 18.1077$ days, and we will assume that the true value of the population standard deviation σ for the new billing system is 4.2 days (as discussed on page 280 of Chapter 7). Then, because we previously showed that the normal point corresponding to 99 percent confidence is $z_{\alpha/2} = z_{.005} = 2.575$, a 99 percent confidence interval for μ is

$$\left[\bar{x} \pm z_{.005} \frac{\sigma}{\sqrt{n}} \right] = \left[18.1077 \pm 2.575 \frac{4.2}{\sqrt{65}} \right]$$
$$= [18.1077 \pm 1.3414]$$
$$= [16.8, 19.4]$$

Recalling that the mean payment time using the old billing system is 39 days, this interval says that we are 99 percent confident that the population mean payment time using the new billing system is between 16.8 days and 19.4 days. Therefore, we are 99 percent confident that the new billing system reduces the mean payment time by at most $39 - 16.8 = 22.2$ days and by at least $39 - 19.4 = 19.6$ days.

Exercises for Section 8.1

CONCEPTS

connect

8.1   Explain why it is important to calculate a confidence interval.

8.2   Explain the meaning of the term "95 percent confidence."

8.3   Under what conditions is the confidence interval $[\bar{x} \pm z_{\alpha/2}(\sigma/\sqrt{n})]$ for μ valid?

8.4   For a fixed sample size, what happens to a confidence interval for μ when we increase the level of confidence?

8.5   For a fixed level of confidence, what happens to a confidence interval for μ when we increase the sample size?

METHODS AND APPLICATIONS

8.6   Suppose that, for a sample of size $n = 100$ measurements, we find that $\bar{x} = 50$. Assuming that σ equals 2, calculate confidence intervals for the population mean μ with the following confidence levels:

    a 95%   **b** 99%   **c** 97%   **d** 80%   **e** 99.73%   **f** 92%

8.7   **THE TRASH BAG CASE** 🖵 TrashBag

Consider the trash bag problem. Suppose that an independent laboratory has tested trash bags and has found that no 30-gallon bags that are currently on the market have a mean breaking strength of 50 pounds or more. On the basis of these results, the producer of the new, improved trash bag feels sure that its 30-gallon bag will be the strongest such bag on the market if the new trash bag's mean breaking strength can be shown to be at least 50 pounds. The mean of the sample of 40 trash bag breaking strengths in Table 1.9 is $\bar{x} = 50.575$. If we let μ denote the mean of the breaking strengths of all possible trash bags of the new type and assume that σ equals 1.65:

    a Calculate 95 percent and 99 percent confidence intervals for μ.

    b Using the 95 percent confidence interval, can we be 95 percent confident that μ is at least 50 pounds? Explain.

    c Using the 99 percent confidence interval, can we be 99 percent confident that μ is at least 50 pounds? Explain.

    d Based on your answers to parts b and c, how convinced are you that the new 30-gallon trash bag is the strongest such bag on the market?

8.8   **THE BANK CUSTOMER WAITING TIME CASE** 🖵 WaitTime

Recall that a bank manager has developed a new system to reduce the time customers spend waiting to be served by tellers during peak business hours. The mean waiting time during peak business hours under the current system is roughly 9 to 10 minutes. The bank manager hopes that the new system will have a mean waiting time that is less than six minutes. The mean of the sample of 100 bank customer waiting times in Table 1.8 is $\bar{x} = 5.46$. If we let μ denote the mean of all possible bank customer waiting times using the new system and assume that σ equals 2.47:

    a Calculate 95 percent and 99 percent confidence intervals for μ.

    b Using the 95 percent confidence interval, can the bank manager be 95 percent confident that μ is less than six minutes? Explain.

    c Using the 99 percent confidence interval, can the bank manager be 99 percent confident that μ is less than six minutes? Explain.

    d Based on your answers to parts b and c, how convinced are you that the new mean waiting time is less than six minutes?

8.9   **THE VIDEO GAME SATISFACTION RATING CASE** 🖵 VideoGame

The mean of the sample of 65 customer satisfaction ratings in Table 1.7 is $\bar{x} = 42.95$. If we let μ denote the mean of all possible customer satisfaction ratings for the XYZ Box video game system, and assume that σ equals 2.64:

    a Calculate 95 percent and 99 percent confidence intervals for μ.

    b Using the 95 percent confidence interval, can we be 95 percent confident that μ is at least 42 (recall that a very satisfied customer gives a rating of at least 42)? Explain.

    c Using the 99 percent confidence interval, can we be 99 percent confident that μ is at least 42? Explain.

    d Based on your answers to parts b and c, how convinced are you that the mean satisfaction rating is at least 42?

8.10 In an article in *Marketing Science*, Silk and Berndt investigate the output of advertising agencies. They describe ad agency output by finding the shares of dollar billing volume coming from various media categories such as network television, spot television, newspapers, radio, and so forth.

  a Suppose that a random sample of 400 U.S. advertising agencies gives an average percentage share of billing volume from network television equal to 7.46 percent, and assume that σ equals 1.42 percent. Calculate a 95 percent confidence interval for the mean percentage share of billing volume from network television for the population of all U.S. advertising agencies.

  b Suppose that a random sample of 400 U.S. advertising agencies gives an average percentage share of billing volume from spot television commercials equal to 12.44 percent, and assume that σ equals 1.55 percent. Calculate a 95 percent confidence interval for the mean percentage share of billing volume from spot television commercials for the population of all U.S. advertising agencies.

  c Compare the confidence intervals in parts *a* and *b*. Does it appear that the mean percentage share of billing volume from spot television commercials for U.S. advertising agencies is greater than the mean percentage share of billing volume from network television? Explain.

8.11 In an article in *Accounting and Business Research*, Carslaw and Kaplan investigate factors that influence "audit delay" for firms in New Zealand. Audit delay, which is defined to be the length of time (in days) from a company's financial year-end to the date of the auditor's report, has been found to affect the market reaction to the report. This is because late reports often seem to be associated with lower returns and early reports often seem to be associated with higher returns.

  Carslaw and Kaplan investigated audit delay for two kinds of public companies—owner-controlled and manager-controlled companies. Here a company is considered to be owner controlled if 30 percent or more of the common stock is controlled by a single outside investor (an investor not part of the management group or board of directors). Otherwise, a company is considered manager controlled. It was felt that the type of control influences audit delay. To quote Carslaw and Kaplan:

  > Large external investors, having an acute need for timely information, may be expected to pressure the company and auditor to start and to complete the audit as rapidly as practicable.

  a Suppose that a random sample of 100 public owner-controlled companies in New Zealand is found to give a mean audit delay of $\bar{x} = 82.6$ days, and assume that σ equals 33 days. Calculate a 95 percent confidence interval for the population mean audit delay for all public owner-controlled companies in New Zealand.

  b Suppose that a random sample of 100 public manager-controlled companies in New Zealand is found to give a mean audit delay of $\bar{x} = 93$ days, and assume that σ equals 37 days. Calculate a 95 percent confidence interval for the population mean audit delay for all public manager-controlled companies in New Zealand.

  c Use the confidence intervals you computed in parts *a* and *b* to compare the mean audit delay for all public owner-controlled companies versus that of all public manager-controlled companies. How do the means compare? Explain.

8.12 In an article in the *Journal of Marketing*, Bayus studied the differences between "early replacement buyers" and "late replacement buyers" in making consumer durable good replacement purchases. Early replacement buyers are consumers who replace a product during the early part of its lifetime, while late replacement buyers make replacement purchases late in the product's lifetime. In particular, Bayus studied automobile replacement purchases. Consumers who traded in cars with ages of zero to three years and mileages of no more than 35,000 miles were classified as early replacement buyers. Consumers who traded in cars with ages of seven or more years and mileages of more than 73,000 miles were classified as late replacement buyers. Bayus compared the two groups of buyers with respect to demographic variables such as income, education, age, and so forth. He also compared the two groups with respect to the amount of search activity in the replacement purchase process. Variables compared included the number of dealers visited, the time spent gathering information, and the time spent visiting dealers.

  a Suppose that a random sample of 800 early replacement buyers yields a mean number of dealers visited of $\bar{x} = 3.3$, and assume that σ equals .71. Calculate a 99 percent confidence interval for the population mean number of dealers visited by early replacement buyers.

  b Suppose that a random sample of 500 late replacement buyers yields a mean number of dealers visited of $\bar{x} = 4.3$, and assume that σ equals .66. Calculate a 99 percent confidence interval for the population mean number of dealers visited by late replacement buyers.

  c Use the confidence intervals you computed in parts *a* and *b* to compare the mean number of dealers visited by early replacement buyers with the mean number of dealers visited by late replacement buyers. How do the means compare? Explain.

LO8-2 Describe the properties of the *t* distribution and use a *t* table.

8.2 *t*-Based Confidence Intervals for a Population Mean: σ Unknown ● ● ●

If we do not know σ (which is usually the case), we can use the sample standard deviation s to help construct a confidence interval for μ. The interval is based on the sampling distribution of

$$t = \frac{\bar{x} - \mu}{s/\sqrt{n}}$$

If the sampled population is normally distributed, then for any sample size n this sampling distribution is what is called a *t* **distribution.**

The curve of the *t* distribution has a shape similar to that of the standard normal curve. Two *t* curves and a standard normal curve are illustrated in Figure 8.6. A *t* curve is symmetrical about zero, which is the mean of any *t* distribution. However, the *t* distribution is more spread out, or variable, than the standard normal distribution. Because the *t* statistic above is a function of two random variables, $\bar{x}$ and s, it is logical that the sampling distribution of this statistic is more variable than the sampling distribution of the z statistic, which is a function of only one random variable, $\bar{x}$. The exact spread, or standard deviation, of the *t* distribution depends on a parameter that is called the **number of degrees of freedom (denoted *df*).** The number of degrees of freedom *df* varies depending on the problem. In the present situation the sampling distribution of *t* has a number of degrees of freedom that equals the sample size minus 1. We say that this sampling distribution is a *t* **distribution with** $n - 1$ **degrees of freedom.** As the sample size n (and thus the number of degrees of freedom) increases, the spread of the *t* distribution decreases (see Figure 8.6). Furthermore, as the number of degrees of freedom approaches infinity, the curve of the *t* distribution approaches (that is, becomes shaped more and more like) the curve of the standard normal distribution.

In order to use the *t* distribution, we employ a *t* **point that is denoted** t_α. As illustrated in Figure 8.7, t_α **is the point on the horizontal axis under the curve of the *t* distribution that gives a right-hand tail area equal to α.** The value of t_α in a particular situation depends upon the right-hand tail area α and the number of degrees of freedom of the *t* distribution. Values of t_α are tabulated in a *t* **table.** Such a table is given in Table A.4 of Appendix A (pages 792 and 793) and a portion of Table A.4 is reproduced in this chapter as Table 8.3. In this *t* table, the rows correspond to the different numbers of degrees of freedom (which are denoted as *df*). The values of *df* are listed down the left side of the table, while the columns designate the right-hand tail area α. For example, suppose we wish to find the *t* point that gives a right-hand tail area of .025 under a *t* curve having $df = 14$ degrees of freedom. To do this, we look in Table 8.3 at the row labeled 14 and the column labeled $t_{.025}$. We find that this $t_{.025}$ point is 2.145 (also see Figure 8.8). Similarly, when there are $df = 14$ degrees of freedom, we find that $t_{.005} = 2.977$ (see Table 8.3 and Figure 8.9).

FIGURE 8.6   **As the Number of Degrees of Freedom Increases, the Spread of the *t* Distribution Decreases and the *t* Curve Approaches the Standard Normal Curve**

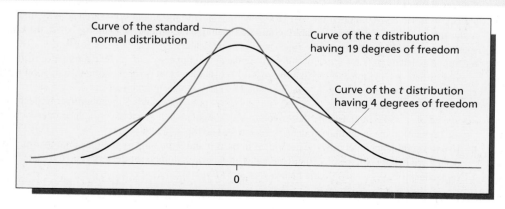

FIGURE 8.7   **An Example of a *t* Point Giving a Specified Right-Hand Tail Area (This *t* Point Gives a Right-Hand Tail Area Equal to α).**

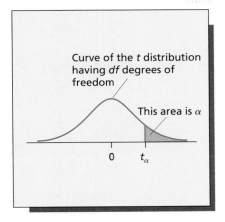

FIGURE 8.8   **The *t* Point Giving a Right-Hand Tail Area of .025 under the *t* Curve Having 14 Degrees of Freedom: $t_{.025} = 2.145$**

TABLE 8.3   **A *t* Table**

df	$t_{.100}$	$t_{.050}$	$t_{.025}$	$t_{.01}$	$t_{.005}$	$t_{.001}$	$t_{.0005}$
1	3.078	6.314	12.706	31.821	63.657	318.31	636.62
2	1.886	2.920	4.303	6.965	9.925	22.326	31.598
3	1.638	2.353	3.182	4.541	5.841	10.213	12.924
4	1.533	2.132	2.776	3.747	4.604	7.173	8.610
5	1.476	2.015	2.571	3.365	4.032	5.893	6.869
6	1.440	1.943	2.447	3.143	3.707	5.208	5.959
7	1.415	1.895	2.365	2.998	3.499	4.785	5.408
8	1.397	1.860	2.306	2.896	3.355	4.501	5.041
9	1.383	1.833	2.262	2.821	3.250	4.297	4.781
10	1.372	1.812	2.228	2.764	3.169	4.144	4.587
11	1.363	1.796	2.201	2.718	3.106	4.025	4.437
12	1.356	1.782	2.179	2.681	3.055	3.930	4.318
13	1.350	1.771	2.160	2.650	3.012	3.852	4.221
14	1.345	1.761	2.145	2.624	2.977	3.787	4.140
15	1.341	1.753	2.131	2.602	2.947	3.733	4.073
16	1.337	1.746	2.120	2.583	2.921	3.686	4.015
17	1.333	1.740	2.110	2.567	2.898	3.646	3.965
18	1.330	1.734	2.101	2.552	2.878	3.610	3.922
19	1.328	1.729	2.093	2.539	2.861	3.579	3.883
20	1.325	1.725	2.086	2.528	2.845	3.552	3.850
21	1.323	1.721	2.080	2.518	2.831	3.527	3.819
22	1.321	1.717	2.074	2.508	2.819	3.505	3.792
23	1.319	1.714	2.069	2.500	2.807	3.485	3.767
24	1.318	1.711	2.064	2.492	2.797	3.467	3.745
25	1.316	1.708	2.060	2.485	2.787	3.450	3.725
26	1.315	1.706	2.056	2.479	2.779	3.435	3.707
27	1.314	1.703	2.052	2.473	2.771	3.421	3.690
28	1.313	1.701	2.048	2.467	2.763	3.408	3.674
29	1.311	1.699	2.045	2.462	2.756	3.396	3.659
30	1.310	1.697	2.042	2.457	2.750	3.385	3.646
40	1.303	1.684	2.021	2.423	2.704	3.307	3.551
60	1.296	1.671	2.000	2.390	2.660	3.232	3.460
120	1.289	1.658	1.980	2.358	2.617	3.160	3.373
∞	1.282	1.645	1.960	2.326	2.576	3.090	3.291

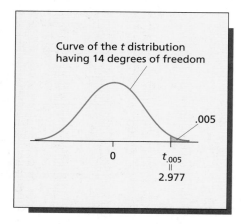

FIGURE 8.9 The *t* Point Giving a Right-Hand Tail Area of .005 Under the *t* Curve Having 14 Degrees of Freedom: $t_{.005} = 2.977$

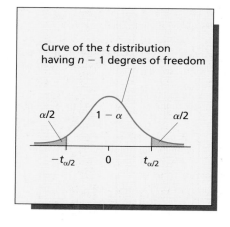

FIGURE 8.10 The Point $t_{\alpha/2}$ with $n - 1$ Degrees of Freedom

Table 8.3 gives *t* points for degrees of freedom *df* from 1 to 30. The table also gives *t* points for 40, 60, 120, and an infinite number of degrees of freedom. Looking at this table, it is useful to realize that the normal points giving the various right-hand tail areas are listed in the row of the *t* table corresponding to an infinite (∞) number of degrees of freedom. Looking at the row corresponding to ∞, we see that, for example, $z_{.025} = 1.96$. Therefore, we can use this row in the *t* table as an alternative to using the normal table when we need to find normal points (such as $z_{\alpha/2}$ in Section 8.1).

LO8-3 Calculate and interpret a *t*-based confidence interval for a population mean when σ is unknown.

Table A.4 of Appendix A (pages 792 and 793) gives *t* points for values of *df* from 1 to 100. We can use a computer to find *t* points based on values of *df* greater than 100. Alternatively, because a *t* curve based on more than 100 degrees of freedom is approximately the shape of the standard normal curve, *t* points based on values of *df* greater than 100 can be approximated by their corresponding *z* points. That is, when performing hand calculations, it is reasonable to approximate values of t_α by z_α when *df* is greater than 100.

We now present the formula for a $100(1 - \alpha)$ percent confidence interval for a population mean μ based on the *t* distribution.

A *t*-Based Confidence Interval for a Population Mean μ: σ Unknown

If the sampled population is normally distributed with mean μ, then a **$100(1 - \alpha)$ percent confidence interval for μ is**

$$\left[\bar{x} \pm t_{\alpha/2} \frac{s}{\sqrt{n}} \right]$$

Here *s* is the sample standard deviation, $t_{\alpha/2}$ is the *t* point giving a right-hand tail area of $\alpha/2$ under the *t* curve having $n - 1$ degrees of freedom, and *n* is the sample size. This confidence interval is also approximately valid for non-normal populations if the sample size is large (at least 30).

Before presenting an example, we need to make a few comments. First, it has been shown that, even if the sample size is not large, this confidence interval is approximately valid for many populations that are not exactly normally distributed. In particular, this interval is approximately valid for a mound-shaped, or single-peaked, population, even if the population is somewhat skewed to the right or left. Second, this interval employs the point $t_{\alpha/2}$, which as shown in Figure 8.10, gives a right-hand tail area equal to $\alpha/2$ under the *t* curve having $n - 1$ degrees of freedom. Here $\alpha/2$ is determined from the desired confidence level $100(1 - \alpha)$ percent.

EXAMPLE 8.2 The Commercial Loan Case: Mean Debt-to-Equity Ratio

One measure of a company's financial health is its *debt-to-equity ratio*. This quantity is defined to be the ratio of the company's corporate debt to the company's equity. If this ratio is too high, it is one indication of financial instability. For obvious reasons, banks often monitor the financial health of companies to which they have extended commercial loans. Suppose that, in order to reduce risk, a large bank has decided to initiate a policy limiting the mean debt-to-equity ratio for its portfolio of commercial loans to being less than 1.5. In order to estimate the mean debt-to-equity ratio of its (current) commercial loan portfolio, the bank randomly selects a sample of 15 of its commercial loan accounts. Audits of these companies result in the following debt-to-equity ratios:

1.31	1.05	1.45	1.21	1.19
1.78	1.37	1.41	1.22	1.11
1.46	1.33	1.29	1.32	1.65

DS DebtEq

A stem-and-leaf display of these ratios is given on the page margin and looks reasonably bell-shaped and symmetrical. Furthermore, the sample mean and standard deviation of the ratios can be calculated to be $\bar{x} = 1.3433$ and $s = .1921$.

1.0	5
1.1	1 9
1.2	1 2 9
1.3	1 2 3 7
1.4	1 5 6
1.5	
1.6	5
1.7	8

Suppose the bank wishes to calculate a 95 percent confidence interval for the loan portfolio's mean debt-to-equity ratio, μ. The reasonably bell-shaped and symmetrical stem-and-leaf display in the page margin implies that the population of all debt-to-equity ratios is (approximately) normally distributed. Thus, we can base the confidence interval on the *t*-distribution. Because the bank has taken a sample of size $n = 15$, we have $n - 1 = 15 - 1 = 14$ degrees of freedom, and the level of confidence $100(1 - \alpha)\% = 95\%$ implies that $1 - \alpha = .95$ and $\alpha = .05$. Therefore, we use the *t* point $t_{\alpha/2} = t_{.05/2} = t_{.025}$, which is the *t* point giving a right-hand tail area of .025 under the *t* curve having 14 degrees of freedom. This *t* point is illustrated in the figure below:

Using Table 8.3 (page 311), we find that $t_{.025}$ with 14 degrees of freedom is 2.145. It follows that the 95 percent confidence interval for μ is

$$\left[\bar{x} \pm t_{.025}\frac{s}{\sqrt{n}}\right] = \left[1.3433 \pm 2.145\frac{.1921}{\sqrt{15}}\right]$$

$$= [1.3433 \pm 0.1064]$$

$$= [1.2369, 1.4497]$$

This interval says the bank is 95 percent confident that the mean debt-to-equity ratio for its portfolio of commercial loan accounts is between 1.2369 and 1.4497. Based on this interval, the bank has strong evidence that the portfolio's mean ratio is less than 1.5 (or that the bank is in compliance with its new policy).

Recall that in the two cases discussed in Section 8.1 we calculated *z*-based confidence intervals for μ by assuming that the population standard deviation σ is known. If σ is actually not known (which would probably be true), we should compute *t*-based confidence intervals. Furthermore, recall that in each of these cases the sample size is large (at least 30). As stated in the summary box, **if the sample size is large, the *t*-based confidence interval for μ is approximately valid even if the sampled population is not normally distributed.** Therefore, consider the car mileage case and the sample of 50 mileages in Table 1.6, which has mean $\bar{x} = 31.56$ and standard deviation $s = .7977$. The 95 percent t-based confidence interval for the population mean mileage μ of the new midsize model is

$$\left[\bar{x} \pm t_{.025} \frac{s}{\sqrt{n}} \right] = \left[31.56 \pm 2.010 \frac{.7977}{\sqrt{50}} \right] = [31.33, 31.79]$$

where $t_{.025} = 2.010$ is based on $n - 1 = 50 - 1 = 49$ degrees of freedom—see Table A.4 (page 792). This interval says we are 95 percent confident that the model's population mean mileage μ is between 31.33 mpg and 31.79 mpg. Based on this interval, the model's EPA mileage estimate is 31 mpg, and the automaker will receive the tax credit.

As another example, the sample of 65 payment times in Table 2.4 has mean $\bar{x} = 18.1077$ and standard deviation $s = 3.9612$. The 99 percent t-based confidence interval for the population mean payment time using the new electronic billing system is

$$\left[\bar{x} \pm t_{.005} \frac{s}{\sqrt{n}} \right] = \left[18.1077 \pm 2.655 \frac{3.9612}{\sqrt{65}} \right] = [16.8, 19.4]$$

where $t_{.005} = 2.655$ is based on $n - 1 = 65 - 1 = 64$ degrees of freedom—see Table A.4 (page 792). Recalling that the mean payment time using the old billing system is 39 days, the interval says that we are 99 percent confident that the population mean payment time using the new billing system is between 16.8 days and 19.4 days. Therefore, we are 99 percent confident that the new billing system reduces the mean payment time by at most 22.2 days and by at least 19.6 days.

EXAMPLE 8.3 The Marketing Research Case: Rating A Bottle Design

Recall that a brand group is considering a new bottle design for a popular soft drink and that Table 1.5 (page 10) gives a random sample of $n = 60$ consumer ratings of this new bottle design. Let μ denote the mean rating of the new bottle design that would be given by all consumers. In order to assess whether μ exceeds the minimum standard composite score of 25 for a successful bottle design, the brand group will calculate a 95 percent confidence interval for μ. The mean and the standard deviation of the 60 bottle design ratings are $\bar{x} = 30.35$ and $s = 3.1073$. It follows that a 95 percent confidence interval for μ is

$$\left[\bar{x} \pm t_{.025} \frac{s}{\sqrt{n}} \right] = \left[30.35 \pm 2.001 \frac{3.1073}{\sqrt{60}} \right] = [29.5, 31.2]$$

where $t_{.025} = 2.001$ is based on $n - 1 = 60 - 1 = 59$ degrees of freedom—see Table A.4 (page 792). Because the interval says we are 95 percent confident that the population mean rating of the new bottle design is between 29.5 and 31.2, we are 95 percent confident that this mean rating exceeds the minimum standard of 25 by at least 4.5 points and by at most 6.2 points.

Confidence intervals for μ can be computed using Excel and MINITAB. For example, the MINITAB output in Figure 8.11 tells us that the t-based 95 percent confidence interval for the mean debt-to-equity ratio is [1.2370, 1.4497]. This result is, within rounding, the same interval calculated in Example 8.2. The MINITAB output also gives the sample mean $\bar{x} = 1.3433$, as well as the sample standard deviation $s = .1921$ and the quantity $s/\sqrt{n} = .0496$, which is called the **standard error of the estimate $\bar{x}$** and denoted "SE Mean" on the MINITAB output. Finally, the MINITAB output gives a box plot of the sample of 15 debt-to-equity ratios and graphically illustrates under the box plot the 95 percent confidence interval for the mean debt-to-equity ratio. Figure 8.12 gives the Excel output of the information needed to calculate the t-based 95 percent confidence interval for the mean debt-to-equity ratio. If we consider the Excel output, we see that $\bar{x} = 1.3433$ (see "Mean"), $s = .1921$ (see "Standard Deviation"), $s/\sqrt{n} = .0496$ (see "Standard Error"), and $t_{.025}(s/\sqrt{n}) = .1064$ [see "Confidence Level (95.0%)"]. The interval, which must be hand calculated (or calculated by using Excel cell formulas), is $[1.3433 \pm .1064] = [1.2369, 1.4497]$.

FIGURE 8.11 **MINITAB Output of a *t*-Based 95 Percent Confidence Interval for the Mean Debt-to-Equity Ratio**

```
Variable   N     Mean    StDev   SE Mean       95% CI
Ratio      15   1.3433  0.1921   0.0496   (1.2370, 1.4497)
```

FIGURE 8.12 **The Excel Output for the Debt-to-Equity Ratio Example**

	A	B	C
1	*Descriptive Statistics*		
2			
3	Mean	1.3433	
4	Standard Error	0.0496	
5	Median	1.32	
6	Mode	#N/A	
7	Standard Deviation	0.1921	
8	Sample Variance	0.0369	
9	Kurtosis	0.8334	
10	Skewness	0.8050	
11	Range	0.73	
12	Minimum	1.05	
13	Maximum	1.78	
14	Sum	20.15	
15	Count	15	
16	Confidence Level(95.0%)	0.1064	

FIGURE 8.13 **A Comparison of a Confidence Interval and a Tolerance Interval**

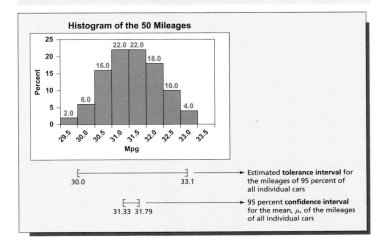

Finally, if the sample size *n* is small and the sampled population is not mound-shaped or is highly skewed, then the *t*-based confidence interval for the population mean might not be valid. In this case we can use a **nonparametric method**—a method that makes no assumption about the shape of the sampled population and is valid for any sample size. In Chapter 18 we discuss nonparametric methods.

Making the correct interpretations: The difference between a confidence interval and a tolerance interval

Recall in the car mileage case that the mean and the standard deviation of the sample of 50 mileages are $\bar{x} = 31.56$ and $s = .7977$. Also, we have seen on the previous page that a 95 percent *t*-based confidence interval for the mean, μ, of the mileages of all individual cars is $[\bar{x} \pm 2.010 (s/\sqrt{50})] = [31.33, 31.79]$. A correct interpretation of this confidence interval says that we are 95 percent confident that the population mean mileage μ is between 31.33 mpg and 31.79 mpg. An incorrect interpretation—and one that is sometimes made by beginning statistics students—is that we estimate that 95 percent of all individual cars would (if tested) get between 31.33 mpg and 31.79 mpg. In general, an interval that contains a specified percentage of the individual measurements in a population is a *tolerance interval* (as previously discussed in Chapter 3). A tolerance interval is of the form $[\mu \pm z_{\alpha/2}\sigma]$ if the population of all individual measurements is normally distributed. For example, the histogram in Figure 8.13 suggests that the population of the mileages of all individual cars is normally distributed. Therefore, consider estimating a tolerance interval that contains the mileages of 95 percent of all individual cars. To do this, we first find the normal point $z_{\alpha/2}$ such that the area under the standard normal curve between $-z_{\alpha/2}$ and $z_{\alpha/2}$ is .95. As shown in the page margin, the appropriate normal point $z_{\alpha/2}$ is $z_{.025} = 1.96$. Estimating μ and σ in the tolerance interval $[\mu \pm 1.96\sigma]$ by $\bar{x} = 31.56$ and $s = .7977$, we then obtain an estimated tolerance interval of $[31.56 \pm 1.96(.7977)] = [30.0, 33.1]$. This estimated tolerance interval implies that approximately 95 percent of all individual cars would (if tested) get between 30.0 mpg and 33.1 mpg. Furthermore, Figure 8.13 shows that the estimated tolerance interval, which is meant to contain the *many mileages* that would be obtained by 95 percent of all individual cars, is much longer than the 95 percent confidence interval, which is meant to contain the *single population mean* μ.

Exercises for Section 8.2

connect

CONCEPTS

8.13 Explain how each of the following changes as *the number of degrees of freedom* describing a *t* curve *increases:*

  a The standard deviation of the *t* curve.   **b** The points t_α and $t_{\alpha/2}$.

8.14 Discuss when it is appropriate to use the *t*-based confidence interval for μ.

METHODS AND APPLICATIONS

8.15 Using Table A.4 (page 792), find $t_{.100}$, $t_{.025}$, and $t_{.001}$ based on 11 degrees of freedom. Also, find these *t* points based on 6 degrees of freedom.

8.16 Suppose that for a sample of $n = 11$ measurements, we find that $\bar{x} = 72$ and $s = 5$. Assuming normality, compute confidence intervals for the population mean μ with the following levels of confidence:

  a 95%   **b** 99%   **c** 80%   **d** 90%   **e** 98%   **f** 99.8%

8.17 The *bad debt ratio* for a financial institution is defined to be the dollar value of loans defaulted divided by the total dollar value of all loans made. Suppose a random sample of seven Ohio banks is selected and that the bad debt ratios (written as percentages) for these banks are 7 percent, 4 percent, 6 percent, 7 percent, 5 percent, 4 percent, and 9 percent. Assuming the bad debt ratios are approximately normally distributed, the MINITAB output of a 95 percent confidence interval for the mean bad debt ratio of all Ohio banks is given below. Using the $\bar{x}$ and s on the MINITAB output, demonstrate the calculation of the 95 percent confidence interval, and calculate a 99 percent confidence interval for the mean debt-to-equity ratio. **DS** BadDebt

Variable	N	Mean	StDev	SE Mean	95% CI
D-Ratio	7	6.00000	1.82574	0.69007	(4.31147, 7.68853)

8.18 In Exercise 8.17, suppose bank officials claim that the mean bad debt ratio for all banks in the Midwest region is 3.5 percent and that the mean bad debt ratio for Ohio banks is higher. Using the 95 percent confidence interval (given by MINITAB), can we be 95 percent confident that this claim is true? Using the 99 percent confidence interval you calculated, can we be 99 percent confident that this claim is true?

8.19 THE AIR SAFETY CASE

Air traffic controllers have the crucial task of ensuring that aircraft don't collide. To do this, they must quickly discern when two planes are about to enter the same air space at the same time. They are aided by video display panels that track the aircraft in their sector and alert the controller when two flight paths are about to converge. The display panel currently in use has a mean "alert time" of 15 seconds. (The alert time is the time elapsing between the instant when two aircraft enter into a collision course and when a controller initiates a call to reroute the planes.) According to Ralph Rudd, a supervisor of air traffic controllers at the Greater Cincinnati International Airport, a new display panel has been developed that uses artificial intelligence to project a plane's current flight path into the future. This new panel provides air traffic controllers with an earlier warning that a collision is likely. It is hoped that the mean "alert time," μ, for the new panel is less than 8 seconds. In order to test the new panel, 15 randomly selected air traffic controllers are trained to use the panel and their alert times for a simulated collision course are recorded. The sample alert times (in seconds) are: 7.2, 7.5, 8.0, 6.8, 7.2, 8.4, 5.3, 7.3, 7.6, 7.1, 9.4, 6.4, 7.9, 6.2, 8.7.   **DS** AlertTimes

  a Using the fact that $\bar{x} = 7.4$ and $s = 1.026$, find a 95 percent confidence interval for the population mean alert time, μ, for the new panel.

  b Can we be 95 percent confident that μ is less than 8 seconds?

8.20 Whole Foods is an all-natural grocery chain that has 50,000 square foot stores, up from the industry average of 34,000 square feet. Sales per square foot of supermarkets average just under $400 per square foot, as reported by *USA Today* in an article on "A whole new ballgame in grocery shopping." Suppose that sales per square foot in the most recent fiscal year are recorded for a random sample of 10 Whole Foods supermarkets. The data (sales dollars per square foot) are as follows: 854, 858, 801, 892, 849, 807, 894, 863, 829, 815. Using the fact that $\bar{x} = 846.2$ and $s = 32.866$, find a 95 percent confidence interval for the population mean sales dollars per square foot for all Whole Foods supermarkets during the most recent fiscal year. Are we 95 percent confident that this mean is greater than $800, the historical average for Whole Foods?   **DS** WholeFoods

FIGURE 8.14   **Excel Output for Exercise 8.21**

	A	B	C
1	**Descriptive Statistics for Yield**		
2			
3	Mean	811	
4	Standard Error	8.7864	
5	Median	814	
6	Mode	#N/A	
7	Standard Deviation	19.6469	
8	Sample Variance	386	
9	Kurtosis	-0.1247	
10	Skewness	-0.2364	
11	Range	52	
12	Minimum	784	
13	Maximum	836	
14	Sum	4055	
15	Count	5	
16	Confidence Level(95.0%)	24.3948	

FIGURE 8.15   **Excel Output for Exercise 8.24**

	A	B	C
1	**Descriptive Statistics for Strength**		
2			
3	Mean	50.575	
4	Standard Error	0.2599	
5	Median	50.65	
6	Mode	50.9	
7	Standard Deviation	1.6438	
8	Sample Variance	2.7019	
9	Kurtosis	-0.2151	
10	Skewness	-0.0549	
11	Range	7.2	
12	Minimum	46.8	
13	Maximum	54	
14	Sum	2023	
15	Count	40	
16	Confidence Level(95.0%)	0.5257	

8.21 A production supervisor at a major chemical company wishes to determine whether a new catalyst, catalyst XA-100, increases the mean hourly yield of a chemical process beyond the current mean hourly yield, which is known to be roughly equal to, but no more than, 750 pounds per hour. To test the new catalyst, five trial runs using catalyst XA-100 are made. The resulting yields for the trial runs (in pounds per hour) are 801, 814, 784, 836, and 820. Assuming that all factors affecting yields of the process have been held as constant as possible during the test runs, it is reasonable to regard the five yields obtained using the new catalyst as a random sample from the population of all possible yields that would be obtained by using the new catalyst. Furthermore, we will assume that this population is approximately normally distributed.   **DS** ChemYield
- **a** Using the Excel output in Figure 8.14, find a 95 percent confidence interval for the mean of all possible yields obtained using catalyst XA-100.
- **b** Based on the confidence interval, can we be 95 percent confident that the mean yield using catalyst XA-100 exceeds 750 pounds per hour? Explain.

8.22 **THE VIDEO GAME SATISFACTION RATING CASE**   **DS** VideoGame

The mean and the standard deviation of the sample of $n = 65$ customer satisfaction ratings in Table 1.7 are $\bar{x} = 42.95$ and $s = 2.6424$. Calculate a t-based 95 percent confidence interval for μ, the mean of all possible customer satisfaction ratings for the XYZ-Box video game system. Are we 95 percent confident that μ is at least 42, the minimal rating given by a very satisfied customer?

8.23 **THE BANK CUSTOMER WAITING TIME CASE**   **DS** WaitTime

The mean and the standard deviation of the sample of 100 bank customer waiting times in Table 1.8 are $\bar{x} = 5.46$ and $s = 2.475$. Calculate a t-based 95 percent confidence interval for μ, the mean of all possible bank customer waiting times using the new system. Are we 95 percent confident that μ is less than six minutes?

8.24 **THE TRASH BAG CASE**   **DS** TrashBag

The mean and the standard deviation of the sample of 40 trash bag breaking strengths in Table 1.9 are $\bar{x} = 50.575$ and $s = 1.6438$.
- **a** Use the Excel output in Figure 8.15 to calculate a t-based 95 percent confidence interval for μ, the mean of the breaking strengths of all possible new trash bags. Are we 95 percent confident that μ is at least 50 pounds?
- **b** Assuming that the population of all individual trash bag breaking strengths is normally distributed, estimate tolerance intervals of the form $[\mu \pm z_{\alpha/2}\, \sigma]$ that contain (1) 95 percent of all individual trash bag breaking strengths and (2) 99.8 percent of all individual trash bag breaking strengths.

8.3 Sample Size Determination ● ● ●

In Section 8.1 we used a sample of 50 mileages to construct a 95 percent confidence interval for the midsize model's mean mileage μ. The size of this sample was not arbitrary—it was planned. To understand this, suppose that before the automaker selected the random sample of 50 mileages, it randomly selected the following sample of five mileages: 30.7, 31.9, 30.3, 32.0,

LO8-4 Determine the appropriate sample size when estimating a population mean.

and 31.6. This sample has mean $\bar{x} = 31.3$. Assuming that the population of all mileages is normally distributed and that the population standard deviation σ is known to equal .8, it follows that a 95 percent confidence interval for μ is

$$\left[\bar{x} \pm z_{.025} \frac{\sigma}{\sqrt{n}} \right] = \left[31.3 \pm 1.96 \frac{.8}{\sqrt{5}} \right]$$
$$= [31.3 \pm .701]$$
$$= [30.6, 32.0]$$

Although the sample mean $\bar{x} = 31.3$ is at least 31, the lower limit of the 95 percent confidence interval for μ is less than 31. Therefore, the midsize model's EPA mileage estimate would be 30 mpg, and the automaker would not receive its tax credit. One reason that the lower limit of this 95 percent interval is less than 31 is that the sample size of 5 is not large enough to make the interval's margin of error

$$z_{.025} \frac{\sigma}{\sqrt{n}} = 1.96 \frac{.8}{\sqrt{5}} = .701$$

small enough. We can attempt to make the margin of error in the interval smaller by increasing the sample size. If we feel that the mean $\bar{x}$ of the larger sample will be at least 31.3 mpg (the mean of the small sample we have already taken), then the lower limit of a $100(1 - \alpha)$ percent confidence interval for μ will be at least 31 if the margin of error is .3 or less.

We will now explain how to find the size of the sample that will be needed to make the margin of error in a confidence interval for μ as small as we wish. In order to develop a formula for the needed sample size, we will initially assume that we know σ. Then, if the population is normally distributed or the sample size is large, the z-based $100(1 - \alpha)$ percent confidence interval for μ is $[\bar{x} \pm z_{\alpha/2} (\sigma/\sqrt{n})]$. To find the needed sample size, we set $z_{\alpha/2} (\sigma/\sqrt{n})$ equal to the desired margin of error and solve for n. Letting E denote the desired margin of error, we obtain

$$z_{\alpha/2} \frac{\sigma}{\sqrt{n}} = E$$

Multiplying both sides of this equation by $\sqrt{n}$ and dividing both sides by E, we obtain

$$\sqrt{n} = \frac{z_{\alpha/2}\sigma}{E}$$

Squaring both sides of this result gives us the formula for n.

Determining the Sample Size for a Confidence Interval for μ: σ Known

A sample of size

$$n = \left(\frac{z_{\alpha/2}\sigma}{E} \right)^2$$

makes the margin of error in a $100(1 - \alpha)$ percent confidence interval for μ equal to E. That is, this sample size makes us $100(1 - \alpha)$ percent confident that $\bar{x}$ is within E units of μ. If the calculated value of n is not a whole number, round this value up to the next whole number (so that the margin of error is at least as small as desired).

If we consider the formula for the sample size n, it intuitively follows that the value E is the farthest that the user is willing to allow $\bar{x}$ to be from μ at a given level of confidence, and the normal point $z_{\alpha/2}$ follows directly from the given level of confidence. Furthermore, because the population standard deviation σ is in the numerator of the formula for n, it follows that the more variable that the individual population measurements are, the larger is the sample size needed to estimate μ with a specified accuracy.

In order to use this formula for n, we must either know σ (which is unlikely) or we must compute an estimate of σ. We first consider the case where we know σ. For example, suppose in the car mileage situation we wish to find the sample size that is needed to make the margin of error in a 95 percent confidence interval for μ equal to .3. Assuming that σ is known to equal .8, and using $z_{.025} = 1.96$, the appropriate sample size is

$$n = \left(\frac{z_{.025}\,\sigma}{E}\right)^2 = \left(\frac{1.96(.8)}{.3}\right)^2 = 27.32$$

Rounding up, we would employ a sample of size 28.

In most real situations, of course, we do not know the true value of σ. If σ is not known, we often estimate σ by using a preliminary sample. In this case we modify the above formula for n by replacing σ by the standard deviation s of the preliminary sample and by replacing $z_{\alpha/2}$ by $t_{\alpha/2}$. This approach usually gives a sample at least as large as we need. Thus, we obtain:

$$n = \left(\frac{t_{\alpha/2}\,s}{E}\right)^2$$

where the number of degrees of freedom for the $t_{\alpha/2}$ point is the size of the preliminary sample minus 1. Intuitively, using $t_{\alpha/2}$ compensates for the fact that the preliminary sample's value of s might underestimate σ, and, therefore, give a sample size that is too small.

EXAMPLE 8.4 The Car Mileage Case: Estimating Mean Mileage

Suppose that in the car mileage situation we wish to find the sample size that is needed to make the margin of error in a 95 percent confidence interval for μ equal to .3. Assuming we do not know σ, we regard the previously discussed sample of five mileages (see the bottom of page 317) as a preliminary sample. Therefore, we replace σ by the standard deviation of the preliminary sample, which can be calculated to be $s = .7583$, and we replace $z_{\alpha/2} = z_{.025} = 1.96$ by $t_{.025} = 2.776$, which is based on $n - 1 = 4$ degrees of freedom. We find that the appropriate sample size is

$$n = \left(\frac{t_{.025}\,s}{E}\right)^2 = \left(\frac{2.776(.7583)}{.3}\right)^2 = 49.24$$

Rounding up, we employ a sample of size 50.

When we make the margin of error in our 95 percent confidence interval for μ equal to .3, we can say we are 95 percent confident that the sample mean $\bar{x}$ is within .3 of μ. To understand this, suppose the true value of μ is 31.6. Recalling that the mean of the sample of 50 mileages is $\bar{x} = 31.56$, we see that this sample mean is within .3 of μ. Other samples of 50 mileages would give different sample means that would be different distances from μ. When we say that our sample of 50 mileages makes us 95 percent confident that $\bar{x}$ is within .3 of μ, we mean that **95 percent of all possible sample means based on 50 mileages are within .3 of μ** and 5 percent of such sample means are not.

EXAMPLE 8.5 The Car Mileage Case: Estimating Mean Mileage

To see that the sample of 50 mileages has actually produced a 95 percent confidence interval with a margin of error that is as small as we requested, recall that the 50 mileages have mean $\bar{x} = 31.56$ and standard deviation $s = .7977$. Therefore, the t-based 95 percent confidence interval for μ is

$$\left[\bar{x} \pm t_{.025}\frac{s}{\sqrt{n}}\right] = \left[31.56 \pm 2.010\frac{.7977}{\sqrt{50}}\right]$$

$$= [31.56 \pm .227]$$

$$= [31.33, 31.79]$$

where $t_{.025} = 2.010$ is based on $n - 1 = 50 - 1 = 49$ degrees of freedom—see Table A.4 (page 792). We see that the margin of error in this interval is .227, which is smaller than the .3 we asked for. Furthermore, as the automaker had hoped, the sample mean $\bar{x} = 31.56$ of the sample of 50 mileages turned out to be at least 31.3. Therefore, because the margin of error is less than .3, the lower limit of the 95 percent confidence interval is above 31 mpg, and the midsize model's EPA mileage estimate is 31 mpg. Because of this, the automaker will receive its tax credit.

Finally, sometimes we do not know σ and we do not have a preliminary sample that can be used to estimate σ. In this case it can be shown that, if we can make a reasonable guess of the range of the population being studied, then a conservatively large estimate of σ is this estimated range divided by 4. For example, if the automaker's design engineers feel that almost all of its midsize cars should get mileages within a range of 5 mpg, then a conservatively large estimate of σ is $5/4 = 1.25$ mpg. When employing such an estimate of σ, it is sufficient to use the z-based sample size formula $n = (z_{\alpha/2}\sigma/E)^2$, because a conservatively large estimate of σ will give us a conservatively large sample size.

Exercises for Section 8.3

connect

CONCEPTS

8.25 Explain what is meant by the margin of error for a confidence interval. What error are we talking about in the context of an interval for μ?

8.26 Explain exactly what we mean when we say that a sample of size n makes us 99 percent confident that $\bar{x}$ is within E units of μ.

8.27 Why do we often need to take a preliminary sample when determining the size of the sample needed to make the margin of error of a confidence interval equal to E?

METHODS AND APPLICATIONS

8.28 Consider a population having a standard deviation equal to 10. We wish to estimate the mean of this population.
  a How large a random sample is needed to construct a 95 percent confidence interval for the mean of this population with a margin of error equal to 1?
  b Suppose that we now take a random sample of the size we have determined in part a. If we obtain a sample mean equal to 295, calculate the 95 percent confidence interval for the population mean. What is the interval's margin of error?

8.29 Referring to Exercise 8.11a (page 309), assume that σ equals 33. How large a random sample of public owner-controlled companies is needed to make us:
  a 95 percent confident that $\bar{x}$, the sample mean audit delay, is within a margin of error of four days of μ, the population mean audit delay?
  b 99 percent confident that $\bar{x}$ is within a margin of error of four days of μ?

8.30 Referring to Exercise 8.12b (page 309), assume that σ equals .66. How large a sample of late replacement buyers is needed to make us:
  a 99 percent confident that $\bar{x}$, the sample mean number of dealers visited, is within a margin of error of .04 of μ, the population mean number of dealers visited?
  b 99.73 percent confident that $\bar{x}$ is within a margin of error of .05 of μ?

8.31 Referring to Exercise 8.21 (page 317), regard the sample of five trial runs for which $s = 19.65$ as a preliminary sample. Determine the number of trial runs of the chemical process needed to make us:
  a 95 percent confident that $\bar{x}$, the sample mean hourly yield, is within a margin of error of eight pounds of the population mean hourly yield μ when catalyst XA-100 is used.
  b 99 percent confident that $\bar{x}$ is within a margin of error of five pounds of μ.   **DS** ChemYield

8.32 Referring to Exercise 8.20 (page 316), regard the sample of 10 sales figures for which $s = 32.866$ as a preliminary sample. How large a sample of sales figures is needed to make us 95 percent confident that $\bar{x}$, the sample mean sales dollars per square foot, is within a margin of error of $10 of μ, the population mean sales dollars per square foot for all Whole Foods supermarkets.   **DS** WholeFoods

8.33 **THE AIR SAFETY CASE**   **DS** AlertTimes

  Referring to Exercise 8.19 (page 316), regard the sample of 15 alert times for which $s = 1.026$ as a preliminary sample. Determine the sample size needed to make us 95 percent confident that $\bar{x}$, the sample mean alert time, is within a margin of error of .3 second of μ, the population mean alert time using the new display panel.

8.4 Confidence Intervals for a Population Proportion ● ● ●

LO8-5 Calculate and interpret a large sample confidence interval for a population proportion.

In Chapter 7, the soft cheese spread producer decided to replace its current spout with the new spout if p, the true proportion of all current purchasers who would stop buying the cheese spread if the new spout were used, is less than .10. Suppose that when 1,000 current purchasers are randomly selected and are asked to try the new spout, 63 say they would stop buying the spread if the new spout were used. The point estimate of the population proportion p is the sample proportion $\hat{p} = 63/1{,}000 = .063$. This sample proportion says we estimate that 6.3 percent of all current purchasers would stop buying the cheese spread if the new spout were used. Since $\hat{p}$ equals .063, we have some evidence that p is less than .10.

In order to see if there is strong evidence that p is less than .10, we can calculate a confidence interval for p. As explained in Chapter 7, if the sample size n is large, then the sampling distribution of the sample proportion $\hat{p}$ is approximately a normal distribution with mean $\mu_{\hat{p}} = p$ and standard deviation $\sigma_{\hat{p}} = \sqrt{p(1-p)/n}$. By using the same logic we used in developing confidence intervals for μ, it follows that a $100(1-\alpha)$ percent confidence interval for p is

$$\left[\hat{p} \pm z_{a/2} \sqrt{\frac{p(1-p)}{n}} \right]$$

Estimating $p(1-p)$ by $\hat{p}(1-\hat{p})$, it follows that a $100(1-\alpha)$ percent confidence interval for p can be calculated as summarized below.

A Large Sample Confidence Interval for a Population Proportion p

If the sample size n is large, a **$100(1-\alpha)$ percent confidence interval for the population proportion p** is

$$\left[\hat{p} \pm z_{\alpha/2} \sqrt{\frac{\hat{p}(1-\hat{p})}{n}} \right]$$

Here n should be considered large if both $n\hat{p}$ and $n(1-\hat{p})$ are at least 5.[2]

EXAMPLE 8.6 The Cheese Spread Case: Improving Profitability

Suppose that the cheese spread producer wishes to calculate a 99 percent confidence interval for p, the population proportion of purchasers who would stop buying the cheese spread if the new spout were used. To determine whether the sample size $n = 1{,}000$ is large enough to enable us to use the confidence interval formula just given, recall that the point estimate of p is $\hat{p} = 63/1{,}000 = .063$. Therefore, because $n\hat{p} = 1{,}000(.063) = 63$ and $n(1-\hat{p}) = 1{,}000(.937) = 937$ are both greater than 5, we can use the confidence interval formula. It follows that the 99 percent confidence interval for p is

$$\left[\hat{p} \pm z_{.005} \sqrt{\frac{\hat{p}(1-\hat{p})}{n}} \right] = \left[.063 \pm 2.575 \sqrt{\frac{(.063)(.937)}{1000}} \right]$$

$$= [.063 \pm .0198]$$

$$= [.0432, .0828]$$

This interval says that we are 99 percent confident that between 4.32 percent and 8.28 percent of all current purchasers would stop buying the cheese spread if the new spout were used. Moreover, because the upper limit of the 99 percent confidence interval is less than .10, we have very strong evidence that the true proportion p of all current purchasers who would stop buying the cheese spread is less than .10. Based on this result, it seems reasonable to use the new spout.

---

[2]Some statisticians suggest using the more conservative rule that both $n\hat{p}$ and $n(1-\hat{p})$ must be at least 10. Furthermore, because $\hat{p}(1-\hat{p})/(n-1)$ is an unbiased point estimate of $p(1-p)/n$, a more correct $100(1-\alpha)$ percent confidence interval for p is $[\hat{p} \pm z_{\alpha/2}\sqrt{\hat{p}(1-\hat{p})/(n-1)}]$. However, because n is large, there is little difference between intervals obtained by using this formula and those obtained by using the formula in the box above.

In order to compare the 99 percent confidence interval for p with a 95 percent confidence interval, we compute the 95 percent confidence interval as follows:

$$\left[\hat{p} \pm z_{.025}\sqrt{\frac{\hat{p}(1-\hat{p})}{n}} \right] = \left[.063 \pm 1.96\sqrt{\frac{(.063)(.937)}{1000}} \right]$$

$$= [.063 \pm .0151]$$

$$= [.0479, .0781]$$

Although the 99 percent confidence interval is somewhat longer than the 95 percent confidence interval, the fairly large sample size of $n = 1,000$ produces intervals that differ only slightly.

In the cheese spread example, a sample of 1,000 purchasers gives us a 99 percent confidence interval for p that has a margin of error of .0198 and a 95 percent confidence interval for p that has a margin of error of .0151. Both of these margins of errors are reasonably small. Generally, however, quite a large sample is needed in order to make the margin of error in a confidence interval for p reasonably small. The next two examples demonstrate that a sample size of 200, which most people would consider quite large, does not necessarily give a 95 percent confidence interval for p with a small margin of error.

EXAMPLE 8.7 The Phe-Mycin Case: Drug Side Effects

Antibiotics occasionally cause nausea as a side effect. Scientists working for a major drug company have developed a new antibiotic called Phe-Mycin. The company wishes to estimate p, the proportion of all patients who would experience nausea as a side effect when being treated with Phe-Mycin. Suppose that a sample of 200 patients is randomly selected. When these patients are treated with Phe-Mycin, 35 patients experience nausea. The point estimate of the population proportion p is the sample proportion $\hat{p} = 35/200 = .175$. This sample proportion says that we estimate that 17.5 percent of all patients would experience nausea as a side effect of taking Phe-Mycin. Furthermore, because $n\hat{p} = 200(.175) = 35$ and $n(1 - \hat{p}) = 200(.825) = 165$ are both at least 5, we can use the previously given formula to calculate a confidence interval for p. Doing this, we find that a 95 percent confidence interval for p is

$$\left[\hat{p} \pm z_{.025}\sqrt{\frac{\hat{p}(1-\hat{p})}{n}} \right] = \left[.175 \pm 1.96\sqrt{\frac{(.175)(.825)}{200}} \right]$$

$$= [.175 \pm .053]$$

$$= [.122, .228]$$

This interval says we are 95 percent confident that between 12.2 percent and 22.8 percent of all patients would experience nausea as a side effect of taking Phe-Mycin. Notice that the margin of error (.053) in this interval is rather large. Therefore, this interval is fairly long, and it does not provide a very precise estimate of p.

EXAMPLE 8.8 The Marketing Ethics Case: Confidentiality

In the book *Essentials of Marketing Research,* William R. Dillon, Thomas J. Madden, and Neil H. Firtle discuss a survey of marketing professionals, the results of which were originally published by Ishmael P. Akoah and Edward A. Riordan in the *Journal of Marketing Research.* In the study, randomly selected marketing researchers were presented with various scenarios involving ethical issues such as confidentiality, conflict of interest, and social acceptability. The marketing researchers were asked to indicate whether they approved or disapproved of the actions described in each scenario. For instance, one scenario that involved the issue of confidentiality was described as follows:

> **Use of ultraviolet ink**   A project director went to the marketing research director's office and requested permission to use an ultraviolet ink to precode a questionnaire for a mail survey. The project director pointed out that although the cover letter promised confidentiality, respondent identification was needed to permit adequate cross-tabulations of the data. The marketing research director gave approval.

Of the 205 marketing researchers who participated in the survey, 117 said they disapproved of the actions taken in the scenario. It follows that a point estimate of p, the proportion of all marketing researchers who disapprove of the actions taken in the scenario, is $\hat{p} = 117/205 = .5707$. Furthermore, because $n\hat{p} = 205(.5707) = 117$ and $n(1 - \hat{p}) = 205(.4293) = 88$ are both at least 5, a 95 percent confidence interval for p is

$$\left[\hat{p} \pm z_{.025}\sqrt{\frac{\hat{p}(1 - \hat{p})}{n}} \right] = \left[.5707 \pm 1.96\sqrt{\frac{(.5707)(.4293)}{205}} \right]$$

$$= [.5707 \pm .0678]$$

$$= [.5029, .6385]$$

This interval says we are 95 percent confident that between 50.29 percent and 63.85 percent of all marketing researchers disapprove of the actions taken in the ultraviolet ink scenario. Notice that because the margin of error (.0678) in this interval is rather large, this interval does not provide a very precise estimate of p. Below we show the MINITAB output of this interval.

```
CI for One Proportion
    X     N     Sample p              95% CI
   117   205    0.570732      (0.502975, 0.638488)
```

In order to find the size of the sample needed to estimate a population proportion, we consider the theoretically correct interval

$$\left[\hat{p} \pm z_{\alpha/2}\sqrt{\frac{p(1 - p)}{n}} \right]$$

To obtain the sample size needed to make the margin of error in this interval equal to E, we set

$$z_{\alpha/2}\sqrt{\frac{p(1 - p)}{n}} = E$$

and solve for n. When we do this, we get the following result:

LO8-6 Determine the appropriate sample size when estimating a population proportion.

Determining the Sample Size for a Confidence Interval for p

A sample of size

$$n = p(1 - p)\left(\frac{z_{\alpha/2}}{E}\right)^2$$

makes the margin of error in a $100(1 - \alpha)$ percent confidence interval for p equal to E. That is, this sample size makes us $100(1 - \alpha)$ percent confident that $\hat{p}$ is within E units of p. If the calculated value of n is not a whole number, round this value up to the next whole number.

Looking at this formula, we see that the larger $p(1 - p)$ is, the larger n will be. To make sure n is large enough, consider Figure 8.16 on the next page, which is a graph of $p(1 - p)$ versus p. This figure shows that $p(1 - p)$ equals .25 when p equals .5. Furthermore, $p(1 - p)$ is never larger than .25. Therefore, if the true value of p could be near .5, we should set $p(1 - p)$ equal to .25. This will ensure that n is as large as needed to make the margin of error as small as desired. For

FIGURE 8.16   The Graph of $p(1 - p)$ versus p

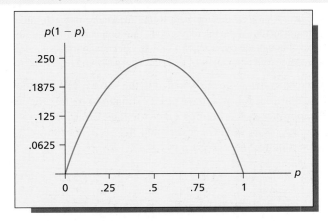

example, suppose we wish to estimate the proportion p of all registered voters who currently favor a particular candidate for president of the United States. If this candidate is the nominee of a major political party, or if the candidate enjoys broad popularity for some other reason, then p could be near .5. Furthermore, suppose we wish to make the margin of error in a 95 percent confidence interval for p equal to .02. If the sample to be taken is random, it should consist of

$$n = p(1 - p)\left(\frac{z_{\alpha/2}}{E}\right)^2 = .25\left(\frac{1.96}{.02}\right)^2 = 2,401$$

registered voters. In reality, a list of all registered voters in the United States is not available to polling organizations. Therefore, it is not feasible to take a (technically correct) random sample of registered voters. For this reason, polling organizations actually employ other (more complicated) kinds of samples. We have explained some of the basic ideas behind these more complex samples in optional Section 7.4. For now, we consider the samples taken by polling organizations to be approximately random. Suppose, then, that when the sample of voters is actually taken, the proportion $\hat{p}$ of sampled voters who favor the candidate turns out to be greater than .52. It follows, because the sample is large enough to make the margin of error in a 95 percent confidence interval for p equal to .02, that the lower limit of such an interval is greater than .50. This says we have strong evidence that a majority of all registered voters favor the candidate. For instance, if the sample proportion $\hat{p}$ equals .53, we are 95 percent confident that the proportion of all registered voters who favor the candidate is between .51 and .55.

Major polling organizations conduct public opinion polls concerning many kinds of issues. While making the margin of error in a 95 percent confidence interval for p equal to .02 requires a sample size of 2,401, making the margin of error in such an interval equal to .03 requires a sample size of only

$$n = p(1 - p)\left(\frac{z_{\alpha/2}}{E}\right)^2 = .25\left(\frac{1.96}{.03}\right)^2 = 1,067.1$$

or 1,068 (rounding up). Of course, these calculations assume that the proportion p being estimated could be near .5. However, for any value of p, increasing the margin of error from .02 to .03 substantially decreases the needed sample size and thus saves considerable time and money. For this reason, although the most accurate public opinion polls use a margin of error of .02, the vast majority of public opinion polls use a margin of error of .03 or larger.

When the news media report the results of a public opinion poll, they express the margin of error in a 95 percent confidence interval for p *in percentage points.* For instance, if the margin of error is .03, the media would say the poll's margin of error is 3 percentage points. The media seldom report the level of confidence, but almost all polling results are based on 95 percent confidence. Sometimes the media make a vague reference to the level of confidence. For instance, if the margin of error is 3 percentage points, the media might say that "the sample result will be within 3 percentage points of the population value in 19 out of 20 samples." Here

FIGURE 8.17   As *p* Gets Closer to .5, *p*(1 − *p*) Increases

the "19 out of 20 samples" is a reference to the level of confidence, which is $100(19/20) = 100(.95) = 95$ percent.

As an example, suppose a news report says a recent poll finds that 34 percent of the public favors military intervention in an international crisis, and suppose the poll's margin of error is reported to be 3 percentage points. This means the sample taken is large enough to make us 95 percent confident that the sample proportion $\hat{p} = .34$ is within .03 (that is, 3 percentage points) of the true proportion p of the entire public that favors military intervention. That is, we are 95 percent confident that p is between .31 and .37.

If the population proportion we are estimating is substantially different from .5, setting p equal to .5 will give a sample size that is much larger than is needed. In this case, we should use our intuition or previous sample information (along with Figure 8.17) to determine the largest reasonable value for $p(1 - p)$. Figure 8.17 implies that as p gets closer to .5, $p(1 - p)$ increases. It follows that $p(1 - p)$ is maximized by the reasonable value of p that is closest to .5. Therefore, **when we are estimating a proportion that is substantially different from .5, we use the reasonable value of p that is closest to .5 to calculate the sample size needed to obtain a specified margin of error.**

EXAMPLE 8.9 The Phe-Mycin Case: Drug Side Effects

Again consider estimating the proportion of all patients who would experience nausea as a side effect of taking the new antibiotic Phe-Mycin. Suppose the drug company wishes to find the size of the random sample that is needed in order to obtain a 2 percent margin of error with 95 percent confidence. In Example 8.7 we employed a sample of 200 patients to compute a 95 percent confidence interval for p. This interval, which is [.122, .228], makes us very confident that p is between .122 and .228. Because .228 is the reasonable value of p that is closest to .5, the largest reasonable value of $p(1 - p)$ is $.228(1 - .228) = .1760$, and thus the drug company should take a sample of

$$n = p(1 - p)\left(\frac{z_{\alpha/2}}{E}\right)^2 = .1760\left(\frac{1.96}{.02}\right)^2 = 1{,}691 \text{ (rounded up)}$$

patients.

Finally, as a last example of choosing p for sample size calculations, suppose that experience indicates that a population proportion p is at least .75. Then, .75 is the reasonable value of p that is closest to .5, and we would use the largest reasonable value of $p(1 - p)$, which is $.75(1 - .75) = .1875$.

Exercises for Section 8.4

CONCEPTS

connect™

8.34 **a** What does a population proportion tell us about the population?
b Explain the difference between p and $\hat{p}$.
c What is meant when a public opinion poll's *margin of error* is 3 percent?

8.35 Suppose we are using the sample size formula in the box on page 323 to find the sample size needed to make the margin of error in a confidence interval for p equal to E. In each of the following situations, explain what value of p would be used in the formula for finding n:
a We have no idea what value p is—it could be any value between 0 and 1.
b Past experience tells us that p is no more than .3.
c Past experience tells us that p is at least .8.

METHODS AND APPLICATIONS

8.36 In each of the following cases, determine whether the sample size n is large enough to use the large sample formula presented in the box on page 321 to compute a confidence interval for p.
a $\hat{p} = .1,\quad n = 30$ **d** $\hat{p} = .8,\quad n = 400$
b $\hat{p} = .1,\quad n = 100$ **e** $\hat{p} = .9,\quad n = 30$
c $\hat{p} = .5,\quad n = 50$ **f** $\hat{p} = .99,\quad n = 200$

8.37 In each of the following cases, compute 95 percent, 98 percent, and 99 percent confidence intervals for the population proportion p.
a $\hat{p} = .4$ and $n = 100$ **c** $\hat{p} = .9$ and $n = 100$
b $\hat{p} = .1$ and $n = 300$ **d** $\hat{p} = .6$ and $n = 50$

8.38 In a news story distributed by the *Washington Post,* Lew Sichelman reports that a substantial fraction of mortgage loans that go into default within the first year of the mortgage were approved on the basis of falsified applications. For instance, loan applicants often exaggerate their income or fail to declare debts. Suppose that a random sample of 1,000 mortgage loans that were defaulted within the first year reveals that 410 of these loans were approved on the basis of falsified applications.
a Find a point estimate of and a 95 percent confidence interval for p, the proportion of all first-year defaults that are approved on the basis of falsified applications.
b Based on your interval, what is a reasonable estimate of the minimum percentage of all first-year defaults that are approved on the basis of falsified applications?

8.39 Suppose that 60 percent of 1000 randomly selected U.S. adults say that they take part in some form of daily activity to keep physically fit. Based on this finding, find a 95 percent confidence interval for the proportion of all U.S. adults who would say they take part in some form of daily activity to keep physically fit. Based on this interval, is it reasonable to conclude that more than 50 percent of all U.S. adults would say they take part in some form of daily activity to keep physically fit?

8.40 In an article in the *Journal of Advertising,* Weinberger and Spotts compare the use of humor in television ads in the United States and the United Kingdom. They found that a substantially greater percentage of U.K. ads use humor.
a Suppose that a random sample of 400 television ads in the United Kingdom reveals that 142 of these ads use humor. Find a point estimate of and a 95 percent confidence interval for the proportion of all U.K. television ads that use humor.
b Suppose a random sample of 500 television ads in the United States reveals that 122 of these ads use humor. Find a point estimate of and a 95 percent confidence interval for the proportion of all U.S. television ads that use humor.
c Do the confidence intervals you computed in parts *a* and *b* suggest that a greater percentage of U.K. ads use humor? Explain. How might an ad agency use this information?

8.41 **THE MARKETING ETHICS CASE: CONFLICT OF INTEREST**

Consider the marketing ethics case described in Example 8.8. One of the scenarios presented to the 205 marketing researchers is as follows:

> A marketing testing firm to which X company gives most of its business recently went public. The marketing research director of X company had been looking for a good investment and proceeded to buy some $20,000 of their stock. The firm continues as X company's leading supplier for testing.

Of the 205 marketing researchers who participated in the ethics survey, 111 said that they disapproved of the actions taken in the scenario. Use this sample result to show that the 95 percent confidence interval for the proportion of all marketing researchers who disapprove of the actions taken in the conflict of interest scenario is as given in the MINITAB output below. Interpret this interval.

CI for One Proportion

X	N	Sample p	95% CI
111	205	0.541463	(0.473254, 0.609673)

8.42 On the basis of the confidence interval given in Exercise 8.41, is there convincing evidence that a majority of all marketing researchers disapprove of the actions taken in the conflict of interest scenario? Explain.

8.43 In an article in *CA Magazine*, Neil Fitzgerald surveyed Scottish business customers concerning their satisfaction with aspects of their banking relationships. Fitzgerald reports that, in 418 telephone interviews conducted by George Street Research, 67 percent of the respondents gave their banks a high rating for overall satisfaction.

   a Assuming that the sample is randomly selected, calculate a 99 percent confidence interval for the proportion of all Scottish business customers who give their banks a high rating for overall satisfaction.

   b Based on this interval, can we be 99 percent confident that more than 60 percent of all Scottish business customers give their banks a high rating for overall satisfaction?

8.44 The manufacturer of the ColorSmart-5000 television set claims 95 percent of its sets last at least five years without needing a single repair. In order to test this claim, a consumer group randomly selects 400 consumers who have owned a ColorSmart-5000 television set for five years. Of these 400 consumers, 316 say their ColorSmart-5000 television sets did not need a repair, whereas 84 say their ColorSmart-5000 television sets did need at least one repair.

   a Find a 99 percent confidence interval for the proportion of all ColorSmart-5000 television sets that have lasted at least five years without needing a single repair.

   b Does this confidence interval provide strong evidence that the percentage of all ColorSmart-5000 television sets that last at least five years without a single repair is less than the 95 percent claimed by the manufacturer? Explain.

8.45 *Consumer Reports* (January 2005) indicates that profit margins on extended warranties are much greater than on the purchase of most products.[3] In this exercise we consider a major electronics retailer that wishes to increase the proportion of customers who buy extended warranties on digital cameras. Historically, 20 percent of digital camera customers have purchased the retailer's extended warranty. To increase this percentage, the retailer has decided to offer a new warranty that is less expensive and more comprehensive. Suppose that three months after starting to offer the new warranty, a random sample of 500 customer sales invoices shows that 152 out of 500 digital camera customers purchased the new warranty. Find a 95 percent confidence interval for the proportion of all digital camera customers who have purchased the new warranty. Are we 95 percent confident that this proportion exceeds .20?

8.46 Consider Exercise 8.39 and suppose we wish to find the sample size n needed in order to be 95 percent confident that $\hat{p}$, the sample proportion of respondents who said they took part in some sort of daily activity to keep physically fit, is within a margin of error of .02 of p, the proportion of all U.S. adults who say that they take part in such activity. In order to find an appropriate value for $p(1 - p)$, note that the 95 percent confidence interval for p that you calculated in Exercise 8.39 was [.57, .63]. This indicates that the reasonable value for p that is closest to .5 is .57, and thus the largest reasonable value for $p(1 - p)$ is $.57(1 - .57) = .2451$. Calculate the required sample size n.

8.47 Referring to Exercise 8.44, determine the sample size needed in order to be 99 percent confident that $\hat{p}$, the sample proportion of ColorSmart-5000 television sets that last at least five years without a single repair, is within a margin of error of .03 of p, the proportion of all sets that last at least five years without a single repair.

8.48 Suppose we conduct a poll to estimate the proportion of voters who favor a major presidential candidate. Assuming that 50 percent of the electorate could be in favor of the candidate, determine the sample size needed so that we are 95 percent confident that $\hat{p}$, the sample proportion of voters who favor the candidate, is within a margin of error of .01 of p, the proportion of all voters who are in favor of the candidate.

---

[3]*Consumer Reports*, January 2005, page 51.

LO8-7 Find and
interpret
confidence intervals
for parameters of
finite populations
(Optional).

8.5 Confidence Intervals for Parameters
of Finite Populations (Optional) ● ● ●

Random sampling   Companies in financial trouble have sometimes falsified their accounts receivable invoices in order to mislead stockholders. For this reason, independent auditors are often asked to estimate a company's true total sales for a given period. To illustrate this, consider a company that sells home theaters. The company accumulated 2,418 sales invoices last year. The total of the sales amounts listed on these invoices (that is, the total sales claimed by the company) is $5,127,492.17. In order to estimate the true total sales for last year, an independent auditor randomly selects 242 of the invoices without replacement and determines the actual sales amounts by contacting the purchasers. The mean and the standard deviation of the actual sales amounts for these invoices are $\bar{x} = \$1,843.93$ and $s = \$516.42$. To use this sample information to estimate the company's true total sales, note that the mean μ of a finite population is the **population total** τ, which is the sum of the values of all of the population measurements, divided by the number, N, of population measurements. That is, we have $\mu = \tau/N$, which implies that $\tau = N\mu$. Because a point estimate of the population mean μ is the sample mean $\bar{x}$, it follows that *a point estimate of the population total τ is $N\bar{x}$.* In the context of estimating the true total sales τ for the home theater company's population of $N = 2,418$ sales invoices, the sample mean invoice amount is $\bar{x} = \$1,843.93$, and thus the point estimate of τ is $N\bar{x} = 2,418(\$1,843.93) = \$4,458,622.74$. This point estimate is considerably lower than the claimed total sales of $5,127,492.17. However, we cannot expect the point estimate of τ to exactly equal the true total sales, so we need to calculate a confidence interval for τ before drawing any unwarranted conclusions.

In general, consider randomly selecting without replacement a large sample of n measurements from a finite population consisting of N measurements and having mean μ and standard deviation σ. It can then be shown that the sampling distribution of the sample mean $\bar{x}$ is approximately a normal distribution with mean $\mu_{\bar{x}} = \mu$ and standard deviation $\sigma_{\bar{x}} = (\sigma/\sqrt{n})\sqrt{(N - n)/(N - 1)}$. Estimating σ by the sample standard deviation s, it can also be shown that the appropriate point estimate of $\sigma_{\bar{x}}$ is $(s/\sqrt{n})\sqrt{(N - n)/N}$, which is used in the following result.

Confidence Intervals for the Population Mean and Population Total for a Finite Population

Suppose we randomly select a sample of n measurements **without replacement from a finite population of N measurements.** Then, if n is large (say, at least 30)

1 A 100(1 — α) percent confidence interval for the population mean μ is

$$\left[\bar{x} \pm z_{\alpha/2} \frac{s}{\sqrt{n}} \sqrt{\frac{N - n}{N}} \right]$$

2 A 100(1 — α) percent confidence interval for the population total τ is found by multiplying the lower and upper limits of the 100(1 — α) percent confidence interval for μ by N.

The quantity $\sqrt{(N - n)/N}$ in the confidence intervals for μ and τ is called the **finite population correction** and is always less than 1. If the population size N is much larger than the sample size n, then the finite population correction is only slightly less than 1. For example, if we randomly select (without replacement) a sample of 1,000 from a population of 1 million, then the finite population correction is $\sqrt{(1,000,000 - 1,000)/1,000,000} = .9995$. In such a case, the finite population correction is not enough less than 1 to meaningfully shorten the confidence intervals for μ and τ and thus can be set equal to 1. However, **if the population size N is not much larger than the sample size n (say, if n is more than 5 percent of N), then the finite population correction is substantially less than 1 and should be included** in the confidence interval calculations.

EXAMPLE 8.10 The Home Theater Case: Auditing Total Sales

Recall that when the independent auditor randomly selects a sample of $n = 242$ invoices, the mean and standard deviation of the actual sales amounts for these invoices are $\bar{x} = 1,843.93$ and $s = 516.42$. Here the sample size $n = 242$ is $(242/2,418) \times 100 = 10.008$ percent of the population size $N = 2,418$. Because n is more than 5 percent of N, we should include the finite population correction in our confidence interval calculations. It follows that a 95 percent confidence interval for the true mean sales amount μ per invoice is

$$\left[\bar{x} \pm z_{.025} \frac{s}{\sqrt{n}} \sqrt{\frac{N-n}{N}} \right] = \left[1,843.93 \pm 1.96 \frac{516.42}{\sqrt{242}} \sqrt{\frac{2,418 - 242}{2,418}} \right]$$

$$= [1,843.93 \pm 61.723812]$$

or [\$1,782.21, \$1,905.65]. Moreover, multiplying the lower and upper limits of this interval by $N = 2,418$, we find that a 95 percent confidence interval for the true total sales τ is $[1,782.21(2,418), 1,905.65(2,418)]$, or [\$4,309,383.80, \$4,607,861.70]. Because the upper limit of this interval is more than \$500,000 below the claimed total sales amount of \$5,127,492.17, we have strong evidence that the claimed total sales amount is overstated.

We sometimes estimate the total number, τ, of population units that fall into a particular category. For instance, the auditor of Example 8.10 might wish to estimate the total number of the 2,418 invoices having incorrect sales amounts. Here the proportion, p, of the population units that fall into a particular category is the total number, τ, of population units that fall into the category divided by the number, N, of population units. That is, $p = \tau/N$, which implies that $\tau = Np$. Therefore, because a point estimate of the population proportion p is the sample proportion $\hat{p}$, a point estimate of the population total τ is $N\hat{p}$. For example, suppose that 34 of the 242 sampled invoices have incorrect sales amounts. Because the sample proportion is $\hat{p} = 34/242 = .1405$, a point estimate of the total number of the 2,418 invoices that have incorrect sales amounts is $N\hat{p} = 2,418(.1405) = 339.729$.

Confidence Intervals for the Proportion of and Total Number of Units in a Category When Sampling a Finite Population

Suppose that we randomly select a sample of n units **without replacement from a finite population of N units.** Then, if n is large

1 A 100(1 — α) percent confidence interval for the population proportion p is

$$\left[\hat{p} \pm z_{\alpha/2} \sqrt{\frac{\hat{p}(1-\hat{p})}{n} \left(\frac{N-n}{N} \right)} \right]$$

2 A 100(1 — α) percent confidence interval for the population total τ is found by multiplying the lower and upper limits of the 100(1 — α) percent confidence interval for p by N.

EXAMPLE 8.11 The Home Theater Case: Auditing Sales Invoices

Recall that we found that 34 of the 242 sampled invoices have incorrect sales amounts. Because $\hat{p} = 34/242 = .1405$, a 95 percent confidence interval for the true proportion of the 2,418 invoices that have incorrect sales amounts is

$$\left[\hat{p} \pm z_{.025} \sqrt{\frac{\hat{p}(1-\hat{p})}{n} \left(\frac{N-n}{N} \right)} \right] = \left[.1405 \pm 1.96 \sqrt{\frac{(.1405)(.8595)}{242} \left(\frac{2,418 - 242}{2,418} \right)} \right]$$

$$= [.1405 \pm .0416]$$

or [.0989, .1821]. Moreover, multiplying the lower and upper limits of this interval by $N = 2{,}418$, we find that a 95 percent confidence interval for the true total number, τ, of the 2,418 sales invoices that have incorrect sales amounts is $[.0989(2{,}418), .1821(2{,}418)]$, or [239.14, 440.32]. Therefore, we are 95 percent confident that between (roughly) 239 and 440 of the 2,418 invoices have incorrect sales amounts.

Stratified random sampling　Recall from Section 7.4 (page 287) that in order to select a *stratified random sample*, we partition the population into nonoverlapping subpopulations called *strata*. Then, we select a random sample from each *stratum*. Also, recall that we have considered a department store chain that proposes to open a new store in a location that would serve a geographical region consisting of three strata: an industrial city, a suburban community, and a rural area. In order to estimate (1) the mean household income in this region and (2) the total number of households in the region that would be likely to patronize the new store, the department store chain randomly selects without replacement 1 percent of the households from each stratum. Each household is asked to (1) report its total household income for the previous year, and (2) indicate whether at least one member of the household would be likely to shop at the new store. Table 8.4 summarizes the size of each stratum (N_i): the size of the sample selected from each stratum (n_i); the mean, variance, and standard deviation of the household incomes sampled from each stratum ($\bar{x}_i$, s_i^2, and s_i); and the proportion of sampled households in each stratum indicating that at least one member of the household would be likely to shop at the new store ($\hat{p}_i$). We now consider the following results.

Estimation in Stratified Random Sampling

Assume that a population is partitioned into k strata, and assume that we randomly select without replacement a sample of n_i measurements from the N_i measurements in the ith stratum. If $\bar{x}_i$, s_i^2, and $\hat{p}_i$ denote the sample mean, sample variance, and sample proportion for the sample selected from the ith stratum, then it can be shown that:

1 A point estimate of the total, τ, of the values of all of the measurements in the entire population is $\hat{\tau} = N_1\bar{x}_1 + N_2\bar{x}_2 + \cdots + N_k\bar{x}_k$. Moreover, if each n_i is large (say, at least 30), a $100(1 - \alpha)$ percent confidence interval for τ is

$$\left[\hat{\tau} \pm z_{\alpha/2} \sqrt{\sum_{i=1}^{k} N_i^2 \left(\frac{N_i - n_i}{N_i} \right) \frac{s_i^2}{n_i}} \right]$$

2 Noting that the total population size is $N = N_1 + N_2 + \cdots + N_k$, a **point estimate of the population mean μ** is $\hat{\mu} = \hat{\tau}/N$, and a $100(1 - \alpha)$ percent confidence interval for μ is found by dividing the lower and upper limits of the $100(1 - \alpha)$ percent confidence interval for τ by N.

3 A point estimate of the total, τ, of the units in the entire population that fall into a category of interest is $\hat{\tau} = N_1\hat{p}_1 + N_2\hat{p}_2 + \cdots + N_k\hat{p}_k$. Moreover, if each n_i is large, a $100(1 - \alpha)$ percent confidence interval for τ is

$$\left[\hat{\tau} \pm z_{\alpha/2} \sqrt{\sum_{i=1}^{k} N_i^2 \left(\frac{N_i - n_i}{N_i} \right) \frac{\hat{p}_i(1 - \hat{p}_i)}{n_i}} \right]$$

4 A point estimate of the population proportion p is $\hat{p} = \hat{\tau}/N$, and a $100(1 - \alpha)$ percent confidence interval for p is found by dividing the lower and upper limits of the $100(1 - \alpha)$ percent confidence interval for τ by N.

TABLE 8.4　A Stratified Random Sample in the Department Store Chain Example

Stratum	N_i	n_i	$\bar{x}_i$	s_i^2	s_i	$\hat{p}_i$
1. Industrial city	12,172	122	$47,287	9,294,621	3048.7	66/122 = .5410
2. Suburb	6,914	69	68,719	25,486,211	5048.4	52/69 = .7536
3. Rural area	3,281	33	56,218	17,186,592	4145.7	22/33 = .6667
	$N = 22{,}367$					

EXAMPLE 8.12 The Department Store Case: Studying Market Demographics

The department store chain has concluded that it should open the new store in the geographical region if (1) it is 95 percent confident that the mean income per household is at least $50,000 and (2) it is 95 percent confident that the total number of households for which at least one household member would be likely to shop at the new store is at least 10,000. Using the information in Table 8.4, a point estimate of the total income, τ, of all households in the geographical region is $\hat{\tau} = N_1\bar{x}_1 + N_2\bar{x}_2 + N_3\bar{x}_3 = 12{,}172(47{,}287) + 6{,}914(68{,}719) + 3{,}281(56{,}218) = 1{,}235{,}150{,}000$ (dollars). To compute a 95 percent confidence interval for τ, we first compute the margin of error in this interval, which is

$$z_{.025}\sqrt{\sum_{i=1}^{k} N_i^2 \left(\frac{N_i - n_i}{N_i}\right)\frac{s_i^2}{n_i}}$$

$$= 1.96\sqrt{(12{,}172)^2\left(\frac{9{,}294{,}621}{122}\right) + (6{,}914)^2\left(\frac{25{,}486{,}211}{69}\right) + (3{,}281)^2\left(\frac{17{,}186{,}592}{33}\right)}$$

$$= 11{,}520{,}869.50$$

Here, we have set each $(N_i - n_i)/N_i$ equal to 1, because each n_i is only 1 percent of N_i. It follows that the 95 percent confidence interval for τ is [1,235,150,000 ± 11,520,869.50], or [$1,223,629,130.50, $1,246,670,869.50]. Dividing the point estimate of τ, $\hat{\tau} = $1,235,150,000, by the population size $N = 22{,}367$ (see Table 8.4), we find that the point estimate of μ, the mean income per household, is $\hat{\mu} = $55,222. Dividing the lower and upper limits of the 95 percent confidence interval for τ by $N = 22{,}367$, we find that the 95 percent confidence interval for μ is [$54,707, $55,737]. This interval makes the department store chain 95 percent confident that the mean income per household is at least $50,000. Therefore, the first condition for opening the new store is met.

Now considering the second condition for opening the new store, note that the point estimate of the true total number, τ, of households in the geographical region for which at least one household member would be likely to shop at the new store is $\hat{\tau} = N_1\hat{p}_1 + N_2\hat{p}_2 + N_3\hat{p}_3 = 12{,}172(.5410) + 6{,}914(.7536) + 3{,}281(.6667) = 13{,}983$. In addition, the margin of error in the 95 percent confidence interval for τ is

$$z_{.025}\sqrt{\sum_{i=1}^{k} N_i^2 \left(\frac{N_i - n_i}{N_i}\right)\frac{\hat{p}_i(1 - \hat{p}_i)}{n_i}}$$

$$= 1.96\sqrt{(12{,}172)^2\frac{(.5410)(.4590)}{122} + (6{,}914)^2\frac{(.7536)(.2464)}{69} + (3{,}281)^2\frac{(.6667)(.3333)}{33}} = 1{,}399$$

where we again have set each $(N_i - n_i)/N_i$ equal to 1. It follows that the 95 percent confidence interval for τ is [13,983 ± 1399], or [12,584, 15,382]. This interval makes the department store chain 95 percent confident that the true total number of households in the geographical region for which at least one household member would be likely to shop at the new store is between 12,584 households and 15,382 households. Because the department store chain is 95 percent confident that this total is at least 10,000, the second condition for opening the new store is met, and the new store will be opened.

To conclude this example, we will find a point estimate of and a 95 percent confidence interval for the true proportion, p, of households in the geographical region for which at least one household member would be likely to shop at the new store. Dividing the previously calculated point estimate of τ, $\hat{\tau} = 13{,}983$, by the total number of households in the geographical region, $N = 22{,}367$, we find that the point estimate of p is .6252. Dividing the lower and upper limits of the previously calculated 95 percent confidence interval for τ, [12,584, 15,832], by $N = 22{,}367$, we find that the 95 percent confidence interval for p is [.5626, .6877].

Exercises for Section 8.5

CONCEPTS

8.49 Define a population total. Give an example of a population total that will interest you in your career when you graduate from college.

8.50 Explain why the finite population correction $\sqrt{(N - n)/N}$ is unnecessary when the population is at least 20 times as large as the sample. Give an example using numbers.

METHODS AND APPLICATIONS

8.51 A retailer that sells audio and video equipment accumulated 10,451 sales invoices during the previous year. The total of the sales amounts listed on these invoices (that is, the total sales claimed by the company) is $6,384,675. In order to estimate the true total sales for last year, an independent auditor randomly selects 350 of the invoices and determines the actual sales amounts by contacting the purchasers. The mean and the standard deviation of the 350 sampled sales amounts are $\bar{x} = \$532$ and $s = \$168$.

    a Find a 95 percent confidence interval for μ, the true mean sales amount per invoice on the 10,451 invoices.

    b Find a point estimate of and a 95 percent confidence interval for τ, the true total sales for the previous year.

    c What does this interval say about the company's claim that the true total sales were $6,384,675? Explain.

8.52 A personnel manager is estimating the total number of person-days lost to unexcused absences by hourly workers in the last year. In a random sample of 50 employees drawn without replacement from the 687 hourly workers at the company, records show that the 50 sampled workers had an average of $\bar{x} = 4.3$ days of unexcused absences over the past year with a standard deviation of $s = 1.26$.

    a Find a point estimate of and a 95 percent confidence interval for the total number of unexcused absences by hourly workers in the last year.

    b Can the personnel manager be 95 percent confident that more than 2,500 person-days were lost to unexcused absences last year? Can the manager be 95 percent confident that more than 3,000 person-days were lost to unexcused absences last year? Explain.

8.53 A company's manager is considering simplification of a travel voucher form. In order to assess the costs associated with erroneous travel vouchers, the manager must estimate the total number of such vouchers that were filled out incorrectly in the last month. In a random sample of 100 vouchers drawn without replacement from the 1,323 travel vouchers submitted in the last month, 31 vouchers were filled out incorrectly.

    a Find a point estimate of and a 95 percent confidence interval for the true proportion of travel vouchers that were filled out incorrectly in the last month.

    b Find a point estimate of and a 95 percent confidence interval for the total number of travel vouchers that were filled out incorrectly in the last month.

    c If it costs the company $10 to correct an erroneous travel voucher, find a reasonable estimate of the minimum cost of correcting all of last month's erroneous travel vouchers. Would it be worthwhile to spend $5,000 to design a simplified travel voucher that could be used for at least a year?

8.54 SAMPLE SIZES WHEN RANDOM SAMPLING FINITE POPULATIONS

    a *Estimating μ and τ*

        Consider randomly selecting a sample of n measurements without replacement from a finite population consisting of N measurements and having variance σ^2. Also consider the sample size given by the formula $n = N\sigma^2/[(N - 1)D + \sigma^2]$. It can be shown that this sample size makes the margin of error in a $100(1 - \alpha)$ percent confidence interval for μ equal to E if we set D equal to $(E/z_{\alpha/2})^2$. It can also be shown that this sample size makes the margin of error in a $100(1 - \alpha)$ percent confidence interval for τ equal to E if we set D equal to $[E/(z_{\alpha/2}N)]^2$. Now consider Exercise 8.52. Using $s^2 = (1.26)^2 = 1.5876$ as an estimate of σ^2, determine the sample size that makes the margin of error in a 95 percent confidence interval for the *total number* of person-days lost to unexcused absences last year equal to 100 days.

    b *Estimating p and τ*

        Consider randomly selecting a sample of n units without replacement from a finite population consisting of N units and having a proportion p of these units fall into a particular category.

Also, consider the sample size given by the formula $n = Np(1 - p)/[(N - 1)D + p(1 - p)]$. It can be shown that this sample size makes the margin of error in a $100(1 - \alpha)$ percent confidence interval for p equal to E if we set D equal to $(E/z_{\alpha/2})^2$. It can also be shown that this sample size makes the margin of error in a $100(1 - \alpha)$ percent confidence interval for τ equal to E if we set D equal to $[E/(z_{\alpha/2}N)]^2$. Now consider Exercise 8.53. Using $\hat{p} = .31$ as an estimate of p, determine the sample size that makes the margin of error in a 95 percent confidence interval for the *proportion* of the 1,323 vouchers that were filled out incorrectly equal to .04.

8.55 The accounts of an investment firm have been classified into 143 large accounts, 4,780 medium-sized accounts, and 20,973 small accounts. The investment firm provides an auditor with each account's *book value*. This is the amount of money that the firm claims is in the account. The auditor determines an account's *audit value* by contacting the owner of the account. This is the amount of money that is actually in the account.

The auditor wishes to detect discrepancies between the stated book values and the audit values. Because it is time consuming and expensive to obtain the audit values, a stratified random sample of accounts is selected, and the difference between the book value and the audit value is determined for each sampled account. The following results are obtained.

Stratum	Number of Accounts in Stratum	Sample Size	Sample Mean Difference	Sample Standard Deviation	Sample Proportion of Accounts Overstated
Large	143	72	$10,661	$5,056	.83
Medium-sized	4,780	239	1,213	671	.94
Small	20,973	210	19	159	.37

a Find point estimates of and 95 percent confidence intervals for the true total, τ, and the true mean, μ, of the differences between the book values and the audit values for the population of all of the investment firm's accounts.

b Find point estimates of and 95 percent confidence intervals for the true total number, τ, and the true proportion, p, of overstated accounts among all of the investment firm's accounts.

c What do you conclude? Why was stratified random sampling important in this situation?

8.56 SAMPLE SIZES IN STRATIFIED RANDOM SAMPLING

Although the department store chain in Example 8.12 has randomly selected 1 percent of the homes in each stratum, there is a more precise way to determine how to sample the strata. The first step is to determine the **optimal fraction,** f_i, of the total sample size, n, that will be **allocated** to the ith stratum. This optimal fraction can be proven to give the shortest confidence intervals for a fixed sample size and can be proven to equal

$$f_i = \frac{N_i\sigma_i/\sqrt{c_i}}{N_1\sigma_1/\sqrt{c_1} + N_2\sigma_2/\sqrt{c_2} + \cdots + N_k\sigma_k/\sqrt{c_k}}$$

Here, c_i is the cost of sampling the ith stratum, and σ_i is the true standard deviation of the measurements in the ith stratum. If the sampling costs are equal (as they might be when conducting telephone interviews), $f_i = N_i\sigma_i/(N_1\sigma_1 + N_2\sigma_2 + \cdots + N_k\sigma_k)$. In the department store example, we will assume that the sampling costs are equal, and we will estimate σ_1, σ_2, and σ_3 by s_1, s_2, and s_3. We can then estimate $N_1\sigma_1$, $N_2\sigma_2$, and $N_3\sigma_3$ to be $N_1s_1 = 37,108,776$, $N_2s_2 = 34,904,638$, and $N_3s_3 = 13,602,042$. Here, we have used the N_i and s_i values in Table 8.4 on page 330. The sum $(N_1s_1 + N_2s_2 + N_3s_3)$ is 85,615,456. Therefore, the optimal sampling fractions are: $f_1 = 37,108,776/85,615,456 = .4334$, $f_2 = 34,904,638/85,615,456 = .4077$, and $f_3 = 13,602,042/85,615,456 = .1589$. Next, consider the sample size formula

$$n = \frac{\sum_{i=1}^{k} N_i^2\sigma_i^2/f_i}{N^2D + \sum_{i=1}^{k} N_i\sigma_i^2}$$

It can be shown that this sample size makes the margin of error in a $100(1 - \alpha)$ percent confidence interval for μ equal to E if we set D equal to $(E/z_{\alpha/2})^2$. It can also be shown that this sample size makes the margin of error in a $100(1 - \alpha)$ percent confidence interval for τ equal to E if we set D equal to $[E/(z_{\alpha/2}N)]^2$. For example, consider the department store chain situation and determining the sample size that makes the margin of error in a 95 percent confidence interval for the mean income per household equal to \$200. In this case, $D = (E/z_{\alpha/2})^2 = (200/1.96)^2 = 10,412.328$. Then, using the previously obtained optimal sampling fractions $f_1, f_2,$ and f_3, and using $s_1^2, s_2^2,$ and s_3^2 in Table 8.4 as estimates of $\sigma_1^2, \sigma_2^2,$ and σ_3^2, we can make the following calculations:

$$\sum_{i=1}^{3} N_i^2 s_i^2 / f_i = 7.3299917 \times 10^{15} \qquad \left(N^2 D + \sum_{i=1}^{3} N_i s_i^2\right) = 5.5548425 \times 10^{12}$$

The needed sample size n is the ratio of these numbers. That is:

$$n = 7.3299917/5.5548425 \times 10^3 = 1320$$

The sizes of the samples to be selected from strata 1, 2, and 3 are then $n_1 = .4334n, n_2 = .4077n$, and $n_3 = .1589n$. Find these sample sizes.

Note: We have given the optimal allocation formulas and the sample size formulas for estimating μ and τ. When estimating p and τ, we use the same formulas that are used for μ and τ, except that we replace σ_i by $\sqrt{p_i(1 - p_i)}$ and σ_i^2 by $p_i(1 - p_i)$, where p_i is the true proportion for the ith stratum. Here, we can estimate $p_i(1 - p_i)$ by the results of a previously taken sample. For example, consider the department store chain situation and Table 8.4. Then, because $\hat{p}_1 = .5410, \hat{p}_2 = .7536$, and $\hat{p}_3 = .6667$, estimates of $p_1(1 - p_1), p_2(1 - p_2),$ and $p_3(1 - p_3)$ are, respectively, .5410(.4590), .7536(.2464), and .6667(.3333).

Chapter Summary

In this chapter we discussed **confidence intervals** for population **means** and **proportions.** First, we studied how to compute a confidence interval for a **population mean.** We saw that when the population standard deviation σ is known, we can use the **normal distribution** to compute a confidence interval for a population mean. When σ is not known, if the population is normally distributed (or at least mound-shaped) or if the sample size n is large, we use the t **distribution** to compute this interval. We also studied how to find the size of the sample needed if we wish to compute a confidence interval for a mean with a prespecified *confidence level* and with a prespecified *margin of error.* Figure 8.18 is a flowchart summarizing our discussions concerning how to compute an appropriate confidence interval for a population mean.

Next we saw that we are often interested in estimating the proportion of population units falling into a category of interest. We showed how to compute a large sample confidence interval for a **population proportion,** and we saw how to find the sample size needed to estimate a population proportion. We concluded this chapter with an optional section that discusses how to estimate means, proportions, and totals for finite populations.

Glossary of Terms

confidence coefficient: The (before sampling) probability that a confidence interval for a population parameter will contain the population parameter. (page 304)

confidence interval: An interval of numbers computed so that we can be very confident (say, 95 percent confident) that a population parameter is contained in the interval. (page 301)

confidence level: The percentage of time that a confidence interval would contain a population parameter if all possible samples were used to calculate the interval. (pages 301, 303, and 306)

degrees of freedom (for a t curve): A parameter that describes the exact spread of the curve of a t distribution. (page 310)

margin of error: The quantity that is added to and subtracted from a point estimate of a population parameter to obtain a confidence interval for the parameter. (page 306)

population total: The sum of the values of all the population measurements. (page 328)

standard error of the estimate $\bar{x}$: The point estimate of $\sigma_{\bar{x}}$. (page 314)

t distribution: A commonly used continuous probability distribution that is described by a distribution curve similar to a normal curve. The t curve is symmetrical about zero and is more spread out than a standard normal curve. (pages 310 and 311)

t point, t_α: The point on the horizontal axis under a t curve that gives a right-hand tail area equal to α. (page 310)

t table: A table of t point values listed according to the area in the tail of the t curve and according to values of the degrees of freedom. (pages 310–312)

FIGURE 8.18 Computing an Appropriate Confidence Interval for a Population Mean

Important Formulas

A z-based confidence interval for a population mean μ with σ known: page 307

A t-based confidence interval for a population mean μ with σ unknown: page 312

Sample size when estimating μ: page 318

A large sample confidence interval for a population proportion p: page 321

Sample size when estimating p: page 323

Confidence intervals for the population mean and total of a finite population: page 328

Confidence intervals for the proportion of and total number of units in a category (finite populations): page 329

Estimation in stratified random sampling: page 330

Supplementary Exercises

connect

8.57 In an article in the *Journal of Accounting Research,* Ashton, Willingham, and Elliott studied audit delay (the length of time from a company's fiscal year-end to the date of the auditor's report) for industrial and financial companies. In the study, a random sample of 250 industrial companies yielded a mean audit delay of 68.04 days with a standard deviation of 35.72 days, while a random sample of 238 financial companies yielded a mean audit delay of 56.74 days with a standard deviation of 34.87 days. Use these sample results to do the following:

   a Calculate a 95 percent confidence interval for the mean audit delay for all industrial companies. Note: $t_{.025} = 1.97$ when $df = 249$.

   b Calculate a 95 percent confidence interval for the mean audit delay for all financial companies. Note: $t_{.025} = 1.97$ when $df = 237$.

c By comparing the 95 percent confidence intervals you calculated in parts *a* and *b*, is there strong evidence that the mean audit delay for financial companies is shorter than the mean audit delay for industrial companies? Explain.

8.58 In an article in *Accounting and Business Research,* Beattie and Jones investigate the use and abuse of graphic presentations in the annual reports of United Kingdom firms. The authors found that 65 percent of the sampled companies graph at least one key financial variable, but that 30 percent of the graphics are materially distorted (nonzero vertical axis, exaggerated trend, or the like). Results for U.S. firms have been found to be similar.

a Suppose that in a random sample of 465 graphics from the annual reports of United Kingdom firms, 142 of the graphics are found to be distorted. Find a point estimate of and a 95 percent confidence interval for the proportion of all U.K. annual report graphics that are distorted.

b Based on this interval, can we be 95 percent confident that more than 25 percent of all graphics appearing in the annual reports of U.K. firms are distorted? Explain. Does this suggest that auditors should understand proper graphing methods?

c Determine the sample size needed in order to be 95 percent confident that $\hat{p}$, the sample proportion of U.K. annual report graphics that are distorted, is within a margin of error of .03 of *p*, the population proportion of all U.K. annual report graphics that are distorted.

8.59 THE DISK BRAKE CASE

National Motors has equipped the ZX-900 with a new disk brake system. We define the stopping distance for a ZX-900 to be the distance (in feet) required to bring the automobile to a complete stop from a speed of 35 mph under normal driving conditions using this new brake system. In addition, we define μ to be the mean stopping distance of all ZX-900s. One of the ZX-900's major competitors is advertised to achieve a mean stopping distance of 60 feet. National Motors would like to claim in a new advertising campaign that the ZX-900 achieves a shorter mean stopping distance.

Suppose that National Motors randomly selects a sample of $n = 81$ ZX-900s. The company records the stopping distance of each automobile and calculates the mean and standard deviation of the sample of $n = 81$ stopping distances to be $\bar{x} = 57.8$ ft and $s = 6.02$ ft.

a Calculate a 95 percent confidence interval for μ. Can National Motors be 95 percent confident that μ is less than 60 ft? Explain.

b Using the sample of $n = 81$ stopping distances as a preliminary sample, find the sample size necessary to make National Motors 95 percent confident that $\bar{x}$ is within a margin of error of one foot of μ.

8.60 In an article in the *Journal of Retailing,* J. G. Blodgett, D. H. Granbois, and R. G. Walters investigated negative word-of-mouth consumer behavior. In a random sample of 201 consumers, 150 reported that they engaged in negative word-of-mouth behavior (for instance, they vowed never to patronize a retailer again). In addition, the 150 respondents who engaged in such behavior, on average, told 4.88 people about their dissatisfying experience (with a standard deviation equal to 6.11).

a Use these sample results to compute a 95 percent confidence interval for the proportion of all consumers who engage in negative word-of-mouth behavior. On the basis of this interval, would it be reasonable to claim that more than 70 percent of all consumers engage in such behavior? Explain.

b Use the sample results to compute a 95 percent confidence interval for the population mean number of people who are told about a dissatisfying experience by consumers who engage in negative word-of-mouth behavior. On the basis of this interval, would it be reasonable to claim that these dissatisfied consumers tell, on average, at least three people about their bad experience? Explain. Note: $t_{.025} = 1.98$ when $df = 149$.

8.61 THE CIGARETTE ADVERTISEMENT CASE   DS ModelAge

A random sample of 50 perceived age estimates for a model in a cigarette advertisement showed that $\bar{x} = 26.22$ years and that $s = 3.7432$ years.

a Use this sample to calculate a 95 percent confidence interval for the population mean age estimate for all viewers of the ad.

b Remembering that the cigarette industry requires that models must appear at least 25 years old, does the confidence interval make us 95 percent confident that the population mean perceived age estimate is at least 25? Is the mean perceived age estimate much more than 25? Explain.

8.62   How safe are child car seats? *Consumer Reports* (May 2005) tested the safety of child car seats in 30 mph crashes. They found "slim safety margins" for some child car seats. Suppose that *Consumer Reports* simulates the safety of the market-leading child car seat. Their test consists of placing the maximum claimed weight in the car seat and simulating crashes at higher and higher miles per hour until a problem occurs. The following data identify the speed at which a problem with the car seat (such as the strap breaking, seat shell cracked, strap adjuster broke, detached from base, etc.) first appeared: 31.0, 29.4, 30.4, 28.9, 29.7, 30.1, 32.3, 31.7, 35.4, 29.1, 31.2, 30.2. Using the fact that $\bar{x} = 30.7833$ and $s = 1.7862$, find a 95 percent confidence interval for the mean speed at which a problem with the car seat first appears. Are we 95 percent confident that this mean is at least 30 mph? **DS** CarSeat

8.63   The manager of a chain of discount department stores wishes to estimate the total number of erroneous discounts allowed by sales clerks during the last month. A random sample of 1000 of the chain's 57,532 transactions for the last month reveals that erroneous discounts were allowed on 41 of the transactions. Use this sample information to find a point estimate of and a 95 percent confidence interval for the total number of erroneous discounts allowed during the last month.

Appendix 8.1 ■ Confidence Intervals Using Excel

Confidence interval for a population mean in Figure 8.12 on page 315 (data file: DebtEq.xlsx):

- Enter the debt-to-equity ratio data from Example 8.2 (page 313) into cells A2 to A16 with the label Ratio in cell A1.
- Select **Data : Data Analysis : Descriptive Statistics**.
- Click OK in the Data Analysis dialog box.
- In the Descriptive Statistics dialog box, enter A1:A16 into the Input Range window.
- Place a checkmark in the "Labels in first row" checkbox.
- Under output options, select "New Worksheet Ply" to have the output placed in a new worksheet and enter the name Output for the new worksheet.
- Place checkmarks in the Summary Statistics and "Confidence Level for Mean" checkboxes. This produces a *t*-based margin of error for a confidence interval.
- Type 95 in the "Confidence Level for Mean" box.
- Click OK in the Descriptive Statistics dialog box.
- A descriptive statistics summary will be displayed in cells A3 through B16 in the Output worksheet. Drag the column borders to reveal complete labels for all of the descriptive statistics.
- Type the heading "95% Confidence Interval" into cells D13 through E13.
- Compute the lower bound of the interval by typing the cell formula = B3 − B16 into cell D14. This subtracts the margin of error of the interval (labeled "Confidence Level (95%)") from the sample mean.
- Compute the upper bound of the interval by typing the formula = B3 + B16 into cell E14.

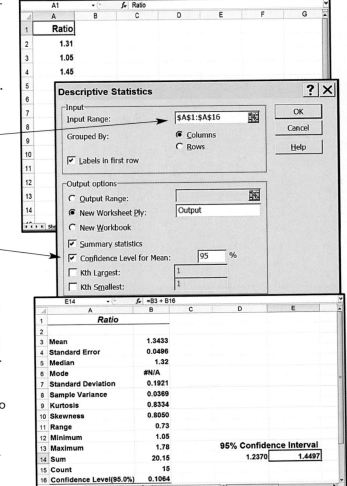

Appendix 8.2 ■ Confidence Intervals Using MegaStat

Confidence interval for the population mean debt-to-equity ratio in Example 8.2 on page 313:

- Select **Add-Ins : MegaStat : Confidence Intervals / Sample Size**

- In the "Confidence Intervals / Sample Size" dialog box, click on the "Confidence Interval—mean" tab.

- Enter the sample mean (here equal to 1.3433) into the Mean window.

- Enter the sample standard deviation (here equal to .1921) into the "Std Dev" window.

- Enter the sample size (here equal to 15) into the "n" window.

- Select a level of confidence from the pull-down menu or type a desired percentage.

- Select a *t*-based or *z*-based interval by clicking on "t" or "z." Here we request a *t*-based interval.

- Click OK in the "Confidence Intervals / Sample Size" dialog box.

Confidence interval for a population proportion in the cheese spread situation of Example 8.6 on page 321:

- In the "Confidence Intervals / Sample Size" dialog box, click on the "Confidence interval—p" tab.

- Enter the sample proportion (here equal to .063) into the "p" window.

- Enter the sample size (here equal to 1000) into the "n" window.

- Select a level of confidence from the pull-down menu or type a desired percentage.

- Click OK in the "Confidence Intervals / Sample Size" dialog box.

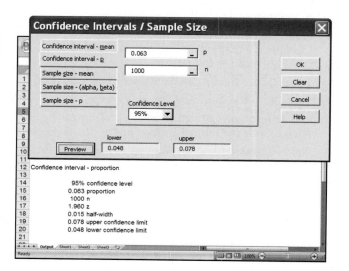

Sample size determination for a proportion problem on page 324:

- In the "Confidence Intervals / Sample Size" dialog box, click on the "Sample size—p" tab.

- Enter the desired margin of error (here equal to 0.02) into the "E" window and enter an estimate of the population proportion into the "p" window.

- Select a level of confidence from the pull-down menu or type a desired percentage.

- Click OK in the "Confidence Intervals / Sample Size" dialog box.

Sample size determination for a population mean problem is done by clicking on the "Sample Size—mean" tab. Then enter a desired margin of error, an estimate of the population standard deviation, and the desired level of confidence. Click OK.

Appendix 8.3 ■ Confidence Intervals Using MINITAB

Confidence interval for a population mean in Figure 8.11 on page 315 (data file: DebtEq.MTW):

- In the Data window, enter the debt-to-equity ratio data from Example 8.2 (page 313) into a single column with variable name Ratio.
- Select **Stat : Basic Statistics : 1-Sample t.**
- In the "1-Sample t (Test and Confidence Interval)" dialog box, select "Samples in columns."
- Select the variable name Ratio into the "Samples in columns" window.
- Click the Options... button.
- In the "1-Sample t—Options" dialog box, enter the desired level of confidence (here 95.0) into the "Confidence level" window.
- Select "not equal" from the Alternative drop-down menu, and click OK in the "1-Sample t—Options" dialog box.
- To produce a boxplot of the data with a graphical representation of the confidence interval, click the Graphs... button, check the "Boxplot of data" checkbox, and click OK in the "1-Sample t—Graphs" dialog box.
- Click OK in "1-Sample t (Test and Confidence Interval)" dialog box.
- The confidence interval is given in the Session window, and the boxplot appears in a graphics window.

A "1-Sample Z" interval requiring a user-specified value of the population standard deviation is also available under Basic Statistics.

Confidence interval for a population proportion in the marketing ethics situation of Example 8.8 on pages 322 and 323:

- Select **Stat : Basic Statistics : 1 Proportion**
- In the "1 Proportion (Test and Confidence Interval)" dialog box, select "Summarized data."
- Enter the number of trials (here equal to 205) and the number of successes (or events) (here equal to 117) into the appropriate windows.
- Click on the Options... button.
- In the "1 Proportion—Options" dialog box, enter the desired level of confidence (here 95.0) into the "Confidence level" window.
- Select "not equal" from the Alternative drop-down menu.
- Check the "Use test and interval based on normal distribution" checkbox.
- Click OK in the "1 Proportion—Options" dialog box.
- Click OK in the "1 Proportion (Test and Confidence Interval)" dialog box.
- The confidence interval will be displayed in the Session window.

CHAPTER 9

Hypothesis Testing

Learning Objectives

After mastering the material in this chapter, you will be able to:

LO9-1 Set up appropriate null and alternative hypotheses.

LO9-2 Describe Type I and Type II errors and their probabilities.

LO9-3 Use critical values and *p*-values to perform a *z* test about a population mean when σ is known.

LO9-4 Use critical values and *p*-values to perform a *t* test about a population mean when σ is unknown.

LO9-5 Use critical values and *p*-values to perform a large sample *z* test about a population proportion.

LO9-6 Calculate Type II error probabilities and the power of a test, and determine sample size (Optional).

Chapter Outline

Hypothesis testing is a statistical procedure used to provide evidence in favor of some statement (called a *hypothesis*). For instance, hypothesis testing might be used to assess whether a population parameter, such as a population mean, differs from a specified standard or previous value. In this chapter we discuss testing hypotheses about population means and proportions.

In order to illustrate how hypothesis testing works, we revisit several cases introduced in previous chapters and also introduce some new cases:

The e-billing Case: The consulting firm uses hypothesis testing to provide strong evidence that the new electronic billing system has reduced the mean payment time by more than 50 percent.

The Cheese Spread Case: The cheese spread producer uses hypothesis testing to supply extremely strong evidence that fewer than 10 percent of all current purchasers would stop buying the cheese spread if the new spout were used.

The Commercial Loan Case: The bank uses hypothesis testing to provide strong evidence that the mean debt-to-equity ratio for its portfolio of commercial loans is less than 1.5.

The Trash Bag Case: A marketer of trash bags uses hypothesis testing to support its claim that the mean breaking strength of its new trash bag is greater than 50 pounds. As a result, a television network approves use of this claim in a commercial.

The Valentine's Day Chocolate Case: A candy company projects that this year's sales of its special valentine box of assorted chocolates will be 10 percent higher than last year. The candy company uses hypothesis testing to assess whether it is reasonable to plan for a 10 percent increase in sales of the valentine box.

9.1 The Null and Alternative Hypotheses and Errors in Hypothesis Testing ● ● ●

LO9-1 Set up appropriate null and alternative hypotheses.

One of the authors' former students is employed by a major television network in the standards and practices division. One of the division's responsibilities is to reduce the chances that advertisers will make false claims in commercials run on the network. Our former student reports that the network uses a statistical methodology called **hypothesis testing** to do this.

To see how this might be done, suppose that a company wishes to advertise a claim, and suppose that the network has reason to doubt that this claim is true. The network assumes for the sake of argument that **the claim is not valid.** This assumption is called the **null hypothesis.** The statement that **the claim is valid** is called the **alternative,** or **research, hypothesis.** The network will run the commercial only if the company making the claim provides **sufficient sample evidence** to reject the null hypothesis that the claim is not valid in favor of the alternative hypothesis that the claim is valid. Explaining the exact meaning of *sufficient sample evidence* is quite involved and will be discussed as we proceed through this chapter.

The Null Hypothesis and the Alternative Hypothesis

In hypothesis testing:

1 The **null hypothesis,** denoted H_0, is the statement being tested. Often, the null hypothesis is a statement of "no difference" or "no effect." The null hypothesis is not rejected unless there is convincing sample evidence that it is false.

2 The **alternative,** or **research, hypothesis,** denoted H_a, is a statement that will be accepted only if there is convincing sample evidence that it is true.

Setting up the null and alternative hypotheses in a practical situation can be tricky. In some situations there is a statement about a population parameter (such as a population mean) for which we need to attempt to find supportive evidence. If the statement says that the parameter is "greater than" a particular number, or if the statement says that the parameter is "less than" a particular number, then (for reasons to be discussed later) we make the statement the *alternative hypothesis, H_a,* and we make the opposite of the statement the *null hypothesis, H_0.* We illustrate these ideas in the following two cases.

EXAMPLE 9.1   The Trash Bag Case[1]: Testing An Advertising Claim

A leading manufacturer of trash bags produces the strongest trash bags on the market. The company has developed a new 30-gallon bag using a specially formulated plastic that is stronger and more biodegradable than other plastics. This plastic's increased strength allows the bag's thickness to be reduced, and the resulting cost savings will enable the company to lower its bag price by 25 percent. The company also believes the new bag is stronger than its current 30-gallon bag.

The manufacturer wants to advertise the new bag on a major television network. In addition to promoting its price reduction, the company also wants to claim the new bag is better for the environment and stronger than its current bag. The network is convinced of the bag's environmental advantages on scientific grounds. However, the network questions the company's claim of increased strength and requires statistical evidence to justify this claim. Although there are various measures of bag strength, the manufacturer and the network agree to employ "breaking strength." A bag's breaking strength is the amount of a representative trash mix (in pounds) that, when loaded into a bag suspended in the air, will cause the bag to rip or tear. Tests show that the current bag has a mean breaking strength that is very close to (but does not exceed) 50 pounds. The new bag's mean breaking strength μ is unknown and in question. Because the trash bag manufacturer wishes to show that *μ is greater than 50 pounds,* we make the statement that *μ is greater than 50 pounds* the alternative hypothesis, H_a, and we make the statement that *μ is less than or equal to 50 pounds* the null hypothesis, H_0. (Note that the *null hypothesis* says that the new trash bag is *not stronger* than the current bag.) We summarize the null and alternative hypotheses by saying that we are testing

$$H_0: \mu \leq 50 \quad \text{versus} \quad H_a: \mu > 50$$

The network will run the manufacturer's commercial if a random sample of n new bags provides sufficient evidence to reject $H_0: \mu \leq 50$ in favor of $H_a: \mu > 50$.

EXAMPLE 9.2   The e-billing Case: Reducing Mean Bill Payment Time

Recall that a management consulting firm has installed a new computer-based electronic billing system for a Hamilton, Ohio, trucking company. Because of the system's advantages, and because the trucking company's clients are receptive to using this system, the management consulting firm believes that the new system will reduce the mean bill payment time by more than 50 percent. The mean payment time using the old billing system was approximately equal to, but no less than, 39 days. Therefore, if μ denotes the mean payment time using the new system, the consulting firm believes and wishes to show that *μ is less than 19.5 days.* It follows that we make the statement that *μ is less than 19.5 days* the alternative hypothesis, H_a, and we make the statement that *μ is greater than or equal to 19.5 days* the null hypothesis, H_0. The consulting firm will randomly select a sample of n invoices and determine if their payment times provide sufficient evidence to reject $H_0: \mu \geq 19.5$ in favor of $H_a: \mu < 19.5$. If such evidence exists, the consulting firm will conclude that the new electronic billing system has reduced the Hamilton trucking company's mean bill payment time by more than 50 percent. This conclusion will be used to help demonstrate the benefits of the new billing system both to the Hamilton company and to other trucking companies that are considering using such a system.

---

[1]This case is based on conversations by the authors with several employees working for a leading producer of trash bags. For purposes of confidentiality, we have agreed to withhold the company's name.

In some situations we need to evaluate a statement that says that a population parameter exactly equals a particular number. It then follows that we make the statement that the population parameter *equals* the particular number the *null hypothesis, H_0*, and we make the statement that the population parameter *does not equal* the particular number the *alternative hypothesis, H_a*. We demonstrate this in the following case.

EXAMPLE 9.3 The Valentine's Day Chocolate Case[2]: Production Planning   C

A candy company annually markets a special 18 ounce box of assorted chocolates to large retail stores for Valentine's Day. This year the candy company has designed an extremely attractive new valentine box and will fill the box with an especially appealing assortment of chocolates. For this reason, the candy company subjectively projects—based on past experience and knowledge of the candy market—that sales of its valentine box will be 10 percent higher than last year. However, because the candy company must decide how many valentine boxes to produce, the company needs to assess whether it is reasonable to plan for a 10 percent increase in sales.

Before the beginning of each Valentine's Day sales season, the candy company sends large retail stores information about its newest valentine box of assorted chocolates. This information includes a description of the box of chocolates, as well as a preview of advertising displays that the candy company will provide to help retail stores sell the chocolates. Each retail store then places a single (nonreturnable) order of valentine boxes to satisfy its anticipated customer demand for the Valentine's Day sales season. Last year the mean order quantity of large retail stores was 300 boxes per store. If the projected 10 percent sales increase will occur, the mean order quantity, μ, of large retail stores this year will *equal* 330 boxes per store. Therefore, the candy company will test the *null hypothesis H_0: $\mu = 330$* versus the *alternative hypothesis H_a*: $\mu \neq 330$. Here, the alternative hypothesis, H_a says that μ might be greater than or less than 330 boxes. If μ turns out to be greater than 330 boxes and the candy company bases its production on a projected mean order quantity of 330 boxes, the company will fail to satisfy demand for its valentine box. If μ turns out to be less than 330 boxes and the candy company bases its production on a projected mean order quantity of 330 boxes, the company will produce more valentine boxes than it can sell.

To perform the hypothesis test, the candy company will randomly select a sample of n large retail stores and will make an early mailing to these stores promoting this year's valentine box. The candy company will then ask each retail store to report how many valentine boxes it anticipates ordering. If the sample data do not provide sufficient evidence to reject H_0: $\mu = 330$ in favor of H_a: $\mu \neq 330$, the candy company will base its production on the projected 10 percent sales increase. On the other hand, if there is sufficient evidence to reject H_0: $\mu = 330$, the candy company will change its production plans.

We next summarize the sets of null and alternative hypotheses that we have thus far considered.

$$H_0: \mu \leq 50 \qquad H_0: \mu \geq 19.5 \qquad H_0: \mu = 330$$
$$\text{versus} \qquad \text{versus} \qquad \text{versus}$$
$$H_a: \mu > 50 \qquad H_a: \mu < 19.5 \qquad H_a: \mu \neq 330$$

The alternative hypothesis H_a: $\mu > 50$ is called a **one-sided, greater than alternative** hypothesis, whereas H_a: $\mu < 19.5$ is called a **one-sided, less than alternative** hypothesis, and H_a: $\mu \neq 330$ is called a **two-sided, not equal to alternative** hypothesis. Many of the alternative hypotheses we consider in this book are one of these three types. Also, note that each null hypothesis we have considered involves an **equality.** For example, the null hypothesis H_0: $\mu \leq 50$ says that μ is either less than or **equal to** 50. We will see that, in general, the approach we use to test a null hypothesis versus an alternative hypothesis requires that the null hypothesis involve an equality. For this reason, **we always formulate the null and alternative hypotheses so that the null hypothesis involves an equality.**

[2]Thanks to Krogers of Oxford, Ohio, for helpful discussions concerning this case.

The idea of a test statistic   Suppose that in the trash bag case the manufacturer randomly selects a sample of $n = 40$ new trash bags. Each of these bags is tested for breaking strength, and the sample mean $\bar{x}$ of the 40 breaking strengths is calculated. In order to test $H_0: \mu \leq 50$ versus $H_a: \mu > 50$, we utilize the **test statistic**

$$z = \frac{\bar{x} - 50}{\sigma_{\bar{x}}} = \frac{\bar{x} - 50}{\sigma/\sqrt{n}}$$

The test statistic z measures the distance between $\bar{x}$ and 50. The division by $\sigma_{\bar{x}}$ says that this distance is measured in units of the standard deviation of all possible sample means. For example, a value of z equal to, say, 2.4 would tell us that $\bar{x}$ is 2.4 such standard deviations above 50. In general, a value of the test statistic that is less than or equal to zero results when $\bar{x}$ is less than or equal to 50. This provides no evidence to support rejecting H_0 in favor of H_a because the point estimate $\bar{x}$ indicates that μ is probably less than or equal to 50. However, a value of the test statistic that is greater than zero results when $\bar{x}$ is greater than 50. This provides evidence to support rejecting H_0 in favor of H_a because the point estimate $\bar{x}$ indicates that μ might be greater than 50. Furthermore, the farther the value of the test statistic is above 0 (the farther $\bar{x}$ is above 50), the stronger is the evidence to support rejecting H_0 in favor of H_a.

Hypothesis testing and the legal system   If the value of the test statistic z is far enough above zero, we reject H_0 in favor of H_a. To see how large z must be in order to reject H_0, we must understand that **a hypothesis test rejects a null hypothesis H_0 only if there is strong statistical evidence against H_0.** This is similar to our legal system, which rejects the innocence of the accused only if evidence of guilt is beyond a reasonable doubt. For instance, the network will reject $H_0: \mu \leq 50$ and run the trash bag commercial only if the test statistic z is far enough above zero to show beyond a reasonable doubt that $H_0: \mu \leq 50$ is false and $H_a: \mu > 50$ is true. A test statistic that is only slightly greater than zero might not be convincing enough. However, because such a test statistic would result from a sample mean $\bar{x}$ that is slightly greater than 50, it would provide some evidence to support rejecting $H_0: \mu \leq 50$, and it certainly would not provide strong evidence supporting $H_0: \mu \leq 50$. Therefore, if the value of the test statistic is not large enough to convince us to reject H_0, **we do not say that we accept H_0. Rather we say that we do not reject H_0** because the evidence against H_0 is not strong enough. Again, this is similar to our legal system, where the lack of evidence of guilt beyond a reasonable doubt results in a verdict of **not guilty,** but does not prove that the accused is innocent.

<table>
<tr><td>LO9-2 Describe
Type I and
Type II errors and
their probabilities.</td><td>**Type I and Type II errors and their probabilities**   To determine exactly how much statistical evidence is required to reject H_0, we consider the errors and the correct decisions that can be made in hypothesis testing. These errors and correct decisions, as well as their implications in the trash bag advertising example, are summarized in Tables 9.1 and 9.2. Across the top of each table are listed the two possible "states of nature." Either $H_0: \mu \leq 50$ is true, which says the manufacturer's claim that μ is greater than 50 is false, or H_0 is false, which says the claim is true. Down the left side of each table are listed the two possible decisions we can make in the hypothesis test. Using the sample data, we will either reject $H_0: \mu \leq 50$, which implies that the claim will be advertised, or we will not reject H_0, which implies that the claim will not be advertised.</td></tr>
</table>

In general, the two types of errors that can be made in hypothesis testing are defined as follows:

Type I and Type II Errors

If we reject H_0 when it is true, this is a **Type I error.**
If we do not reject H_0 when it is false, this is a **Type II error.**

As can be seen by comparing Tables 9.1 and 9.2, if we commit a Type I error, we will advertise a false claim. If we commit a Type II error, we will fail to advertise a true claim.

We now let the symbol α (pronounced **alpha**) **denote the probability of a Type I error,** and we let β (pronounced **beta**) **denote the probability of a Type II error.** Obviously, we would like both α and β to be small. A common (but not the only) procedure is to base a hypothesis test on taking a sample of a fixed size (for example, $n = 40$ trash bags) and on setting

TABLE 9.1   Type I and Type II Errors

Decision	State of Nature	
	$H_0: \mu \leq 50$ True	$H_0: \mu \leq 50$ False
Reject $H_0: \mu \leq 50$	Type I error	Correct decision
Do not reject $H_0: \mu \leq 50$	Correct decision	Type II error

TABLE 9.2   The Implications of Type I and Type II Errors in the Trash Bag Example

Decision	State of Nature	
	Claim False	Claim True
Advertise the claim	Advertise a false claim	Advertise a true claim
Do not advertise the claim	Do not advertise a false claim	Do not advertise a true claim

α equal to a small prespecified value. Setting α low means there is only a small chance of rejecting H_0 when it is true. This implies that we are requiring strong evidence against H_0 before we reject it.

We sometimes choose α as high as .10, but we usually choose α between .05 and .01. A frequent choice for α is .05. In fact, our former student tells us that the network often tests advertising claims by setting the probability of a Type I error equal to .05. That is, the network will run a commercial making a claim if the sample evidence allows it to reject a null hypothesis that says the claim is not valid in favor of an alternative hypothesis that says the claim is valid with α set equal to .05. Because a Type I error is deciding that the claim is valid when it is not, the policy of setting α equal to .05 says that, in the long run, the network will advertise only 5 percent of all invalid claims made by advertisers.

One might wonder why the network does not set α lower—say at .01. One reason is that **it can be shown that, for a fixed sample size, the lower we set α, the higher is β, and the higher we set α, the lower is β.** Setting α at .05 means that β, the probability of failing to advertise a true claim (a Type II error), will be smaller than it would be if α were set at .01. As long as (1) the claim to be advertised is plausible and (2) the consequences of advertising the claim even if it is false are not terribly serious, then it is reasonable to set α equal to .05. However, if either (1) or (2) is not true, then we might set α lower than .05. For example, suppose a pharmaceutical company wishes to advertise that it has developed an effective treatment for a disease that has been very resistant to treatment. Such a claim is (perhaps) difficult to believe. Moreover, if the claim is false, patients suffering from the disease would be subjected to false hope and needless expense. In such a case, it might be reasonable for the network to set α at .01 because this would lower the chance of advertising the claim if it is false. We usually do not set α lower than .01 because doing so often leads to an unacceptably large value of β. We explain some methods for computing the probability of a Type II error in optional Section 9.5. However, β can be difficult or impossible to calculate in many situations, and we often must rely on our intuition when deciding how to set α.

Exercises for Section 9.1

CONCEPTS

9.1   Define each of the following: Type I error, α, Type II error, β.

9.2   When testing a hypothesis, why don't we set the probability of a Type I error to be extremely small? Explain.

METHODS AND APPLICATIONS

9.3   THE VIDEO GAME SATISFACTION RATING CASE   ⑤ VideoGame

Recall that "very satisfied" customers give the XYZ-Box video game system a rating that is at least 42. Suppose that the manufacturer of the XYZ-Box wishes to use the 65 satisfaction ratings to provide evidence supporting the claim that the mean composite satisfaction rating for the XYZ-Box exceeds 42.

a　Letting μ represent the mean composite satisfaction rating for the XYZ-Box, set up the null and alternative hypotheses needed if we wish to attempt to provide evidence supporting the claim that μ exceeds 42.

b　In the context of this situation, interpret making a Type I error; interpret making a Type II error.

9.4　**THE BANK CUSTOMER WAITING TIME CASE**　🔵 WaitTime

Recall that a bank manager has developed a new system to reduce the time customers spend waiting for teller service during peak hours. The manager hopes the new system will reduce waiting times from the current 9 to 10 minutes to less than 6 minutes.

　Suppose the manager wishes to use the 100 waiting times to support the claim that the mean waiting time under the new system is shorter than six minutes.

a　Letting μ represent the mean waiting time under the new system, set up the null and alternative hypotheses needed if we wish to attempt to provide evidence supporting the claim that μ is shorter than six minutes.

b　In the context of this situation, interpret making a Type I error; interpret making a Type II error.

9.5　An automobile parts supplier owns a machine that produces a cylindrical engine part. This part is supposed to have an outside diameter of three inches. Parts with diameters that are too small or too large do not meet customer requirements and must be rejected. Lately, the company has experienced problems meeting customer requirements. The technical staff feels that the mean diameter produced by the machine is off target. In order to verify this, a special study will randomly sample 100 parts produced by the machine. The 100 sampled parts will be measured, and if the results obtained cast a substantial amount of doubt on the hypothesis that the mean diameter equals the target value of three inches, the company will assign a problem-solving team to intensively search for the causes of the problem.

a　The parts supplier wishes to set up a hypothesis test so that the problem-solving team will be assigned when the null hypothesis is rejected. Set up the null and alternative hypotheses for this situation.

b　In the context of this situation, interpret making a Type I error; interpret making a Type II error.

9.6　The Crown Bottling Company has just installed a new bottling process that will fill 16-ounce bottles of the popular Crown Classic Cola soft drink. Both overfilling and underfilling bottles are undesirable: Underfilling leads to customer complaints and overfilling costs the company considerable money. In order to verify that the filler is set up correctly, the company wishes to see whether the mean bottle fill, μ, is close to the target fill of 16 ounces. To this end, a random sample of 36 filled bottles is selected from the output of a test filler run. If the sample results cast a substantial amount of doubt on the hypothesis that the mean bottle fill is the desired 16 ounces, then the filler's initial setup will be readjusted.

a　The bottling company wants to set up a hypothesis test so that the filler will be readjusted if the null hypothesis is rejected. Set up the null and alternative hypotheses for this hypothesis test.

b　In the context of this situation, interpret making a Type I error; interpret making a Type II error.

9.7　Consolidated Power, a large electric power utility, has just built a modern nuclear power plant. This plant discharges waste water that is allowed to flow into the Atlantic Ocean. The Environmental Protection Agency (EPA) has ordered that the waste water may not be excessively warm so that thermal pollution of the marine environment near the plant can be avoided. Because of this order, the waste water is allowed to cool in specially constructed ponds and is then released into the ocean. This cooling system works properly if the mean temperature of waste water discharged is 60°F or cooler. Consolidated Power is required to monitor the temperature of the waste water. A sample of 100 temperature readings will be obtained each day, and if the sample results cast a substantial amount of doubt on the hypothesis that the cooling system is working properly (the mean temperature of waste water discharged is 60°F or cooler), then the plant must be shut down and appropriate actions must be taken to correct the problem.

a　Consolidated Power wishes to set up a hypothesis test so that the power plant will be shut down when the null hypothesis is rejected. Set up the null and alternative hypotheses that should be used.

b　In the context of this situation, interpret making a Type I error; interpret making a Type II error.

c　The EPA periodically conducts spot checks to determine whether the waste water being discharged is too warm. Suppose the EPA has the power to impose very severe penalties (for example, very heavy fines) when the waste water is excessively warm. Other things being equal, should Consolidated Power set the probability of a Type I error equal to $\alpha = .01$ or $\alpha = .05$? Explain.

9.2 z Tests about a Population Mean: σ Known ◉ ● ●

LO9-3 Use critical values and p-values to perform a z test about a population mean when σ is known.

In this section we discuss hypothesis tests about a population mean that are *based on the normal distribution*. These tests are called z **tests,** and they require that the *true value of the population standard deviation σ is known*. Of course, in most real-world situations the true value of σ is not known. However, the concepts and calculations of hypothesis testing are most easily illustrated using the normal distribution. Therefore, in this section we will assume that—through theory or history related to the population under consideration—we know σ. When σ is unknown, we test hypotheses about a population mean by using the *t distribution*. In Section 9.3 we study *t tests*, and we will revisit the examples of this section assuming that σ is unknown.

Testing a "greater than" alternative hypothesis by using a critical value rule   In Section 9.1 we explained how to set up appropriate null and alternative hypotheses. We also discussed how to specify a value for α, the probability of a Type I error (also called the **level of significance**) of the hypothesis test, and we introduced the idea of a test statistic. We can use these concepts to begin developing a five-step hypothesis-testing procedure. We will introduce these steps in the context of the trash bag case and testing a "greater than" alternative hypothesis.

Step 1: State the null hypothesis H_0 and the alternative hypothesis H_a. In the trash bag case, we will test $H_0: \mu \le 50$ versus $H_a: \mu > 50$. Here, μ is the mean breaking strength of the new trash bag.

Step 2: Specify the level of significance α. The television network will run the commercial stating that the new trash bag is stronger than the current bag if we can reject $H_0: \mu \le 50$ in favor of $H_a: \mu > 50$ by setting α equal to .05.

Step 3: Select the test statistic. In order to test $H_0: \mu \le 50$ versus $H_a: \mu > 50$, we will test the modified null hypothesis $H_0: \mu = 50$ versus $H_a: \mu > 50$. The idea here is that if there is sufficient evidence to reject the hypothesis that μ equals 50 in favor of $\mu > 50$, then there is certainly also sufficient evidence to reject the hypothesis that μ is less than or equal to 50. In order to test $H_0: \mu = 50$ versus $H_a: \mu > 50$, we will randomly select a sample of $n = 40$ new trash bags and calculate the mean $\bar{x}$ of the breaking strengths of these bags. We will then utilize the **test statistic** illustrated below.

$$z = \frac{\bar{x} - 50}{\sigma/\sqrt{n}}$$

Sample mean →   Hypothesized population mean →   Population standard deviation →   Sample size →

A positive value of this test statistic results from an $\bar{x}$ that is greater than 50 and thus provides evidence against $H_0: \mu = 50$ and in favor of $H_a: \mu > 50$. Moreover, the manufacturer has improved its trash bags multiple times in the past. Studies show that the population standard deviation σ of individual trash bag breaking strengths has remained constant for each of these updates and equals 1.65 pounds.

Step 4: Determine the critical value rule for deciding whether to reject H_0. To decide how large the test statistic z must be to reject H_0 in favor of H_a by setting the probability of a Type I error equal to α, we note that different samples would give different sample means and thus different values of z. **Because the sample size $n = 40$ is large, the Central Limit Theorem tells us that the sampling distribution of z is (approximately) a standard normal distribution if the null hypothesis $H_0: \mu = 50$ is true.** Therefore, we do the following:

- Place the probability of a Type I error, α, in the right-hand tail of the standard normal curve and use the normal table (see Table A.3, page 790) to find the normal point z_α. Here z_α, which we call a **critical value,** is the point on the horizontal axis under the standard normal curve that gives a right-hand tail area equal to α.

- **Reject $H_0: \mu = 50$ in favor of $H_a: \mu > 50$ if and only if the test statistic z is greater than the critical value z_α.** (This is called a **right tailed critical value rule.**)

FIGURE 9.1   A Right Tailed Critical Value Rule for Testing H_0: $\mu = 50$ versus H_a: $\mu > 50$ by Setting $\alpha = .05$

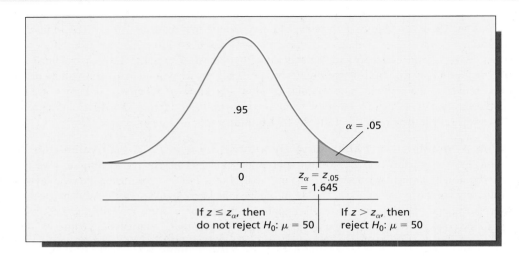

Figure 9.1 illustrates that because we have set α equal to .05, we should use the critical value $z_\alpha = z_{.05} = 1.645$ (see Table A.3). This says that we should reject H_0 if $z > 1.645$ and we should not reject H_0 if $z \le 1.645$. Moreover, the α of .05 says that there is only a 5 percent chance of z being greater than 1.645 if H_0: $\mu = 50$ is true. Therefore, if the sample that we will actually select gives a value of z that is greater than 1.645 and thus causes us to reject H_0: $\mu = 50$, we can be intuitively confident that we have made the right decision. This is because we will have rejected H_0 by using a test that allows only a 5 percent chance of wrongly rejecting H_0. In general, if we can reject a null hypothesis in favor of an alternative hypothesis by setting the probability of a Type I error equal to α, we say that we have **statistical significance at the α level.**

Step 5: Collect the sample data, compute the value of the test statistic, and decide whether to reject H_0. Interpret the statistical results. When the sample of $n = 40$ new trash bags is randomly selected, the mean of the breaking strengths is calculated to be $\bar{x} = 50.575$ pounds. Assuming that σ is 1.65 pounds, the value of the test statistic is

$$z = \frac{\bar{x} - 50}{\sigma/\sqrt{n}} = \frac{50.575 - 50}{1.65/\sqrt{40}} = 2.20$$

Because $z = 2.20$ is greater than the critical value $z_{.05} = 1.645$, we can reject H_0: $\mu = 50$ in favor of H_a: $\mu > 50$ by setting α equal to .05. Therefore, we conclude (at an α of .05) that the population mean breaking strength of the new trash bag exceeds 50 pounds. Furthermore, this conclusion has **practical importance** to the trash bag manufacturer because it means that the television network will approve running commercials claiming that the new trash bag is stronger than the current bag. Note, however, that the point estimate of μ, $\bar{x} = 50.575$, indicates that μ is not much larger than 50. Therefore, the trash bag manufacturer can claim only that its new bag is slightly stronger than its current bag. Of course, this might be practically important to consumers who feel that, because the new bag is 25 percent less expensive and is more environmentally sound, it is definitely worth purchasing if it has any strength advantage. However, to customers who are looking only for a substantial increase in bag strength, the statistical results would not be practically important. Notice that the point estimate of the parameter involved in a hypothesis test can help us to assess practical importance.

A p-value for testing a "greater than" alternative hypothesis   To decide whether to reject the null hypothesis H_0 at level of significance α, steps 4 and 5 of the five-step critical value procedure compare the test statistic value to a critical value. Another way to make this decision is to calculate a ***p*-value,** which measures the likelihood of the sample results if the null hypothesis H_0 is true. **Sample results that are not likely if H_0 is true are evidence that H_0 is not true.** To test H_0 by using a p-value procedure, we use the same first three steps used by the critical value procedure and the new steps 4 and 5:

FIGURE 9.2   The *p*-Value for Testing H_0: $\mu = 50$ versus H_a: $\mu > 50$.

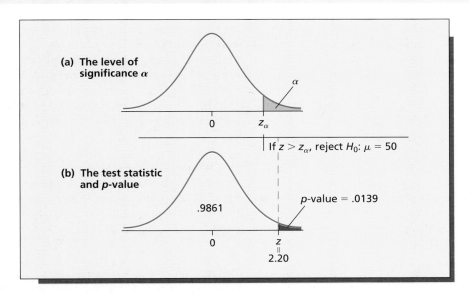

Step 4: Collect the sample data, compute the value of the test statistic, and compute the *p*-value. The *p*-value for testing a null hypothesis H_0 versus an alternative hypothesis H_a is defined as follows:

> The ***p*-value** is the probability, computed assuming that the null hypothesis H_0 is true, of observing a value of the test statistic that is at least as contradictory to H_0 and supportive of H_a as the value actually computed from the sample data.

In the trash bag case, the value of the test statistic computed from the sample data is $z = 2.20$. Because we are testing H_0: $\mu = 50$ versus the **greater than** alternative hypothesis H_a: $\mu > 50$, this positive test statistic value contradicts H_0 and supports H_a. A value of the test statistic that is at least as contradictory to H_0 and supportive of H_a as $z = 2.20$ is a value of the test statistic that is **greater than or equal to** $z = 2.20$. Therefore, the *p*-value is the probability, computed assuming that H_0: $\mu = 50$ is true, of observing a value of the test statistic that is greater than or equal to $z = 2.20$. As illustrated in Figure 9.2(b), this ***p*-value is the area under the standard normal curve to the right of $z = 2.20$** and equals $1 - .9861 = .0139$ (see Table A.3, page 790). The *p*-value of .0139 says that, if H_0: $\mu = 50$ is true, then only 139 in 10,000 of all possible test statistic values are at least as large, or contradictory to H_0, as the value $z = 2.20$. That is, if we are to believe that H_0 is true, we must believe that we have observed a test statistic value that can be described as having a 139 in 10,000 chance. It is difficult to believe that we have observed such a small chance, but is this evidence strong enough to reject H_0: $\mu = 50$ and run the trash bag commercial? As discussed in step 5, this depends on the level of significance α used by the television network.

Step 5: Reject H_0 if the *p*-value is less than α. Interpret the statistical results. Consider the two normal curves in Figures 9.2(a) and (b). These normal curves show that if the *p*-value of .0139 is less than a particular level of significance α, the test statistic value $z = 2.20$ is greater than the critical value z_α, and thus we can reject H_0: $\mu = 50$ at level of significance α. For example, recall that the television network has set α equal to .05. Then, **because the *p*-value of .0139 is less than the α of .05, we would reject H_0: $\mu = 50$ at level of significance .05** and thus run the trash bag commercial on the network.

Comparing the critical value and *p*-value methods   Thus far we have seen that we can reject H_0: $\mu = 50$ in favor of H_a: $\mu > 50$ at level of significance α if **the test statistic z is greater than the critical value z_α**, or equivalently, **the *p*-value is less than α**. Because different television networks sometimes have different policies for evaluating an advertising claim, different television networks sometimes use different values of α when evaluating the same advertising claim. For example, while the network of the previous example used an α value of .05 to evaluate the trash bag claim, three other networks might use three different α values (say, .04, .025, and .01) to evaluate this claim. If we use the critical value method to test H_0: $\mu = 50$ versus H_a: $\mu > 50$ at each of these α values, we would have to look up a different critical value z_α for each different α value. On the other hand, the p-value of .0139 is **more efficient** because it immediately tells us whether we can reject H_0 at each different α value. Specifically, because the p-value of .0139 is less than each of the α values .05, .04, and .025, we would reject H_0 and thus run the trash bag commercial on the networks using these α values. However, because the p-value of .0139 is greater than the α value .01, we would not reject H_0 and thus not run the trash bag commercial on the network using this α value.

A summary of the five steps of hypothesis testing　　In the real world, in spite of the greater efficiency of the p-value, both critical values and p-values are used to test hypotheses. For example, NBC uses critical value rules, whereas CBS uses p-values, to evaluate advertising claims statistically. Throughout this book we will (formally or informally) use the following five steps to implement the critical value and p-value approaches to hypothesis testing.

The Five Steps of Hypothesis Testing

1 State the null hypothesis H_0 and the alternative hypothesis H_a.

2 Specify the level of significance α.

3 Select the test statistic.

Using a critical value rule:

4 Determine the critical value rule for deciding whether to reject H_0.

5 Collect the sample data, compute the value of the test statistic, and decide whether to reject H_0 by using the critical value rule. Interpret the statistical results.

Using a p-value:

4 Collect the sample data, compute the value of the test statistic, and compute the p-value.

5 Reject H_0 at level of significance α if the p-value is less than α. Interpret the statistical results.

Testing a "less than" alternative hypothesis by using a critical value rule　　Consider the e-billing case. In order to study whether the new electronic billing system reduces the mean bill payment time by more than 50 percent, the management consulting firm will test H_0: $\mu \geq 19.5$ versus H_a: $\mu < 19.5$ **(step 1)**. A Type I error (concluding that H_a: $\mu < 19.5$ is true when H_0: $\mu \geq 19.5$ is true) would result in the consulting firm overstating the benefits of the new billing system, both to the company in which it has been installed and to other companies that are considering installing such a system. Because the consulting firm desires to have only a 1 percent chance of doing this, the firm will set α **equal to .01 (step 2)**.

To perform the hypothesis test, we will test the modified null hypothesis H_0: $\mu = 19.5$ versus H_a: $\mu < 19.5$. We will randomly select a sample of $n = 65$ invoices paid using the new billing system and calculate the mean $\bar{x}$ of the payment times of these invoices. Then, because the sample size is large, the Central Limit Theorem applies, and we will utilize the **test statistic (step 3)**

$$z = \frac{\bar{x} - 19.5}{\sigma/\sqrt{n}}$$

A value of the test statistic z that is less than zero results when $\bar{x}$ is less than 19.5. This provides evidence to support rejecting H_0 in favor of H_a because the point estimate $\bar{x}$ indicates that μ might be less than 19.5. To decide how much less than zero the test statistic must be to reject H_0 in favor

FIGURE 9.3 Testing $H_0: \mu = 19.5$ versus $H_a: \mu < 19.5$ by Using a Critical Value and a p-Value

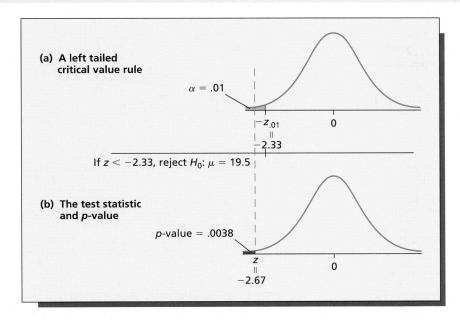

of H_a at significance level α, we will use the **left tailed critical value rule** illustrated in Figure 9.3(a). Specifically, we will place α in the left-hand tail of the standard normal curve and **reject $H_0: \mu = 19.5$ in favor of $H_a: \mu < 19.5$ if and only if the test statistic z is less than the critical value $-z_\alpha$ (step 4).** Here, $-z_\alpha$ is the point on the horizontal axis under the standard normal curve that gives a left-hand tail area equal to α. Because α equals .01, the critical value $-z_\alpha$ is $-z_{.01} = -2.33$ [see Figure 9.3(a)].

When the sample of $n = 65$ invoices is randomly selected, the mean of the payment times of these invoices is calculated to be $\bar{x} = 18.1077$ days. Assuming that the population standard deviation σ of payment times for the new electronic billing system is 4.2 days (as discussed on page 280 of Chapter 7), the **value of the test statistic** is

$$z = \frac{\bar{x} - 19.5}{\sigma/\sqrt{n}} = \frac{18.1077 - 19.5}{4.2/\sqrt{65}} = -2.67$$

Because $z = -2.67$ is less than the critical value $-z_{.01} = -2.33$, we can reject $H_0: \mu = 19.5$ in favor of $H_a: \mu < 19.5$ by setting α equal to .01 (step 5). Therefore, we conclude (at an α of .01) that the population mean payment time for the new electronic billing system is less than 19.5 days. This, along with the fact that the sample mean $\bar{x} = 18.1077$ is slightly less than 19.5, implies that it is reasonable for the management consulting firm to conclude (and claim) that the new electronic billing system has reduced the population mean payment time by slightly more than 50 percent.

A p-value for testing a "less than" alternative hypothesis The value of the test statistic computed from the sample data is $z = -2.67$. Because we are testing $H_0: \mu = 19.5$ versus the **less than** alternative hypothesis $H_a: \mu < 19.5$, a value of the test statistic that is at least as contradictory to H_0 and supportive of H_a as $z = -2.67$ is a value of the test statistic that is **less than or equal to** $z = -2.67$. Therefore, the p-value is the probability, computed assuming that $H_0: \mu = 19.5$ is true, of observing a value of the test statistic that is less than or equal to $z = -2.67$. As illustrated in Figure 9.3(b), this **p-value is the area under the standard normal curve to the left of $z = -2.67$ (step 4)** and equals .0038 (see Table A.3, page 790). The p-value of .0038 says that, if $H_0: \mu = 19.5$ is true, then only 38 in 10,000 of all possible test statistic values are at least as negative, or contradictory to H_0, as the value $z = -2.67$. Moreover, recall that the management consulting firm has set α equal to .01. **Because the p-value of .0038 is less than the α of .01, we can reject $H_0: \mu = 19.5$ in favor of $H_a: \mu < 19.5$ by setting α equal to .01 (step 5).**

F I G U R E 9 . 4   Testing H_0: $\mu = 330$ versus H_a: $\mu \neq 330$ by Using Critical Values and the p-Value

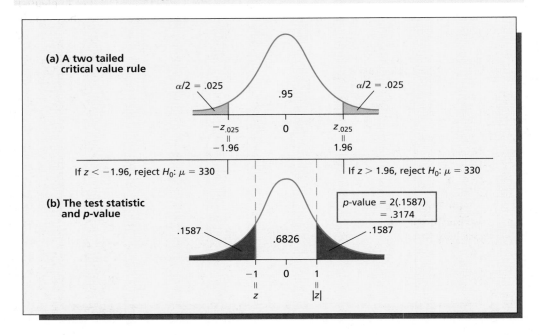

Testing a "not equal to" alternative hypothesis by using a critical value rule   Consider the Valentine's Day chocolate case. To assess whether this year's sales of its valentine box of assorted chocolates will be 10 percent higher than last year's, the candy company will test H_0: $\mu = 330$ versus H_a: $\mu \neq 330$ (step 1). Here, μ is the mean order quantity of this year's valentine box by large retail stores. If the candy company does not reject H_0: $\mu = 330$ and H_0: $\mu = 330$ is false (a Type II error) the candy company will base its production of valentine boxes on a 10 percent projected sales increase that is not correct. Because the candy company wishes to have a reasonably small probability of making this Type II error, the company will set α **equal to .05** (step 2). Setting α equal to .05 rather than .01 makes the probability of a Type II error smaller than it would be if α were set at .01. (See Section 9.5 for more on Type II errors.)

To perform the hypothesis test, the candy company will randomly select $n = 100$ large retail stores and will make an early mailing to these stores promoting this year's valentine box of assorted chocolates. The candy company will then ask each sampled retail store to report its anticipated order quantity of valentine boxes and will calculate the mean $\bar{x}$ of the reported order quantities. Because the sample size is large, the Central Limit Theorem applies, and we will utilize the **test statistic** (step 3)

$$z = \frac{\bar{x} - 330}{\sigma / \sqrt{n}}$$

A value of the test statistic that is greater than 0 results when $\bar{x}$ is greater than 330. This provides evidence to support rejecting H_0 in favor of H_a because the point estimate $\bar{x}$ indicates that μ might be greater than 330. Similarly, a value of the test statistic that is less than 0 results when $\bar{x}$ is less than 330. This also provides evidence to support rejecting H_0 in favor of H_a because the point estimate $\bar{x}$ indicates that μ might be less than 330. To decide how different from zero (positive or negative) the test statistic must be in order to reject H_0 in favor of H_a at significance level α, we will use the **two tailed critical value rule** illustrated in Figure 9.4(a). Specifically, we will divide α into two equal parts and **reject H_0: $\mu = 330$ in favor of H_a: $\mu \neq 330$ if and only if the test statistic z is greater than the critical value $z_{\alpha/2}$ or less than the critical value $-z_{\alpha/2}$ (step 4)**. Note that this is equivalent to saying that we should **reject H_0 if and only if the absolute value of the test statistic, $|z|$, is greater than the critical value $z_{\alpha/2}$**. Because $\alpha/2 = .05/2 = .025$, it follows that the critical values $z_{\alpha/2}$ and $-z_{\alpha/2}$ are $z_{.025} = 1.96$ and $-z_{.025} = -1.96$ [see Figure 9.4(a)].

When the sample of $n = 100$ large retail stores is randomly selected, the mean of their reported order quantities is calculated to be $\bar{x} = 326$ boxes. Assuming that the population standard deviation σ of large retail store order quantities for this year's valentine box will be 40 boxes (the same as it was for previous years' valentine boxes), the value of the test statistic is

$$z = \frac{\bar{x} - 330}{\sigma/\sqrt{n}} = \frac{326 - 330}{40/\sqrt{100}} = -1$$

Because $z = -1$ is between the critical values $-z_{.025} = -1.96$ and $z_{.025} = 1.96$ (or, equivalently, because $|z| = 1$ is less than $z_{.025} = 1.96$), we cannot reject H_0: $\mu = 330$ in favor of H_a: $\mu \neq 330$ by setting α equal to .05 (step 5). Therefore, we cannot conclude (at an α of .05) that the population mean order quantity of this year's valentine box by large retail stores will differ from 330 boxes. It follows that the candy company will base its production of valentine boxes on the ten percent projected sales increase.

A p-value for testing a "not equal to" alternative hypothesis   The value of the test statistic computed from the sample data is $z = -1$. Because the alternative hypothesis H_a: $\mu \neq 330$ says that μ might be greater or less than 330, both positive and negative test statistic values contradict H_0: $\mu = 330$ and support H_a: $\mu \neq 330$. It follows that a value of the test statistic that is at least as contradictory to H_0 and supportive of H_a as $z = -1$ is a value of the test statistic that is greater than or equal to 1 or less than or equal to -1. Therefore, the p-value is the probability, computed assuming that H_0: $\mu = 330$ is true, of observing a value of the test statistic that is greater than or equal to 1 or less than or equal to -1. As illustrated in Figure 9.4 (b), this p-value equals the area under the standard normal curve to the right of 1, plus the area under this curve to the left of -1. But, by the symmetry of the normal curve, the sum of these two areas, and thus the **p-value, is twice the area under the standard normal curve to the right of $|z| = 1$, the absolute value of the test statistic (step 4).** Because the area under the standard normal curve to the right of $|z| = 1$ is $1 - .8413 = .1587$ (see Table A.3, page 790), the p-value is $2(.1587) = .3174$. The p-value of .3174 says that, if H_0: $\mu = 330$ is true, then 31.74 percent of all possible test statistic values are at least as contradictory to H_0 as $z = -1$. Moreover, recall that the candy company has set α equal to .05. **Because the p-value of .3174 is greater than the α of .05, we cannot reject H_0: $\mu = 330$ in favor of H_a: $\mu \neq 330$ by setting α equal to .05 (step 5).**

A general procedure for testing a hypothesis about a population mean   In general, let μ_0 be the value for μ specified in the null hypothesis. Then, the following summary box gives the critical value and p-value procedures for performing (1) a right tailed test of H_0: $\mu = \mu_0$ versus H_a: $\mu > \mu_0$ (for example, H_0: $\mu = 50$ versus H_a: $\mu > 50$); (2) a left tailed test of H_0: $\mu = \mu_0$ versus H_a: $\mu < \mu_0$ (for example, H_0: $\mu = 19.5$ versus H_a: $\mu < 19.5$); and (3) a two tailed test of H_0: $\mu = \mu_0$ versus H_a: $\mu \neq \mu_0$ (for example, H_0: $\mu = 330$ versus H_a: $\mu \neq 330$).

Testing a Hypothesis about a Population Mean When σ Is Known

| Null Hypothesis H_0: $\mu = \mu_0$ | Test Statistic $z = \dfrac{\bar{x} - \mu_0}{\sigma/\sqrt{n}}$ | Assumptions | Normal population or Large sample size |

Using confidence intervals to test hypotheses   Confidence intervals can be used to test hypotheses. Specifically, it can be proven that we can reject $H_0: \mu = \mu_0$ in favor of $H_a: \mu \neq \mu_0$ by setting the probability of a Type I error equal to α if and only if the $100(1 - \alpha)$ percent confidence interval for μ does not contain μ_0. For example, consider the Valentine's Day chocolate case and testing $H_0: \mu = 330$ versus $H_a: \mu \neq 330$ by setting α equal to .05. To do this, we use the mean $\bar{x} = 326$ of the sample of $n = 100$ reported order quantities to calculate the 95 percent confidence interval for μ to be

$$\left[\bar{x} \pm z_{\alpha/2} \frac{\sigma}{\sqrt{n}} \right] = \left[326 \pm 1.96 \frac{40}{\sqrt{100}} \right] = [318.2, 333.8]$$

Because this interval does contain 330, we cannot reject $H_0: \mu = 330$ in favor of $H_a: \mu \neq 330$ by setting α equal to .05.

While we can use **two-sided confidence intervals** to test "not equal to" alternative hypotheses, we must use **one-sided confidence intervals** to test "greater than" or "less than" alternative hypotheses. We will not study one-sided confidence intervals in this book. However, it should be emphasized that we do not need to use confidence intervals (one-sided or two-sided) to test hypotheses. We can test hypotheses by using test statistics and critical values or p-values, and these are the approaches that we will feature throughout this book.

Measuring the weight of evidence against the null hypothesis   As originally defined, the p-value is a probability that measures the likelihood of the sample results if the null hypothesis H_0 is true. **The smaller the p-value is, the less likely are the sample results if the null hypothesis H_0 is true. Therefore, the stronger is the evidence that H_0 is false and that the alternative hypothesis H_a is true.** Interpreted in this way, the p-value can be regarded as a measure of the **weight of evidence** against the null hypothesis and in favor of the alternative hypothesis. Through statistical practice, statisticians have concluded (somewhat subjectively) that:

Interpreting the Weight of Evidence against the Null Hypothesis

If the p-value for testing H_0 is less than

- .10, we have **some evidence** that H_0 is false.
- .05, we have **strong evidence** that H_0 is false.

- .01, we have **very strong evidence** that H_0 is false.
- .001, we have **extremely strong evidence** that H_0 is false.

We will frequently use these conclusions in future examples. Understand, however, that there are really no sharp borders between different weights of evidence. Rather, there is really only increasingly strong evidence against the null hypothesis as the p-value decreases. For example, the trash bag manufacturer, in addition to deciding whether $H_0: \mu = 50$ can be rejected in favor of $H_a: \mu > 50$ at each television network's chosen value of α, would almost certainly wish to know how much evidence there is that its new trash bag is stronger than its current trash bag. The p-value for testing $H_0: \mu = 50$ is .0139, which is less than .05 but not less than .01. Therefore, we have strong evidence, but not very strong evidence, that $H_0: \mu = 50$ is false and $H_a: \mu > 50$ is true. As another example, the p-value in the e-billing case is .0038. This provides very strong evidence, but not extremely strong evidence, that $H_0: \mu = 19.5$ is false and $H_a: \mu < 19.5$ is true. Finally, the p-value in the Valentine's Day chocolate case is .3174. This provides little evidence that $H_0: \mu = 330$ is false and $H_a: \mu \neq 330$ is true.

Exercises for Section 9.2

CONCEPTS

connect

9.8   Explain what a critical value is, and explain how it is used to test a hypothesis.

9.9   Explain what a p-value is, and explain how it is used to test a hypothesis.

METHODS AND APPLICATIONS

9.10 Suppose that we wish to test $H_0: \mu = 80$ versus $H_a: \mu > 80$, where σ is known to equal 20. Also, suppose that a sample of $n = 100$ measurements randomly selected from the population has a mean of $\bar{x} = 85$.
   a Calculate the value of the test statistic z.
   b By comparing z with a critical value, test H_0 versus H_a at $\alpha = .05$.
   c Calculate the p-value for testing H_0 versus H_a.
   d Use the p-value to test H_0 versus H_a at each of $\alpha = .10, .05, .01,$ and $.001$.
   e How much evidence is there that $H_0: \mu = 80$ is false and $H_a: \mu > 80$ is true?

9.11 Suppose that we wish to test $H_0: \mu = 20$ versus $H_a: \mu < 20$, where σ is known to equal 7. Also, suppose that a sample of $n = 49$ measurements randomly selected from the population has a mean of $\bar{x} = 18$.
   a Calculate the value of the test statistic z.
   b By comparing z with a critical value, test H_0 versus H_a at $\alpha = .01$.
   c Calculate the p-value for testing H_0 versus H_a.
   d Use the p-value to test H_0 versus H_a at each of $\alpha = .10, .05, .01,$ and $.001$.
   e How much evidence is there that $H_0: \mu = 20$ is false and $H_a: \mu < 20$ is true?

9.12 Suppose that we wish to test $H_0: \mu = 40$ versus $H_a: \mu \neq 40$, where σ is known to equal 18. Also, suppose that a sample of $n = 81$ measurements randomly selected from the population has a mean of $\bar{x} = 35$.
   a Calculate the value of the test statistic z.
   b By comparing z with critical values, test H_0 versus H_a at $\alpha = .05$.
   c Calculate the p-value for testing H_0 versus H_a.
   d Use the p-value to test H_0 versus H_a at each of $\alpha = .10, .05, .01,$ and $.001$.
   e How much evidence is there that $H_0: \mu = 40$ is false and $H_a: \mu \neq 40$ is true?

9.13 THE VIDEO GAME SATISFACTION RATING CASE DS VideoGame

Recall that "very satisfied" customers give the XYZ-Box video game system a rating that is at least 42. Suppose that the manufacturer of the XYZ-Box wishes to use the random sample of 65 satisfaction ratings to provide evidence supporting the claim that the mean composite satisfaction rating for the XYZ-Box exceeds 42.
   a Letting μ represent the mean composite satisfaction rating for the XYZ-Box, set up the null hypothesis H_0 and the alternative hypothesis H_a needed if we wish to attempt to provide evidence supporting the claim that μ exceeds 42.
   b The random sample of 65 satisfaction ratings yields a sample mean of $\bar{x} = 42.954$. Assuming that σ equals 2.64, use critical values to test H_0 versus H_a at each of $\alpha = .10, .05, .01,$ and $.001$.
   c Using the information in part b, calculate the p-value and use it to test H_0 versus H_a at each of $\alpha = .10, .05, .01,$ and $.001$.
   d How much evidence is there that the mean composite satisfaction rating exceeds 42?

9.14 THE BANK CUSTOMER WAITING TIME CASE DS WaitTime

Recall that a bank manager has developed a new system to reduce the time customers spend waiting for teller service during peak hours. The manager hopes the new system will reduce waiting times from the current 9 to 10 minutes to less than 6 minutes.
   Suppose the manager wishes to use the random sample of 100 waiting times to support the claim that the mean waiting time under the new system is shorter than six minutes.
   a Letting μ represent the mean waiting time under the new system, set up the null and alternative hypotheses needed if we wish to attempt to provide evidence supporting the claim that μ is shorter than six minutes.
   b The random sample of 100 waiting times yields a sample mean of $\bar{x} = 5.46$ minutes. Assuming that $\sigma = 2.47$ minutes, use critical values to test H_0 versus H_a at each of $\alpha = .10, .05, .01,$ and $.001$.
   c Using the information in part b, calculate the p-value and use it to test H_0 versus H_a at each of $\alpha = .10, .05, .01,$ and $.001$.
   d How much evidence is there that the new system has reduced the mean waiting time to below six minutes?

9.15 Consolidated Power, a large electric power utility, has just built a modern nuclear power plant. This plant discharges waste water that is allowed to flow into the Atlantic Ocean. The Environmental Protection Agency (EPA) has ordered that the waste water may not be excessively warm so that thermal pollution of the marine environment near the plant can be avoided. Because of this order, the waste water is allowed to cool in specially constructed ponds and is then released into the ocean. This cooling system works properly if the mean temperature of waste water discharged is 60°F or cooler. Consolidated Power is required to monitor the temperature of the waste water. A sample of 100 temperature readings will be obtained each day, and if the sample results cast a substantial amount of doubt on the hypothesis that the cooling system is working properly (the mean temperature of waste water discharged is 60°F or cooler), then the plant must be shut down and appropriate actions must be taken to correct the problem.

a Consolidated Power wishes to set up a hypothesis test so that the power plant will be shut down when the null hypothesis is rejected. Set up the null hypothesis H_0 and the alternative hypothesis H_a that should be used.

b Suppose that Consolidated Power decides to use a level of significance of $\alpha = .05$, and suppose a random sample of 100 temperature readings is obtained. If the sample mean of the 100 temperature readings is $\bar{x} = 60.482$, test H_0 versus H_a and determine whether the power plant should be shut down and the cooling system repaired. Perform the hypothesis test by using a critical value and a p-value. Assume $\sigma = 2$.

9.16 Do part b of Exercise 9.15 if $\bar{x} = 60.262$.

9.17 Do part b of Exercise 9.15 if $\bar{x} = 60.618$.

9.18 An automobile parts supplier owns a machine that produces a cylindrical engine part. This part is supposed to have an outside diameter of three inches. Parts with diameters that are too small or too large do not meet customer requirements and must be rejected. Lately, the company has experienced problems meeting customer requirements. The technical staff feels that the mean diameter produced by the machine is off target. In order to verify this, a special study will randomly sample 100 parts produced by the machine. The 100 sampled parts will be measured, and if the results obtained cast a substantial amount of doubt on the hypothesis that the mean diameter equals the target value of three inches, the company will assign a problem-solving team to intensively search for the causes of the problem.

a The parts supplier wishes to set up a hypothesis test so that the problem-solving team will be assigned when the null hypothesis is rejected. Set up the null and alternative hypotheses for this situation.

b A sample of 40 parts yields a sample mean diameter of $\bar{x} = 3.006$ inches. Assuming σ equals .016: **(1)** Use a critical value to test H_0 versus H_a by setting α equal to .05. **(2)** Should the problem-solving team be assigned? **(3)** Use a p-value to test H_0 versus H_a with $\alpha = .05$.

9.19 The Crown Bottling Company has just installed a new bottling process that will fill 16-ounce bottles of the popular Crown Classic Cola soft drink. Both overfilling and underfilling bottles are undesirable: Underfilling leads to customer complaints and overfilling costs the company considerable money. In order to verify that the filler is set up correctly, the company wishes to see whether the mean bottle fill, μ, is close to the target fill of 16 ounces. To this end, a random sample of 36 filled bottles is selected from the output of a test filler run. If the sample results cast a substantial amount of doubt on the hypothesis that the mean bottle fill is the desired 16 ounces, then the filler's initial setup will be readjusted.

a The bottling company wants to set up a hypothesis test so that the filler will be readjusted if the null hypothesis is rejected. Set up the null and alternative hypotheses for this hypothesis test.

b Suppose that Crown Bottling Company decides to use a level of significance of $\alpha = .01$, and suppose a random sample of 36 bottle fills is obtained from a test run of the filler. For each of the following four sample means—$\bar{x} = 16.05$, $\bar{x} = 15.96$, $\bar{x} = 16.02$, and $\bar{x} = 15.94$—determine whether the filler's initial setup should be readjusted. In each case, use **(1)** a critical value, **(2)** a p-value, and **(3)** a confidence interval. Assume that σ equals .1.

9.20 THE DISK BRAKE CASE

National Motors has equipped the ZX-900 with a new disk brake system. We define μ to be the mean stopping distance (from a speed of 35 mph) of all ZX-900s. National Motors would like to claim that the ZX-900 achieves a shorter mean stopping distance than the 60 ft claimed by a competitor.

a Set up the null and alternative hypotheses needed to support National Motors' claim.

b A television network will allow National Motors to advertise its claim if the appropriate null hypothesis can be rejected at $\alpha = .05$. If a random sample of 81 ZX-900s have a mean stopping distance of $\bar{x} = 57.8$ ft, will National Motors be allowed to advertise the claim? Assume that $\sigma = 6.02$ ft and justify your answer using both a critical value and a p-value.

9.3 t Tests about a Population Mean: σ Unknown ● ● ●

LO9-4 Use critical values and p-values to perform a t test about a population mean when σ is unknown.

If we do not know σ (which is usually the case), we can base a hypothesis test about μ on the sampling distribution of

$$\frac{\bar{x} - \mu}{s/\sqrt{n}}$$

If the sampled population is normally distributed (or if the sample size is large—at least 30), then this sampling distribution is exactly (or approximately) a **t distribution having $n - 1$ degrees of freedom.** This leads to the following results:

A t Test about a Population Mean: σ Unknown

Null Hypothesis $H_0: \mu = \mu_0$ **Test Statistic** $t = \dfrac{\bar{x} - \mu_0}{s/\sqrt{n}}$ $df = n - 1$ **Assumptions**   Normal population or Large sample size

Critical Value Rule			p-Value (Reject H_0 if p-Value < α)		
$H_a: \mu > \mu_0$	$H_a: \mu < \mu_0$	$H_a: \mu \neq \mu_0$	$H_a: \mu > \mu_0$	$H_a: \mu < \mu_0$	$H_a: \mu \neq \mu_0$
Reject H_0 if $t > t_\alpha$	Reject H_0 if $t < -t_\alpha$	Reject H_0 if $|t| > t_{\alpha/2}$—that is, $t > t_{\alpha/2}$ or $t < -t_{\alpha/2}$	p-value = area to the right of t	p-value = area to the left of t	p-value = twice the area to the right of $|t|$

EXAMPLE 9.4   The Commercial Loan Case: Mean Debt-to-Equity Ratio   Ⓒ

One measure of a company's financial health is its *debt-to-equity ratio*. This quantity is defined to be the ratio of the company's corporate debt to the company's equity. If this ratio is too high, it is one indication of financial instability. For obvious reasons, banks often monitor the financial health of companies to which they have extended commercial loans. Suppose that, in order to reduce risk, a large bank has decided to initiate a policy limiting the mean debt-to-equity ratio for its portfolio of commercial loans to being less than 1.5. In order to assess whether the mean debt-to-equity ratio μ of its (current) commercial loan portfolio is less than 1.5, the bank will test the **null hypothesis $H_0: \mu = 1.5$ versus the alternative hypothesis $H_a: \mu < 1.5$.** In this situation, a Type I error (rejecting $H_0: \mu = 1.5$ when $H_0: \mu = 1.5$ is true) would result in the bank concluding that the mean debt-to-equity ratio of its commercial loan portfolio is less than 1.5 when it is not. Because the bank wishes to be very sure that it does not commit this Type I error, it will test H_0 versus H_a by using a **.01 level of significance.** To perform the hypothesis test, the bank randomly selects a sample of 15 of its commercial loan accounts. Audits of these companies result in the following debt-to-equity ratios (arranged in increasing order): 1.05, 1.11, 1.19, 1.21, 1.22, 1.29, 1.31, 1.32, 1.33, 1.37, 1.41, 1.45, 1.46, 1.65, and 1.78. The mound-shaped stem-and-leaf display of these ratios is given on the page margin and indicates that the population of all debt-to-equity ratios is (approximately) normally distributed. It follows that it is appropriate to calculate the value of the **test statistic t in the summary box.** Furthermore, because $H_a: \mu < 1.5$ implies a left tailed test, we should **reject $H_0: \mu = 1.5$ if the value of t is less than the critical value $-t_\alpha = -t_{.01} = -2.624$.** Here, $-t_{.01} = -2.624$ is based on $n - 1 = 15 - 1 = 14$ degrees of freedom (see Table A.4, on page 792), and this critical value is illustrated in Figure 9.5(a). The mean and the standard deviation of the random sample of $n = 15$ debt-to-equity ratios are $\bar{x} = 1.3433$ and $s = .1921$. This implies that the **value of the test statistic is**

1.0	5
1.1	1 9
1.2	1 2 9
1.3	1 2 3 7
1.4	1 5 6
1.5	
1.6	5
1.7	8

DS DebtEq

$$t = \frac{\bar{x} - 1.5}{s/\sqrt{n}} = \frac{1.3433 - 1.5}{.1921/\sqrt{15}} = -3.1589$$

FIGURE 9.5   Testing H_0: $\mu = 1.5$ versus H_a: $\mu < 1.5$ by Using a Critical Value and the *p*-Value

```
Test of mu = 1.5 vs < 1.5

                                            95% Upper
Variable    N     Mean    StDev   SE Mean      Bound       T       P
Ratio      15   1.3433   0.1921   0.0496      1.4307    -3.16   0.003
```

Because $t = -3.1589$ is less than $-t_{.01} = -2.624$, we reject H_0: $\mu = 1.5$ in favor of H_a: $\mu < 1.5$. That is, we conclude (at an α of .01) that the population mean debt-to-equity ratio of the bank's commercial loan portfolio is less than 1.5. This, along with the fact that the sample mean $\bar{x} = 1.3433$ is slightly less than 1.5, implies that it is reasonable for the bank to conclude that the population mean debt-to-equity ratio of its commercial loan portfolio is slightly less than 1.5.

The *p*-value for testing H_0: $\mu = 1.5$ versus H_a: $\mu < 1.5$ is the area under the curve of the *t* distribution having 14 degrees of freedom to the left of $t = -3.1589$. Tables of *t* points (such as Table A.4) are not complete enough to give such areas for most *t* statistic values, so we use computer software packages to calculate *p*-values that are based on the *t* distribution. For example, Excel tells us that the *p*-value for testing H_0: $\mu = 1.5$ versus H_a: $\mu < 1.5$ is .00348, which is given in the rounded form .003 on the MINITAB output at the bottom of Figure 9.5. The *p*-value of .00348 says that if we are to believe that H_0 is true, we must believe that we have observed a test statistic value that can be described as having a 348 in 100,000 chance. Moreover, because the *p*-value of .00348 is between .01 and .001, we have very strong evidence, but not extremely strong evidence, that H_0: $\mu = 1.5$ is false and H_a: $\mu < 1.5$ is true. That is, we have very strong evidence that the mean debt-to-equity ratio of the bank's commercial loan portfolio is less than 1.5.

Recall that in three cases discussed in Section 9.2 we tested hypotheses by assuming that the population standard deviation σ is known and by using *z* tests. If σ is actually not known in these cases (which would probably be true), we should test the hypotheses under consideration by using *t* tests. Furthermore, recall that in each case the sample size is large (at least 30). **In general, it can be shown that if the sample size is large, the *t* test is approximately valid even if the sampled population is not normally distributed (or mound shaped).** Therefore, consider the Valentine's Day chocolate case and testing H_0: $\mu = 330$ versus H_a: $\mu \neq 330$ at the **.05 level of significance.** To perform the hypothesis test, assume that we will randomly select $n = 100$ large

FIGURE 9.6   Testing H_0: $\mu = 330$ versus H_a: $\mu \neq 330$ by Using Critical Values and the *p*-Value

```
Test of mu = 330 vs not = 330

Variable    N     Mean    StDev  SE Mean      95% CI          T       P
Boxes      100   326.00   39.10    3.91   (318.24, 333.76)  -1.02   0.309
```

retail stores and use their anticipated order quantities to calculate the value of the **test statistic** *t* **in the summary box.** Then, because the alternative hypothesis H_a: $\mu \neq 330$ implies a two tailed test, we will **reject** H_0: $\mu = 330$ **if the absolute value of** *t* **is greater than** $t_{\alpha/2} = t_{.025} = 1.984$ (based on $n - 1 = 99$ degrees of freedom)—see Figure 9.6(a). Suppose that when the sample is randomly selected, the mean and the standard deviation of the $n = 100$ reported order quantities are calculated to be $\bar{x} = 326$ and $s = 39.1$. The **value of the test statistic** is

$$t = \frac{\bar{x} - 330}{s/\sqrt{n}} = \frac{326 - 330}{39.1/\sqrt{100}} = -1.023$$

Because $|t| = 1.023$ **is less than** $t_{.025} = 1.984$, **we cannot reject** H_0: $\mu = 330$ **by setting** α **equal to .05.** It follows that we cannot conclude (at an α of .05) that this year's population mean order quantity of the valentine box by large retail stores will differ from 330 boxes. Therefore, the candy company will base its production of valentine boxes on the 10 percent projected sales increase. The *p*-value for the hypothesis test is twice the area under the *t* distribution curve having 99 degrees of freedom to the right of $|t| = 1.023$. Using a computer, we find that this *p*-value is .3088 (see Figure 9.6(b)), which provides little evidence against H_0: $\mu = 330$ and in favor of H_a: $\mu \neq 330$. In Exercises 9.24 and 9.25, the reader will assume that σ is unknown in the e-billing and trash bag cases and will perform appropriate *t* tests in these cases.

To conclude this section, note that if the sampled population is not approximately normally distributed and the sample size is not large, it might be appropriate to use a **nonparametric test about the population median** (see Chapter 18).

Exercises for Section 9.3

CONCEPTS

9.21   What assumptions must be met in order to carry out a *t* test about a population mean?

9.22   How do we decide whether to use a *z* test or a *t* test when testing a hypothesis about a population mean?

METHODS AND APPLICATIONS

9.23   Suppose that a random sample of nine measurements from a normally distributed population gives a sample mean of $\bar{x} = 2.57$ and a sample standard deviation of $s = .3$. Use critical values to test H_0: $\mu = 3$ versus H_a: $\mu \neq 3$ using levels of significance $\alpha = .10$, $\alpha = .05$, $\alpha = .01$, and $\alpha = .001$.

9.24   Consider the e-billing case. The mean and the standard deviation of the sample of $n = 65$ payment times are $\bar{x} = 18.1077$ and $s = 3.9612$. (**1**) Test H_0: $\mu = 19.5$ versus H_a: $\mu < 19.5$ by setting α equal to .01 and using a critical value rule. (**2**) Interpret the (computer calculated) p-value of .0031 for the test. That is, explain how much evidence there is that H_0 is false.   **DS** PayTime

9.25   Consider the trash bag case. The mean and the standard deviation of the sample of $n = 40$ trash bag breaking strengths are $\bar{x} = 50.575$ and $s = 1.6438$. (**1**) Test H_0: $\mu = 50$ versus H_a: $\mu > 50$ by setting α equal to .05 and using a critical value rule. (**2**) Interpret the (computer calculated) p-value of .0164 for the test. That is, explain how much evidence there is that H_0 is false.   **DS** TrashBag

9.26   **THE AIR SAFETY CASE**   **DS** AlertTimes

Recall that it is hoped that the mean alert time, μ, using the new display panel is less than eight seconds. (**1**) Formulate the null hypothesis H_0 and the alternative hypothesis H_a that would be used to attempt to provide evidence that μ is less than eight seconds. (**2**) Discuss the meanings of a Type I error and a Type II error in this situation. (**3**) The mean and the standard deviation of the sample of $n = 15$ alert times are $\bar{x} = 7.4$ and $s = 1.0261$. Test H_0 versus H_a by setting α equal to .05 and using a critical value. Assume that the population of all alert times using the new display panel is approximately normally distributed. (**4**) Interpret the p-value of .02 for the test.

9.27   The *bad debt ratio* for a financial institution is defined to be the dollar value of loans defaulted divided by the total dollar value of all loans made. Suppose that a random sample of seven Ohio banks is selected and that the bad debt ratios (written as percentages) for these banks are 7%, 4%, 6%, 7%, 5%, 4%, and 9%.   **DS** BadDebt

   a   Banking officials claim that the mean bad debt ratio for all Midwestern banks is 3.5 percent and that the mean bad debt ratio for Ohio banks is higher. (**1**) Set up the null and alternative hypotheses needed to attempt to provide evidence supporting the claim that the mean bad debt ratio for Ohio banks exceeds 3.5 percent. (**2**) Discuss the meanings of a Type I error and a Type II error in this situation.

   b   Assuming that bad debt ratios for Ohio banks are approximately normally distributed: (**1**) Use a critical value and the given sample information to test the hypotheses you set up in part *a* by setting α equal to .01. (**2**) Interpret the p-value of .006 for the test.

9.28   How might practical importance be defined for the situation in Exercise 9.27?

9.29   **THE VIDEO GAME SATISFACTION RATING CASE**   **DS** VideoGame

Recall that "very satisfied" customers give the XYZ-Box video game system a composite satisfaction rating that is at least 42.

   a   Letting μ represent the mean composite satisfaction rating for the XYZ-Box, set up the null and alternative hypotheses needed if we wish to attempt to provide evidence supporting the claim that μ exceeds 42.

   b   The mean and the standard deviation of a sample of $n = 65$ customer satisfaction ratings are $\bar{x} = 42.95$ and $s = 2.6424$. (**1**) Use a critical value to test the hypotheses you set up in part *a* by setting α equal to .01. (**2**) Interpret the p-value of .0025 for the test.

9.30   **THE BANK CUSTOMER WAITING TIME CASE**   **DS** WaitTime

Recall that a bank manager has developed a new system to reduce the time customers spend waiting for teller service during peak hours. The manager hopes the new system will reduce waiting times from the current 9 to 10 minutes to less than 6 minutes.

   a   Letting μ represent the mean waiting time under the new system, set up the null and alternative hypotheses needed if we wish to attempt to provide evidence supporting the claim that μ is shorter than six minutes.

   b   The mean and the standard deviation of a sample of 100 bank customer waiting times are $\bar{x} = 5.46$ and $s = 2.475$. (**1**) Use a critical value to test the hypotheses you set up in part *a* by setting α equal to .05. (**2**) Interpret the p-value of .0158 for the test.

9.31   Consider a chemical company that wishes to determine whether a new catalyst, catalyst XA-100, changes the mean hourly yield of its chemical process from the historical process mean of 750 pounds per hour. When five trial runs are made using the new catalyst, the following yields (in pounds per hour) are recorded: 801, 814, 784, 836, and 820.   **DS** ChemYield

a   Letting μ be the mean of all possible yields using the new catalyst, set up the null and alternative hypotheses needed if we wish to attempt to provide evidence that μ differs from 750 pounds.

b   The mean and the standard deviation of the sample of 5 catalyst yields are $\bar{x} = 811$ and $s = 19.647$. **(1)** Using a critical value and assuming approximate normality, test the hypotheses you set up in part *a* by setting α equal to .01. **(2)** The *p*-value for the hypothesis test is given in the Excel output on the page margin. Interpret this *p*-value.

t-statistic
6.942585
p-value
0.002261

9.32   Recall from Exercise 8.12 that Bayus (1991) studied the mean numbers of auto dealers visited by early and late replacement buyers. **(1)** Letting μ be the mean number of dealers visited by all late replacement buyers, set up the null and alternative hypotheses needed if we wish to attempt to provide evidence that μ differs from 4 dealers. **(2)** A random sample of 100 late replacement buyers yields a mean and a standard deviation of the number of dealers visited of $\bar{x} = 4.32$ and $s = .67$. Use critical values to test the hypotheses you set up by setting α equal to .10, .05, .01, and .001. **(3)** Do we estimate that μ is less than 4 or greater than 4?

9.33   In 1991 the average interest rate charged by U.S. credit card issuers was 18.8 percent. Since that time, there has been a proliferation of new credit cards affiliated with retail stores, oil companies, alumni associations, professional sports teams, and so on. A financial officer wishes to study whether the increased competition in the credit card business has reduced interest rates. To do this, the officer will test a hypothesis about the current mean interest rate, μ, charged by all U.S. credit card issuers. To perform the hypothesis test, the officer randomly selects $n = 15$ credit cards and obtains the following interest rates (arranged in increasing order): 14.0, 14.6, 15.3, 15.6, 15.8, 16.4, 16.6, 17.0, 17.3, 17.6, 17.8, 18.1, 18.4, 18.7, and 19.2. A stem-and-leaf display of the interest rates is given on the page margin, and the MINITAB and Excel outputs for testing H_0: $\mu = 18.8$ versus H_a: $\mu < 18.8$ follow.

14	06
15	368
16	46
17	0368
18	147
19	2

DS CreditCd

Test of mu = 18.8 vs < 18.8						t-statistic
						−4.97
Variable	N	Mean	StDev	SE Mean	T P	p-value
Rate	15	16.8267	1.5378	0.3971	−4.97 0.000	0.000103

a   Set up the null and alternative hypotheses needed to provide evidence that mean interest rates have decreased since 1991.

b   Use the MINITAB and Excel outputs and critical values to test the hypotheses you set up in part (a) at the .05, .01, and .001 levels of significance.

c   Use the MINITAB and Excel outputs and a *p*-value to test the hypotheses you set up in part (a) at the .05, .01, and .001 levels of significance.

d   Based on your results in parts (b) and (c), how much evidence is there that mean interest rates have decreased since 1991?

LO9-5 Use critical values and *p*-values to perform a large sample *z* test about a population proportion.

9.4 *z* Tests about a Population Proportion ● ● ●

In this section we study a large sample hypothesis test about a population proportion (that is, about the fraction of population elements that possess some characteristic). We begin with an example.

EXAMPLE 9.5 The Cheese Spread Case: Improving Profitability

C

Recall that the soft cheese spread producer has decided that replacing the current spout with the new spout is profitable only if p, the true proportion of all current purchasers who would stop buying the cheese spread if the new spout were used, is less than .10. The producer feels that it is unwise to change the spout unless it has very strong evidence that p is less than .10. Therefore, the spout will be changed if and only if the null hypothesis H_0: $p = .10$ can be rejected in favor of the alternative hypothesis H_a: $p < .10$ at the .01 level of significance.

In order to see how to test this kind of hypothesis, remember that when n is large, the sampling distribution of

$$\frac{\hat{p} - p}{\sqrt{\dfrac{p(1-p)}{n}}}$$

is approximately a standard normal distribution. Let p_0 denote a specified value between 0 and 1 (its exact value will depend on the problem), and consider testing the null hypothesis $H_0: p = p_0$. We then have the following result:

A Large Sample Test about a Population Proportion

Null Hypothesis $H_0: p = p_0$

Test Statistic $z = \dfrac{\hat{p} - p_0}{\sqrt{\dfrac{p_0(1 - p_0)}{n}}}$

Assumptions[3] $np_0 \geq 5$ and $n(1 - p_0) \geq 5$

Critical Value Rule			p-Value (Reject H_0 if p-Value $< \alpha$)		
$H_a: p > p_0$	$H_a: p < p_0$	$H_a: p \neq p_0$	$H_a: p > p_0$	$H_a: p < p_0$	$H_a: p \neq p_0$
Reject H_0 if $z > z_\alpha$	Reject H_0 if $z < -z_\alpha$	Reject H_0 if $|z| > z_{\alpha/2}$ —that is, $z > z_{\alpha/2}$ or $z < -z_{\alpha/2}$	p-value = area to the right of z	p-value = area to the left of z	p-value = twice the area to the right of $|z|$

EXAMPLE 9.6 The Cheese Spread Case: Improving Profitability

We have seen that the cheese spread producer wishes to test $H_0: p = .10$ versus $H_a: p < .10$, where p is the proportion of all current purchasers who would stop buying the cheese spread if the new spout were used. The producer will use the new spout if H_0 can be rejected in favor of H_a at the **.01 level of significance.** To perform the hypothesis test, we will randomly select $n = 1,000$ current purchasers of the cheese spread, find the proportion ($\hat{p}$) of these purchasers who would stop buying the cheese spread if the new spout were used, and calculate the value of the **test statistic z in the summary box.** Then, because the alternative hypothesis $H_a: p < .10$ implies a left tailed test, we will **reject $H_0: p = .10$ if the value of z is less than $-z_\alpha = -z_{.01} = -2.33$.** (Note that using this procedure is valid because $np_0 = 1,000(.10) = 100$ and $n(1 - p_0) = 1,000(1 - .10) = 900$ are both at least 5.) Suppose that when the sample is randomly selected, we find that 63 of the 1,000 current purchasers say they would stop buying the cheese spread if the new spout were used. Because $\hat{p} = 63/1,000 = .063$, the **value of the test statistic** is

$$z = \frac{\hat{p} - p_0}{\sqrt{\dfrac{p_0(1 - p_0)}{n}}} = \frac{.063 - .10}{\sqrt{\dfrac{.10(1 - .10)}{1,000}}} = -3.90$$

Because $z = -3.90$ is less than $-z_{.01} = -2.33$, we reject $H_0: p = .10$ in favor of $H_a: p < .10$. That is, we conclude (at an α of .01) that the proportion of all current purchasers who would stop buying the cheese spread if the new spout were used is less than .10. It follows that the company will use the new spout. Furthermore, the point estimate $\hat{p} = .063$ says we estimate that 6.3 percent of all current customers would stop buying the cheese spread if the new spout were used.

Although the cheese spread producer has made its decision by setting α equal to a single, pre-chosen value (.01), it would probably also wish to know the weight of evidence against H_0 and in favor of H_a. The p-value is the area under the standard normal curve to the left of $z = -3.90$. Table A.3 (page 790) tells us that this area is .00005. Because this p-value is less than .001, we

---

[3]Some statisticians suggest using the more conservative rule that both np_0 and $n(1 - p_0)$ must be at least 10.

have extremely strong evidence that H_a: $p < .10$ is true. That is, we have extremely strong evidence that fewer than 10 percent of all current purchasers would stop buying the cheese spread if the new spout were used.

EXAMPLE 9.7 The Phantol Case: Testing the Effectiveness of a Drug

Recent medical research has sought to develop drugs that lessen the severity and duration of viral infections. Virol, a relatively new drug, has been shown to provide relief for 70 percent of all patients suffering from viral upper respiratory infections. A major drug company is developing a competing drug called Phantol. The drug company wishes to investigate whether Phantol is more effective than Virol. To do this, the drug company will test a hypothesis about the proportion, p, of all patients whose symptoms would be relieved by Phantol. **The null hypothesis to be tested is H_0: $p = .70$, and the alternative hypothesis is H_a: $p > .70$.** If H_0 can be rejected in favor of H_a at the **.05 level of significance,** the drug company will conclude that Phantol helps more than the 70 percent of patients helped by Virol. To perform the hypothesis test, we will randomly select $n = 300$ patients having viral upper respiratory infections, find the proportion ($\hat{p}$) of these patients whose symptoms are relieved by Phantol and calculate the value of the **test statistic z in the summary box.** Then, because the alternative hypothesis H_a: $p > .70$ implies a right tailed test, we will **reject H_0: $p = .70$ if the value of z is greater than $z_\alpha = z_{.05} = 1.645$.** (Note that using this procedure is valid because $np_0 = 300(.70) = 210$ and $n(1 - p_0) = 300(1 - .70) = 90$ are both at least 5.) Suppose that when the sample is randomly selected, we find that Phantol provides relief for 231 of the 300 patients. Because $\hat{p} = 231/300 = .77$, the **value of the test statistic** is

$$z = \frac{\hat{p} - p_0}{\sqrt{\dfrac{p_0(1 - p_0)}{n}}} = \frac{.77 - .70}{\sqrt{\dfrac{(.70)(1 - .70)}{300}}} = 2.65$$

Because $z = 2.65$ is greater than $z_{.05} = 1.645$, we reject H_0: $p = .70$ in favor of H_a: $p > .70$. That is, we conclude (at an α of .05) that Phantol will provide relief for more than 70 percent of all patients suffering from viral upper respiratory infections. More specifically, the point estimate $\hat{p} = .77$ of p says that we estimate that Phantol will provide relief for 77 percent of all such patients. Comparing this estimate to the 70 percent of all patients whose symptoms are relieved by Virol, we conclude that Phantol is somewhat more effective.

The p-value for testing H_0: $p = .70$ versus H_a: $p > .70$ is the area under the standard normal curve to the right of $z = 2.65$. This p-value is $(1.0 - .9960) = .004$ (see Table A.3, page 790), and it provides very strong evidence against H_0: $p = .70$ and in favor of H_a: $p > .70$. That is, we have very strong evidence that Phantol will provide relief for more than 70 percent of all patients suffering from viral upper respiratory infections.

EXAMPLE 9.8 The Electronic Article Surveillance Case: False Alarms

A sports equipment discount store is considering installing an electronic article surveillance device and is concerned about the proportion, p, of all consumers who would never shop in the store again if the store subjected them to a false alarm. Suppose that industry data for general discount stores says that 15 percent of all consumers say that they would never shop in a store again if the store subjected them to a false alarm. To determine whether this percentage is different for the sports equipment discount store, the store will test the **null hypothesis H_0: $p = .15$ versus the alternative hypothesis H_a: $p \neq .15$** at the **.05 level of significance.** To perform the hypothesis test, the store will randomly select $n = 500$ consumers, find the proportion $\hat{p}$ of these consumers who say that they would never shop in the store again if the store subjected them to a false alarm, and calculate the value of the **test statistic z in the summary box.** Then, because the alternative hypothesis H_a: $p \neq .15$ implies a two tailed test, we will **reject H_0: $p = .15$ if $|z|$, the absolute value of the test statistic z, is greater than $z_{\alpha/2} = z_{.025} = 1.96$.** (Note that using this procedure is valid because $np_0 = (500)(.15) = 75$ and $n(1 - p_0) = (500)(1 - .15) = 425$ are both at least 5.)

Suppose that when the sample is randomly selected, we find that 70 out of 500 consumers say that they would never shop in the store again if the store subjected them to a false alarm. Because $\hat{p} = 70/500 = .14$, the **value of the test statistic** is

$$z = \frac{\hat{p} - p_0}{\sqrt{\dfrac{p_0(1 - p_0)}{n}}} = \frac{.14 - .15}{\sqrt{\dfrac{.15(1 - .15)}{500}}} = -.63$$

Because $|z| = .63$ is less than $z_{.025} = 1.96$, we cannot reject $H_0: p = .15$ in favor of $H_a: p \neq .15$. That is, we cannot conclude (at an α of .05) that the percentage of all people who would never shop in the sports discount store again if the store subjected them to a false alarm differs from the general discount store percentage of 15 percent.

The p-value for testing $H_0: p = .15$ versus $H_a: p \neq .15$ is twice the area under the standard normal curve to the right of $|z| = .63$. Because the area under the standard normal curve to the right of $|z| = .63$ is $(1 - .7357) = .2643$ (see Table A.3, page 790), the p-value is $2(.2643) = .5286$. As can be seen on the output below, MINITAB calculates this p-value to be 0.531 (this value is slightly more accurate than our (hand- and table-) calculated result.

```
Test of p = 0.15 vs p not = 0.15

  X     N   Sample p      95% CI       Z-Value   P-Value
 70   500     0.14    (0.1096, 0.1704)   -0.63     0.531
```

This p-value is large and provides little evidence against $H_0: p = .15$ and in favor of $H_a: p \neq .15$. That is, we have little evidence that the percentage of people who would never shop in the sports discount store again if the store subjected them to a false alarm differs from the general discount store percentage of 15 percent.

Exercises for Section 9.4

CONCEPTS

9.34 If we wish to test a hypothesis to provide evidence supporting the claim that fewer than 5 percent of the units produced by a process are defective, formulate the null and alternative hypotheses.

9.35 What condition must be satisfied in order for the methods of this section to be appropriate?

METHODS AND APPLICATIONS

9.36 Suppose we test $H_0: p = .3$ versus $H_a: p \neq .3$ and that a random sample of $n = 100$ gives a sample proportion $\hat{p} = .20$.
  a Test H_0 versus H_a at the .01 level of significance by using critical values. What do you conclude?
  b Find the p-value for this test.
  c Use the p-value to test H_0 versus H_a by setting α equal to .10, .05, .01, and .001. What do you conclude at each value of α?

9.37 **THE MARKETING ETHICS CASE: CONFLICT OF INTEREST**

Recall that a conflict of interest scenario was presented to a sample of 205 marketing researchers and that 111 of these researchers disapproved of the actions taken.
  a Let p be the proportion of all marketing researchers who disapprove of the actions taken in the conflict of interest scenario. Set up the null and alternative hypotheses needed to attempt to provide evidence supporting the claim that a majority (more than 50 percent) of all marketing researchers disapprove of the actions taken.
  b Assuming that the sample of 205 marketing researchers has been randomly selected, use critical values and the previously given sample information to test the hypotheses you set up in part a at the .10, .05, .01, and .001 levels of significance. How much evidence is there that a majority of all marketing researchers disapprove of the actions taken?
  c Suppose a random sample of 1,000 marketing researchers reveals that 540 of the researchers disapprove of the actions taken in the conflict of interest scenario. Use critical values to determine how much evidence there is that a majority of all marketing researchers disapprove of the actions taken.

d Note that in parts *b* and *c* the sample proportion $\hat{p}$ is (essentially) the same. Explain why the results of the hypothesis tests in parts *b* and *c* differ.

9.38 Last year, television station WXYZ's share of the 11 P.M. news audience was approximately equal to, but no greater than, 25 percent. The station's management believes that the current audience share is higher than last year's 25 percent share. In an attempt to substantiate this belief, the station surveyed a random sample of 400 11 P.M. news viewers and found that 146 watched WXYZ.

    a Let *p* be the current proportion of all 11 P.M. news viewers who watch WXYZ. Set up the null and alternative hypotheses needed to attempt to provide evidence supporting the claim that the current audience share for WXYZ is higher than last year's 25 percent share.

    b Use critical values and the following MINITAB output to test the hypotheses you set up in part *a* at the .10, .05, .01, and .001 levels of significance. How much evidence is there that the current audience share is higher than last year's 25 percent share?

```
Test of p = 0.25 vs p > 0.25

Sample     X     N     Sample p     Z-Value     P-Value
1        146    400    0.365000       5.31        0.000
```

    c Find the *p*-value for the hypothesis test in part *b*. Use the *p*-value to carry out the test by setting α equal to .10, .05, .01, and .001. Interpret your results.

    d Do you think that the result of the station's survey has practical importance? Why or why not?

9.39 In the book *Essentials of Marketing Research,* William R. Dillon, Thomas J. Madden, and Neil H. Firtle discuss a marketing research proposal to study day-after recall for a brand of mouthwash. To quote the authors:

> The ad agency has developed a TV ad for the introduction of the mouthwash. The objective of the ad is to create awareness of the brand. The objective of this research is to evaluate the awareness generated by the ad measured by aided- and unaided-recall scores.
>
> A minimum of 200 respondents who claim to have watched the TV show in which the ad was aired the night before will be contacted by telephone in 20 cities.
>
> The study will provide information on the incidence of unaided and aided recall.

Suppose a random sample of 200 respondents shows that 46 of the people interviewed were able to recall the commercial without any prompting (unaided recall).

    a In order for the ad to be considered successful, the percentage of unaided recall must be above the category norm for a TV commercial for the product class. If this norm is 18 percent, set up the null and alternative hypotheses needed to attempt to provide evidence that the ad is successful.

    b Use the previously given sample information to: **(1)** Compute the *p*-value for the hypothesis test you set up in part *a*. **(2)** Use the *p*-value to carry out the test by setting α equal to .10, .05, .01, and .001. **(3)** How much evidence is there that the TV commercial is successful?

    c Do you think the result of the ad agency's survey has practical importance? Explain your opinion.

9.40 An airline's data indicate that 50 percent of people who begin the online process of booking a flight never complete the process and pay for the flight. To reduce this percentage, the airline is considering changing its website so that the entire booking process, including flight and seat selection and payment, can be done on two simple pages rather than the current four pages. A random sample of 300 customers who begin the booking process are exposed to the new system, and 117 of them do not complete the process. **(1)** Formulate the null and alternative hypotheses needed to attempt to provide evidence that the new system has reduced the noncompletion percentage. **(2)** Use critical values and a *p*-value to perform the hypothesis test by setting α equal to .10, .05, .01, and .001.

9.41 Suppose that a national survey finds that 73 percent of restaurant employees say that work stress has a negative impact on their personal lives. A random sample of 200 employees of a large restaurant chain finds that 141 employees say that work stress has a negative impact on their personal lives. **(1)** Formulate the null and alternative hypotheses needed to attempt to provide evidence that the percentage of work-stressed employees for the restaurant chain differs from the national percentage. **(2)** Use critical values and a *p*-value to perform the hypothesis test by setting α equal to .10, .05, .01, and .001.

9.42 The manufacturer of the ColorSmart-5000 television set claims that 95 percent of its sets last at least five years without needing a single repair. In order to test this claim, a consumer group randomly selects 400 consumers who have owned a ColorSmart-5000 television set for five years. Of these 400 consumers, 316 say that their ColorSmart-5000 television sets did not need repair, while 84 say that their ColorSmart-5000 television sets did need at least one repair.

    a   Letting p be the proportion of ColorSmart-5000 television sets that last five years without a single repair, set up the null and alternative hypotheses that the consumer group should use to attempt to show that the manufacturer's claim is false.

    b   Use critical values and the previously given sample information to test the hypotheses you set up in part a by setting α equal to .10, .05, .01, and .001. How much evidence is there that the manufacturer's claim is false?

    c   Do you think the results of the consumer group's survey have practical importance? Explain your opinion.

LO9-6 Calculate Type II error probabilities and the power of a test, and determine sample size (Optional).

9.5 Type II Error Probabilities and Sample Size Determination (Optional) ● ● ●

As we have seen, we often take action (for example, advertise a claim) on the basis of having rejected the null hypothesis. In this case, we know the chances that the action has been taken erroneously because we have prespecified α, the probability of rejecting a true null hypothesis. However, sometimes we must act (for example, decide how many Valentine's Day boxes of chocolates to produce) on the basis of *not* rejecting the null hypothesis. If we must do this, it is best to know the probability of not rejecting a false null hypothesis (a Type II error). If this probability is not small enough, we may change the hypothesis testing procedure. In order to discuss this further, we must first see how to compute the probability of a Type II error.

As an example, the Federal Trade Commission (FTC) often tests claims that companies make about their products. Suppose coffee is being sold in cans that are labeled as containing three pounds, and also suppose that the FTC wishes to determine if the mean amount of coffee μ in all such cans is at least three pounds. To do this, the FTC tests $H_0: \mu \geq 3$ (or $\mu = 3$) versus $H_a: \mu < 3$ by setting $\alpha = .05$. Suppose that a sample of 35 coffee cans yields $\bar{x} = 2.9973$. Assuming that σ is known to equal .0147, we see that because

$$z = \frac{2.9973 - 3}{.0147/\sqrt{35}} = -1.08$$

is not less than $-z_{.05} = -1.645$, we cannot reject $H_0: \mu \geq 3$ by setting $\alpha = .05$. Because we cannot reject H_0, we cannot have committed a Type I error, which is the error of rejecting a true H_0. However, we might have committed a Type II error, which is the error of not rejecting a false H_0. Therefore, before we make a final conclusion about μ, we should calculate the probability of a Type II error.

A Type II error is not rejecting $H_0: \mu \geq 3$ when H_0 is false. Because any value of μ that is less than 3 makes H_0 false, there is a different Type II error (and, therefore, a different Type II error probability) associated with each value of μ that is less than 3. In order to demonstrate how to calculate these probabilities, we will calculate the probability of not rejecting $H_0: \mu \geq 3$ when in fact μ equals 2.995. This is the probability of failing to detect an average underfill of .005 pound. For a fixed sample size (for example, $n = 35$ coffee can fills), the value of β, the probability of a Type II error, depends upon how we set α, the probability of a Type I error. Because we have set $\alpha = .05$, we reject H_0 if

$$\frac{\bar{x} - 3}{\sigma/\sqrt{n}} < -z_{.05}$$

or, equivalently, if

$$\bar{x} < 3 - z_{.05}\frac{\sigma}{\sqrt{n}} = 3 - 1.645\frac{.0147}{\sqrt{35}} = 2.9959126$$

Therefore, we do not reject H_0 if $\bar{x} \geq 2.9959126$. It follows that β, the probability of not rejecting $H_0: \mu \geq 3$ when μ equals 2.995, is

$$\beta = P(\bar{x} \geq 2.9959126 \text{ when } \mu = 2.995)$$

$$= P\left(z \geq \frac{2.9959126 - 2.995}{.0147/\sqrt{35}}\right)$$

$$= P(z \geq .37) = 1 - .6443 = .3557$$

> **FIGURE 9.7   Calculating β When μ Equals 2.995**

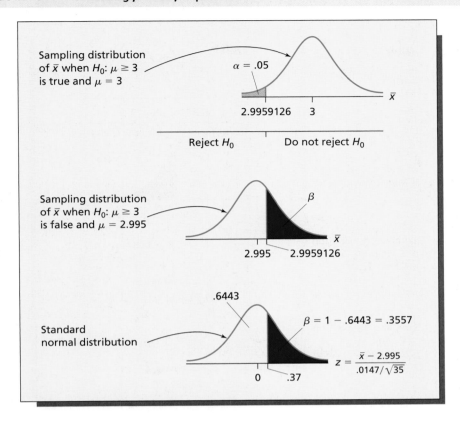

This calculation is illustrated in Figure 9.7. Similarly, it follows that β, the probability of not rejecting H_0: $\mu \geq 3$ when μ equals 2.99, is

$$\beta = P(\bar{x} \geq 2.9959126 \text{ when } \mu = 2.99)$$

$$= P\left(z \geq \frac{2.9959126 - 2.99}{.0147/\sqrt{35}}\right)$$

$$= P(z \geq 2.38) = 1 - .9913 = .0087$$

It also follows that β, the probability of not rejecting H_0: $\mu \geq 3$ when μ equals 2.985, is

$$\beta = P(\bar{x} \geq 2.9959126 \text{ when } \mu = 2.985)$$

$$= P\left(z \geq \frac{2.9959126 - 2.985}{.0147/\sqrt{35}}\right)$$

$$= P(z \geq 4.39)$$

This probability is less than .00003 (because z is greater than 3.99).

In Figure 9.8 we illustrate the values of β that we have calculated. Notice that the closer an alternative value of μ is to 3 (the value specified by H_0: $\mu = 3$), the larger is the associated value of β. Although alternative values of μ that are closer to 3 have larger associated probabilities of Type II errors, these values of μ have associated Type II errors with less serious consequences. For example, we are more likely not to reject H_0: $\mu = 3$ when $\mu = 2.995$ ($\beta = .3557$) than we are not to reject H_0: $\mu = 3$ when $\mu = 2.99$ ($\beta = .0087$). However, not rejecting H_0: $\mu = 3$ when $\mu = 2.995$, which means that we are failing to detect an average underfill of .005 pound, is less serious than not rejecting H_0: $\mu = 3$ when $\mu = 2.99$, which means that we are failing to detect a larger average underfill of .01 pound. In order to decide whether a particular hypothesis test adequately controls the probability of a Type II error, we must determine which Type II errors are serious, and then we must decide whether the probabilities of these errors are small enough. For

FIGURE 9.8   How β Changes as the Alternative Value of μ Changes

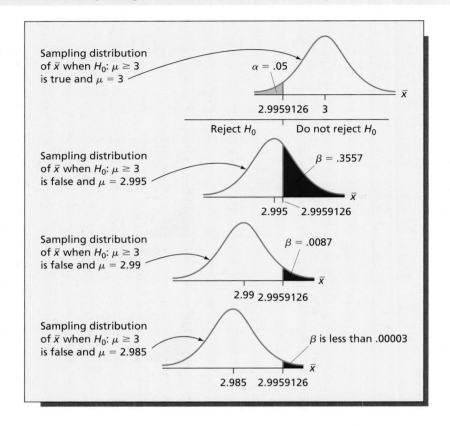

example, suppose that the FTC and the coffee producer agree that failing to reject H_0: $\mu = 3$ when μ equals 2.99 is a serious error, but that failing to reject H_0: $\mu = 3$ when μ equals 2.995 is not a particularly serious error. Then, because the probability of not rejecting H_0: $\mu = 3$ when μ equals 2.99 is .0087, which is quite small, we might decide that the hypothesis test adequately controls the probability of a Type II error. To understand the implication of this, recall that the sample of 35 coffee cans, which has $\bar{x} = 2.9973$, does not provide enough evidence to reject H_0: $\mu \geq 3$ by setting $\alpha = .05$. We have just shown that the probability that we have failed to detect a serious underfill is quite small (.0087), so the FTC might decide that no action should be taken against the coffee producer. Of course, this decision should also be based on the variability of the fills of the individual cans. Because $\bar{x} = 2.9973$ and $\sigma = .0147$, we estimate that 99.73 percent of all individual coffee can fills are contained in the interval $[\bar{x} \pm 3\sigma] = [2.9973 \pm 3(.0147)] = [2.9532, 3.0414]$. If the FTC believes it is reasonable to accept fills as low as (but no lower than) 2.9532 pounds, this evidence also suggests that no action against the coffee producer is needed.

Suppose, instead, that the FTC and the coffee producer had agreed that failing to reject H_0: $\mu \geq 3$ when μ equals 2.995 is a serious mistake. The probability of this Type II error is .3557, which is large. Therefore, we might conclude that the hypothesis test is not adequately controlling the probability of a serious Type II error. In this case, we have two possible courses of action. First, we have previously said that, for a fixed sample size, the lower we set α, the higher is β, and the higher we set α, the lower is β. Therefore, if we keep the sample size fixed at $n = 35$ coffee cans, we can reduce β by increasing α. To demonstrate this, suppose we increase α to .10. In this case we reject H_0 if

$$\frac{\bar{x} - 3}{\sigma/\sqrt{n}} < -z_{.10}$$

or, equivalently, if

$$\bar{x} < 3 - z_{.10} \frac{\sigma}{\sqrt{n}} = 3 - 1.282 \frac{.0147}{\sqrt{35}} = 2.9968145$$

Therefore, we do not reject H_0 if $\bar{x} \geq 2.9968145$. It follows that β, the probability of not rejecting H_0: $\mu \geq 3$ when μ equals 2.995, is

$$\beta = P(\bar{x} \geq 2.9968145 \text{ when } \mu = 2.995)$$

$$= P\left(z \geq \frac{2.9968145 - 2.995}{.0147/\sqrt{35}}\right)$$

$$= P(z \geq .73) = 1 - .7673 = .2327$$

We thus see that increasing α from .05 to .10 reduces β from .3557 to .2327. However, β is still too large, and, besides, we might not be comfortable making α larger than .05. Therefore, if we wish to decrease β and maintain α at .05, we must increase the sample size. We will soon present a formula we can use to find the sample size needed to make both α and β as small as we wish.

Once we have computed β, we can calculate what we call the *power* of the test.

The **power** of a statistical test is the probability of rejecting the null hypothesis when it is false.

Just as β depends upon the alternative value of μ, so does the power of a test. In general, **the power associated with a particular alternative value of μ equals $1 - \beta$,** where β is the probability of a Type II error associated with the same alternative value of μ. For example, we have seen that, when we set $\alpha = .05$, the probability of not rejecting H_0: $\mu \geq 3$ when μ equals 2.99 is .0087. Therefore, the power of the test associated with the alternative value 2.99 (that is, the probability of rejecting H_0: $\mu \geq 3$ when μ equals 2.99) is $1 - .0087 = .9913$.

Thus far we have demonstrated how to calculate β when testing a *less than* alternative hypothesis. In the following box we present (without proof) a method for calculating the probability of a Type II error when testing a *less than*, a *greater than*, or a *not equal to* alternative hypothesis:

Calculating the Probability of a Type II Error

Assume that the sampled population is normally distributed, or that a large sample will be taken. Consider testing H_0: $\mu = \mu_0$ versus one of H_a: $\mu > \mu_0$, H_a: $\mu < \mu_0$, or H_a: $\mu \neq \mu_0$. Then, if we set the probability of a Type I error equal to α and randomly select a sample of size n, the probability, β, of a Type II error corresponding to the alternative value μ_a of μ is (exactly or approximately) equal to the area under the standard normal curve to the left of

$$z^* - \frac{|\mu_0 - \mu_a|}{\sigma/\sqrt{n}}$$

Here z^* equals z_α if the alternative hypothesis is one-sided ($\mu > \mu_0$ or $\mu < \mu_0$), in which case the method for calculating β is exact. Furthermore, z^* equals $z_{\alpha/2}$ if the alternative hypothesis is two-sided ($\mu \neq \mu_0$), in which case the method for calculating β is approximate.

EXAMPLE 9.9 The Valentine's Day Chocolate Case: Production Planning   C

In the Valentine's Day chocolate case we are testing H_0: $\mu = 330$ versus H_a: $\mu \neq 330$ by setting $\alpha = .05$. We have seen that the mean of the reported order quantities of a random sample of $n = 100$ large retail stores is $\bar{x} = 326$. Assuming that σ equals 40, it follows that because

$$z = \frac{326 - 330}{40/\sqrt{100}} = -1$$

is between $-z_{.025} = -1.96$ and $z_{.025} = 1.96$, we cannot reject H_0: $\mu = 330$ by setting $\alpha = .05$. Because we cannot reject H_0, we might have committed a Type II error. Suppose that the candy company decides that failing to reject H_0: $\mu = 330$ when μ differs from 330 by as many as 15 valentine boxes (that is, when μ is 315 or 345) is a serious Type II error. Because we have set α

equal to .05, β for the alternative value $\mu_a = 315$ (that is, the probability of not rejecting H_0: $\mu = 330$ when μ equals 315) is the area under the standard normal curve to the left of

$$z^* - \frac{|\mu_0 - \mu_a|}{\sigma/\sqrt{n}} = z_{.025} - \frac{|\mu_0 - \mu_a|}{\sigma/\sqrt{n}}$$

$$= 1.96 - \frac{|330 - 315|}{40/\sqrt{100}}$$

$$= -1.79$$

Here $z^* = z_{\alpha/2} = z_{.05/2} = z_{.025}$ because the alternative hypothesis ($\mu \neq 330$) is two-sided. The area under the standard normal curve to the left of -1.79 is .0367. Therefore, β for the alternative value $\mu_a = 315$ is .0367. Similarly, it can be verified that β for the alternative value $\mu_a = 345$ is .0367. It follows, because we cannot reject H_0: $\mu = 330$ by setting $\alpha = .05$, and because we have just shown that there is a reasonably small (.0367) probability that we have failed to detect a serious (that is, a 15 valentine box) deviation of μ from 330, that it is reasonable for the candy company to base this year's production of valentine boxes on the projected mean order quantity of 330 boxes per large retail store.

In the following box we present (without proof) a formula that tells us the sample size needed to make both the probability of a Type I error and the probability of a Type II error as small as we wish:

Calculating the Sample Size Needed to Achieve Specified Values of α and β

Assume that the sampled population is normally distributed, or that a large sample will be taken. Consider testing H_0: $\mu = \mu_0$ versus one of H_a: $\mu > \mu_0$, H_a: $\mu < \mu_0$, or H_a: $\mu \neq \mu_0$. Then, in order to make the probability of a Type I error equal to α and the probability of a Type II error corresponding to the alternative value μ_a of μ equal to β, we should take a sample of size

$$n = \frac{(z^* + z_\beta)^2 \sigma^2}{(\mu_0 - \mu_a)^2}$$

Here z^* equals z_α if the alternative hypothesis is one-sided ($\mu > \mu_0$ or $\mu < \mu_0$), and z^* equals $z_{\alpha/2}$ if the alternative hypothesis is two-sided ($\mu \neq \mu_0$). Also, z_β is the point on the scale of the standard normal curve that gives a right-hand tail area equal to β.

EXAMPLE 9.10 Finding A Sample Size

Again consider the coffee fill example and suppose we wish to test H_0: $\mu \geq 3$ (or $\mu = 3$) versus H_a: $\mu < 3$. If we wish α to be .05 and β for the alternative value $\mu_a = 2.995$ of μ to be .05, we should take a sample of size

$$n = \frac{(z^* + z_\beta)^2 \sigma^2}{(\mu_0 - \mu_a)^2} = \frac{(z_\alpha + z_\beta)^2 \sigma^2}{(\mu_0 - \mu_a)^2}$$

$$= \frac{(z_{.05} + z_{.05})^2 \sigma^2}{(\mu_0 - \mu_a)^2}$$

$$= \frac{(1.645 + 1.645)^2 (.0147)^2}{(3 - 2.995)^2}$$

$$= 93.5592 = 94 \text{ (rounding up)}$$

Here, $z^* = z_\alpha = z_{.05} = 1.645$ because the alternative hypothesis ($\mu < 3$) is one-sided, and $z_\beta = z_{.05} = 1.645$.

Although we have set both α and β equal to the same value in the coffee fill situation, it is not necessary for α and β to be equal. As an example, again consider the Valentine's Day chocolate case, in which we are testing H_0: $\mu = 330$ versus H_a: $\mu \neq 330$. Suppose that the candy company decides that failing to reject H_0: $\mu = 330$ when μ differs from 330 by as many as 15 valentine boxes (that is, when μ is 315 or 345) is a serious Type II error. Furthermore, suppose that it is also decided that this Type II error is more serious than a Type I error. Therefore, α will be set equal to .05 and β for the alternative value $\mu_a = 315$ (or $\mu_a = 345$) of μ will be set equal to .01. It follows that the candy company should take a sample of size

$$
\begin{aligned}
n &= \frac{(z^* + z_\beta)^2 \sigma^2}{(\mu_0 - \mu_a)^2} = \frac{(z_{\alpha/2} + z_\beta)^2 \sigma^2}{(\mu_0 - \mu_a)^2} \\[2mm]
&= \frac{(z_{.025} + z_{.01})^2 \sigma^2}{(\mu_0 - \mu_a)^2} \\[2mm]
&= \frac{(1.96 + 2.326)^2 (40)^2}{(330 - 315)^2} \\[2mm]
&= 130.62 = 131 \ (\text{rounding up})
\end{aligned}
$$

Here, $z^* = z_{\alpha/2} = z_{.05/2} = z_{.025} = 1.96$ because the alternative hypothesis ($\mu \neq 330$) is two-sided, and $z_\beta = z_{.01} = 2.326$ (see the bottom row of the t table on page 311).

To conclude this section, we point out that the methods we have presented for calculating the probability of a Type II error and determining sample size can be extended to other hypothesis tests that utilize the normal distribution. We will not, however, present the extensions in this book.

Exercises for Section 9.5

CONCEPTS

connect

9.43 We usually take action on the basis of having rejected the null hypothesis. When we do this, we know the chances that the action has been taken erroneously because we have prespecified α, the probability of rejecting a true null hypothesis. Here, it is obviously important to know (prespecify) α, the probability of a Type I error. When is it important to know the probability of a Type II error? Explain why.

9.44 Explain why we are able to compute many different values of β, the probability of a Type II error, for a single hypothesis test.

9.45 Explain what is meant by
   a A serious Type II error.
   b The power of a statistical test.

9.46 In general, do we want the power corresponding to a serious Type II error to be near 0 or near 1? Explain.

METHODS AND APPLICATIONS

9.47 Again consider the Consolidated Power waste water situation. Remember that the power plant will be shut down and corrective action will be taken on the cooling system if the null hypothesis H_0: $\mu \leq 60$ is rejected in favor of H_a: $\mu > 60$. In this exercise we calculate probabilities of various Type II errors in the context of this situation.
   a Recall that Consolidated Power's hypothesis test is based on a sample of $n = 100$ temperature readings and assume that σ equals 2. If the power company sets $\alpha = .025$, calculate the probability of a Type II error for each of the following alternative values of μ: 60.1, 60.2, 60.3, 60.4, 60.5, 60.6, 60.7, 60.8, 60.9, 61.
   b If we want the probability of making a Type II error when μ equals 60.5 to be very small, is Consolidated Power's hypothesis test adequate? Explain why or why not. If not, and if we wish to maintain the value of α at .025, what must be done?
   c The **power curve** for a statistical test is a plot of the power $= 1 - \beta$ on the vertical axis versus values of μ that make the null hypothesis false on the horizontal axis. Plot the power curve for Consolidated Power's test of H_0: $\mu \leq 60$ versus H_a: $\mu > 60$ by plotting power $= 1 - \beta$ for each of the alternative values of μ in part a. What happens to the power of the test as the alternative value of μ moves away from 60?

9.48 Again consider the automobile parts supplier situation. Remember that a problem-solving team will be assigned to rectify the process producing the cylindrical engine parts if the null hypothesis $H_0: \mu = 3$ is rejected in favor of $H_a: \mu \neq 3$. In this exercise we calculate probabilities of various Type II errors in the context of this situation.

 a Suppose that the parts supplier's hypothesis test is based on a sample of $n = 100$ diameters and that σ equals .023. If the parts supplier sets $\alpha = .05$, calculate the probability of a Type II error for each of the following alternative values of μ: 2.990, 2.995, 3.005, 3.010.

 b If we want both the probabilities of making a Type II error when μ equals 2.995 and when μ equals 3.005 to be very small, is the parts supplier's hypothesis test adequate? Explain why or why not. If not, and if we wish to maintain the value of α at .05, what must be done?

 c Plot the power of the test versus the alternative values of μ in part a. What happens to the power of the test as the alternative value of μ moves away from 3?

9.49 In each of the following situations, find the necessary sample size.

 a In the Consolidated Power hypothesis test of $H_0: \mu \leq 60$ versus $H_a: \mu > 60$ (as discussed in Exercise 9.47) find the sample size needed to make the probability of a Type I error equal to .025 and the probability of a Type II error corresponding to the alternative value $\mu_a = 60.5$ equal to .025. Here, assume σ equals 2.

 b In the automobile parts supplier's hypothesis test of $H_0: \mu = 3$ versus $H_a: \mu \neq 3$ (as discussed in Exercise 9.48) find the sample size needed to make the probability of a Type I error equal to .05 and the probability of a Type II error corresponding to the alternative value $\mu_a = 3.005$ equal to .05. Here, assume σ equals .023.

Chapter Summary

We began this chapter by learning about the two hypotheses that make up the structure of a hypothesis test. The **null hypothesis** is the statement being tested. The null hypothesis is often a statement of "no difference" or "no effect," and it is not rejected unless there is convincing sample evidence that it is false. The **alternative,** or, **research, hypothesis** is a statement that is accepted only if there is convincing sample evidence that it is true and that the null hypothesis is false. In some situations, the alternative hypothesis is a statement for which we wish to find supportive evidence. We also learned that two types of errors can be made in a hypothesis test. A **Type I error** occurs when we reject a true null hypothesis, and a **Type II error** occurs when we do not reject a false null hypothesis.

We studied two commonly used ways to conduct a hypothesis test. The first involves comparing the value of a test statistic with what is called a **critical value,** and the second employs what is called a **p-value.** The p-value measures the weight of evidence against the null hypothesis. The smaller the p-value, the more we doubt the null hypothesis.

The specific hypothesis tests we covered in this chapter all dealt with a hypothesis about one population parameter. First, we studied a test about a **population mean** that is based on the assumption that the population standard deviation σ **is known.** This test employs the **normal distribution.** Second, we studied a test about a population mean that assumes that σ **is unknown.** We learned that this test is based on the t **distribution.** Figure 9.9 presents a flowchart summarizing how to select an appropriate test statistic to test a hypothesis about a population mean. Then we presented a test about a **population proportion** that is based on the **normal distribution.** We concluded this chapter by studying Type II error probabilities, and we showed how we can find the sample size needed to make both the probability of a Type I error and the probability of a serious Type II error as small as we wish.

Glossary of Terms

alternative (research) hypothesis: A statement that will be accepted only if there is convincing sample evidence that it is true. Sometimes it is a statement for which we wish to find supportive evidence. (page 341)

critical value: The value of the test statistic is compared with a critical value in order to decide whether the null hypothesis can be rejected. (pages 347, 350, 352)

FIGURE 9.9 Selecting an Appropriate Test Statistic to Test a Hypothesis about a Population Mean

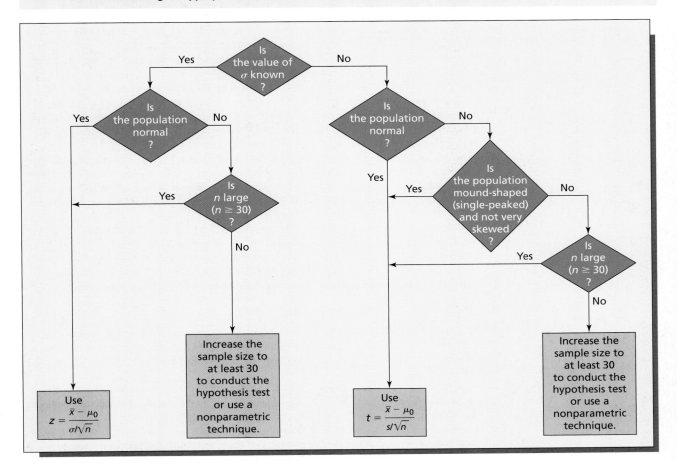

greater than alternative: An alternative hypothesis that is stated as a *greater than* (>) inequality. (page 343)

less than alternative: An alternative hypothesis that is stated as a *less than* (<) inequality. (page 343)

not equal to alternative: An alternative hypothesis that is stated as a *not equal to* (≠) inequality. (page 343)

null hypothesis: The statement being tested in a hypothesis test. It is often a statement of "no difference" or "no effect." (page 341)

p-value (probability value): The probability, computed assuming that the null hypothesis H_0 is true, of observing a value of the test statistic that is at least as contradictory to H_0 and supportive

of H_a as the value actually computed from the sample data. The p-value measures how much doubt is cast on the null hypothesis by the sample data. The smaller the p-value, the more we doubt the null hypothesis. (pages 349, 351, 353)

test statistic: A statistic computed from sample data in a hypothesis test. It is either compared with a critical value or used to compute a p-value. (page 347)

two-sided alternative hypothesis: An alternative hypothesis that is stated as a *not equal to* (≠) inequality. (page 343)

Type I error: Rejecting a true null hypothesis. (page 344)

Type II error: Failing to reject a false null hypothesis. (page 344)

Important Formulas and Tests

Hypothesis Testing steps: page 350

A hypothesis test (z test) about a population mean (σ known): page 353

A hypothesis test (t test) about a population mean (σ unknown): page 357

A large sample hypothesis test about a population proportion: page 362

Calculating the probability of a Type II error: page 369

Sample size determination to achieve specified values of α and β: page 370

Supplementary Exercises

connect

9.50 The auditor for a large corporation routinely monitors cash disbursements. As part of this process, the auditor examines check request forms to determine whether they have been properly approved. Improper approval can occur in several ways. For instance, the check may have no approval, the check request might be missing, the approval might be written by an unauthorized person, or the dollar limit of the authorizing person might be exceeded.

a Last year the corporation experienced a 5 percent improper check request approval rate. Because this was considered unacceptable, efforts were made to reduce the rate of improper approvals. Letting p be the proportion of all checks that are now improperly approved, set up the null and alternative hypotheses needed to attempt to demonstrate that the current rate of improper approvals is lower than last year's rate of 5 percent.

b Suppose that the auditor selects a random sample of 625 checks that have been approved in the last month. The auditor finds that 18 of these 625 checks have been improperly approved. Use critical values and this sample information to test the hypotheses you set up in part a at the .10, .05, .01, and .001 levels of significance. How much evidence is there that the rate of improper approvals has been reduced below last year's 5 percent rate?

c Find the p-value for the test of part b. Use the p-value to carry out the test by setting α equal to .10, .05, .01, and .001. Interpret your results.

d Suppose the corporation incurs a $10 cost to detect and correct an improperly approved check. If the corporation disburses at least 2 million checks per year, does the observed reduction of the rate of improper approvals seem to have practical importance? Explain your opinion.

9.51 **THE CIGARETTE ADVERTISEMENT CASE** 🅳🅢 ModelAge

Recall that the cigarette industry requires that models in cigarette ads must appear to be at least 25 years old. Also recall that a sample of 50 people is randomly selected at a shopping mall. Each person in the sample is shown a "typical cigarette ad" and is asked to estimate the age of the model in the ad.

a Let μ be the mean perceived age estimate for all viewers of the ad, and suppose we consider the industry requirement to be met if μ is at least 25. Set up the null and alternative hypotheses needed to attempt to show that the industry requirement is not being met.

b Suppose that a random sample of 50 perceived age estimates gives a mean of $\bar{x} = 23.663$ years and a standard deviation of $s = 3.596$ years. Use these sample data and critical values to test the hypotheses of part a at the .10, .05, .01, and .001 levels of significance.

c How much evidence do we have that the industry requirement is not being met?

d Do you think that this result has practical importance? Explain your opinion.

9.52 **THE CIGARETTE ADVERTISEMENT CASE** 🅳🅢 ModelAge

Consider the cigarette ad situation discussed in Exercise 9.51. Using the sample information given in that exercise, the p-value for testing H_0 versus H_a can be calculated to be .0057.

a Determine whether H_0 would be rejected at each of $\alpha = .10$, $\alpha = .05$, $\alpha = .01$, and $\alpha = .001$.

b Describe how much evidence we have that the industry requirement is not being met.

9.53 In an article in the *Journal of Retailing,* Kumar, Kerwin, and Pereira study factors affecting merger and acquisition activity in retailing. As part of the study, the authors compare the characteristics of "target firms" (firms targeted for acquisition) and "bidder firms" (firms attempting to make acquisitions). Among the variables studied in the comparison were earnings per share, debt-to-equity ratio, growth rate of sales, market share, and extent of diversification.

a Let μ be the mean growth rate of sales for all target firms (firms that have been targeted for acquisition in the last five years and that have not bid on other firms), and assume growth rates are approximately normally distributed. Furthermore, suppose a random sample of 25 target firms yields a sample mean sales growth rate of $\bar{x} = 0.16$ with a standard deviation of $s = 0.12$. Use critical values and this sample information to test $H_0: \mu \le .10$ versus $H_a: \mu > .10$ by setting α equal to .10, .05, .01, and .001. How much evidence is there that the mean growth rate of sales for target firms exceeds .10 (that is, exceeds 10 percent)?

b Now let μ be the mean growth rate of sales for all firms that are bidders (firms that have bid to acquire at least one other firm in the last five years), and again assume growth rates are approximately normally distributed. Furthermore, suppose a random sample of 25 bidders yields a sample mean sales growth rate of $\bar{x} = 0.12$ with a standard deviation of $s = 0.09$. Use critical values and this sample information to test $H_0: \mu \le .10$ versus $H_a: \mu > .10$ by setting α equal to .10, .05, .01, and .001. How much evidence is there that the mean growth rate of sales for bidders exceeds .10 (that is, exceeds 10 percent)?

9.54   A consumer electronics firm has developed a new type of remote control button that is designed to operate longer before becoming intermittent. A random sample of 35 of the new buttons is selected and each is tested in continuous operation until becoming intermittent. The resulting lifetimes are found to have a sample mean of $\bar{x} = 1{,}241.2$ hours and a sample standard deviation of $s = 110.8$.

   a   Independent tests reveal that the mean lifetime (in continuous operation) of the best remote control button on the market is 1,200 hours. Letting μ be the mean lifetime of the population of all new remote control buttons that will or could potentially be produced, set up the null and alternative hypotheses needed to attempt to provide evidence that the new button's mean lifetime exceeds the mean lifetime of the best remote button currently on the market.

   b   Using the previously given sample results, use critical values to test the hypotheses you set up in part *a* by setting α equal to .10, .05, .01, and .001. What do you conclude for each value of α?

   c   Suppose that $\bar{x} = 1{,}241.2$ and $s = 110.8$ had been obtained by testing a sample of 100 buttons. Use critical values to test the hypotheses you set up in part *a* by setting α equal to .10, .05, .01, and .001. Which sample (the sample of 35 or the sample of 100) gives a more statistically significant result? That is, which sample provides stronger evidence that H_a is true?

   d   If we define practical importance to mean that μ exceeds 1,200 by an amount that would be clearly noticeable to most consumers, do you think that the result has practical importance? Explain why the samples of 35 and 100 both indicate the same degree of practical importance.

   e   Suppose that further research and development effort improves the new remote control button and that a random sample of 35 buttons gives $\bar{x} = 1{,}524.6$ hours and $s = 102.8$ hours. Test your hypotheses of part *a* by setting α equal to .10, .05, .01, and .001.

   (1)   Do we have a highly statistically significant result? Explain.

   (2)   Do you think we have a practically important result? Explain.

9.55   Again consider the remote control button lifetime situation discussed in Exercise 9.54. Using the sample information given in the introduction to Exercise 9.54, the *p*-value for testing H_0 versus H_a can be calculated to be .0174.

   a   Determine whether H_0 would be rejected at each of $\alpha = .10$, $\alpha = .05$, $\alpha = .01$, and $\alpha = .001$.

   b   Describe how much evidence we have that the new button's mean lifetime exceeds the mean lifetime of the best remote button currently on the market.

9.56   Several industries located along the Ohio River discharge a toxic substance called carbon tetrachloride into the river. The state Environmental Protection Agency monitors the amount of carbon tetrachloride pollution in the river. Specifically, the agency requires that the carbon tetrachloride contamination must average no more than 10 parts per million. In order to monitor the carbon tetrachloride contamination in the river, the agency takes a daily sample of 100 pollution readings at a specified location. If the mean carbon tetrachloride reading for this sample casts substantial doubt on the hypothesis that the average amount of carbon tetrachloride contamination in the river is at most 10 parts per million, the agency must issue a shutdown order. In the event of such a shutdown order, industrial plants along the river must be closed until the carbon tetrachloride contamination is reduced to a more acceptable level. Assume that the state Environmental Protection Agency decides to issue a shutdown order if a sample of 100 pollution readings implies that H_0: $\mu \leq 10$ can be rejected in favor of H_a: $\mu > 10$ by setting $\alpha = .01$. If σ equals 2, calculate the probability of a Type II error for each of the following alternative values of μ: 10.1, 10.2, 10.3, 10.4, 10.5, 10.6, 10.7, 10.8, 10.9, and 11.0.

9.57   Suppose that a spokesman for U.S. travel agencies claims that more than 65 percent of all U.S. passengers who booked cruises last year used travel agencies to book their cruises. In the October 2, 2011, issue of the *Hamilton Journal News,* an actual survey of U.S. passengers who booked cruises last year found that 68 percent of those sampled used travel agencies to book their cruises. Assuming that the survey was based on 1,500 randomly selected U.S. passengers who booked cruises last year, calculate a *p*-value that shows the evidence supporting the spokesman's claim. Interpret your results.

9.58   Assume that an insurance survey is based on 1,000 randomly selected U.S. households in a particular income class and finds that 640 of these households bought life insurance last year.

   a   If p denotes the proportion of all U.S. households in the income class that bought life insurance last year, set up the null and alternative hypotheses needed to attempt to justify the claim that more than 60 percent of U.S. households in the income class bought life insurance last year.

b　Test the hypotheses you set up in part *a* by setting α = .10, .05, .01, and .001. How much evidence is there that more than 60 percent of U.S. households in the income class bought life insurance last year?

9.59　How safe are child car seats? *Consumer Reports* (May 2005) tested the safety of child car seats in 30 mph crashes. They found "slim safety margins" for some child car seats. Suppose that *Consumer Reports* simulates the safety of the market-leading child car seat. Their test consists of placing the maximum claimed weight in the car seat and simulating crashes at higher and higher speeds until a problem occurs. The following data identify the speed (in miles per hour) at which a problem with the car seat (such as the strap breaking, seat shell cracked, strap adjuster broke, detached from base, etc.) first appeared: 31.0, 29.4, 30.4, 28.9, 29.7, 30.1, 32.3, 31.7, 35.4, 29.1, 31.2, 30.2. Let μ denote the true mean speed at which a problem with the car seat first appears. The following MINITAB output gives the results of using the sample data to test H_0: μ = 30 versus H_a: $\mu >$ 30.　**DS** CarSeat

```
Test of mu = 30 vs > 30

Variable    N      Mean    StDev   SE Mean     T      P
mph        12   30.7833   1.7862   0.5156    1.52   0.078
```

How much evidence is there that μ exceeds 30 mph?

9.60　*Consumer Reports* (January 2005) indicates that profit margins on extended warranties are much greater than on the purchase of most products.[4] In this exercise we consider a major electronics retailer that wishes to increase the proportion of customers who buy extended warranties on digital cameras. Historically, 20 percent of digital camera customers have purchased the retailer's extended warranty. To increase this percentage, the retailer has decided to offer a new warranty that is less expensive and more comprehensive. Suppose that three months after starting to offer the new warranty, a random sample of 500 customer sales invoices shows that 152 out of 500 digital camera customers purchased the new warranty. **(1)** Letting *p* denote the proportion of all digital camera customers who have purchased the new warranty, calculate the *p*-value for testing H_0: *p* = .20 versus H_a: *p* > .20. **(2)** How much evidence is there that *p* exceeds .20? **(3)** Does the difference between $\hat{p}$ and .2 seem to be practically important? Explain your opinion.

9.61　*Fortune* magazine has periodically reported on the rise of fees and expenses charged by stock funds.

a　Suppose that 10 years ago the average annual expense for stock funds was 1.19 percent. Let μ be the current mean annual expense for all stock funds, and assume that stock fund annual expenses are approximately normally distributed. If a random sample of 12 stock funds gives a sample mean annual expense of $\bar{x}$ = 1.63% with a standard deviation of *s* = .31%, use critical values and this sample information to test H_0: $\mu \le$ 1.19% versus H_a: $\mu >$ 1.19% by setting α equal to .10, .05, .01, and .001. How much evidence is there that the current mean annual expense for stock funds exceeds the average of 10 years ago?

b　Do you think that the result in part *a* has practical importance? Explain your opinion.

9.62　Internet Exercise

Are American consumers comfortable using their credit cards to make purchases over the Internet? Suppose that a noted authority suggests that credit cards will be firmly established on the Internet once the "80 percent barrier" is broken; that is, as soon as more than 80 percent of those who make purchases over the Internet are willing to use a credit card to pay for their transactions. A recent Gallup Poll (story, survey results, and analysis can be found at http://www.gallup.com/poll/releases/pr000223.asp) found that, out of *n* = 302 Internet purchasers surveyed, 267 have paid for Internet purchases using a credit card. Based on the results of the Gallup survey, is there sufficient evidence to conclude that the proportion of Internet purchasers willing to

use a credit card now exceeds 0.80? Set up the appropriate null and alternative hypotheses, test at the 0.05 and 0.01 levels of significance, and calculate a *p*-value for your test.

Go to the Gallup Organization website (http://www.gallup.com). Select an interesting current poll and prepare a brief written summary of the poll or some aspect thereof. Include a statistical test for the significance of a proportion (you may have to make up your own value for the hypothesized proportion p_0) as part of your report. For example, you might select a political poll and test whether a particular candidate is preferred by a majority of voters (*p* > 0.50).

---

[4]*Consumer Reports,* January 2005, page 51.

Appendix 9.1 ■ One-Sample Hypothesis Testing Using Excel

Hypothesis test for a population mean in Exercise 9.33 on page 361 (data file: CreditCd.xlsx):

The Data Analysis ToolPak in Excel does not explicitly provide for one-sample tests of hypotheses. A one-sample test can be conducted using the Descriptive Statistics component of the Analysis ToolPak and a few additional computations using Excel.

Descriptive statistics:

- Enter the interest rate data from Exercise 9.33 (page 361) into cells A2:A16 with the label Rate in cell A1.
- Select **Data : Data Analysis : Descriptive Statistics.**
- Click OK in the Data Analysis dialog box.
- In the Descriptive Statistics dialog box, enter A1:A16 into the Input Range box.
- Place checkmarks in the "Labels in first row" and Summary Statistics checkboxes.
- Under output options, select "New Worksheet Ply" and enter Output for the worksheet's name.
- Click OK in the Descriptive Statistics dialog box.

The resulting block of descriptive statistics is displayed in the Output worksheet and entries needed to carry out the *t* test have been entered into the cell range D3:E6.

Computation of the test statistic and *p*-value:

- In cell E7, type the formula
  = (E3 − E4)/(E5/SQRT(E6))
  to compute the test statistic t ($= -4.970$).
- Click on cell E8 and then select the Insert Function button f_x on the Excel toolbar.
- In the Insert Function dialog box, select Statistical from the "Or select a category:" menu, select T.DIST from the "Select a function:" menu, and click OK.
- In the T.DIST Function Arguments dialog box, enter E7 into the X window.
- Enter 14 into the Deg_freedom window and Enter 1 into the Cumulative window.
- Click OK in the T.DIST Function Arguments dialog box.
- The *p*-value for the test will be placed in cell E8.

The T.DIST function returns the left tail area under the appropriate *t* curve. Because we are testing a "less than" alternative hypothesis in this example, the desired *p*-value is a left tail area. If we are testing a **"greater than" alternative,** the *p*-value (which is a right tail area) is found by using a cell formula to subtract the left tail area provided by Excel from one. In the case of a **"not equal to" alternative,** we use the T.DIST function to find the area under the *t*-curve to the left of the absolute value (abs) of the *t*-statistic. We then use cell formula(s) to subtract this area from one and to multiply the resulting right tail area by two.

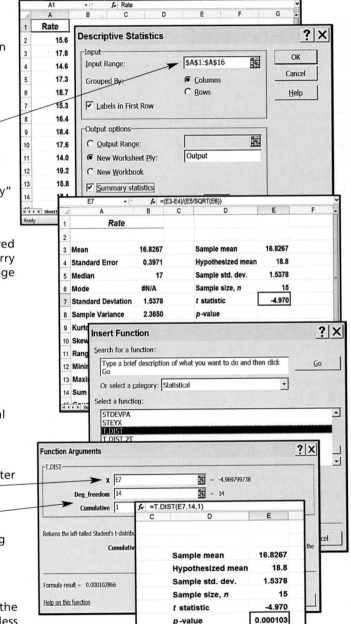

Appendix 9.2 ■ One-Sample Hypothesis Testing Using MegaStat

Hypothesis test for a population mean in Exercise 9.33 on page 361 (data file: CreditCd.xlsx):

- Enter the interest rate data from Exercise 9.33 (page 361) into cells A2:A16 with the label Rate in cell A1.

- Select **Add-Ins : MegaStat : Hypothesis Tests : Mean vs. Hypothesized Value**

- In the "Hypothesis Test: Mean vs. Hypothesized Value" dialog box, click on "data input" and use the AutoExpand feature to enter the range A1: A16 into the Input Range window.

- Enter the hypothesized value (here equal to 18.8) into the Hypothesized Mean window.

- Select the desired alternative (here "less than") from the drop-down menu in the Alternative box.

- Click on t-test and click OK in the "Hypothesis Test: Mean vs. Hypothesized Value" dialog box.

- A hypothesis test employing summary data can be carried out by clicking on "summary data," and by entering a range into the Input Range window that contains the following— label; sample mean; sample standard deviation; sample size n.

A z test can be carried out (in the unlikely event that the population standard deviation is known) by clicking on "z-test."

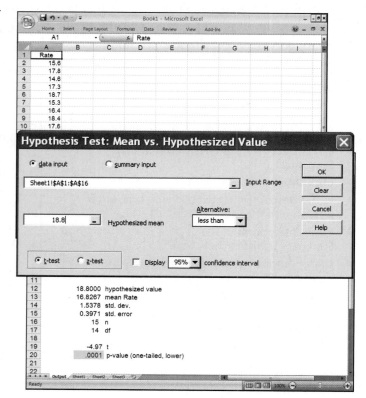

Hypothesis test for a population proportion. Consider testing H_0: $p = .05$ versus H_a: $p > .05$, where $n = 250$ and $\hat{p} = .16$.

- Select **Add-Ins : MegaStat : Hypothesis Tests : Proportion vs. Hypothesized Value**

- In the "Hypothesis Test: Proportion vs. Hypothesized Value" dialog box, enter the hypothesized value (here equal to 0.05) into the "Hypothesized p" window.

- Enter the observed sample proportion (here equal to 0.16) into the "Observed p" window.

- Enter the sample size (here equal to 250) into the "n" window.

- Select the desired alternative (here "greater than") from the drop-down menu in the Alternative box.

- Check the "Display confidence interval" checkbox (if desired), and select or type the appropriate level of confidence.

- Click OK in the "Hypothesis Test: Proportion vs. Hypothesized Value" dialog box.

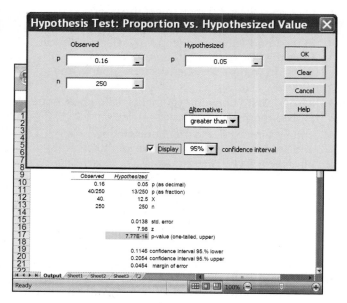

Appendix 9.3 ■ One-Sample Hypothesis Testing Using MINITAB

Hypothesis test for a population mean in Exercise 9.33 on page 361 (data file: CreditCd.MTW):

- In the Data window, enter the interest rate data from Exercise 9.33 (page 361) into a single column with variable name Rate.
- Select **Stat : Basic Statistics : 1-Sample t.**
- In the "1-Sample t (Test and Confidence Interval)" dialog box, select the "Samples in columns" option.
- Select the variable name Rate into the "Samples in columns" window.
- Place a checkmark in the "Perform hypothesis test" checkbox.
- Enter the hypothesized mean (here 18.8) into the "Hypothesized mean" window.
- Click the Options . . . button, select the desired alternative (in this case "less than") from the Alternative drop-down menu, and click OK in the "1-Sample t-Options" dialog box.
- To produce a boxplot of the data with a graphical representation of the hypothesis test, click the Graphs . . . button in the "1-Sample t (Test and Confidence Interval)" dialog box, check the "Boxplot of data" checkbox, and click OK in the "1-Sample t—Graphs" dialog box.
- Click OK in the "1-Sample t (Test and Confidence Interval)" dialog box.
- The *t* test results are given in the Session window, and the boxplot is displayed in a graphics window.

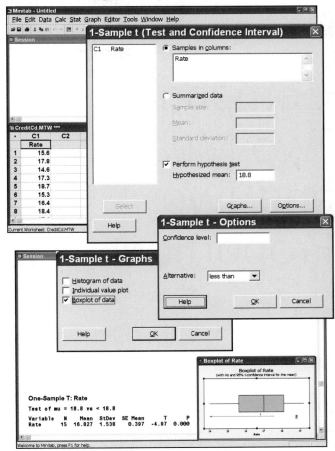

Hypothesis test for a population proportion in Exercise 9.38 on page 365:

- Select **Stat : Basic Statistics : 1 Proportion**
- In the "1 Proportion (Test and Confidence Interval)" dialog box, select the "Summarized data" option.
- Enter the sample number of successes (here equal to 146) into the "Number of events" window.
- Enter the sample size (here equal to 400) into the "Number of trials" window.
- Place a checkmark in the "Perform hypothesis test" checkbox.
- Enter the hypothesized proportion (here equal to 0.25) into the "Hypothesized proportion" window.
- Click on the Options . . . button.
- In the "1 Proportion—Options" dialog box, select the desired alternative (in this case "greater than") from the Alternative drop-down menu.
- Place a checkmark in the "Use test and interval based on normal distribution" checkbox.
- Click OK in the "1 Proportion—Options" dialog box and click OK in the "1 Proportion (Test and Confidence Interval)" dialog box.
- The hypothesis test results are given in the Session window.

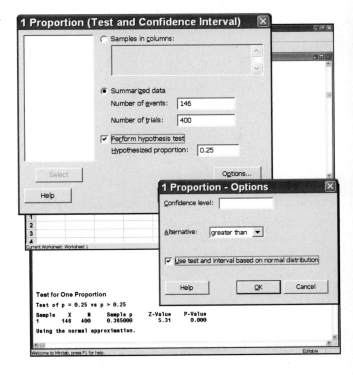

CHAPTER 10

Comparing Two Means and Two Proportions

Learning Objectives

After mastering the material in this chapter, you will be able to:

LO10-1 Compare two population means when the samples are independent.

LO10-2 Recognize when data come from independent samples and when they are paired.

LO10-3 Compare two population means when the data are paired.

LO10-4 Compare two population proportions using large independent samples.

Chapter Outline

10.1 Comparing Two Population Means by Using Independent Samples

10.2 Paired Difference Experiments

10.3 Comparing Two Population Proportions by Using Large, Independent Samples

B usiness improvement often requires making comparisons. For example, to increase consumer awareness of a product or service, it might be necessary to compare different types of advertising campaigns. Or to offer more profitable investments to its customers, an investment firm might compare the profitability of different investment portfolios. As a third example, a manufacturer might compare different production methods in order to minimize or eliminate out-of-specification product.

In this chapter we discuss using confidence intervals and hypothesis tests to **compare two populations.** Specifically, we compare two

population means and two population proportions. We make these comparisons by studying **differences.** For instance, to compare two population means, say μ_1 and μ_2, we consider the difference between these means, $\mu_1 - \mu_2$. If, for example, we use a confidence interval or hypothesis test to conclude that $\mu_1 - \mu_2$ is a positive number, then we conclude that μ_1 is greater than μ_2. On the other hand, if a confidence interval or hypothesis test shows that $\mu_1 - \mu_2$ is a negative number, then we conclude that μ_1 is less than μ_2.

We explain many of this chapter's methods in the context of three new cases:

The Catalyst Comparison Case: The production supervisor at a chemical plant uses confidence intervals and hypothesis tests for the difference between two population means to determine which of two catalysts maximizes the hourly yield of a chemical process. By maximizing yield, the plant increases its productivity and improves its profitability.

The Auto Insurance Case: In order to reduce the costs of automobile accident claims, an insurance company uses confidence intervals and hypothesis

tests for the difference between two population means to compare repair cost estimates for damaged cars at two different garages.

The Test Market Case: An advertising agency is test marketing a new product by using one advertising campaign in Des Moines, Iowa, and a different campaign in Toledo, Ohio. The agency uses confidence intervals and hypothesis tests for the difference between two population proportions to compare the effectiveness of the two advertising campaigns.

10.1 Comparing Two Population Means by Using Independent Samples ● ● ●

LO10-1 Compare two population means when the samples are independent.

A bank manager has developed a new system to reduce the time customers spend waiting to be served by tellers during peak business hours. We let μ_1 denote the population mean customer waiting time during peak business hours under the current system. To estimate μ_1, the manager randomly selects $n_1 = 100$ customers and records the length of time each customer spends waiting for service. The manager finds that the mean and the variance of the waiting times for these 100 customers are $\bar{x}_1 = 8.79$ minutes and $s_1^2 = 4.8237$. We let μ_2 denote the population mean customer waiting time during peak business hours for the new system. During a trial run, the manager finds that the mean and the variance of the waiting times for a random sample of $n_2 = 100$ customers are $\bar{x}_2 = 5.14$ minutes and $s_2^2 = 1.7927$.

In order to compare μ_1 and μ_2, the manager estimates $\mu_1 - \mu_2$, the difference between μ_1 and μ_2. Intuitively, a logical point estimate of $\mu_1 - \mu_2$ is the difference between the sample means

$$\bar{x}_1 - \bar{x}_2 = 8.79 - 5.14 = 3.65 \text{ minutes}$$

This says we estimate that the current population mean waiting time is 3.65 minutes longer than the population mean waiting time under the new system. That is, we estimate that the new system reduces the mean waiting time by 3.65 minutes.

To compute a confidence interval for $\mu_1 - \mu_2$ (or to test a hypothesis about $\mu_1 - \mu_2$), we need to know the properties of the sampling distribution of $\bar{x}_1 - \bar{x}_2$. To understand this sampling distribution, consider randomly selecting a sample[1] of n_1 measurements from a population having mean μ_1 and variance σ_1^2. Let $\bar{x}_1$ be the mean of this sample. Also consider randomly selecting a

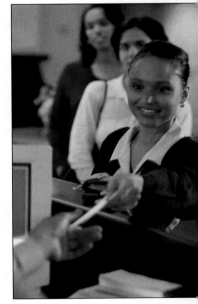

[1]Each sample in this chapter is a *random* sample. As has been our practice throughout this book, for brevity we sometimes refer to "random samples" as "samples."

FIGURE 10.1   The Sampling Distribution of $\overline{x}_1 - \overline{x}_2$ Has Mean $\mu_1 - \mu_2$ and Standard Deviation $\sigma_{\overline{x}_1 - \overline{x}_2}$

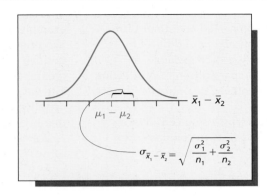

sample of n_2 measurements from another population having mean μ_2 and variance σ_2^2. Let $\overline{x}_2$ be the mean of this sample. Different samples from the first population would give different values of $\overline{x}_1$, and different samples from the second population would give different values of $\overline{x}_2$—so different pairs of samples from the two populations would give different values of $\overline{x}_1 - \overline{x}_2$. In the following box we describe the **sampling distribution of $\overline{x}_1 - \overline{x}_2$**, which is the probability distribution of all possible values of $\overline{x}_1 - \overline{x}_2$. Here we assume that the randomly selected samples from the two populations are independent of each other. This means that there is no relationship between the measurements in one sample and the measurements in the other sample. In such a case, we say that we are performing an **independent samples experiment.**

The Sampling Distribution of $\overline{x}_1 - \overline{x}_2$

If the randomly selected samples are **independent** of each other, then the population of all possible values of $\overline{x}_1 - \overline{x}_2$

1 Has a normal distribution if each sampled population has a normal distribution, or has approximately a normal distribution if the sampled populations are not normally distributed and each of the sample sizes n_1 and n_2 is large.

2 Has mean $\mu_{\overline{x}_1 - \overline{x}_2} = \mu_1 - \mu_2$

3 Has standard deviation $\sigma_{\overline{x}_1 - \overline{x}_2} = \sqrt{\dfrac{\sigma_1^2}{n_1} + \dfrac{\sigma_2^2}{n_2}}$

Figure 10.1 illustrates the sampling distribution of $\overline{x}_1 - \overline{x}_2$. Using this sampling distribution, we can find a confidence interval for and test a hypothesis about $\mu_1 - \mu_2$ by using the normal distribution. However, the interval and test assume that the true values of the population variances σ_1^2 and σ_2^2 are known, which is very unlikely. Therefore, we will estimate σ_1^2 and σ_2^2 by using s_1^2 and s_2^2, the variances of the samples randomly selected from the populations being compared, and base a confidence interval and a hypothesis test on the t distribution. There are two approaches to doing this. The first approach gives theoretically correct confidence intervals and hypothesis tests but assumes that the population variances σ_1^2 and σ_2^2 are equal. The second approach does not require that σ_1^2 and σ_2^2 are equal but gives only approximately correct confidence intervals and hypothesis tests. In the bank customer waiting time situation, the sample variances are $s_1^2 = 4.8237$ and $s_2^2 = 1.7927$. The difference in these sample variances makes it questionable to assume that the population variances are equal. More will be said later about deciding whether we can assume that two population variances are equal and about choosing between the two t-distribution approaches in a particular situation. For now, we will first consider the case where the population variances σ_1^2 and σ_2^2 can be assumed to be equal. Denoting the common value of these variances as σ^2, it follows that

$$\sigma_{\bar{x}_1 - \bar{x}_2} = \sqrt{\frac{\sigma_1^2}{n_1} + \frac{\sigma_2^2}{n_2}} = \sqrt{\frac{\sigma^2}{n_1} + \frac{\sigma^2}{n_2}} = \sqrt{\sigma^2 \left(\frac{1}{n_1} + \frac{1}{n_2} \right)}$$

Because we are assuming that $\sigma_1^2 = \sigma_2^2 = \sigma^2$, we do not need separate estimates of σ_1^2 and σ_2^2. Instead, we combine the results of the two independent random samples to compute a single estimate of σ^2. This estimate is called the **pooled estimate** of σ^2, and it is a weighted average of the two sample variances s_1^2 and s_2^2. Denoting the pooled estimate as s_p^2, it is computed using the formula

$$s_p^2 = \frac{(n_1 - 1)s_1^2 + (n_2 - 1)s_2^2}{n_1 + n_2 - 2}$$

Using s_p^2, the estimate of $\sigma_{\bar{x}_1 - \bar{x}_2}$ is

$$\sqrt{s_p^2 \left(\frac{1}{n_1} + \frac{1}{n_2} \right)}$$

and we form the statistic

$$\frac{(\bar{x}_1 - \bar{x}_2) - (\mu_1 - \mu_2)}{\sqrt{s_p^2 \left(\frac{1}{n_1} + \frac{1}{n_2} \right)}}$$

It can be shown that, if we have randomly selected independent samples from two normally distributed populations having equal variances, then the sampling distribution of this statistic is a t distribution having $(n_1 + n_2 - 2)$ degrees of freedom. Therefore, we can obtain the following confidence interval for $\mu_1 - \mu_2$:

A t-Based Confidence Interval for the Difference between Two Population Means: Equal Variances

Suppose we have randomly selected independent samples from two normally distributed populations having equal variances. Then, a **100(1 − α) percent confidence interval for $\mu_1 - \mu_2$** is

$$\left[(\bar{x}_1 - \bar{x}_2) \pm t_{\alpha/2} \sqrt{s_p^2 \left(\frac{1}{n_1} + \frac{1}{n_2} \right)} \right] \quad \text{where} \quad s_p^2 = \frac{(n_1 - 1)s_1^2 + (n_2 - 1)s_2^2}{n_1 + n_2 - 2}$$

and $t_{\alpha/2}$ is based on $(n_1 + n_2 - 2)$ degrees of freedom.

EXAMPLE 10.1 The Catalyst Comparison Case: Process Improvement

A production supervisor at a major chemical company must determine which of two catalysts, catalyst XA-100 or catalyst ZB-200, maximizes the hourly yield of a chemical process. In order to compare the mean hourly yields obtained by using the two catalysts, the supervisor runs the process using each catalyst for five one-hour periods. The resulting yields (in pounds per hour)

TABLE 10.1   **Yields of a Chemical Process Obtained Using Two Catalysts**   Catalyst

Catalyst XA-100	Catalyst ZB-200
801	752
814	718
784	776
836	742
820	763
$\bar{x}_1 = 811$	$\bar{x}_2 = 750.2$
$s_1^2 = 386$	$s_2^2 = 484.2$

for each catalyst, along with the means, variances, and box plots[2] of the yields, are given in Table 10.1. Assuming that all other factors affecting yields of the process have been held as constant as possible during the test runs, it seems reasonable to regard the five observed yields for each catalyst as a random sample from the population of all possible hourly yields for the catalyst. Furthermore, because the sample variances $s_1^2 = 386$ and $s_2^2 = 484.2$ do not differ substantially (notice that $s_1 = 19.65$ and $s_2 = 22.00$ differ by even less), it might be reasonable to conclude that the population variances are approximately equal.[3] It follows that the pooled estimate

$$s_p^2 = \frac{(n_1 - 1)s_1^2 + (n_2 - 1)s_2^2}{n_1 + n_2 - 2}$$

$$= \frac{(5 - 1)(386) + (5 - 1)(484.2)}{5 + 5 - 2} = 435.1$$

is a point estimate of the common variance σ^2.

We define μ_1 as the mean hourly yield obtained by using catalyst XA-100, and we define μ_2 as the mean hourly yield obtained by using catalyst ZB-200. If the populations of all possible hourly yields for the catalysts are normally distributed, then a 95 percent confidence interval for $\mu_1 - \mu_2$ is

$$\left[(\bar{x}_1 - \bar{x}_2) \pm t_{.025} \sqrt{s_p^2 \left(\frac{1}{n_1} + \frac{1}{n_2} \right)} \right]$$

$$= \left[(811 - 750.2) \pm 2.306 \sqrt{435.1 \left(\frac{1}{5} + \frac{1}{5} \right)} \right]$$

$$= [60.8 \pm 30.4217]$$

$$= [30.38, \ 91.22]$$

Here $t_{.025} = 2.306$ is based on $n_1 + n_2 - 2 = 5 + 5 - 2 = 8$ degrees of freedom. This interval tells us that we are 95 percent confident that the mean hourly yield obtained by using catalyst XA-100 is between 30.38 and 91.22 pounds higher than the mean hourly yield obtained by using catalyst ZB-200.

Suppose we wish to test a hypothesis about $\mu_1 - \mu_2$. In the following box we describe how this can be done. Here we test the null hypothesis $H_0: \mu_1 - \mu_2 = D_0$, where D_0 is a number whose value varies depending on the situation. Often D_0 will be the number 0. In such a case, the null hypothesis $H_0: \mu_1 - \mu_2 = 0$ says there is **no difference** between the population means μ_1 and μ_2. In this case, each alternative hypothesis in the box implies that the population means μ_1 and μ_2 differ in a particular way.

---

[2]All of the box plots presented in this chapter and in Chapter 12 have been obtained using MINITAB.
[3]We describe how to test the equality of two variances in Chapter 11 (although, as we will explain, this test has drawbacks).

A t-Test about the Difference between Two Population Means: Equal Variances

Null Hypothesis $H_0: \mu_1 - \mu_2 = D_0$

Test Statistic $t = \dfrac{(\bar{x}_1 - \bar{x}_2) - D_0}{\sqrt{s_p^2\left(\dfrac{1}{n_1} + \dfrac{1}{n_2}\right)}}$

Assumptions   Independent samples
and
Equal variances
and either
Normal populations
or
Large sample sizes

Critical Value Rule			p-Value (Reject H_0 if p-Value $< \alpha$)		
$H_a: \mu_1 - \mu_2 > D_0$	$H_a: \mu_1 - \mu_2 < D_0$	$H_a: \mu_1 - \mu_2 \neq D_0$	$H_a: \mu_1 - \mu_2 > D_0$	$H_a: \mu_1 - \mu_2 < D_0$	$H_a: \mu_1 - \mu_2 \neq D_0$

Reject H_0 if $t > t_\alpha$

Reject H_0 if $t < -t_\alpha$

Reject H_0 if $|t| > t_{\alpha/2}$—that is, $t > t_{\alpha/2}$ or $t < -t_{\alpha/2}$

p-value = area to the right of t

p-value = area to the left of t

p-value = twice the area to the right of $|t|$

Here t_α, $t_{\alpha/2}$, and the p-values are based on $n_1 + n_2 - 2$ degrees of freedom.

EXAMPLE 10.2 The Catalyst Comparison Case: Process Improvement

In order to compare the mean hourly yields obtained by using catalysts XA-100 and ZB-200, we will test $H_0: \mu_1 - \mu_2 = 0$ versus $H_a: \mu_1 - \mu_2 \neq 0$ at the **.05 level of significance.** To perform the hypothesis test, we will use the sample information in Table 10.1 to calculate the value of the **test statistic t in the summary box.** Then, because $H_a: \mu_1 - \mu_2 \neq 0$ implies a two tailed test, we will **reject $H_0: \mu_1 - \mu_2 = 0$ if the absolute value of t is greater than $t_{\alpha/2} = t_{.025} = 2.306$.** Here the $t_{\alpha/2}$ point is based on $n_1 + n_2 - 2 = 5 + 5 - 2 = 8$ degrees of freedom. Using the data in Table 10.1, the **value of the test statistic** is

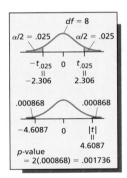

$$t = \frac{(\bar{x}_1 - \bar{x}_2) - D_0}{\sqrt{s_p^2\left(\dfrac{1}{n_1} + \dfrac{1}{n_2}\right)}} = \frac{(811 - 750.2) - 0}{\sqrt{435.1\left(\dfrac{1}{5} + \dfrac{1}{5}\right)}} = 4.6087$$

Because $|t| = 4.6087$ **is greater than $t_{.025} = 2.306$, we can reject $H_0: \mu_1 - \mu_2 = 0$ in favor of $H_a: \mu_1 - \mu_2 \neq 0$.** We conclude (at an α of .05) that the mean hourly yields obtained by using the two catalysts differ. Furthermore, the point estimate $\bar{x}_1 - \bar{x}_2 = 811 - 750.2 = 60.8$ says we estimate that the mean hourly yield obtained by using catalyst XA-100 is 60.8 pounds higher than the mean hourly yield obtained by using catalyst ZB-200.

Figure 10.2(a) gives the Excel output for using the equal variance t statistic to test H_0 versus H_a. The output tells us that $t = 4.6087$ and that the associated p-value is .001736. This very small p-value tells us that we have very strong evidence against $H_0: \mu_1 - \mu_2 = 0$ and in favor of $H_a: \mu_1 - \mu_2 \neq 0$. In other words, we have very strong evidence that the mean hourly yields obtained by using the two catalysts differ. (Note that in Figure 10.2(b) we give the Excel output for using an *unequal variances t statistic,* which is discussed on the following pages, to perform the hypothesis test.)

FIGURE 10.2   **Excel Outputs for Testing the Equality of Means in the Catalyst Comparison Case**

(a) The Excel Output Assuming Equal Variances

t-Test: Two-Sample Assuming Equal Variances

	XA-100	ZB-200
Mean	811	750.2
Variance	386	484.2
Observations	5	5
Pooled Variance	435.1	
Hypothesized Mean Diff	0	
df	8	
t Stat	4.608706	
P(T<=t) one-tail	0.000868	
t Critical one-tail	1.859548	
P(T<=t) two-tail	0.001736	
t Critical two-tail	2.306004	

(b) The Excel Output Assuming Unequal Variances

t-Test: Two-Sample Assuming Unequal Variances

	XA-100	ZB-200
Mean	811	750.2
Variance	386	484.2
Observations	5	5
Hypothesized Mean Diff	0	
df	8	
t Stat	4.608706	
P(T<=t) one-tail	0.000868	
t Critical one-tail	1.859548	
P(T<=t) two-tail	0.001736	
t Critical two-tail	2.306004	

When the sampled populations are normally distributed and the population variances σ_1^2 and σ_2^2 differ, the following can be shown.

t-Based Confidence Intervals for $\mu_1 - \mu_2$, and t-Tests about $\mu_1 - \mu_2$: Unequal Variances

1 When the sample sizes n_1 and n_2 are equal, the "equal variances" t-based confidence interval and hypothesis test given in the preceding two boxes are approximately valid even if the population variances σ_1^2 and σ_2^2 differ substantially. As a rough rule of thumb, if the larger sample variance is not more than three times the smaller sample variance when the sample sizes are equal, we can use the equal variances interval and test.

2 Suppose that the larger sample variance is more than three times the smaller sample variance when the sample sizes are equal or suppose that both the sample sizes and the sample variances differ substantially. Then, we can use an approximate procedure that is sometimes called an "unequal variances" procedure. This procedure says that an **approximate 100(1 − α) percent confidence interval for $\mu_1 - \mu_2$** is

$$\left[(\bar{x}_1 - \bar{x}_2) \pm t_{\alpha/2} \sqrt{\frac{s_1^2}{n_1} + \frac{s_2^2}{n_2}} \right]$$

Furthermore, we can test $H_0: \mu_1 - \mu_2 = D_0$ by using the test statistic

$$t = \frac{(\bar{x}_1 - \bar{x}_2) - D_0}{\sqrt{\dfrac{s_1^2}{n_1} + \dfrac{s_2^2}{n_2}}}$$

and by using the previously given critical value and p-value conditions.

For both the interval and the test, the degrees of freedom are equal to

$$df = \frac{(s_1^2/n_1 + s_2^2/n_2)^2}{\dfrac{(s_1^2/n_1)^2}{n_1 - 1} + \dfrac{(s_2^2/n_2)^2}{n_2 - 1}}$$

Here, if df is not a whole number, we can round df down to the next smallest whole number.

In general, both the "equal variances" and the "unequal variances" procedures have been shown to be approximately valid when the sampled populations are only approximately normally distributed (say, if they are mound-shaped). Furthermore, although the above summary box might seem to imply that we should use the unequal variances procedure only if we cannot use the equal variances procedure, this is not necessarily true. In fact, because the unequal variances procedure can be shown to be a very accurate approximation whether or not the population variances are equal and for most sample sizes (here, both n_1 and n_2 should be at least 5), **many statisticians believe that it is best to use the unequal variances procedure in almost every situation.** If each of n_1 and n_2 is large (at least 30), both the equal variances procedure and the unequal variances procedure are approximately valid, no matter what probability distributions describe the sampled populations.

To illustrate the unequal variances procedure, consider the bank customer waiting time situation, and recall that $\mu_1 - \mu_2$ is the difference between the mean customer waiting time under the current system and the mean customer waiting time under the new system. Because of cost considerations, the bank manager wants to implement the new system only if it reduces the mean waiting time by more than three minutes. Therefore, the manager will test the **null hypothesis H_0: $\mu_1 - \mu_2 = 3$ versus the alternative hypothesis H_a: $\mu_1 - \mu_2 > 3$.** If H_0 can be rejected in favor of H_a at the **.05 level of significance,** the manager will implement the new system. Recall that a random sample of $n_1 = 100$ waiting times observed under the current system gives a sample mean $\bar{x}_1 = 8.79$ and a sample variance $s_1^2 = 4.8237$. Also, recall that a random sample of $n_2 = 100$ waiting times observed during the trial run of the new system yields a sample mean $\bar{x}_2 = 5.14$ and a sample variance $s_2^2 = 1.7927$. Because each sample is large, we can use the **unequal variances test statistic t in the summary box.** The degrees of freedom for this statistic are

$$df = \frac{(s_1^2/n_1 + s_2^2/n_2)^2}{\dfrac{(s_1^2/n_1)^2}{n_1 - 1} + \dfrac{(s_2^2/n_2)^2}{n_2 - 1}}$$

$$= \frac{[(4.8237/100) + (1.7927/100)]^2}{\dfrac{(4.8237/100)^2}{99} + \dfrac{(1.7927/100)^2}{99}}$$

$$= 163.657$$

which we will round down to 163. Therefore, because H_a: $\mu_1 - \mu_2 > 3$ implies a right tailed test, we will **reject H_0: $\mu_1 - \mu_2 = 3$ if the value of the test statistic t is greater than $t_\alpha = t_{.05} = 1.65$** (which is based on 163 degrees of freedom and has been found using a computer). Using the sample data, the **value of the test statistic** is

$$t = \frac{(\bar{x}_1 - \bar{x}_2) - 3}{\sqrt{\dfrac{s_1^2}{n_1} + \dfrac{s_2^2}{n_2}}} = \frac{(8.79 - 5.14) - 3}{\sqrt{\dfrac{4.8237}{100} + \dfrac{1.7927}{100}}} = \frac{.65}{.25722} = 2.53$$

Because $t = 2.53$ is greater than $t_{.05} = 1.65$, we reject H_0: $\mu_1 - \mu_2 = 3$ in favor of H_a: $\mu_1 - \mu_2 > 3$. We conclude (at an α of .05) that $\mu_1 - \mu_2$ is greater than 3 and, therefore, that the new system reduces the population mean customer waiting time by more than 3 minutes. Therefore, the bank manager will implement the new system. Furthermore, the point estimate $\bar{x}_1 - \bar{x}_2 = 3.65$ says that we estimate that the new system reduces mean waiting time by 3.65 minutes.

Figure 10.3 gives the MINITAB output of using the unequal variances procedure to test H_0: $\mu_1 - \mu_2 = 3$ versus H_a: $\mu_1 - \mu_2 > 3$. The output tells us that $t = 2.53$ and that the associated p-value is .006. The very small p-value tells us that we have very strong evidence against H_0: $\mu_1 - \mu_2 = 3$ and in favor of H_a: $\mu_1 - \mu_2 > 3$. That is, we have very strong evidence that $\mu_1 - \mu_2$ is greater than 3 and, therefore, that the new system reduces the mean customer waiting time by more than 3 minutes. To find a 95 percent confidence interval for $\mu_1 - \mu_2$, note that we can use a computer to find that $t_{.025}$ based on 163 degrees of freedom is 1.97. It follows that the 95 percent confidence interval for $\mu_1 - \mu_2$ is

$$\left[(\bar{x}_1 - \bar{x}_2) \pm t_{.025}\sqrt{\frac{s_1^2}{n_1} + \frac{s_2^2}{n_2}}\right] = \left[(8.79 - 5.14) \pm 1.97\sqrt{\frac{4.8237}{100} + \frac{1.7927}{100}}\right]$$

$$= [3.65 \pm .50792]$$

$$= [3.14, 4.16]$$

This interval says that we are 95 percent confident that the new system reduces the mean of all customer waiting times by between 3.14 minutes and 4.16 minutes.

FIGURE 10.3   MINITAB Output of the Unequal Variances Procedure for the Bank Customer Waiting Time Situation

Two-Sample T-Test and CI

```
Sample     N     Mean    StDev   SE Mean
Current   100    8.79    2.20     0.22
New       100    5.14    1.34     0.13

Difference = mu(1) - mu(2)
Estimate for difference:  3.650
95% lower bound for difference:  3.224
T-Test of difference = 3 (vs >):
T-Value = 2.53     P-Value = 0.006   DF = 163
```

FIGURE 10.4   MINITAB Output of the Unequal Variances Procedure for the Catalyst Comparison Case

Two-Sample T-Test and CI: XA-100, ZB-200

```
           N     Mean    StDev   SE Mean
XA-100     5    811.0    19.6     8.8
ZB-200     5    750.2    22.0     9.8

Difference = mu (XA-100) - mu (ZB-200)
Estimate for difference:  60.8000
95% CI for difference:  (29.6049, 91.9951)
T-Test of difference = 0 (vs not =):
 T-Value = 4.61     P-Value = 0.002   DF = 7
```

In general, the degrees of freedom for the unequal variances procedure will always be less than or equal to $n_1 + n_2 - 2$, the degrees of freedom for the equal variances procedure. For example, if we use the unequal variances procedure to analyze the catalyst comparison data in Table 10.1, we can calculate df to be 7.9. This is slightly less than $n_1 + n_2 - 2 = 5 + 5 - 2 = 8$, the degrees of freedom for the equal variances procedure. Figure 10.2(b) gives the Excel output, and Figure 10.4 gives the MINITAB output, of the unequal variances analysis of the catalyst comparison data. Note that the Excel unequal variances procedure rounds $df = 7.9$ up to 8 and obtains the same results as did the equal variances procedure (see Figure 10.2(a)). On the other hand, MINITAB rounds $df = 7.9$ down to 7 and finds that a 95 percent confidence interval for $\mu_1 - \mu_2$ is [29.6049, 91.9951]. MINITAB also finds that the test statistic for testing $H_0: \mu_1 - \mu_2 = 0$ versus $H_a: \mu_1 - \mu_2 \neq 0$ is $t = 4.61$ and that the associated p-value is .002. These results do not differ by much from the results given by the equal variances procedure.

To conclude this section, it is important to point out that if the sample sizes n_1 and n_2 are not large (at least 30), and if we fear that the sampled populations might be far from normally distributed, we can use a **nonparametric method.** One nonparametric method for comparing populations when using independent samples is the **Wilcoxon rank sum test.** This test is discussed in Chapter 18.

Exercises for Section 10.1

CONCEPTS

connect™

For each of the formulas described below, list all of the assumptions that must be satisfied in order to validly use the formula.

10.1   The confidence interval in the formula box on page 383.

10.2   The hypothesis test described in the formula box on page 385.

10.3   The confidence interval and hypothesis test described in the formula box on page 386.

METHODS AND APPLICATIONS

Suppose we have taken independent, random samples of sizes $n_1 = 7$ and $n_2 = 7$ from two normally distributed populations having means μ_1 and μ_2, and suppose we obtain $\bar{x}_1 = 240$, $\bar{x}_2 = 210$, $s_1 = 5$, and $s_2 = 6$. Using the equal variances procedure, do Exercises 10.4, 10.5, and 10.6.

10.4   Calculate a 95 percent confidence interval for $\mu_1 - \mu_2$. Can we be 95 percent confident that $\mu_1 - \mu_2$ is greater than 20? Explain why we can use the equal variances procedure here.

10.5   Use critical values to test the null hypothesis $H_0: \mu_1 - \mu_2 \leq 20$ versus the alternative hypothesis $H_a: \mu_1 - \mu_2 > 20$ by setting α equal to .10, .05, .01, and .001. How much evidence is there that the difference between μ_1 and μ_2 exceeds 20?

10.6   Use critical values to test the null hypothesis $H_0: \mu_1 - \mu_2 = 20$ versus the alternative hypothesis $H_a: \mu_1 - \mu_2 \neq 20$ by setting α equal to .10, .05, .01, and .001. How much evidence is there that the difference between μ_1 and μ_2 is not equal to 20?

10.7   Repeat Exercises 10.4 through 10.6 using the unequal variances procedure. Compare your results to those obtained using the equal variances procedure.

10.8 An article in *Fortune* magazine reported on the rapid rise of fees and expenses charged by mutual funds. Assuming that stock fund expenses and municipal bond fund expenses are each approximately normally distributed, suppose a random sample of 12 stock funds gives a mean annual expense of 1.63 percent with a standard deviation of .31 percent, and an independent random sample of 12 municipal bond funds gives a mean annual expense of 0.89 percent with a standard deviation of .23 percent. Let μ_1 be the mean annual expense for stock funds, and let μ_2 be the mean annual expense for municipal bond funds. Do parts a, b, and c by using the equal variances procedure. Then repeat a, b, and c using the unequal variances procedure. Compare your results.

a Set up the null and alternative hypotheses needed to attempt to establish that the mean annual expense for stock funds is larger than the mean annual expense for municipal bond funds. Test these hypotheses at the .05 level of significance. What do you conclude?

b Set up the null and alternative hypotheses needed to attempt to establish that the mean annual expense for stock funds exceeds the mean annual expense for municipal bond funds by more than .5 percent. Test these hypotheses at the .05 level of significance. What do you conclude?

c Calculate a 95 percent confidence interval for the difference between the mean annual expenses for stock funds and municipal bond funds. Can we be 95 percent confident that the mean annual expense for stock funds exceeds that for municipal bond funds by more than .5 percent? Explain.

10.9 In the book *Business Research Methods,* Donald R. Cooper and C. William Emory (1995) discuss a manager who wishes to compare the effectiveness of two methods for training new salespeople. The authors describe the situation as follows:

> The company selects 22 sales trainees who are randomly divided into two experimental groups—one receives type A and the other type B training. The salespeople are then assigned and managed without regard to the training they have received. At the year's end, the manager reviews the performances of salespeople in these groups and finds the following results:

	A Group	B Group
Average Weekly Sales	$\bar{x}_1 = \$1,500$	$\bar{x}_2 = \$1,300$
Standard Deviation	$s_1 = 225$	$s_2 = 251$

a Set up the null and alternative hypotheses needed to attempt to establish that type A training results in higher mean weekly sales than does type B training.

b Because different sales trainees are assigned to the two experimental groups, it is reasonable to believe that the two samples are independent. Assuming that the normality assumption holds, and using the equal variances procedure, test the hypotheses you set up in part a at levels of significance .10, .05, .01, and .001. How much evidence is there that type A training produces results that are superior to those of type B?

c Use the equal variances procedure to calculate a 95 percent confidence interval for the difference between the mean weekly sales obtained when type A training is used and the mean weekly sales obtained when type B training is used. Interpret this interval.

10.10 A marketing research firm wishes to compare the prices charged by two supermarket chains—Miller's and Albert's. The research firm, using a standardized one-week shopping plan (grocery list), makes identical purchases at 10 of each chain's stores. The stores for each chain are randomly selected, and all purchases are made during a single week.

The shopping expenses obtained at the two chains, along with box plots of the expenses, are as follows:　**DS** ShopExp

Miller's

| $119.25 | $121.32 | $122.34 | $120.14 | $122.19 |
| $123.71 | $121.72 | $122.42 | $123.63 | $122.44 |

Albert's

| $111.99 | $114.88 | $115.11 | $117.02 | $116.89 |
| $116.62 | $115.38 | $114.40 | $113.91 | $111.87 |

Because the stores in each sample are different stores in different chains, it is reasonable to assume that the samples are independent, and we assume that weekly expenses at each chain are normally distributed.

a Letting μ_M be the mean weekly expense for the shopping plan at Miller's, and letting μ_A be the mean weekly expense for the shopping plan at Albert's, Figure 10.5 gives the MINITAB output of the test of $H_0: \mu_M - \mu_A = 0$ (that is, there is no difference between μ_M and μ_A) versus $H_a: \mu_M - \mu_A \neq 0$ (that is, μ_M and μ_A differ). Note that MINITAB has employed the

FIGURE 10.5   **MINITAB Output of Testing the Equality of Mean Weekly Expenses at Miller's and Albert's Supermarket Chains (for Exercise 10.10)**

```
Two-sample T for Millers vs Alberts

           N      Mean     StDev    SE Mean
Millers    10    121.92     1.40      0.44
Alberts    10    114.81     1.84      0.58

Difference = mu(Millers)- mu(Alberts)    Estimate for difference: 7.10900
95% CI for difference:  (5.57350, 8.64450)
T-Test of diff = 0 (vs not =): T-Value = 9.73    P-Value = 0.000   DF = 18
Both use Pooled StDev = 1.6343
```

equal variances procedure. Use the sample data to show that $\bar{x}_M = 121.92$, $s_M = 1.40$, $\bar{x}_A = 114.81$, $s_A = 1.84$, and $t = 9.73$.

  b Using the t statistic given on the output and critical values, test H_0 versus H_a by setting α equal to .10, .05, .01, and .001. How much evidence is there that the mean weekly expenses at Miller's and Albert's differ?

  c Figure 10.5 gives the p-value for testing H_0: $\mu_M - \mu_A = 0$ versus H_a: $\mu_M - \mu_A \neq 0$. Use the p-value to test H_0 versus H_a by setting α equal to .10, .05, .01, and .001. How much evidence is there that the mean weekly expenses at Miller's and Albert's differ?

  d Figure 10.5 gives a 95 percent confidence interval for $\mu_M - \mu_A$. Use this confidence interval to describe the size of the difference between the mean weekly expenses at Miller's and Albert's. Do you think that these means differ in a practically important way?

  e Set up the null and alternative hypotheses needed to attempt to establish that the mean weekly expense for the shopping plan at Miller's exceeds the mean weekly expense at Albert's by more than $5. Test the hypotheses at the .10, .05, .01, and .001 levels of significance. How much evidence is there that the mean weekly expense at Miller's exceeds that at Albert's by more than $5?

10.11 A large discount chain compares the performance of its credit managers in Ohio and Illinois by comparing the mean dollar amounts owed by customers with delinquent charge accounts in these two states. Here a small mean dollar amount owed is desirable because it indicates that bad credit risks are not being extended large amounts of credit. Two independent, random samples of delinquent accounts are selected from the populations of delinquent accounts in Ohio and Illinois, respectively. The first sample, which consists of 10 randomly selected delinquent accounts in Ohio, gives a mean dollar amount of $524 with a standard deviation of $68. The second sample, which consists of 20 randomly selected delinquent accounts in Illinois, gives a mean dollar amount of $473 with a standard deviation of $22.

  a Set up the null and alternative hypotheses needed to test whether there is a difference between the population mean dollar amounts owed by customers with delinquent charge accounts in Ohio and Illinois.

  b Figure 10.6 gives the MINITAB output of using the unequal variances procedure to test the equality of mean dollar amounts owed by customers with delinquent charge accounts in Ohio and Illinois. Assuming that the normality assumption holds, test the hypotheses you set up in part a by setting α equal to .10, .05, .01, and .001. How much evidence is there that the mean dollar amounts owed in Ohio and Illinois differ?

  c Assuming that the normality assumption holds, calculate a 95 percent confidence interval for the difference between the mean dollar amounts owed in Ohio and Illinois. Based on this interval, do you think that these mean dollar amounts differ in a practically important way?

10.12 A loan officer compares the interest rates for 48-month fixed-rate auto loans and 48-month variable-rate auto loans. Two independent, random samples of auto loan rates are selected. A sample of eight 48-month fixed-rate auto loans had the following loan rates: **DS** AutoLoan

4.29%   3.75%   3.50%   3.99%   3.75%   3.99%   5.40%   4.00%

while a sample of five 48-month variable-rate auto loans had loan rates as follows:

3.59%   2.75%   2.99%   2.50%   3.00%

  a Set up the null and alternative hypotheses needed to determine whether the mean rates for 48-month fixed-rate and variable-rate auto loans differ.

  b Figure 10.7 gives the Excel output of using the equal variances procedure to test the hypotheses you set up in part a. Assuming that the normality and equal variances assumptions hold, use the Excel output and critical values to test these hypotheses by setting α equal to

FIGURE 10.6	**MINITAB Output of Testing the Equality of Mean Dollar Amounts Owed for Ohio and Illinois (for Exercise 10.11)**

Two-Sample T-Test and CI

```
Sample      N     Mean    StDev    SE Mean
Ohio       10    524.0     68.0        22
Illinois   20    473.0     22.0       4.9

Difference = mu(1) - mu(2)
Estimate for difference:   51.0
95% CI for difference:  (1.1, 100.9)
T-Test of difference = 0 (vs not =):
   T-Value = 2.31    P-Value = 0.046   DF = 9
```

FIGURE 10.7	**Excel Output of Testing the Equality of Mean Loan Rates for Fixed and Variable 48-Month Auto Loans (for Exercise 10.12)**

t-Test: Two-Sample Assuming Equal Variances

	Fixed-Rate (%)	Variable-Rate (%)
Mean	4.0838	2.966
Variance	0.3376	0.1637
Observations	8	5
Pooled Variance	0.2744	
Hypothesized Mean Difference	0	
df	11	
t Stat	3.7431	
P(T<=t) one-tail	0.0016	
t Critical one-tail	1.7959	
P(T<=t) two-tail	0.0032	
t Critical two-tail	2.2010	

.10, .05, .01, and .001. How much evidence is there that the mean rates for 48-month fixed- and variable-rate auto loans differ?

c Figure 10.7 gives the *p*-value for testing the hypotheses you set up in part *a*. Use the *p*-value to test these hypotheses by setting α equal to .10, .05, .01, and .001. How much evidence is there that the mean rates for 48-month fixed- and variable-rate auto loans differ?

d Calculate a 95 percent confidence interval for the difference between the mean rates for fixed- and variable-rate 48-month auto loans. Can we be 95 percent confident that the difference between these means exceeds .4 percent? Explain.

e Use a hypothesis test to establish that the difference between the mean rates for fixed- and variable-rate 48-month auto loans exceeds .4 percent. Use α equal to .05.

10.2 Paired Difference Experiments ● ● ●

EXAMPLE 10.3 The Auto Insurance Case: Comparing Mean Repair Costs

Home State Casualty, specializing in automobile insurance, wishes to compare the repair costs of moderately damaged cars (repair costs between $700 and $1,400) at two garages. One way to study these costs would be to take two independent samples (here we arbitrarily assume that each sample is of size $n = 7$). First we would randomly select seven moderately damaged cars that have recently been in accidents. Each of these cars would be taken to the first garage (garage 1), and repair cost estimates would be obtained. Then we would randomly select seven *different* moderately damaged cars, and repair cost estimates for these cars would be obtained at the second garage (garage 2). This sampling procedure would give us independent samples because the cars taken to garage 1 differ from those taken to garage 2. However, because the repair costs for moderately damaged cars can range from $700 to $1,400, there can be substantial differences in damages to moderately damaged cars. These differences might tend to conceal any real differences between repair costs at the two garages. For example, suppose the repair cost estimates for the cars taken to garage 1 are higher than those for the cars taken to garage 2. This difference might exist because garage 1 charges customers more for repair work than does garage 2. However, the difference could also arise because the cars taken to garage 1 are more severely damaged than the cars taken to garage 2.

To overcome this difficulty, we can perform a **paired difference experiment.** Here we could randomly select one sample of $n = 7$ moderately damaged cars. The cars in this sample would be taken to both garages, and a repair cost estimate for each car would be obtained at each garage. The advantage of the paired difference experiment is that the repair cost estimates at the two garages are obtained for the same cars. Thus, any true differences in the repair cost estimates would not be concealed by possible differences in the severity of damages to the cars.

Suppose that when we perform the paired difference experiment, we obtain the repair cost estimates in Table 10.2 (these estimates are given in units of $100). To analyze these data, we

LO10-2 Recognize when data come from independent samples and when they are paired.

TABLE 10.2   A Sample of $n = 7$ Paired Differences of the Repair Cost Estimates at Garages 1 and 2 (Cost Estimates in Hundreds of Dollars)   DS Repair

Sample of $n = 7$ Damaged Cars	Repair Cost Estimates at Garage 1	Repair Cost Estimates at Garage 2	Sample of $n = 7$ Paired Differences
Car 1	$ 7.1	$ 7.9	$d_1 = -.8$
Car 2	9.0	10.1	$d_2 = -1.1$
Car 3	11.0	12.2	$d_3 = -1.2$
Car 4	8.9	8.8	$d_4 = .1$
Car 5	9.9	10.4	$d_5 = -.5$
Car 6	9.1	9.8	$d_6 = -.7$
Car 7	10.3	11.7	$d_7 = -1.4$
	$\bar{x}_1 = 9.329$	$\bar{x}_2 = 10.129$	$\bar{d} = -.8 = \bar{x}_1 - \bar{x}_2$
			$s_d^2 = .2533$
			$s_d = .5033$

calculate the difference between the repair cost estimates at the two garages for each car. The resulting **paired differences** are given in the last column of Table 10.2. The mean of the sample of $n = 7$ paired differences is

$$\bar{d} = \frac{-.8 + (-1.1) + (-1.2) + \cdots + (-1.4)}{7} = -.8$$

which equals the difference between the sample means of the repair cost estimates at the two garages

$$\bar{x}_1 - \bar{x}_2 = 9.329 - 10.129 = -.8$$

Furthermore, $\bar{d} = -.8$ (that is, $-\$80$) is the point estimate of

$$\mu_d = \mu_1 - \mu_2$$

the mean of the population of all possible paired differences of the repair cost estimates (for all possible moderately damaged cars) at garages 1 and 2 (which is equivalent to μ_1, the mean of all possible repair cost estimates at garage 1, minus μ_2, the mean of all possible repair cost estimates at garage 2). This says we estimate that the mean of all possible repair cost estimates at garage 1 is $80 less than the mean of all possible repair cost estimates at garage 2.

In addition, the variance and standard deviation of the sample of $n = 7$ paired differences

$$s_d^2 = \frac{\sum_{i=1}^{7} (d_i - \bar{d})^2}{7 - 1} = .2533$$

and

$$s_d = \sqrt{.2533} = .5033$$

are the point estimates of σ_d^2 and σ_d, the variance and standard deviation of the population of all possible paired differences.

LO10-3 Compare two population means when the data are paired.

In general, suppose we wish to compare two population means, μ_1 and μ_2. Also suppose that we have obtained two different measurements (for example, repair cost estimates) on the same n units (for example, cars), and suppose we have calculated the n paired differences between these measurements. Let $\bar{d}$ and s_d be the mean and the standard deviation of these n paired differences. If it is reasonable to assume that the paired differences have been randomly selected from a normally distributed (or at least mound-shaped) population of paired differences with mean μ_d and standard deviation σ_d, then the sampling distribution of

$$\frac{\bar{d} - \mu_d}{s_d / \sqrt{n}}$$

is a t distribution having $n - 1$ degrees of freedom. This implies that we have the following confidence interval for μ_d:

A Confidence Interval for the Mean, μ_d, of a Population of Paired Differences

Let μ_d be the mean of a **normally distributed population of paired differences**, and let $\bar{d}$ and s_d be the mean and standard deviation of a sample of n paired differences that have been randomly selected from the population. Then, a **100(1 − α) percent** confidence interval for $\mu_d = \mu_1 - \mu_2$ is

$$\left[\bar{d} \pm t_{\alpha/2}\frac{s_d}{\sqrt{n}}\right]$$

Here $t_{\alpha/2}$ is based on $(n - 1)$ degrees of freedom.

EXAMPLE 10.4 The Auto Insurance Case: Comparing Mean Repair Costs

Using the data in Table 10.2, and assuming that the population of paired repair cost differences is normally distributed, a 95 percent confidence interval for $\mu_d = \mu_1 - \mu_2$ is

$$\left[\bar{d} \pm t_{.025}\frac{s_d}{\sqrt{n}}\right] = \left[-.8 \pm 2.447\frac{.5033}{\sqrt{7}}\right]$$
$$= [-.8 \pm .4654]$$
$$= [-1.2654, -.3346]$$

Here $t_{.025} = 2.447$ is based on $n - 1 = 7 - 1 = 6$ degrees of freedom. This interval says that Home State Casualty can be 95 percent confident that μ_d, the mean of all possible paired differences of the repair cost estimates at garages 1 and 2, is between −$126.54 and −$33.46. That is, we are 95 percent confident that μ_1, the mean of all possible repair cost estimates at garage 1, is between $126.54 and $33.46 less than μ_2, the mean of all possible repair cost estimates at garage 2.

We can also test a hypothesis about μ_d, the mean of a population of paired differences. We show how to test the null hypothesis

$$H_0: \mu_d = D_0$$

in the following box. Here the value of the constant D_0 depends on the particular problem. Often D_0 equals 0, and the null hypothesis $H_0: \mu_d = 0$ says that μ_1 and μ_2 do not differ.

Testing a Hypothesis about the Mean, μ_d, of a Population of Paired Differences

| **Null Hypothesis** $H_0: \mu_d = D_0$ | **Test Statistic** $t = \dfrac{\bar{d} - D_0}{s_d/\sqrt{n}}$ $df = n - 1$ | **Assumptions** | Normal population of paired differences or Large sample size |

EXAMPLE 10.5 The Auto Insurance Case: Comparing Mean Repair Costs

Home State Casualty currently contracts to have moderately damaged cars repaired at garage 2. However, a local insurance agent suggests that garage 1 provides less expensive repair service that is of equal quality. Because it has done business with garage 2 for years, Home State has decided to give some of its repair business to garage 1 only if it has very strong evidence that μ_1, the mean repair cost estimate at garage 1, is smaller than μ_2, the mean repair cost estimate at garage 2—that is, if $\mu_d = \mu_1 - \mu_2$ is less than zero. Therefore, we will test $H_0: \mu_d = 0$ or, equivalently, $H_0: \mu_1 - \mu_2 = 0$, versus $H_a: \mu_d < 0$ or, equivalently, $H_a: \mu_1 - \mu_2 < 0$, at the **.01 level of significance**. To perform the hypothesis test, we will use the sample data in Table 10.2 to calculate the value of the **test statistic t in the summary box**. Because $H_a: \mu_d < 0$ implies a left tailed test, we will **reject $H_0: \mu_d = 0$ if the value of t is less than** $-t_\alpha = -t_{.01} = -3.143$. Here the t_α point is based on $n - 1 = 7 - 1 = 6$ degrees of freedom. Using the data in Table 10.2, the **value of the test statistic is**

$$t = \frac{\bar{d} - D_0}{s_d/\sqrt{n}} = \frac{-.8 - 0}{.5033/\sqrt{7}} = -4.2053$$

Because $t = -4.2053$ is less than $-t_{.01} = -3.143$, we can reject $H_0: \mu_d = 0$ in favor of H_a: $\mu_d < 0$. We conclude (at an α of .01) that μ_1, the mean repair cost estimate at garage 1, is less than μ_2, the mean repair cost estimate at garage 2. As a result, Home State will give some of its repair business to garage 1. Furthermore, Figure 10.8 gives the MINITAB output of this hypothesis test and shows us that the p-value for the test is .003. Because this p-value is very small, we have very strong evidence that H_0 should be rejected and that μ_1 is less than μ_2.

Figure 10.9 shows the Excel output for testing $H_0: \mu_d = 0$ versus $H_a: \mu_d < 0$ (the "one-tail" test) and for testing $H_0: \mu_d = 0$ versus $H_a: \mu_d \neq 0$ (the "two-tail" test). The Excel p-value for testing $H_0: \mu_d = 0$ versus $H_a: \mu_d < 0$ is .002826, which in the rounded form .003 is the same as

FIGURE 10.8   MINITAB Output of Testing $H_0: \mu_d = 0$ versus $H_a: \mu_d < 0$

```
Paired T for Garage1 - Garage2

              N      Mean      StDev     SE Mean
Garage1       7     9.3286     1.2500    0.4724
Garage2       7    10.1286     1.5097    0.5706
Difference    7    -0.800000   0.503322  0.190238

T-Test of mean difference = 0 (vs < 0):
              T-Value = -4.21      P-Value = 0.003
```

FIGURE 10.9   Excel Output of Testing $H_0: \mu_d = 0$

t-Test: Paired Two Sample for Means

	Garage1	Garage2
Mean	9.328571	10.12857
Variance	1.562381	2.279048
Observations	7	7
Pearson Correlation	0.950744	
Hypothesized Mean	0	
df	6	
t Stat	−4.20526	
P(T<=t) one-tail	0.002826	
t Critical one-tail	1.943181	
P(T<=t) two-tail	0.005653	
t Critical two-tail	2.446914	

the MINITAB p-value. This very small p-value tells us that Home State has very strong evidence that the mean repair cost at garage 1 is less than the mean repair cost at garage 2. The Excel p-value for testing H_0: $\mu_d = 0$ versus H_a: $\mu_d \neq 0$ is .005653.

In general, an experiment in which we have obtained two different measurements on the same n units is called a **paired difference experiment.** The idea of this type of experiment is to remove the variability due to the variable (for example, the amount of damage to a car) on which the observations are paired. In many situations, a paired difference experiment will provide more information than an independent samples experiment. As another example, suppose that we wish to assess which of two different machines produces a higher hourly output. If we randomly select 10 machine operators and randomly assign 5 of these operators to test machine 1 and the others to test machine 2, we would be performing an independent samples experiment. This is because different machine operators test machines 1 and 2. However, any difference in machine outputs could be obscured by differences in the abilities of the machine operators. For instance, if the observed hourly outputs are higher for machine 1 than for machine 2, we might not be able to tell whether this is due to (1) the superiority of machine 1 or (2) the possible higher skill level of the operators who tested machine 1. Because of this, it might be better to randomly select five machine operators, thoroughly train each operator to use both machines, and have each operator test both machines. We would then be **pairing on the machine operator,** and this would remove the variability due to the differing abilities of the operators.

The formulas we have given for analyzing a paired difference experiment are based on the t distribution. These formulas assume that the population of all possible paired differences is normally distributed (or at least mound-shaped). If the sample size is large (say, at least 30), the t-based interval and tests of this section are approximately valid no matter what the shape of the population of all possible paired differences. If the sample size is small, and if we fear that the population of all paired differences might be far from normally distributed, we can use a nonparametric method. One nonparametric method for comparing two populations when using a paired difference experiment is the **Wilcoxon signed ranks test.** This nonparametric test is discussed in Chapter 18.

Exercises for Section 10.2

CONCEPTS

connect

10.13 Explain how a paired difference experiment differs from an independent samples experiment in terms of how the data for these experiments are collected.

10.14 Why is a paired difference experiment sometimes more informative than an independent samples experiment? Give an example of a situation in which a paired difference experiment might be advantageous.

10.15 Suppose a company wishes to compare the hourly output of its employees before and after vacations. Explain how you would collect data for a paired difference experiment to make this comparison.

METHODS AND APPLICATIONS

10.16 Suppose a sample of 49 paired differences that have been randomly selected from a normally distributed population of paired differences yields a sample mean of $\bar{d} = 5$ and a sample standard deviation of $s_d = 7$.

    a Calculate a 95 percent confidence interval for $\mu_d = \mu_1 - \mu_2$. Can we be 95 percent confident that the difference between μ_1 and μ_2 is not equal to 0?

    b Test the null hypothesis H_0: $\mu_d = 0$ versus the alternative hypothesis H_a: $\mu_d \neq 0$ by setting α equal to .10, .05, .01, and .001. How much evidence is there that μ_d differs from 0? What does this say about how μ_1 and μ_2 compare?

    c The p-value for testing H_0: $\mu_d \leq 3$ versus H_a: $\mu_d > 3$ equals .0256. Use the p-value to test these hypotheses with α equal to .10, .05, .01, and .001. How much evidence is there that μ_d exceeds 3? What does this say about the size of the difference between μ_1 and μ_2?

10.17 Suppose a sample of 11 paired differences that has been randomly selected from a normally distributed population of paired differences yields a sample mean of $\bar{d} = 103.5$ and a sample standard deviation of $s_d = 5$.

   a Calculate 95 percent and 99 percent confidence intervals for $\mu_d = \mu_1 - \mu_2$.

   b Test the null hypothesis $H_0: \mu_d \leq 100$ versus $H_a: \mu_d > 100$ by setting α equal to .05 and .01. How much evidence is there that $\mu_d = \mu_1 - \mu_2$ exceeds 100?

   c Test the null hypothesis $H_0: \mu_d \geq 110$ versus $H_a: \mu_d < 110$ by setting α equal to .05 and .01. How much evidence is there that $\mu_d = \mu_1 - \mu_2$ is less than 110?

10.18 In the book *Essentials of Marketing Research*, William R. Dillon, Thomas J. Madden, and Neil H. Firtle (1993) present preexposure and postexposure attitude scores from an advertising study involving 10 respondents. The data for the experiment are given in Table 10.3. Assuming that the differences between pairs of postexposure and preexposure scores are normally distributed: Ⓓ AdStudy

   a Set up the null and alternative hypotheses needed to attempt to establish that the advertisement increases the mean attitude score (that is, that the mean postexposure attitude score is higher than the mean preexposure attitude score).

   b Test the hypotheses you set up in part *a* at the .10, .05, .01, and .001 levels of significance. How much evidence is there that the advertisement increases the mean attitude score?

   c Estimate the minimum difference between the mean postexposure attitude score and the mean preexposure attitude score. Justify your answer.

10.19 National Paper Company must purchase a new machine for producing cardboard boxes. The company must choose between two machines. The machines produce boxes of equal quality, so the company will choose the machine that produces (on average) the most boxes. It is known that there are substantial differences in the abilities of the company's machine operators. Therefore National Paper has decided to compare the machines using a paired difference experiment. Suppose that eight randomly selected machine operators produce boxes for one hour using machine 1 and for one hour using machine 2, with the following results: Ⓓ BoxYield

	Machine Operator							
	1	**2**	**3**	**4**	**5**	**6**	**7**	**8**
Machine 1	53	60	58	48	46	54	62	49
Machine 2	50	55	56	44	45	50	57	47

   a Assuming normality, perform a hypothesis test to determine whether there is a difference between the mean hourly outputs of the two machines. Use $\alpha = .05$.

   b Estimate the minimum and maximum differences between the mean outputs of the two machines. Justify your answer.

10.20 During 2011 a company implemented a number of policies aimed at reducing the ages of its customers' accounts. In order to assess the effectiveness of these measures, the company randomly selects 10 customer accounts. The average age of each account is determined for the years 2010 and 2011. These data are given in Table 10.4. Assuming that the population of paired differences between the average ages in 2011 and 2010 is normally distributed: Ⓓ AcctAge

TABLE 10.3 **Preexposure and Postexposure Attitude Scores (for Exercise 10.18)** Ⓓ AdStudy

Subject	Preexposure Attitudes (A_1)	Postexposure Attitudes (A_2)	Attitude Change (d_i)
1	50	53	3
2	25	27	2
3	30	38	8
4	50	55	5
5	60	61	1
6	80	85	5
7	45	45	0
8	30	31	1
9	65	72	7
10	70	78	8

Source: W. R. Dillon, T. J. Madden, and N. H. Firtle, *Essentials of Marketing Research* (Burr Ridge, IL: Richard D. Irwin, 1993), p. 435. Copyright © 1993. Reprinted by permission of McGraw-Hill Companies, Inc.

TABLE 10.4 **Average Account Ages in 2010 and 2011 for 10 Randomly Selected Accounts (for Exercise 10.20)** Ⓓ AcctAge

Account	Average Age of Account in 2011 (Days)	Average Age of Account in 2010 (Days)
1	27	35
2	19	24
3	40	47
4	30	28
5	33	41
6	25	33
7	31	35
8	29	51
9	15	18
10	21	28

FIGURE 10.10   Excel Output of a Paired Difference Analysis of the Account Age Data (for Exercise 10.20)

t-Test: Paired Two Sample for Means

	2011 Age	2010 Age
Mean	27	34
Variance	53.55556	104.2222
Observations	10	10
Pearson Correlation	0.804586	
Hypothesized Mean	0	
df	9	
t Stat	−3.61211	
P(T<=t) one-tail	0.00282	
t Critical one-tail	1.833114	
P(T<=t) Two-tail	0.005641	
t Critical two-tail	2.262159	

TABLE 10.5   Weekly Study Time Data for Students Who Perform Well on the MidTerm   🗅 StudyTime

Students	1	2	3	4	5	6	7	8
Before	15	14	17	17	19	14	13	16
After	9	9	11	10	19	10	14	10

   a Set up the null and alternative hypotheses needed to establish that the mean average account age has been reduced by the company's new policies.
   b Figure 10.10 gives the Excel output needed to test the hypotheses of part *a*. Use critical values to test these hypotheses by setting α equal to .10, .05, .01, and .001. How much evidence is there that the mean average account age has been reduced?
   c Figure 10.10 gives the *p*-value for testing the hypotheses of part *a*. Use the *p*-value to test these hypotheses by setting α equal to .10, .05, .01, and .001. How much evidence is there that the mean average account age has been reduced?
   d Calculate a 95 percent confidence interval for the mean difference in the average account ages between 2011 and 2010. Estimate the minimum reduction in the mean average account ages from 2010 to 2011.

10.21 Do students reduce study time in classes where they achieve a higher midterm score? In a *Journal of Economic Education* article (Winter 2005), Gregory Krohn and Catherine O'Connor studied student effort and performance in a class over a semester. In an intermediate macroeconomics course, they found that "students respond to higher midterm scores by reducing the number of hours they subsequently allocate to studying for the course."[4] Suppose that a random sample of $n = 8$ students who performed well on the midterm exam was taken and weekly study times before and after the exam were compared. The resulting data are given in Table 10.5. Assume that the population of all possible paired differences is normally distributed.
   a Set up the null and alternative hypotheses to test whether there is a difference in the population mean study time before and after the midterm exam.
   b Below we present the MINITAB output for the paired differences test. Use the output and critical values to test the hypotheses at the .10, .05, and .01 levels of significance. Has the population mean study time changed?

Paired T-Test and CI: StudyBefore, StudyAfter

```
Paired T for StudyBefore - StudyAfter
              N     Mean    StDev   SE Mean
StudyBefore   8  15.6250   1.9955    0.7055
StudyAfter    8  11.5000   3.4226    1.2101
Difference    8   4.12500  2.99702   1.05961

95% CI for mean difference: (1.61943, 6.63057)
T-Test of mean difference = 0 (vs not = 0): T-Value = 3.89   P-Value = 0.006
```

   c Use the *p*-value to test the hypotheses at the .10, .05, and .01 levels of significance. How much evidence is there against the null hypothesis?

[4]Source: "Student Effort and Performance over the Semester," *Journal of Economic Education*, Winter 2005, pages 3–28.

10.3 Comparing Two Population Proportions by Using Large, Independent Samples ● ● ●

EXAMPLE 10.6 The Test Market Case: Comparing Advertising Media

LO10-4 Compare two population proportions using large independent samples.

Suppose a new product was test marketed in the Des Moines, Iowa, and Toledo, Ohio, metropolitan areas. Equal amounts of money were spent on advertising in the two areas. However, different advertising media were employed in the two areas. Advertising in the Des Moines area was done entirely on television, while advertising in the Toledo area consisted of a mixture of television, radio, newspaper, and magazine ads. Two months after the advertising campaigns commenced, surveys are taken to estimate consumer awareness of the product. In the Des Moines area, 631 out of 1,000 randomly selected consumers are aware of the product, while in the Toledo area 798 out of 1,000 randomly selected consumers are aware of the product. We define p_1 to be the proportion of all consumers in the Des Moines area who are aware of the product and p_2 to be the proportion of all consumers in the Toledo area who are aware of the product. It follows that, because the sample proportions of consumers who are aware of the product in the Des Moines and Toledo areas are

$$\hat{p}_1 = \frac{631}{1,000} = .631$$

and

$$\hat{p}_2 = \frac{798}{1,000} = .798$$

then a point estimate of $p_1 - p_2$ is

$$\hat{p}_1 - \hat{p}_2 = .631 - .798 = -.167$$

This says we estimate that p_1 is .167 less than p_2. That is, we estimate that the percentage of all consumers who are aware of the product in the Toledo area is 16.7 percentage points higher than the percentage in the Des Moines area.

In order to find a confidence interval for and to carry out a hypothesis test about $p_1 - p_2$, we need to know the properties of the **sampling distribution of $\hat{p}_1 - \hat{p}_2$.** In general, therefore, consider randomly selecting n_1 elements from a population, and assume that a proportion p_1 of all the elements in the population fall into a particular category. Let $\hat{p}_1$ denote the proportion of elements in the sample that fall into the category. Also, consider randomly selecting a sample of n_2 elements from a second population, and assume that a proportion p_2 of all the elements in this population fall into the particular category. Let $\hat{p}_2$ denote the proportion of elements in the second sample that fall into the category.

The Sampling Distribution of $\hat{p}_1 - \hat{p}_2$

I f the randomly selected samples are independent of each other, then the population of all possible values of $\hat{p}_1 - \hat{p}_2$:

1 Approximately has a normal distribution if each of the sample sizes n_1 and n_2 is large. Here n_1 and n_2 are large enough if $n_1 p_1$, $n_1(1 - p_1)$, $n_2 p_2$, and $n_2(1 - p_2)$ are all at least 5.

2 Has mean $\mu_{\hat{p}_1 - \hat{p}_2} = p_1 - p_2$

3 Has standard deviation $\sigma_{\hat{p}_1 - \hat{p}_2} = \sqrt{\dfrac{p_1(1 - p_1)}{n_1} + \dfrac{p_2(1 - p_2)}{n_2}}$

If we estimate p_1 by $\hat{p}_1$ and p_2 by $\hat{p}_2$ in the expression for $\sigma_{\hat{p}_1 - \hat{p}_2}$, then the sampling distribution of $\hat{p}_1 - \hat{p}_2$ implies the following $100(1 - \alpha)$ percent confidence interval for $p_1 - p_2$.

A Large Sample Confidence Interval for the Difference between Two Population Proportions[5]

$\mathbf{S}$uppose we randomly select a sample of size n_1 from a population, and let $\hat{p}_1$ denote the proportion of elements in this sample that fall into a category of interest. Also suppose we randomly select a sample of size n_2 from another population, and let $\hat{p}_2$ denote the proportion of elements in this second sample that fall into the category of interest. Then, if each of the sample sizes n_1 and n_2 is large (n_1 and n_2 are considered to be large if $n_1\hat{p}_1$, $n_1(1 - \hat{p}_1)$, $n_2\hat{p}_2$, and $n_2(1 - \hat{p}_2)$ are all at least 5), and if the random samples are independent of each other, a **100(1 − α) percent confidence interval for $p_1 - p_2$** is

$$\left[(\hat{p}_1 - \hat{p}_2) \pm z_{\alpha/2}\sqrt{\frac{\hat{p}_1(1 - \hat{p}_1)}{n_1} + \frac{\hat{p}_2(1 - \hat{p}_2)}{n_2}} \right]$$

EXAMPLE 10.7 The Test Market Case: Comparing Advertising Media

Recall that in the advertising media situation described at the beginning of this section, 631 of 1,000 randomly selected consumers in Des Moines are aware of the new product, while 798 of 1,000 randomly selected consumers in Toledo are aware of the new product. Also recall that

$$\hat{p}_1 = \frac{631}{1,000} = .631$$

and

$$\hat{p}_2 = \frac{798}{1,000} = .798$$

Because $n_1\hat{p}_1 = 1,000(.631) = 631$, $n_1(1 - \hat{p}_1) = 1,000(1 - .631) = 369$, $n_2\hat{p}_2 = 1,000(.798) = 798$, and $n_2(1 - \hat{p}_2) = 1,000(1 - .798) = 202$ are all at least 5, both n_1 and n_2 can be considered large. It follows that a 95 percent confidence interval for $p_1 - p_2$ is

$$\left[(\hat{p}_1 - \hat{p}_2) \pm z_{.025}\sqrt{\frac{\hat{p}_1(1 - \hat{p}_1)}{n_1} + \frac{\hat{p}_2(1 - \hat{p}_2)}{n_2}} \right]$$

$$= \left[(.631 - .798) \pm 1.96\sqrt{\frac{(.631)(.369)}{1,000} + \frac{(.798)(.202)}{1,000}} \right]$$

$$= [-.167 \pm .0389]$$

$$= [-.2059, \ -.1281]$$

This interval says we are 95 percent confident that p_1, the proportion of all consumers in the Des Moines area who are aware of the product, is between .2059 and .1281 less than p_2, the proportion of all consumers in the Toledo area who are aware of the product. Thus, we have substantial evidence that advertising the new product by using a mixture of television, radio, newspaper, and magazine ads (as in Toledo) is more effective than spending an equal amount of money on television commercials only.

[5]More correctly, because $\hat{p}_1(1 - \hat{p}_1)/(n_1 - 1)$ and $\hat{p}_2(1 - \hat{p}_2)/(n_2 - 1)$ are unbiased point estimates of $p_1(1 - p_1)/n_1$ and $p_2(1 - p_2)/n_2$, a point estimate of $\sigma_{\hat{p}_1 - \hat{p}_2}$ is

$$s_{\hat{p}_1 - \hat{p}_2} = \sqrt{\frac{\hat{p}_1(1 - \hat{p}_1)}{n_1 - 1} + \frac{\hat{p}_2(1 - \hat{p}_2)}{n_2 - 1}}$$

and a 100(1 − α) percent confidence interval for $p_1 - p_2$ is $[(\hat{p}_1 - \hat{p}_2) \pm z_{\alpha/2}s_{\hat{p}_1 - \hat{p}_2}]$. Because both n_1 and n_2 are large, there is little difference between the interval obtained by using this formula and those obtained by using the formula in the box above.

To test the null hypothesis H_0: $p_1 - p_2 = D_0$, we use the test statistic

$$z = \frac{(\hat{p}_1 - \hat{p}_2) - D_0}{\sigma_{\hat{p}_1 - \hat{p}_2}}$$

A commonly employed special case of this hypothesis test is obtained by setting D_0 equal to 0. In this case, the null hypothesis H_0: $p_1 - p_2 = 0$ says there is **no difference** between the population proportions p_1 and p_2. When $D_0 = 0$, the best estimate of the common population proportion $p = p_1 = p_2$ is obtained by computing

$$\hat{p} = \frac{\text{the total number of elements in the two samples that fall into the category of interest}}{\text{the total number of elements in the two samples}}$$

Therefore, the point estimate of $\sigma_{\hat{p}_1 - \hat{p}_2}$ is

$$s_{\hat{p}_1 - \hat{p}_2} = \sqrt{\frac{\hat{p}(1 - \hat{p})}{n_1} + \frac{\hat{p}(1 - \hat{p})}{n_2}}$$

$$= \sqrt{\hat{p}(1 - \hat{p})\left(\frac{1}{n_1} + \frac{1}{n_2}\right)}$$

For the case where $D_0 \neq 0$, the point estimate of $\sigma_{\hat{p}_1 - \hat{p}_2}$ is obtained by estimating p_1 by $\hat{p}_1$ and p_2 by $\hat{p}_2$. With these facts in mind, we present the following procedure for testing H_0: $p_1 - p_2 = D_0$:

A Hypothesis Test about the Difference between Two Population Proportions

Null Hypothesis H_0: $p_1 - p_2 = D_0$

Test Statistic $z = \dfrac{(\hat{p}_1 - \hat{p}_2) - D_0}{\sigma_{\hat{p}_1 - \hat{p}_2}}$

Assumptions Independent samples and Large sample sizes

Note:

1 If $D_0 = 0$, we estimate $\sigma_{\hat{p}_1 - \hat{p}_2}$ by

$$s_{\hat{p}_1 - \hat{p}_2} = \sqrt{\hat{p}(1 - \hat{p})\left(\frac{1}{n_1} + \frac{1}{n_2}\right)}$$

2 If $D_0 \neq 0$, we estimate $\sigma_{\hat{p}_1 - \hat{p}_2}$ by

$$s_{\hat{p}_1 - \hat{p}_2} = \sqrt{\frac{\hat{p}_1(1 - \hat{p}_1)}{n_1} + \frac{\hat{p}_2(1 - \hat{p}_2)}{n_2}}$$

EXAMPLE 10.8 The Test Market Case: Comparing Advertising Media

Recall that p_1 is the proportion of all consumers in the Des Moines area who are aware of the new product and that p_2 is the proportion of all consumers in the Toledo area who are aware of the new product. To test for the equality of these proportions, we will test $H_0: p_1 - p_2 = 0$ versus $H_a: p_1 - p_2 \neq 0$ at the **.05 level of significance.** Because both of the Des Moines and Toledo samples are large (see Example 10.7), we will calculate the value of the **test statistic z in the summary box** (where $D_0 = 0$). Since $H_a: p_1 - p_2 \neq 0$ implies a two tailed test, we will **reject $H_0: p_1 - p_2 = 0$ if the absolute value of z is greater than** $z_{\alpha/2} = z_{.05/2} = z_{.025} = 1.96$. Because 631 out of 1,000 randomly selected Des Moines residents were aware of the product and 798 out of 1,000 randomly selected Toledo residents were aware of the product, the estimate of $p = p_1 = p_2$ is

$$\hat{p} = \frac{631 + 798}{1,000 + 1,000} = \frac{1,429}{2,000} = .7145$$

and the **value of the test statistic is**

$$z = \frac{(\hat{p}_1 - \hat{p}_2) - D_0}{\sqrt{\hat{p}(1 - \hat{p})(\frac{1}{n_1} + \frac{1}{n_2})}} = \frac{(.631 - .798) - 0}{\sqrt{(.7145)(.2855)(\frac{1}{1,000} + \frac{1}{1,000})}} = \frac{-.167}{.0202} = -8.2673$$

Because $|z| = 8.2673$ is greater than 1.96, we can reject $H_0: p_1 - p_2 = 0$ in favor of $H_a: p_1 - p_2 \neq 0$. We conclude (at an α of .05) that the proportions of all consumers who are aware of the product in Des Moines and Toledo differ. Furthermore, the point estimate $\hat{p}_1 - \hat{p}_2 = .631 - .798 = -.167$ says we estimate that the percentage of all consumers who are aware of the product in Toledo is 16.7 percentage points higher than the percentage of all consumers who are aware of the product in Des Moines. The p-value for this test is twice the area under the standard normal curve to the right of $|z| = 8.2673$. Because the area under the standard normal curve to the right of 3.99 is .00003, the p-value for testing H_0 is less than $2(.00003) = .00006$. It follows that we have extremely strong evidence that $H_0: p_1 - p_2 = 0$ should be rejected in favor of $H_a: p_1 - p_2 \neq 0$. That is, this small p-value provides extremely strong evidence that p_1 and p_2 differ. Figure 10.11 presents the MINITAB output of the hypothesis test of $H_0: p_1 - p_2 = 0$ versus $H_a: p_1 - p_2 \neq 0$ and of a 95 percent confidence interval for $p_1 - p_2$. Note that the MINITAB output gives a value of the test statistic z (that is, the value -8.41) that is slightly different from the value -8.2673 calculated above. The reason is that, even though we are testing $H_0: p_1 - p_2 = 0$, MINITAB uses the second formula in the summary box (rather than the first formula) to calculate $s_{\hat{p}_1 - \hat{p}_2}$.

FIGURE 10.11   MINITAB Output of Statistical Inference in the Test Market Case

Test and CI for Two Proportions

```
Sample    X      N    Sample p
1        631   1000   0.631000
2        798   1000   0.798000

Difference = p(1) - p(2)
Estimate for difference: -0.167
95% CI for difference: (-0.205906, -0.128094)
Test of difference = 0 (vs not = 0): Z = -8.41, P-value = 0.000
```

Exercises for Section 10.3

CONCEPTS

10.22 Explain what population is described by the sampling distribution of $\hat{p}_1 - \hat{p}_2$.

10.23 What assumptions must be satisfied in order to use the methods presented in this section?

METHODS AND APPLICATIONS

In Exercises 10.24 through 10.26 we assume that we have selected two independent random samples from populations having proportions p_1 and p_2 and that $\hat{p}_1 = 800/1,000 = .8$ and $\hat{p}_2 = 950/1,000 = .95$.

10.24 Calculate a 95 percent confidence interval for $p_1 - p_2$. Interpret this interval. Can we be 95 percent confident that $p_1 - p_2$ is less than 0? That is, can we be 95 percent confident that p_1 is less than p_2? Explain.

10.25 Test $H_0: p_1 - p_2 = 0$ versus $H_a: p_1 - p_2 \neq 0$ by using critical values and by setting α equal to .10, .05, .01, and .001. How much evidence is there that p_1 and p_2 differ? Explain.

10.26 Test $H_0: p_1 - p_2 \geq -.12$ versus $H_a: p_1 - p_2 < -.12$ by using a p-value and by setting α equal to .10, .05, .01, and .001. How much evidence is there that p_2 exceeds p_1 by more than .12? Explain.

10.27 In an article in the *Journal of Advertising*, Weinberger and Spotts compare the use of humor in television ads in the United States and in the United Kingdom. Suppose that independent random samples of television ads are taken in the two countries. A random sample of 400 television ads in the United Kingdom reveals that 142 use humor, while a random sample of 500 television ads in the United States reveals that 122 use humor.

   a Set up the null and alternative hypotheses needed to determine whether the proportion of ads using humor in the United Kingdom differs from the proportion of ads using humor in the United States.

   b Test the hypotheses you set up in part *a* by using critical values and by setting α equal to .10, .05, .01, and .001. How much evidence is there that the proportions of U.K. and U.S. ads using humor are different?

   c Set up the hypotheses needed to attempt to establish that the difference between the proportions of U.K. and U.S. ads using humor is more than .05 (five percentage points). Test these hypotheses by using a p-value and by setting α equal to .10, .05, .01, and .001. How much evidence is there that the difference between the proportions exceeds .05?

   d Calculate a 95 percent confidence interval for the difference between the proportion of U.K. ads using humor and the proportion of U.S. ads using humor. Interpret this interval. Can we be 95 percent confident that the proportion of U.K. ads using humor is greater than the proportion of U.S. ads using humor?

10.28 In the book *Essentials of Marketing Research*, William R. Dillon, Thomas J. Madden, and Neil H. Firtle discuss a research proposal in which a telephone company wants to determine whether the appeal of a new security system varies between homeowners and renters. Independent samples of 140 homeowners and 60 renters are randomly selected. Each respondent views a TV pilot in which a test ad for the new security system is embedded twice. Afterward, each respondent is interviewed to find out whether he or she would purchase the security system.

   Results show that 25 out of the 140 homeowners definitely would buy the security system, while 9 out of the 60 renters definitely would buy the system.

   a Letting p_1 be the proportion of homeowners who would buy the security system, and letting p_2 be the proportion of renters who would buy the security system, set up the null and alternative hypotheses needed to determine whether the proportion of homeowners who would buy the security system differs from the proportion of renters who would buy the security system.

   b Find the test statistic z and the p-value for testing the hypotheses of part *a*. Use the p-value to test the hypotheses with α equal to .10, .05, .01, and .001. How much evidence is there that the proportions of homeowners and renters differ?

   c Calculate a 95 percent confidence interval for the difference between the proportions of homeowners and renters who would buy the security system. On the basis of this interval, can we be 95 percent confident that these proportions differ? Explain.

   Note: An Excel add-in (MegaStat) output of the hypothesis test and confidence interval in parts *b* and *c* is given in Appendix 10.2 on page 409.

10.29 In the book *Cases in Finance*, Nunnally and Plath present a case in which the estimated percentage of uncollectible accounts varies with the age of the account. Here the age of an unpaid account is the number of days elapsed since the invoice date.

   An accountant believes that the percentage of accounts that will be uncollectible increases as the ages of the accounts increase. To test this theory, the accountant randomly selects independent samples of 500 accounts with ages between 31 and 60 days and 500 accounts with ages between 61 and 90 days from the accounts receivable ledger dated one year ago. When the sampled accounts are examined, it is found that 10 of the 500 accounts with ages between 31 and 60 days were eventually classified as uncollectible, while 27 of the 500 accounts with ages between 61 and 90 days were eventually classified as uncollectible. Let p_1 be the proportion of accounts with ages between 31 and 60 days that will be uncollectible, and let p_2 be the proportion of accounts with ages between 61 and 90 days that will be uncollectible.

a Use the MINITAB output below to determine how much evidence there is that we should reject $H_0: p_1 - p_2 = 0$ in favor of $H_a: p_1 - p_2 \neq 0$.

b Identify a 95 percent confidence interval for $p_1 - p_2$, and estimate the smallest that the difference between p_1 and p_2 might be.

Test and CI for Two Proportions

```
Sample                 X     N     Sample p
1 (31 to 60 days)      10    500   0.020000     Difference = p(1) - p(2)
2 (61 to 90 days       27    500   0.054000     Estimate for difference:  -0.034

95% CI for difference:    (-0.0573036, -0.0106964)
Test for difference = 0 (vs not = 0):   Z = -2.85    P-Value = 0.004
```

10.30 On January 7, 2000, the Gallup Organization released the results of a poll comparing the lifestyles of today with yesteryear. The survey results were based on telephone interviews with a randomly selected national sample of 1,031 adults, 18 years and older, conducted December 20–21, 1999. The poll asked several questions and compared the 1999 responses with the responses given in polls taken in previous years. Below we summarize some of the poll's results.[6]

Percentage of respondents who

1	Had taken a vacation lasting six days or more within the last 12 months:	December 1999 42%	December 1968 62%
2	Took part in some sort of daily activity to keep physically fit:	December 1999 60%	September 1977 48%
3	Watched TV more than four hours on an average weekday:	December 1999 28%	April 1981 25%
4	Drove a car or truck to work:	December 1999 87%	April 1971 81%

Assuming that each poll was based on a randomly selected national sample of 1,031 adults and that the samples in different years are independent:

a Let p_1 be the December 1999 population proportion of U.S. adults who had taken a vacation lasting six days or more within the last 12 months, and let p_2 be the December 1968 population proportion who had taken such a vacation. Calculate a 99 percent confidence interval for the difference between p_1 and p_2. Interpret what this interval says about how these population proportions differ.

b Let p_1 be the December 1999 population proportion of U.S. adults who took part in some sort of daily activity to keep physically fit, and let p_2 be the September 1977 population proportion who did the same. Carry out a hypothesis test to attempt to justify that the proportion who took part in such daily activity increased from September 1977 to December 1999. Use $\alpha = .05$ and explain your result.

c Let p_1 be the December 1999 population proportion of U.S. adults who watched TV more than four hours on an average weekday, and let p_2 be the April 1981 population proportion who did the same. Carry out a hypothesis test to determine whether these population proportions differ. Use $\alpha = .05$ and interpret the result of your test.

d Let p_1 be the December 1999 population proportion of U.S. adults who drove a car or truck to work, and let p_2 be the April 1971 population proportion who did the same. Calculate a 95 percent confidence interval for the difference between p_1 and p_2. On the basis of this interval, can it be concluded that the 1999 and 1971 population proportions differ?

Chapter Summary

This chapter has explained **how to compare two populations** by using confidence intervals and hypothesis tests. First we discussed how to compare **two population means** by using **independent samples.** Here the measurements in one sample are not related to the measurements in the other sample. When the population variances are unknown, *t*-based inferences are appropriate if the populations are normally distributed or the sample sizes are large. Both **equal variances and unequal variances** *t*-based procedures exist. We learned that, because it can be difficult to compare the population variances, many statisticians

believe that it is almost always best to use the unequal variances procedure.

Sometimes samples are not independent. We learned that one such case is what is called a **paired difference experiment.** Here we obtain two different measurements on the same sample units, and we can compare two population means by using a confidence interval or by conducting a hypothesis test that employs the differences between the pairs of measurements. We concluded this chapter by discussing how to compare **two population proportions** by using **large, independent samples.**

Glossary of Terms

independent samples experiment: An experiment in which there is no relationship between the measurements in the different samples. (page 382)

paired difference experiment: An experiment in which two different measurements are taken on the same units and inferences are made using the differences between the pairs of measurements. (page 395)

sampling distribution of $\hat{p}_1 - \hat{p}_2$: The probability distribution that describes the population of all possible values of $\hat{p}_1 - \hat{p}_2$,

where $\hat{p}_1$ is the sample proportion for a random sample taken from one population and $\hat{p}_2$ is the sample proportion for a random sample taken from a second population. (page 398)

sampling distribution of $\overline{x}_1 - \overline{x}_2$: The probability distribution that describes the population of all possible values of $\overline{x}_1 - \overline{x}_2$, where $\overline{x}_1$ is the sample mean of a random sample taken from one population and $\overline{x}_2$ is the sample mean of a random sample taken from a second population. (page 382)

Important Formulas and Tests

Sampling distribution of $\overline{x}_1 - \overline{x}_2$ (independent random samples): page 382

t-based confidence interval for $\mu_1 - \mu_2$ when $\sigma_1^2 = \sigma_2^2$: page 383

t-based confidence interval for $\mu_1 - \mu_2$ when $\sigma_1^2 \neq \sigma_2^2$: page 386

t-test about $\mu_1 - \mu_2$ when $\sigma_1^2 = \sigma_2^2$: page 385

t-test about $\mu_1 - \mu_2$ when $\sigma_1^2 \neq \sigma_2^2$: page 386

Confidence interval for μ_d: page 393

A hypothesis test about μ_d: page 393

Sampling distribution of $\hat{p}_1 - \hat{p}_2$ (independent random samples): page 398

Large sample confidence interval for $p_1 - p_2$: page 399

Large sample hypothesis test about $p_1 - p_2$: page 400

Supplementary Exercises

connect

Exercises 10.31 and 10.32 deal with the following situation:

In an article in the *Journal of Retailing,* Kumar, Kerwin, and Pereira study factors affecting merger and acquisition activity in retailing by comparing "target firms" and "bidder firms" with respect to several financial and marketing-related variables. If we consider two of the financial variables included in the study, suppose a random sample of 36 "target firms" gives a mean earnings per share of $1.52 with a standard deviation of $0.92, and that this sample gives a mean debt-to-equity ratio of 1.66 with a standard deviation of 0.82. Furthermore, an independent random sample of 36 "bidder firms" gives a mean earnings per share of $1.20 with a standard deviation of $0.84, and this sample gives a mean debt-to-equity ratio of 1.58 with a standard deviation of 0.81.

10.31   **a**   Set up the null and alternative hypotheses needed to test whether the mean earnings per share for all "target firms" differs from the mean earnings per share for all "bidder firms." Test these hypotheses at the .10, .05, .01, and .001 levels of significance. How much evidence is there that these means differ? Explain.

       b   Calculate a 95 percent confidence interval for the difference between the mean earnings per share for "target firms" and "bidder firms." Interpret the interval.

10.32 **a** Set up the null and alternative hypotheses needed to test whether the mean debt-to-equity ratio for all "target firms" differs from the mean debt-to-equity ratio for all "bidder firms." Test these hypotheses at the .10, .05, .01, and .001 levels of significance. How much evidence is there that these means differ? Explain.

b Calculate a 95 percent confidence interval for the difference between the mean debt-to-equity ratios for "target firms" and "bidder firms." Interpret the interval.

c Based on the results of this exercise and Exercise 10.31, does a firm's earnings per share or the firm's debt-to-equity ratio seem to have the most influence on whether a firm will be a "target" or a "bidder"? Explain.

10.33 What impact did the September 11 terrorist attack have on U.S. airline demand? An analysis was conducted by Ito and Lee, "Assessing the impact of the September 11 terrorist attacks on U.S. airline demand," in the *Journal of Economics and Business* (January–February 2005). They found a negative short-term effect of over 30 percent and an ongoing negative impact of over 7 percent. Suppose that we wish to test the impact by taking a random sample of 12 airline routes before and after 9/11. Passenger miles (millions of passenger miles) for the same routes were tracked for the 12 months prior to and the 12 months immediately following 9/11. Assume that the population of all possible paired differences is normally distributed.

a Set up the null and alternative hypotheses needed to determine whether there was a reduction in mean airline passenger demand.

b Below we present the MINITAB output for the paired differences test. Use the output and critical values to test the hypotheses at the .10, .05, and .01 levels of significance. Has the population mean airline demand been reduced?

Paired T-Test and CI: Before911, After911

```
Paired T for Before911 - After911
              N      Mean     StDev    SE Mean
Before911    12   117.333    26.976     7.787
After911     12    87.583    25.518     7.366
Difference   12   29.7500    10.3056    2.9750

T-Test of mean difference = 0 (vs > 0): T-Value = 10.00   P-Value = 0.000
```

c Use the *p*-value to test the hypotheses at the .10, .05, and .01 levels of significance. How much evidence is there against the null hypothesis?

10.34 In the book *Essentials of Marketing Research,* William R. Dillon, Thomas J. Madden, and Neil H. Firtle discuss evaluating the effectiveness of a test coupon. Samples of 500 test coupons and 500 control coupons were randomly delivered to shoppers. The results indicated that 35 of the 500 control coupons were redeemed, while 50 of the 500 test coupons were redeemed.

a In order to consider the test coupon for use, the marketing research organization required that the proportion of all shoppers who would redeem the test coupon be statistically shown to be greater than the proportion of all shoppers who would redeem the control coupon. Assuming that the two samples of shoppers are independent, carry out a hypothesis test at the .01 level of significance that will show whether this requirement is met by the test coupon. Explain your conclusion.

b Use the sample data to find a point estimate and a 95 percent interval estimate of the difference between the proportions of all shoppers who would redeem the test coupon and the control coupon. What does this interval say about whether the test coupon should be considered for use? Explain.

c Carry out the test of part *a* at the .10 level of significance. What do you conclude? Is your result statistically significant? Compute a 90 percent interval estimate instead of the 95 percent interval estimate of part *b*. Based on the interval estimate, do you feel that this result is practically important? Explain.

10.35 A marketing manager wishes to compare the mean prices charged for two brands of CD players. The manager conducts a random survey of retail outlets and obtains independent random samples of prices with the following results:

	Onkyo	JVC
Sample mean, $\bar{x}$	$189	$145
Sample standard deviation, s	$ 12	$ 10
Sample size	6	12

Assuming normality and equal variances:

a Use an appropriate hypothesis test to determine whether the mean prices for the two brands differ. How much evidence is there that the mean prices differ?

b Use an appropriate 95 percent confidence interval to estimate the difference between the mean prices of the two brands of CD players. Do you think that the difference has practical importance?

c Use an appropriate hypothesis test to provide evidence supporting the claim that the mean price of the Onkyo CD player is more than $30 higher than the mean price for the JVC CD player. Set α equal to .05.

10.36 In its February 2, 1998, issue, *Fortune* magazine published the results of a Yankelovich Partners survey of 600 adults that investigated their ideas about marriage and divorce. (All respondents had incomes of $50,000 or more.). For each statement below, the proportions of men and women who agreed with the statement are given.

People were magnanimous on the general proposition:

- In a divorce in a long-term marriage where the husband works outside the home and the wife is not employed for pay, the wife should be entitled to half the assets accumulated during the marriage.
  93% of women agree
  85% of men agree

But when we got to the goodies, a gender gap began to appear . . .

- The pension accumulated during the marriage should be split evenly.
  80% of women agree
  68% of men agree

- Stock options granted during the marriage should be split evenly.
  77% of women agree
  62% of men agree

Source: Reprinted from the February 2, 1998, issue of *Fortune*. Copyright 1998 Time, Inc. Reprinted by permission.

Assuming that the survey results were obtained from independent random samples of 300 men and 300 women:

a For each statement, carry out a hypothesis test that tests the equality of the population proportions of men and women who agree with the statement. Use α equal to .10, .05, .01, and .001. How much evidence is there that the population proportions of men and women who agree with each statement differ?

b For each statement, calculate a 95 percent confidence interval for the difference between the population proportion of men who agree with the statement and the population proportion of women who agree with the statement. Use the interval to help assess whether you feel that the difference between population proportions has practical importance.

10.37   Internet Exercise

a A prominent issue of the 2000 U.S. presidential campaign was campaign finance reform. A *Washington Post*/ABC News poll (reported April 4, 2000) found that 63 percent of 1,083 American adults surveyed believed that stricter campaign finance laws would be effective (a lot or somewhat) in reducing the influence of money in politics. Was this view uniformly held or did it vary by gender, race, or political party affiliation? A summary of survey responses, broken down by gender, is given in the table below.

Summary of Responses	Male	Female	All
Believe reduce influence, p	59%	66%	63%
Number surveyed, n	520	563	1,083

[Source: *Washington Post* website: www.washington-post.com/wp-srv/politics/polls/vault/vault.htm.

Is there sufficient evidence in this survey to conclude that the proportion of individuals who believed that campaign finance laws can reduce the influence of money in politics differs between females and males? Set up the appropriate null and alternative hypotheses. Conduct your test at the .05 and .01 levels of significance and calculate the p-value for your test. Make sure your conclusion is clearly stated.

b Search the World Wide Web for an interesting recent political poll dealing with an issue or political candidates, where responses are broken down by gender or some other two-category classification. (A list of high-potential websites is given below.) Use a difference in proportions test to determine whether political preference differs by gender or other two-level grouping.

Political polls on the World Wide Web:

ABC News:	www.abcnews.go.com/pollingunit
Washington Post:	www.washingtonpost.com/wp-dyn/content/politics/polls/?nid=roll_polls
Gallup:	www.gallup.com/Home.aspx
Polling Report:	www.pollingreport.com
Rasmussen Reports:	www.rasmussenreports.com/public_content/politics
Zogby International:	www.zogby.com/features/zogbytables3.cfm
CBS News Poll Database:	www.cbsnews.com/stories/2007/10/12/politics/main3362530.shtml?tag=cbsnewsMainColumnArea;cbsnewsMainColumnArea.0

Appendix 10.1 ■ Two-Sample Hypothesis Testing Using Excel

Test for the difference between means, equal variances, in Figure 10.2(a) on page 386 (data file: Catalyst.xlsx):

- Enter the data from Table 10.1 (page 384) into two columns: yields for catalyst XA-100 in column A and yields for catalyst ZB-200 in column B, with labels XA-100 and ZB-200.

- Select **Data : Data Analysis : t-Test: Two-Sample Assuming Equal Variances** and click OK in the Data Analysis dialog box.

- In the t-Test dialog box, enter A1: A6 in the "Variable 1 Range" window.

- Enter B1:B6 in the "Variable 2 Range" window.

- Enter 0 (zero) in the "Hypothesized Mean Difference" box.

- Place a checkmark in the Labels checkbox.

- Enter 0.05 into the Alpha box.

- Under output options, select "New Worksheet Ply" to have the output placed in a new worksheet and enter the name Output for the new worksheet.

- Click OK in the t-Test dialog box.

- The output will be displayed in a new worksheet.

Note: The *t*-test assuming unequal variances can be done by selecting **Data : Data Analysis : t-Test : Two-Sample Assuming Unequal Variances.**

Test for paired differences in Figure 10.9 on page 394 (data file: Repair.xlsx):

- Enter the data from Table 10.2 (page 392) into two columns: costs for Garage 1 in column A and costs for Garage 2 in column B, with labels Garage1 and Garage2.

- Select **Data : Data Analysis : t-Test: Paired Two Sample for Means** and click OK in the Data Analysis dialog box.

- In the t-Test dialog box, enter A1:A8 into the "Variable 1 Range" window.

- Enter B1:B8 into the "Variable 2 Range" window.

- Enter 0 (zero) in the "Hypothesized Mean Difference" box.

- Place a checkmark in the Labels checkbox.

- Enter 0.05 into the Alpha box.

- Under output options, select "New Worksheet Ply" to have the output placed in a new worksheet and enter the name Output for the new worksheet.

- Click OK in the t-Test dialog box.

- The output is displayed in a new worksheet.

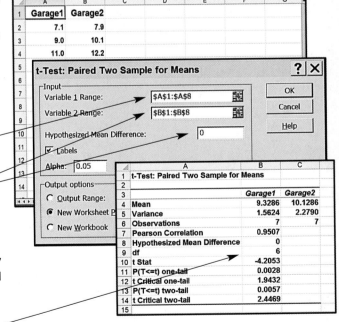

Appendix 10.2 ■ Two-Sample Hypothesis Testing Using MegaStat

Test for the difference between means, equal variances, similar to Figure 10.2(a) on page 386 (data file: Catalyst.xlsx):

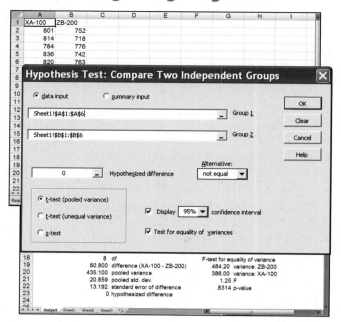

- Enter the data from Table 10.1 (page 384) into two columns: yields for catalyst XA-100 in column A and yields for catalyst ZB-200 in column B, with labels XA-100 and ZB-200.

- Select **MegaStat : Hypothesis Tests : Compare Two Independent Groups**

- In the "Hypothesis Test: Compare Two Independent Groups" dialog box, click on "data input."

- Click in the Group 1 window and use the autoexpand feature to enter the range A1:A6.

- Click in the Group 2 window and use the AutoExpand feature to enter the range B1:B6.

- Enter the Hypothesized Difference (here equal to 0) into the so labeled window.

- Select an Alternative (here "not equal") from the drop-down menu in the Alternative box.

- Click on "t-test (pooled variance)" to request the equal variances test described on page 385.

- Check the "Display confidence interval" checkbox, and select or type a desired level of confidence.

- Check the "Test for equality of variances" checkbox to request the *F*-test that will be discussed in Chapter 11.

- Click OK in the "Hypothesis Test: Compare Two Independent Groups" dialog box.

- The *t*-test assuming unequal variances described on page 386 can be done by clicking "t-test (unequal variance)."

Test for paired differences similar to Figure 10.9 on page 394 (data file: Repair.xlsx):

- Enter the data from Table 10.2 (page 392) into two columns: costs for Garage 1 in column A and costs for Garage 2 in column B, with labels Garage1 and Garage2.

- Select **Add-Ins : MegaStat : Hypothesis Tests : Paired Observations.**

- In the "Hypothesis Test: Paired Observations" dialog box, click on "data input."

- Click in the Group 1 window, and use the AutoExpand feature to enter the range A1:A8.

- Click in the Group 2 window, and use the AutoExpand feature to enter the range B1:B8.

- Enter the Hypothesized difference (here equal to 0) into the so labeled window.

- Select an Alternative (here "not equal") from the drop-down menu in the Alternative box.

- Click on "t-test."

- Click OK in the "Hypothesis Test: Paired Observations" dialog box.

- If the sample sizes are large, a test based on the normal distribution can be done by clicking on "z-test."

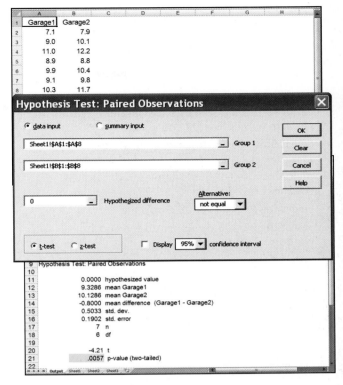

Hypothesis Test and Confidence Interval for Two Independent Proportions in Exercise 10.28 on page 402:

- Select **Add-Ins : MegaStat : Hypothesis Tests: Compare Two Independent Proportions.**

- In the "Hypothesis Test: Compare Two Proportions" dialog box, enter the number of successes x (here equal to 25) and the sample size n (here equal to 140) for homeowners in the "x" and "n" Group 1 windows.

- Enter the number of successes x (here equal to 9) and the sample size n (here equal to 60) for renters in the "x" and "n" Group 2 windows.

- Enter the Hypothesized difference (here equal to 0) into the so labeled window.

- Select an Alternative (here "not equal") from the drop-down menu in the Alternative box.

- Check the "Display confidence interval" checkbox, and select or type a desired level of confidence (here equal to 95%).

- Click OK in the "Hypothesis Test: Compare Two Proportions" dialog box.

Appendix 10.3 ■ Two-Sample Hypothesis Testing Using MINITAB

Test for the difference between means, unequal variances, in Figure 10.4 on page 388 (data file: Catalyst.MTW):

- In the data window, enter the data from Table 10.1 (page 384) into two columns with variable names XA-100 and ZB-200.

- Select **Stat : Basic Statistics : 2-Sample t**.

- In the "2-Sample t (Test and Confidence Interval)" dialog box, select the "Samples in different columns" option.

- Select the XA-100 variable into the First window.

- Select the ZB-200 variable into the Second window.

- Click on the Options . . . button, enter the desired level of confidence (here, 95.0) in the "Confidence level" window, enter 0.0 in the "Test difference" window, and select "not equal" from the Alternative pull-down menu. Click OK in the "2-Sample t—Options" dialog box.

- To produce yield by catalyst type boxplots, click the Graphs . . . button, check the "Boxplots of data" checkbox, and click OK in the "2 Sample t—Graphs" dialog box.

- Click OK in the "2-Sample t (Test and Confidence Interval)" dialog box.

- The results of the two-sample *t*-test (including the *t* statistic and *p*-value) and the confidence interval for the difference between means appear in the Session window, while the boxplots will be displayed in a graphics window.

- A test for the difference between two means when the **variances are equal** can be performed by placing a checkmark in the "Assume Equal Variances" checkbox in the "2-Sample t (Test and Confidence Interval)" dialog box.

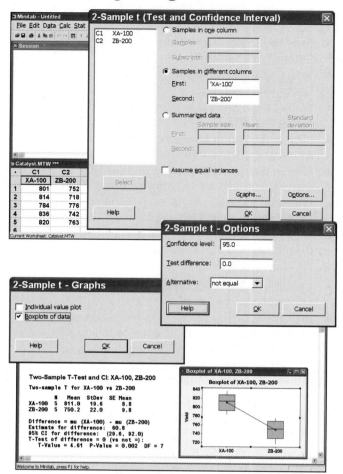

Test for paired differences in Figure 10.8 on page 394 (data file: Repair.MTW):

- In the Data window, enter the data from Table 10.2 (page 392) into two columns with variable names Garage1 and Garage2.

- Select **Stat : Basic Statistics : Paired t.**

- In the "Paired t (Test and Confidence Interval)" dialog box, select the "Samples in columns" option.

- Select Garage1 into the "First sample" window and Garage2 into the "Second sample" window.

- Click the Options . . . button.

- In the "Paired t—Options" dialog box, enter the desired level of confidence (here, 95.0) in the "Confidence level" window, enter 0.0 in the "Test mean" window, select "less than" from the Alternative pull-down menu, and click OK.

- To produce a boxplot of differences with a graphical summary of the test, click the Graphs . . . button, check the "Boxplot of differences" checkbox, and click OK in the "Paired t—Graphs" dialog box.

- Click OK in the "Paired t (Test and Confidence Interval)" dialog box. The results of the paired *t*-test are given in the Session window, and graphical output is displayed in a graphics window.

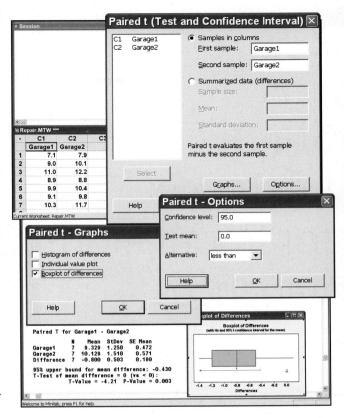

Hypothesis test and confidence interval for two Independent proportions in Figure 10.11 on page 401:

- Select **Stat : Basic Statistics : 2 Proportions.**

- In the "2 Proportions (Test and Confidence Interval)" dialog box, select the "Summarized data" option.

- Enter the sample size for Des Moines (equal to 1000) into the "First—Trials" window, and enter the number of successes for Des Moines (equal to 631) into the "First—Events" window.

- Enter the sample size for Toledo (equal to 1000) into the "Second—Trials" window, and enter the number of successes for Toledo (equal to 798) into the "Second—Events" window.

- Click on the Options . . . button.

- In the "2 Proportions—Options" dialog box, enter the desired level of confidence (here 95.0) into the "Confidence level" window.

- Enter 0.0 into the "Test difference" window because we are testing that the difference between the two proportions equals zero.

- Select the desired alternative hypothesis (here "not equal") from the Alternative drop-down menu.

- Check the "Use pooled estimate of p for test" checkbox because "Test difference" equals zero. Do not check this box in cases where "Test difference" does not equal zero.

- Click OK in the "2 Proportions—Options" dialog box.

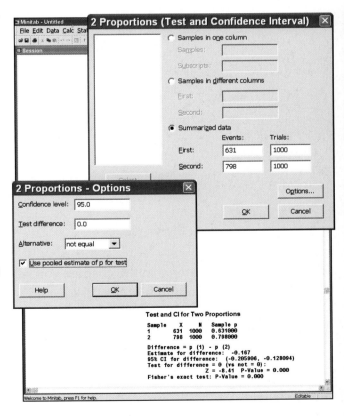

- Click OK in the "2 Proportions (Test and Confidence Interval)" dialog box to obtain results for the test in the Session window.

CHAPTER 11

Statistical Inferences for Population Variances

Learning Objectives

After mastering the material in this chapter, you will be able to:

LO11-1 Describe the properties of the chi-square distribution and use a chi-square table.

LO11-2 Use the chi-square distribution to make statistical inferences about a population variance.

LO11-3 Describe the properties of the F distribution and use an F table.

LO11-4 Compare two population variances when the samples are independent.

Chapter Outline

11.1 The Chi-Square Distribution

11.2 Statistical Inference for a Population Variance

11.3 The F Distribution

11.4 Comparing Two Population Variances by Using Independent Samples

I n Chapters 7 through 10, we have studied making statistical inferences about population means and proportions. In this chapter we discuss making statistical inferences about population variances. For example, consider a jelly and jam producer that has a filling process that is supposed to fill jars with 16 ounces of grape jelly. Even if the mean of all jar fills produced by the process is 16 ounces, the jar fills will vary somewhat and thus not every jar will contain exactly 16 ounces of grape jelly. However, we can use confidence intervals for, and hypothesis testing about, a population variance to assess whether the variation of the jar fills is small enough to meet the jelly and jam producer's requirements for the jar fills. As another example, we can use a hypothesis test concerning two population variances to compare the variance of the output of a currently used industrial process with the variance of the output obtained by using a newly improved process. If the variance of the newly improved process is less than the variance of the currently used process, then the improved process produces output that is more consistent than the current output.

11.1 The Chi-Square Distribution ● ● ●

LO11-1 Describe the properties of the chi-square distribu-tion and use a chi-square table.

Sometimes we can make statistical inferences by using the **chi-square distribution.** The proba-bility curve of the χ^2 (pronounced *chi-square*) distribution is skewed to the right. Moreover, the exact shape of this probability curve depends on a parameter that is called the **number of degrees of freedom (denoted *df*).** Figure 11.1 illustrates chi-square distributions having 2, 5, and 10 degrees of freedom.

In order to use the chi-square distribution, we employ a **chi-square point,** which is denoted χ_{α}^2. As illustrated in the upper portion of Figure 11.2, χ_{α}^2 **is the point on the horizontal axis under the curve of the chi-square distribution that gives a right-hand tail area equal to α.** The value of χ_{α}^2 in a particular situation depends on the right-hand tail area α and the number of degrees of freedom (*df*) of the chi-square distribution. Values of χ_{α}^2 are tabulated in a **chi-square table.** Such a table is given in Table A.5 of Appendix A (page 794); a portion of this table is re-produced as Table 11.1 on the next page. Looking at the chi-square table, the rows correspond to the appropriate number of degrees of freedom (values of which are listed down the left side of the table), while the columns designate the right-hand tail area α. For example, suppose we wish to find the chi-square point that gives a right-hand tail area of .05 under a chi-square curve having 5 degrees of freedom. To do this, we look in Table 11.1 at the row labeled 5 and the col-umn labeled $\chi_{.05}^2$. We find that this $\chi_{.05}^2$ point is 11.0705 (see the shaded area in Table 11.1 and lower portion of Figure 11.2).

| FIGURE 11.1 | Chi-Square Distributions with 2, 5, and 10 Degrees of Freedom |

| FIGURE 11.2 |
| Chi-Square Points |

TABLE 11.1	A Portion of the Chi-Square Table				
Degrees of Freedom (df)	$\chi^2_{.10}$	$\chi^2_{.05}$	$\chi^2_{.025}$	$\chi^2_{.01}$	$\chi^2_{.005}$
1	2.70554	3.84146	5.02389	6.63490	7.87944
2	4.60517	5.99147	7.37776	9.21034	10.5966
3	6.25139	7.81473	9.34840	11.3449	12.8381
4	7.77944	9.48773	11.1433	13.2767	14.8602
5	9.23635	11.0705	12.8325	15.0863	16.7496
6	10.6446	12.5916	14.4494	16.8119	18.5476

LO11-2 Use the chi-square distribution to make statistical inferences about a population variance.

11.2 Statistical Inference for a Population Variance ● ● ●

A jelly and jam producer has a filling process that is supposed to fill jars with 16 ounces of grape jelly. Through long experience with the filling process, the producer knows that the population of all fills produced by the process is normally distributed with a mean of 16 ounces, a variance of .000625, and a standard deviation of .025 ounce. Using the Empirical Rule, it follows that 99.73 percent of all jar fills produced by the process are in the tolerance interval $[16 \pm 3(.025)] =$ [15.925, 16.075]. In order to be competitive with the tightest specifications in the jelly and jam industry, the producer has decided that at least 99.73 percent of all jar fills must be between 15.95 ounces and 16.05 ounces. Because the tolerance limits [15.925, 16.075] of the current filling process are not inside the specification limits [15.95, 16.05], the jelly and jam producer designs a new filling process that will hopefully reduce the variance of the jar fills. A random sample of $n = 30$ jars filled by the new process is selected, and the mean and the variance of the corresponding jar fills are found to be $\bar{x} = 16$ ounces and $s^2 = .000121$. In order to attempt to show that the variance, σ^2, of the population of all jar fills that would be produced by the new process is less than .000625, we can use the following result:

Statistical Inference for a Population Variance

Suppose that s^2 is the variance of a sample of n measurements randomly selected from a normally distributed population having variance σ^2. The sampling distribution of the statistic $(n-1)s^2/\sigma^2$ is a chi-square distribution having $n-1$ degrees of freedom. This implies that

1 A $100(1 - \alpha)$ percent confidence interval for σ^2 is

$$\left[\frac{(n-1)s^2}{\chi^2_{\alpha/2}}, \frac{(n-1)s^2}{\chi^2_{1-(\alpha/2)}} \right]$$

Here $\chi^2_{\alpha/2}$ and $\chi^2_{1-(\alpha/2)}$ are the points under the curve of the chi-square distribution having $n-1$ degrees of freedom that give right-hand tail areas of, respectively, $\alpha/2$ and $1 - (\alpha/2)$.

2 We can test $H_0: \sigma^2 = \sigma_0^2$ at level of significance α by using the test statistic

$$\chi^2 = \frac{(n-1)s^2}{\sigma_0^2}$$

and by using the critical value rule or p-value that is positioned under the appropriate alternative hypothesis. **We reject H_0 if the p-value is less than α.**

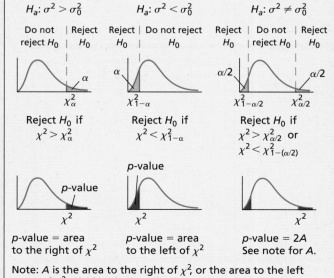

$H_a: \sigma^2 > \sigma_0^2$

Do not reject H_0 | Reject H_0

Reject H_0 if $\chi^2 > \chi^2_\alpha$

p-value = area to the right of χ^2

$H_a: \sigma^2 < \sigma_0^2$

Reject H_0 | Do not reject H_0

Reject H_0 if $\chi^2 < \chi^2_{1-\alpha}$

p-value = area to the left of χ^2

$H_a: \sigma^2 \neq \sigma_0^2$

Reject H_0 | Do not reject H_0 | Reject H_0

Reject H_0 if $\chi^2 > \chi^2_{\alpha/2}$ or $\chi^2 < \chi^2_{1-(\alpha/2)}$

p-value = 2A See note for A.

Note: A is the area to the right of χ^2, or the area to the left of χ^2, whichever is smaller.

FIGURE 11.3　Testing H_0: $\sigma^2 = .000625$ versus H_a: $\sigma^2 < .000625$ by Setting $\alpha = .05$

FIGURE 11.4　The Chi-Square Points $\chi^2_{.025}$ and $\chi^2_{.975}$

The assumption that the sampled population is normally distributed must hold fairly closely for the statistical inferences just given about σ^2 to be valid. When we check this assumption in the jar fill situation, we find that a histogram (not given here) of the sample of $n = 30$ jar fills is bell-shaped and symmetrical. In order to assess whether the jar fill variance σ^2 for the new filling process is less than .000625, we test **the null hypothesis H_0: $\sigma^2 = .000625$ versus the alternative hypothesis H_a: $\sigma^2 < .000625$.** If H_0 can be rejected in favor of H_a at the **.05 level of significance,** we will conclude that the new process has reduced the variance of the jar fills. Because the histogram of the sample of $n = 30$ jar fills is bell-shaped and symmetrical, **the appropriate test statistic is given in the summary box.** Furthermore, because H_a: $\sigma^2 < .000625$ implies a left tailed test, we should **reject H_0: $\sigma^2 = .000625$ if the value of χ^2 is less than the critical value $\chi^2_{1-\alpha} = \chi^2_{.95} = 17.7083$.** Here $\chi^2_{.95} = 17.7083$ is based on $n - 1 = 30 - 1 = 29$ degrees of freedom, and this critical value is illustrated in Figure 11.3. Because the sample variance is $s^2 = .000121$, the **value of the test statistic** is

p-value $< .001$

$df = 29$

0　5.6144

MINITAB output

```
Statistics

N    StDev    Variance
30   0.0110   0.000121

Tests

Method         Chi-Square
Standard       5.61

      DF    P-Value
      29    0.000
```

$$\chi^2 = \frac{(n-1)s^2}{\sigma_0^2} = \frac{(29)(.000121)}{.000625} = 5.6144$$

Because $\chi^2 = 5.6144$ is less than $\chi^2_{.95} = 17.7083$, we reject H_0: $\sigma^2 = .000625$ in favor of H_a: $\sigma^2 < .000625$. That is, we conclude (at an α of .05) that the new process has reduced the population variance of the jar fills. Moreover, the p-value for the test is less than .001 (see the figure on the page margin). Therefore, we have extremely strong evidence that the population jar fill variance has been reduced.

In order to compute a 95 percent confidence interval for σ^2, we note that $\alpha = .05$. Therefore, $\chi^2_{\alpha/2}$ is $\chi^2_{.025}$ and $\chi^2_{1-(\alpha/2)}$ is $\chi^2_{.975}$. Table A.5 (page 794) tells us that these points (based on $n - 1 = 29$ degrees of freedom) are $\chi^2_{.025} = 45.7222$ and $\chi^2_{.975} = 16.0471$ (see Figure 11.4). It follows that a 95 percent confidence interval for σ^2 is

$$\left[\frac{(n-1)s^2}{\chi^2_{\alpha/2}}, \frac{(n-1)s^2}{\chi^2_{1-(\alpha/2)}} \right] = \left[\frac{(29)(.000121)}{45.7222}, \frac{(29)(.000121)}{16.0471} \right]$$

$$= [.000076746, .00021867]$$

Moreover, taking square roots of both ends of this interval, we find that a 95 percent confidence interval for σ is [.008760, .01479]. The upper end of this interval, .01479, is an estimate of the largest that σ for the new process might reasonably be. Recalling that the estimate of the population mean jar fill μ for the new process is $\bar{x} = 16$, and using .01479 as the estimate of σ, we estimate that (at the worst) 99.73 percent of all jar fills that would be produced with the new process are in the tolerance interval $[16 \pm 3(.01479)] = [15.956, 16.044]$. This tolerance interval is narrower than the tolerance interval of [15.925, 16.075] for the old jar filling process and is within the specification limits of [15.95, 16.05].

Exercises for Sections 11.1 and 11.2

CONCEPTS

11.1 What assumption must hold to make statistical inferences about a population variance?

11.2 Define the meaning of the chi-square points $\chi^2_{\alpha/2}$ and $\chi^2_{1-(\alpha/2)}$. Hint: Draw a picture.

METHODS AND APPLICATIONS

11.3 **a** If $df = 8$, find the chi-square points χ^2_{025}, χ^2_{01}, and χ^2_{005} (see Table A.5 on page 794).

   b If $df = 16$, find the chi-square points χ^2_{99}, χ^2_{975}, χ^2_{10}, and χ^2_{005} (see Table A.5 on page 794).

11.4 Suppose that $n = 10$ and $s^2 = 9$. Assume normality.

   a Compute a 95 percent confidence interval for σ^2.

   b Test the null hypothesis $H_0 : \sigma^2 = 15$ versus $H_a : \sigma^2 < 15$ at the .05 level of significance.

11.5 Suppose that $n = 20$ and $s^2 = 25$. Assume normality.

   a Compute a 99 percent confidence interval for σ^2.

   b Test the null hypothesis $H_0 : \sigma^2 = 35$ versus $H_a : \sigma^2 \neq 35$ at the .01 level of significance.

11.6 Suppose that $n = 25$ and $s^2 = 49$. Assume normality.

   a Compute a 98 percent confidence interval for σ^2.

   b Compute a 98 percent confidence interval for σ.

   c Test the null hypothesis $H_0 : \sigma^2 = 25$ versus $H_a : \sigma^2 > 25$ at the .05 level of significance.

11.7 A random sample of $n = 30$ metal hardness depths has an s^2 of .0885 and a bell-shaped and symmetrical histogram. If σ^2 denotes the corresponding population variance, test $H_0 : \sigma^2 = .2209$ versus $H_a : \sigma^2 < .2209$ by setting α equal to .05.

Exercises 11.8 and 11.9 relate to the following situation: Consider an engine parts supplier and suppose the supplier has determined that the mean and the variance of the population of all cylindrical engine part outside diameters produced by the current machine are, respectively, 3 inches and .0005. To reduce this variance, a new machine is designed, and a random sample of $n = 25$ outside diameters produced by this new machine has a mean of $\bar{x} = 3$ inches, a variance of $s^2 = .00014$, and a bell-shaped and symmetrical histogram.

11.8 In order for a cylindrical engine part to give an engine long life, the outside diameter of the part must be between the specification limits of 2.95 inches and 3.05 inches. Assuming normality, determine whether 99.73 percent of the outside diameters produced by the current machine are within the specification limits.

11.9 If σ^2 denotes the variance of the population of all outside diameters that would be produced by the new machine: **(1)** Test $H_0 : \sigma^2 = .0005$ versus $H_a : \sigma^2 < .0005$ by setting α equal to .05. **(2)** Find 95 percent confidence intervals for σ^2 and σ. **(3)** Using the upper end of the 95 percent confidence interval for σ, and assuming $\mu = 3$, determine whether 99.73 percent of the outside diameters produced by the new machine are within the specification limits.

11.10 A manufacturer of coffee vending machines has designed a new, less expensive machine. The current machine is known to dispense (into cups) an average of 6 fl. oz., with a standard deviation of .2 fl. oz. When the new machine is tested using 15 cups, the mean and the standard deviation of the fills are found to be 6 fl. oz. and .214 fl. oz. Test $H_0 : \sigma = .2$ versus $H_a : \sigma \neq .2$ at levels of significance .05 and .01. Assume normality.

11.11 In Exercise 11.10, test $H_0 : \sigma = .2$ versus $H_a : \sigma > .2$ at levels of significance .05 and .01.

LO11-3 Describe the properties of the F distribution and use an F table.

11.3 The *F* Distribution ● ● ●

In this and upcoming chapters we will make statistical inferences by using what is called an **F distribution.** In general, as illustrated in Figure 11.5, the curve of the F distribution is skewed to the right. Moreover, the exact shape of this curve depends on two parameters that are called the **numerator degrees of freedom (denoted df_1)** and the **denominator degrees of freedom (denoted df_2)**. In order to use the F distribution, we employ an **F point,** which is denoted F_α. As illustrated in Figure 11.5(a), F_α **is the point on the horizontal axis under the curve of the F distribution that gives a right-hand tail area equal to α.** The value of F_α in a particular situation depends on the size of the right-hand tail area (the size of α) and on the numerator degrees of freedom (df_1) and the denominator degrees of freedom (df_2). Values of F_α are given in an **F table.** Tables A.6, A.7, A.8, and

FIGURE 11.5 *F* **Distribution Curves and** *F* **Points**

(a) The point F_α **corresponding to** df_1 **and** df_2 **degrees of freedom**

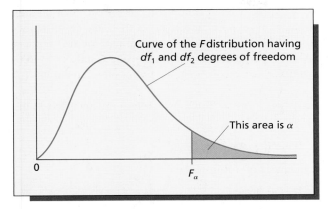

(b) The point $F_{.05}$ **corresponding to 4 and 7 degrees of freedom**

A.9 (pages 795–798) give values of $F_{.10}$, $F_{.05}$, $F_{.025}$, and $F_{.01}$, respectively. Each table tabulates values of F_α according to the appropriate numerator degrees of freedom (values listed across the top of the table) and the appropriate denominator degrees of freedom (values listed down the left side of the table). A portion of Table A.7, which gives values of $F_{.05}$, is reproduced in this chapter as Table 11.2. For instance, suppose we wish to find the *F* point that gives a right-hand tail area of .05 under the curve of the *F* distribution having 4 numerator and 7 denominator degrees of freedom. To do this, we scan across the top of Table 11.2 until we find the column corresponding to 4 numerator degrees of freedom, and we scan down the left side of the table until we find the row corresponding to 7 denominator degrees of freedom. The table entry in this column and row is the desired *F* point. We find that the $F_{.05}$ point is 4.12 (see Figure 11.5(b) and Table 11.2).

TABLE 11.2 **A Portion of an** *F* **Table: Values of** $F_{.05}$

df_2 \ df_1	Numerator Degrees of Freedom (df_1)													
	1	2	3	4	5	6	7	8	9	10	12	15	20	24
1	161.4	199.5	215.7	224.6	230.2	234.0	236.8	238.9	240.5	241.9	243.9	245.9	248.0	249.1
2	18.51	19.00	19.16	19.25	19.30	19.33	19.35	19.37	19.38	19.40	19.41	19.43	19.45	19.45
3	10.13	9.55	9.28	9.12	9.01	8.94	8.89	8.85	8.81	8.79	8.74	8.70	8.66	8.64
4	7.71	6.94	6.59	6.39	6.26	6.16	6.09	6.04	6.00	5.96	5.91	5.86	5.80	5.77
5	6.61	5.79	5.41	5.19	5.05	4.95	4.88	4.82	4.77	4.74	4.68	4.62	4.56	4.53
6	5.99	5.14	4.76	4.53	4.39	4.28	4.21	4.15	4.10	4.06	4.00	3.94	3.87	3.84
7	5.59	4.71	4.25	4.12	3.97	3.87	3.79	3.73	3.68	3.64	3.57	3.51	3.44	3.41
8	5.32	4.46	4.07	3.84	3.69	3.58	3.50	3.44	3.39	3.35	3.28	3.22	3.15	3.12
9	5.12	4.26	3.86	3.63	3.48	3.37	3.29	3.23	3.18	3.14	3.07	3.01	2.94	2.90
10	4.96	4.10	3.71	3.48	3.33	3.22	3.14	3.07	3.02	2.98	2.91	2.85	2.77	2.74
11	4.84	3.98	3.59	3.36	3.20	3.09	3.01	2.95	2.90	2.85	2.79	2.72	2.65	2.61
12	4.75	3.89	3.49	3.26	3.11	3.00	2.91	2.85	2.80	2.75	2.69	2.62	2.54	2.51
13	4.67	3.81	3.41	3.18	3.03	2.92	2.83	2.77	2.71	2.67	2.60	2.53	2.46	2.42
14	4.60	3.74	3.34	3.11	2.96	2.85	2.76	2.70	2.65	2.60	2.53	2.46	2.39	2.35
15	4.54	3.68	3.29	3.06	2.90	2.79	2.71	2.64	2.59	2.54	2.48	2.40	2.33	2.29

(Denominator Degrees of Freedom (df_2) is labeled down the left side.)

LO11-4 Compare
two popu-
lation variances
when the samples
are independent.

11.4 Comparing Two Population Variances by Using Independent Samples ● ● ●

We have seen that we often wish to compare two population means. In addition, it is often useful to compare two population variances. For example, we might compare the variances of the fills that would be produced by two processes that are supposed to fill jars with 16 ounces of strawberry preserves. Or, as another example, we might wish to compare the variance of the chemical yields obtained when using Catalyst XA-100 with that obtained when using Catalyst ZB-200. Here the catalyst that produces yields with the smaller variance is giving more consistent (or predictable) results.

If σ_1^2 and σ_2^2 are the population variances that we wish to compare, one approach is to test the null hypothesis

$$H_0: \sigma_1^2 = \sigma_2^2$$

We might test H_0 versus an alternative hypothesis of, for instance,

$$H_a: \sigma_1^2 > \sigma_2^2$$

Dividing by σ_2^2, we see that testing these hypotheses is equivalent to testing

$$H_0: \frac{\sigma_1^2}{\sigma_2^2} = 1 \qquad \text{versus} \qquad H_a: \frac{\sigma_1^2}{\sigma_2^2} > 1$$

Intuitively, we would reject H_0 in favor of H_a if s_1^2/s_2^2 is significantly larger than 1. Here s_1^2 is the variance of a random sample of n_1 observations from the population with variance σ_1^2, and s_2^2 is the variance of a random sample of n_2 observations from the population with variance σ_2^2. To decide exactly how large s_1^2/s_2^2 must be in order to reject H_0, we need to consider the sampling distribution of s_1^2/s_2^2.[1]

It can be shown that, if the null hypothesis $H_0: \sigma_1^2/\sigma_2^2 = 1$ is true, then the population of all possible values of s_1^2/s_2^2 is described by an F distribution. The values of df_1 and df_2 that describe the sampling distribution of s_1^2/s_2^2 are given in the following result:

The Sampling Distribution of s_1^2/s_2^2

Suppose we randomly select independent samples from two normally distributed populations having variances σ_1^2 and σ_2^2. Then, if the null hypothesis $H_0: \sigma_1^2/\sigma_2^2 = 1$ is true, the population of all possible values of s_1^2/s_2^2 has an **F distribution** with **$df_1 = (n_1 - 1)$ numerator degrees of freedom** and with **$df_2 = (n_2 - 1)$ denominator degrees of freedom**.

In the box on the next page, we present the procedure for testing the equality of two population variances when the alternative hypothesis is *one-sided*.

EXAMPLE 11.1 The Jar Fill Case: Comparing Process Consistencies

A jelly and jam producer has decided to purchase one of two jar-filling processes—process 1 or process 2—to fill 16-ounce jars with strawberry preserves. Process 1 is slightly more expensive than process 2, but the maker of process 1 claims that σ_1^2, the variance of all fills that would be produced by process 1, is less than σ_2^2, the variance of all fills that would be produced by process 2. To test $H_0: \sigma_1^2 = \sigma_2^2$ versus $H_a: \sigma_1^2 < \sigma_2^2$ the jelly and jam producer measures the fills

---

[1]Note that we divide by σ_2^2 to form a null hypothesis of the form $H_0: \dfrac{\sigma_1^2}{\sigma_2^2} = 1$ rather than subtracting σ_2^2 to form a null hypothesis of the form $H_0: \sigma_1^2 - \sigma_2^2 = 0$. This is because the population of all possible values of $s_1^2 - s_2^2$ has no known sampling distribution.

Testing the Equality of Two Population Variances versus a One-Tailed Alternative Hypothesis

Suppose we randomly select independent samples from two normally distributed populations—populations 1 and 2. Let s_1^2 be the variance of the random sample of n_1 observations from population 1, and let s_2^2 be the variance of the random sample of n_2 observations from population 2.

1 In order to test $H_0: \sigma_1^2 = \sigma_2^2$ versus $H_a: \sigma_1^2 > \sigma_2^2$, define the test statistic

$$F = \frac{s_1^2}{s_2^2}$$

and define the corresponding p-value to be the area to the right of F under the curve of the F distribution having $df_1 = n_1 - 1$ numerator degrees of freedom and $df_2 = n_2 - 1$ denominator degrees of freedom. We can reject H_0 at level of significance α if and only if

a $F > F_\alpha$ or, equivalently,

b   p-value $< \alpha$.

Here F_α is based on $df_1 = n_1 - 1$ and $df_2 = n_2 - 1$ degrees of freedom.

2 In order to test $H_0: \sigma_1^2 = \sigma_2^2$ versus $H_a: \sigma_1^2 < \sigma_2^2$, define the test statistic

$$F = \frac{s_2^2}{s_1^2}$$

and define the corresponding p-value to be the area to the right of F under the curve of the F distribution having $df_1 = n_2 - 1$ numerator degrees of freedom and $df_2 = n_1 - 1$ denominator degrees of freedom. We can reject H_0 at level of significance α if and only if

a $F > F_\alpha$ or, equivalently,

b   p-value $< \alpha$.

Here F_α is based on $df_1 = n_2 - 1$ and $df_2 = n_1 - 1$ degrees of freedom.

Reject H_0 if $F > F_\alpha$

---

of 25 randomly selected jars produced by each process. The jar fill measurements for each process are given in the page margin. A histogram (not shown here) for each sample is bell-shaped and symmetrical, the sample sizes are $n_1 = 25$ and $n_2 = 25$, and the sample variances are $s_1^2 = .0001177$ and $s_2^2 = .0004847$. Therefore, we compute the test statistic

$$F = \frac{s_2^2}{s_1^2} = \frac{.0004847}{.0001177} = 4.1168$$

and we compare this value with F_α based on $df_1 = n_2 - 1 = 25 - 1 = 24$ numerator degrees of freedom and $df_2 = n_1 - 1 = 25 - 1 = 24$ denominator degrees of freedom. If we test H_0 versus H_a at the .05 level of significance, then Table A.7 on page 796 (a portion of which is shown below) tells us that when $df_1 = 24$ and $df_2 = 24$, we have $F_{.05} = 1.98$.

df_2 \ df_1	1	2	3	4	5	6	7	8	9	10	12	15	20	24
22	4.30	3.44	3.05	2.82	2.66	2.55	2.46	2.40	2.34	2.30	2.23	2.15	2.07	2.03
23	4.28	3.42	3.03	2.80	2.64	2.53	2.44	2.37	2.32	2.27	2.20	2.13	2.05	2.01
24	4.26	3.40	3.01	2.78	2.62	2.51	2.42	2.36	2.30	2.25	2.18	2.11	2.03	1.98
25	4.24	3.39	2.99	2.76	2.60	2.49	2.40	2.34	2.28	2.24	2.16	2.09	2.01	1.96
26	4.23	3.37	2.98	2.74	2.59	2.47	2.39	2.32	2.27	2.22	2.15	2.07	1.99	1.95
27	4.21	3.35	2.96	2.73	2.57	2.46	2.37	2.31	2.25	2.20	2.13	2.06	1.97	1.93

Process 1	Process 2
15.9841	15.9622
16.0150	15.9736
15.9964	15.9753
15.9916	15.9802
15.9949	15.9820
16.0003	15.9860
15.9884	15.9885
16.0016	15.9897
16.0260	15.9903
16.0216	15.9920
16.0065	15.9928
15.9997	15.9934
15.9909	15.9973
16.0043	16.0014
15.9881	16.0016
16.0078	16.0053
15.9934	16.0053
16.0150	16.0098
16.0057	16.0102
15.9928	16.0252
15.9987	16.0316
16.0131	16.0331
15.9981	16.0384
16.0025	16.0386
15.9898	16.0401

DS Preserves

Because $F = 4.1168$ is greater than $F_{.05} = 1.98$, we can reject $H_0: \sigma_1^2 = \sigma_2^2$ in favor of $H_a: \sigma_1^2 < \sigma_2^2$. That is, we conclude (at an α of .05) that the variance of all fills that would be produced by process 1 is less than the variance of all fills that would be produced by process 2. That is, process 1 produces more consistent fills.

$F_{.05} = 1.98$

BI

FIGURE 11.6 **Excel Output for Testing** H_0: $\sigma_1^2 = \sigma_2^2$ **versus** H_a: $\sigma_1^2 < \sigma_2^2$

F-Test Two-Sample for Variances

	Process 2	Process 1
Mean	16.001756	16.00105
Variance	0.0004847	0.0001177
Observations	25	25
df	24	24
F	4.1167856	
P(F<=f) one-tail	0.0004787	
F Critical one-tail	1.9837596	

The p-value for testing H_0 versus H_a is the area to the right of $F = 4.1168$ under the curve of the F distribution having 24 numerator degrees of freedom and 24 denominator degrees of freedom. The Excel output in Figure 11.6 tells us that this p-value equals 0.0004787. Because this p-value is less than .001, we have extremely strong evidence to support rejecting H_0 in favor of H_a. That is, there is extremely strong evidence that process 1 produces jar fills that are more consistent (less variable) than the jar fills produced by process 2.

We now present a procedure for testing the null hypothesis H_0: $\sigma_1^2 = \sigma_2^2$ versus the two-sided alternative hypothesis H_a: $\sigma_1^2 \neq \sigma_2^2$.

Testing the Equality of Two Population Variances (Two-Tailed Alternative)

Suppose we randomly select independent samples from two normally distributed populations and define all notation as in the previous box. Then, in order to test H_0: $\sigma_1^2 = \sigma_2^2$ versus H_a: $\sigma_1^2 \neq \sigma_2^2$, define the test statistic

$$F = \frac{\text{the larger of } s_1^2 \text{ and } s_2^2}{\text{the smaller of } s_1^2 \text{ and } s_2^2}$$

and let

df_1 = {the size of the sample having the larger variance} − 1

df_2 = {the size of the sample having the smaller variance} − 1

Also, define the corresponding p-value to be twice the area to the right of F under the curve of the F distribution having df_1 numerator degrees of freedom and df_2 denominator degrees of freedom. We can reject H_0 at level of significance α if and only if

1 $F > F_{\alpha/2}$ or, equivalently,

2 p-value $< \alpha$.

Here $F_{\alpha/2}$ is based on df_1 and df_2 degrees of freedom.

EXAMPLE 11.2 The Catalyst Comparison Case: Process Improvement

Consider the catalyst comparison situation and suppose the production supervisor wishes to use the sample data in Table 10.1 on page 384 to determine whether σ_1^2, the variance of the chemical yields obtained by using Catalyst XA-100, differs from σ_2^2, the variance of the chemical yields obtained by using Catalyst ZB-200. Table 10.1 tells us that $n_1 = 5$, $n_2 = 5$, $s_1^2 = 386$, and $s_2^2 = 484.2$.

FIGURE 11.7   Testing $H_0: \sigma_1^2 = \sigma_2^2$ versus $H_a: \sigma_1^2 \neq \sigma_2^2$ in the Catalyst Comparison Case with $\alpha = .05$

.025

0 $F = 1.2544$ $F_{.025} = 9.60$

MINITAB Output for catalyst comparison

Test for Equal Variances: ZB-200, XA-100

```
F-Test (Normal Distribution)
Test Statistic = 1.25,
p-value = 0.831
```

Therefore, we can reject $H_0: \sigma_1^2 = \sigma_2^2$ in favor of $H_a: \sigma_1^2 \neq \sigma_2^2$ at the .05 level of significance if

$$F = \frac{\text{the larger of } s_1^2 \text{ and } s_2^2}{\text{the smaller of } s_1^2 \text{ and } s_2^2} = \frac{484.2}{386} = 1.2544$$

is greater than $F_{\alpha/2} = F_{.05/2} = F_{.025}$. Here the degrees of freedom are

$$df_1 = \{\text{the size of the sample having the larger variance}\} - 1$$
$$= n_2 - 1 = 5 - 1 = 4$$

and

$$df_2 = \{\text{the size of the sample having the smaller variance}\} - 1$$
$$= n_1 - 1 = 5 - 1 = 4$$

Table A.8 (page 797) tells us that the appropriate $F_{.025}$ point equals 9.60 (see Figure 11.7). Because $F = 1.2544$ is not greater than 9.60, we cannot reject H_0 at the .05 level of significance. Furthermore, the MINITAB output at the top of the page tells us that the p-value for this hypothesis test is 0.831. Because the p-value is large, we have little evidence that the variabilities of the yields produced by Catalysts XA-100 and ZB-200 differ.

It has been suggested that the F test of $H_0: \sigma_1^2 = \sigma_2^2$ be used to choose between the equal variances and unequal variances t-based procedures when comparing two means (as described in Section 10.1). Certainly the F-test is one approach to making this choice. However, studies have shown that the validity of the F-test is very sensitive to violations of the normality assumption—much more sensitive, in fact, than the equal variances procedure is to violations of the equal variances assumption. While opinions vary, some statisticians believe that this is a serious problem and that the F test should never be used to choose between the equal variances and unequal variances procedures. Others feel that performing the test for this purpose is reasonable if the test's limitations are kept in mind.

As an example for those who believe that using the F-test is reasonable, we found in Example 11.2 that we do not reject $H_0: \sigma_1^2 = \sigma_2^2$ at the .05 level of significance in the context of the catalyst comparison situation. Further, the p-value related to the F-test, which equals 0.831, tells us that there is little evidence to suggest that the population variances differ. It follows that it might be reasonable to compare the mean yields of the catalysts by using the equal variances procedures (as we have done in Examples 10.1 and 10.2).

Exercises for Sections 11.3 and 11.4

CONCEPTS

11.12 Explain what population is described by the sampling distribution of s_1^2/s_2^2.

11.13 Intuitively explain why a value of s_1^2/s_2^2 that is substantially greater than 1 provides evidence that σ_1^2 is not equal to σ_2^2.

METHODS AND APPLICATIONS

11.14 Use Table 11.2 on page 417 to find the $F_{.05}$ point for each of the following:
a $df_1 = 3$ numerator degrees of freedom and $df_2 = 14$ denominator degrees of freedom.
b $df_1 = 6$ and $df_2 = 10$.
c $df_1 = 2$ and $df_2 = 11$.
d $df_1 = 7$ and $df_2 = 5$.

11.15 Use Tables A.6, A.7, A.8, and A.9 (pages 795–798) to find the following F_α points:
a $F_{.10}$ with $df_1 = 4$ numerator degrees of freedom and $df_2 = 7$ denominator degrees of freedom.
b $F_{.01}$ with $df_1 = 3$ and $df_2 = 25$.
c $F_{.025}$ with $df_1 = 7$ and $df_2 = 17$.
d $F_{.05}$ with $df_1 = 9$ and $df_2 = 3$.

11.16 Suppose two independent random samples of sizes $n_1 = 9$ and $n_2 = 7$ that have been taken from two normally distributed populations having variances σ_1^2 and σ_2^2 give sample variances of $s_1^2 = 100$ and $s_2^2 = 20$.
a Test $H_0: \sigma_1^2 = \sigma_2^2$ versus $H_a: \sigma_1^2 \neq \sigma_2^2$ with $\alpha = .05$. What do you conclude?
b Test $H_0: \sigma_1^2 = \sigma_2^2$ versus $H_a: \sigma_1^2 > \sigma_2^2$ with $\alpha = .05$. What do you conclude?

11.17 The stopping distances of a random sample of $n_1 = 16$ Fire-Hawk compact cars have a mean of $\bar{x}_1 = 57.2$ feet and a standard deviation of $s_1 = 4.81$ feet. The stopping distances of a random sample of $n_2 = 16$ Lance compact cars have a mean of $\bar{x}_2 = 62.7$ feet and a standard deviation of $s_2 = 7.56$ feet. Here, each stopping distance is measured from a speed of 35 mph. If σ_1^2 and σ_2^2 denote the corresponding population variances, test $H_0: \sigma_1^2 = \sigma_2^2$ versus $H_a: \sigma_1^2 < \sigma_2^2$ by setting α equal to .05 and using a critical value (assume normality).

11.18 The National Golf Association's consumer advocacy group wishes to compare the variabilities in durability of two brands of golf balls: Champ golf balls and Master golf balls. The advocacy group randomly selects 10 balls of each brand and places each ball into a machine that exerts the force produced by a 250-yard drive. The number of simulated drives needed to crack or chip each ball is recorded, and the results are given below. 🅓🅢 GolfBrands

Champ Golf Balls					Master Golf Balls				
270	334	301	307	298	364	302	350	348	396
290	315	305	325	331	325	342	359	327	355

Assuming normality, test to see if the variabilities in durability differ for the two brands at the .10, .05, and .01 levels of significance. What do you conclude?

11.19 A marketing research firm wishes to compare the prices charged by two supermarket chains— Miller's and Albert's. The research firm, using a standardized one-week shopping plan (grocery list), makes identical purchases at 10 of each chain's stores. The stores for each chain are randomly selected, and all purchases are made during a single week. It is found that the mean and the standard deviation of the shopping expenses at the 10 Miller's stores are $\bar{x}_1 = \$121.92$ and $s_1 = \$1.40$. It is also found that the mean and the standard deviation of the shopping expenses at the 10 Albert's stores are $\bar{x}_2 = \$114.81$ and $s_2 = \$1.84$. Assuming normality, test to see if the corresponding population standard deviations differ by setting α equal to .05. Is it reasonable to use the equal variances procedure of Chapter 10 to compare population means? Explain.

Chapter Summary

We began this chapter by presenting the **chi-square distribution.** We then saw how to use this distribution to make **statistical inferences about a population variance.** Next, we presented the **F distribution.** Then we concluded this chapter by discussing how to compare **two population variances** by using independent samples, and we learned that this comparison is done by using a test based on the F distribution.

Glossary of Terms

chi-square distribution: A useful continuous probability distribution. Its probability curve is skewed to the right, and the exact shape of the probability curve depends on the number of degrees of freedom associated with the curve. (pages 413–414)

F distribution: A continuous probability curve having a shape that depends on two parameters—the numerator degrees of freedom, df_1, and the denominator degrees of freedom, df_2. (pages 416–417)

sampling distribution of s_1^2/s_2^2: The probability distribution that describes the population of all possible values of s_1^2/s_2^2, where s_1^2 is the sample variance of a random sample taken from one population and s_2^2 is the sample variance of a random sample taken from a second population. (page 418)

Important Formulas and Tests

Statistical inferences about a population variance: page 414

Confidence Interval: page 414

Hypothesis Test: page 414

Testing the equality of two population variances: pages 419 and 420

One-Tailed Alternative: page 419

Two-Tailed Alternative: page 420

Supplementary Exercises

11.20 A company is studying the productivity of a machine that produces an automobile part. The times (in seconds) needed to produce 100 parts for each of eight test production runs were: 40.77, 36.38, 36.82, 52.94, 48.33, 28.31, 60.56, and 28.92. Use these data to compute a 95 percent confidence interval for the standard deviation of all times needed to produce 100 such automobile parts using the machine. **DS PrdnTimes**

11.21 Consider Exercise 11.20. At the .05 level of significance, determine whether the data given support the claim that the variance of all times needed to produce 100 of the auto parts is less than 150 seconds.

11.22 Standard deviation of returns is often used as a measure of a mutual fund's volatility (risk). A larger standard deviation of returns is an indication of higher risk. According to Morningstar.com (June 17, 2010), the American Century Equity Income Institutional Fund, a large cap fund, has a standard deviation of returns equal to 14.11 percent. Morningstar.com also reported that the Fidelity Small Cap Discovery Fund has a standard deviation of returns equal to 28.44 percent. Each standard deviation was computed using a sample of size 36. Perform a hypothesis test to determine if the variance of returns for the Fidelity Small Cap Discovery Fund is larger than the variance of returns for the American Century Equity Income Institutional Fund. Perform the test at the .05 level of significance, and assume normality.

11.23 Hoping to reduce the variability of the final exam scores in his business statistics classes, an instructor at Miami University in Oxford, Ohio, developed a new set of PowerPoint presentations to use in his classes. One business statistics section was taught using the instructor's old notes and a second section was taught using the new PowerPoint presentations. The final exam scores earned by the students in the two sections are given in the following table. **DS FinalExams**

Section1: Using Old Notes									Section 2: Using New PowerPoint Slides							
60	70	83	69	83	80				62	78	84	65	74	78	93	96
82	90	57	72	89	76				83	64	98	64	96	88	96	80
62	70	84	91	79	76				86	66	78	89	97	79	58	76
54	80								73	69	75	63	73	82		

Assuming that these two sections represent approximately independent random samples of students, and assuming approximate normality, test to see if the new PowerPoint presentations have reduced the variability of the final exam scores at the .05 level of significance. Explain your conclusion.

11.24 In Exercise 10.11 on page 390, we used the unequal variances procedure on page 386 to compare population means. The sample standard deviations involved in the comparison were $s_1 = 68$ and $s_2 = 22$. Each sample size was 10.

a Assuming normality, test to see if the corresponding population standard deviations differ by setting α equal to .05.

b Was it reasonable to use the unequal variances procedure to compare population means? Explain.

Appendix 11.1 ■ A Two-Sample Hypothesis Test for the Equality of Two Variances Using Excel

Hypothesis test for the equality of two variances in Figure 11.6 on page 420 (data file: Preserves.xlsx):

- Enter the Preserves data (on page 419) into columns A and B with the label "Process 1" in cell A1 and the label "Process 2" in cell B1.

- Select **Data : Data Analysis : F-Test Two-Sample for Variances.**

- In the F-Test dialog box, enter B1:B26 in the "Variable 1 Range" window. (because Process 2 has the higher sample standard deviation).

- Enter A1:A26 in the "Variable 2 Range" window.

- Place a checkmark in the Labels checkbox.

- Enter .05 in the Alpha box.

- Under output options, select "New Worksheet Ply" and enter the name "Output" to have the output placed in a new worksheet with name "Output."

- Click OK in the F-test dialog box to obtain the results in a new worksheet.

Appendix 11.2 ■ One- and Two-Sample Hypothesis Tests for Variances Using MegaStat

Hypothesis test for a population variance in Exercise 11.7 on page 416:

- Enter a label (in this case Depth) into cell A1, the sample variance (here equal to .0885) into cell A2, and the sample size (here equal to 30) into cell A3.

- Select **Add-Ins : MegaStat : Hypothesis Tests : Chi-square Variance Test.**

- Click on "summary input."

- Enter the range A1:A3 into the Input Range window—that is, enter the range containing the data label, the sample variance, and the sample size.

- Enter the hypothesized value (here equal to 0.2209) into the "Hypothesized variance" window.

- Select the desired alternative (in this case "less than") from the drop-down menu in the Alternative box.

- Check the "Display confidence interval" checkbox (if desired) and select or type the appropriate level of confidence.

- Click OK in the "Chi-square Variance Test" dialog box.

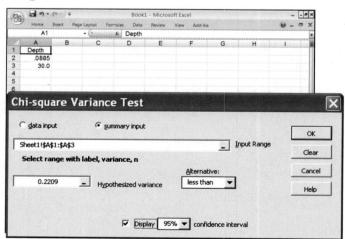

- A chi-square variance test may be carried out using **data input** by entering the observed sample values into a column in the Excel worksheet, and by then using the autoexpand feature to enter the range containing the label and sample values into the Input Range window.

MegaStat performs an F-test for the equality of variances when it carries out the t-test for the equality of two means assuming equal variances. See Appendix 10.2 (page 408).

Appendix 11.3 ■ One- and Two-Sample Inferences for Variances Using MINITAB

Hypothesis test and confidence intervals for a population variance in the example on pages 414 and 415, where the hypothesized variance is .000625 and the hypothesized standard deviation is .025.

- Select **Stat : Basic Statistics : 1 Variance.**
- In the "1 Variance" dialog box, click on "Summarized data."
- Place a check mark in the "Perform hypothesis test" checkbox.
- Enter the sample size (here 30), the sample standard deviation (here .011—that is, $(.011)^2 = .000121$), and the hypothesized standard deviation (here .025—that is, $(.025)^2 = .000625$) in the appropriate windows.
- Click the Options . . . button, enter the desired level of confidence (here, 95.0), select the desired alternative (in this case "less than"), and click OK.
- Click OK in the "1 Variance" dialog box.
- The results are given in the Session window.
- Because we have chosen a one-sided alternative (less than), we get a one-sided confidence interval (not discussed in this book). To obtain a two-sided confidence interval, repeat the steps above and change the alternative to "not equal".

Test for equality of variances in Figure 11.7 on page 421 (data file: Catalyst.MTW):

- Enter the labels XA-100 and ZB-200 into columns C1 and C2. Then enter the catalyst comparison data in Table 10.1 (page 384) into columns C1 and C2—yields for catalyst XA-100 in column C1 and yields for catalyst ZB-200 in column C2.
- Select **Stat : Basic Statistics : 2 Variances.**
- In the "2 Variances" dialog box, select the "Samples in different columns" option.
- In the "2 Variances" dialog box, enter 'ZB-200' into the "First" window (because the ZB-200 yields have the larger sample variance) and enter 'XA-100' into the "Second" window (because the XA-100 yields have the smaller sample variance).
- Click OK in the "2 Variances" dialog box.
- The *F* statistic and the *p*-value for the two-sided test will be displayed in the session window (along with additional output that we do not describe in this book). A graphical summary of the test is shown in a graphics window. (We will not show or explain this graphical summary here.)

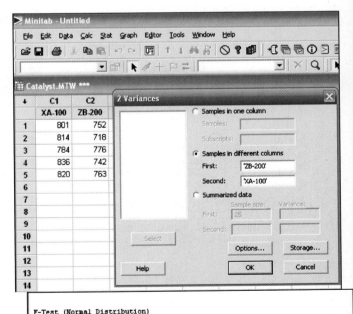

CHAPTER 12

Experimental Design and Analysis of Variance

Learning Objectives

After mastering the material in this chapter, you will be able to:

LO12-1 Explain the basic terminology and concepts of experimental design.

LO12-2 Compare several different population means by using a one-way analysis of variance.

LO12-3 Compare treatment effects and block effects by using a randomized block design.

LO12-4 Assess the effects of two factors on a response variable by using a two-way analysis of variance.

LO12-5 Describe what happens when two factors interact.

Chapter Outline

I n Chapter 10 we learned that business improvement often involves making **comparisons.** In that chapter we presented several confidence intervals and several hypothesis testing procedures for comparing two population means. However, business improvement often requires that we compare more than two population means. For instance, we might compare the mean sales obtained by using three different advertising campaigns in order to improve a company's marketing process. Or, we might compare the mean production output obtained by using four different manufacturing process designs to improve productivity.

In this chapter we extend the methods presented in Chapter 10 by considering statistical procedures for **comparing two or more population means.** Each of the methods we discuss is called an **analysis of variance (ANOVA)** procedure. We also present some basic concepts of **experimental design,** which involves deciding how to collect data in a way that allows us to most effectively compare population means.

We explain the methods of this chapter in the context of three cases:

The Oil Company Case: An oil company wishes to develop a reasonably priced gasoline that will deliver improved mileages. The company uses **one-way analysis of variance** to compare the effects of three types of gasoline on mileage in order to find the gasoline type that delivers the highest mean mileage.

The Cardboard Box Case: A paper company performs an experiment to investigate the effects of four production methods on the number of defective cardboard boxes produced in an hour. The company uses a **randomized block ANOVA** to determine which production method yields the smallest mean number of defective boxes.

The Supermarket Case: A commercial bakery supplies many supermarkets. In order to improve the effectiveness of its supermarket shelf displays the company wishes to compare the effects of shelf display height (bottom, middle, or top) and width (regular or wide) on monthly demand. The bakery employs **two-way analysis of variance** to find the display height and width combination that produces the highest monthly demand.

12.1 Basic Concepts of Experimental Design ● ● ●

LO12-1 Explain the basic terminology and concepts of experimental design.

In many statistical studies a variable of interest, called the **response variable** (or **dependent variable**), is identified. Then data are collected that tell us about how one or more **factors** (or **independent variables**) influence the variable of interest. If we cannot control the factor(s) being studied, we say that the data obtained are **observational.** For example, suppose that in order to study how the size of a home relates to the sales price of the home, a real estate agent randomly selects 50 recently sold homes and records the square footages and sales prices of these homes. Because the real estate agent cannot control the sizes of the randomly selected homes, we say that the data are observational.

If we can control the factors being studied, we say that the data are **experimental.** Furthermore, in this case the values, or **levels,** of the factor (or combination of factors) are called **treatments.** The purpose of most experiments is **to compare and estimate the effects of the different treatments on the response variable.** For example, suppose that an oil company wishes to study how three different gasoline types (A, B, and C) affect the mileage obtained by a popular compact automobile model. Here the response variable is gasoline mileage, and the company will study a single factor—gasoline type. Because the oil company can control which gasoline type is used in the compact automobile, the data that the oil company will collect are experimental. Furthermore, the treatments—the levels of the factor gasoline type—are gasoline types A, B, and C.

In order to collect data in an experiment, the different treatments are assigned to objects (people, cars, animals, or the like) that are called **experimental units.** For example, in the gasoline mileage situation, gasoline types A, B, and C will be compared by conducting mileage tests using a compact automobile. The automobiles used in the tests are the experimental units.

In general, when a treatment is applied to more than one experimental unit, it is said to be **replicated.** Furthermore, when the analyst controls the treatments employed and how they are applied to the experimental units, a **designed experiment** is being carried out. A commonly used, simple experimental design is called the **completely randomized experimental design.**

In a **completely randomized experimental design,** independent random samples of experimental units are assigned to the treatments.

As illustrated in the following examples, we can sometimes assign *independent* random samples of experimental units to the treatments by assigning *different* random samples of experimental units to different treatments.

EXAMPLE 12.1 The Oil Company Case: Comparing Gasoline Types

North American Oil Company is attempting to develop a reasonably priced gasoline that will deliver improved gasoline mileages. As part of its development process, the company would like to compare the effects of three types of gasoline (*A*, *B*, and *C*) on gasoline mileage. For testing purposes, North American Oil will compare the effects of gasoline types *A*, *B*, and *C* on the gasoline mileage obtained by a popular compact model called the Lance. Suppose the company has access to 1,000 Lances that are representative of the population of all Lances, and suppose the company will utilize a completely randomized experimental design that employs samples of size five. In order to accomplish this, five Lances will be randomly selected from the 1,000 available Lances. These autos will be assigned to gasoline type *A*. Next, five *different* Lances will be randomly selected from the remaining 995 available Lances. These autos will be assigned to gasoline type *B*. Finally, five *different* Lances will be randomly selected from the remaining 990 available Lances. These autos will be assigned to gasoline type *C*.

Each randomly selected Lance is test driven using the appropriate gasoline type (treatment) under normal conditions for a specified distance, and the gasoline mileage for each test drive is measured. We let x_{ij} denote the jth mileage obtained when using gasoline type *i*. The mileage data obtained are given in Table 12.1. Here we assume that the set of gasoline mileage observations obtained by using a particular gasoline type is a sample randomly selected from the infinite population of all Lance mileages that could be obtained using that gasoline type. Examining the box plots shown next to the mileage data, we see some evidence that gasoline type *B* yields the highest gasoline mileages.

TABLE 12.1   The Gasoline Mileage Data   GasMile2

Gasoline Type *A*	Gasoline Type *B*	Gasoline Type *C*
$x_{A1} = 34.0$	$x_{B1} = 35.3$	$x_{C1} = 33.3$
$x_{A2} = 35.0$	$x_{B2} = 36.5$	$x_{C2} = 34.0$
$x_{A3} = 34.3$	$x_{B3} = 36.4$	$x_{C3} = 34.7$
$x_{A4} = 35.5$	$x_{B4} = 37.0$	$x_{C4} = 33.0$
$x_{A5} = 35.8$	$x_{B5} = 37.6$	$x_{C5} = 34.9$

EXAMPLE 12.2 The Supermarket Case: Studying the Effect of Display Height

The Tastee Bakery Company supplies a bakery product to many supermarkets in a metropolitan area. The company wishes to study the effect of the shelf display height employed by the supermarkets on monthly sales (measured in cases of 10 units each) for this product. Shelf display height, the factor to be studied, has three levels—bottom (*B*), middle (*M*), and top (*T*)—which are the treatments. To compare these treatments, the bakery uses a completely randomized experimental design. For each shelf height, six supermarkets (the experimental units) of equal sales potential are randomly selected, and each supermarket displays the product using its assigned shelf height for a month. At the end of the month, sales of the bakery product (the response variable) at the 18 participating stores are recorded, giving the data in Table 12.2. Here we assume that the set of sales amounts for each display height is a sample randomly selected from the population of all sales amounts that could be obtained (at supermarkets of the given sales potential) at that display height. Examining the box plots that are shown next to the sales data, we seem to have evidence that a middle display height gives the highest bakery product sales.

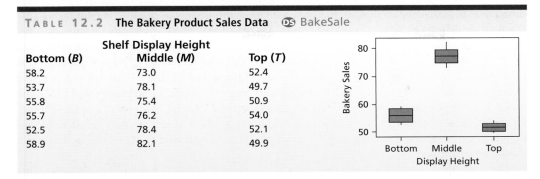

TABLE 12.2   **The Bakery Product Sales Data**   DS BakeSale

Shelf Display Height		
Bottom (*B*)	Middle (*M*)	Top (*T*)
58.2	73.0	52.4
53.7	78.1	49.7
55.8	75.4	50.9
55.7	76.2	54.0
52.5	78.4	52.1
58.9	82.1	49.9

12.2 One-Way Analysis of Variance ● ● ●

LO12-2 Compare several different population means by using a one-way analysis of variance.

Suppose we wish to study the effects of p **treatments** (treatments 1, 2, . . . , p) on a **response variable.** For any particular treatment, say treatment i, we define μ_i and σ_i to be the mean and standard deviation of the population of all possible values of the response variable that could potentially be observed when using treatment i. Here we refer to μ_i as **treatment mean i.** The goal of **one-way analysis of variance** (often called **one-way ANOVA**) is to estimate and compare the effects of the different treatments on the response variable. We do this by **estimating and comparing the treatment means** $\mu_1, \mu_2, \ldots, \mu_p$. Here we assume that a sample has been randomly selected for each of the p treatments by employing a completely randomized experimental design. We let n_i denote the size of the sample that has been randomly selected for treatment i, and we let x_{ij} denote the jth value of the response variable that is observed when using treatment i. It then follows that the point estimate of μ_i is $\bar{x}_i$, the average of the sample of n_i values of the response variable observed when using treatment i. It further follows that the point estimate of σ_i is s_i, the standard deviation of the sample of n_i values of the response variable observed when using treatment i.

For example, consider the gasoline mileage situation. We let μ_A, μ_B, and μ_C denote the means and σ_A, σ_B, and σ_C denote the standard deviations of the populations of all possible gasoline mileages using gasoline types A, B, and C. To estimate these means and standard deviations, North American Oil has employed a completely randomized experimental design and has obtained the samples of mileages in Table 12.1. The means of these samples—$\bar{x}_A = 34.92$, $\bar{x}_B = 36.56$, and $\bar{x}_C = 33.98$—are the point estimates of μ_A, μ_B, and μ_C. The standard deviations of these samples—$s_A = .7662$, $s_B = .8503$, and $s_C = .8349$—are the point estimates of σ_A, σ_B, and σ_C. Using these point estimates, we will (later in this section) test to see whether there are any statistically significant differences between the treatment means μ_A, μ_B, and μ_C. If such differences exist, we will estimate the magnitudes of these differences. This will allow North American Oil to judge whether these differences have practical importance.

The one-way ANOVA formulas allow us to test for significant differences between treatment means and allow us to estimate differences between treatment means. The validity of these formulas requires that the following assumptions hold:

Assumptions for One-Way Analysis of Variance

1 **Constant variance**—the p populations of values of the response variable associated with the treatments have equal variances.

2 **Normality**—the p populations of values of the response variable associated with the treatments all have normal distributions.

3 **Independence**—the samples of experimental units associated with the treatments are randomly selected, independent samples.

The one-way ANOVA results are not very sensitive to violations of the equal variances assumption. Studies have shown that this is particularly true when the sample sizes employed are equal (or nearly equal). Therefore, a good way to make sure that unequal variances will not be a problem is to take samples that are the same size. In addition, it is useful to compare the sample standard deviations $s_1, s_2, \ldots, s_p$ to see if they are reasonably equal. As a general rule, *the one-way ANOVA results will be approximately correct if the largest sample standard deviation is no more than twice the smallest sample standard deviation.* The variations of the samples can also be compared by constructing a box plot for each sample (as we have done for the gasoline mileage data in Table 12.1). Several statistical tests also employ the sample variances to test the equality of the population variances [see Bowerman and O'Connell (1990) for two of these tests]. However, these tests have some drawbacks—in particular, their results are very sensitive to violations of the normality assumption. Because of this, there is controversy as to whether these tests should be performed.

The normality assumption says that each of the p populations is normally distributed. This assumption is not crucial. It has been shown that the one-way ANOVA results are approximately valid for mound-shaped distributions. It is useful to construct a box plot and/or a stem-and-leaf display for each sample. If the distributions are reasonably symmetric, and if there are no outliers, the ANOVA results can be trusted for sample sizes as small as 4 or 5. As an example, consider the gasoline mileage study of Example 12.1. The box plots of Table 12.1 suggest that the variability of the mileages in each of the three samples is roughly the same. Furthermore, the sample standard deviations $s_A = .7662$, $s_B = .8503$, and $s_C = .8349$ are reasonably equal (the largest is not even close to twice the smallest). Therefore, it is reasonable to believe that the constant variance assumption is satisfied. Moreover, because the sample sizes are the same, unequal variances would probably not be a serious problem anyway. Many small, independent factors influence gasoline mileage, so the distributions of mileages for gasoline types A, B, and C are probably mound-shaped. In addition, the box plots of Table 12.1 indicate that each distribution is roughly symmetric with no outliers. Thus, the normality assumption probably approximately holds. Finally, because North American Oil has employed a completely randomized design, the independence assumption probably holds. This is because the gasoline mileages in the different samples were obtained for *different* Lances.

Testing for significant differences between treatment means   As a preliminary step in one-way ANOVA, we wish to determine whether there are any statistically significant differences between the treatment means $\mu_1, \mu_2, \ldots, \mu_p$. To do this, we test the null hypothesis

$$H_0: \mu_1 = \mu_2 = \cdots = \mu_p$$

This hypothesis says that all the treatments have the same effect on the mean response. We test H_0 versus the alternative hypothesis

$$H_a: \text{At least two of } \mu_1, \mu_2, \ldots, \mu_p \text{ differ}$$

This alternative says that at least two treatments have different effects on the mean response.

To carry out such a test, we compare what we call the **between-treatment variability** to the **within-treatment variability.** For instance, suppose we wish to study the effects of three gasoline types (X, Y, and Z) on mean gasoline mileage, and consider Figure 12.1(a). This figure depicts three independent random samples of gasoline mileages obtained using gasoline types X, Y, and Z. Observations obtained using gasoline type X are plotted as blue dots ($\bullet$), observations obtained using gasoline type Y are plotted as red dots ($\bullet$), and observations obtained using gasoline type Z are plotted as green dots ($\bullet$). Furthermore, the sample treatment means are labeled as "type X mean," "type Y mean," and "type Z mean." We see that the variability of the sample treatment means—that is, the **between-treatment variability**—is not large compared to the variability within each sample (the **within-treatment variability**). In this case, the differences between the sample treatment means could quite easily be the result of sampling variation. Thus we would not have sufficient evidence to reject

$$H_0: \mu_X = \mu_Y = \mu_Z$$

Next look at Figure 12.1(b), which depicts a different set of three independent random samples of gasoline mileages. Here the variability of the sample treatment means (the between-treatment variability) is large compared to the variability within each sample. This would probably provide

FIGURE 12.1   Comparing Between-Treatment Variability and Within-Treatment Variability

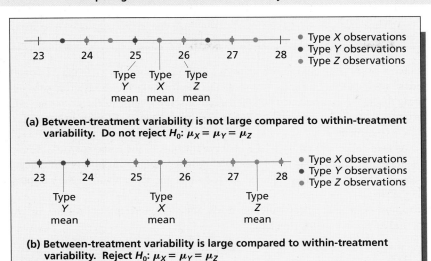

(a) Between-treatment variability is not large compared to within-treatment variability. Do not reject H_0: $\mu_X = \mu_Y = \mu_Z$

(b) Between-treatment variability is large compared to within-treatment variability. Reject H_0: $\mu_X = \mu_Y = \mu_Z$

enough evidence to tell us to reject H_0: $\mu_X = \mu_Y = \mu_Z$ in favor of H_a: At least two of μ_X, μ_Y, and μ_Z differ. We would conclude that at least two of gasoline types X, Y, and Z have different effects on mean mileage.

In order to numerically compare the between-treatment and within-treatment variability, we can define several **sums of squares** and **mean squares.** To begin, we define n to be the total number of experimental units employed in the one-way ANOVA, and we define $\bar{x}$ to be the overall mean of all observed values of the response variable. Then we define the following:

The **treatment sum of squares** is

$$SST = \sum_{i=1}^{p} n_i(\bar{x}_i - \bar{x})^2$$

In order to compute SST, we calculate the difference between each sample treatment mean $\bar{x}_i$ and the overall mean $\bar{x}$, we square each of these differences, we multiply each squared difference by the number of observations for that treatment, and we sum over all treatments. The SST measures the variability of the sample treatment means. For instance, if all the sample treatment means ($\bar{x}_i$ values) were equal, then the treatment sum of squares would be equal to 0. The more the $\bar{x}_i$ values vary, the larger will be SST. In other words, the **treatment sum of squares** measures the amount of **between-treatment variability.**

As an example, consider the gasoline mileage data in Table 12.1. In this experiment we employ a total of

$$n = n_A + n_B + n_C = 5 + 5 + 5 = 15$$

experimental units. Furthermore, the overall mean of the 15 observed gasoline mileages is

$$\bar{x} = \frac{34.0 + 35.0 + \cdots + 34.9}{15} = \frac{527.3}{15} = 35.153$$

Then

$$SST = \sum_{i=A,B,C} n_i(\bar{x}_i - \bar{x})^2$$
$$= n_A(\bar{x}_A - \bar{x})^2 + n_B(\bar{x}_B - \bar{x})^2 + n_C(\bar{x}_C - \bar{x})^2$$
$$= 5(34.92 - 35.153)^2 + 5(36.56 - 35.153)^2 + 5(33.98 - 35.153)^2$$
$$= 17.0493$$

In order to measure the within-treatment variability, we define the following quantity:

The **error sum of squares** is

$$SSE = \sum_{j=1}^{n_1}(x_{1j} - \bar{x}_1)^2 + \sum_{j=1}^{n_2}(x_{2j} - \bar{x}_2)^2 + \cdots + \sum_{j=1}^{n_p}(x_{pj} - \bar{x}_p)^2$$

Here x_{1j} is the jth observed value of the response in the first sample, x_{2j} is the jth observed value of the response in the second sample, and so forth. The formula above says that we compute SSE by calculating the squared difference between each observed value of the response and its corresponding sample treatment mean and by summing these squared differences over all the observations in the experiment.

The SSE measures the variability of the observed values of the response variable around their respective sample treatment means. For example, if there were no variability within each sample, the error sum of squares would be equal to 0. The more the values within the samples vary, the larger will be SSE.

As an example, in the gasoline mileage study, the sample treatment means are $\bar{x}_A = 34.92$, $\bar{x}_B = 36.56$, and $\bar{x}_C = 33.98$. It follows that

$$\begin{aligned} SSE &= \sum_{j=1}^{n_A}(x_{Aj} - \bar{x}_A)^2 + \sum_{j=1}^{n_B}(x_{Bj} - \bar{x}_B)^2 + \sum_{j=1}^{n_C}(x_{Cj} - \bar{x}_C)^2 \\ &= [(34.0 - 34.92)^2 + (35.0 - 34.92)^2 + (34.3 - 34.92)^2 + (35.5 - 34.92)^2 + (35.8 - 34.92)^2] \\ &\quad + [(35.3 - 36.56)^2 + (36.5 - 36.56)^2 + (36.4 - 36.56)^2 + (37.0 - 36.56)^2 + (37.6 - 36.56)^2] \\ &\quad + [(33.3 - 33.98)^2 + (34.0 - 33.98)^2 + (34.7 - 33.98)^2 + (33.0 - 33.98)^2 + (34.9 - 33.98)^2] \\ &= 8.028 \end{aligned}$$

Finally, we define a sum of squares that measures the total amount of variability in the observed values of the response:

The **total sum of squares** is

$$SSTO = SST + SSE$$

The variability in the observed values of the response must come from one of two sources—the between-treatment variability or the within-treatment variability. It follows that the total sum of squares equals the sum of the treatment sum of squares and the error sum of squares. Therefore, the **SST and SSE are said to partition the total sum of squares.** For the gasoline mileage study

$$SSTO = SST + SSE = 17.0493 + 8.028 = 25.0773$$

In order to decide whether there are any statistically significant differences between the treatment means, it makes sense to compare the amount of between-treatment variability to the amount of within-treatment variability. This comparison suggests the following F-test:

An *F*-Test for Differences between Treatment Means

Suppose that we wish to compare p treatment means $\mu_1, \mu_2, \ldots, \mu_p$ and consider testing

$H_0: \mu_1 = \mu_2 = \cdots = \mu_p$ versus H_a: At least two of $\mu_1, \mu_2, \ldots, \mu_p$ differ
(all treatment means are equal)   (at least two treatment means differ)

To perform the hypothesis test, define the **treatment mean square** to be $MST = SST/(p - 1)$ and define the **error mean square** to be $MSE = SSE/(n - p)$. Also, define the F statistic

$$F = \frac{MST}{MSE} = \frac{SST/(p - 1)}{SSE/(n - p)}$$

and its p-value to be the area under the F curve with $p - 1$ and $n - p$ degrees of freedom to the right of F. We can reject H_0 in favor of H_a at level of significance α if either of the following equivalent conditions holds:

1 $F > F_\alpha$ **2** p-value $< \alpha$

Here the F_α point is based on $p - 1$ numerator and $n - p$ denominator degrees of freedom.

A large value of F results when SST, which measures the between-treatment variability, is large compared to SSE, which measures the within-treatment variability. If F is large enough, this implies that H_0 should be rejected. The rejection point F_α tells us when F is large enough to allow us to reject H_0 at level of significance α. When F is large, the associated p-value is small. If this p-value is less than α, we can reject H_0 at level of significance α.

EXAMPLE 12.3 The Oil Company Case: Comparing Gasoline Types   C

Consider the North American Oil Company data in Table 12.1. The company wishes to determine whether any of gasoline types A, B, and C have different effects on mean Lance gasoline mileage. That is, we wish to see whether there are any statistically significant differences between μ_A, μ_B, and μ_C. To do this, we test the null hypothesis H_0: $\mu_A = \mu_B = \mu_C$, which says that gasoline types A, B, and C have the same effects on mean gasoline mileage. We test H_0 versus the alternative H_a: At least two of μ_A, μ_B, and μ_C differ, which says that at least two of gasoline types A, B, and C have different effects on mean gasoline mileage.

Because we have previously computed SST to be 17.0493 and SSE to be 8.028, and because we are comparing $p = 3$ treatment means, we have

$$MST = \frac{SST}{p-1} = \frac{17.0493}{3-1} = 8.525$$

and

$$MSE = \frac{SSE}{n-p} = \frac{8.028}{15-3} = 0.669$$

It follows that

$$F = \frac{MST}{MSE} = \frac{8.525}{0.669} = 12.74$$

In order to test H_0 at the .05 level of significance, we use $F_{.05}$ with $p - 1 = 3 - 1 = 2$ numerator and $n - p = 15 - 3 = 12$ denominator degrees of freedom. Table A.7 (page 796) tells us that this F point equals 3.89, so we have

$$F = 12.74 > F_{.05} = 3.89$$

Therefore, we reject H_0 at the .05 level of significance. This says we have strong evidence that at least two of the treatment means μ_A, μ_B, and μ_C differ. In other words, we conclude that at least two of gasoline types A, B, and C have different effects on mean gasoline mileage.

The results of an analysis of variance are often summarized in what is called an **analysis of variance table.** This table gives the sums of squares (SST, SSE, $SSTO$), the mean squares (MST and MSE), and the F statistic and its related p-value for the ANOVA. The table also gives the degrees of freedom associated with each source of variation—treatments, error, and total. Table 12.3 gives the ANOVA table for the gasoline mileage problem. Notice that in the column labeled "Sums of Squares," the values of SST and SSE sum to $SSTO$.

Figure 12.2 gives the MINITAB and Excel output of an analysis of variance of the gasoline mileage data. Note that the upper portion of the MINITAB output and the lower portion of the Excel output give the ANOVA table of Table 12.3. Also, note that each output gives the value $F = 12.74$ and the related p-value, which equals .001 (rounded). Because this p-value is less than .05, we reject H_0 at the .05 level of significance.

Pairwise comparisons If the one-way ANOVA F test says that at least two treatment means differ, then we investigate which treatment means differ and we estimate how large the differences are. We do this by making what we call **pairwise comparisons** (that is, we compare treatment means *two at a time*). One way to make these comparisons is to compute point estimates of and confidence intervals for **pairwise differences.** For example, in the oil company case we might estimate the pairwise differences $\mu_A - \mu_B$, $\mu_A - \mu_C$, and $\mu_B - \mu_C$. Here, for instance, the pairwise difference $\mu_A - \mu_B$ can be interpreted as the change in mean mileage achieved by changing from using gasoline type B to using gasoline type A.

TABLE 12.3   Analysis of Variance (ANOVA) Table for Testing $H_0: \mu_A = \mu_B = \mu_C$ in the Oil Company Case ($p = 3$ Gasoline Types, $n = 15$ Observations)

Source	Degrees of Freedom	Sums of Squares	Mean Squares	F Statistic	p-Value
Treatments	$p - 1 = 3 - 1$ $= 2$	$SST = 17.0493$	$MST = \dfrac{SST}{p-1}$ $= \dfrac{17.0493}{3-1}$ $= 8.525$	$F = \dfrac{MST}{MSE}$ $= \dfrac{8.525}{0.669}$ $= 12.74$	0.001
Error	$n - p = 15 - 3$ $= 12$	$SSE = 8.028$	$MSE = \dfrac{SSE}{n-p}$ $= \dfrac{8.028}{15-3}$ $= 0.669$		
Total	$n - 1 = 15 - 1$ $= 14$	$SSTO = 25.0773$			

FIGURE 12.2   MINITAB and Excel Output of an Analysis of Variance of the Oil Company Gasoline Mileage Data in Table 12.1

(a) The MINITAB output

```
One-way   ANOVA:   Type A,   Type B,   Type C                    Tukey 95% Simultaneous
Source    DF        SS        MS        F         P               Confidence Intervals
Gas Type  2 [1]   17.049 [4]  8.525 [7]  12.74 [9]  0.001 [10]
Error     12 [2]   8.028 [5]  0.669 [8]                          Type A subtracted from:
Total     14 [3]   25.077 [6]                                               Lower    Center    Upper
                              Individual 95%                      Type B    0.2610   1.6400    3.0190
                        CIs For Mean Based on Pooled StDev        Type C   -2.3190  -0.9400    0.439
Level   N   Mean       StDev  ---+---------+---------+---------+------
Type A  5   34.920 [11]  0.766           (------*------)          Type B subtracted from:
Type B  5   36.560 [12]  0.850                    (------*-----)            Lower    Center    Upper
Type C  5   33.980 [13]  0.835  (-----*------)                    Type C   -3.9590  -2.5800  -1.2010

Pooled StDev = 0.818          ---+---------+---------+---------+------
                              33.6      34.8      36.0      37.2
```

(b) The Excel output

SUMMARY

Groups	Count	Sum	Average	Variance
Type A	5	174.6	34.92 [11]	0.587
Type B	5	182.8	36.56 [12]	0.723
Type C	5	169.9	33.98 [13]	0.697

ANOVA

Source of Variation	SS	df	MS	F	P-value	F crit
Between Groups	17.0493 [4]	2 [1]	8.5247 [7]	12.7424 [9]	0.0011 [10]	3.8853 [14]
Within Groups	8.0280 [5]	12 [2]	0.6690 [8]			
Total	25.0773 [6]	14 [3]				

[1] $p-1$ [2] $n-p$ [3] $n-1$ [4] SST [5] SSE [6] $SSTO$ [7] MST [8] MSE [9] F statistic   [10] p-value related to F [11] $\bar{x}_A$ [12] $\bar{x}_B$ [13] $\bar{x}_C$ [14] $F_{.05}$

There are two approaches to calculating confidence intervals for pairwise differences. The first involves computing the usual, or **individual, confidence interval** for each pairwise difference. Here, if we are computing $100(1 - \alpha)$ percent confidence intervals, we are $100(1 - \alpha)$ percent confident that each individual pairwise difference is contained in its respective interval. That is, the confidence level associated with each (individual) comparison is $100(1 - \alpha)$ percent, and we refer to α as the **comparisonwise error rate.** However, we are less than $100(1 - \alpha)$ percent confident that all of the pairwise differences are simultaneously contained in their respective intervals. A more conservative approach is to compute **simultaneous confidence intervals.** Such intervals make us $100(1 - \alpha)$ percent confident that all of the pairwise differences are simultaneously contained in their respective intervals. That is, when we compute simultaneous intervals, the overall confidence level associated with all the comparisons being made in the experiment is $100(1 - \alpha)$ percent, and we refer to α as the **experimentwise error rate.**

Several kinds of simultaneous confidence intervals can be computed. In this book we present what is called the **Tukey formula** for simultaneous intervals. We do this because, *if we are interested in studying all pairwise differences between treatment means, the Tukey formula yields the most precise (shortest) simultaneous confidence intervals.*

Estimation in One-Way ANOVA

1 Consider the **pairwise difference** $\mu_i - \mu_h$, which can be interpreted to be the change in the mean value of the response variable associated with changing from using treatment h to using treatment i. Then, a **point estimate of the difference** $\mu_i - \mu_h$ is $\bar{x}_i - \bar{x}_h$, where $\bar{x}_i$ and $\bar{x}_h$ are the sample treatment means associated with treatments i and h.

2 A **Tukey simultaneous** $100(1 - \alpha)$ **percent confidence interval for** $\mu_i - \mu_h$ is

$$\left[(\bar{x}_i - \bar{x}_h) \pm q_\alpha \sqrt{\frac{MSE}{m}} \right]$$

Here, the value q_α is obtained from Table A.10 (pages 799–800), which is a **table of percentage**

points of the studentized range. In this table q_α is listed corresponding to values of p and $n - p$. Furthermore, we assume that the sample sizes n_i and n_h are equal to the same value, which we denote as m. If n_i and n_h are not equal, we replace $q_\alpha \sqrt{MSE/m}$ by $(q_\alpha/\sqrt{2})\sqrt{MSE[(1/n_i) + (1/n_h)]}$.

3 A **point estimate of the treatment mean** μ_i is $\bar{x}_i$ and an **individual** $100(1 - \alpha)$ **percent confidence interval for** μ_i is

$$\left[\bar{x}_i \pm t_{\alpha/2} \sqrt{\frac{MSE}{n_i}} \right]$$

Here, the $t_{\alpha/2}$ point is based on $n - p$ degrees of freedom.

EXAMPLE 12.4 The Oil Company Case: Comparing Gasoline Types

Part 1: Using confidence intervals   In the gasoline mileage study, we are comparing $p = 3$ treatment means (μ_A, μ_B, and μ_C). Furthermore, each sample is of size $m = 5$, there are a total of $n = 15$ observed gas mileages, and the *MSE* found in Table 12.3 is .669. Because $q_{.05} = 3.77$ is the entry found in Table A.10 (page 799) corresponding to $p = 3$ and $n - p = 12$, a Tukey simultaneous 95 percent confidence interval for $\mu_B - \mu_A$ is

$$\left[(\bar{x}_B - \bar{x}_A) \pm q_{.05} \sqrt{\frac{MSE}{m}} \right] = \left[(36.56 - 34.92) \pm 3.77 \sqrt{\frac{.669}{5}} \right]$$
$$= [1.64 \pm 1.379]$$
$$= [.261, 3.019]$$

Similarly, Tukey simultaneous 95 percent confidence intervals for $\mu_A - \mu_C$ and $\mu_B - \mu_C$ are, respectively,

$$[(\bar{x}_A - \bar{x}_C) \pm 1.379] \qquad \text{and} \qquad [(\bar{x}_B - \bar{x}_C) \pm 1.379]$$
$$= [(34.92 - 33.98) \pm 1.379] \qquad\qquad = [(36.56 - 33.98) \pm 1.379]$$
$$= [-0.439, 2.319] \qquad\qquad\qquad = [1.201, 3.959]$$

These intervals make us simultaneously 95 percent confident that (1) changing from gasoline type A to gasoline type B increases mean mileage by between .261 and 3.019 mpg, (2) changing from gasoline type C to gasoline type A might decrease mean mileage by as much as .439 mpg or might increase mean mileage by as much as 2.319 mpg, *and* (3) changing from gasoline type C to gasoline type B increases mean mileage by between 1.201 and 3.959 mpg. The first and third of these intervals make us 95 percent confident that μ_B is at least .261 mpg greater than μ_A and at least 1.201 mpg greater than μ_C. Therefore, we have strong evidence that gasoline type B yields the highest mean mileage of the gasoline types tested. Furthermore, noting that $t_{.025}$ based on

$n - p = 12$ degrees of freedom is 2.179, it follows that an individual 95 percent confidence interval for μ_B is

$$\left[\bar{x}_B \pm t_{.025}\sqrt{\frac{MSE}{n_B}}\right] = \left[36.56 \pm 2.179\sqrt{\frac{.669}{5}}\right]$$

$$= [35.763, 37.357]$$

This interval says we can be 95 percent confident that the mean mileage obtained by using gasoline type B is between 35.763 and 37.357 mpg. Notice that this confidence interval is graphed on the MINITAB output of Figure 12.2. This output also shows the 95 percent confidence intervals for μ_A and μ_C and gives Tukey simultaneous 95 percent intervals for $\mu_B - \mu_A$, $\mu_C - \mu_A$, and $\mu_C - \mu_B$. Note that the last two Tukey intervals on the output are the "negatives" of the Tukey intervals that we hand calculated for $\mu_A - \mu_C$ and $\mu_B - \mu_C$.

Part 2: Using hypothesis testing (optional)   We next consider testing $H_0: \mu_i - \mu_h = 0$ versus $H_a: \mu_i - \mu_h \neq 0$. The test statistic t for performing this test is calculated by dividing $\bar{x}_i - \bar{x}_h$ by $\sqrt{MSE[(1/n_i) + (1/n_h)]}$. For example, consider testing $H_0: \mu_B - \mu_A = 0$ versus $H_a: \mu_B - \mu_A \neq 0$. Since $\bar{x}_B - \bar{x}_A = 36.56 - 34.92 = 1.64$ and $\sqrt{MSE[(1/n_B) + (1/n_A)]} = \sqrt{.669[(1/5) + (1/5)]} = .5173$, the test statistic t equals $1.64/.5173 = 3.17$. This test statistic value is given in the leftmost portion of the following Excel add-in (MegaStat) output, as is the test statistic value for testing $H_0: \mu_B - \mu_C = 0$ ($t = 4.99$) and the test statistic value for testing $H_0: \mu_A - \mu_C = 0$ ($t = 1.82$):

Tukey simultaneous comparison t-values (d.f. = 12)

		Type C 33.98	Type A 34.92	Type B 36.56	critical values for experimentwise error rate:	
Type C	33.98				0.05	2.67
Type A	34.92	1.82			0.01	3.56
Type B	36.56	4.99	3.17			

If we wish to use the **Tukey simultaneous comparison procedure** having an experimentwise error rate of α, we reject $H_0: \mu_i - \mu_h = 0$ in favor of $H_a: \mu_i - \mu_h \neq 0$ if the absolute value of t is greater than the critical value $q_\alpha/\sqrt{2}$. Table A.10 (page 799) tells us that $q_{.05}$ is 3.77 and $q_{.01}$ is 5.04. Therefore, the critical values for experimentwise error rates of .05 and .01 are, respectively, $3.77/\sqrt{2} = 2.67$ and $5.04/\sqrt{2} = 3.56$ (see the right portion of the MegaStat output). Suppose we set α equal to .05. Then, since the test statistic value for testing $H_0: \mu_B - \mu_A = 0$ ($t = 3.17$) and the test statistic value for testing $H_0: \mu_B - \mu_C = 0$ ($t = 4.99$) are greater than the critical value 2.67, we reject both null hypotheses. This, along with the fact that $\bar{x}_B = 36.56$ is greater than $\bar{x}_A = 34.92$ and $\bar{x}_C = 33.98$, leads us to conclude that gasoline type B yields the highest mean mileage.

In general, when we use a completely randomized experimental design, it is important to compare the treatments by using experimental units that are essentially the same with respect to the characteristic under study. For example, in the oil company case we have used cars of the same type (Lances) to compare the different gasoline types, and in the supermarket case we have used grocery stores of the same sales potential for the bakery product to compare the shelf display heights (the reader will analyze the data for this case in the exercises). Sometimes, however, it is not possible to use experimental units that are essentially the same with respect to the characteristic under study. One approach to dealing with this situation is to employ **a randomized block design.** This experimental design is discussed in Section 12.3.

To conclude this section, we note that if we fear that the normality and/or equal variances assumptions for one-way analysis of variance do not hold, we can use a nonparametric approach to compare several populations. See Section 18.4 of Chapter 18.

Exercises for Section 12.2

CONCEPTS

connect

12.1   Define the meaning of the terms *response variable, factor, treatments,* and *experimental units.*

12.2   Explain the assumptions that must be satisfied in order to validly use the one-way ANOVA formulas.

FIGURE 12.3   MINITAB Output of a One-Way ANOVA of the Bakery Sales Data in Table 12.2

```
One-way ANOVA: Bakery Sales versus Display Height          Tukey 95% Simultaneous
                                                            Confidence Intervals
Source         DF      SS      MS      F      P
Display Height  2  2273.88  1136.94  184.57  0.000          Bottom subtracted from:
Error          15    92.40     6.16                                  Lower    Center   Upper
Total          17  2366.28                                 Middle   17.681   21.400  25.119
                           Individual 95%                  Top      -8.019   -4.300  -0.581
                           CIs For Mean Based on Pooled StDev
Level    N    Mean   StDev   --------+---------+---------+---------+-   Middle subtracted from:
Bottom   6  55.800   2.477       (--*-)                                     Lower    Center   Upper
Middle   6  77.200   3.103                            (--*-)         Top    -29.419  -25.700 -21.981
Top      6  51.500   1.648   (-*--)
                           --------+---------+---------+---------+-
Pooled StDev = 2.482           56.0      64.0      72.0      80.0
```

FIGURE 12.4   MINITAB Output of a One-Way ANOVA of the Display Panel Study Data in Table 12.4

```
One-way ANOVA: Time versus Display                         Tukey 95% Simultaneous
                                                            Confidence Intervals
Source    DF      SS      MS      F      P
Display    2   500.17  250.08  30.11  0.000                 A subtracted from:
Error      9    74.75    8.31                                      Lower    Center   Upper
Total     11   574.92                                       B     -9.692    -4.000   1.692
                          Individual 95%                    C      5.558    11.250  16.942
                          CIs For Mean Based on Pooled StDev
Level   N    Mean   StDev   -+---------+---------+---------+--------
A       4  24.500   2.646            (-----*----)                    B subtracted from:
B       4  20.500   2.646   (----*-----)                                  Lower    Center   Upper
C       4  35.750   3.304                       (-----*----)        C      9.558    15.250  20.942
                          -+---------+---------+---------+--------
Pooled StDev = 2.882      18.0      24.0      30.0      36.0
```

12.3 Explain the difference between the between-treatment variability and the within-treatment variability when performing a one-way ANOVA.

12.4 Explain why we conduct pairwise comparisons of treatment means.

METHODS AND APPLICATIONS

12.5 **THE SUPERMARKET CASE** ⟳ BakeSale

Consider Example 12.2, and let μ_B, μ_M, and μ_T represent the mean monthly sales when using the bottom, middle, and top shelf display heights, respectively. Figure 12.3 gives the MINITAB output of a one-way ANOVA of the bakery sales study data in Table 12.2 (page 429).

a Test the null hypothesis that μ_B, μ_M, and μ_T are equal by setting $\alpha = .05$. On the basis of this test, can we conclude that the bottom, middle, and top shelf display heights have different effects on mean monthly sales?

b Consider the pairwise differences $\mu_M - \mu_B$, $\mu_T - \mu_B$, and $\mu_T - \mu_M$. Find a point estimate of and a Tukey simultaneous 95 percent confidence interval for each pairwise difference. Interpret the meaning of each interval in practical terms. Which display height maximizes mean sales?

c Find 95 percent confidence intervals for μ_B, μ_M, and μ_T. Interpret each interval.

12.6 A study compared three different display panels for use by air traffic controllers. Each display panel was tested in a simulated emergency condition; 12 highly trained air traffic controllers took part in the study. Four controllers were randomly assigned to each display panel. The time (in seconds) needed to stabilize the emergency condition was recorded. The results of the study are given in Table 12.4. Let μ_A, μ_B, and μ_C represent the mean times to stabilize the emergency condition when using display panels A, B, and C, respectively. Figure 12.4 gives the MINITAB output of a one-way ANOVA of the display panel data ⟳ Display

a Test the null hypothesis that μ_A, μ_B, and μ_C are equal by setting $\alpha = .05$. On the basis of this test, can we conclude that display panels A, B, and C have different effects on the mean time to stabilize the emergency condition?

b Consider the pairwise differences $\mu_B - \mu_A$, $\mu_C - \mu_A$, and $\mu_C - \mu_B$. Find a point estimate of and a Tukey simultaneous 95 percent confidence interval for each pairwise difference. Interpret the

TABLE 12.4
Display Panel Study Data
⟳ Display

Display Panel		
A	B	C
21	24	40
27	21	36
24	18	35
26	19	32

TABLE 12.5
Bottle Design Study Data
🗂 BottleDes

Bottle Design		
A	B	C
16	33	23
18	31	27
19	37	21
17	29	28
13	34	25

FIGURE 12.5   **Excel Output of a One-Way ANOVA of the Bottle Design Study Data**

SUMMARY

Groups	Count	Sum	Average	Variance
DESIGN A	5	83	16.6	5.3
DESIGN B	5	164	32.8	9.2
DESIGN C	5	124	24.8	8.2

ANOVA

Source of Variation	SS	df	MS	F	P-Value	F crit
Between Groups	656.1333	2	328.0667	43.35683	3.23E-06	3.88529
Within Groups	90.8	12	7.566667			
Total	746.9333	14				

FIGURE 12.6   **Excel Output of a One-Way ANOVA of the Golf Ball Durability Data**

SUMMARY

Groups	Count	Sum	Average	Variance
Alpha	5	1268	253.6	609.3
Best	5	1532	306.4	740.3
Century	5	1209	241.8	469.7
Divot	5	1683	336.6	605.3

Tukey simultaneous comparison t-values (d.f. = 16)

		Century 241.8	Alpha 253.6	Best 306.4	Divot 336.6
Century	241.8				
Alpha	253.6	0.76			
Best	306.4	4.15	3.39		
Divot	336.6	6.09	5.33	1.94	

Critical values for experimentwise error rate:

0.05	2.86
0.01	3.67

ANOVA

Source of Variation	SS	df	MS	F	P-Value	F crit
Between Groups	29860.4	3	9953.4667	16.420798	3.853E-05	3.2388715
Within Groups	9698.4	16	606.15			
Total	39558.8	19				

results by describing the effects of changing from using each display panel to using each of the other panels. Which display panel minimizes the time required to stabilize the emergency condition?

12.7   A consumer preference study compares the effects of three different bottle designs (A, B, and C) on sales of a popular fabric softener. A completely randomized design is employed. Specifically, 15 supermarkets of equal sales potential are selected, and 5 of these supermarkets are randomly assigned to each bottle design. The number of bottles sold in 24 hours at each supermarket is recorded. The data obtained are displayed in Table 12.5. Let μ_A, μ_B, and μ_C represent mean daily sales using bottle designs A, B, and C, respectively. Figure 12.5 gives the Excel output of a one-way ANOVA of the bottle design study data.   🗂 BottleDes

TABLE 12.6
Golf Ball Durability Test Results
🗂 GolfBall

Brand	
Alpha	Best
281	270
220	334
274	307
242	290
251	331

Century	Divot
218	364
244	302
225	325
273	337
249	355

   a   Test the null hypothesis that μ_A, μ_B, and μ_C are equal by setting $\alpha = .05$. That is, test for statistically significant differences between these treatment means at the .05 level of significance. Based on this test, can we conclude that bottle designs A, B, and C have different effects on mean daily sales?

   b   Consider the pairwise differences $\mu_B - \mu_A$, $\mu_C - \mu_A$, and $\mu_C - \mu_B$. Find a point estimate of and a Tukey simultaneous 95 percent confidence interval for each pairwise difference. Interpret the results in practical terms. Which bottle design maximizes mean daily sales?

   c   Find and interpret a 95 percent confidence interval for each of the treatment means μ_A, μ_B, and μ_C.

12.8   In order to compare the durability of four different brands of golf balls (ALPHA, BEST, CENTURY, and DIVOT), the National Golf Association randomly selects five balls of each brand and places each ball into a machine that exerts the force produced by a 250-yard drive. The number of simulated drives needed to crack or chip each ball is recorded. The results are given in Table 12.6. The Excel output of a one-way ANOVA of these data is shown in Figure 12.6. Test for statistically significant differences between the treatment means μ_{ALPHA}, μ_{BEST}, $\mu_{CENTURY}$, and μ_{DIVOT}. Set $\alpha = .05$.   🗂 GolfBall

12.9   Perform pairwise comparisons of the treatment means in Exercise 12.8 by (1) Using Tukey simultaneous 95 percent confidence intervals (2) Optionally using t statistics and critical values (see the right side of Figure 12.6 and page 436). Which brands are most durable? Find and interpret a 95 percent confidence interval for each of the treatment means.

12.3 The Randomized Block Design ● ● ●

Not all experiments employ a completely randomized design. For instance, suppose that when we employ a completely randomized design, we fail to reject the null hypothesis of equality of treatment means because the within-treatment variability (which is measured by the *SSE*) is large. This could happen because differences between the experimental units are concealing true differences between the treatments. We can often remedy this by using what is called a **randomized block design.**

LO12-3 Compare treatment effects and block effects by using a randomized block design.

EXAMPLE 12.5 The Cardboard Box Case: Comparing Production Methods

The Universal Paper Company manufactures cardboard boxes. The company wishes to investigate the effects of four production methods (methods 1, 2, 3, and 4) on the number of defective boxes produced in an hour. To compare the methods, the company could utilize a completely randomized design. For each of the four production methods, the company would select several (say, as an example, three) machine operators, train each operator to use the production method to which he or she has been assigned, have each operator produce boxes for one hour, and record the number of defective boxes produced. The three operators using any one production method would be *different* from those using any other production method. That is, the completely randomized design would utilize a total of 12 machine operators. However, the abilities of the machine operators could differ substantially. These differences might tend to conceal any real differences between the production methods. To overcome this disadvantage, the company will employ a **randomized block experimental design.** This involves randomly selecting three machine operators and training each operator thoroughly to use all four production methods. Then each operator will produce boxes for one hour using each of the four production methods. The order in which each operator uses the four methods should be random. We record the number of defective boxes produced by each operator using each method. The advantage of the randomized block design is that the defective rates obtained by using the four methods result from employing the *same* three operators. Thus any true differences in the effectiveness of the methods would not be concealed by differences in the operators' abilities.

When Universal Paper employs the randomized block design, it obtains the 12 defective box counts in Table 12.7. We let x_{ij} denote the number of defective boxes produced by machine operator j using production method i. For example, $x_{32} = 5$ says that 5 defective boxes were produced by machine operator 2 using production method 3 (see Table 12.7). In addition to the 12 defective box counts, Table 12.7 gives the sample mean of these 12 observations, which is $\bar{x} = 7.5833$, and also gives **sample treatment means** and **sample block means.** The sample treatment means are the average defective box counts obtained when using production methods 1, 2, 3, and 4. Denoting these sample treatment means as $\bar{x}_{1\bullet}, \bar{x}_{2\bullet}, \bar{x}_{3\bullet}$, and $\bar{x}_{4\bullet}$, we see from Table 12.7 that $\bar{x}_{1\bullet} = 10.3333$, $\bar{x}_{2\bullet} = 10.3333$, $\bar{x}_{3\bullet} = 5.0$, and $\bar{x}_{4\bullet} = 4.6667$. Because $\bar{x}_{3\bullet}$ and $\bar{x}_{4\bullet}$ are less than $\bar{x}_{1\bullet}$ and $\bar{x}_{2\bullet}$, we estimate that the mean number of defective boxes produced per hour by production method 3 or 4 is less than the mean number of defective boxes produced per hour by production method 1 or 2. The sample block means are the average defective box counts obtained by machine operators 1, 2, and 3. Denoting these sample block means as $\bar{x}_{\bullet 1}, \bar{x}_{\bullet 2}$, and $\bar{x}_{\bullet 3}$, we see from Table 12.7 that $\bar{x}_{\bullet 1} = 6.0$, $\bar{x}_{\bullet 2} = 7.75$, and $\bar{x}_{\bullet 3} = 9.0$. Because $\bar{x}_{\bullet 1}, \bar{x}_{\bullet 2}$, and $\bar{x}_{\bullet 3}$ differ, we have evidence that the abilities of the machine operators differ and thus that using the machine operators as blocks is reasonable.

TABLE 12.7   Numbers of Defective Cardboard Boxes Obtained by Production Methods 1, 2, 3, and 4 and Machine Operators 1, 2, and 3   DS CardBox

Treatment (Production Method)	Block (Machine Operator) 1	2	3	Sample Treatment Mean
1	9	10	12	10.3333
2	8	11	12	10.3333
3	3	5	7	5.0
4	4	5	5	4.6667
Sample Block Mean	6.0	7.75	9.0	$\bar{x} = 7.5833$

In general, a **randomized block design** compares p treatments (for example, production methods) by using b blocks (for example, machine operators). Each block is used exactly once to measure the effect of each and every treatment. The advantage of the randomized block design over the completely randomized design is that we are comparing the treatments by using the *same* experimental units. Thus any true differences in the treatments will not be concealed by differences in the experimental units.

In order to analyze the data obtained in a randomized block design, we define

x_{ij} = the value of the response variable observed when block j uses treatment i

$\bar{x}_{i\bullet}$ = the mean of the b values of the response variable observed when using treatment i

$\bar{x}_{\bullet j}$ = the mean of the p values of the response variable observed when using block j

$\bar{x}$ = the mean of the total of the bp values of the response variable that we have observed in the experiment

The ANOVA procedure for a randomized block design partitions the **total sum of squares (SSTO)** into three components: the **treatment sum of squares (SST)**, the **block sum of squares (SSB)**, and the **error sum of squares (SSE)**. The formula for this partitioning is

$$SSTO = SST + SSB + SSE$$

We define each of these sums of squares and show how they are calculated for the defective cardboard box data as follows (note that $p = 4$ and $b = 3$):

Step 1: Calculate SST, which measures the amount of between-treatment variability:

$$
\begin{aligned}
SST &= b \sum_{i=1}^{p} (\bar{x}_{i\bullet} - \bar{x})^2 \\
&= 3[(\bar{x}_{1\bullet} - \bar{x})^2 + (\bar{x}_{2\bullet} - \bar{x})^2 + (\bar{x}_{3\bullet} - \bar{x})^2 + (\bar{x}_{4\bullet} - \bar{x})^2] \\
&= 3[(10.3333 - 7.5833)^2 + (10.3333 - 7.5833)^2 \\
&\quad + (5.0 - 7.5833)^2 + (4.6667 - 7.5833)^2] \\
&= 90.9167
\end{aligned}
$$

Step 2: Calculate SSB, which measures the amount of variability due to the blocks:

$$
\begin{aligned}
SSB &= p \sum_{j=1}^{b} (\bar{x}_{\bullet j} - \bar{x})^2 \\
&= 4[(\bar{x}_{\bullet 1} - \bar{x})^2 + (\bar{x}_{\bullet 2} - \bar{x})^2 + (\bar{x}_{\bullet 3} - \bar{x})^2] \\
&= 4[(6.0 - 7.5833)^2 + (7.75 - 7.5833)^2 + (9.0 - 7.5833)^2] \\
&= 18.1667
\end{aligned}
$$

Step 3: Calculate $SSTO$, which measures the total amount of variability:

$$
\begin{aligned}
SSTO &= \sum_{i=1}^{p} \sum_{j=1}^{b} (x_{ij} - \bar{x})^2 \\
&= (9 - 7.5833)^2 + (10 - 7.5833)^2 + (12 - 7.5833)^2 \\
&\quad + (8 - 7.5833)^2 + (11 - 7.5833)^2 + (12 - 7.5833)^2 \\
&\quad + (3 - 7.5833)^2 + (5 - 7.5833)^2 + (7 - 7.5833)^2 \\
&\quad + (4 - 7.5833)^2 + (5 - 7.5833)^2 + (5 - 7.5833)^2 \\
&= 112.9167
\end{aligned}
$$

Step 4: Calculate SSE, which measures the amount of variability due to the error:

$$
\begin{aligned}
SSE &= SSTO - SST - SSB \\
&= 112.9167 - 90.9167 - 18.1667 \\
&= 3.8333
\end{aligned}
$$

These sums of squares are shown in Table 12.8, which is the ANOVA table for a randomized block design. This table also gives the degrees of freedom, mean squares, and F statistics used to

TABLE 12.8 Randomized Block ANOVA Table for the Defective Box Data

Source of Variation	Degrees of Freedom	Sum of Squares	Mean Square	F
Treatments	$p - 1 = 3$	$SST = 90.9167$	$MST = \dfrac{SST}{p-1} = 30.3056$	$F(\text{treatments}) = \dfrac{MST}{MSE} = 47.4348$
Blocks	$b - 1 = 2$	$SSB = 18.1667$	$MSB = \dfrac{SSB}{b-1} = 9.0833$	$F(\text{blocks}) = \dfrac{MSB}{MSE} = 14.2174$
Error	$(p-1)(b-1) = 6$	$SSE = 3.8333$	$MSE = \dfrac{SSE}{(p-1)(b-1)} = .6389$	
Total	$pb - 1 = 11$	$SSTO = 112.9167$		

test the hypotheses of interest in a randomized block experiment, as well as the values of these quantities for the defective cardboard box data.

Of main interest is the test of the null hypothesis H_0 that **no differences exist between the treatment effects** on the mean value of the response variable versus the alternative hypothesis H_a that **at least two treatment effects differ.** We can reject H_0 in favor of H_a at level of significance α if $F(\text{treatments})$ is greater than the F_α point based on $p - 1$ numerator and $(p - 1)(b - 1)$ denominator degrees of freedom. In the defective cardboard box case, $F_{.05}$ based on $p - 1 = 3$ numerator and $(p - 1)(b - 1) = 6$ denominator degrees of freedom is 4.76 (see Table A.7, page 796). Because $F(\text{treatments}) = 47.4348$ (see Table 12.8) is greater than $F_{.05} = 4.76$, we reject H_0 at the .05 level of significance. Therefore, we have strong evidence that at least two production methods have different effects on the mean number of defective boxes produced per hour.

It is also of interest to test the null hypothesis H_0 that **no differences exist between the block effects** on the mean value of the response variable versus the alternative hypothesis H_a that **at least two block effects differ.** We can reject H_0 in favor of H_a at level of significance α if $F(\text{blocks})$ is greater than the F_α point based on $b - 1$ numerator and $(p - 1)(b - 1)$ denominator degrees of freedom. In the defective cardboard box case, $F_{.05}$ based on $b - 1 = 2$ numerator and $(p - 1)(b - 1) = 6$ denominator degrees of freedom is 5.14 (see Table A.7, page 796). Because $F(\text{blocks}) = 14.2174$ (see Table 12.8) is greater than $F_{.05} = 5.14$, we reject H_0 at the .05 level of significance. Therefore, we have strong evidence that at least two machine operators have different effects on the mean number of defective boxes produced per hour.

Figure 12.7 gives the MINITAB and Excel outputs of a randomized block ANOVA of the defective cardboard box data. The p-value of .000 ($<.001$) related to $F(\text{treatments})$ provides extremely strong evidence of differences in production method effects. The p-value of .0053 related to $F(\text{blocks})$ provides very strong evidence of differences in machine operator effects.

If, in a randomized block design, we conclude that at least two treatment effects differ, we can perform pairwise comparisons to determine how they differ.

Point Estimates and Confidence Intervals in a Randomized Block ANOVA

Consider the **difference between the effects of treatments i and h on the mean value of the response variable.** Then:

1 A **point estimate** of this difference is $\bar{x}_{i\cdot} - \bar{x}_{h\cdot}$.

2 A **Tukey simultaneous $100(1 - \alpha)$ percent confidence interval** for this difference is

$$\left[(\bar{x}_{i\cdot} - \bar{x}_{h\cdot}) \pm q_\alpha \frac{s}{\sqrt{b}} \right]$$

Here the value q_α is obtained from Table A.10 (pages 799–800), which is a table of percentage points of the studentized range. In this table q_α is listed corresponding to values of p and $(p - 1)(b - 1)$.

FIGURE 12.7   MINITAB and Excel Outputs of a Randomized Block ANOVA of the Defective Box Data

(a) The MINITAB Output

```
 Rows: Method   Columns: Operator
              1          2          3        All      Method      Mean            Operator   Mean
   1       9.000     10.000     12.000     10.333       1       10.3333 [12]        1        6.00 [16]
   2       8.000     11.000     12.000     10.333       2       10.3333 [13]        2        7.75 [17]
   3       3.000      5.000      7.000      5.000       3        5.0000 [14]        3        9.00 [18]
   4       4.000      5.000      5.000      4.667       4        4.6667 [15]
  All      6.000      7.750      9.000      7.583
```

Two-way ANOVA: Rejects versus Method, Operator

Source	DF	SS	MS	F	P
Method	3	90.917 [1]	30.3056 [5]	47.43 [8]	0.000 [9]
Operator	2	18.167 [2]	9.0833 [6]	14.22 [10]	0.005 [11]
Error	6	3.833 [3]	0.6389 [7]		
Total	11	112.917 [4]			

(b) The Excel output

ANOVA: Two-Factor Without Replication

Summary	Count	Sum	Average	Variance
Method1	3	31	10.3333 [12]	2.3333
Method2	3	31	10.3333 [13]	4.3333
Method3	3	5	5 [14]	4
Method4	3	14	4.6667 [15]	0.3333
Operator1	4	24	6 [16]	8.6667
Operator2	4	31	7.75 [17]	10.25
Operator3	4	36	9 [18]	12.6667

ANOVA

Source of Variation	SS	df	MS	F	P-value	F crit
Method	90.9167 [1]	3	30.3056 [5]	47.4348 [8]	0.0001 [9]	4.7571
Operator	18.1667 [2]	2	9.0833 [6]	14.2174 [10]	0.0053 [11]	5.1433
Error	3.8333 [3]	6	0.6389 [7]			
Total	112.9167 [4]	11				

[1] SST	[2] SSB	[3] SSE	[4] SSTO	[5] MST	[6] MSB	[7] MSE	[8] F(treatments)	[9] p-value for F(treatments)
[10] F(blocks)	[11] p-value for F(blocks)	[12] $\bar{x}_{1\bullet}$	[13] $\bar{x}_{2\bullet}$	[14] $\bar{x}_{3\bullet}$	[15] $\bar{x}_{4\bullet}$	[16] $\bar{x}_{\bullet 1}$	[17] $\bar{x}_{\bullet 2}$	[18] $\bar{x}_{\bullet 3}$

EXAMPLE 12.6 The Cardboard Box Case: Comparing Production Methods

We have previously concluded that we have extremely strong evidence that at least two production methods have different effects on the mean number of defective boxes produced per hour. We have also seen that the sample treatment means are $\bar{x}_{1\bullet} = 10.3333$, $\bar{x}_{2\bullet} = 10.3333$, $\bar{x}_{3\bullet} = 5.0$, and $\bar{x}_{4\bullet} = 4.6667$. Because $\bar{x}_{4\bullet}$ is the smallest sample treatment mean, we will use Tukey simultaneous 95 percent confidence intervals to compare the effect of production method 4 with the effects of production methods 1, 2, and 3. To compute these intervals, we first note that $q_{.05} = 4.90$ is the entry in Table A.10 (page 799) corresponding to $p = 4$ and $(p - 1)(b - 1) = 6$. Also, note that the *MSE* found in the randomized block ANOVA table is .6389 (see Figure 12.7), which implies that $s = \sqrt{.6389} = .7993$. It follows that a Tukey simultaneous 95 percent confidence interval for the difference between the effects of production methods 4 and 1 on the mean number of defective boxes produced per hour is

$$\left[(\bar{x}_{4\bullet} - \bar{x}_{1\bullet}) \pm q_{.05} \frac{s}{\sqrt{b}} \right] = \left[(4.6667 - 10.3333) \pm 4.90 \left(\frac{.7993}{\sqrt{3}} \right) \right]$$

$$= [-5.6666 \pm 2.2615]$$

$$= [-7.9281, -3.4051]$$

Furthermore, it can be verified that a Tukey simultaneous 95 percent confidence interval for the difference between the effects of production methods 4 and 2 on the mean number of defective boxes produced per hour is also $[-7.9281, -3.4051]$. Therefore, we can be 95 percent confident that changing from production method 1 or 2 to production method 4 decreases the mean number of defective boxes produced per hour by a machine operator by between 3.4051 and 7.9281 boxes. A Tukey simultaneous 95 percent confidence interval for the difference between the effects of production methods 4 and 3 on the mean number of defective boxes produced per hour is

$$[(\bar{x}_{4\cdot} - \bar{x}_{3\cdot}) \pm 2.2615] = [(4.6667 - 5) \pm 2.2615]$$
$$= [-2.5948, \ 1.9282]$$

This interval tells us (with 95 percent confidence) that changing from production method 3 to production method 4 might decrease the mean number of defective boxes produced per hour by as many as 2.5948 boxes or might increase this mean by as many as 1.9282 boxes. In other words, because this interval contains 0, we cannot conclude that the effects of production methods 4 and 3 differ.

Exercises for Section 12.3

CONCEPTS

12.10 In your own words, explain why we sometimes employ the randomized block design.

12.11 Describe what *SSTO*, *SST*, *SSB*, and *SSE* measure.

12.12 How can we test to determine if the blocks we have chosen are reasonable?

METHODS AND APPLICATIONS

12.13 A marketing organization wishes to study the effects of four sales methods on weekly sales of a product. The organization employs a randomized block design in which three salesman use each sales method. The results obtained are given in Figure 12.8, along with the Excel output of a randomized block ANOVA of these data.   ⟁ SaleMeth

    a Test the null hypothesis H_0 that no differences exist between the effects of the sales methods (treatments) on mean weekly sales. Set $\alpha = .05$. Can we conclude that the different sales methods have different effects on mean weekly sales?

    b Test the null hypothesis H_0 that no differences exist between the effects of the salesmen (blocks) on mean weekly sales. Set $\alpha = .05$. Can we conclude that the different salesmen have different effects on mean weekly sales?

    c Use Tukey simultaneous 95 percent confidence intervals to make pairwise comparisons of the sales method effects on mean weekly sales. Which sales method(s) maximize mean weekly sales?

FIGURE 12.8   **The Sales Method Data and the Excel Output of a Randomized Block ANOVA**   ⟁ SaleMeth

ANOVA: Two-Factor without Replication

Sales Method, *i*	Salesman, *j* A	B	C	SUMMARY	Count	Sum	Average	Variance
1	32	29	30	Method 1	3	91	30.3333	2.3333
2	32	30	28	Method 2	3	90	30	4
3	28	25	23	Method 3	3	76	25.3333	6.3333
4	25	24	23	Method 4	3	72	24	1
				Salesman A	4	117	29.25	11.5833
				Salesman B	4	108	27	8.6667
				Salesman C	4	104	26	12.6667

ANOVA

Source of Variation	SS	df	MS	F	P-value	F crit
Rows	93.5833	3	31.1944	36.2258	0.0003	4.7571
Columns	22.1667	2	11.0833	12.8710	0.0068	5.1433
Error	5.1667	6	0.8611			
Total	120.9167	11				

TABLE 12.9 **Results of a Bottle Design Experiment**
ⒹⓈ BottleDes2

Bottle Design, i	Supermarket, j			
	1	**2**	**3**	**4**
A	16	14	1	6
B	33	30	19	23
C	23	21	8	12

TABLE 12.10 **Results of a Keyboard Experiment**
ⒹⓈ Keyboard

Data Entry Specialist	Keyboard Brand		
	A	**B**	**C**
1	77	67	63
2	71	62	59
3	74	63	59
4	67	57	54

12.14 A consumer preference study involving three different bottle designs (A, B, and C) for the jumbo size of a new liquid laundry detergent was carried out using a randomized block experimental design, with supermarkets as blocks. Specifically, four supermarkets were supplied with all three bottle designs, which were priced the same. Table 12.9 gives the number of bottles of each design sold in a 24-hour period at each supermarket. If we use these data, SST, SSB, and SSE can be calculated to be 586.1667, 421.6667, and 1.8333, respectively.   ⒹⓈ BottleDes2

   a Test the null hypothesis H_0 that no differences exist between the effects of the bottle designs on mean daily sales. Set $\alpha = .05$. Can we conclude that the different bottle designs have different effects on mean sales?

   b Test the null hypothesis H_0 that no differences exist between the effects of the supermarkets on mean daily sales. Set $\alpha = .05$. Can we conclude that the different supermarkets have different effects on mean sales?

   c Use Tukey simultaneous 95 percent confidence intervals to make pairwise comparisons of the bottle design effects on mean daily sales. Which bottle design(s) maximize mean sales?

12.15 To compare three brands of computer keyboards, four data entry specialists were randomly selected. Each specialist used all three keyboards to enter the same kind of text material for 10 minutes, and the number of words entered per minute was recorded. The data obtained are given in Table 12.10. If we use these data, SST, SSB, and SSE can be calculated to be 392.6667, 143.5833, and 2.6667, respectively.   ⒹⓈ Keyboard

   a Test the null hypothesis H_0 that no differences exist between the effects of the keyboard brands on the mean number of words entered per minute. Set $\alpha = .05$.

   b Test the null hypothesis H_0 that no differences exist between the effects of the data entry specialists on the mean number of words entered per minute. Set $\alpha = .05$.

   c Use Tukey simultaneous 95 percent confidence intervals to make pairwise comparisons of the keyboard brand effects on the mean number of words entered per minute. Which keyboard brand maximizes the mean number of words entered per minute?

12.16 The Coca-Cola Company introduced New Coke in 1985. Within three months of this introduction, negative consumer reaction forced Coca-Cola to reintroduce the original formula of Coke as Coca-Cola Classic. Suppose that two years later, in 1987, a marketing research firm in Chicago compared the sales of Coca-Cola Classic, New Coke, and Pepsi in public building vending machines. To do this, the marketing research firm randomly selected 10 public buildings in Chicago having both a Coke machine (selling Coke Classic and New Coke) and a Pepsi machine.

FIGURE 12.9 **The Coca-Cola Data and a MINITAB Output of a Randomized Block ANOVA of the Data**

	Building									
	1	**2**	**3**	**4**	**5**	**6**	**7**	**8**	**9**	**10**
Coke Classic	45	136	134	41	146	33	71	224	111	87
New Coke	6	114	56	14	39	20	42	156	61	140
Pepsi	24	90	100	43	51	42	68	131	74	107

Two-way ANOVA: Cans versus Drink, Building

Source	DF	SS	MS	F	P
Drink	2	7997.6	3998.80	5.78	0.011
Building	9	55573.5	6174.83	8.93	0.000
Error	18	12443.7	691.32		
Total	29	76014.8			

Descriptive Statistics: Cans

Variable	Drink	Mean
Cans	Coke Classic	102.8
	New Coke	64.8
	Pepsi	73.0

The data—in number of cans sold over a given period of time—and a MINITAB randomized block ANOVA of the data are given in Figure 12.9. **DS** Coke

a Test the null hypothesis H_0 that no differences exist between the mean sales of Coca-Cola Classic, New Coke, and Pepsi in Chicago public building vending machines. Set $\alpha = .05$.

b Make pairwise comparisons of the mean sales of Coca-Cola Classic, New Coke, and Pepsi in Chicago public building vending machines by using Tukey simultaneous 95 percent confidence intervals.

c By the mid-1990s the Coca-Cola Company had discontinued making New Coke and had returned to making only its original product. Is there evidence in the 1987 study that this might happen? Explain your answer.

12.4 Two-Way Analysis of Variance ● ● ●

LO12-4 Assess the effects of two factors on a response variable by using a two-way analysis of variance.

Many response variables are affected by more than one factor. Because of this we must often conduct experiments in which we study the effects of several factors on the response. In this section we consider studying the effects of **two factors** on a response variable. To begin, recall that in Example 12.2 we discussed an experiment in which the Tastee Bakery Company investigated the effect of shelf display height on monthly demand for one of its bakery products. This one-factor experiment is actually a simplification of a two-factor experiment carried out by the Tastee Bakery Company. We discuss this two-factor experiment in the following example.

EXAMPLE 12.7 The Supermarket Case: Comparing Display Heights and Widths

The Tastee Bakery Company supplies a bakery product to many metropolitan supermarkets. The company wishes to study the effects of two factors—**shelf display height** and **shelf display width**—on **monthly demand** (measured in cases of 10 units each) for this product. The factor "display height" is defined to have three levels: B (bottom), M (middle), and T (top). The factor "display width" is defined to have two levels: R (regular) and W (wide). The **treatments** in this experiment are **display height and display width combinations.** These treatments are

$$BR \quad BW \quad MR \quad MW \quad TR \quad TW$$

Here, for example, the notation BR denotes the treatment "bottom display height and regular display width." For each display height and width combination the company randomly selects a sample of $m = 3$ metropolitan area supermarkets (all supermarkets used in the study will be of equal sales potential). Each supermarket sells the product for one month using its assigned display height and width combination, and the month's demand for the product is recorded. The six samples obtained in this experiment are given in Table 12.11 on the next page. We let $x_{ij,k}$ denote the monthly demand obtained at the kth supermarket that used display height i and display width j. For example, $x_{MW,2} = 78.4$ is the monthly demand obtained at the second supermarket that used a middle display height and a wide display.

In addition to giving the six samples, Table 12.11 gives the **sample treatment mean** for each display height and display width combination. For example, $\bar{x}_{BR} = 55.9$ is the mean of the sample of three demands observed at supermarkets using a bottom display height and a regular display width. The table also gives the sample mean demand for each level of display height (B, M, and T) and for each level of display width (R and W). Specifically,

$\bar{x}_{B\cdot} = 55.8 =$ the mean of the six demands observed when using a bottom display height

$\bar{x}_{M\cdot} = 77.2 =$ the mean of the six demands observed when using a middle display height

$\bar{x}_{T\cdot} = 51.5 =$ the mean of the six demands observed when using a top display height

$\bar{x}_{\cdot R} = 60.8 =$ the mean of the nine demands observed when using a regular display width

$\bar{x}_{\cdot W} = 62.2 =$ the mean of the nine demands observed when using a wide display

Finally, Table 12.11 gives $\bar{x} = 61.5$, which is the overall mean of the total of 18 demands observed in the experiment. Because $\bar{x}_{M\cdot} = 77.2$ is considerably larger than $\bar{x}_{B\cdot} = 55.8$ and $\bar{x}_{T\cdot} = 51.5$, we estimate that mean monthly demand is highest when using a middle display height. Because $\bar{x}_{\cdot R} = 60.8$ and $\bar{x}_{\cdot W} = 62.2$ do not differ by very much, we estimate there is little difference between the effects of a regular display width and a wide display on mean monthly demand.

| TABLE 12.11 | Six Samples of Monthly Demands for a Bakery Product ⒹⓈ BakeSale2 |

	Display Width		
Display Height	**R**	**W**	
B	58.2	55.7	
	53.7	52.5	
	55.8	58.9	
	$\bar{x}_{BR} = 55.9$	$\bar{x}_{BW} = 55.7$	$\bar{x}_{B\cdot} = 55.8$
M	73.0	76.2	
	78.1	78.4	
	75.4	82.1	
	$\bar{x}_{MR} = 75.5$	$\bar{x}_{MW} = 78.9$	$\bar{x}_{M\cdot} = 77.2$
T	52.4	54.0	
	49.7	52.1	
	50.9	49.9	
	$\bar{x}_{TR} = 51.0$	$\bar{x}_{TW} = 52.0$	$\bar{x}_{T\cdot} = 51.5$
	$\bar{x}_{\cdot R} = 60.8$	$\bar{x}_{\cdot W} = 62.2$	$\bar{x} = 61.5$

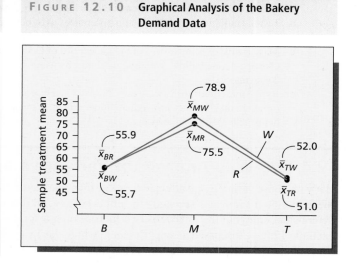

FIGURE 12.10 Graphical Analysis of the Bakery Demand Data

Figure 12.10 presents a graphical analysis of the bakery demand data. In this figure we plot, for each display width (R and W), the change in the sample treatment mean demand associated with changing the display height from bottom (B) to middle (M) to top (T). Note that, for either a regular display width (R) or a wide display (W), the middle display height (M) gives the highest mean monthly demand. Also, note that, for either a bottom, middle, or top display height, there is little difference between the effects of a regular display width and a wide display on mean monthly demand. This sort of graphical analysis is useful for determining whether a condition called **interaction** exists. In general, for two factors that might affect a response variable, we say that **interaction exists if the relationship between the mean response and one factor depends on the other factor.** This is clearly true in the leftmost figure below:

 LO12-5 Describe what happens when two factors interact.

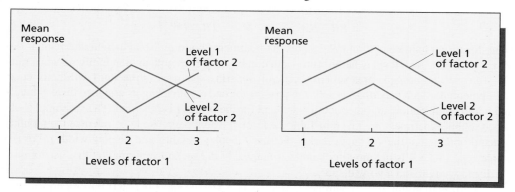

Specifically, this figure shows that at levels 1 and 3 of factor 1, level 1 of factor 2 gives the highest mean response, while at level 2 of factor 1, level 2 of factor 2 gives the highest mean response. On the other hand, the **parallel** line plots in the rightmost figure indicate a lack of interaction between factors 1 and 2. Because the sample mean plots in Figure 12.10 look nearly parallel, we might intuitively conclude that there is little or no interaction between display height and display width.

Suppose we wish to study the effects of two factors on a response variable. We assume that the first factor, which we refer to as **factor 1,** has *a* **levels** (levels $1, 2, \ldots, a$). Further, we assume that the second factor, which we will refer to as **factor 2,** has *b* **levels** (levels $1, 2, \ldots, b$). Here a **treatment** is considered to be a **combination of a level of factor 1 and a level of factor 2.** It follows that there are a total of ab treatments, and we assume that we will employ a *completely randomized experimental design* in which we will assign m randomly selected experimental units to each treatment. This procedure results in our observing m values of the response variable for each of the ab treatments, and in this case we say that we are performing a **two-factor factorial experiment.**

In addition to graphical analysis, **two-way analysis of variance (two-way ANOVA)** is a useful tool for analyzing the data from a two-factor factorial experiment. To explain the ANOVA approach for analyzing such an experiment, we define

$x_{ij,k}$ = the kth value of the response variable observed when using level i of factor 1 and level j of factor 2

$\bar{x}_{ij}$ = the mean of the m values observed when using the ith level of factor 1 and the jth level of factor 2

$\bar{x}_{i\bullet}$ = the mean of the bm values observed when using the ith level of factor 1

$\bar{x}_{\bullet j}$ = the mean of the am values observed when using the jth level of factor 2

$\bar{x}$ = the mean of the abm values that we have observed in the experiment

The ANOVA procedure for a two-factor factorial experiment partitions the **total sum of squares (SSTO)** into four components: the **factor 1 sum of squares–SS(1)**, the **factor 2 sum of squares–SS(2)**, the **interaction sum of squares–SS(int)**, and the **error sum of squares–SSE.** The formula for this partitioning is as follows:

$$SSTO = SS(1) + SS(2) + SS(\text{int}) + SSE$$

We define each of these sums of squares and show how they are calculated for the bakery demand data as follows (note that $a = 3$, $b = 2$, and $m = 3$):

Step 1: Calculate $SSTO$, which measures the total amount of variability:

$$SSTO = \sum_{i=1}^{a} \sum_{j=1}^{b} \sum_{k=1}^{m} (x_{ij,k} - \bar{x})^2$$

$$= (58.2 - 61.5)^2 + (53.7 - 61.5)^2 + \cdots + (49.9 - 61.5)^2 = 2{,}366.28$$

Step 2: Calculate $SS(1)$, which measures the amount of variability due to the different levels of factor 1:

$$SS(1) = bm \sum_{i=1}^{a} (\bar{x}_{i\bullet} - \bar{x})^2$$

$$= 2 \cdot 3[(\bar{x}_{B\bullet} - \bar{x})^2 + (\bar{x}_{M\bullet} - \bar{x})^2 + (\bar{x}_{T\bullet} - \bar{x})^2]$$

$$= 6[(55.8 - 61.5)^2 + (77.2 - 61.5)^2 + (51.5 - 61.5)^2] = 2{,}273.88$$

Step 3: Calculate $SS(2)$, which measures the amount of variability due to the different levels of factor 2:

$$SS(2) = am \sum_{j=1}^{b} (\bar{x}_{\bullet j} - \bar{x})^2$$

$$= 3 \cdot 3[(\bar{x}_{\bullet R} - \bar{x})^2 + (\bar{x}_{\bullet W} - \bar{x})^2]$$

$$= 9[(60.8 - 61.5)^2 + (62.2 - 61.5)^2] = 8.82$$

Step 4: Calculate $SS(\text{int})$, which measures the amount of variability due to the interaction between factors 1 and 2:

$$SS(\text{int}) = m \sum_{i=1}^{a} \sum_{j=1}^{b} (\bar{x}_{ij} - \bar{x}_{i\bullet} - \bar{x}_{\bullet j} + \bar{x})^2$$

$$= 3[(\bar{x}_{BR} - \bar{x}_{B\bullet} - \bar{x}_{\bullet R} + \bar{x})^2 + (\bar{x}_{BW} - \bar{x}_{B\bullet} - \bar{x}_{\bullet W} + \bar{x})^2$$

$$+ (\bar{x}_{MR} - \bar{x}_{M\bullet} - \bar{x}_{\bullet R} + \bar{x})^2 + (\bar{x}_{MW} - \bar{x}_{M\bullet} - \bar{x}_{\bullet W} + \bar{x})^2$$

$$+ (\bar{x}_{TR} - \bar{x}_{T\bullet} - \bar{x}_{\bullet R} + \bar{x})^2 + (\bar{x}_{TW} - \bar{x}_{T\bullet} - \bar{x}_{\bullet W} + \bar{x})^2]$$

$$= 3[(55.9 - 55.8 - 60.8 + 61.5)^2 + (55.7 - 55.8 - 62.2 + 61.5)^2$$

$$+ (75.5 - 77.2 - 60.8 + 61.5)^2 + (78.9 - 77.2 - 62.2 + 61.5)^2$$

$$+ (51.0 - 51.5 - 60.8 + 61.5)^2 + (52.0 - 51.5 - 62.2 + 61.5)^2] = 10.08$$

TABLE 12.12   Two-Way ANOVA Table for the Bakery Demand Data

Source of Variation	Degrees of Freedom	Sum of Squares	Mean Square	F
Factor 1	$a - 1 = 2$	$SS(1) = 2{,}273.88$	$MS(1) = \dfrac{SS(1)}{a-1} = 1136.94$	$F(1) = \dfrac{MS(1)}{MSE} = 185.6229$
Factor 2	$b - 1 = 1$	$SS(2) = 8.82$	$MS(2) = \dfrac{SS(2)}{b-1} = 8.82$	$F(2) = \dfrac{MS(2)}{MSE} = 1.44$
Interaction	$(a-1)(b-1) = 2$	$SS(\text{int}) = 10.08$	$MS(\text{int}) = \dfrac{SS(\text{int})}{(a-1)(b-1)} = 5.04$	$F(\text{int}) = \dfrac{MS(\text{int})}{MSE} = .8229$
Error	$ab(m-1) = 12$	$SSE = 73.50$	$MSE = \dfrac{SSE}{ab(m-1)} = 6.125$	
Total	$abm - 1 = 17$	$SSTO = 2{,}366.28$		

Step 5: Calculate SSE, which measures the amount of variability due to the error:

$$SSE = SSTO - SS(1) - SS(2) - SS(\text{int})$$
$$= 2{,}366.28 - 2{,}273.88 - 8.82 - 10.08 = 73.50$$

These sums of squares are shown in Table 12.12, which is called a **two-way analysis of variance (ANOVA) table.** This table also gives the degrees of freedom, mean squares, and F statistics used to test the hypotheses of interest in a two-factor factorial experiment, as well as the values of these quantities for the shelf display data.

We first test the null hypothesis H_0 that **no interaction exists between factors 1 and 2** versus the alternative hypothesis H_a that **interaction does exist.** We can reject H_0 in favor of H_a at level of significance α if $F(\text{int})$ is greater than the F_α point based on $(a-1)(b-1)$ numerator and $ab(m-1)$ denominator degrees of freedom. In the supermarket case, $F_{.05}$ based on $(a-1)(b-1) = 2$ numerator and $ab(m-1) = 12$ denominator degrees of freedom is 3.89 (see Table A.7, page 796). Because $F(\text{int}) = .8229$ (see Table 12.12) is less than $F_{.05} = 3.89$, we cannot reject H_0 at the .05 level of significance. We conclude that little or no interaction exists between shelf display height and shelf display width. That is, we conclude that the relationship between mean demand for the bakery product and shelf display height depends little (or not at all) on the shelf display width. Further, we conclude that the relationship between mean demand and shelf display width depends little (or not at all) on the shelf display height. Therefore, we can test the significance of each factor separately.

To test the significance of factor 1, we test the null hypothesis H_0 that **no differences exist between the effects of the different levels of factor 1** on the mean response versus the alternative hypothesis H_a that **at least two levels of factor 1 have different effects.** We can reject H_0 in favor of H_a at level of significance α if $F(1)$ is greater than the F_α point based on $a - 1$ numerator and $ab(m-1)$ denominator degrees of freedom. In the supermarket case, $F_{.05}$ based on $a - 1 = 2$ numerator and $ab(m-1) = 12$ denominator degrees of freedom is 3.89. Because $F(1) = 185.6229$ (see Table 12.12) is greater than $F_{.05} = 3.89$, we can reject H_0 at the .05 level of significance. Therefore, we have strong evidence that at least two of the bottom, middle, and top display heights have different effects on mean monthly demand.

To test the significance of factor 2, we test the null hypothesis H_0 that **no differences exist between the effects of the different levels of factor 2** on the mean response versus the alternative hypothesis H_a that **at least two levels of factor 2 have different effects.** We can reject H_0 in favor of H_a at level of significance α if $F(2)$ is greater than the F_α point based on $b - 1$ numerator and $ab(m-1)$ denominator degrees of freedom. In the supermarket case, $F_{.05}$ based on $b - 1 = 1$ numerator and $ab(m-1) = 12$ denominator degrees of freedom is 4.75. Because $F(2) = 1.44$ (see Table 12.12) is less than $F_{.05} = 4.75$, we cannot reject H_0 at the .05 level of significance. Therefore, we do not have strong evidence that the regular display width and the wide display have different effects on mean monthly demand.

FIGURE 12.11   MINITAB and Excel Outputs of a Two-Way ANOVA of the Bakery Demand Data

(a) The MINITAB Output

```
Rows : Height    Columns : Width
 Cell Contents : Demand   : Mean
```

	Regular	Wide	All	Height	Mean	Width	Mean
Bottom	55.90	55.70	55.80	Bottom	55.8 [16]	Regular	60.8 [19]
Middle	75.50	78.90	77.20	Middle	77.2 [17]	Wide	62.2 [20]
Top	51.00	52.00	51.50	Top	51.5 [18]		
All	60.80	62.20	61.50				

Two-way ANOVA: Demand versus Height, Width

Source	DF	SS	MS	F	P
Height	2	2273.88 [1]	1136.94 [6]	185.62 [10]	0.000 [11]
Width	1	8.82 [2]	8.82 [7]	1.44 [12]	0.253 [13]
Interaction	2	10.08 [3]	5.04 [8]	0.82 [14]	0.462 [15]
Error	12	73.50 [4]	6.12 [9]		
Total	17	2366.28 [5]			

(b) The Excel Output

ANOVA: Two-Factor With Replication

SUMMARY	Regular	Wide	Total
Bottom			
Count	3	3	6
Sum	167.7	167.1	334.8
Average	55.9	55.7	55.8 [16]
Variance	5.07	10.24	6.136
Middle			
Count	3	3	6
Sum	226.5	236.7	463.2
Average	75.5	78.9	77.2 [17]
Variance	6.51	8.89	9.628
Top			
Count	3	3	6
Sum	153.0	156.0	309.0
Average	51.0	52.0	51.5 [18]
Variance	1.8	4.2	2.7
Total			
Count	9	9	
Sum	547.2	559.8	
Average	60.8 [19]	62.2 [20]	
Variance	129.405	165.277	

ANOVA

Source of Variation	SS	df	MS	F	P-value	F crit
Height	2273.88 [1]	2	1136.94 [6]	185.6229 [10]	0.0000 [11]	3.8853
Width	8.82 [2]	1	8.82 [7]	1.4400 [12]	0.2533 [13]	4.7472
Interaction	10.08 [3]	2	5.04 [8]	0.8229 [14]	0.4625 [15]	3.8853
Within	73.5 [4]	12	6.125 [9]			
Total	2366.28 [5]	17				

[1] SS(1) [2] SS(2) [3] SS(int) [4] SSE [5] SSTO [6] MS(1) [7] MS(2) [8] MS(int) [9] MSE [10] $F(1)$ [11] p-value for $F(1)$
[12] $F(2)$ [13] p-value for $F(2)$ [14] F(int) [15] p-value for F(int) [16] $\bar{x}_{B\cdot}$ [17] $\bar{x}_{M\cdot}$ [18] $\bar{x}_{T\cdot}$ [19] $\bar{x}_{\cdot R}$ [20] $\bar{x}_{\cdot W}$

Noting that Figure 12.11 gives MINITAB and Excel outputs of a two-way ANOVA for the bakery demand data, we next discuss how to make pairwise comparisons.

Point Estimates and Confidence Intervals in Two-Way ANOVA

1 Consider the **difference between the effects of levels i and i' of factor 1 on the mean value of the response variable.**

a A **point estimate** of this difference is $\bar{x}_{i\cdot} - \bar{x}_{i'\cdot}$.

b A **Tukey simultaneous $100(1 - \alpha)$ percent confidence interval** for this difference (in the set of all possible paired differences between the effects of the different levels of factor 1) is

$$\left[(\bar{x}_{i\cdot} - \bar{x}_{i'\cdot}) \pm q_\alpha \sqrt{MSE\left(\frac{1}{bm}\right)} \right]$$

where q_α is obtained from Table A.10 (pages 799–800), which is a table of percentage points of the studentized range. Here q_α is listed corresponding to values of a and $ab(m - 1)$.

2 Consider the **difference between the effects of levels j and j' of factor 2 on the mean value of the response variable.**

a A **point estimate** of this difference is $\bar{x}_{\cdot j} - \bar{x}_{\cdot j'}$

b A **Tukey simultaneous $100(1 - \alpha)$ percent confidence interval** for this difference (in the set of all possible paired differences between the effects of the different levels of factor 2) is

$$\left[(\bar{x}_{\cdot j} - \bar{x}_{\cdot j'}) \pm q_\alpha \sqrt{MSE\left(\frac{1}{am}\right)} \right]$$

where q_α is obtained from Table A.10 and is listed corresponding to values of b and $ab(m - 1)$.

3 Let μ_{ij} denote the **mean value of the response variable obtained when using level i of factor 1 and level j of factor 2. A point estimate** of μ_{ij} is $\bar{x}_{ij}$, and an **individual $100(1 - \alpha)$ percent confidence interval** for μ_{ij} is

$$\left[\bar{x}_{ij} \pm t_{\alpha/2} \sqrt{\frac{MSE}{m}} \right]$$

where the $t_{\alpha/2}$ point is based on $ab(m - 1)$ degrees of freedom.

EXAMPLE 12.8 The Supermarket Case: Comparing Display Heights and Widths

We have previously concluded that at least two of the bottom, middle, and top display heights have different effects on mean monthly demand. Because $\bar{x}_{M\cdot} = 77.2$ is greater than $\bar{x}_{B\cdot} = 55.8$ and $\bar{x}_{T\cdot} = 51.5$, we will use Tukey simultaneous 95 percent confidence intervals to compare the effect of a middle display height with the effects of the bottom and top display heights. To compute these intervals, we first note that $q_{.05} = 3.77$ is the entry in Table A.10 (page 799) corresponding to $a = 3$ and $ab(m - 1) = 12$. Also note that the *MSE* found in the two-way ANOVA table is 6.125 (see Table 12.12 on page 448). It follows that a Tukey simultaneous 95 percent confidence interval for the difference between the effects of a middle and bottom display height on mean monthly demand is

$$\left[(\bar{x}_{M\cdot} - \bar{x}_{B\cdot}) \pm q_{.05} \sqrt{MSE\left(\frac{1}{bm}\right)} \right] = \left[(77.2 - 55.8) \pm 3.77 \sqrt{6.125\left(\frac{1}{2(3)}\right)} \right]$$

$$= [21.4 \pm 3.8091]$$

$$= [17.5909, 25.2091]$$

This interval says we are 95 percent confident that changing from a bottom display height to a middle display height will increase the mean demand for the bakery product by between 17.5909 and 25.2091 cases per month. Similarly, a Tukey simultaneous 95 percent confidence interval for the difference between the effects of a middle and top display height on mean monthly demand is

$$[(\bar{x}_{M\cdot} - \bar{x}_{T\cdot}) \pm 3.8091] = [(77.2 - 51.5) \pm 3.8091]$$

$$= [21.8909, 29.5091]$$

This interval says we are 95 percent confident that changing from a top display height to a middle display height will increase mean demand for the bakery product by between 21.8909 and 29.5091 cases per month. Together, these intervals make us 95 percent confident that a middle shelf display height is, on average, at least 17.5909 cases sold per month better than a bottom shelf display height and at least 21.8909 cases sold per month better than a top shelf display height.

Next, recall that previously conducted *F*-tests suggest that there is little or no interaction between display height and display width and that there is little difference between using a regular display width and a wide display. However, noting that $\bar{x}_{MW} = 78.9$ is slightly larger than $\bar{x}_{MR} = 75.5$, we now find an individual 95 percent confidence interval for μ_{MW}, the mean demand obtained when using a middle display height and a wide display:

$$\left[\bar{x}_{MW} \pm t_{.025}\sqrt{\frac{MSE}{m}} \right] = \left[78.9 \pm 2.179\sqrt{\frac{6.125}{3}} \right]$$

$$= [75.7865, 82.0135]$$

Here $t_{.025} = 2.179$ is based on $ab(m - 1) = 12$ degrees of freedom. This interval says that, when we use a middle display height and a wide display, we can be 95 percent confident that mean demand for the bakery product will be between 75.7865 and 82.0135 cases per month.

If we conclude that (substantial) interaction exists between factors 1 and 2, the effects of changing the level of one factor will depend on the level of the other factor. In this case, we cannot analyze the levels of the two factors separately. One simple alternative procedure is to use one-way ANOVA (see Section 12.2) to compare all of the treatment means (the μ_{ij}'s) with the possible purpose of finding the best combination of levels of factors 1 and 2.

Exercises for Section 12.4

CONCEPTS

connect

12.17 What is a treatment in the context of a two-factor factorial experiment?

12.18 Explain what we mean when we say that interaction exists between two factors.

METHODS AND APPLICATIONS

12.19 A study compared three display panels used by air traffic controllers. Each display panel was tested for four different simulated emergency conditions. Twenty-four highly trained air traffic controllers were used in the study. Two controllers were randomly assigned to each display panel–emergency condition combination. The time (in seconds) required to stabilize the emergency condition was recorded. Figure 12.12 gives the resulting data and the MINITAB output of a two-way ANOVA of the data.   **DS** Display2
   a Interpret the interaction plot in Figure 12.12. Then test for interaction with $\alpha = .05$.
   b Test the significance of display panel effects with $\alpha = .05$.
   c Test the significance of emergency condition effects with $\alpha = .05$.
   d Make pairwise comparisons of display panels A, B, and C by using Tukey simultaneous 95 percent confidence intervals.
   e Make pairwise comparisons of emergency conditions 1, 2, 3, and 4 by using Tukey simultaneous 95 percent confidence intervals.
   f Which display panel minimizes the time required to stabilize an emergency condition? Does your answer depend on the emergency condition? Why?
   g Calculate a 95 percent (individual) confidence interval for the mean time required to stabilize emergency condition 4 using display panel B.

12.20 A telemarketing firm has studied the effects of two factors on the response to its television advertisements. The first factor is the time of day at which the ad is run, while the second is the position of the ad within the hour. The data in Figure 12.13, which were obtained by using a completely randomized experimental design, give the number of calls placed to an 800 number following a sample broadcast of the advertisement. If we use Excel to analyze these data, we obtain the output in Figure 12.13.   **DS** TelMktResp
   a Perform graphical analysis to check for interaction between time of day and position of advertisement. Explain your conclusion. Then test for interaction with $\alpha = .05$.
   b Test the significance of time of day effects with $\alpha = .05$.
   c Test the significance of position of advertisement effects with $\alpha = .05$.
   d Make pairwise comparisons of the morning, afternoon, and evening times by using Tukey simultaneous 95 percent confidence intervals.
   e Make pairwise comparisons of the four ad positions by using Tukey simultaneous 95 percent confidence intervals.
   f Which time of day and advertisement position maximizes consumer response? Compute a 95 percent (individual) confidence interval for the mean number of calls placed for this time of day/ad position combination.

FIGURE 12.12   The Display Panel Data and the MINITAB Output of a Two-Way ANOVA ⏺ Display2

Emergency Condition

Display Panel	1	2	3	4
A	17	25	31	14
	14	24	34	13
B	15	22	28	9
	12	19	31	10
C	21	29	32	15
	24	28	37	19

Two-way ANOVA: Time versus Panel, Condition

Source	DF	SS	MS	F	P
Panel	2	218.58	109.292	26.49	0.000
Condition	3	1247.46	415.819	100.80	0.000
Interaction	6	16.42	2.736	0.66	0.681
Error	12	49.50	4.125		
Total	23	1531.96			

Tabulated statistics: Panel, Condition

```
Rows:    Panel     Columns:   Condition

           1      2       3        4       All
A        15.50  24.50   32.50    13.50    21.50
B        13.50  20.50   29.50     9.50    18.25
C        22.50  28.50   34.50    17.00    25.63
All      17.17  24.50   32.17    13.33    21.79
Cell Contents:     Time   :    Mean
```

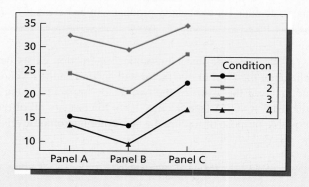

FIGURE 12.13   The Telemarketing Data and the Excel Output of a Two-Way ANOVA ⏺ TelMktResp

Position of Advertisement

Time of Day	On the Hour	On the Half-Hour	Early in Program	Late in Program
10:00 morning	42	36	62	51
	37	41	68	47
	41	38	64	48
4:00 afternoon	62	57	88	67
	60	60	85	60
	58	55	81	66
9:00 evening	100	97	127	105
	96	96	120	101
	103	101	126	107

ANOVA: Two-Factor With Replication

Summary	Hour	Half-Hour	Early	Late	Total
Morning					
Count	3	3	3	3	12
Sum	120	115	194	146	575
Average	40	38.3	64.7	48.7	47.9
Variance	7	6.3	9.3	4.3	123.7
Afternoon					
Count	3	3	3	3	12
Sum	180	172	254	193	799
Average	60	57.3	84.7	64.3	66.6
Variance	4	6.3	12.3	14.3	132.4
Evening					
Count	3	3	3	3	12
Sum	299	294	373	313	1279
Average	99.67	98	124.3	104.3	106.6
Variance	12.33	7	14.3	9.3	128.3
Total					
Count	9	9	9	9	
Sum	599	581	821	652	
Average	66.56	64.56	91.22	72.44	
Variance	697.53	701.78	700.69	625.03	

ANOVA

Source of Variation	SS	df	MS	F	P-value	F crit
Sample	21560.89	2	10780.444	1209.02	8.12E-25	3.403
Columns	3989.42	3	1329.B06	149.14	1.19E-15	3.009
Interaction	25.33	6	4.222	0.47	0.8212	2.508
Within	214	24	8.917			
Total	25789.64	35				

Chapter Summary

We began this chapter by introducing some basic concepts of **experimental design.** We saw that we carry out an experiment by setting the values of one or more **factors** before the values of the **response variable** are observed. The different values (or levels) of a factor are called **treatments,** and the purpose of most experiments is to compare and estimate the effects of the various treatments on the response variable. We saw that the different treatments are assigned to **experimental units,** and we discussed the **completely randomized experimental design.** This design assigns independent, random samples of experimental units to the treatments.

We began studying how to analyze experimental data by discussing **one-way analysis of variance (one-way ANOVA).** Here we study how one factor (having *p* levels) affects the response variable. In particular, we learned how to use this methodology to test for differences between the **treatment means** and to estimate the size of pairwise differences between the treatment means.

Sometimes, even if we randomly select the experimental units, differences between the experimental units conceal differences between the treatments. In such a case, we learned that we can employ a **randomized block design.** Each **block** (experimental unit or set of experimental units) is used exactly once to measure the effect of each and every treatment. Because we are comparing the treatments by using the same experimental units, any true differences between the treatments will not be concealed by differences between the experimental units.

The last technique we studied in this chapter was **two-way analysis of variance (two-way ANOVA).** Here we study the effects of two factors by carrying out a **two-factor factorial experiment.** If there is little or no interaction between the two factors, then we are able to study the significance of each of the two factors separately. On the other hand, if substantial interaction exists between the two factors, we study the nature of the differences between the treatment means.

Glossary of Terms

analysis of variance table: A table that summarizes the sums of squares, mean squares, *F* statistic(s), and *p*-value(s) for an analysis of variance. (pages 434, 441, and 448)

completely randomized experimental design: An experimental design in which independent, random samples of experimental units are assigned to the treatments. (page 428)

experimental units: The entities (objects, people, and so on) to which the treatments are assigned. (page 427)

factor: A variable that might influence the response variable; an independent variable. (page 427)

interaction: When the relationship between the mean response and one factor depends on the level of the other factor. (page 446)

one-way ANOVA: A method used to estimate and compare the effects of the different levels of a single factor on a response variable. (page 429)

randomized block design: An experimental design that compares *p* treatments by using *b* blocks (experimental units or sets of

experimental units). Each block is used exactly once to measure the effect of each and every treatment. (page 439)

replication: When a treatment is applied to more than one experimental unit. (page 427)

response variable: The variable of interest in an experiment; the dependent variable. (page 427)

treatment: A value (or level) of a factor (or combination of factors). (page 427)

treatment mean: The mean value of the response variable obtained by using a particular treatment. (page 429)

two-factor factorial experiment: An experiment in which we randomly assign *m* experimental units to each combination of levels of two factors. (page 446)

two-way ANOVA: A method used to study the effects of two factors on a response variable. (page 447)

Important Formulas and Tests

One-way ANOVA sums of squares: pages 431–432

One-way ANOVA *F*-test: page 432

One-way ANOVA table: page 434

Estimation in one-way ANOVA: page 435

Randomized block sums of squares: page 440

Randomized block ANOVA table: page 441

Estimation in a randomized block ANOVA: page 441

Two-way ANOVA sums of squares: pages 447–448

Two-way ANOVA table: page 448

Estimation in two-way ANOVA: page 450

Supplementary Exercises

12.21   An experiment is conducted to study the effects of two sales approaches—high-pressure (*H*) and low-pressure (*L*)—and to study the effects of two sales pitches (1 and 2) on the weekly sales of a product. The data in Table 12.13 on the next page are obtained by using a completely randomized

TABLE 12.13   Results of the Sales Approach Experiment DS SaleMeth2

	Sales Pitch	
Sales Pressure	1	2
H	32	32
	29	30
	30	28
L	28	25
	25	24
	23	23

FIGURE 12.14   Excel Output of a Two-Way ANOVA of the Sales Approach Data

ANOVA: Two-Factor With Replication

SUMMARY	Pitch 1	Pitch 2	Total
High Pressure			
Count	3	3	6
Sum	91	90	181
Average	30.3333	30	30.1667
Variance	2.3333	4	2.5667
Low Pressure			
Count	3	3	6
Sum	76	72	148
Average	25.3333	24	24.6667
Variance	6.3333	1	3.4667
Total			
Count	6	6	
Sum	167	162	
Average	27.8333	27	
Variance	10.9667	12.8	

ANOVA

Source of Variation	SS	df	MS	F	P-value	F crit
Pressure	90.75	1	90.75	26.5610	0.0009	5.3177
Pitch	2.0833	1	2.0833	0.6098	0.4574	5.3177
Interaction	0.75	1	0.75	0.2195	0.6519	5.3177
Within	27.3333	8	3.4167			
Total	120.917	11				

TABLE 12.14
Reduction of Cholesterol Levels
DS CholRed

	Drug	
X	Y	Z
22	40	15
31	35	9
19	47	14
27	41	11
25	39	21
18	33	5

FIGURE 12.15   An Interaction Plot for the House Profitability Data

TABLE 12.15   Results of the House Profitability Study DS HouseProf

Foreman	House Design					
	A		B		C	
1	10.2	10.65	12.2	11.95	19.4	18.80
	11.1		11.7		18.2	
2	9.7	10.25	11.6	11.80	13.6	13.15
	10.8		12.0		12.7	

design, and Figure 12.14 gives the Excel output of a two-way ANOVA of the sales experiment data. DS SaleMeth2

a Perform graphical analysis to check for interaction between sales pressure and sales pitch.

b Test for interaction by setting $\alpha = .05$.

c Test for differences in the effects of the levels of sales pressure by setting $\alpha = .05$.

d Test for differences in the effects of the levels of sales pitch by setting $\alpha = .05$.

12.22 A drug company wishes to compare the effects of three different drugs (X, Y, and Z) that are being developed to reduce cholesterol levels. Each drug is administered to six patients at the recommended dosage for six months. At the end of this period the reduction in cholesterol level is recorded for each patient. The results are given in Table 12.14. Using these data we obtain $SSTO = 2547.8$, $SSE = 395.7$, $\bar{x}_X = 23.67$, $\bar{x}_Y = 39.17$, and $\bar{x}_Z = 12.50$. Completely analyze these data using one-way ANOVA. DS CholRed

12.23 A small builder of speculative homes builds three basic house designs and employs two foremen. The builder has used each foreman to build two houses of each design and has obtained the profits given in Table 12.15 (the profits are given in thousands of dollars, and the sample means are enclosed in blue rectangles). If we use two-way ANOVA, we find that the p-value related to $F(\text{int})$ is .001. Is this consistent with what you see in Figure 12.15? Explain your answer. Using the fact that $MSE = .39$, find an individual 95 percent confidence interval for the true mean profit when foreman 1 builds house design 3. DS HouseProf

Appendix 12.1 ■ Experimental Design and Analysis of Variance Using Excel

One-way ANOVA in Figure 12.2(b) on page 434 (data file: GasMile2.xlsx):

- Enter the gasoline mileage data from Table 12.1 (page 428) as follows: type the label "Type A" in cell A1 with its five mileage values in cells A2 to A6; type the label "Type B" in cell B1 with its five mileage values in cells B2 to B6; type the label "Type C" in cell C1 with its five mileage values in cells C2 to C6.

- Select **Data : Data Analysis : Anova : Single Factor** and click OK in the Data Analysis dialog box.

- In the "Anova: Single Factor" dialog box, enter A1:C6 into the "Input Range" window.

- Select the "Grouped by: Columns" option.

- Place a checkmark in the "Labels in first row" checkbox.

- Enter 0.05 into the Alpha box.

- Under output options, select "New Worksheet Ply" to have the output placed in a new worksheet and enter the name "Output" for the new worksheet.

- Click OK in the "Anova: Single Factor" dialog box.

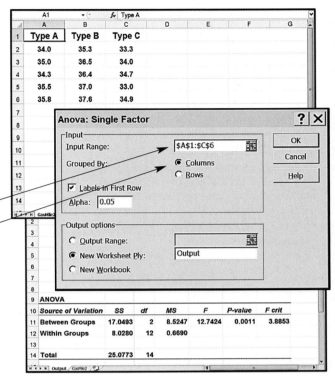

Randomized block ANOVA in Figure 12.8 on page 443 (data file: SaleMeth.xlsx):

- Enter the sales methods data from Figure 12.8 (page 443) as shown in the screen.

- Select **Data : Data Analysis : Anova: Two-Factor Without Replication** and click OK in the Data Analysis dialog box.

- In the "Anova: Two Factor Without Replication" dialog box, enter A1:D5 into the "Input Range" window.

- Place a checkmark in the "Labels" checkbox.

- Enter 0.05 in the Alpha box.

- Under output options, select "New Worksheet Ply" to have the output placed in a new worksheet and enter the name "Output" for the new worksheet.

- Click OK in the "Anova: Two-Factor Without Replication" dialog box.

Two-way ANOVA in Figure 12.14 on page 454 (data file: SaleMeth2.xlsx):

- Enter the sales approach experiment data from Table 12.13 (page 454) as shown in the screen.

- Select **Data : Data Analysis : Anova : Two-Factor With Replication** and click OK in the Data Analysis dialog box.

- In the "Anova: Two-Factor With Replication" dialog box, enter A1:C7 into the "Input Range" window.

- Enter the value 3 into the "Rows per Sample" box (this indicates the number of replications).

- Enter 0.05 in the Alpha box.

- Under output options, select "New Worksheet Ply" to have the output placed in a new worksheet and enter the name "Output" for the new worksheet.

- Click OK in the "Anova: Two-Factor With Replication" dialog box.

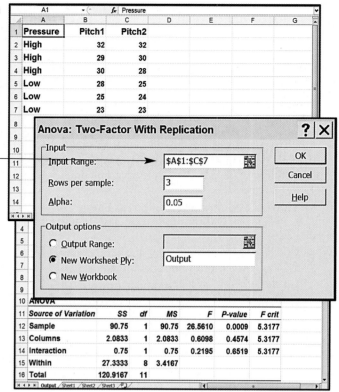

Appendix 12.2 ■ Experimental Design and Analysis of Variance Using MegaStat

One-way ANOVA similar to Figure 12.2(b) on page 434 (data file: GasMile2.xlsx):

- Enter the gas mileage data in Table 12.1 (page 428) into columns A, B, and C—Type A mileages in column A (with label "Type A"), Type B mileages in column B (with label "Type B"), and Type C mileages in column C (with label "Type C"). Note that the input columns for the different groups must be side by side. However, the number of observations in each group can be different.

- Select **Add-Ins : MegaStat : Analysis of Variance : One-Factor ANOVA.**

- In the One-Factor ANOVA dialog box, use the AutoExpand feature to enter the range A1:C6 into the Input Range window.

- If desired, request "Post-hoc Analysis" to obtain Tukey simultaneous comparisons and pairwise t tests. Select from the options: "Never," "Always," or "When $p < .05$." The option "When $p < .05$" gives post-hoc analysis when the p-value for the F statistic is less than .05.

- Check the Plot Data checkbox to obtain a plot comparing the groups.

- Click OK in the One-Factor ANOVA dialog box.

Randomized block ANOVA similar to Figure 12.7(b) on page 442 (data file: CardBox.xlsx):

- Enter the cardboard box data in Table 12.7 (page 439) in the arrangement shown in the screen. Here each column corresponds to a **treatment** (in this case, a production method) and each row corresponds to a **block** (in this case, a machine operator). Identify the production methods using the labels Method 1, Method 2, Method 3, and Method 4 in cells B1, C1, D1, and E1. Identify the blocks using the labels Operator 1, Operator 2, and Operator 3 in cells A2, A3, and A4.

- Select **Add-Ins : MegaStat : Analysis of Variance : Randomized Blocks ANOVA.**

- In the Randomized Blocks ANOVA dialog box, click in the Input Range window and enter the range A1:E4.

- If desired, request "Post-hoc Analysis" to obtain Tukey simultaneous comparisons and pairwise *t*-tests. Select from the options: "Never," "Always," or "When $p < .05$." The option "When $p < .05$" gives post-hoc analysis when the *p*-value related to the *F* statistic for the treatments is less than .05.

- Check the Plot Data checkbox to obtain a plot comparing the treatments.

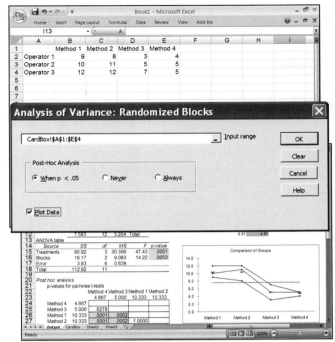

- Click OK in the Randomized Blocks ANOVA dialog box.

Two-way ANOVA similar to Figure 12.11(b) on page 449 (data file: BakeSale2.xlsx):

- Enter the bakery demand data in Table 12.11 (page 446) in the arrangement shown in the screen. Here the row labels Bottom, Middle, and Top are the levels of factor 1 (in this case, shelf display height) and the column labels Regular and Wide are the levels of factor 2 (in this case, shelf display width). The arrangement of the data is as laid out in Table 12.11.

- Select **Add-Ins : MegaStat : Analysis of Variance: Two-Factor ANOVA.**

- In the Two-Factor ANOVA dialog box, enter the range A1:C10 into the Input Range window.

- Type 3 into the "Replications per Cell" window.

- Check the "Interaction Plot by Factor 1" and "Interaction Plot by Factor 2" checkboxes to obtain interaction plots.

- If desired, request "Post-hoc Analysis" to obtain Tukey simultaneous comparisons and pairwise *t*-tests. Select from the options: "Never," "Always," and "When $p < .05$." The option "When $p < .05$" gives post-hoc analysis when the *p*-value related to the *F* statistic for a factor is less than .05. Here we have selected "Always."

- Click OK in the Two-Factor ANOVA dialog box.

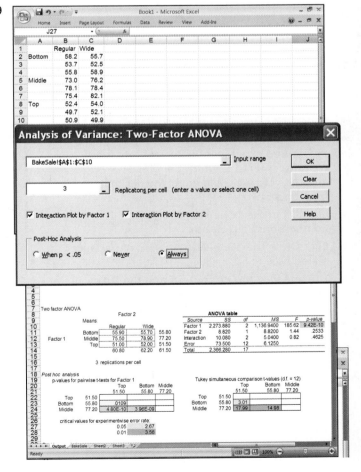

Appendix 12.3 ■ Experimental Design and Analysis of Variance Using MINITAB

One-way ANOVA in Figure 12.2(a) on page 434 (data file: GasMile2.MTW):

- In the Data window, enter the data from Table 12.1 (page 428) into three columns with variable names Type A, Type B, and Type C.

- Select **Stat : ANOVA : One-way (Unstacked)**.

- In the "One-Way Analysis of Variance" dialog box, enter 'Type A' 'Type B' 'Type C' into the "Responses (in separate columns)" window. (The single quotes are necessary because of the blank spaces in the variable names. The quotes will be added automatically if the names are selected from the variable list or if they are selected by double clicking.)

- Click OK in the "One-Way Analysis of Variance" dialog box.

To produce mileage by gasoline type boxplots similar to those shown in Table 12.1 (page 428):

- Click the Graphs . . . button in the "One-Way Analysis of Variance" dialog box.

- Check the "Boxplots of data" checkbox and click OK in the "One-Way Analysis of Variance— Graphs" dialog box.

- Click OK in the "One-Way Analysis of Variance" dialog box.

To produce Tukey pairwise comparisons:

- Click on the Comparisons . . . button in the "One-Way Analysis of Variance" dialog box.

- Check the "Tukey's family error rate" checkbox.

- In the "Tukey's family error rate" box, enter the desired experimentwise error rate (here we have entered 5, which denotes 5%— alternatively, we could enter the decimal fraction .05).

- Click OK in the "One-Way Multiple Comparisons" dialog box.

- Click OK in the "One-Way Analysis of Variance" dialog box.

- The one-way ANOVA output and the Tukey multiple comparisons will be given in the Session window, and the box plots will appear in a graphics window.

Randomized Block ANOVA in Figure 12.7(a) on page 442 (data File: CardBox.MTW):

- In the data window, enter the observed number of defective boxes from Table 12.7 (page 439) into column C1 with variable name "Rejects"; enter the corresponding production method (1,2,3,or 4) into column C2 with variable name "Method"; and enter the corresponding machine operator (1,2,or 3) into column C3 with variable name "Operator."

- Select **Stat : ANOVA : Two-way.**

- In the "Two-Way Analysis of Variance" dialog box, select Rejects into the Response window.

- Select Method into the Row Factor window and check the "Display Means" checkbox.

- Select Operator into the Column Factor window and check the "Display Means" checkbox.

- Check the "Fit additive model" checkbox.

- Click OK in the "Two-way Analysis of Variance" dialog box to display the randomized block ANOVA in the Session window.

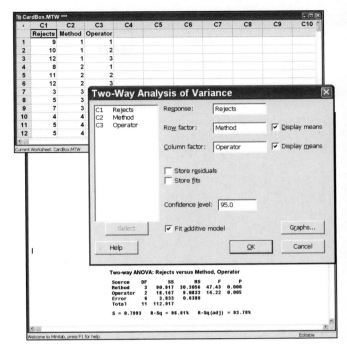

Two-way ANOVA in Figure 12.11(a) on page 449 (data file: BakeSale2.MTW):

- In the data window, enter the observed demands from Table 12.11 (page 446) into column C1 with variable name "Demand"; enter the corresponding shelf display heights (Bottom, Middle, or Top) into column C2 with variable name "Height"; and enter the corresponding shelf display widths (Regular or Wide) into column C3 with variable name "Width."

- Select **Stat : ANOVA : Two-Way.**

- In the "Two-Way Analysis of Variance" dialog box, select Demand into the Response window.

- Select Height into the "Row Factor" window.

- Select Width into the "Column Factor" window.

- To produce tables of means by Height and Width, check the "Display means" checkboxes next to the "Row factor" and "Column factor" windows. This will also produce individual confidence intervals for each level of the row factor and each level of the column factor—these intervals are not shown in Figure 12.11.

- Enter the desired level of confidence for the individual confidence intervals in the "Confidence level" box.

- Click OK in the "Two-Way Analysis of Variance" dialog box.

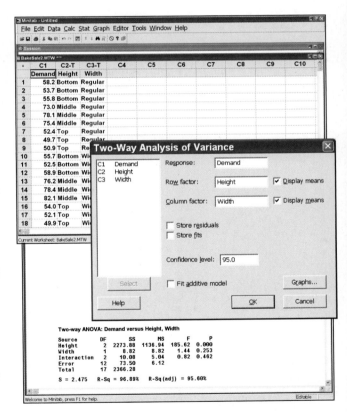

To produce an interaction plot similar to the one in Figure 12.10 on page 446:

- Select **Stat : ANOVA : Interactions plot.**

- In the Interactions Plot dialog box, select Demand into the Responses window.

- Select Width and Height into the Factors window.

- Click OK in the Interactions Plot dialog box to obtain the plot in a graphics window.

CHAPTER 13

Chi-Square Tests

Learning Objectives

After mastering the material in this chapter, you will be able to:

LO13-1 Test hypotheses about multinomial probabilities by using a chi-square goodness-of-fit test.

LO13-2 Perform a goodness-of-fit test for normality.

LO13-3 Decide whether two qualitative variables are independent by using a chi-square test for independence.

Chapter Outline

n this chapter we present two useful hypothesis tests based on the **chi-square distribution.** (We have discussed the chi-square distribution in Section 11.1). First, we consider the **chi-square test of goodness of fit.** This test evaluates whether data falling into several categories do so with a hypothesized set of probabilities. Second, we discuss the **chi-square test for independence.**

Here data are classified on two dimensions and are summarized in a **contingency table.** The test for independence then evaluates whether the cross-classified variables are independent of each other. If we conclude that the variables are not independent, then we have established that the variables in question are related, and we must then investigate the nature of the relationship.

13.1 Chi-Square Goodness-of-Fit Tests ● ● ●

Multinomial probabilities   Sometimes we collect count data in order to study how the counts are distributed among several **categories** or **cells.** As an example, we might study consumer preferences for four different brands of a product. To do this, we select a random sample of consumers, and we ask each survey participant to indicate a brand preference. We then count the number of consumers who prefer each of the four brands. Here we have four categories (brands), and we study the distribution of the counts in each category in order to see which brands are preferred.

LO13-1 Test hypotheses about multinomial probabilities by using a chi-square goodness-of-fit test.

We often use categorical data to carry out a statistical inference. For instance, suppose that a major wholesaler in Cleveland, Ohio, carries four different brands of microwave ovens. Historically, consumer behavior in Cleveland has resulted in the market shares shown in Table 13.1. The wholesaler plans to begin doing business in a new territory—Milwaukee, Wisconsin. To study whether its policies for stocking the four brands of ovens in Cleveland can also be used in Milwaukee, the wholesaler compares consumer preferences for the four ovens in Milwaukee with the historical market shares observed in Cleveland. A random sample of 400 consumers in Milwaukee gives the preferences shown in Table 13.2.

To compare consumer preferences in Cleveland and Milwaukee, we must consider a **multinomial experiment.** This is similar to the binomial experiment. However, a binomial experiment concerns count data that can be classified into two categories, while a multinomial experiment is more general and concerns count data that are classified into two or more categories. Specifically, the assumptions for the multinomial experiment are as follows:

The Multinomial Experiment

1 We perform an experiment in which we carry out n identical trials and in which there are k possible outcomes on each trial.

2 The probabilities of the k outcomes are denoted $p_1, p_2, \ldots, p_k$ where $p_1 + p_2 + \cdots + p_k = 1$. These probabilities stay the same from trial to trial.

3 The trials in the experiment are independent.

4 The results of the experiment are observed frequencies (counts) of the number of trials that result in each of the k possible outcomes. The frequencies are denoted $f_1, f_2, \ldots, f_k$. That is, f_1 is the number of trials resulting in the first possible outcome, f_2 is the number of trials resulting in the second possible outcome, and so forth.

TABLE 13.1 **Market Shares for Four Microwave Oven Brands in Cleveland, Ohio** ⓒⓢ MicroWav

Brand	Market Share
1	20%
2	35%
3	30%
4	15%

TABLE 13.2 **Brand Preferences for Four Microwave Ovens in Milwaukee, Wisconsin** ⓒⓢ MicroWav

Brand	Observed Frequency (Number of Consumers Sampled Who Prefer the Brand)
1	102
2	121
3	120
4	57

Notice that the scenario that defines a multinomial experiment is similar to the one that defines a binomial experiment. In fact, a binomial experiment is simply a multinomial experiment where k equals 2 (there are two possible outcomes on each trial).

In general, the probabilities $p_1, p_2, \ldots, p_k$ are unknown, and we estimate their values. Or, we compare estimates of these probabilities with a set of specified values. We now look at such an example.

EXAMPLE 13.1 The Microwave Oven Case: Studying Consumer Preferences

Suppose the microwave oven wholesaler wishes to compare consumer preferences in Milwaukee with the historical market shares in Cleveland. If the consumer preferences in Milwaukee are substantially different, the wholesaler will consider changing its policies for stocking the ovens. Here we will define

p_1 = the proportion of Milwaukee consumers who prefer brand 1

p_2 = the proportion of Milwaukee consumers who prefer brand 2

p_3 = the proportion of Milwaukee consumers who prefer brand 3

p_4 = the proportion of Milwaukee consumers who prefer brand 4

Remembering that the historical market shares for brands 1, 2, 3, and 4 in Cleveland are 20 percent, 35 percent, 30 percent, and 15 percent, we test the null hypothesis

$$H_0: p_1 = .20, \quad p_2 = .35, \quad p_3 = .30, \quad \text{and} \quad p_4 = .15$$

which says that consumer preferences in Milwaukee are consistent with the historical market shares in Cleveland. We test H_0 versus

$$H_a: \text{the previously stated null hypothesis is not true}$$

To test H_0 we must compare the "observed frequencies" given in Table 13.2 with the "expected frequencies" for the brands calculated on the assumption that H_0 is true. For instance, if H_0 is true, we would expect $400(.20) = 80$ of the 400 Milwaukee consumers surveyed to prefer brand 1. Denoting this expected frequency for brand 1 as E_1, the expected frequencies for brands 2, 3, and 4 when H_0 is true are $E_2 = 400(.35) = 140$, $E_3 = 400(.30) = 120$, and $E_4 = 400(.15) = 60$. Recalling that Table 13.2 gives the observed frequency for each brand, we have $f_1 = 102$, $f_2 = 121$, $f_3 = 120$, and $f_4 = 57$. We now compare the observed and expected frequencies by computing a **chi-square statistic** as follows:

$$\chi^2 = \sum_{i=1}^{k=4} \frac{(f_i - E_i)^2}{E_i}$$

$$= \frac{(102 - 80)^2}{80} + \frac{(121 - 140)^2}{140} + \frac{(120 - 120)^2}{120} + \frac{(57 - 60)^2}{60}$$

$$= \frac{484}{80} + \frac{361}{140} + \frac{0}{120} + \frac{9}{60} = 8.7786$$

Clearly, the more the observed frequencies differ from the expected frequencies, the larger χ^2 will be and the more doubt will be cast on the null hypothesis. If the chi-square statistic is large enough (beyond a critical value), then we reject H_0.

To find an appropriate critical value, it can be shown that, when the null hypothesis is true, the sampling distribution of χ^2 is approximately a χ^2 distribution with $k - 1 = 4 - 1 = 3$ degrees of freedom. If we wish to test H_0 at the .05 level of significance, we reject H_0 if and only if

$$\chi^2 > \chi^2_{.05}$$

FIGURE 13.1   **Output of a MINITAB Session That Computes the Chi-Square Statistic and Its Related *p*-Value for the Microwave Oven Case**

```
Minitab - Chi Square Example.MPJ                                    _ □ ✕
File  Edit  Data  Calc  Stat  Graph  Editor  Tools  Window  Help

Session


Sum of ChiSq                         Data Display

Sum of ChiSq = 8.77857                  PValue
                                          0.0323845


Worksheet 1 ***
```

↓	C1	C2	C3	C4	C5	C6	C7	C8
	Frequency	MarketShr	Expected	ChiSq	PValue			
1	102	0.20	80	6.05000	0.0323845			
2	121	0.35	140	2.57857				
3	120	0.30	120	0.00000				
4	57	0.15	60	0.15000				
5								
6								

Because Table A.5 (page 794) tells us that the $\chi^2_{.05}$ point corresponding to $k - 1 = 3$ degrees of freedom equals 7.81473, we find that

$$\chi^2 = 8.7786 > \chi^2_{.05} = 7.81473$$

and we reject H_0 at the .05 level of significance. Alternatively, the *p*-value for this hypothesis test is the area under the curve of the chi-square distribution having 3 degrees of freedom to the right of $\chi^2 = 8.7786$. This *p*-value can be calculated to be .0323845. Because this *p*-value is less than .05, we can reject H_0 at the .05 level of significance. Although there is no single MINITAB dialog box that produces a chi-square goodness-of-fit test, Figure 13.1 shows the output of a MINITAB session that computes the chi-square statistic and its related *p*-value for the microwave oven case.

  We conclude that the preferences of all consumers in Milwaukee for the four brands of ovens are not consistent with the historical market shares in Cleveland. Based on this conclusion, the wholesaler should consider changing its stocking policies for microwave ovens when it enters the Milwaukee market. To study how to change its policies, the wholesaler might compute a 95 percent confidence interval for, say, the proportion of consumers in Milwaukee who prefer brand 2. Because $\hat{p}_2 = 121/400 = .3025$, this interval is (see Section 8.4, page 321)

$$\left[\hat{p}_2 \pm z_{.025} \sqrt{\frac{\hat{p}_2(1 - \hat{p}_2)}{n_2}} \right] = \left[.3025 \pm 1.96 \sqrt{\frac{.3025(1 - .3025)}{400}} \right]$$

$$= [.2575, .3475]$$

Because this entire interval is below .35, it suggests that (1) the market share for brand 2 ovens in Milwaukee will be smaller than the 35 percent market share that this brand commands in Cleveland, and (2) fewer brand 2 ovens (on a percentage basis) should be stocked in Milwaukee. Notice here that by restricting our attention to one particular brand (brand 2), we are essentially combining the other brands into a single group. It follows that we now have two possible outcomes—"brand 2" and "all other brands." Therefore, we have a binomial experiment, and we can employ the methods of Section 8.4, which are based on the binomial distribution.

In the following box we give a general chi-square goodness-of-fit test for multinomial probabilities:

A Goodness-of-Fit Test for Multinomial Probabilities

Consider a **multinomial experiment** in which each of n randomly selected items is classified into one of k groups. We let

f_i = the number of items classified into group i (that is, the ith observed frequency)

$E_i = np_i$

= the expected number of items that would be classified into group i if p_i is the probability of a randomly selected item being classified into group i (that is, the ith expected frequency)

If we wish to test

H_0: the values of the multinomial probabilities are $p_1, p_2, \ldots, p_k$—that is, the probability of a randomly selected item being classified into group 1 is p_1, the probability of a randomly selected item being classified into group 2 is p_2, and so forth

versus

H_a: at least one of the multinomial probabilities is not equal to the value stated in H_0

we define the **chi-square goodness-of-fit statistic** to be

$$\chi^2 = \sum_{i=1}^{k} \frac{(f_i - E_i)^2}{E_i}$$

Also, define the p-value related to χ^2 to be the area under the curve of the chi-square distribution having $k - 1$ degrees of freedom to the right of χ^2.

Then, we can reject H_0 in favor of H_a at level of significance α if either of the following equivalent conditions holds:

1 $\chi^2 > \chi_\alpha^2$

2 p-value $< \alpha$

Here the χ_α^2 point is based on $k - 1$ degrees of freedom.

This test is based on the fact that it can be shown that, when H_0 is true, the sampling distribution of χ^2 is approximately a chi-square distribution with $k - 1$ degrees of freedom, if the sample size n is large. **It is generally agreed that n should be considered large if all of the "expected cell frequencies" (E_i values) are at least 5.** Furthermore, recent research implies that this condition on the E_i values can be somewhat relaxed. For example, Moore and McCabe (1993) indicate that **it is reasonable to use the chi-square approximation if the number of groups (k) exceeds 4, the average of the E_i values is at least 5, and the smallest E_i value is at least 1.** Notice that in Example 13.1 all of the E_i values are much larger than 5. Therefore, the chi-square test is valid.

A special version of the chi-square goodness-of-fit test for multinomial probabilities is called a **test for homogeneity.** This involves testing the null hypothesis that all of the multinomial probabilities are equal. For instance, in the microwave oven case we would test

$$H_0: p_1 = p_2 = p_3 = p_4 = .25$$

which would say that no single brand of microwave oven is preferred to any of the other brands (equal preferences). If this null hypothesis is rejected in favor of

$$H_a: \text{At least one of } p_1, p_2, p_3, \text{ and } p_4 \text{ exceeds } .25$$

we would conclude that there is a preference for one or more of the brands. Here each of the expected cell frequencies equals $.25(400) = 100$. Remembering that the observed cell frequencies are $f_1 = 102, f_2 = 121, f_3 = 120,$ and $f_4 = 57$, the chi-square statistic is

$$\chi^2 = \sum_{i=1}^{4} \frac{(f_i - E_i)^2}{E_i}$$

$$= \frac{(102 - 100)^2}{100} + \frac{(121 - 100)^2}{100} + \frac{(120 - 100)^2}{100} + \frac{(57 - 100)^2}{100}$$

$$= .04 + 4.41 + 4 + 18.49 = 26.94$$

Because $\chi^2 = 26.94$ is greater than $\chi_{.05}^2 = 7.81473$ (see Table A.5 on page 794 with $k - 1 = 4 - 1 = 3$ degrees of freedom), we reject H_0 at level of significance .05. We conclude that preferences for the four brands are not equal and that at least one brand is preferred to the others.

Normal distributions   We have seen that many statistical methods are based on the assumption that a random sample has been selected from a normally distributed population. We can check the validity of the normality assumption by using frequency distributions, stem-and-leaf displays, histograms, and normal plots. Another approach is to use a chi-square goodness-of-fit test to check the normality assumption. We show how this can be done in the following example.

LO13-2 Perform a goodness-of-fit test for normality.

EXAMPLE 13.2 The Car Mileage Case: Testing Normality

Consider the sample of 50 gas mileages given in Table 1.6 (page 11). A histogram of these mileages (see Figure 2.9, page 46) is symmetrical and bell-shaped. This suggests that the sample of mileages has been randomly selected from a normally distributed population. In this example we use a chi-square goodness-of-fit test to check the normality of the mileages.

To perform this test, we first divide the number line into intervals (or categories). One way to do this is to use the class boundaries of the histogram in Figure 2.9. Table 13.3 gives these intervals and also gives observed frequencies (counts of the number of mileages in each interval), which have been obtained from the histogram of Figure 2.9. The chi-square test is done by comparing these observed frequencies with the expected frequencies in the rightmost column of Table 13.3. To explain how the expected frequencies are calculated, we first use the sample mean $\bar{x} = 31.56$ and the sample standard deviation $s = .798$ of the 50 mileages as point estimates of the population mean μ and population standard deviation σ. Then, for example, consider p_1, the probability that a randomly selected mileage will be in the first interval (less than 30.0) in Table 13.3, if the population of all mileages is normally distributed. We estimate p_1 to be

$$p_1 = P(\text{mileage} < 30.0) = P\left(z < \frac{30.0 - 31.56}{.798}\right)$$
$$= P(z < -1.95) = .0256$$

It follows that $E_1 = 50p_1 = 50(.0256) = 1.28$ is the expected frequency for the first interval under the normality assumption. Next, if we consider p_2, the probability that a randomly selected mileage will be in the second interval in Table 13.3 if the population of all mileages is normally distributed, we estimate p_2 to be

$$p_2 = P(30.0 \leq \text{mileage} < 30.5) = P\left(\frac{30.0 - 31.56}{.798} \leq z < \frac{30.5 - 31.56}{.798}\right)$$
$$= P(-1.95 \leq z < -1.33) = .0918 - .0256 = .0662$$

It follows that $E_2 = 50p_2 = 50(.0662) = 3.31$ is the expected frequency for the second interval under the normality assumption. The other expected frequencies are computed similarly. In general, p_i is the probability that a randomly selected mileage will be in interval i if the population of all possible mileages is normally distributed with mean 31.56 and standard deviation .798, and E_i is the expected number of the 50 mileages that would be in interval i if the population of all possible mileages has this normal distribution.

It seems reasonable to reject the null hypothesis

H_0: the population of all mileages is normally distributed

in favor of the alternative hypothesis

H_a: the population of all mileages is not normally distributed

TABLE 13.3   **Observed and Expected Cell Frequencies for a Chi-Square Goodness-of-Fit Test for Testing the Normality of the Population of Gasoline Mileages**   📀 GasMiles

Interval	Observed Frequency (f_i)	p_i If the Population of Mileages Is Normally Distributed	Expected Frequency, $E_i = np_i = 50p_i$
Less than 30.0	1	$p_1 = P(\text{mileage} < 30.0) = .0256$	$E_1 = 50(.0256) = 1.28$
$30.0 < 30.5$	3	$p_2 = P(30.0 \leq \text{mileage} < 30.5) = .0662$	$E_2 = 50(.0662) = 3.31$
$30.5 < 31.0$	8	$p_3 = P(30.5 \leq \text{mileage} < 31.0) = .1502$	$E_3 = 50(.1502) = 7.51$
$31.0 < 31.5$	11	$p_4 = P(31.0 \leq \text{mileage} < 31.5) = .2261$	$E_4 = 50(.2261) = 11.305$
$31.5 < 32.0$	11	$p_5 = P(31.5 \leq \text{mileage} < 32.0) = .2407$	$E_5 = 50(.2407) = 12.035$
$32.0 < 32.5$	9	$p_6 = P(32.0 \leq \text{mileage} < 32.5) = .1722$	$E_6 = 50(.1722) = 8.61$
$32.5 < 33.0$	5	$p_7 = P(32.5 \leq \text{mileage} < 33.0) = .0831$	$E_7 = 50(.0831) = 4.155$
Greater than 33.0	2	$p_8 = P(\text{mileage} > 33.0) = .0359$	$E_8 = 50(.0359) = 1.795$

if the observed frequencies in Table 13.3 differ substantially from the corresponding expected frequencies in Table 13.3. We compare the observed frequencies with the expected frequencies under the normality assumption by computing the chi-square statistic

Chi-square curve with 5 degrees of freedom

p-value = .994

0   $\chi^2 = .43242$

$$\chi^2 = \sum_{i=1}^{8} \frac{(f_i - E_i)^2}{E_i}$$

$$= \frac{(1 - 1.28)^2}{1.28} + \frac{(3 - 3.31)^2}{3.31} + \frac{(8 - 7.51)^2}{7.51} + \frac{(11 - 11.305)^2}{11.305}$$

$$+ \frac{(11 - 12.035)^2}{12.035} + \frac{(9 - 8.61)^2}{8.61} + \frac{(5 - 4.155)^2}{4.155} + \frac{(2 - 1.795)^2}{1.795}$$

$$= .43242$$

Because we have estimated $m = 2$ parameters (μ and σ) in computing the expected frequencies (E_i values), it can be shown that the sampling distribution of χ^2 is approximately a chi-square distribution with $k - 1 - m = 8 - 1 - 2 = 5$ degrees of freedom. Therefore, we can reject H_0 at level of significance α if

$$\chi^2 > \chi_\alpha^2$$

where the χ_α^2 point is based on $k - 1 - m = 8 - 1 - 2 = 5$ degrees of freedom. If we wish to test H_0 at the .05 level of significance, Table A.5 (page 794) tells us that $\chi_{.05}^2 = 11.0705$. Therefore, because

$$\chi^2 = .43242 < \chi_{.05}^2 = 11.0705$$

we cannot reject H_0 at the .05 level of significance, and we cannot reject the hypothesis that the population of all mileages is normally distributed. Therefore, for practical purposes it is probably reasonable to assume that the population of all mileages is approximately normally distributed and that inferences based on this assumption are valid. Finally, the p-value for this test, which is the area under the chi-square curve having 5 degrees of freedom to the right of $\chi^2 = .43242$, can be shown to equal .994. Because this p-value is large (much greater than .05), we have little evidence to support rejecting the null hypothesis (normality).

Note that although some of the expected cell frequencies in Table 13.3 are not at least 5, the number of classes (groups) is 8 (which exceeds 4), the average of the expected cell frequencies is at least 5, and the smallest expected cell frequency is at least 1. Therefore, it is probably reasonable to consider the result of this chi-square test valid. If we choose to base the chi-square test on the more restrictive assumption that all of the expected cell frequencies are at least 5, then we can combine adjacent cell frequencies as follows:

Original f_i Values	Original p_i Values	Original E_i Values	Combined E_i Values	Combined p_i Values	Combined f_i Values
1	.0256	1.28			
3	.0662	3.31	12.1	.2420	12
8	.1502	7.51			
11	.2261	11.305	11.305	.2261	11
11	.2407	12.035	12.035	.2407	11
9	.1722	8.61	8.61	.1722	9
5	.0831	4.155			
2	.0359	1.795	5.95	.1190	7

When we use these combined cell frequencies, the chi-square approximation is based on $k - 1 - m = 5 - 1 - 2 = 2$ degrees of freedom. We find that $\chi^2 = .30102$ and that the p-value = .860. Because this p-value is much greater than .05, we cannot reject the hypothesis of normality at the .05 level of significance.

In Example 13.2 we based the intervals employed in the chi-square goodness-of-fit test on the class boundaries of a histogram for the observed mileages. Another way to establish intervals for such a test is to compute the sample mean $\bar{x}$ and the sample standard deviation s and to use intervals based on the Empirical Rule as follows:

Interval 1: less than $\bar{x} - 2s$

Interval 2: $\bar{x} - 2s < \bar{x} - s$

Interval 3: $\bar{x} - s < \bar{x}$

Interval 4: $\bar{x} < \bar{x} + s$

Interval 5: $\bar{x} + s < \bar{x} + 2s$

Interval 6: greater than $\bar{x} + 2s$

However, care must be taken to ensure that each of the expected frequencies is large enough (using the previously discussed criteria).

No matter how the intervals are established, we use $\bar{x}$ as an estimate of the population mean μ and we use s as an estimate of the population standard deviation σ when we calculate the expected frequencies (E_i values). Because we are estimating $m = 2$ population parameters, the critical value χ_α^2 is based on $k - 1 - m = k - 1 - 2 = k - 3$ degrees of freedom, where k is the number of intervals employed.

In the following box we summarize how to carry out this chi-square test:

A Goodness-of-Fit Test for a Normal Distribution

1 We will test the following null and alternative hypotheses:

H_0: the population has a normal distribution

H_a: the population does not have a normal distribution

2 Select a random sample of size n and compute the sample mean $\bar{x}$ and sample standard deviation s.

3 Define k intervals for the test. Two reasonable ways to do this are to use the classes of a histogram of the data or to use intervals based on the Empirical Rule.

4 Record the observed frequency (f_i) for each interval.

5 Calculate the expected frequency (E_i) for each interval under the normality assumption. Do this by computing the probability that a normal variable having mean $\bar{x}$ and standard deviation s

is within the interval and by multiplying this probability by n. Make sure that each expected frequency is large enough. If necessary, combine intervals to make the expected frequencies large enough.

6 Calculate the chi-square statistic

$$\chi^2 = \sum_{i=1}^{k} \frac{(f_i - E_i)^2}{E_i}$$

and define the p-value for the test to be the area under the curve of the chi-square distribution having $k - 3$ degrees of freedom to the right of χ^2.

7 Reject H_0 in favor of H_a at level of significance α if either of the following equivalent conditions holds:

a $\chi^2 > \chi_\alpha^2$ **b** p-value $< \alpha$

Here, the χ_α^2 point is based on $k - 3$ degrees of freedom.

While chi-square goodness-of-fit tests are often used to verify that it is reasonable to assume that a random sample has been selected from a normally distributed population, such tests can also check other distribution forms. For instance, we might verify that it is reasonable to assume that a random sample has been selected from a Poisson distribution. In general, **the number of degrees of freedom for the chi-square goodness-of-fit test will equal $k - 1 - m$,** where k is the number of intervals or categories employed in the test and m is the number of population parameters that must be estimated to calculate the needed expected frequencies.

Exercises for Section 13.1

CONCEPTS

connect

13.1 Describe the characteristics that define a multinomial experiment.

13.2 Give the conditions that the expected cell frequencies must meet in order to validly carry out a chi-square goodness-of-fit test.

13.3 Explain the purpose of a goodness-of-fit test.

13.4 When performing a chi-square goodness-of-fit test, explain why a large value of the chi-square statistic provides evidence that H_0 should be rejected.

13.5 Explain two ways to obtain intervals for a goodness-of-fit test of normality.

METHODS AND APPLICATIONS

13.6 The shares of the U.S. automobile market held in 1990 by General Motors, Japanese manufacturers, Ford, Chrysler, and other manufacturers were, respectively, 36%, 26%, 21%, 9%, and 8%. Suppose that a new survey of 1,000 new-car buyers shows the following purchase frequencies:

GM	Japanese	Ford	Chrysler	Other
193	384	170	90	163

a Show that it is appropriate to carry out a chi-square test using these data.   DS AutoMkt
b Test to determine whether the current market shares differ from those of 1990. Use $\alpha = .05$.

13.7 Last rating period, the percentages of viewers watching several channels between 11 P.M. and 11:30 P.M. in a major TV market were as follows: DS TVRate

WDUX (News)	WWTY (News)	WACO (*Cheers* Reruns)	WTJW (News)	Others
15%	19%	22%	16%	28%

Suppose that in the current rating period, a survey of 2,000 viewers gives the following frequencies:

WDUX (News)	WWTY (News)	WACO (*Cheers* Reruns)	WTJW (News)	Others
182	536	354	151	777

a Show that it is appropriate to carry out a chi-square test using these data.
b Test to determine whether the viewing shares in the current rating period differ from those in the last rating period at the .10 level of significance. What do you conclude?

13.8 In the *Journal of Marketing Research* (November 1996), Gupta studied the extent to which the purchase behavior of **scanner panels** is representative of overall brand preferences. A scanner panel is a sample of households whose purchase data are recorded when a magnetic identification card is presented at a store checkout. The table below gives peanut butter purchase data collected by the A. C. Nielson Company using a panel of 2,500 households in Sioux Falls, South Dakota. The data were collected over 102 weeks. The table also gives the market shares obtained by recording all peanut butter purchases at the same stores during the same period.   DS ScanPan
a Show that it is appropriate to carry out a chi-square test.
b Test to determine whether the purchase behavior of the panel of 2,500 households is consistent with the purchase behavior of the population of all peanut butter purchasers. Assume here that purchase decisions by panel members are reasonably independent, and set $\alpha = .05$.

Brand	Size	Number of Purchases by Household Panel	Market Shares					
Jif	18 oz.	3,165	20.10%					
Jif	28	1,892	10.10					
Jif	40	726	5.42					
Peter Pan	10	4,079	16.01					
Skippy	18	6,206	28.56					
Skippy	28	1,627	12.33					
Skippy	40	1,420	7.48					
Total		19,115						

Goodness-of-Fit Test

obs	expected	O − E	(O − E)²/E	% of chisq
3165	3842.115	−677.115	119.331	13.56
1892	1930.615	−38.615	0.772	0.09
726	1036.033	−310.033	92.777	10.54
4079	3060.312	1018.689	339.092	38.52
6206	5459.244	746.756	102.147	11.60
1627	2356.880	−729.880	226.029	25.68
1420	1429.802	−9.802	0.067	0.01
19115	19115.000	0.000	880.216	100.00

880.22 chisquare   6 df   0.0000   p-value

Source: Reprinted with permission from *The Journal of Marketing Research*, published by the American Marketing Association, Vol. 33, S. Gupta et al., "Do Household Scanner Data Provide Representative Inferences from Brand Choices? A Comparison with Store Data," p. 393 (Table 6).

13.9 The purchase frequencies for six different brands of a digital camera are observed at a discount store over one month: DS DigCam

Brand	1	2	3	4	5	6
Purchase Frequency	131	273	119	301	176	200

a Carry out a test of homogeneity for these data with $\alpha = .025$.
b Interpret the result of your test.

13.10 A wholesaler has recently developed a computerized sales invoicing system. Prior to implementing this system, a manual system was used. The distribution of the number of errors per invoice for the manual system is as follows: DS Invoice2

Errors per Invoice	0	1	2	3	More Than 3
Percentage of Invoices	87%	8%	3%	1%	1%

After implementation of the computerized system, a random sample of 500 invoices gives the following error distribution:

Errors per Invoice	0	1	2	3	More Than 3
Number of Invoices	479	10	8	2	1

a Show that it is appropriate to carry out a chi-square test using these data.
b Use the following Excel output to determine whether the error percentages for the computerized system differ from those for the manual system at the .05 level of significance. What do you conclude?

pi	Ei	fi	$(f - E)^2/E$
0.87	435	479	4.4506
0.08	40	10	22.5000
0.03	15	8	3.2667
0.01	5	2	1.8000
0.01	5	1	3.2000

Chi-Square 35.21724   p-value 0.0000001096

13.11   THE e-billing CASE

Consider the sample of 65 payment times given in Table 2.4 (page 42). Use these data to carry out a chi-square goodness-of-fit test to test whether the population of all payment times is normally distributed by doing the following: DS PayTime

a It can be shown that $\bar{x} = 18.1077$ and that $s = 3.9612$ for the payment time data. Use these values to compute the intervals
   (1) Less than $\bar{x} - 2s$ (4) $\bar{x} < \bar{x} + s$
   (2) $\bar{x} - 2s < \bar{x} - s$ (5) $\bar{x} + s < \bar{x} + 2s$
   (3) $\bar{x} - s < \bar{x}$ (6) Greater than $\bar{x} + 2s$

b Assuming that the population of all payment times is normally distributed, find the probability that a randomly selected payment time will be contained in each of the intervals found in part a. Use these probabilities to compute the expected frequency under the normality assumption for each interval.

c Verify that the average of the expected frequencies is at least 5 and that the smallest expected frequency is at least 1. What does this tell us?

d Formulate the null and alternative hypotheses for the chi-square test of normality.

e For each interval given in part a, find the observed frequency. Then calculate the chi-square statistic needed for the chi-square test of normality.

f Use the chi-square statistic to test normality at the .05 level of significance. What do you conclude?

13.12   THE MARKETING RESEARCH CASE

Consider the sample of 60 bottle design ratings given in Table 1.5 (page 10). Use these data to carry out a chi-square goodness-of-fit test to determine whether the population of all bottle design ratings is normally distributed. Use $\alpha = .05$, and note that $\bar{x} = 30.35$ and $s = 3.1073$ for the 60 bottle design ratings.   DS Design

13.13   THE BANK CUSTOMER WAITING TIME CASE

Consider the sample of 100 waiting times given in Table 1.8 (page 13). Use these data to carry out a chi-square goodness-of-fit test to determine whether the population of all waiting times is normally distributed. Use $\alpha = .10$, and note that $\bar{x} = 5.46$ and $s = 2.475$ for the 100 waiting times.   DS WaitTime

13.14 The table on the next page gives a frequency distribution describing the number of errors found in thirty 1,000-line samples of computer code. Suppose that we wish to determine whether the number of errors can be described by a Poisson distribution with mean $\mu = 4.5$. Using the Poisson probability tables, fill in the table. Then perform an appropriate chi-square goodness-of-fit test at the .05 level of significance. What do you conclude about whether the number of errors can be described by a Poisson distribution with $\mu = 4.5$? Explain.   **DS** CodeErr

Number of Errors	Observed Frequency	Probability Assuming Errors Are Poisson Distributed with $\mu = 4.5$	Expected Frequency
0–1	6		
2–3	5		
4–5	7		
6–7	8		
8 or more	4		

LO13-3 Decide whether two qualitative variables are independent by using a chi-square test for independence.

13.2 A Chi-Square Test for Independence ● ● ●

We have spent considerable time in previous chapters studying relationships between variables. One way to study the relationship between two variables is to classify multinomial count data on two scales (or dimensions) by setting up a *contingency table*.

EXAMPLE 13.3 The Brokerage Firm Case: Studying Client Satisfaction

A brokerage firm sells several kinds of investment products—a stock fund, a bond fund, and a tax-deferred annuity. The company is examining whether customer satisfaction depends on the type of investment product purchased. To do this, 100 clients are randomly selected from the population of clients who have purchased shares in exactly one of the funds. The company records the fund type purchased by these clients and asks each sampled client to rate his or her level of satisfaction with the fund as high, medium, or low. Table 13.4 on page 472 gives the survey results.

We can look at the data in Table 13.4 in an organized way by constructing a **contingency table** (also called a **two-way cross-tabulation or cross-classification table**). Such a table classifies the data on two dimensions—type of fund and degree of client satisfaction. Figure 13.2 gives Excel and MINITAB outputs of a contingency table of fund type versus level of satisfaction. This table consists of a row for each fund type and a column for each level of satisfaction. Together, the rows and columns form a "cell" for each fund type–satisfaction level combination. That is, there is a cell for each "contingency" with respect to fund type and satisfaction level. Both the Excel and MINITAB outputs give a **cell frequency** for each cell. On the MINITAB output, this is the top number given in the cell. The cell frequency is a count (observed frequency) of the number of surveyed clients with the cell's fund type–satisfaction level combination. For instance, 15 of the surveyed clients invest in the bond fund and report high satisfaction, while 24 of the surveyed clients invest in the tax-deferred annuity and report medium satisfaction. In addition to the cell frequencies, each output also gives:

Row totals (at the far right of each table): These are counts of the numbers of clients who invest in each fund type. These row totals tell us that

1 30 clients invest in the bond fund.

2 30 clients invest in the stock fund.

3 40 clients invest in the tax-deferred annuity.

Column totals (at the bottom of each table): These are counts of the numbers of clients who report high, medium, and low satisfaction. These column totals tell us that

1 40 clients report high satisfaction.

2 40 clients report medium satisfaction.

3 20 clients report low satisfaction.

Overall total (the bottom-right entry in each table): This tells us that a total of 100 clients were surveyed.

Besides the row and column totals, the MINITAB output gives **row and column percentages** (below the row and column totals). For example, 30.00 percent of the surveyed clients invest in the bond fund, and 20.00 percent of the surveyed clients report low satisfaction. Furthermore, in

FIGURE 13.2   **Excel and MINITAB Outputs of a Contingency Table of Fund Type versus Level of Client Satisfaction (See the Survey Results in Table 13.4)**   Invest

(a) The Excel Output

ᵃChi-square statistic.
ᵇp-value for chi-square.

(b) The MINITAB Output

```
Rows: FundType    Columns: SatRating

                High       Med       Low       All

Bond              15        12         3        30
                50.00     40.00     10.00    100.00
                37.50     30.00     15.00     30.00
                   12        12         6        30

Stock             24         4         2        30
                80.00     13.33      6.67    100.00
                60.00     10.00     10.00     30.00
                   12        12         6        30

TaxDef             1        24        15        40
                 2.50     60.00     37.50    100.00
                 2.50     60.00     75.00     40.00
                   16        16         8        40

All               40        40        20       100
                40.00     40.00     20.00    100.00
               100.00    100.00    100.00    100.00
                   40        40        20       100

Pearson Chi-Square = 46.438, DF = 4
          P-Value = 0.000

Cell Contents:        Count
                      % of Row
                      % of Column
                      Expected count
```

addition to a cell frequency, the MINITAB output gives a **row percentage** and a **column percentage** for each cell (these are below the cell frequency in each cell). For instance, looking at the "bond fund–high satisfaction cell," we see that the 15 clients in this cell make up 50.0 percent of the 30 clients who invest in the bond fund, and they make up 37.5 percent of the 40 clients who report high satisfaction. We will explain the last number that appears in each cell of the MINITAB output later in this section.

Looking at the contingency tables, it appears that the level of client satisfaction may be related to the fund type. We see that higher satisfaction ratings seem to be reported by stock and bond fund investors, while holders of tax-deferred annuities report lower satisfaction ratings. To carry out a formal statistical test we can test the null hypothesis

$$H_0\text{: fund type and level of client satisfaction are independent}$$

versus

$$H_a\text{: fund type and level of client satisfaction are dependent}$$

In order to perform this test, we compare the counts (or **observed cell frequencies**) in the contingency table with the counts we would expect if we assume that fund type and level of satisfaction are independent. Because these latter counts are computed by assuming independence, we call them the **expected cell frequencies under the independence assumption.** We illustrate how to calculate these expected cell frequencies by considering the cell corresponding to the bond fund and high client satisfaction. We first use the data in the contingency table to compute an estimate of the probability that a randomly selected client invests in the bond fund. Denoting this probability as p_B, we estimate p_B by dividing the row total for the bond fund by the total number of clients surveyed. That is, denoting the row total for the bond fund as r_B and letting n denote the total number of clients surveyed, the estimate of p_B is $r_B / n = 30/100 = .3$. Next we compute an estimate of the probability that a randomly selected client will report high satisfaction. Denoting this probability as p_H, we estimate p_H by dividing the column total for high

TABLE 13.4 Results of a Customer Satisfaction Survey Given to 100 Randomly Selected Clients Who Invest in One of Three Fund Types—a Bond Fund, a Stock Fund, or a Tax-Deferred Annuity ⊙Ⓢ Invest

Client	Fund Type	Level of Satisfaction	Client	Fund Type	Level of Satisfaction	Client	Fund Type	Level of Satisfaction
1	BOND	HIGH	35	STOCK	HIGH	69	BOND	MED
2	STOCK	HIGH	36	BOND	MED	70	TAXDEF	MED
3	TAXDEF	MED	37	TAXDEF	MED	71	TAXDEF	MED
4	TAXDEF	MED	38	TAXDEF	LOW	72	BOND	HIGH
5	STOCK	LOW	39	STOCK	HIGH	73	TAXDEF	MED
6	STOCK	HIGH	40	TAXDEF	MED	74	TAXDEF	LOW
7	STOCK	HIGH	41	BOND	HIGH	75	STOCK	HIGH
8	BOND	MED	42	BOND	HIGH	76	BOND	HIGH
9	TAXDEF	LOW	43	BOND	LOW	77	TAXDEF	LOW
10	TAXDEF	LOW	44	TAXDEF	LOW	78	BOND	MED
11	STOCK	MED	45	STOCK	HIGH	79	STOCK	HIGH
12	BOND	LOW	46	BOND	HIGH	80	STOCK	HIGH
13	STOCK	HIGH	47	BOND	MED	81	BOND	MED
14	TAXDEF	MED	48	STOCK	HIGH	82	TAXDEF	MED
15	TAXDEF	MED	49	TAXDEF	MED	83	BOND	HIGH
16	TAXDEF	LOW	50	TAXDEF	MED	84	STOCK	MED
17	STOCK	HIGH	51	STOCK	HIGH	85	STOCK	HIGH
18	BOND	HIGH	52	TAXDEF	MED	86	BOND	MED
19	BOND	MED	53	STOCK	HIGH	87	TAXDEF	MED
20	TAXDEF	MED	54	TAXDEF	MED	88	TAXDEF	LOW
21	TAXDEF	MED	55	STOCK	LOW	89	STOCK	HIGH
22	BOND	HIGH	56	BOND	HIGH	90	TAXDEF	MED
23	TAXDEF	MED	57	STOCK	HIGH	91	BOND	HIGH
24	TAXDEF	LOW	58	BOND	MED	92	TAXDEF	HIGH
25	STOCK	HIGH	59	TAXDEF	LOW	93	TAXDEF	LOW
26	BOND	HIGH	60	TAXDEF	LOW	94	TAXDEF	LOW
27	TAXDEF	LOW	61	STOCK	MED	95	STOCK	HIGH
28	BOND	MED	62	BOND	LOW	96	BOND	HIGH
29	STOCK	HIGH	63	STOCK	HIGH	97	BOND	MED
30	STOCK	HIGH	64	TAXDEF	MED	98	STOCK	HIGH
31	BOND	MED	65	TAXDEF	MED	99	TAXDEF	MED
32	TAXDEF	MED	66	TAXDEF	LOW	100	TAXDEF	MED
33	BOND	HIGH	67	STOCK	HIGH			
34	STOCK	MED	68	BOND	HIGH			

satisfaction by the total number of clients surveyed. That is, denoting the column total for high satisfaction as c_H, the estimate of p_H is $c_H/n = 40/100 = .4$. Next, assuming that investing in the bond fund and reporting high satisfaction are **independent,** we compute an estimate of the probability that a randomly selected client invests in the bond fund and reports high satisfaction. Denoting this probability as p_{BH}, we can compute its estimate by recalling from Section 4.4 that if two events A and B are statistically independent, then $P(A \cap B)$ equals $P(A)P(B)$. It follows that, if we assume that investing in the bond fund and reporting high satisfaction are independent, we can compute an estimate of p_{BH} by multiplying the estimate of p_B by the estimate of p_H. That is, the estimate of p_{BH} is $(r_B/n)(c_H/n) = (.3)(.4) = .12$. Finally, we compute an estimate of the expected cell frequency under the independence assumption. Denoting the expected cell frequency as E_{BH}, the estimate of E_{BH} is

$$\hat{E}_{BH} = n \left(\frac{r_B}{n} \right) \left(\frac{c_H}{n} \right) = 100(.3)(.4) = 12$$

This estimated expected cell frequency is given in the MINITAB output of Figure 13.2(b) as the last number under the observed cell frequency for the bond fund–high satisfaction cell.

Noting that the expression for $\hat{E}_{BH}$ can be written as

$$\hat{E}_{BH} = n\left(\frac{r_B}{n}\right)\left(\frac{c_H}{n}\right) = \frac{r_B c_H}{n}$$

we can generalize to obtain a formula for the estimated expected cell frequency for any cell in the contingency table. Letting $\hat{E}_{ij}$ denote the estimated expected cell frequency corresponding to row i and column j in the contingency table, we see that

$$\hat{E}_{ij} = \frac{r_i c_j}{n}$$

where r_i is the row total for row i and c_j is the column total for column j. For example, for the fund type–satisfaction level contingency table, we obtain

$$\hat{E}_{SL} = \frac{r_S c_L}{n} = \frac{30(20)}{100} = \frac{600}{100} = 6$$

and

$$\hat{E}_{TM} = \frac{r_T c_M}{n} = \frac{40(40)}{100} = \frac{1,600}{100} = 16$$

These (and the other estimated expected cell frequencies under the independence assumption) are the last numbers below the observed cell frequencies in the MINITAB output of Figure 13.2(b). Intuitively, these estimated expected cell frequencies tell us what the contingency table would look like if fund type and level of client satisfaction were independent. A table of estimated expected cell frequencies is also given below the contingency table on the Excel output of Figure 13.2(a).

To test the null hypothesis of independence, we will compute a chi-square statistic that compares the observed cell frequencies with the estimated expected cell frequencies calculated assuming independence. Letting f_{ij} denote the observed cell frequency for cell ij, we compute

$$\chi^2 = \sum_{\text{all cells}} \frac{(f_{ij} - \hat{E}_{ij})^2}{\hat{E}_{ij}}$$

$$= \frac{(f_{BH} - \hat{E}_{BH})^2}{\hat{E}_{BH}} + \frac{(f_{BM} - \hat{E}_{BM})^2}{\hat{E}_{BM}} + \cdots + \frac{(f_{TL} - \hat{E}_{TL})^2}{\hat{E}_{TL}}$$

$$= \frac{(15 - 12)^2}{12} + \frac{(12 - 12)^2}{12} + \frac{(3 - 6)^2}{6} + \frac{(24 - 12)^2}{12} + \frac{(4 - 12)^2}{12}$$

$$+ \frac{(2 - 6)^2}{6} + \frac{(1 - 16)^2}{16} + \frac{(24 - 16)^2}{16} + \frac{(15 - 8)^2}{8}$$

$$= 46.4375$$

If the value of the chi-square statistic is large, this indicates that the observed cell frequencies differ substantially from the expected cell frequencies calculated by assuming independence. Therefore, the larger the value of chi-square, the more doubt is cast on the null hypothesis of independence.

To find an appropriate critical value, we let r denote the number of rows in the contingency table and we let c denote the number of columns. Then, it can be shown that, when the null hypothesis of independence is true, the sampling distribution of χ^2 is approximately a χ^2 distribution with $(r-1)(c-1) = (3-1)(3-1) = 4$ degrees of freedom. If we test H_0 at the .05 level of significance, we reject H_0 if and only if

$$\chi^2 > \chi^2_{.05}$$

Because Table A.5 (page 794) tells us that the $\chi^2_{.05}$ point corresponding to $(r-1)(c-1) = 4$ degrees of freedom equals 9.48773, we have

$$\chi^2 = 46.4375 > \chi^2_{.05} = 9.48773$$

and we reject H_0 at the .05 level of significance. We conclude that fund type and level of client satisfaction are not independent.

In the following box we summarize how to carry out a chi-square test for independence:

A Chi-Square Test for Independence

Suppose that each of n randomly selected elements is classified on two dimensions, and suppose that the result of the two-way classification is a **contingency table having r rows and c columns.** Let

　f_{ij} = the cell frequency corresponding to row i and column j of the contingency table (that is, the number of elements classified in row i and column j)

　r_i = the row total for row i in the contingency table

　c_j = the column total for column j in the contingency table

　$\hat{E}_{ij} = \dfrac{r_i c_j}{n}$

　　= the estimated expected number of elements that would be classified in row i and column j of the contingency table if the two classifications are statistically independent

If we wish to test

　H_0: the two classifications are statistically independent

versus

　H_a: the two classifications are statistically dependent

we define the test statistic

$$\chi^2 = \sum_{\text{all cells}} \frac{(f_{ij} - \hat{E}_{ij})^2}{\hat{E}_{ij}}$$

Also, define the p-value related to χ^2 to be the area under the curve of the chi-square distribution having $(r-1)(c-1)$ degrees of freedom to the right of χ^2. Then, we can reject H_0 in favor of H_a at level of significance α if either of the following equivalent conditions holds:

1　$\chi^2 > \chi^2_\alpha$

2　p-value $< \alpha$

Here the χ^2_α point is based on $(r-1)(c-1)$ degrees of freedom.

This test is based on the fact that it can be shown that, when the null hypothesis of independence is true, the sampling distribution of χ^2 is approximately a chi-square distribution with $(r-1)(c-1)$ degrees of freedom, if the sample size n is large. **It is generally agreed that n should be considered large if all of the estimated expected cell frequencies ($\hat{E}_{ij}$ values) are at least 5.** Moore and McCabe (1993) indicate that **it is reasonable to use the chi-square approximation if the number of cells (rc) exceeds 4, the average of the $\hat{E}_{ij}$ values is at least 5, and the smallest $\hat{E}_{ij}$ value is at least 1.** Notice that in Figure 13.2 all of the estimated expected cell frequencies are greater than 5.

EXAMPLE 13.4　The Brokerage Firm Case: Studying Client Satisfaction

Again consider the Excel and MINITAB outputs of Figure 13.2, which give the contingency table of fund type versus level of client satisfaction. Both outputs give the chi-square statistic ($= 46.438$) for testing the null hypothesis of independence, as well as the related p-value. We see that this p-value is less than .001. It follows, therefore, that we can reject

　H_0: fund type and level of client satisfaction are independent

at the .05 level of significance, because the p-value is less than .05.

　In order to study the nature of the dependency between the classifications in a contingency table, it is often useful to plot the row and/or column percentages. As an example, Figure 13.3 gives plots of the row percentages in the contingency table of Figure 13.2(b). For instance, looking at the column in this contingency table corresponding to a high level of satisfaction, the contingency table tells us that 40.00 percent of the surveyed clients report a high level of satisfaction. If fund type and level of satisfaction really are independent, then we would expect roughly 40 percent of the clients in each of the three categories—bond fund participants, stock fund participants, and tax-deferred annuity holders—to report a high level of satisfaction. That is, we would expect the row percentages in the "high satisfaction" column to be roughly 40 percent in each row.

FIGURE 13.3   Plots of Row Percentages versus Investment Type for the Contingency
               Tables in Figure 13.2

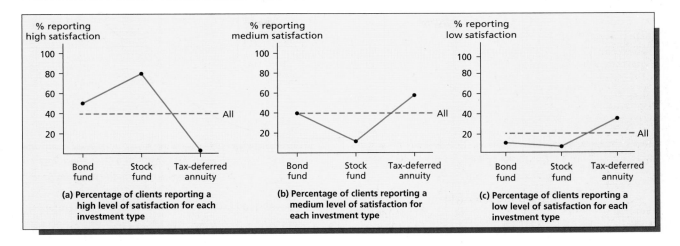

However, Figure 13.3(a) gives a plot of the percentages of clients reporting a high level of satisfaction for each investment type (that is, the figure plots the three row percentages in the column corresponding to "high satisfaction"). We see that these percentages vary considerably. Noting that the dashed line in the figure is the 40 percent reporting a high level of satisfaction for the overall group, we see that the percentage of stock fund participants reporting high satisfaction is 80 percent. This is far above the 40 percent we would expect if independence exists. On the other hand, the percentage of tax-deferred annuity holders reporting high satisfaction is only 2.5 percent—way below the expected 40 percent if independence exists. In a similar fashion, Figures 13.3(b) and (c) plot the row percentages for the medium and low satisfaction columns in the contingency table. These plots indicate that stock fund participants report medium and low levels of satisfaction less frequently than the overall group of clients, and that tax-deferred annuity participants report medium and low levels of satisfaction more frequently than the overall group of clients.

To conclude this section, we note that the chi-square test for independence can be used to test the equality of several population proportions. We will show how this is done in Exercise 13.21.

Exercises for Section 13.2

CONCEPTS

13.15 What is the purpose behind summarizing data in the form of a two-way contingency table?

13.16 When performing a chi-square test for independence, explain how the "cell frequencies under the independence assumption" are calculated. For what purpose are these frequencies calculated?

METHODS AND APPLICATIONS

13.17 A marketing research firm wishes to study the relationship between wine consumption and whether a person likes to watch professional tennis on television. One hundred randomly selected people are asked whether they drink wine and whether they watch tennis. The following results are obtained: DS WineCons

	Watch Tennis	Do Not Watch Tennis	Totals
Drink Wine	16	24	40
Do Not Drink Wine	4	56	60
Totals	20	80	100

a For each row and column total, calculate the corresponding row or column percentage.
b For each cell, calculate the corresponding cell, row, and column percentages.

TABLE 13.5   **Depreciation Methods Used by a Sample of 78 Firms**   DS DeprMeth

Depreciation Methods	France	Germany	UK	Total
A. Straight line (S)	15	0	25	40
B. Declining Bal (D)	1	1	1	3
C. (D & S)	10	25	0	35
Total companies	26	26	26	78

Source: E. N. Emenyonu and S. J. Gray, "EC Accounting Harmonisation: An Empirical Study of Measurement Practices in France, Germany, and the UK," *Accounting and Business Research* 23, no. 89 (1992), pp. 49–58. Reprinted by permission of the author.

Chi-Square Test for Independence

	France	Germany	UK	Total
A. Straight line (S)	15	0	25	40
B. Declining Bal (D)	1	1	1	3
C. (D & S)	10	25	0	35
Total	26	26	26	78
50.89 chisquare	4 df	0.0000	p-value	

TABLE 13.6   **A Contingency Table of the Results of the Accidents Study**   DS Accident

	On-the-Job Accident		
Smoker	Yes	No	Row Total
Heavy	12	4	16
Moderate	9	6	15
Nonsmoker	13	22	35
Column total	34	32	66

Source: D. R. Cooper and C. W. Emory, *Business Research Methods* (5th ed.) (Burr Ridge, IL: Richard D. Irwin, 1995), p. 451.

FIGURE 13.4   **MINITAB Output of a Chi-Square Test for Independence in the Accident Study**

```
Expected counts are below observed counts

            Accident  No Accident  Total
Heavy            12            4     16
               8.24         7.76

Moderate          9            6     15
               7.73         7.27

Nonsmoker        13           22     35
              18.03        16.97

Total            34           32     66

Chi-Sq = 6.860, DF = 2, P-Value = 0.032
```

c   Test the hypothesis that whether people drink wine is independent of whether people watch tennis. Set $\alpha = .05$.

d   Given the results of the chi-square test, does it make sense to advertise wine during a televised tennis match (assuming that the ratings for the tennis match are high enough)? Explain.

13.18   In recent years major efforts have been made to standardize accounting practices in different countries; this is called *harmonization*. In an article in *Accounting and Business Research,* Emmanuel N. Emenyonu and Sidney J. Gray studied the extent to which accounting practices in France, Germany, and the UK are harmonized.   DS DeprMeth

     a   Depreciation method is one of the accounting practices studied by Emenyonu and Gray. Three methods were considered—the straight-line method (S), the declining balance method (D), and a combination of D & S (sometimes European firms start with the declining balance method and then switch over to the straight-line method when the figure derived from straight line exceeds that from declining balance). The data in Table 13.5 summarize the depreciation methods used by a sample of 78 French, German, and U.K. firms. Use these data and the results of the chi-square analysis in Table 13.5 to test the hypothesis that depreciation method is independent of a firm's location (country) at the .05 level of significance.

     b   Perform a graphical analysis to study the relationship between depreciation method and country. What conclusions can be made about the nature of the relationship?

13.19   In the book *Business Research Methods* (5th ed.), Donald R. Cooper and C. William Emory discuss studying the relationship between on-the-job accidents and smoking. Cooper and Emory describe the study as follows: DS Accident

     Suppose a manager implementing a smoke-free workplace policy is interested in whether smoking affects worker accidents. Since the company has complete reports of on-the-job accidents, she draws a sample of names of workers who were involved in accidents during the last year. A similar sample from among workers who had no reported accidents in the last year is drawn. She interviews members of both groups to determine if they are smokers or not.

     The sample results are given in Table 13.6.

     a   For each row and column total in Table 13.6, find the corresponding row/column percentage.

     b   For each cell in Table 13.6, find the corresponding cell, row, and column percentages.

TABLE 13.7   A Contingency Table Relating Delivery Time and Computer-Assisted Ordering
ⒹⓈ DelTime

Computer-Assisted Ordering	Below Industry Average	Delivery Time Equal to Industry Average	Above Industry Average	Row Total
No	4	12	8	24
Yes	10	4	2	16
Column total	14	16	10	40

TABLE 13.8   A Summary of the Results of a TV Viewership Study   ⒹⓈ TVView

Watch 11 P.M. News?	18 or Less	Age Group 19 to 35	36 to 54	55 or Older	Total
Yes	37	48	56	73	214
No	213	202	194	177	786
Total	250	250	250	250	1,000

   c Use the MINITAB output in Figure 13.4 to test the hypothesis that the incidence of on-the-job accidents is independent of smoking habits. Set $\alpha = .01$.

   d Is there a difference in on-the-job accident occurrences between smokers and nonsmokers? Explain.

13.20 In the book *Essentials of Marketing Research,* William R. Dillon, Thomas J. Madden, and Neil A. Firtle discuss the relationship between delivery time and computer-assisted ordering. A sample of 40 firms shows that 16 use computer-assisted ordering, while 24 do not. Furthermore, past data are used to categorize each firm's delivery times as below the industry average, equal to the industry average, or above the industry average. The results obtained are given in Table 13.7.

   a Test the hypothesis that delivery time performance is independent of whether computer-assisted ordering is used. What do you conclude by setting $\alpha = .05$?   ⒹⓈ DelTime

   b Verify that a chi-square test is appropriate.

   c Is there a difference between delivery-time performance between firms using computer-assisted ordering and those not using computer-assisted ordering?

   d Carry out graphical analysis to investigate the relationship between delivery-time performance and computer-assisted ordering. Describe the relationship.

13.21 A television station wishes to study the relationship between viewership of its 11 P.M. news program and viewer age (18 years or less, 19 to 35, 36 to 54, 55 or older). A sample of 250 television viewers in each age group is randomly selected, and the number who watch the station's 11 P.M. news is found for each sample. The results are given in Table 13.8.   ⒹⓈ TVView

   a Let $p_1, p_2, p_3,$ and p_4 be the proportions of all viewers in each age group who watch the station's 11 P.M. news. If these proportions are equal, then whether a viewer watches the station's 11 P.M. news is independent of the viewer's age group. Therefore, we can test the null hypothesis H_0 that $p_1, p_2, p_3,$ and p_4 are equal by carrying out a chi-square test for independence. Perform this test by setting $\alpha = .05$.

   b Compute a 95 percent confidence interval for the difference between p_1 and p_4.

Chapter Summary

In this chapter we presented two hypothesis tests that employ the **chi-square distribution.** In Section 13.1 we discussed a **chi-square test of goodness-of-fit.** Here we considered a situation in which we study how count data are distributed among various categories. In particular, we considered a **multinomial experiment** in which randomly selected items are classified into several groups, and we saw how to perform a goodness-of-fit test for the multinomial probabilities associated with these groups. We also explained how to perform a goodness-of-fit test for normality. In Section 13.2 we presented a **chi-square test for independence.** Here we classify count data on two dimensions, and we summarize the cross-classification in the form of a **contingency table.** We use the cross-classified data to test whether the two classifications are **statistically independent,** which is really a way to see whether the classifications are related. We also learned that we can use graphical analysis to investigate the nature of the relationship between the classifications.

Glossary of Terms

chi-square test for independence: A test to determine whether two classifications are independent. (page 474)

contingency table: A table that summarizes data that have been classified on two dimensions or scales. (page 470)

goodness-of-fit test for multinomial probabilities: A test to determine whether multinomial probabilities are equal to a specific set of values. (page 464)

goodness-of-fit test for normality: A test to determine if a sample has been randomly selected from a normally distributed population. (page 467)

homogeneity (test for): A test of the null hypothesis that all multinomial probabilities are equal. (page 464)

multinomial experiment: An experiment that concerns count data that are classified into more than two categories. (page 461)

Important Formulas and Tests

A goodness-of-fit test for multinomial probabilities: page 464

A test for homogeneity: page 464

A goodness-of-fit test for a normal distribution: page 467

A chi-square test for independence: page 474

Supplementary Exercises

connect

13.22 A large supermarket conducted a consumer preference study by recording the brand of wheat bread purchased by customers in its stores. The supermarket carries four brands of wheat bread. In a random sample of 200 purchasers, the numbers of purchasers preferring Brands *A*, *B*, *C*, and *D* of the wheat bread were, respectively, 51, 82, 27, and 40. **(1)** Test the null hypothesis that the four brands are equally preferred by setting α equal to .05. **(2)** Find a 95 percent confidence interval for the proportion of all purchasers who prefer Brand *B*. 🖸 BreadPref

13.23 An occupant traffic study was carried out to aid in the remodeling of a large building on a university campus. The building has five entrances, and the choice of entrance was recorded for a random sample of 300 persons entering the building. The numbers of persons using Entrances 1, 2, 3, 4, and 5 were, respectively, 30, 91, 97, 40, and 42. **(1)** Test the null hypothesis that the five entrances are equally used by setting α equal to .05. **(2)** Find a 95 percent confidence interval for the proportion of all people who use Entrance 3. 🖸 EntrPref

13.24 In an article in *Accounting and Business Research,* Meier, Alam, and Pearson studied auditor lobbying on several proposed U.S. accounting standards that affect banks and savings and loan associations. As part of this study, the authors investigated auditors' positions regarding proposed changes in accounting standards that would increase client firms' reported earnings. It was hypothesized that auditors would favor such proposed changes because their clients' managers would receive higher compensation (salary, bonuses, and so on) when client earnings were reported to be higher. Table 13.9 summarizes auditor and client positions (in favor or opposed) regarding proposed changes in accounting standards that would increase client firms' reported earnings. Here the auditor and client positions are cross-classified versus the size of the client firm. 🖸 AuditPos

  a Test to determine whether auditor positions regarding earnings-increasing changes in accounting standards depend on the size of the client firm. Use $\alpha = .05$.

  b Test to determine whether client positions regarding earnings-increasing changes in accounting standards depend on the size of the client firm. Use $\alpha = .05$.

  c Carry out a graphical analysis to investigate a possible relationship between (1) auditor positions and the size of the client firm and (2) client positions and the size of the client firm.

  d Does the relationship between position and the size of the client firm seem to be similar for both auditors and clients? Explain.

13.25 In the book *Business Research Methods* (5th ed.), Donald R. Cooper and C. William Emory discuss a market researcher for an automaker who is studying consumer preferences for styling features of larger sedans. Buyers, who were classified as "first-time" buyers or "repeat" buyers, were asked to express their preference for one of two types of styling—European styling or Japanese styling. Of 40 first-time buyers, 8 preferred European styling and 32 preferred Japanese styling. Of 60 repeat buyers, 40 preferred European styling, and 20 preferred Japanese styling.

  a Set up a contingency table for these data.

  b Test the hypothesis that buyer status (repeat versus first-time) and styling preference are independent at the .05 level of significance. What do you conclude?

  c Carry out a graphical analysis to investigate the nature of any relationship between buyer status and styling preference. Describe the relationship.

TABLE 13.9 Auditor and Client Positions Regarding Earnings-Increasing Changes in Accounting Standards ⒟S AuditPos

(a) Auditor Positions

	Large Firms	Small Firms	Total
In Favor	13	130	143
Opposed	10	24	34
Total	23	154	177

(b) Client Positions

	Large Firms	Small Firms	Total
In Favor	12	120	132
Opposed	11	34	45
Total	23	154	177

Source: Heidi Hylton Meier, Pervaiz Alam, and Michael A. Pearson, "Auditor Lobbying for Accounting Standards: The Case of Banks and Savings and Loan Associations," *Accounting and Business Research* 23, no. 92 (1993), pp. 477–487.

TABLE 13.10 Auditor Positions Regarding Earnings-Decreasing Changes in Accounting Standards ⒟S AuditPos2

	Large Firms	Small Firms	Total
In Favor	27	152	179
Opposed	29	154	183
Total	56	306	362

Source: Heidi Hylton Meier, Pervaiz Alam, and Michael A. Pearson, "Auditor Lobbying for Accounting Standards: The Case of Banks and Savings and Loan Associations," *Accounting and Business Research* 23, no. 92 (1993), pp. 477–487.

TABLE 13.11 Results of the Coupon Redemption Study ⒟S Coupon

Coupon Redemption Level	Store Location			Total
	Midtown	North Side	South Side	
High	69	97	52	218
Medium	101	93	76	270
Low	30	10	72	112
Total	200	200	200	600

TABLE 13.12 A Sample of 65 Customer Satisfaction Ratings ⒟S VideoGame

39	46	42	40	45	44	44	44	45
45	44	46	46	46	41	46	46	
38	40	40	41	43	38	48	39	
42	39	47	43	47	43	44	41	
42	40	44	39	43	36	41	44	
41	42	43	43	41	44	45	42	
38	45	45	46	40	44	44	47	
42	44	45	45	43	45	44	43	

FIGURE 13.5 MINITAB Output of a Chi-Square Test for Independence in the Coupon Redemption Study

```
Expected counts are below observed counts

            Midtown    North    South    Total
High            69        97       52      218
             72.67     72.67    72.67

Medium         101        93       76      270
             90.00     90.00    90.00

Low             30        10       72      112
             37.33     37.33    37.33

Total          200       200      200      600

Chi-Sq = 71.476, DF = 4, P-Value = 0.000
```

13.26 Again consider the situation of Exercise 13.24. Table 13.10 summarizes auditor positions regarding proposed changes in accounting standards that would decrease client firms' reported earnings. Determine whether the relationship between auditor position and the size of the client firm is the same for earnings-decreasing changes in accounting standards as it is for earnings-increasing changes in accounting standards. Justify your answer using both a statistical test and a graphical analysis. ⒟S AuditPos2

13.27 The manager of a chain of three discount drug stores wishes to investigate the level of discount coupon redemption at its stores. All three stores have the same sales volume. Therefore, the manager will randomly sample 200 customers at each store with regard to coupon usage. The survey results are given in Table 13.11. Test the hypothesis that redemption level and location are independent with $\alpha = .01$. Use the MINITAB output in Figure 13.5. ⒟S Coupon

13.28 THE VIDEO GAME SATISFACTION RATING CASE

Consider the sample of 65 customer satisfaction ratings given in Table 13.12. Carry out a chi-square goodness-of-fit test of normality for the population of all customer satisfaction ratings. Recall that we previously calculated $\bar{x} = 42.95$ and $s = 2.6424$ for the 65 ratings. ⒟S VideoGame

Note: An Internet exercise for this chapter is on page 485.

Appendix 13.1 ■ Chi-Square Tests Using Excel

Chi-square goodness-of-fit test in Exercise 13.10 on page 469 (data file: Invoice2.xlsx):

- In the first row of the spreadsheet, enter the following column headings in order—Percent, Expected, Number, and ChiSqContribution. Also enter the heading *P*-Value in cell C11.

- Beginning in cell A2, enter the "percentage of invoice figures" from Exercise 13.10 as decimal fractions into column A.

- Compute expected values. Enter the formula =500*A2 into cell B2 and press Enter. Copy this formula through cell B6 by double-clicking the drag handle (in the lower right corner) of cell B2.

- Enter the "number of invoice figures" from Exercise 13.10 into cells C2 through C6.

- Compute cell chi-square contributions. In cell D2, enter the formula =(C2 − B2)^2/B2 and press Enter. Copy this formula through cell D6 by double-clicking the drag handle (in the lower right corner) of cell D2.

- Compute the chi-square statistic in cell D8. Use the mouse to select the range of cells D2:D8 and click the Σ button on the Excel ribbon.

- Click on an empty cell, say cell A12, and select the Insert Function button f_x on the Excel ribbon.

- In the Insert Function dialog box, select Statistical from the "Or select a category:" menu, select CHISQ.DIST from the "Select a function:" menu, and click OK.

- In the "CHISQ.DIST Function Arguments" dialog box, enter D8 into the "X" window, enter 3 into the "Deg_freedom" window, and enter 1 into the Cumulative window.

- Click OK in the "CHISQ.DIST Function Arguments" dialog box. The left tail area related to the value of the chi-square statistic is entered into cell A12.

- To calculate the *p*-value related to the chi-square statistic, enter the cell formula = 1.0 − A12 into cell C12. This produces the *p*-value in cell C12.

Contingency table and chi-square test of independence in Figure 13.2(a) on page 471 (data file: Invest. xlsx):

- Follow the instructions given in Appendix 2.1 for using a PivotTable to construct a contingency table of fund type versus level of customer satisfaction and place the table in a new worksheet.

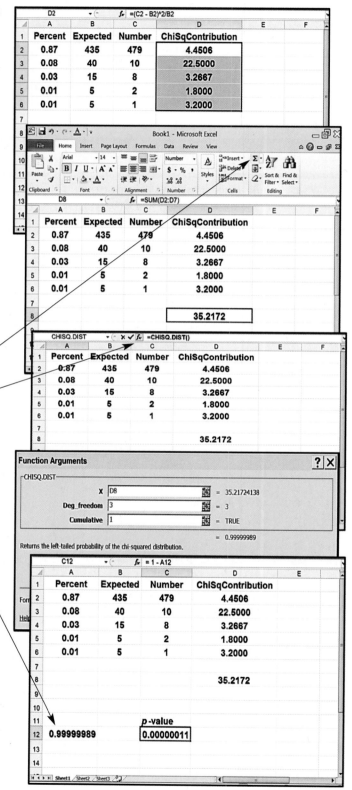

To compute a table of expected values:

- In cell B9, type the formula =$E4*B$7/$E$7 (be very careful to include the $ in all the correct places) and press the Enter key (to obtain the expected value 12 in cell B9).

- Click on cell B9 and use the mouse to point the cursor to the drag handle (in the lower right corner) of the cell. The cursor will change to a black cross. Using the black cross, drag the handle right to cell D9 and release the mouse button to fill cells C9:D9. With B9:D9 still selected, use the black cross to drag the handle down to cell D11. Release the mouse button to fill cells B10:D11.

- To add marginal totals, select the range B9:E12 and click the Σ button on the Excel ribbon.

To compute the chi-square statistic:

- In cell B14, type the formula = (B4 – B9)^2/B9 and press the Enter key to obtain the cell contribution 0.75 in cell B14.

- Click on cell B14 and (using the procedure described above) use the "black cross cursor" to drag the cell handle right to cell D14 and then down to cell D16 (obtaining the cell contributions in cells B14:D16).

- To add marginal totals, select the cell range B14:E17 and click the Σ button on the Excel ribbon.

- The chi-square statistic is in cell E17 (= 46.4375).

To compute the *p*-value for the chi-square test of independence:

- Click on an empty cell, say C19.

- Select the Insert Function button f_x on the Excel ribbon.

- In the Insert Function dialog box, select Statistical from the "Or select a category:" menu, select CHISQ.DIST from the "Select a function:" menu, and click OK.

- In the "CHISQ.DIST Function Arguments" dialog box, enter E17 (the cell location of the chi-square statistic) into the "X" window, 4 into the "Deg_freedom" window, and 1 into the "Cumulative" window.

- Click OK in the "CHISQ.DIST Function Arguments" dialog box.

- To produce the *p*-value related to the chi-square statistic, type the cell formula = 1.0 − C19 into cell C20.

The *p*-value related to the chi-square statistic can also be obtained by using the CHISQ.TEST function. To do this, we enter the range of the values of the observed cell frequencies (here, B4:D6) into the "Actual_range" window, and we enter the range of the expected cell frequencies (here, B9:D11) into the "Expected_range" window. When we click OK in the CHISQ.TEST Function Arguments

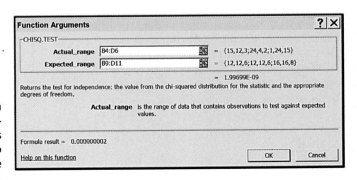

dialog box, this function returns the *p*-value in a single spreadsheet cell.

Appendix 13.2 ■ Chi-Square Tests Using MegaStat

Contingency table and chi-square test of independence similar to Figure 13.2(a) on page 471 (data file: Invest.xlsx):

- Follow the instructions given in Appendix 2.2 for using MegaStat to construct a contingency table of fund type versus level of customer satisfaction.

- After having made entries to specify the row and column variables for the table, in the list of Output Options place a checkmark in the "chi-square" checkbox.

- If desired, row, column, and cell percentages can be obtained by placing checkmarks in the "% of row," "% of column," and "% of total" checkboxes in the list of Output Options. Here we have elected to not request these percentages.

- Click OK in the Crosstabulation dialog box.

- The value of the chi-square statistic (= 46.44) and its related *p*-value (= 0.000000002) are given below the contingency table.

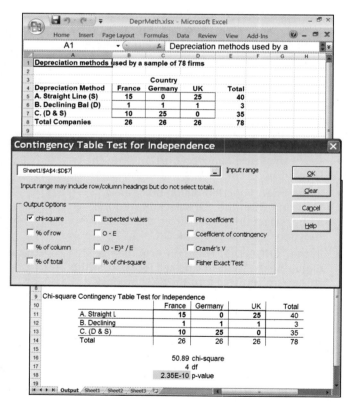

Chi-square test for independence with contingency table input data in the depreciation situation of Exercise 13.18 on page 476 (data file: DeprMeth.xlsx):

- Enter the depreciation method contingency table data in Table 13.5 on page 476 as shown in the screen—depreciation methods in rows and countries in columns.

- Select **Add-Ins : MegaStat : Chi-square/ Crosstab : Contingency Table.**

- In the "Contingency Table Test for Independence" dialog box, click in the Input Range window and (by dragging the mouse) enter the range A4:D7. Note that the entered range may contain row and column labels, but the range should not include the "Total" row or "Total" column.

- In the list of Output Options, check the chi-square checkbox to obtain the results of the chi-square test for independence.

- If desired, row, column, and cell percentages can be obtained by placing checkmarks in the "% of row," "% of column," and "% of total" checkboxes in the list of Output Options. Here we have elected to not request these percentages.

- Click OK in the "Contingency Table Test for Independence" dialog box.

Chi-square goodness-of-fit test for the scanner panel data in Exercise 13.8 on page 468 (data file: ScanPan.xlsx):

- Enter the scanner panel data in Exercise 13.8 (page 468) as shown in the screen with the number of purchases for each brand in column C and with the market share for each brand (expressed as a percentage) in column D. Note that the total number of purchases for all brands equals 19,115 (which is in cell C11).

- In cell E4, type the cell formula =D4*19115 and press Enter to compute the expected frequency for the Jif—18 ounce brand/size combination. Copy this cell formula (by double-clicking the drag handle in the lower right corner of cell E4) to compute the expected frequencies for each of the other brands in cells E5 through E10.

- Select **Add-Ins : MegaStat : Chi-square/ Crosstab : Goodness of Fit Test.**

- In the "Goodness of Fit Test" dialog box, click in the "Observed values Input range" window and enter the range C4:C10. Enter this range by dragging with the mouse—the AutoExpand feature cannot be used in the "Goodness of Fit Test" dialog box.

- Click in the "Expected values Input range" window, and enter the range E4:E10. Again, enter this range by dragging with the mouse.

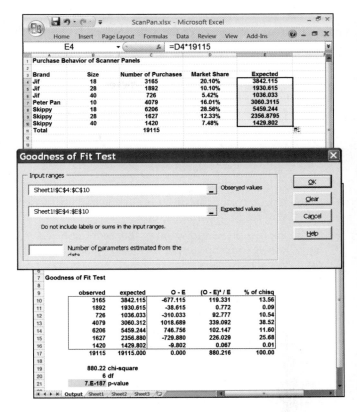

- Click OK in the "Goodness of Fit Test" dialog box.

Appendix 13.3 ■ Chi-Square Tests Using MINITAB

Contingency table and chi-square test of independence for the client satisfaction data as in Figure 13.2(b) on page 471 (data file: Invest.MTW):

- Follow the instructions for constructing a contingency table of fund type versus level of client satisfaction as given in Appendix 2.3.

- After entering the categorical variables into the "Cross Tabulation and Chi-Square" dialog box, click on the Chi-Square... button.

- In the "Cross Tabulation—Chi-Square" dialog box, place checkmarks in the "Chi-Square analysis" and "Expected cell counts" check boxes and click OK.

- Click OK in the "Cross Tabulation and Chi-Square" dialog box to obtain results in the Session window.

The chi-square statistic can also be calculated from summary data by entering the cell counts from Figure 13.2 and by selecting "Chi-Square Test (Table in Worksheet)" from the Stat : Tables submenu.

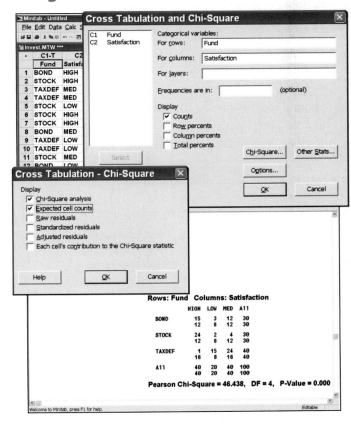

Chi-square test for goodness-of-fit in Figure 13.1 on page 463 (data file: MicroWav.MTW):

- Enter the microwave oven data from Tables 13.1 and 13.2 on page 461—observed frequencies in column C1 with variable name Frequency and market shares (entered as decimal fractions) in column C2 with variable name MarketShr.

To compute the chi-square statistic:

- Select **Calc : Calculator.**
- In the Calculator dialog box, enter Expected into the "Store result in variable" box.
- In the Expression window, enter 400*MarketShr and click OK to compute the expected values.
- Select **Calc : Calculator.**
- Enter ChiSq into the "Store result in variable" box.
- In the Expression window enter the formula (Frequency − Expected)**2/Expected and click OK to compute the cell chi-square contributions.
- Select **Calc : Column Statistics.**
- In the Column Statistics dialog box, click on Sum.
- Enter ChiSq in the "Input variable" box.
- Enter k1 in the "Store result in" box and click OK to compute the chi-square statistic and to store it as the constant k1.
- The chi-square statistic will be displayed in the session window.

To compute the *p*-value for the test:

We first compute the probability of obtaining a value of the chi-square statistic that is less than or equal to the computed value (= 8.77857):

- Select **Calc : Probability Distributions : Chi-Square.**
- In the Chi-Square Distribution dialog box, click on "Cumulative probability."
- Enter 3 in the "Degrees of freedom" box.
- Click the "Input constant" option and enter k1 into the corresponding box.
- Enter k2 into the "Optional storage" box.
- Click OK in the Chi-Square Distribution dialog box. This computes the needed probability and stores its value as a constant, k2.

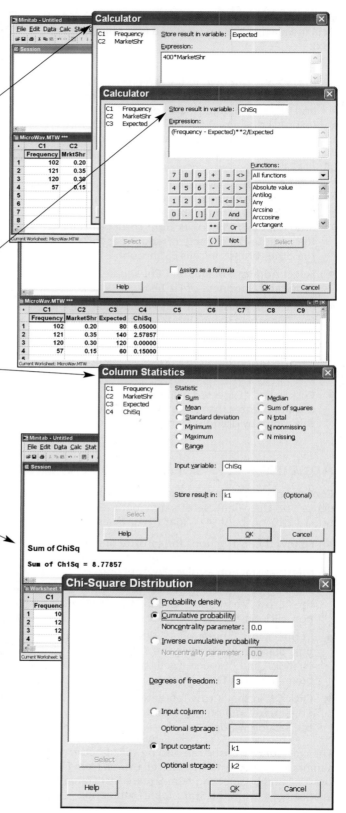

- Select **Calc : Calculator.**
- In the Calculator dialog box, enter PValue into the "Store result in variable" box.
- In the Expression window, enter the formula $1 - k2$, and click OK to compute the p-value related to the chi-square statistic.

To display the p-value:

- Select **Data : Display Data.**
- Enter PValue in the "Columns, constants, and matrices to display" window and click OK.

Sum of ChiSq (= 8.77857) is the chi-square statistic, and PValue (= 0.0323845) is the corresponding p-value.

13.29   Internet Exercise

A report on the 1995 National Health Risk Behavior Survey, conducted by the Centers for Disease Control and Prevention, can be found at the CDC website [http://www.cdc.gov: More Data & Statistics: CDC Data & Statistics Resources, Surveys Tab: CDC Surveys, Youth Risk Behavior Surveillance System (YRBSS): Publications and Data Files, YRBSS Publications: MMWR: Youth Risk Behavior Surveillance – National College Health Risk Behavior Survey – United States, 1995, or, directly, go to www.cdc.gov/mmwr/PDF/SS/SS4504.pdf]. Among the issues addressed in the survey was whether the subjects had, in the prior 30 days, ridden with a driver who had been drinking alcohol. Does the proportion of students exhibiting this selected risk behavior vary by ethnic group? The report includes tables summarizing the "Ridden Drinking" risk behavior by ethnic group (Table 3) and the ethnic composition (Table 1) for a sample of $n = 4,609$ college students. The "Ridden Drinking" and ethnic group information is extracted from Tables 1 and 3 and is displayed as proportions or probabilities in the leftmost panel of the table below. Note that the values in the body of the leftmost panel are given as conditional prob-

abilities, the probabilities of exhibiting the "Ridden Drinking" risk behavior, given ethnic group. These conditional probabilities can be multiplied by the appropriate marginal probabilities to compute the joint probabilities for all the risk behavior by ethnic group combinations to obtain the summaries in the center panel. Finally, the joint probabilities are multiplied by the sample size to obtain projected counts for the number of students in each "Ridden Drinking" by ethnic group combination. The "Other" ethnic group was omitted from the Table 3 summaries and is thus not included in this analysis.

Is there sufficient evidence to conclude that the proportion of college students exhibiting the "Ridden Drinking" behavior varies by ethnic group? Conduct a chi-square test for independence using the projected count data provided in the rightmost panel of the summary table. (Data are available in MINITAB and Excel files, YouthRisk.MTW and YouthRisk.xlsx.) Test at the 0.01 level of significance and report an approximate p-value for your test. Be sure to clearly state your hypotheses and conclusion. **DS** YouthRisk

	Conditional Probabilities [Table 3: P(R|E). Table 1: P(E)]			Joint Probabilities [P(ER) = P(R|E)P(E)]			Projected Counts [n = 4609] [n(ER) = P(ER) × 4609]		
	Ridden Drinking?			Ridden Drinking?			Ridden Drinking?		
Ethnic	%Y|Eth	%N|Eth	% Ethnic	Yes	No	Total	Yes	No	Total
White	0.383	0.617	0.728	0.2788	0.4492	0.7280	1,285	2,070	3,355
Black	0.275	0.725	0.103	0.0283	0.0747	0.1030	131	344	475
Hispanic	0.307	0.693	0.071	0.0218	0.0492	0.0710	100	227	327

Simple Linear Regression Analysis

Learning Objectives

After mastering the material in this chapter, you will be able to:

LO14-1 Explain the simple linear regression model.

LO14-2 Find the least squares point estimates of the slope and y-intercept.

LO14-3 Describe the assumptions behind simple linear regression and calculate the standard error.

LO14-4 Test the significance of the slope and y-intercept.

LO14-5 Calculate and interpret a confidence interval for a mean value and a prediction interval for an individual value.

LO14-6 Calculate and interpret the simple coefficients of determination and correlation.

LO14-7 Test hypotheses about the population correlation coefficient.

LO14-8 Test the significance of a simple linear regression model by using an F-test.

LO14-9 Use residual analysis to check the assumptions of simple linear regression.

Chapter Outline

anagers often make decisions by studying the relationships between variables, and process improvements can often be made by understanding how changes in one or more variables affect the process output. **Regression analysis** is a statistical technique in which we use observed data to relate a variable of interest, which is called the **dependent** (or **response**) **variable,** to one or more **independent** (or **predictor**) **variables.** The objective is to build a **regression model,** or **prediction equation,** that can be used to **describe, predict,** and **control** the dependent variable on the basis of the independent variables. For example, a company might wish to improve its marketing process. After collecting data concerning the demand for a product, the product's price, and the advertising

expenditures made to promote the product, the company might use regression analysis to develop an equation to predict demand on the basis of price and advertising expenditure. Predictions of demand for various price–advertising expenditure combinations can then be used to evaluate potential changes in the company's marketing strategies.

In the next two chapters we give a thorough presentation of regression analysis. We begin in this chapter by presenting **simple linear regression** analysis. Using this technique is appropriate when we are relating a dependent variable to a single independent variable and when *a straight-line model* describes the relationship between these two variables. We explain many of the methods of this chapter in the context of two new cases:

The Tasty Sub Shop Case: A business entrepreneur uses simple linear regression analysis to predict the yearly revenue for a potential restaurant site on the basis of the number of residents living near the site. The entrepreneur then uses the prediction to assess the profitability of the potential restaurant site.

The QHIC Case: The marketing department at Quality Home Improvement Center (QHIC) uses simple linear regression analysis to predict home upkeep expenditure on the basis of home value. Predictions of home upkeep expenditures are used to help determine which homes should be sent advertising brochures promoting QHIC's products and services.

14.1 The Simple Linear Regression Model and the Least Squares Point Estimates ● ● ●

LO14-1 Explain the simple linear regression model.

The simple linear regression model   The **simple linear regression model** assumes that the relationship between the **dependent variable, which is denoted y,** and the **independent variable, denoted x,** can be approximated by a straight line. We can tentatively decide whether there is an approximate straight-line relationship between y and x by making a **scatter diagram,** or **scatter plot,** of y versus x. First, data concerning the two variables are observed in pairs. To construct the scatter plot, each value of y is plotted against its corresponding value of x. If the y values tend to increase or decrease in a straight-line fashion as the x values increase, and if there is a scattering of the (x, y) points around the straight line, then it is reasonable to describe the relationship between y and x by using the simple linear regression model. We illustrate this in the following case study.

EXAMPLE 14.1 The Tasty Sub Shop Case: Predicting Yearly Revenue for a Potential Restaurant Site

Part 1: Purchasing a Tasty Sub Shop franchise   The Tasty Sub Shop is a restaurant chain that sells franchises to business entrepreneurs. Like Quiznos and Subway, the Tasty Sub Shop does not construct a standard, recognizable building to house each of its restaurants. Instead, the entrepreneur wishing to purchase a Tasty Sub franchise finds a suitable site, which consists of a suitable geographical location and suitable store space to rent. Then, when Tasty Sub approves the site, an architect and a contractor are hired to remodel the store rental space and thus "build" the Tasty Sub Shop restaurant. Franchise regulations allow Tasty Sub (and other chains) to help entrepreneurs understand the factors that affect restaurant profitability and to provide basic guidance in evaluating potential restaurant sites. However, in order to prevent restaurant chains from overpredicting profits and thus misleading potential franchise owners, these regulations

TABLE 14.1	The Tasty Sub Shop Revenue Data

DS TastySub1

Restaurant	Population Size, x (Thousands of Residents)	Yearly Revenue, y (Thousands of Dollars)
1	20.8	527.1
2	27.5	548.7
3	32.3	767.2
4	37.2	722.9
5	39.6	826.3
6	45.1	810.5
7	49.9	1040.7
8	55.4	1033.6
9	61.7	1090.3
10	64.6	1235.8

FIGURE 14.1 Excel Output of a Scatter Plot of y versus x

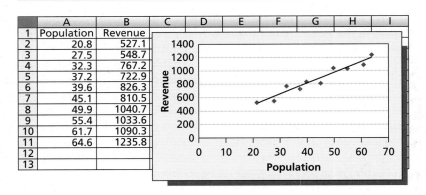

make each individual entrepreneur responsible for predicting the profits of his or her potential restaurant sites.

In this case study we consider a business entrepreneur who has found several potential sites for a Tasty Sub Shop restaurant. Similar to most existing Tasty Sub restaurant sites, each of the entrepreneur's sites is a store rental space located in an outdoor shopping area that is close to one or more residential areas. For a Tasty Sub restaurant built on such a site, yearly revenue is known to partially depend on (1) the number of residents living near the site and (2) the amount of business and shopping near the site. Referring to the number of residents living near a site as *population size* and to the yearly revenue for a Tasty Sub restaurant built on the site as *yearly revenue,* the entrepreneur will—in this chapter—try to predict the **dependent (response) variable** yearly revenue (y) on the basis of the **independent (predictor) variable** population size (x). (In the next chapter the entrepreneur will also use the amount of business and shopping near a site to help predict yearly revenue.) To predict yearly revenue on the basis of population size, the entrepreneur randomly selects 10 existing Tasty Sub restaurants that are built on sites similar to the sites that the entrepreneur is considering. The entrepreneur then asks the owner of each existing restaurant what the restaurant's revenue y was last year and estimates—with the help of the owner and published demographic information—the number of residents, or population size x, living near the site. The values of y (measured in thousands of dollars) and x (measured in thousands of residents) that are obtained are given in Table 14.1. In Figure 14.1 we give an Excel output of a scatter plot of y versus x. This plot shows (1) a tendency for the yearly revenues to increase in a straight-line fashion as the population sizes increase and (2) a scattering of points around the straight line. A **regression model** describing the relationship between y and x must represent these two characteristics. We now develop such a model.

Part 2: The simple linear regression model The **simple linear regression model** relating y to x can be expressed as follows:

$$y = \beta_0 + \beta_1 x + \varepsilon$$

This model says that the values of y can be represented by a *mean level* ($\mu_y = \beta_0 + \beta_1 x$) that changes in a straight line fashion as x changes, combined with random fluctuations (described by the error term ε) that cause the values of y to deviate from the mean level. Here:

1 The **mean level** $\mu_y = \beta_0 + \beta_1 x$ is the mean yearly revenue corresponding to a particular population size x. That is, noting that different Tasty Sub restaurants could potentially be built near different populations of the same size x, the mean level $\mu_y = \beta_0 + \beta_1 x$ is the mean of the yearly revenues that would be obtained by all such restaurants. In addition, because $\mu_y = \beta_0 + \beta_1 x$ is the equation of a straight line, the mean yearly revenues that correspond to increasing values of the population size x lie on a straight line. For example,

FIGURE 14.2   The Simple Linear Regression Model Relating Yearly Revenue (*y*) to Population (*x*)

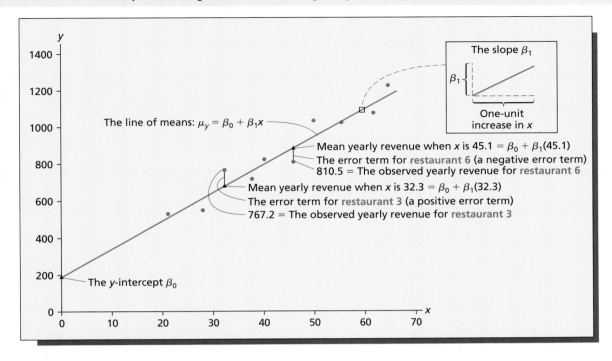

Table 14.1 tells us that 32,300 residents live near restaurant 3 and 45,100 residents live near restaurant 6. It follows that the mean yearly revenue for all Tasty Sub restaurants that could potentially be built near populations of 32,300 residents is $\beta_0 + \beta_1(32.3)$. Similarly, the mean yearly revenue for all Tasty Sub restaurants that could potentially be built near populations of 45,100 residents is $\beta_0 + \beta_1(45.1)$. Figure 14.2 depicts these two mean yearly revenues as triangles that lie on the straight line $\mu_y = \beta_0 + \beta_1 x$, which we call the **line of means.** The unknown parameters β_0 and β_1 are the **y-intercept** and the **slope** of the line of means. When we estimate β_0 and β_1 in the next subsection, we will be able to estimate mean yearly revenue μ_y on the basis of the population size x.

2   The **y-intercept** β_0 of the line of means can be understood by considering Figure 14.2. As illustrated in this figure, the y-intercept β_0 is the mean yearly revenue for all Tasty Sub restaurants that could potentially be built near populations of zero residents. However, because it is unlikely that a Tasty Sub restaurant would be built near a population of zero residents, this interpretation of β_0 is of dubious practical value. There are many regression situations where the y-intercept β_0 lacks a practical interpretation. In spite of this, statisticians have found that β_0 is almost always an important component of the line of means and thus of the simple linear regression model.

3   The **slope** β_1 of the line of means can also be understood by considering Figure 14.2. As illustrated in this figure, the slope β_1 is the change in mean yearly revenue that is associated with a one-unit increase (that is, a 1,000 resident increase) in the population size x.

4   The **error term** ε of the simple linear regression model accounts for any factors affecting yearly revenue other than the population size x. Such factors would include the amount of business and shopping near a restaurant and the skill of the owner as an operator of the restaurant. For example, Figure 14.2 shows that the error term for restaurant 3 is positive. Therefore, the observed yearly revenue $y = 767.2$ for restaurant 3 is above the corresponding mean yearly revenue for all restaurants that have $x = 32.3$. As another example, Figure 14.2 also shows that the error term for restaurant 6 is negative. Therefore, the observed yearly revenue $y = 810.5$ for restaurant 6 is below the corresponding mean yearly revenue for all restaurants that have $x = 45.1$. Of course, because we do not know the true values of β_0 and β_1, the relative positions of the quantities pictured in Figure 14.2 are only hypothetical.

FIGURE 14.3   The Simple Linear Regression Model (Here the Slope β_1 Is Positive)

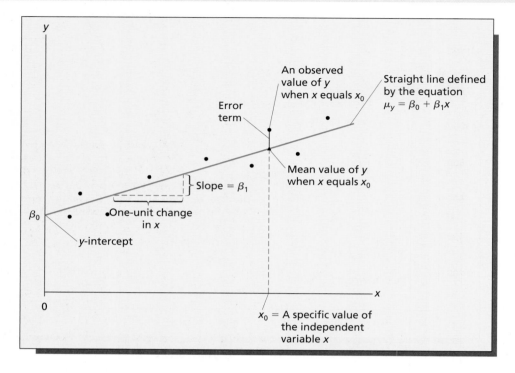

With the Tasty Sub Shop example as background, we are ready to define the **simple linear regression model relating the dependent variable y to the independent variable x.** We suppose that we have gathered n observations—each observation consists of an observed value of x and its corresponding value of y. Then:

The Simple Linear Regression Model

The **simple linear (or straight line) regression model** is: $y = \beta_0 + \beta_1 x + \varepsilon$
Here

1 $\mu_y = \beta_0 + \beta_1 x$ is the **mean value** of the dependent variable y when the value of the independent variable is x.

2 β_0 is the **y-intercept.** β_0 is the mean value of y when x equals zero.

3 β_1 is the **slope.** β_1 is the change (amount of increase or decrease) in the mean value of y associated with a one-unit increase in x. If β_1 is positive, the mean value of y increases as x increases. If β_1 is negative, the mean value of y decreases as x increases.

4 ε is an **error term** that describes the effects on y of all factors other than the value of the independent variable x.

This model is illustrated in Figure 14.3 (note that x_0 in this figure denotes a specific value of the independent variable x). The y-intercept β_0 and the slope β_1 are called **regression parameters.** In addition, we have interpreted the slope β_1 to be the change in the mean value of y associated with a one-unit increase in x. We sometimes refer to this change as *the effect of the independent variable x on the dependent variable y.* However, we cannot prove that a *change in an independent variable causes a change in the dependent variable.* Rather, regression can be used only to establish that the two variables move together and that the independent variable contributes information for predicting the dependent variable. For instance, regression analysis might be used to establish that as liquor sales have increased over the years, college professors' salaries have also increased. However, this does not prove that increases in liquor sales cause increases in college professors' salaries. Rather, both variables are influenced by a third variable—long-run growth in the national economy.

FIGURE 14.4   **An Estimated Regression Line Drawn through the Tasty Sub Shop Revenue Data**

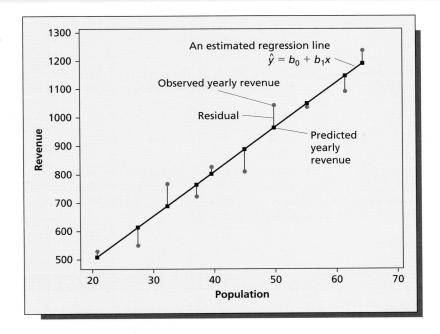

The least squares point estimates   Suppose that we have gathered n observations (x_1, y_1), $(x_2, y_2), \ldots, (x_n, y_n)$, where each observation consists of a value of an independent variable x and a corresponding value of a dependent variable y. Also, suppose that a scatter plot of the n observations indicates that the simple linear regression model relates y to x. In order to estimate the y-intercept β_0 and the slope β_1 of the line of means of this model, we could visually draw a line—called an **estimated regression line**—through the scatter plot. Then, we could read the y-intercept and slope off the estimated regression line and use these values as the point estimates of β_0 and β_1. Unfortunately, if different people visually drew lines through the scatter plot, their lines would probably differ from each other. What we need is the "best line" that can be drawn through the scatter plot. Although there are various definitions of what this best line is, one of the most useful best lines is the *least squares line*.

To understand the least squares line, we let

$$\hat{y} = b_0 + b_1 x$$

denote the general equation of an estimated regression line drawn through a scatter plot. Here, because we will use this line to predict y on the basis of x, we call $\hat{y}$ *the predicted value of y* when the value of the independent variable is x. In addition, b_0 is the y-intercept and b_1 is the slope of the estimated regression line. When we determine numerical values for b_0 and b_1, these values will be the point estimates of the y-intercept β_0 and the slope β_1 of the line of means. To explain which estimated regression line is the least squares line, we begin with the Tasty Sub Shop situation. Figure 14.4 shows an estimated regression line drawn through a scatter plot of the Tasty Sub Shop revenue data. In this figure the red dots represent the 10 observed yearly revenues and the black squares represent the 10 predicted yearly revenues given by the estimated regression line. Furthermore, the line segments drawn between the red dots and black squares represent *residuals,* which are the differences between the observed and predicted yearly revenues. Intuitively, if a particular estimated regression line provides a good "fit" to the Tasty Sub Shop revenue data, it will make the predicted yearly revenues "close" to the observed yearly revenues, and thus the residuals given by the line will be small. The *least squares line* is the line that minimizes the sum of squared residuals. That is, the least squares line is the line positioned on the scatter plot so as to minimize the sum of the squared vertical distances between the observed and predicted yearly revenues.

LO14-2 Find the least squares point estimates of the slope and y-intercept.

To define the least squares line in a general situation, consider an arbitrary observation (x_i, y_i) in a sample of n observations. For this observation, the **predicted value of the dependent variable y** given by an estimated regression line is

$$\hat{y}_i = b_0 + b_1 x_i$$

Furthermore, the difference between the observed and predicted values of y, $y_i - \hat{y}_i$, is the **residual** for the observation, and the **sum of squared residuals** for all n observations is

$$SSE = \sum_{i=1}^{n} (y_i - \hat{y}_i)^2$$

The **least squares line** is the line that minimizes SSE. To find this line, we find the values of the y-intercept b_0 and slope b_1 that give values of $\hat{y}_i = b_0 + b_1 x_i$ that minimize SSE. These values of b_0 and b_1 are called the **least squares point estimates** of β_0 and β_1. Using calculus, it can be shown that these estimates are calculated as follows:[1]

The Least Squares Point Estimates

For the simple linear regression model:

1 The **least squares point estimate of the slope β_1** is

$$b_1 = \frac{SS_{xy}}{SS_{xx}} \quad \text{where}$$

$$SS_{xy} = \sum (x_i - \bar{x})(y_i - \bar{y}) = \sum x_i y_i - \frac{\left(\sum x_i\right)\left(\sum y_i\right)}{n} \quad \text{and} \quad SS_{xx} = \sum (x_i - \bar{x})^2 = \sum x_i^2 - \frac{\left(\sum x_i\right)^2}{n}$$

2 The **least squares point estimate of the y-intercept β_0** is

$$b_0 = \bar{y} - b_1 \bar{x} \quad \text{where}$$

$$\bar{y} = \frac{\sum y_i}{n} \quad \text{and} \quad \bar{x} = \frac{\sum x_i}{n}$$

Here n is the number of observations (an observation is an observed value of x and its corresponding value of y).

The following example illustrates how to calculate these point estimates and how to use these point estimates to estimate mean values and predict individual values of the dependent variable. Note that the quantities SS_{xy} and SS_{xx} used to calculate the least squares point estimates are also used throughout this chapter to perform other important calculations.

---

[1]In order to simplify notation, we will often drop the limits on summations in this and subsequent chapters. That is, instead of using the summation $\sum_{i=1}^{n}$ we will simply write $\sum$.

EXAMPLE 14.2 The Tasty Sub Shop Case: The Least Squares Estimates   C

Part 1: Calculating the least squares point estimates   Again consider the Tasty Sub Shop problem. To compute the least squares point estimates of the regression parameters β_0 and β_1 we first calculate the following preliminary summations:

y_i	x_i	x_i^2	$x_i y_i$
527.1	20.8	$(20.8)^2 = 432.64$	$(20.8)(527.1) = 10963.68$
548.7	27.5	$(27.5)^2 = 756.25$	$(27.5)(548.7) = 15089.25$
767.2	32.3	$(32.3)^2 = 1,043.29$	$(32.3)(767.2) = 24780.56$
722.9	37.2	$(37.2)^2 = 1,383.84$	$(37.2)(722.9) = 26891.88$
826.3	39.6	$(39.6)^2 = 1,568.16$	$(39.6)(826.3) = 32721.48$
810.5	45.1	$(45.1)^2 = 2,034.01$	$(45.1)(810.5) = 36553.55$
1040.7	49.9	$(49.9)^2 = 2,490.01$	$(49.9)(1040.7) = 51930.93$
1033.6	55.4	$(55.4)^2 = 3,069.16$	$(55.4)(1033.6) = 57261.44$
1090.3	61.7	$(61.7)^2 = 3,806.89$	$(61.7)(1090.3) = 67271.51$
1235.8	64.6	$(64.6)^2 = 4,173.16$	$(64.6)(1235.8) = 79832.68$
$\sum y_i = 8603.1$	$\sum x_i = 434.1$	$\sum x_i^2 = 20,757.41$	$\sum x_i y_i = 403,296.96$

Using these summations, we calculate SS_{xy} and SS_{xx} as follows.

$$SS_{xy} = \sum x_i y_i - \frac{\left(\sum x_i\right)\left(\sum y_i\right)}{n}$$

$$= 403,296.96 - \frac{(434.1)(8603.1)}{10}$$

$$= 29,836.389$$

$$SS_{xx} = \sum x_i^2 - \frac{\left(\sum x_i\right)^2}{n}$$

$$= 20,757.41 - \frac{(434.1)^2}{10}$$

$$= 1913.129$$

It follows that the least squares point estimate of the slope β_1 is

$$b_1 = \frac{SS_{xy}}{SS_{xx}} = \frac{29,836.389}{1913.129} = 15.596$$

Furthermore, because

$$\bar{y} = \frac{\sum y_i}{n} = \frac{8603.1}{10} = 860.31 \quad \text{and} \quad \bar{x} = \frac{\sum x_i}{n} = \frac{434.1}{10} = 43.41$$

the least squares point estimate of the y-intercept β_0 is

$$b_0 = \bar{y} - b_1\bar{x} = 860.31 - (15.596)(43.41) = 183.31$$

(where we have used more decimal place accuracy than shown to obtain the result 183.31).

Because $b_1 = 15.596$, we estimate that mean yearly revenue at Tasty Sub restaurants increases by 15.596 (that is by \$15,596) for each one-unit (1,000 resident) increase in the population size x. Because $b_0 = 183.31$, we estimate that mean yearly revenue for all Tasty Sub restaurants that could potentially be built near populations of zero residents is \$183,310. However, because it is unlikely that a Tasty Sub restaurant would be built near a population of zero residents, this interpretation is of dubious practical value.

The least squares line

$$\hat{y} = b_0 + b_1 x = 183.31 + 15.596x$$

is sometimes called the *least squares prediction equation*. In Table 14.2 (on the next page) we summarize using this prediction equation to calculate the predicted yearly revenues and the

TABLE 14.2   Calculation of *SSE* Obtained by Using the Least Squares Point Estimates

y_i	x_i	$\hat{y}_i = 183.31 + 15.596x_i$	$y_i - \hat{y}_i$
527.1	20.8	$183.31 + 15.596(20.8) = 507.69$	19.41
548.7	27.5	$183.31 + 15.596(27.5) = 612.18$	-63.48
767.2	32.3	687.04	80.16
722.9	37.2	763.46	-40.56
826.3	39.6	800.89	25.41
810.5	45.1	886.67	-76.17
1040.7	49.9	961.53	79.17
1033.6	55.4	1047.30	-13.70
1090.3	61.7	1145.55	-55.25
1235.8	64.6	1190.78	45.02

$$SSE = \sum (y_i - \hat{y}_i)^2 = (19.41)^2 + (-63.48)^2 + \cdots + (45.02)^2 = 30{,}460.21$$

Note: The predictions and residuals in this table are taken from MINITAB, which uses values of b_0 and b_1 that are more precise than the rounded values we have calculated by hand. If you use the formula $\hat{y}_i = 183.31 + 15.596x_i$, your figures may differ slightly from those given here.

FIGURE 14.5   The MINITAB Output of the Least Squares Line

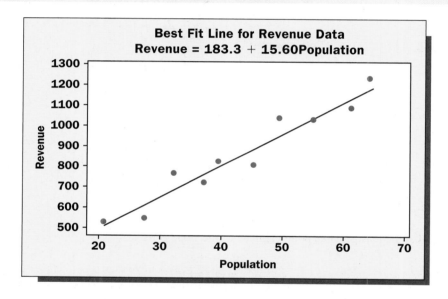

residuals for the 10 observed Tasty Sub restaurants. For example, because the population size for restaurant 1 was 20.8, the predicted yearly revenue for restaurant 1 is

$$\hat{y}_1 = 183.31 + 15.596(20.8) = 507.69$$

It follows, because the observed yearly revenue for restaurant 1 was $y_1 = 527.1$, that the residual for restaurant 1 is

$$y_1 - \hat{y}_1 = 527.1 - 507.69 = 19.41$$

If we consider all of the residuals in Table 14.2 and add their squared values, we find that *SSE*, the sum of squared residuals, is 30,460.21. This *SSE* value will be used throughout this chapter. Figure 14.5 gives the MINITAB output of the least squares line. Note that this output gives (within rounding) the least squares estimates we have calculated ($b_0 = 183.3$ and $b_1 = 15.60$). In general, we will rely on Excel and MINITAB to compute the least squares estimates (and to perform many other regression calculations).

Part 2: Estimating a mean yearly revenue and predicting an individual yearly revenue   We define the **experimental region** to be the range of the previously observed population sizes. Referring to Table 14.2, we see that the experimental region consists of the range

FIGURE 14.6   Point Estimation and Point Prediction, and the Danger of Extrapolation

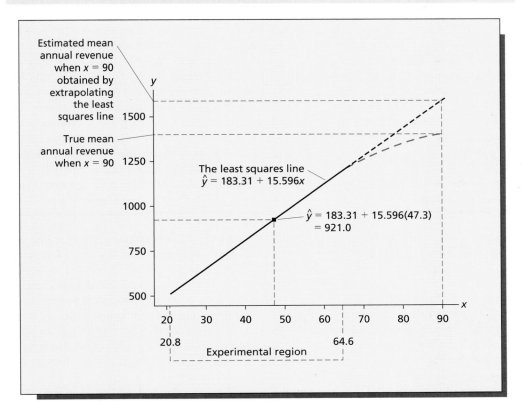

of population sizes from 20.8 to 64.6. The simple linear regression model relates yearly revenue y to population size x for values of x that are in the experimental region. For such values of x, the least squares line is the estimate of the line of means. It follows that the point on the least squares line corresponding to a population size of x

$$\hat{y} = b_0 + b_1 x$$

is the point estimate of $\beta_0 + \beta_1 x$, the mean yearly revenue for all Tasty Sub restaurants that could potentially be built near populations of size x. In addition, we predict the error term ε to be 0. Therefore, $\hat{y}$ is also the *point prediction* of an *individual value* $y = \beta_0 + \beta_1 x + \varepsilon$, which is the yearly revenue for a single (individual) Tasty Sub restaurant that is built near a population of size x. Note that the reason we predict the error term ε to be zero is that, because of several *regression assumptions* to be discussed in the next section, ε has a 50 percent chance of being positive and a 50 percent chance of being negative.

For example, suppose that one of the business entrepreneur's potential restaurant sites is near a population of 47,300 residents. Because $x = 47.3$ is in the experimental region,

$$\hat{y} = 183.31 + 15.596(47.3)$$
$$= 921.0 \text{ (that is, \$921,000)}$$

is

1   The **point estimate** of the mean yearly revenue for all Tasty Sub restaurants that could potentially be built near populations of 47,300 residents.

2   The **point prediction** of the yearly revenue for a single Tasty Sub restaurant that is built near a population of 47,300 residents.

Figure 14.6 illustrates $\hat{y} = 921.0$ as a square on the least squares line. Moreover, suppose that the yearly rent and other fixed costs for the entrepreneur's potential restaurant will be $257,550 and that (according to Tasty Sub corporate headquarters) the yearly food and other variable costs for the restaurant will be 60 percent of the yearly revenue. Because we predict that the yearly revenue for the restaurant will be \$921,000, it follows that we predict that the yearly total operating cost for the restaurant will be \$257,550 + .6(\$921,000) = \$810,150. In addition, if we subtract this predicted yearly operating cost from the predicted yearly revenue of \$921,000, we predict that the yearly profit for the restaurant will be \$110,850. Of course, these predictions are point predictions. In Section 14.4 we will predict the restaurant's yearly revenue and profit *with confidence*.

To conclude this example, note that Figure 14.6 illustrates the potential danger of using the least squares line to predict outside the experimental region. In the figure, we extrapolate the least squares line beyond the experimental region to obtain a prediction for a population size of $x = 90$. As shown in Figure 14.6, for values of x in the experimental region (that is, between 20.8 and 64.6) the observed values of y tend to increase in a straight-line fashion as the values of x increase. However, for population sizes greater than $x = 64.6$, we have no data to tell us whether the relationship between y and x continues as a straight-line relationship or, possibly, becomes a curved relationship. If, for example, this relationship becomes the sort of curved relationship shown in Figure 14.6, then extrapolating the straight-line prediction equation to obtain a prediction for $x = 90$ would overestimate mean yearly revenue (see Figure 14.6).

The previous example illustrates that when we are using a least squares regression line, we should not estimate a mean value or predict an individual value unless the corresponding value of x is in the **experimental region**—the range of the previously observed values of x. Often the value $x = 0$ is not in the experimental region. In such a situation, it would not be appropriate to interpret the y-intercept b_0 as the estimate of the mean value of y when x equals 0. For example, consider the Tasty Sub Shop problem. Figure 14.6 illustrates that the population size $x = 0$ is not in the experimental region. Therefore, it would not be appropriate to use $b_0 = 183.31$ as the point estimate of the mean yearly revenue for all Tasty Sub restaurants that could potentially be built near populations of zero residents. Because it is not meaningful to interpret the y-intercept in many regression situations, we often omit such interpretations.

We now present a general procedure for estimating a mean value and predicting an individual value:

Point Estimation and Point Prediction in Simple Linear Regression

Let b_0 and b_1 be the least squares point estimates of the y-intercept β_0 and the slope β_1 in the simple linear regression model, and suppose that x_0, a specified value of the independent variable x, is inside the experimental region. Then

$$\hat{y} = b_0 + b_1 x_0$$

1 is the **point estimate** of the **mean value of the dependent variable** when the value of the independent variable is x_0.

2 is the **point prediction** of an **individual value of the dependent variable** when the value of the independent variable is x_0. Here we predict the error term to be 0.

Exercises for Section 14.1

CONCEPTS

connect

14.1 What is the least squares regression line, and what are the least squares point estimates?

14.2 Why is it dangerous to extrapolate outside the experimental region?

METHODS AND APPLICATIONS

In Exercises 14.3 through 14.8 we present six data sets involving a dependent variable y and an independent variable x. For each data set, assume that the simple linear regression model

$$y = \beta_0 + \beta_1 x + \varepsilon$$

relates y to x.

14.3   THE NATURAL GAS CONSUMPTION CASE 🟢 GasCon1

On the next page we give the average hourly outdoor temperature (x) in a city during a week and the city's natural gas consumption (y) during the week for each of eight weeks (the temperature readings are expressed in degrees Fahrenheit and the natural gas consumptions are expressed in

Week	Average Hourly Temperature, x (°F)	Natural Gas Consumption, y (MMcf)
1	28.0	12.4
2	28.0	11.7
3	32.5	12.4
4	39.0	10.8
5	45.9	9.4
6	57.8	9.5
7	58.1	8.0
8	62.5	7.5

DS GasCon1

millions of cubic feet of natural gas—denoted MMcf). The output to the right of the data is obtained when MINITAB is used to fit a least squares line to the natural gas consumption data.

a Find the least squares point estimates b_0 and b_1 on the computer output and report their values. Interpret b_0 and b_1. Is an average hourly temperature of 0°F in the experimental region? What does this say about the interpretation of b_0?

b Use the facts that $SS_{xy} = -179.6475$; $SS_{xx} = 1{,}404.355$; $\bar{y} = 10.2125$; and $\bar{x} = 43.98$ to hand calculate (within rounding) b_0 and b_1.

c Use the least squares line to compute a point estimate of the mean natural gas consumption for all weeks having an average hourly temperature of 40°F and a point prediction of the natural gas consumption for an individual week having an average hourly temperature of 40°F.

14.4   THE STARTING SALARY CASE   DS StartSal

The chairman of the marketing department at a large state university undertakes a study to relate starting salary (y) after graduation for marketing majors to grade point average (GPA) in major courses. To do this, records of seven recent marketing graduates are randomly selected, and the data shown below on the left are obtained. The MINITAB output obtained by fitting a least squares regression line to the data is below on the right.

Marketing Graduate	GPA, x	Starting Salary, y (Thousands of Dollars)
1	3.26	33.8
2	2.60	29.8
3	3.35	33.5
4	2.86	30.4
5	3.82	36.4
6	2.21	27.6
7	3.47	35.3

DS StartSal

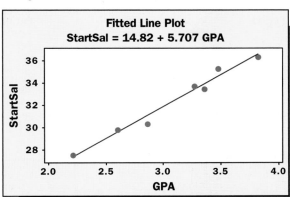

a Find the least squares point estimates b_0 and b_1 on the computer output and report their values. Interpret b_0 and b_1. Does the interpretation of b_0 make practical sense?

b Use the least squares line to compute a point estimate of the mean starting salary for all marketing graduates having a grade point average of 3.25 and a point prediction of the starting salary for an individual marketing graduate having a grade point average of 3.25.

14.5   THE SERVICE TIME CASE   DS SrvcTime

Accu-Copiers, Inc., sells and services the Accu-500 copying machine. As part of its standard service contract, the company agrees to perform routine service on this copier. To obtain information about the time it takes to perform routine service, Accu-Copiers has collected data for 11 service calls. The data and Excel output from fitting a least squares regression line to the data follow on the next page.

Service Call	Number of Copiers Serviced, x	Number of Minutes Required, y
1	4	109
2	2	58
3	5	138
4	7	189
5	1	37
6	3	82
7	4	103
8	5	134
9	2	68
10	4	112
11	6	154

DS SrvcTime

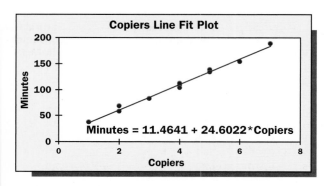

a Find the least squares point estimates b_0 and b_1 on the computer output and report their values. Interpret b_0 and b_1. Does the interpretation of b_0 make practical sense?

b Use the least squares line to compute a point estimate of the mean time to service four copiers and a point prediction of the time to service four copiers on a single call.

14.6   THE FRESH DETERGENT CASE   DS Fresh

Enterprise Industries produces Fresh, a brand of liquid laundry detergent. In order to study the relationship between price and demand for the large bottle of Fresh, the company has gathered data concerning demand for Fresh over the last 30 sales periods (each sales period is four weeks). Here, for each sales period,

   y = demand for the large bottle of Fresh (in hundreds of thousands of bottles) in the sales period, and

   x = the difference between the average industry price (in dollars) of competitors' similar detergents and the price (in dollars) of Fresh as offered by Enterprise Industries in the sales period.

The data and MINITAB output from fitting a least squares regression line to the data follow below.

Fresh Detergent Demand Data

Sales Period	y	x	Sales Period	y	x
1	7.38	−.05	24	8.50	.10
2	8.51	.25	25	8.75	.50
3	9.52	.60	26	9.21	.60
4	7.50	0	27	8.27	−.05
5	9.33	.25	28	7.67	0
6	8.28	.20	29	7.93	.05
7	8.75	.15	30	9.26	.55
8	7.87	.05			
9	7.10	−.15			
10	8.00	.15			
11	7.89	.20			
12	8.15	.10			
13	9.10	.40			
14	8.86	.45			
15	8.90	.35			
16	8.87	.30			
17	9.26	.50			
18	9.00	.50			
19	8.75	.40			
20	7.95	−.05			
21	7.65	−.05			
22	7.27	−.10			
23	8.00	.20			

DS Fresh

a Find the least squares point estimates b_0 and b_1 on the computer output and report their values.

b Interpret b_0 and b_1. Does the interpretation of b_0 make practical sense?

c Write the equation of the least squares line.

d Use the least squares line to compute a point estimate of the mean demand in all sales periods when the price difference is .10 and a point prediction of the actual demand in an individual sales period when the price difference is .10.

14.7 THE DIRECT LABOR COST CASE ⊙S DirLab

An accountant wishes to predict direct labor cost (y) on the basis of the batch size (x) of a product produced in a job shop. Data for 12 production runs are given in the table below, along with the Excel output from fitting a least squares regression line to the data.

Direct Labor Cost Data ⊙S DirLab

Direct Labor Cost, y ($100s)	Batch Size, x
71	5
663	62
381	35
138	12
861	83
145	14
493	46
548	52
251	23
1024	100
435	41
772	75

Batch Size Line Fit Plot

LaborCost = 18.488 + 10.146*BSize

a By using the formulas illustrated in Example 14.2 (see page 493) and the data provided, verify that (within rounding) $b_0 = 18.488$ and $b_1 = 10.146$, as shown on the Excel output.

b Interpret the meanings of b_0 and b_1. Does the interpretation of b_0 make practical sense?

c Write the least squares prediction equation.

d Use the least squares line to obtain a point estimate of the mean direct labor cost for all batches of size 60 and a point prediction of the direct labor cost for an individual batch of size 60.

14.8 THE REAL ESTATE SALES PRICE CASE ⊙S RealEst

A real estate agency collects data concerning y = the sales price of a house (in thousands of dollars), and x = the home size (in hundreds of square feet). The data are given in the table below. The MINITAB output from fitting a least squares regression line to the data is on the next page.

Real Estate Sales Price Data ⊙S RealEst

Sales Price (y)	Home Size (x)	Sales Price (y)	Home Size (x)
180	23	165.9	21
98.1	11	193.5	24
173.1	20	127.8	13
136.5	17	163.5	19
141	15	172.5	25

Source: Reprinted with permission from *The Real Estate Appraiser and Analyst,* Spring 1986 issue. Copyright 1986 by the Appraisal Institute, Chicago, Illinois.

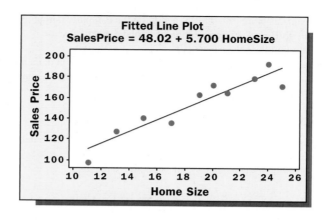

a   By using the formulas illustrated in Example 14.2 (see page 493) and the data provided, verify that (within rounding) $b_0 = 48.02$ and $b_1 = 5.700$, as shown on the MINITAB output.

b   Interpret the meanings of b_0 and b_1. Does the interpretation of b_0 make practical sense?

c   Write the least squares prediction equation.

d   Use the least squares line to obtain a point estimate of the mean sales price of all houses having 2,000 square feet and a point prediction of the sales price of an individual house having 2,000 square feet.

LO14-3 Describe the assumptions behind simple linear regression and calculate the standard error.

14.2 Model Assumptions and the Standard Error ● ● ●

Model assumptions   In order to perform hypothesis tests and set up various types of intervals when using the simple linear regression model

$$y = \beta_0 + \beta_1 x + \varepsilon$$

we need to make certain assumptions about the error term ε. At any given value of x, there is a population of error term values that could potentially occur. These error term values describe the different potential effects on y of all factors other than the value of x. Therefore, these error term values explain the variation in the y values that could be observed when the independent variable is x. Our statement of the simple linear regression model assumes that μ_y, the mean of the population of all y values that could be observed when the independent variable is x, is $\beta_0 + \beta_1 x$. This model also implies that $\varepsilon = y - (\beta_0 + \beta_1 x)$, so this is equivalent to assuming that the mean of the corresponding population of potential error term values is 0. In total, we make four assumptions (called the **regression assumptions**) about the simple linear regression model. These assumptions can be stated in terms of potential y values or, equivalently, in terms of potential error term values. Following tradition, we begin by stating these assumptions in terms of potential error term values:

The Regression Assumptions

1   At any given value of x, the population of potential error term values has a **mean equal to 0**.

2   **Constant Variance Assumption**
At any given value of x, the population of potential error term values has a variance that does not depend on the value of x. That is, the different populations of potential error term values corresponding to different values of x have **equal variances**. We denote the **constant variance** as σ^2.

3   **Normality Assumption**
At any given value of x, the population of potential error term values has a **normal distribution**.

4   **Independence Assumption**
Any one value of the error term ε is **statistically independent** of any other value of ε. That is, the value of the error term ε corresponding to an observed value of y is statistically independent of the value of the error term corresponding to any other observed value of y.

FIGURE 14.7   An Illustration of the Model Assumptions

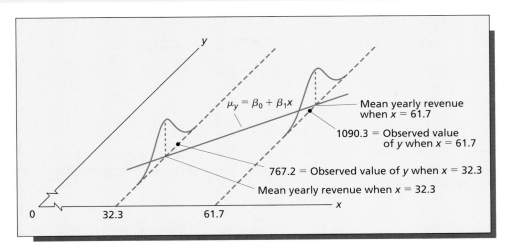

Taken together, the first three assumptions say that, at any given value of x, the population of potential error term values is **normally distributed** with **mean zero** and a **variance σ^2 that does not depend on the value of x.** Because the potential error term values cause the variation in the potential y values, these assumptions imply that the population of all y values that could be observed when the independent variable is x is **normally distributed** with **mean $\beta_0 + \beta_1 x$ and a variance σ^2 that does not depend on x.** These three assumptions are illustrated in Figure 14.7 in the context of the Tasty Sub Shop problem. Specifically, this figure depicts the populations of yearly revenues corresponding to two values of the population size x—32.3 and 61.7. Note that these populations are shown to be normally distributed with different means (each of which is on the line of means) and with the same variance (or spread).

The independence assumption is most likely to be violated when time series data are being utilized in a regression study. For example, the natural gas consumption data in Exercise 14.3 are time series data. Intuitively, the independence assumption says that there is no pattern of positive error terms being followed (in time) by other positive error terms, and there is no pattern of positive error terms being followed by negative error terms. That is, there is no pattern of higher-than-average y values being followed by other higher-than-average y values, and there is no pattern of higher-than-average y values being followed by lower-than-average y values.

It is important to point out that the regression assumptions very seldom, if ever, hold exactly in any practical regression problem. However, it has been found that regression results are not extremely sensitive to mild departures from these assumptions. In practice, only pronounced departures from these assumptions require attention. In Section 14.9 we show how to check the regression assumptions. Prior to doing this, we will suppose that the assumptions are valid in our examples.

In Section 14.1 we stated that, when we predict an individual value of the dependent variable, we predict the error term to be 0. To see why we do this, note that the regression assumptions state that, at any given value of the independent variable, the population of all error term values that can potentially occur is normally distributed with a mean equal to 0. Because we also assume that successive error terms (observed over time) are statistically independent, each error term has a 50 percent chance of being positive and a 50 percent chance of being negative. Therefore, it is reasonable to predict any particular error term value to be 0.

The mean square error and the standard error   To present statistical inference formulas in later sections, we need to be able to compute point estimates of σ^2 and σ, the constant variance and standard deviation of the error term populations. The point estimate of σ^2 is called the **mean square error** and the point estimate of σ is called the **standard error.** In the following box, we show how to compute these estimates:

The Mean Square Error and the Standard Error

I f the regression assumptions are satisfied and *SSE* is the sum of squared residuals:

1 The point estimate of σ^2 is the **mean square error**

$$s^2 = \frac{SSE}{n-2}$$

2 The point estimate of σ is the **standard error**

$$s = \sqrt{\frac{SSE}{n-2}}$$

In order to understand these point estimates, recall that σ^2 is the variance of the population of *y* values (for a given value of *x*) around the mean value μ_y. Because $\hat{y}$ is the point estimate of this mean, it seems natural to use

$$SSE = \sum (y_i - \hat{y}_i)^2$$

to help construct a point estimate of σ^2. We divide *SSE* by $n - 2$ because it can be proven that doing so makes the resulting s^2 an unbiased point estimate of σ^2. Here we call $n - 2$ the **number of degrees of freedom** associated with *SSE*.

EXAMPLE 14.3 The Tasty Sub Shop Case: The Standard Error

Consider the Tasty Sub Shop situation, and recall that in Table 14.2 (page 494) we have calculated the sum of squared residuals to be $SSE = 30{,}460.21$. It follows, because we have observed $n = 10$ yearly revenues, that the point estimate of σ^2 is the mean square error

$$s^2 = \frac{SSE}{n-2} = \frac{30{,}460.21}{10-2} = 3807.526$$

This implies that the point estimate of σ is the standard error

$$s = \sqrt{s^2} = \sqrt{3807.526} = 61.7052$$

To conclude this section, note that in optional Section 14.10 we present a shortcut formula for calculating *SSE*. The reader may study Section 14.10 now or at any later point.

Exercises for Section 14.2

CONCEPTS

14.9 What four assumptions do we make about the simple linear regression model?

14.10 What is estimated by the mean square error, and what is estimated by the standard error?

METHODS AND APPLICATIONS

14.11 THE NATURAL GAS CONSUMPTION CASE   **DS** GasCon1

When a least squares line is fit to the 8 observations in the natural gas consumption data, we obtain $SSE = 2.568$. Calculate s^2 and s.

14.12 THE STARTING SALARY CASE   **DS** StartSal

When a least squares line is fit to the 7 observations in the starting salary data, we obtain $SSE = 1.438$. Calculate s^2 and s.

14.13 THE SERVICE TIME CASE   **DS** SrvcTime

When a least squares line is fit to the 11 observations in the service time data, we obtain $SSE = 191.7017$. Calculate s^2 and s.

14.14　THE FRESH DETERGENT CASE　DS Fresh

When a least squares line is fit to the 30 observations in the Fresh detergent data, we obtain $SSE = 2.806$. Calculate s^2 and s.

14.15　THE DIRECT LABOR COST CASE　DS DirLab

When a least squares line is fit to the 12 observations in the labor cost data, we obtain $SSE = 746.7624$. Calculate s^2 and s.

14.16　THE REAL ESTATE SALES PRICE CASE　DS RealEst

When a least squares line is fit to the 10 observations in the real estate sales price data, we obtain $SSE = 896.8$. Calculate s^2 and s.

14.17　Ten sales regions of equal sales potential for a company were randomly selected. The advertising expenditures (in units of $10,000) in these 10 sales regions were purposely set during July of last year at, respectively, 5, 6, 7, 8, 9, 10, 11, 12, 13 and 14. The sales volumes (in units of $10,000) were then recorded for the 10 sales regions and found to be, respectively, 89, 87, 98, 110, 103, 114, 116, 110, 126, and 130. Assuming that the simple linear regression model is appropriate, it can be shown that $b_0 = 66.2121$, $b_1 = 4.4303$, and $SSE = 222.8242$. Calculate s^2 and s.　DS SalesPlot

14.3 Testing the Significance of the Slope and y-Intercept ● ● ●

LO14-4 Test the significance of the slope and y-intercept.

Testing the significance of the slope　A simple linear regression model is not likely to be useful unless there is a **significant relationship between y and x.** In order to judge the significance of the relationship between y and x, we test the null hypothesis

$$H_0: \beta_1 = 0$$

which says that there is no change in the mean value of y associated with an increase in x, versus the alternative hypothesis

$$H_a: \beta_1 \neq 0$$

which says that there is a (positive or negative) change in the mean value of y associated with an increase in x. It would be reasonable to conclude that x is significantly related to y if we can be quite certain that we should reject H_0 in favor of H_a.

In order to test these hypotheses, recall that we compute the least squares point estimate b_1 of the true slope β_1 by using a sample of n observed values of the dependent variable y. Different samples of n observed y values would yield different values of the least squares point estimate b_1. It can be shown that, if the regression assumptions hold, then the population of all possible values of b_1 is normally distributed with a mean of β_1 and with a standard deviation of

$$\sigma_{b_1} = \frac{\sigma}{\sqrt{SS_{xx}}}$$

The standard error s is the point estimate of σ, so it follows that a point estimate of σ_{b_1} is

$$s_{b_1} = \frac{s}{\sqrt{SS_{xx}}}$$

which is called the **standard error of the estimate b_1.** Furthermore, if the regression assumptions hold, then the population of all values of

$$\frac{b_1 - \beta_1}{s_{b_1}}$$

has a t distribution with $n - 2$ degrees of freedom. It follows that, if the null hypothesis $H_0: \beta_1 = 0$ is true, then the population of all possible values of the test statistic

$$t = \frac{b_1}{s_{b_1}}$$

has a t distribution with $n - 2$ degrees of freedom. Therefore, we can test the significance of the regression relationship as follows:

Testing the Significance of the Regression Relationship: Testing the Significance of the Slope

Null Hypothesis $H_0: \beta_1 = 0$ **Test Statistic** $t = \dfrac{b_1}{s_{b_1}}$ where $s_{b_1} = \dfrac{s}{\sqrt{SS_{xx}}}$ **Assumptions** The regression assumptions

Here $t_{\alpha/2}$, t_α, and all p-values are based on $n - 2$ degrees of freedom. **If we can reject H_0: $\beta_1 = 0$ at a given value of α, then we conclude that the slope (or, equivalently, the regression relationship) is significant at the α level.**

We usually use the two-sided alternative H_a: $\beta_1 \neq 0$ for this test of significance. However, sometimes a one-sided alternative is appropriate. For example, in the Tasty Sub Shop problem we can say that if the slope β_1 is not 0, then it must be positive. A positive β_1 would say that mean yearly revenue increases as the population size x increases. Because of this, it would be appropriate to decide that x is significantly related to y if we can reject H_0: $\beta_1 = 0$ in favor of the one-sided alternative H_a: $\beta_1 > 0$. Although this test would be slightly more effective than the usual two tailed test, there is little practical difference between using the one tailed or two tailed test. Furthermore, computer packages (such as Excel and MINITAB) present results for the two tailed test. For these reasons we will emphasize the two tailed test in future discussions.

It should also be noted that

1   **If we can decide that the slope is significant at the .05 significance level,** then we have concluded that x is significantly related to y by using a test that allows only a .05 probability of concluding that x is significantly related to y when it is not. **This is usually regarded as strong evidence that the regression relationship is significant.**

2   **If we can decide that the slope is significant at the .01 significance level, this is usually regarded as very strong evidence that the regression relationship is significant.**

3   **The smaller the significance level α at which H_0 can be rejected, the stronger is the evidence that the regression relationship is significant.**

EXAMPLE 14.4 The Tasty Sub Shop Case: Testing the Significance of the Slope

Again consider the Tasty Sub Shop revenue model. For this model $SS_{xx} = 1913.129$, $b_1 = 15.596$, and $s = 61.7052$ [see Examples 14.2 (page 493) and 14.3 (page 502)]. Therefore,

$$s_{b_1} = \frac{s}{\sqrt{SS_{xx}}} = \frac{61.7052}{\sqrt{1913.129}} = 1.411$$

and

$$t = \frac{b_1}{s_{b_1}} = \frac{15.596}{1.411} = 11.05$$

FIGURE 14.8   **Excel and MINITAB Outputs of a Simple Linear Regression Analysis of the Tasty Sub Shop Revenue Data**

(a) The Excel Output

Regression Statistics

Multiple R	0.9688
R Square	0.9386 [9]
Adjusted R Square	0.9309
Standard Error	61.7052 [8]
Observations	10

ANOVA	df	SS	MS	F	Significance F
Regression	1	465316.3004 [10]	465316.3004	122.2096 [13]	0.0000 [14]
Residual	8	30460.2086 [11]	3807.5261		
Total	9	495776.5090 [12]			

	Coefficients	Standard Error	t Stat	P-value [7]	Lower 95%	Upper 95%
Intercept	183.3051 [1]	64.2741 [3]	2.8519 [5]	0.0214	35.0888	331.5214
Population	15.5956 [2]	1.4107 [4]	11.0548 [6]	0.0000	12.3424 [19]	18.8488 [19]

(b) The MINITAB Output

```
The regression equation is
Revenue = 183 + 15.6 Population

Predictor          Coef          SE Coef               T             P 7
Constant         183.31 1        64.27 3           2.85 5        0.021
Population        15.596 2        1.411 4          11.05 6        0.000

S = 61.7052 8                  R-Sq = 93.9% 9        R-Sq(adj) = 93.1%

Analysis of Variance
Source             DF            SS              MS             F        P-value
Regression          1        465316 10         465316      122.21 13    0.000 14
Residual Error      8         30460 11           3808
Total               9        495777 12

 Predicted Values for New Observations
    New Obs         Fit 15      SE Fit 16          95% CI 17          95% PI 18
        1           921.0         20.3        (874.2, 967.7)    (771.2, 1070.7)

Values of Predictors for New Observations
    New Obs     Population
        1           47.3
```

---

[1] b_0 = point estimate of the y-intercept   [2] b_1 = point estimate of the slope   [3] s_{b_0} = standard error of the estimate b_0 [4] s_{b_1} = standard error of the estimate b_1 [5] t for testing significance of the y-intercept   [6] t for testing significance of the slope   [7] p-values for t statistics   [8] s = standard error   [9] r^2 [10] Explained variation   [11] SSE = Unexplained variation   [12] Total variation   [13] F(model) statistic   [14] p-value for F(model)   [15] $\hat{y}$ = point prediction when $x = 47.3$ [16] $s_{\hat{y}}$ = standard error of the estimate $\hat{y}$ [17] 95% confidence interval when $x = 47.3$ [18] 95% prediction interval when $x = 47.3$ [19] 95% confidence interval for the slope β_1

Figure 14.8 presents the Excel and MINITAB outputs of a simple linear regression analysis of the Tasty Sub Shop revenue data. Note that b_0 (labeled as [1] on the outputs), b_1 (labeled [2]), s (labeled [8]), s_{b_1} (labeled [4]), and t (labeled [6]) are given on each of these outputs. (The other quantities on the outputs will be discussed later.) In order to test $H_0: \beta_1 = 0$ versus $H_a: \beta_1 \neq 0$ at the $\alpha = .05$ level of significance, we compare $|t| = 11.05$ with $t_{\alpha/2} = t_{.025} = 2.306$, which is based on $n - 2 = 10 - 2 = 8$ degrees of freedom. Because $|t| = 11.05$ is greater than $t_{.025} = 2.306$, we reject $H_0: \beta_1 = 0$ and conclude that there is strong evidence that the slope (regression relationship) is significant. The p-value for testing H_0 versus H_a is twice the area to the right of $|t| = 11.05$ under the curve of the t distribution having $n - 2 = 8$ degrees of freedom. Both the Excel and MINITAB outputs in Figure 14.8 tell us that this p-value is less than .001 (see [7] on the outputs). It follows that we can reject H_0 in favor of H_a at level of significance .05, .01, or .001, which implies that we have extremely strong evidence that the regression relationship between x and y is significant.

A Confidence Interval for the Slope

I f the regression assumptions hold, a **100(1 − α) percent confidence interval for the true slope β_1 is** $[b_1 \pm t_{\alpha/2}s_{b_1}]$. Here $t_{\alpha/2}$ is based on $n - 2$ degrees of freedom.

EXAMPLE 14.5 The Tasty Sub Shop Case: A Confidence Interval for the Slope

The Excel and MINITAB outputs in Figure 14.8 tell us that $b_1 = 15.596$ and $s_{b_1} = 1.411$. Thus, for instance, because $t_{.025}$ based on $n - 2 = 10 - 2 = 8$ degrees of freedom equals 2.306, a 95 percent confidence interval for β_1 is

$$[b_1 \pm t_{.025}s_{b_1}] = [15.596 \pm 2.306(1.411)]$$

$$= [12.342, 18.849]$$

(where we have used more decimal place accuracy than shown to obtain the final result). This interval says we are 95 percent confident that, if the population size increases by one thousand residents, then mean yearly revenue will increase by at least $12,342 and by at most $18,849. Also, because the 95 percent confidence interval for β_1 does not contain 0, we can reject $H_0: \beta_1 = 0$ in favor of $H_a: \beta_1 \neq 0$ at level of significance .05. Note that the 95 percent confidence interval for β_1 is given on the Excel output but not on the MINITAB output (see Figure 14.8).

Testing the significance of the y-intercept We can also test the significance of the y-intercept β_0. We do this by testing the null hypothesis $H_0: \beta_0 = 0$ versus the alternative hypothesis $H_a: \beta_0 \neq 0$. **If we can reject H_0 in favor of H_a by setting the probability of a Type I error equal to α, we conclude that the intercept β_0 is significant at the α level.** To carry out the hypothesis test, we use the test statistic

$$t = \frac{b_0}{s_{b_0}} \quad \text{where} \quad s_{b_0} = s\sqrt{\frac{1}{n} + \frac{\bar{x}^2}{SS_{xx}}}$$

Here the critical value and p-value conditions for rejecting H_0 are the same as those given previously for testing the significance of the slope, except that t is calculated as b_0/s_{b_0}. For example, if we consider the Tasty Sub Shop problem and the Excel and MINITAB outputs in Figure 14.8, we see that $b_0 = 183.31$, $s_{b_0} = 64.27$, $t = 2.85$, and p-value $= .021$. Because $t = 2.85 > t_{.025} = 2.306$ and p-value $< .05$, we can reject $H_0: \beta_0 = 0$ in favor of $H_a: \beta_0 \neq 0$ at the .05 level of significance. This provides strong evidence that the y-intercept β_0 of the line of means does not equal 0 and thus is significant. Therefore, we should include β_0 in the Tasty Sub Shop revenue model.

In general, if we fail to conclude that the intercept is significant at a level of significance of .05, it might be reasonable to drop the y-intercept from the model. However, it is common practice to include the y-intercept whether or not $H_0: \beta_0 = 0$ is rejected. In fact, experience suggests that it is definitely safest, when in doubt, to include the intercept β_0.

Exercises for Section 14.3

CONCEPTS

connect

14.18 What do we conclude if we can reject $H_0: \beta_1 = 0$ in favor of $H_a: \beta_1 \neq 0$ by setting
     a α equal to .05?   **b** α equal to .01?

14.19 Give an example of a practical application of the confidence interval for β_1.

METHODS AND APPLICATIONS

In Exercises 14.20 through 14.25, we refer to Excel and MINITAB outputs of simple linear regression analyses of the data sets related to the six case studies introduced in the exercises for Section 14.1. Using the appropriate output for each case study,
     a   Find the least squares point estimates b_0 and b_1 of β_0 and β_1 on the output and report their values.
     b   Find SSE and s on the computer output and report their values.

c Find s_{b_1} and the *t* statistic for testing the significance of the slope on the output and report their values. Show (within rounding) how *t* has been calculated by using b_1 and s_{b_1} from the computer output.

d Using the *t* statistic and an appropriate critical value, test H_0: $\beta_1 = 0$ versus H_a: $\beta_1 \neq 0$ by setting α equal to .05. Is the slope (regression relationship) significant at the .05 level?

e Using the *t* statistic and an appropriate critical value, test H_0: $\beta_1 = 0$ versus H_a: $\beta_1 \neq 0$ by setting α equal to .01. Is the slope (regression relationship) significant at the .01 level?

f Find the *p*-value for testing H_0: $\beta_1 = 0$ versus H_a: $\beta_1 \neq 0$ on the output and report its value. Using the *p*-value, determine whether we can reject H_0 by setting α equal to .10, .05, .01, and .001. How much evidence is there that the slope (regression relationship) is significant?

g Calculate the 95 percent confidence interval for β_1 using numbers on the output. Interpret the interval.

h Calculate the 99 percent confidence interval for β_1 using numbers on the output.

i Find s_{b_0} and the *t* statistic for testing the significance of the *y* intercept on the output and report their values. Show (within rounding) how *t* has been calculated by using b_0 and s_{b_0} from the computer output.

j Find the *p*-value for testing H_0: $\beta_0 = 0$ versus H_a: $\beta_0 \neq 0$ on the computer output and report its value. Using the *p*-value, determine whether we can reject H_0 by setting α equal to .10, .05, .01, and .001. What do you conclude about the significance of the *y* intercept?

k Using the data set and *s* from the computer output, hand calculate (within rounding) SS_{xx}, s_{b_0}, and s_{b_1}.

14.20 THE NATURAL GAS CONSUMPTION CASE   🌐 GasCon1

The Excel and MINITAB outputs of a simple linear regression analysis of the data set for this case (see Exercise 14.3 on pages 496 and 497) are given in Figures 14.9 and 14.10. Recall that labeled Excel and MINITAB outputs are on page 505. Note that gas consumption is called FuelCons on the MINITAB output of Figure 14.10.

14.21 THE STARTING SALARY CASE   🌐 StartSal

The MINITAB output of a simple linear regression analysis of the data set for this case (see Exercise 14.4 on page 497) is given in Figure 14.11. Recall that a labeled MINITAB regression output is on page 505.

FIGURE 14.9   Excel Output of a Simple Linear Regression Analysis of the Natural Gas Consumption Data

Regression Statistics

Multiple R	0.9484
R Square	0.8995
Adjusted R Square	0.8827
Standard Error	0.6542
Observations	8

ANOVA	df	SS	MS	F	Significance F
Regression	1	22.9808	22.9808	53.6949	0.0003
Residual	6	2.5679	0.4280		
Total	7	25.5488			

	Coefficients	Standard Error	t Stat	P-value	Lower 95%	Upper 95%
Intercept	15.8379	0.8018	19.7535	1.09E-06	13.8760	17.7997
TEMP	–0.1279	0.0175	–7.3277	0.0003	–0.1706	–0.0852

FIGURE 14.10   MINITAB Output of a Simple Linear Regression Analysis of the Natural Gas Consumption Data

```
The regression equation is
FuelCons = 15.8 - 0.128 Temp

Predictor        Coef       SE Coef          T          P
Constant      15.8379        0.8018      19.75      0.000
Temp         -0.12792        0.01746      -7.33      0.000

S = 0.654209      R-Sq = 89.9%        R-Sq(adj) = 88.3%

Analysis of Variance
Source            DF         SS          MS          F          P
Regression         1     22.981      22.981      53.69      0.000
Residual Error     6      2.568       0.428
Total              7     25.549

Values of Predictors for New Obs    Predicted Values for New Observations
New Obs   Temp                       New Obs     Fit    SE Fit        95% CI            95% PI
     1    40.0                             1  10.721     0.241  (10.130, 11.312)  (9.015, 12.427)
```

FIGURE 14.11   MINITAB Output of a Simple Linear Regression Analysis of the
                Starting Salary Data

```
The regression equation is
StartSal = 14.8 + 5.71 GPA

Predictor    Coef   SE Coef      T       P
Constant   14.816     1.235   12.00   0.000
GPA        5.7066    0.3953   14.44   0.000

S = 0.536321   R-Sq = 97.7%   R-Sq(adj) = 97.2%

Analysis of Variance
Source          DF      SS       MS       F       P
Regression       1   59.942   59.942   208.39  0.000
Residual Error   5    1.438    0.288
Total            6   61.380

Values of Predictors for New Obs    Predicted Values for New Observations
New Obs   GPA                       New Obs     Fit   SE Fit       95% CI            95% PI
      1  3.25                             1  33.362    0.213  (32.813, 33.911)  (31.878, 34.846)
```

FIGURE 14.12   Excel Output of a Simple Linear Regression Analysis of the
                Service Time Data

Regression Statistics	
Multiple R	0.9952
R Square	0.9905
Adjusted R Square	0.9894
Standard Error	4.6152
Observations	11

ANOVA	df	SS	MS	F	Significance F
Regression	1	19918.8438	19918.844	935.149	2.094E-10
Residual	9	191.7017	21.300184		
Total	10	20110.5455			

	Coefficients	Standard Error	t Stat	P-value	Lower 95%	Upper 95%
Intercept	11.4641	3.4390	3.3335	0.0087	3.6845	19.2437
Copiers	24.6022	0.8045	30.5802	2.09E-10	22.7823	26.4221

14.22   THE SERVICE TIME CASE   DS SrvcTime

The Excel output of a simple linear regression analysis of the data set for this case (see Exercise 14.5 on pages 497 and 498) is given in Figure 14.12. Recall that a labeled Excel regression output is on page 505.

14.23   THE FRESH DETERGENT CASE   DS Fresh

The MINITAB output of a simple linear regression analysis of the data set for this case (see Exercise 14.6 on page 498) is given in Figure 14.13. Recall that a labeled MINITAB regression output is on page 505.

14.24   THE DIRECT LABOR COST CASE   DS DirLab

The Excel output of a simple linear regression analysis of the data set for this case (see Exercise 14.7 on page 499) is given in Figure 14.14. Recall that a labeled Excel regression output is on page 505.

14.25   THE REAL ESTATE SALES PRICE CASE   DS RealEst

The MINITAB output of a simple linear regression analysis of the data set for this case (see Exercise 14.8 on pages 499 and 500) is given in Figure 14.15. Recall that a labeled MINITAB regression output is on page 505.

14.26 Find and interpret a 95 percent confidence interval for the slope β_1 of the simple linear regression model describing the sales volume data in Exercise 14.17 (page 503).   DS SalesPlot

FIGURE 14.13　　MINITAB Output of a Simple Linear Regression Analysis of the Fresh
　　　　　　　　　Detergent Demand Data

```
The regression equation is
Demand = 7.81 + 2.67 PriceDif

Predictor      Coef   SE Coef      T      P
Constant    7.81409   0.07988  97.82  0.000
PriceDif     2.6652    0.2585  10.31  0.000

S = 0.316561   R-Sq = 79.2%   R-Sq(adj) = 78.4%

Analysis of Variance
Source         DF       SS      MS      F      P
Regression      1   10.653  10.653  106.30  0.000
Residual Error  28   2.806   0.100
Total           29  13.459

Values of Predictors for New Obs    Predicted Values for New Observations
New Obs   PriceDif                  New Obs    Fit   SE Fit     95% CI           95% PI
    1      0.100                        1    8.0806  0.0648  (7.9479, 8.2133)  (7.4187, 8.7425)
    2      0.250                        2    8.4804  0.0586  (8.3604, 8.6004)  (7.8209, 9.1398)
```

FIGURE 14.14　　Excel Output of a Simple Linear Regression Analysis of the
　　　　　　　　　Direct Labor Cost Data

Regression Statistics

Multiple R	0.9996
R Square	0.9993
Adjusted R Square	0.9992
Standard Error	8.6415
Observations	12

ANOVA	df	SS	MS	F	Significance F
Regression	1	1024592.9043	1024592.9043	13720.4677	5.04E-17
Residual	10	746.7624	74.6762		
Total	11	1025339.6667			

	Coefficients	Standard Error	t Stat	P-value	Lower 95%	Upper 95%
Intercept	18.4875	4.6766	3.9532	0.0027	8.0674	28.9076
BatchSize (x)	10.1463	0.0866	117.1344	5.04E-17	9.9533	10.3393

FIGURE 14.15　　MINITAB Output of a Simple Linear Regression Analysis of the Real Estate
　　　　　　　　　Sales Price Data

```
The regression equation is
SPrice = 48.0 + 5.70 HomeSize

Predictor     Coef   SE Coef     T      P
Constant     48.02    14.41    3.33  0.010
HomeSize    5.7003   0.7457    7.64  0.000

S = 10.5880      R-Sq = 88.0%     R-Sq(adj) = 86.5%

Analysis of Variance
Source         DF       SS      MS      F      P
Regression      1    6550.7  6550.7  58.43  0.000
Residual Error  8     896.8   112.1
Total           9    7447.5

Values of Predictors for New Obs    Predicted Values for New Observations
New Obs   HomeSize                  New Obs    Fit   SE Fit     95% CI           95% PI
    1       20.0                        1   162.03   3.47  (154.04, 170.02)  (136.34, 187.72)
```

F I G U R E 1 4 . 1 6   **Excel Output of a Simple Linear Regression Analysis of the Fast-Food Restaurant Rating Data**

Regression Statistics						
Multiple R	0.9873					
R Square	0.9747					
Adjusted R Square	0.9684					
Standard Error	0.1833					
Observations	6					

ANOVA	df	SS	MS	F	Significance F	
Regression	1	5.1817	5.1817	154.2792	0.0002	
Residual	4	0.1343	0.0336			
Total	5	5.3160				

	Coefficients	Standard Error	t Stat	P-value	Lower 95%	Upper 95%
Intercept	−0.1602	0.3029	−0.5289	0.6248	−1.0011	0.6807
MeanTaste (x)	1.2731	0.1025	12.4209	0.0002	0.9885	1.5577

14.27 THE FAST-FOOD RESTAURANT RATING CASE   ⒟ⓢ FastFood

In the early 1990s researchers at The Ohio State University studied consumer ratings of six fast-food restaurants: Borden Burger, Hardee's, Burger King, McDonald's, Wendy's, and White Castle. Each of 406 randomly selected individuals gave each restaurant a rating of 1, 2, 3, 4, 5, or 6 on the basis of taste, and then ranked the restaurants from 1 through 6 on the basis of overall preference. In each case, 1 is the best rating and 6 the worst. The mean ratings given by the 406 individuals are given in the following table:

Restaurant	Mean Taste	Mean Preference
Borden Burger	3.5659	4.2552
Hardee's	3.329	4.0911
Burger King	2.4231	3.0052
McDonald's	2.0895	2.2429
Wendy's	1.9661	2.5351
White Castle	3.8061	4.7812

Figure 14.16 gives the Excel output of a simple linear regression analysis of this data. Here, mean preference is the dependent variable and mean taste is the independent variable. Recall that a labeled Excel regression output is given on page 505.

a Find the least squares point estimate b_1 of β_1 on the computer output. Report and interpret this estimate.

b Find the 95 percent confidence interval for β_1 on the output. Report and interpret the interval.

LO14-5 Calculate and interpret a confidence interval for a mean value and a prediction interval for an individual value.

14.4 Confidence and Prediction Intervals ● ● ●

If the regression relationship between y and x is significant, then

$$\hat{y} = b_0 + b_1 x_0$$

is the **point estimate of the mean value of y** when the value of the independent variable x is x_0. We have also seen that $\hat{y}$ is the **point prediction of an individual value of y** when the value of the independent variable x is x_0. In this section we will assess the accuracy of $\hat{y}$ as both a point estimate and a point prediction. To do this, we will find a **confidence interval for the mean value of y** and a **prediction interval for an individual value of y.**

Because each possible sample of n values of the dependent variable gives values of b_0 and b_1 that differ from the values given by other samples, different samples give different values of

$\hat{y} = b_0 + b_1 x_0$. If the regression assumptions hold, a confidence interval for the mean value of y is based on the estimated standard deviation of the normally distributed population of all possible values of $\hat{y}$. This estimated standard deviation is called the **standard error of $\hat{y}$,** is denoted $s_{\hat{y}}$, and is given by the formula

$$s_{\hat{y}} = s\sqrt{\frac{1}{n} + \frac{(x_0 - \bar{x})^2}{SS_{xx}}}$$

Here, s is the standard error (see Section 14.2), $\bar{x}$ is the average of the n previously observed values of x, and $SS_{xx} = \Sigma x_i^2 - (\Sigma x_i)^2/n$.

As explained above, a confidence interval for the mean value of y is based on the standard error $s_{\hat{y}}$. A prediction interval for an individual value of y is based on a more complex standard error: the estimated standard deviation of the population of all possible values of $y - \hat{y}$, the prediction error obtained when predicting y by $\hat{y}$. We refer to this estimated standard deviation as the **standard error of $y - \hat{y}$** and denote it as $s_{(y-\hat{y})}$. If the regression assumptions hold, the formula for $s_{(y-\hat{y})}$ is

$$s_{(y-\hat{y})} = s\sqrt{1 + \frac{1}{n} + \frac{(x_0 - \bar{x})^2}{SS_{xx}}}$$

Intuitively, the "extra 1" under the radical in the formula for $s_{(y-\hat{y})}$ accounts for the fact that there is *more uncertainty* in predicting an individual value $y = \beta_0 + \beta_1 x_0 + \varepsilon$ than in estimating the mean value $\beta_0 + \beta_1 x_0$ (because we must predict the error term ε when predicting an individual value). Therefore, as shown in the following summary box, the prediction interval for an individual value of y is longer than the confidence interval for the mean value of y.

A Confidence Interval and a Prediction Interval

I f the regression assumptions hold,

1 A **100($1 - \alpha$) percent confidence interval for the mean value of y** when x equals x_0 is

$$\left[\hat{y} \pm t_{\alpha/2}s\sqrt{\frac{1}{n} + \frac{(x_0 - \bar{x})^2}{SS_{xx}}} \right]$$

2 A **100($1 - \alpha$) percent prediction interval for an individual value of y** when x equals x_0 is

$$\left[\hat{y} \pm t_{\alpha/2}s\sqrt{1 + \frac{1}{n} + \frac{(x_0 - \bar{x})^2}{SS_{xx}}} \right]$$

Here, $t_{\alpha/2}$ is based on ($n - 2$) degrees of freedom.

The summary box tells us that both the formula for the confidence interval and the formula for the prediction interval use the quantity $1/n + (x_0 - \bar{x})^2/SS_{xx}$. We will call this quantity the **distance value,** because it is a measure of the distance between x_0, the value of x for which we will make a point estimate or a point prediction, and $\bar{x}$, the average of the previously observed values of x. The farther that x_0 is from $\bar{x}$, which represents the center of the experimental region, the larger is the distance value, and thus the longer are both the confidence interval $[\hat{y} \pm t_{\alpha/2}s\sqrt{\text{distance value}}]$ and the prediction interval $[\hat{y} \pm t_{\alpha/2}s\sqrt{1 + \text{distance value}}]$. Said another way, when x_0 is farther from the center of the data, $\hat{y} = b_0 + b_1 x_0$ is likely to be less accurate as both a point estimate and a point prediction.

EXAMPLE 14.6 The Tasty Sub Shop Case: Predicting Revenue and Profit

In the Tasty Sub Shop problem, recall that one of the business entrepreneur's potential sites is near a population of 47,300 residents. Also, recall that

$$\hat{y} = b_0 + b_1 x_0$$

$$= 183.31 + 15.596(47.3)$$

$$= 921.0 \text{ (that is, \$921,000)}$$

is the point estimate of the mean yearly revenue for all Tasty Sub restaurants that could potentially be built near populations of 47,300 residents and is the point prediction of the yearly revenue for a single Tasty Sub restaurant that is built near a population of 47,300 residents. Using the information in Example 14.2 (page 493), we compute

$$\text{distance value} = \frac{1}{n} + \frac{(x_0 - \bar{x})^2}{SS_{xx}}$$

$$= \frac{1}{10} + \frac{(47.3 - 43.41)^2}{1913.129}$$

$$= .1079$$

Because $s = 61.7052$ (see Example 14.3 on page 502) and because $t_{\alpha/2} = t_{.025}$ based on $n - 2 = 10 - 2 = 8$ degrees of freedom equals 2.306, it follows that a 95 percent confidence interval for the mean yearly revenue when $x = 47.3$ is

$$[\hat{y} \pm t_{\alpha/2} s \sqrt{\text{distance value}}]$$

$$= [921.0 \pm 2.306(61.7052)\sqrt{.1079}]$$

$$= [921.0 \pm 46.74]$$

$$= [874.3, 967.7]$$

This interval says we are 95 percent confident that the mean yearly revenue for all Tasty Sub restaurants that could potentially be built near populations of 47,300 residents is between $874,300 and $967,700.

Because the entrepreneur would be operating a single Tasty Sub restaurant that is built near a population of 47,300 residents, the entrepreneur is interested in obtaining a prediction interval for the yearly revenue of such a restaurant. A 95 percent prediction interval for this revenue is

$$[\hat{y} \pm t_{\alpha/2} s \sqrt{1 + \text{distance value}}]$$

$$= [921.0 \pm 2.306(61.7052)\sqrt{1.1079}]$$

$$= [921.0 \pm 149.77]$$

$$= [771.2, 1070.8]$$

This interval says that we are 95 percent confident that the yearly revenue for a single Tasty Sub restaurant that is built near a population of 47,300 residents will be between $771,200 and $1,070,800. Moreover, recall that the yearly rent and other fixed costs for the entrepreneur's potential restaurant will be $257,550 and that (according to Tasty Sub corporate headquarters) the yearly food and other variable costs for the restaurant will be 60 percent of the yearly revenue. Using the lower end of the 95 percent prediction interval [771.2, 1070.8], we predict that (1) the restaurant's yearly operating cost will be $257,550 + .6($771,200) = $720,270 and (2) the restaurant's yearly profit will be $771,200 − $720,270 = $50,930. Using the upper end of the 95 percent prediction interval [771.2, 1070.8], we predict that (1) the restaurant's yearly

FIGURE 14.17   MINITAB Output of 95% Confidence and Prediction Intervals for the Tasty
                Sub Shop Case

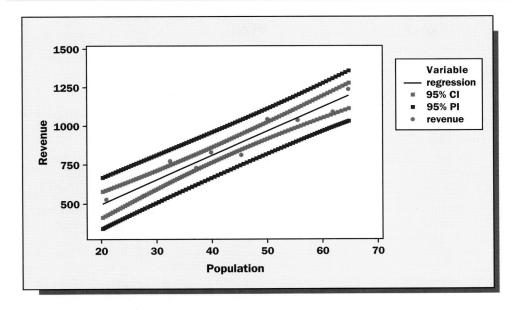

operating cost will be $257,550 + .6($1,070,800) = $900,030 and (2) the restaurant's yearly profit will be $1,070,800 − $900,030 = $170,770. Combining the two predicted profits, it follows that we are 95 percent confident that the potential restaurant's yearly profit will be between $50,930 and $170,770. If the entrepreneur decides that this is an acceptable range of potential yearly profits, then the entrepreneur might decide to purchase a Tasty Sub franchise for the potential restaurant site. In Chapter 15 we will use a *multiple regression model* to reduce the range of the predicted yearly profits for the potential Tasty Sub restaurant.

Below we repeat the bottom of the MINITAB output in Figure 14.8(b) on page 505. This output gives (within rounding) the point estimate and prediction $\hat{y} = 921.0$, the 95 percent confidence interval for the mean value of y when x equals 47.3, and the 95 percent prediction interval for an individual value of y when x equals 47.3.

```
Predicted Values for New Observations
New Obs      Fit   SE Fit       95% CI          95% PI
      1    921.0     20.3   (874.2, 967.7)  (771.2, 1070.7)
```

Although the MINITAB output does not directly give the distance value, it does give $s_{\hat{y}} = s\sqrt{\text{distance value}}$ under the heading "SE Fit." A little algebra shows that this implies that the distance value equals $(s_{\hat{y}}/s)^2$. Specifically, because $s_{\hat{y}} = 20.3$ and $s = 61.7052$, the distance value equals $(20.3/61.7052)^2 = .1082$. Note that, because MINITAB rounds $s_{\hat{y}}$, this calculation of the distance value is slightly less accurate than the previous hand calculation that obtained a distance value of .1079.

To conclude this example, note that Figure 14.17 illustrates the MINITAB output of the 95 percent confidence and prediction intervals corresponding to all values of x in the experimental region. Here $\bar{x} = 43.41$ can be regarded as the center of the experimental region. Notice that the farther x_0 is from $\bar{x} = 43.41$, the larger is the distance value and, therefore, the longer are the 95 percent confidence and prediction intervals. These longer intervals are undesirable because they give us less information about mean and individual values of y.

Exercises for Section 14.4

CONCEPTS

connect

14.28   What is the difference between a confidence interval and a prediction interval?

14.29   What does the distance value measure? How does the distance value affect a confidence or prediction interval?

METHODS AND APPLICATIONS

14.30   **THE NATURAL GAS CONSUMPTION CASE**   GasCon1

The following partial MINITAB regression output for the natural gas consumption data relates to predicting the city's natural gas consumption (in MMcf) in a week that has an average hourly temperature of 40°F.

```
Predicted Values for New Observations
New Obs       Fit    SE Fit        95% CI              95% PI
      1    10.721     0.241   (10.130, 11.312)   (9.015, 12.427)
```

a   Report (as shown on the computer output) a point estimate of and a 95 percent confidence interval for the mean natural gas consumption for all weeks having an average hourly temperature of 40°F.

b   Report (as shown on the computer output) a point prediction of and a 95 percent prediction interval for the natural gas consumption in a single week that has an average hourly temperature of 40°F.

c   Remembering that $s = .6542$; $SS_{xx} = 1,404.355$; $\bar{x} = 43.98$; and $n = 8$, hand calculate the distance value when $x_0 = 40$. Remembering that the distance value equals $(s_{\hat{y}}/s)^2$, use s and $s_{\hat{y}}$ from the computer output to calculate (within rounding) the distance value using this formula. Note that, because MINITAB rounds $s_{\hat{y}}$, the first hand calculation is the more accurate calculation of the distance value.

d   Remembering that for the natural gas consumption data $b_0 = 15.84$ and $b_1 = -.1279$, calculate (within rounding) the confidence interval of part a and the prediction interval of part b.

e   Suppose that next week the city's average hourly temperature will be 40°F. Also, suppose that the city's natural gas company will use the point prediction $\hat{y} = 10.721$ and order 10.721 MMcf of natural gas to be shipped to the city by a pipeline transmission system. The company will have to pay a fine to the transmission system if the city's actual gas usage y differs from the order of 10.721 MMcf by more than 10.5 percent—that is, is outside of the range $[10.721 \pm .105(10.721)] = [9.595, 11.847]$. Discuss why the 95 percent prediction interval for y, [9.015, 12.427], says that y might be outside of the allowable range and thus does not make the company 95 percent confident that it will avoid paying a fine.
Note: In the exercises of Chapter 15, we will use multiple regression analysis to predict y accurately enough so that the company is likely to avoid paying a fine.

14.31   **THE STARTING SALARY CASE**   StartSal

The following partial MINITAB regression output for the starting salary data relates to predicting the starting salary of a marketing graduate having a grade point average of 3.25.

```
Predicted Values for New Observations
New Obs      Fit    SE Fit        95% CI              95% PI
      1   33.362     0.213   (32.813, 33.911)   (31.878, 34.846)
```

a   Report (as shown on the computer output) a point estimate of and a 95 percent confidence interval for the mean starting salary of all marketing graduates having a grade point average of 3.25.

b   Report (as shown on the computer output) a point prediction of and a 95 percent prediction interval for the starting salary of an individual marketing graduate having a grade point average of 3.25.

c   Remembering that $s = .536321$ and that the distance value equals $(s_{\hat{y}}/s)^2$, use $s_{\hat{y}}$ from the computer output to hand calculate the distance value when $x = 3.25$.

d   Remembering that for the starting salary data $n = 7$, $b_0 = 14.816$, and $b_1 = 5.7066$, hand calculate (within rounding) the confidence interval of part a and the prediction interval of part b.

14.32   THE SERVICE TIME CASE   ⦿ SrvcTime

The following partial Excel add-in (MegaStat) regression output for the service time data relates to predicting service times for 1, 2, 3, 4, 5, 6, and 7 copiers.

Predicted values for: Minutes (y)

Copiers (x)	Predicted	95% Confidence Intervals		95% Prediction Intervals		Leverage
		lower	upper	lower	upper	
1	36.066	29.907	42.226	23.944	48.188	0.348
2	60.669	55.980	65.357	49.224	72.113	0.202
3	85.271	81.715	88.827	74.241	96.300	0.116
4	109.873	106.721	113.025	98.967	120.779	0.091
5	134.475	130.753	138.197	123.391	145.559	0.127
6	159.077	154.139	164.016	147.528	170.627	0.224
7	183.680	177.233	190.126	171.410	195.950	0.381

a Report (as shown on the computer output) a point estimate of and a 95 percent confidence interval for the mean time to service four copiers.

b Report (as shown on the computer output) a point prediction of and a 95 percent prediction interval for the time to service four copiers on a single call.

c For this case: $n = 11$, $b_0 = 11.4641$, $b_1 = 24.6022$, and $s = 4.615$. Using this information and a distance value (called **Leverage** on the add-in output), hand calculate (within rounding) the confidence interval of part a and the prediction interval of part b.

d If we examine the service time data, we see that there was at least one call on which Accu-Copiers serviced each of 1, 2, 3, 4, 5, 6, and 7 copiers. The 95 percent confidence intervals for the mean service times on these calls might be used to schedule future service calls. To understand this, note that a person making service calls will (in, say, a year or more) make a very large number of service calls. Some of the person's individual service times will be below, and some will be above, the corresponding mean service times. However, because the very large number of individual service times will average out to the mean service times, it seems fair to both the efficiency of the company and to the person making service calls to schedule service calls by using estimates of the mean service times. Therefore, suppose we wish to schedule a call to service five copiers. Examining the computer output, we see that a 95 percent confidence interval for the mean time to service five copiers is [130.753, 138.197]. Because the mean time might be 138.197 minutes, it would seem fair to allow 138 minutes to make the service call. Now suppose we wish to schedule a call to service four copiers. Determine how many minutes to allow for the service call.

14.33   THE FRESH DETERGENT CASE   ⦿ Fresh

The following partial MINITAB regression output for the Fresh detergent data relates to predicting demand for future sales periods in which the price difference will be .10 (see New Obs 1) and .25 (see New Obs 2).

```
Predicted Values for New Observations
New Obs      Fit  SE Fit       95% CI              95% PI
      1   8.0806  0.0648  (7.9479, 8.2133)   (7.4187, 8.7425)
      2   8.4804  0.0586  (8.3604, 8.6004)   (7.8209, 9.1398)
```

a Report (as shown on the computer output) a point estimate of and a 95 percent confidence interval for the mean demand for Fresh in all sales periods when the price difference is .10.

b Report (as shown on the computer output) a point prediction of and a 95 percent prediction interval for the actual demand for Fresh in an individual sales period when the price difference is .10.

c Remembering that $s = .316561$ and that the distance value equals $(s_{\hat{y}}/s)^2$, use $s_{\hat{y}}$ from the computer output to hand calculate the distance value when $x = .10$.

d For this case: $n = 30$, $b_0 = 7.81409$, $b_1 = 2.6652$, and $s = .316561$. Using this information, and your result from part c, find 99 percent confidence and prediction intervals for mean and individual demands when $x = .10$.

e Repeat parts a, b, c, and d when $x = .25$.

14.34   THE DIRECT LABOR COST CASE   DS DirLab

The following partial Excel add-in (MegaStat) regression output for the direct labor cost data relates to predicting direct labor cost when the batch size is 60.

Predicted values for: LaborCost (y)

BatchSize (x)	Predicted	95% Confidence Interval		95% Prediction Interval		Leverage
		lower	upper	lower	upper	
60	627.263	621.054	633.472	607.032	647.494	0.104

a   Report (as shown on the computer output) a point estimate of and a 95 percent confidence interval for the mean direct labor cost of all batches of size 60.

b   Report (as shown on the computer output) a point prediction of and a 95 percent prediction interval for the actual direct labor cost of an individual batch of size 60.

c   For this case: $n = 12$, $b_0 = 18.4875$, $b_1 = 10.1463$, and $s = 8.6415$. Use this information and the distance value (called **Leverage**) on the computer output to compute 99 percent confidence and prediction intervals for the mean and individual labor costs when $x = 60$.

14.35   THE REAL ESTATE SALES PRICE CASE   DS RealEst

The following partial MINITAB regression output for the real estate sales price data relates to predicting the sales price of a home having 2,000 square feet.

```
Predicted Values for New Observations
New Obs     Fit   SE Fit        95% CI              95% PI
      1  162.03    3.47  (154.04, 170.02)  (136.34, 187.72)
```

a   Report (as shown on the MINITAB output) a point estimate of and a 95 percent confidence interval for the mean sales price of all houses having 2,000 square feet.

b   Report (as shown on the MINITAB output) a point prediction of and a 95 percent prediction interval for the sales price of an individual house having 2,000 square feet.

c   If you were purchasing a home having 2,000 square feet, which of the above intervals would you find to be most useful? Explain.

LO14-6 Calculate and interpret the simple coefficients of determination and correlation.

14.5 Simple Coefficients of Determination and Correlation ● ● ●

The simple coefficient of determination   The **simple coefficient of determination** is a measure of the usefulness of a simple linear regression model. To introduce this quantity, which is denoted r^2 (pronounced r **squared**), suppose we have observed n values of the dependent variable y. However, we choose to predict y without using a predictor (independent) variable x. In such a case the only reasonable prediction of a specific value of y, say y_i, would be $\bar{y}$, which is simply the average of the n observed values $y_1, y_2, \ldots, y_n$. Here the error of prediction in predicting y_i would be $y_i - \bar{y}$. For example, Figure 14.18(a) illustrates the prediction errors obtained for the Tasty Sub Shop revenue data when we do not use the information provided by the independent variable x, population size.

Next, suppose we decide to employ the predictor variable x and observe the values $x_1, x_2, \ldots, x_n$ corresponding to the observed values of y. In this case the prediction of y_i is

$$\hat{y}_i = b_0 + b_1 x_i$$

and the error of prediction is $y_i - \hat{y}_i$. For example, Figure 14.18(b) illustrates the prediction errors obtained in the Tasty Sub Shop case when we use the predictor variable x. Together, Figures 14.18(a) and (b) show the reduction in the prediction errors accomplished by employing the predictor variable x (and the least squares line).

Using the predictor variable x decreases the prediction error in predicting y_i from $(y_i - \bar{y})$ to $(y_i - \hat{y}_i)$, or by an amount equal to

$$(y_i - \bar{y}) - (y_i - \hat{y}_i) = (\hat{y}_i - \bar{y})$$

FIGURE 14.18   **The Reduction in the Prediction Errors Accomplished by Employing the Predictor Variable** *x*

(a) Prediction errors for the Tasty Sub Shop case when we do not use the information contributed by x

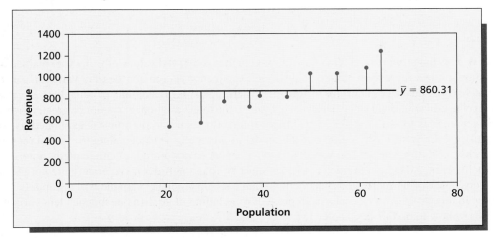

(b) Prediction errors for the Tasty Sub Shop case when we use the information contributed by x by using the least squares line

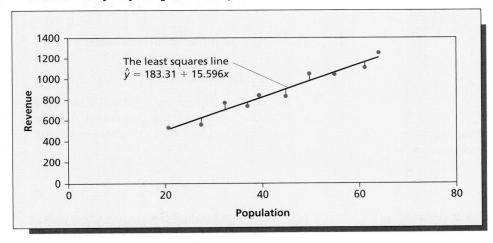

It can be shown that in general

$$\sum (y_i - \bar{y})^2 - \sum (y_i - \hat{y}_i)^2 = \sum (\hat{y}_i - \bar{y})^2$$

The sum of squared prediction errors obtained when we do not employ the predictor variable x, $\sum (y_i - \bar{y})^2$, is called the **total variation.** Intuitively, this quantity measures the total amount of variation exhibited by the observed values of y. The sum of squared prediction errors obtained when we use the predictor variable x, $\sum (y_i - \hat{y}_i)^2$, is called the **unexplained variation (this is another name for SSE).** Intuitively, this quantity measures the amount of variation in the values of y that is not explained by the predictor variable. The quantity $\sum (\hat{y}_i - \bar{y})^2$ is called the **explained variation.** Using these definitions and the above equation involving these summations, we see that

Total variation − Unexplained variation = Explained variation

It follows that the explained variation is the reduction in the sum of squared prediction errors that has been accomplished by using the predictor variable x to predict y. It also follows that

Total variation = Explained variation + Unexplained variation

Intuitively, this equation implies that the explained variation represents the amount of the total variation in the observed values of y that is explained by the predictor variable x (and the simple linear regression model).

We now define the **simple coefficient of determination** to be

$$r^2 = \frac{\text{Explained variation}}{\text{Total variation}}$$

That is, r^2 is the proportion of the total variation in the n observed values of y that is explained by the simple linear regression model. Neither the explained variation nor the total variation can be negative (both quantities are sums of squares). Therefore, r^2 is greater than or equal to 0. Because the explained variation must be less than or equal to the total variation, r^2 cannot be greater than 1. The nearer r^2 is to 1, the larger is the proportion of the total variation that is explained by the model, and the greater is the utility of the model in predicting y. If the value of r^2 is not reasonably close to 1, the independent variable in the model does not provide accurate predictions of y. In such a case, a different predictor variable must be found in order to accurately predict y. It is also possible that no regression model employing a single predictor variable will accurately predict y. In this case the model must be improved by including more than one independent variable. We show how to do this in Chapter 15.

The Simple Coefficient of Determination, r^2

For the simple linear regression model

1   **Total variation** $= \sum (y_i - \bar{y})^2$

2   **Explained variation** $= \sum (\hat{y}_i - \bar{y})^2$

3   **Unexplained variation** $= \sum (y_i - \hat{y}_i)^2$

4   **Total variation = Explained variation + Unexplained variation**

5   **The simple coefficient of determination is**

$$r^2 = \frac{\text{Explained variation}}{\text{Total variation}}$$

6 r^2 is the proportion of the total variation in the n observed values of the dependent variable that is explained by the simple linear regression model.

EXAMPLE 14.7 The Tasty Sub Shop Case: Calculating and Interpreting r^2

For the Tasty Sub data we have seen that $\bar{y} = 860.31$ (see Example 14.2 on page 493). It follows that the total variation is

$$\sum (y_i - \bar{y})^2 = (527.1 - 860.31)^2 + (548.7 - 860.31)^2 + \cdots + (1235.8 - 860.31)^2$$

$$= 495{,}776.51$$

Furthermore, we found in Table 14.2 (page 494) that the unexplained variation is $SSE = 30{,}460.21$. Therefore, we can compute the explained variation and r^2 as follows:

$$\text{Explained variation} = \text{Total variation} - \text{Unexplained variation}$$

$$= 495{,}776.51 - 30{,}460.21 = 465{,}316.30$$

$$r^2 = \frac{\text{Explained variation}}{\text{Total variation}} = \frac{465{,}316.30}{495{,}776.51} = .939$$

This value of r^2 says that the regression model explains 93.9 percent of the total variation in the 10 observed yearly revenues.

FIGURE 14.19   **An Illustration of Different Values of the Simple Correlation Coefficient**

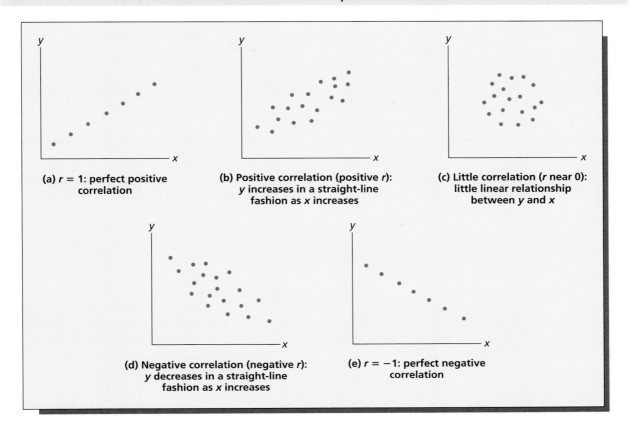

(a) $r = 1$: perfect positive correlation

(b) Positive correlation (positive r): y increases in a straight-line fashion as x increases

(c) Little correlation (r near 0): little linear relationship between y and x

(d) Negative correlation (negative r): y decreases in a straight-line fashion as x increases

(e) $r = -1$: perfect negative correlation

The simple correlation coefficient, r   People often claim that two variables are correlated. For example, a college admissions officer might feel that the academic performance of college students (measured by grade point average) is correlated with the students' scores on a standardized college entrance examination. This means that college students' grade point averages are related to their college entrance exam scores. One measure of the relationship between two variables y and x is the **simple correlation coefficient.** We define this quantity as follows:

The Simple Correlation Coefficient

The **simple correlation coefficient between y and x,** denoted by r, is

$$r = +\sqrt{r^2} \quad \text{if } b_1 \text{ is positive} \qquad \text{and} \qquad r = -\sqrt{r^2} \quad \text{if } b_1 \text{ is negative}$$

where b_1 is the slope of the least squares line relating y to x. This correlation coefficient **measures the strength of the linear relationship between y and x.**

Because r^2 is always between 0 and 1, the correlation coefficient r is between -1 and 1. A value of r near 0 implies little linear relationship between y and x. A value of r close to 1 says that y and x have a strong tendency to move together in a straight-line fashion with a positive slope and, therefore, that y and x are highly related and **positively correlated.** A value of r close to -1 says that y and x have a strong tendency to move together in a straight-line fashion with a negative slope and, therefore, that y and x are highly related and **negatively correlated.** Figure 14.19 illustrates these relationships. Notice that when $r = 1$, y and x have a perfect linear relationship with a positive slope, whereas when $r = -1$, y and x have a perfect linear relationship with a negative slope.

EXAMPLE 14.8 The Tasty Sub Shop Case: Simple Correlation Coefficient

In the Tasty Sub Shop case, we found that $b_1 = 15.596$ and $r^2 = .939$. It follows that the simple correlation coefficient between y (yearly revenue) and x (population size) is

$$ r = +\sqrt{r^2} = +\sqrt{.939} = .969 $$

This simple correlation coefficient says that x and y have a strong tendency to move together in a linear fashion with a positive slope. We have seen this tendency in Figure 14.1 (page 488), which indicates that y and x are positively correlated.

If we have computed the least squares slope b_1 and r^2, the method given in the previous box provides the easiest way to calculate r. The simple correlation coefficient can also be calculated using the formula

$$ r = \frac{SS_{xy}}{\sqrt{SS_{xx} SS_{yy}}} $$

Here SS_{xy} and SS_{xx} have been defined in Section 14.1 on page 492, and SS_{yy} denotes the total variation, which has been defined in this section. Furthermore, this formula for r automatically gives r the correct (+ or −) sign. For instance, in the Tasty Sub Shop case, $SS_{xy} = 29,836.389$, $SS_{xx} = 1913.129$, and $SS_{yy} = 495,776.51$ (see Examples 14.2 on page 493 and 14.7 on page 518). Therefore

$$ r = \frac{SS_{xy}}{\sqrt{SS_{xx} SS_{yy}}} $$

$$ = \frac{29,836.389}{\sqrt{(1,913.129)(495,776.51)}} = .969 $$

It is important to make two points. First, **the value of the simple correlation coefficient is not the slope of the least squares line.** If we wish to find this slope, we should use the previously given formula for b_1.[2] Second, **high correlation does not imply that a cause-and-effect relationship exists.** When r indicates that y and x are highly correlated, this says that y and x have a strong tendency to move together in a straight-line fashion. The correlation does not mean that changes in x cause changes in y. Instead, some other variable (or variables) could be causing the apparent relationship between y and x. For example, suppose that college students' grade point averages and college entrance exam scores are highly positively correlated. This does not mean that earning a high score on a college entrance exam causes students to receive a high grade point average. Rather, other factors such as intellectual ability, study habits, and attitude probably determine both a student's score on a college entrance exam and a student's college grade point average. In general, while the simple correlation coefficient can show that variables tend to move together in a straight-line fashion, scientific theory must be used to establish cause-and-effect relationships.

A technical note   In optional Section 14.10 we present some shortcut formulas for calculating the total, explained, and unexplained variations. Also, for those who have already read Section 14.3, r^2, the explained variation, the unexplained variation, and the total variation are calculated by Excel and MINITAB. These quantities are identified on the Excel and MINITAB outputs of Figure 14.8 (page 505) by, respectively, the labels 9 , 10 , 11 , and 12 . These outputs also give an "adjusted r^2." We will explain the meaning of this quantity in Chapter 15.

---

[2]Essentially, the difference between r and b_1 is a change of scale. It can be shown that b_1 and r are related by the equation $b_1 = (SS_{yy}/SS_{xx})^{1/2} r$.

Exercises for Section 14.5

CONCEPTS

14.36 Discuss the meanings of the total variation, the unexplained variation, and the explained variation.

14.37 What does the simple coefficient of determination measure?

METHODS AND APPLICATIONS

In Exercises 14.38 through 14.43, we give the total variation, the unexplained variation (SSE), and the least squares point estimate b_1 that are obtained when simple linear regression is used to analyze the data set related to each of six previously discussed case studies. Using the information given in each exercise, find the explained variation, the simple coefficient of determination (r^2), and the simple correlation coefficient (r). Interpret r^2.

14.38 THE NATURAL GAS CONSUMPTION CASE ⓓⓢ GasCon1

Total variation = 25.549; SSE = 2.568; $b_1 = -.12792$

14.39 THE STARTING SALARY CASE ⓓⓢ StartSal

Total variation = 61.380; SSE = 1.438; $b_1 = 5.7066$

14.40 THE SERVICE TIME CASE ⓓⓢ SrvcTime

Total variation = 20,110.5455; SSE = 191.7017; $b_1 = 24.6022$

14.41 THE FRESH DETERGENT CASE ⓓⓢ Fresh

Total variation = 13.459; SSE = 2.806; $b_1 = 2.6652$

14.42 THE DIRECT LABOR COST CASE ⓓⓢ DirLab

Total variation = 1,025,339.6667; SSE = 746.7624; $b_1 = 10.1463$

14.43 THE REAL ESTATE SALES PRICE CASE ⓓⓢ RealEst

Total variation = 7447.5; SSE = 896.8; $b_1 = 5.7003$

14.6 Testing the Significance of the Population Correlation Coefficient (Optional) ● ● ●

LO14-7 Test hypotheses about the population correlation coefficient.

We have seen that the simple correlation coefficient measures the linear relationship between the observed values of x and the observed values of y that make up the sample. A similar coefficient of linear correlation can be defined for the population of *all possible combinations of observed values of x and y*. We call this coefficient the **population correlation coefficient** and denote it by the symbol ρ (pronounced **rho**). We use r as the point estimate of ρ. In addition, we can carry out a hypothesis test. Here we test the null hypothesis H_0: $\rho = 0$, which says there is no linear relationship between x and y, against the alternative H_a: $\rho \neq 0$, which says there is a positive or negative linear relationship between x and y. This test employs the test statistic

$$t = \frac{r\sqrt{n-2}}{\sqrt{1-r^2}}$$

and is based on the assumption that the population of all possible observed combinations of values of x and y has a **bivariate normal probability distribution.** See Wonnacott and Wonnacott (1981) for a discussion of this distribution. It can be shown that the preceding test statistic t and the p-value used to test H_0: $\rho = 0$ versus H_a: $\rho \neq 0$ are equal to, respectively, the test statistic $t = b_1/s_{b_1}$ and the p-value used to test H_0: $\beta_1 = 0$ versus H_a: $\beta_1 \neq 0$, where β_1 is the slope in the simple linear regression model. Keep in mind, however, that although the mechanics involved in these hypothesis tests are the same, these tests are based on different assumptions (remember that the test for significance of the slope is based on the regression assumptions). If the bivariate normal distribution assumption for the test concerning ρ is badly violated, we can use a nonparametric approach to correlation. One such approach is **Spearman's rank correlation coefficient.** This approach is discussed in Chapter 18.

EXAMPLE 14.9 The Tasty Sub Shop Case: The Correlation Between x and y

Again consider testing the significance of the slope in the Tasty Sub Shop problem. Recall that in Example 14.4 (page 504) we found that $t = 11.05$ and that the p-value related to this t statistic is less than .001. We therefore (if the regression assumptions hold) can reject H_0: $\beta_1 = 0$ at level of significance .05, .01, or .001, and we have extremely strong evidence that x is significantly related to y. This also implies (if the population of all possible observed combinations of x and y has a bivariate normal probability distribution) that we can reject H_0: $\rho = 0$ in favor of H_a: $\rho \neq 0$ at level of significance .05, .01, or .001. It follows that we have extremely strong evidence of a linear relationship, or correlation, between x and y. Furthermore, because we have previously calculated r to be .969, we estimate that x and y are positively correlated.

Exercises for Section 14.6

CONCEPTS

14.44 Explain what is meant by the population correlation coefficient ρ.

14.45 Explain how we test H_0: $\rho = 0$ versus H_a: $\rho \neq 0$. What do we conclude if we reject H_0: $\rho = 0$?

METHODS AND APPLICATIONS

14.46 **THE STARTING SALARY CASE** DS StartSal

Consider testing H_0: $\beta_1 = 0$ versus H_a: $\beta_1 \neq 0$. Figure 14.11 (page 508) tells us that $t = 14.44$ and that the related p-value is less than .001. Assuming that the bivariate normal probability distribution assumption holds, test H_0: $\rho = 0$ versus H_a: $\rho \neq 0$ by setting α equal to .05, .01, and .001. What do you conclude about how x and y are related?

14.47 **THE SERVICE TIME CASE** DS SrvcTime

Consider testing H_0: $\beta_1 = 0$ versus H_a: $\beta_1 \neq 0$. Figure 14.12 (page 508) tells us that $t = 30.5802$ and that the related p-value is less than .001. Assuming that the bivariate normal probability distribution assumption holds, test H_0: $\rho = 0$ versus H_a: $\rho \neq 0$ by setting α equal to .05, .01, and .001. What do you conclude about how x and y are related?

LO14-8 Test the significance of a simple linear regression model by using an F-test.

14.7 An F-Test for the Model ● ● ●

In this section we discuss an F-test that can be used to test the significance of the regression relationship between x and y. Sometimes people refer to this as testing the significance of the simple linear regression model. For simple linear regression, this test is another way to test the null hypothesis H_0: $\beta_1 = 0$ (the relationship between x and y is not significant) versus H_a: $\beta_1 \neq 0$ (the relationship between x and y is significant). If we can reject H_0 at level of significance α, we often say that **the simple linear regression model is significant at level of significance α.**

An F Test for the Simple Linear Regression Model

Suppose that the regression assumptions hold, and define the **overall F statistic** to be

$$F(\text{model}) = \frac{\text{Explained variation}}{(\text{Unexplained variation})/(n-2)}$$

Also define the p-value related to $F(\text{model})$ to be the area under the curve of the F distribution (having 1 numerator and $n-2$ denominator degrees of freedom) to the right of $F(\text{model})$—see Figure 14.20(b).

We can reject H_0: $\beta_1 = 0$ in favor of H_a: $\beta_1 \neq 0$ at level of significance α if either of the following equivalent conditions holds:

1 $F(\text{model}) > F_\alpha$

2 p-value $< \alpha$

Here the point F_α is based on 1 numerator and $n-2$ denominator degrees of freedom.

FIGURE 14.20(a) The *F*-Test Critical Value

FIGURE 14.20(a) **The *F*-Test Critical Value**

FIGURE 14.20(b) **The *F*-Test *p*-Value**

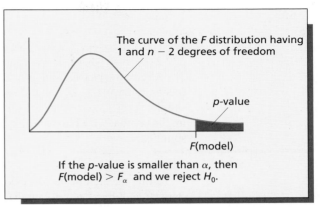

The first condition in the box says we should reject H_0: $\beta_1 = 0$ (and conclude that the relationship between x and y is significant) when F(model) is large. This is intuitive because a large overall F statistic would be obtained when the explained variation is large compared to the unexplained variation. This would occur if x is significantly related to y, which would imply that the slope β_1 is not equal to 0. Figure 14.20(a) illustrates that we reject H_0 when F(model) is greater than F_α. As can be seen in Figure 14.20(b), when F(model) is large, the related p-value is small. When the p-value is small enough [resulting from an F(model) statistic that is large enough], we reject H_0. Figure 14.20(b) illustrates that the second condition in the box (p-value $< \alpha$) is an equivalent way to carry out this test.

EXAMPLE 14.10 The Tasty Sub Shop Case: An *F*-Test for the Model

Consider the Tasty Sub Shop problem and the following partial MINITAB output of the simple linear regression analysis relating yearly revenue y to population size x:

```
Analysis of Variance
Source            DF          SS          MS         F      P-value
Regression         1      465316      465316    122.21        0.000
Residual Error     8       30460        3808
Total              9      495777
```

Looking at this output, we see that the explained variation is 465,316 and the unexplained variation is 30,460. It follows that

$$F(\text{model}) = \frac{\text{Explained variation}}{(\text{Unexplained variation})/(n-2)}$$

$$= \frac{465,316}{30,460/(10-2)} = \frac{465,316}{3808}$$

$$= 122.21$$

Note that this overall F statistic is given on the MINITAB output and is also given on the following partial Excel output:

ANOVA	df	SS	MS	F	Significance F
Regression	1	465316.3004	465316.3004	122.2096	0.0000
Residual	8	30460.2086	3807.5261		
Total	9	495776.5090			

The p-value related to F(model) is the area to the right of 122.21 under the curve of the F distribution having 1 numerator and 8 denominator degrees of freedom. This p-value is given on both the MINITAB output (labeled "p") and the Excel output (labeled "Significance F") and is less than .001. If we wish to test the significance of the regression relationship with level of significance $\alpha = .05$, we use the critical value $F_{.05}$ based on 1 numerator and 8 denominator degrees of freedom. Using Table A.7 (page 796), we find that $F_{.05} = 5.32$. Because F(model) = 122.21 > $F_{.05} = 5.32$, we can reject $H_0: \beta_1 = 0$ in favor of $H_a: \beta_1 \neq 0$ at level of significance .05. Alternatively, because the p-value is smaller than .05, .01, and .001, we can reject H_0 at level of significance .05, .01, or .001. Therefore, we have extremely strong evidence that $H_0: \beta_1 = 0$ should be rejected and that the regression relationship between x and y is significant. That is, we might say that we have extremely strong evidence that the simple linear model relating y to x is significant.

Testing the significance of the regression relationship between y and x by using the overall F statistic and its related p-value is equivalent to doing this test by using the t statistic and its related p-value. Specifically, it can be shown that $(t)^2 = F$(model) and that $(t_{\alpha/2})^2$ based on $n - 2$ degrees of freedom equals F_α based on 1 numerator and $n - 2$ denominator degrees of freedom. It follows that the critical value conditions

$$|t| > t_{\alpha/2} \quad \text{and} \quad F(\text{model}) > F_\alpha$$

are equivalent. Furthermore, the p-values related to t and F(model) can be shown to be equal. Because these tests are equivalent, it would be logical to ask why we have presented the F-test. There are two reasons. First, most standard regression computer packages include the results of the F-test as a part of the regression output. Second, the F-test has a useful generalization in multiple regression analysis (where we employ more than one predictor variable). The F-test in multiple regression is not equivalent to a t test. This is further explained in Chapter 15.

Exercises for Section 14.7

CONCEPTS

connect

14.48   What are the null and alternative hypotheses for the F-test in simple linear regression?

14.49   The F-test in simple linear regression is equivalent to what other test?

METHODS AND APPLICATIONS

In Exercises 14.50 through 14.55, we give MINITAB and Excel outputs of simple linear regression analyses of the data sets related to six previously discussed case studies. Using the appropriate computer output,
a Use the explained variation and the unexplained variation as given on the computer output to calculate (within rounding) the F(model) statistic.
b Utilize the F(model) statistic and the appropriate critical value to test $H_0: \beta_1 = 0$ versus $H_a: \beta_1 \neq 0$ by setting α equal to .05. What do you conclude about the regression relationship between y and x?
c Utilize the F(model) statistic and the appropriate critical value to test $H_0: \beta_1 = 0$ versus $H_a: \beta_1 \neq 0$ by setting α equal to .01. What do you conclude about the regression relationship between y and x?
d Find the p-value related to F(model) on the computer output and report its value. Using the p-value, test the significance of the regression model at the .10, .05, .01, and .001 levels of significance. What do you conclude?
e Show that the F(model) statistic is (within rounding) the square of the t statistic for testing $H_0: \beta_1 = 0$ versus $H_a: \beta_1 \neq 0$. Also, show that the $F_{.05}$ critical value is the square of the $t_{.025}$ critical value.

Note that in the lower right hand corner of each output we give (in parentheses) the number of observations, n, used to perform the regression analysis and the t statistic for testing $H_0: \beta_1 = 0$ versus $H_a: \beta_1 \neq 0$.

14.50   THE NATURAL GAS CONSUMPTION CASE   🅳🅢 GasCon1

ANOVA	df	SS	MS	F	Significance F
Regression	1	22.9808	22.9808	53.6949	0.0003
Residual	6	2.5679	0.4280		
Total	7	25.5488			(n=8; t=-7.33)

14.51 THE STARTING SALARY CASE Ⓓ StartSal

```
Analysis of Variance
Source              DF      SS       MS        F       P
Regression           1   59.942   59.942   208.39   0.000
Residual Error       5    1.438    0.288
Total                6   61.380            (n=7; t=14.44)
```

14.52 THE SERVICE TIME CASE Ⓓ SrvcTime

ANOVA	SS	df	MS	F	p-value
Regression	19,918.8438	1	19,918.8438	935.15	2.09E-10
Residual	191.7017	9	21.3002		
Total	20,110.5455	10		(n=11; t=30.580)	

14.53 THE FRESH DETERGENT CASE Ⓓ Fresh

```
Analysis of Variance
Source              DF      SS       MS        F       P
Regression           1   10.653   10.653   106.30   0.000
Residual Error      28    2.806    0.100
Total               29   13.459            (n=30; t=10.31)
```

14.54 THE DIRECT LABOR COST CASE Ⓓ DirLab

ANOVA	df	SS	MS	F	Significance F
Regression	1	1024592.9043	1024592.9043	13720.4677	5.04E-17
Residual	10	746.7624	74.6762		
Total	11	1025339.6667		(n=12; t=117.1344)	

14.55 THE REAL ESTATE SALES PRICE CASE Ⓓ RealEst

```
Analysis of Variance
Source              DF      SS       MS        F       P
Regression           1   6550.7   6550.7   58.43   0.000
Residual Error       8    896.8    112.1
Total                9   7447.5            (n=10; t=7.64)
```

14.8 The QHIC Case: Developing An Advertising Strategy ● ● ●

Quality Home Improvement Center (QHIC) operates five stores in a large metropolitan area. The marketing department at QHIC wishes to study the relationship between x, home value (in thousands of dollars), and y, yearly expenditure on home upkeep (in dollars). A random sample of 40 homeowners is taken and survey participants are asked to estimate their expenditures during the previous year on the types of home upkeep products and services offered by QHIC. Public records of the county auditor are used to obtain the previous year's assessed values of the homeowner's homes. The resulting x and y values, as well as a scatter plot of these values, are given in Figure 14.21. The Excel output included in this figure tells us that the least squares point estimates of the y-intercept β_0 and the slope β_1 are $b_0 = -348.3921$ and $b_1 = 7.2583$. The p-value associated with b_1 implies there is a significant linear relationship between x and y. In addition, because $b_1 = 7.2583$, we estimate that mean yearly upkeep expenditure increases by \$7.26 for each additional \$1,000 increase in home value. Consider a home worth \$220,000, and note that $x_0 = 220$ is in the range of previously observed values of x: 48.9 to 286.18. It follows that

$$\hat{y} = b_0 + b_1 x_0$$

$$= -348.3921 + 7.2583(220)$$

$$= 1,248.43 \text{ (or } \$1,248.43)$$

FIGURE 14.21   The QHIC Upkeep Expenditure Data, Scatterplot, and Excel Output   ⊙ QHIC

Home	Value of Home, x (Thousands of Dollars)	Upkeep Expenditure, y (Dollars)	Home	Value of Home, x (Thousands of Dollars)	Upkeep Expenditure, y (Dollars)
1	237.00	1,412.08	21	153.04	849.14
2	153.08	797.20	22	232.18	1,313.84
3	184.86	872.48	23	125.44	602.06
4	222.06	1,003.42	24	169.82	642.14
5	160.68	852.90	25	177.28	1,038.80
6	99.68	288.48	26	162.82	697.00
7	229.04	1,288.46	27	120.44	324.34
8	101.78	423.08	28	191.10	965.10
9	257.86	1,351.74	29	158.78	920.14
10	96.28	378.04	30	178.50	950.90
11	171.00	918.08	31	272.20	1,670.32
12	231.02	1,627.24	32	48.90	125.40
13	228.32	1,204.76	33	104.56	479.78
14	205.90	857.04	34	286.18	2,010.64
15	185.72	775.00	35	83.72	368.36
16	168.78	869.26	36	86.20	425.60
17	247.06	1,396.00	37	133.58	626.90
18	155.54	711.50	38	212.86	1,316.94
19	224.20	1,475.18	39	122.02	390.16
20	202.04	1,413.32	40	198.02	1,090.84

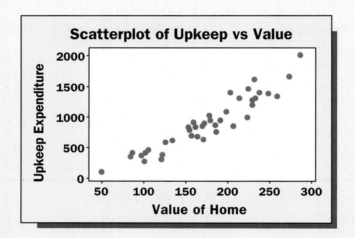

Regression Statistics	
Multiple R	0.9430
R Square	0.8892
Adjusted R Square	0.8863
Standard Error	146.8973
Observations	40

ANOVA	df	SS	MS	F	Significance F
Regression	1	6582759.6972	6582759.6972	305.0564	0.0000
Residual	38	819995.5427	21578.8301		
Total	39	7402755.2399			

	Coefficients	Standard Error	t Stat	P-value	Lower 95%	Upper 95%
Intercept	−348.3921	76.1410	−4.5756	0.0000	−502.5314	−194.2527
Value	7.2583	0.4156	17.4659	0.0000	6.4170	8.0995

is the point estimate of the mean yearly upkeep expenditure for all homes worth $220,000 and is the point prediction of a yearly upkeep expenditure for an individual home worth $220,000.

The marketing department at QHIC wishes to determine which homes should be sent advertising brochures promoting QHIC's products and services. If the marketing department has decided to send an advertising brochure to any home that has a predicted yearly upkeep expenditure of at least $500, then a home worth $220,000 would be sent an advertising brochure. This is because the predicted yearly upkeep expenditure for such a home is (as calculated above) $1,248.43. Other homes can be evaluated in a similar fashion.

14.9 Residual Analysis ● ● ●

LO14-9 Use residual analysis to check the assumptions of simple linear regression.

In this section we explain how to check the validity of the regression assumptions. The required checks are carried out by analyzing the **regression residuals.** The residuals are defined as follows:

> For any particular observed value of y, the corresponding **residual** is
>
> $$e = y - \hat{y} = (\text{observed value of } y - \text{predicted value of } y)$$
>
> where the predicted value of y is calculated using the **least squares prediction equation**
>
> $$\hat{y} = b_0 + b_1 x$$

The linear regression model $y = \beta_0 + \beta_1 x + \varepsilon$ implies that the error term ε is given by the equation $\varepsilon = y - (\beta_0 + \beta_1 x)$. Because $\hat{y}$ in the previous box is clearly the point estimate of $\beta_0 + \beta_1 x$, we see that the residual $e = y - \hat{y}$ is the point estimate of the error term ε. If the regression assumptions are valid, then, for any given value of the independent variable, the population of potential error term values will be normally distributed with mean 0 and variance σ^2 (see the regression assumptions in Section 14.2 on page 500). Furthermore, the different error terms will be statistically independent. Because the residuals provide point estimates of the error terms, it follows that

> If the regression assumptions hold, the residuals should look like they have been randomly and independently selected from normally distributed populations having mean 0 and variance σ^2.

In any real regression problem, the regression assumptions will not hold exactly. In fact, it is important to point out that mild departures from the regression assumptions do not seriously hinder our ability to use a regression model to make statistical inferences. Therefore, we are looking for pronounced, rather than subtle, departures from the regression assumptions. Because of this, we will require that the residuals only approximately fit the description just given.

Residual plots   One useful way to analyze residuals is to plot them versus various criteria. The resulting plots are called **residual plots.** To construct a residual plot, we compute the residual for each observed y value. The calculated residuals are then plotted versus some criterion. To validate the regression assumptions, we make residual plots against (1) values of the independent variable x; (2) values of $\hat{y}$, the predicted value of the dependent variable; and (3) the time order in which the data have been observed (if the regression data are time series data).

We next look at an example of constructing residual plots. Then we explain how to use these plots to check the regression assumptions.

EXAMPLE 14.11 The QHIC Case: Constructing Residual Plots

Figure 14.21 gives the QHIC upkeep expenditure data and a scatterplot of the data. If we use a simple linear regression model to describe the QHIC data, we find that the least squares point estimates of β_0 and β_1 are $b_0 = -348.3921$ and $b_1 = 7.2583$. The Excel add-in (MegaStat) output in

FIGURE 14.22   **Residuals and Residual Plots for the QHIC Simple Linear Regression Model**

(a) Excel add-in (MegaStat) output of the residuals

Observation	Upkeep	Predicted	Residual	Observation	Upkeep	Predicted	Residual
1	1,412.080	1,371.816	40.264	21	849.140	762.413	86.727
2	797.200	762.703	34.497	22	1,313.840	1,336.832	−22.992
3	872.480	993.371	−120.891	23	602.060	562.085	39.975
4	1,003.420	1,263.378	−259.958	24	642.140	884.206	−242.066
5	852.900	817.866	35.034	25	1,038.800	938.353	100.447
6	288.480	375.112	−86.632	26	697.000	833.398	−136.398
7	1,288.460	1,314.041	−25.581	27	324.340	525.793	−201.453
8	423.080	390.354	32.726	28	965.100	1,038.662	−73.562
9	1,351.740	1,523.224	−171.484	29	920.140	804.075	116.065
10	378.040	350.434	27.606	30	950.900	947.208	3.692
11	918.080	892.771	25.309	31	1,670.320	1,627.307	43.013
12	1,627.240	1,328.412	298.828	32	125.400	6.537	118.863
13	1,204.760	1,308.815	−104.055	33	479.780	410.532	69.248
14	857.040	1,146.084	−289.044	34	2,010.640	1,728.778	281.862
15	775.000	999.613	−224.613	35	368.360	259.270	109.090
16	869.260	876.658	−7.398	36	425.600	277.270	148.330
17	1,396.000	1,444.835	−48.835	37	626.900	621.167	5.733
18	711.500	780.558	−69.058	38	1,316.940	1,196.602	120.338
19	1,475.180	1,278.911	196.269	39	390.160	537.261	−147.101
20	1,413.320	1,118.068	295.252	40	1,090.840	1,088.889	1.951

(b) MINITAB output of a residual plot versus x

(c) MINITAB output of a residual plot versus $\hat{y}$

Figure 14.22(a) presents the predicted home upkeep expenditures and residuals that are given by the simple linear regression model. Here each residual is computed as

$$e = y - \hat{y} = y - (b_0 + b_1 x) = y - (-348.3921 + 7.2583x)$$

For instance, for the first observation (home) when $y = 1{,}412.08$ and $x = 237.00$ (see Figure 14.21 on page 526), the residual is

$$e = 1{,}412.08 - (-348.3921 + 7.2583(237))$$
$$= 1{,}412.08 - 1{,}371.816 = 40.264$$

The MINITAB output in Figure 14.22(b) and (c) gives plots of the residuals for the QHIC simple linear regression model against values of x and $\hat{y}$. To understand how these plots are constructed, recall that for the first observation (home) $y = 1{,}412.08$, $x = 237.00$, $\hat{y} = 1{,}371.816$, and the residual is 40.264. It follows that the point plotted in Figure 14.22(b) corresponding to the first observation has a horizontal axis coordinate of the x value 237.00 and a vertical axis coordinate of the residual 40.264. It also follows that the point plotted in Figure 14.22(c) corresponding to the first observation has a horizontal axis coordinate of the $\hat{y}$ value 1,371.816, and a vertical axis coordinate of the residual 40.264. Finally, note that the QHIC data are cross-sectional data, not time series data. Therefore, we cannot make a residual plot versus time.

FIGURE 14.23   **Residual Plots and the Constant Variance Assumption**

The constant variance assumption   To check the validity of the constant variance assumption, we examine plots of the residuals against values of x, $\hat{y}$, and time (if the regression data are time series data). When we look at these plots, the pattern of the residuals' fluctuation around 0 tells us about the validity of the constant variance assumption. A residual plot that "fans out" [as in Figure 14.23(a)] suggests that the error terms are becoming more spread out as the horizontal plot value increases and that the constant variance assumption is violated. Here we would say that an **increasing error variance** exists. A residual plot that "funnels in" [as in Figure 14.23(b)] suggests that the spread of the error terms is decreasing as the horizontal plot value increases and that again the constant variance assumption is violated. In this case we would say that a **decreasing error variance** exists. A residual plot with a "horizontal band appearance" [as in Figure 14.23(c)] suggests that the spread of the error terms around 0 is not changing much as the horizontal plot value increases. Such a plot tells us that the constant variance assumption (approximately) holds.

As an example, consider the QHIC case and the residual plot in Figure 14.22(b). This plot appears to fan out as x increases, indicating that the spread of the error terms is increasing as x increases. That is, an increasing error variance exists. This is equivalent to saying that the variance of the population of potential yearly upkeep expenditures for houses worth x (thousand dollars) appears to increase as x increases. The reason is that the model $y = \beta_0 + \beta_1 x + \varepsilon$ says that the variation of y is the same as the variation of ε. For example, the variance of the population of potential yearly upkeep expenditures for houses worth \$200,000 would be larger than the variance of the population of potential yearly upkeep expenditures for houses worth \$100,000. Increasing variance makes some intuitive sense because people with more expensive homes generally have more discretionary income. These people can choose to spend either a substantial amount or a much smaller amount on home upkeep, thus causing a relatively large variation in upkeep expenditures.

Another residual plot showing the increasing error variance in the QHIC Case is Figure 14.22(c). This plot tells us that the residuals appear to fan out as $\hat{y}$ (predicted y) increases, which is logical because $\hat{y}$ is an increasing function of x. Also, note that the scatter plot of y versus x in Figure 14.21 (page 526) shows the increasing error variance—the y values appear to fan out as x increases. In fact, one might ask why we need to consider residual plots when we can simply look at scatter plots of y versus x. One answer is that, in general, because of possible differences in scaling between residual plots and scatter plots of y versus x, one of these types of plots might be more informative in a particular situation. Therefore, we should always consider both types of plots.

When the constant variance assumption is violated, we cannot use the formulas of this chapter to make statistical inferences. Later in this section we discuss how we can make statistical inferences when a nonconstant error variance exists.

The assumption of correct functional form   If the functional form of a regression model is incorrect, the residual plots constructed by using the model often display a pattern suggesting the form of a more appropriate model. For instance, if we use a simple linear regression model when the true relationship between y and x is curved, the residual plot will have a curved appearance. For example, the scatter plot of upkeep expenditure, y, versus home value, x, in Figure 14.21 (page 526) has either a straight-line or slightly curved appearance. We used a simple linear regression model to describe the relationship between y and x, but note that there is a "dip," or slightly curved appearance, in the upper left portion of each residual plot in Figure 14.22 (page 528). Therefore, both the scatter plot and residual plots indicate that there might be a slightly curved relationship between y and x. Later in this section we discuss one way to model curved relationships.

The normality assumption   If the normality assumption holds, a histogram and/or stem-and-leaf display of the residuals should look reasonably bell-shaped and reasonably symmetric about 0. Figure 14.24(a) gives the MINITAB output of a stem-and-leaf display of the residuals from the simple linear regression model describing the QHIC data. The stem-and-leaf display looks fairly bell-shaped and symmetric about 0. However, the tails of the display look somewhat long and "heavy" or "thick," indicating a possible violation of the normality assumption.

Another way to check the normality assumption is to construct a **normal plot** of the residuals. To make a normal plot, we first arrange the residuals in order from smallest to largest. Letting the ordered residuals be denoted as $e_{(1)}, e_{(2)}, \ldots, e_{(n)}$ we denote the ith residual in the ordered listing as $e_{(i)}$. We plot $e_{(i)}$ on the vertical axis against a point called $z_{(i)}$ on the horizontal axis. Here $z_{(i)}$ is defined to be the point on the horizontal axis under the standard normal curve so that the area under this curve to the left of $z_{(i)}$ is $(3i - 1)/(3n + 1)$. For example, recall in the QHIC case that there are $n = 40$ residuals given in Figure 14.22(a). It follows that, when $i = 1$, then

$$\frac{3i - 1}{3n + 1} = \frac{3(1) - 1}{3(40) + 1} = \frac{2}{121} = .0165$$

Therefore, $z_{(1)}$ is the normal point having an area of .0165 under the standard normal curve to its left. Thus, as illustrated in Figure 14.24(b), $z_{(1)}$ equals -2.13. Because the smallest residual in Figure 14.22(a) is -289.044, the first point plotted is $e_{(1)} = -289.044$ on the vertical scale versus $z_{(1)} = -2.13$ on the horizontal scale. When $i = 2$, it can be verified that $(3i - 1)/(3n + 1)$ equals .0413 and thus that $z_{(2)} = -1.74$. Therefore, because the second-smallest residual in Figure 14.24(a) is -259.958, the second point plotted is $e_{(2)} = -259.958$ on the vertical scale versus $z_{(2)} = -1.74$ on the horizontal scale. This process is continued until the entire normal plot is constructed. The Excel add-in (MegaStat) output of this plot is given in Figure 14.24(c).

An equivalent plot is shown in Figure 14.24(d), which is a MINITAB output. In this figure, we plot the percentage $p_{(i)}$ of the area under the standard normal curve to the left of $z_{(i)}$ on the vertical axis. Thus, the first point plotted in this normal plot is $e_{(1)} = -289.044$ on the horizontal scale versus $p_{(1)} = (.0165)(100) = 1.65$ on the vertical scale, and the second point plotted is $e_{(2)} = -259.958$ on the horizontal scale versus $p_{(2)} = (.0413)(100) = 4.13$ on the vertical scale. It is important to note that the scale on the vertical axis does not have the usual spacing between the percentages. The spacing reflects the distance between the z-scores that correspond to the percentages in the standard normal distribution. Hence, if we wished to create the plot in Figure 14.24(d) by hand, we would need special graphing paper with this vertical scale.

It can be proven that, if the normality assumption holds, then the expected value of the ith ordered residual $e_{(i)}$ is proportional to $z_{(i)}$. Therefore, a plot of the $e_{(i)}$ values on the horizontal scale versus the $z_{(i)}$ values on the vertical scale (or equivalently, the $e_{(i)}$ values on the horizontal scale versus the $p_{(i)}$ values on the vertical scale) should have a straight-line appearance. That is, if the normality assumption holds, then the normal plot should have a straight-line appearance. A normal plot that does not look like a straight line (admittedly, a subjective decision) indicates that the normality assumption is violated. Because the normal plots in Figure 14.24 have some curvature (particularly in the upper right portion), there is a possible violation of the normality assumption.

F I G U R E   1 4 . 2 4   **Stem-and-Leaf Display and Normal Plots of the Residuals from the Simple Linear Regression Model Describing the QHIC Data**

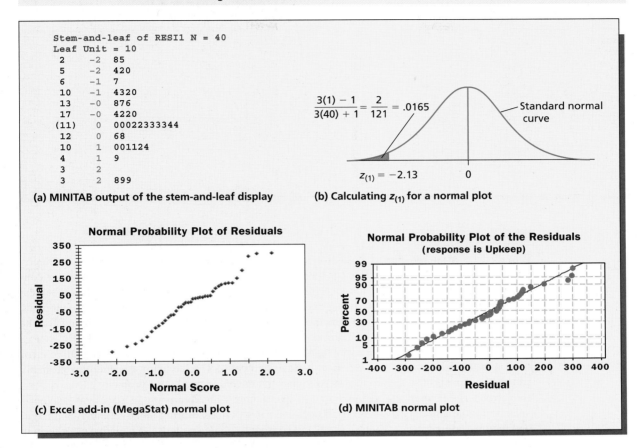

(a) MINITAB output of the stem-and-leaf display

(b) Calculating $z_{(1)}$ for a normal plot

(c) Excel add-in (MegaStat) normal plot

(d) MINITAB normal plot

It is important to realize that violations of the constant variance and correct functional form assumptions can often cause a histogram and/or stem-and-leaf display of the residuals to look nonnormal and can cause the normal plot to have a curved appearance. Because of this, it is usually a good idea to use residual plots to check for nonconstant variance and incorrect functional form before making any final conclusions about the normality assumption. Later in this section we discuss a procedure that sometimes remedies simultaneous violations of the constant variance, correct functional form, and normality assumptions.

The independence assumption   The independence assumption is most likely to be violated when the regression data are **time series data**—that is, data that have been collected in a time sequence. For such data the time-ordered error terms can be **autocorrelated.** Intuitively, we say that error terms occurring over time have **positive autocorrelation** if a positive error term in time period i tends to produce, or be followed by, another positive error term in time period $i + k$ (some later time period) and if a negative error term in time period i tends to produce, or be followed by, another negative error term in time period $i + k$. In other words, positive autocorrelation exists when positive error terms tend to be followed over time by positive error terms and when negative error terms tend to be followed over time by negative error terms. Positive autocorrelation in the error terms is depicted in Figure 14.25(a), which illustrates that **positive autocorrelation can produce a cyclical error term pattern over time.** The simple linear regression model implies that a positive error term produces a greater-than-average value of y and a negative error term produces a smaller-than-average value of y. It follows that positive autocorrelation in the error terms means that greater-than-average values of y tend to be followed by greater-than-average values of y, and smaller-than-average values of y tend to be followed by smaller-than-average values of y. An example of positive autocorrelation could hypothetically be

FIGURE 14.25   **Positive and Negative Autocorrelation**

**(a) Positive Autocorrelation in the Error
     Terms: Cyclical Pattern**

**(b) Negative Autocorrelation in the Error
     Terms: Alternating Pattern**

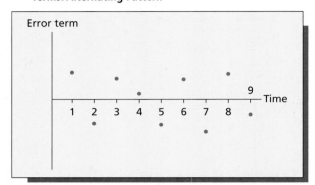

provided by a simple linear regression model relating demand for a product to advertising expenditure. Here we assume that the data are time series data observed over a number of consecutive sales periods. One of the factors included in the error term of the simple linear regression model is competitors' advertising expenditure for their similar products. If, for the moment, we assume that competitors' advertising expenditure significantly affects the demand for the product, then a higher-than-average competitors' advertising expenditure probably causes demand for the product to be lower than average and hence probably causes a negative error term. On the other hand, a lower-than-average competitors' advertising expenditure probably causes the demand for the product to be higher than average and hence probably causes a positive error term. If, then, competitors tend to spend money on advertising in a cyclical fashion—spending large amounts for several consecutive sales periods (during an advertising campaign) and then spending lesser amounts for several consecutive sales periods—a negative error term in one sales period will tend to be followed by a negative error term in the next sales period, and a positive error term in one sales period will tend to be followed by a positive error term in the next sales period. In this case the error terms would display positive autocorrelation, and thus these error terms would not be statistically independent.

Intuitively, error terms occurring over time have **negative autocorrelation** if a positive error term in time period i tends to produce, or be followed by, a negative error term in time period $i + k$ and if a negative error term in time period i tends to produce, or be followed by, a positive error term in time period $i + k$. In other words, negative autocorrelation exists when positive error terms tend to be followed over time by negative error terms and negative error terms tend to be followed over time by positive error terms. An example of negative autocorrelation in the error terms is depicted in Figure 14.25(b), which illustrates that **negative autocorrelation in the error terms can produce an alternating pattern over time.** It follows that negative autocorrelation in the error terms means that greater-than-average values of y tend to be followed by smaller-than-average values of y and smaller-than-average values of y tend to be followed by greater-than-average values of y. An example of negative autocorrelation might be provided by a retailer's weekly stock orders. Here a larger-than-average stock order one week might result in an oversupply and hence a smaller-than-average order the next week.

The **independence assumption** basically says that the time-ordered error terms display no positive or negative autocorrelation. This says that **the error terms occur in a random pattern over time.** Such a random pattern would imply that the error terms (and their corresponding y values) are statistically independent.

Because the residuals are point estimates of the error terms, a residual plot versus time is used to check the independence assumption. If a residual plot versus the data's time sequence has a cyclical appearance, the error terms are positively autocorrelated, and the independence assumption is violated. If a plot of the time-ordered residuals has an alternating pattern, the error terms are negatively autocorrelated, and again the independence assumption is violated.

However, if a plot of the time-ordered residuals displays a random pattern, the error terms have little or no autocorrelation. In such a case, it is reasonable to conclude that the independence assumption holds.

EXAMPLE 14.12 Pages Bookstore: Positive Autocorrelation

Figure 14.26(a) presents data concerning weekly sales at Pages Bookstore (Sales), Pages weekly advertising expenditure (Adver), and the weekly advertising expenditure of Pages main competitor (Compadv). Here the sales values are expressed in thousands of dollars, and the advertising expenditure values are expressed in hundreds of dollars. Figure 14.26(a) also gives the MINITAB output of the residuals that are obtained when a simple linear regression analysis is performed relating Pages sales to Pages advertising expenditure. These residuals are plotted versus time in Figure 14.26(b). We see that the residual plot has a cyclical pattern. This tells us that the error terms for the model are positively autocorrelated and the independence assumption is violated. Furthermore, there tend to be positive residuals when the competitor's advertising expenditure is lower (in weeks 1 through 8 and weeks 14, 15, and 16) and negative residuals when the competitor's advertising expenditure is higher (in weeks 9 through 13). Therefore, the competitor's advertising expenditure seems to be causing the positive autocorrelation.

FIGURE 14.26   **Pages Bookstore Sales and Advertising Data, and Residual Analysis**

(a) **The data and the MINITAB output of the residuals from a simple linear regression relating Pages sales to Pages advertising expenditure**   ◗Ⓢ BookSales

Observation	Adver	Compadv	Sales	Predicted	Residual
1	18	10	22	18.7	3.3
2	20	10	27	23.0	4.0
3	20	15	23	23.0	−0.0
4	25	15	31	33.9	−2.9
5	28	15	45	40.4	4.6
6	29	20	47	42.6	4.4
7	29	20	45	42.6	2.4
8	28	25	42	40.4	1.6
9	30	35	37	44.7	−7.7
10	31	35	39	46.9	−7.9
11	34	35	45	53.4	−8.4
12	35	30	52	55.6	−3.6
13	36	30	57	57.8	−0.8
14	38	25	62	62.1	−0.1
15	41	20	73	68.6	4.4
16	45	20	84	77.3	6.7

Durbin-Watson = 0.65

(b) **A plot of the residuals in Figure 14.26(a) versus time**

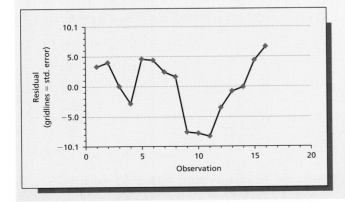

To conclude this example, note that the simple linear regression model relating Pages sales to Pages advertising expenditure has a standard error, s, of 5.038. The residual plot in Figure 14.26(b) includes grid lines that are placed one and two standard errors above and below the residual mean of 0. Such grid lines help us to better diagnose potential violations of the regression assumptions.

When the independence assumption is violated, various remedies can be employed. One approach is to identify which independent variable left in the error term (for example, competitors' advertising expenditure) is causing the error terms to be autocorrelated. We can then remove this independent variable from the error term and insert it directly into the regression model, forming a **multiple regression model.** (Multiple regression models are discussed in Chapter 15.)

The Durbin–Watson test   One type of positive or negative autocorrelation is called **first-order autocorrelation.** It says that ε_t, the error term in time period t, is related to ε_{t-1}, the error term in time period $t-1$. To check for first-order autocorrelation, we can use the **Durbin–Watson statistic**

$$d = \frac{\sum_{t=2}^{n} (e_t - e_{t-1})^2}{\sum_{t=1}^{n} e_t^2}$$

where $e_1, e_2, \ldots, e_n$ are the time-ordered residuals.

Intuitively, small values of d lead us to conclude that there is positive autocorrelation. This is because, if d is small, the differences $(e_t - e_{t-1})$ are small. This indicates that the adjacent residuals e_t and e_{t-1} are of the same magnitude, which in turn says that the adjacent error terms ε_t and ε_{t-1} are positively correlated. Consider testing the null hypothesis H_0 **that the error terms are not autocorrelated** versus the alternative hypothesis H_a **that the error terms are positively autocorrelated.** Durbin and Watson have shown that there are points (denoted $d_{L,\alpha}$ and $d_{U,\alpha}$) such that, if α is the probability of a Type I error, then

1 If $d < d_{L,\alpha}$, we reject H_0.

2 If $d > d_{U,\alpha}$, we do not reject H_0.

3 If $d_{L,\alpha} \leq d \leq d_{U,\alpha}$, the test is inconclusive.

Reject H_0 $d_{L,\alpha}$ Test inconclusive $d_{U,\alpha}$ Do not reject H_0

So that the Durbin–Watson test may be easily done, tables containing the points $d_{L,\alpha}$ and $d_{U,\alpha}$ have been constructed. These tables give the appropriate $d_{L,\alpha}$ and $d_{U,\alpha}$ points for various values of α; k, the number of independent variables used by the regression model; and n, the number of observations. Tables A.11, A.12, and A.13 (pages 801–802) give these points for $\alpha = .05$, $\alpha = .025$, and $\alpha = .01$. A portion of Table A.11 is given in Table 14.3. Note that when we are considering a simple linear regression model, which uses *one* independent variable, we look up the points $d_{L,\alpha}$ and $d_{U,\alpha}$ under the heading "$k = 1$." Other values of k are used when we study multiple regression models in Chapter 15. Using the residuals in Figure 14.26(a), the Durbin–Watson statistic for the simple linear regression model relating Pages sales to Pages advertising expenditure is calculated to be

$$d = \frac{\sum_{t=2}^{16} (e_t - e_{t-1})^2}{\sum_{t=1}^{16} e_t^2}$$

$$= \frac{(4.0 - 3.3)^2 + (0.0 - 4.0)^2 + \cdots + (6.7 - 4.4)^2}{(3.3)^2 + (4.0)^2 + \cdots + (6.7)^2}$$

$$= .65$$

A MINITAB output of the Durbin–Watson statistic is given at the bottom of Figure 14.26(a). To test for positive autocorrelation, we note that there are $n = 16$ observations and the regression

TABLE 14.3   **Critical Values for the Durbin–Watson d Statistic ($\alpha = .05$)**

n	k = 1		k = 2		k = 3		k = 4	
	$d_{L,.05}$	$d_{U,.05}$	$d_{L,.05}$	$d_{U,.05}$	$d_{L,.05}$	$d_{U,.05}$	$d_{L,.05}$	$d_{U,.05}$
15	1.08	1.36	0.95	1.54	0.82	1.75	0.69	1.97
16	1.10	1.37	0.98	1.54	0.86	1.73	0.74	1.93
17	1.13	1.38	1.02	1.54	0.90	1.71	0.78	1.90
18	1.16	1.39	1.05	1.53	0.93	1.69	0.82	1.87
19	1.18	1.40	1.08	1.53	0.97	1.68	0.86	1.85
20	1.20	1.41	1.10	1.54	1.00	1.68	0.90	1.83

model uses $k = 1$ independent variable. Therefore, if we set $\alpha = .05$, Table 14.3 tells us that $d_{L,.05} = 1.10$ and $d_{U,.05} = 1.37$. Because $d = .65$ is less than $d_{L,.05} = 1.10$, we reject the null hypothesis of no autocorrelation. That is, we conclude (at an α of .05) that there is positive (first-order) autocorrelation.

It can be shown that the Durbin–Watson statistic d is always between 0 and 4. Large values of d (and hence small values of $4 - d$) lead us to conclude that there is negative autocorrelation because if d is large, this indicates that the differences $(e_t - e_{t-1})$ are large. This says that the adjacent error terms ε_t and ε_{t-1} are negatively autocorrelated. Consider testing the null hypothesis H_0 **that the error terms are not autocorrelated** versus the alternative hypothesis H_a **that the error terms are negatively autocorrelated.** Durbin and Watson have shown that based on setting the probability of a Type I error equal to α, the points $d_{L,\alpha}$ and $d_{U,\alpha}$ are such that

1   If $(4 - d) < d_{L,\alpha}$, we reject H_0.

2   If $(4 - d) > d_{U,\alpha}$, we do not reject H_0.

3   If $d_{L,\alpha} \leq (4 - d) \leq d_{U,\alpha}$, the test is inconclusive.

Reject H_0 $d_{L,\alpha}$ Test inconclusive $d_{U,\alpha}$ Do not reject H_0

As an example, for the Pages sales simple linear regression model, we see that

$$(4 - d) = (4 - .65) = 3.35 > d_{U,.05} = 1.37$$

Therefore, on the basis of setting α equal to .05, we do not reject the null hypothesis of no autocorrelation. That is, there is no evidence of negative (first-order) autocorrelation.

We can also use the Durbin–Watson statistic to test for positive or negative autocorrelation. Specifically, consider testing the null hypothesis H_0 **that the error terms are not autocorrelated** versus the alternative hypothesis H_a **that the error terms are positively or negatively autocorrelated.** Durbin and Watson have shown that, based on setting the probability of a Type I error equal to α, we perform both the above described test for positive autocorrelation and the above described test for negative autocorrelation by using the critical values $d_{L,\alpha/2}$ and $d_{U,\alpha/2}$ for each test. If **either test** says to reject H_0, then we reject H_0. If **both tests** say to not reject H_0, then we do not reject H_0. Finally, if **either test** is inconclusive, then the overall test is inconclusive. For example, consider testing for positive or negative autocorrelation in the Pages sales model. If we set α equal to .05, then $\alpha/2 = .025$, and we need to find the points $d_{L,.025}$ and $d_{U,.025}$ when $n = 16$ and $k = 1$. Looking up these points in Table A.12 (page 801), we find that $d_{L,.025} = .98$ and $d_{U,.025} = 1.24$. Because $d = .65$ is less than $d_{L,.025} = .98$, we reject the null hypothesis of no autocorrelation. That is, we conclude (at an α of .05) that there is first-order autocorrelation.

Although we have used the Pages sales model in these examples to demonstrate the Durbin–Watson tests for (1) positive autocorrelation, (2) negative autocorrelation, and (3) positive or negative autocorrelation, we must in practice choose one of these Durbin–Watson tests in a particular situation. Because positive autocorrelation is more common in real time series data than negative autocorrelation, the Durbin–Watson test for positive autocorrelation is used more often than the other two tests. Also, note that each Durbin–Watson test assumes that the population of all possible residuals at any time t has a normal distribution.

Transforming the dependent variable: A possible remedy for violations of the constant variance, correct functional form, and normality assumptions   In general, if a data or residual plot indicates that the error variance of a regression model increases as an independent variable or the predicted value of the dependent variable increases, then we can sometimes remedy the situation by transforming the dependent variable. One transformation that works well is to take each y value to a fractional power. As an example, we might use a transformation in which we take the square root (or one-half power) of each y value. Letting y^* denote the value obtained when the transformation is applied to y, we would write the **square root transformation** as

$$y^* = \sqrt{y} = y^{.5}$$

Another commonly used transformation is the **quartic root transformation.** Here we take each y value to the one-fourth power. That is,

$$y^* = y^{.25}$$

If we consider a transformation that takes each y value to a fractional power (such as .5, .25, or the like), as the power approaches 0, the transformed value y^* approaches the natural logarithm of y (commonly written ln y). In fact, we sometimes use the **logarithmic transformation**

$$y^* = \ln y$$

which takes the natural logarithm of each y value. In general, when we take a fractional power (including the natural logarithm) of the dependent variable, the transformation not only tends to equalize the error variance but also tends to "straighten out" certain types of nonlinear data plots. Specifically, if a data plot indicates that the dependent variable is increasing at an increasing rate, then a fractional power transformation tends to straighten out the data plot. A fractional power transformation can also help to remedy a violation of the normality assumption. Because we cannot know which fractional power to use before we actually take the transformation, we recommend taking all of the square root, quartic root, and natural logarithm transformations and seeing which one best equalizes the error variance and (possibly) straightens out a nonlinear data plot.

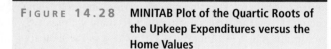

EXAMPLE 14.13 The QHIC Case: Using a Data Transformation

Consider the QHIC upkeep expenditures in Figure 14.21. In Figures 14.27, 14.28, and 14.29 we show the plots that result when we take the square root, quartic root, and natural logarithmic transformations of the upkeep expenditures and plot the transformed values versus the home values. The square root transformation seems to best equalize the error variance and straighten out the curved data plot in Figure 14.21. Note that the natural logarithm transformation seems to

FIGURE 14.27	MINITAB Plot of the Square Roots of the Upkeep Expenditures versus the Home Values

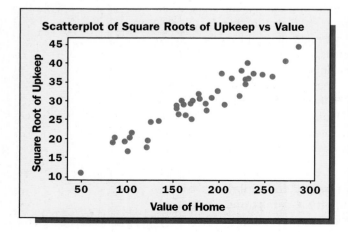

FIGURE 14.28	MINITAB Plot of the Quartic Roots of the Upkeep Expenditures versus the Home Values

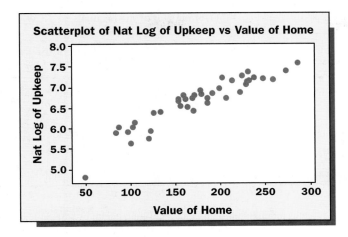

FIGURE 14.29 MINITAB Plot of the Natural Logarithms of the Upkeep Expenditures versus the Home Values

FIGURE 14.30 MINITAB Output of a Regression Analysis of the Upkeep Expenditure Data by Using the Model $y^* = \beta_0 + \beta_1 x + \varepsilon$ where $y^* = y^{.5}$, and a Residual Plot versus x

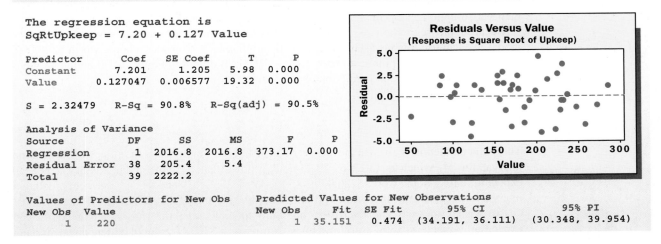

```
The regression equation is
SqRtUpkeep = 7.20 + 0.127 Value

Predictor      Coef    SE Coef      T       P
Constant      7.201     1.205    5.98   0.000
Value      0.127047   0.006577   19.32   0.000

S = 2.32479   R-Sq = 90.8%   R-Sq(adj) = 90.5%

Analysis of Variance
Source           DF       SS       MS       F       P
Regression        1    2016.8   2016.8   373.17   0.000
Residual Error   38     205.4      5.4
Total            39    2222.2
```

```
Values of Predictors for New Obs      Predicted Values for New Observations
New Obs   Value                       New Obs     Fit   SE Fit       95% CI              95% PI
      1     220                             1  35.151    0.474   (34.191, 36.111)   (30.348, 39.954)
```

"overtransform" the data—the error variance tends to decrease as the home value increases and the data plot seems to "bend down." The plot of the quartic roots indicates that the quartic root transformation also seems to overtransform the data (but not by as much as the logarithmic transformation). In general, as the fractional power gets smaller, the transformation gets stronger. Different fractional powers are best in different situations.

Because the plot in Figure 14.27 of the square roots of the upkeep expenditures versus the home values has a straight-line appearance, we consider the model

$$y^* = \beta_0 + \beta_1 x + \varepsilon \quad \text{where } y^* = y^{.5}$$

The MINITAB output of a regression analysis using this transformed model is given in Figure 14.30, along with a plot of the transformed model's residuals versus x. Note that this residual plot has a horizontal band appearance. It can also be verified that the transformed model's residual plot versus $\hat{y}$, which we do not give here, has a similar horizontal band appearance.

FIGURE 14.31   MINITAB Output of Normality Assumption Analysis for the Upkeep Expenditure Model
$y^* = \beta_0 + \beta_1 x + \varepsilon$ where $y^* = y^{.5}$

(a) Histogram of the residuals

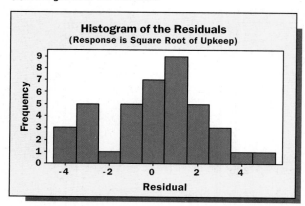

(b) Normal plot of the residuals

Therefore, we conclude that the constant variance and the correct functional form assumptions approximately hold for the transformed model. Next, note that the histogram of the transformed model's residuals in Figure 14.31(a) looks reasonably bell-shaped and symmetric, and note that the normal plot of these residuals in Figure 14.31(b) looks straighter than the normal plots for the untransformed model (see Figure 14.24 on page 531). Therefore, we also conclude that the normality assumption approximately holds for the transformed model.

Because the regression assumptions approximately hold for the transformed regression model, we can use this model to make statistical inferences. Consider a home worth $220,000. Using the least squares point estimates on the MINITAB output in Figure 14.30 on the previous page, it follows that a point prediction of y^* for such a home is

$$\hat{y}^* = 7.201 + .127047(220)$$
$$= 35.151$$

This point prediction is given at the bottom of the MINITAB output, as is the 95 percent prediction interval for y^*, which is [30.348, 39.954]. It follows that a point prediction of the upkeep expenditure for a home worth $220,000 is $(35.151)^2 = \$1,235.59$ and that a 95 percent prediction interval for this upkeep expenditure is $[(30.348)^2, (39.954)^2] = [\$921.00, \$1596.32]$. Suppose that QHIC wishes to send an advertising brochure to any home that has a predicted upkeep expenditure of at least $500. It follows that a home worth $220,000 would be sent an advertising brochure. This is because the predicted yearly upkeep expenditure for such a home is (as just calculated) $1,235.59. Other homes can be evaluated in a similar fashion.

Exercises for Section 14.9

 connect

CONCEPTS

14.56 In regression analysis, what variables should the residuals be plotted against?

14.57 What patterns in residual plots indicate violations of the regression assumptions?

14.58 In regression analysis, how do we check the normality assumption?

METHODS AND APPLICATIONS

14.59 THE SERVICE TIME CASE 🔵 SrvcTime

The residuals given by the service time prediction equation $\hat{y} = 11.4641 + 24.6022x$ are listed in Table 14.4(a), and residual plots versus x and $\hat{y}$ are given in Figures 14.32(a) and (b). Do the plots indicate any violations of the regression assumptions? Explain.

TABLE 14.4	Service Time Model Residuals and Normal Plot Calculations

(a) Predicted values and residuals using
$$\hat{y} = 11.4641 + 24.6022x$$

Observation	Copiers	Minutes	Predicted	Residual
1	4	109.0	109.9	−0.9
2	2	58.0	60.7	−2.7
3	5	138.0	134.5	3.5
4	7	189.0	183.7	5.3
5	1	37.0	36.1	0.9
6	3	82.0	85.3	−3.3
7	4	103.0	109.9	−6.9
8	5	134.0	134.5	−0.5
9	2	68.0	60.7	7.3
10	6	112.0	109.9	2.1
11	4	154.0	159.1	−5.1

(b) Ordered residuals and normal plot calculations

i	Ordered Residual, $e_{(i)}$	$\dfrac{3i-1}{3n+1}$	$z_{(i)}$
1	−6.9	.0588	−1.565
2	−5.1	.1470	−1.05
3	−3.3	.2353	−.72
4	−2.7	.3235	−.46
5	−0.9	.4118	−.22
6	−0.5	.5000	0
7	0.9	.5882	.22
8	2.1	.6765	.46
9	3.5	.7647	.72
10	5.3	.8529	1.05
11	7.3	.9412	1.565

FIGURE 14.32	Service Time Model Residual and Normal Plots

(a) Residual plot versus x

(b) Residual plot versus $\hat{y}$

(c) Normal plot

14.60   THE SERVICE TIME CASE ⊙ SrvcTime

The residuals given by the service time prediction equation $\hat{y} = 11.4641 + 24.6022x$ are listed in Table 14.4(a).

a In this exercise we construct a normal plot of these residuals. To construct this plot, we must first arrange the residuals in order from smallest to largest. These ordered residuals are given in Table 14.4(b). Denoting the ith ordered residual as $e_{(i)}$ ($i = 1, 2, \ldots, 11$), we next compute for each value of i the point $z_{(i)}$. These computations are summarized in Table 14.4(b). Show how $z_{(4)} = -.46$ and $z_{(10)} = 1.05$ have been obtained.

b The ordered residuals (the $e_{(i)}$'s) are plotted against the $z_{(i)}$'s in Figure 14.32(c). Does this figure indicate a violation of the normality assumption? Explain.

14.61 A simple linear regression model is employed to analyze the 24 monthly observations given in Table 14.5 on the next page. Residuals are computed and are plotted versus time. The resulting residual plot is shown in Figure 14.33 on the next page. **(1)** Discuss why the residual plot suggests the existence of positive autocorrelation. **(2)** The Durbin–Watson statistic d can be calculated to be .473. Test for positive (first-order) autocorrelation at $\alpha = .05$, and test for negative (first-order) autocorrelation at $\alpha = .05$ ⊙ SalesAdv

14.62   THE LAPTOP SERVICE TIME CASE ⊙ SrvcTime2

The page margin shows data concerning the time, y, required to perform service (in minutes) and the number of laptop computers serviced, x, for 15 service calls. Figure 14.34 on the next page gives a plot of y versus x, and Figure 14.35(a) gives the Excel output of a plot of the residuals versus x for a simple linear regression model. What regression assumption appears to be violated? Explain.

The Laptop Service Time Data

Service Time, y	Laptops Serviced, x
92	3
63	2
126	6
247	8
49	2
90	4
119	5
114	6
67	2
115	4
188	6
298	11
77	3
151	10
27	1

TABLE 14.5   Sales and Advertising Data for Exercise 14.61   DS SalesAdv

Month	Monthly Total Sales, y	Advertising Expenditures, x
1	202.66	116.44
2	232.91	119.58
3	272.07	125.74
4	290.97	124.55
5	299.09	122.35
6	296.95	120.44
7	279.49	123.24
8	255.75	127.55
9	242.78	121.19
10	255.34	118.00
11	271.58	121.81
12	268.27	126.54
13	260.51	129.85
14	266.34	122.65
15	281.24	121.64
16	286.19	127.24
17	271.97	132.35
18	265.01	130.86
19	274.44	122.90
20	291.81	117.15
21	290.91	109.47
22	264.95	114.34
23	228.40	123.72
24	209.33	130.33

Source: *Forecasting Methods and Applications,* "Sales and Advertising Data," by S. Makridakis, S. C. Wheelwright, and V. E. McGee, *Forecasting: Methods and Applications* (Copyright © 1983 John Wiley & Sons, Inc.). Reprinted by permission of John Wiley & Sons, Inc.

FIGURE 14.33   Residual Plot for Exercise 14.61

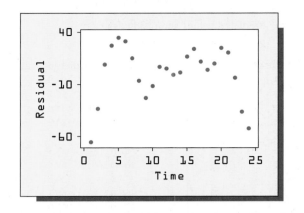

FIGURE 14.34   The Laptop Service Time Scatter Plot (for Exercise 14.62)   DS SrvcTime2

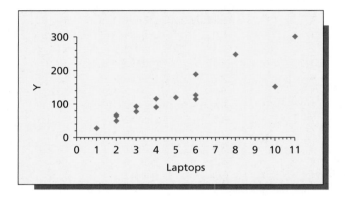

FIGURE 14.35   Residual Plots in the Laptop Service Time Case (for Exercises 14.62 and 14.63).

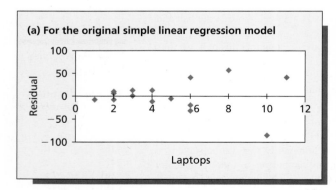

(a) For the original simple linear regression model

(b) For the transformed regression model

14.63   THE LAPTOP SERVICE TIME CASE   DS SrvcTime2

Figure 14.35(a) shows the residual plot versus x for the simple linear regression of the laptop service time data. This plot fans out, indicating that the error term ε tends to become larger in magnitude as x increases. To remedy this violation of the constant variance assumption, we divide all terms in the simple linear regression model by x. This gives the transformed model

$$\frac{y}{x} = \beta_0\left(\frac{1}{x}\right) + \beta_1 + \frac{\varepsilon}{x} \quad \text{or, equivalently,} \quad \frac{y}{x} = \beta_0 + \beta_1\left(\frac{1}{x}\right) + \frac{\varepsilon}{x}$$

FIGURE 14.36 **MINITAB Output of a Regression Analysis of the Laptop Service Time Data Using the Model $y/x = \beta_0 + \beta_1(1/x) + \varepsilon/x$**

```
The regression equation is
Y/X = 24.0 + 6.76 1/X

Predictor        Coef      SE Coef         T         P
Constant        24.041       2.246     10.70     0.000
1/X              6.764       5.794      1.17     0.264

        S = 5.15816      R-Sq = 9.50%     R-Sq(adj) = 2.5%

Analysis of Variance
Source             DF         SS        MS        F        P
Regression          1      36.27     36.27     1.36    0.264
Residual Error     13     345.89     26.61
Total              14     382.15

Values of Predictors for New Obs  Predicted Values for New Observations
New Obs          1/X             Obs       Fit    SE Fit        95% CI              95% PI
   1           0.143              1     25.01      1.65    (21.43, 28.58)     (13.30, 36.71)
```

Figure 14.36 and Figure 14.35(b) give a regression output and a residual plot versus x for this model. Does the residual plot indicate that the constant variance assumption holds for the transformed model? Explain.

14.64 THE LAPTOP SERVICE TIME CASE DS SrvcTime2

Consider a future service call on which seven laptops will be serviced. Let μ_0 represent the mean service time for all service calls on which seven laptops will be serviced, and let y_0 represent the actual service time for an individual service call on which seven laptops will be serviced. The bottom of the MINITAB output in Figure 14.36 tells us that $\hat{y}/7 = 24.041 + 6.764(1/7) = 25.01$ is a point estimate of $\mu_0/7$ and a point prediction of $y_0/7$. **(1)** Multiply this result by 7 to obtain $\hat{y}$. **(2)** Multiply the ends of the confidence interval and prediction interval shown on the MINITAB output by 7. This will give a 95 percent confidence interval for μ_0 and a 95 percent prediction interval for y_0. **(3)** If the number of minutes we will allow for the future service call is the upper limit of the 95 percent confidence interval for μ_0, how many minutes will we allow?

14.65 USING A NATURAL LOGARITHM TRANSFORMATION DS WestStk

Western Steakhouses, a fast-food chain, opened 15 years ago. Each year since then the number of steakhouses in operation, y, was recorded. An analyst for the firm wishes to use these data to predict the number of steakhouses that will be in operation next year. The data are given in the page margin, and a plot of the data is given in Figure 14.37(a) on the next page. Examining the data plot, we see that the number of steakhouse openings has increased over time at an increasing rate and with increasing variation. A plot of the natural logarithms of the steakhouse values versus time (see Figure 14.37(b) on the next page) has a straight-line appearance with constant variation. Therefore, we consider the model $\ln y_t = \beta_0 + \beta_1 t + \varepsilon_t$. If we use MINITAB, we find that the least squares point estimates of β_0 and β_1 are $b_0 = 2.07012$ and $b_1 = .256880$. We also find that a point prediction of and a 95 percent prediction interval for the natural logarithm of the number of steakhouses in operation next year (year 16) are 6.1802 and [5.9945, 6.3659]. See the MINITAB output in Figure 14.38 on the next page.

a Use the least squares point estimates to calculate the point prediction.

b By exponentiating the point prediction and prediction interval—that is, by calculating $e^{6.1802}$ and $[e^{5.9945}, e^{6.3659}]$—find a point prediction of and a 95 percent prediction interval for the number of steakhouses in operation next year.

c The model $\ln y_t = \beta_0 + \beta_1 t + \varepsilon_t$ is called a **growth curve model** because it implies that

$$y_t = e^{(\beta_0 + \beta_1 t + \varepsilon_t)} = (e^{\beta_0})(e^{\beta_1 t})(e^{\varepsilon_t}) = \alpha_0 \alpha_1^t \eta_t$$

where $\alpha_0 = e^{\beta_0}$, $\alpha_1 = e^{\beta_1}$, and $\eta_t = e^{\varepsilon_t}$. Here $\alpha_1 = e^{\beta_1}$ is called the **growth rate** of the y values. Noting that the least squares point estimate of β_1 is $b_1 = .256880$, estimate the growth rate α_1.

d We see that $y_t = \alpha_0 \alpha_1^t \eta_t = (\alpha_0 \alpha_1^{t-1})\alpha_1 \eta_t \approx (y_{t-1})\alpha_1 \eta_t$. This says that y_t is expected to be approximately α_1 times y_{t-1}. Noting this, interpret the growth rate of part (c).

The Steakhouse Data	
Year, t	Steakhouses, y
1	11
2	14
3	16
4	22
5	28
6	36
7	46
8	67
9	82
10	99
11	119
12	156
13	257
14	284
15	403

(a) Time Series Plot of y versus t

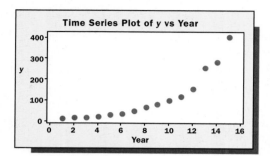

(b) Time Series Plot of Natural Logarithm of y versus t

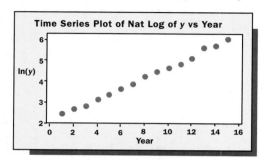

F I G U R E 1 4 . 3 8   **MINITAB Output of a Regression Analysis of the Steakhouse Data Using the Model ln $y_t = \beta_0 + \beta_1 t + \varepsilon_t$ (for Exercise 14.65)**

```
The regression equation is
ln(y) = 2.07 + 0.257 Year

Predictor        Coef      SE Coef        T        P
Constant      2.07012      0.04103    50.45    0.000
Year          0.256880     0.004513   56.92    0.000

S = 0.0755161   R-Sq = 99.6%   R-Sq(adj) = 99.6%    Durbin-Watson statistic = 1.87643

Analysis of Variance
Source          DF        SS        MS         F        P
Regression       1    18.477    18.477   3239.97    0.000
Residual Error  13     0.074     0.006
Total           14    18.551

Values of Predictors for New Obs    Predicted Values for New Observations
New Obs   Year                      Obs     Fit   SE Fit      95% CI            95% PI
      1     16                        1  6.1802   0.0410  (6.0916, 6.2689)  (5.9945, 6.3659)
```

14.10 Some Shortcut Formulas (Optional) ●●●

Calculating the sum of squared residuals   A shortcut formula for the sum of squared residuals is

$$SSE = SS_{yy} - \frac{SS_{xy}^2}{SS_{xx}}$$

where

$$SS_{yy} = \sum (y_i - \bar{y})^2 = \sum y_i^2 - \frac{\left(\sum y_i\right)^2}{n}$$

For example, consider the Tasty Sub Shop case. If we square each of the ten observed yearly revenues in Table 14.1 (page 488) and add up the resulting squared values, we find that $\sum y_i^2 = 7{,}897{,}109.47$. We have also found in Example 14.2 (page 493) that $\sum y_i = 8603.1$, $SS_{xy} = 29{,}836.389$ and $SS_{xx} = 1{,}913.129$. It follows that

$$SS_{yy} = \sum y_i^2 - \frac{\left(\sum y_i\right)^2}{n} = 7{,}897{,}109.47 - \frac{(8603.1)^2}{10} = 495{,}776.51$$

and

$$SSE = SS_{yy} - \frac{SS_{xy}^2}{SS_{xx}} = 495{,}776.51 - \frac{(29{,}836.389)^2}{1913.129}$$

$$= 495{,}776.51 - 465{,}316.30 = 30{,}460.21$$

Finally, note that SS_{xy}^2/SS_{xx} equals $b_1 SS_{xy}$. However, we recommend using the first of these expressions, because doing so usually gives less round-off error.

Calculating the total, explained, and unexplained variations   The **unexplained variation** is SSE, and thus the shortcut formula for SSE is a shortcut formula for the unexplained variation. The quantity SS_{yy} defined on page 542 is the **total variation,** and thus the shortcut formula for SS_{yy} is a shortcut formula for the total variation. Lastly, it can be shown that the expression SS_{xy}^2/SS_{xx} equals the **explained variation** and thus is a shortcut formula for this quantity.

Chapter Summary

This chapter has discussed **simple linear regression analysis,** which relates a **dependent variable** to a single **independent** (predictor) **variable.** We began by considering the **simple linear regression model,** which employs two parameters: the **slope** and **y intercept.** We next discussed how to compute the **least squares point estimates** of these parameters and how to use these estimates to calculate a **point estimate of the mean value of the dependent variable** and a **point prediction of an individual value** of the dependent variable. Then, after considering the assumptions behind the simple linear regression model, we discussed **testing the significance of the regression relationship** (slope), calculating a **confidence interval** for the mean value of the dependent variable, and calculating a **prediction interval** for an individual value of the dependent variable. We next explained several measures of the utility of the simple linear regression model. These include the **simple coefficient of determination** and an **F-test for the simple linear model.** We concluded this chapter by giving a discussion of using **residual analysis** to detect violations of the regression assumptions. We learned that we can sometimes remedy violations of these assumptions by **transforming** the dependent variable.

Glossary of Terms

dependent variable: The variable that is being described, predicted, or controlled. (page 487)

distance value: A measure of the distance between a particular value x_0 of the independent variable x and $\bar{x}$, the average of the previously observed values of x (the center of the experimental region). (page 511)

error term: The difference between an individual value of the dependent variable and the corresponding mean value of the dependent variable. (page 490)

experimental region: The range of the previously observed values of the independent variable. (page 494)

explained variation: A quantity that measures the amount of the total variation in the observed values of y that is explained by the predictor variable x. (pages 517 and 518)

independent variable: A variable used to describe, predict, and control the dependent variable. (page 487)

least squares point estimates: The point estimates of the slope and y intercept of the simple linear regression model that minimize the sum of squared residuals. (pages 492–493)

negative autocorrelation: The situation in which positive error terms tend to be followed over time by negative error terms and negative error terms tend to be followed over time by positive error terms. (page 532)

normal plot: A residual plot that is used to check the normality assumption. (page 530)

positive autocorrelation: The situation in which positive error terms tend to be followed over time by positive error terms and negative error terms tend to be followed over time by negative error terms. (page 531)

residual: The difference between the observed value of the dependent variable and the corresponding predicted value of the dependent variable. (pages 492, 527)

residual plot: A plot of the residuals against some criterion. The plot is used to check the validity of one or more regression assumptions. (page 527)

simple coefficient of determination r^2: The proportion of the total variation in the observed values of the dependent variable that is explained by the simple linear regression model. (page 518)

simple correlation coefficient: A measure of the linear association between two variables. (page 519)

simple linear regression model: An equation that describes the straight-line relationship between a dependent variable and an independent variable. (page 490)

slope (of the simple linear regression model): The change in the mean value of the dependent variable that is associated with a one-unit increase in the value of the independent variable. (page 490)

total variation: A quantity that measures the total amount of variation exhibited by the observed values of the dependent variable y. (pages 517 and 518)

unexplained variation: A quantity that measures the amount of of the total variation in the observed values of y that is not explained by the predictor variable x. (pages 517 and 518)

y-intercept (of the simple linear regression model): The mean value of the dependent variable when the value of the independent variable is 0. (page 490)

Important Formulas and Tests

Simple linear regression model: page 490

Least squares point estimates of β_0 and β_1: pages 492 and 493

Least squares line (prediction equation): page 492

The predicted value of y: page 492

The residual: pages 492 and 527

Sum of squared residuals: pages 492 and 502

Point estimate of a mean value of y: pages 496 and 510

Point prediction of an individual value of y: pages 496 and 510

Mean square error: page 502

Standard error: page 502

Standard error of the estimate b_1: page 503

Testing the significance of the slope: page 504

Testing the significance of the y-intercept: page 506

Confidence interval for the slope: page 506

Standard error of $\hat{y}$: page 511

Confidence interval for a mean value of y: page 511

Prediction interval for an individual value of y: page 511

Explained variation: page 518

Unexplained variation: page 518

Total variation: page 518

Simple coefficient of determination r^2: page 518

Simple correlation coefficient: page 519

Testing the significance of the population correlation coefficient: page 521

An F-test for the simple linear regression model: page 522

Normal plot calculations: page 530

Durbin–Watson test: pages 534–535

Shortcut formulas: pages 542–543

Supplementary Exercises

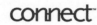

14.66 Consider the following data concerning the demand (y) and price (x) of a consumer product. **DS** Demand

Demand, y	252	244	241	234	230	223
Price, x	$2.00	$2.20	$2.40	$2.60	$2.80	$3.00

a Plot y versus x. Does it seem reasonable to use the simple linear regression model to relate y to x?

b Calculate the least squares point estimates of the parameters in the simple linear regression model.

c Write the least squares prediction equation. Graph this equation on the plot of y versus x.

d Test the significance of the regression relationship between y and x.

e Find a point prediction of and a 95 percent prediction interval for the demand corresponding to each of the prices $2.10, $2.75, and $3.10.

14.67 In an article in *Public Roads* (1983), Bissell, Pilkington, Mason, and Woods study bridge safety (measured in accident rates per 100 million vehicles) and the **difference** between the width of the bridge and the width of the roadway approach (road plus shoulder):[3] **DS** AutoAcc

WidthDiff.	−6	−4	−2	0	2	4	6	8	10	12
Accident	120	103	87	72	58	44	31	20	12	7

The MINITAB output of a simple linear regression analysis relating accident to width difference is as follows:

```
The regression equation is
Accident Rate = 74.7 - 6.44 WidthDif

Predictor        Coef      SE Coef          T          P
Constant       74.727        1.904      39.25      0.000
WidthDif      -6.4424       0.2938     -21.93      0.000

S = 5.33627    R-Sq = 98.4%    R-Sq(adj) = 98.2%

Analysis of Variance
Source          DF           SS          MS          F          P
Regression       1        13697       13697     480.99      0.000
Residual Error   8          228          28
Total            9        13924
```

[3]Source: H. H. Bissell, G. B. Pilkington II, J. M. Mason, and D. L. Woods, "Roadway Cross Section and Alignment," *Public Roads* 46 (March 1983), pp. 132–41.

Using the MINITAB output

a Identify and interpret the least squares point estimate of the slope of the simple linear regression model.

b Identify and interpret the p-value for testing H_0: $\beta_1 = 0$ versus H_a: $\beta_1 \neq 0$.

c Identify and interpret r^2.

14.68 The data in Table 14.6 concerning the relationship between smoking and lung cancer death are presented in a course of The Open University, *Statistics in Society,* Unit C4, The Open University Press, Milton Keynes, England, 1983. The original source of the data is *Occupational Mortality: The Registrar General's Decennial Supplement for England and Wales, 1970–1972,* Her Majesty's Stationery Office, London, 1978. In the table, a smoking index greater (less) than 100 indicates that men in the occupational group smoke more (less) than average when compared to all men of the same age. Similarly, a lung cancer death index greater (less) than 100 indicates that men in the occupational group have a greater (less) than average lung cancer death rate when compared to all men of the same age. In Figure 14.39 we present a portion of a MINITAB output of a simple linear regression analysis relating the lung cancer death index to the smoking index. In Figure 14.40 we present a plot of the lung cancer death index versus the smoking index. ⓓⓢ Smoking

TABLE 14.6 The Smoking and Lung Cancer Death Data ⓓⓢ Smoking

Occupational Group	Smoking Index	Lung Cancer Death Index
Farmers, foresters, and fisherman	77	84
Miners and quarrymen	137	116
Gas, coke, and chemical makers	117	123
Glass and ceramics makers	94	128
Furnace, forge, foundry, and rolling mill workers	116	155
Electrical and electronics workers	102	101
Engineering and allied trades	111	118
Woodworkers	93	113
Leather workers	88	104
Textile workers	102	88
Clothing workers	91	104
Food, drink, and tobacco workers	104	129
Paper and printing workers	107	86
Makers of other products	112	96
Construction workers	113	144
Painters and decorators	110	139
Drivers of stationary engines, cranes, etc.	125	113
Laborers not included elsewhere	133	146
Transport and communications workers	115	128
Warehousemen, storekeepers, packers, and bottlers	105	115
Clerical workers	87	79
Sales workers	91	85
Service, sport, and recreation workers	100	120
Administrators and managers	76	60
Professionals, technical workers, and artists	66	51

FIGURE 14.39 MINITAB Output of a Simple Linear Regression Analysis of the Data in Table 14.6

```
The regression equation is
Death Index = - 2.9 + 1.09 Smoking Index

Predictor        Coef      SE Coef         T          P
Constant        -2.89        23.03     -0.13      0.901
Smoking Index   1.0875       0.2209      4.92       0.00

S = 18.6154    R-Sq = 51.3%    R-Sq(adj) = 49.2%
```

FIGURE 14.40   **A Plot of the Lung Cancer Death Index versus the Smoking Index**

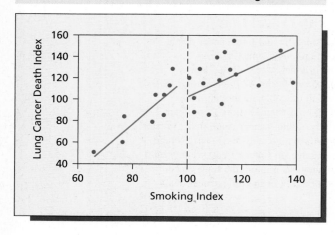

TABLE 14.7   **Return Length Estimates of β_1**

Average Estimate of β_1   Ⓓ Beta

Return Length Time	Aggressive Stocks	Defensive Stocks	Neutral Stocks
1	1.37	.50	.98
3	1.42	.44	.95
6	1.53	.41	.94
9	1.69	.39	1.00
12	1.83	.40	.98
15	1.67	.38	1.00
18	1.78	.39	1.02
24	1.86	.35	1.14
30	1.83	.33	1.22

Source: Reprinted by permission from H. Levy, "Measuring Risk and Performance over Alternative Investment Horizons," *Financial Analysts Journal* (March–April 1984), pp. 61–68. Copyright © 1984, CFA Institute. Reproduced and modified from Financial Analysts Journal with permission of CFA Institute.

a   Although the data do not prove that smoking increases your chance of getting lung cancer, can you think of a third factor that would cause the two indexes to move together?

b   Does the slope of the hypothetical line relating the two indexes when the smoking index is less than 100 seem to equal the slope of the hypothetical line relating the two indexes when the smoking index is greater than 100? If you wish, use simple linear regression to make a more precise determination. What practical conclusion might you make?

14.69   In analyzing the stock market, we sometimes use the model $y = \beta_0 + \beta_1 x + \varepsilon$ to relate y, the rate of return on a particular stock, to x, the rate of return on the overall stock market. When using the preceding model, we can interpret β_1 to be the percentage point change in the mean (or expected) rate of return on the particular stock that is associated with an increase of one percentage point in the rate of return on the overall stock market.

   If regression analysis can be used to conclude (at a high level of confidence) that β_1 is greater than 1 (for example, if the 95 percent confidence interval for β_1 were [1.1826, 1.4723]), this indicates that the mean rate of return on the particular stock changes more quickly than the rate of return on the overall stock market. Such a stock is called an *aggressive stock* because gains for such a stock tend to be greater than overall market gains (which occur when the market is bullish). However, losses for such a stock tend to be greater than overall market losses (which occur when the market is bearish). Aggressive stocks should be purchased if you expect the market to rise and avoided if you expect the market to fall.

   If regression analysis can be used to conclude (at a high level of confidence) that β_1 is less than 1 (for example, if the 95 percent confidence interval for β_1 were [.4729, .7861]), this indicates that the mean rate of return on the particular stock changes more slowly than the rate of return on the overall stock market. Such a stock is called a *defensive stock.* Losses for such a stock tend to be less than overall market losses, whereas gains for such a stock tend to be less than overall market gains. Defensive stocks should be held if you expect the market to fall and sold off if you expect the market to rise.

   If the least squares point estimate b_1 of β_1 is nearly equal to 1, and if the 95 percent confidence interval for β_1 contains 1, this might indicate that the mean rate of return on the particular stock changes at roughly the same rate as the rate of return on the overall stock market. Such a stock is called a *neutral stock.*

   In an article in *Financial Analysts Journal,* Haim Levy considers how a stock's value of β_1 depends on the length of time for which the rate of return is calculated. Levy calculated estimated values of β_1 for return length times varying from 1 to 30 months for each of 38 aggressive stocks, 38 defensive stocks, and 68 neutral stocks. In Table 14.7 we present the average estimate of β_1 for each stock type for different return length times.

a   Let y = average estimate of β_1 and x = return length time, and consider relating y to x for each stock type by using the simple linear regression model $y = \beta_0^* + \beta_1^* x + \varepsilon$. Here β_0^* and β_1^* are regression parameters relating y to x. We use the asterisks to indicate that these regression parameters are different from β_0 and β_1. Calculate a 95 percent confidence interval for β_1^* for each stock type.

b   Carefully interpret the meaning of each interval that you found in part(a).

14.70 On January 28, 1986, the space shuttle *Challenger* exploded soon after takeoff, killing all eight astronauts aboard. The temperature at the Kennedy Space Center at liftoff was 31°F. Before the launch, several scientists argued that the launch should be delayed because the shuttle's O-rings might harden in the cold and leak. Other scientists used the data plot in Figure 14.41 to argue that there was no relationship between temperature and O-ring failure. On the basis of this figure and other considerations, *Challenger* was launched to its disastrous, last flight.

Scientists using the data plot in Figure 14.41 made a horrible mistake. They relied on a data plot that was created by using only the seven previous launches where there was at least one O-ring failure. A plot based on all 24 previous launches—17 of which had no O-ring failures—is given in Figure 14.42.

a Intuitively, do you think that Figure 14.42 indicates that there is a relationship between temperature and O-ring failure? Use simple linear regression to justify your answer.

b Even though the figure using only seven launches is incomplete, what about it should have cautioned the scientists not to make the launch?

14.71 In New Jersey, banks have been charged with withdrawing from counties having a high percentage of minorities. To substantiate this charge, P. D'Ambrosio and S. Chambers (1995) present the data in Table 14.8 concerning the percentage, x, of minority population and the number of county residents, y, per bank branch in each of New Jersey's 21 counties. If we use Excel to perform a simple linear regression analysis of this data, we obtain the output given in Figure 14.43 on the next page. ⓓⓢ NJBank

a Determine if there is a significant relationship between x and y.

b Describe the exact nature of any relationship that exists between x and y. (Hint: Estimate β_1 by a point estimate and a confidence interval.)

Note: The Internet exercise for this chapter is on page 553.

FIGURE 14.41	A Data Plot Based on Seven Launches

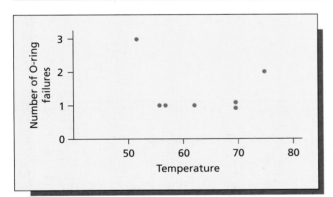

TABLE 14.8	The New Jersey Bank Data
	ⓓⓢ NJBank

County	Percentage of Minority Population, *x*	Number of Residents Per Bank Branch, *y*
Atlantic	23.3	3,073
Bergen	13.0	2,095
Burlington	17.8	2,905
Camden	23.4	3,330
Cape May	7.3	1,321
Cumberland	26.5	2,557
Essex	48.8	3,474
Gloucester	10.7	3,068
Hudson	33.2	3,683
Hunterdon	3.7	1,998
Mercer	24.9	2,607
Middlesex	18.1	3,154
Monmouth	12.6	2,609
Morris	8.2	2,253
Ocean	4.7	2,317
Passaic	28.1	3,307
Salem	16.7	2,511
Somerset	12.0	2,333
Sussex	2.4	2,568
Union	25.6	3,048
Warren	2.8	2,349

Source: P. D'Ambrosio and S. Chambers, "No Checks and Balances," *Asbury Park Press*, September 10, 1995. Copyright © 1995 Asbury Park Press. Used with permission.

FIGURE 14.42	A Data Plot Based on All 24 Launches

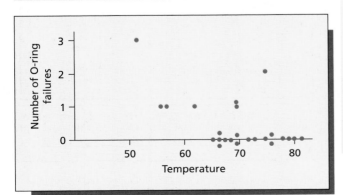

FIGURE 14.43   Excel Output of a Simple Linear Regression Analysis of the New Jersey Bank Data

Regression Statistics

Multiple R	0.7256
R Square	0.5265
Adjusted R Square	0.5016
Standard Error	400.2546
Observations	21

ANOVA	df	SS	MS	F	Significance F
Regression	1	3385090.234	3385090	21.1299	0.0002
Residual	19	3043870.432	160203.7		
Total	20	6428960.667			

	Coefficients	Standard Error	t Stat	P-value	Lower 95%	Upper 95%
Intercept	2082.0153	159.1070	13.0856	5.92E-11	1749.0005	2415.0301
% Minority Pop (x)	35.2877	7.6767	4.5967	0.0002	19.2202	51.3553

Appendix 14.1 ■ Simple Linear Regression Analysis Using Excel

Simple linear regression in Figure 14.9 on page 507 (data file: GasCon1.xlsx):

- Enter the natural gas consumption data (page 497)—the temperatures in column A with label Temp and the gas consumptions in column B with label FuelCons.

- Select **Data : Data Analysis : Regression** and click OK in the Data Analysis dialog box.

- In the Regression dialog box:

  Enter B1:B9 into the "Input Y Range" box.

  Enter A1:A9 into the "Input X Range" box.

- Place a checkmark in the Labels checkbox.

- Be sure that the "Constant is Zero" checkbox is NOT checked.

- Select the "New Worksheet Ply" option and enter the name Output into the New Worksheet window.

- Click OK in the Regression dialog box to obtain the regression results in a new worksheet.

To produce residual plots similar to Figures 14.22(b) and 14.22(c) on page 528:

- In the Regression dialog box, place a checkmark in the Residuals checkbox to request predicted values and residuals.

- Place a checkmark in the Residual Plots checkbox.

- Place a checkmark in the Normal Probability Plots checkbox.

- Click OK in the Regression dialog box.

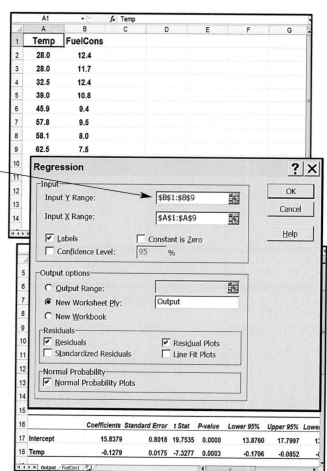

- Move the plots to chart sheets to format them for effective viewing. Additional residual plots—residuals versus predicted values and residuals versus time—can be produced using the Excel charting features.

To compute a point prediction of gas consumption when temperature is 40°F (data file: GasCon1.xlsx):

- The Excel Analysis ToolPak does not provide an option for computing point or interval predictions. A point prediction can be computed from the regression results using Excel cell formulas.

- In the regression output, the estimated intercept and slope parameters from cells A17:B18 have been copied to cells D2:E3 and the predictor value 40 has been placed in cell E5.

- In cell E6, enter the Excel formula = E2 + E3*E5 (= 10.721) to compute the prediction.

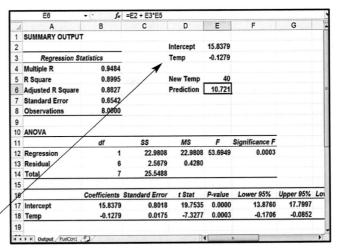

Simple linear regression with a transformed response similar to Figure 14.30 on page 537 (data file: QHIC.xlsx):

- Enter the QHIC upkeep expenditure data from Figure 14.21 (page 526). Enter the label Value in cell A1 with the home values in cells A2 to A41 and enter the label Upkeep in cell B1 with the upkeep expenditures in cells B2 to B41.

- Enter the label SqUpkeep in cell C1.

- Click on cell C2 and then select the Insert Function button f_x on the Excel ribbon.

- Select **Math & Trig** from the "Or select a category:" menu, select **SQRT** from the "Select a function:" menu, and click OK in the Insert Function dialog box.

- In the "SQRT Function Arguments" dialog box, enter B2 in the Number box and click OK to compute the square root of the value in cell B2.

- Copy the cell formula of C2 through cell C41 by double-clicking the drag handle (in the lower right corner) of cell C2 to compute the square roots of the remaining upkeep values.

- Follow the steps for **simple linear regression** (on page 548) using cells C1:C41 as the response (Input Y Range) and cells A1:A41 as the predictor (Input X Range).

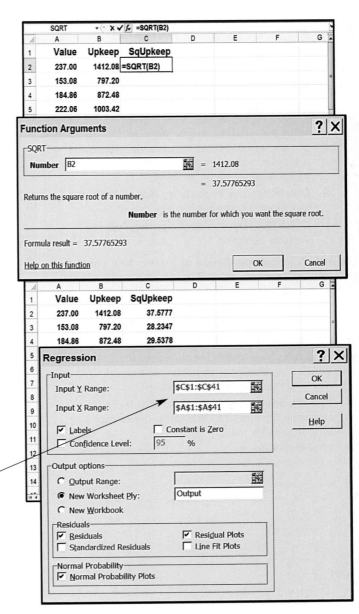

Appendix 14.2 ■ Simple Linear Regression Analysis Using MegaStat

Simple linear regression for the service time data in Exercise 14.5 on page 497 (data file: SrvcTime.xlsx):

- Enter the service time data (page 498) with the numbers of copiers serviced in column A with label Copiers and with the service times in column B with label Minutes.

- Select **Add-Ins : MegaStat : Correlation/ Regression : Regression Analysis.**

- In the Regression Analysis dialog box, click in the Independent Variables window and use the autoexpand feature to enter the range A1:A12.

- Click in the Dependent Variable window and use the AutoExpand feature to enter the range B1:B12.

- Check the appropriate Options and Residuals checkboxes as follows:

    1 Check "Test Intercept" to include a *y*-intercept and to test its significance.

    2 Check "Output Residuals" to obtain a list of the model residuals.

    3 Check "Plot Residuals by Observation," and "Plot Residuals by Predicted Y and X" to obtain residual plots versus time, versus the predicted values of *y*, and versus the values of the independent variable.

    4 Check "Normal Probability Plot of Residuals" to obtain a normal plot.

    5 Check "Durbin-Watson" for the Durbin–Watson statistic.

To obtain a **point prediction** of *y* when four computers will be serviced (as well as a confidence interval and prediction interval):

- Click on the drop-down menu above the Predictor Values window and select "Type in predictor values."

- Type the value of the independent variable for which a prediction is desired (here equal to 4) into the Predictor Values window.

- Select a desired level of confidence (here 95%) from the Confidence Level drop-down menu or type in a value.

- Click OK in the Regression Analysis dialog box.

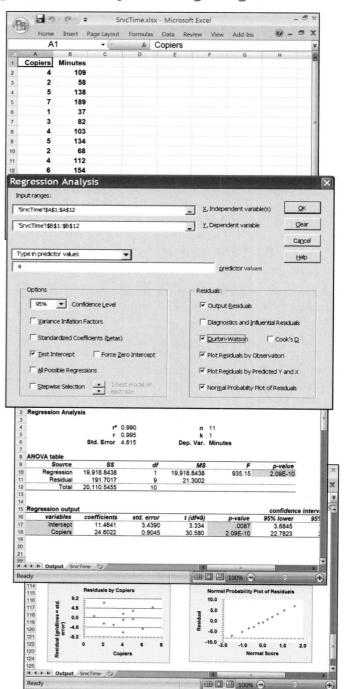

To compute several point predictions of *y*—say, when 1, 2, 3, and 4 computers will be serviced—(and to compute corresponding confidence and prediction intervals):

- Enter the values of *x* for which predictions are desired into a column in the spreadsheet—these values can be in any column. Here we have entered the values 1, 2, 3, and 4 into cells E1 through E4.

- Click on the drop-down menu above the predictor values window and select "Predictor values from spreadsheet cells."

- Enter the range E1:E4 into the predictor values window.

- Click OK in the Regression Analysis dialog box.

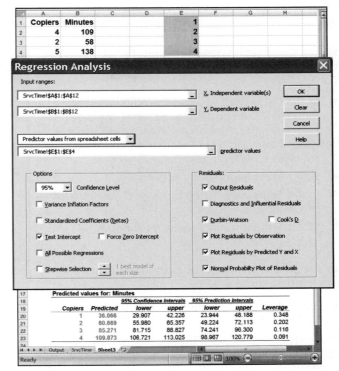

Predicted values for: Minutes						
		95% Confidence Intervals		95% Prediction Intervals		
Copiers	Predicted	lower	upper	lower	upper	Leverage
1	36.066	29.907	42.226	23.944	48.188	0.348
2	60.669	55.980	65.357	49.224	72.113	0.202
3	85.271	81.715	88.827	74.241	96.300	0.116
4	109.873	106.721	113.025	98.967	120.779	0.091

Simple linear regression with a transformed response similar to Figure 14.30 on page 537 (data file: QHIC.xlsx):

- Enter the QHIC data from Figure 14.21 (page 526)—the home values in column A (with label Value) and the upkeep expenditures in column B (with label Upkeep).

- Follow the instructions on page 549 in Appendix 14.1 to calculate the square roots of the upkeep expenditures in column C (with label SRUpkeep).

- Select **Add-Ins : MegaStat : Correlation/Regression : Regression Analysis.**

- In the Regression Analysis dialog box, click in the Independent variables window, and use the AutoExpand feature to enter the range A1:A41.

- Click in the Dependent variable window and use the AutoExpand feature to enter the range C1:C41.

- Check the "Test Intercept" checkbox to include a *y*-intercept and test its significance.

To compute a **point prediction of the square root of *y*** (as well as a confidence interval and prediction interval) for a house having a value of $220,000:

- Select "Type in predictor values" from the drop-down menu above the predictor values window.

- Type 220 into the predictor values window.

- Select a desired level of confidence (here 95%) from the drop-down menu in the Confidence Level box or type in a value.

- Click OK in the Regression Analysis dialog box.

Appendix 14.3 ■ Simple Linear Regression Analysis Using MINITAB

Simple linear regression of the natural gas consumption data in Figure 14.10 on page 507 (data file: Gas-Con1.MTW):

- In the Data window, enter the gas consumption data from Exercise 14.3 (page 497)—average hourly temperatures in column C1 with variable name Temp and weekly gas consumptions in column C2 with variable name FuelCons.
- Select **Stat : Regression : Regression.**
- In the Regression dialog box, select FuelCons into the Response window.
- Select Temp into the Predictors window.

To compute a **prediction** of natural gas consumption when temperature is 40°F:

- In the Regression dialog box, click on the Options... button.
- In the "Regression—Options" dialog box, type 40 in the "Prediction intervals for new observations" window.
- Click OK in the "Regression—Options" dialog box.

To produce **residual analysis** similar to Figure 14.32 on page 539:

- In the Regression dialog box, click on the Graphs... button.
- In the "Regression—Graphs" dialog box, select the "Residuals for Plots: Regular" option.
- To obtain a histogram and normal plot of the residuals, a plot of the residuals versus the fitted values, and a plot of the residuals versus time order, select "Four in one" in the list of options under Residual Plots. (Note that the plot versus time order is generally informative only if the data are in time sequence order.)
- Enter Temp in the "Residuals versus the variables" window to obtain a plot of the residuals versus the values of average hourly temperature.
- Click OK in the "Regression—Graphs" dialog box.
- To see the regression results in the Session window and high-resolution graphs in two graphics windows, click OK in the Regression dialog box.

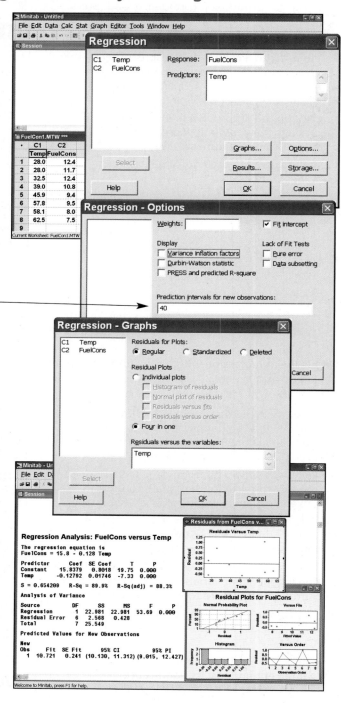

Simple linear regression with a transformed response in Figure 14.30 on page 537 (data file: QHIC.MTW):

- In the Data window, enter the QHIC upkeep expenditure data from Figure 14.21 (page 526)—home values in column C1 with variable name Value and upkeep expenditures in column C2 with variable name Upkeep.

- Select **Calc : Calculator.**

- In the Calculator dialog box, enter SqRtUpkeep in the "Store result in variable" window.

- From the Functions menu list, double-click on "Square root," giving SQRT(number) in the Expression window.

- Replace "number" in the Expression window with Upkeep by double-clicking Upkeep in the variables list.

- Click OK in the Calculator dialog box to obtain a new column, SqRtUpkeep, containing the square roots of the Upkeep values.

- Follow the steps for **simple linear regression** on page 552 using SqRtUpkeep as the response and Value as the predictor.

Calculator

C1   Value
C2   Upkeep

Store result in variable: SqRtUpkeep

Expression:

SQRT('Upkeep')

Functions: All functions

	C1	C2	C3	C4	C5	C6	C7
	Value	Upkeep	SqRtUpkeep				
1	237.00	1412.08	37.5777				
2	153.08	797.20	28.2347				
3	184.86	872.48	29.5378				
4	222.06	1003.42	31.6768				
5	160.68	852.90	29.2045				
6	99.68	288.48	16.9847				
7	229.04	1288.46	35.8951				

14.72   Internet Exercise

The *U.S. News & World Report* website provides rankings of the best colleges and universities in the United States. The free version of "Best Colleges" gives information such as number of students enrolled, tuition rates, and so forth. Among the data provided are the percentage acceptance rate and the average freshman retention rate.

One might wonder if there is a statistically significant relationship between average freshman percentage retention rate and the percentage acceptance rate at colleges and universities in the United States. To investigate this possible relationship, go to the *U.S. News & World Report* website (www.usnews.com). Then make selections as follows: Education; Best Colleges; National Universities; View National Universities Rankings. From the rankings, randomly select a list of the ranked universities and their most recent acceptance rates. Note that following the list of ranked universities is a list of unranked schools. Omit these unranked schools from your analysis. Next, return to the National Universities

page and select "Freshman Retention Rate" from the "National Universities Quick Comparison" list. Compile a list of average retention rates for the schools in your list of ranked universities. Finally, enter the ranked universities and their corresponding acceptance rates and average freshman retention rates into a spreadsheet.

Using Excel or MINITAB, construct a scatter plot of average freshman retention rate versus acceptance rate. Describe any apparent relationship between these variables. Develop a simple linear regression model expressing average freshman retention rate as a linear function of acceptance rate. Then use Excel or MINITAB to fit the model. Using the computer output, identify the key summary measures—r^2, the standard error, and the F-statistic from the ANOVA table. Identify and interpret the estimated regression coefficients. Suppose that a university has an acceptance rate of 90 percent. Use your regression model to predict the average freshman retention rate for this school. Prepare a brief report summarizing your analysis and conclusions.

CHAPTER 15

Multiple Regression and Model Building

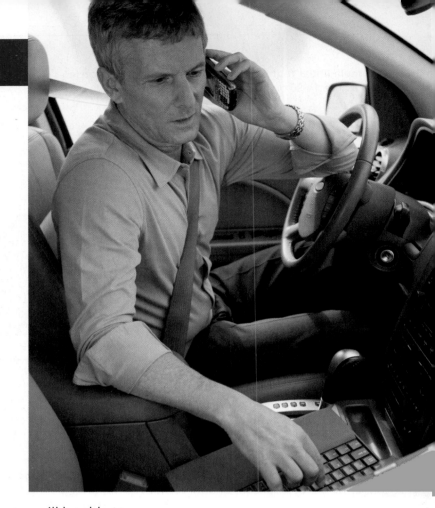

Learning Objectives

After mastering the material in this chapter, you will be able to:

LO15-1 Explain the multiple regression model and the related least squares point estimates.

LO15-2 Explain the assumptions behind multiple regression and calculate the standard error.

LO15-3 Calculate and interpret the multiple and adjusted multiple coefficients of determination.

LO15-4 Test the significance of a multiple regression model by using an F-test.

LO15-5 Test the significance of a single independent variable.

LO15-6 Find and interpret a confidence interval for a mean value of the dependent variable and a prediction interval for an individual value.

LO15-7 Use dummy variables to model qualitative independent variables.

LO15-8 Use squared and interaction variables.

LO15-9 Describe multicollinearity and build a multiple regression model.

LO15-10 Use residual analysis to check the assumptions of multiple regression.

LO15-11 Use a logistic model to estimate probabilities and odds ratios.

Chapter Outline

Note: After completing Section 15.7, the reader may study Sections 15.8, 15.9, 15.10, 15.11, and 15.12 in any order without loss of continuity.

O ften we can more accurately describe, predict, and control a dependent variable by using a regression model that employs more than one independent variable. Such a model is called a **multiple regression model,** which is the subject of this chapter.

In order to explain the ideas of this chapter, we consider the following cases:

The Tasty Sub Shop Case: The business entrepreneur more accurately predicts the yearly revenue for a potential restaurant site by using a multiple regression model that employs as independent variables (1) the number of residents living near the site and (2) a rating of the amount of business and shopping near the site. The entrepreneur uses the more accurate predictions given by the multiple regression model to more accurately assess the profitability of the potential restaurant site.

The Sales Representative Case: A sales manager evaluates the performance of sales representatives by using a multiple regression model that predicts sales performance on the basis of five independent variables. Salespeople whose actual performance is far worse than predicted performance will get extra training to help improve their sales techniques.

15.1 The Multiple Regression Model and the Least Squares Point Estimates ● ● ●

LO15-1 Explain the multiple regression model and the related least squares point estimates.

Regression models that employ more than one independent variable are called **multiple regression models.** We begin our study of these models by considering the following example.

EXAMPLE 15.1 The Tasty Sub Shop Case: A Multiple Regression Model

Part 1: The data and a regression model Consider the Tasty Sub Shop problem in which the business entrepreneur wishes to predict yearly revenue for potential Tasty Sub restaurant sites. In Chapter 14 we used the number of residents, or population size x, living near a site to predict y, the yearly revenue for a Tasty Sub Shop built on the site. We now consider predicting y on the basis of the population size and a second predictor variable—the business rating. The business rating for a restaurant site reflects the amount of business and shopping near the site. This rating is expressed as a whole number between 1 and 10. Sites having only limited business and shopping nearby do not provide many potential customers—shoppers or local employees likely to eat in a Tasty Sub Shop—so they receive ratings near 1. However, sites located near substantial business and shopping activity do provide many potential customers for a Tasty Sub Shop, so they receive much higher ratings. The best possible rating for business activity is 10.

The business entrepreneur has collected data concerning yearly revenue (y), population size (x_1), and business rating (x_2) for 10 existing Tasty Sub restaurants that are built on sites similar to the site the entrepreneur is considering. These data are given in Table 15.1.

TABLE 15.1 The Tasty Sub Shop Revenue Data ⊙Ⓢ TastySub2

Restaurant	Population Size, x_1 (Thousands of Residents)	Business Rating, x_2	Yearly Revenue, y (Thousands of Dollars)
1	20.8	3	527.1
2	27.5	2	548.7
3	32.3	6	767.2
4	37.2	5	722.9
5	39.6	8	826.3
6	45.1	3	810.5
7	49.9	9	1040.5
8	55.4	5	1033.6
9	61.7	4	1090.3
10	64.6	7	1235.8

FIGURE 15.1   Plot of *y* (Yearly Revenue) versus
                           x₁ (Population Size)

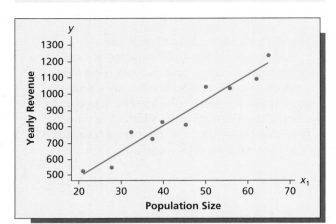

FIGURE 15.2   Plot of *y* (Yearly Revenue) versus
                           x₂ (Business Rating)

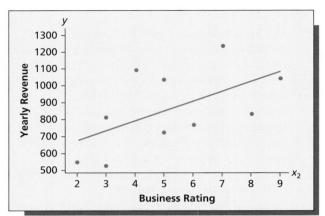

Figure 15.1 presents a scatter plot of y versus x_1. This plot shows that y tends to increase in a straight-line fashion as x_1 increases. Figure 15.2 shows a scatter plot of y versus x_2. This plot shows that y tends to increase in a straight-line fashion as x_2 increases. Together, the scatter plots in Figures 15.1 and 15.2 imply that a reasonable multiple regression model relating y (yearly revenue) to x_1 (population size) and x_2 (business rating) is

$$y = \beta_0 + \beta_1 x_1 + \beta_2 x_2 + \varepsilon$$

This model says that the values of y can be represented by a **mean level** ($\mu_y = \beta_0 + \beta_1 x_1 + \beta_2 x_2$) that changes as x_1 and x_2 change, combined with random fluctuations (described by the **error term** ε) that cause the values of y to deviate from the mean level. Here:

1   The mean level $\mu_y = \beta_0 + \beta_1 x_1 + \beta_2 x_2$ is the mean yearly revenue for all Tasty Sub restaurants that could potentially be built near populations of size x_1 and business/shopping areas having a rating of x_2. Furthermore, the equation

$$\mu_y = \beta_0 + \beta_1 x_1 + \beta_2 x_2$$

is the equation of a plane—called the **plane of means**—in three-dimensional space. The plane of means is the shaded plane illustrated in Figure 15.3. Different mean yearly revenues corresponding to different population size–business rating combinations lie on the plane of means. For example, Table 15.1 tells us that restaurant 3 is built near a population of 32,300 residents and a business/shopping area having a rating of 6. It follows that

$$\beta_0 + \beta_1(32.3) + \beta_2(6)$$

is the mean yearly revenue for all Tasty Sub restaurants that could potentially be built near populations of 32,300 residents and business/shopping areas having a rating of 6.

2   β_0, β_1, and β_2 are (unknown) regression parameters that relate mean yearly revenue to x_1 and x_2. Specifically:

- β_0 (the *intercept of the model*) is the mean yearly revenue for all Tasty Sub restaurants that could potentially be built near populations of zero residents and business/shopping areas having a rating of 0. This interpretation, however, is of dubious practical value, because we have not observed any Tasty Sub restaurants that are built near populations of zero residents and business/shopping areas having a rating of zero. (The lowest business rating is 1.)

FIGURE 15.3   A Geometrical Interpretation of the Regression Model Relating y to x_1 and x_2

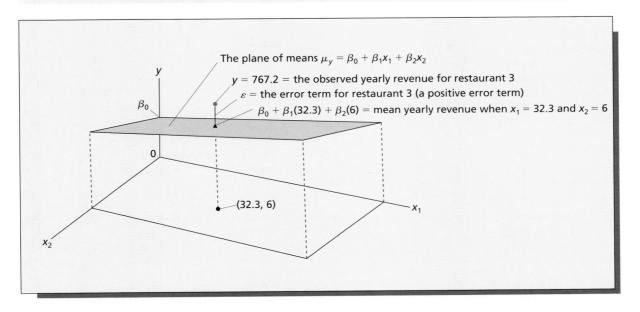

The plane of means $\mu_y = \beta_0 + \beta_1 x_1 + \beta_2 x_2$

$y = 767.2 =$ the observed yearly revenue for restaurant 3

$\varepsilon =$ the error term for restaurant 3 (a positive error term)

$\beta_0 + \beta_1(32.3) + \beta_2(6) =$ mean yearly revenue when $x_1 = 32.3$ and $x_2 = 6$

(32.3, 6)

- β_1 (the **regression parameter for the variable x_1**) is the change in mean yearly revenue that is associated with a one-unit (1000 resident) increase in the population size (x_1) when the business rating (x_2) does not change. Intuitively, β_1 is the slope of the plane of means in the x_1 direction.

- β_2 (the **regression parameter for the variable x_2**) is the change in mean yearly revenue that is associated with a one-unit increase in the business rating (x_2) when the population size (x_1) does not change. Intuitively, β_2 is the slope of the plane of means in the x_2 direction.

3   ε is an error term that describes the effect on y of all factors other than x_1 and x_2. One such factor is the skill of the owner as an operator of the restaurant under consideration. For example, Figure 15.3 shows that the error term for restaurant 3 is positive. This implies that the observed yearly revenue for restaurant 3, $y = 767.2$, is greater than the mean yearly revenue for all Tasty Sub restaurants that could potentially be built near populations of 32,300 residents and business/shopping areas having a rating of 6. In general, positive error terms cause their respective observed yearly revenues to be greater than the corresponding mean yearly revenues. On the other hand, negative error terms cause their respective observed yearly revenues to be less than the corresponding mean yearly revenues.

Part 2: The least squares point estimates   If b_0, b_1, and b_2 denote point estimates of β_0, β_1, and β_2, then the point prediction of an observed yearly revenue $y = \beta_0 + \beta_1 x_1 + \beta_2 x_2 + \varepsilon$ is

$$\hat{y} = b_0 + b_1 x_1 + b_2 x_2$$

which we call a *predicted yearly revenue*. Here, because the regression assumptions (to be discussed in Section 15.2) imply that the error term ε has a 50 percent chance of being positive and a 50 percent chance of being negative, we predict ε to be zero. Now, consider the 10 Tasty Sub restaurants in Table 15.1. If any particular values of b_0, b_1, and b_2 are good point estimates, they will make the predicted yearly revenue for each restaurant fairly close to the observed yearly revenue for the restaurant. This will make the restaurant's *residual*—the difference between the restaurant's observed and predicted yearly revenues—fairly small (in magnitude). We define the **least squares point estimates** to be the values of b_0, b_1, and b_2 that minimize *SSE*, the sum of squared residuals for the 10 restaurants.

FIGURE 15.4 Excel and MINITAB Outputs of a Regression Analysis of the Tasty Sub Shop Revenue Data in Table 15.1 Using the Model $y = \beta_0 + \beta_1 x_1 + \beta_2 x_2 + \varepsilon$

(a) The Excel output

Regression Statistics

Multiple R	0.9905
R Square	0.9810 [8]
Adjusted R Square	0.9756 [9]
Standard Error	36.6856 [7]
Observations	10

ANOVA	df	SS	MS	F	Significance F
Regression	2	486355.7 [10]	243177.8	180.689 [13]	9.46E-07 [14]
Residual	7	9420.8 [11]	1345.835		
Total	9	495776.5 [12]			

	Coefficients	Standard Error [4]	t Stat [5]	P-value [6]	Lower 95% [19]	Upper 95% [19]
Intercept	125.289 [1]	40.9333	3.06	0.0183	28.4969	222.0807
population	14.1996 [2]	0.9100	15.60	1.07E-06	12.0478	16.3517
bus_rating	22.8107 [3]	5.7692	3.95	0.0055	9.1686	36.4527

(b) The MINITAB output

```
The regression equation is
revenue = 125 + 14.2 population + 22.8 bus_rating
```

Predictor	Coef	SE Coef [4]	T [5]	P [6]
Constant	125.29 [1]	40.93	3.06	0.018
population	14.1996 [2]	0.91	15.6	0.000
bus_rating	22.811 [3]	5.769	3.95	0.006

S = 36.6856 [7]   R-Sq = 98.10% [8]   R-Sq(adj) = 97.6% [9]

Analysis of Variance

Source	DF	SS	MS	F	P
Regression	2	486356 [10]	243178	180.69 [13]	0.000 [14]
Residual Error	7	9421 [11]	1346		
Total	9	495777 [12]			

Predicted Values for New Observations

New Obs	Fit [15]	SE Fit [16]	95% CI [17]	95% PI [18]
1	956.6	15	(921.0, 992.2)	(862.8, 1050.4)

Values of Predictors for New Observations

New Obs	population	bus_rating
1	47.3	7

[1] b_0 [2] b_1 [3] b_2 [4] s_{b_j} = standard error of the estimate b_j	[5] t statistics	[6] p-values for t statistics	[7] s = standard error
[8] R^2 [9] Adjusted R^2 [10] Explained variation	[11] SSE = Unexplained variation	[12] Total variation	[13] F(model) statistic
[14] p-value for F(model) [15] $\hat{y}$ = point prediction when $x_1 = 47.3$ and $x_2 = 7$	[16] $s_{\hat{y}}$ = standard error of the estimate $\hat{y}$		
[17] 95% confidence interval when $x_1 = 47.3$ and $x_2 = 7$	[18] 95% prediction interval when $x_1 = 47.3$ and $x_2 = 7$	[19] 95% confidence interval for β_j	

The formula for the least squares point estimates of the parameters in a multiple regression model is expressed using a branch of mathematics called **matrix algebra.** This formula is presented in Bowerman, O'Connell, and Koehler (2005). In the main body of the book, we will rely on Excel and MINITAB to compute the needed estimates. For example, consider the Excel and MINITAB outputs in Figure 15.4. These outputs tell us that the least squares point estimates of β_0, β_1, and β_2 in the Tasty Sub Shop revenue model are $b_0 = 125.29$, $b_1 = 14.1996$, and $b_2 = 22.811$ (see [1], [2], and [3]). The point estimate $b_1 = 14.1996$ of β_1 says we estimate that mean yearly revenue increases by \$14,199.60 when the population size increases by 1,000 residents and the business rating does not change. The point estimate $b_2 = 22.811$ of β_2 says we estimate that mean yearly revenue increases by \$22,811 when there is a one-unit increase in the business rating and the population size does not change.

TABLE 15.2 The Point Predictions and Residuals Using the Least Squares Point Estimates, $b_0 = 125.29$, $b_1 = 14.1996$, and $b_2 = 22.811$

Restaurant	Population Size, x_1 (Thousands of Residents)	Business Rating, x_2	Yearly Revenue, y (Thousands of Dollars)	Predicted Yearly Revenue $\hat{y} = 125.29 + 14.1996x_1 + 22.811x_2$	Residual, $y - \hat{y}$
1	20.8	3	527.1	489.07	38.03
2	27.5	2	548.7	561.40	−12.70
3	32.3	6	767.2	720.80	46.40
4	37.2	5	722.9	767.57	−44.67
5	39.6	8	826.3	870.08	−43.78
6	45.1	3	810.5	834.12	−23.62
7	49.9	9	1040.7	1039.15	1.55
8	55.4	5	1033.6	1026.00	7.60
9	61.7	4	1090.3	1092.65	−2.35
10	64.6	7	1235.8	1202.26	33.54

$$SSE = (38.03)^2 + (-12.70)^2 + \cdots + (33.54)^2 = 9420.8$$

The equation

$$\hat{y} = b_0 + b_1x_1 + b_2x_2$$
$$= 125.29 + 14.1996x_1 + 22.811x_2$$

is called the **least squares prediction equation.** In Table 15.2 we summarize using this prediction equation to calculate the predicted yearly revenues and the residuals for the 10 observed Tasty Sub restaurants. For example, because the population size and business rating for restaurant 1 were 20.8 and 3, the predicted yearly revenue for restaurant 1 is

$$\hat{y} = 125.29 + 14.1996(20.8) + 22.811(3)$$
$$= 489.07$$

It follows, because the observed yearly revenue for restaurant 1 was $y = 527.1$, that the residual for restaurant 1 is

$$y - \hat{y} = 527.1 - 489.07 = 38.03$$

If we consider all of the residuals in Table 15.2 and add their squared values, we find that **SSE, the sum of squared residuals,** is 9420.8. This *SSE* value is given on the Excel and MINITAB outputs in Figure 15.4 (see ⑪) and will be used throughout this chapter.

Part 3: Estimating means and predicting individual values   The least squares prediction equation is the equation of a plane—called the **least squares plane**—in three-dimensional space. The least squares plane is the estimate of the plane of means. It follows that the point on the least squares plane corresponding to the population size x_1 and the business rating x_2

$$\hat{y} = b_0 + b_1x_1 + b_2x_2$$
$$= 125.29 + 14.1996x_1 + 22.811x_2$$

is the point estimate of $\beta_0 + \beta_1x_1 + \beta_2x_2$, the mean yearly revenue for all Tasty Sub restaurants that could potentially be built near populations of size x_1 and business/shopping areas having a rating of x_2. In addition, because we predict the error term to be 0, $\hat{y}$ is also the point prediction of $y = \beta_0 + \beta_1x_1 + \beta_2x_2 + \varepsilon$, the yearly revenue for a single Tasty Sub restaurant that is built near a population of size x_1 and a business/shopping area having a rating of x_2.

For example, suppose that one of the business entrepreneur's potential restaurant sites is near a population of 47,300 residents and a business/shopping area having a rating of 7. It follows that

$$\hat{y} = 125.29 + 14.1996(47.3) + 22.811(7)$$
$$= 956.6 \text{ (that is, \$956,600)}$$

is

1   The **point estimate** of the mean yearly revenue for all Tasty Sub restaurants that could potentially be built near populations of 47,300 residents and business/shopping areas having a rating of 7, and

2   The **point prediction** of the yearly revenue for a single Tasty Sub restaurant that is built near a population of 47,300 residents and a business/shopping area having a rating of 7.

Notice that $\hat{y} = 956.6$ is given at the bottom of the MINITAB output in Figure 15.4 on page 558 (see 15). Moreover, recall that the yearly rent and other fixed costs for the entrepreneur's potential restaurant will be $257,550 and that (according to Tasty Sub corporate headquarters) the yearly food and other variable costs for the restaurant will be 60 percent of the yearly revenue. Because we predict that the yearly revenue for the restaurant will be $956,600, it follows that we predict that the yearly total operating cost for the restaurant will be $257,550 + .6($956,600) = $831,510. In addition, if we subtract this predicted yearly operating cost from the predicted yearly revenue of $956,600, we predict that the yearly profit for the restaurant will be $125,090. Of course, these predictions are point predictions. In Section 15.6 we will predict the restaurant's yearly revenue and profit *with confidence*.

The Tasty Sub Shop revenue model expresses the dependent variable as a function of two independent variables. In general, we can use a multiple regression model to express a dependent variable as a function of any number of independent variables. For example, in the past, natural gas utilities serving the Cincinnati, Ohio, area have predicted daily natural gas consumption by using four independent (predictor) variables—average temperature, average wind velocity, average sunlight, and change in average temperature from the previous day. The general form of a multiple regression model expresses the dependent variable y as a function of k independent variables $x_1, x_2, \ldots, x_k$. We express this general form in the following box.

The Multiple Regression Model

The **multiple regression model relating y to $x_1, x_2, \ldots, x_k$** is

$$y = \beta_0 + \beta_1 x_1 + \beta_2 x_2 + \cdots + \beta_k x_k + \varepsilon$$

Here

1 $\mu_y = \beta_0 + \beta_1 x_1 + \beta_2 x_2 + \cdots + \beta_k x_k$ is the mean value of the dependent variable y when the values of the independent variables are $x_1, x_2, \ldots, x_k$.

2 $\beta_0, \beta_1, \beta_2, \ldots, \beta_k$ are (unknown) **regression parameters** relating the mean value of y to $x_1, x_2, \ldots, x_k$.

3 ε is an **error term** that describes the effects on y of all factors other than the values of the independent variables $x_1, x_2, \ldots, x_k$.

If $b_0, b_1, b_2, \ldots, b_k$ denote point estimates of $\beta_0, \beta_1, \beta_2, \ldots, \beta_k$, then

$$\hat{y} = b_0 + b_1 x_1 + b_2 x_2 + \cdots + b_k x_k$$

is the **point estimate of the mean value of the dependent variable** when the values of the independent variables are $x_1, x_2, \ldots, x_k$. In addition, because we predict the error term ε to be 0, $\hat{y}$ is also the **point prediction of an individual value of the dependent variable** when the values of the independent variables are $x_1, x_2, \ldots, x_k$. Now, assume that we have obtained n observations, where each observation consists of an observed value of the dependent variable y and corresponding observed values of the independent variables $x_1, x_2, \ldots, x_k$. For the ith observation, let y_i and $\hat{y}_i$ denote the observed and predicted values of the dependent variable, and define the residual to be $e_i = y_i - \hat{y}_i$. It then follows that the **least squares point estimates** are the values of $b_0, b_1, b_2, \ldots, b_k$ that minimize the sum of squared residuals:

$$SSE = \sum_{i=1}^{n} (y_i - \hat{y}_i)^2$$

As illustrated in Example 15.1, we use Excel and MINITAB to find the least squares point estimates.

To conclude this section, consider an arbitrary independent variable, which we will denote as x_j, in a multiple regression model. We can then interpret the parameter β_j to be the change in the mean value of the dependent variable that is associated with a one-unit increase in x_j when the other independent variables in the model do not change. This interpretation is based, however, on the assumption that x_j can increase by one unit without the other independent variables in the model changing. In some situations (as we will see) this assumption is not reasonable.

Exercises for Section 15.1

CONCEPTS

15.1   In the multiple regression model, what sum of squared deviations do the least squares point estimates minimize?

15.2   When using the multiple regression model, how do we obtain a point estimate of the mean value of the dependent variable and a point prediction of an individual value of the dependent variable?

METHODS AND APPLICATIONS

15.3   THE NATURAL GAS CONSUMPTION CASE   Ⓞ GasCon2

Consider the situation in which a gas company wishes to predict weekly natural gas consumption for its city. In the exercises of Chapter 14, we used the single predictor variable x, average hourly temperature, to predict y, weekly natural gas consumption. We now consider predicting y on the basis of average hourly temperature and a second predictor variable—the chill index. The chill index for a given average hourly temperature expresses the combined effects of all other major weather-related factors that influence natural gas consumption, such as wind velocity, sunlight, cloud cover, and the passage of weather fronts. The chill index is expressed as a whole number between 0 and 30. A weekly chill index near 0 indicates that, given the average hourly temperature during the week, all other major weather-related factors will only slightly increase weekly natural gas consumption. A weekly chill index near 30 indicates that, given the average hourly temperature during the week, other weather-related factors will greatly increase weekly natural gas consumption. The natural gas company has collected data concerning weekly natural gas consumption (y, in MMcF), average hourly temperature (x_1, in degrees Fahrenheit), and the chill index (x_2) for the last eight weeks. The data are given in Table 15.3, and scatter plots of y versus x_1 and y versus x_2 are given below the data. Moreover, Figure 15.5 on the next page gives Excel and MINITAB outputs of a regression analysis of these data using the model

$$y = \beta_0 + \beta_1 x_1 + \beta_2 x_2 + \varepsilon$$

a   Using the Excel or MINITAB output (depending on the package used in your class), find (on the output) b_1 and b_2, the least squares point estimates of β_1 and β_2, and report their values. Then interpret b_1 and b_2.

b   Calculate a point estimate of the mean natural gas consumption for all weeks that have an average hourly temperature of 40 and a chill index of 10, and a point prediction of the amount of natural gas consumed in a single week that has an average hourly temperature of 40 and a chill index of 10. Find this point estimate (prediction), which is given at the bottom of the MINITAB output, and verify that it equals (within rounding) your calculated value.

15.4   THE REAL ESTATE SALES PRICE CASE   Ⓞ RealEst2

A real estate agency collects the data in Table 15.4 concerning

y = sales price of a house (in thousands of dollars)

x_1 = home size (in hundreds of square feet)

x_2 = rating (an overall "niceness rating" for the house expressed on a scale
          from 1 [worst] to 10 [best], and provided by the real estate agency)

Scatter plots of y versus x_1 and y versus x_2 are as follows:

TABLE 15.3
The Natural Gas Consumption Data
Ⓞ GasCon2

y	x_1	x_2
12.4	28.0	18
11.7	28.0	14
12.4	32.5	24
10.8	39.0	22
9.4	45.9	8
9.5	57.8	16
8.0	58.1	1
7.5	62.5	0

TABLE 15.4
The Real Estate Sales Price Data
Ⓞ RealEst2

y	x_1	x_2
180	23	5
98.1	11	2
173.1	20	9
136.5	17	3
141	15	8
165.9	21	4
193.5	24	7
127.8	13	6
163.5	19	7
172.5	25	2

Source: R. L. Andrews and J. T. Ferguson, "Integrating Judgement with a Regression Appraisal," *The Real Estate Appraiser and Analyst* 52, no. 2 (1986). Reprinted by permission.

FIGURE 15.5   Excel and MINITAB Outputs of a Regression Analysis of the Natural Gas Consumption Data
Using the Model $y = \beta_0 + \beta_1 x_1 + \beta_2 x_2 + \varepsilon$

(a) The Excel output

Regression Statistics

Multiple R	0.9867
R Square	0.9736
Adjusted R Square	0.9631
Standard Error	0.3671
Observations	8

ANOVA	df	SS	MS	F	Significance F
Regression	2	24.8750	12.4375	92.3031	0.0001
Residual	5	0.6737	0.1347		
Total	7	25.5488			

	Coefficients	Standard Error	t Stat	P-value	Lower 95%	Upper 95%
Intercept	13.1087	0.8557	15.3193	2.15E-05	10.9091	15.3084
TEMP	-0.0900	0.0141	-6.3942	0.0014	-0.1262	-0.0538
CHILL	0.0825	0.0220	3.7493	0.0133	0.0259	0.1391

(b) The MINITAB output

```
The regression equation is
FuelCons = 13.1 - 0.0900 Temp + 0.0825 Chill

Predictor        Coef        SE Coef           T          P
Constant      13.1087         0.8557       15.32      0.000
Temp         -0.09001        0.01408       -6.39      0.001
Chill         0.08249        0.02200        3.75      0.013

s = 0.367078      R-Sq = 97.4%       R-Sq(adj) = 96.3%

Analysis of Variance
Source           DF           SS          MS          F          P
Regression        2       24.875      12.438      92.30      0.000
Residual Error    5        0.674       0.135
Total             7       25.549

Values of Predictors for New Obs    Predicted Values for New Observations
New Obs Temp Chill                  New Obs      Fit     SE Fit       95% CI            95% PI
     1  40.0  10.0                       1   10.333      0.170  (9.895, 10.771)  (9.293, 11.374)
```

FIGURE 15.6   MINITAB Output of a Regression Analysis of the Real Estate Sales Price Data Using
the Model $y = \beta_0 + \beta_1 x_1 + \beta_2 x_2 + \varepsilon$

```
The regression equation is
SalesPrice = 29.3 + 5.61 HomeSize + 3.83 Rating

Predictor     Coef    SE Coef       T       P
Constant    29.347      4.891    6.00   0.001
HomeSize    5.6128     0.2285   24.56   0.000
Rating      3.8344     0.4332    8.85   0.000

S = 3.24164    R-Sq = 99.0%    R-Sq(adj) = 98.7%

Analysis of Variance
Source           DF        SS        MS        F       P
Regression        2    7374.0    3687.0   350.87   0.000
Residual Error    7      73.6      10.5
Total             9    7447.5

Values of Predictors for New Obs    Predicted Values for New Observations
New Obs   HomeSize   Rating         New Obs     Fit    SE Fit       95% CI             95% PI
      1     20.0     8.00                1   172.28      1.57  (168.56, 175.99)  (163.76, 180.80)
```

The agency wishes to develop a regression model that can be used to predict the sales prices of future houses it will list. Figure 15.6 gives the MINITAB output of a regression analysis of the real estate sales price data in Table 15.4 using the model

$$y = \beta_0 + \beta_1 x_1 + \beta_2 x_2 + \varepsilon$$

a Using the MINITAB output, identify and interpret b_1 and b_2, the least squares point estimates of β_1 and β_2.

b Calculate a point estimate of the mean sales price of all houses having 2,000 square feet and a rating of 8, and a point prediction of the sales price of a single house having 2,000 square feet and a rating of 8. Find this point estimate (prediction), which is given at the bottom of the MINITAB output, and verify that it equals (within rounding) your calculated value.

15.5 THE FRESH DETERGENT CASE ⓓⓢ Fresh2

Enterprise Industries produces Fresh, a brand of liquid laundry detergent. In order to manage its inventory more effectively and make revenue projections, the company would like to better predict demand for Fresh. To develop a prediction model, the company has gathered data concerning demand for Fresh over the last 30 sales periods (each sales period is defined to be a four-week period). The demand data are presented in Table 15.5. Here, for each sales period,

y = the demand for the large size bottle of Fresh (in hundreds of thousands of bottles) in the sales period

x_1 = the price (in dollars) of Fresh as offered by Enterprise Industries in the sales period

x_2 = the average industry price (in dollars) of competitors' similar detergents in the sales period

x_3 = Enterprise Industries' advertising expenditure (in hundreds of thousands of dollars) to promote Fresh in the sales period

Figure 15.7 on the next page gives the Excel output of a regression analysis of the Fresh Detergent demand data in Table 15.5 using the model

$$y = \beta_0 + \beta_1 x_1 + \beta_2 x_2 + \beta_3 x_3 + \varepsilon$$

a Find (on the output) and report the values of b_1, b_2, and b_3, the least squares point estimates of β_1, β_2, and β_3. Interpret b_1, b_2, and b_3.

TABLE 15.5 **Historical Data Concerning Demand for Fresh Detergent** ⓓⓢ Fresh2

Sales Period	Price for Fresh, x_1	Average Industry Price, x_2	Advertising Expenditure for Fresh, x_3	Demand for Fresh, y	Sales Period	Price for Fresh, x_1	Average Industry Price, x_2	Advertising Expenditure for Fresh, x_3	Demand for Fresh, y
1	3.85	3.80	5.50	7.38	16	3.80	4.10	6.80	8.87
2	3.75	4.00	6.75	8.51	17	3.70	4.20	7.10	9.26
3	3.70	4.30	7.25	9.52	18	3.80	4.30	7.00	9.00
4	3.70	3.70	5.50	7.50	19	3.70	4.10	6.80	8.75
5	3.60	3.85	7.00	9.33	20	3.80	3.75	6.50	7.95
6	3.60	3.80	6.50	8.28	21	3.80	3.75	6.25	7.65
7	3.60	3.75	6.75	8.75	22	3.75	3.65	6.00	7.27
8	3.80	3.85	5.25	7.87	23	3.70	3.90	6.50	8.00
9	3.80	3.65	5.25	7.10	24	3.55	3.65	7.00	8.50
10	3.85	4.00	6.00	8.00	25	3.60	4.10	6.80	8.75
11	3.90	4.10	6.50	7.89	26	3.65	4.25	6.80	9.21
12	3.90	4.00	6.25	8.15	27	3.70	3.65	6.50	8.27
13	3.70	4.10	7.00	9.10	28	3.75	3.75	5.75	7.67
14	3.75	4.20	6.90	8.86	29	3.80	3.85	5.80	7.93
15	3.75	4.10	6.80	8.90	30	3.70	4.25	6.80	9.26

FIGURE 15.7   **Excel Output of a Regression Analysis of the Fresh Detergent Demand Data Using the Model $y = \beta_0 + \beta_1x_1 + \beta_2x_2 + \beta_3x_3 + \varepsilon$**

(a) The Excel output

Regression Statistics

Multiple R	0.9453
R Square	0.8936
Adjusted R Square	0.8813
Standard Error	0.2347
Observations	30

ANOVA	df	SS	MS	F	Significance F
Regression	3	12.0268	4.0089	72.797	8.883E-13
Residual	26	1.4318	0.0551		
Total	29	13.4586			

	Coefficients	Standard Error	t Stat	P-value	Lower 95%	Upper 95%
Intercept	7.5891	2.4450	3.1039	0.0046	2.5633	12.6149
Price (X1)	-2.3577	0.6379	-3.6958	0.0010	-3.6690	-1.0464
IndPrice (X2)	1.6122	0.2954	5.4586	0.0000	1.0051	2.2193
AdvExp (X3)	0.5012	0.1259	3.9814	0.0005	0.2424	0.7599

(b) Prediction using an Excel add-in (MegaStat)

Predicted values for: Demand (y)

Price (x1)	IndPrice (x2)	AdvExp (x3)	Predicted	95% Confidence Interval lower	95% Confidence Interval upper	95% Prediction Interval lower	95% Prediction Interval upper	Leverage
3.7	3.9	6.5	8.4107	8.3143	8.5070	7.9188	8.9025	0.040

TABLE 15.6   **Hospital Labor Needs Data**   DS HospLab

Hospital	Monthly X-Ray Exposures, x_1	Monthly Occupied Bed Days, x_2	Average Length of Stay, x_3	Monthly Labor Hours Required, y
1	2,463	472.92	4.45	566.52
2	2,048	1,339.75	6.92	696.82
3	3,940	620.25	4.28	1,033.15
4	6,505	568.33	3.90	1,603.62
5	5,723	1,497.60	5.50	1,611.37
6	11,520	1,365.83	4.60	1,613.27
7	5,779	1,687.00	5.62	1,854.17
8	5,969	1,639.92	5.15	2,160.55
9	8,461	2,872.33	6.18	2,305.58
10	20,106	3,655.08	6.15	3,503.93
11	13,313	2,912.00	5.88	3,571.89
12	10,771	3,921.00	4.88	3,741.40
13	15,543	3,865.67	5.50	4,026.52
14	34,703	12,446.33	10.78	11,732.17
15	39,204	14,098.40	7.05	15,414.94
16	86,533	15,524.00	6.35	18,854.45

Source: *Procedures and Analysis for Staffing Standards Development Regression Analysis Handbook* (San Diego, CA: Navy Manpower and Material Analysis Center, 1979).

b Consider the demand for Fresh Detergent in a future sales period when Enterprise Industries' price for Fresh will be $x_1 = 3.70$, the average price of competitors' similar detergents will be $x_2 = 3.90$ and Enterprise Industries' advertising expenditure for Fresh will be $x_3 = 6.50$. The point prediction of this demand is given at the bottom of the Excel add-in output. Report this point prediction and show (within rounding) how it has been calculated.

15.6 THE HOSPITAL LABOR NEEDS CASE   DS HospLab

Table 15.6 presents data concerning the need for labor in 16 U.S. Navy hospitals. Here, y = monthly labor hours required; x_1 = monthly X-ray exposures; x_2 = monthly occupied bed

FIGURE 15.8   **Excel Output of a Regression Analysis of the Hospital Labor Needs Data Using the Model $y = \beta_0 + \beta_1 x_1 + \beta_2 x_2 + \beta_3 x_3 + \varepsilon$**

(a) The Excel output

Regression Statistics

Multiple R	0.9981
R Square	0.9961
Adjusted R Square	0.9952
Standard Error	387.1598
Observations	16

ANOVA	df	SS	MS	F	Significance F
Regression	3	462327889.4	154109296.5	1028.1309	9.92E-15
Residual	12	1798712.2	149892.7		
Total	15	464126601.6			

	Coefficients	Standard Error	t Stat	P-value	Lower 95%	Upper 95%
Intercept	1946.8020	504.1819	3.8613	0.0023	848.2840	3045.3201
XRay (x1)	0.0386	0.0130	2.9579	0.0120	0.0102	0.0670
BedDays (x2)	1.0394	0.0676	15.3857	2.91E-09	0.8922	1.1866
LengthStay (x3)	-413.7578	98.5983	-4.1964	0.0012	-628.5850	-198.9306

(b) Prediction Using an Excel add-in (MegaStat)

Predicted values for: LaborHours

XRay (x1)	BedDays (x2)	LengthStay (x3)	Predicted	95% Confidence Interval lower	95% Confidence Interval upper	95% Prediction Interval lower	95% Prediction Interval upper	Leverage
56194	14077.88	6.89	15,896.2473	15,378.0313	16,414.4632	14,906.2361	16,886.2584	0.3774

days (a hospital has one occupied bed day if one bed is occupied for an entire day); and x_3 = average length of patients' stay (in days). Figure 15.8 gives the Excel output of a regression analysis of the data using the model

$$y = \beta_0 + \beta_1 x_1 + \beta_2 x_2 + \beta_3 x_3 + \varepsilon$$

Note that the variables x_1, x_2, and x_3 are denoted as XRay, BedDays, and LengthStay on the output.

a Find (on the output) and report the values of b_1, b_2, and b_3, the least squares point estimates of β_1, β_2, and β_3. Interpret b_1, b_2, and b_3. Note that the negative value of b_3 ($= -413.7578$) might say that, when XRay and BedDays stay constant, an increase in LengthStay implies less patient turnover and thus fewer start-up hours needed for the initial care of new patients.

b Consider a questionable hospital for which XRay = 56,194, BedDays = 14,077.88, and LengthStay = 6.89. A point prediction of the labor hours corresponding to this combination of values of the independent variables is given on the Excel add-in output. Report this point prediction and show (within rounding) how it has been calculated.

c If the actual number of labor hours used by the questionable hospital was $y = 17,207.31$, how does this y value compare with the point prediction?

15.2 Model Assumptions and the Standard Error ●●●

Model assumptions   In order to perform hypothesis tests and set up various types of intervals when using the multiple regression model

$$y = \beta_0 + \beta_1 x_1 + \beta_2 x_2 + \cdots + \beta_k x_k + \varepsilon$$

we need to make certain assumptions about the error term ε. At any given combination of values of $x_1, x_2, \ldots, x_k$, there is a population of error term values that could potentially occur. These error term values describe the different potential effects on y of all factors other than the combination of values of $x_1, x_2, \ldots, x_k$. Therefore, these error term values explain the variation in the y values that could be observed at the combination of values of $x_1, x_2, \ldots, x_k$. We make the following four assumptions about the potential error term values.

LO15-2 Explain the assumptions behind multiple regression and calculate the standard error.

Assumptions for the Multiple Regression Model

1 At any given combination of values of x_1, $x_2, \ldots, x_k$, the population of potential error term values has a mean equal to 0.

2 **Constant variance assumption:** At any given combination of values of $x_1, x_2, \ldots, x_k$, the population of potential error term values has a variance that does not depend on the combination of values of $x_1, x_2, \ldots, x_k$. That is, the different populations of potential error term values corresponding to different combinations of values of $x_1, x_2, \ldots, x_k$ have equal variances. We denote the constant variance as σ^2.

3 **Normality assumption:** At any given combination of values of $x_1, x_2, \ldots, x_k$, the population of potential error term values has a **normal distribution**.

4 **Independence assumption:** Any one value of the error term ε is **statistically independent** of any other value of ε. That is, the value of the error term ε corresponding to an observed value of y is statistically independent of the error term corresponding to any other observed value of y.

Taken together, the first three assumptions say that, at any given combination of values of $x_1, x_2, \ldots, x_k$, the population of potential error term values is normally distributed with mean 0 and a variance σ^2 that does not depend on the combination of values of $x_1, x_2, \ldots, x_k$. Because the potential error term values cause the variation in the potential y values, the first three assumptions imply that, at any given combination of values of $x_1, x_2, \ldots, x_k$, the population of y values that could be observed is normally distributed with mean $\beta_0 + \beta_1 x_1 + \beta_2 x_2 + \cdots + \beta_k x_k$ and a variance σ^2 that does not depend on the combination of values of $x_1, x_2, \ldots, x_k$. Furthermore, the independence assumption says that, when time series data are utilized in a regression study, there are no patterns in the error term values. In Section 15.11 we show how to check the validity of the regression assumptions. That section can be read at any time after Section 15.7. As in simple linear regression, only pronounced departures from the assumptions must be remedied.

The mean square error and the standard error   To present statistical inference formulas in later sections, we need to be able to compute point estimates of σ^2 and σ (the constant variance and standard deviation of the different error term populations). We show how to do this in the following box:

The Mean Square Error and the Standard Error

Suppose that the multiple regression model

$$y = \beta_0 + \beta_1 x_1 + \beta_2 x_2 + \cdots + \beta_k x_k + \varepsilon$$

utilizes k independent variables and thus has $(k + 1)$ parameters $\beta_0, \beta_1, \beta_2, \ldots, \beta_k$. Then, if the regression assumptions are satisfied, and if SSE denotes the sum of squared residuals for the model:

1 A point estimate of σ^2 is the **mean square error**

$$s^2 = \frac{SSE}{n - (k + 1)}$$

2 A point estimate of σ is the **standard error**

$$s = \sqrt{\frac{SSE}{n - (k + 1)}}$$

In order to explain these point estimates, recall that σ^2 is the variance of the population of y values (for given values of $x_1, x_2, \ldots, x_k$) around the mean value μ_y. Because $\hat{y}$ is the point estimate of this mean, it seems natural to use $SSE = \Sigma(y_i - \hat{y}_i)^2$ to help construct a point estimate of σ^2. We divide SSE by $n - (k + 1)$ because it can be proven that doing so makes the resulting s^2 an unbiased point estimate of σ^2. We call $n - (k + 1)$ the **number of degrees of freedom** associated with SSE.

We will see in Section 15.6 that if a particular regression model gives a small standard error, then the model will give short prediction intervals and thus accurate predictions of individual y values. For example, Table 15.2 (page 559) shows that SSE for the Tasty Sub Shop revenue model

$$y = \beta_0 + \beta_1 x_1 + \beta_2 x_2 + \varepsilon$$

is 9420.8. Because this model utilizes $k = 2$ independent variables and thus has $k + 1 = 3$ parameters (β_0, β_1, and β_2), a point estimate of σ^2 is the mean square error

$$s^2 = \frac{SSE}{n - (k + 1)} = \frac{9420.8}{10 - 3} = \frac{9420.8}{7} = 1345.835$$

and a point estimate of σ is the standard error $s = \sqrt{1345.835} = 36.6856$. Note that $SSE = 9420.8$, $s^2 = 1345.835$, and $s = 36.6856$ are given on the Excel and MINITAB outputs in Figure 15.4 (page 558). Also note that the s of 36.6856 for the two independent variable model is less than the s of 61.7052 for the simple linear regression model that uses only the population size to predict yearly revenue (see Example 14.3, page 502).

15.3 R^2 and Adjusted R^2 ● ● ●

The multiple coefficient of determination, R^2   In this section we discuss several ways to assess the utility of a multiple regression model. We first discuss a quantity called the **multiple coefficient of determination**, which is denoted R^2. The formulas for R^2 and several other related quantities are given in the following box:

LO15-3 Calculate and interpret the multiple and adjusted multiple coefficients of determination.

The Multiple Coefficient of Determination, R^2

For the multiple regression model:

1 **Total variation** $= \sum (y_i - \bar{y})^2$

2 **Explained variation** $= \sum (\hat{y}_i - \bar{y})^2$

3 **Unexplained variation** $= \sum (y_i - \hat{y}_i)^2$

4 **Total variation = Explained variation + Unexplained variation**

5 The **multiple coefficient of determination** is

$$R^2 = \frac{\text{Explained variation}}{\text{Total variation}}$$

6 R^2 is the proportion of the total variation in the n observed values of the dependent variable that is explained by the overall regression model.

7 **Multiple correlation coefficient** $= R = \sqrt{R^2}$

As an example, consider the Tasty Sub Shop revenue model

$$y = \beta_0 + \beta_1 x_1 + \beta_2 x_2 + \varepsilon$$

and the following MINITAB output:

```
S = 36.6856    R-Sq = 98.10%   R-Sq(adj) = 97.6%

Analysis of Variance
Source            DF      SS       MS       F       P
Regression         2   486356   243178   180.69   0.000
Residual Error     7     9421     1346
Total              9   495777
```

This output tells us that the total variation (SS Total), explained variation (SS Regression), and unexplained variation (SS Residual Error) for the model are, respectively, 495,777, 486,356, and 9,421. The output also tells us that the multiple coefficient of determination is

$$R^2 = \frac{\text{Explained variation}}{\text{Total variation}} = \frac{486,356}{495,777} = .981 \quad (98.1\% \text{ on the output})$$

which implies that the multiple correlation coefficient is $R = \sqrt{.981} = .9905$. The value of $R^2 = .981$ says that the two independent variable Tasty Sub Shop revenue model explains 98.1 percent of the total variation in the 10 observed yearly revenues. Note this R^2 value is larger than the r^2 of .939 for the simple linear regression model that uses only the population size to predict yearly revenue. Also note that the quantities given on the MINITAB output are given on the following Excel output.

Regression Statistics

Multiple R	0.9905
R Square	0.9810
Adjusted R Square	0.9756
Standard Error	36.6856
Observations	10

ANOVA	df	SS	MS	F	Significance F
Regression	2	486355.7	243177.8	180.689	9.46E-07
Residual	7	9420.8	1345.835		
Total	9	495776.5			

Adjusted R^2   Even if the independent variables in a regression model are unrelated to the dependent variable, they will make R^2 somewhat greater than 0. To avoid overestimating the importance of the independent variables, many analysts recommend calculating an *adjusted* multiple coefficient of determination.

Adjusted R^2

The **adjusted multiple coefficient of determination (adjusted R^2)** is

$$\overline{R}^2 = \left(R^2 - \frac{k}{n-1}\right)\left(\frac{n-1}{n-(k+1)}\right)$$

where R^2 is the multiple coefficient of determination, n is the number of observations, and k is the number of independent variables in the model under consideration.

To briefly explain this formula, note that it can be shown that subtracting $k/(n-1)$ from R^2 helps avoid overestimating the importance of the k independent variables. Furthermore, multiplying $[R^2 - (k/(n-1))]$ by $(n-1)/(n-(k+1))$ makes $\overline{R}^2$ equal to 1 when R^2 equals 1.

As an example, consider the Tasty Sub Shop revenue model

$$y = \beta_0 + \beta_1 x_1 + \beta_2 x_2 + \varepsilon$$

Because we have seen that $R^2 = .981$, it follows that

$$\overline{R}^2 = \left(R^2 - \frac{k}{n-1}\right)\left(\frac{n-1}{n-(k+1)}\right)$$
$$= \left(.981 - \frac{2}{10-1}\right)\left(\frac{10-1}{10-(2+1)}\right)$$
$$= .9756$$

which is given on the MINITAB and Excel outputs.

If R^2 is less than $k/(n-1)$, which can happen, then $\overline{R}^2$ will be negative. In this case, statistical software systems set $\overline{R}^2$ equal to 0. Historically, R^2 and $\overline{R}^2$ have been popular measures of model utility—possibly because they are unitless and between 0 and 1. In general, we desire R^2 and $\overline{R}^2$ to be near 1. However, sometimes even if a regression model has an R^2 and an $\overline{R}^2$ that are near 1, the model is still not able to predict accurately. We will discuss assessing a model's ability to predict accurately, as well as using R^2 and $\overline{R}^2$ to help choose a regression model, as we proceed through the rest of this chapter.

15.4 The Overall *F*-Test ● ● ●

LO15-4 Test the significance of a multiple regression model by using an *F*-test.

Another way to assess the utility of a regression model is to test the significance of the regression relationship between y and $x_1, x_2, \ldots, x_k$. For the multiple regression model, we test the null hypothesis $H_0: \beta_1 = \beta_2 = \cdots = \beta_k = 0$, which says that **none of the independent variables x_1, $x_2, \ldots, x_k$ is significantly related to y (the regression relationship is not significant)**, versus the alternative hypothesis H_a: At least one of $\beta_1, \beta_2, \ldots, \beta_k$ does not equal 0, which says that **at least one of the independent variables is significantly related to y (the regression relationship is significant)**. If we can reject H_0 at level of significance α, we say that **the multiple regression model is significant at level of significance α.** We carry out the test as follows:

An *F*-Test for the Multiple Regression Model

Suppose that the regression assumptions hold and that the multiple regression model has $(k + 1)$ parameters, and consider testing

$$H_0: \beta_1 = \beta_2 = \cdots = \beta_k = 0$$

versus

H_a: At least one of $\beta_1, \beta_2, \ldots, \beta_k$ does not equal 0.

We define the **overall *F* statistic** to be

$$F(\text{model}) = \frac{(\text{Explained variation})/k}{(\text{Unexplained variation})/[n - (k + 1)]}$$

Also define the *p*-value related to $F(\text{model})$ to be the area under the curve of the *F* distribution (having k and $[n - (k + 1)]$ degrees of freedom) to the right of $F(\text{model})$. Then, we can reject H_0 in favor of H_a at level of significance α if either of the following equivalent conditions holds:

1 $F(\text{model}) > F_\alpha$

2 *p*-value $< \alpha$

Here the point F_α is based on k numerator and $n - (k + 1)$ denominator degrees of freedom.

Condition 1 is intuitively reasonable because a large value of $F(\text{model})$ would be caused by an explained variation that is large relative to the unexplained variation. This would occur if at least one independent variable in the regression model significantly affects y, which would imply that H_0 is false and H_a is true.

EXAMPLE 15.2 The Tasty Sub Shop Case: The Overall *F*-Test   C

Consider the Tasty Sub Shop revenue model

$$y = \beta_0 + \beta_1 x_1 + \beta_2 x_2 + \varepsilon$$

and the following MINITAB output

```
Analysis of Variance
Source            DF        SS       MS        F       P
Regression         2    486356   243178   180.69   0.000
Residual Error     7      9421     1346
Total              9    495777
```

This output tells us that the explained and unexplained variations for this model are, respectively, 486,356 and 9,421. It follows, because there are $k = 2$ independent variables, that

$$F(\text{model}) = \frac{(\text{Explained variation})/k}{(\text{Unexplained variation})/[n - (k + 1)]}$$

$$= \frac{486{,}356/2}{9421/[10 - (2 + 1)]} = \frac{243{,}178}{1345.8}$$

$$= 180.69$$

Note that this overall F statistic is given on the MINITAB output and is also given on the following Excel output:

ANOVA	df	SS	MS	F	Significance F
Regression	2	486355.7	243177.8	180.689	9.46E-07
Residual	7	9420.8	1345.835		
Total	9	495776.5			

The p-value related to F(model) is the area to the right of 180.69 under the curve of the F distribution having $k = 2$ numerator and $n - (k + 1) = 10 - 3 = 7$ denominator degrees of freedom. Both the MINITAB and Excel outputs say this p-value is less than .001.

If we wish to test the significance of the regression model at level of significance $\alpha = .05$, we use the critical value $F_{.05}$ based on 2 numerator and 7 denominator degrees of freedom. Using Table A.7 (page 796), we find that $F_{.05} = 4.74$. Because F(model) $= 180.69 > F_{.05} = 4.74$, we can reject H_0 in favor of H_a at level of significance .05. Alternatively, because the p-value is smaller than .05, .01, and .001, we can reject H_0 at level of significance .05, .01, and .001. Therefore, we have extremely strong evidence that the Tasty Sub Shop revenue model is significant. That is, we have extremely strong evidence that at least one of the independent variables x_1 and x_2 in the model is significantly related to y.

If the overall F-test tells us that at least one independent variable in a regression model is significant, we next attempt to decide which independent variables are significant. In the next section we discuss one way to do this.

Exercises for Sections 15.2, 15.3, and 15.4

CONCEPTS

connect

15.7   What is estimated by the mean square error, and what is estimated by the standard error?

15.8   **a** What do R^2 and $\overline{R}^2$ measure?   **b** How do R^2 and $\overline{R}^2$ differ?

15.9   What is the purpose of the overall F-test?

METHODS AND APPLICATIONS

In Exercises 15.10 to 15.13 we give Excel and MINITAB outputs of regression analyses of the data sets related to four case studies introduced in Section 15.1. Above each output we give the regression model and the number of observations, n, used to perform the regression analysis under consideration. Using the appropriate model, sample size n, and output:

1   Report SSE, s^2, and s as shown on the output. Calculate s^2 from SSE and other numbers.

2   Report the total variation, unexplained variation, and explained variation as shown on the output.

3   Report R^2 and $\overline{R}^2$ as shown on the output. Interpret R^2 and $\overline{R}^2$. Show how $\overline{R}^2$ has been calculated from R^2 and other numbers.

4   Calculate the F(model) statistic by using the explained and unexplained variations (as shown on the output) and other relevant quantities. Find F(model) on the output to check your answer (within rounding).

5   Use the F(model) statistic and the appropriate critical value to test the significance of the linear regression model under consideration by setting α equal to .05.

6   Use the F(model) statistic and the appropriate critical value to test the significance of the linear regression model under consideration by setting α equal to .01.

7   Find the p-value related to F(model) on the output. Using the p-value, test the significance of the linear regression model by setting $\alpha = .10, .05, .01,$ and $.001$. What do you conclude?

15.10   THE NATURAL GAS CONSUMPTION CASE   **DS** GasCon2

Model: $y = \beta_0 + \beta_1 x_1 + \beta_2 x_2 + \varepsilon$ Sample size: $n = 8$

The output follows on the next page:

```
S = 0.367078    R-Sq = 97.4%    R-Sq(adj) = 96.3%

Analysis of Variance
Source             DF      SS      MS       F      P
Regression          2   24.875  12.438   92.30  0.000
Residual Error      5    0.674   0.135
Total               7   25.549
```

15.11 **THE REAL ESTATE SALES PRICE CASE**   DS RealEst2

Model: $y = \beta_0 + \beta_1 x_1 + \beta_2 x_2 + \varepsilon$ Sample size: $n = 10$

```
S = 3.24164    R-Sq = 99.0%    R-Sq(adj) = 98.7%

Analysis of Variance
Source             DF      SS      MS       F       P
Regression          2   7374.0  3687.0   350.87  0.000
Residual Error      7     73.6    10.5
Total               9   7447.5
```

15.12 **THE FRESH DETERGENT CASE**   DS Fresh2

Model: $y = \beta_0 + \beta_1 x_1 + \beta_2 x_2 + \beta_3 x_3 + \varepsilon$ Sample size: $n = 30$

Regression Statistics	
Multiple R	0.9453
R Square	0.8936
Adjusted R Square	0.8813
Standard Error	0.2347
Observations	30

ANOVA	df	SS	MS	F	Significance F
Regression	3	12.0268	4.0089	72.7973	0.0000
Residual	26	1.4318	0.0551		
Total	29	13.4586			

15.13 **THE HOSPITAL LABOR NEEDS CASE**   DS HospLab

Model: $y = \beta_0 + \beta_1 x_1 + \beta_2 x_2 + \beta_3 x_3 + \varepsilon$ Sample size: $n = 16$

Regression Statistics	
Multiple R	0.9981
R Square	0.9961
Adjusted R Square	0.9952
Standard Error	387.1598
Observations	16

ANOVA	df	SS	MS	F	Significance F
Regression	3	462327889.4	154109296.5	1028.1309	9.92E-15
Residual	12	1798712.2	149892.7		
Total	15	464126601.6			

15.5 Testing the Significance of an Independent Variable ●●●

LO15-5 Test the significance of a single independent variable.

Consider the multiple regression model

$$y = \beta_0 + \beta_1 x_1 + \beta_2 x_2 + \cdots + \beta_k x_k + \varepsilon$$

In order to gain information about which independent variables significantly affect y, we can test the significance of a single independent variable. We arbitrarily refer to this variable as x_j and assume that it is multiplied by the parameter β_j. For example, if $j = 1$, we are testing the significance of x_1, which is multiplied by β_1; if $j = 2$, we are testing the significance of x_2, which is multiplied by β_2. To test the significance of x_j, we test the null hypothesis $H_0: \beta_j = 0$. We usually test H_0 versus the alternative hypothesis $H_a: \beta_j \neq 0$. **It is reasonable to conclude that x_j is significantly related to y in the regression model under consideration if H_0 can be rejected in favor of H_a at a small level of significance.** Here the phrase *in the regression model under consideration* is very important. This is because it can be shown that whether x_j is significantly related to y in a particular regression model can depend on what other independent variables are included in the model. This issue will be discussed in detail in Section 15.10.

Testing the significance of x_j in a multiple regression model is similar to testing the significance of the slope in the simple linear regression model (recall we test $H_0: \beta_1 = 0$ in simple regression). It can be proved that, if the regression assumptions hold, the population of all possible values of the least squares point estimate b_j is normally distributed with mean β_j and standard deviation σ_{b_j}. The point estimate of σ_{b_j} is called the **standard error of the estimate b_j** and is denoted s_{b_j}. The formula for s_{b_j} involves matrix algebra and is discussed in Bowerman, O'Connell, and Koehler (2005). In our discussion here, we will rely on Excel and MINITAB to compute s_{b_j}. It can be shown that, if the regression assumptions hold, then the population of all possible values of

$$\frac{b_j - \beta_j}{s_{b_j}}$$

has a t distribution with $n - (k + 1)$ degrees of freedom. It follows that, if the null hypothesis $H_0: \beta_j = 0$ is true, then the population of all possible values of the test statistic

$$t = \frac{b_j}{s_{b_j}}$$

has a t distribution with $n - (k + 1)$ degrees of freedom. Therefore, we can test the significance of x_j as follows:

Testing the Significance of the Independent Variable x_j

Null Hypothesis $H_0: \beta_j = 0$	Test Statistic $t = \dfrac{b_j}{s_{b_j}}$ $df = n - (k + 1)$	Assumptions The regression assumptions

As in testing $H_0: \beta_1 = 0$ in simple linear regression, we usually use the two-sided alternative hypothesis $H_a: \beta_j \neq 0$. Excel and MINITAB present the results for the two-sided test.

It is customary to test the significance of each and every independent variable in a regression model. Generally speaking,

1   If we can reject $H_0: \beta_j = 0$ at the .05 level of significance, we have strong evidence that the independent variable x_j is significantly related to y in the regression model.

2   If we can reject $H_0: \beta_j = 0$ at the .01 level of significance, we have very strong evidence that x_j is significantly related to y in the regression model.

3   The smaller the significance level α at which H_0 can be rejected, the stronger is the evidence that x_j is significantly related to y in the regression model.

TABLE 15.7 t Statistics and p-Values for Testing the Significance of the Intercept, x_1, and x_2 in the Tasty Sub Shop Revenue Model $y = \beta_0 + \beta_1 x_1 + \beta_2 x_2 + \varepsilon$

(a) Calculation of the t statistics

Independent Variable	Null Hypothesis	b_j	s_{b_j}	$t = \dfrac{b_j}{s_{b_j}}$	p-Value
Intercept	$H_0: \beta_0 = 0$	$b_0 = 125.29$	$s_{b_0} = 40.93$	$t = \dfrac{b_0}{s_{b_0}} = \dfrac{125.29}{40.93} = 3.06$	.0183
x_1	$H_0: \beta_1 = 0$	$b_1 = 14.1996$	$s_{b_1} = 0.91$	$t = \dfrac{b_1}{s_{b_1}} = \dfrac{14.1996}{.91} = 15.6$	$< .001$
x_2	$H_0: \beta_2 = 0$	$b_2 = 22.811$	$s_{b_2} = 5.769$	$t = \dfrac{b_2}{s_{b_2}} = \dfrac{22.811}{5.769} = 3.95$	.0055

(b) The MINITAB output

```
Predictor     Coef   SE Coef      T      P
Constant    125.29     40.93   3.06  0.018
population  14.1996      0.91  15.6   0.000
bus_rating  22.811      5.769  3.95  0.006
```

(c) The Excel output

	Coefficients	Standard Error	t Stat	P-value	Lower 95%	Upper 95%
Intercept	125.289	40.9333	3.06	0.0183	28.4969	222.0807
population	14.1996	0.9100	15.60	1.07E-06	12.0478	16.3515
bus_rating	22.8107	5.7692	3.95	0.0055	9.1686	36.4527

EXAMPLE 15.3 The Tasty Sub Shop Case: t statistics and related p-values

Again consider the Tasty Sub Shop revenue model

$$y = \beta_0 + \beta_1 x_1 + \beta_2 x_2 + \varepsilon$$

Table 15.7(a) summarizes the calculation of the t statistics and related p-values for testing the significance of the intercept and each of the independent variables x_1 and x_2. Here the values of b_j, s_{b_j}, t, and the p-value have been obtained from the MINITAB and Excel outputs of Table 15.7(b) and (c). If we wish to carry out tests at the .05 level of significance, we use the critical value $t_{.05/2} = t_{.025} = 2.365$, which is based on $n - (k + 1) = 10 - 3 = 7$ degrees of freedom. Looking at Table 15.7 (a), we see that

1   For the intercept, $|t| = 3.06 > 2.365$.
2   For x_1, $|t| = 15.6 > 2.365$.
3   For x_2, $|t| = 3.95 > 2.365$.

Because in each case $|t| > t_{.025}$, we reject each of the null hypotheses in Table 15.7(a) at the .05 level of significance. Furthermore, because the p-value related to x_1 is less than .001, we can reject $H_0: \beta_1 = 0$ at the .001 level of significance. Also, because the p-value related to x_2 is less than .01, we can reject $H_0: \beta_2 = 0$ at the .01 level of significance. On the basis of these results, we have extremely strong evidence that in the above model x_1 (population size) is significantly related to y. We also have very strong evidence that in this model x_2 (business rating) is significantly related to y.

We next consider how to calculate a confidence interval for a regression parameter.

A Confidence Interval for the Regression Parameter β_j

If the regression assumptions hold, a **100(1 − α) percent confidence interval** for β_j is

$$[b_j \pm t_{\alpha/2}s_{b_j}]$$

Here $t_{\alpha/2}$ is based on $n - (k + 1)$ degrees of freedom.

EXAMPLE 15.4 The Tasty Sub Shop Case: A Confidence Interval for β_1

Consider the Tasty Sub Shop revenue model

$$y = \beta_0 + \beta_1 x_1 + \beta_2 x_2 + \varepsilon$$

The MINITAB and Excel outputs in Table 15.7 tell us that $b_1 = 14.1996$ and $s_{b_1} = .91$. It follows, because $t_{.025}$ based on $n - (k + 1) = 10 - 3 = 7$ degrees of freedom equals 2.365, that a 95 percent confidence interval for β_1 is (see the Excel output)

$$[b_1 \pm t_{.025}s_{b_1}] = [14.1996 \pm 2.365(.91)]$$

$$= [12.048, 16.352]$$

This interval says we are 95 percent confident that, if the population size increases by 1,000 residents and the business rating does not change, then mean yearly revenue will increase by between $12,048 and $16,352. Furthermore, because this 95 percent confidence interval does not contain 0, we can reject H_0: $\beta_1 = 0$ in favor of H_a: $\beta_1 \neq 0$ at the .05 level of significance.

Exercises for Section 15.5

CONCEPTS

connect™

15.14 What do we conclude about x_j if we can reject H_0: $\beta_j = 0$ in favor of H_a: $\beta_j \neq 0$ by setting
    a α equal to .05?
    b α equal to .01?

15.15 Give an example of a practical application of the confidence interval for β_j.

METHODS AND APPLICATIONS

In Exercises 15.16 through 15.19 we refer to Excel and MINITAB outputs of regression analyses of the data sets related to four case studies introduced in Section 15.1. The outputs are given in Figure 15.9. Using the appropriate output, do the following for **each parameter** β_j in the model under consideration:

1. Find b_j, s_{b_j}, and the t statistic for testing H_0: $\beta_j = 0$ on the output and report their values. Show how t has been calculated by using b_j and s_{b_j}.

2. Using the t statistic and appropriate critical values, test H_0: $\beta_j = 0$ versus H_a: $\beta_j \neq 0$ by setting α equal to .05. Which independent variables are significantly related to y in the model with $\alpha = .05$?

3. Using the t statistic and appropriate critical values, test H_0: $\beta_j = 0$ versus H_a: $\beta_j \neq 0$ by setting α equal to .01. Which independent variables are significantly related to y in the model with $\alpha = .01$?

4. Find the p-value for testing H_0: $\beta_j = 0$ versus H_a: $\beta_j \neq 0$ on the output. Using the p-value, determine whether we can reject H_0 by setting α equal to .10, .05, .01, and .001. What do you conclude about the significance of the independent variables in the model?

5. Calculate the 95 percent confidence interval for β_j. Discuss one practical application of this interval.

6. Calculate the 99 percent confidence interval for β_j.

15.16 THE NATURAL GAS CONSUMPTION CASE ⑤ GasCon2

Use the MINITAB output in Figure 15.9(a) to do (1) through (6) for each of β_0, β_1, and β_2.

FIGURE 15.9 *t* Statistics and *p*-Values for Four Case Studies

(a) MINITAB output for the natural gas consumption case (sample size : *n* = 8)

Predictor	Coef	SE Coef	T	P
Constant	13.1087	0.8557	15.32	0.000
Temp	-0.09001	0.01408	-6.39	0.001
Chill	0.08249	0.02200	3.75	0.013

(b) MINITAB output for the real estate sales price case (sample size: *n* = 10)

Predictor	Coef	SE Coef	T	P
Constant	29.347	4.891	6.00	0.001
HomeSize	5.6128	0.2285	24.56	0.000
Rating	3.8344	0.4332	8.85	0.000

(c) Excel output for the Fresh detergent case (sample size: *n* = 30)

	Coefficients	Standard Error	t Stat	P-value	Lower 95%	Upper 95%
Intercept	7.5891	2.4450	3.1039	0.0046	2.5633	12.6149
Price (x1)	-2.3577	0.6379	-3.6958	0.0010	-3.6690	-1.0464
IndPrice (x2)	1.6122	0.2954	5.4586	0.0000	1.0051	2.2193
AdvExp (x3)	0.5012	0.1259	3.9814	0.0005	0.2424	0.7599

(d) Excel output for the hospital labor needs case (sample size: *n* = 16)

	Coefficients	Standard Error	t Stat	P-value	Lower 95%	Upper 95%
Intercept	1946.8020	504.1819	3.8613	0.0023	848.2840	3045.3201
XRay (x1)	0.0386	0.0130	2.9579	0.0120	0.0102	0.0670
BedDays (x2)	1.0394	0.0676	15.3857	2.91E-09	0.8922	1.1866
LengthStay (x3)	-413.7578	98.5983	-4.1964	0.0012	-628.5850	-198.9306

15.17   THE REAL ESTATE SALES PRICE CASE ⒹⓈ RealEst2

Use the MINITAB output in Figure 15.9(b) to do (1) through (6) for each of β_0, β_1, and β_2.

15.18   THE FRESH DETERGENT CASE ⒹⓈ Fresh2

Use the Excel output in Figure 15.9(c) to do (1) through (6) for each of β_0, β_1, β_2, and β_3.

15.19   THE HOSPITAL LABOR NEEDS CASE ⒹⓈ HospLab

Use the Excel output in Figure 15.9(d) to do (1) through (6) for each of β_0, β_1, β_2, and β_3.

15.6 Confidence and Prediction Intervals ● ● ●

LO15-6 Find and interpret a confidence interval for a mean value and a prediction interval for an individual value.

In this section we show how to use the multiple regression model to find a **confidence interval for a mean value of *y*** and a **prediction interval for an individual value of *y*.** We first present an example of these intervals, and we then discuss (in an optional technical note) the formulas used to compute the intervals.

EXAMPLE 15.5 The Tasty Sub Shop Case: Estimating Mean Revenue and Predicting Revenue and Profit

In the Tasty Sub Shop problem, recall that one of the business entrepreneur's potential sites is near a population of 47,300 residents and a business/shopping area having a rating of 7. Also, recall that

$$\hat{y} = b_0 + b_1 x_1 + b_2 x_2$$
$$= 125.29 + 14.1996 (47.3) + 22.811(7)$$
$$= 956.6 \text{ (that is, \$956,600)}$$

is:

1   The **point estimate** of the mean yearly revenue for all Tasty Sub restaurants that could po-
    tentially be built near populations of 47,300 residents and business/shopping areas having a
    rating of 7, and
2   The **point prediction** of the yearly revenue for a single Tasty Sub restaurant that is built
    near a population of 47,300 residents and a business/shopping area having a rating of 7.

This point estimate and prediction are given at the bottom of the MINITAB output in Figure 15.4,
which we repeat here as follows:

```
New Obs      Fit   SE Fit       95% CI              95% PI
    1       956.6       15   (921.0, 992.2)    (862.8, 1050.4)
```

In addition to giving $\hat{y} = 956.6$, the MINITAB output also gives a 95 percent confidence interval
and a 95 percent prediction interval. The 95 percent confidence interval, [921.0, 992.2], says that
we are 95 percent confident that the mean yearly revenue for all Tasty Sub restaurants that could
potentially be built near populations of 47,300 residents and business/shopping areas having a
rating of 7 is between $921,000 and $992,200. The 95 percent prediction interval, [862.8, 1050.4],
says that we are 95 percent confident that the yearly revenue for a single Tasty Sub restaurant that
is built near a population of 47,300 residents and a business/shopping area having a rating of 7
will be between $862,800 and $1,050,400.

Now, recall that the yearly rent and other fixed costs for the entrepreneur's potential restaurant
will be $257,550 and that (according to Tasty Sub corporate headquarters) the yearly food and
other variable costs for the restaurant will be 60 percent of the yearly revenue. Using the lower end
of the 95 percent prediction interval [862.8, 1050.4], we predict that (1) the restaurant's yearly operating cost will be $257,550 + .6(862,800) = $775,230 and (2) the restaurant's yearly profit will
be $862,800 − $775,230 = $87,570. Using the upper end of the 95 percent prediction interval
[862.8, 1050.4], we predict that (1) the restaurant's yearly operating cost will be $257,550 +
.6(1,050,400) = $887,790 and (2) the restaurant's yearly profit will be $1,050,400 − $887,790 =
$162,610. Combining the two predicted profits, it follows that we are 95 percent confident that the
potential restaurant's yearly profit will be between $87,570 and $162,610. If the entrepreneur decides that this is an acceptable range of potential yearly profits, then the entrepreneur might decide
to purchase a Tasty Sub franchise for the potential restaurant site.

A technical note (optional)   In general

$$\hat{y} = b_0 + b_1x_1 + b_2x_2 + \cdots + b_kx_k$$

is the **point estimate of the mean value of the dependent variable y** when the values of the
independent variables are $x_1, x_2, \ldots, x_k$ and is the **point prediction of an individual value of
the dependent variable y** when the values of the independent variables are $x_1, x_2, \ldots, x_k$.
Furthermore:

A Confidence Interval and a Prediction Interval

If the regression assumptions hold,

1   A 100$(1 - \alpha)$ percent confidence interval for the mean value of y when the values of the
    independent variables are $x_1, x_2, \ldots, x_k$ is

$$[\hat{y} \pm t_{\alpha/2}s\sqrt{\text{distance value}}]$$

2   A 100$(1 - \alpha)$ percent prediction interval for an individual value of y when the values of the
    independent variables are $x_1, x_2, \ldots, x_k$ is

$$[\hat{y} \pm t_{\alpha/2}s\sqrt{1 + \text{distance value}}]$$

Here $t_{\alpha/2}$ is based on $n - (k + 1)$ degrees of freedom and s is the standard error (see page 566). Furthermore,
the formula for the **distance value** (also sometimes called the **leverage value**) involves matrix algebra and is
given in Bowerman, O'Connell, and Koehler (2005). In practice, we can obtain the distance value from the
outputs of statistical software packages (such as MINITAB and an Excel add-in).

Intuitively, the **distance value** is a measure of the distance of the combination of values x_1, $x_2, \ldots, x_k$ from the center of the observed data. The farther that this combination is from the center of the observed data, the larger is the distance value, and thus the longer are both the confidence interval and the prediction interval.

MINITAB gives $s_{\hat{y}} = s\sqrt{\text{distance value}}$ under the heading "SE Fit." Because the MINITAB output also gives s, the distance value can be found by calculating $(s_{\hat{y}}/s)^2$. For example, the MINITAB output in Figure 15.4 (page 558) tells us that $\hat{y} = 956.6$ (see "Fit") and $s_{\hat{y}} = 15$ (see "SE Fit"). Therefore, because s for the two-variable Tasty Sub Shop revenue model equals 36.6856 (see Figure 15.4), the distance value equals $(15/36.6856)^2 = .1671826$. It follows that the 95 percent confidence and prediction intervals given on the MINITAB output of Figure 15.4 have been calculated (within rounding) as follows:

$[\hat{y} \pm t_{.025} s\sqrt{\text{distance value}}]$ $[\hat{y} \pm t_{.025} s\sqrt{1 + \text{distance value}}]$

$= [956.6 \pm 2.365(36.6856)\sqrt{.1671826}]$ $= [956.6 \pm 2.365(36.6856)\sqrt{1.1671826}]$

$= [956.6 \pm 35.47]$ $= [956.6 \pm 93.73]$

$= [921.1, 992.1]$ $= [862.9, 1050.3]$

Here $t_{\alpha/2} = t_{.025} = 2.365$ is based on $n - (k + 1) = 10 - 3 = 7$ degrees of freedom.

Exercises for Section 15.6

CONCEPTS

15.20 What is the difference between a confidence interval and a prediction interval?

15.21 What does the distance value measure? How does the distance value affect a confidence or prediction interval? (Note: You must read the optional technical note to answer this question.)

METHODS AND APPLICATIONS

15.22 **THE NATURAL GAS CONSUMPTION CASE**   DS GasCon2

The following partial MINITAB regression output for the natural gas consumption data relates to predicting the city's natural gas consumption (in MMcF) in a week that has an average hourly temperature of 40°F and a chill index of 10.

New Obs	Fit	SE Fit	95% CI	95% PI
1	10.333	0.170	(9.895, 10.771)	(9.293, 11.374)

a Report (as shown on the computer output) a point estimate of and a 95 percent confidence interval for the mean natural gas consumption for all weeks having an average hourly temperature of 40°F and a chill index of 10.

b Report (as shown on the computer output) a point prediction of and a 95 percent prediction interval for the natural gas consumption in a single week that has an average hourly temperature of 40°F and a chill index of 10.

c Suppose that next week the city's average hourly temperature will be 40°F and the city's chill index will be 10. Also, suppose the city's natural gas company will use the point prediction $\hat{y} = 10.333$ and order 10.333 MMcF of natural gas to be shipped to the city by a pipeline transmission system. The gas company will have to pay a fine to the transmission system if the city's actual gas usage y differs from the order of 10.333 MMcF by more than 10.5 percent— that is, is outside of the range $[10.333 \pm .105(10.333)] = [9.248, 11.418]$. Discuss why the 95 percent prediction interval for y, [9.293, 11.374], says that y is likely to be inside the allowable range and thus makes the gas company 95 percent confident that it will avoid paying a fine.

d Find 99 percent confidence and prediction intervals for the mean and actual natural gas consumption referred to in parts a and b. Hint: $n = 8$ and $s = .367078$. Optional technical note needed.

15.23 **THE REAL ESTATE SALES PRICE CASE**   DS RealEst2

The following MINITAB output relates to a house having 2,000 square feet and a rating of 8.

New Obs	Fit	SE Fit	95% CI	95% PI
1	172.28	1.57	(168.56, 175.99)	(163.76, 180.80)

connect

a Report (as shown on the output) a point estimate of and a 95 percent confidence interval for the mean sales price of all houses having 2,000 square feet and a rating of 8.

b Report (as shown on the output) a point prediction of and a 95 percent prediction interval for the actual sales price of an individual house having 2,000 square feet and a rating of 8.

c Find 99 percent confidence and prediction intervals for the mean and actual sales prices referred to in parts *a* and *b*. Hint: $n = 10$ and $s = 3.24164$. Optional technical note needed.

15.24 THE FRESH DETERGENT CASE   Fresh2

Consider the demand for Fresh Detergent in a future sales period when Enterprise Industries' price for Fresh will be $x_1 = 3.70$, the average price of competitors' similar detergents will be $x_2 = 3.90$, and Enterprise Industries' advertising expenditure for Fresh will be $x_3 = 6.50$. A 95 percent prediction interval for this demand is given on the following Excel add-in (MegaStat) output:

	95% Confidence Interval		95% Prediction Interval		
Predicted	lower	upper	lower	upper	Leverage
8.4107	8.3143	8.5070	7.9188	8.9025	0.040

a Find and report the 95 percent prediction interval on the output. If Enterprise Industries plans to have in inventory the number of bottles implied by the upper limit of this interval, it can be very confident that it will have enough bottles to meet demand for Fresh in the future sales period. How many bottles is this? If we multiply the number of bottles implied by the lower limit of the prediction interval by the price of Fresh ($3.70), we can be very confident that the resulting dollar amount will be the minimum revenue from Fresh in the future sales period. What is this dollar amount?

b Calculate a 99 percent prediction interval for the demand for Fresh in the future sales period. Hint: $n = 30$ and $s = .235$. Optional technical note needed. Note that the distance value equals **Leverage.**

15.25 THE HOSPITAL LABOR NEEDS CASE   HospLab

Consider a questionable hospital for which XRay = 56,194, BedDays = 14,077.88, and LengthStay = 6.89. A 95 percent prediction interval for the labor hours corresponding to this combination of values of the independent variables is given in the following Excel add-in (MegaStat) output:

	95% Confidence Interval		95% Prediction Interval		
Predicted	lower	upper	lower	upper	Leverage
15,896.2473	15,378.0313	16,414.4632	14,906.2361	16,886.2584	0.3774

Find and report the prediction interval on the output. Then, use this interval to determine if the actual number of labor hours used by the questionable hospital ($y = 17,207.31$) is unusually low or high.

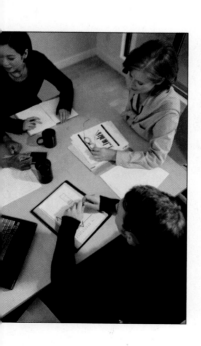

15.7 The Sales Representative Case: Evaluating Employee Performance ● ● ●

Suppose the sales manager of a company wishes to evaluate the performance of the company's sales representatives. Each sales representative is solely responsible for one sales territory, and the manager decides that it is reasonable to measure the performance, y, of a sales representative by using the yearly sales of the company's product in the representative's sales territory. The manager feels that sales performance y substantially depends on five independent variables:

x_1 = number of months the representative has been employed by the company

x_2 = sales of the company's product and competing products in the sales territory (a measure of sales potential)

x_3 = dollar advertising expenditure in the territory

x_4 = weighted average of the company's market share in the territory for the previous four years

x_5 = change in the company's market share in the territory over the previous four years

FIGURE 15.10   Sales Representative Performance Study Data   ⒹⓈ SalePerf

	Sales, y	Time with Company, x_1	Market Potential, x_2	Advertising, x_3	Market Share, x_4	Market Share Change, x_5
	3,669.88	43.10	74,065.11	4,582.88	2.51	0.34
	3,473.95	108.13	58,117.30	5,539.78	5.51	0.15
	2,295.10	13.82	21,118.49	2,950.38	10.91	−0.72
	4,675.56	186.18	68,521.27	2,243.07	8.27	0.17
	6,125.96	161.79	57,805.11	7,747.08	9.15	0.50
	2,134.94	8.94	37,806.94	402.44	5.51	0.15
	5,031.66	365.04	50,935.26	3,140.62	8.54	0.55
	3,367.45	220.32	35,602.08	2,086.16	7.07	−0.49
	6,519.45	127.64	46,176.77	8,846.25	12.54	1.24
	4,876.37	105.69	42,053.24	5,673.11	8.85	0.31
	2,468.27	57.72	36,829.71	2,761.76	5.38	0.37
	2,533.31	23.58	33,612.67	1,991.85	5.43	−0.65
	2,408.11	13.82	21,412.79	1,971.52	8.48	0.64
	2,337.38	13.82	20,416.87	1,737.38	7.80	1.01
	4,586.95	86.99	36,272.00	10,694.20	10.34	0.11
	2,729.24	165.85	23,093.26	8,618.61	5.15	0.04
	3,289.40	116.26	26,878.59	7,747.89	6.64	0.68
	2,800.78	42.28	39,571.96	4,565.81	5.45	0.66
	3,264.20	52.84	51,866.15	6,022.70	6.31	−0.10
	3,453.62	165.04	58,749.82	3,721.10	6.35	−0.03
	1,741.45	10.57	23,990.82	860.97	7.37	−1.63
	2,035.75	13.82	25,694.86	3,571.51	8.39	−0.43
	1,578.00	8.13	23,736.35	2,845.50	5.15	0.04
	4,167.44	58.54	34,314.29	5,060.11	12.88	0.22
	2,799.97	21.14	22,809.53	3,552.00	9.14	−0.74

Source: This data set is from a research study published in "An Analytical Approach for Evaluation of Sales Territory Performance," *Journal of Marketing*, January 1972, 31–37 (authors are David W. Cravens, Robert B. Woodruff, and Joseph C. Stamper). We have updated the situation in our case study to be more modern.

In Figure 15.10 we present values of y and x_1 through x_5 for 25 randomly selected sales representatives. To understand the values of y and x_2 in the table, note that sales of the company's product or any competing product are measured in hundreds of units of the product sold. Therefore, for example, the first sales figure of 3,669.88 in Figure 15.10 means that the first randomly selected sales representative sold 366,988 units of the company's product during the year.

Plots of y versus x_1 through x_5 are given in Figure 15.10. Because each plot has an approximate straight-line appearance, it is reasonable to relate y to x_1 through x_5 by using the regression model

$$y = \beta_0 + \beta_1 x_1 + \beta_2 x_2 + \beta_3 x_3 + \beta_4 x_4 + \beta_5 x_5 + \varepsilon$$

The main objective of the regression analysis is to help the sales manager evaluate sales performance by comparing actual performance to predicted performance. The manager has randomly selected the 25 representatives from all the representatives the company considers to be effective and wishes to use a regression model based on effective representatives to evaluate questionable representatives.

Figure 15.11 on the next page gives the Excel output of a regression analysis of the sales representative performance data using the five independent variable model. This output tells us that the least squares point estimates of the model parameters are $b_0 = -1,113.7879$, $b_1 = 3.6121$, $b_2 = .0421$, $b_3 = .1289$, $b_4 = 256.9555$, and $b_5 = 324.5334$. In addition, because the output tells us that the p-values associated with Time, MktPoten, Adver, and MktShare are all less than .01, we have very strong evidence that these variables are significantly related to y and, thus, are important in this model. Because the p-value associated with Change is .0530, we have close to strong evidence that this variable is also important.

FIGURE 15.11   **Excel Output of a Regression Analysis of the Sales Representative Performance Data Using the Model** $y = \beta_0 + \beta_1 x_1 + \beta_2 x_2 + \beta_3 x_3 + \beta_4 x_4 + \beta_5 x_5 + \varepsilon$

(a) The Excel output

Regression Statistics

Multiple R	0.9566
R Square	0.9150
Adjusted R Square	0.8926
Standard Error	430.2319
Observations	25

ANOVA	df	SS	MS	F	Significance F
Regression	5	37862658.9002	7572531.7800	40.9106	0.0000
Residual	19	3516890.0266	185099.4751		
Total	24	41379548.9269			

	Coefficients	Standard Error	t Stat	P-value	Lower 95%	Upper 95%
Intercept	-1113.7879	419.8869	-2.6526	0.0157	-1992.6213	-234.9545
Time	3.6121	1.1817	3.0567	0.0065	1.1388	6.0854
MktPoten	0.0421	0.0067	6.2527	0.0000	0.0280	0.0562
Adver	0.1289	0.0370	3.4792	0.0025	0.0513	0.2064
MktShare	256.9555	39.1361	6.5657	0.0000	175.0428	338.8683
Change	324.5334	157.2831	2.0634	0.0530	-4.6638	653.7307

(b) Prediction using an Excel add-in (MegaStat)

Predicted values for: Sales

	95% Confidence Interval		95% Prediction Interval		
Predicted	lower	upper	lower	upper	Leverage
4,181.74333	3,884.90651	4,478.58015	3,233.59431	5,129.89235	0.109

Consider a questionable sales representative for whom Time = 85.42, MktPoten = 35,182.73, Adver = 7,281.65, MktShare = 9.64, and Change = .28. The point prediction of the sales, y, corresponding to this combination of values of the independent variables is

$$\hat{y} = -1,113.7879 + 3.6121(85.42) + .0421(35,182.73)$$
$$+ .1289(7,281.65) + 256.9555(9.64) + 324.5334(.28)$$
$$= 4,181.74 \text{ (that is, } 418,174 \text{ units)}$$

In addition to giving this point prediction, the Excel output tells us that a 95 percent prediction interval for y is [3233.59, 5129.89]. Furthermore, suppose that the actual sales y for the questionable representative were 3,087.52. This actual sales figure is less than the point prediction $\hat{y} = 4,181.74$ and is less than the lower bound of the 95 percent prediction interval for y, [3233.59, 5129.89]. Therefore, we conclude that there is strong evidence that the actual performance of the questionable representative is less than predicted performance. We should investigate the reason for this. Perhaps the questionable representative needs special training.

LO15-7 Use dummy variables to model qualitative independent variables.

15.8 Using Dummy Variables to Model Qualitative Independent Variables ● ● ●

While the levels (or values) of a quantitative independent variable are numerical, the levels of a **qualitative** independent variable are defined by describing them. For instance, the type of sales technique used by a door-to-door salesperson is a qualitative independent variable. Here we might define three different levels—high pressure, medium pressure, and low pressure.

	Number of Households,		Sales Volume,
Store	x	Location	y
1	161	Street	157.27
2	99	Street	93.28
3	135	Street	136.81
4	120	Street	123.79
5	164	Street	153.51
6	221	Mall	241.74
7	179	Mall	201.54
8	204	Mall	206.71
9	214	Mall	229.78
10	101	Mall	135.22

TABLE 15.8   The Electronics World Sales Volume Data
Electronics1

FIGURE 15.12   Plot of the Sales Volume Data and a Geometrical Interpretation of the Model $y = \beta_0 + \beta_1 x + \beta_2 D_M + \varepsilon$

We can model the effects of the different levels of a qualitative independent variable by using what we call **dummy variables** (also called **indicator variables**). Such variables are usually defined so that they take on two values—either 0 or 1. To see how we use dummy variables, we begin with an example.

EXAMPLE 15.6 The Electronics World Case: Comparing Three Kinds of Store Locations

Part 1: The data and data plots   Suppose that Electronics World, a chain of stores that sells audio and video equipment, has gathered the data in Table 15.8. These data concern store sales volume in July of last year (y, measured in thousands of dollars), the number of households in the store's area (x, measured in thousands), and the location of the store (on a suburban street or in a suburban shopping mall—a qualitative independent variable). Figure 15.12 gives a data plot of y versus x. Stores having a street location are plotted as solid dots, while stores having a mall location are plotted as asterisks. Notice that the line relating y to x for mall locations has a higher y-intercept than does the line relating y to x for street locations.

Part 2: A dummy variable model   In order to model the effects of the street and shopping mall locations, we define a dummy variable denoted D_M as follows:

$$D_M = \begin{cases} 1 & \text{if a store is in a mall location} \\ 0 & \text{otherwise} \end{cases}$$

Using this dummy variable, we consider the regression model

$$y = \beta_0 + \beta_1 x + \beta_2 D_M + \varepsilon$$

This model and the definition of D_M imply that

1   For a street location, mean sales volume equals

$$\beta_0 + \beta_1 x + \beta_2 D_M = \beta_0 + \beta_1 x + \beta_2(0)$$
$$= \beta_0 + \beta_1 x$$

2   For a mall location, mean sales volume equals

$$\beta_0 + \beta_1 x + \beta_2 D_M = \beta_0 + \beta_1 x + \beta_2(1)$$
$$= (\beta_0 + \beta_2) + \beta_1 x$$

FIGURE 15.13   **Excel Output of a Regression Analysis of the Sales Volume Data Using the Model**
$y = \beta_0 + \beta_1 x + \beta_2 D_M + \varepsilon$

Regression Statistics

Multiple R	0.9913
R Square	0.9827
Adjusted R Square	0.9778
Standard Error	7.3288
Observations	10

ANOVA	df	SS	MS	F	Significance F
Regression	2	21411.7977	10705.8989	199.3216	6.75E-07
Residual	7	375.9817	53.7117		
Total	9	21787.7795			

	Coefficients	Standard Error	t Stat	P-value	Lower 95%	Upper 95%
Intercept	17.3598	9.4470	1.8376	0.1087	-4.9788	39.6985
Households (x)	0.8510	0.0652	13.0439	3.63E-06	0.6968	1.0053
DummyMall	29.2157	5.5940	5.2227	0.0012	15.9881	42.4434

Thus, the dummy variable allows us to model the situation illustrated in Figure 15.12. Here, the lines relating mean sales volume to x for street and mall locations have different y intercepts, β_0 and $(\beta_0 + \beta_2)$, and the same slope β_1. Note that β_2 is the difference between the mean monthly sales volume for stores in mall locations and the mean monthly sales volume for stores in street locations, when all these stores have the same number of households in their areas. That is, we can say that β_2 represents the effect on mean sales of a mall location compared to a street location. The Excel output in Figure 15.13 tells us that the least squares point estimate of β_2 is $b_2 = 29.2157$. This says that for any given number of households in a store's area, we estimate that the mean monthly sales volume in a mall location is \$29,215.70 greater than the mean monthly sales volume in a street location.

Part 3: A dummy variable model for comparing three locations   In addition to the data concerning street and mall locations in Table 15.8, Electronics World has also collected data concerning downtown locations. The complete data set is given in Table 15.9 and plotted in Figure 15.14. Here stores having a downtown location are plotted as open circles. A model describing these data is

$$y = \beta_0 + \beta_1 x + \beta_2 D_M + \beta_3 D_D + \varepsilon$$

Here the dummy variable D_M is as previously defined and the dummy variable D_D is defined as follows

$$D_D = \begin{cases} 1 & \text{if a store is in a downtown location} \\ 0 & \text{otherwise} \end{cases}$$

It follows that

1   For a street location, mean sales volume equals

$$\beta_0 + \beta_1 x + \beta_2 D_M + \beta_3 D_D = \beta_0 + \beta_1 x + \beta_2(0) + \beta_3(0)$$
$$= \beta_0 + \beta_1 x$$

2   For a mall location, mean sales volume equals

$$\beta_0 + \beta_1 x + \beta_2 D_M + \beta_3 D_D = \beta_0 + \beta_1 x + \beta_2(1) + \beta_3(0)$$
$$= (\beta_0 + \beta_2) + \beta_1 x$$

	Number of Households,		Sales Volume,
Store	x	Location	y
1	161	Street	157.27
2	99	Street	93.28
3	135	Street	136.81
4	120	Street	123.79
5	164	Street	153.51
6	221	Mall	241.74
7	179	Mall	201.54
8	204	Mall	206.71
9	214	Mall	229.78
10	101	Mall	135.22
11	231	Downtown	224.71
12	206	Downtown	195.29
13	248	Downtown	242.16
14	107	Downtown	115.21
15	205	Downtown	197.82

TABLE 15.9   **The Complete Electronics World Sales Volume Data**
Electronics2

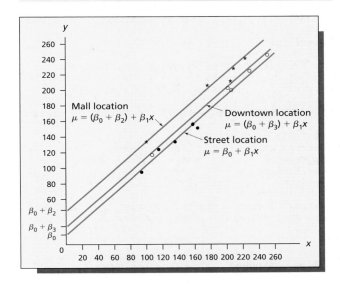

FIGURE 15.14   **Plot of the Complete Electronics World Sales Volume Data and a Geometrical Interpretation of the Model**
$y = \beta_0 + \beta_1 x + \beta_2 D_M + \beta_3 D_D + \varepsilon$

3   For a downtown location, mean sales volume equals

$$\beta_0 + \beta_1 x + \beta_2 D_M + \beta_3 D_D = \beta_0 + \beta_1 x + \beta_2(0) + \beta_3(1)$$
$$= (\beta_0 + \beta_3) + \beta_1 x$$

Thus, the dummy variables allow us to model the situation illustrated in Figure 15.14. Here the lines relating mean sales volume to x for street, mall, and downtown locations have different y-intercepts, β_0, $(\beta_0 + \beta_2)$, and $(\beta_0 + \beta_3)$, and the same slope β_1. Note that β_2 represents the effect on mean sales of a mall location compared to a street location, and β_3 represents the effect on mean sales of a downtown location compared to a street location. Furthermore, the difference between β_2 and β_3, $\beta_2 - \beta_3$, represents the effect on mean sales of a mall location compared to a downtown location.

Part 4: Comparing the three locations   Figure 15.15 on the next page gives the MINITAB and Excel outputs of a regression analysis of the sales volume data using the dummy variable model. These outputs tell us that the least squares point estimate of β_2 is $b_2 = 28.374$. This says that for any given number of households in a store's area, we estimate that the mean monthly sales volume in a mall location is \$28,374 greater than the mean monthly sales volume in a street location. Furthermore, because the Excel output tells us that a 95 percent confidence interval for β_2 is [18.5545, 38.193], we are 95 percent confident that for any given number of households in a store's area, the mean monthly sales volume in a mall location is between \$18,554.50 and \$38,193 greater than the mean monthly sales volume in a street location. The MINITAB and Excel outputs also show that the t statistic for testing $H_0: \beta_2 = 0$ versus $H_a: \beta_2 \neq 0$ equals 6.36 and that the related p-value is less than .001. Therefore, we have very strong evidence that there is a difference between the mean monthly sales volumes in mall and street locations.

We next note that the outputs in Figure 15.15 show that the least squares point estimate of β_3 is $b_3 = 6.864$. Therefore, we estimate that for any given number of households in a store's area, the mean monthly sales volume in a downtown location is \$6,864 greater than the mean monthly sales volume in a street location. Furthermore, the Excel output shows that a 95 percent confidence interval for β_3 is $[-3.636, 17.3635]$. This says we are 95 percent confident that for any given number of households in a store's area, the mean monthly sales volume in a downtown

FIGURE 15.15 **MINITAB and Excel Outputs of a Regression Analysis of the Complete Sales Volume Data Using the Model $y = \beta_0 + \beta_1 x + \beta_2 D_M + \beta_3 D_D + \varepsilon$**

(a) The MINITAB output

```
The regression equation is
Sales = 15.0 + 0.869 Households + 28.4 DMall + 6.86 DDowntown

Predictor      Coef   SE Coef      T      P
Constant     14.978     6.188    2.42  0.034
Households  0.86859   0.04049   21.45  0.000
DMall        28.374     4.461    6.36  0.000
DDowntown     6.864     4.770    1.44  0.178

S = 6.34941   R-Sq = 98.7%   R-Sq(adj) = 98.3%

Analysis of Variance
Source            DF      SS     MS       F      P
Regression         3   33269  11090  275.07  0.000
Residual Error    11     443     40
Total             14   33712

Values of Predictors for New Obs        Predicted Values for New Observations
New Obs  Households  DMall DDowntown     New Obs     Fit  SE Fit       95% CI             95% PI
      1         200      1         0           1  217.07    2.91  (210.65, 223.48)  (201.69, 232.45)
```

(b) The Excel output

Regression Statistics

Multiple R	0.9934
R Square	0.9868
Adjusted R Square	0.9833
Standard Error	6.3494
Observations	15

ANOVA	df	SS	MS	F	Significance F
Regression	3	33268.6953	11089.5651	275.0729	1.27E-10
Residual	11	443.4650	40.3150		
Total	14	33712.1603			

	Coefficients	Standard Error	t Stat	P-value	Lower 95%	Upper 95%
Intercept	14.9777	6.1884	2.4203	0.0340	1.3570	28.5984
Households (x)	0.8686	0.0405	21.4520	2.52E-10	0.7795	0.9577
DummyMall	28.3738	4.4613	6.3600	5.37E-05	18.5545	38.1930
DummyDtown	6.8638	4.7705	1.4388	0.1780	-3.6360	17.3635

location is between \$3,636 less than and \$17,363.50 greater than the mean monthly sales volume in a street location. The MINITAB and Excel outputs also show that the t statistic and p-value for testing H_0: $\beta_3 = 0$ versus H_a: $\beta_3 \neq 0$ are $t = 1.44$ and p-value $= .178$. Therefore, we do not have strong evidence that there is a difference between the mean monthly sales volumes in downtown and street locations.

Finally, note that, because $b_2 = 28.374$ and $b_3 = 6.864$, the point estimate of $\beta_2 - \beta_3$ is $b_2 - b_3 = 28.374 - 6.864 = 21.51$. Therefore, we estimate that mean monthly sales volume in a mall location is \$21,510 higher than mean monthly sales volume in a downtown location. Near the end of this section we show how to compare the mall and downtown locations by using a confidence interval and a hypothesis test. We will find that there is very strong evidence that the mean monthly sales volume in a mall location is higher than the mean monthly sales volume in a downtown location. In summary, the mall location seems to give a higher mean monthly sales volume than either the street or downtown location.

Part 5: Predicting a future sales volume   Suppose that Electronics World wishes to predict the sales volume in a future month for an individual store that has 200,000 households in its area and is located in a shopping mall. The point prediction of this sales volume is (note $D_M = 1$

FIGURE 15.16   Geometrical Interpretation of the Sales Volume Model
$$y = \beta_0 + \beta_1 x + \beta_2 D_M + \beta_3 x D_M + \varepsilon$$

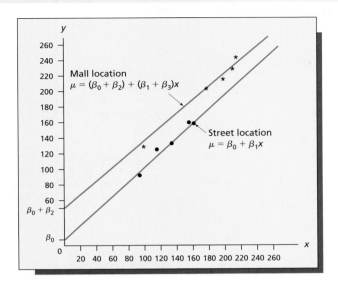

and $D_D = 0$ when a store is in a shopping mall)

$$\hat{y} = b_0 + b_1(200) + b_2(1) + b_3(0)$$
$$= 14.978 + .8686(200) + 28.374(1)$$
$$= 217.07$$

This point prediction is given at the bottom of the MINITAB output in Figure 15.15(a). The corresponding 95 percent prediction interval, which is [201.69, 232.45], says we are 95 percent confident that the sales volume in a future sales period for an individual mall store that has 200,000 households in its area will be between \$201,690 and \$232,450.

Part 6: Interaction models   Consider the Electronics World data for street and mall locations given in Table 15.8 (page 581) and the model

$$y = \beta_0 + \beta_1 x + \beta_2 D_M + \beta_3 x D_M + \varepsilon$$

This model uses the *cross-product,* or *interaction, term* $x D_M$ and implies that

1   For a street location, mean sales volume equals (because $D_M = 0$)

$$\beta_0 + \beta_1 x + \beta_2(0) + \beta_3 x(0) = \beta_0 + \beta_1 x$$

2   For a mall location, mean sales volume equals (because $D_M = 1$)

$$\beta_0 + \beta_1 x + \beta_2(1) + \beta_3 x(1) = (\beta_0 + \beta_2) + (\beta_1 + \beta_3)x$$

As illustrated in Figure 15.16, if we use this model, then the straight lines relating mean sales volume to x for street and mall locations have *different y-intercepts* and *different slopes*. The *different slopes* imply that this model assumes *interaction* between x and store location. Such a model is appropriate if the relationship between mean sales volume and x depends on (that is, is different for) the street and mall store locations. In general, **interaction** exists between two independent variables if the relationship between (for example, the slope of the line relating) the mean value of the dependent variable and one of the independent variables depends upon the value (or level) of the other independent variable. Figure 15.17 gives the Excel output of a regression analysis of the sales volume data using the interaction model. Here D_M and $x D_M$ are labeled as DM and XDM, respectively, on the output. The Excel output tells us that the p-value related to the significance of $x D_M$ is .5886. This large p-value tells us that the interaction term is not significant. It follows that the no-interaction model on page 581 seems best.

FIGURE 15.17　**Excel Output Using the Interaction Model**
$$y = \beta_0 + \beta_1 x + \beta_2 D_M + \beta_3 x D_M + \varepsilon$$

Regression Statistics

Multiple R	0.9918
R Square	0.9836
Adjusted R Square	0.9755
Standard Error	7.7092
Observations	10

ANOVA

	df	SS	MS	F	Significance F
Regression	3	21431.1861	7143.7287	120.1995988	9.531E-06
Residual	6	356.5933	59.4322		
Total	9	21787.7795			

	Coefficients	Standard Error	t Stat	P-value	Lower 95%	Upper 95%
Intercept	7.9004	19.3142	0.4090	0.6967	-39.3598	55.1606
Households	0.9207	0.1399	6.5792	0.0006	0.5783	1.2631
DM	42.7297	24.3812	1.7526	0.1302	-16.9289	102.3884
XDM	-0.0917	0.1606	-0.5712	0.5886	-0.4846	0.3012

Next, consider the Electronics World data for street, mall, and downtown locations given in Table 15.9 (page 583). In modeling these data, if we believe that interaction exists between the number of households in a store's area and store location, we might consider using the model

$$y = \beta_0 + \beta_1 x + \beta_2 D_M + \beta_3 D_D + \beta_4 x D_M + \beta_5 x D_D + \varepsilon$$

Similar to Figure 15.16, this model implies that the straight lines relating mean sales volume to x for the street, mall, and downtown locations have *different y-intercepts* and *different slopes*. If we perform a regression analysis of the sales volume data using this interaction model, we find that the p-values related to the significance of $x D_M$ and $x D_D$ are large (.5334 and .8132, respectively). Because these interaction terms are not significant, it seems best to employ the no-interaction model on page 582.

In general, if we wish to model the effect of a qualitative independent variable having a levels, we use $a - 1$ dummy variables. Consider the kth such dummy variable D_k ($k =$ one of the values $1, 2, \ldots, a - 1$). The parameter β_k multiplying D_k represents the mean difference between the level of y when the qualitative variable assumes level k and when it assumes the level a. For example, if we wish to compare the effects on sales, y, of four different types of advertising campaigns—television (T), radio (R), magazine (M), and mailed coupons (C)—we might employ the model

$$y = \beta_0 + \beta_1 D_T + \beta_2 D_R + \beta_3 D_M + \varepsilon$$

Because this model does not use a dummy variable to represent the mailed coupon advertising campaign, the parameter β_1 is the difference between mean sales when a television advertising campaign is used and mean sales when a mailed coupon advertising campaign is used. The interpretations of β_2 and β_3 follow similarly. As another example, if we wish to employ a confidence interval and a hypothesis test to compare the mall and downtown locations in the Electronics World example, we can use the model

$$y = \beta_0 + \beta_1 x + \beta_2 D_S + \beta_3 D_M + \varepsilon$$

Here the dummy variable D_M is as previously defined, and

$$D_S = \begin{cases} 1 & \text{if a store is in a street location} \\ 0 & \text{otherwise} \end{cases}$$

Because this model does not use a dummy variable to represent the downtown location, the parameter β_2 expresses the effect on mean sales of a street location compared to a downtown location, and the parameter β_3 expresses the effect on mean sales of a mall location compared to a downtown location.

The Excel output of the least squares point estimates of the parameters of this model is as follows:

	Coefficients	Standard Error	t Stat	P-value	Lower 95%	Upper 95%
Intercept	21.8415	8.5585	2.5520	0.0269	3.0044	40.6785
Households (x)	0.8686	0.0405	21.4520	2.52E-10	0.7795	0.9577
DummyStreet	-6.8638	4.7705	-1.4388	0.1780	-17.3635	3.6360
DummyMall	21.5100	4.0651	5.2914	0.0003	12.5628	30.4572

Because the least squares point estimate of β_3 is $b_3 = 21.51$, we estimate that for any given number of households in a store's area, the mean monthly sales volume in a mall location is \$21,510 higher than the mean monthly sales volume in a downtown location. The Excel output tells us that a 95 percent confidence interval for β_3 is [12.5628, 30.4572]. Therefore, we are 95 percent confident that for any given number of households in a store's area, the mean monthly sales volume in a mall location is between \$12,562.80 and \$30,457.20 greater than the mean monthly sales volume in a downtown location. The Excel output also shows that the t statistic and p-value for testing $H_0: \beta_3 = 0$ versus $H_a: \beta_3 \neq 0$ in this model are, respectively, 5.2914 and .0003. Therefore, we have very strong evidence that there is a difference between the mean monthly sales volumes in mall and downtown locations.

In some situations dummy variables represent the effects of unusual events or occurrences that may have an important impact on the dependent variable. For instance, suppose we wish to build a regression model relating quarterly sales of automobiles (y) to automobile prices (x_1), fuel prices (x_2), and personal income (x_3). If an autoworkers' strike occurred in a particular quarter that had a major impact on automobile sales, then we might define a dummy variable D_S to be equal to 1 if an autoworkers' strike occurs and to be equal to 0 otherwise. The least squares point estimate of the regression parameter multiplied by D_S would estimate the effect of the strike on mean auto sales. Finally, dummy variables can be used to model the impact of regularly occuring *seasonal* influences on time series data—for example, the impact of the hot summer months on soft drink sales. This is discussed in Supplementary Exercise 15.58 at the end of this chapter.

Exercises for Section 15.8

CONCEPTS

15.26   What is a qualitative independent variable?

15.27   How do we use dummy variables to model the effects of a qualitative independent variable?

15.28   What does the parameter multiplied by a dummy variable express?

METHODS AND APPLICATIONS

15.29   Neter, Kutner, Nachtsheim, and Wasserman (1996) relate the speed, y, with which a particular insurance innovation is adopted to the size of the insurance firm, x, and the type of firm. The dependent variable y is measured by the number of months elapsed between the time the first firm adopted the innovation and the time the firm being considered adopted the innovation. The size of the firm, x, is measured by the total assets of the firm, and the type of firm—a qualitative independent variable—is either a mutual company or a stock company. The data in Table 15.10 on the next page are observed.   **DS** InsInnov

    a   Discuss why the data plot in the page margin indicates that the model

$$y = \beta_0 + \beta_1 x + \beta_2 D_S + \varepsilon$$

       might appropriately describe the observed data. Here D_S equals 1 if the firm is a stock company and 0 if the firm is a mutual company.

    b   The model of part *a* implies that the mean adoption time of an insurance innovation by mutual companies having an asset size x equals

$$\beta_0 + \beta_1 x + \beta_2(0) = \beta_0 + \beta_1 x$$

connect

Plot of the Insurance Innovation Data

- Mutual
× Stock
— Linear (Mutual)
— Linear (Stock)

TABLE 15.10 The Insurance Innovation Data ⒹⓈ InsInnov

Firm	Number of Months Elapsed, y	Size of Firm (Millions of Dollars), x	Type of Firm	Firm	Number of Months Elapsed, y	Size of Firm (Millions of Dollars), x	Type of Firm
1	17	151	Mutual	11	28	164	Stock
2	26	92	Mutual	12	15	272	Stock
3	21	175	Mutual	13	11	295	Stock
4	30	31	Mutual	14	38	68	Stock
5	22	104	Mutual	15	31	85	Stock
6	0	277	Mutual	16	21	224	Stock
7	12	210	Mutual	17	20	166	Stock
8	19	120	Mutual	18	13	305	Stock
9	4	290	Mutual	19	30	124	Stock
10	16	238	Mutual	20	14	246	Stock

FIGURE 15.18 Excel Output of a Regression Analysis of the Insurance Innovation Data Using the Model $y = \beta_0 + \beta_1 x + \beta_2 D_S + \varepsilon$

Regression Statistics

Multiple R	0.9461
R Square	0.8951
Adjusted R Square	0.8827
Standard Error	3.2211
Observations	20

ANOVA	df	SS	MS	F	Significance F
Regression	2	1,504.4133	752.2067	72.4971	4.77E-09
Residual	17	176.3867	10.3757		
Total	19	1,680.8			

	Coefficients	Standard Error	t Stat	P-value	Lower 95%	Upper 95%
Intercept	33.8741	1.8139	18.6751	9.15E-13	30.0472	37.7010
Size of Firm (x)	-0.1017	0.0089	-11.4430	2.07E-09	-0.1205	-0.0830
DummyStock	8.0555	1.4591	5.5208	3.74E-05	4.9770	11.1339

and that the mean adoption time by stock companies having an asset size x equals

$$\beta_0 + \beta_1 x + \beta_2(1) = \beta_0 + \beta_1 x + \beta_2$$

The difference between these two means equals the model parameter β_2. In your own words, interpret the practical meaning of β_2.

c Figure 15.18 presents the Excel output of a regression analysis of the insurance innovation data using the model of part a. (1) Using the output, test H_0: $\beta_2 = 0$ versus H_a: $\beta_2 \neq 0$ by setting $\alpha = .05$ and .01. (2) Interpret the practical meaning of the result of this test. (3) Also, use the computer output to find, report, and interpret a 95 percent confidence interval for β_2.

d If we add the interaction term xD_S to the model of part a, we find that the p-value related to this term is .9821. What does this imply?

15.30 THE FLORIDA POOL HOME CASE ⒹⓈ PoolHome

Table 3.11 (page 143) gives the selling price (Price, expressed in thousands of dollars), the square footage (SqrFt), the number of bathrooms (Bathrms), and the niceness rating (Niceness, expressed as an integer from 1 to 7) of 80 homes randomly selected from all homes sold in a Florida city during the last six months. (The random selections were made from homes having between 2,000 and 3,500 square feet.) Table 3.11 also gives values of the dummy variable Pool?, which equals 1 if a home has a pool and 0 otherwise. Figure 15.19 presents the MINITAB output of a regression analysis of these data using the model

$$\text{Price} = \beta_0 + \beta_1 \times \text{SqrFt} + \beta_2 \times \text{Bathrms} + \beta_3 \times \text{Niceness} + \beta_4 \times \text{Pool?} + \varepsilon$$

a Noting that β_4 is the effect on mean sales price of a home having a pool, find (on the output) a point estimate of this effect. If the average current purchase price of the pools in the sample is

FIGURE 15.19   MINITAB Output of a Regression Analysis of the Florida Pool Home Data Using the Model Price $= \beta_0 + \beta_1 \times$ SqrFt $+ \beta_2 \times$ Bathrms $+ \beta_3 \times$ Niceness $+ \beta_4 \times$ Pool? $+ \varepsilon$

```
The regression equation is
Price = 25.0 + 0.0526 SqrFt + 10.0 Bathrms + 10.0 Niceness + 25.9 Pool?

Predictor      Coef    SE Coef       T      P
Constant      24.98      16.63    1.50  0.137
SqrFt       0.05264    0.00659    7.98  0.000
Bathrms      10.043      3.729    2.69  0.009
Niceness     10.042     0.7915   12.69  0.000
Pool?        25.862      3.575    7.23  0.000


S = 13.532    R-Sq = 87.40%   R-Sq(adj) = 86.80%

Analysis of Variance
Source          DF        SS      MS       F      P
Regression       4     95665   23916  130.61  0.000
Residual Error  75     13734     183
Total           79    109399
```

$32,500, find a point estimate of the percentage of a pool's cost that a customer buying a pool can expect to recoup when selling his (or her) home.

b If we add various combinations of the interaction terms SqrFt × Pool?, Bathrooms × Pool?, and Niceness × Pool? to the above model, we find that the p-values related to these terms are greater than .05. What does this imply?

15.31 THE SUPERMARKET CASE   ⑤ BakeSale

The Tastee Bakery Company supplies a bakery product to many supermarkets in a metropolitan area. The company wishes to study the effect of the height of the shelf display employed by the supermarkets on monthly sales, y (measured in cases of 10 units each), for this product. Shelf display height has three levels—bottom (B), middle (M), and top (T). For each shelf display height, six supermarkets of equal sales potential will be randomly selected, and each supermarket will display the product using its assigned shelf height for a month. At the end of the month, sales of the bakery product at the 18 participating stores will be recorded. When the experiment is carried out, the data in Table 15.11 are obtained. Here we assume that the set of sales amounts for each display height is a sample that has been randomly selected from the population of all sales amounts that could be obtained (at supermarkets of the given sales potential) when using that display height. To compare the population mean sales amounts μ_B, μ_M, and μ_T that would be obtained by using the bottom, middle, and top display heights, we use the following dummy variable regression model:

$$y = \beta_B + \beta_M D_M + \beta_T D_T + \varepsilon$$

Here D_M equals 1 if a middle display height is used and 0 otherwise; D_T equals 1 if a top display height is used and 0 otherwise. Figure 15.20 on the next page presents the MINITAB output of a regression analysis of the bakery sales study data using this model.[1]

a By using the definitions of the dummy variables, show that

$$\mu_B = \beta_B \qquad \mu_M = \beta_B + \beta_M \qquad \mu_T = \beta_B + \beta_T$$

b Use the overall F statistic to test H_0: $\beta_M = \beta_T = 0$, or, equivalently, H_0: $\mu_B = \mu_M = \mu_T$. Interpret the practical meaning of the result of this test.

c Use your results in part a to do the following: (1) Show that

$$\mu_M - \mu_B = \beta_M \qquad \mu_T - \mu_B = \beta_T \qquad \mu_M - \mu_T = \beta_M - \beta_T$$

TABLE 15.11
Bakery Sales Study Data (Sales in Cases)
⑤ BakeSale

Shelf Display Height		
Bottom (B)	Middle (M)	Top (T)
58.2	73.0	52.4
53.7	78.1	49.7
55.8	75.4	50.9
55.7	76.2	54.0
52.5	78.4	52.1
58.9	82.1	49.9

---

[1]In general, the regression approach of this exercise produces the same comparisons of several population means that are produced by **one-way analysis of variance** (see Section 12.2).

FIGURE 15.20   **MINITAB Output of a Dummy Variable Regression Analysis of the Bakery Sales Data in Table 15.11**

```
The regression equation is
Bakery Sales = 55.8 + 21.4 DMiddle - 4.30 DTop

Predictor    Coef   SE Coef      T      P
Constant   55.800     1.013  55.07  0.000
DMiddle    21.400     1.433  14.93  0.000
DTop       -4.300     1.433  -3.00  0.009

S = 2.48193   R-Sq = 96.1%   R-Sq(adj) = 95.6%

Analysis of Variance
Source          DF      SS      MS      F      P
Regression       2  2273.9  1136.9  184.57  0.000
Residual Error  15    92.4     6.2
Total           17  2366.3

Values of Predictors for New Obs     Predicted Values for New Observations
New Obs  DMiddle  DTop              New Obs    Fit  SE Fit        95% CI              95% PI
      1        1     0                    1  77.200   1.013  (75.040, 79.360)  (71.486, 82.914)
```

TABLE 15.12

Advertising Campaigns Used by Enterprise Industries

DS Fresh3

Sales Period	Advertising Campaign
1	B
2	B
3	B
4	A
5	C
6	A
7	C
8	C
9	B
10	C
11	A
12	C
13	C
14	A
15	B
16	B
17	B
18	A
19	B
20	B
21	C
22	A
23	A
24	A
25	A
26	B
27	C
28	B
29	C
30	C

(2) Use the least squares point estimates of the model parameters to find a point estimate of each of the three differences in means. (3) Find a 95 percent confidence interval for and test the significance of each of the first two differences in means. Interpret your results.

d Find (1) a point estimate of mean sales when using a middle display height, (2) a 95 percent confidence interval for mean sales when using a middle display height, and (3) a 95 percent prediction interval for sales at an individual supermarket that employs a middle display height. Hint: See the bottom of the MINITAB output in Figure 15.20.

e Consider the following alternative model

$$y = \beta_T + \beta_B D_B + \beta_M D_M + \varepsilon$$

Here D_B equals 1 if a bottom display height is used and 0 otherwise. The MINITAB output of the least squares point estimates of the parameters of this model is as follows:

Predictor	Coef	SE Coef	T	P
Constant	51.500	1.013	50.83	0.000
DBottom	4.300	1.433	3.00	0.009
DMiddle	25.700	1.433	17.94	0.000

Because β_M expresses the effect of the middle display height with respect to the effect of the top display height, β_M equals $\mu_M - \mu_T$. Use the MINITAB output to calculate a 95 percent confidence interval for and test the significance of $\mu_M - \mu_T$. Interpret your results.

15.32 THE FRESH DETERGENT CASE DS Fresh3

Recall from Exercise 15.5 that Enterprise Industries has observed the historical data in Table 15.5 (page 563) concerning y (demand for Fresh liquid laundry detergent), x_1 (the price of Fresh), x_2 (the average industry price of competitors' similar detergents), and x_3 (Enterprise Industries' advertising expenditure for Fresh). To ultimately increase the demand for Fresh, Enterprise Industries' marketing department is comparing the effectiveness of three different advertising campaigns. These campaigns are denoted as campaigns A, B, and C. Campaign A consists entirely of television commercials, campaign B consists of a balanced mixture of television and radio commercials, and campaign C consists of a balanced mixture of television, radio, newspaper, and magazine ads. To conduct the study, Enterprise Industries has randomly selected one advertising campaign to be used in each of the 30 sales periods in Table 15.5. Although logic would indicate that each of campaigns A, B, and C should be used in 10 of the 30 sales periods, Enterprise Industries has made previous commitments to the advertising media involved in the study. As a result, campaigns A, B, and C were randomly assigned to, respectively, 9, 11, and 10 sales periods. Furthermore, advertising was done in only the first three weeks of each sales period, so that the carryover effect of the campaign used in a sales period to the next sales period would be minimized. Table 15.12 lists the campaigns used in the sales periods.

To compare the effectiveness of advertising campaigns A, B, and C, we define two dummy variables. Specifically, we define the dummy variable D_B to equal 1 if campaign B is used in a

FIGURE 15.21   **Excel Output of a Dummy Variable Regression Model Analysis of the Fresh Demand Data**

Regression Statistics

Multiple R	0.9797
R Square	0.9597
Adjusted R Square	0.9513
Standard Error	0.1503
Observations	30

ANOVA	df	SS	MS	F	Significance F
Regression	5	12.9166	2.5833	114.3862	6.237E-16
Residual	24	0.5420	0.0226		
Total	29	13.4586			

	Coefficients	Standard Error	t Stat	P-value	Lower 95%	Upper 95%
Intercept	8.7154	1.5849	5.4989	1.1821E-05	5.4443	11.9866
Price (X1)	-2.7680	0.4144	-6.6790	6.5789E-07	-3.6234	-1.9127
Ind Price (X2)	1.6667	0.1913	8.7110	6.7695E-09	1.2718	2.0616
AdvExp (X3)	0.4927	0.0806	6.1100	2.6016E-06	0.3263	0.6592
DB	0.2695	0.0695	3.8804	0.0007	0.1262	0.4128
DC	0.4396	0.0703	6.2496	1.8506E-06	0.2944	0.5847

Predicted values for: Demand using an Excel add-in (MegaStat)

	95% Confidence Interval		95% Prediction Interval		
Predicted	lower	upper	lower	upper	Leverage
8.61621	8.51380	8.71862	8.28958	8.94285	0.109

sales period and 0 otherwise. Furthermore, we define the dummy variable D_C to equal 1 if campaign C is used in a sales period and 0 otherwise. Figure 15.21 presents the Excel add-in (MegaStat) output of a regression analysis of the Fresh demand data by using the model

$$y = \beta_0 + \beta_1 x_1 + \beta_2 x_2 + \beta_3 x_3 + \beta_4 D_B + \beta_5 D_C + \varepsilon$$

a In this model the parameter β_4 represents the effect on mean demand of advertising campaign B compared to advertising campaign A, and the parameter β_5 represents the effect on mean demand of advertising campaign C compared to advertising campaign A. **(1)** Use the regression output to find and report a point estimate of each of the above effects and to test the significance of each of the above effects. **(2)** Find and report a 95 percent confidence interval for each of the above effects. **(3)** Interpret your results.

b The prediction results at the bottom of the output correspond to a future period when Fresh's price will be $x_1 = 3.70$, the average price of similar detergents will be $x_2 = 3.90$, Fresh's advertising expenditure will be $x_3 = 6.50$, and advertising campaign C will be used. **(1)** Show (within rounding) how $\hat{y} = 8.61621$ is calculated. **(2)** Find, report, and interpret a 95 percent confidence interval for mean demand and a 95 percent prediction interval for an individual demand when $x_1 = 3.70$, $x_2 = 3.90$, $x_3 = 6.50$, and campaign C is used.

c Consider the alternative model

$$y = \beta_0 + \beta_1 x_1 + \beta_2 x_2 + \beta_3 x_3 + \beta_4 D_A + \beta_5 D_C + \varepsilon$$

Here D_A equals 1 if advertising campaign A is used and equals 0 otherwise. Describe the effect represented by the regression parameter β_5.

d The Excel output of the least squares point estimates of the parameters of the model of part c is as follows.

	Coefficients	Standard Error	t Stat	P-value	Lower 95%	Upper 95%
Intercept	8.9849	1.5971	5.6259	8.61E-06	5.6888	12.2811
Price (X1)	-2.7680	0.4144	-6.6790	6.58E-07	-3.6234	-1.9127
Ind Price (X2)	1.6667	0.1913	8.7110	6.77E-09	1.2718	2.0616
AdvExp (X3)	0.4927	0.0806	6.1100	2.60E-06	0.3263	0.6592
DA	-0.2695	0.0695	-3.8804	0.0007	-0.4128	-0.1262
DC	0.1701	0.0669	2.5429	0.0179	0.0320	0.3081

Use the Excel output to (1) test the significance of the effect represented by β_5 and (2) find a 95 percent confidence interval for β_5. (3) Interpret your results.

15.33   THE FRESH DETERGENT CASE   ⓓⓢ Fresh3

If we add the independent variables x_3D_B and x_3D_C to the first model of Exercise 15.32, we find that the p-values related to these independent variables are .2797 and .2486. What does this imply?

LO15-8 Use squared and interaction variables.

15.9 Using Squared and Interaction Variables ◐ ● ●

Using squared variables   One useful form of the multiple regression model is what we call the **quadratic regression model.** Assuming that we have obtained n observations—each consisting of an observed value of y and a corresponding value of x—the model is as follows:

The Quadratic Regression Model

The **quadratic regression model** relating y to x is

$$y = \beta_0 + \beta_1 x + \beta_2 x^2 + \varepsilon$$

where

1 $\beta_0 + \beta_1 x + \beta_2 x^2$ is μ_y, the mean value of the dependent variable y when the value of the independent variable is x.

2 β_0, β_1, and β_2 are (unknown) **regression parameters** relating the mean value of y to x.

3 ε is an error term that describes the effects on y of all factors other than x and x^2.

The quadratic equation $\mu_y = \beta_0 + \beta_1 x + \beta_2 x^2$ that relates μ_y to x is the equation of a **parabola.** Two parabolas are shown in Figure 15.22(a) and (b) and help to explain the meanings of the parameters β_0, β_1, and β_2. Here β_0 is the **y-intercept** of the parabola (the value of μ_y when x = 0). Furthermore, β_1 is the **shift parameter** of the parabola: the value of β_1 shifts the parabola to the left or right. Specifically, increasing the value of β_1 shifts the parabola to the left. Lastly, β_2 is the **rate of curvature** of the parabola. If β_2 is greater than 0, the parabola opens upward [see Figure 15.22(a)]. If β_2 is less than 0, the parabola opens downward [see Figure 15.22(b)]. If a scatter plot of y versus x shows points scattered around a parabola, or a part of a parabola [some typical parts are shown in Figure 15.22(c), (d), (e), and (f)], then the quadratic regression model might appropriately relate y to x.

FIGURE 15.22   **The Mean Value of the Dependent Variable Changing in a Quadratic Fashion as x Increases ($\mu_y = \beta_0 + \beta_1 x + \beta_2 x^2$)**

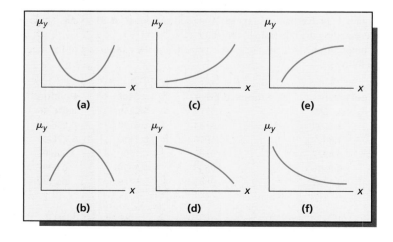

EXAMPLE 15.7 The Gasoline Additive Case: Maximizing Mileage

An oil company wishes to improve the gasoline mileage obtained by cars that use its regular un-leaded gasoline. Company chemists suggest that an additive, ST-3000, be blended with the gaso-line. In order to study the effects of this additive, mileage tests are carried out in a laboratory using test equipment that simulates driving under prescribed conditions. The amount of additive ST-3000 blended with the gasoline is varied, and the gasoline mileage for each test run is recorded. Table 15.13 gives the results of the test runs. Here the dependent variable y is gasoline mileage (in miles per gallon) and the independent variable x is the amount of additive ST-3000 used (measured as the number of units of additive added to each gallon of gasoline). One of the study's goals is to determine the number of units of additive that should be blended with the gaso-line to maximize gasoline mileage. The company would also like to predict the maximum mileage that can be achieved using additive ST-3000.

Figure 15.23(a) gives a scatter plot of y versus x. Because the scatter plot has the appearance of a quadratic curve (that is, part of a parabola), it seems reasonable to relate y to x by using the quadratic model

$$y = \beta_0 + \beta_1 x + \beta_2 x^2 + \varepsilon$$

Figure 15.23(b) and (c) gives the MINITAB output of a regression analysis of the data using this quadratic model. Here the squared term x^2 is denoted as UnitsSq on the output. The MINITAB output tells us that the least squares point estimates of the model parameters are $b_0 = 25.7152$, $b_1 = 4.9762$, and $b_2 = -1.01905$. These estimates give us the least squares prediction equation

$$\hat{y} = 25.7152 + 4.9762x - 1.01905x^2$$

Intuitively, this is the equation of the best quadratic curve that can be fitted to the data plotted in Figure 15.23(a). The MINITAB output also tells us that the p-values related to x and x^2 are less than .001. This implies that we have very strong evidence that each of these model components is significant. The fact that x^2 seems significant confirms the graphical evidence that there is a quadratic relationship between y and x. Once we have such confirmation, we usually retain the linear term x in the model no matter what the size of its p-value. The reason is that geometrical considerations indicate that it is best to use both x and x^2 to model a quadratic relationship.

The oil company wishes to find the value of x that results in the highest predicted mileage. Using calculus, it can be shown that the value $x = 2.44$ maximizes predicted gas mileage. There-fore, the oil company can maximize predicted mileage by blending 2.44 units of additive

TABLE 15.13
The Gasoline Additive Data
DS GasAdd

Additive Units (x)	Gasoline Mileage (y)
0	25.8
0	26.1
0	25.4
1	29.6
1	29.2
1	29.8
2	32.0
2	31.4
2	31.7
3	31.7
3	31.5
3	31.2
4	29.4
4	29.0
4	29.5

BI

FIGURE 15.23   **MINITAB Scatter Plot and Quadratic Model Regression Analysis of the Gasoline Additive Data**

(a) The scatter plot

(b) The least squares point estimates

```
The regression equation is
Mileage = 25.7 + 4.98 Units - 1.02 UnitsSq

Predictor        Coef    SE Coef        T       P
Constant      25.7152     0.1554   165.43   0.000
Units          4.9762     0.1841    27.02   0.000
UnitsSq      -1.01905    0.04414   -23.09   0.000

S = 0.286079    R-Sq = 98.6%    R-Sq(adj) = 98.3%

Analysis of Variance
Source           DF       SS       MS       F       P
Regression        2   67.915   33.958  414.92   0.000
Residual Error   12    0.982    0.082
Total            14   68.897
```

(c) Prediction

```
Values of Predictors for New Obs      Predicted Values for New Observations
New Obs   Unit    UnitsSq             New Obs      Fit   SE Fit        95% CI               95% PI
   1      2.44     5.9536                  1   31.7901   0.1111   (31.5481, 32.0322)   (31.1215, 32.4588)
```

ST-3000 with each gallon of gasoline. This will result in a predicted gas mileage equal to

$$\hat{y} = 25.7152 + 4.9762(2.44) - 1.01905(2.44)^2$$
$$= 31.7901 \text{ miles per gallon}$$

This predicted mileage is the point estimate of the mean mileage that would be obtained by all gallons of the gasoline (when blended as just described) and is the point prediction of the mileage that would be obtained by an individual gallon of the gasoline. Note that $\hat{y} = 31.7901$ is given at the bottom of the MINITAB output in Figure 15.23(c). In addition, the MINITAB output tells us that a 95 percent confidence interval for the mean mileage that would be obtained by all gallons of the gasoline is [31.5481, 32.0322]. If the test equipment simulates driving conditions in a particular automobile, this confidence interval implies that an owner of the automobile can be 95 percent confident that he or she will average between 31.5481 mpg and 32.0322 mpg when using a very large number of gallons of the gasoline. The MINITAB output also tells us that a 95 percent prediction interval for the mileage that would be obtained by an individual gallon of the gasoline is [31.1215, 32.4588].

Using interaction variables   Multiple regression models often contain **interaction variables.** We form an interaction variable by multiplying two independent variables together. For instance, if a regression model includes the independent variables x_1 and x_2, then we can form the interaction variable x_1x_2. It is appropriate to employ an interaction variable if the relationship between the dependent variable y and one of the independent variables depends upon the value of the other independent variable. In the following example we consider a multiple regression model that uses a linear variable, a squared variable, and an interaction variable.

EXAMPLE 15.8 The Fresh Detergent Case: Predicting Demand   Ⓒ

Price Difference,
$x_4 = x_2 - x_1$
(Dollars)

−.05
.25
.60
0
.25
.20
.15
.05
−.15
.15
.20
.10
.40
.45
.35
.30
.50
.50
.40
−.05
−.05
−.10
.20
.10
.50
.60
−.05
0
.05
.55

Enterprise Industries produces Fresh, a brand of liquid laundry detergent. In order to manage its inventory more effectively and make revenue projections, the company would like to better predict demand for Fresh. To develop a prediction model, the company has gathered data concerning demand for Fresh over the last 30 sales periods (each sales period is defined to be a four-week period). For each sales period, these data consist of recorded values of the demands (in hundreds of thousands of bottles) for the large size bottle of Fresh (y), the price (in dollars) of Fresh as offered by Enterprise Industries (x_1), the average industry price (in dollars) of competitors' similar detergents (x_2), and Enterprise Industries' advertising expenditure (in hundreds of thousands of dollars) to promote Fresh (x_3). The data have been given in Table 15.5 on page 563. To begin our analysis, suppose that Enterprise Industries believes on theoretical grounds that the difference between x_1 and x_2 (the *price difference* $x_4 = x_2 - x_1$) adequately describes the effects of x_1 and x_2 on y. That is, perhaps demand for Fresh depends more on how the price for Fresh compares to competitors' prices than it does on the absolute levels of the prices for Fresh and other competing detergents. This makes sense because most consumers must buy a certain amount of detergent no matter what the price might be. The values of the price difference $x_4 = x_2 - x_1$, calculated from the data in Table 15.5, are given in the page margin. Now, consider the following plots:

Ⓓ Fresh2

Because the plot on the left shows a linear relationship between y and x_4, we should use x_4 to predict y. Because the plot on the right shows a quadratic relationship between y and x_3, we

FIGURE 15.24 Excel and Excel add-in (MegaStat) Output of a Regression Analysis of the Fresh Demand Data by Using the Interaction Model $y = \beta_0 + \beta_1 x_4 + \beta_2 x_3 + \beta_3 x_3^2 + \beta_4 x_4 x_3 + \varepsilon$

(a) The Excel output

Regression Statistics

Multiple R	0.9596	Adjusted R Square	0.9083	Observations	30
R Square	0.9209	Standard Error	0.2063		

ANOVA	df	SS	MS	F	Significance F
Regression	4	12.3942	3.0985	72.7771	2.11E-13
Residual	25	1.0644	0.0426		
Total	29	13.4586			

	Coefficients	Standard Error	t Stat	P-value	Lower 95%	Upper 95%
Intercept	29.1133	7.4832	3.8905	0.0007	13.7013	44.5252
PriceDif (x4)	11.1342	4.4459	2.5044	0.0192	1.9778	20.2906
AdvExp (x3)	-7.6080	2.4691	-3.0813	0.0050	-12.6932	-2.5228
x3sq	0.6712	0.2027	3.3115	0.0028	0.2538	1.0887
x4x3	-1.4777	0.6672	-2.2149	0.0361	-2.8518	-0.1037

(b) Prediction using an Excel add-in (MegaStat)

Predicted values for: Y

Predicted	95% Confidence Interval		95% Prediction Interval		Leverage
	lower	upper	lower	upper	
8.32725	8.21121	8.44329	7.88673	8.76777	0.075

should use x_3 and x_3^2 to predict y. Moreover, if x_4 and x_3 interact, then we should use the interaction variable $x_4 x_3$ to predict y. This gives the model

$$y = \beta_0 + \beta_1 x_4 + \beta_2 x_3 + \beta_3 x_3^2 + \beta_4 x_4 x_3 + \varepsilon.$$

Figure 15.24 presents the Excel output obtained when this model is fit to the Fresh demand data. The p-values for testing the significance of the intercept and the independent variables are all below .05. Therefore, we have strong evidence that each of these terms should be included in the model. In particular, because the p-value related to $x_4 x_3$ is .0361, we have strong evidence that x_4 and x_3 interact. We will examine the nature of this interaction in the discussion to come.

Suppose that Enterprise Industries wishes to predict demand for Fresh in a future sales period when the price difference will be $.20 (that is, 20 cents) and when advertising expenditure will be $650,000. Using the least squares point estimates in Figure 15.24(a), the point prediction is

$$\hat{y} = 29.1133 + 11.1342(.20) - 7.6080(6.50) + 0.6712(6.50)^2 - 1.4777(.20)(6.50)$$
$$= 8.32725 \quad (832,725 \text{ bottles}).$$

Figure 15.24(b) gives this point prediction along with the 95 percent confidence interval for mean demand and the 95 percent prediction interval for the actual demand when x_4 equals 0.20 and x_3 equals 6.50.

To investigate the nature of the interaction between x_3 and x_4, consider the prediction equation

$$\hat{y} = 29.1133 + 11.1342 x_4 - 7.6080 x_3 + 0.6712 x_3^2 - 1.4777 x_4 x_3$$

obtained from the least squares point estimates in Figure 15.24(a). Also, consider the six combinations of price difference x_4 and advertising expenditure x_3 obtained by combining the x_4 values .10 and .30 with the x_3 values 6.0, 6.4, and 6.8. When we use the prediction equation to predict the demands for Fresh corresponding to these six combinations, we obtain the predicted demands ($\hat{y}$ values) shown in Figure 15.25(a) on the next page. (Note that we consider *two* x_4 values because there is a *linear* relationship between y and x_4, and we consider *three* x_3 values because there is a *quadratic* relationship between y and x_3.) Now:

1   If we fix x_3 at 6.0 in Figure 15.25(a) and plot the corresponding $\hat{y}$ values 7.86 and 8.31 versus the x_4 values .10 and .30, we obtain the two squares connected by the lowest line in

FIGURE 15.25   Interaction between x_4 and x_3

(a) Predicted demands   **(b) Plots of $\hat{y}$ versus x_4 for different x_3 values**   **(c) Plots of $\hat{y}$ versus x_3 for different x_4 values**
   ($\hat{y}$ values)

	x_4	
x_3	.10	.30
6.0	7.86	8.31
6.4	8.08	8.42
6.8	8.52	8.74

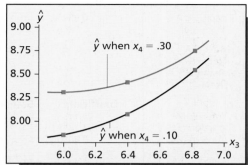

Figure 15.25(b). Similarly, if we fix x_3 at 6.4 and plot the corresponding $\hat{y}$ values 8.08 and 8.42 versus the x_4 values .10 and .30, we obtain the two squares connected by the middle line in Figure 15.25(b). Also, if we fix x_3 at 6.8 and plot the corresponding $\hat{y}$ values 8.52 and 8.74 versus the x_4 values .10 and .30, we obtain the two squares connected by the highest line in Figure 15.25(b). Examining the three lines relating $\hat{y}$ to x_4, we see that the slopes of these lines decrease as x_3 increases from 6.0 to 6.4 to 6.8. This says that as the price difference x_4 increases from .10 to .30 (that is, as Fresh becomes less expensive compared to its competitors), the *rate of increase* of predicted demand $\hat{y}$ is slower when advertising expenditure x_3 is higher than when advertising expenditure x_3 is lower. Moreover, this might be logical because it says that when a higher advertising expenditure makes more customers aware of Fresh's cleaning abilities and thus causes customer demand for Fresh to be higher, there is less opportunity for an increased price difference to increase demand for Fresh.

2   If we fix x_4 at .10 in Figure 15.25(a) and plot the corresponding $\hat{y}$ values 7.86, 8.08, and 8.52 versus the x_3 values 6.0, 6.4, and 6.8, we obtain the three squares connected by the lower quadratic curve in Figure 15.25(c). Similarly, if we fix x_4 at .30 and plot the corresponding $\hat{y}$ values 8.31, 8.42, and 8.74 versus the x_3 values 6.0, 6.4, and 6.8, we obtain the three squares connected by the higher quadratic curve in Figure 15.25(c). The non-parallel quadratic curves in Figure 15.25(c) say that as advertising expenditure x_3 increases from 6.0 to 6.8, the rate of increase of predicted demand $\hat{y}$ is slower when the price difference x_4 is larger (that is, $x_4 = .30$) than when the price difference x_4 is smaller (that is, $x_4 = .10$). Moreover, this might be logical because it says that when a larger price difference causes customer demand for Fresh to be higher, there is less opportunity for an increased advertising expenditure to increase demand for Fresh.

To summarize the nature of the interaction between x_4 and x_3, we might say that a higher value of each of these independent variables somewhat weakens the impact of the other independent variable on predicted demand. In Exercise 15.37 we will consider a situation where a higher value of each of two independent variables somewhat strengthens the impact of the other independent variable on the predicted value of the dependent variable. Moreover, if the *p*-value related to $x_4 x_3$ in the Fresh detergent situation had been large and thus we had removed $x_4 x_3$ from the model (that is, *no interaction*), then the plotted lines in Figure 15.25(b) would have been *parallel* and the plotted quadratic curves in Figure 15.25(c) would have been *parallel*. This would say that as each independent variable increases, predicted demand increases at the same rate whether the other independent variable is larger or smaller.

Exercises for Section 15.9

CONCEPTS

15.34 When does a scatter plot suggest the use of the quadratic regression model?

15.35 How do we model the interaction between two independent variables?

connect

METHODS AND APPLICATIONS

15.36 United Oil Company is attempting to develop a reasonably priced unleaded gasoline that will deliver higher gasoline mileages than can be achieved by its current unleaded gasolines. As part of its development process, United Oil wishes to study the effect of two independent variables—x_1, amount of gasoline additive RST (0, 1, or 2 units), and x_2, amount of gasoline additive XST (0, 1, 2, or 3 units), on gasoline mileage, y. Mileage tests are carried out using equipment that simulates driving under prescribed conditions. The combinations of x_1 and x_2 used in the experiment, along with the corresponding values of y, are given on the page margin.

    a   Discuss why the data plots given on the page margin indicate that the model $y = \beta_0 + \beta_1 x_1 + \beta_2 x_1^2 + \beta_3 x_2 + \beta_4 x_2^2 + \varepsilon$ might appropriately relate y to x_1 and x_2. If we fit this model to the data on the page margin, we find that the least squares point estimates of the model parameters and their associated p-values (given in parentheses) are $b_0 = 28.1589$ ($<.001$), $b_1 = 3.3133$ ($<.001$), $b_2 = -1.4111$ ($<.001$), $b_3 = 5.2752$ ($<.001$), and $b_4 = -1.3964$ ($<.001$). Moreover, consider the mean mileage obtained by all gallons of the gasoline when it is made with one unit of RST and two units of XST (a combination that the data on the page margin indicates would maximize mean mileage). A point estimate of and a 95 percent confidence interval for this mean mileage are 35.0261 and [34.4997, 35.5525]. Using the above model, show how the point estimate is calculated.

    b   If we add the independent variable $x_1 x_2$ to the model in part(a), we find that the p-value related to $x_1 x_2$ is .9777. What does this imply?

15.37 If we fit the model $y = \beta_0 + \beta_1 x_1 + \beta_2 x_2 + \beta_3 x_2^2 + \beta_4 x_1 x_2 + \varepsilon$ to the real estate sales price data in Table 15.4 (page 561), we find that the least squares point estimates of the model parameters and their associated p-values (given in parentheses) are $b_0 = 27.438$ ($<.001$), $b_1 = 5.0813$ ($<.001$), $b_2 = 7.2899$ ($<.001$), $b_3 = -.5311$ (.001), and $b_4 = .11473$ (.014).

    a   A point prediction of and a 95 percent prediction interval for the sales price of a house having 2000 square feet ($x_1 = 20$) and a niceness rating of 8 ($x_2 = 8$) are 171.751 ($\$171,751$) and [168.836, 174.665]. Using the above model, show how the point prediction is calculated.

    b   Below we give model predictions of sales prices of houses for six combinations of x_1 and x_2, along with plots of the predictions needed to interpret the interaction between x_1 and x_2. Carefully interpret this interaction. **DS** RealEst2

RST Units (x_1)	XST Units (x_2)	Gas Mileage (y, mpg)
0	0	27.4
0	0	28.0
0	0	28.6
1	0	29.6
1	0	30.6
2	0	28.6
2	0	29.8
0	1	32.0
0	1	33.0
1	1	33.3
1	1	34.5
0	2	32.3
0	2	33.5
1	2	34.4
1	2	35.0
1	2	35.6
2	2	33.3
2	2	34.0
2	2	34.7
1	3	33.4
2	3	32.0
2	3	33.0

DS UnitedOil

Predicted Sales Prices

x_2 \ x_1	13	22
2	108.933	156.730
5	124.124	175.019
8	129.756	183.748

15.10 Model Building and the Effects of Multicollinearity ● ● ●

Multicollinearity   Recall the sales representative performance data in Figure 15.10 (page 579). These data consist of values of the dependent variable y (SALES) and of the independent variables x_1 (TIME), x_2 (MKTPOTEN), x_3 (ADVER), x_4 (MKTSHARE), and x_5 (CHANGE). The complete sales representative performance data analyzed by Cravens, Woodruff, and Stomper (1972) consist of the data presented in Figure 15.10 and data concerning three additional independent variables. These three additional variables are x_6 = number of accounts handled by the representative (ACCTS); x_7 = average workload per account, measured by using a weighting

LO15-9 Describe multicollinearity and build a multiple regression model.

based on the sizes of the orders by the accounts and other workload-related criteria (WKLOAD); and x_8 = an aggregate rating on eight dimensions of the representative's performance, made by a sales manager and expressed on a 1–7 scale (RATING).

Table 15.14 gives the observed values of x_6, x_7, and x_8, and Figure 15.26(a) presents the MINITAB output of a **correlation matrix** for the sales representative performance data. Examining the first column of this matrix, we see that the simple correlation coefficient between SALES and WKLOAD is −.117 and that the p-value for testing the significance of the relationship between SALES and WKLOAD is .577. This indicates that there is little or no relationship between SALES and WKLOAD. However, the simple correlation coefficients between SALES and the other seven independent variables range from .402 to .754, with associated p-values ranging from .046 to .000. This indicates the existence of potentially useful relationships between SALES and these seven independent variables.

While simple correlation coefficients (and scatter plots) give us a preliminary understanding of the data, they cannot be relied upon alone to tell us which independent variables are significantly related to the dependent variable. One reason for this is a condition called *multicollinearity*. **Multicollinearity** is said to exist among the independent variables in a regression situation if these independent variables are related to or dependent upon each other. One way to investigate multicollinearity is to examine the correlation matrix. To understand this, note that all of the simple correlation coefficients not located in the first column of this matrix measure the **simple correlations between the independent variables.** For example, the simple correlation coefficient between ACCTS and TIME is .758, which says that the ACCTS values increase as the TIME values increase. Such a relationship makes sense because it is logical that the longer a sales representative has been with the company, the more accounts he or she handles. Statisticians often regard multicollinearity in a data set to be severe if at least one simple correlation coefficient between the independent variables is at least .9. Because the largest such simple correlation coefficient in Figure 15.26(a) is .758, this is not true for the sales representative performance data. Note, however, that even moderate multicollinearity can be a potential problem. This will be demonstrated later using the sales representative performance data.

Another way to measure multicollinearity is to use **variance inflation factors.** Consider a regression model relating a dependent variable y to a set of independent variables $x_1, \ldots, x_{j-1}, x_j, x_{j+1}, \ldots, x_k$. The **variance inflation factor for the independent variable x_j** in this set is denoted VIF_j and is defined by the equation

$$VIF_j = \frac{1}{1 - R_j^2}$$

where R_j^2 is the multiple coefficient of determination for the regression model that relates x_j to all the other independent variables $x_1, \ldots, x_{j-1}, x_{j+1}, \ldots, x_k$ in the set. For example, Figure 15.26(b) gives the MINITAB output of the t statistics, p-values, and variance inflation factors

TABLE 15.14

Values of ACCTS, WKLOAD, and RATING

💿 SalePerf2

Accounts, x_6	Work-load, x_7	Rating, x_8
74.86	15.05	4.9
107.32	19.97	5.1
96.75	17.34	2.9
195.12	13.40	3.4
180.44	17.64	4.6
104.88	16.22	4.5
256.10	18.80	4.6
126.83	19.86	2.3
203.25	17.42	4.9
119.51	21.41	2.8
116.26	16.32	3.1
142.28	14.51	4.2
89.43	19.35	4.3
84.55	20.02	4.2
119.51	15.26	5.5
80.49	15.87	3.6
136.58	7.81	3.4
78.86	16.00	4.2
136.58	17.44	3.6
138.21	17.98	3.1
75.61	20.99	1.6
102.44	21.66	3.4
76.42	21.46	2.7
136.58	24.78	2.8
88.62	24.96	3.9

FIGURE 15.26   MINITAB Output of the Correlation Matrix and a Regression Analysis for the Sales Representative Performance Situation

(a) The correlation matrix

	Sales	Time	MktPoten	Adver	MktShare	Change	Accts	WkLoad
Time	0.623							
	0.001							
MktPoten	0.598	0.454						
	0.002	0.023						
Adver	0.596	0.249	0.174					
	0.002	0.230	0.405					
MktShare	0.484	0.106	-0.211	0.264				
	0.014	0.613	0.312	0.201				
Change	0.489	0.251	0.268	0.377	0.085			
	0.013	0.225	0.195	0.064	0.685			
Accts	0.754	0.758	0.479	0.200	0.403	0.327		
	0.000	0.000	0.016	0.338	0.046	0.110		
WkLoad	-0.117	-0.179	-0.259	-0.272	0.349	-0.288	-0.199	
	0.577	0.391	0.212	0.188	0.087	0.163	0.341	
Rating	0.402	0.101	0.359	0.411	-0.024	0.549	0.229	-0.277
	0.046	0.631	0.078	0.041	0.911	0.004	0.272	0.180

Cell contents: Pearson correlation
P-Value

(b) The t statistics, p-values, and variance inflation factors for the eight-independent-variables model.

Predictor	Coef	SE Coef	T	P	VIF
Constant	-1507.8	778.6	-1.94	0.071	
Time	2.010	1.931	1.04	0.313	3.343
MktPoten	0.037205	0.008202	4.54	0.000	1.978
Adver	0.15099	0.04711	3.21	0.006	1.910
MktShare	199.02	67.03	2.97	0.009	3.236
Change	290.9	186.8	1.56	0.139	1.602
Accts	5.551	4.776	1.16	0.262	5.639
WkLoad	19.79	33.68	0.59	0.565	1.818
Rating	8.2	128.5	0.06	0.950	1.809

for the sales representative performance model that relates y to all eight independent variables. The largest variance inflation factor is $VIF_6 = 5.639$. To calculate VIF_6, MINITAB first calculates the multiple coefficient of determination for the regression model that relates x_6 to x_1, x_2, x_3, x_4, x_5, x_7, and x_8 to be $R_6^2 = .822673$. It then follows that

$$VIF_6 = \frac{1}{1 - R_6^2} = \frac{1}{1 - .822673} = 5.639$$

In general, if $R_j^2 = 0$, which says that x_j is not related to the other independent variables, then the variance inflation factor VIF_j equals 1. On the other hand, if $R_j^2 > 0$, which says that x_j is related to the other independent variables, then $(1 - R_j^2)$ is less than 1, making VIF_j greater than 1. Generally, the multicollinearity between independent variables is considered **(1)** severe if the largest variance inflation factor is greater than 10 and **(2)** moderately strong if the largest variance inflation factor is greater than 5. Moreover, if the mean of the variance inflation factors is substantially greater than 1 (sometimes a difficult criterion to assess), multicollinearity might be problematic. In the sales representative performance model, the largest variance inflation factor, $VIF_6 = 5.639$, is greater than 5. Therefore, we might classify the multicollinearity as being moderately strong.

The reason that VIF_j is called the variance inflation factor is that it can be shown that, when VIF_j is greater than 1, then the standard deviation σ_{b_j} of the population of all possible values of the least squares point estimate b_j is likely to be inflated beyond its value when $R_j^2 = 0$. If σ_{b_j} is greatly inflated, two slightly different samples of values of the dependent variable can yield two substantially different values of b_j. To intuitively understand why strong multicollinearity can significantly affect the least squares point estimates, consider the so-called "picket fence" display in the page margin. This figure depicts two independent variables (x_1 and x_2) exhibiting strong multicollinearity (note that as x_1 increases, x_2 increases). The heights of the pickets on the fence represent the y observations. If we assume that the model $y = \beta_0 + \beta_1 x_1 + \beta_2 x_2 + \varepsilon$ adequately describes this data, then calculating the least squares point estimates amounts to fitting a plane to the points on the top of the picket fence. Clearly, this plane would be quite unstable. That is, a slightly different height of one of the pickets (a slightly different y value) could cause the slant of the fitted plane (and the least squares point estimates that determine this slant) to change radically. It follows that, when strong multicollinearity exists, sampling variation can result in least squares point estimates that differ substantially from the true values of the regression parameters. In fact, some of the least squares point estimates may have a sign (positive or negative) that differs from the sign of the true value of the parameter (we will see an example of this in the exercises). Therefore, when strong multicollinearity exists, it is dangerous to interpret the individual least squares point estimates.

The most important problem caused by multicollinearity is that, even when multicollinearity is not severe, it can hinder our ability to use the t statistics and related p-values to assess the importance of the independent variables. Recall that we can reject $H_0: \beta_j = 0$ in favor of $H_a: \beta_j \neq 0$ at level of significance α if and only if the absolute value of the corresponding t statistic is greater than $t_{\alpha/2}$ based on $n - (k + 1)$ degrees of freedom, or, equivalently, if and only if the related p-value is less than α. Thus the larger (in absolute value) the t statistic is and the smaller the p-value is, the stronger is the evidence that we should reject $H_0: \beta_j = 0$ and the stronger is the evidence that the independent variable x_j is significant. When multicollinearity exists, the sizes of the t statistic and of the related p-value **measure the additional importance of the independent variable x_j over the combined importance of the other independent variables in the regression model.** Because two or more correlated independent variables contribute redundant information, multicollinearity often causes the t statistics obtained by relating a dependent variable to a set of correlated independent variables to be smaller (in absolute value) than the t statistics that would be obtained if separate regression analyses were run, where each separate regression analysis relates the dependent variable to a smaller set (for example, only one) of the correlated independent variables. Thus multicollinearity can cause some of the correlated independent variables to appear less important—in terms of having small absolute t statistics and large p-values—than they really are. Another way to understand this is to note that because multicollinearity inflates σ_{b_j}, it inflates the point estimate s_{b_j} of σ_{b_j}. Because $t = b_j/s_{b_j}$, an inflated value of s_{b_j} can (depending on the

The Picket Fence Display

size of b_j) cause t to be small (and the related p-value to be large). This would suggest that x_j is not significant even though x_j may really be important.

For example, Figure 15.26(b) on page 598 tells us that when we perform a regression analysis of the sales representative performance data using a model that relates y to all eight independent variables, the p-values related to TIME, MKTPOTEN, ADVER, MKTSHARE, CHANGE, ACCTS, WKLOAD, and RATING are, respectively, .313, .000, .006, .009, .139, .262, .565, and .950. By contrast, recall from Figure 15.11 (page 580) that when we perform a regression analysis of the sales representative performance data using a model that relates y to the first five independent variables, the p-values related to TIME, MKTPOTEN, ADVER, MKTSHARE, and CHANGE are, respectively, .0065, .0001, .0025, .0001, and .0530. Note that TIME (p-value = .0065) is significant at the .01 level and CHANGE (p-value = .0530) is significant at the .06 level in the five independent variable model. However, when we consider the model that uses all eight independent variables, neither TIME (p-value = .313) nor CHANGE (p-value = .139) is significant at the .10 level. The reason that TIME and CHANGE seem more significant in the five independent variable model is that, because this model uses fewer variables, TIME and CHANGE contribute less overlapping information and thus have more additional importance in this model.

Comparing regression models on the basis of R^2, s, adjusted R^2, prediction interval length, and the C statistic

We have seen that when multicollinearity exists in a model, the p-value associated with an independent variable in the model measures the additional importance of the variable over the combined importance of the other variables in the model. Therefore, it can be difficult to use the p-values to determine which variables to retain and which variables to remove from a model. The implication of this is that we need to evaluate more than the *additional importance* of each independent variable in a regression model. We also need to evaluate how well the independent variables *work together* to accurately describe, predict, and control the dependent variable. One way to do this is to determine if the *overall* model gives a high R^2 and $\overline{R}^2$, a small s, and short prediction intervals.

It can be proved that **adding any independent variable to a regression model, even an unimportant independent variable, will decrease the unexplained variation and will increase the explained variation.** Therefore, because the total variation $\Sigma(y_i - \overline{y})^2$ depends only on the observed y values and thus remains unchanged when we add an independent variable to a regression model, it follows that **adding any independent variable to a regression model will increase R^2,** which equals the explained variation divided by the total variation. This implies that R^2 cannot tell us (by decreasing) that adding an independent variable is undesirable. That is, although we wish to obtain a model with a large R^2, there are better criteria than R^2 that can be used to *compare* regression models.

One better criterion is the standard error $s = \sqrt{SSE/[n - (k + 1)]}$. When we add an independent variable to a regression model, the number of model parameters $(k + 1)$ increases by one, and thus the number of degrees of freedom $n - (k + 1)$ decreases by one. If the decrease in $n - (k + 1)$, which is used in the denominator to calculate s, is proportionally more than the decrease in SSE (the unexplained variation) that is caused by adding the independent variable to the model, then s will increase. **If s increases, this tells us that we should not add the independent variable to the model,** because the new model would give longer prediction intervals and thus less accurate predictions. If s decreases, the new model is likely to give shorter prediction intervals but (as we will see) is not guaranteed to do so. Thus, it can be useful to compare the lengths of prediction intervals for different models. Also, it can be shown that the standard error s decreases if and only if $\overline{R}^2$ (adjusted R^2) increases. It follows that, if we are comparing regression models, the model that gives the smallest s gives the largest $\overline{R}^2$.

EXAMPLE 15.9 The Sales Representative Case: Model Comparisons

Figure 15.27 gives the MINITAB output resulting from calculating R^2, $\overline{R}^2$, and s for **all possible regression models** based on all possible combinations of the eight independent variables in the sales representative performance situation (the values of C-p on the output will be explained after we complete this example). The MINITAB output gives the two best models of each size in terms

FIGURE 15.27   **MINITAB Output of the Best Two Sales Representative Performance Regression Models of Each Size**

Vars	R-Sq	R-Sq(adj)	Mallows C-p	S	Time	MktPoten	Adver	MktShare	Change	Accts	WkLoad	Rating
1	56.8	55.0	67.6	881.09						X		
1	38.8	36.1	104.6	1049.3	X							
2	77.5	75.5	27.2	650.39			X			X		
2	74.6	72.3	33.1	691.10		X		X				
3	84.9	82.7	14.0	545.51		X	X	X				
3	82.8	80.3	18.4	582.64		X	X			X		
4	90.0	88.1	5.4	453.84		X	X	X		X		
4	89.6	87.5	6.4	463.95	X	X	X	X				
5	91.5	89.3	4.4	430.23	X	X	X	X	X			
5	91.2	88.9	5.0	436.75		X	X	X	X	X		
6	92.0	89.4	5.4	428.00	X	X	X	X	X	X		
6	91.6	88.9	6.1	438.20		X	X	X	X	X	X	
7	92.2	89.0	7.0	435.67	X	X	X	X	X	X	X	
7	92.0	88.8	7.3	440.30	X	X	X	X	X	X		X
8	92.2	88.3	9.0	449.03	X	X	X	X	X	X	X	X

of s and $\overline{R}^2$—the two best one-variable models, the two best two-variable models, the two best three-variable models, and so on. Examining the output, we see that the three models having the smallest values of s and largest values of $\overline{R}^2$ are

1. The six-variable model that contains

    TIME, MKTPOTEN, ADVER, MKTSHARE, CHANGE, ACCTS

    and has $s = 428.00$ and $\overline{R}^2 = 89.4$; we refer to this model as Model 1.

2. The five-variable model that contains

    TIME, MKTPOTEN, ADVER, MKTSHARE, CHANGE

    and has $s = 430.23$ and $\overline{R}^2 = 89.3$; we refer to this model as Model 2.

3. The seven-variable model that contains

    TIME, MKTPOTEN, ADVER, MKTSHARE, CHANGE, ACCTS, WKLOAD

    and has $s = 435.67$ and $\overline{R}^2 = 89.0$; we refer to this model as Model 3.

To see that s can increase when we add an independent variable to a regression model, note that s increases from 428.00 to 435.67 when we add WKLOAD to Model 1 to form Model 3. In this case, although it can be verified that adding WKLOAD decreases the unexplained variation from 3,297,279.3342 to 3,226,756.2751, this decrease has not been enough to offset the change in the denominator of $s^2 = SSE/[n - (k + 1)]$, which decreases from $25 - 7 = 18$ to $25 - 8 = 17$. To see that prediction interval lengths might increase even though s decreases, consider adding ACCTS to Model 2 to form Model 1. This decreases s from 430.23 to 428.00. However, consider a questionable sales representative for whom TIME = 85.42, MKTPOTEN = 35,182.73, ADVER = 7,281.65, MKTSHARE = 9.64, CHANGE = .28, and ACCTS = 120.61. The 95 percent prediction interval given by Model 2 for sales corresponding to this combination of values of the independent variables is [3,233.59, 5,129.89] and has length $5,129.89 - 3,233.59 = 1896.3$. The 95 percent prediction interval given by Model 1 for such sales is [3,193.86, 5,093.14] and has length $5,093.14 - 3,193.86 = 1,899.28$. In other words, even though Model 2 has a slightly larger s, it gives a slightly shorter prediction interval. (For those who have studied the formula for a prediction interval, $[\hat{y} \pm t_{\alpha/2}s\sqrt{1 + \text{distance value}}]$, Model 2 gives a slightly shorter 95 percent prediction interval because it uses one less variable and thus can be verified to give slightly smaller values of $t_{.025}$ and the distance value.) In addition, the extra independent variable ACCTS in Model 1 can be verified to have a p-value of .2881. Therefore, we conclude that Model 2 is better than Model 1 and is, in fact, the "best" sales representative performance model (using only linear independent variables).

Another quantity that can be used for comparing regression models is called the **C statistic** (also often called the C_p **statistic**). To show how to calculate the C statistic, suppose that we wish to choose an appropriate set of independent variables from p potential independent variables. We first calculate the mean square error, which we denote as s_p^2, for the model using all p potential independent variables. Then, if SSE denotes the unexplained variation for another particular model that has k independent variables, it follows that the C statistic for this model is

$$C = \frac{SSE}{s_p^2} - [n - 2(k + 1)]$$

For example, consider the sales representative case. It can be verified that the mean square error for the model using all $p = 8$ independent variables is 201,621.21 and that the SSE for the model using the first $k = 5$ independent variables (Model 2 in the previous example) is 3,516,812.7933. It follows that the C statistic for this latter model is

$$C = \frac{3{,}516{,}812.7933}{201{,}621.21} - [25 - 2(5 + 1)] = 4.4$$

Because the C statistic for a given model is a function of the model's SSE, and because we want SSE to be small, **we want C to be small.** Although adding an unimportant independent variable to a regression model will decrease SSE, adding such a variable can increase C. This can happen when the decrease in SSE caused by the addition of the extra independent variable is not enough to offset the decrease in $n - 2(k + 1)$ caused by the addition of the extra independent variable (which increases k by 1). It should be noted that although adding an unimportant independent variable to a regression model can increase both s^2 and C, there is no exact relationship between s^2 and C.

While we want C to be small, it can be shown from the theory behind the C statistic that **we also wish to find a model for which the C statistic roughly equals $k + 1$,** the number of parameters in the model. **If a model has a C statistic substantially greater than $k + 1$, it can be shown that this model has substantial *bias* and is undesirable.** Thus, although we want to find a model for which C is as small as possible, if C for such a model is substantially greater than $k + 1$, we may prefer to choose a different model for which C is slightly larger and more nearly equal to the number of parameters in that (different) model. **If a particular model has a small value of C and C for this model is less than $k + 1$, then the model should be considered desirable.** Finally, it should be noted that for the model that includes all p potential independent variables (and thus utilizes $p + 1$ parameters), it can be shown that $C = p + 1$.

If we examine Figure 15.27, we see that Model 2 of the previous example has the smallest C statistic. The C statistic for this model (denoted C-p on the MINITAB output) equals 4.4. Because $C = 4.4$ is less than $k + 1 = 6$, the model is not biased. Therefore, this model should be considered best with respect to the C statistic.

Stepwise regression   In some situations it is useful to employ an **iterative model selection procedure,** where at each step a single independent variable is added to or deleted from a regression model, and a new regression model is evaluated. We now discuss one such procedure—**stepwise regression.**

Stepwise regression begins by considering all of the one-independent-variable models and choosing the model for which the p-value related to the independent variable in the model is the smallest. If this p-value is less than α_{entry}, an α value for "entering" a variable, the independent variable is the first variable entered into the stepwise regression model and stepwise regression continues. Stepwise regression then considers the remaining independent variables not in the stepwise model and chooses the independent variable which, when paired with the first independent variable entered, has the smallest p-value. If this p-value is less than α_{entry}, the new variable is entered into the stepwise model. Moreover, the stepwise procedure checks to see if the p-value

FIGURE 15.28   The MINITAB Output of the Sales Representative Case Stepwise Regression

$(\alpha_{entry} = \alpha_{stay} = .10)$

Step	1	2	3	4
Constant	709.32	50.30	-327.23	-1441.94
Accts	21.7	19.0	15.6	9.2
T-Value	5.50	6.41	5.19	3.22
P-Value	0.000	0.000	0.000	0.004
Adver		0.227	0.216	0.175
T-Value		4.50	4.77	4.74
P-Value		0.000	0.000	0.000
MktPoten			0.0219	0.0382
T-Value			2.53	4.79
P-Value			0.019	0.000
MktShare				190
T-Value				3.82
P-Value				0.001
S	881	650	583	454
R-Sq	56.85	77.51	82.77	90.04
R-Sq(adj)	54.97	75.47	80.31	88.05
Mallows C-p	67.6	27.2	18.4	5.4

TABLE 15.15   Squared Variables and Interaction Variables in the Sales Representative Case

SQT	=	TIME*TIME
SQMP	=	MKTPOTEN*MKTPOTEN
SQA	=	ADVER*ADVER
SQMS	=	MKTSHARE*MKTSHARE
SQC	=	CHANGE*CHANGE
TMP	=	TIME*MKTPOTEN
TA	=	TIME*ADVER
TMS	=	TIME*MKTSHARE
TC	=	TIME*CHANGE
MPA	=	MKTPOTEN*ADVER
MPMS	=	MKTPOTEN*MKTSHARE
MPC	=	MKTPOTEN*CHANGE
AMS	=	ADVER*MKTSHARE
AC	=	ADVER*CHANGE
MSC	=	MKTSHARE*CHANGE

related to the first variable entered into the stepwise model is less than α_{stay}, an α value for allowing a variable to stay in the stepwise model. This is done because multicollinearity could have changed the p-value of the first variable entered into the stepwise model. The stepwise procedure continues this process and concludes when no new independent variable can be entered into the stepwise model. It is common practice to set both α_{entry} and α_{stay} equal to .05 or .10.

For example, again consider the sales representative performance data. We let $x_1, x_2, x_3, x_4, x_5,$ $x_6, x_7,$ and x_8 be the eight potential independent variables employed in the stepwise procedure. Figure 15.28 gives the MINITAB output of the stepwise regression employing these independent variables where both α_{entry} and α_{stay} have been set equal to .10. The stepwise procedure (1) adds ACCTS (x_6) on the first step; (2) adds ADVER (x_3) and retains ACCTS on the second step; (3) adds MKTPOTEN (x_2) and retains ACCTS and ADVER on the third step; and (4) adds MKTSHARE (x_4) and retains ACCTS, ADVER, and MKTPOTEN on the fourth step. The procedure terminates after step 4 when no more independent variables can be added. Therefore, the stepwise procedure arrives at the model that utilizes $x_2, x_3, x_4,$ and x_6. Note that this model is not the model using $x_1, x_2, x_3, x_4,$ and x_5 that was obtained by evaluating all possible regression models and that has the smallest C statistic of 4.4. In general, stepwise regression can miss finding the best regression model but is useful in **data mining,** where a massive number of independent variables exist and all possible regression models cannot be evaluated.

Some advanced model-building methods: Using squared and interaction variables and the partial *F*-test   We have concluded that perhaps the best sales representative performance model using only linear independent variables is the model using TIME, MKTPOTEN, ADVER, MKTSHARE, and CHANGE. We have also seen in Section 15.9 that using squared variables (which model quadratic curvature) and interaction variables can improve a regression model. In Table 15.15 we present the five squared variables and the ten (pairwise) interaction variables that can be formed using TIME, MKTPOTEN, ADVER, MKTSHARE, and CHANGE. Consider having MINITAB evaluate all possible models involving these squared and interaction variables, where the five linear variables are included in each possible model. If we have MINITAB do this and find the best model of each size in terms of s, we obtain the output in Figure 15.29 on the next page. (Note that we do not include values of the C statistic on the output because it can be shown that this statistic can give misleading results when using squared and interaction variables.) Examining the output, we see that the model that uses 12 squared and interaction variables (or a total of

FIGURE 15.29   MINITAB Comparisons Using Additional Squared and Interaction Variables

```
Note: all models include the 5 linear variables

                                             S     S                           M
          Squared and                        S  Q  S  Q  S  T     T     M  P  M  A     M
  Total   Interaction                        Q  M  Q  M  Q  M  T  M  T  P  M  P  M  A  S
  Vars    Vars      R-Sq  R-Sq(adj)     S    T  P  A  S  C  P  A  S  C  A  S  C  S  C  C
    6        1      94.2     92.2    365.87                            x
    7        2      95.8     94.1    318.19  x                         x
    8        3      96.5     94.7    301.61  x                         x     x
    9        4      97.0     95.3    285.53  x                x  x     x
   10        5      97.5     95.7    272.05  x                x  x     x     x
   11        6      98.1     96.5    244.00  x     x          x  x     x           x
   12        7      98.7     97.4    210.70  x  x             x  x     x        x  x
   13        8      99.0     97.8    193.95  x  x          x  x  x     x        x  x
   14        9      99.2     98.0    185.44  x  x       x     x  x     x        x  x  x
   15       10      99.3     98.2    175.70  x  x       x     x  x     x  x  x  x  x
   16       11      99.4     98.2    177.09  x  x       x  x  x  x     x  x  x  x  x
   17       12      99.5     98.2    174.60  x  x       x  x  x  x  x  x  x  x  x  x
   18       13      99.5     98.1    183.22  x  x  x       x  x  x  x  x  x  x  x  x  x
   19       14      99.6     97.9    189.77  x  x       x  x  x  x  x  x  x  x  x  x  x
   20       15      99.6     97.4    210.78  x  x  x  x  x  x  x  x  x  x  x  x  x  x  x
```

17 variables, including the 5 linear variables) has the smallest s ($= 174.6$) of any model. Unfortunately, although we would like to test the significance of the independent variables in this model, extreme multicollinearity (relationships between the independent variables) exists when using squared and interaction variables. Thus, the usual t tests for assessing the significance of individual independent variables might not be reliable. As an alternative, we will use a *partial F-test*. Specifically, considering the model with the smallest s of 174.6 and a total of 17 variables to be a *complete model*, we will use this test to assess whether at least one variable in the *subset* of 12 squared and interaction variables in this model is significant.

The Partial *F*-Test: An *F*-Test for a Portion of a Regression Model

Suppose that the regression assumptions hold, and consider a **complete model** that uses k independent variables. To assess whether at least one of the independent variables in a subset of k^* independent variables in this model is significant, we test the null hypothesis

H_0: All of the β_j coefficients corresponding to the independent variables in the subset are zero

which says that none of the independent variables in the subset are significant. We test H_0 versus

H_a: At least one of the β_j coefficients corresponding to the independent variables in the subset is not equal to zero

which says that at least one of the independent variables in the subset is significant. Let SSE_C denote the unexplained variation for the complete model, and let SSE_R denote the unexplained variation for the

reduced model that uses all k independent variables **except** for the k^* independent variables in the subset. Also, define

$$F(\text{partial}) = \frac{(SSE_R - SSE_C)/k^*}{SSE_C/[n - (k + 1)]}$$

and define the *p*-value related to $F(\text{partial})$ to be the area under the curve of the F distribution (having k^* and $[n - (k + 1)]$ degrees of freedom) to the right of $F(\text{partial})$. Then, we can reject H_0 in favor of H_a at level of significance α if either of the following equivalent conditions holds:

1 $F(\text{partial}) > F_\alpha$

2 $p\text{-value} < \alpha$

Here the point F_α is based on k^* numerator and $n - (k + 1)$ denominator degrees of freedom.

Using Excel or MINITAB, we find that the unexplained variation for the *complete model* that uses all $k = 17$ variables is $SSE_C = 213{,}396.12$ and the unexplained variation for the *reduced model* that does not use the $k^* = 12$ squared and interaction variables (and thus uses only the 5 linear variables) is $SSE_R = 3{,}516{,}859.2$. It follows that

$$F(\text{partial}) = \frac{(SSE_R - SSE_C)/k^*}{SSE_C/[n - (k + 1)]}$$

$$= \frac{(3{,}516{,}859.2 \, - \, 213{,}396.12)/12}{213{,}396.12/[25 \, - \, (17 \, + \, 1)]}$$

$$= \frac{3{,}303{,}463.1/12}{213{,}396.12/7} = 9.03$$

Because $F_{.05}$ based on $k^* = 12$ numerator and $n-(k + 1) = 7$ denominator degrees of freedom is 3.57 (see Table A.7 on page 796), and because F(partial) = 9.03 is greater than $F_{.05} = 3.57$, we conclude (at an α of .05) that at least one of the 12 squared and interaction variables in the 17-variable model is significant. In the exercises, the reader will do further analysis and use another partial F-test to pick a model that is perhaps better than the 17-variable model.

Exercises for Section 15.10

CONCEPTS

15.38 What is multicollinearity? What problems can be caused by multicollinearity?

15.39 Discuss how we compare regression models.

METHODS AND APPLICATIONS

15.40 THE HOSPITAL LABOR NEEDS CASE ⊙S HospLab2

Load	Pop
15.57	18.0
44.02	9.5
20.42	12.8
18.74	36.7
49.20	35.7
44.92	24.0
55.48	43.3
59.28	46.7
94.39	78.7
128.02	180.5
96.00	60.9
131.42	103.7
127.21	126.8
409.20	169.4
463.70	331.4
510.22	371.6

Recall that Table 15.6 (page 564) presents data concerning the need for labor in 16 U.S. Navy hospitals. This table gives values of the dependent variable Hours (monthly labor hours) and of the independent variables Xray (monthly X-ray exposures), BedDays (monthly occupied bed days—a hospital has one occupied bed day if one bed is occupied for an entire day), and Length (average length of patients' stay, in days). The data in Table 15.6 are part of a larger data set analyzed by the Navy. The complete data set consists of two additional independent variables— Load (average daily patient load) and Pop (eligible population in the area, in thousands)—values of which are given on the page margin. Figures 15.30 and 15.31 (on the next page) give Excel and MINITAB outputs of multicollinearity analysis and model building for the complete hospital labor needs data set.

a **(1)** Find the three largest simple correlation coefficients among the independent variables and the three largest variance inflation factors in Figure 15.30. **(2)** Discuss why these statistics imply that the independent variables BedDays, Load, and Pop are most strongly involved in multicollinearity and thus contribute possibly redundant information for predicting Hours. Note that, although we have reasoned in Exercise 15.6(a) on page 565 that a negative coefficient (that is, least squares point estimate) for Length might be intuitively reasonable, the negative coefficients for Load and Pop [see Figure 15.30(b)] are not intuitively reasonable and are a

---

FIGURE 15.30   **Multicollinearity and a Regression Analysis in the Hospital Labor Needs Situation**

(a) Excel output of the correlation matrix

	Hours(y)	Xray(x1)	BedDays(x2)	Length(x3)	Load(x4)	Pop(x5)
Hours(y)	1					
Xray(x1)	0.9425	1				
BedDays(x2)	0.9889	0.9048	1			
Length(x3)	0.5603	0.4243	0.6609	1		
Load(x4)	0.9886	0.9051	0.9999	0.6610	1	
Pop(x5)	0.9465	0.9124	0.9328	0.4515	0.9353	1

(b) A MINITAB regression analysis

Predictor	Coef	SE Coef	T	P	VIF
Constant	2270.4	670.8	3.38	0.007	
Xray(x1)	0.04112	0.01368	3.01	0.013	8.1
BedDays(x2)	1.413	1.925	0.73	0.48	8684.2
Length(x3)	-467.9	131.6	-3.55	0.005	4.2
Load(x4)	-9.30	60.81	-0.15	0.882	9334.5
Pop(x5)	-3.223	4.474	-0.72	0.488	23.0

FIGURE 15.31   The MINITAB Output of Model Building for the Hospital Labor Needs Data

(a) The two best models of each size

Vars	R-Sq	R-Sq(adj)	Mallows C-p	S
1	97.8	97.6	52.3	856.71
1	97.7	97.6	54	867.67
2	99.3	99.2	9.5	489.13
2	99.3	99.2	11.1	509.82
3	99.6	99.5	3.3	387.16
3	99.6	99.4	5	415.47
4	99.7	99.5	4	381.56
4	99.6	99.5	4.5	390.88
5	99.7	99.5	6	399.71

X r a y 1	D a y s 2	L g t h 3	L o a d 4	P o p 5
X				
				X
	X	X		
		X	X	
X	X	X		
X			X	X
X	X	X		X
X	X	X	X	
X	X	X	X	X

(b) Stepwise regression ($\alpha_{\text{entry}} = \alpha_{\text{stay}} = .10$)

Step	1	2	3
Constant	-70.23	2741.24	1946.80
BedDays	1.101	1.223	1.039
T-Value	24.87	36.30	15.39
P-Value	0.000	0.000	0.000
Length		-572	-414
T-Value		-5.47	-4.20
P-Value		0.000	0.001
XRay			0.039
T-Value			2.96
P-Value			0.012
S	857	489	387
R-Sq	97.79	99.33	99.61

further indication of strong multicollinearity. We conclude that a final regression model for predicting Hours may not need all three of the potentially redundant independent variables Bed-Days, Load, and Pop.

b   Figure 15.31(a) indicates that the two best hospital labor needs models are the model using Xray, BedDays, Pop, and Length, which we will call Model 1, and the model using Xray, BedDays, and Length, which we will call Model 2. **(1)** Which model gives the smallest value of *s* and the largest value of $\bar{R}^2$? **(2)** Which model gives the smallest value of *C*? **(3)** Consider a questionable hospital for which Xray = 56,194, BedDays = 14,077.88, Pop = 329.7, and Length = 6.89. The 95 percent prediction intervals given by Models 1 and 2 for labor hours corresponding to this combination of values of the independent variables are, respectively, [14,888.43, 16,861.30] and [14,906.24, 16,886.26]. Which model gives the shortest prediction interval?

c   **(1)** Which model is chosen by stepwise regression in Figure 15.31(b)? **(2)** Overall, which model seems best? **(3)** Which of BedDays, Load, and Pop does this best model use?

15.41   THE SALES REPRESENTATIVE CASE

Consider Figure 15.29 on page 604. The model using 12 squared and interaction variables has the smallest *s*. However, if we desire a somewhat simpler model, note that *s* does not increase substantially until we move from a model having seven squared and interaction variables to a model having six such variables. Moreover, we might subjectively conclude that the *s* of 210.70 for the model using 7 squared and interaction variables is not that much larger than the *s* of 174.6 for the model using 12 squared and interaction variables. Using the fact that the unexplained variations for these respective models are 532,733.88 and 213,396.12, perform a partial *F*-test to assess whether at least one of the extra five squared and interaction variables is significant. If none of the five extra variables are significant, we might consider the simpler model to be best.   ⑤ SalePerf

LO15-10 Use residual analysis to check the assumptions of multiple regression.

15.11 Residual Analysis in Multiple Regression ● ● ●

Basic residual analysis   For a multiple regression model we plot the residuals given by the model against (1) values of each independent variable, (2) values of the predicted value of the dependent variable, and (3) the time order in which the data have been observed (if the regression data are time series data). A fanning-out pattern on a residual plot indicates an increasing error variance; a funneling-in pattern indicates a decreasing error variance. Both violate the constant variance assumption. A curved pattern on a residual plot indicates that the functional form of the regression model is incorrect. If the regression data are time series data, a cyclical pattern on the residual plot versus time suggests positive autocorrelation, while an alternating pattern suggests negative autocorrelation. Both violate the independence assumption. On the other hand, if all residual plots have (at least approximately) a horizontal band appearance, then it is reasonable to believe that the constant variance, correct functional form, and independence assumptions approximately hold. To check the normality assumption, we can construct a histogram, stem-and-leaf display, and normal plot of the residuals. The histogram and stem-and-leaf display should look bell-shaped and symmetric about 0; the normal plot should have a straight-line appearance.

FIGURE 15.32   Residual Plots for the Sales Representative Performance Model

(a) Normal plot of the residuals   (b) Plot of the residuals versus predicted sales

FIGURE 15.33   Outlying Observations

To illustrate these ideas, consider the sales representative performance data in Figure 15.10 (page 579). Figure 15.11 (page 580) gives the Excel output of a regression analysis of these data using the model that relates y to $x_1, x_2, x_3, x_4,$ and x_5. The least squares point estimates on the output give the prediction equation

$$\hat{y} = -1,113.7879 + 3.6121x_1 + .0421x_2 + .1289x_3 + 256.9555x_4 + 324.5334x_5$$

Using this prediction equation, we can calculate the predicted sales values and residuals given on the page margin. For example, observation 10 corresponds to a sales representative for whom $x_1 = 105.69$, $x_2 = 42,053.24$, $x_3 = 5,673.11$, $x_4 = 8.85$, and $x_5 = .31$. If we insert these values into the prediction equation, we obtain a predicted sales value of $\hat{y}_{10} = 4,143.597$. Because the actual sales for the sales representative are $y_{10} = 4,876.370$, the residual e_{10} equals the difference between $y_{10} = 4,876.370$ and $\hat{y}_{10} = 4,143.597$, which is 732.773. The normal plot of the residuals in Figure 15.32(a) has an approximate straight-line appearance. The plot of the residuals versus predicted sales in Figure 15.32(b) has a horizontal band appearance, as do the plots of the residuals versus the independent variables (these plots are not given here). We conclude that the regression assumptions approximately hold for the sales representative performance model.

Outliers   An observation that is well separated from the rest of the data is called an **outlier,** and an observation may be an outlier with respect to its y value and/or its x values. We illustrate these ideas by considering Figure 15.33, which is a hypothetical plot of the values of a dependent variable y against an independent variable x. Observation 1 in this figure is outlying with respect to its y value, but not with respect to its x value. Observation 2 is outlying with respect to its x value, but because its y value is consistent with the regression relationship displayed by the nonoutlying observations, it is not outlying with respect to its y value. Observation 3 is an outlier with respect to its x value and its y value.

It is important to identify outliers because (as we will see) outliers can have adverse effects on a regression analysis and thus are candidates for removal from a data set. Moreover, in addition to using data plots, we can use more sophisticated procedures to detect outliers. For example, suppose that the U.S. Navy wishes to develop a regression model based on efficiently run Navy hospitals to evaluate the labor needs of questionably run Navy hospitals. Figure 15.34(a) on the next page gives labor needs data for 17 Navy hospitals. Specifically, this table gives values of the dependent variable Hours (y, monthly labor hours required) and of the independent variables Xray (x_1, monthly X-ray exposures), BedDays (x_2, monthly occupied bed days—a hospital has one occupied bed day if one bed is occupied for an entire day), and Length (x_3, average length of patients' stay, in days). When we perform a regression analysis of these data using the model relating y to $x_1, x_2,$ and x_3, we obtain the Excel add-in (MegaStat) output of residuals and outlier diagnostics shown in Figure 15.34(b), as well as the residual plot shown in Figure 15.34(c). (MINITAB gives the same diagnostics, and at the end of this section we will give formulas for most of these diagnostics). We now explain the meanings of the diagnostics.

Obs	Predicted	Residual
1	3,504.990	164.890
2	3,901.180	−427.230
3	2,774.866	−479.766
4	4,911.872	−236.312
5	5,415.196	710.764
6	2,026.090	108.850
7	5,126.127	−94.467
8	3,106.925	260.525
9	6,055.297	464.153
10	4,143.597	732.773
11	2,503.165	−34.895
12	1,827.065	706.245
13	2,478.083	−69.973
14	2,351.344	−13.964
15	4,797.688	−210.738
16	2,904.099	−174.859
17	3,362.660	−73.260
18	2,907.376	−106.596
19	3,625.026	−360.826
20	4,056.443	−602.823
21	1,409.835	331.615
22	2,494.101	−458.351
23	1,617.561	−39.561
24	4,574.903	−407.463
25	2,488.700	311.270

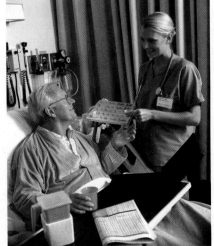

FIGURE 15.34　**Hospital Labor Needs Data, Outlier Diagnostics, and Residual Plots**

(a) The data 💿 HospLab3

Hospital	Hours y	Xray x_1	BedDays x_2	Length x_3
1	566.52	2463	472.92	4.45
2	696.82	2048	1339.75	6.92
3	1033.15	3940	620.25	4.28
4	1603.62	6505	568.33	3.90
5	1611.37	5723	1497.60	5.50
6	1613.27	11520	1365.83	4.60
7	1854.17	5779	1687.00	5.62
8	2160.55	5969	1639.92	5.15
9	2305.58	8461	2872.33	6.18
10	3503.93	20106	3655.08	6.15
11	3571.89	13313	2912.00	5.88
12	3741.40	10771	3921.00	4.88
13	4026.52	15543	3865.67	5.50
14	10343.81	36194	7684.10	7.00
15	11732.17	34703	12446.33	10.78
16	15414.94	39204	14098.40	7.05
17	18854.45	86533	15524.00	6.35

(b) Excel add-in (MegaStat) outlier diagnostics for the model $y = \beta_0 + \beta_1 x_1 + \beta_2 x_2 + \beta_3 x_3 + \epsilon$

Observation	Residual	Leverage	Studentized Residual	Studentized Deleted Residual
1	-121.889	0.121	-0.211	-0.203
2	-25.028	0.226	-0.046	-0.044
3	67.757	0.130	0.118	0.114
4	431.156	0.159	0.765	0.752
5	84.590	0.085	0.144	0.138
6	-380.599	0.112	-0.657	-0.642
7	177.612	0.084	0.302	0.291
8	369.145	0.083	0.627	0.612
9	-493.181	0.085	-0.838	-0.828
10	-687.403	0.120	-1.192	-1.214
11	380.933	0.077	0.645	0.630
12	-623.102	0.177	-1.117	-1.129
13	-337.709	0.064	-0.568	-0.553
14	1,630.503	0.146	2.871	4.558
15	-348.694	0.682	-1.005	-1.006
16	281.914	0.785	0.990	0.989
17	-406.003	0.863	-1.786	-1.975

Source: Hospital Labor Needs Data from Procedures and Analysis for Staffing Standards Development: Regression Analysis Handbook, © 1979.

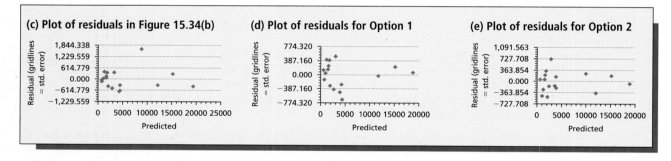

(c) Plot of residuals in Figure 15.34(b)

(d) Plot of residuals for Option 1

(e) Plot of residuals for Option 2

Leverage values　The **leverage value** for an observation is the **distance value** that has been discussed in the optional technical note at the end of Section 15.6 (page 576). This value is a measure of the distance between the observation's x values and the center of all of the observed x values. **If the leverage value for an observation is large, the observation is outlying with respect to its x values and thus would have substantial leverage in determining the least squares prediction equation.** For example, each of observations 2 and 3 in Figure 15.33 on the previous page is an outlier with respect to its x value and thus would have substantial leverage in determining the position of the least squares line. Moreover, because observations 2 and 3 have inconsistent y values, they would pull the least squares line in opposite directions. A **leverage value is considered to be large if it is greater than twice the average of all of the leverage values,** which can be shown to be equal to $2(k + 1)/n$. [The Excel add-in (MegaStat) shades such a leverage value in dark blue.] For example, because there are $n = 17$ observations in Figure 15.34(a) and because the model relating y to x_1, x_2, and x_3 utilizes $k = 3$ independent variables, twice the average leverage value is $2(k + 1)/n = 2(3 + 1)/17 = .4706$. Looking at Figure 15.34(b), we see that the leverage values for hospitals 15, 16, and 17 are, respectively, .682, .785, and .863. Because these leverage values are greater than .4706, we conclude that **hospitals 15, 16, and 17 are outliers with respect to their x values.** Intuitively, this is because Figure 15.34(a) indicates that x_2 (monthly occupied bed days) is substantially larger for hospitals 15, 16, and 17 than for hospitals 1 through 14. Also note that both x_1 (monthly X-ray exposures) and x_2 (monthly occupied bed days) are substantially larger for hospital 14 than for hospitals 1 through 13. To summarize, we might classify, hospitals 1 through 13 as small to medium sized hospitals and hospitals 14, 15, 16, and 17 as larger hospitals.

Residuals and studentized residuals To identify outliers with respect to their y values, we can use residuals. Any residual that is substantially different from the others is suspect. For example, note from Figure 15.34(b) that the residual for hospital 14, $e_{14} = 1630.503$, seems much larger than the other residuals. Assuming that the labor hours of 10,343.81 for hospital 14 has not been misrecorded, the residual of 1630.503 says that the labor hours are 1630.503 hours more than predicted by the regression model. If we divide an observation's residual by the residual's standard error, we obtain a **studentized residual.** For example, Figure 15.34(b) tells us that the studentized residual for hospital 14 is 2.871. If the studentized residual for an observation is greater than 2 in absolute value, we have some evidence that the observation is an outlier with respect to its y value.

Deleted residuals and studentized deleted residuals Consider again Figure 15.33 on page 607, and suppose that we use observation 3 to help determine the least squares line. Doing this might draw the least squares line toward observation 3, causing the point prediction $\hat{y}_3$ given by the line to be near y_3 and thus the usual residual $y_3 - \hat{y}_3$ to be small. This would falsely imply that observation 3 is not an outlier with respect to its y value. Moreover, this sort of situation shows the need for computing a **deleted residual.** For a particular observation, observation i, the deleted residual is found by subtracting from y_i the point prediction $\hat{y}_{(i)}$ computed using least squares point estimates based on all n observations except for observation i. Standard statistical software packages calculate the deleted residual for each observation and divide this residual by its standard error to form the **studentized deleted residual.** The experience of the authors leads us to suggest that one should conclude that an observation is an outlier with respect to its y value if (and only if) the studentized deleted residual is greater in absolute value than $t_{.005}$, which is based on $n - k - 2$ degrees of freedom. [The Excel add-in (MegaStat) shades such a studentized deleted residual in dark blue.] For the hospital labor needs model, $n - k - 2 = 17 - 3 - 2 = 12$, and therefore $t_{.005} = 3.055$. The studentized deleted residual for hospital 14, which equals 4.558 [see Figure 15.34(b)], is greater in absolute value than $t_{.005} = 3.055$. Therefore, we conclude that **hospital 14 is an outlier with respect to its y value.**

An example of dealing with outliers One option for dealing with the fact that hospital 14 is an outlier with respect to its y value is to assume that hospital 14 has been run inefficiently. Because we need to develop a regression model using efficiently run hospitals, based on this assumption we would remove hospital 14 from the data set. If we perform a regression analysis using a model relating y to x_1, x_2, and x_3 with hospital 14 removed from the data set (we call this **Option 1**), we obtain a standard error of $s = 387.16$. This s is considerably smaller than the large standard error of 614.779 caused by hospital 14's large residual when we use all 17 hospitals to relate y to x_1, x_2, and x_3.

A second option is motivated by the fact that *large organizations sometimes exhibit inherent inefficiencies.* To assess whether there might be a *general large hospital inefficiency,* we define a dummy variable D_L that equals 1 for the larger hospitals 14–17 and 0 for the smaller hospitals 1–13. If we fit the resulting regression model $y = \beta_0 + \beta_1 x_1 + \beta_2 x_2 + \beta_3 x_3 + \beta_4 D_L + \varepsilon$ to all 17 hospitals (we call this **Option 2**), we obtain a b_4 of 2871.78 and a p-value for testing $H_0: \beta_4 = 0$ of .0003. This indicates the existence of a large hospital inefficiency that is estimated to be an extra 2871.78 hours per month. In addition, the dummy variable model's s is 363.854, which is slightly smaller than the s of 387.16 obtained using Option 1. The studentized deleted residual for hospital 14 using the dummy variable model tells us what would happen if we removed hospital 14 from the data set and predicted y_{14} by using a newly fitted dummy variable model. In the exercises the reader will show that **the prediction obtained, which uses a large hospital inefficiency estimate based on the remaining large hospitals 15, 16, and 17, indicates that hospital 14's labor hours are not unusually large.** This justifies leaving hospital 14 in the data set when using the dummy variable model. In summary, both Options 1 and 2 seem reasonable. The reader will further compare these options in the exercises.

Cook's D, Dfbetas, and Dffits (Optional) If a particular observation, observation i, is an outlier with respect to its y and/or x values, it might significantly *influence* the least squares point estimates of the model parameters. To detect such influence, we compute **Cook's distance measure** (or **Cook's D**) for observation i, which we denote as D_i. To understand D_i, let $F_{.50}$

Obs	Cook's D
1	0.002
2	0.000
3	0.001
4	0.028
5	0.000
6	0.014
7	0.002
8	0.009
9	0.016
10	0.049
11	0.009
12	0.067
13	0.006
14	0.353
15	0.541
16	0.897
17	5.033

denote the 50th percentile of the F distribution based on $(k + 1)$ numerator and $n - (k + 1)$ denominator degrees of freedom. It can be shown that **if D_i is greater than $F_{.50}$, then removing observation i from the data set would significantly change (as a group) the least squares point estimates of the model parameters.** In this case we say that **observation i is influential.** For example, suppose that we relate y to x_1, x_2, and x_3 using all $n = 17$ observations in Figure 15.34(a). Noting that $k + 1 = 4$ and $n - (k + 1) = 13$, we find (using Excel) that $F_{.50} = .8845$. The Excel add-in (MegaStat) output in the page margin tells us that both $D_{16} = .897$ and $D_{17} = 5.033$ are greater than $F_{.50} = .8845$ (see the dark blue shading). It follows that removing either hospital 16 or 17 from the data set would significantly change (as a group) the least squares estimates of the model parameters.

To assess whether a particular least squares point estimate would significantly change, we can use an advanced statistical software package such as SAS, which gives the following **difference in estimate of β_j statistics (Dfbetas)** for hospitals 16 and 17:

	INTERCEP	X1	X2	X3
Obs	Dfbetas	Dfbetas	Dfbetas	Dfbetas
16	0.9880	−1.4289	1.7339	−1.1029
17	0.0294	−3.0114	1.2688	0.3155

Hosp	Dffits
1	−0.07541
2	−0.02404
3	0.04383
4	0.32657
5	0.04213
6	−0.22799
7	0.08818
8	0.18406
9	−0.25179
10	−0.44871
11	0.18237
12	−0.52368
13	−0.14509
14	1.88820
15	−1.47227
16	1.89295
17	−4.96226

Examining the Dfbetas statistics, we see that hospital 17's Dfbetas for the independent variable x_1 (monthly X-ray exposures) equals $−3.0114$, which is *negative and greater in absolute value than 2*, a sometimes used critical value for Dfbetas statistics. This implies that removing hospital 17 from the data set would *significantly decrease* the least squares point estimate of the effect, β_1, of monthly X-ray exposures on monthly labor hours. One possible consequence might then be that our model would *significantly underpredict* the monthly labor hours for a hospital which [like hospital 17—see Figure 15.34(a)] has a particularly large number of monthly X-ray exposures. In fact, consider the MINITAB output in the page margin of the **difference in fits statistic (Dffits)**. Dffits for hospital 17 equals $−4.96226$, which is *negative and greater in absolute value than the critical value 2*. This implies that removing hospital 17 from the data set would *significantly decrease* the point prediction of the monthly labor hours for a hospital that has the same values of $x_1, x_2,$ and x_3 as does hospital 17. Moreover, although it can be verified that using the previously discussed Option 1 or Option 2 to deal with hospital 14's large residual substantially reduces Cook's D, Dfbetas for x_1, and Dffits for hospital 17, these or similar statistics remain or become somewhat significant for the large hospitals 15, 16, and 17. The practical implication is that if we wish to predict monthly labor hours for questionably run *large* hospitals, it is very important to keep all of the efficiently run large hospitals 15, 16, and 17 in the data set. (Furthermore, it would be desirable to add information for additional efficiently run large hospitals to the data set.)

A technical note (Optional)   Let h_i and e_i denote the leverage value and residual for observation i based on a regression model using k independent variables. Then, for observation i, the studentized residual is e_i divided by $s\sqrt{1 - h_i}$, the studentized deleted residual (denoted t_i) is $e_i\sqrt{n - k - 2}$ divided by $\sqrt{SSE(1 - h_i) - e_i^2}$, Cook's distance measure is $e_i^2 h_i$ divided by $(k + 1)s^2(1 - h_i)^2$, and the difference in fits statistic is $t_i[h_i/(1 - h_i)]^{1/2}$. The formula for the difference in estimate of β_j statistics is very complicated and will not be given here.

Exercises for Section 15.11

CONCEPTS

15.42 Discuss how we use residual plots to check the regression assumptions for multiple regression.

15.43 Discuss how we identify an outlier with respect to its y value and/or x values.

METHODS AND APPLICATIONS

15.44 For each of the following cases, use the indicated residual plots to check for any violations of the regression assumptions.

a   The Tasty Sub Shop Case: For the model relating *Revenue* to *Population* and *Business Rating,* use the following plots: TastySub2

(a) Plot of residuals versus Population

(b) Plot of residuals versus Business rating

Obs	SDR1	SDR2
1	−0.333	−1.439
2	0.404	0.233
3	0.161	−0.750
4	1.234	0.202
5	0.425	0.213
6	−0.795	−1.490
7	0.677	0.617
8	1.117	1.010
9	−1.078	−0.409
10	−1.359	−0.400
11	1.461	2.571
12	−2.224	−0.624
13	−0.685	0.464
14		1.406
15	−0.137	−2.049
16	1.254	1.108
17	0.597	−0.639

b   The Natural Gas Consumption Case: For the model relating *GasCons* to *Temp* and *Chill,* use the plots shown on pages 623 (in Appendix 15.2) and 626 (in Appendix 15.3).   GasCon2

15.45   THE HOSPITAL LABOR NEEDS CASE   HospLab   HospLab4

(1) Analyze the studentized deleted residuals on the page margin for Options 1 and 2 (see **SDR1** and **SDR2**). (2) Is hospital 14 an outlier with respect to its *y* value when using Option 2? (3) Consider a questionable large hospital ($D_L = 1$) for which Xray $= 56,194$, BedDays $= 14,077.88$, and Length $= 6.89$. Also, consider the labor needs in an efficiently run large hospital described by this combination of values of the independent variables. The 95 percent prediction intervals for these labor needs given by the models of Options 1 and 2 are, respectively, [14,906.24, 16,886.26] and [15,175.04, 17,030.01]. By comparing these prediction intervals, by analyzing the residual plots for Options 1 and 2 given in Figure 15.34(d) and (e) on page 608, and by using your conclusions regarding the studentized deleted residuals, recommend which option should be used. (4) What would you conclude if the questionable large hospital used 17,207.31 monthly labor hours?

15.46   Recall that Figure 14.26 (a) on page 533 gives $n = 16$ weekly values of Pages Bookstore sales (y), Pages advertising expenditure (x_1), and competitor's advertising expenditure (x_2). When we fit the model $y = \beta_0 + \beta_1 x_1 + \beta_2 x_2 + \varepsilon$ to the data, we find that the Durbin–Watson statistic is $d = 1.6\overline{3}$. Use the partial Durbin–Watson table on the page margin to test for positive autocorrelation by setting α equal to .05.

	k = 2	
n	$d_{L,.05}$	$d_{U,.05}$
15	0.95	1.54
16	0.98	1.54
17	1.02	1.54
18	1.05	1.53

LO15-11 Use a logistic model to estimate probabilities and odds ratios.

15.12 Logistic Regression ●●●

Suppose that in a study of the effectiveness of offering a price reduction on a given product, 300 households having similar incomes were selected. A coupon offering a price reduction, x, on the product, as well as advertising material for the product, was sent to each household. The coupons offered different price reductions (10, 20, 30, 40, 50, and 60 dollars), and 50 homes were assigned at random to each price reduction. The table in the page margin summarizes the number, y, and proportion, $\hat{p}$, of households redeeming coupons for each price reduction, x (expressed in units of 10). On the left side of Figure 15.35 we plot the $\hat{p}$ values versus the

x	y	$\hat{p}$
1	4	.08
2	7	.14
3	20	.40
4	35	.70
5	44	.88
6	46	.92

 PrcRed

FIGURE 15.35   MINITAB Output of a Logistic Regression of the Price Reduction Data

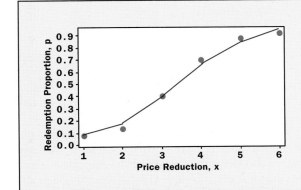

```
Logistic Regression Table
Predictor        Coef       SE Coef        Z        P
Constant      -3.7456     0.434355    -8.62    0.000
x              1.1109     0.119364     9.31    0.000
```

Price Reduction, x	Probability Estimate	Price Reduction, x	Probability Estimate
1	0.066943	4	0.667791
2	0.178920	5	0.859260
3	0.398256	6	0.948831

Group	Test 1	Test 2
1	96	85
1	96	88
1	91	81
1	95	78
1	92	85
1	93	87
1	98	84
1	92	82
1	97	89
1	95	96
1	99	93
1	89	90
1	94	90
1	92	94
1	94	84
1	90	92
1	91	70
1	90	81
1	86	81
1	90	76
1	91	79
1	88	83
1	87	82
0	93	74
0	90	84
0	91	81
0	91	78
0	88	78
0	86	86
0	79	81
0	83	84
0	79	77
0	88	75
0	81	85
0	85	83
0	82	72
0	82	81
0	81	77
0	86	76
0	81	84
0	85	78
0	83	77
0	81	71

x values and draw a hypothetical curve through the plotted points. A theoretical curve having the shape of the curve in Figure 15.35 is the **logistic curve**

$$p(x) = \frac{e^{(\beta_0 + \beta_1 x)}}{1 + e^{(\beta_0 + \beta_1 x)}}$$

where $p(x)$ denotes the probability that a household receiving a coupon having a price reduction of x will redeem the coupon. The MINITAB output in Figure 15.35 tells us that the point estimates of β_0 and β_1 are $b_0 = -3.7456$ and $b_1 = 1.1109$. (The point estimates in logistic regression are usually obtained by an advanced statistical procedure called *maximum likelihood estimation.*) Using these estimates, it follows that, for example,

$$\hat{p}(5) = \frac{e^{(-3.7456 + 1.1109(5))}}{1 + e^{(-3.7456 + 1.1109(5))}} = \frac{6.1037}{1 + 6.1037} = .8593$$

That is, $\hat{p}(5) = .8593$ is the point estimate of the probability that a household receiving a coupon having a price reduction of $50 will redeem the coupon. The MINITAB output in Figure 15.35 gives the values of $\hat{p}(x)$ for $x = 1, 2, 3, 4, 5,$ and 6.

The **general logistic regression model** relates the probability that an event (such as redeeming a coupon) will occur to k independent variables $x_1, x_2, \ldots, x_k$. This general model is

$$p(x_1, x_2, \ldots, x_k) = \frac{e^{(\beta_0 + \beta_1 x_1 + \beta_2 x_2 + \cdots + \beta_k x_k)}}{1 + e^{(\beta_0 + \beta_1 x_1 + \beta_2 x_2 + \cdots + \beta_k x_k)}}$$

where $p(x_1, x_2, \ldots, x_k)$ is the probability that the event will occur when the values of the independent variables are $x_1, x_2, \ldots, x_k$. In order to estimate $\beta_0, \beta_1, \beta_2, \ldots, \beta_k$ we obtain n observations, with each observation consisting of observed values of $x_1, x_2, \ldots, x_k$ and of a dependent variable y. Here, y is a **dummy variable** that equals 1 if the event has occurred and 0 otherwise.

For example, suppose that the personnel director of a firm has developed two tests to help determine whether potential employees would perform successfully in a particular position. To help estimate the usefulness of the tests, the director gives both tests to 43 employees that currently hold the position. Table 15.16 gives the scores of each employee on both tests and indicates whether the employee is currently performing successfully or unsuccessfully in the position. If the employee is performing successfully, we set the dummy variable *Group* equal to 1; if the employee is performing unsuccessfully, we set *Group* equal to 0. Let x_1 and x_2 denote the scores of a potential employee on tests 1 and 2, and let $p(x_1, x_2)$ denote the probability that a potential employee having the scores x_1 and x_2 will perform successfully in the position. We can estimate the relationship between $p(x_1, x_2)$ and x_1 and x_2 by using the logistic regression model

$$p(x_1, x_2) = \frac{e^{(\beta_0 + \beta_1 x_1 + \beta_2 x_2)}}{1 + e^{(\beta_0 + \beta_1 x_1 + \beta_2 x_2)}}$$

The MINITAB output in Figure 15.36 tells us that the point estimates of $\beta_0, \beta_1,$ and β_2 are $b_0 = -56.17, b_1 = .4833,$ and $b_2 = .1652$. Consider, therefore, a potential employee who scores a 93 on test 1 and an 84 on test 2. It follows that a point estimate of the probability that the potential employee will perform successfully in the position is

$$\hat{p}(93, 84) = \frac{e^{(-56.17 + .4833(93) + .1652(84))}}{1 + e^{(-56.17 + .4833(93) + .1652(84))}} = \frac{14.206506}{15.206506} = .9342$$

If we *classify* a potential employee into *group 1* ("will perform successfully"), as opposed to *group 2* ("will not perform successfully"), if and only if $\hat{p}(x_1, x_2)$ is greater than .5, this potential employee is classified into group 1.

To further analyze the logistic regression output, we consider several hypothesis tests that are based on the chi-square distribution. We first consider testing $H_0: \beta_1 = \beta_2 = 0$ versus H_a: At least one of β_1 or β_2 does not equal 0. The p-value for this test is the area under the chi-square curve having $k = 2$ degrees of freedom to the right of the test statistic value $G = 31.483$. Although the

FIGURE 15.36   **MINITAB Output of a Logistic Regression of the Performance Data**

```
Response Information

Variable  Value  Count
Group       1      23    (Event)
            0      20
          Total    43

Logistic Regression Table
                                                   Odds      95% CI
Predictor       Coef   SE Coef      Z      P     Ratio   Lower   Upper
Constant      -56.17   17.4516   -3.22  0.001
Test 1         0.4833   0.1578    3.06  0.002   1.62    1.19    2.21
Test 2         0.1652   0.1021    1.62  0.106   1.18    0.97    1.44

Log-Likelihood = -13.959
Test that all slopes are zero: G = 31.483, DF = 2, P-Value = 0.000
```

calculation of G is too complicated to demonstrate in this book, the MINITAB output gives the value of G and the related p-value, which is less than .001. This p-value implies that we have extremely strong evidence that at least one of β_1 or β_2 does not equal zero. The p-value for testing H_0: $\beta_1 = 0$ versus H_a: $\beta_1 \neq 0$ is the area under the chi-square curve having one degree of freedom to the right of the square of $z = (b_1/s_{b_1}) = (.4833/.1578) = 3.06$. The MINITAB output tells us that this p-value is .002, which implies that we have very strong evidence that the score on test 1 is related to the probability of a potential employee's success. The p-value for testing H_0: $\beta_2 = 0$ versus H_a: $\beta_2 \neq 0$ is the area under the chi-square curve having one degree of freedom to the right of the square of $z = (b_2/s_{b_2}) = (.1652/.1021) = 1.62$. The MINITAB output tells us that this p-value is .106, which implies that we do not have strong evidence that the score on test 2 is related to the probability of a potential employee's success. In Exercise 15.49 we will consider a logistic regression model that uses only the score on test 1 to estimate the probability of a potential employee's success.

The **odds** of success for a potential employee is defined to be the probability of success divided by the probability of failure for the employee. That is,

$$\text{odds} = \frac{p(x_1, x_2)}{1 - p(x_1, x_2)}$$

For the potential employee who scores a 93 on test 1 and an 84 on test 2, we estimate that the odds of success are $.9342/(1 - .9342) = 14.22$. That is, we estimate that the odds of success for the potential employee are about 14 to 1. It can be shown that $e^{b_1} = e^{.4833} = 1.62$ is a point estimate of the **odds ratio for x_1,** which is the proportional change in the odds (for any potential employee) that is associated with an increase of one in x_1 when x_2 stays constant. This point estimate of the odds ratio for x_1 is shown on the MINITAB output and says that, for every one point increase in the score on test 1 when the score on test 2 stays constant, we estimate that a potential employee's odds of success increase by 62 percent. Furthermore, the 95 percent confidence interval for the odds ratio for x_1, [1.19, 2.21], does not contain 1. Therefore, as with the (equivalent) chi-square test of H_0: $\beta_1 = 0$, we conclude that there is strong evidence that the score on test 1 is related to the probability of success for a potential employee. Similarly, it can be shown that $e^{b_2} = e^{.1652} = 1.18$ is a point estimate of the **odds ratio for x_2,** which is the proportional change in the odds (for any potential employee) that is associated with an increase of one in x_2 when x_1 stays constant. This point estimate of the odds ratio for x_2 is shown on the MINITAB output and says that, for every one point increase in the score on test 2 when the score on test 1 stays constant, we estimate that a potential employee's odds of success increases by 18 percent. However, the 95 percent confidence interval for the odds ratio for x_2, [.97, 1.44], contains 1. Therefore, as with the equivalent chi-square test of H_0: $\beta_2 = 0$, we cannot conclude that there is strong evidence that the score on test 2 is related to the probability of success for a potential employee.

To conclude this section, consider the **general logistic regression model**

$$p(x_1, x_2, \ldots, x_k) = \frac{e^{(\beta_0 + \beta_1 x_1 + \beta_2 x_2 + \cdots + \beta_k x_k)}}{1 + e^{(\beta_0 + \beta_1 x_1 + \beta_2 x_2 + \cdots + \beta_k x_k)}}$$

where $p(x_1, x_2, \ldots, x_k)$ is the probability that the event under consideration will occur when the values of the independent variables are $x_1, x_2, \ldots, x_k$. The **odds** of the event occurring is defined to be $p(x_1, x_2, \ldots, x_k)/(1 - p(x_1, x_2, \ldots, x_k))$, which is the probability that the event will occur divided by the probability that the event will not occur. It can be shown that the odds equals $e^{(\beta_0 + \beta_1 x_1 + \beta_2 x_2 + \cdots + \beta_k x_k)}$. The natural logarithm of the odds is $(\beta_0 + \beta_1 x_1 + \beta_2 x_2 + \cdots + \beta_k x_k)$, which is called the **logit**. If $b_0, b_1, b_2, \ldots, b_k$ are the point estimates of $\beta_0, \beta_1, \beta_2, \ldots, \beta_k$, the point estimate of the logit, denoted $\widehat{\ell g}$, is $(b_0 + b_1 x_1 + b_2 x_2 + \cdots + b_k x_k)$. It follows that the point estimate of the probability that the event will occur is

$$\hat{p}(x_1, x_2, \ldots, x_k) = \frac{e^{\widehat{\ell g}}}{1 + e^{\widehat{\ell g}}} = \frac{e^{(b_0 + b_1 x_1 + b_2 x_2 + \cdots + b_k x_k)}}{1 + e^{(b_0 + b_1 x_1 + b_2 x_2 + \cdots + b_k x_k)}}$$

Finally, consider an arbitrary independent variable x_j. It can be shown that e^{b_j} is the point estimate of the **odds ratio for x_j**, which is the proportional change in the odds that is associated with a one unit increase in x_j when the other independent variables stay constant.

Exercises for Section 15.12

connect

y	x_1	x_2	x_3
0	6	2	0
0	4	0	1
1	6	6	1
1	6	3	1
0	4	1	0
1	8	3	0
0	4	2	1
0	4	4	0
0	6	1	0
1	8	10	0
0	4	2	1
0	8	5	0
0	4	2	0
0	6	7	0
1	4	5	1
0	6	4	0
0	8	0	1
1	6	1	1
0	4	7	0
0	4	1	1
0	4	5	0
0	6	0	1
1	8	5	1
0	4	9	0
0	8	1	0
0	6	1	1
1	4	10	1
1	6	12	0

DS Gender

Source: William Mendenhall and Terry Sincich, *A Second Course in Business Statistics: Regression Analysis,* Fourth edition, © 1993. Reprinted with permission of Prentice Hall.

CONCEPTS

15.47 What two values does the dependent variable equal in logistic regression? What do these values represent?

15.48 Define the odds of an event, and the odds ratio for x_j.

METHODS AND APPLICATIONS

15.49 If we use the logistic regression model

$$p(x_1) = \frac{e^{(\beta_0 + \beta_1 x_1)}}{1 + e^{(\beta_0 + \beta_1 x_1)}}$$

to analyze the performance data in Table 15.16 on page 612, we find that the point estimates of the model parameters and their associated p-values (given in parentheses) are $b_0 = -43.37(.001)$ and $b_1 = .4897(.001)$. **(1)** Find a point estimate of the probability of success for a potential employee who scores a 93 on test 1. **(2)** Using $b_1 = .4897$, find a point estimate of the odds ratio for x_1. **(3)** Interpret this point estimate.

15.50 Mendenhall and Sincich (1993) present data that can be used to investigate allegations of gender discrimination in the hiring practices of a particular firm. These data are given in the page margin. In this table, y is a dummy variable that equals 1 if a potential employee was hired and 0 otherwise; x_1 is the number of years of education of the potential employee; x_2 is the number of years of experience of the potential employee; and x_3 is a dummy variable that equals 1 if the potential employee was a male and 0 if the potential employee was a female. If we use the logistic regression model

$$p(x_1, x_2, x_3) = \frac{e^{(\beta_0 + \beta_1 x_1 + \beta_2 x_2 + \beta_3 x_3)}}{1 + e^{(\beta_0 + \beta_1 x_1 + \beta_2 x_2 + \beta_3 x_3)}}$$

to analyze these data, we find that the point estimates of the model parameters and their associated p-values (given in parentheses) are $b_0 = -14.2483(.0191)$, $b_1 = 1.1549(.0552)$, $b_2 = .9098 (.0341)$, and $b_3 = 5.6037(.0313)$.

a Consider a potential employee having 4 years of education and 5 years of experience. Find **(1)** a point estimate of the probability that the potential employee will be hired if the potential employee is a male, and **(2)** a point estimate of the probability that the potential employee will be hired if the potential employee is a female.

b **(1)** Using $b_3 = 5.6037$, find a point estimate of the odds ratio for x_3. **(2)** Interpret this odds ratio. **(3)** Using the p-value describing the importance of x_3, can we conclude that there is strong evidence that gender is related to the probability that a potential employee will be hired?

Chapter Summary

This chapter has discussed **multiple regression analysis.** We began by considering the **multiple regression model** and the assumptions behind this model. We next discussed the **least squares point estimates** of the model parameters and some ways to judge **overall model utility**—the **standard error,** the **multiple coefficient of determination,** the **adjusted multiple coefficient of determination,** and the **overall F-test.** Then we considered testing the significance of a single independent variable in a multiple regression model, calculating a **confidence interval** for the mean value of the dependent variable, and calculating a **prediction interval** for an individual value of the dependent variable. We continued this chapter by explaining the use of **dummy variables** to model **qualitative** independent variables and the use of

squared and interaction variables. We then considered **multicollinearity,** which can adversely affect the ability of the t statistics and associated p-values to assess the importance of the independent variables in a regression model. For this reason, we need to determine if the overall model gives a **high R^2,** a **small s,** a **high adjusted R^2, short prediction intervals,** and a **small C.** We explained how to compare regression models on the basis of these criteria, and we discussed **stepwise regression** and the **partial F-test.** We then considered using **residual analysis** (including the detection of **outliers**) to check the assumptions for multiple regression models. We concluded this chapter by discussing how to use **logistic regression** to estimate the probability of an event.

Glossary of Terms

dummy variable: A variable that takes on the values 0 or 1 and is used to describe the effects of the different levels of a qualitative independent variable in a regression model. (page 581)
interaction: The situation in which the relationship between the mean value of the dependent variable and an independent variable is dependent on the value of another independent variable. (pages 585 and 594)

multicollinearity: The situation in which the independent variables used in a regression analysis are related to each other. (page 598)
multiple regression model: An equation that describes the relationship between a dependent variable and more than one independent variable. (page 560)
stepwise regression: An iterative model building technique for selecting important predictor variables (page 602)

Important Formulas and Tests

The least squares point estimates: page 557

The multiple regression model: page 560

Point estimate of a mean value of y: page 560

Point prediction of an individual value of y: page 560

Mean square error: page 566

Standard error: page 566

Total variation: page 567

Explained variation: page 567

Unexplained variation: page 567

Multiple coefficient of determination: page 567

Multiple correlation coefficient: page 567

Adjusted multiple coefficient of determination: page 568

An F test for the multiple regression model: page 569

Testing the significance of an independent variable: page 572

Confidence interval for β_j: page 574

Confidence interval for a mean value of y: pages 575 and 576

Prediction interval for an individual value of y: pages 575 and 576

Distance value (in multiple regression): page 576

The quadratic regression model: page 592

Variance inflation factor: page 598

C statistic: page 602

Partial F test: page 604

Studentized deleted residual: page 609

Cook's D, Dfbetas, and Dffits: pages 609–610

Logistic curve: page 612

Logistic regression model: page 612

Odds and odds ratio: page 613

Supplementary Exercises

15.51 The trend in home building in recent years has been to emphasize open spaces and great rooms, rather than smaller living rooms and family rooms. A builder of speculative homes in the college community of Oxford, Ohio, had been building such homes, but his homes had been taking many months to sell and selling for substantially less than the asking price. In order to determine what types of homes would attract residents of the community, the builder contacted a statistician at a local college. The statistician went to a local real estate agency and obtained the data in Table 15.17. This table presents the sales price y, square footage x_1, number of rooms x_2, number of bedrooms x_3, and age x_4 for each of 63 single-family residences recently sold in the community. When we perform a regression analysis of these data using the model

$$y = \beta_0 + \beta_1 x_1 + \beta_2 x_2 + \beta_3 x_3 + \beta_4 x_4 + \varepsilon$$

we find that the least squares point estimates of the model parameters and their associated p-values (given in parentheses) are as shown in Table 15.18. Discuss why the estimates $b_2 = 6.3218$ and $b_3 = -11.1032$ suggest that it might be more profitable when building a house of a

TABLE 15.17   Measurements Taken on 63 Single-Family Residences   OxHome

Residence	Sales Price, y (× $1,000)	Square Feet, x_1	Rooms, x_2	Bedrooms, x_3	Age, x_4	Residence	Sales Price, y (× $1,000)	Square Feet, x_1	Rooms, x_2	Bedrooms, x_3	Age, x_4
1	53.5	1,008	5	2	35	33	63.0	1,053	5	2	24
2	49.0	1,290	6	3	36	34	60.0	1,728	6	3	26
3	50.5	860	8	2	36	35	34.0	416	3	1	42
4	49.9	912	5	3	41	36	52.0	1,040	5	2	9
5	52.0	1,204	6	3	40	37	75.0	1,496	6	3	30
6	55.0	1,204	5	3	10	38	93.0	1,936	8	4	39
7	80.5	1,764	8	4	64	39	60.0	1,904	7	4	32
8	86.0	1,600	7	3	19	40	73.0	1,080	5	2	24
9	69.0	1,255	5	3	16	41	71.0	1,768	8	4	74
10	149.0	3,600	10	5	17	42	83.0	1,503	6	3	14
11	46.0	864	5	3	37	43	90.0	1,736	7	3	16
12	38.0	720	4	2	41	44	83.0	1,695	6	3	12
13	49.5	1,008	6	3	35	45	115.0	2,186	8	4	12
14	105.0	1,950	8	3	52	46	50.0	888	5	2	34
15	152.5	2,086	7	3	12	47	55.2	1,120	6	3	29
16	85.0	2,011	9	4	76	48	61.0	1,400	5	3	33
17	60.0	1,465	6	3	102	49	147.0	2,165	7	3	2
18	58.5	1,232	5	2	69	50	210.0	2,353	8	4	15
19	101.0	1,736	7	3	67	51	60.0	1,536	6	3	36
20	79.4	1,296	6	3	11	52	100.0	1,972	8	3	37
21	125.0	1,996	7	3	9	53	44.5	1,120	5	3	27
22	87.9	1,874	5	2	14	54	55.0	1,664	7	3	79
23	80.0	1,580	5	3	11	55	53.4	925	5	3	20
24	94.0	1,920	5	3	14	56	65.0	1,288	5	3	2
25	74.0	1,430	9	3	16	57	73.0	1,400	5	3	2
26	69.0	1,486	6	3	27	58	40.0	1,376	6	3	103
27	63.0	1,008	5	2	35	59	141.0	2,038	12	4	62
28	67.5	1,282	5	3	20	60	68.0	1,572	6	3	29
29	35.0	1,134	5	2	74	61	139.0	1,545	6	3	9
30	142.5	2,400	9	4	15	62	140.0	1,993	6	3	4
31	92.2	1,701	5	3	15	63	55.0	1,130	5	2	21
32	56.0	1,020	6	3	16						

TABLE 15.18

The Least Squares Point Estimates for Exercise 15.51

$b_0 = 10.3676$
    (.3710)
$b_1 = .0500$
    (<.001)
$b_2 = 6.3218$
    (.0152)
$b_3 = -11.1032$
    (.0635)
$b_4 = -.4319$
    (.0002)

specified square footage (1) to include both a (smaller) living room and family room rather than a (larger) great room and (2) to not increase the number of bedrooms (at the cost of another type of room) that would normally be included in a house of the specified square footage. Note: Based on the statistical results, the builder realized that there are many families with children in a college town and that the parents in such families would rather have one living area for the children (the family room) and a separate living area for themselves (the living room). The builder started modifying his open-space homes accordingly and greatly increased his profits.

15.52   THE FRESH DETERGENT CASE   Fresh3

Recall from Exercise 15.32 (page 590) that Enterprise Industries has advertised Fresh liquid laundry detergent by using three different advertising campaigns—advertising campaign *A* (television commercials), advertising campaign *B* (a balanced mixture of television and radio commercials) and advertising campaign *C* (a balanced mixture of television, radio, newspaper, and magazine ads). To compare the effectiveness of these advertising campaigns, consider using two models, Model 1 and Model 2, that are shown with corresponding partial Excel outputs in Figure 15.37. In these models y is demand for Fresh; x_4 is the price difference; x_3 is Enterprise Industries' advertising expenditure for Fresh; D_A equals 1 if advertising campaign *A* is used in a sales period and 0 otherwise; D_B equals 1 if advertising campaign *B* is used in a sales period and 0 otherwise; and D_C equals 1 if advertising campaign *C* is used in a sales period and 0 otherwise. Moreover, in Model 1 the parameter β_5 represents the effect on mean demand of advertising campaign *B* compared to advertising campaign *A*, and the parameter β_6 represents the effect on mean demand of advertising campaign *C* compared to advertising campaign *A*. In Model 2 the

FIGURE 15.37 Excel Output for the Fresh Detergent Case

(a) Partial Excel output for the model $y = \beta_0 + \beta_1 x_4 + \beta_2 x_3 + \beta_3 x_3^2 + \beta_4 x_4 x_3 + \beta_5 D_B + \beta_6 D_C + \varepsilon$

	Coefficients	Standard Error	t Stat	P-value	Lower 95%	Upper 95%
Intercept	25.612696	4.7938	5.3429	2.00E-05	15.6960	35.5294
X4	9.0587	3.0317	2.9880	0.0066	2.7871	15.3302
X3	−6.5377	1.5814	−4.1342	0.0004	−9.8090	−3.2664
X3SQ	0.5844	0.1299	4.5001	0.0002	0.3158	0.8531
X4X3	−1.1565	0.4557	−2.5376	0.0184	−2.0992	−0.2137
DB	0.2137	0.0622	3.4380	0.0022	0.0851	0.3423
DC	0.3818	0.0613	6.2328	2.33E-06	0.2551	0.5085

(b) Partial Excel output for the model $y = \beta_0 + \beta_1 x_4 + \beta_2 x_3 + \beta_3 x_3^2 + \beta_4 x_4 x_3 + \beta_5 D_A + \beta_6 D_C + \varepsilon$

	Coefficients	Standard Error	t Stat	P-value	Lower 95%	Upper 95%
Intercept	25.8264	4.7946	5.3866	1.80E-05	15.9081	35.7447
X4	9.05868	3.0317	2.9880	0.0066	2.7871	15.3302
X3	−6.5377	1.5814	−4.1342	0.0004	−9.8090	−3.2664
X3SQ	0.58444	0.1299	4.5001	0.0002	0.3158	0.8531
X4X3	−1.1565	0.4557	−2.5376	0.0184	−2.0992	−0.2137
DA	−0.2137	0.0622	−3.4380	0.0022	−0.3423	−0.0851
DC	0.16809	0.0637	2.6385	0.0147	0.0363	0.2999

parameter β_6 represents the effect on mean demand of advertising campaign C compared to advertising campaign B.

a Compare advertising compaigns A, B, and C by finding 95 percent confidence intervals for (1) β_5 and β_6 in Model 1 and (2) β_6 in Model 2. Interpret the intervals.

b Using Model 1 or Model 2, a point prediction of Fresh demand when $x_4 = .20$, $x_3 = 6.50$, and campaign C will be used is 8.50068 (that is, 850,068 bottles). Show (by hand calculation) that Model 1 and Model 2 give the same point prediction.

c Consider the alternative model

$$y = \beta_0 + \beta_1 x_4 + \beta_2 x_3 + \beta_3 x_3^2 + \beta_4 x_4 x_3 + \beta_5 D_B + \beta_6 D_C + \beta_7 x_3 D_B + \beta_8 x_3 D_C + \varepsilon$$

which we will call Model 3. The Excel output of the least squares point estimates of the parameters of this model is as follows:

	Coefficients	Standard Error	t Stat	P-value	Lower 95%	Upper 95%
Intercept	28.6873	5.1285	5.5937	1.5E-05	18.0221	39.3526
X4	10.8253	3.2988	3.2816	0.0036	3.9651	17.6855
X3	−7.4115	1.6617	−4.4602	0.0002	−10.8671	−3.9558
X3SQ	0.6458	0.1346	4.7984	9.66E-05	0.3659	0.9257
X4X3	−1.4156	0.4929	−2.8722	0.00912	−2.4406	−0.3907
DB	−0.4807	0.7309	−0.6577	0.517904	−2.0007	1.0393
DC	−0.9351	0.8357	−1.1189	0.2758	−2.6731	0.8029
X3DB	0.10722	0.1117	0.9600	0.3480	−0.1251	0.3395
X3DC	0.20349	0.1288	1.5797	0.1291	−0.0644	0.4714

Let $\mu_{[d,a,A]}$, $\mu_{[d,a,B]}$, and $\mu_{[d,a,C]}$ denote the mean demands for Fresh when the price difference is d, the advertising expenditure is a, and we use advertising campaigns A, B, and C, respectively. The model of this part implies that

$$\mu_{[d,a,A]} = \beta_0 + \beta_1 d + \beta_2 a + \beta_3 a^2 + \beta_4 da + \beta_5(0) + \beta_6(0) + \beta_7 a(0) + \beta_8 a(0)$$

$$\mu_{[d,a,B]} = \beta_0 + \beta_1 d + \beta_2 a + \beta_3 a^2 + \beta_4 da + \beta_5(1) + \beta_6(0) + \beta_7 a(1) + \beta_8 a(0)$$

$$\mu_{[d,a,C]} = \beta_0 + \beta_1 d + \beta_2 a + \beta_3 a^2 + \beta_4 da + \beta_5(0) + \beta_6(1) + \beta_7 a(0) + \beta_8 a(1)$$

(1) Using these equations, verify that $\mu_{[d,a,C]} - \mu_{[d,a,A]}$ equals $\beta_6 + \beta_8 a$. **(2)** Using the least squares point estimates, show that a point estimate of $\mu_{[d,a,C]} - \mu_{[d,a,A]}$ equals .3266 when $a = 6.2$ and equals .4080 when $a = 6.6$. **(3)** Verify that $\mu_{[d,a,C]} - \mu_{[d,a,B]}$ equals $\beta_6 - \beta_5 + \beta_8 a - \beta_7 a$. **(4)** Using the least squares point estimates, show that a point estimate of $\mu_{[d,a,C]} - \mu_{[d,a,B]}$ equals .14266 when $a = 6.2$ and equals .18118 when $a = 6.6$. **(5)** Discuss why these results imply that the larger that advertising expenditure a is, then the larger is the improvement in mean sales that is obtained by using advertising campaign C rather than advertising campaign A or B.

d If we use an Excel add-in (MegaStat), we can use Models 1, 2, and 3 to predict demand for Fresh in a future sales period when the price difference will be $x_4 = .20$, the advertising expenditure will be $x_3 = 6.50$, and campaign C will be used. The prediction results using Model 1 or Model 2 are as follows:

Predicted	95% Confidence Interval		95% Prediction Interval		Leverage
	lower	upper	lower	upper	
8.50068	8.40370	8.59765	8.21322	8.78813	0.128

The prediction results using Model 3 are as follows:

Predicted	95% Confidence Interval		95% Prediction Interval		Leverage
	lower	upper	lower	upper	
8.51183	8.41229	8.61136	8.22486	8.79879	0.137

e Which model gives the shortest 95 percent prediction interval for Fresh demand?

f Using all of the results in this exercise, discuss why there might be a small amount of interaction between advertising expenditure and advertising campaign.

15.53 THE FRESH DETERGENT CASE 🖸 Fresh3

The unexplained variation for Model 1 of the previous exercise

$$y = \beta_0 + \beta_1 x_4 + \beta_2 x_3 + \beta_3 x_3^2 + \beta_4 x_4 x_3 + \beta_5 D_B + \beta_6 D_C + \varepsilon$$

is .3936. If we set both β_5 and β_6 in this model equal to 0 (that is, if we eliminate the dummy variable portion of this model), the resulting reduced model has an unexplained variation of 1.0644. Using an α of .05, perform a partial F-test (see page 604) of $H_0: \beta_5 = \beta_6 = 0$. (Hint: $n = 30$, $k = 6$, and $k^* = 2$.) If we reject H_0, we conclude that at least two of advertising campaigns A, B, and C have different effects on mean demand. Many statisticians believe that rejection of H_0 by using the partial F-test makes it more legitimate to make pairwise comparisons of advertising campaigns A, B, and C, as we did in part a of the previous exercise. Here, the partial F-test is regarded as a *preliminary test of significance*.

15.54 In the article "The Effect of Promotion Timing on Major League Baseball Attendance" (*Sport Marketing Quarterly,* December 1999), T. C. Boyd and T. C. Krehbiel use data from six major league baseball teams having outdoor stadiums to study the effect of promotion timing on major league baseball attendance. One of their regression models describes game attendance in 1996 as follows (*p*-values less than .10 are shown in parentheses under the appropriate independent variables):

$$\text{Attendance} = 2{,}521 + 106.5 \; \textit{Temperature} + 12.33 \; \textit{Winning \%} + .2248 \; \textit{OpWin \%}$$
$$(<.001) \qquad\qquad (<.001) \qquad\qquad (<.001)$$
$$- \; 424.2 \; \textit{DayGame} + 4{,}845 \; \textit{Weekend} + 1{,}192 \; \textit{Rival} + 4{,}745 \; \textit{Promotion}$$
$$(<.001) \qquad\qquad (<.10) \qquad\qquad (<.001)$$
$$+ \; 5{,}059 \; \textit{Promo*DayGame} - 4{,}690 \; \textit{Promo*Weekend} + 696.5 \; \textit{Promo*Rival}$$
$$(<.001) \qquad\qquad\qquad (<.001)$$

In this model, *Temperature* is the high temperature recorded in the city on game day; *Winning %* is the home team's winning percentage at the start of the game; *OpWin %* is a dummy variable that equals 1 if the opponent's winning percentage was .500 or higher and 0 otherwise; *DayGame* is a dummy variable that equals 1 if the game was a day game and 0 otherwise; *Weekend* is a dummy variable that equals 1 if the game was on a Friday, Saturday, or Sunday and 0 otherwise; *Rival* is a dummy variable that equals 1 if the opponent was a rival and 0 otherwise; *Promotion* is a dummy variable that equals 1 if the home team ran a promotion during the game and 0 otherwise. Using the model, which is based on 475 games and has an R^2 of .6221, Boyd and Krehbiel conclude that "promotions run during day games and on weekdays are likely to result in greater attendance increases." Carefully explain why the following part of their model justifies this conclusion: $+ 5,059\ Promo*DayGame - 4,690\ Promo*Weekend$.

15.55 Table 15.19 in the page margin gives the number of bathrooms for each of the 63 homes in Table 15.17. Using the following MINITAB output of the best single model of each size in terms of $\overline{R}^2$, s, and C, determine which overall model seems best: **DS** OxHome2

```
                                              R
                                      S  O  B     B
                                      Q  O  E  A  A
                        Mallows       F  M  D  G  T
Vars  R-Sq  R-Sq(adj)    C-p      S   T  S  S  E  H
  1   63.3    62.7      18.9   21.382  X
  2   69.1    68.1       8.6   19.782  X     X
  3   70.9    69.4       6.9   19.372  X  X  X
  4   72.6    70.7       5.3   18.962  X  X  X  X
  5   73.2    70.8       6.0   18.917  X  X  X  X  X
```

15.56 THE QHIC CASE

Consider the QHIC data in Figure 14.21 (page 526). When we performed a regression analysis of these data by using the simple linear regression model, plots of the model's residuals versus x (home value) and $\hat{y}$ (predicted upkeep expenditure) both fanned out and had a "dip," or slightly curved appearance (see Figure 14.22, page 528). In order to remedy the indicated violations of the constant variance and correct functional form assumptions, we transformed the dependent variable by taking the square roots of the upkeep expenditures. An alternative approach consists of two steps. First, the slightly curved appearance of the residual plots implies that it is reasonable to add the squared term x^2 to the simple linear regression model. This gives the **quadratic regression model** $y = \beta_0 + \beta_1 x + \beta_2 x^2 + \varepsilon$. The upper residual plot in the MINITAB output that follows shows that a plot of the model's residuals versus x fans out, indicating a violation of the constant variance assumption.

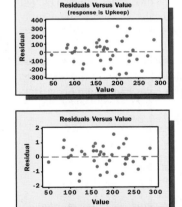

```
Predictor       Coef     SE Coef        T        P
Noconstant
1/Value        -53.50      83.20     -0.64    0.524
One             3.409       1.321     2.58    0.014
Value         0.011224   0.004627     2.43    0.020

Predicted Values for New Observations
                Fit         95% CI              95% PI
              5.635    (5.306, 5.964)    (3.994, 7.276)
```

$$\frac{\hat{y}}{220} = \frac{-53.50}{220} + 3.409 + .011224(220) = 5.635$$

To remedy this violation, we (in the second step) divide all terms in the quadratic model by x. This gives the transformed model

$$\frac{y}{x} = \beta_0 \left(\frac{1}{x}\right) + \beta_1 + \beta_2 x + \frac{\varepsilon}{x}$$

The lower residual plot in the MINITAB output is the residual plot versus x for this transformed model, and the MINITAB output of a regression analysis using the transformed model is given to the right of the residual plots.

a Does the residual plot indicate the constant variance assumption holds for the transformed model?

TABLE 15.19
Number of Bathrooms
DS OxHome2

Bath	Bath
1.0	2.0
1.0	1.5
1.0	1.0
1.0	1.5
1.0	2.0
1.5	1.5
1.5	1.0
2.0	1.5
2.0	1.5
2.5	2.0
1.0	2.5
1.0	2.0
2.0	2.5
1.5	1.0
2.0	1.0
1.5	1.0
1.0	2.0
1.5	2.5
1.0	2.0
1.5	2.0
2.5	1.0
2.0	2.0
1.0	1.0
2.5	1.5
2.0	1.5
2.0	1.0
1.0	2.0
2.0	1.0
1.0	2.0
2.5	2.0
2.0	2.0
1.0	

TABLE 15.20

Quarterly Sales of the TRK-50 Mountain Bike

DS BikeSales

t	Sales, y_t
1 (Winter)	10
2 (Spring)	31
3 (Summer)	43
4 (Fall)	16
5	11
6	33
7	45
8	17
9	13
10	34
11	48
12	19
13	15
14	37
15	51
16	21

b Consider a home worth \$220,000. We let μ_0 represent the mean yearly upkeep expenditure for all homes worth \$220,000, and we let y_0 represent the yearly upkeep expenditure for an individual home worth \$220,000. **(1)** The bottom of the MINITAB regression output on the previous page tells us that $\hat{y}/220 = 5.635$ is a point estimate of $\mu_0/220$ and a point prediction of $y_0/220$. Multiply this result by 220 to obtain $\hat{y}$. **(2)** Multiply the ends of the confidence interval and prediction interval shown on the MINITAB output by 220. This will give a 95 percent confidence interval for μ_0 and a 95 percent prediction interval for y_0. **(3)** Suppose that QHIC has decided to send a special, more expensive advertising brochure to any home whose value makes QHIC 95 percent confident that the mean upkeep expenditure for all homes having this value is at least \$1,000. Should QHIC send a special brochure to a home worth \$220,000?

15.57 BACKWARD ELIMINATION DS OxHome2

Backward elimination is an iterative model selection procedure that begins by considering the model that contains all of the potential independent variables and then attempts to remove independent variables one at a time from this model. On each step, an independent variable is removed from the model if it has the largest *p*-value of any independent variable remaining in the model and if its *p*-value is greater than α_{stay}, an α value for allowing a variable to stay in the model. Backward elimination terminates when all the *p*-values for the independent variables remaining in the model are less than α_{stay}. For example, Figure 15.38 shows the MINITAB output of a backward elimination for the residential sales data in Tables 15.17 and 15.19 on pages 616 and 619. Here, α_{stay} has been set equal to .05. Interpret the steps in the output and write out the model that is found by the backward elimination procedure.

15.58 TREND AND SEASONAL PATTERNS DS BikeSales

Time Series Plot of Bike Sales

Table 15.20 in the page margin presents quarterly sales of the TRK-50 mountain bike for the previous 16 quarters at a bicycle shop in Switzerland. The time series plot under the sales data shows that the bike sales exhibit an upward *linear trend* (that is, an upward straight line movement over time) and a strong *seasonal pattern*, with bike sales being higher in the spring and summer quarters than in the winter and fall quarters. If we let y_t denote the number of TRK-50 mountain bikes sold in time period t at the Swiss bike shop, then a regression model describing y_t is

$$y_t = \beta_0 + \beta_1 t + \beta_{Q2}Q_2 + \beta_{Q3}Q_3 + \beta_{Q4}Q_4 + \varepsilon_t$$

Here the expression $(\beta_0 + \beta_1 t)$ models the linear trend evident in the time series plot, and Q_2, Q_3, and Q_4 are dummy variables defined for quarters 2, 3, and 4. Specifically, Q_2 equals 1 if quarterly bike sales were observed in quarter 2 (spring) and 0 otherwise; Q_3 equals 1 if quarterly bike sales

---

FIGURE 15.38　MINITAB Output of the Residential Sales Data Backward Elimination

Step	1	2	3	4
Constant	2.27061	10.36762	-0.08788	10.31302
Sqfeet	0.0448	0.0500	0.0427	0.0530
T-Value	4.82	6.17	5.87	10.66
P-Value	0.000	0.000	0.000	0.000
Rooms	5.8	6.3	4.5	
T-Value	2.26	2.50	1.89	
P-Value	0.027	0.015	0.064	
Bdrms	-9.4	-11.1		
T-Value	-1.56	-1.89		
P-Value	0.124	0.063		
Age	-0.37	-0.43	-0.43	-0.36
T-Value	-3.01	-3.94	-3.87	-3.36
P-Value	0.004	0.000	0.000	0.001
Bathrms	7.7			
T-Value	1.13			
P-Value	0.264			
S	18.9	19.0	19.4	19.8
R-Sq	73.17	72.57	70.88	69.12
R-Sq(adj)	70.82	70.68	69.40	68.09
Mallows Cp	6.0	5.3	6.9	8.6

FIGURE 15.39　MINITAB Output of the Quarterly Bike Sales Regression Analysis

```
The regression equation is
BikeSales = 8.75 + 0.500 Time + 21.0 Q2
                 + 33.5 Q3 + 4.50 Q4

Predictor    Coef    SE Coef      T      P
Constant    8.7500    0.4281   20.44  0.000
Time        0.50000   0.03769  13.27  0.000
Q2         21.0000    0.4782   43.91  0.000
Q3         33.5000    0.4827   69.41  0.000
Q4          4.5000    0.4900    9.18  0.000


S = 0.674200    R-Sq = 99.8%

            R-Sq(adj) = 99.8%

Predicted Values for New Observations
New Obs    Fit   SE Fit      95%  PI
   1    17.250   0.506   (15.395, 19.105)
   2    38.750   0.506   (36.895, 40.605)
   3    51.750   0.506   (49.895, 53.605)
   4    23.250   0.506   (21.395, 25.105)
```

were observed in quarter 3 (summer) and 0 otherwise; Q_4 equals 1 if quarterly bike sales were observed in quarter 4 (fall) and 0 otherwise. Note that we have not defined a dummy variable for quarter 1 (winter). It follows that the regression parameters β_{Q2}, β_{Q3}, and β_{Q4} compare quarters 2, 3, and 4 with quarter 1. Intuitively, for example, β_{Q4} is the difference, excluding trend, between the level of the time series in quarter 4 (fall) and the level of the time series in quarter 1 (winter). A positive β_{Q4} would imply that, excluding trend, bike sales in the fall can be expected to be higher than bike sales in the winter. A negative β_{Q4} would imply that, excluding trend, bike sales in the fall can be expected to be lower than bike sales in the winter.

Figure 15.39 gives the MINITAB output of a regression analysis of the quarterly bike sales by using the dummy variable model. **(1)** Interpret the least squares point estimates $b_{Q2} = 21$, $b_{Q3} = 33.5$, and $b_{Q4} = 4.5$ of β_{Q2}, β_{Q3}, and β_{Q4}. **(2)** Also note that at the bottom of the MINITAB output there are point predictions of and 95 percent prediction intervals for y_{17}, y_{18}, y_{19}, and y_{20}, bike sales in periods 17, 18, 19, and 20 (quarters 1, 2, 3 and 4 of next year). Hand calculate these point predictions.

Appendix 15.1 ■ Multiple Regression Analysis Using Excel

Multiple regression in Figure 15.5(a) on page 562 (data file: GasCon2.xlsx):

- Enter the gas consumption data from Table 15.3 (page 561)—temperatures (with label Temp) in column A, chill indexes (with label Chill) in column B, and gas consumptions (with label FuelCons) in column C.

- Select **Data : Data Analysis : Regression** and click OK in the Data Analysis dialog box.

- In the Regression dialog box:
  Enter C1 : C9 into the "Input Y Range" window.
  Enter A1 : B9 into the "Input X Range" window.

- Place a checkmark in the Labels checkbox.

- Be sure that the "Constant is Zero" checkbox is NOT checked.

- Select the "New Worksheet Ply" Output option.

- Click OK in the Regression dialog box to obtain the regression output in a new worksheet.

Note: The independent variables must be in adjacent columns because the "Input X Range" must span the range of the values for all of the independent variables.

To compute a point prediction for natural gas consumption when temperature is 40°F and the chill index is 10:

- The Excel Analysis ToolPak does not provide an option for computing point or interval predictions. A point prediction can be computed from the regression results using Excel cell formulas as follows.

- The estimated regression coefficients and their labels are in cells A17:B19 of the output worksheet and the predictor values 40 and 10 have been placed in cells G3 and G4.

- In cell G5, enter the Excel formula
  = B17+B18*G3+B19*G4
  to compute the point prediction (=10.3331).

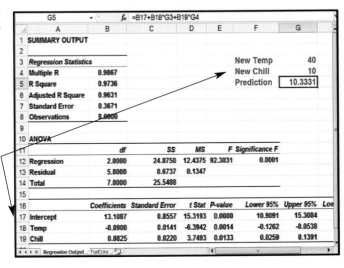

Sales volume multiple regression with indicator (dummy) variables in Figure 15.15(b) on page 584 (data file: Electronics2.xlsx):

- Enter the sales volume data from Table 15.9 (page 583)—sales volumes (with label Sales) in column A, store locations (with label Location) in column B, and number of households (with label Households) in column C. (The order of the columns is chosen to arrange for an adjacent block of predictor variables.)

- Enter the labels DM and DD in cells D1 and E1.

- Following the definition of the dummy variables DM and DD in Example 15.6 (pages 581 and 582), enter the appropriate values of 0 and 1 for these two variables into columns D and E.

- Select **Data : Data Analysis : Regression** and click OK in the Data Analysis dialog box.

- In the Regression dialog box:

  Enter A1:A16 into the "Input Y Range" window. Enter C1:E16 into the "Input X Range" window.

- Place a checkmark in the Labels checkbox.

- Select the "New Worksheet Ply" Output option.

- Click OK in the Regression dialog box to obtain the regression results in a new worksheet.

Gasoline additive multiple linear regression with a quadratic term similar to Figure 15.23 on page 593 (data file: GasAdd.xlsx):

- Enter the gas mileage data from Table 15.13 (page 593)—mileages (with label Mileage) in column A and units of additive (with label Units) in column B. (Units are listed second in order to be adjacent to the squared units predictor.)

- Enter UnitsSq into cell C1.

- Click on cell C2, and enter the formula =B2*B2. Press "Enter" to compute the squared value of Units for the first observation.

- Copy the cell formula of C2 through cell C16 (by double-clicking the drag handle in the lower right corner of cell C2) to compute the squared units for the remaining observations.

- Select **Data : Data Analysis : Regression** and click OK in the Data Analysis dialog box.

- In the Regression dialog box:

  Enter A1:A16 into the "Input Y Range" window.
  Enter B1:C16 into the "Input X Range" window.

- Place a checkmark in the Labels checkbox.

- Select the "New Worksheet Ply" Output option.

- Click OK in the Regression dialog box to obtain the regression output in a new worksheet.

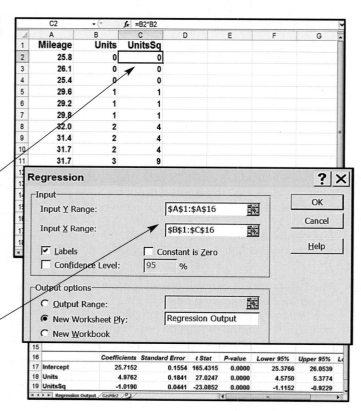

Appendix 15.2 ■ Multiple Regression Analysis Using MegaStat

Multiple regression similar to Figure 15.5 on page 562 (data file: GasCon2.xlsx):

- Enter the gas consumption data in Table 15.3 (page 561) as shown—temperature (with label Temp) in column A, chill index (with label Chill) in column B, and gas consumption (with label FuelCons) in column C. Note that Temp and Chill are contiguous columns (that is, they are next to each other). This is not necessary, but it makes selection of the independent variables (as described below) easiest.

- Select **Add-Ins : MegaStat : Correlation/ Regression : Regression Analysis**

- In the Regression Analysis dialog box, click in the Independent Variables window and use the AutoExpand feature to enter the range A1:B9. Note that if the independent variables are not next to each other, hold the CTRL key down while making selections and then autoexpand.

- Click in the Dependent Variable window and enter the range C1:C9.

- Check the appropriate Options and Residuals checkboxes as follows:

    1 Check "Test Intercept" to include a *y*-intercept and to test its significance.

    2 Check "Output Residuals" to obtain a list of the model residuals.

    3 Check "Plot Residuals by Observation" and "Plot Residuals by Predicted Y and X" to obtain residual plots versus time, versus the predicted values of *y*, and versus the values of each independent variable (see Section 15.11).

    4 Check "Normal Probability Plot of Residuals" to obtain a normal plot (see Section 14.9).

    5 Check "Diagnostics and Influential Residuals" to obtain diagnostics (see Section 15.11).

    6 Check "Durbin-Watson" to obtain the Durbin–Watson statistic (see Section 14.9) and check "Variance Inflation Factors" (see Section 15.10).

To obtain a **point prediction** of *y* when temperature equals 40 and chill index equals 10 (as well as a confidence interval and prediction interval):

- Click on the drop-down menu above the Predictor Values window and select "Type in predictor values."

- Type 40 and 10 (separated by at least one blank space) into the Predictor Values window.

(Continues across page)

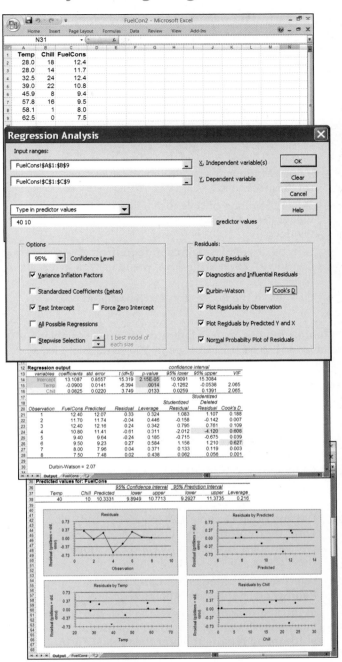

- Select a desired level of confidence (here 95%) from the Confidence Level drop-down menu or type in a value.

- Click OK in the Regression Analysis dialog box.

Predictions can also be obtained by placing the values of the predictor variables into spreadsheet cells. For example, suppose that we wish to compute predictions of *y* for each of the following three temperature—chill index combinations: 50 and 15; 55 and 20; 30 and 12. To do this:

- Enter the values for which predictions are desired in spreadsheet cells as illustrated in the screenshot—here temperatures are entered in column F and chill indexes are entered in column G. However, the values could be entered in any contiguous columns.

- In the drop-down menu above the Predictor Values window, select "Predictor values from spreadsheet cells."

- Select the range of cells containing the Predictor Values (here F1:G3) into the predictor values window.

- Select a desired level of confidence from the Confidence Level drop-down menu or type in a value.

- Click OK in the Regression Analysis dialog box.

Multiple regression with indicator (dummy) variables similar to Figure 15.15 on page 584 (data file: Electronics2.xlsx):

- Enter the sales volume data from Table 15.9 (page 583)—sales volume (with label Sales) in column A, store location (with label Location) in column B, and number of households (with label Households) in column C. Again note that the order of the variables is chosen to allow for a contiguous block of predictor variables.

- Enter the labels DM and DD into cells D1 and E1.

- Following the definitions of the dummy variables DM and DD in Example 15.6 (pages 581 and 582), enter the appropriate values of 0 and 1 for these two variables into columns D and E as shown in the screen.

- Select **Add-Ins : MegaStat : Correlation/ Regression : Regression Analysis.**

- In the Regression Analysis dialog box, click in the Independent Variables window and use the autoexpand feature to enter the range C1:E16.

- Click in the Dependent Variable window and enter the range A1:A16.

To compute a prediction of sales volume for 200,000 households and a mall location:

- Select "Type in predictor values" from the drop-down menu above the Predictor Values window.

- Type 200 1 0 into the Predictor Values window.

- Select or type a desired level of confidence (here 95%) in the Confidence Level box.

- Click the Options and Residuals checkboxes as shown (or as desired).

- Click OK in the Regression Analysis dialog box.

Multiple linear regression with a quadratic term similar to Figure 15.23 on page 593 (data file: GasAdd.xlsx):

- Enter the gasoline additive data from Table 15.13 (page 593)—mileages (with label Mileage) in column A and units of additive (with label Units) in column B.

- Enter the label UnitsSq in cell C1.

- Click on cell C2 and type the cell formula =B2*B2. Press enter to compute the squared value of Units for the first observation.

- Copy the cell formula of C2 through cell C16 (by double-clicking the drag handle in the lower right corner of cell C2) to compute the squared units for the remaining observations.

- Select **Add-Ins : MegaStat : Correlation/ Regression : Regression Analysis.**

- In the Regression Analysis dialog box, click in the Independent Variables window and use the AutoExpand feature to enter the range B1:C16.

- Click in the Dependent Variable window and enter the range A1:A16.

To compute a prediction for mileage when Units equals 2.44:

- Select "Type in predictor values" from the drop-down menu above the Predictor Values window.

- Type 2.44 5.9536 in the Predictor Values window. Note that (2.44)**2=5.9536 must first be hand calculated.

- Select or type the desired level of confidence (here 95%) in the Confidence Level box.

- Check the Options and Residuals checkboxes as desired.

- Click OK in the Regression Analysis dialog box.

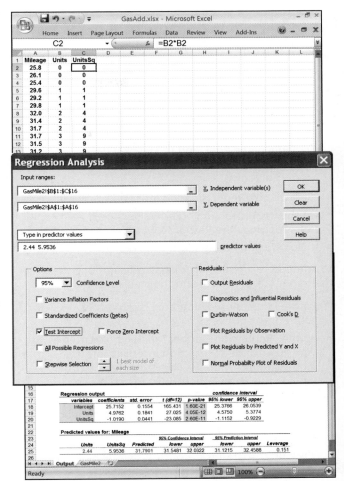

Stepwise selection similar to Figure 15.27 on page 601 (data file: SalePerf2.xlsx):

- Enter the sales performance data in Figure 15.10 (page 579) and Table 15.14 (page 598) into columns A through I with labels as shown in the screen.

- Select **Add-Ins : MegaStat : Correlation/ Regression : Regression Analysis.**

- In the Regression Analysis dialog box, click in the Independent Variables window and use the AutoExpand feature to enter the range B1:I26.

- Click in the Dependent Variable window and use the AutoExpand feature to enter the range A1:A26.

- Check the "Stepwise Selection" checkbox.

- Click OK in the Regression Analysis dialog box.

Stepwise selection will give the best model of each size (1, 2, 3, etc. independent variables). The default gives one model of each size. For more models, use the arrow buttons to request the desired number of models of each size.

- Check the "All Possible Regressions" checkbox to obtain the results for all possible regressions. This option will handle up to 12 independent variables.

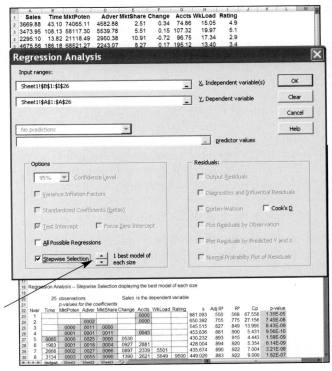

Appendix 15.3 ■ Multiple Regression Analysis Using MINITAB

Multiple regression in Figure 15.5(b) on page 562 (data file: GasCon2.MTW):

- In the Data window, enter the gas consumption data from Table 15.3 (page 561)—the average hourly temperatures in column C1 with variable name Temp, the chill indexes in column C2 with variable name Chill, and the weekly gas consumptions in column C3 with variable name FuelCons.

- Select **Stat : Regression : Regression.**

- In the Regression dialog box, select FuelCons into the Response window.

- Select Temp and Chill into the Predictors window.

To compute a prediction for gas consumption when the temperature is 40° F and the chill index is 10:

- In the Regression dialog box, click on the Options . . . button.

- In the "Regression Options" dialog box, enter 40 and 10 into the "Prediction intervals for new observations" window. (The number and order of values in this window must match the Predictors list in the Regression dialog box.)

- Click OK in the Regression—Options dialog box.

To obtain residual plots:

- Click on the Graphs . . . button, select the desired plots (see Appendix 14.3), and click OK in the Regression—Graphs dialog box.

To obtain variance inflation factors (VIF):

- Place a checkmark in the Variance inflation factors checkbox in the Regression—Options dialog box.

To obtain outlying and influential observation diagnostics:

- Click the Storage button, and in the Regression—Storage dialog box, place checkmarks in the following checkboxes: Fits (for predicted values), Residuals, Standardized residuals (for studentized residuals), Deleted *t* residuals (for studentized deleted residuals), Hi (for leverages), and Cook's distance. Click OK in the Regression—Storage dialog box.

- Click OK in the Regression dialog box.

Multiple regression with indicator (dummy) variables in Figure 15.15(a) on page 584 (data file: Electronics2. MTW):

- In the Data window, enter the sales volume data from Table 15.9 on page 583 with sales volume in column C1, location in column C2, and number of households in column C3 with variable names Sales, Location, and Households.

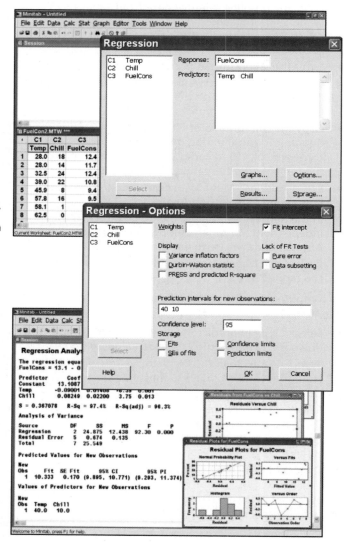

To create indicator/dummy variable predictors:

- Select **Calc : Make Indicator Variables.**
- In the "Make Indicator Variables" dialog box, enter Location into the "Indicator variables for" window.
- The "Store indicator variables in columns" window lists the distinct values of Location in alphabetical order. Corresponding to each distinct value, enter the variable name to be used for that value's indicator variable—here we have used the names DDowntown, DMall, and DStreet (or you can use default names that are supplied by MINITAB if you wish). The first indicator variable (DDowntown) will have 1's in all rows where the Location equals Downtown and 0's elsewhere. The second indicator variable (DMall) will have 1's in all rows where Location equals Mall and 0's elsewhere. The third indicator variable (DStreet) will have 1's in all rows where Location equals Street and 0's elsewhere.
- Click OK in the "Make Indicator Variables" dialog box to create the indicator variables in the Data window.

To fit the multiple regression model:

- Select **Stat : Regression : Regression.**
- In the Regression dialog box, select Sales into the Response window.
- Select Households DMall DDowntown into the Predictors window.

To compute a prediction of sales volume for 200,000 households and a mall location:

- Click on the Options . . . button.
- In the "Regression—Options" dialog box, type 200 1 0 into the "Prediction intervals for new observations" window.
- Click OK in the "Regression—Options" dialog box.
- Click OK in the Regression dialog box.

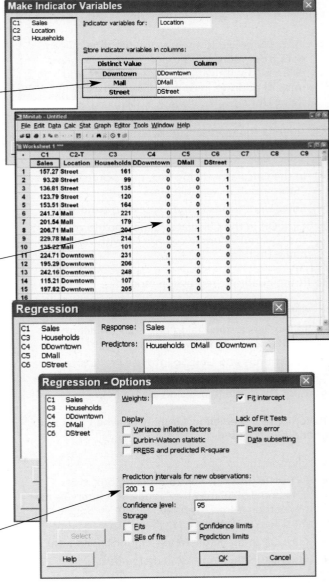

Correlation matrix in Figure 15.26(a) on page 598 (data file: SalePerf2.MTW):

- In the Data window, enter the sales representative performance data from Figure 15.10 (page 579) and Table 15.14 (page 598) into columns C1–C9 with variable names Sales, Time, MktPoten, Adver, MktShare, Change, Accts, WkLoad, and Rating.
- Select **Stat : Basic Statistics : Correlation.**
- In the Correlation dialog box, enter all variable names into the Variables window.
- If *p*-values are desired, make sure that the "Display *p*-values" checkbox is checked.
- Click OK in the Correlation dialog box.

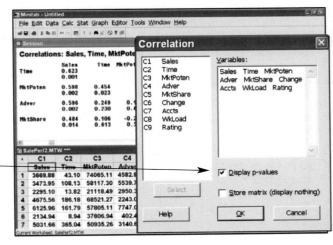

Multiple linear regression with a quadratic term in Figure 15.23 on page 593 (data file: GasAdd.MTW):

- In the Data window, enter the gasoline mileage data from Table 15.13 (page 593)—mileages in column C1 with variable name Mileage and units of additive in column C2 with variable name Units.

To compute the **quadratic predictor**, UnitsSq:

- Select **Calc : Calculator.**
- In the Calculator dialog box, enter UnitsSq in the "Store result in variable" box.
- Enter Units*Units in the Expression window.
- Click OK in the Calculator dialog box to obtain the squared values in column C3 with variable name UnitsSq.

To fit the quadratic regression model:

- Select **Stat : Regression : Regression.**
- In the Regression dialog box, select Mileage into the Response window.
- Select Units and UnitsSq into the Predictors window.
- Click OK in the Regression dialog box.

To compute a **prediction** for mileage when 2.44 units of additive are used:

- Click on the Options . . . button.
- In the Regression—Options dialog box, type 2.44 and 5.9536 into the "Prediction intervals for new observations" window. [$(2.44)^2 = 5.9536$ must first be calculated by hand.]
- Click OK in the Regression—Options dialog box.
- Click OK in the Regression dialog box.

Logistic regression in Figure 15.36 on page 613 (data file: PerfTest.MTW):

- In the data window, enter the performance data in Table 15.16 on page 612—Group (either 1 or 0) in column C1 with variable name Group, the score on test 1 in column C2 with variable name Test1, and the score on test 2 in column C3 with variable name Test2.
- Select **Stat : Regression : Binary Logistic Regression.**
- In the "Binary Logistic Regression" dialog box, enter Group into the Response window.
- Enter Test1 and Test2 into the model window.
- Click OK in the "Binary Logistic Regression" dialog box.

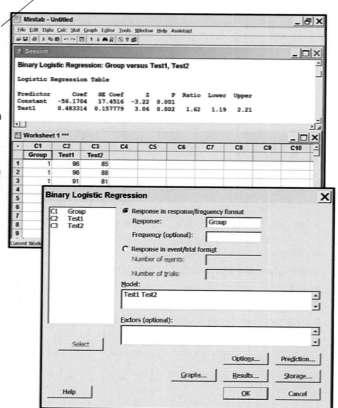

Best subsets regression in Figure 15.27 on page 601 (data file: SalePerf2.MTW):

- In the Data window, enter the sales territory performance data from Figure 15.10 (page 579) and Table 15.14 (page 598) into columns C1–C9 with variable names Sales, Time, MktPoten, Adver, MktShare, Change, Accts, WkLoad, and Rating.

- Select **Stat : Regression : Best Subsets.**

- In the Best Subsets Regression dialog box, enter Sales into the Response window.

- Enter the remaining variable names into the "Free predictors" window.

- Click on the Options . . . button.

- In the "Best Subsets Regression—Options" dialog box, enter 2 in the "Models of each size to print" window.

- Click OK in the "Best Subsets Regression—Options" dialog box.

- Click OK in the Best Subsets Regression dialog box.

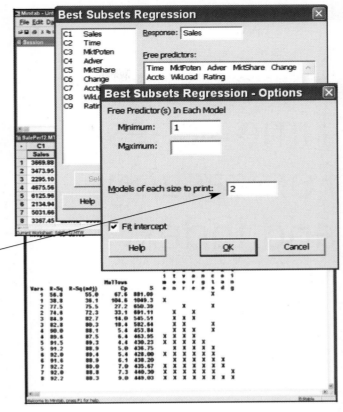

Stepwise regression in Figure 15.28 on page 603 (data file: SalePerf2.MTW):

- In the Data window, enter the sales territory performance data from Figure 15.10 (page 579) and Table 15.14 (page 598) into columns C1–C9 with variable names Sales, Time, MktPoten, Adver, MktShare, Change, Accts, WkLoad, and Rating.

- Select **Stat : Regression : Stepwise.**

- In the Stepwise Regression dialog box, enter Sales into the Response window.

- Enter the remaining variable names into the Predictors window.

- Click on the Methods . . . button.

- In the Stepwise—Methods dialog box, select the "Use alpha values" option.

- Select the "Stepwise (Forward and Backward)" option.

- Enter 0.10 in the "Alpha to enter" and "Alpha to remove" boxes.

- Click OK in the Stepwise—Methods dialog box.

- Click OK in the Stepwise Regression dialog box.

- The results of the stepwise regression are given in the Session window.

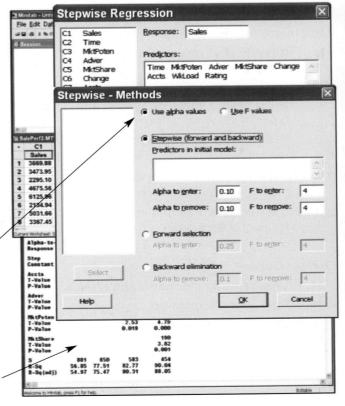

CHAPTER 16

Time Series Forecasting and Index Numbers

Learning Objectives

After mastering the material in this chapter, you will be able to:

LO16-1 Identify the components of a time series.

LO16-2 Use time series regression to forecast time series having linear, quadratic, and certain types of seasonal patterns.

LO16-3 Use data transformations to forecast time series having increasing seasonal variation.

LO16-4 Use multiplicative decomposition and moving averages to forecast a time series.

LO16-5 Use simple exponential smoothing to forecast a time series.

LO16-6 Use double exponential smoothing to forecast a time series.

LO16-7 Use multiplicative Winters' method to forecast a time series.

LO16-8 Appreciate some of the basic concepts of Box–Jenkins forecasting models.

LO16-9 Compare time series models by using forecast errors.

L16-10 Use index numbers to compare economic data over time.

Chapter Outline

Note: After completing Section 16.2, the reader may study Sections 16.3, 16.4, 16.6, 16.7, and 16.8 in any order without loss of continuity. Section 16.5 requires background from Sections 16.1, 16.2, and 16.4. Section 16.8 may be covered at any time.

A **time series** is a set of observations on a variable of interest that has been collected in **time order.** In this chapter we discuss developing and using **univariate time series models,** which forecast future values of a time series **solely on the basis of past values of the time series.** Often univariate time series models forecast future time series values by extrapolating the **trend** and/or **seasonal patterns** exhibited by the past values of the time series. To illustrate these ideas, we consider several cases in this chapter, including:

The Calculator Sales Case: By extrapolating an upward trend in past sales of the Bismark X-12 electronic calculator, Smith's Department Stores, Inc., forecasts future sales of this calculator. The forecasts help the department store chain to better implement its inventory and financial policies.

The Traveler's Rest Case: By extrapolating an upward trend and the seasonal behavior of its past hotel room occupancies, Traveler's Rest, Inc., forecasts future hotel room occupancies. The forecasts help the hotel chain to more effectively hire help and acquire supplies.

16.1 Time Series Components and Models ● ● ●

LO16-1 Identify the components of a time series.

In order to identify patterns in time series data, it is often convenient to think of such data as consisting of several components: **trend, cycle, seasonal variations,** and **irregular fluctuations. Trend** refers to the upward or downward movement that characterizes a time series over time. Thus trend reflects the long-run growth or decline in the time series. Trend movements can represent a variety of factors. For example, long-run movements in the sales of a particular industry might be determined by changes in consumer tastes, increases in total population, and increases in per capita income. **Cycle** refers to recurring up-and-down movements around trend levels. These fluctuations can last from 2 to 10 years or even longer measured from peak to peak or trough to trough. One of the common cyclical fluctuations found in time series data is the *business cycle,* which is represented by fluctuations in the time series caused by recurrent periods of prosperity and recession. **Seasonal variations** are periodic patterns in a time series that complete themselves within a calendar year or less and then are repeated on a regular basis. Often seasonal variations occur yearly. For example, soft drink sales and hotel room occupancies are annually higher in the summer months, while department store sales are annually higher during the winter holiday season. Seasonal variations can also last less than one year. For example, daily restaurant patronage might exhibit within-week seasonal variation, with daily patronage higher on Fridays and Saturdays. **Irregular fluctuations** are erratic time series movements that follow no recognizable or regular pattern. Such movements represent what is "left over" in a time series after trend, cycle, and seasonal variations have been accounted for.

Time series that exhibit trend, seasonal, and cyclical components are illustrated in Figure 16.1. In Figure 16.1(a) a time series of sales observations that has an essentially straight-line or linear trend is plotted. Figure 16.1(b) portrays a time series of sales observations that contains a

FIGURE 16.1   Time Series Exhibiting Trend, Seasonal, and Cyclical Components

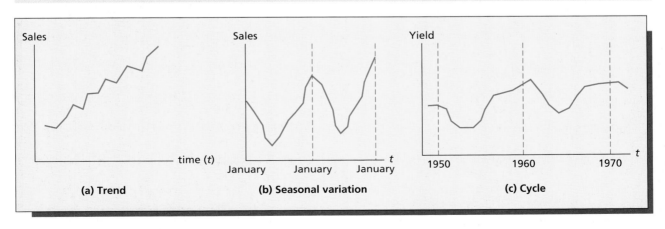

(a) Trend   (b) Seasonal variation   (c) Cycle seasonal pattern that repeats annually. Figure 16.1(c) exhibits a time series of agricultural yields that is cyclical, repeating a cycle about once every 10 years.

Time series models attempt to identify significant patterns in the components of a time series. Then, assuming that these patterns will continue into the future, time series models extrapolate these patterns to forecast future time series values. In Section 16.2 we discuss forecasting by **time series regression models,** and in Section 16.3 we discuss forecasting by using an intuitive method called **multiplicative decomposition.** Both of these approaches assume that the time series components remain essentially constant over time. If the time series components might be changing slowly over time, it is appropriate to forecast by using **exponential smoothing.** This approach is discussed in Sections 16.4 and 16.5. If the time series components might be changing fairly quickly over time, it is appropriate to forecast by using the **Box–Jenkins methodology.** This more advanced approach is discussed in (Optional) Section 16.6.

LO16-2 Use time series regression to forecast time series having linear, quadratic, and certain types of seasonal patterns.

16.2 Time Series Regression ●●●

Modeling trend components   We begin this section with two examples.

EXAMPLE 16.1 The Cod Catch Case: No Trend Regression

TABLE 16.1

Cod Catch (in Tons)

CodCatch

Month	Year 1	Year 2
Jan.	362	276
Feb.	381	334
Mar.	317	394
Apr.	297	334
May	399	384
June	402	314
July	375	344
Aug.	349	337
Sept.	386	345
Oct.	328	362
Nov.	389	314
Dec.	343	365

The Bay City Seafood Company owns a fleet of fishing trawlers and operates a fish processing plant. In order to forecast its minimum and maximum possible revenues from cod sales and plan the operations of its fish processing plant, the company desires to make both point forecasts and prediction interval forecasts of its monthly cod catch (measured in tons). The company has recorded monthly cod catch for the previous two years (years 1 and 2). The cod history is given in Table 16.1. A time series plot shows that the cod catches appear to randomly fluctuate around a constant average level. (See the plot in Figure 16.2.) Because the company subjectively believes that this data pattern will continue in the future, it seems reasonable to use the **"no trend"** regression model

$$y_t = \beta_0 + \varepsilon_t$$

to forecast cod catch in future months. It can be shown that for the no trend regression model the least squares point estimate b_0 of β_0 is $\bar{y}$, the average of the n observed time series values. Because the average $\bar{y}$ of the $n = 24$ observed cod catches is 351.29, it follows that $\hat{y}_t = b_0 = 351.29$ is the point prediction of the cod catch (y_t) in any future month. Furthermore, it can be shown that a $100(1 - \alpha)$ percent prediction interval for any future y_t value described by the no trend model is $[\hat{y}_t \pm t_{\alpha/2} s\sqrt{1 + (1/n)}]$. Here s is the sample standard deviation of the n observed time series values, and $t_{\alpha/2}$ is based on $n - 1$ degrees of freedom. For example, because s can be calculated to be

FIGURE 16.2   **Plot of Cod Catch versus Time**

FIGURE 16.3   **Plot of Calculator Sales versus Time**

33.82 for the $n = 24$ cod catches, and because $t_{.025}$ based on $n - 1 = 23$ degrees of freedom is 2.069, it follows that a 95 percent prediction interval for the cod catch in any future month is $[351.29 \pm 2.069(33.82)\sqrt{1 + (1/24)}]$, or $[279.92, 422.66]$.

EXAMPLE 16.2 The Calculator Sales Case: Inventory Policy

For the last two years Smith's Department Stores, Inc., has carried a new type of electronic calculator called the Bismark X-12. Sales of this calculator have generally increased over these two years. Smith's inventory policy attempts to ensure that stores will have enough Bismark X-12 calculators to meet practically all demand for the Bismark X-12, while at the same time ensuring that Smith's does not needlessly tie up its money by ordering many more calculators than can be sold. In order to implement this inventory policy in future months, Smith's requires both point predictions and prediction intervals for total monthly Bismark X-12 demand.

The monthly calculator demand data for the last two years are given in Table 16.2. A time series plot of the demand data is shown in Figure 16.3. The demands appear to randomly fluctuate around an average level that increases over time in a linear fashion. Furthermore, Smith's believes that this trend will continue for at least the next year. Thus it is reasonable to use the **"linear trend"** regression model

$$y_t = \beta_0 + \beta_1 t + \varepsilon_t$$

to forecast calculator sales in future months. Notice that this model is just a simple linear regression model where the time period t plays the role of the independent variable. The least squares point estimates of β_0 and β_1 can be calculated to be $b_0 = 198.0290$ and $b_1 = 8.0743$. [see Figure 16.4(a).] Therefore, for example, point forecasts of Bismark X-12 demand in January and February of year 3 (time periods 25 and 26) are, respectively,

$$\hat{y}_{25} = 198.0290 + 8.0743(25) = 399.9 \quad \text{and}$$

$$\hat{y}_{26} = 198.0290 + 8.0743(26) = 408.0$$

Note that Figure 16.4(b) gives these point forecasts. In addition, it can be shown using either the formulas for simple linear regression or a computer software package [see Figure 16.4(c)] that a 95 percent prediction interval for demand in time period 25 is $[328.6, 471.2]$ and that a 95 percent prediction interval for demand in time period 26 is $[336.0, 479.9]$. These prediction intervals can help Smith's implement its inventory policy. For instance, if Smith's stocks 471 Bismark X-12 calculators in January of year 3, we can be reasonably sure that monthly demand will be met.

TABLE 16.2
Calculator Sales
Data DS CalcSale

Month	Year 1	Year 2
Jan.	197	296
Feb.	211	276
Mar.	203	305
Apr.	247	308
May	239	356
June	269	393
July	308	363
Aug.	262	386
Sept.	258	443
Oct.	256	308
Nov.	261	358
Dec.	288	384

FIGURE 16.4   Excel Analysis of the Calculator Sales Data Using the Linear Trend Regression Model

(a) The Excel Output

ANOVA

	df	SS	MS	F	Significance F
Regression	1	74974.3567	74974.3567	74.7481	1.5893E-08
Residual	22	22066.6016	1003.0273		
Total	33	97040.9583			

	Coefficients	Standard Error	t Stat	P-value	Lower 95%	Upper 95%
Intercept	198.0290	13.3444	14.8398	6.0955E-13	170.3543	225.7036
T	8.0743	8.9339	8.6457	1.5893E-08	6.1375	10.0112

(b) Prediction using Excel

	A	B	C	D
24	358	23		
25	384	24		
26	399.8877	25	USING TREND	
27	407.962	26		

(c) Prediction using an Excel add-in (MegaStat)

Predicted values for: Sales

		95% Confidence Intervals		95% Prediction Intervals	
t	Predicted	lower	upper	lower	upper
25	399.9	372.2	427.6	328.6	471.2
26	408.0	378.6	437.3	336.0	479.9

Example 16.1 illustrates that the intercept β_0 can be used to model a lack of trend over time, and Example 16.2 illustrates that the expression $(\beta_0 + \beta_1 t)$ can model a linear trend over time. In addition, as will be illustrated in Exercise 16.42, the expression $(\beta_0 + \beta_1 t + \beta_2 t^2)$ can model a quadratic trend over time.

Modeling seasonal components We next consider how to forecast time series described by trend and seasonal components.

EXAMPLE 16.3 The Bike Sales Case: Inventory Policy

Table 16.3 presents quarterly sales of the TRK-50 mountain bike for the previous four years at a bicycle shop in Switzerland. The time series plot in Figure 16.5 shows that the bike sales exhibit a linear trend and a strong seasonal pattern, with bike sales being higher in the spring and summer quarters than in the winter and fall quarters. If we let y_t denote the number of TRK-50 mountain bikes sold in time period t at the Swiss bike shop, then a regression model describing y_t is

$$y_t = \beta_0 + \beta_1 t + \beta_{Q2}Q_2 + \beta_{Q3}Q_3 + \beta_{Q4}Q_4 + \varepsilon_t$$

Here the expression $(\beta_0 + \beta_1 t)$ models the linear trend evident in Figure 16.5. Q_2, Q_3, and Q_4 are dummy variables defined for quarters 2, 3, and 4. Specifically, Q_2 equals 1 if quarterly bike sales were observed in quarter 2 (spring) and 0 otherwise; Q_3 equals 1 if quarterly bike sales were observed in quarter 3 (summer) and 0 otherwise; Q_4 equals 1 if quarterly bike sales were observed in quarter 4 (fall) and 0 otherwise. Note that we have not defined a dummy variable for quarter 1 (winter). It follows that the regression parameters β_{Q2}, β_{Q3}, and β_{Q4} compare quarters 2, 3, and 4 with quarter 1. Intuitively, for example, β_{Q4} is the difference, excluding trend, between the level of the time series (y_t) in quarter 4 (fall) and the level of the time series in quarter 1 (winter). A positive β_{Q4} would imply that, excluding trend, bike sales in the fall can be expected to be higher than bike sales in the winter. A negative β_{Q4} would imply that, excluding trend, bike sales in the fall can be expected to be lower than bike sales in the winter.

Figure 16.6 gives the MINITAB output of a regression analysis of the quarterly bike sales by using the dummy variable model. The MINITAB output tells us that the linear trend and the seasonal dummy variables are significant (every t statistic has a related p-value less than .01). Also, notice that the least squares point estimates of β_{Q2}, β_{Q3}, and β_{Q4} are, respectively, $b_{Q2} = 21$, $b_{Q3} = 33.5$, and $b_{Q4} = 4.5$. It follows that, excluding trend, expected bike sales in quarter 2 (spring), quarter 3 (summer), and quarter 4 (fall) are estimated to be, respectively, 21, 33.5, and 4.5 bikes greater than expected bike sales in quarter 1 (winter). Furthermore, using all of the least squares point estimates in Figure 16.6, we can compute point forecasts of bike sales in quarters

TABLE 16.3	Quarterly Sales of the TRK-50 Mountain Bike BikeSales		
Year	Quarter	t	Sales, y_t
1	1 (Winter)	1	10
	2 (Spring)	2	31
	3 (Summer)	3	43
	4 (Fall)	4	16
2	1	5	11
	2	6	33
	3	7	45
	4	8	17
3	1	9	13
	2	10	34
	3	11	48
	4	12	19
4	1	13	15
	2	14	37
	3	15	51
	4	16	21

FIGURE 16.5 Time Series Plot of TRK-50 Bike Sales

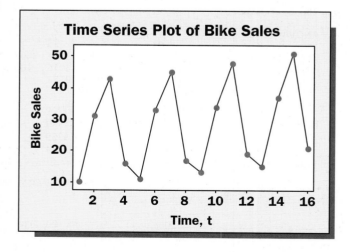

FIGURE 16.6   **MINITAB Output of an Analysis of the Quarterly Bike Sales by Using Dummy Variable Regression**

```
The regression equation is
BikeSales = 8.75 + 0.500 Time + 21.0 Q2 + 33.5 Q3 + 4.50 Q4


Predictor        Coef   SE Coef       T       P
Constant       8.7500    0.4281   20.44   0.000
Time          0.50000   0.03769   13.27   0.000
Q2            21.0000    0.4782   43.91   0.000
Q3            33.5000    0.4827   69.41   0.000
Q4             4.5000    0.4900    9.18   0.000


S = 0.674200   R-Sq = 99.8%   R-Sq(adj) = 99.8%


Values of Predictors for New Obs    Predicted Values for New Observations
New Obs   Time    Q2    Q3    Q4    New Obs     Fit   SE Fit        95% CI              95% PI
      1   17.0     0     0     0          1   17.250   0.506   (16.137, 18.363)   (15.395, 19.105)
      2   18.0     1     0     0          2   38.750   0.506   (37.637, 39.863)   (36.895, 40.605)
      3   19.0     0     1     0          3   51.750   0.506   (50.637, 52.863)   (49.895, 53.605)
      4   20.0     0     0     1          4   23.250   0.506   (22.137, 24.363)   (21.395, 25.105)
```

1 through 4 of next year (periods 17 through 20) as follows:

$$\hat{y}_{17} = b_0 + b_1(17) + b_{Q2}(0) + b_{Q3}(0) + b_{Q4}(0) = 8.75 + .5(17) = 17.250$$

$$\hat{y}_{18} = b_0 + b_1(18) + b_{Q2}(1) + b_{Q3}(0) + b_{Q4}(0) = 8.75 + .5(18) + 21 = 38.750$$

$$\hat{y}_{19} = b_0 + b_1(19) + b_{Q2}(0) + b_{Q3}(1) + b_{Q4}(0) = 8.75 + .5(19) + 33.5 = 51.750$$

$$\hat{y}_{20} = b_0 + b_1(20) + b_{Q2}(0) + b_{Q3}(0) + b_{Q4}(1) = 8.75 + .5(20) + 4.5 = 23.250$$

These point forecasts are given at the bottom of the MINITAB output, as are 95 percent prediction intervals for y_{17}, y_{18}, y_{19}, and y_{20}. The upper limits of these prediction intervals suggest that the bicycle shop can be reasonably sure that it will meet demand for the TRK-50 mountain bike if the numbers of bikes it stocks in quarters 1 through 4 are, respectively, 19, 41, 54, and 25 bikes.

EXAMPLE 16.4 The Traveler's Rest Case: Predicting Hotel Room Occupancy

Table 16.4 presents a time series of hotel room occupancies observed by Traveler's Rest, Inc., a corporation that operates four hotels in a midwestern city. The analysts in the operating division of the corporation were asked to develop a model that could be used to obtain short-term forecasts (up to one year) of the number of occupied rooms in the hotels. These forecasts were needed by various personnel to assist in hiring additional help during the summer months, ordering materials that have long delivery lead times, budgeting of local advertising expenditures, and so on. The available historical data consisted of the number of occupied rooms during each day for the previous 14 years. Because it was desired to obtain monthly forecasts, these data were reduced to monthly averages by dividing each monthly total by the number of days in the month. The monthly room averages for the previous 14 years are the time series values given in Table 16.4. A time series plot of these values in Figure 16.7(a) shows that the monthly room averages follow a strong trend and have a seasonal pattern with one major and several minor peaks during the year. Note that the major peak each year occurs during the high summer travel months of June, July, and August.

Although the quarterly bike sales and monthly hotel room averages both exhibit seasonal variation, they exhibit different kinds of seasonal variation. The quarterly bike sales plotted in Figure 16.5 exhibit *constant seasonal variation*. In general, **constant seasonal variation** is seasonal variation where the magnitude of the seasonal swing does not depend on the level of the time series. On the other hand, **increasing seasonal variation** is seasonal variation where the magnitude of the seasonal swing increases as the level of the time series increases. Figure 16.7(a) shows that the monthly hotel room averages exhibit increasing seasonal variation. If a time series exhibits increasing seasonal variation, one approach is to first use a **fractional power transformation** (see Section 14.9) that produces a transformed time series that exhibits constant seasonal

TABLE 16.4		**Monthly Hotel Room Averages** 🔵 TravRest										
Year	Jan.	Feb.	Mar.	Apr.	May	June	July	Aug.	Sept.	Oct.	Nov.	Dec.
1	501	488	504	578	545	632	728	725	585	542	480	530
2	518	489	528	599	572	659	739	758	602	587	497	558
3	555	523	532	623	598	683	774	780	609	604	531	592
4	578	543	565	648	615	697	785	830	645	643	551	606
5	585	553	576	665	656	720	826	838	652	661	584	644
6	623	553	599	657	680	759	878	881	705	684	577	656
7	645	593	617	686	679	773	906	934	713	710	600	676
8	645	602	601	709	706	817	930	983	745	735	620	698
9	665	626	649	740	729	824	937	994	781	759	643	728
10	691	649	656	735	748	837	995	1040	809	793	692	763
11	723	655	658	761	768	885	1067	1038	812	790	692	782
12	758	709	715	788	794	893	1046	1075	812	822	714	802
13	748	731	748	827	788	937	1076	1125	840	864	717	813
14	811	732	745	844	833	935	1110	1124	868	860	762	877

FIGURE 16.7   Plots for the Monthly Hotel Room Averages in Table 16.4

(a) Plot of the monthly hotel room averages versus time

(b) Plot of the quartic roots of the monthly hotel averages versus time

LO16-3 Use data transformations to forecast time series having increasing seasonal variation.

variation. Therefore, consider taking the square roots, quartic roots, and natural logarithms of the monthly hotel room averages in Table 16.4. If we do this and plot the resulting three sets of transformed values versus time, we find that the quartic root transformation best equalizes the seasonal variation. Figure 16.7(b) presents a plot of the quartic roots of the monthly hotel room averages versus time. Letting y_t denote the hotel room average observed in time period t, it follows that a regression model describing the quartic root of y_t is

$$y_t^{.25} = \beta_0 + \beta_1 t + \beta_{M1}M_1 + \beta_{M2}M_2 + \cdots + \beta_{M11}M_{11} + \varepsilon_t$$

The expression $(\beta_0 + \beta_1 t)$ models the linear trend evident in Figure 16.7(b). Furthermore, M_1, $M_2, \ldots, M_{11}$ are dummy variables defined for months January (month 1) through November (month 11). For example, M_1 equals 1 if a monthly room average was observed in January, and 0 otherwise; M_2 equals 1 if a monthly room average was observed in February, and 0 otherwise. Note that we have not defined a dummy variable for December (month 12). It follows that the regression parameters $\beta_{M1}, \beta_{M2}, \ldots, \beta_{M11}$ compare January through November with December. Intuitively, for example, β_{M1} is the difference, excluding trend, between the level of the time series $(y_t^{.25})$ in January and the level of the time series in December. A positive β_{M1} would imply that, excluding trend, the value of the time series in January can be expected to be greater than the value in December. A negative β_{M1} would imply that, excluding trend, the value of the time series in January can be expected to be smaller than the value in December.

Figure 16.8 gives relevant portions of the Excel output of a regression analysis of the hotel room data using the quartic root dummy variable model. The Excel output tells us that the linear trend and the seasonal dummy variables are significant (every t statistic has a related p-value less than .05). In addition, although not shown on the output, $R^2 = .988$. Now consider time period 169, which is January of next year and which therefore implies that $M_1 = 1$ and that all the other

FIGURE 16.8　Excel Output of an Analysis of the Quartic Roots of the Room Averages Using Dummy Variable Regression

(a) The Excel output

	Coefficients	Standard Error	t Stat	P-value
Intercept	4.8073	0.0085	568.0695	4.06E-259
t	0.0035	0.0000	79.0087	3.95E-127
M1	-0.0525	0.0106	-4.9709	1.75E-06
M2	-0.1408	0.0106	-13.3415	1.59E-27
M3	-0.1071	0.0106	-10.1509	7.016E-19
M4	0.0499	0.0105	4.7284	5.05E-06
M5	0.0254	0.0105	2.4096	0.0171
M6	0.1902	0.0105	18.0311	6.85E-40
M7	0.3825	0.0105	36.2663	1.28E-77
M8	0.4134	0.0105	39.2009	2.41E-82
M9	0.0714	0.0105	6.7731	2.47E-10
M10	0.0506	0.0105	4.8029	3.66E-06
M11	-0.1419	0.0105	-13.4626	7.47E-28

(b) Prediction of $y_t^{.25}$ using an Excel add-in (MegaStat)

		95% Prediction Intervals	
t	Predicted	lower	upper
169	5.3489	5.2913	5.4065
170	5.2641	5.2065	5.3217
171	5.3013	5.2437	5.3589
172	5.4618	5.4042	5.5194
173	5.4409	5.3833	5.4984
174	5.6091	5.5515	5.6667
175	5.8049	5.7473	5.8625
176	5.8394	5.7818	5.8969
177	5.5009	5.4433	5.5585
178	5.4837	5.4261	5.5412
179	5.2946	5.2370	5.3522
180	5.4400	5.3825	5.4976

dummy variables equal 0. Using the least squares point estimates in Figure 16.8(a), we compute a point forecast of $y_{169}^{.25}$ to be

$$b_0 + b_1(169) + b_{M1}(1) = 4.8073 + 0.0035(169) + (-.0525)(1)$$
$$= 5.3489$$

Note that this point forecast is given in Figure 16.8(b) [see time period 169]. It follows that a point forecast of y_{169} is

$$(5.3489)^4 = 818.57$$

Furthermore, Figure 16.8(b) shows that a 95 percent prediction interval for $y_{169}^{.25}$ is [5.2913, 5.4065]. It follows that a 95 percent prediction interval for y_{169} is

$$[(5.2913)^4, (5.4065)^4] = [783.88, 854.41]$$

This interval says that Traveler's Rest, Inc., can be 95 percent confident that the monthly hotel room average in period 169 will be no less than 783.88 rooms per day and no more than 854.41 rooms per day. Lastly, note that Figure 16.8(b) also gives point forecasts of and 95 percent prediction intervals for the quartic roots of the hotel room averages in February through December of next year (time periods 170 through 180).

The validity of the regression methods just illustrated requires that the independence assumption be satisfied. However, when time series data are analyzed, this assumption is often violated. It is quite common for the time-ordered error terms to exhibit **positive or negative autocorrelation.** In Section 14.9 we discussed positive and negative autocorrelation, and we saw that we can use the **Durbin–Watson statistic d** to check for such autocorrelation. For example, it can be verified that this statistic shows no evidence of positive or negative first-order autocorrelation in the error terms of the calculator sales model or in the error terms of the bike sales model. However, the Durbin–Watson statistic for the dummy variable regression model describing the quartic roots of the hotel room averages can be calculated to be $d = 1.26$. Because the dummy variable regression model uses $k = 12$ independent variables, and because Tables A.11, A.12, and A.13 (pages 801 and 802) do not give the **Durbin–Watson critical points** corresponding to $k = 12$, we cannot test for autocorrelation using these tables. However, it can be shown that $d = 1.26$ is quite small and indicates **positive autocorrelation** in the error terms. One approach to dealing with autocorrelation in the error terms is to predict a future error term ε_t by using an **autoregressive model** that relates ε_t to past error terms $\varepsilon_{t-1}, \varepsilon_{t-2}, \ldots$. A better way (in the authors' opinion) is to use the Box–Jenkins methodology to forecast the time series. This methodology is presented in Section 16.6.

Exercises for Section 16.2

CONCEPTS

16.1 Discuss how we model no trend and a linear trend.

16.2 Discuss the difference between constant seasonal variation and increasing seasonal variation.

METHODS AND APPLICATIONS

16.3 **THE LUMBER PRODUCTION CASE** DS LumberProd

In this exercise we consider annual U.S. lumber production over 30 years. The data were obtained from the U.S. Department of Commerce *Survey of Current Business* and are presented in Table 16.5. (The lumber production values are given in millions of board feet.) Plot the lumber production values versus time and discuss why the plot indicates that the model $y_t = \beta_0 + \varepsilon_t$ might appropriately describe these values.

16.4 **THE LUMBER PRODUCTION CASE** DS LumberProd

Referring to the situation of Exercise 16.3, the mean and the standard deviation of the lumber production values can be calculated to be $\bar{y} = 35{,}651.9$ and $s = 2{,}037.3599$. Find a point forecast of and a 95 percent prediction interval for any future lumber production value.

16.5 **THE WATCH SALES CASE** DS WatchSale

The past 20 monthly sales figures for a new type of watch sold at Lambert's Discount Stores are given in Table 16.6.

a Plot the watch sales values versus time and discuss why the plot indicates that the model

$$y_t = \beta_0 + \beta_1 t + \varepsilon_t$$

might appropriately describe these values.

b The least squares point estimates of β_0 and β_1 can be calculated to be $b_0 = 290.0895$ and $b_1 = 8.6677$. Use b_0 and b_1 to show (calculate) that a point forecast of watch sales in period 21 is $\hat{y}_{21} = 472.1$. Use the formulas of simple linear regression analysis or a computer software package to show that a 95 percent prediction interval for watch sales in period 21 is [421.5, 522.7].

16.6 **THE AIR CONDITIONER SALES CASE** DS ACSales

Bargain Department Stores, Inc., is a chain of department stores in the Midwest. Quarterly sales of the "Bargain 8000-Btu Air Conditioner" over the past three years are as given in the lefthand portion of Table 16.7.

a Plot sales versus time and discuss why the plot indicates that the model

$$y_t = \beta_0 + \beta_1 t + \beta_2 t^2 + \beta_{Q2} Q_2 + \beta_{Q3} Q_3 + \beta_{Q4} Q_4 + \varepsilon_t$$

might appropriately describe the sales values. In this model Q_2, Q_3, and Q_4 are appropriately defined dummy variables for quarters 2, 3, and 4.

TABLE 16.5
Annual Total U.S. Lumber Production
DS LumberProd

35,404	35,733
37,462	35,791
32,901	34,592
33,178	38,902
34,449	37,858
38,044	32,926
36,762	35,697
36,742	34,548
33,385	32,087
34,171	37,515
36,124	38,629
38,658	32,019
32,901	35,710
36,356	36,693
37,166	37,153

TABLE 16.6
Watch Sales Values
DS WatchSale

298	356
302	371
301	399
351	392
336	425
361	411
407	455
351	457
357	465
346	481

TABLE 16.7 **Air Conditioner Sales and A Dummy Variable Regression Analysis of the Sales Data** DS ACSales

Year	Quarter	Sales	
1	1	2,915	The regression equation is
	2	8,032	Sales = 2625 + 383 T - 11.4 TSq + 4630 Q2 + 6739 Q3 - 1565 Q4
	3	10,411	
	4	2,427	

```
Predictor    Coef    SE Coef      T       P
Constant    2624.5    100.4     26.15   0.000     S = 92.4244
T           382.82     34.03    11.25   0.000     R-Sq = 100.0%
TSq         -11.354     2.541   -4.47   0.004     R-Sq(adj)= 99.9%
Q2         4629.74     76.08    60.86   0.000
Q3         6738.85     77.38    87.09   0.000
Q4        -1565.32     79.34   -19.73   0.000
```

Year	Quarter	Sales
2	1	4,381
	2	9,138
	3	11,386
	4	3,382
3	1	5,105
	2	9,894
	3	12,300
	4	4,013

```
Time     Fit    SE Fit         95% CI                 95% PI
 13    5682.4   112.6   ( 5406.9,  5957.9)    ( 5325.9,  6038.8)
 14   10388.4   142.8   (10039.0, 10737.8)    ( 9972.2, 10804.6)
 15   12551.0   177.2   (12117.4, 12984.7)    (12061.9, 13040.2)
 16    4277.7   213.9   ( 3754.4,  4801.1)    ( 3707.6,  4847.8)
```

b The right-hand portion of Table 16.7 is the MINITAB output of a regression analysis of the air conditioner sales data using the model in part *a*. (**1**) Define the dummy variables Q_2, Q_3, and Q_4. (**2**) Use the MINITAB output to find, report, and interpret the least squares point estimates of β_{Q2}, β_{Q3}, and β_{Q4}.

c At the bottom of the MINITAB output are point and prediction interval forecasts of air conditioner sales in the four quarters of year 4. Find and report these forecasts and hand calculate the point forecasts.

16.7 Table 16.8 gives the monthly international passenger totals over the last 11 years for an airline company. A plot of these passenger totals reveals an upward trend with increasing seasonal variation, and the natural logarithmic transformation is found to best equalize the seasonal variation [see Figure 16.9(a) and (b)]. Figure 16.9(c) gives the MINITAB output of a regression analysis of the monthly international passenger totals by using the model

$$\ln y_t = \beta_0 + \beta_1 t + \beta_{M1}M_1 + \beta_{M2}M_2 + \cdots + \beta_{M11}M_{11} + \varepsilon_t$$

Here $M_1, M_2, \ldots, M_{11}$ are appropriately defined dummy variables for January (month 1) through November (month 11). Let y_{133} denote the international passenger totals in month 133 (January of next year). The MINITAB output tells us that a point forecast of and a 95 percent prediction interval for $\ln y_{133}$ are, respectively, 6.08610 and [5.96593, 6.20627]. (**1**) Using the least squares point estimates on the MINITAB output, calculate the point forecast. (**2**) By calculating $e^{6.08610}$ and $[e^{5.96593}, e^{6.20627}]$, find a point forecast of and a 95 percent prediction interval for y_{133}. **DS** AirPass

16.8 Use the Durbin–Watson statistic given at the bottom of the MINITAB output in Figure 16.9(c) to assess whether there is positive autocorrelation.

TABLE 16.8   Monthly International Passenger Totals (Thousands of Passengers)   DS AirPass

Year	Jan.	Feb.	Mar.	Apr.	May	June	July	Aug.	Sept.	Oct.	Nov.	Dec.
1	112	118	132	129	121	135	148	148	136	119	104	118
2	115	126	141	135	125	149	170	170	158	133	114	140
3	145	150	178	163	172	178	199	199	184	162	146	166
4	171	180	193	181	183	218	230	242	209	191	172	194
5	196	196	236	235	229	243	264	272	237	211	180	201
6	204	188	235	227	234	264	302	293	259	229	203	229
7	242	233	267	269	270	315	364	347	312	274	237	278
8	284	277	317	313	318	374	413	405	355	306	271	306
9	315	301	356	348	355	422	465	467	404	347	305	336
10	340	318	362	348	363	435	491	505	404	359	310	337
11	360	342	406	396	420	472	548	559	463	407	362	405

Source: *FAA Statistical Handbook of Civil Aviation* (several annual issues). These data were originally presented by Box and Jenkins (1976). We have updated the situation in this exercise to be more modern.

FIGURE 16.9   Analysis of the Monthly International Passenger Totals

(a) Plot of the passenger totals

(b) Plot of the natural logarithms of the passenger totals

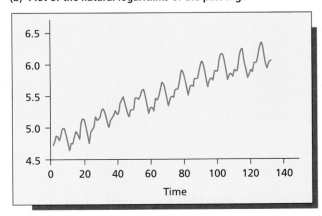

FIGURE 16.9   Analysis of the Monthly International Passenger Totals (*continued*)

(c) MINITAB Output of a Regression Analysis of the Monthly International Passenger Totals Using the Dummy Variable Model

```
Predictor       Coef    SE Coef        T      P    Predicted Values for New Observations
Constant     4.69618    0.01973   238.02  0.000    Time      Fit   SE Fit          95% PI
Time       0.0103075  0.0001316    78.30  0.000     133   6.08610  0.01973   (5.96593, 6.20627)
Jan          0.01903    0.02451     0.78  0.439     134   6.07888  0.01973   (5.95871, 6.19905)
Feb          0.00150    0.02451     0.06  0.951     135   6.22564  0.01973   (6.10547, 6.34581)
March        0.13795    0.02450     5.63  0.000     136   6.19383  0.01973   (6.07366, 6.31400)
April        0.09583    0.02449     3.91  0.000     137   6.20008  0.01973   (6.07991, 6.32025)
May          0.09178    0.02449     3.75  0.000     138   6.33292  0.01973   (6.21276, 6.45309)
June         0.21432    0.02448     8.75  0.000     139   6.44360  0.01973   (6.32343, 6.56377)
July         0.31469    0.02448    12.85  0.000     140   6.44682  0.01973   (6.32665, 6.56699)
Aug          0.30759    0.02448    12.57  0.000     141   6.31605  0.01973   (6.19588, 6.43622)
Sept         0.16652    0.02448     6.80  0.000     142   6.18515  0.01973   (6.06498, 6.30531)
Oct          0.02531    0.02447     1.03  0.303     143   6.05455  0.01973   (5.93438, 6.17472)
Nov         -0.11559    0.02447    -4.72  0.000     144   6.18045  0.01973   (6.06028, 6.30062)

S = 0.0573917    R-Sq = 98.3%    R-Sq(adj) = 98.1%    Durbin-Watson statistic = 0.420944
```

LO16-4 Use multiplicative decomposition and moving averages to forecast a time series.

16.3 Multiplicative Decomposition ●●●

When a time series exhibits increasing (or decreasing) seasonal variation, we can use the **multiplicative decomposition method** to decompose the time series into its **trend, seasonal, cyclical,** and **irregular** components. This is illustrated in the following example.

EXAMPLE 16.5 The Tasty Cola Case: Predicting Soft Drink Sales

The Discount Soda Shop, Inc., owns and operates 10 drive-in soft drink stores. Discount Soda has been selling Tasty Cola, a soft drink introduced just three years ago and gaining in popularity. Periodically, Discount Soda orders Tasty Cola from the regional distributor. To better implement its inventory policy, Discount Soda needs to forecast monthly Tasty Cola sales (in hundreds of cases).

Discount Soda has recorded monthly Tasty Cola sales for the previous three years. This time series is given in Table 16.9 and plotted in Figure 16.10. Notice that, in addition to having a linear trend, the Tasty Cola sales time series possesses seasonal variation, with sales of the soft drink

TABLE 16.9   Monthly Sales of Tasty Cola (in Hundreds of Cases)   DS TastyCola

Year	Month	t	Sales, y_t	Year	Month	t	Sales, y_t
1	1 (Jan.)	1	189	2	7	19	831
	2 (Feb.)	2	229		8	20	960
	3 (Mar.)	3	249		9	21	1,152
	4 (Apr.)	4	289		10	22	759
	5 (May)	5	260		11	23	607
	6 (June)	6	431		12	24	371
	7 (July)	7	660	3	1	25	298
	8 (Aug.)	8	777		2	26	378
	9 (Sept.)	9	915		3	27	373
	10 (Oct.)	10	613		4	28	443
	11 (Nov.)	11	485		5	29	374
	12 (Dec.)	12	277		6	30	660
2	1	13	244		7	31	1,004
	2	14	296		8	32	1,153
	3	15	319		9	33	1,388
	4	16	370		10	34	904
	5	17	313		11	35	715
	6	18	556		12	36	441

FIGURE 16.10   Time Series Plot of the Tasty Cola Sales Data

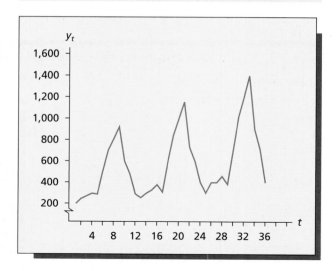

greatest in the summer and early fall months and lowest in the winter months. Because the seasonal variation seems to be increasing, we will see as we progress through this example that it might be reasonable to conclude that y_t, the sales of Tasty Cola in period t, is described by the **multiplicative model**

$$y_t = TR_t \times SN_t \times CL_t \times IR_t$$

Here TR_t, SN_t, CL_t, and IR_t represent the trend, seasonal, cyclical, and irregular components of the time series in time period t.

Table 16.10 summarizes the calculations needed to find estimates—denoted tr_t, sn_t, cl_t, and ir_t—of TR_t, SN_t, CL_t, and IR_t. As shown in the table, we begin by calculating **moving averages** and **centered moving averages.** The purpose behind computing these averages is to eliminate seasonal variations and irregular fluctuations from the data. The first moving average of the first 12 Tasty Cola sales values is

$$\frac{189 + 229 + 249 + 289 + 260 + 431 + 660 + 777 + 915 + 613 + 485 + 277}{12}$$

$$= 447.833$$

TABLE 16.10   Tasty Cola Sales and the Multiplicative Decomposition Method

t Time Period	y_t Tasty Cola Sales	First Step: 12-Period Moving Average	$tr_t \times cl_t$: Centered Moving Average	$sn_t \times ir_t$: $\frac{y_t}{tr_t \times cl_t}$	sn_t: Table 16.11	d_t: $\frac{y_t}{sn_t}$	tr_t: 380.163 +9.489t	$tr_t \times sn_t$: Multiply tr_t by sn_t	$cl_t \times ir_t$: $\frac{y_t}{tr_t \times sn_t}$	cl_t: 3-Period Moving Average	ir_t: $\frac{cl_t \times ir_t}{cl_t}$
1 (Jan)	189				.493	383.37	389.652	192.10	.9839		
2	229				.596	384.23	399.141	237.89	.9626	.9902	.9721
3	249				.595	418.49	408.630	243.13	1.0241	1.0010	1.0231
4	289				.680	425	418.119	284.32	1.0165	1.0396	.9778
5	260				.564	460.99	427.608	241.17	1.0781	1.0315	1.0452
6	431	447.833			.986	437.12	437.097	430.98	1.0000	1.0285	.9723
7	660	452.417	450.125	1.466	1.467	449.9	446.586	655.14	1.0074	1.0046	1.0028
8	777	458	455.2085	1.707	1.693	458.95	456.075	772.13	1.0063	1.0004	1.0059
9	915	563.833	460.9165	1.985	1.990	459.79	465.564	926.47	.9876	.9937	.9939
10	613	470.583	467.208	1.312	1.307	469.01	475.053	620.89	.9873	.9825	1.0049
11	485	475	472.7915	1.026	1.029	471.33	489.542	498.59	.9727	.9648	1.0082
12	277	485.417	480.2085	.577	.600	461.67	494.031	296.42	.9345	.9634	.9700
13 (Jan)	244	499.667	492.542	.495	.493	494.97	503.520	248.24	.9829	.9618	1.0219
14	296	514.917	507.292	.583	.596	496.64	513.009	305.75	.9681	.9924	.9755
15	319	534.667	524.792	.608	.595	536.13	522.498	310.89	1.0261	1.0057	1.0203
16	370	546.833	540.75	.684	.680	544.12	531.987	361.75	1.0228	1.0246	.9982
17	313	557	551.9165	.567	.564	554.97	541.476	305.39	1.0249	1.0237	1.0012
18	556	564.833	560.9165	.991	.986	563.89	550.965	543.25	1.0235	1.0197	1.0037
19	831	569.333	567.083	1.465	1.467	566.46	560.454	822.19	1.0107	1.0097	1.0010
20	960	576.167	572.75	1.676	1.693	567.04	569.943	964.91	.9949	1.0016	.9933
21	1,152	580.667	578.417	1.992	1.990	578.89	579.432	1,153.07	.9991	.9934	1.0057
22	759	586.75	583.7085	1.300	1.307	580.72	588.921	769.72	.9861	.9903	.9958
23	607	591.833	589.2915	1.030	1.029	589.89	598.410	615.76	.9858	.9964	.9894
24	371	600.5	596.1665	.622	.600	618.33	607.899	364.74	1.0172	.9940	1.0233
25 (Jan)	298	614.917	607.7085	.490	.493	604.46	617.388	304.37	.9791	1.0027	.9765
26	378	631	622.9585	.607	.596	634.23	626.877	373.62	1.0117	.9920	1.0199
27	373	650.667	640.8335	.582	.595	626.89	636.366	378.64	.9851	1.0018	.9833
28	443	662.75	656.7085	.675	.680	651.47	645.855	439.18	1.0087	1.0030	1.0057
29	374	671.75	667.25	.561	.564	663.12	655.344	369.61	1.0119	1.0091	1.0028
30	660	677.583	674.6665	.978	.986	669.37	664.833	655.53	1.0068	1.0112	.9956
31	1,004				1.467	684.39	674.322	989.23	1.0149	1.0059	1.0089
32	1,153				1.693	681.04	683.811	1,157.69	.9959	1.0053	.9906
33	1,388				1.990	697.49	693.300	1,379.67	1.0060	.9954	1.0106
34	904				1.307	691.66	702.789	918.55	.9842	.9886	.9955
35	715				1.029	694.85	712.278	732.93	.9755	.9927	.9827
36	441				.600	735	721.707	433.06	1.0183		

Here we use a "12-period moving average" because the Tasty Cola time series data are monthly (12 time periods or "seasons" per year). If the data were quarterly, we would compute a "4-period moving average." The second moving average is obtained by dropping the first sales value (y_1) from the average and by including the next sales value (y_{13}) in the average. Thus we obtain

$$\frac{229 + 249 + 289 + 260 + 431 + 660 + 777 + 915 + 613 + 485 + 277 + 244}{12}$$

$$= 452.417$$

The third moving average is obtained by dropping y_2 from the average and by including y_{14} in the average. We obtain

$$\frac{249 + 289 + 260 + 431 + 660 + 777 + 915 + 613 + 485 + 277 + 244 + 296}{12}$$

$$= 458$$

Successive moving averages are computed similarly until we include y_{36} in the last moving average. Note that we use the term *moving average* here because, as we calculate these averages, we move along by dropping the most remote observation in the previous average and by including the "next" observation in the new average.

The first moving average corresponds to a time that is midway between periods 6 and 7, the second moving average corresponds to a time that is midway between periods 7 and 8, and so forth. In order to obtain averages corresponding to time periods in the original Tasty Cola time series, we calculate **centered moving averages.** The centered moving averages are two-period moving averages of the previously computed 12-period moving averages. Thus the first centered moving average is

$$\frac{447.833 + 452.417}{2} = 450.125$$

The second centered moving average is

$$\frac{452.417 + 458}{2} = 455.2085$$

Successive centered moving averages are calculated similarly. The 12-period moving averages and centered moving averages for the Tasty Cola sales time series are given in Table 16.10.

If the original moving averages had been computed using an odd number of time series values, the centering procedure would not have been necessary. For example, if we had three seasons per year, we would compute three-period moving averages. Then, the first moving average would correspond to period 2, the second moving average would correspond to period 3, and so on. However, most seasonal time series are quarterly, monthly, or weekly, so the centering procedure is necessary.

The centered moving average in time period t is considered to equal $tr_t \times cl_t$, the estimate of $TR_t \times CL_t$, because the averaging procedure is assumed to have removed seasonal variations (note that each moving average is computed using exactly one observation from each season) and (short-term) irregular fluctuations. The (longer-term) trend effects and cyclical effects—that is, $tr_t \times cl_t$—remain.

Because the model

$$y_t = TR_t \times SN_t \times CL_t \times IR_t$$

implies that

$$SN_t \times IR_t = \frac{y_t}{TR_t \times CL_t}$$

it follows that the estimate $sn_t \times ir_t$ of $SN_t \times IR_t$ is

$$sn_t \times ir_t = \frac{y_t}{tr_t \times cl_t}$$

TABLE 16.11		Estimation of the Seasonal Factors			
		$sn_t \times ir_t = y_t/(tr_t \times cl_t)$			$sn_t =$
		Year 1	Year 2	$\overline{sn}_t$	$1.0008758(\overline{sn}_t)$
1	Jan.	.495	.490	.4925	.493
2	Feb.	.583	.607	.595	.596
3	Mar.	.608	.582	.595	.595
4	Apr.	.684	.675	.6795	.680
5	May	.567	.561	.564	.564
6	June	.991	.978	.9845	.986
7	July	1.466	1.465	1.4655	1.467
8	Aug.	1.707	1.676	1.6915	1.693
9	Sep.	1.985	1.992	1.9885	1.990
10	Oct.	1.312	1.300	1.306	1.307
11	Nov.	1.026	1.030	1.028	1.029
12	Dec.	.577	.622	.5995	.600

FIGURE 16.11 Plot of Tasty Cola Sales and Deseasonalized Sales

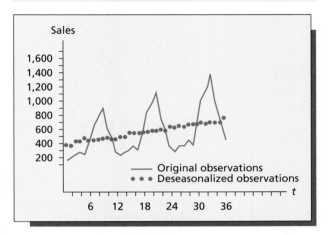

Noting that the values of $sn_t \times ir_t$ are calculated in Table 16.10, we can find sn_t by grouping the values of $sn_t \times ir_t$ by months and calculating an average, $\overline{sn}_t$, for each month. These monthly averages are given for the Tasty Cola data in Table 16.11. The monthly averages are then normalized so that they sum to the number of time periods in a year. Denoting the number of time periods in a year by L (for instance, $L = 4$ for quarterly data, $L = 12$ for monthly data), we accomplish the normalization by multiplying each value of $\overline{sn}_t$ by the quantity

$$\frac{L}{\sum \overline{sn}_t} = \frac{12}{.4925 + .595 + \cdots + .5995}$$

$$= \frac{12}{11.9895} = 1.0008758$$

This normalization process results in the estimate $sn_t = 1.0008758(\overline{sn}_t)$, which is the estimate of SN_t. These calculations are summarized in Table 16.11.

Having calculated the values of sn_t and placed them in Table 16.10, we next define the **deseasonalized observation** in time period t to be

$$d_t = \frac{y_t}{sn_t}$$

Deseasonalized observations are computed to better estimate the trend component TR_t. Dividing y_t by the estimated seasonal factor removes the seasonality from the data and allows us to better understand the nature of the trend. The deseasonalized observations are calculated in Table 16.10 and are plotted in Figure 16.11. Because the deseasonalized observations have a straight-line appearance, it seems reasonable to assume a linear trend

$$TR_t = \beta_0 + \beta_1 t$$

We estimate TR_t by fitting a straight line to the deseasonalized observations. That is, we compute the least squares point estimates of the parameters in the simple linear regression model relating the dependent variable d_t to the independent variable t:

$$d_t = \beta_0 + \beta_1 t + \varepsilon_t$$

We obtain $b_0 = 380.163$ and $b_1 = 9.489$. It follows that the estimate of TR_t is

$$tr_t = b_0 + b_1 t = 380.163 + 9.489t$$

The values of tr_t are calculated in Table 16.10. Note that, for example, although $y_{22} = 759$, Tasty Cola sales in period 22 (October of year 2), are larger than $tr_{22} = 588.921$ (the estimated trend in period 22), $d_{22} = 580.72$ is smaller than $tr_{22} = 588.921$. This implies that, on a deseasonalized basis, Tasty Cola sales were slightly down in October of year 2. This might have been caused by a slightly colder October than usual.

Thus far, we have found estimates sn_t and tr_t of SN_t and TR_t. Because the model

$$y_t = TR_t \times SN_t \times CL_t \times IR_t$$

implies that

$$CL_t \times IR_t = \frac{y_t}{TR_t \times SN_t}$$

it follows that the estimate of $CL_t \times IR_t$ is

$$cl_t \times ir_t = \frac{y_t}{tr_t \times sn_t}$$

Moreover, experience has shown that, when considering either monthly or quarterly data, we can average out ir_t and thus calculate the estimate cl_t of CL_t by computing a three-period moving average of the $cl_t \times ir_t$ values.

Finally, we calculate the estimate ir_t of IR_t by using the equation

$$ir_t = \frac{cl_t \times ir_t}{cl_t}$$

The calculations of the values cl_t and ir_t for the Tasty Cola data are summarized in Table 16.10. Because there are only three years of data, and because most of the values of cl_t are near 1, we cannot discern a well-defined cycle. Furthermore, examining the values of ir_t, we cannot detect a pattern in the estimates of the irregular factors.

Traditionally, the estimates tr_t, sn_t, cl_t, and ir_t obtained by using the multiplicative decomposition method are used to describe the time series. However, we can also use these estimates to forecast future values of the time series. If there is no pattern in the irregular component, we predict IR_t to equal 1. Therefore, the point forecast of y_t is

$$\hat{y}_t = tr_t \times sn_t \times cl_t$$

if a well-defined cycle exists and can be predicted. The point forecast is

$$\hat{y}_t = tr_t \times sn_t$$

if a well-defined cycle does not exist or if CL_t cannot be predicted, as in the Tasty Cola example. Because values of $tr_t \times sn_t$ have been calculated in column 9 of Table 16.10, these values are the point forecasts of the $n = 36$ historical Tasty Cola sales values. Furthermore, we present in Table 16.12 point forecasts of future Tasty Cola sales in the 12 months of year 4. Recalling that

TABLE 16.12   **Forecasts of Future Values of Tasty Cola Sales Calculated Using the Multiplicative Decomposition Method**

t	sn_t	$tr_t = 380.163 + 9.489t$	Point Prediction, $\hat{y}_t = tr_t \times sn_t$	Approximate 95% Prediction Interval	y_t
37	.493	731.273	360.52	[333.72, 387.32]	352
38	.596	740.762	441.48	[414.56, 468.40]	445
39	.595	750.252	446.40	[419.36, 473.44]	453
40	.680	759.741	516.62	[489.45, 543.79]	541
41	.564	769.231	433.85	[406.55, 461.15]	457
42	.986	778.720	767.82	[740.38, 795.26]	762
43	1.467	788.209	1,156.30	[1,128.71, 1,183.89]	1,194
44	1.693	797.699	1,350.50	[1,322.76, 1,378.24]	1,361
45	1.990	807.188	1,606.30	[1,578.41, 1,634.19]	1,615
46	1.307	816.678	1,067.40	[1,039.35, 1,095.45]	1,059
47	1.029	826.167	850.12	[821.90, 878.34]	824
48	.600	835.657	501.39	[473, 529.78]	495

the estimated trend equation is $tr_t = 380.163 + 9.489t$ and that the estimated seasonal factor for August is 1.693 (see Table 16.11), it follows, for example, that the point forecast of Tasty Cola sales in period 44 (August of year 4) is

$$\hat{y}_{44} = tr_{44} \times sn_{44}$$
$$= (380.163 + 9.489(44))(1.693)$$
$$= 797.699(1.693)$$
$$= 1,350.50$$

Although there is no theoretically correct prediction interval for y_t, a fairly accurate **approximate 100(1 − α) percent prediction interval for y_t** is obtained by computing an interval that is centered at $\hat{y}_t$ and that has a length equal to the length of the $100(1 - \alpha)$ percent prediction interval for the **deseasonalized observation d_t**. Here the interval for d_t is obtained by using the model

$$d_t = TR_t + \varepsilon_t$$
$$= \beta_0 + \beta_1 t + \varepsilon_t$$

For instance, using MINITAB to predict d_t on the basis of this model, we find that a 95 percent prediction interval for d_{44} is [769.959, 825.439]. Because this interval has a **half-length** equal to $(825.439 - 769.959)/2 = 55.48/2 = 27.74$, it follows that an approximate 95 percent prediction interval for y_{44} is

$$[\hat{y}_{44} \pm 27.74] = [1,350.50 \pm 27.74]$$
$$= [1,322.76, 1,378.24]$$

In Table 16.12 we give the approximate 95 percent prediction intervals (calculated by the above method) for Tasty Cola sales in the 12 months of year 4.

Next, suppose we actually observe Tasty Cola sales in year 4, and these sales are as given in Table 16.12. In Figure 16.12 we plot the observed and forecasted sales for all 48 sales periods. In practice, the comparison of the observed and forecasted sales in years 1 through 3 would be used by the analyst to determine whether the forecasting equation adequately fits the historical data. An adequate fit (as indicated by Figure 16.12, for example) might prompt an analyst to use this equation to calculate forecasts for future time periods. One reason that the Tasty Cola forecasting equation

$$\hat{y}_t = tr_t \times sn_t$$
$$= (380.163 + 9.489t)sn_t$$

FIGURE 16.12   **A Plot of the Observed and Forecasted Tasty Cola Sales Values**

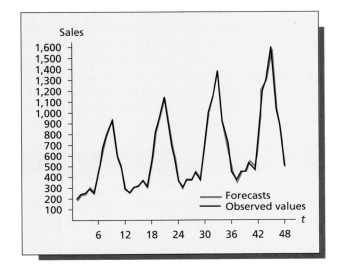

provides reasonable forecasts is that this equation *multiplies tr*$_t$ by *sn*$_t$. Therefore, as the average level of the time series (determined by the trend) increases, the seasonal swing of the time series increases, which is consistent with the data plots in Figures 16.10 and 16.12. For example, note from Table 16.11 that the estimated seasonal factor for August is 1.693. The forecasting equation yields a prediction of Tasty Cola sales in August of year 1 equal to

$$\hat{y}_8 = [380.163 + 9.489(8)]1.693$$
$$= (456.075)(1.693)$$
$$= 772.13$$

This implies a seasonal swing of $772.13 - 456.075 = 316.055$ (hundreds of cases) above 456.075, the estimated trend level. The forecasting equation yields a prediction of Tasty Cola sales in August of year 2 equal to

$$\hat{y}_{20} = [380.163 + 9.489(20)]1.693$$
$$= (569.943)(1.693)$$
$$= 964.91$$

which implies an increased seasonal swing of $964.91 - 569.943 = 394.967$ (hundreds of cases) above 569.943, the estimated trend level. In general, then, the forecasting equation is appropriate for forecasting a time series with a seasonal swing that is proportional to the average level of the time series as determined by the trend—that is, a time series exhibiting increasing seasonal variation.

We next note that the U.S. Bureau of the Census has developed the **Census II method,** which is a sophisticated version of the multiplicative decomposition method discussed in this section. The initial version of Census II was primarily developed by Julius Shiskin in the late 1950s when a computer program was written to perform the rather complex calculations. Several modifications have been made to the first version of the method over the years. Census II continues to be widely used by a variety of businesses and government agencies.

Census II first adjusts the original data for "trading day variations." That is, the data are adjusted to account for the fact that, for example, different months or quarters will consist of different numbers of business days or "trading days." The method then uses an iterative procedure to obtain estimates of the seasonal component (SN_t), the trading day component, the so-called trend-cycle component ($TR_t \times CL_t$), and the irregular component (IR_t). The iterative procedure makes extensive use of moving averages and a method for identifying and replacing extreme values in order to eliminate randomness. For a good explanation of the details involved here and in the Census II method as a whole, see Makridakis, Wheelwright, and McGee (1983). After carrying out a number of tests to check the correctness of the estimates, the method estimates the trend-cycle, seasonal, and irregular components.

MINITAB carries out a modified version of the multiplicative decomposition method discussed in this section. We believe that MINITAB's modified version (at the time of the writing of this book) makes some conceptual errors that can result in biased estimates of the time series components. Therefore, we will not present MINITAB output of multiplicative decomposition. The Excel add-in (MegaStat) estimates the seasonal factors and the trend line exactly as described in this section. MegaStat does not estimate the cyclical and irregular components. However, because it is often reasonable to make forecasts by using estimates of the seasonal factors and trend line, MegaStat can be used to do this. In Appendix 16.2, we show a MegaStat output that estimates the seasonal factors and trend line for the Tasty Cola data.

Exercises for Section 16.3

CONCEPTS

connect

16.9   Explain how the multiplicative decomposition model estimates seasonal factors.

16.10 Explain how the multiplicative decomposition method estimates the trend effect.

16.11 Discuss how the multiplicative decomposition method makes point forecasts of future time series values.

METHODS AND APPLICATIONS

Exercises 16.12 through 16.16 are based on the following situation: International Machinery, Inc., produces a tractor and wishes to use **quarterly** tractor sales data observed in the last four years to predict quarterly tractor sales next year. The following MegaStat output gives the tractor sales data and the estimates of the seasonal factors and trend line for the data: Ⓓ IntMach

t	Year	Quarter	Sales, y	Centered Moving Average	Ratio to CMA	Seasonal Indexes	Sales, y Deseasonalized
1	1	1	293			1.191	245.9
2	1	2	392			1.521	257.7
3	1	3	221	275.125	0.803	0.804	275.0
4	1	4	147	302.000	0.487	0.484	303.9
5	2	1	388	325.250	1.193	1.191	325.7
6	2	2	512	338.125	1.514	1.521	336.6
7	2	3	287	354.125	0.810	0.804	357.1
8	2	4	184	381.500	0.482	0.484	380.4
9	3	1	479	405.000	1.183	1.191	402.0
10	3	2	640	417.375	1.533	1.521	420.7
11	3	3	347	435.000	0.798	0.804	431.8
12	3	4	223	462.125	0.483	0.484	461.0
13	4	1	581	484.375	1.199	1.191	487.7
14	4	2	755	497.625	1.517	1.521	496.3
15	4	3	410			0.804	510.2
16	4	4	266			0.484	549.9

Calculation of Seasonal Indexes

	1	2	3	4	
1			0.803	0.487	
2	1.193	1.514	0.810	0.482	
3	1.183	1.533	0.798	0.483	
4	1.199	1.517			
mean:	1.192	1.522	0.804	0.484	4.001
adjusted:	1.191	1.521	0.804	0.484	4.000

16.12   Find and identify the four seasonal factors for quarters 1, 2, 3, and 4.

16.13   What type of trend is indicated by the plot of the deseasonalized data?

16.14   What is the equation of the estimated trend that has been calculated using the deseasonalized data?

16.15   Compute a point forecast of tractor sales (based on trend and seasonal factors) for each of the quarters next year.

16.16   Compute an approximate 95 percent prediction interval forecast of tractor sales for each of the quarters next year. Use the fact that the half-lengths of 95 percent prediction intervals for the deseasonalized sales values in the four quarters of next year are, respectively, 14, 14.4, 14.6, and 15.

16.17   If we use the multiplicative decomposition method to analyze the quarterly bicycle sales data given in Table 16.3 (page 634), we find that the quarterly seasonal factors are .46, 1.22, 1.68, and .64. Furthermore, if we use a statistical software package to fit a straight line to the deseasonalized sales values, we find that the estimate of the trend is $tr_t = 22.61 + .59t$.

In addition, we find that the half-lengths of 95 percent prediction intervals for the deseasonalized sales values in the four quarters of the next year are, respectively, 2.80, 2.85, 2.92, and 2.98.
Ⓓ BikeSales

a   Calculate point predictions of bicycle sales in the four quarters of the next year.

b   Calculate approximate 95 percent prediction intervals for bicycle sales in the four quarters of the next year.

16.4 Simple Exponential Smoothing ● ● ●

LO16-5 Use simple exponential smoothing to forecast a time series.

In ongoing forecasting systems, forecasts of future time series values are made each period for succeeding periods. At the end of each period the estimates of the time series parameters and the forecasting equation need to be updated to account for the most recent observation. This updating accounts for possible changes in the parameters that may occur over time. In addition, such changes may imply that unequal weights should be applied to the time series observations when the estimates of the parameters are updated.

In this section we assume that a time series is appropriately described by the no trend equation

$$y_t = \beta_0 + \varepsilon_t$$

When the parameter β_0 remains constant over time, we have seen that it is reasonable to forecast future values of y_t by using regression analysis (see Example 16.1 on page 632). In such a case, the least squares point estimate of β_0 is

$$b_0 = \bar{y} = \text{the average of the observed time series values}$$

When we compute the point estimate b_0 we are **equally weighting** each of the previously observed time series values $y_1, y_2, \ldots, y_n$.

When the value of the parameter β_0 is slowly changing over time, the equal weighting scheme may not be appropriate. Instead, it may be desirable to weight recent observations more heavily than remote observations. **Simple exponential smoothing** is a forecasting method that applies unequal weights to the time series observations. This unequal weighting is accomplished by using a **smoothing constant** that determines how much weight is attached to each observation. The most recent observation is given the most weight. More distantly past observations are given successively smaller weights. The procedure allows the forecaster to update the estimate of β_0 so that changes in the value of this parameter can be detected and incorporated into the forecasting equation. We illustrate simple exponential smoothing in the following example.

EXAMPLE 16.6 The Cod Catch Case: Simple Exponential Smoothing

Consider the cod catch data of Example 16.1, which are given in Table 16.1 (page 632). The plot of these data (in Figure 16.2 on page 632) suggests that the no trend model

$$y_t = \beta_0 + \varepsilon_t$$

may appropriately describe the cod catch series. It is also possible that the parameter β_0 could be slowly changing over time.

We begin the simple exponential smoothing procedure by calculating an initial estimate of the average level β_0 of the series. This estimate is denoted S_0 and is computed by averaging the first six time series values. We obtain

$$S_0 = \frac{\sum_{t=1}^{6} y_t}{6} = \frac{362 + 381 + \cdots + 402}{6} = 359.667$$

Note that, because simple exponential smoothing attempts to track changes over time in the average level β_0 by using newly observed values to update the estimates of β_0, we use only six of the $n = 24$ time series observations to calculate the initial estimate of β_0. If we do this, then 18 observations remain to tell us how β_0 may be changing over time. Experience has shown that, in general, it is reasonable to calculate initial estimates in exponential smoothing procedures by using half of the historical data. However, it can be shown that, in simple exponential smoothing, using six observations is reasonable (it would not, however, be reasonable to use a very small number of observations because doing so might make the initial estimate so different from the true value of β_0 that the exponential smoothing procedure would be adversely affected).

Next, assume that at the end of time period $T - 1$ we have an estimate S_{T-1} of β_0. Then, assuming that in time period T we obtain a new observation y_T, we can update S_{T-1} to S_T, which is an estimate made in period T of β_0. We compute the updated estimate by using the so-called **smoothing equation**

$$S_T = \alpha y_T + (1 - \alpha)S_{T-1}$$

Here α is a smoothing constant between 0 and 1 (α will be discussed in more detail later). The updating equation says that S_T, the estimate made in time period T of β_0, equals a fraction α (for example, .1) of the newly observed time series observation y_T plus a fraction $(1 - \alpha)$ (for example, .9) of S_{T-1}, the estimate made in time period $T - 1$ of β_0. The more the average level of the process is changing, the more a newly observed time series value should influence our estimate, and thus the larger the smoothing constant α should be set. We will soon see how to use historical data to determine an appropriate value of α.

		Actual Cod	**Smoothed**	**Forecast Made**	**Forecast**
Year	**Month**	**Catch, y_T**	**Estimate, S_T**	**Last Period**	**Error**
			($S_0 = 359.667$)		
1	Jan.	362	359.713	359.667	2.333
	Feb.	381	360.139	359.713	21.287
	Mar.	317	359.276	360.139	−43.139
	Apr.	297	358.031	359.276	−62.276
	May	399	358.850	358.031	40.969
	June	402	359.713	358.850	43.150
	July	375	360.019	359.713	15.287
	Aug.	349	359.799	360.019	−11.019
	Sept.	386	360.323	359.799	26.201
	Oct.	328	359.676	360.323	−32.323
	Nov.	389	360.263	359.676	29.324
	Dec.	343	359.917	360.263	−17.263
2	Jan.	276	358.239	359.917	−83.917
	Feb.	334	357.754	358.239	−24.239
	Mar.	394	358.479	357.754	36.246
	Apr.	334	357.990	358.479	−24.479
	May	384	358.510	357.990	26.010
	June	314	357.620	358.510	−44.510
	July	344	357.347	357.620	−13.620
	Aug.	337	356.940	357.347	−20.347
	Sept.	345	356.701	356.940	−11.940
	Oct.	362	356.807	356.701	5.299
	Nov.	314	355.951	356.807	−42.807
	Dec.	365	356.132	355.951	9.049

TABLE 16.13 One-Period-Ahead Forecasting of the Historical Cod Catch Time Series Using Simple Exponential Smoothing with $\alpha = .02$

We will now begin with the initial estimate $S_0 = 359.667$ and update this initial estimate by applying the smoothing equation to the 24 observed cod catches. To do this, we arbitrarily set α equal to .02, and to judge the appropriateness of this choice of α we calculate "one-period-ahead" forecasts of the historical cod catches as we carry out the smoothing procedure. Because the initial estimate of β_0 is $S_0 = 359.667$, it follows that 359.667 is the forecast made at time 0 for y_1, the value of the time series in period 1. Because we see from Table 16.13 that $y_1 = 362$, we have a forecast error of $362 - 359.667 = 2.333$. Using $y_1 = 362$, we can update S_0 to S_1, an estimate made in period 1 of the average level of the time series, by using the equation

$$S_1 = \alpha y_1 + (1 - \alpha)S_0$$
$$= .02(362) + .98(359.667) = 359.713$$

Because this implies that 359.713 is the forecast made in period 1 for y_2, and because we see from Table 16.13 that $y_2 = 381$, we have a forecast error of $381 - 359.713 = 21.287$. Using $y_2 = 381$, we can update S_1 to S_2, an estimate made in period 2 of β_0, by using the equation

$$S_2 = \alpha y_2 + (1 - \alpha)S_1$$
$$= .02(381) + .98(359.713) = 360.139$$

Because this implies that 360.139 is the forecast made in period 2 for y_3, and because we see from Table 16.13 that $y_3 = 317$, we have a forecast error of $317 - 360.139 = -43.139$. This procedure is continued through the entire 24 periods of historical data. The results are summarized in Table 16.13. Using the results in this table, we find that, for $\alpha = .02$, the mean of the squared forecast errors is 1161.14. To find a "good" value of α, we evaluate the mean of the squared forecast errors for values of α ranging from .02 to .30 in increments of .02. (In most exponential smoothing applications, the value of the smoothing constant used is between .01 and .30.) When we do this, we find that $\alpha = .02$ minimizes the mean of the squared forecast errors. Because this minimizing value of α is small, it appears to be best to apply small weights to new observations, which tells us that the level of the time series is not changing very much.

In general, simple exponential smoothing is carried out as follows:

Simple Exponential Smoothing

1 Suppose that the time series $y_1, \ldots, y_n$ is described by the equation

$$y_t = \beta_0 + \varepsilon_t$$

where the average level β_0 of the process may be slowly changing over time. Then the estimate S_T of β_0 made in time period T is given by the **smoothing equation**

$$S_T = \alpha y_T + (1 - \alpha)S_{T-1}$$

where α is a smoothing constant between 0 and

1 and S_{T-1} is the estimate of β_0 made in time period $T - 1$.

2 A point forecast made in time period T for any future value of the time series is S_T.

3 If we observe y_{T+1} in time period $T + 1$, we can update S_T to S_{T+1} by using the equation

$$S_{T+1} = \alpha y_{T+1} + (1 - \alpha)S_T$$

and a point forecast made in time period $T + 1$ for any future value of the time series is S_{T+1}.

EXAMPLE 16.7 The Cod Catch Case: Forecasting

In Example 16.6 we saw that $\alpha = .02$ is a "good" value of the smoothing constant when forecasting the 24 observed cod catches in Table 16.13. Therefore, we will use simple exponential smoothing with $\alpha = .02$ to forecast future monthly cod catches. From Table 16.13 we see that $S_{24} = 356.132$ is the estimate made in month 24 of the average level β_0 of the monthly cod catches. It follows that the point forecast made in month 24 of any future monthly cod catch is 356.132 tons of cod. Now, assuming that we observe a cod catch in January of year 3 of $y_{25} = 384$, we can update S_{24} to S_{25} by using the equation

$$
\begin{aligned}
S_{25} &= \alpha y_{25} + (1 - \alpha)S_{24} \\
&= .02(384) + .98(356.132) \\
&= 356.689
\end{aligned}
$$

This implies that the point forecast made in month 25 of any future monthly cod catch is 356.689 tons of cod.

By using the smoothing equation

$$S_T = \alpha y_T + (1 - \alpha)S_{T-1}$$

it can be shown that S_T, the estimate made in time period T of the average level β_0 of the time series, can be expressed as

$$
\begin{aligned}
S_T &= \alpha y_T + \alpha(1 - \alpha)y_{T-1} + \alpha(1 - \alpha)^2 y_{T-2} \\
&\quad + \cdots + \alpha(1 - \alpha)^{T-1}y_1 + (1 - \alpha)^T S_0
\end{aligned}
$$

The coefficients measuring the contributions of the observations $y_T, y_{T-1}, y_{T-2}, \ldots, y_1$—that is, $\alpha, \alpha(1 - \alpha), \alpha(1 - \alpha)^2, \ldots, \alpha(1 - \alpha)^{T-1}$—decrease *exponentially* with age. For this reason we refer to this procedure as simple *exponential* smoothing.

Because the coefficients measuring the contributions of $y_T, y_{T-1}, y_{T-2}, \ldots, y_1$ are decreasing exponentially, the most recent observation y_T makes the largest contribution to the current estimate of β_0. Older observations make smaller and smaller contributions to this estimate. Thus remote observations are "dampened out" of the current estimate of β_0 as time advances. The rate at which remote observations are dampened out depends on the smoothing constant α. For values of α near 1, remote observations are dampened out quickly. For example, if $\alpha = .9$ we obtain coefficients .9, .09, .009, .0009, ... For values of α near 0, remote observations are dampened out more slowly (if $\alpha = .1$, we obtain coefficients .1, .09, .081, .0729, . . .). The choice of a smoothing constant α is usually made by simulated forecasting of a historical data set as illustrated in Example 16.6.

Computer software packages can be used to implement exponential smoothing. These packages choose the smoothing constant (or constants) in different ways and also compute approximate

FIGURE 16.13   MINITAB Output of Using Simple Exponential Smoothing to Forecast
                the Cod Catches

(a) The graphical forecasts

(b) The numerical forecasts of the cod catch in month 25 (and any other future month)

	Forecasts		
Period	Forecast	Lower	Upper
25	348.168	276.976	419.360

prediction intervals in different ways. Optimally, the user should carefully investigate how the computer software package implements exponential smoothing. At a minimum, the user should not trust the forecasts given by the software package if they seem illogical.

Figure 16.13 gives the MINITAB output of using simple exponential smoothing to forecast in month 24 the cod catches in future months. Note that MINITAB has selected the smoothing constant $\alpha = .0703909$ and tells us that the point forecast and the 95 percent prediction interval forecast of the cod catch in any future month are, respectively, 348.168 and [276.976, 419.360]. Looking at Figure 16.13(a), these forecasts seem intuitively reasonable. An Excel add-in (MegaStat) output of simple exponential smoothing for the cod catch data is given in Appendix 16.1.

Exercises for Section 16.4

CONCEPTS

connect

16.18   In general, when is it appropriate to use exponential smoothing?

16.19   What is the purpose of a smoothing constant in exponential smoothing?

METHODS AND APPLICATIONS

16.20   **THE COD CATCH CASE**   🖸 CodCatch

Consider Table 16.13 (page 649). Verify (calculate) that S_3, an estimate made in period 3 of β_0, is 359.276. Also verify (calculate) that the one-period-ahead forecast error for period 4 is -62.276, as shown in Table 16.13.

FIGURE 16.14   **MINITAB Output of Using Simple Exponential Smoothing to Forecast Lumber Production**

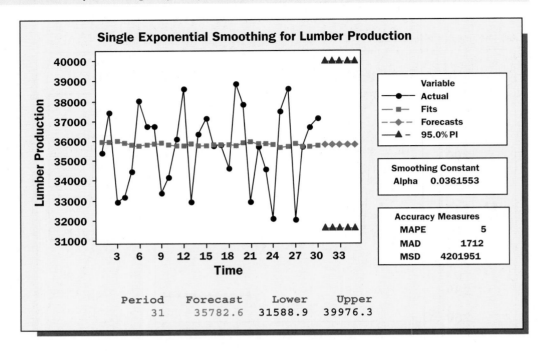

Period	Forecast	Lower	Upper
31	35782.6	31588.9	39976.3

16.21   THE COD CATCH CASE   DS CodCatch

Consider Example 16.7 (page 650). Suppose that we observe a cod catch in February of year 3 of $y_{26} = 328$. Update $S_{25} = 356.689$ to S_{26}, a point forecast made in month 26 of any future monthly cod catch. Use $\alpha = .02$ as in Example 16.7.

16.22   THE LUMBER PRODUCTION CASE   DS LumberProd

Figure 16.14 gives the MINITAB output of using simple exponential smoothing to forecast yearly U.S. lumber production. Here MINITAB has estimated the smoothing constant alpha to be .0361553. Use the MINITAB output to find and report the point prediction of and the 95 percent prediction interval for the total U.S. lumber production in a future year.

LO16-6 Use double exponential smoothing to forecast a time series.

16.5 Holt–Winters' Models ● ● ●

Holt–Winters' double exponential smoothing   Various extensions of simple exponential smoothing can be used to forecast time series that are described by models that are different from the model $y_t = \beta_0 + \varepsilon_t$. For example, **Holt–Winters' double exponential smoothing** can be used to forecast time series that are described by the linear trend model

$$y_t = \beta_0 + \beta_1 t + \varepsilon_t$$

Here we assume that β_0 and β_1 (and thus the linear trend) may be changing slowly over time. To implement Holt–Winters' double exponential smoothing, we let ℓ_{T-1} denote the estimate of the level $\beta_0 + \beta_1(T - 1)$ of the time series in time period $T - 1$, and we let b_{T-1} denote the estimate of the slope β_1 of the time series in time period $T - 1$. Then, if we observe a new time series value y_T in time period T, the estimate of the level $\beta_0 + \beta_1 T$ of the time series in time period T uses the **smoothing constant α** and is

$$\ell_T = \alpha y_T + (1 - \alpha)[\ell_{T-1} + b_{T-1}]$$

This equation says that ℓ_T equals a fraction α of the newly observed time series value y_T plus a fraction $(1 - \alpha)$ of $[\ell_{T-1} + b_{T-1}]$, which is the estimate of the level of the time series in time period T, as calculated using the estimates ℓ_{T-1} and b_{T-1} computed in time period $T - 1$. Furthermore, the estimate of the slope β_1 of the time series in time period T uses the **smoothing constant γ** and is

$$b_T = \gamma[\ell_T - \ell_{T-1}] + (1 - \gamma)b_{T-1}$$

This equation says that b_T equals a fraction γ of $[\ell_T - \ell_{T-1}]$, which is an estimate of the difference between the levels of the time series in periods T and $T - 1$, plus a fraction $(1 - \gamma)$ of b_{T-1}, the estimate of the slope made in time period $T - 1$.

To use the updating equations, we first obtain initial estimates ℓ_0 and b_0 of the level and the slope of the time series in time period 0. One way to do this is to fit a least squares trend line to part (say, one-half) of the historical data and let the y-intercept and slope of the trend line be ℓ_0 and b_0. For example, consider the 24 observed calculator sales values in Table 16.2 (page 633). If we fit a least squares trend line to the first 12 of those values, we obtain

$$\hat{y}_t = 204.803 + 6.9406t$$

This would imply that $\ell_0 = 204.803$ and $b_0 = 6.9406$. MINITAB uses a more complicated method to find initial estimates and obtains $\ell_0 = 198.0290$ and $b_0 = 8.0743$. Starting with the MINITAB initial estimates ℓ_0 and b_0, we calculate a point forecast of y_1 from time origin 0 to be

$$\hat{y}_1(0) = \ell_0 + b_0 = 198.0290 + 8.0743 = 206.103$$

This point forecast is shown on the MINITAB output of Figure 16.15(a) [it is the first number under the column headed $\hat{y}_T(T - 1)$]. Also shown on the output are the actual calculator sales value $y_1 = 197$ and the forecast error, which is

$$y_1 - \hat{y}_1(0) = 197 - 206.103 = -9.103$$

FIGURE 16.15　The MINITAB Output of Double Exponential Smoothing for the Calculator Sales Data

(a) The updated level and slope estimates when $\alpha = .2$ and $\gamma = .2$

$\ell_0 = 198.0290 \quad b_0 = 8.0743$

Time T	Sales y_T	Level ℓ_T	Slope b_T	Forecast $\hat{y}_T(T-1)$	Error $y_T - \hat{y}_T(T-1)$
1	197	204.283	7.7102	206.103	-9.1033
2	211	211.794	7.6705	211.993	-0.9929
3	203	216.172	7.0119	219.465	-16.4648
4	247	227.947	7.9646	223.184	23.8162
5	239	236.529	8.0881	235.912	3.0884
6	269	249.494	9.0634	244.617	24.3827
7	308	268.446	11.0411	258.557	49.4427
8	262	275.990	10.3416	279.487	-17.4869
9	258	280.665	9.2084	286.331	-28.3312
10	256	283.099	7.8535	289.873	-33.8733
11	261	284.962	6.6554	290.952	-29.9521
12	288	290.894	6.5107	291.617	-3.6171
13	296	297.123	6.4545	297.404	-1.4043
14	276	298.062	5.3514	303.578	-27.5780
15	305	303.731	5.4148	303.414	1.5862
16	308	308.917	5.3690	309.146	-1.1459
17	356	322.629	7.0376	314.286	41.7143
18	393	342.333	9.5709	329.666	63.3339
19	363	354.123	10.0148	351.904	11.0962
20	386	368.510	10.8893	364.138	21.8621
21	443	392.120	13.4333	379.400	63.6004
22	308	386.042	9.5312	405.553	-97.5529
23	358	388.059	8.0282	395.574	-37.5735
24	384	393.670	7.5447	396.087	-12.0870

(b) Point and 95 percent prediction interval forecasts when $\alpha = .2$ and $\gamma = .2$

Period	Forecast	Lower	Upper
25	401.214	337.813	464.616
26	408.759	344.037	473.482
27	416.304	350.159	482.449
28	423.849	356.186	491.512
29	431.393	362.124	500.663
30	438.938	367.979	509.898

(c) Point and 95 percent prediction interval forecasts when $\alpha = .496$ and $\gamma = .142$

Period	Forecast	Lower	Upper
25	383.677	319.135	448.220
26	389.121	316.066	462.177
27	394.565	312.109	477.022
28	400.010	307.534	492.486
29	405.454	302.521	508.386
30	410.898	297.191	524.604

We next choose values of the smoothing constants α and γ. A reasonable choice (and the default option of MINITAB) is to let each of α and γ be .2. Then, using $y_1 = 197$ and the equation for ℓ_T, it follows that the estimate of the level of the time series in time period 1 is

$$\ell_1 = \alpha y_1 + (1 - \alpha)[\ell_0 + b_0]$$
$$= .2(197) + .8[198.0290 + 8.0743]$$
$$= 204.283$$

Furthermore, using the equation for b_T, the estimate of the slope of the time series in time period 1 is

$$b_1 = \gamma[\ell_1 - \ell_0] + (1 - \gamma)b_0$$
$$= .2[204.283 - 198.0290] + .8(8.0743)$$
$$= 7.7102$$

It follows that a point forecast made in time period 1 of y_2 is

$$\hat{y}_2(1) = \ell_1 + b_1 = 204.283 + 7.7102 = 211.993$$

Because the actual calculator sales value in period 2 is $y_2 = 211$, the forecast error is

$$y_2 - \hat{y}_2(1) = 211 - 211.933 = -.993$$

The MINITAB output in Figure 16.15(a) on the previous page shows the entire process of using the double exponential smoothing updating equations to find new period-by-period estimates of the level and slope of the time series. The output also shows the one-period-ahead forecasts and forecast errors, which are utilized to evaluate the effectiveness of the double exponential smoothing procedure. At the end of the updating process, MINITAB uses $\ell_{24} = 393.670$ and $b_{24} = 7.5447$ to calculate point forecasts of future calculator sales values. For example, point forecasts of y_{25} and y_{26} made from time origin 24 are

$$\hat{y}_{25}(24) = \ell_{24} + b_{24} = 393.670 + 7.5447 = 401.214$$

and

$$\hat{y}_{26}(24) = \ell_{24} + 2b_{24} = 393.670 + 2(7.5447) = 408.759$$

These point forecasts, as well as point forecasts of y_{27} through y_{30}, are shown on the MINITAB output in Figure 16.15(b). Also shown are 95 percent prediction interval forecasts of y_{25} through y_{30}.

Figure 16.16 shows a MINITAB output that graphically illustrates the forecasts when $\alpha = .2$ and $\gamma = .2$. Generally speaking, choosing $\alpha = .2$ and $\gamma = .2$ gives reasonable results, but MINITAB will choose its own values of α and γ. If we have MINITAB do this, it chooses $\alpha = .496$ and $\gamma = .142$. The forecasts given by this choice of α and γ are given in Figure 16.15(c) and graphically illustrated in Figure 16.17. To evaluate the choice of a particular set of values for α and γ, MINITAB gives the **mean of the absolute forecast errors (the MAD)** and the **mean of the squared forecast errors (the MSD)** for the 24 historical calculator sales values. Comparing Figures 16.16 and 16.17, we see that $\alpha = .2$ and $\gamma = .2$ give a smaller MAD and MSD than do $\alpha = .496$ and $\gamma = .142$. Therefore, we might conclude that we should use the forecasts of y_{25} through y_{30} based on $\alpha = .2$ and $\gamma = .2$. On the other hand, we might believe that the lower sales values at the end of the observed data signal that the sales values will not continue to increase as fast as they have been increasing. In this case, we might use the lower forecasts given by $\alpha = .496$ and $\gamma = .142$ (see Figure 16.17).

LO16-7 Use multiplicative Winters' method to forecast a time series.

Multiplicative Winters' method (requires material from Section 16.3)

The **Multiplicative Winters' method** can be used to forecast time series that are described by the model

$$y_t = (\beta_0 + \beta_1 t) \times SN_t + \varepsilon_t$$

Here we assume that β_0 and β_1 (and thus the linear trend) and SN_t (which represents the seasonal pattern) may be changing slowly over time. To implement the multiplicative Winters' method, we let ℓ_{T-1} denote the estimate of the deseasonalized level $\beta_0 + \beta_1(T - 1)$ of the time series in time period $T - 1$, and we let b_{T-1} denote the estimate of the slope β_1 of the time series in time period $T - 1$. Then, suppose that we observe a new time series value y_T in time period T, and let sn_{T-L} denote the "most recent" estimate of the seasonal factor for the season corresponding to time period T. Here L denotes the number of seasons in a year ($L = 12$ for monthly data, and $L = 4$ for quarterly data),

FIGURE 16.16   The MINITAB Graphical Forecasts of Calculator Sales When $\alpha = .2$ and $\gamma = .2$

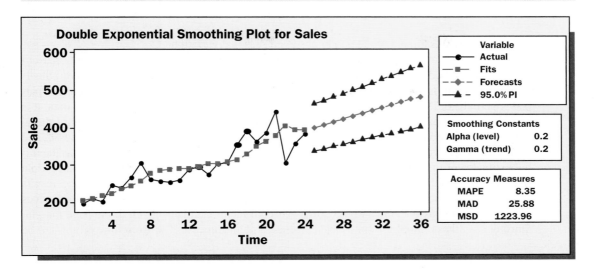

FIGURE 16.17   The MINITAB Graphical Forecasts When $\alpha = .496$ and $\gamma = .142$

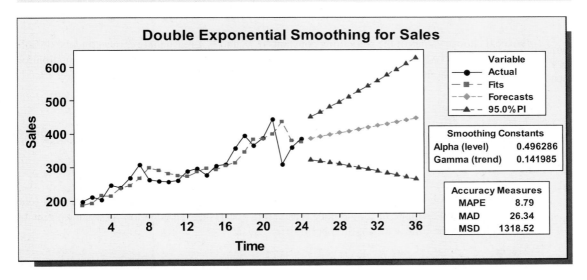

and thus $T - L$ denotes the time period occurring one year prior to time period T. Furthermore, the subscript $T - L$ of sn_{T-L} denotes the fact that the time series value observed in time period $T - L$ was the most recent time series value observed in the season being analyzed and thus was the most recent time series value used to help find sn_{T-L}. Then, the estimate of the deseasonalized level $\beta_0 + \beta_1 T$ of the time series in time period T uses the smoothing constant α and is

$$\ell_T = \alpha \frac{y_T}{sn_{T-L}} + (1 - \alpha)[\ell_{T-1} + b_{T-1}]$$

where y_T/sn_{T-L} is the deseasonalized observation in time period T. The estimate of the slope β_1 of the time series in time period T uses the smoothing constant γ and is

$$b_T = \gamma[\ell_T - \ell_{T-1}] + (1 - \gamma)b_{T-1}$$

The new estimate of the seasonal factor SN_T in time period T uses the smoothing constant δ and is

$$sn_T = \delta \frac{y_T}{\ell_T} + (1 - \delta)sn_{T-L}$$

where y_T/ℓ_T is an estimate of the newly observed seasonal variation.

To use the updating equations, we first obtain initial estimates ℓ_0, b_0, and sn_0 of the deseasonalized level, slope, and seasonal factors of the time series in time period 0. One way to do this is to use the multiplicative decomposition method (see Section 16.3 on page 640) to analyze part (say, one-half) of the historical data. Here, if there are less than five years of historical data, it is probably best to base the initial estimates on all of the historical data. Then, we regard the y-intercept and slope of the trend line fit to the deseasonalized data as the initial estimates ℓ_0 and b_0. Furthermore, we regard the multiplicative decomposition method's seasonal factors as the initial estimates of the seasonal factors in time period 0. For example, consider the 36 Tasty Cola sales values in Table 16.9 (page 640). Using the multiplicative decomposition method results summarized in Tables 16.10 (page 641) and 16.11 (page 643), we obtain the initial estimates $\ell_0 = 380.163$ and $b_0 = 9.489$ and the initial seasonal factor estimates given in the page margin. Starting with these initial estimates, we calculate a point forecast of y_1 from time origin 0 to be

Initial Seasonal Factor Estimates

Month	sn_0
Jan.	.493
Feb.	.596
Mar.	.595
Apr.	.680
May	.564
June	.986
July	1.467
Aug.	1.693
Sept.	1.990
Oct.	1.307
Nov.	1.029
Dec.	.600

$$\hat{y}_1(0) = (\ell_0 + b_0)sn_0$$
$$= (380.163 + 9.489)(.493)$$
$$= 192.098$$

Here we have used the initial January seasonal factor estimate $sn_0 = .493$ because y_1 is Tasty Cola sales in January of year 1. The actual value of y_1 is 189, so the forecast error is

$$y_1 - \hat{y}_1(0) = 189 - 192.098 = -3.098$$

We next choose values of the smoothing constants α, γ, and δ. A reasonable choice (and the default option of MINITAB) is to let each of α, γ, and δ be .2. Then, using $y_1 = 189$ and the equation for ℓ_T, it follows that the estimate of the deseasonalized level of the time series in time period 1 is

$$\ell_1 = \alpha \frac{y_1}{sn_0} + (1 - \alpha)[\ell_0 + b_0]$$
$$= .2\left[\frac{189}{.493}\right] + .8[380.163 + 9.489]$$
$$= 388.395$$

Here we have used the initial January seasonal factor estimate $sn_0 = .493$ as the most recent Winters' method estimate of the January seasonal factor. Using the equation for b_T, the estimate of the slope of the time series in time period 1 is

$$b_1 = \gamma[\ell_1 - \ell_0] + (1 - \gamma)b_0$$
$$= .2[388.395 - 380.163] + .8(9.489)$$
$$= 9.238$$

Using the equation for sn_T, the new estimate of the January seasonal factor in time period 1 is

$$sn_1 = \delta \frac{y_1}{\ell_1} + (1 - \delta)sn_0$$
$$= .2\left[\frac{189}{388.395}\right] + .8(.493)$$
$$= .492$$

It follows that a point forecast made in period 1 of y_2 is

$$\hat{y}_2(1) = (\ell_1 + b_1)sn_0$$
$$= (388.395 + 9.238)(.596)$$
$$= 236.989$$

Here we have used the initial February seasonal factor estimate $sn_0 = .596$ because y_2 is the Tasty Cola sales in February of year 1. The actual value of y_2 is 229, so the forecast error is

$$y_2 - \hat{y}_2(1) = 229 - 236.989 = -7.989$$

The MINITAB output in Figure 16.18(a) on the next page shows the entire process of using the Winters' method updating equations to find new period-by-period estimates of the level, slope, and seasonal factors of the time series. The output also shows the one-period-ahead forecasts and forecast errors, which are utilized to evaluate the effectiveness of the Winters' method procedure. MINITAB does not find initial estimates by using the multiplicative decomposition method. We will not discuss how MINITAB obtains initial estimates, but note from Figure 16.18(a) that the values of ℓ_1 and b_1 obtained by MINITAB ($\ell_1 = 278.768$ and $b_1 = 44.9736$) are very different from the values that we obtained by hand calculation ($\ell_1 = 388.395$ and $b_1 = 9.238$). In addition, the one-period-ahead forecast errors obtained by MINITAB are generally quite large in periods 1 through 12 but then become reasonably small for periods 13 through 36. To further illustrate the Winters' method updating equations, note from Figure 16.18(a) that $\ell_{35} = 725.603$ and $b_{35} = 8.9026$. Because the most recent estimate of the December seasonal factor is $sn_{24} = .60767$, the point forecast made in period 35 of y_{36} (sales in December of year 3) is

$$\hat{y}_{36}(35) = (\ell_{35} + b_{35})sn_{24}$$
$$= (725.603 + 8.9026)(.60767)$$
$$= 446.34$$

The actual sales value in period 36 is $y_{36} = 441$, so the forecast error is

$$y_{36} - \hat{y}_{36}(35) = 441 - 446.34 = -5.34$$

The updated estimates ℓ_{36}, b_{36}, and sn_{36} are calculated as follows:

$$\ell_{36} = \alpha \frac{y_{36}}{sn_{24}} + (1 - \alpha)[\ell_{35} + b_{35}]$$
$$= .2\left[\frac{441}{.60767}\right] + .8[725.603 + 8.9026]$$
$$= 732.75$$
$$b_{36} = \gamma[\ell_{36} - \ell_{35}] + (1 - \gamma)b_{35}$$
$$= .2[732.75 - 725.603] + .8(8.9026)$$
$$= 8.5514$$

and

$$sn_{36} = \delta \frac{y_{36}}{\ell_{36}} + (1 - \delta)sn_{24}$$
$$= .2\left[\frac{441}{732.75}\right] + .8(.60767)$$
$$= .6065$$

We are now at the end of the historical data, so we can forecast future Tasty Cola sales values. Figure 16.18(b) gives the point and 95 percent prediction interval forecasts of future sales values in periods 37 through 48, and Figure 16.19 graphically portrays the forecasts. To see how the point forecasts are calculated, note that, for example, the most recent estimates of the January and July seasonal factors are $sn_{25} = .48019$ and $sn_{31} = 1.42891$. Therefore, point forecasts made in period 36 of Tasty Cola sales in periods 37 and 43 (January and July of year 4) are

$$\hat{y}_{37}(36) = (\ell_{36} + b_{36})sn_{25} = (732.75 + 8.5514)(.48019) = 355.96$$

and

$$\hat{y}_{43}(36) = (\ell_{36} + 7b_{36})sn_{31} = [732.75 + 7(8.5514)](1.42891) = 1{,}132.57$$

FIGURE 16.18   The MINITAB Output of Winters' Method for the Tasty Cola Sales Data,
When $\alpha = .2$, $\gamma = .2$, and $\delta = .2$

(a) The updated level, slope, and seasonal factor estimates

Time T	Sales y_T	Level ℓ_T	Slope b_T	Seasonal sn_T	Forecast $\hat{y}_T(T-1)$	Error $y_T - \hat{y}_T(T-1)$
1	189	278.768	44.9736	0.48896	106.67	82.334
2	229	343.270	48.8794	0.56818	175.93	53.065
3	249	401.836	50.8167	0.57606	221.63	27.371
4	289	449.774	50.2409	0.65605	298.49	-9.492
5	260	492.009	48.6398	0.55787	282.62	-22.624
6	431	520.567	44.6235	0.94880	529.30	-98.301
7	660	541.448	39.8750	1.42638	835.48	-175.485
8	777	556.089	34.8280	1.64516	992.39	-215.395
9	915	562.722	29.1891	1.95207	1201.68	-286.680
10	613	565.315	23.8699	1.28544	790.62	-177.623
11	485	563.116	18.6561	1.01787	622.78	-137.777
12	277	552.752	12.8521	0.60770	369.04	-92.044
13	244	552.287	10.1887	0.47953	276.56	-32.557
14	296	554.174	8.5282	0.56137	319.59	-23.586
15	319	560.914	8.1706	0.57459	324.15	-5.151
16	370	568.063	7.9664	0.65511	373.35	-3.349
17	313	573.035	7.3675	0.55554	321.35	-8.352
18	556	581.523	7.5916	0.95026	550.68	5.315
19	831	587.811	7.3308	1.42385	840.30	-9.301
20	960	592.820	6.8664	1.64000	979.10	-19.101
21	1152	597.777	6.4846	1.94709	1170.63	-18.631
22	759	601.501	5.9325	1.28072	776.74	-17.742
23	607	605.216	5.4890	1.01488	618.29	-11.287
24	371	610.664	5.4807	0.60767	371.13	-0.126
25	298	617.205	5.6927	0.48019	295.46	2.542
26	378	632.989	7.7111	0.56853	349.67	28.326
27	373	642.391	8.0493	0.57580	368.14	4.859
28	443	655.597	9.0806	0.65923	426.11	16.891
29	374	666.385	9.4222	0.55668	369.26	4.743
30	660	679.556	10.1717	0.95445	642.19	17.807
31	1004	692.808	10.7879	1.42891	982.07	21.934
32	1153	703.487	10.7660	1.63980	1153.90	-0.898
33	1388	713.974	10.7103	1.94648	1390.71	-2.712
34	904	720.918	9.9571	1.27537	928.12	-24.118
35	715	725.603	8.9026	1.00898	741.75	-26.753
36	441	732.750	8.5514	0.60650	446.34	-5.336

(b) Point and 95 percent prediction interval forecasts

Period	Forecast	Lower	Upper
37	355.96	240.98	470.95
38	426.31	309.52	543.10
39	436.69	317.90	555.49
40	505.60	384.60	626.60
41	431.71	308.32	555.10
42	748.35	622.39	874.31
43	1132.57	1003.88	1261.26
44	1313.74	1182.16	1445.32
45	1576.09	1441.48	1710.70
46	1043.59	905.81	1181.37
47	834.24	693.17	975.32
48	506.65	362.17	651.14

FIGURE 16.19   MINITAB Output of Using Winters' Method to Forecast Tasty Cola Sales

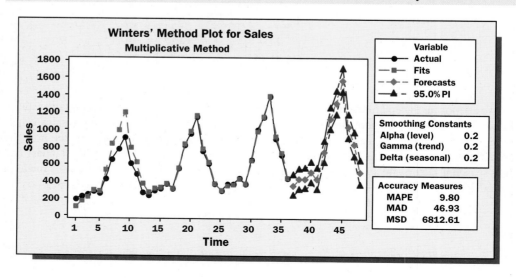

The reason that the 95 percent prediction intervals are so wide is that they can be shown to be functions of the historical forecast errors, which are very large in periods 1 through 12. The mean absolute forecast error in periods 13 through 36 can be calculated to be 12.98 and is more representative of the Winters' method's accuracy than is the mean absolute forecast error in all 36 periods, which is 46.93 (see Figure 16.19). Therefore, to obtain more reasonable prediction intervals, we might multiply the lengths of the prediction intervals by $12.98/46.93 \approx .28$. For example, Figure 16.18(b) tells us that the 95 percent prediction interval for y_{37} is [240.98, 470.95], which has length $470.95 - 240.98 = 229.97$. Multiplying this length by .28, we obtain $(229.97)(.28) = 64.39$. Surrounding the point forecast 355.96 by a new half-length of $64.39/2 = 32.2$, we obtain a new 95 percent prediction interval of $[355.96 \pm 32.2] = [323.76, 388.16]$. The other 95 percent prediction intervals can be modified similarly.

The wide prediction intervals in Figure 16.18(b) result from a combination of a short historical series (36 sales values) and MINITAB obtaining inaccurate initial estimates of the level, slope, and seasonal factors. When the historical series is long (for example, see Exercise 16.28, page 660), MINITAB usually obtains reasonable prediction intervals. Finally, note that MINITAB will not choose its own values of α, γ, and δ. However, the user can simply experiment with different combinations of values of these smoothing constants until a combination is found that produces the "best" results.

Exercises for Section 16.5

CONCEPTS

16.23 When do we use double exponential smoothing?

16.24 When do we use the multiplicative Winters' method?

METHODS AND APPLICATIONS

16.25 Consider Figure 16.15 on page 653. Calculate ℓ_2 and b_2 from ℓ_1, b_1, and y_2. Also, calculate $\hat{y}_{27}(24)$ from ℓ_{24} and b_{24}.

16.26 Consider Figure 16.18 on page 658. Calculate ℓ_{35}, b_{35}, and sn_{35} from ℓ_{34}, b_{34}, y_{35}, and sn_{23}. Also, calculate $\hat{y}_{38}(36)$ from ℓ_{36}, b_{36}, and sn_{26}.

16.27 THE WATCH SALES CASE   DS WatchSale

Figure 16.20 gives the MINITAB output of using double exponential smoothing in month 20 to forecast watch sales in months 21 through 26. Here we have used MINITAB's default option that sets each of the smoothing constants alpha and gamma equal to .2. Find and report the point prediction of and a 95 percent prediction interval for watch sales in month 21.

FIGURE 16.20   **MINITAB Output of Using Double Exponential Smoothing to Forecast Watch Sales**

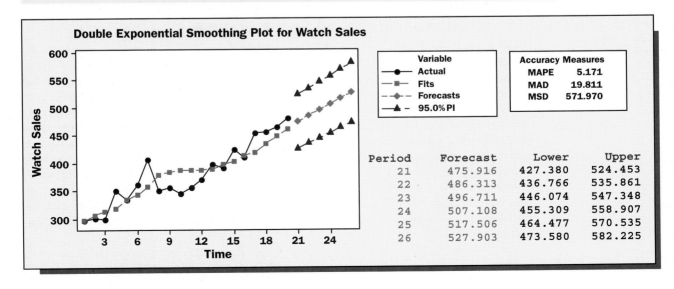

Period	Forecast	Lower	Upper
21	475.916	427.380	524.453
22	486.313	436.766	535.861
23	496.711	446.074	547.348
24	507.108	455.309	558.907
25	517.506	464.477	570.535
26	527.903	473.580	582.225

FIGURE 16.21   MINITAB Output of Using Winters' Method to Forecast the Monthly
Hotel Room Averages

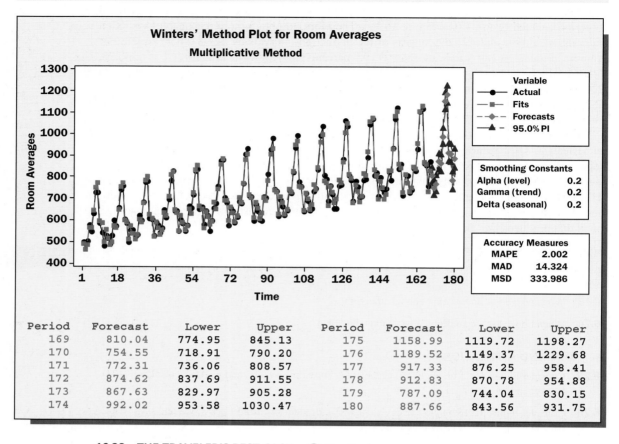

Period	Forecast	Lower	Upper	Period	Forecast	Lower	Upper
169	810.04	774.95	845.13	175	1158.99	1119.72	1198.27
170	754.55	718.91	790.20	176	1189.52	1149.37	1229.68
171	772.31	736.06	808.57	177	917.33	876.25	958.41
172	874.62	837.69	911.55	178	912.83	870.78	954.88
173	867.63	829.97	905.28	179	787.09	744.04	830.15
174	992.02	953.58	1030.47	180	887.66	843.56	931.75

16.28   THE TRAVELER'S REST CASE DS TravRest

Figure 16.21 gives the MINITAB output of using multiplicative Winters' method in month 168 to forecast the monthly hotel room averages in months 169 through 180. Here we have used MINITAB's default option that sets each of the smoothing constants alpha, gamma, and delta equal to .2. Use the MINITAB output to find and report the point prediction of and a 95 percent prediction interval for the monthly hotel room average in period 169.

LO16-8 Appreciate some of the basic concepts of Box–Jenkins forecasting models.

16.6 A Brief Introduction to Box–Jenkins Models (Optional Advanced Section) ● ● ●

In this section we discuss the **Box–Jenkins methodology.** This methodology, developed by G. E. P. Box and G. M. Jenkins (1976), uses an approach to describe the trend and seasonal effects in time series data that is quite different from the approach taken by regression (or exponential smoothing). The Box–Jenkins methodology begins by determining if the time series under consideration is *stationary*. Intuitively, a time series is **stationary** if the statistical properties (for example, the level and the variance) of the time series are essentially constant through time. If we have observed n values $y_1, y_2, \ldots, y_n$ of a time series, we can use a plot of these values (against time) to help us determine whether the time series is stationary. If the n values seem to fluctuate with constant variation around a constant level, then it is reasonable to believe that the time series is stationary. If the n values do not fluctuate around a constant level or do not fluctuate with constant variation, then it is reasonable to believe that the time series is nonstationary. In this case, the Box–Jenkins methodology tells us to *transform* the nonstationary time series values into stationary time series values.

For example, recall that Table 16.8 on page 639 gives monthly international passenger totals for the past 11 years for an airline. The partial MINITAB output in Figure 16.22(a) gives the first 15 and the last 2 of these monthly passenger totals (see Pass). The plot of these passenger totals is

FIGURE 16.22   The Passenger Totals, Natural Logarithms, and Differences Data, and Time Series Plots of the Passenger Totals and Natural Logarithms

(a) Partial MINITAB data output

t	Pass	LnPass	Reg	Seas	RegSeas
1	112	4.71850	*	*	*
2	118	4.77068	0.052186	*	*
3	132	4.88280	0.112117	*	*
4	129	4.85981	−0.022990	*	*
5	121	4.79579	−0.064022	*	*
6	135	4.90527	0.109484	*	*
7	148	4.99721	0.091937	*	*
8	148	4.99721	0.000000	*	*
9	136	4.91265	−0.084557	*	*
10	119	4.77912	−0.133531	*	*
11	104	4.64439	−0.134733	*	*
12	118	4.77068	0.126294	*	*
13	115	4.74493	−0.025752	0.026433	*
14	126	4.83628	0.091350	0.065597	0.039164
15	141	4.94876	0.112478	0.065958	0.000361
131	362	5.89164	−0.117169	0.155072	0.029581
132	405	6.00389	0.112243	0.183804	0.028732

(b) Passenger totals plot

Time Series Plot of Pass

(c) Natural logarithm plot

Time Series Plot of LnPass

shown in Figure 16.22(b) and indicates that the passenger totals exhibit an upward linear trend with seasonal variation that increases with the level of the totals. In terms of Box–Jenkins modeling, the **increasing seasonal variation** implies that the time series is **nonstationary with respect to its variance** and we should use a variance stabilizing transformation. Figure 16.22(a) gives the natural logarithms (see LnPass) of the monthly passenger totals for the time periods shown in the figure, and Figure 16.22(c) shows that the natural logarithms exhibit an upward linear trend with constant (variance-stabilized) seasonal variation. That is, letting y_t^* denote the variance-stabilized passenger total in month t, it follows that $y_t^* = \ln y_t$. The linear trend and seasonal variation in the y_t^* values indicate that, although these values are stationary with respect to their variance, they are **nonstationary with respect to their level.** To transform these values into stationary values with respect to their level, the Box–Jenkins methodology uses one of three types of *differencing: regular differencing*, *seasonal differencing*, or *combined regular and seasonal differencing*.

The **regular difference** of the passenger totals' natural logarithms in time period t, denoted z_t, is the difference between y_t^*, the natural logarithm in time period t, and y_{t-1}^*, the natural logarithm in time period $t-1$. That is, $z_t = y_t^* - y_{t-1}^*$. For example, Figure 16.22(a) tells us that the natural logarithms in months 1, 2, 3, 131, and 132 are $y_1^* = 4.71850$, $y_2^* = 4.77068$, $y_3^* = 4.88280$, $y_{131}^* = 5.89164$, and $y_{132}^* = 6.00389$. Therefore, the regular differences of the natural logarithms are:

$$z_2 = y_2^* - y_1^* = 4.77068 - 4.71850 = .05218$$
$$z_3 = y_3^* - y_2^* = 4.88280 - 4.77068 = .11212$$
$$\vdots$$
$$z_{132} = y_{132}^* - y_{131}^* = 6.00389 - 5.89164 = .11225$$

Figure 16.22(a) gives the regular differences (see Reg) of the natural logarithms for the time periods shown in the figure. Note that, because MINITAB does calculations using more precise decimal place accuracy than it sometimes shows, the results in Figure 16.22(a) are slightly different from the results that we hand calculate. To calculate the **seasonal differences** of the natural logarithms in time period t, we use the equation $z_t = y_t^* - y_{t-L}^*$, where L is the number of seasons in a year. Because the passenger totals data is monthly, L equals 12, and thus we use the equation $z_t = y_t^* - y_{t-12}^*$. Figure 16.22(a) tells us that $y_1^* = 4.71850$, $y_2^* = 4.77068$, $y_{13}^* = 4.74493$, and $y_{14}^* = 4.83628$. It follows that the first two seasonal differences are:

$$z_{13} = y_{13}^* - y_1^* = 4.74493 - 4.71850 \quad \text{and} \quad z_{14} = y_{14}^* - y_2^* = 4.83628 - 4.77068$$
$$= .02643 \quad\quad\quad\quad\quad\quad\quad = .0656$$

To carry out **combined regular and seasonal differencing,** we take the regular differences of the seasonal differences. For example, the regular difference of the just calculated two seasonal

FIGURE 16.23   **Time Series Plots for Analyzing the Passenger Totals' Natural Logarithms**

(a) Regular difference plot   **(b) Seasonal difference plot**   **(c) Combined difference plot**

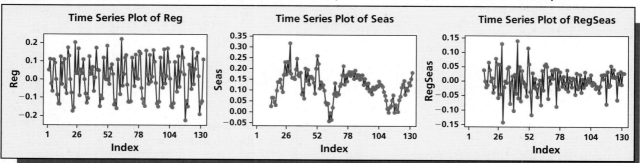

differences is $.0656 - .02643 = .03917$. Figure 16.22(a) gives the seasonal differences (see Seas) and the combined regular and seasonal differences (see RegSeas) of the natural logarithms for the time periods shown in the figure. Moreover, Figure 16.23 shows time series plots of the regular differences, the seasonal differences, and the combined regular and seasonal differences of the natural logarithms. Examining the plot in Figure 16.23(a), it might seem at first glance that the regular differences are fluctuating with constant variation around a constant level. However, the periodic "dips" in the plot indicate that the regular differences exhibit a seasonal pattern and thus are nonstationary. The plot in Figure 16.23(b) shows that the seasonal differences do not exhibit any long term upward or downward trend movements or any seasonal pattern. However, because these seasonal differences exhibit repeated, short term upward and downward trend movements, we say that they exhibit **changing (or stochastic) trend effects.** These stochastic trend effects imply that the seasonal differences are nonstationary. Finally, Figure 16.23(c) shows that the combined regular and seasonal differences do not seem to exhibit either trend effects or a seasonal pattern. Because these combined differences seem to fluctuate with (approximately) constant variation around a constant level, we will regard them as being stationary.

A Box–Jenkins model   Because the combined regular and seasonal differences are stationary, we will find a Box–Jenkins model describing them. The combined regular and seasonal difference in time period t, z_t, is the regular difference of the seasonal difference $y_t^* - y_{t-12}^*$ and thus can be expressed as

$$z_t = y_t^* - y_{t-12}^* - (y_{t-1}^* - y_{t-13}^*)$$

The simplest Box–Jenkins model describing z_t would set z_t equal to an error term ε_t. This would give

$$y_t^* - y_{t-12}^* - (y_{t-1}^* - y_{t-13}^*) = \varepsilon_t$$

Solving for y_t^*, we would have the following Box–Jenkins model describing y_t^*:

$$y_t^* = y_{t-12}^* + (y_{t-1}^* - y_{t-13}^*) + \varepsilon_t$$

If we temporarily ignore the error term ε_t, this model says that y_t^*, the passenger totals' natural logarithm in time period t, equals y_{t-12}^*, the passenger totals' natural logarithm one year ago, plus $(y_{t-1}^* - y_{t-13}^*)$, the difference between the passenger totals' natural logarithm last month and the passenger totals' natural logarithm one year ago last month. Of course, this and all Box–Jenkins models describe the time series value y_t^* by using ε_t, the error term in time period t, and in fact some Box–Jenkins models also describe y_t^* by using $\varepsilon_{t-1}, \varepsilon_{t-2}, \ldots$, the error terms in previous time periods. Such previous error terms are called *moving average terms.* Later in this section we

FIGURE 16.24   Analysis of the Passenger Totals' Box–Jenkins Model

(a) Estimation and diagnostic checking

Type		Coef	SE Coef	T	P
MA	1	0.3407	0.0868	3.93	0.000
SMA	12	0.6299	0.0766	8.23	0.000

Modified Box-Pierce (Ljung-Box)
Chi-Square statistic

Lag	12	24	36	48
Chi-Square	7.5	19.6	30.5	38.7
DF	10	22	34	46
P-Value	0.679	0.607	0.638	0.770

(b) Residuals

t	LnPass	FITS	RESI
120	5.82008	5.86184	−0.041754
121	5.88610	5.85600	0.030104
122	5.83481	5.83182	0.002987
123	6.00635	5.98014	0.026218
124	5.98141	5.97049	0.010927
125	6.04025	6.00109	0.039167
126	6.15698	6.18944	−0.032462
127	6.30628	6.27991	0.026361
128	6.32615	6.30195	0.024195
129	6.13773	6.15349	−0.015763
130	6.00881	6.01104	−0.002232
131	5.89164	5.87364	0.018005
132	6.00389	5.99133	0.012558

(c) Forecasting

Period	Forecast	95% Limits Lower	Upper
133	6.03771	5.96718	6.10823
134	5.99099	5.90652	6.07546
135	6.14666	6.05023	6.24308
136	6.12046	6.01341	6.22751
137	6.15698	6.04026	6.27369
138	6.30256	6.17692	6.42819
139	6.42828	6.29432	6.56224
140	6.43857	6.29677	6.58037
141	6.26527	6.11604	6.41450
142	6.13438	5.97807	6.29069
143	6.00539	5.84231	6.16846
144	6.11358	5.94401	6.28316

will see that the appropriate Box–Jenkins model describing the logged passenger total y_t^* uses the moving average terms ε_{t-1}, ε_{t-2}, and ε_{t-13} and is

$$y_t^* = y_{t-12}^* + (y_{t-1}^* - y_{t-13}^*) + \varepsilon_t - \theta_1\varepsilon_{t-1} - \theta_{12}\varepsilon_{t-12} + \theta_1\theta_{12}\varepsilon_{t-13}$$

Here, θ_1 and θ_{12} are unknown parameters that must be estimated from sample data, and the minus signs are used because of the theory behind the Box–Jenkins methodology. The procedure for finding such a model is quite complex. For this reason we will first give the reader an intuitive understanding of the model by using it to forecast future time series values.

The MINITAB output in Figure 16.24(a) tells us that the least squares point estimates of θ_1 and θ_{12} are $\hat{\theta}_1 = .3407$ and $\hat{\theta}_{12} = .6299$. Moreover, because the p-values for testing $H_0 : \theta_1 = 0$ and $H_0 : \theta_{12} = 0$ are each less than .001, we conclude that each of θ_1 and θ_{12} is important in the model. (The lower half of Figure 16.24(a) provides a *Chi-square analysis* that is used to *diagnostically check* the adequacy of the model. This will be explained later.) To compute a point forecast of y_{133}^*, next month's logged passenger total, we insert $t = 133$, as well as the least squares point estimates $\hat{\theta}_1 = .3407$ and $\hat{\theta}_{12} = .6299$, into the model. This gives the point forecast

$$\hat{y}_{133}^*(132) = y_{121}^* + (y_{132}^* - y_{120}^*) + \hat{\varepsilon}_{133} - .3407\,\hat{\varepsilon}_{132} - .6299\,\hat{\varepsilon}_{121} + (.3407)(.6299)\,\hat{\varepsilon}_{120}$$

To compute this point forecast, we use the natural logarithms (see LnPass in Figure 16.24(b)) $y_{120}^* = 5.82008$, $y_{121}^* = 5.88610$, and $y_{132}^* = 6.00389$ of the passenger totals in months 120, 121, and 132. In addition, we predict the future error term ε_{133} to be $\hat{\varepsilon}_{133} = 0$, and we predict the past error terms ε_{132}, ε_{121}, and ε_{120} by using MINITAB computed residuals for time periods 132, 121, and 120. To obtain the residuals, MINITAB uses an advanced technique and the Box–Jenkins model that it has fit to the 132 logged passenger totals to calculate a point prediction of each logged passenger total. The residual for a particular month is then the difference between the observed logged passenger total and the predicted logged passenger total for the month. Figure 16.24(b) shows the residuals for months 120 through 132. For month 120, for example, the observed logged passenger total is $y_{120}^* = 5.82008$ (see LnPass), the predicted logged passenger total is $\hat{y}_{120}^* = 5.86184$ (see FITS), and the residual $\hat{\varepsilon}_{120}$ is $y_{120}^* - \hat{y}_{120}^* = 5.82008 - 5.86184 = -.041754$ (see RESI). Figure 16.24(b) tells us that the residuals for time periods 132, 121, and 120 are $\hat{\varepsilon}_{132} = .012558$, $\hat{\varepsilon}_{121} = .030104$, and $\hat{\varepsilon}_{120} = -.041754$. Inserting all of the needed quantities into the above equation for the point forecast $\hat{y}_{133}^*(132)$, we find that

$$\hat{y}_{133}^*(132) = 5.88610 + (6.00389 - 5.82008) + 0$$
$$- .3407(.012558) - .6299(.030104)$$
$$+ (.3407)(.6299)(-.041754)$$
$$= 6.03771$$

This point forecast and a 95 percent prediction interval for y_{133}^* are given in Figure 16.24(c). Exponentiating the point forecast and the ends of the prediction interval, we obtain $e^{6.03771} = 418,933$ and $[e^{5.96718}, e^{6.10823}] = [390,403, 449,542]$. Therefore, the airline forecasts that it will fly 418,933 customers in month 133 (January of year 12). The airline is 95 percent confident it will fly between 390,403 and 449,542 customers in month 133.

FIGURE 16.25   The SAC and SPAC of the Combined Regular and Seasonal Differences

(a) The SAC   (b) The SPAC

FIGURE 16.26   SAC of the Passenger Totals' Natural Logarithms

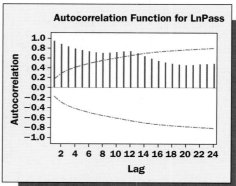

The sample autocorrelation function   In order to help find a Box–Jenkins model describing a time series of z_t values, we use the *sample autocorrelation function (SAC)* and the *sample partial autocorrelation (SPAC)* of the z_t values. To explain the sample autocorrelation function, we first define the **sample autocorrelation at lag k,** denoted r_k, to be the simple correlation coefficient between z_t values separated by k time units. For example, r_1, r_2, and r_3 are the simple correlation coefficients between z_t values separated by, respectively, one, two, and three time units. To illustrate calculating (for instance) r_3, consider the combined regular and seasonal differences of the passenger totals' natural logarithms. In Figure 16.22(a) we have computed these combined differences to be $z_{14} = .039164$, $z_{15} = .000361, \ldots, z_{131} = .029581$, and $z_{132} = .028732$. The mean of these combined differences can be shown to equal $\bar{z} = .001322$. Inserting these z_t values and $\bar{z}$ into the following equation

$$r_3 = \frac{(z_{14} - \bar{z})(z_{17} - \bar{z}) + (z_{15} - \bar{z})(z_{18} - \bar{z}) + \cdots + (z_{129} - \bar{z})(z_{132} - \bar{z})}{(z_{14} - \bar{z})^2 + (z_{15} - \bar{z})^2 + \cdots + (z_{132} - \bar{z})^2}$$

it follows that r_3, the simple correlation coefficient between z_t values separated by three time units, can be calculated to be $-.216$. In general, we define the **sample autocorrelation function (SAC)** to be a listing, or graph, of the sample autocorrelations at lags $k = 1, 2, \ldots$. Figure 16.25(a) presents the MINITAB output of the SAC of the combined differences of the passenger totals' natural logarithms. The vertical lines on the output represent the sample autocorrelations. For example, the vertical lines at lags 1, 2, and 3 represent r_1, r_2, and r_3, which can be computed to be $-.317, .109$, and (as just demonstrated) $-.216$. In order to begin to interpret the meaning of these and the other sample autocorrelations in the SAC, we identify the existence of **spikes** in the SAC. We say that **a spike exists at lag k in the SAC** if the sample autocorrelation r_k is large enough in magnitude to conclude that ρ_k, the population autocorrelation of all possible z_t values separated by k time units, does not equal 0. One frequently used convention is to conclude that a spike exists at lag k in the SAC if r_k is at least as large in magnitude as twice its estimated standard deviation. If we examine the MINITAB output of the SAC in Figure 16.25(a), we see that the "center line" on the plot of the r_k values is positioned at 0. Furthermore, for any lag k the dashed line above the center line is two estimated standard deviations greater than 0, and the dashed line below the center line is two estimated standard deviations less than 0. If the vertical line representing r_k extends at least as far up or down as the two standard deviation dashed lines corresponding to lag k, then we conclude that a spike exists at lag k in the SAC. Examining Figure 16.25(a), we conclude that spikes exist at lags 1, 3, and 12 in the SAC.

The sample partial autocorrelation function   The **sample partial autocorrelation function (SPAC)** of a time series of z_t values is a listing, or graph, of the **sample partial autocorrelations** at lags $k = 1, 2, \ldots$. It is beyond the scope of this text to give a precise definition of the **sample partial autocorrelation at lag k.** However, this quantity, which is denoted r_{kk}, may intuitively be thought of as the sample autocorrelation of z_t values separated by k time units **with the effects of the intervening z_t values eliminated.** Figure 16.25(b) gives the MINITAB output of the SPAC of the combined differences of the passenger totals' natural logarithms. Examining this output, we see that, for example, the vertical lines at lags 1 and 2 represent r_{11} and r_{22}, the sample partial autocorrelations of the combined differences separated by, respectively, one and two time units. In general, if r_{kk} is at least as large in magnitude as twice its estimated standard deviation, we say that **a spike exists at lag k in the SPAC.** This implies that ρ_{kk}, the population partial autocorrelation of all possible z_t values separated by k time units, does not equal 0. The r_{kk} values are plotted in the MINITAB output of Figure 16.25(b). We conclude that a spike exists at lag k in the SPAC if the vertical line representing r_{kk} extends at least as far up or down as the two standard deviation dashed lines corresponding to lag k. Because this occurs at lags 1, 3, 9, 12, and 23, we conclude that spikes occur at these lags in the SPAC. We will now see that the spikes in the SAC and SPAC, as well as the overall behavior of the SAC and SPAC, help us to **tentatively identify** a Box–Jenkins model.

Moving average terms   We have previously seen that some Box–Jenkins models describe the **future time series value z_t** by using **past error terms ε_{t-1}, ε_{t-2}, . . . ,** which are called **moving average terms.** The following guidelines tell us when to use *nonseasonal moving average terms* and *seasonal moving average terms.* [See Bowerman, O'Connell, and Koehler (2005) for the theory behind the guidelines.] To use the guidelines, we define (for monthly seasonal data) the **nonseasonal level** of the SAC and the SPAC to be lags 1 through 9 and the **seasonal level** of the SAC and the SPAC to be lags 12 and 24.

Guideline 1: Using nonseasonal moving average terms   Suppose that, at the nonseasonal level, the SAC has **a spike at one or more lags and then abruptly cuts off** (that is, has no spikes) after a certain lag, and the **SPAC dies down fairly quickly** (that is, has sample partial autocorrelations that steadily decrease fairly quickly). In this case, we should describe the time series value z_t by using **past error terms (nonseasonal moving average terms) that correspond to the lags at which spikes exist in the SAC.** For example, we have seen that Figure 16.25 gives the SAC and SPAC of the combined differences of the passenger totals' natural logarithms. At the nonseasonal level, the SAC has spikes at lags 1 and 3 and then cuts off after lag 3, and the SPAC dies down fairly quickly. Here, in concluding that the SPAC dies down fairly quickly, we have ignored a spike at lag 9 in the SPAC. In general, it is a common practice to ignore spikes at higher nonseasonal lags in the SAC and SPAC. Because the SAC has spikes at lags 1 and 3, this guideline says that we should describe the combined difference z_t by using ε_{t-1} and ε_{t-3}. However, because the spike at lag 3 is barely a spike, and because the Box–Jenkins methodology seeks to find simple (*parsimonious*) models, we will begin by attempting to describe z_t by using ε_{t-1} (and not ε_{t-3}). Then, we will *diagnostically check* the model to see if we made the right decision.

Guideline 2: Using a seasonal moving average term   Suppose that, at the **seasonal level,** the **SAC has a spike at lag 12 and cuts off after lag 12** (that is, has a small sample autocorrelation at lag 24), and the **SPAC dies down fairly quickly (at lags 12 and 24).** In this case, we should describe the time series value z_t by using the **past error term ε_{t-12}** (which is called a **seasonal moving average term**). For example, consider Figure 16.25. At the seasonal level, the SAC has a spike at lag 12 and cuts off after lag 12, and the SPAC dies down fairly quickly. Therefore, we should describe z_t by using the seasonal moving average term ε_{t-12}. Because we have also concluded in Guideline 1 that we should describe z_t by using ε_{t-1}, it follows that a tentative Box–Jenkins model describing z_t is

$$z_t = \varepsilon_t - \theta_1 \varepsilon_{t-1} - \theta_{12} \varepsilon_{t-12} + \theta_1 \theta_{12} \varepsilon_{t-13}$$

Here, theory behind the Box–Jenkins methodology tells us to use the **multiplicative component** $\theta_1 \theta_{12} \varepsilon_{t-13}$. Moreover, if we insert the expression for the combined difference, $z_t = y_t^* - y_{t-12}^* - (y_{t-1}^* - y_{t-13}^*)$, into this model and solve for y_t^*, we obtain

$$y_t^* = y_{t-12}^* + (y_{t-1}^* - y_{t-13}^*) + \varepsilon_t - \theta_1 \varepsilon_{t-1} - \theta_{12} \varepsilon_{t-12} + \theta_1 \theta_{12} \varepsilon_{t-13}$$

Before using this tentative model to calculate forecasts (as we have done on page 663), we should check to see if the model is *adequate*. In general, it can be shown that if a tentative model is **adequate,** then the sample autocorrelations of the tentative model's residuals will not be unusually large, and thus the model's **Chi-square statistic *p*-values** will be greater than .05. Because the Chi-square statistic *p*-values in Figure 16.24(a) for the tentative passenger totals model are greater than .05, we conclude that this model is adequate.

We have seen that if a time series fluctuates with constant variation around a constant level, then the time series should be considered to be stationary. It can also be shown that if the SAC cuts off or dies down fairly quickly at both the nonseasonal and seasonal levels, then the time series should be considered to be stationary. However, if the SAC has large sample autocorrelations that die down very slowly at either level, or at both levels (for example, see Figure 16.26 on page 664), then the time series should be considered to be nonstationary.

Autoregressive Terms   Some Box–Jenkins models describe the **future time series value** z_t, by using **past time series values** $z_{t-1}, z_{t-2}, \ldots$, which are called **autoregressive terms.** The following guidelines tell us when to use *nonseasonal autoregressive terms* and *seasonal autoregressive terms.*

Guideline 3: Using nonseasonal autoregressive terms   Suppose that, at the nonseasonal level, the **SAC dies down fairly quickly** (that is, has sample autocorrelations that steadily decrease fairly quickly), and the **SPAC has a spike at one or more lags and then abruptly cuts off** (that is, has no spikes) after a certain lag. In this case we should describe the time series value z_t by using **past time series values (nonseasonal autoregressive terms) that correspond to the lags at which spikes exist in the SPAC.** For example, consider the seasonal differences ($z_t = y_t^* - y_{t-12}^*$) of the quartic roots ($y_t^* = y_t^{.25}$) of the hotel room averages in Table 16.4 on page 636. It can be verified that these seasonal differences fluctuate with constant variation around a constant level and are, therefore, stationary. Figure 16.27 gives the SAC and SPAC of these seasonal differences. At the nonseasonal level, the SAC dies down fairly quickly, and the SPAC has spikes at lags 1 and 3 and (with the exception of a smaller spike at lag 5) cuts off after lag 3. Because the SPAC has spikes at lags 1 and 3, this guideline says that we should describe the seasonal difference z_t by using z_{t-1} and z_{t-3}. Moreover, MINITAB requires us to use the **intervening term** z_{t-2} because we use z_{t-1} and z_{t-3}.

Guideline 4: Using a seasonal autoregressive term   Suppose that, at the **seasonal level**, the **SAC dies down fairly quickly (at lags 12 and 24),** and the **SPAC has a spike at lag 12 and cuts off after lag 12** (that is, has a small sample partial autocorrelation at lag 24). In this case, we should describe the time series value z_t by using the **past time series value** z_{t-12} (which is called a **seasonal autoregressive term**). In practice, the behavior described in this guideline does not occur frequently.

Examining Figure 16.27, we see that at the seasonal level, the SAC has a spike at lag 12 and cuts off after lag 12, and the SPAC dies down fairly quickly. This is the behavior described in Guideline 2, and thus Guideline 2 says that we should describe z_t by using the seasonal moving average term z_{t-12}. Because Guideline 3 says that we should also describe z_t by using z_{t-1}, z_{t-2}, and z_{t-3}, a tentative Box–Jenkins model describing z_t is

$$z_t = \delta + \phi_1 z_{t-1} + \phi_2 z_{t-2} + \phi_3 z_{t-3} - \theta_{12} \varepsilon_{t-12} + \varepsilon_t$$

Here, we have included a **constant term** δ (to be explained momentarily) in the model, and δ, as well as ϕ_1, ϕ_2, ϕ_3, and θ_{12} are unknown parameters that must be estimated from sample data. Inserting the seasonal difference $z_t = y_t^* - y_{t-12}^*$ into this model and solving for y_t^*, we find that a tentative Box–Jenkins model describing y_t^* is

$$y_t^* = \delta + y_{t-12}^* + \phi_1(y_{t-1}^* - y_{t-13}^*) + \phi_2(y_{t-2}^* - y_{t-14}^*) + \phi_3(y_{t-3}^* - y_{t-15}^*) - \theta_{12}\varepsilon_{t-12} + \varepsilon_t$$

The constant term δ in the tentative model says that there is a **deterministic trend** of δ as we move from y_{t-12}^*, the quartic root of the hotel room average one year ago, to y_t^*, the quartic root of the current hotel room average. In the exercises, the reader will assess the appropriateness of the tentative model (δ will be found to be important) and will use the model to forecast. (It can be verified that a constant term δ is not needed in the passenger totals model.)

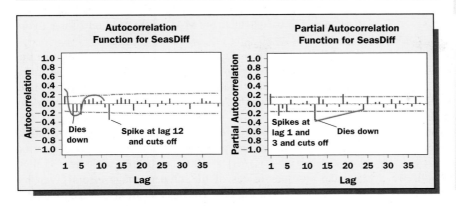

FIGURE 16.27   The SAC and SPAC of the Hotel Room Seasonal Differences

FIGURE 16.28   Forecasting (for Exercise 16.31)

Period	Forecast	95% Limits Lower	Upper
169	5.38091	5.33070	5.43111
170	5.26784	5.21622	5.31946
171	5.27552	5.22303	5.32801
172	5.42917	5.37584	5.48249
173	5.40940	5.35592	5.46289
174	5.59285	5.53915	5.64654
175	5.82033	5.76663	5.87404
176	5.85258	5.79888	5.90629
177	5.47779	5.42406	5.53152
178	5.47843	5.42470	5.53215
179	5.28889	5.23516	5.34262
180	5.46090	5.40717	5.51463

To conclude this section, note that the reason we did not use any multiplicative terms in the hotel room average model is that the nonseasonal components $\phi_1 z_{t-1}$, $\phi_2 z_{t-2}$, and $\phi_3 z_{t-3}$ are autoregressive components and the seasonal component $-\theta_{12}\varepsilon_{t-12}$ is a moving average component. If the SAC at the seasonal level had told us to use the seasonal autoregressive term z_{t-12} (Guideline 4), then $-\theta_{12}\varepsilon_{t-12}$ would be replaced by $\phi_{12} z_{t-12} - \phi_1\phi_{12} z_{t-13} - \phi_2\phi_{12} z_{t-14} - \phi_3\phi_{12} z_{t-15}$. This model uses three multiplicative terms, which are appropriate when *both* the nonseasonal and seasonal components of the model are autoregressive.

Exercises for Section 16.6

CONCEPTS

connect

16.29   Discuss the purpose of differencing.

16.30   Explain how we use the SAC and SPAC.

METHODS AND APPLICATIONS

16.31   The least squares point estimates of the parameters of the tentative hotel room average model are $\hat{\delta} = .038056\ (.000)$, $\hat{\phi}_1 = .2392\ (.003)$, $\hat{\phi}_2 = .1322\ (.104)$, $\hat{\phi}_3 = -.2642\ (.001)$, and $\hat{\theta}_{12} = .5271\ (.000)$, where the MINITAB calculated p-values for the importance of the model parameters are given in parentheses. The chi-square statistic p-values for the diagnostic checking of model adequacy are .242 (lag 12), .186 (lag 24), .276 (lag 36), and .461 (lag 48). (1) Assess the appropriateness of the tentative model. (2) Use the model to write out an expression for y^{*}_{169}. (3) Hand calculate the point forecast of y^{*}_{169} to be $\hat{y}^{*}_{169}(168) = 5.38091$ (see Figure 16.28). Hint: Recalling that $y^{*}_t = y^{.25}_t$, use the facts that $y^{*}_{157} = 5.33648$, $y^{*}_{168} - y^{*}_{156} = .10212$, $y^{*}_{167} - y^{*}_{155} = .07934$, $y^{*}_{166} - y^{*}_{154} = -.00628$, and the residual for period 157 is .057297.

16.32   Find a point forecast and a 95 percent prediction interval for y_{169}.

Note: For an exercise on tentative identification, see Supplemental Exercise 16.44 on page 675.

16.7 Forecast Error Comparisons ● ● ●

LO16-9 Compare time series models by using forecast errors.

Consider comparing the forecasting accuracies of two particular forecasting methods—Method 1 and Method 2. To do this, we use each method to compute point forecasts ($\hat{y}_t$) of the future values (y_t) of a time series. We then wait for the future values to occur, record them, and compute the forecast errors ($y_t - \hat{y}_t$). Specifically, suppose that the results we obtain when we use Method 1 and Method 2 to forecast 12 future values of a time series are as shown in Tables 16.14 and 16.15 on the next page. Three criteria by which to compare Method 1 and Method 2 are the **mean absolute deviation (MAD),** the **mean squared deviation (MSD),** and the **mean absolute percentage error (MAPE).**

TABLE 16.14

Method 1 Forecast Errors

y_t	$\hat{y}_t$	$y_t - \hat{y}_t$
352	360.52	−8.52
445	441.48	3.52
453	446.40	6.6
541	516.62	24.38
457	433.85	23.15
762	767.82	−5.82
1,194	1,156.30	37.7
1,361	1,350.50	10.5
1,615	1,606.30	8.7
1,059	1,067.40	−8.4
824	850.12	−26.12
495	501.39	−6.39

TABLE 16.15

Method 2 Forecast Errors

y_t	$\hat{y}_t$	$y_t - \hat{y}_t$
352	355.96	−3.96
445	426.31	18.69
453	436.69	16.31
541	505.60	35.4
457	431.71	25.29
762	748.35	13.65
1,194	1,132.57	61.43
1,361	1,313.74	47.26
1,615	1,576.09	38.91
1,059	1,043.59	15.41
824	834.24	−10.24
495	506.65	−11.65

To calculate the MAD, we find the absolute value of each forecast error and then average the resulting absolute values. For example, if we find the absolute value of each of the 12 forecast errors given by Method 1 in Table 16.14, sum the 12 absolute values, and divide the sum by 12, we find that the MAD is 14.15. By contrast, if we calculate the MAD of the Method 2 forecast errors in Table 16.15, we find that the MAD is 25.6.

To calculate the MSD, we find the squared value of each forecast error and then average the resulting squared values. For example, if we find the squared value of each of the 12 forecast errors given by Method 1 in Table 16.14, sum the 12 squared values, and divide the sum by 12, we find that the MSD is 307.80. By contrast, if we calculate the MSD of the Method 2 forecast errors in Table 16.15, we find that the MSD is 892.44.

To calculate the MAPE, we find the percentage error for each forecast, $[(y_t - \hat{y}_t)/y_t] \times 100\%$, and we then average the absolute values of the percentage errors. For example, the percentage error for the first forecast given by Method 1 is $[(y_1 - \hat{y}_1)/y_1] \times 100\% = [(352 - 360.52)/352] \times 100\% = -2.42\%$. If we average the absolute values of the 12 percentage errors given by Method 1, we find that the MAPE is 2.06%. By contrast, if we calculate the MAPE of the Method 2 forecast errors, we find that the MAPE is 3.24%.

In general, we want a forecasting method that gives small values of the MAD, MSD, and MAPE. Note, however, that the MSD is the average of the *squared forecast errors*. It follows that the MSD, unlike the MAD and MAPE, penalizes a forecasting method much more for large forecast errors than for small forecast errors. Therefore, the forecasting method that gives the smallest MSD may not be the forecasting method that gives the smallest MAD, or MAPE. Furthermore, the forecaster who uses the MSD to choose a forecasting method would prefer several smaller forecast errors to one large error. In our example, Method 1 gives smaller values of the MAD, MSD, and MAPE than does Method 2. Moreover, for those who have studied Sections 16.3 and 16.5, the point forecasts in Tables 16.14 and 16.15 are point forecasts given by the multiplicative decomposition method (Method 1) and multiplicative Winters' method (Method 2). These point forecasts are point forecasts of future Tasty Cola sales in months 37 through 48. Although the multiplicative decomposition method does better in this situation, the multiplicative Winters' method would do better in other situations.

Exercises for Section 16.7

CONCEPTS

16.33 What is the MAD? What is the MSD? What is the MAPE? How do we use these quantities?

16.34 Why does the MSD penalize a forecasting method much more for large forecast errors than for small forecast errors?

METHODS AND APPLICATIONS

Exercises 16.35 and 16.36 compare two forecasting methods—method A and method B. Suppose that method A gives the point forecasts 57, 61, and 70 of three future time series values. Method B gives the point forecasts 59, 65, and 73 of these three future values. The three future values turn out to be 60, 64, and 67.

16.35 Calculate the MAD, MSD, and MAPE for method A. Calculate the MAD, MSD, and MAPE for method B.

16.36 Which method—method A or method B—gives the smallest MAD? The smallest MSD? The smallest MAPE?

LO16-10 Use index numbers to compare economic data over time.

16.8 Index Numbers ● ● ●

We often wish to compare a value of a time series relative to another value of the time series. For instance, according to the U.S. Bureau of Labor Statistics, energy prices increased by 4.7 percent from 1995 to 1996, while apparel prices decreased by .2 percent from 1995 to 1996. In order to make such comparisons, we must describe the time series. We have seen (in Section 16.3) that time series decomposition can be employed to describe a time series. Another way to describe time-related data is to use *index numbers*.

When we compare time series values to the same previous value, we say that the previous value is in the **base time period,** and successive comparisons of time series values to the value in the base period form a sequence of **index numbers.** More formally, a **simple index number** (or **simple index**) is defined as follows:

A **simple index** is obtained by dividing the current value of a time series by the value of the time series in the base time period and by multiplying this ratio by 100. That is, if y_t denotes the current value and if y_0 denotes the value in the base time period, then the **simple index number** is

$$\frac{y_t}{y_0} \times 100$$

The time series values used to construct an index are often *quantities* or *prices*. For instance, in Table 16.16 we give the price of a gallon of regular gasoline in the United States (in dollars) for the years 2003 through 2011. If we consider 2003 to be the base year, we compute an index for each succeeding year by dividing the price per gallon for each year by 1.59 (the price per gallon for the base year 2003) and by multiplying by 100. For example, for 2007 the simple index is $(2.80/1.59) \times 100 = 176.10$, while the simple index for 2008 is $(3.27/1.59) \times 100 = 205.66$. Table 16.16 gives the remaining index values for 2003 through 2011. Notice that (by definition) the index for the base year will always equal 100.0 (as it does here).

Although the simple index is not written with a percentage sign, comparisons of the index with the base year are percentage comparisons. For instance, the index of 205.66 for 2008 tells us that the price per gallon in 2008 was up 105.66 percent compared to the 2003 base year. In general, *if we are comparing the index to the base year*, the difference between the index and 100 gives the percentage change from the base year. It is important to point out that other period-to-period percentage comparisons cannot be made by subtracting indexes. For instance, the percentage difference between the prices per gallon in 2007 and 2008 is *not* $205.66 - 176.10 = 29.56$ percent. Rather, the percentage difference is

$$\frac{205.66 - 176.10}{176.10} \times 100 = 16.79$$

This says that the price per gallon in 2008 was up 16.79 percent relative to 2007.

A simple index is computed by using the values of one time series. Often, however, we compute an index based on the accumulated values of more than one time series. Such an index is called an **aggregate index.** As an example, food prices are often compared with an aggregate index based on a "market basket" of commonly bought grocery items. For instance, consider a market basket consisting of six items—a gallon of whole milk, a one pound jar of peanut butter, a pound of red delicious apples, a dozen eggs, a pound loaf of white bread, and a pound of ground beef. Table 16.17 on the next page lists average city prices for these items in June 2006 and in June 2011 according to the Consumer Price Index Detailed Report.

One way to compare prices would be to compute a simple index for each individual item in the market basket. However, we can create an aggregate price index by totaling the prices for each year and by then computing a simple index of the yearly price totals. Using the data in

---

TABLE 16.16 **Price of a Gallon of Regular Gasoline (in Dollars): 2003 to 2011**
                 DS PriceGas1

Year	2003	2004	2005	2006	2007	2008	2009	2010	2011
Price per Gallon	1.59	1.88	2.30	2.59	2.80	3.27	2.35	2.78	3.63
Index (Base Year = 2003)	100.0	118.24	144.65	162.89	176.10	205.66	147.80	174.84	228.30

Source: U.S. Energy Information Administration.

TABLE 16.17   2006 and 2011 Prices for a Market Basket of Grocery Items   ⑤ MkBskt

Grocery Item	2006 Price	2011 Price
1 gal. of whole milk	$3.00	$3.62
1 lb. jar of peanut butter	$1.74	$1.96
1 lb. of red delicious apples	$1.05	$1.32
1 dozen eggs	$1.24	$1.68
1 lb. loaf of white bread	$1.07	$1.49
1 lb. of ground beef	$2.24	$2.77
Totals	$10.34	$12.84

Source: http://www.bls.gov/cpi/cpid1106.pdf

Table 16.17, we obtain $(12.84/10.34) \times 100 = 124.18$. This index tells us that prices of the market basket grocery items in 2011 have increased by 24.18 percent over the prices of these items in the base year 2006. Notice that this percentage increase does not necessarily apply to each individual grocery item, nor does this index necessarily apply to any of the individual grocery items. It applies only to the aggregate of grocery items in the market basket.

In general, we compute an aggregate price index as follows:

An **aggregate price index** is

$$\left(\frac{\sum p_t}{\sum p_0} \right) \times 100$$

where $\sum p_t$ is the sum of the prices in the current time period and $\sum p_0$ is the sum of the prices in the base year.

A disadvantage of this aggregate price index is that it does not take into account the fact that some items in the market basket are purchased more frequently than others. To remedy this deficiency, we can weight each price by the quantity of that item purchased in a given period (say yearly). Then we can total the weighted prices for each year and compute a simple index of the weighted price totals. To illustrate, Table 16.18 gives the 2006 and 2011 prices of the market basket items and also gives estimates of the quantity of each item purchased in a year by a typical family. The table also gives the price multiplied by the quantity for each item, which is simply the total yearly cost of purchasing the item. These costs are totaled for each year. Looking at Table 16.18, we see that a typical family in 2006 spent $824.09 purchasing the market basket items during the year, while the family spent $1049.68 purchasing the market basket items during 2011. We now compute a simple index of the total costs, which is $(1049.68/824.09) \times 100 = 127.37$.

This type of index is called a **weighted aggregate price index.** Two versions of this kind of index are commonly used. The first version is called a **Laspeyres index.** Here the quantities that are specified for the base year are also employed for all succeeding time periods. This is the assumption we have made in Table 16.18. Notice that the quantities for 2011 are the same as those specified for 2006. In general,

A **Laspeyres index** is

$$\frac{\sum p_t q_0}{\sum p_0 q_0} \times 100$$

where p_0 represents a base period price, q_0 represents a base period quantity, and p_t represents a current period price.

Because the Laspeyres index employs the base period quantities in all succeeding time periods, this index allows for ready comparison of prices for identical quantities of goods purchased. Such an index is useful as long as the base quantities provide a reasonable representation of consumption patterns in succeeding time periods. However, sometimes purchasing patterns can change drastically as consumer preferences change or as dramatic price changes occur. If

TABLE 16.18   **2006 and 2011 Prices and Quantities for a Market Basket of Grocery Items**   Ⓓ MkBskt

Grocery Item	2006 (Base Year) Price, p_0	Quantity, q	$p_0 \times q$ = cost	2011 Price, p_t	Quantity, q	$p_t \times q$ = cost
1 gal. of whole milk	$3.00	52	$156.00	$3.62	52	$188.24
1 lb. jar of peanut butter	$1.74	13	$22.62	$1.96	13	$25.48
1 lb. of red delicious apples	$1.05	55	$57.75	$1.32	55	$72.60
1 dozen eggs	$1.24	72	$89.28	$1.68	72	$120.96
1 lb. loaf of white bread	$1.07	156	$166.92	$1.49	156	$232.44
1 lb. of ground beef	$2.24	148	$331.52	$2.77	148	$409.96
Totals	$10.34		$824.09	$12.84		$1049.68

TABLE 16.19   **2006 and 2011 Prices and 2011 Quantities for a Market Basket of Grocery Items**   Ⓓ MkBsktR

Grocery Item	2006 Price, p_0	2011 Quantity, q_t	$p_0 \times q_t$ = cost	2011 Price, p_t	2011 Quantity, q_t	$p_t \times q_t$ = cost
1 gal. of whole milk	$3.00	40	$120.00	$3.62	40	$144.80
1 lb. jar of peanut butter	$1.74	21	$36.54	$1.96	21	$41.16
1 lb. of red delicious apples	$1.05	82	$86.10	$1.32	82	$108.24
1 dozen eggs	$1.24	60	$74.40	$1.68	60	$100.80
1 lb. loaf of white bread	$1.07	175	$187.25	$1.49	175	$260.75
1 lb. of ground beef	$2.24	148	$331.52	$2.77	148	$409.96
Totals	$10.34	Total	$835.81	$12.84	Total	$1065.71

consumption patterns in the current period are very different from the quantities specified in the base period, then a Laspeyres index can be misleading because it relates to quantities of goods that few people would purchase.

A second version of the weighted aggregate price index is called a **Paasche index.** Here we update the quantities so that they reflect consumption patterns in the current time period.

A **Paasche index** is

$$\frac{\sum p_t q_t}{\sum p_0 q_t} \times 100$$

where p_0 represents a base period price, p_t represents a current period price, and q_t represents a current period quantity.

As an example, Table 16.19 presents revised quantities for the grocery items in our previously discussed market basket. These quantities reflect increased consumption of apples, peanut butter, and bread, and decreased consumption of milk and eggs. We calculate a 2006 cost of $835.81 for the items in the market basket and a 2011 cost of $1065.71 for the items in the market basket. Therefore, the Paasche index is $(1065.71/835.81) \times 100 = 127.51$.

Because the Paasche index uses quantities from the current period, it reflects current buying habits. However, quantity data for the current period can be difficult to obtain. Furthermore, although each period is compared to the base period, it is difficult to compare the index at other points in time. This is because different quantities are used in different periods, and thus changes in the index are affected by changes in both prices and quantities.

Economic indexes   Several commonly quoted economic indexes are compiled monthly by the U.S. Bureau of Labor Statistics. Two important indexes are the **Consumer Price Index** (the **CPI**) and the **Producer Price Index** (the **PPI**). These are both *Laspeyres indexes.*

The CPI monitors the price of a market basket of goods and services that would be purchased by typical nonfarm consumers. Actually, there are two Consumer Price Indexes. The CPI-U, the

FIGURE 16.29   Plot of the Monthly CPI-U from February 1947 until April 2011

Source: www.data360.org/pdf_print_group.aspx?Print_Group_Id=169.

Consumer Price Index for all Urban Workers, is often reported by the press as an indicator of price changes. Figure 16.29, which gives a plot of the monthly CPI-U from February 1947 until April 2011, shows the general increasing trend in prices over this period. The U.S. Bureau of the Census periodically changes the base period for the CPI. The plot in Figure 16.29 uses a base period of 1982–1984. Here, assume that the base period cost used to compute the CPI-U is the average of the 36 monthly market basket costs over the 1982–1984 base period. The April 2011 CPI-U, computed with a 1982–1984 base index of 100, was 224.91. This says that the cost of purchasing the market basket of goods and services was 124.91 percent higher in April 2011 than it was in the 1982–1984 base period. A second CPI, the CPI-W (Consumer Price Index for Urban Wage Earners and Clerical Workers) is often used to determine wage increases that are written into labor contracts.

The PPI tracks the prices of goods sold by wholesalers. An increase in the PPI is often regarded as an indication that retail prices will soon rise.

Exercises for Section 16.8

connect

CONCEPTS

16.37 Explain the difference between a simple index and an aggregate index.

16.38 Explain the difference between a Laspeyres index and a Paasche index.

METHODS AND APPLICATIONS

16.39 Referring to the discussion of Figure 16.29, the CPI-U for March 2011 was 223.47, and the CPI-U for October 1963 was 30. Interpret these CPI-U's.

16.40 Recall that Table 16.16 (page 669) gives the price of a gallon of regular gasoline in the United States (in dollars) for the years 2003 through 2011. Table 16.20 gives the price of a gallon of regular gasoline in the United States (in dollars) for the years 1990 through 2002.
DS PriceGas2

  a By using 1990 as the base year, construct a simple index for the prices of a gallon of regular gasoline in Tables 16.20 and 16.16.

  b Plot the indices you have constructed versus time (1990 through 2011). Describe the pattern that you see.

16.41 Suppose that Table 16.21 gives the yearly automobile operating expenses in a particular region of the United States for the years 1990, 2000, and 2011.   DS AutoExp

  a Using 1990 as the base year, construct the Laspeyres index for these operating expenses. Describe how the operating expenses have changed over time.

TABLE 16.20
Gas Prices
DS PriceGas2

Year	Price per Gallon ($)
1990	1.16
1991	1.14
1992	1.13
1993	1.11
1994	1.11
1995	1.15
1996	1.23
1997	1.23
1998	1.06
1999	1.17
2000	1.51
2001	1.46
2002	1.36

TABLE 16.21   **Yearly Automobile Operating Expenses in 1990, 2000, and 2011**   ⊙ₛ Autoexp

	1990		2000		2011	
Item	Price	Quantity	Price	Quantity	Price	Quantity
Gallon of gasoline	$1.16	1000	$1.51	882	$3.63	682
Quart of oil	$2.00	15	$3.50	15	$5.75	15
Tire	$125.00	2	$132.00	2	$142.00	2
Insurance	$750.00	1	$900.00	1	$1,100.00	1

Note: The quantities are based on 15,000 miles driven per year and a 30,000 mile tire lifetime.

b Using 1990 as the base year, construct the Paasche index for the operating expenses.

c Another index, the **value index,** is given by the formula $(\Sigma p_t\, q_t / \Sigma p_0\, q_0) \times 100$. This index measures the changes in both the prices and quantities involved. Using 1990 as the base year, construct the value index for the operating expenses. Compare the three indices you have constructed.

Chapter Summary

In this chapter we have discussed using **univariate time series** models to forecast future time series values. We began by seeing that it can be useful to think of a time series as consisting of **trend, seasonal, cyclical, and irregular components.** If these components remain *constant* over time, then it is appropriate to describe and forecast the time series by using a **time series regression model.** We discussed using such models to describe **no trend,** a **linear trend,** and **constant seasonal variation** (by utilizing dummy variables). We also considered various transformations that transform **increasing seasonal variation** into constant seasonal variation. As an alternative to using a transformation and dummy variables to model increasing seasonal variation, we discussed using the **multiplicative decomposition method.** We then turned to a consideration of **exponential smoothing,** which is appropriate to use if the components of a time series may be *changing slowly* over time. Specifically, we discussed **simple exponential smoothing, Holt–Winters' double exponential smoothing, and multiplicative Winters' method.** We next considered how to use the Box–Jenkins methodology to forecast a time series having components that may be *changing fairly quickly* over time. We also explained how to compare forecasting methods by using the **mean absolute deviation (MAD),** the **mean squared deviation (MSD),** and the **mean absolute percentage error (MAPE).** We concluded this chapter by showing how to use **index numbers** to describe time-related data. Our discussion included the construction of a **simple index,** an **aggregate index,** a **Laspeyres index,** and a **Paasche index.**

Glossary of Terms

autoregressive terms: Past time series values used in Box–Jenkins models. (page 664)

cyclical variation: Recurring up-and-down movements of a time series around trend levels that last more than one calendar year (often 2 to 10 years) from peak to peak or trough to trough. (page 631)

deseasonalized time series: A time series that has had the effect of seasonal variation removed. (page 645)

double exponential smoothing: An exponential smoothing procedure that can be used to forecast a time series described by a linear trend model with parameters that may be slowly changing over time. (pages 652–654)

exponential smoothing: A forecasting method that weights recent observations more heavily than distantly past observations. (page 648)

index number: A number that compares a value of a time series relative to another value of the time series. (pages 668–672)

irregular component: What is "left over" in a time series after trend, cycle, and seasonal variations have been accounted for. (page 631)

MAD: The mean of the absolute values of a set of forecast errors. (pages 667–668)

MAPE: The mean of the absolute values of the percentage errors of a set of forecasts. (pages 667–668)

MSD: The mean of the squares of a set of forecast errors. (pages 667–668)

moving averages: Averages of successive groups of time series observations. (page 641)

moving average terms: Past error terms used in Box–Jenkins models. (page 665)

multiplicative Winters' method: An exponential smoothing procedure that can be used to forecast a time series described by a linear trend and increasing (or decreasing) seasonal variation with parameters that may be slowly changing over time. (pages 654–659)

seasonal variation: Periodic patterns in a time series that repeat themselves within a calendar year and are then repeated yearly. (page 631)

simple exponential smoothing: An exponential smoothing procedure that can be used to forecast a time series described by a no trend model with an average level that may be slowly changing over time. (pages 647–651)

smoothing constant: A number that determines how much weight is attached to each observation when using exponential smoothing. (page 648)

time series: A set of observations that has been collected in time order. (page 631)

trend: The long-run upward or downward movement that characterizes a time series over a period of time. (page 631)

univariate time series model: A model that predicts future values of a time series solely on the basis of past values of the time series. (page 631)

Important Formulas and Tests

No trend: page 632

Linear trend: page 633

Modeling constant seasonal variation by using dummy variables: pages 634–637

The multiplicative decomposition model: pages 640–646

Simple exponential smoothing: page 650

Double exponential smoothing: pages 652–654

Multiplicative Winters' method: pages 654–659

Mean absolute deviation (MAD): pages 654, 667–668

Mean absolute percentage error (MAPE): pages 667–668

Mean squared deviation (MSD): pages 654, 667–668

Simple index: page 669

Aggregate price index: page 670

Laspeyres index: page 670

Paasche index: page 671

Supplementary Exercises

connect

TABLE 16.22

Absorbent Paper Towels Sales

DS Towels

y_t	y_t	y_t
15.0000	9.2835	11.4986
14.4064	7.7219	13.2778
14.9383	6.8300	13.5910
16.0374	8.2046	13.4297
15.6320	8.5289	13.3125
14.3975	8.8733	12.7445
13.8959	8.7948	11.7979
14.0765	8.1577	11.7319
16.3750	7.9128	11.6523
16.5342	8.7978	11.3718
16.3839	9.0775	10.5502
17.1006	9.3234	11.4741
17.7876	10.4739	11.5568
17.7354	10.6943	11.7986
17.0010	9.8367	11.8867
17.7485	8.1803	11.2951
18.1888	7.2509	12.7847
18.5997	5.0814	13.9435
17.5859	1.8313	13.6859
15.7389	−0.9127	14.1136
13.6971	−1.3173	13.8949
15.0059	−0.6021	14.2853
16.2574	0.1400	16.3867
14.3506	1.4030	17.0884
11.9515	1.9280	15.8861
12.0328	3.5626	14.8227
11.2142	1.9615	15.9479
11.7023	4.8463	15.0982
12.5905	6.5454	13.8770
12.1991	8.0141	14.2746
10.7752	7.9746	15.1682
10.1129	8.4959	15.3818
9.9330	8.4539	14.1863
11.7435	8.7114	13.9996
12.2590	7.3780	15.2463
12.5009	8.1905	17.0179
11.5378	9.9720	17.2929
9.6649	9.6930	16.6366
10.1043	9.4506	15.3410
10.3452	11.2088	15.6453

16.42 The State University Credit Union, a savings institution open to the faculty and staff of State University, handles savings accounts and makes loans to members. In order to plan its investment strategies, the credit union requires both point and prediction interval forecasts of monthly loan requests (in thousands of dollars) to be made by the faculty and staff in future months. The credit union has recorded monthly loan requests for its past two years of operation. These loan requests are as follows: DS Loans

Year 1	297	249	340	406	464	481	549	553	556	642	670	712
Year 2	808	809	867	855	965	921	956	990	1019	1021	1033	1127

If we use MINITAB to fit the **quadratic trend model**

$$y_t = \beta_0 + \beta_1 t + \beta_2 t^2 + \varepsilon_t$$

to these data, we obtain the following partial MINITAB output.

```
The regression equation is
Y = 200 + 50.9 Time - 0.568 TimeSQ

Predictor        Coef      SE Coef         T          P
Constant       199.62        20.85      9.58      0.000
Time           50.937         3.842     13.26      0.000
TimeSQ         -0.5677        0.1492    -3.80      0.001

S = 31.2469   R-Sq = 98.7%   R-Sq(adj) = 98.6%

Predicted Values for New Observations

New Obs Time TimeSQ     Fit SE Fit         95% CI              95% PI
   1    25.0    625  1118.21  20.85  (1074.85, 1161.56)  (1040.09, 1196.32)
   2    26.0    676  1140.19  24.44  (1089.37, 1191.01)  (1057.70, 1222.68)
```

a Does the quadratic term t^2 seem important in the model? Justify your answer.

b At the bottom of the MINITAB output are point and prediction interval forecasts of loan requests in months 25 and 26. (**1**) Find and report these forecasts. (**2**) Then (using the least squares point estimates of β_0, β_1, and β_2 on the computer output) calculate the point forecasts.

16.43 The Olympia Paper Company, Inc., makes Absorbent Paper Towels. The company would like to develop a prediction model that can be used to give point forecasts and prediction interval forecasts of weekly sales over 100,000 rolls, in units of 10,000 rolls, of Absorbent Paper Towels. With a reliable model, Olympia Paper can more effectively plan its production schedule, plan its budget, and estimate requirements for producing and storing this product. For the past 120 weeks the company has recorded weekly sales of Absorbent Paper Towels. The 120 sales figures, $y_1, y_2, \ldots y_{120}$, are given in Table 16.22, and the MINITAB output resulting from using simple exponential smoothing to forecast future values of the sales figures is given in Figure 16.30, on the next page. Note that MINITAB chooses a smoothing constant of 1.35442, which is not (as is the usual case) between 0 and 1. In general, if the trend effects in a time series are changing fairly quickly (as the plot of the sales values in Figure 16.30 indicates is true) MINITAB will often choose a smoothing constant greater than 1. Use the MINITAB output to find a point forecast of and a 95 percent prediction interval for the number of rolls of Absorbent Paper Towels that will be sold in a future week.

FIGURE 16.30   **MINITAB Output of Simple Exponential Smoothing for the Absorbent Paper Towels Sales Time Series** ⓓⓢ Towels

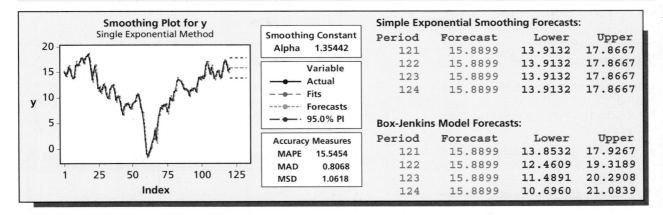

16.44   Figure 16.30 shows that the sales values in Table 16.22 are nonstationary and nonseasonal. At the nonseasonal level (lags 1 through 9), the SAC of the regular differences of the sales values has a spike at lag 1 and cuts off after lag 1, and the SPAC of these regular differences dies down fairly quickly. Discuss why the guidelines in Section 16.6 say that a tentative Box–Jenkins model describing the regular differences $z_t = y_t - y_{t-1}$ is $z_t = \varepsilon_t - \theta_1 \varepsilon_{t-1}$ and thus that a tentative model describing y_t is $y_t = y_{t-1} + \varepsilon_t - \theta_1 \varepsilon_{t-1}$. Estimation shows that θ_1 is important in the tentative model and that a constant term δ does not belong in the model. Diagnostic checking shows that the tentative model is adequate. Because the adequate Box–Jenkins model can be shown to be equivalent to simple exponential smoothing, it gives the same point forecasts. However, MINITAB calculates the Box–Jenkins model prediction intervals differently and obtains increasingly wide intervals (see Figure 16.30).

Appendix 16.1 ■ Time Series Analysis Using Excel

Point forecasts from a linear trend line for the calculator sales data in Table 16.2 on page 633 (data file: CalcSale.xlsx):

- Enter the calculator sales data from Table 16.2 with the label "Sales" in cell A1 and the values of sales in cells A2 through A25.
- Enter the label "Month" in cell B1 and the values 1 to 28 in cells B2 through B29.
- Click on cell A26.
- Click the Insert Function button $\boxed{f_x}$ on the Excel ribbon.
- In the Insert Function dialog box, select Statistical from the "Or select a category:" menu and select TREND from the "Select a function:" menu. Then click OK in the Insert Function dialog box.
- In the "TREND Function Arguments" dialog box, enter $A$2:$A$25 into the "Known_y's" window. Don't forget the dollar signs—this must be an absolute cell reference.
- Enter $B$2:$B$25 into the "Known_x's" window. Again, don't forget the dollar signs.
- Enter B26 into the "New_x's" window.
- Enter the value 1 into the Const window.

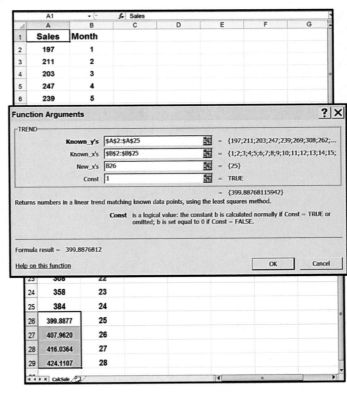

(Continues on the next page.)

- Click OK in the "TREND Function Arguments" dialog box to produce the point forecast for time period 25.

- Double-click on the drag handle in cell A26 to extend the forecasts through time period 28.

Appendix 16.2 ■ Time Series Analysis Using MegaStat

Calculation of seasonal factors and deseasonalization similar to Table 16.10, Table 16.11, and Figure 16.11 on pages 641 and 643 (data file: TastyCola.xlsx):

- Enter the Tasty Cola data in Table 16.9 (page 640) into column A with label Sales. Only the sales values in Table 16.9 need to be entered—the year, month, and time period need not be entered.

- Select **Add-Ins : MegaStat : Time Series/ Forecasting : Deseasonalization.**

- In the Deseasonalization dialog box, enter the range A1:A37 into the "Input Range of Seasonal Data" window. This range can be entered by dragging with the mouse—the AutoExpand feature cannot be used in this dialog box.

- Select the type of seasonal data—"quarterly" or "monthly"—by clicking. Here we have selected "monthly" because the Tasty Cola data consists of monthly sales values.

- In the "First data period" box, specify the month (in this case, January) in which the first time series value was observed by using the up or down arrow buttons.

- In the "First data period" box, enter the year in which the first time series value was observed (here equal to 1) into the Year box.

- Check the Plot Values checkbox to obtain plots of the seasonal observations, the deseasonalized data, and a trend line fit to the deseasonalized data.

- Click OK in the Deseasonalization dialog box.

- The seasonal factors are displayed in the "Seasonal Indexes" column of the "Centered Moving Average and Deseasonalization" table in the output worksheet. They are also given in the "adjusted" row at the bottom of the "Calculation of Seasonal Indexes" table in the output worksheet.

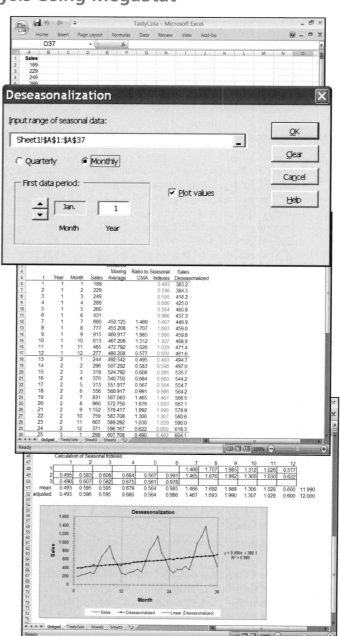

Simple exponential smoothing similar to Table 16.13 on page 649 (data file: CodCatch.xlsx):

- Enter the cod catch data in Table 16.1 (page 632) into column A with label CodCatch.

- Select **Add-Ins : MegaStat : Time Series/ Forecasting : Exponential Smoothing : Simple Exponential Smoothing.**

- In the Simple Exponential Smoothing dialog box, enter the range A1:A25 into the "Input Range for Data" window. Enter this range by dragging with the mouse—the autoexpand feature cannot be used in this dialog box.

- Type the value of the smoothing constant (here equal to .02) into the Alpha window.

- Leave the Initial Value window blank if you wish to use an initial value equal to the average of the first six time series observations. If another initial value is desired, type it into the Initial Value window.

- Click OK in the Simple Exponential Smoothing dialog box.

- The forecast for a future value of the time series is found at the bottom of the "Forecast" column in the output worksheet.

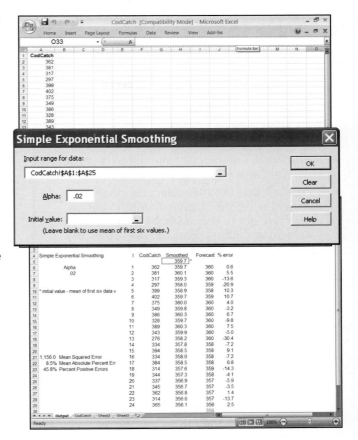

Double exponential smoothing similar to Figure 16.15 on page 653 (data file: CalcSale.xlsx):

- Enter the calculator sales data in Table 16.2 on page 633 into column A with label Sales.

- Select **Add-Ins : MegaStat : Time Series/ Forecasting : Exponential Smoothing : Two-factor Exponential Smoothing.**

- In the Two-Factor Exponential Smoothing dialog box, enter the range A1:A25 into the "Input Range for Data" window. Enter this range by dragging with the mouse—the AutoExpand feature cannot be used in this dialog box.

- Type the desired values of the smoothing constants (here both are set equal to .20) into the Alpha and Beta boxes.

- Leave the "Initial Value" and "Initial Trend" boxes blank if you wish to use initial values that are estimated by the computer using the first six time series observations. If you wish to supply initial values, type an initial value of the intercept into the "Initial Value" box and type an initial value of the slope into the "Initial Trend" box. Here we have supplied the values 198.0 and 8.1.

- Click OK in the Two-Factor Exponential Smoothing dialog box.

- The forecast for the next time series value is found at the bottom of the Forecast column in the output worksheet.

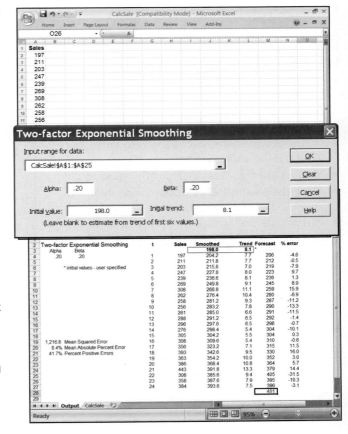

Appendix 16.3 ■ Time Series Analysis Using MINITAB

Simple exponential smoothing in Figure 16.13 on page 651 (data file: CodCatch.MTW):

- In the Data window, enter the cod catch data from Table 16.1 on page 632 into column C1 with variable name CodCatch.

- Select **Stat : Time Series : Single Exp Smoothing.**

- In the Single Exponential Smoothing dialog box, enter CodCatch in the Variable window.

- To request that MINITAB select the smoothing constant, select the "Optimal ARIMA" option under "Weight to Use in Smoothing." To choose your own smoothing constant, select the "Use" option and enter the desired smoothing constant in the window.

- Place a checkmark in the "Generate forecasts" checkbox.

- Enter 12 in the "Number of forecasts" window and enter 24 in the "Starting from origin" window.

- Click OK in the Single Exponential Smoothing dialog box to see the forecast results in the Session window and a graphical summary in a high-resolution graphics window.

Double exponential smoothing can be performed by choosing **Double Exp Smoothing** from the Time Series menu and by following the remainder of the preceding steps.

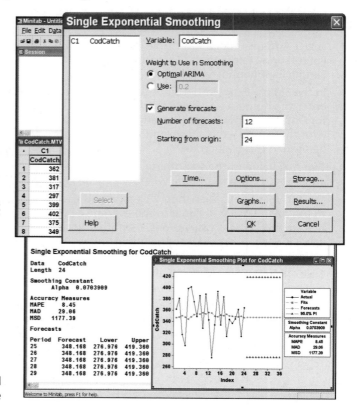

Multiplicative Winters' method in Figure 16.19 on page 658 (data file: TastyCola.MTW):

- In the Data window, enter the Tasty Cola data from Table 16.9 (page 640) into column C1 with variable name Sales.

- Select **Stat : Time Series : Winters' Method.**

- In the Winters' Method dialog box, enter Sales into the Variable window.

- Enter 12 in the "Seasonal length" window.

- Click the Multiplicative option under Method Type.

- Use the default values for "Weights to Use in Smoothing" (0.2 in each of the Level, Trend, and Seasonal windows).

- Click the "Generate forecasts" checkbox.

- Enter 12 in the "Number of forecasts" window and enter 36 in the "Starting from origin" window.

- Click OK in the Winters' Method dialog box to obtain the forecast results in the Session window and a graphical summary in a high-resolution graphics window.

Computing the SAC and SPAC of the combined regular and seasonal differences of the logged passenger totals in Figure 16.25 on page 664 (data file: AirPass. MTW):

- Select **Calc : Calculator** and calculate the natural logarithms of the passenger totals (with variable name LnPassengers) as shown in the calculator dialog box to the right.

- Select **Stat : Time Series : Differences**

- In the Differences dialog box, enter LnPassengers into the Series window.

- Enter 'Seasonal Diff' into the "Store differences in" window.

- Enter 12 into the Lag window.

- Click OK to calculate the first order seasonal differences of the logged passenger totals.

- Select **Stat : Time Series : Differences**

- In the Differences dialog box, enter 'Seasonal Diff' into the series window.

- Enter 'RegSeasonal Diff' into the "Store differences in" window.

- Enter 1 into the Lag window.

- Click OK to calculate the first order regular differences of the first order seasonal differences of the logged passenger totals.

- Select **Stat : Time Series : Autocorrelation**

- In the Autocorrelation Function dialog box, enter 'RegSeasonal Diff' into the series window.

- Enter 24 into the "Number of lags" window.

- Click OK in the Autocorrelation Function dialog box to obtain a graph of the sample autocorrelation function of the combined regular and seasonal differences of the logged passenger totals.

- In a similar fashion, obtain a graph of the sample partial autocorrelation function by selecting **Stat : Time Series : Partial Autocorrelation**

Performing estimation, diagnostic checking, and forecasting using the passenger totals Box–Jenkins model as in Figure 16.24 on page 663 (data file: AirPass. MTW):

- Select **Stat : Time Series : ARIMA**

- Enter "LnPassengers" into the Series window.

- Place a checkmark in the "Fit seasonal model" box and enter 12 into the Period window to specify monthly data.

- Enter 1 into each of the Nonseasonal and Seasonal Difference windows (first order regular and first order seasonal differencing).

- Enter 0 into each of the Nonseasonal Autoregressive and Seasonal Autoregressive windows (the model has no autoregressive terms).

- Enter 1 into each of the Nonseasonal Moving average and Seasonal Moving average windows. (These specify the first-order nonseasonal and first-order seasonal moving average terms.)

- Be sure that the "Include constant term in model" checkbox is not checked (no constant in model).

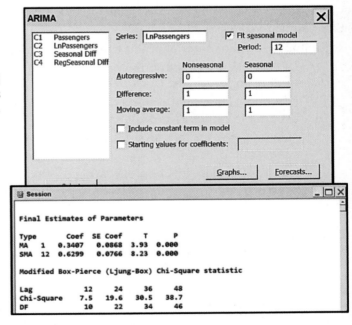

- Click on the Forecasts... button and enter 12 into the "Lead" window to forecast 12 months into the future.

- Click OK in the ARIMA dialog box.

CHAPTER 17

Process Improvement Using Control Charts

Learning Objectives

After mastering the material in this chapter, you will be able to:

LO17-1 Discuss the principles and importance of quality improvement.

LO17-2 Distinguish between common causes and assignable causes of process variation.

LO17-3 Sample a process by using rational subgrouping.

LO17-4 Use $\bar{x}$ and R charts to establish process control.

LO17-5 Detect the presence of assignable causes through pattern analysis.

LO17-6 Decide whether a process is capable of meeting specifications.

LO17-7 Use p charts to monitor process quality.

LO17-8 Use diagrams to discern the causes of quality problems (Optional).

Chapter Outline

17.1 Quality: Its Meaning and a Historical Perspective

17.2 Statistical Process Control and Causes of Process Variation

17.3 Sampling a Process, Rational Subgrouping, and Control Charts

17.4 $\bar{x}$ and R Charts

17.5 Comparison of a Process with Specifications: Capability Studies

17.6 Charts for Fraction Nonconforming

17.7 Cause-and-Effect and Defect Concentration Diagrams (Optional)

his chapter explains how to use **control charts** to improve business processes. Basically, a control chart is a graphical device that helps us determine when a process is not operating consistently and thus is "out of control." The information provided by a control chart helps us discover the causes of unusual process variations. When such causes have been identified, we attempt to remove them in order to reduce the amount of process variation. By doing so, we improve the process.

We begin this chapter by tracing the history of the U.S. quality movement. Then we study control charts for monitoring the level and variability of a process and for monitoring the fraction of nonconforming (or defective) units produced. We also discuss how to evaluate the *process capability.* That is, we show how to assess a process's ability to produce individual items that meet customer requirements (*specifications*). In particular, we explain the concept of six sigma capability, which was introduced by Motorola Inc. In an optional section we discuss cause-and-effect diagrams.

In order to demonstrate the ideas of this chapter, we employ three case studies:

The Hole Location Case: A manufacturer of automobile air conditioner compressors uses control charts to reduce variation in the locations of a hose connection hole that is punched in the outer housing (or shell) of the compressor.

The Hot Chocolate Temperature Case: The food service staff at a university dining hall wishes to avoid possible litigation by making sure that it does not serve excessively hot beverages. The staff uses control charts to find and eliminate causes of unusual variations in hot chocolate temperatures.

The Camshaft Case: An automobile manufacturer wishes to improve the process it uses to harden a part in a camshaft assembly. The manufacturer uses control charts and process capability studies to reduce the sources of process variation that are responsible for a 12 percent rework rate and a 9 percent scrap rate. After the process variation is reduced, virtually all of the hardened parts meet specifications. (Note: This case is included in the supplementary exercises.)

17.1 Quality: Its Meaning and a Historical Perspective ● ● ●

LO17-1 Discuss the principles and importance of quality improvement.

What is quality? It is not easy to define quality, and a number of different definitions have been proposed. One definition that makes sense is **fitness for use.** Here the user of a product or service can be an individual, a manufacturer, a retailer, or the like. For instance, an individual who purchases a High Definition television set or a DVD recorder expects the unit to be defect free and to provide years of reliable, high-performance service. If the TV or DVD recorder performs as desired, it is fit for use. Another definition of quality that makes sense says that **quality is the extent to which customers feel that a product or service exceeds their needs and expectations.** For instance, if the DVD recorder's purchaser believes the unit exceeds all the needs and expectations he or she had for the recorder when it was purchased, then the customer is satisfied with the unit's quality.

Three types of quality can be considered: **quality of design, quality of conformance,** and **quality of performance. Quality of design** has to do with intentional differences between goods and services with the same basic purpose. For instance, all DVD recorders are built to perform the same function—record and play back DVDs. However, DVD recorders differ with respect to various design characteristics—picture sharpness, sound quality, digital effects, ease of use, and so forth. A given level of design quality may satisfy some consumers and may not satisfy others. The product design will specify a set of **tolerances (specifications)** that must be met. For example, the design of a DVD recorder sets forth many specifications regarding electronic and physical characteristics that must be met if the unit is to operate acceptably. **Quality of conformance** is the ability of a process to meet the specifications set forth by the design. **Quality of performance** is how well the product or service actually performs in the marketplace. Companies must find out how well customers' needs are met and how reliable products are by conducting after-sales research.

The marketing research arm of a company must determine what the customer seeks in each of these dimensions. Consumer research is used to develop a product or service concept—a combination of design characteristics that exceeds the expectations of a large number of consumers. This concept is translated into a design. The design includes specifications that, if met, will satisfy consumer wants and needs. A production process is then developed to meet the design specifications. In order to do this, variables that can control the process must be identified, and the relationships between input variables and final quality characteristics must be understood. The manufacturer expresses quality characteristics as measurable variables that can be tracked and used to monitor and improve the performance of the process. Service call analysis often leads to product or service redesigns in order to improve the product or service concept. It is extremely important that the initial design be a good one so that excessive redesigns and customer dissatisfaction can be avoided.

History of the quality movement In the 1700s and 1800s, master craftsmen and their apprentices were responsible for designing and building products. Quantities of goods produced were small, and product quality was controlled by expert workmanship. Master craftsmen had a great deal of pride in their work, and quality was not a problem. However, the introduction of mass production in the late 1800s and early 1900s changed things. Production processes became very complex, with many workers (rather than one skilled craftsman) responsible for the final product. Inevitably, product quality characteristics displayed variation. In particular, Henry Ford developed the moving assembly line at Ford Motor Company. As assembly line manufacturing spread, quality became a problem. Production managers were rewarded for meeting production quotas, and quality suffered. To make mass-produced products more consistent, inspectors were hired to check product quality. However, 100 percent inspection proved to be costly, and people started to look for alternatives.

Much of the early work in quality control was done at Bell Telephone (now known as American Telephone and Telegraph or AT&T). The Bell System and Western Electric, the manufacturing arm of Bell Telephone, formed the Inspection Engineering Department to deal with quality problems. In 1924 Walter Shewhart of Bell Telephone Laboratories introduced the concept of statistical quality control—controlling quality of mass-produced goods. Shewhart believed that variation always exists in manufactured products, and that the variation can be studied, monitored, and controlled using statistics. In particular, Shewhart developed a statistical tool called the **control chart.** Such a chart is a graph that can tell a company when a process needs to be adjusted and when the process should be left alone. In the late 1920s Harold F. Dodge and Harold G. Romig, also of Bell Telephone Laboratories, introduced **statistical acceptance sampling,** a statistical sampling technique that enables a company to accept or reject a quantity of goods (called a **lot**) without inspecting the entire lot. By the mid-1930s, Western Electric was heavily using **statistical quality control (SQC)** to improve quality, increase productivity, and reduce inspection costs. However, these statistical methods were not widely adopted outside Bell Telephone.

During World War II statistical quality control became widespread. Faced with the task of producing large quantities of high-quality war matériel, industry turned to statistical methods, failure analysis, vendor certification, and early product design. The U.S. War Department required that suppliers of war matériel employ acceptance sampling, and its use became commonplace. Statistical control charts were also used, although not as widely as acceptance sampling.

In 1946 the **American Society for Quality Control (ASQC)** was established to encourage the use of quality improvement methods. The organization sponsors training programs, seminars, and publications dealing with quality issues. In spite of the efforts of the ASQC, however, interest in quality in American industry diminished after the war. American business had little competition in the world market—Europe and Japan were rebuilding their shattered economies. Tremendous emphasis was placed on increased production because firms were often unable to meet the demand for their products. Profits were high, and the concern for quality waned. As a result, postwar American managers did not understand the importance of quality and process improvement, and they were not informed about quality improvement techniques.

However, events in Japan took a different turn. After the war, Japanese industrial capacity was crippled. Productivity was very low, and products were of notoriously bad quality. In those days, products stamped "Made in Japan" were generally considered to be "cheap junk." The man credited with turning this situation around is W. Edwards Deming. Deming, born in 1900, earned a Ph.D. in mathematical physics from Yale University in 1927. He then went to work in a Department of Agriculture–affiliated laboratory. Deming, who had learned statistics while studying physics, applied statistics to experiments conducted at the laboratory. Through this work, Deming was introduced to Walter Shewhart, who explained his theories about using statistical control charts to improve quality and productivity. During World War II, Deming was largely responsible for teaching 35,000 American engineers and technical people how to use statistics to improve the quality of war matériel. After the war, the Allied command sent a group of these engineers to Japan. Their mission was to improve the Japanese communication system. In doing so, the engineers employed the statistical methods they had learned, and Deming's work was brought to the attention of the **Union of Japanese Scientists and Engineers (JUSE).** Deming, who had started his own consulting firm in 1946, was asked by the JUSE to help increase Japanese productivity. In July 1950 Deming traveled to Japan and gave a series of lectures titled "Elementary Principles of the Statistical Control of Quality" to a group of 230 Japanese managers. Deming taught the Japanese how to use statistics to determine how well a system can perform, and taught them how to design process improvements to make the system operate better and more efficiently. He also taught the Japanese that the more quality a producer builds into a product, the less it costs. Realizing the serious nature of their economic crisis, the Japanese adopted Deming's ideas as a philosophy of doing business. Through Deming, the Japanese found that by listening to the wants and needs of consumers and by using statistical methods for process improvement in production, they could export high-quality products to the world market.

Although American business was making only feeble attempts to improve product quality in the 1950s and 1960s, it was able to maintain a dominant competitive position. Many U.S. companies focused more on marketing and financial strategies than on product and production. But the Japanese and other foreign competitors were making inroads. By the 1970s, the quality of many Japanese and European products (for instance, automobiles, television sets, and electronic equipment) became far superior to their American-made counterparts. Also, rising prices made consumers more quality conscious—people expected high quality if they were going to pay high prices. As a result, the market shares of U.S. firms rapidly decreased. Many U.S. firms were severely injured or went out of business.

Meanwhile, Deming continued teaching and preaching quality improvement. While Deming was famous in Japan, he was relatively unknown in the United States until 1980. In June 1980 Deming was featured in an NBC television documentary titled "If Japan Can, Why Can't We?" This program, written and narrated by then–NBC correspondent Lloyd Dobyns, compared Japanese and American industrial productivity and credited Deming for Japan's success. Within days, demand for Deming's consulting services skyrocketed. Deming consulted with many major U.S. firms. Among these firms are The Ford Motor Company, General Motors Corporation, and The Procter & Gamble Company. Ford, for instance, began consulting with Deming in 1981. Donald Petersen, who was Ford's chairman and chief executive officer at the time, became a Deming disciple. By following the Deming philosophy, Ford, which was losing 2 billion dollars yearly in 1980, attempted to create a quality culture. Quality of Ford products was greatly improved, and the company again became profitable. The 1980s saw many U.S. companies adopt a philosophy of continuous improvement of quality and productivity in all areas of their businesses—manufacturing, accounting, sales, finance, personnel, marketing, customer service, maintenance, and so forth. This overall approach of applying quality principles to all company activities is called **total quality management (TQM)** or **total quality control (TQC).** It is becoming an important management strategy in American business. Dr. Deming taught seminars on quality improvement for managers and statisticians until his death on December 20, 1993. Deming's work resulted in widespread changes in both the structure of the world economy and the ways in which American businesses are managed.

The fundamental ideas behind Deming's approach to quality and productivity improvement are contained in his "**14 points.**" These are a set of managerial principles that, if followed, Deming believed would enable a company to improve quality and productivity, reduce costs, and compete effectively in the world market. We briefly summarize the 14 points in Table 17.1 on the next page. For more complete discussions of these points, see Bowerman and O'Connell (1996), Deming (1986), Walton (1986), Scherkenbach (1987), or Gitlow, Gitlow, Oppenheim, and Oppenheim (1989). Deming stressed that implementation of the 14 points requires both changes in management philosophy and the use of statistical methods. In addition, Deming believed that it is necessary to follow all of the points, not just some of them.

In 1988 the first **Malcolm Baldrige National Quality Awards** were presented. These awards, presented by the U.S. Commerce Department, are named for the late Malcolm Baldrige, who was Commerce Secretary during the Reagan administration. The awards were established to promote

TABLE 17.1   W. Edwards Deming's 14 Points

1   **Create constancy of purpose toward improvement of product and service with a plan to become competitive, stay in business, and provide jobs.**
    Devise a plan for the long-term success of the company based on quality improvement.

2   **Adopt a new philosophy.**
    Do not tolerate commonly accepted mistakes, delays, defective materials, and defective workmanship.

3   **Cease dependence on mass inspection.**
    Quality cannot be inspected into a product. It must be built into the product through process improvement.

4   **End the practice of awarding business on the basis of price tag.**
    Do not buy from the lowest bidder without taking the quality of goods purchased into account. Purchasing should be based on lowest total cost (including the cost of bad quality).

5   **Improve constantly and forever the system of production and service to improve quality and productivity, and thus constantly decrease costs.**
    Constantly seek to improve every aspect of the business.

6   **Institute training.**
    Workers should know how to do their jobs and should know how their jobs affect quality and the success of the company.

7   **Institute leadership.**
    The job of management is leadership, not mere supervision. Leadership involves understanding the work that needs to be done and fostering process improvement.

8   **Drive out fear, so that everyone may work more effectively for the company.**
    Workers should not be afraid to express ideas, to ask questions, or to take appropriate action.

9   **Break down organizational barriers.**
    Barriers that damage the company performance (such as competition between staff areas, poor communication, disputes between labor and management, and so on) must be removed so that everyone can work for the good of the company.

10 **Eliminate slogans, exhortations, and arbitrary numerical goals and targets for the workforce that urge the workers to achieve new levels of productivity and quality without providing methods.**
    Slogans and numerical goals (such as production quotas) are counterproductive unless management provides methods for achieving them.

11 **Eliminate work standards and numerical quotas.**
    Work standards and numerical quotas that specify the quantity of goods to be produced while quality is ignored are counterproductive and should be eliminated.

12 **Remove barriers that rob employees of their pride of workmanship.**
    While workers want to do a good job and have pride in their work, bad management practices often rob workers of their pride. Barriers that rob workers of pride (such as inadequate instructions, cheap materials, poor maintenance, and so on) must be removed.

13 **Institute a vigorous program of education and self-improvement.**
    Education and training are necessary for everyone if continuous improvement is to be achieved.

14 **Take action to accomplish the transformation.**
    A management structure that is committed to continuous improvement must be put in place.

Source: W. Edwards Deming, "Deming's 14 Points, condensed version" from *Out of Crisis*. Copyright © MIT Press. Used with permission.

quality awareness, to recognize quality achievements by U.S. companies, and to publicize successful quality strategies. The Malcolm Baldrige National Quality Award Consortium, formed by the ASQC (now known as the ASQ) and the American Productivity and Quality Center, administers the award. The Baldrige award has become one of the most prestigious honors in American business. Annual awards are given in three categories—manufacturing, service, and small business. Winners include companies such as Motorola Inc., Xerox Corporation Business Products and Systems, the Commercial Nuclear Fuel Division of Westinghouse Electric Corporation, Milliken and Company, Cadillac Division, General Motors Corporation, Ritz Carlton Hotels, and AT&T Consumer Communications.

Finally, the 1990s saw the adoption of an international quality standards system called **ISO 9000.** More than 90 countries around the globe have adopted the ISO 9000 series of standards for their companies, as have many multinational corporations (including AT&T, 3M, IBM, Motorola, and DuPont). As a brief introduction to ISO 9000, we quote "Is ISO 9000 for You?" published by CEEM Information Systems:

What Is ISO 9000?
ISO 9000 is a series of international standards for quality assurance management systems. It establishes the organizational structure and processes for assuring that the production of goods or services meets a consistent and agreed-upon level of quality for a company's customers.

The ISO 9000 series is unique in that it applies to a very wide range of organizations and industries encompassing both the manufacturing and service sectors.

Why Is ISO 9000 Important?

ISO 9000 is important for two reasons. First . . . the discipline imposed by the standard for processes influencing your quality management systems can enhance your company's quality consistency.

Second . . . more and more companies, both here at home and internationally, are requiring their suppliers to be ISO 9000 registered.[1]

Clearly, quality has finally become a crucially important issue in American business. The quality revolution now affects every area in business. But the Japanese continue to mount new challenges. For years, the Japanese have used **designed statistical experiments** to develop new processes, find and remedy process problems, improve product performance, and improve process efficiency. Much of this work is based on the insights of Genichi Taguchi, a Japanese engineer. His methods of experimental design, the so-called **Taguchi methods,** have been heavily used in Japan since the 1960s. Although Taguchi's methodology is controversial in statistical circles, the use of experimental design gives the Japanese a considerable advantage over U.S. competitors because it enables them to design a high level of quality into a product before production begins. Some U.S. manufacturers have begun to use experimental design techniques to design quality into their products. It will be necessary for many more U.S. companies to do so in order to remain competitive in the future—a challenge for the 21st century.

17.2 Statistical Process Control and Causes of Process Variation ● ● ●

LO17-2 Distinguish between common causes and assignable causes of process variation.

Statistical process control **Statistical process control (SPC)** is a systematic method for analyzing process data (quality characteristics) in which we monitor and study the **process variation.** The goal is to stabilize the process and to reduce the amount of process variation. When a process has been stabilized, we say that the process is in *statistical control.* That is, more formally:

> A process is in **statistical control** when the process measurements display a constant amount of variation around a constant mean (or *level*).

The ultimate goal of SPC is **continuous process improvement.** While we often use SPC to monitor and improve manufacturing processes, SPC is also commonly used to improve service quality. For instance, we might use SPC to reduce the time it takes to process a loan application, or to improve the accuracy of an order entry system.

Before the widespread use of SPC, quality control was based on an **inspection** approach. Here the product is first made, and then the final product is inspected to eliminate defective items. This is called **action on the output** of the process. The emphasis here is on detecting defective product that has already been produced. This is costly and wasteful because, if defective product is produced, the bad items must be (1) **scrapped,** (2) **reworked or reprocessed** (that is, fixed), or (3) **downgraded** (sold off at a lower price). In fact, the cost of bad quality (scrap, rework, and so on) can be tremendously high. It is not unusual for this cost to be as high as 10 to 30 percent or more of a company's dollar sales.

In contrast to the inspection approach, SPC emphasizes integrating quality improvement into the process. Here the goal is **preventing bad quality by taking appropriate action on the process.** In order to accomplish this goal, we must decide when actions on the process are needed. The focus of much of this chapter is to show how such decisions can be made.

Causes of process variation In order to understand SPC methodology, we must realize that the variations we observe in quality characteristics are caused by different sources. These sources include factors such as equipment (machines or the like), materials, people, methods and procedures, the environment, and so forth. Here we must distinguish between **usual process variation** and **unusual process variation.** Usual process variation results from what we call **common causes of process variation.**

> **Common causes** are sources of variation that have the potential to influence all process observations. That is, these sources of variation are inherent to the current process design.

[1]CEEM Information Services, "Is ISO 9000 for You?" 1993.

Common cause variation can be substantial. For instance, obsolete or poorly maintained equipment, a poorly designed process, and inadequate instructions for workers are examples of common causes that might significantly influence all process output. As an example, suppose that we are filling 16-ounce jars with grape jelly. A 25-year-old, obsolete filler machine might be a common cause of process variation that influences all the jar fills. While (in theory) it might be possible to replace the filler machine with a new model, we might have chosen not to do so, and the obsolete filler causes all the jar fills to exhibit substantial variation.

Common causes also include small influences that would cause slight variation even if all conditions are held as constant as humanly possible. For example, in the jar fill situation, small variations in the speed at which jars move under the filler valves, slight floor vibrations, and small differences between filler valve settings would always influence the jar fills even when conditions are held as constant as possible. Sometimes these small variations are described as being due to "chance."

Together, the important and unimportant common causes of variation determine the **usual process variability.** That is, these causes determine the amount of variation that exists when the process is operating routinely. We can reduce the amount of common cause variation by removing some of the important common causes. **Reducing common cause variation is usually a management responsibility.** For instance, replacing obsolete equipment, redesigning a plant or process, or improving plant maintenance would require management action.

In addition to common cause variation, processes are affected by a different kind of variation called **assignable cause variation** (sometimes also called **special cause** or **specific cause variation).**

Assignable causes are sources of **unusual process variation.** These are intermittent or permanent changes in the process that are not common to all process observations and that may cause important process variation. Assignable causes are usually of short duration, but they can be persistent or recurring conditions.

For example, in the jar filling situation, one of the filler valves may become clogged so that some jars are being substantially underfilled (or perhaps are not filled at all). Or a relief operator might incorrectly set the filler so that all jars are being substantially overfilled for a short period of time. As another example, suppose that a bank wishes to study the length of time customers must wait before being served by a teller. If a customer fills out a banking form incorrectly, this might cause a temporary delay that increases the waiting time for other customers. Notice that **assignable causes** such as these can often be remedied by local supervision—for instance, by a production line foreman, a machine operator, a head bank teller, or the like. **One objective of SPC is to detect and eliminate assignable causes of process variation.** By doing this, we reduce the amount of process variation. This results in improved quality.

It is important to point out that an assignable cause could be beneficial—that is, it could be an unusual process variation resulting in unusually good process performance. In such a situation, we wish to discover the root cause of the variation, and then we wish to incorporate this condition into the process if possible. For instance, suppose we find that a process performs unusually well when a raw material purchased from a particular supplier is used. It might be desirable to purchase as much of the raw material as possible from this supplier.

When a process exhibits only common cause variation, it will operate in a stable, or consistent, fashion. That is, in the absence of any unusual process variations, **the process will display a constant amount of variation around a constant mean.** On the other hand, if assignable causes are affecting the process, then the process will not be stable—unusual variations will cause the process mean or variability to change over time. It follows that

1   When a process is influenced only by **common cause variation, the process will be in statistical control.**

2   When a process is influenced by **one or more assignable causes, the process will not be in statistical control.**

In general, in order to bring a process into statistical control, we must find and eliminate undesirable assignable causes of process variation, and we should (if feasible) build desirable assignable causes into the process. When we have done these things, the process is what we call a **stable, common cause system.** This means that the process operates in a **consistent** fashion and is **predictable.** Because there are no unusual process variations, the process (as currently configured) is doing all it can be expected to do.

When a process is in statistical control, management can evaluate the **process capability.** That is, it can assess whether the process can produce output meeting customer or producer requirements. If it does not, action by local supervision will not remedy the situation—remember, the assignable causes (the sources of process variation that can be dealt with by local supervision) have already been removed. Rather, some fundamental change will be needed in order to reduce common cause variation. For instance, perhaps a new, more modern filler machine must be purchased and installed. This will require action by management.

Finally, the SPC approach is really a philosophy of doing business. It is an entire firm or organization that is focused on a single goal: continuous quality and productivity improvement. The impetus for this philosophy must come from management. Unless management is supportive and directly involved in the ongoing quality improvement process, the SPC approach will not be successful.

Exercises for Sections 17.1 and 17.2

CONCEPTS

17.1 Write an essay comparing the management philosophy that Dr. Deming advocated in his 14 points to the management styles you have been exposed to in your personal work experiences. Do you think Dr. Deming's philosophy is preferable to the management styles you have seen in practice? Which of the 14 points do you agree with? Which do you disagree with?

17.2 Write a paragraph explaining how common causes of process variation differ from assignable causes of process variation.

METHODS AND APPLICATIONS

17.3 In this exercise we consider several familiar processes. In each case, describe several common causes and several assignable causes that might result in variation of the given quality characteristic.

     a   Process: getting ready for school or work in the morning.
         Quality characteristic: the time it takes to get ready.
     b   Process: driving, walking, or otherwise commuting from your home or apartment to school or work.
         Quality characteristic: the time it takes to commute.
     c   Process: studying for and taking a statistics exam.
         Quality characteristic: the score received on the exam.
     d   Process: starting your car in the morning.
         Quality characteristic: the time it takes to start your car.

17.4 Form a group of three or four students in your class. As a group project, select a familiar process and determine a variable that measures the quality of some aspect of the output of this process. Then list some common causes and assignable causes that might result in variation of the variable you have selected for the process. Discuss your lists in class.

17.3 Sampling a Process, Rational Subgrouping, and Control Charts ● ● ●

LO17-3 Sample a process by using rational subgrouping.

In order to find and eliminate assignable causes of process variation, we sample output from the process. To do this, we first decide which **process variables**—that is, which process characteristics—will be studied. Several graphical techniques (sometimes called *prestatistical tools*) are used here. Pareto charts (see Section 2.1 on page 38) help identify problem areas and opportunities for improvement. Cause-and-effect diagrams (see optional Section 17.7 on page 721) help uncover sources of process variation and potentially important process variables. The goal is to identify process variables that can be studied in order to decrease the gap between customer expectations and process performance.

Whenever possible and economical, it is best to study a **quantitative,** rather than a **categorical,** process variable. For example, suppose we are filling 16-ounce jars with grape jelly, and suppose specifications state that each jar should contain between 15.95 and 16.05 ounces of jelly. If we record the fill of each sampled jar by simply noting that the jar either "meets specifications" (the fill is between 15.95 and 16.05 ounces) or "does not meet the specifications," then we are studying a **categorical process variable.** However, if we measure and record the amount of grape jelly contained in the jar (say, to the nearest one-hundredth of an ounce), then we are studying a **quantitative process variable.** Actually measuring the fill is best because this tells us **how close** we are to the specification limits and thus provides more information. As we will soon see, this additional information often allows us to decide whether to take action on a process by using a relatively small number of measurements.

When we study a quantitative process variable, we say that we are employing **measurement data.** To analyze such data, we take a series of samples (usually called **subgroups**) over time. Each subgroup consists of a set of several measurements; subgroup sizes between 2 and 6 are often used. Summary statistics (for example, means and ranges) for each subgroup are calculated and are plotted versus time. By comparing plot points, we hope to discover when unusual process variations are taking place.

Each subgroup is typically observed over a short period of time—a period of time in which the process operating characteristics do not change much. That is, we employ **rational subgroups.**

Rational Subgroups

R ational subgroups are selected so that, **if process changes of practical importance exist, the chance that these changes will occur between subgroups is maximized and the chance that these changes will occur within subgroups is minimized.**

In order to obtain rational subgroups, we must determine the frequency with which subgroups will be selected. For example, we might select a subgroup once every 15 minutes, once an hour, or once a day. In general, we should observe subgroups often enough to detect important process changes. For instance, suppose we wish to study a process, and suppose we feel that workers' shift changes (that take place every eight hours) may be an important source of process variation. In this case, rational subgroups can be obtained by selecting a subgroup during each eight-hour shift. Here shift changes will occur **between** subgroups. Therefore, if shift changes are an important source of variation, the rational subgroups will enable us to observe the effects of these changes by comparing plot points for different subgroups (shifts). However, in addition, suppose hourly machine resets are made, and we feel that these resets may also be an important source of process variation. In this case, rational subgroups can be obtained by selecting a subgroup during each hour. Here machine resets will occur **between** subgroups, and we will be able to observe their effects by comparing plot points for different subgroups (hours). If in this situation we selected one subgroup each eight-hour shift, we would not obtain rational subgroups. This is because hourly machine resets would occur **within** subgroups, and we would not be able to observe the effects of these resets by comparing plot points for different shifts. In general, it is very important to try to identify important sources of variation (potential assignable causes such as shift changes, resets, and so on) before deciding how subgroups will be selected. As previously stated, constructing a cause-and-effect diagram helps uncover these sources of variation (see optional Section 17.7 on page 721).

Once we determine the sampling frequency, we need to determine the **subgroup size**—that is, the number of measurements that will be included in each subgroup—and how we will actually select the measurements in each subgroup. It is recommended that the **subgroup size be held constant.** Denoting this constant subgroup size as n, we typically choose n to be from 2 to 6, with $n = 4$ or 5 being a frequent choice. To illustrate how we can actually select the subgroup measurements, suppose we select a subgroup of 5 units every hour from the output of a machine that produces 100 units per hour. We can select these units by using a **consecutive, periodic,** or **random** sampling process. If we employ consecutive sampling, we would select 5 consecutive units produced by the machine at the beginning of (or at some time during) each hour. Here **production conditions**—machine operator, machine setting, raw material batch, and so forth—**will be as constant as possible within the subgroup.** Such a subgroup provides a "freeze-frame picture" of the process at a particular point in time. Thus the **chance of variations occurring within the subgroups is minimized.** If we use periodic sampling, we would select 5 units periodically through each hour. For example, because the machine produces 100 units per hour, we could select the 1st, 21st, 41st, 61st, and 81st units produced. If we use random sampling, we would use a random number table to randomly select 5 of the 100 units produced during each hour. If production conditions are really held fairly constant during each hour, then consecutive, periodic, and random sampling will each provide a similar representation of the process. If production conditions vary considerably during each hour, and if we are able to recognize this variation by using a periodic or random sampling procedure, this would tell us that we should be sampling the process more often than once an hour. Of course, if we are using periodic or random sampling every hour, we might not realize that the process operates with considerably less variation during shorter periods (perhaps because we have not used a consecutive sampling procedure). We therefore might not recognize the extent of the hourly variation.

Lastly, it is important to point out that we **must also take subgroups for a period of time that is long enough to give potential sources of variation a chance to show up.** If, for instance, different batches of raw materials are suspected to be a significant source of process variation, and if we receive new batches every few days, we may need to collect subgroups for several weeks in order to assess the effects of the batch-to-batch variation. **A statistical rule of thumb says that we require at least 20 subgroups of size 4 or 5 in order to judge statistical control and in order to obtain reasonable estimates of the process mean and variability.** However, practical considerations may require the collection of much more data.

We now look at a more concrete example of subgrouped data.

EXAMPLE 17.1 The Hole Location Case[2]: Subgrouped Process Data   C

A manufacturer produces automobile air conditioner compressor shells. The compressor shell is basically the outer metal housing of the compressor. Several holes of various sizes must be punched into the shell to accommodate hose connections that must be made to the compressor. If any one of these holes is punched in the wrong location, the compressor shell becomes a piece of scrap metal (at considerable cost to the manufacturer). Figure 17.1(a) illustrates a compressor shell (note the holes that have been punched in the housing). Experience with the hole-punching process suggests that substantial changes (machine resets, equipment lubrication, and so forth)

FIGURE 17.1   **The Compressor Shell and the Hole Location Data**   DS HoleLoc

(a) Holes punched in a compressor shell for hose connections

(b) Twenty subgroups of 5 hole location measurements (measurement from trim edge to the bottom of hole; target value is 3.00 inches)

Time	Subgroup	1	2	3	4	5	Mean	Range
8:00 AM	1	3.05	3.02	3.04	3.09	3.05	3.05	0.07
8:20 AM	2	3.00	3.04	2.98	2.99	2.99	3.00	0.06
8:40 AM	3	3.07	3.06	2.94	2.97	3.01	3.01	0.13
9:00 AM	4	3.02	2.96	3.01	2.98	3.02	2.998	0.06
9:20 AM	5	3.01	2.98	3.04	3.01	3.01	3.01	0.06
9:40 AM	6	3.01	3.02	2.99	2.97	2.96	2.99	0.06
10:00 AM	7	3.03	2.98	2.92	3.17	2.96	3.012	0.25
10:20 AM	8	3.05	3.03	2.96	3.01	2.97	3.004	0.09
10:40 AM	9	2.99	2.96	3.01	3.00	2.95	2.982	0.06
11:00 AM	10	3.02	3.02	2.98	3.03	3.02	3.014	0.05
11:20 AM	11	2.97	2.96	2.96	3.00	3.04	2.986	0.08
11:40 AM	12	3.06	3.04	3.02	3.10	3.05	3.054	0.08
12:00 PM	13	2.99	3.00	3.04	2.96	3.02	3.002	0.08
12:20 PM	14	3.00	3.01	2.99	3.00	3.01	3.002	0.02
12:40 PM	15	3.02	2.96	3.04	2.95	2.97	2.988	0.09
1:00 PM	16	3.02	3.02	3.04	2.98	3.03	3.018	0.06
1:20 PM	17	3.01	2.87	3.09	3.02	3.00	2.998	0.22
1:40 PM	18	3.05	2.96	3.01	2.97	2.98	2.994	0.09
2:00 PM	19	3.02	2.99	3.00	2.98	3.00	2.998	0.04
2:20 PM	20	3.00	3.00	3.01	3.05	3.01	3.014	0.05

[2]The data for this case were obtained from a metal fabrication plant located in the Cincinnati, Ohio, area. For confidentiality, we have agreed to withhold the company's name.

can occur quite frequently—as often as two or three times an hour. Because we wish to observe the impact of these changes if and when they occur, rational subgroups are obtained by selecting a subgroup every 20 minutes or so. Specifically, about every 20 minutes five compressor shells are consecutively selected from the process output. For each shell selected, a measurement that helps to specify the location of a particular hole in the compressor shell is made. The measurement is taken by measuring from one of the edges of the compressor shell (called the trim edge) to the bottom of the hole [see Figure 17.1(a)]. Obviously, it is not possible to measure to the center of the hole because you cannot tell where it is! The target value for the measured dimension is 3.00 inches. Of course, the manufacturer would like as little variation around the target as possible. Figure 17.1(b) gives the measurements obtained for 20 subgroups that were selected between 8 A.M. and 2:20 P.M. on a particular day. Here a subgroup consists of the five measurements labeled 1 through 5 in a single row in the table. Notice that Figure 17.1(b) also gives the mean, $\bar{x}$, and the range, R, of the measurements in each subgroup. In the next section we will see how to use the subgroup means and ranges to detect when unusual process variations have taken place.

Subgrouped data are used to determine when assignable causes of process variation exist. Typically, we analyze subgrouped data by plotting summary statistics for the subgroups versus time. The resulting plots are often called **graphs of process performance.** For example, the subgroup means and the subgroup ranges of the hole location measurements in Figure 17.1(b) are plotted in time order on graphs of process performance in the Excel output of Figure 17.2. The subgroup means ($\bar{x}$ values) and ranges (R values) are plotted on the vertical axis, while the time sequence (in this case, the subgroup number) is plotted on the horizontal axis. The $\bar{x}$ values and R values for corresponding subgroups are lined up vertically. The plot points on each graph are connected by line segments as a visual aid. However, the lines between the plot points do not really say anything about the process performance between the observed subgroups. Notice that the subgroup means and ranges vary over time.

If we consider the plot of subgroup means, very high and very low points are undesirable—they represent large deviations from the target hole location dimension (3 inches). If we consider the plot of subgroup ranges, very high points are undesirable (high variation in the hole location dimensions), while very low points are desirable (little variation in the hole location dimensions).

FIGURE 17.2   Excel Output of Graphs of Performance (Subgroup Means and Ranges) for the Hole Location Data in Figure 17.1(b)

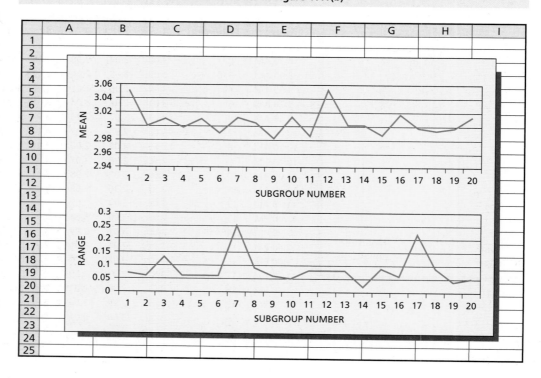

We now wish to answer a very basic question. **Is the variation that we see on the graphs of performance due to the usual process variation (that is, due to common causes), or is the variation due to one or more assignable causes (unusual variations)?** It is possible that unusual variations have occurred and that action should be taken to reduce the variation in production conditions. It is also possible that the variation in the plot points is caused by common causes and that (given the current configuration of the process) production conditions have been held as constant as possible. For example, do the high points on the $\bar{x}$ plot in Figure 17.2 suggest that one or more assignable causes have increased the hole location dimensions enough to warrant corrective action? As another example, do the high points on the R plot suggest that excess variability in the hole location dimensions exists and that corrective action is needed? Or does the lowest point on the R plot indicate that an improvement in process performance (reduction in variation) has occurred due to an assignable cause?

We can answer these questions by converting the graphs of performance shown in Figure 17.2 into **control charts.** In general, by converting graphs of performance into control charts, we can (with only a small chance of being wrong) determine whether observed process variations are unusual (due to assignable causes). That is, the purpose of a control chart is to monitor a process so we can take corrective action in response to assignable causes when it is needed. This is called **statistical process monitoring.** The use of "seat of the pants intuition" is not a particularly effective way to decide whether observed process performance is unusual. By using a control chart, we can reduce our chances of making two possible errors—(1) taking action when none is needed and (2) not taking action when action is needed.

A control chart employs a **center line** (denoted **CNL**) and two control limits—an **upper control limit** (denoted **UCL**) and a **lower control limit** (denoted **LCL**). The center line represents the average performance of the process when it is in a state of statistical control—that is, when only common cause variation exists. The upper and lower control limits are horizontal lines situated above and below the center line. These control limits are established so that, when the process is in control, almost all plot points will be between the upper and lower limits. In practice, the control limits are used as follows:

1   If all observed plot points are **between the LCL and UCL** (and if no unusual patterns of points exist—this will be explained later), we have no evidence that assignable causes exist and we assume that the process is in **statistical control.** In this case, **only common causes of process variation exist,** and **no action to remove assignable causes is taken on the process.** If we were to take such action, we would be **unnecessarily tampering** with the process.

2   If we observe one or more plot points **outside the control limits,** then we have evidence that the process is **out of control due to one or more assignable causes.** Here **we must take action on the process** to remove these assignable causes.

In the next section we begin to discuss how to construct control charts. Before doing this, however, we must emphasize the importance of **documenting** a process while the subgroups of data are being collected. The time at which each subgroup is taken is recorded, and the person who collected the data is also recorded. Any process changes (machine resets, adjustments, shift changes, operator changes, and so on) must be documented. Any potential sources of variation that may significantly affect the process output should be noted. If the process is not well documented, it will be very difficult to identify the root causes of unusual variations that may be detected when we analyze the subgroups of data.

17.4 *x̄* and *R* Charts ● ● ●

LO17-4 Use $\bar{x}$ and R charts to establish process control.

$\bar{x}$ **and R charts** are the most commonly used control charts for **measurement data** (such charts are often called **variables control charts**). **Subgroup means** are plotted versus time on the $\bar{x}$ chart, while **subgroup ranges** are plotted on the R chart. The $\bar{x}$ chart monitors the **process mean** or **level** (we wish to run near a desired target level). The R chart is used to monitor the amount of **variability** around the process level (we desire as little variability as possible around the target). Note here that we employ two control charts, and that **it is important to use the two charts together.** If we do not use both charts, we will not get all the information needed to improve the process.

Before seeing how to construct $\bar{x}$ and R charts, we should mention that it is also possible to monitor the process variability by using a chart for **subgroup standard deviations.** Such a chart is called an **s chart.** However, the overwhelming majority of practitioners use R charts rather than s charts. This is partly due to historical reasons. When control charts were developed, electronic calculators and computers did not exist. It was, therefore, much easier to compute a subgroup range than it was to compute a subgroup standard deviation. For this reason, the use of R charts has persisted. Some people also feel that it is easier for factory personnel (some of whom may have little mathematical background) to understand and relate to the subgroup range. In addition, while the standard deviation (which is computed using all the measurements in a subgroup) is a better measure of variability than the range (which is computed using only two measurements), the R chart usually suffices. This is because $\bar{x}$ and R charts usually employ small subgroups—as mentioned previously, subgroup sizes are often between 2 and 6. For such subgroup sizes, it can be shown that using subgroup ranges is almost as effective as using subgroup standard deviations.

To construct $\bar{x}$ and R charts, suppose we have observed rational subgroups of n measurements over successive time periods (hours, shifts, days, or the like). We first calculate the mean $\bar{x}$ and range R for each subgroup, and we construct graphs of performance for the $\bar{x}$ values and for the R values (as in Figure 17.2). In order to calculate center lines and control limits, let $\bar{x}$ denote the mean of the subgroup of n measurements that is selected in a particular time period. Furthermore, assume that the population of all process measurements that could be observed in any time period is normally distributed with mean μ and standard deviation σ, and also assume successive process measurements are statistically independent.[3] Then, if μ and σ stay constant over time, the sampling distribution of subgroup means in any time period is normally distributed with mean μ and standard deviation $\sigma / \sqrt{n}$. It follows that (in any time period) 99.73 percent of all possible values of the subgroup mean $\bar{x}$ are in the interval

$$[\mu - 3(\sigma/\sqrt{n}), \; \mu + 3(\sigma/\sqrt{n})]$$

This fact is illustrated in Figure 17.3. It follows that we can set a center line and control limits for the $\bar{x}$ chart as

$$\text{Center line} = \mu$$
$$\text{Upper control limit} = \text{UCL}_{\bar{x}} = \mu + 3(\sigma/\sqrt{n})$$
$$\text{Lower control limit} = \text{LCL}_{\bar{x}} = \mu - 3(\sigma/\sqrt{n})$$

If an observed subgroup mean is inside these control limits, we have no evidence to suggest that the process is out of control. However, if the subgroup mean is outside these limits, we conclude that μ and/or σ have changed, and that the process is out of control. The $\bar{x}$ chart limits are illustrated in Figure 17.3.

If the process is in control, and thus μ and σ stay constant over time, it follows that μ and σ are the mean and standard deviation of all possible process measurements. For this reason, we call μ the **process mean** and σ the **process standard deviation.** Because in most real situations we do not know the true values of μ and σ, we must estimate these values. If the process is in control, an appropriate estimate of the process mean μ is

$$\bar{\bar{x}} = \text{the mean of all observed subgroup means}$$

($\bar{\bar{x}}$ is **pronounced "x double bar"**). It follows that the center line for the $\bar{x}$ chart is

$$\text{Center line}_{\bar{x}} = \bar{\bar{x}}$$

To obtain control limits for the $\bar{x}$ chart, we compute

$$\bar{R} = \text{the mean of all observed subgroup ranges}$$

It can be shown that an appropriate estimate of the process standard deviation σ is $(\bar{R}/d_2)$, where d_2 is a constant that depends on the subgroup size n. Although we do not present a development of d_2 here, it intuitively makes sense that, for a given subgroup size, our best estimate of the process standard deviation should be related to the average of the subgroup ranges ($\bar{R}$). The

---

[3]Basically, *statistical independence* here means that successive process measurements do not display any kind of pattern over time.

FIGURE 17.3 An Illustration of $\bar{x}$ Chart Control Limits with the Process Mean μ and Process Standard Deviation σ Known

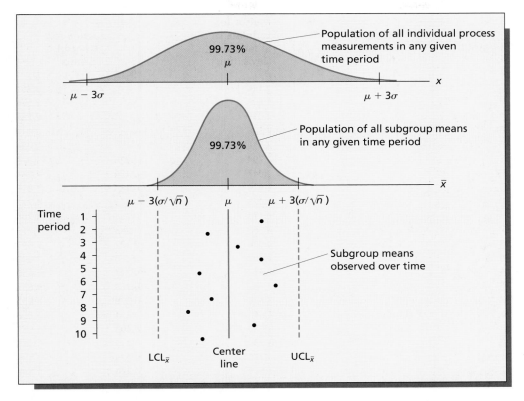

number d_2 relates these quantities. Values of d_2 are given in Table 17.2 (on the next page) for subgroup sizes $n = 2$ through $n = 25$. At the end of this section we further discuss why we use $\bar{R}/d_2$ to estimate the process standard deviation.

Substituting the estimate $\bar{\bar{x}}$ of μ and the estimate $\bar{R}/d_2$ of σ into the limits

$$\mu + 3(\sigma/\sqrt{n}) \quad \text{and} \quad \mu - 3(\sigma/\sqrt{n})$$

we obtain

$$\text{UCL}_{\bar{x}} = \bar{\bar{x}} + 3\left(\frac{\bar{R}/d_2}{\sqrt{n}}\right) = \bar{\bar{x}} + \left(\frac{3}{d_2\sqrt{n}}\right)\bar{R}$$

$$\text{LCL}_{\bar{x}} = \bar{\bar{x}} - 3\left(\frac{\bar{R}/d_2}{\sqrt{n}}\right) = \bar{\bar{x}} - \left(\frac{3}{d_2\sqrt{n}}\right)\bar{R}$$

Finally, we define

$$A_2 = \frac{3}{d_2\sqrt{n}}$$

and rewrite the control limits as

$$\text{UCL}_{\bar{x}} = \bar{\bar{x}} + A_2\bar{R} \quad \text{and} \quad \text{LCL}_{\bar{x}} = \bar{\bar{x}} - A_2\bar{R}$$

Here we call A_2 a **control chart constant.** As the formula for A_2 implies, this control chart constant depends on the subgroup size n. Values of A_2 are given in Table 17.2 for subgroup sizes $n = 2$ through $n = 25$.

The center line for the R chart is

$$\text{Center line}_R = \bar{R}$$

Furthermore, assuming normality, it can be shown that there are control chart constants D_4 and D_3 so that

$$\text{UCL}_R = D_4\bar{R} \quad \text{and} \quad \text{LCL}_R = D_3\bar{R}$$

TABLE 17.2   Control Chart Constants for $\bar{x}$ and R Charts

| | Chart for Averages ($\bar{x}$) | Chart for Ranges (R) | | |
Subgroup Size, n	Factor for Control Limits, A_2	Divisor for Estimate of Standard Deviation, d_2	Factors for Control Limits D_3	D_4
2	1.880	1.128	—	3.267
3	1.023	1.693	—	2.574
4	0.729	2.059	—	2.282
5	0.577	2.326	—	2.114
6	0.483	2.534	—	2.004
7	0.419	2.704	0.076	1.924
8	0.373	2.847	0.136	1.864
9	0.337	2.970	0.184	1.816
10	0.308	3.078	0.223	1.777
11	0.285	3.173	0.256	1.744
12	0.266	3.258	0.283	1.717
13	0.249	3.336	0.307	1.693
14	0.235	3.407	0.328	1.672
15	0.223	3.472	0.347	1.653
16	0.212	3.532	0.363	1.637
17	0.203	3.588	0.378	1.622
18	0.194	3.640	0.391	1.608
19	0.187	3.689	0.403	1.597
20	0.180	3.735	0.415	1.585
21	0.173	3.778	0.425	1.575
22	0.167	3.819	0.434	1.566
23	0.162	3.858	0.443	1.557
24	0.157	3.895	0.451	1.548
25	0.153	3.931	0.459	1.541

Here the control chart constants D_4 and D_3 also depend on the subgroup size n. Values of D_4 and D_3 are given in Table 17.2 for subgroup sizes $n = 2$ through $n = 25$. We summarize the center lines and control limits for $\bar{x}$ and R charts in the following box:

$\bar{x}$ and R Chart Center Lines and Control Limits

Center line$_{\bar{x}}$ = $\bar{\bar{x}}$ Center line$_R$ = $\bar{R}$

$UCL_{\bar{x}} = \bar{\bar{x}} + A_2\bar{R}$ $UCL_R = D_4\bar{R}$

$LCL_{\bar{x}} = \bar{\bar{x}} - A_2\bar{R}$ $LCL_R = D_3\bar{R}$

and A_2, D_4, and D_3 are control chart constants that depend on the subgroup size (see Table 17.2). When D_3 is not listed, the R chart does not have a lower control limit.[4]

where $\bar{\bar{x}}$ = the mean of all subgroup means
    $\bar{R}$ = the mean of all subgroup ranges

EXAMPLE 17.2 The Hole Location Case: Trial Control Limits

Consider the hole location data for air conditioner compressor shells that is given in Figure 17.1 (page 689). In order to calculate $\bar{x}$ and R chart control limits for this data, we compute

$$\bar{\bar{x}} = \text{the average of the 20 subgroup means}$$

$$= \frac{3.05 + 3.00 + \cdots + 3.014}{20} = 3.0062$$

---

[4]When D_3 is not listed, the theoretical lower control limit for the R chart is negative. In this case, some practitioners prefer to say that the LCL_R equals 0. Others prefer to say that the LCL_R does not exist because a range R equal to 0 does not indicate that an assignable cause exists and because it is impossible to observe a negative range below LCL_R. We prefer the second alternative. In practice, it makes no difference.

FIGURE 17.4   MINITAB Output of $\bar{x}$ and R Charts for the Hole Location Data

$$\bar{R} = \text{the average of the 20 subgroup ranges}$$
$$= \frac{.07 + .06 + \cdots + .05}{20} = 0.085$$

Looking at Table 17.2, we see that when the subgroup size is $n = 5$, the control chart constants needed for $\bar{x}$ and R charts are $A_2 = .577$ and $D_4 = 2.114$. It follows that center lines and control limits are

$$\text{Center line}_{\bar{x}} = \bar{\bar{x}} = 3.0062$$

$$\text{UCL}_{\bar{x}} = \bar{\bar{x}} + A_2\bar{R} = 3.0062 + .577(0.085) = 3.0552$$

$$\text{LCL}_{\bar{x}} = \bar{\bar{x}} - A_2\bar{R} = 3.0062 - .577(0.085) = 2.9572$$

$$\text{Center line}_R = \bar{R} = .085$$

$$\text{UCL}_R = D_4\bar{R} = 2.114(.085) = 0.1797$$

Because D_3 is not listed in Table 17.2 for a subgroup size of $n = 5$, the R chart does not have a lower control limit. Figure 17.4 presents the MINITAB output of the $\bar{x}$ and R charts for the hole location data. Note that the center lines and control limits that we have just calculated are shown on the $\bar{x}$ and R charts.

Control limits such as those computed in Example 17.2 are called **trial control limits.** Theoretically, control limits are supposed to be computed using subgroups collected while the process is in statistical control. However, it is impossible to know whether the process is in control until we have constructed the control charts. If, after we have set up the $\bar{x}$ and R charts, we find that the process is in control, we can use the charts to monitor the process.

If the charts show that the process is not in statistical control (for example, there are plot points outside the control limits), we must find and eliminate the assignable causes before we can calculate control limits for monitoring the process. In order to understand how to find and eliminate assignable causes, we must understand how changes in the process mean and the process variation show up on $\bar{x}$ and R charts. To do this, consider Figures 17.5 and 17.6 on the next page. These figures illustrate that, whereas a change in the process mean shows up only on the $\bar{x}$ chart, a change in the process variation shows up on both the $\bar{x}$ and R charts. Specifically, Figure 17.5 shows that, when the process mean increases, the sample means plotted on the $\bar{x}$ chart increase and go out of control. Figure 17.6 shows that, when the process variation

FIGURE 17.5   A Shift of the Process Mean

FIGURE 17.6   An Increase in the Process Variation

(standard deviation, σ) increases,

1   The sample ranges plotted on the R chart increase and go out of control.

2   The sample means plotted on the $\bar{x}$ chart become more variable (because, when σ increases, $\sigma_{\bar{x}} = \sigma/\sqrt{n}$ increases) and go out of control.

Because changes in the process mean and in the process variation show up on the $\bar{x}$ chart, we do not begin by analyzing the $\bar{x}$ chart. This is because, if there were out-of-control sample means on the $\bar{x}$ chart, we would not know whether the process mean or the process variation had changed. Therefore, it might be more difficult to identify the assignable causes of the out-of-control sample means because the assignable causes that would cause the process mean to shift could be very different from the assignable causes that would cause the process variation to increase. For instance, unwarranted frequent resetting of a machine might cause the process level to shift up and down, while improper lubrication of the machine might increase the process variation.

In order to simplify and better organize our analysis procedure, we begin by analyzing the R chart, which reflects only changes in the process variation. Then we analyze the $\bar{x}$ chart.

EXAMPLE 17.3 The Hole Location Case: Establishing Statistical Control

Consider the $\bar{x}$ and R charts for the hole location data that are given in Figure 17.4 on page 695. To develop control limits that can be used for ongoing control, we first examine the R chart. We find two points above the UCL on the R chart. This indicates that excess within-subgroup variability exists at these points. We see that the out-of-control points correspond to subgroups 7 and 17. Investigation reveals that, when these subgroups were selected, an inexperienced, newly hired operator ran the operation while the regular operator was on break. We find that the inexperienced operator is not fully closing the clamps that fasten down the compressor shells during the hole punching operation. This is causing excess variability in the hole locations. This assignable cause can be eliminated by thoroughly retraining the newly hired operator.

Because we have identified and corrected the assignable cause associated with the points that are out of control on the R chart, we can drop subgroups 7 and 17 from the data set. We recalculate center lines and control limits by using the remaining 18 subgroups. We first recompute (omitting $\bar{x}$ and R values for subgroups 7 and 17):

$$\bar{\bar{x}} = \frac{54.114}{18} = 3.0063 \quad \text{and} \quad \bar{R} = \frac{1.23}{18} = .0683$$

Notice here that $\bar{\bar{x}}$ has not changed much (see Figure 17.4), but $\bar{R}$ has been reduced from .085 to .0683. Using the new $\bar{\bar{x}}$ and $\bar{R}$ values, revised control limits for the $\bar{x}$ chart are

$$\text{UCL}_{\bar{x}} = \bar{\bar{x}} + A_2\bar{R} = 3.0063 + .577(.0683) = 3.0457$$

$$\text{LCL}_{\bar{x}} = \bar{\bar{x}} - A_2\bar{R} = 3.0063 - .577(.0683) = 2.9669$$

FIGURE 17.7   MINITAB Output of $\bar{x}$ and R Charts for the Hole Location Data: Subgroups 7 and 17 Omitted

The revised UCL for the R chart is

$$\text{UCL}_R = D_4\overline{R} = 2.114(.0683) = .1444$$

Because D_3 is not listed for subgroups of size 5, the R chart does not have a LCL. Here the reduction in $\overline{R}$ has reduced the UCL on the R chart from .1797 to .1444 and has also narrowed the control limits for the $\bar{x}$ chart. For instance, the UCL for the $\bar{x}$ chart has been reduced from 3.0552 to 3.0457. The MINITAB output of the $\bar{x}$ and R charts employing these revised center lines and control limits is shown in Figure 17.7.

We must now check the revised R chart for statistical control. We find that the chart shows good control: there are no other points outside the control limits or long runs of points on either side of the center line. Because the R chart is in good control, we can analyze the revised $\bar{x}$ chart. We see that two plot points are above the UCL on the $\bar{x}$ chart. Notice that these points were not outside our original trial control limits in Figure 17.4 on page 695. However, the elimination of the assignable cause and the resulting reduction in $\overline{R}$ has narrowed the $\bar{x}$ chart control limits so that these points are now out of control. Because the R chart is in control, the points on the $\bar{x}$ chart that are out of control suggest that the process level has shifted when subgroups 1 and 12 were taken. Investigation reveals that these subgroups were observed immediately after start-up at the beginning of the day and immediately after start-up following the lunch break. We find that, if we allow a five-minute machine warm-up period, we can eliminate the process level problem.

Because we have again found and eliminated an assignable cause, we must compute newly revised center lines and control limits. Dropping subgroups 1 and 12 from the data set, we recompute

$$\bar{\bar{x}} = \frac{48.01}{16} = 3.0006 \qquad \text{and} \qquad \overline{R} = \frac{1.08}{16} = .0675$$

Using the newest $\bar{\bar{x}}$ and $\overline{R}$ values, we compute newly revised control limits as follows:

$$\text{UCL}_{\bar{x}} = \bar{\bar{x}} + A_2\overline{R} = 3.0006 + .577(.0675) = 3.0396$$

$$\text{LCL}_{\bar{x}} = \bar{\bar{x}} - A_2\overline{R} = 3.0006 - .577(.0675) = 2.9617$$

$$\text{UCL}_R = D_4\overline{R} = 2.114(.0675) = .1427$$

Again, the R chart does not have a LCL. We obtain the newly revised $\bar{x}$ and R charts that are shown in the MINITAB output of Figure 17.8 on the next page. We see that all the points on each chart are inside their respective control limits. This says that the actions taken to remove assignable causes have brought the process into statistical control. However, it is important to point out that, although the process is in statistical control, **this does not necessarily mean that the**

FIGURE 17.8   MINITAB Output of $\bar{x}$ and R Charts for the Hole Location Data: Subgroups 1, 7, 12, and 17 Omitted. The Charts Show Good Control.

process is capable of producing products that meet the customer's needs. That is, while the control charts tell us that no assignable causes of process variation remain, the charts do not (directly) tell us anything about how much common cause variation exists. If there is too much common cause variability, the process will not meet customer or manufacturer specifications. We will discuss this further in Section 17.5.

When both the $\bar{x}$ and R charts are in statistical control, we can use the control limits for ongoing process monitoring. New $\bar{x}$ and R values for subsequent subgroups are plotted with respect to these limits. We summarize analyzing $\bar{x}$ and R charts as follows:

Analyzing $\bar{x}$ and R Charts to Establish Process Control

1 Remember that it is important to use both the $\bar{x}$ chart and the R chart to study the process.

2 Begin by analyzing the R chart for statistical control.

   a Find and eliminate assignable causes that are indicated by the R chart.

   b Revise both the $\bar{x}$ and R chart control limits, dropping data for subgroups corresponding to assignable causes that have been found and eliminated in 2a.

   c Check the revised R chart for control.

   d Repeat 2a, b, and c as necessary until the R chart shows statistical control.

3 When the R chart is in statistical control, the $\bar{x}$ chart can be properly analyzed.

   a Find and eliminate assignable causes that are indicated by the $\bar{x}$ chart.

   b Revise both the $\bar{x}$ and R chart control limits, dropping data for subgroups corresponding to assignable causes that have been found and eliminated in 3a.

   c Check the revised $\bar{x}$ chart (and the revised R chart) for control.

   d Repeat 3a, b, and c (or, if necessary, 2a, b, and c and 3a, b, and c) as needed until both the $\bar{x}$ and R charts show statistical control.

4 When both the $\bar{x}$ and R charts are in control, use the control limits for process monitoring.

   a Plot $\bar{x}$ and R points for newly observed subgroups with respect to the established limits.

   b If either the $\bar{x}$ chart or the R chart indicates a lack of control, take corrective action on the process.

5 Periodically update the $\bar{x}$ and R chart control limits using all relevant data (data that describe the process as it now operates).

6 When a major process change is made, develop new control limits if necessary.

With respect to periodically updating the $\bar{x}$ and R chart control limits in ongoing process monitoring, note that employees often seem to be uncomfortable working with control limits that are frequently changing. Therefore, it is probably a good idea to update the control limits only when the new data would substantially change the limits. Of course, if an important process change is implemented, new data must be collected, and we may need to develop new control limits from scratch.

EXAMPLE 17.4 The Hole Location Case: Process Monitoring

We consider the hole location problem and the revised $\bar{x}$ and R charts shown in Figure 17.8. Because the process has been brought into statistical control, we may use the control limits in Figure 17.8 to monitor the process. This would assume that we have used an appropriate subgrouping scheme and have observed enough subgroups to give potential assignable causes a chance to show up. In reality, we probably want to collect considerably more than 20 subgroups before setting control limits for ongoing control of the process.

We assume for this example that the control limits in Figure 17.8 are reasonable. Table 17.3 gives four subsequently observed subgroups of five hole location dimensions. The subgroup means and ranges for these data are plotted with respect to the ongoing control limits in the MINITAB output of Figure 17.9. We see that the R chart remains in control, while the mean for subgroup 24 is above the UCL on the $\bar{x}$ chart. This tells us that an assignable cause has increased the process mean. Therefore, action is needed to reduce the process mean.

TABLE 17.3 **Four Subgroups of Five Hole Location Dimensions Observed after Developing Control Limits for Ongoing Process Monitoring**

	Measurement (Inches)					Mean,	Range,
Subgroup	1	2	3	4	5	$\bar{x}$	R
21	2.98	3.00	2.97	2.99	2.98	2.984	.03
22	3.02	3.06	3.01	2.97	3.03	3.018	.09
23	3.03	3.08	3.01	2.99	3.02	3.026	.09
24	3.05	3.00	3.11	3.07	3.06	3.058	.11

FIGURE 17.9 **MINITAB Output of $\bar{x}$ and R Charts for the Hole Location Data: Ongoing Control**

Having seen how to interpret $\bar{x}$ and R charts, we are now better prepared to understand why we estimate the process standard deviation σ by $\bar{R}/d_2$. Recall that when μ and σ are known, the $\bar{x}$ chart control limits are $[\mu \pm 3(\sigma/\sqrt{n})]$. The standard deviation σ in these limits is the process standard deviation **when the process is in control.** When this standard deviation is unknown, **we estimate σ as if the process is in control, even though the process might not be in control.** The quantity $\bar{R}/d_2$ is an appropriate estimate of σ because $\bar{R}$ **is the average of individual ranges computed from rational subgroups—subgroups selected so that the chances that important process changes occur within a subgroup are minimized.** Thus each subgroup range, and therefore $\bar{R}/d_2$, estimates the process variation as if the process were in control. Of course, we could also compute the standard deviation of the measurements in each subgroup, and employ the average of the subgroup standard deviations to estimate σ. The key is not whether we use ranges or standard deviations to measure the variation within the subgroups. Rather, the key is that we must calculate a measure of variation for each subgroup and then must average the separate measures of subgroup variation in order to estimate the process variation as if the process is in control.

LO17-5 Detect the presence of assignable causes through pattern analysis.

Pattern analysis   When we observe a plot point outside the control limits on a control chart, we have strong evidence that an assignable cause exists. In addition, several other data patterns indicate the presence of assignable causes. Precise description of these patterns is often made easier by **dividing the control band into zones—designated A, B, and C.** Zone boundaries are set at points that are one and two standard deviations (of the plotted statistic) on either side of the center line. We obtain six zones—each zone being one standard deviation wide—with three zones on each side of the center line. The zones that stretch one standard deviation above and below the center line are designated as **C zones.** The zones that extend from one to two standard deviations away from the center line are designated as **B zones.** The zones that extend from two to three standard deviations away from the center line are designated as **A zones.** Figure 17.10 illustrates a control chart with the six zones and shows how the zone boundaries for an $\bar{x}$ chart and an R chart are calculated. This figure also shows the values of the zone boundaries for the hole location $\bar{x}$ and R charts shown in Figure 17.8 (page 698). In calculating these boundaries, we use $\bar{\bar{x}} = 3.0006$ and $\bar{R} = .0675$, which we computed from subgroups 1 through 20 with subgroups 1, 7, 12, and 17 removed from the data set; that is, we are using $\bar{\bar{x}}$ and $\bar{R}$ when the process is in control. For example, the upper A–B boundary for the $\bar{x}$ chart has been calculated as follows:

$$\bar{\bar{x}} + \frac{2}{3}(A_2\bar{R}) = 3.0006 + \frac{2}{3}(.577(.0675)) = 3.0266$$

Finally, Figure 17.10 shows (based on a normal distribution of plot points) the percentages of points that we would expect to observe in each zone when the process is in statistical control. For instance, we would expect to observe 34.13 percent of the plot points in the upper portion of zone C.

For an $\bar{x}$ chart, if the distribution of process measurements is reasonably normal, then the distribution of subgroup means will be approximately normal, and the percentages shown in Figure 17.10 apply. That is, the plotted subgroup means for an "in control" $\bar{x}$ chart should look as if they have been randomly selected from a normal distribution. Any distribution of plot points that looks very different from the expected percentages will suggest the existence of an assignable cause.

Several companies (for example, Western Electric [AT&T] and Ford Motor Company) have established sets of rules for identifying assignable causes; use of such rules is called **pattern analysis.** We summarize some commonly accepted rules on the next page. Note that many of these rules are illustrated in Figures 17.11, 17.12, and 17.13, which show several common out-of-control patterns. Also note that it is tempting to use many rules to decide when an assignable cause exists. However, if we use too many rules, we can end up with an unacceptably high chance of a **false out-of-control signal** (that is, an out-of-control signal when there is no assignable cause present). For most control charts, the use of the rules described on the next page will yield an overall probability of a false signal in the range of 1 to 2 percent.

FIGURE 17.10   **Zone Boundaries**

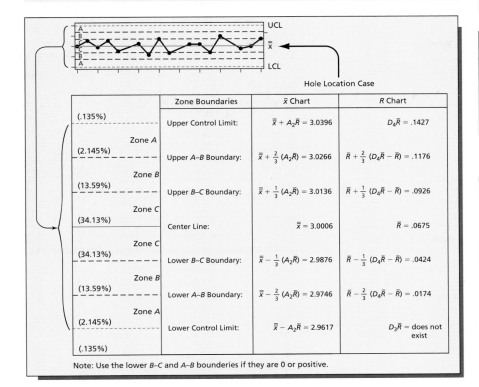

	Zone Boundaries	$\bar{x}$ Chart	R Chart
(.135%)	Upper Control Limit:	$\bar{\bar{x}} + A_2\bar{R} = 3.0396$	$D_4\bar{R} = .1427$
Zone A			
(2.145%)	Upper A–B Boundary:	$\bar{\bar{x}} + \frac{2}{3}(A_2\bar{R}) = 3.0266$	$\bar{R} + \frac{2}{3}(D_4\bar{R} - \bar{R}) = .1176$
Zone B			
(13.59%)	Upper B–C Boundary:	$\bar{\bar{x}} + \frac{1}{3}(A_2\bar{R}) = 3.0136$	$\bar{R} + \frac{1}{3}(D_4\bar{R} - \bar{R}) = .0926$
Zone C			
(34.13%)	Center Line:	$\bar{\bar{x}} = 3.0006$	$\bar{R} = .0675$
Zone C			
(34.13%)	Lower B–C Boundary:	$\bar{\bar{x}} - \frac{1}{3}(A_2\bar{R}) = 2.9876$	$\bar{R} - \frac{1}{3}(D_4\bar{R} - \bar{R}) = .0424$
Zone B			
(13.59%)	Lower A–B Boundary:	$\bar{\bar{x}} - \frac{2}{3}(A_2\bar{R}) = 2.9746$	$\bar{R} - \frac{2}{3}(D_4\bar{R} - \bar{R}) = .0174$
Zone A			
(2.145%)	Lower Control Limit:	$\bar{\bar{x}} - A_2\bar{R} = 2.9617$	$D_3\bar{R} = $ does not exist
(.135%)			

Note: Use the lower B–C and A–B bounderies if they are 0 or positive.

FIGURE 17.11

Two Out of Three Points in Zone A

FIGURE 17.12

Four Out of Five Points in Zone B

Pattern Analysis for $\bar{x}$ and R Charts

If one or more of the following conditions exist, it is reasonable to conclude that one or more assignable causes are present:

1   One plot point beyond zone A (that is, beyond the three standard deviation control limits).

2   Two out of three consecutive plot points in zone A (or beyond) on one side of the center line of the control chart. Sometimes a zone boundary that separates zones A and B is called a **two standard deviation warning limit.** Figure 17.11 illustrates this pattern. Specifically, note that plot points 5 and 6 are two consecutive plot points in zone A and that plot points 19 and 21 are two out of three consecutive plot points in zone A.

3   Four out of five consecutive plot points in zone B (or beyond) on one side of the center line of the control chart. Figure 17.12 illustrates this pattern. Specifically, note that plot points 2, 3, 4, and 5 are four consecutive plot points in zone B and that plot points 12, 13, 15, and 16 are four out of five consecutive plot points in zone B (or beyond).

4   A run of at least eight plot points. Here we define a **run** to be a **sequence of plot points of the same type.** For example, we can have a run of points on one side of (above or below) the center line. Such a run is illustrated in part (a) of Figure 17.13 on the next page, which shows a run above the center line. We might also observe a run of steadily increasing plot points (a **run up**) or a run of steadily decreasing plot points (a **run down**). These patterns are illustrated in parts (b) and (c) of Figure 17.13. Any of the above types of runs consisting of at least eight points is an out-of-control signal.

5   A **nonrandom pattern** of plot points. Such a pattern might be an **increasing** or **decreasing trend, a fanning-out or funneling-in pattern, a cycle, an alternating pattern,** or any other pattern that is very inconsistent with the percentages given in Figure 17.10 (see parts (d) through (h) of Figure 17.13).

If none of the patterns or conditions in 1 through 5 exists, then the process is **in control.**

FIGURE 17.13   Other Out-of-Control Patterns

FIGURE 17.14   Ongoing $\bar{x}$ and R Charts for the Hole Location Data—Zones *A*, *B*, and *C* Included

(a) A run on one side of the center line

(b) A run up

(c) A run down

(d) A trend (here, increasing)

(e) Fanning out

(f) Funneling in

(g) A cycle

(h) An alternating pattern

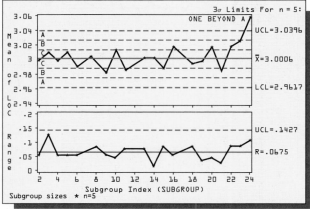

As a specific example, Figure 17.14 shows ongoing $\bar{x}$ and R charts for the hole location problem. Here the $\bar{x}$ chart includes zone boundaries with zones *A*, *B*, and *C* labeled. Notice that the first out-of-control condition (one plot point beyond zone *A*) exists. Looking at the last five plot points on the $\bar{x}$ chart, we see that the third out-of-control condition (four out of five consecutive plot points in zone *B* or beyond) also exists.

Exercises for Sections 17.3 and 17.4

CONCEPTS

17.5   Explain (1) the purpose of an $\bar{x}$ chart, (2) the purpose of an R chart, (3) why both charts are needed.

17.6   Explain why the initial control limits calculated for a set of subgrouped data are called "trial control limits."

17.7   Explain why a change in process variability shows up on both the $\bar{x}$ and R charts.

METHODS AND APPLICATIONS

17.8   A pizza restaurant monitors the size (measured by the diameter) of the 10-inch pizzas that it prepares. Pizza crusts are made from doughs that are prepared and prepackaged in boxes of 15 by a supplier. Doughs are thawed and pressed in a pressing machine. The toppings are added, and the pizzas are baked. The wetness of the doughs varies from box to box, and if the dough is too wet or greasy, it is difficult to press, resulting in a crust that is too small. The first shift of workers begins work at 4 P.M., and a new shift takes over at 9 P.M. and works until closing. The pressing machine

TABLE 17.4   10 Samples of Pizza Crust Diameters   DS PizzaDiam

Subgroup	Time	Pizza Crust Diameter (Inches)					Mean, $\bar{x}$	Range, R
		1	2	3	4	5		
1	4 P.M.	9.8	9.0	9.0	9.2	9.2	9.24	0.8
2	5 P.M.	9.5	10.3	10.2	10.0	10.0	10.00	0.8
3	6 P.M.	10.5	10.3	9.8	10.0	10.3	10.18	0.7
4	7 P.M.	10.7	9.5	9.8	10.0	10.0	10.00	1.2
5	8 P.M.	10.0	10.5	10.0	10.5	10.5	10.30	0.5
6	9 P.M.	10.0	9.0	9.0	9.2	9.3	9.30	1.0
7	10 P.M.	11.0	10.0	10.3	10.3	10.0	10.32	1.0
8	11 P.M.	10.0	10.2	10.1	10.3	11.0	10.32	1.0
9	12 A.M.	10.0	10.4	10.4	10.5	10.0	10.26	0.5
10	1 A.M.	11.0	10.5	10.1	10.2	10.2	10.40	0.9

New shift at 9 P.M., pressing machine adjusted at the start of each shift (4 P.M. and 9 P.M.).

is readjusted at the beginning of each shift. The restaurant takes five consecutive pizzas prepared at the beginning of each hour from opening to closing on a particular day. The diameter of each baked pizza in the subgroups is measured, and the pizza crust diameters obtained are given in Table 17.4. Use the pizza crust diameter data to do the following: DS PizzaDiam

a   Show that $\bar{\bar{x}} = 10.032$ and $\bar{R} = .84$.

b   Find the center lines and control limits for the $\bar{x}$ and R charts for the pizza crust data.

c   Set up the $\bar{x}$ and R charts for the pizza crust data.

d   Is the R chart for the pizza crust data in statistical control? Explain.

e   Is the $\bar{x}$ chart for the pizza crust data in statistical control? If not, use the $\bar{x}$ chart and the information given with the data to try to identify any assignable causes that might exist.

f   Suppose that, based on the $\bar{x}$ chart, the manager of the restaurant decides that the employees do not know how to properly adjust the dough pressing machine. Because of this, the manager thoroughly trains the employees in the use of this equipment. Because an assignable cause (incorrect adjustment of the pressing machine) has been found and eliminated, we can remove the subgroups affected by this unusual process variation from the data set. We therefore drop subgroups 1 and 6 from the data. Use the remaining eight subgroups to show that we obtain revised center lines of $\bar{\bar{x}} = 10.2225$ and $\bar{R} = .825$.

g   Use the revised values of $\bar{\bar{x}}$ and $\bar{R}$ to compute revised $\bar{x}$ and R chart control limits for the pizza crust diameter data. Set up $\bar{x}$ and R charts using these revised limits. Be sure to omit subgroup means and ranges for subgroups 1 and 6 when setting up these charts.

h   Has removing the assignable cause brought the process into statistical control? Explain.

17.9   THE HOT CHOCOLATE TEMPERATURE CASE[5]

Since 1994 a number of consumers have filed and won large claims against national fast-food chains as a result of being scalded by excessively hot beverages such as coffee, tea, and hot chocolate. Because of such litigation, the food service staff at a university dining hall wishes to study the temperature of the hot chocolate dispensed by its hot chocolate machine. The dining hall staff believes that there might be substantial variations in hot chocolate temperatures from meal to meal. Therefore, it is decided that at least one subgroup of hot chocolate temperatures will be observed during each meal—breakfast (6:30 A.M. to 10 A.M.), lunch (11 A.M. to 1:30 P.M.), and dinner (5 P.M. to 7:30 P.M.). In addition, because the hot chocolate machine is heavily used during most meals, the dining hall staff also believes that hot chocolate temperatures might vary substantially from the beginning to the end of a single meal. It follows that the staff will obtain rational subgroups by selecting a subgroup a half hour after the beginning of each meal and by selecting another subgroup a half hour prior to the end of each meal. Specifically, each subgroup will be selected by pouring three cups of hot chocolate over a 10-minute time span using periodic sampling (the second cup will be poured 5 minutes after the first, and the third cup will be poured 5 minutes after the second). The temperature of the hot chocolate will be measured by a candy thermometer (to the nearest degree Fahrenheit) immediately after each cup is poured. Table 17.5 on the next page gives the results for 24 subgroups of three hot chocolate temperatures taken at each meal served at the dining hall over a four-day period. Here a subgroup consists of the three temperatures labeled 1 through 3 in a single

[5]The data for this case were collected for a student's term project with the cooperation of the Food Service at Miami University, Oxford, Ohio.

TABLE 17.5   24 Subgroups of Three Hot Chocolate Temperatures (Measurements to the Nearest Degree Fahrenheit)   DS HotChoc

Day	Meal	Subgroup	Temperature 1	Temperature 2	Temperature 3	Subgroup Mean, $\bar{x}$	Subgroup Range, R
Monday	Breakfast	1	142°	140°	139°	140.33°	3°
		2	141	138	140	139.67	3
	Lunch	3	143	146	147	145.33	4
		4	146	149	147	147.33	3
	Dinner	5	133	142	140	138.33	9
		6	138	139	141	139.33	3
Tuesday	Breakfast	7	145	143	140	142.67	5
		8	139	144	145	142.67	6
	Lunch	9	139	141	147	142.33	8
		10	150	144	147	147.00	6
	Dinner	11	138	135	137	136.67	3
		12	145	141	144	143.33	4
Wednesday	Breakfast	13	138	145	139	140.67	7
		14	145	136	141	140.67	9
	Lunch	15	140	139	140	139.67	1
		16	142	143	145	143.33	3
	Dinner	17	144	142	141	142.33	3
		18	137	140	146	141.00	9
Thursday	Breakfast	19	125	129	135	129.67	10
		20	134	139	136	136.33	5
	Lunch	21	145	141	146	144.00	5
		22	147	146	148	147.00	2
	Dinner	23	140	143	139	140.67	4
		24	139	139	143	140.33	4

FIGURE 17.15   Excel add-in (MegaStat) Output of $\bar{x}$ and R Charts for the Hot Chocolate Temperature Data

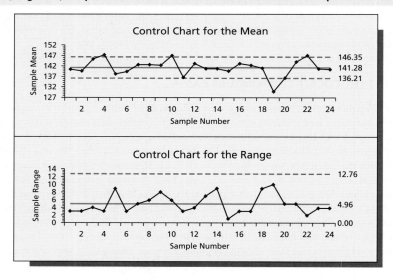

row in the table. The $\bar{x}$ and R charts for these data are given in the Excel add-in (MegaStat) output in Figure 17.15.   DS HotChoc

a   Using the fact that $\bar{\bar{x}} = 141.28$ and $\bar{R} = 4.96$, compute the control limits for the $\bar{x}$ and R charts and verify that they are as shown in Figure 17.15.

b   Is the R chart in statistical control? Explain.

c   Is the $\bar{x}$ chart in statistical control? If not, use the $\bar{x}$ chart to identify any out-of-control points.

FIGURE 17.16   **Excel Add-in (MegaStat) Output of Revised *x̄* and *R* Charts for the Hot Chocolate Temperature Data. The Process Is Now in Control.**

d Looking at the $\bar{x}$ chart, we see that the subgroup means that are above the UCL were observed during lunch (note subgroups 4, 10, and 22). Investigation and process documentation reveal that on these days the hot chocolate machine was not turned off between breakfast and lunch. Discussion among members of the dining hall staff further reveals that, because there is less time between breakfast and lunch than there is between lunch and dinner or dinner and break-fast, the staff often fails to turn off the hot chocolate machine between breakfast and lunch. Apparently, this is the reason behind the higher hot chocolate temperatures observed during lunch. Investigation also shows that the dining hall staff failed to turn on the hot chocolate machine before breakfast on Thursday (see subgroup 19)—in fact, a student had to ask that the machine be turned on. This caused the subgroup mean for subgroup 19 to be far below the $\bar{x}$ chart LCL. The dining hall staff concludes that the hot chocolate machine needs to be turned off after breakfast and then turned back on 15 minutes before lunch (prior experience suggests that it takes the machine 15 minutes to warm up). The staff also concludes that the machine should be turned on 15 minutes before each meal. In order to ensure that these actions are taken, an automatic timer is purchased to turn on the hot chocolate machine at the appropriate times. This brings the process into statistical control. Figure 17.16 shows $\bar{x}$ and R charts with revised control limits calculated using the subgroups that remain after the subgroups for the out-of-control lunches (subgroups 3, 4, 9, 10, 21, and 22) and the out-of-control breakfast (subgroups 19 and 20) are eliminated from the data set. Are these revised control charts in statistical control? Explain.

17.10 A company packages a bulk product in bags with a 50-pound label weight. During a typical day's operation of the fill process, 22 subgroups of five bag fills are observed. Using the observed data, $\bar{\bar{x}}$ and $\bar{R}$ are calculated to be 52.9364 pounds and 1.6818 pounds, respectively. When the 22 $\bar{x}$'s and 22 R's are plotted with respect to the appropriate control limits, the first 6 subgroups are found to be out of control. This is traced to a mechanical start-up problem, which is remedied. Using the remaining 16 subgroups, $\bar{\bar{x}}$ and $\bar{R}$ are calculated to be 52.5875 pounds and 1.2937 pounds, respectively.

a Calculate appropriate revised $\bar{x}$ and R chart control limits.

b When the remaining 16 $\bar{x}$'s and 16 R's are plotted with respect to the appropriate revised control limits, they are found to be within these limits. What does this imply?

17.11 In the book *Tools and Methods for the Improvement of Quality*, Gitlow, Gitlow, Oppenheim, and Oppenheim discuss an example of using $\bar{x}$ and R charts to study tuning knob diameters. In their problem description the authors say this:

A manufacturer of high-end audio components buys metal tuning knobs to be used in the assembly of its products. The knobs are produced automatically by a subcontractor using a single machine that is supposed to produce them with a constant diameter. Nevertheless, because of persistent final assembly problems with the knobs, management has decided to examine this process output by requesting that the subcontractor keep an $\bar{x}$ and R chart for knob diameter.

TABLE 17.6   **25 Subgroups of Tuning Knob Diameters** DS KnobDiam

Time	Subgroup Number	Diameter Measurement 1	2	3	4	Average, $\bar{x}$	Range, R
8:30 A.M.	1	836	846	840	839	840.25	10
9:00	2	842	836	839	837	838.50	6
9:30	3	839	841	839	844	840.75	5
10:00	4	840	836	837	839	838.00	4
10:30	5	838	844	838	842	840.50	6
11:00	6	838	842	837	843	840.00	6
11:30	7	842	839	840	842	840.75	3
12:00	8	840	842	844	836	840.50	8
12:30 P.M.	9	842	841	837	837	839.25	5
1:00	10	846	846	846	845	845.75	1
1:30	11	849	846	848	844	846.75	5
2:00	12	845	844	848	846	845.75	4
2:30	13	847	845	846	846	846.00	2
3:00	14	839	840	841	838	839.50	3
3:30	15	840	839	839	840	839.50	1
4:00	16	842	839	841	837	839.75	5
4:30	17	841	845	839	839	841.00	6
5:00	18	841	841	836	843	840.25	7
5:30	19	845	842	837	840	841.00	8
6:00	20	839	841	842	840	840.50	3
6:30	21	840	840	842	836	839.50	6
7:00	22	844	845	841	843	843.25	4
7:30	23	848	843	844	836	842.75	12
8:00	24	840	844	841	845	842.50	5
8:30	25	843	845	846	842	844.00	4

Source: H. Gitlow, S. Gitlow, A. Oppenheim, and R. Oppenheim, *Tools and Methods for the Improvement of Quality*, p. 301. Copyright © 1989. Reprinted by permission of McGraw-Hill Companies, Inc.

On a particular day the subcontractor selects four knobs every half hour and carefully measures their diameters. Twenty-five subgroups are obtained, and these subgroups (along with their subgroup means and ranges) are given in Table 17.6.   DS KnobDiam

a For these data, show that $\bar{\bar{x}} = 841.45$ and $\bar{R} = 5.16$. Then use these values to calculate control limits and to set up $\bar{x}$ and R charts for the 25 subgroups of tuning knob diameters. Do these $\bar{x}$ and R charts indicate the existence of any assignable causes? Explain.

b An investigation is carried out to find out what caused the large range for subgroup 23. The investigation reveals that a water pipe burst at 7:25 P.M. and that the mishap resulted in water leaking under the machinery used in the tuning knob production process. The resulting disruption is the apparent cause for the out-of-control range for subgroup 23. The water pipe is mended, and because this fix is reasonably permanent, we are justified in removing subgroup 23 from the data set. Using the remaining 24 subgroups, show that revised center lines are $\bar{\bar{x}} = 841.40$ and $\bar{R} = 4.88$.

c Use the revised values of $\bar{\bar{x}}$ and $\bar{R}$ to set up revised $\bar{x}$ and R charts for the remaining 24 subgroups of diameters. Be sure to omit the mean and range for subgroup 23.

d Looking at the revised R chart, is this chart now in statistical control? What does your answer say about whether we can use the $\bar{x}$ chart to decide if the process mean is changing?

e Looking at the revised $\bar{x}$ chart, is this chart in statistical control? What does your answer tell us about the process mean?

f An investigation is now undertaken to find the cause of the very high $\bar{x}$ values for subgroups 10, 11, 12, and 13. We again quote Gitlow, Gitlow, Oppenheim, and Oppenheim:

> The investigation leads to the discovery that . . . a keyway wedge had cracked and needed to be replaced on the machine. The mechanic who normally makes this repair was out to lunch, so the machine operator made the repair. This individual had not been properly trained for the repair; for this reason, the wedge was not properly aligned in the keyway, and the subsequent points were out of control. Both the operator and the mechanic agree that the need for this repair was not unusual. To correct this problem it is decided to train the machine operator and provide the appropriate tools for making

this repair in the mechanic's absence. Furthermore, the maintenance and engineering staffs agree to search for a replacement part for the wedge that will not be so prone to cracking.

Because the assignable causes responsible for the very high $\bar{x}$ values for subgroups 10, 11, 12, and 13 have been found and eliminated, we remove these subgroups from the data set. Show that removing subgroups 10, 11, 12, and 13 (in addition to the previously removed subgroup 23) results in the revised center lines $\bar{\bar{x}} = 840.46$ and $\bar{R} = 5.25$. Then use these revised values to set up revised $\bar{x}$ and R charts for the remaining 20 subgroups.

g Are all of the subgroup means and ranges for these newly revised $\bar{x}$ and R charts inside their respective control limits? Note: See Exercise 17.14 for more on this situation.

17.12 In an issue of *Quality Progress,* Gunter presents several control charts. Four of these charts are reproduced in Figure 17.17. For each chart, find any evidence of a lack of statistical control (that is, for each chart identify any evidence of the existence of one or more assignable causes). In each case, if such evidence exists, clearly explain why the plot points indicate that the process is not in control.

17.13 In the book *Tools and Methods for the Improvement of Quality,* Gitlow, Gitlow, Oppenheim, and Oppenheim present several control charts in a discussion and exercises dealing with pattern analysis. These control charts, which include appropriate A, B, and C zones, are reproduced in Figure 17.18. For each chart, identify any evidence of a lack of statistical control (that is, for each chart identify any evidence suggesting the existence of one or more assignable causes). In each case, if such evidence exists, clearly explain why the plot points indicate that the process is not in control.

17.14 Consider Exercise 7.11. After removing subgroups 10, 11, 12, 13, and 23 from Table 17.6, we found that $\bar{\bar{x}} = 840.46$ and $\bar{R} = 5.25$. Using the formula $\bar{\bar{x}} + (2/3) A_2 \bar{R}$, calculate the upper $A - B$ boundary for performing pattern analysis. Then, using the fact that the last three $\bar{x}$ values are 843.25, 842.50, and 844.0 (see Table 17.6 on page 706, and recall that we removed subgroup 23), identify a condition that indicates a lack of statistical control.

FIGURE 17.17   Charts for Exercise 17.12

FIGURE 17.18   Charts for Exercise 17.13

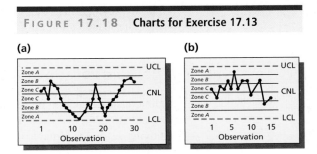

Source: H. Gitlow, S. Gitlow, A. Oppenheim, and R. Oppenheim, *Tools and Methods for the Improvement of Quality*, pp. 191–93, 209–11. Copyright © 1989. Reprinted by permission of McGraw-Hill Companies, Inc.

Source: B. Gunter, "Process Capability Studies Part 3: The Tale of the Charts," *Quality Progress* (June 1991), pp. 77–82. Copyright © 1991. American Society for Quality. Used with permission.

17.5 Comparison of a Process with Specifications: Capability Studies ● ● ●

LO17-6 Decide whether a process is capable of meeting specifications.

If we have a process in **statistical control,** we have found and **eliminated** the **assignable causes of process variation.** Therefore, the individual process measurements fluctuate over time with a **constant standard deviation** σ around a **constant mean** μ. It follows that we can use the individual process measurements to estimate μ and σ. Doing this lets us determine if the process is capable of producing output that meets specifications. Specifications are based on fitness for use criteria—that is. the specifications are established by design engineers or customers. Even if a process is in statistical control, it may exhibit too much **common cause variation** (represented by σ) to meet specifications.

As will be shown in Example 17.5, one way to study the capability of a process that is in statistical control is to construct a **histogram** from a set of individual process measurements. The histogram can then be compared with the product specification limits. In addition, we know that if all possible individual process measurements are normally distributed with mean μ and standard deviation σ, then 99.73 percent of these measurements will be in the interval $[\mu - 3\sigma, \mu + 3\sigma]$. Estimating μ and σ by $\bar{\bar{x}}$ and $\bar{R}/d_2$, we obtain the **natural tolerance limits**[6] for the process.

Natural Tolerance Limits

The **natural tolerance limits** for a normally distributed process that is in statistical control are

$$\left[\bar{\bar{x}} \pm 3\left(\frac{\bar{R}}{d_2}\right) \right] = \left[\bar{\bar{x}} - 3\left(\frac{\bar{R}}{d_2}\right), \quad \bar{\bar{x}} + 3\left(\frac{\bar{R}}{d_2}\right) \right]$$

where d_2 is a constant that depends on the subgroup size n. Values of d_2 are given in Table 17.2 (page 694) for subgroup sizes $n = 2$ to $n = 25$. These limits contain approximately 99.73 percent of the individual process measurements.

If the natural tolerance limits are inside the specification limits, then almost all (99.73 percent) of the individual process measurements are produced within the specification limits. In this case we say that the process is **capable** of meeting specifications. Furthermore, if we use $\bar{x}$ and R charts to monitor the process, then as long as the process remains in statistical control, the process will continue to meet the specifications. If the natural tolerance limits are wider than the specification limits, we say that the process is **not capable.** Here some individual process measurements are outside the specification limits.

EXAMPLE 17.5 The Hole Location Case: Meeting Customer Requirements

Again consider the hole punching process for air conditioner compressor shells. Recall that we were able to get this process into a state of statistical control with $\bar{\bar{x}} = 3.0006$ and $\bar{R} = .0675$ by removing several assignable causes of process variation.

Figure 17.19 gives a relative frequency histogram of the 80 individual hole location measurements used to construct the $\bar{x}$ and R charts of Figure 17.8 (page 698). This histogram

FIGURE 17.19   **A Relative Frequency Histogram of the Hole Location Data (Based on the Data with Subgroups 1, 7, 12, and 17 Omitted)**

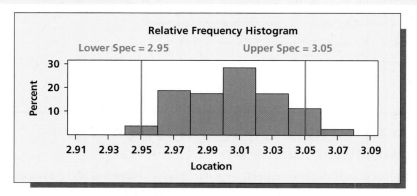

---

[6]There are a number of alternative formulas for the natural tolerance limits. Here we give the version that is the most clearly related to using $\bar{x}$ and R charts. At the end of this section we present an alternative formula.

suggests that the population of all individual hole location dimensions is approximately normally distributed.

Because the process is in statistical control, $\bar{\bar{x}} = 3.0006$ is an estimate of the process mean, and $\bar{R}/d_2 = .0675/2.326 = .0290198$ is an estimate of the process standard deviation. Here $d_2 = 2.326$ is obtained from Table 17.2 (page 694) corresponding to the subgroup size $n = 5$. Furthermore, the natural tolerance limits

$$\left[\bar{\bar{x}} \pm 3\left(\frac{\bar{R}}{d_2}\right)\right] = \left[3.0006 \pm 3\left(\frac{.0675}{2.326}\right)\right]$$

$$= [3.0006 \pm .0871]$$

$$= [2.9135, 3.0877]$$

tell us that almost all (approximately 99.73 percent) of the individual hole location dimensions produced by the hole punching process are between 2.9135 inches and 3.0877 inches.

Suppose a major customer requires that the hole location dimension must meet specifications of $3.00 \pm .05$ inches. That is, the customer requires that every individual hole location dimension must be between 2.95 inches and 3.05 inches. The natural tolerance limits, [2.9135, 3.0877], which contain almost all individual hole location dimensions, are wider than the specification limits [2.95, 3.05]. This says that some of the hole location dimensions are outside the specification limits. Therefore, the process is not capable of meeting the specifications. Note that the histogram in Figure 17.19 also shows that some of the hole location dimensions are outside the specification limits.

Figure 17.20 illustrates the situation, assuming that the individual hole location dimensions are normally distributed. The figure shows that the natural tolerance limits are wider than the

FIGURE 17.20   **Calculating the Fraction out of Specification for the Hole Location Data. Specifications Are 3.00 ± .05.**

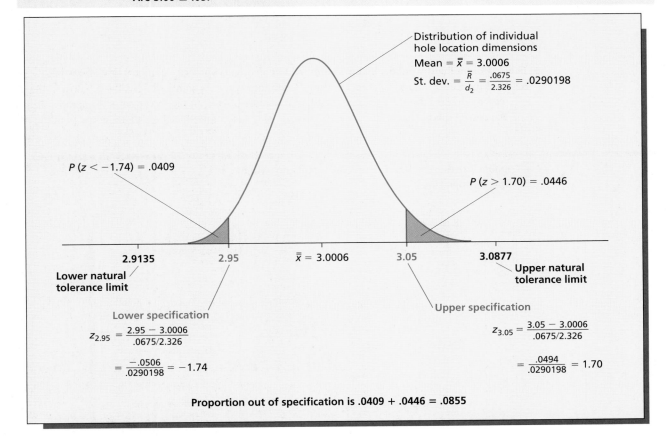

specification limits. The shaded areas under the normal curve make up the fraction of product that is outside the specification limits. Figure 17.20 also shows the calculation of the estimated fraction of hole location dimensions that are out of specification. We estimate that 8.55 percent of the dimensions do not meet the specifications.

Because the process is not capable of meeting specifications, it must be improved by removing common cause variation. This is management's responsibility. Suppose engineering and management conclude that the excessive variation in the hole locations can be reduced by redesigning the machine that punches the holes in the compressor shells. Also suppose that after a research and development program is carried out to do this, the process is run using the new machine and 20 new subgroups of $n = 5$ hole location measurements are obtained. The resulting $\bar{x}$ and R charts (not given here) indicate that the process is in control with $\bar{\bar{x}} = 3.0002$ and $\bar{R} = .0348$. Furthermore, a histogram of the 100 hole location dimensions used to construct the $\bar{x}$ and R charts indicates that all possible hole location measurements are approximately normally distributed. It follows that we estimate that almost all individual hole location dimensions are contained within the new natural tolerance limits

$$\left[\bar{\bar{x}} \pm 3\left(\frac{\bar{R}}{d_2}\right)\right] = \left[3.0002 \pm 3\left(\frac{.0348}{2.326}\right)\right]$$

$$= [3.0002 \pm .0449]$$

$$= [2.9553, 3.0451]$$

As illustrated in Figure 17.21, these tolerance limits are within the specification limits $3.00 \pm .05$. Therefore, the new process is now capable of producing almost all hole location dimensions inside the specifications. The new process is capable because the estimated process standard deviation has been substantially reduced (from $\bar{R}/d_2 = .0675/2.326 = .0290$ for the old process to $\bar{R}/d_2 = .0348/2.326 = .0149613$ for the redesigned process).

Next, note that (for the improved process) the z value corresponding to the lower specification limit (2.95) is

$$z_{2.95} = \frac{2.95 - 3.0002}{.0149613} = -3.36$$

This says that the lower specification limit is 3.36 estimated process standard deviations below $\bar{\bar{x}}$. Because the lower natural tolerance limit is 3 estimated process standard deviations below $\bar{\bar{x}}$, there is a **leeway** of .36 estimated process standard deviations between the lower natural tolerance limit and the lower specification limit (see Figure 17.21). Also, note that the z value corresponding to

---

FIGURE 17.21   **A Capable Process: The Natural Tolerance Limits Are within the Specification Limits**

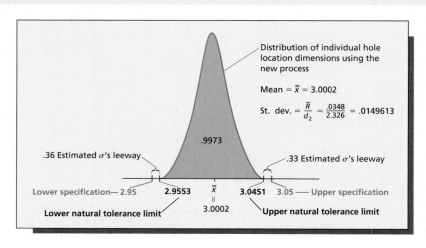

the upper specification limit (3.05) is

$$z_{3.05} = \frac{3.05 - 3.0002}{.0149613} = 3.33$$

This says that the upper specification limit is 3.33 estimated process standard deviations above $\bar{\bar{x}}$. Because the upper natural tolerance limit is 3 estimated process standard deviations above $\bar{\bar{x}}$, there is a **leeway** of .33 estimated process standard deviations between the upper natural tolerance limit and the upper specification limit (see Figure 17.21). Because some leeway exists between the natural tolerance limits and the specification limits, the distribution of process measurements (that is, the curve in Figure 17.21) can shift slightly to the right or left (or can become slightly more spread out) without violating the specifications. Obviously, the more leeway, the better.

To understand why process leeway is important, recall that a process must be in statistical control before we can assess the capability of the process. In fact:

> In order to demonstrate that a company's product meets customer requirements, the company must present
> 1 $\bar{x}$ and R charts that are in statistical control.
> 2   Natural tolerance limits that are within the specification limits.

However, even if a capable process shows good statistical control, the process mean and/or the process variation will occasionally change (due to new assignable causes or unexpected recurring problems). If the process mean shifts and/or the process variation increases, a process will need some leeway between the natural tolerance limits and the specification limits in order to avoid producing out-of-specification product. We can determine the amount of process leeway (if any exists) by defining what we call the **sigma level capability** of the process.

> **Sigma Level Capability**
>
> The **sigma level capability** of a process is the number of estimated process standard deviations between the estimated process mean, $\bar{\bar{x}}$, and the specification limit that is closest to $\bar{\bar{x}}$.

For instance, in the previous example the lower specification limit (2.95) is 3.36 estimated standard deviations below the estimated process mean, $\bar{\bar{x}}$, and the upper specification limit (3.05) is 3.33 estimated process standard deviations above $\bar{\bar{x}}$. It follows that the upper specification limit is closest to the estimated process mean $\bar{\bar{x}}$, and because this specification limit is 3.33 estimated process standard deviations from $\bar{\bar{x}}$, we say that the hole punching process has 3.33 sigma capability.

If a process has a sigma level capability of three or more, then there are at least three estimated process standard deviations between $\bar{\bar{x}}$ and the specification limit that is closest to $\bar{\bar{x}}$. It follows that, if the distribution of process measurements is normally distributed, then the process is capable of meeting the specifications. For instance, Figure 17.22(a) on the next page illustrates a process with three sigma capability. This process is just barely capable—that is, there is no process leeway. Figure 17.22(b) on the next page illustrates a process with six sigma capability. This process has three standard deviations of leeway. In general, we see that if a process is capable, the sigma level capability expresses the amount of process leeway. The higher the sigma level capability, the more process leeway. More specifically, for a capable process, the sigma level capability minus three gives the number of estimated standard deviations of process leeway. For example, because the hole punching process has 3.33 sigma capability, this process has $3.33 - 3 = .33$ estimated standard deviations of leeway.

The difference between three sigma and six sigma capability is dramatic. To illustrate this, look at Figure 17.22(a), which shows that a normally distributed process with three sigma capability produces 99.73 percent good quality (the area under the distribution curve between

FIGURE 17.22   **Sigma Level Capability and Process Leeway**

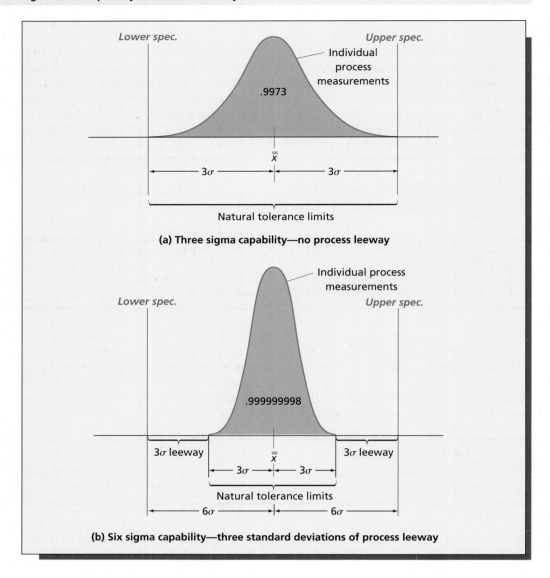

(a) Three sigma capability—no process leeway

(b) Six sigma capability—three standard deviations of process leeway

the specification limits is .9973). On the other hand, Figure 17.22(b) shows that a normally distributed process with six sigma capability produces 99.9999998 percent good quality. Said another way, if the process mean is centered between the specifications, and if we produce large quantities of product, then a normally distributed process with three sigma capability will produce an average of 2,700 defective products per million, while a normally distributed process with six sigma capability will produce an average of only .002 defective products per million.

In the long run, however, process shifts due to assignable causes are likely to occur. It can be shown that, if we monitor the process by using an $\bar{x}$ chart that employs a typical subgroup size of 4 to 6, the largest sustained shift of the process mean that might remain undetected by the $\bar{x}$ chart is a shift of 1.5 process standard deviations. In this worst case, it can be shown that a normally distributed three sigma capable process will produce an average of 66,800 defective products per million (clearly unacceptable), while a normally distributed six sigma capable process will produce an average of only 3.4 defective products per million. Therefore, if a six sigma capable process is monitored by $\bar{x}$ and R charts, then, when a process shift occurs, we can detect the shift (by using the control charts), and we can take immediate corrective action before a substantial number of defective products are produced.

This is, in fact, how control charts are supposed to be used to prevent the production of defective product. That is, our strategy is

Prevention Using Control Charts

1 Reduce common cause variation in order to create leeway between the natural tolerance limits and the specification limits.

2 Use control charts to establish statistical control and to monitor the process.

3 When the control charts give out-of-control signals, take immediate action on the process to reestablish control before out-of-specification product is produced.

A number of U.S. companies have adopted what they call a **six sigma philosophy.** In fact, these companies refer to themselves as **six sigma companies.** It is the goal of these companies to achieve six sigma capability for all processes in the entire organization. For instance, Motorola, Inc., the first company to adopt a six sigma philosophy, began a five-year quality improvement program in 1987. The goal of Motorola's companywide defect reduction program is to achieve six sigma capability for all processes—for instance, manufacturing processes, delivery, information systems, order completeness, accuracy of transactions records, and so forth. As a result of its six sigma plan, Motorola claims to have saved more than $1.5 billion. The corporation won the Malcolm Baldrige National Quality Award in 1988, and Motorola's six sigma plan has become a model for firms that are committed to quality improvement. Other companies that have adopted the six sigma philosophy include IBM, Digital Equipment Corporation, and General Electric.

To conclude this section, we make two comments. First, it has been traditional to measure process capability by using what is called the C_{p_k} **index.** This index is calculated by dividing the sigma level capability by three. For example, because the hole punching process illustrated in Figure 17.21 (page 710) has a sigma level capability of 3.33, the C_{p_k} for this process is 1.11. In general, if C_{p_k} is at least 1, then the sigma level capability of the process is at least 3 and thus the process is capable. Historically, C_{p_k} has been used because its value relative to the number 1 describes the process capability. We prefer using sigma level capability to characterize process capability because we believe that it is more intuitive.

Second, when a process is in control, then the estimates $\overline{R}/d_2$ and s of the process standard deviation will be very similar. This implies that we can compute the natural tolerance limits by using the alternative formula $[\overline{\overline{x}} \pm 3s]$. For example, because the mean and standard deviation of the 80 observations used to construct the $\overline{x}$ and R charts in Figure 17.8 (page 698) are $\overline{\overline{x}} = 3.0006$ and $s = .028875$, we obtain the natural tolerance limits

$$[\overline{\overline{x}} \pm 3s] = [3.0006 \pm 3(.028875)]$$
$$= [2.9140, \ 3.0872]$$

These limits are very close to those obtained in Example 17.5 on pages 708 and 709, [2.9135, 3.0877], which were computed by using the estimate $\overline{R}/d_2 = .0290198$ of the process standard deviation. Use of the alternative formula $[\overline{\overline{x}} \pm 3s]$ is particularly appropriate when there are long-run process variations that are not measured by the subgroup ranges (in which case $\overline{R}/d_2$ underestimates the process standard deviation). Because statistical control in any real application of SPC will not be perfect, some people believe that this version of the natural tolerance limits is the most appropriate.

Exercises for Section 17.5

CONCEPTS

connect

17.15 Write a short paragraph explaining why a process that is in statistical control is not necessarily capable of meeting customer requirements (specifications).

17.16 Explain the interpretation of the natural tolerance limits for a process. What assumptions must be made in order to properly make this interpretation? How do we check these assumptions?

17.17 Explain how the natural tolerance limits compare to the specification limits when
    a A process is capable of meeting specifications.
    b A process is not capable of meeting specifications.

17.18 For each of the following, explain

  a Why it is important to have leeway between the natural tolerance limits and the specification limits.

  b What is meant by the sigma level capability for a process.

  c Two reasons why it is important to achieve six sigma capability.

METHODS AND APPLICATIONS

17.19 THE HOT CHOCOLATE TEMPERATURE CASE

Consider the hot chocolate temperature situation in Exercise 17.9 (page 703). We found that $\bar{x}$ and R charts based on subgroups of size 3 for these data are in statistical control with $\bar{\bar{x}} = 140.73$ and $\bar{R} = 4.75$. **DS** HotChoc

  a Assuming that the hot chocolate temperatures are approximately normally distributed, calculate a range of values that contains almost all (approximately 99.73 percent) of the hot chocolate temperatures.

  b Find reasonable estimates of the maximum and minimum hot chocolate temperatures that would be served at the dining hall.

  c Suppose the dining hall staff has determined that all of the hot chocolate it serves should have a temperature between 130°F and 150°F. Is the process capable of meeting these specifications? Why or why not?

  d Find the sigma level capability of the process.

17.20 Suppose that $\bar{x}$ and R charts based on subgroups of size 3 are used to monitor the moisture content of a type of paper. The $\bar{x}$ and R charts are found to be in statistical control with $\bar{\bar{x}} = 6.0$ percent and $\bar{R} = .4$ percent. Further, a histogram of the individual moisture content readings suggests that these measurements are approximately normally distributed.

  a Compute the natural tolerance limits (limits that contain almost all the individual moisture content readings) for this process.

  b If moisture content specifications are 6.0 percent $\pm .5$ percent, is this process capable of meeting the specifications? Why or why not?

  c Estimate the fraction of paper that is out of specification.

  d Find the sigma level capability of the process.

17.21 A grocer has a contract with a produce wholesaler that specifies that the wholesaler will supply the grocer with grapefruit that weigh at least .75 pounds each. In order to monitor the grapefruit weights, the grocer randomly selects three grapefruit from each of 25 different crates of grapefruit received from the wholesaler. Each grapefruit's weight is determined and, therefore, 25 subgroups of three grapefruit weights are obtained. When $\bar{x}$ and R charts based on these subgroups are constructed, we find that these charts are in statistical control with $\bar{\bar{x}} = .8467$ and $\bar{R} = .11$. Further, a histogram of the individual grapefruit weights indicates that these measurements are approximately normally distributed.

  a Calculate a range of values that contains almost all (approximately 99.73 percent) of the individual grapefruit weights.

  b Find a reasonable estimate of the maximum weight of a grapefruit that the grocer is likely to sell.

  c Suppose that the grocer's contract with its produce supplier specifies that grapefruits are to weigh a minimum of .75 lb. Is this lower specification being met? Explain. Note here that there is no upper specification because we would like grapefruits to be as large as possible.

  d If the lower specification of .75 lb. is not being met, estimate the fraction of grapefruits that weigh less than .75 lb. Hint: Find an estimate of the standard deviation of the individual grapefruit weights.

17.22 Consider the pizza crust diameters for 10-inch pizzas given Exercise 17.8 (pages 702–703). We found that, by removing an assignable cause, we were able to bring the process into statistical control with $\bar{\bar{x}} = 10.2225$ and $\bar{R} = .825$. **DS** PizzaDiam

  a Recalling that the subgroup size for the pizza crust $\bar{x}$ and R charts is 5, and assuming that the pizza crust diameters are approximately normally distributed, calculate the natural tolerance limits for the diameters.

  b Using the natural tolerance limits, estimate the largest diameter likely to be sold by the restaurant as a 10-inch pizza.

  c Using the natural tolerance limits, estimate the smallest diameter likely to be sold by the restaurant as a 10-inch pizza.

  d Are all 10-inch pizzas sold by this restaurant really at least 10 inches in diameter? If not, estimate the fraction of pizzas that are not at least 10 inches in diameter.

17.23 Consider the bag fill situation in Exercise 17.10 (page 705). We found that the elimination of a start-up problem brought the filling process into statistical control with $\bar{\bar{x}} = 52.5875$ and $\bar{R} = 1.2937$.

    a Recalling that the fill weight $\bar{x}$ and R charts are based on subgroups of size 5, and assuming that the fill weights are approximately normally distributed, calculate the natural tolerance limits for the process.

    b Suppose that management wishes to reduce the mean fill weight in order to save money by "giving away" less product. However, because customers expect each bag to contain at least 50 pounds of product, management wishes to leave some process leeway. Therefore, after the mean fill weight is reduced, the lower natural tolerance limit is to be no less than 50.5 lb. Based on the natural tolerance limits, how much can the mean fill weight be reduced? If the product costs $2 per pound, and if 1 million bags are sold per year, what is the yearly cost reduction achieved by lowering the mean fill weight?

17.24 Suppose that a normally distributed process (centered at target) has three sigma capability. If the process shifts 1.5 sigmas to the right, show that the process will produce defective products at a rate of 66,800 per million.

17.25 Suppose that a product is assembled using 10 different components, each of which must meet specifications for five different quality characteristics. Therefore, we have 50 different specifications that potentially could be violated. Further suppose that each component possesses three sigma capability (process centered at target) for each quality characteristic. Then, if we assume normality and independence, find the probability that all 50 specifications will be met.

17.6 Charts for Fraction Nonconforming ● ● ●

LO17-7 Use *p* charts to monitor process quality.

Sometimes, rather than collecting measurement data, we inspect items and simply decide whether each item conforms to some desired criterion (or set of criteria). For example, a fuel tank does or does not leak, an order is correctly or incorrectly processed, a batch of chemical product is acceptable or must be reprocessed, or plastic wrap appears clear or too hazy. When an inspected unit does not meet the desired criteria, it is said to be **nonconforming** (or **defective**). When an inspected unit meets the desired criteria, it is said to be **conforming** (or **nondefective**). Traditionally, the terms *defective* and *nondefective* have been employed. Lately, the terms *nonconforming* and *conforming* have become popular.

The control chart that we set up for this type of data is called a **p chart.** To construct this chart, we observe subgroups of n units over time. We inspect or test the n units in each subgroup and determine the number d of these units that are nonconforming. We then calculate for each subgroup

$$\hat{p} = d/n = \text{the fraction of nonconforming units in the subgroup}$$

and we plot the $\hat{p}$ values versus time on the p chart. If the process being studied is in statistical control and producing a fraction p of nonconforming units, and if the units inspected are independent, then the number of nonconforming units d in a subgroup of n units inspected can be described by a binomial distribution. If, in addition, n is large enough so that np is greater than 2,[7] then both d and the fraction $\hat{p}$ of nonconforming units are approximately described by normal distributions. Furthermore, the population of all possible $\hat{p}$ values has mean $\mu_{\hat{p}} = p$ and standard deviation

$$\sigma_{\hat{p}} = \sqrt{\frac{p(1 - p)}{n}}$$

Therefore, if p is known we can compute three standard deviation control limits for values of $\hat{p}$ by setting

$$\text{UCL} = p + 3\sqrt{\frac{p(1 - p)}{n}} \quad \text{and} \quad \text{LCL} = p - 3\sqrt{\frac{p(1 - p)}{n}}$$

However, because it is unlikely that p will be known, we usually must estimate p from process data. The estimate of p is

$$\bar{p} = \frac{\text{Total number of nonconforming units in all subgroups}}{\text{Total number inspected in all subgroups}}$$

---

[7]Some statisticians believe that this condition should be $np > 5$. However, for p charts many think $np > 2$ is sufficient.

Substituting $\bar{p}$ for p, we obtain the following:

Center Line and Control Limits for a *p* Chart

$$\text{Center line} = \bar{p} \qquad \text{UCL} = \bar{p} + 3\sqrt{\frac{\bar{p}(1 - \bar{p})}{n}} \qquad \text{LCL} = \bar{p} - 3\sqrt{\frac{\bar{p}(1 - \bar{p})}{n}}$$

Note that if the LCL calculates negative, there is no lower control limit for the *p* chart.

The control limits calculated using these formulas are considered to be **trial control limits.** Plot points above the upper control limit suggest that one or more assignable causes have increased the process fraction nonconforming. Plot points below the lower control limit may suggest that an improvement in the process performance has been observed. However, plot points below the lower control limit may also tell us that an inspection problem exists. Perhaps defective items are still being produced, but for some reason the inspection procedure is not finding them. If the chart shows a lack of control, assignable causes must be found and eliminated and the trial control limits must be revised. Here data for subgroups associated with assignable causes that have been eliminated will be dropped, and data for newly observed subgroups will be added when calculating the revised limits. This procedure is carried out until the process is in statistical control. When control is achieved, the limits can be used to monitor process performance. **The process capability for a process that is in statistical control is expressed using $\bar{p}$, the estimated process fraction nonconforming.** When the process is in control and $\bar{p}$ is too high to meet internal or customer requirements, common causes of process variation must be removed in order to reduce $\bar{p}$. This is a management responsibility.

EXAMPLE 17.6 The Sales Invoice Case: Improving Customer Service

To improve customer service, a corporation wishes to study the fraction of incorrect sales invoices that are sent to its customers. Every week a random sample of 100 sales invoices sent during the week is selected, and the number of sales invoices containing at least one error is determined. The data for the last 30 weeks are given in Table 17.7. To construct a *p* chart for these data, we plot the fraction of incorrect invoices versus time. Because the true overall fraction *p* of incorrect invoices is unknown, we estimate *p* by (see Table 17.7)

$$\bar{p} = \frac{1 + 5 + 4 + \cdots + 0}{3,000} = \frac{69}{3,000} = .023$$

Because $n\bar{p} = 100(.023) = 2.3$ is greater than 2, the population of all possible $\hat{p}$ values has an approximate normal distribution if the process is in statistical control. Therefore, we calculate the center line and control limits for the *p* chart as follows:

$$\text{Center line} = \bar{p} = .023$$

$$\text{UCL} = \bar{p} + 3\sqrt{\frac{\bar{p}(1 - \bar{p})}{n}} = .023 + 3\sqrt{\frac{.023(1 - .023)}{100}}$$
$$= .023 + .04497$$
$$= .06797$$

$$\text{LCL} = \bar{p} - 3\sqrt{\frac{\bar{p}(1 - \bar{p})}{n}} = .023 - .04497$$
$$= -.02197$$

Because the LCL calculates negative, there is no lower control limit for this *p* chart. The Excel add-in (MegaStat) output of the *p* chart for these data is shown in Figure 17.23. We note that no plot points are outside the control limits, and we fail to see any nonrandom patterns of points.

TABLE 17.7   Sales Invoice Data—100 Invoices Sampled Weekly Ⓞ Invoice

Week	Number of Incorrect Sales Invoices (d)	Fraction of Incorrect Sales Invoices ($\hat{p} = d/100$)	Week	Number of Incorrect Sales Invoices (d)	Fraction of Incorrect Sales Invoices ($\hat{p} = d/100$)
1	1	.01	16	3	.03
2	5	.05	17	3	.03
3	4	.04	18	2	.02
4	0	.00	19	1	.01
5	3	.03	20	0	.00
6	2	.02	21	4	.04
7	1	.01	22	2	.02
8	3	.03	23	1	.01
9	0	.00	24	2	.02
10	6	.06	25	5	.05
11	4	.04	26	2	.02
12	3	.03	27	3	.03
13	2	.02	28	4	.04
14	0	.00	29	1	.01
15	2	.02	30	0	.00

FIGURE 17.23   Excel Add-in (MegaStat) Output of a *p* Chart for the Sales Invoice Data

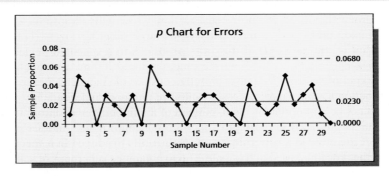

We conclude that the process is in statistical control with a relatively constant process fraction nonconforming of $\bar{p} = .023$. That is, the process is stable with an average of approximately 2.3 incorrect invoices per each 100 invoices processed. Because no assignable causes are present, there is no reason to believe that any of the plot points have been affected by unusual process variations. That is, it will not be worthwhile to look for unusual circumstances that have changed the average number of incorrect invoices per 100 invoices processed. If an average of 2.3 incorrect invoices per each 100 invoices is not acceptable, then management must act to remove common causes of process variation. For example, perhaps sales personnel need additional training or perhaps the invoice itself needs to be redesigned.

In the previous example, subgroups of 100 invoices were randomly selected each week for 30 weeks. In general, subgroups must be taken often enough to detect possible sources of variation in the process fraction nonconforming. For example, if we believe that shift changes may significantly influence the process performance, then we must observe at least one subgroup per shift in order to study the shift-to-shift variation. Subgroups must also be taken long enough to allow the major sources of process variation to show up. As a general rule, at least 25 subgroups will be needed to estimate the process performance and to test for process control.

We have said that the size n of each subgroup should be large enough so that np (which is usually estimated by $n\bar{p}$) is greater than 2 (some practitioners prefer np to be greater than 5). Because we often monitor a p that is quite small (.05 or .01 or less), n must often be quite large. Subgroup sizes of 50 to 200 or more are common. Another suggestion is to choose a subgroup size that is large enough to give a positive lower control limit (often, when employing a p chart, smaller subgroup sizes give a calculated lower control limit that is negative). A positive LCL is desirable because it allows us to detect opportunities for process improvement. Such an opportunity exists when we observe a plot point below the LCL. If there is no LCL, it would obviously be impossible to obtain a plot point below the LCL. It can be shown that

---

A condition that guarantees that the subgroup size is large enough to yield a **positive lower control limit for a p chart is**

$$n > \frac{9(1 - p_0)}{p_0}$$

where p_0 is an initial estimate of the fraction nonconforming produced by the process. This condition is appropriate when three standard deviation control limits are employed.

For instance, suppose experience suggests that a process produces 2 percent nonconforming items. Then, in order to construct a p chart with a positive lower control limit, the subgroup size employed must be greater than

$$\frac{9(1 - p_0)}{p_0} = \frac{9(1 - .02)}{.02} = 441$$

As can be seen from this example, for small values of p_0, the above condition may require very large subgroup sizes. For this reason, it is not crucial that the lower control limit be positive.

We have thus far discussed how often—that is, over what specified periods of time (each hour, shift, day, week, or the like)—we should select subgroups. We have also discussed how large each subgroup should be. We next consider how we actually choose the items in a subgroup. One common procedure—which often yields large subgroup sizes—is to include in a subgroup **all (that is, 100 percent) of the units produced in a specified period of time.** For instance, a subgroup might consist of all the units produced during a particular hour. When employing this kind of scheme, we must carefully consider the independence assumption. The binomial distribution assumes that successive units are produced independently. It follows that a p chart would not be appropriate if the likelihood of a unit being nonconforming depends on whether other units produced in close proximity are nonconforming. Another procedure is to **randomly select the units in a subgroup from all the units produced in a specified period of time.** This was the procedure used in Example 17.6 to obtain the subgroups of sales invoices. As long as the subgroup size is small relative to the total number of units produced in the specified period, the units in the randomly selected subgroup should probably be **independent.** However, if the rate of production is low, it could be difficult to obtain a large enough subgroup when using this method. In fact, even if we inspect 100 percent of the process output over a specified period, and even if the production rate is quite high, it might still be difficult to obtain a large enough subgroup. This is because (as previously discussed) we must select subgroups often enough to detect possible assignable causes of variation. If we must select subgroups fairly often, the production rate may not be high enough to yield the needed subgroup size in the time in which the subgroup must be selected.

In general, the large subgroup sizes that are required can make it difficult to set up useful p charts. For this reason, we sometimes (especially when we are monitoring a very small p) relax the requirement that np be greater than 2. Practice shows that even if np is somewhat smaller than 2, we can still use the three standard deviation p chart control limits. In such a case, we detect assignable causes by looking for points outside the control limits and by looking for runs of points on the same side of the center line. In order for the distribution of all possible $\hat{p}$ values to be sufficiently normal to use the pattern analysis rules we presented for $\bar{x}$ charts, $n\bar{p}$ must be greater than 2. In this case we carry out pattern analysis for a p chart as we do for an $\bar{x}$ chart (see page 701), and we use the following zone boundaries:

Upper A–B boundary: $\bar{p} + 2\sqrt{\dfrac{\bar{p}(1 - \bar{p})}{n}}$ \qquad Lower B–C boundary: $\bar{p} - \sqrt{\dfrac{\bar{p}(1 - \bar{p})}{n}}$

Upper B–C boundary: $\bar{p} + \sqrt{\dfrac{\bar{p}(1 - \bar{p})}{n}}$ \qquad Lower A–B boundary: $\bar{p} - 2\sqrt{\dfrac{\bar{p}(1 - \bar{p})}{n}}$

Here, when the LCL calculates negative, it should not be placed on the control chart. Zone boundaries, however, can still be placed on the control chart as long as they are not negative.

Exercises for Section 17.6

CONCEPTS

17.26 In your own words, define a *nonconforming unit.*

17.27 Describe two situations in your personal life in which you might wish to plot a control chart for fraction nonconforming.

17.28 Explain why it can sometimes be difficult to obtain rational subgroups when using a control chart for fraction nonconforming.

METHODS AND APPLICATIONS

17.29 Suppose that $\bar{p} = .1$ and $n = 100$. Calculate the upper and lower control limits, UCL and LCL, of the corresponding p chart.

17.30 Suppose that $\bar{p} = .04$ and $n = 400$. Calculate the upper and lower control limits, UCL and LCL, of the corresponding p chart.

17.31 In an issue of *Quality Progress,* William J. McCabe discusses using a p chart to study a company's order entry system. The company was experiencing problems meeting the promised 60-day delivery schedule. An investigation found that the order entry system frequently lacked all the information needed to correctly process orders. Figure 17.24 gives a p chart analysis of the percentage of orders having missing information.

   a From Figure 17.24 we see that $\bar{p} = .527$. If the subgroup size for this p chart is $n = 250$, calculate the upper and lower control limits, UCL and LCL.

   b Is the p chart of Figure 17.24 in statistical control? That is, are there any assignable causes affecting the fraction of orders having missing information?

   c On the basis of the p chart in Figure 17.24, McCabe says,

> The process was stable and one could conclude that the cause of the problem was built into the system. The major cause of missing information was salespeople not paying attention to detail, combined with management not paying attention to this problem. Having sold the product, entering the order into the system was generally left to clerical people while the salespeople continued selling.

Can you suggest possible improvements to the order entry system?

17.32 In the book *Tools and Methods for the Improvement of Quality,* Gitlow, Gitlow, Oppenheim, and Oppenheim discuss a data entry operation that makes a large number of entries every day. Over a 24-day period, daily samples of 200 data entries are inspected. Table 17.8 gives the number of erroneous entries per 200 that were inspected each day.   **DS** DataErr

   a Use the data in Table 17.8 to compute $\bar{p}$. Then use this value of $\bar{p}$ to calculate the control limits for a p chart of the data entry operation, and set up the p chart. Include zone boundaries on the chart.

FIGURE 17.24 **A p Chart for the Fraction of Orders with Missing Information**

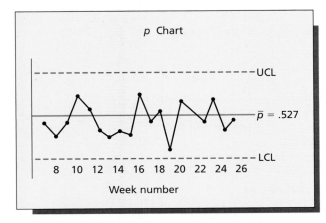

TABLE 17.8 **The Number of Erroneous Entries for 24 Daily Samples of 200 Data Entries**
      DS DataErr

Day	Number of Erroneous Entries	Day	Number of Erroneous Entries
1	6	13	2
2	6	14	4
3	6	15	7
4	5	16	1
5	0	17	3
6	0	18	1
7	6	19	4
8	14	20	0
9	4	21	4
10	0	22	15
11	1	23	4
12	8	24	1

b Is the data entry process in statistical control, or are assignable causes affecting the process? Explain.

c Investigation of the data entry process is described by Gitlow, Gitlow, Oppenheim, and Oppenheim as follows:

> In our example, to bring the process under control, management investigated the observations which were out of control (days 8 and 22) in an effort to discover and remove the special causes of variation in the process. In this case, management found that on day 8 a new operator had been added to the workforce without any training. The logical conclusion was that the new environment probably caused the unusually high number of errors. To ensure that this special cause would not recur, the company added a one-day training program in which data entry operators would be acclimated to the work environment.
>
> A team of managers and workers conducted an investigation of the circumstances occurring on day 22. Their work revealed that on the previous night one of the data entry consoles malfunctioned and was replaced with a standby unit. The standby unit was older and slightly different from the ones currently used in the department. The repairs on the regular console were not expected to be completed until the morning of day 23. To correct this special source of variation, the team recommended purchasing a spare console that would match the existing equipment and disposing of the outdated model presently being used as the backup. Management then implemented the suggestion.

Because the assignable causes on days 8 and 22 have been found and eliminated, we can remove the data for these days from the data set. Remove the data and calculate the new value of $\bar{p}$. Then set up a revised p chart for the remaining 22 subgroups.

d Did the actions taken bring the process into statistical control? Explain.

17.33 In an issue of *Quality Progress,* William J. McCabe discusses using a p chart to study the percentage of errors made by 21 buyers processing purchase requisitions. The p chart presented by McCabe is shown in Figure 17.25. In his explanation of this chart, McCabe says,

> The causes of the errors . . . could include out-of-date procedures, unreliable office equipment, or the perceived level of management concern with errors. These causes are all associated with the system and are all under management control.
>
> Focusing on the 21 buyers, weekly error rates were calculated for a 30-week period (the data existed, but weren't being used). A p-chart was set up for the weekly department error rate. It showed a 5.2 percent average rate for the department. In week 31, the manager called the buyers together and made two statements: "I care about errors because they affect our costs and delivery schedules," and "I am going to start to count errors by individual buyers so I can understand the causes." The p-chart . . . shows an almost immediate drop from 5.2 percent to 3.1 percent.
>
> The explanation is that the common cause system (supervision, in this case) had changed; the improvement resulted from eliminating buyer sloppiness in the execution of orders. The p-chart indicates that buyer errors are now stable at 3.1 percent. The error rate will stay there until the common cause system is changed again.

FIGURE 17.25   ***p* Chart for the Weekly Department Error Rate for 21 Buyers Processing Purchase Requisitions**

a   The *p* chart in Figure 17.25 shows that $\bar{p} = .052$ for weeks 1 through 30. Noting that the subgroup size for this chart is $n = 400$, calculate the control limits UCL and LCL for the *p* chart during weeks 1 through 30.

b   The *p* chart in Figure 17.25 shows that after week 30 the value of $\bar{p}$ is reduced to .031. Assuming that the process has been permanently changed after week 30, calculate new control limits based on $\bar{p} = .031$. If we use these new control limits after week 30, is the improved process in statistical control? Explain.

17.34   The customer service manager of a discount store monitors customer complaints. Each day a random sample of 100 customer transactions is selected. These transactions are monitored, and the number of complaints received concerning these transactions during the next 30 days is recorded. The numbers of complaints received for 20 consecutive daily samples of 100 transactions are, respectively, 2, 5, 10, 1, 5, 6, 9, 4, 1, 7, 1, 5, 7, 4, 5, 4, 6, 3, 10, and 5.
Ⓓ Complaints

a   Use the data to compute $\bar{p}$. Then use this value of $\bar{p}$ to calculate the control limits for a *p* chart of the complaints data. Set up the *p* chart.

b   Are the customer complaints for this 20-day period in statistical control? That is, have any unusual problems caused an excessive number of complaints during this period? Explain why or why not.

c   Suppose the discount store receives 13 complaints in the next 30 days for the 100 transactions that have been randomly selected on day 21. Should the situation be investigated? Explain why or why not.

17.7 Cause-and-Effect and Defect Concentration Diagrams (Optional) ● ● ●

LO17-8 Use diagrams to discern the causes of quality problems (Optional).

We saw in Chapter 2 that Pareto charts are often used to identify quality problems that require attention. When an opportunity for improvement has been identified, it is necessary to examine potential causes of the problem or defect (the undesirable **effect**). Because many processes are complex, there are often a very large number of possible **causes,** and it may be difficult to focus on the important ones. In this section we discuss two diagrams that can be employed to help uncover potential causes of process variation that are resulting in the undesirable effect.

The **cause-and-effect diagram** was initially developed by Japanese quality expert **Professor Kaoru Ishikawa.** In fact, these diagrams are often called **Ishikawa diagrams;** they are also called **fishbone charts** for reasons that will become obvious when we look at an example. Cause-and-effect diagrams are usually constructed by a quality team. For example, the team might consist of product designers and engineers, production workers, inspectors, supervisors and foremen, quality engineers, managers, sales representatives, and maintenance personnel. The team will set up the cause-and-effect diagram during a **brainstorming session.** After the problem (effect) is clearly stated, the team attempts to identify as many potential causes (sources of process variation) as possible. None of the potential causes suggested by team members should be criticized or rejected. The goal is to identify as many potential causes as possible. No attempt is made to actually develop solutions to the problem at this point. After beginning to brainstorm potential causes, it may be useful to observe the process in operation for a period of time before finishing the diagram. It is helpful to focus on finding sources of process variation rather than discussing reasons why these causes cannot be eliminated.

The causes identified by the team are organized into a cause-and-effect diagram as follows:

1   After clearly stating the problem, write it in an effect box at the far right of the diagram. Draw a horizontal (center) line connected to the effect box.

2   Identify major potential cause categories. Write them in boxes that are connected to the center line. Various approaches can be employed in setting up these categories. For example, Figure 17.26 on the next page is a cause-and-effect diagram for "why tables are not cleared quickly" in a restaurant. This diagram employs the categories:

Policy   Procedures   People   Physical Environment

3   Identify subcauses and classify these according to the major potential cause categories identified in step 2. Identify new major categories if necessary. Place subcauses on the diagram as branches. See Figure 17.26.

FIGURE 17.26   A Cause-and-Effect Diagram for "Why Tables Are Not Cleared Quickly" in a Restaurant

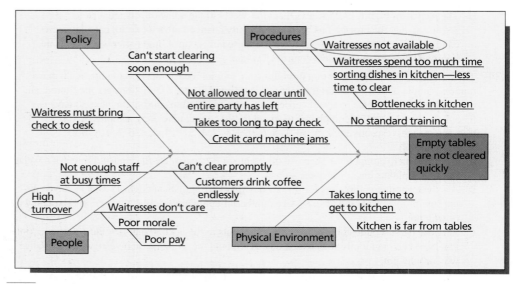

Source: M. Gaudard, R. Coates, and L. Freeman, "Accelerating Improvement," *Quality Progress* (October 1991), pp. 81–88. Copyright © 1991. American Society for Quality. Used with permission.

4   Try to decide which causes are most likely causing the problem or defect. Circle the most likely causes. See Figure 17.26.

After the cause-and-effect diagram has been constructed, the most likely causes of the problem or defect need to be studied. It is usually necessary to collect and analyze data in order to find out if there is a relationship between likely causes and the effect. We have studied various statistical methods (for instance, control charts, scatter plots, ANOVA, and regression) that help in this determination.

A **defect concentration diagram** is a picture of the product. It depicts all views—for example, front, back, sides, bottom, top, and so on. The various kinds of defects are then illustrated on the diagram. Often, by examining the locations of the defects, we can discern information concerning the causes of the defects. For example, in the October 1990 issue of *Quality Progress,* The Juran Institute presents a defect concentration diagram that plots the locations of chips in the enamel finish of a kitchen range. This diagram is shown in Figure 17.27. If the manufacturer of this range plans to use protective packaging to prevent chipping, it appears that the protective packaging should be placed on the corners, edges, and burners of the range.

FIGURE 17.27   Defect Concentration Diagram Showing the Locations of Enamel Chips on Kitchen Ranges

Source: "The Tools of Quality Part V: Check Sheets," from *QI Tools: Data Collection Workbook*, p. 11. Copyright © 1989. Juran Institute, Inc. Reprinted with permission from Juran Institute, Inc.

Exercises for Section 17.7

CONCEPTS

17.35 Explain the purpose behind constructing (a) a cause-and-effect diagram and (b) a defect concentration diagram.

17.36 Explain how to construct (a) a cause-and-effect diagram and (b) a defect concentration diagram.

METHODS AND APPLICATIONS

17.37 In an issue of *Quality Progress,* Hoexter and Julien discuss the quality of the services delivered by law firms. One aspect of such service is the quality of attorney–client communication. Hoexter and Julien present a cause-and-effect diagram for "poor client–attorney telephone communications." This diagram is shown in Figure 17.28.

   a Using this diagram, what (in your opinion) are the most important causes of poor client–attorney telephone communications?

   b Try to improve the diagram. That is, try to add causes to the diagram.

17.38 In an issue of *Quality Progress,* The Juran Institute presents an example that deals with the production of integrated circuits. The article describes the situation as follows:

> The manufacture of integrated circuits begins with silicon slices that, after a sequence of complex operations, will contain hundreds or thousands of chips on their surfaces. Each chip must be tested to establish whether it functions properly. During slice testing, some chips are found to be defective and are rejected. To reduce the number of rejects, it is necessary to know not only the percentage but also the locations and the types of defects. There are normally two major types of defects: functional and parametric. A functional reject occurs when a chip does not perform one of its functions. A parametric reject occurs when the circuit functions properly, but a parameter of the chip, such as speed or power consumption, is not correct.

Figure 17.29 gives a defect concentration diagram showing the locations of rejected chips within the integrated circuit. Only those chips that had five or more defects during the testing of 1,000 integrated circuits are shaded. Describe where parametric rejects tend to be, and describe where functional rejects tend to be.

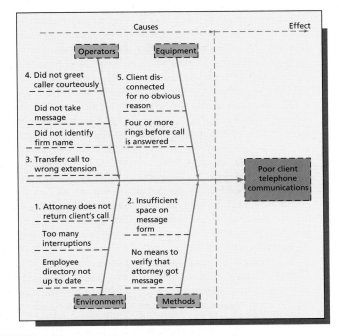

FIGURE 17.28 **A Cause-and-Effect Diagram for "Poor Client–Attorney Telephone Communications"**

FIGURE 17.29 **Defect Concentration Diagram Showing the Locations of Rejected Chips on Integrated Circuits**

■ Parametric rejects
■ Functional rejects

FIGURE 17.30   A Cause-and-Effect Diagram on the "Lack of Quality in Schools"

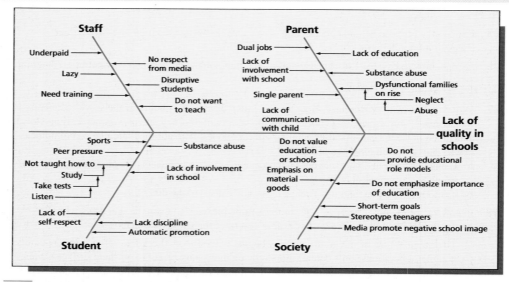

Source: F. P. Schargel, "Teaching TQM in an Inner City High School," *Quality Progress* (September 1994), pp. 87–90. Copyright © 1994 American Society for Quality. Used with permission.

17.39 In an issue of *Quality Progress,* Franklin P. Schargel presents a cause-and-effect diagram for the "lack of quality in schools." We present this diagram in Figure 17.30.
   a Identify and circle the causes that you feel contribute the most to the "lack of quality in schools."
   b Try to improve the diagram. That is, see if you can add causes to the diagram.

Chapter Summary

In this chapter we studied how to improve business processes by using **control charts.** We began by considering several meanings of quality, and we discussed the history of the quality movement in the United States. We saw that Walter Shewhart introduced statistical quality control while working at Bell Telephone Laboratories during the 1920s and 30s, and we also saw that W. Edwards Deming taught the Japanese how to use statistical methods to improve product quality following World War II. When the quality of Japanese products surpassed that of American-made goods, and when, as a result, U.S. manufacturers lost substantial shares of their markets, Dr. Deming consulted and lectured extensively in the United States. This sparked an American reemphasis on quality that continues to this day. We also briefly presented **Deming's 14 Points,** a set of management principles that, if followed, Deming believed would enable a company to improve quality and productivity, reduce costs, and gain competitive advantage.

We next learned that processes are influenced by **common cause variation** (inherent variation) and by **assignable cause variation** (unusual variation), and we saw that a control chart signals when assignable causes exist. Then we discussed how to sample a process. In particular, we explained that effective control charting requires **rational subgrouping.** Such subgroups minimize the chances that important process variations will occur within subgroups, and they maximize the chances that such variations will occur between subgroups.

Next we studied $\bar{x}$ and R **charts** in detail. We saw that $\bar{x}$ charts are used to monitor and stabilize the process mean (level), and that R charts are used to monitor and stabilize the process variability. In particular, we studied how to construct $\bar{x}$ and R charts by using **control chart constants,** how to recognize out-of-control conditions

by employing **zone boundaries** and **pattern analysis,** and how to use $\bar{x}$ and R charts to get a process into statistical control.

While it is important to bring a process into statistical control, we learned that it is also necessary to meet the **customer's** or **manufacturer's requirements** (or **specifications**). Because statistical control does not guarantee that the process output meets specifications, we must carry out a **capability study** after the process has been brought into control. We studied how this is done by computing **natural tolerance limits,** which are limits that contain almost all the individual process measurements. We saw that, if the natural tolerance limits are inside the specification limits, then the process is **capable** of meeting the specifications. We also saw that we can measure how capable a process is by using **sigma level capability,** and we learned that a number of major businesses now orient their management philosophy around the concept of **six sigma capability.** In particular, we learned that, if a process is in statistical control and if the process has six sigma or better capability, then the defective rate will be very low (3.4 per million or less).

We continued by studying **p charts,** which are charts for fraction nonconforming. Such charts are useful when it is not possible (or when it is very expensive) to measure the quality characteristic of interest.

We concluded this chapter with an optional section on how to construct **cause-and-effect diagrams** and **defect concentration diagrams.** These diagrams are used to identify opportunities for process improvement and to discover sources of process variation.

It should be noted that two useful types of control charts not discussed in this chapter are **individuals charts** and **c charts.** These charts are discussed in Appendix L in the Online Learning Center www.mhhe.com/bowerman7e.

Glossary of Terms

acceptance sampling: A statistical sampling technique that enables us to accept or reject a quantity of goods (the lot) without inspecting the entire lot. (page 682)

assignable causes (of process variation): Unusual sources of process variation. Also called **special causes** or **specific causes** of process variation. (page 686)

capable process: A process that has the ability to produce products or services that meet customer or manufacturer requirements (specifications). (page 708)

cause-and-effect diagram: A diagram that enumerates (lists) the potential causes of an undesirable effect. (page 721)

common causes (of process variation): Sources of process variation that are inherent to the process design—that is, sources of usual process variation. (page 685)

conforming unit (nondefective): An inspected unit that meets a set of desired criteria. (page 715)

control chart: A graph of process performance that includes a center line and two control limits—an upper control limit, UCL, and a lower control limit, LCL. Its purpose is to detect assignable causes. (page 691)

C_{p_k} **index:** A process's sigma level capability divided by 3. (page 713)

defect concentration diagram: An illustration of a product that depicts the locations of defects that have been observed. (page 722)

ISO 9000: A series of international standards for quality assurance management systems. (page 684)

natural tolerance limits: Assuming a process is in statistical control and assuming process measurements are normally distributed, limits that contain almost all (approximately 99.73 percent) of the individual process measurements. (page 708)

nonconforming unit (defective): An inspected unit that does not meet a set of desired criteria. (page 715)

pattern analysis: Looking for patterns of plot points on a control chart in order to find evidence of assignable causes. (page 700)

p chart: A control chart on which the proportion nonconforming (in subgroups of size n) is plotted versus time. (page 715)

quality of conformance: How well a process is able to meet the requirements (specifications) set forth by the process design. (page 681)

quality of design: How well the design of a product or service meets and exceeds the needs and expectations of the customer. (page 681)

quality of performance: How well a product or service performs in the marketplace. (page 681)

rational subgroups: Subgroups of process observations that are selected so that the chances that process changes will occur between subgroups is maximized. (page 688)

R chart: A control chart on which subgroup ranges are plotted versus time. It is used to monitor the process variability (or spread). (pages 691 and 694)

run: A sequence of plot points on a control chart that are of the same type—for instance, a sequence of plot points above the center line. (page 701)

sigma level capability: The number of estimated process standard deviations between the estimated process mean, $\bar{\bar{x}}$, and the specification limit that is closest to $\bar{\bar{x}}$. (page 711)

statistical control: A state in which process measurements display a constant amount of variation around a constant mean (or level). (page 685)

statistical process control (SPC): A systematic method for analyzing process data in which we monitor and study the process variation. The goal is continuous process improvement. (page 685)

subgroup: A set of process observations that are grouped together for purposes of control charting. (page 688)

total quality management (TQM): Applying quality principles to all company activities. (page 683)

variables control charts: Control charts constructed by using measurement data. (page 691)

$\bar{x}$ **chart (x-bar chart):** A control chart on which subgroup means are plotted versus time. It is used to monitor the process mean (or level). (pages 691 and 694)

Important Formulas

Center line and control limits for an $\bar{x}$ chart: page 694

Center line and control limits for an R chart: page 694

Zone boundaries for an $\bar{x}$ chart: page 701

Zone boundaries for an R chart: page 701

Natural tolerance limits for normally distributed process measurements: page 708

Sigma level capability: page 711

C_{p_k} index: page 713

Center line and control limits for a p chart: page 716

Zone boundaries for a p chart: page 718

Supplementary Exercises

Exercises 17.40 through 17.43 are based on a case study adapted from an example presented in the paper "Managing with Statistical Models" by James C. Seigel (1982). Seigel's example concerned a problem encountered by Ford Motor Company.

connect

THE CAMSHAFT CASE ⓓⓢ Camshaft

An automobile manufacturer produces the parts for its vehicles in many different locations and transports them to assembly plants. In order to keep the assembly operations running efficiently, it is vital that all parts be within specification limits. One important part used in the assembly of V6 engines is the engine camshaft, and one important quality characteristic of this camshaft is the case hardness depth of its eccentrics. A camshaft eccentric is a metal disk positioned on the camshaft so that as the camshaft turns, the eccentric drives a lifter that opens and closes an engine valve. The V6 engine camshaft and its

FIGURE 17.31   A Camshaft and Related Parts

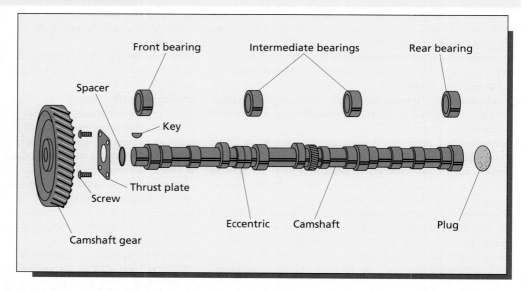

TABLE 17.9   Hardness Depth Data for Camshafts (Coil #1)   **DS** Camshaft

Date	6/7	8	9	10	11	14	15	16	17	18	21	22	23	24	25
READINGS 1	3.7	5.5	4.0	4.5	4.7	4.3	5.1	4.3	4.0	3.7	4.4	5.0	7.2	4.9	4.7
2	4.3	4.0	3.8	4.1	4.7	4.5	4.4	4.1	4.5	4.2	4.6	5.9	6.9	5.1	4.0
3	5.5	4.3	3.0	3.5	5.0	3.6	4.0	3.7	4.1	4.9	5.4	6.5	6.0	4.5	3.9
4	4.6	3.5	1.7	4.2	4.3	3.8	3.6	3.9	3.5	5.5	5.5	9.4	5.4	4.0	4.2
5	4.9	3.6	0	3.9	4.4	4.1	3.7	4.0	3.0	5.9	6.3	10.1	5.5	4.2	3.7
Subgroup Mean $\bar{x}$	4.6	4.2	2.5	4.0	4.6	4.1	4.2	4	3.8	4.8	5.2	7.4	6.2	4.5	4.1
Subgroup Range R	1.8	2.0	4.0	1.0	0.7	0.9	1.5	0.6	1.5	2.2	1.9	5.1	1.8	1.1	1.0

Date	28	29	30	7/1	2	5	6	7	8	9	12	13	14	15	16
READINGS 1	3.7	3.5	4.7	4.0	5.0	5.8	3.6	4.0	3.5	4.1	6.2	5.5	4.4	4.0	3.9
2	3.9	3.8	5.0	3.7	4.1	6.3	3.9	3.6	5.5	4.8	5.1	5.0	4.0	3.6	3.5
3	3.4	3.6	4.1	3.9	4.2	3.8	4.1	3.5	5.0	3.8	5.4	3.9	3.7	3.7	3.3
4	3.0	4.1	3.9	4.4	5.2	5.2	3.0	5.5	4.0	3.9	3.9	4.2	3.9	3.5	1.7
5	0	4.4	4.3	4.2	5.5	3.9	1.7	3.5	3.5	4.4	4.7	4.4	3.6	3.7	0
Subgroup Mean $\bar{x}$	2.8	3.9	4.4	4	4.8	5	3.3	4	4.3	4.2	5.1	4.6	3.9	3.7	2.5
Subgroup Range R	3.9	0.9	1.1	0.7	1.4	2.5	2.4	2.0	2.0	1.0	2.3	1.6	0.8	0.5	3.9

eccentrics are illustrated in Figure 17.31. These eccentrics are hardened by a process that passes the camshaft through an electrical coil that "cooks" or "bakes" the camshaft. Studies indicate that the hardness depth of the eccentric labeled in Figure 17.31 is representative of the hardness depth of all the eccentrics on the camshaft. Therefore, the hardness depth of this representative eccentric is measured at a specific location and is regarded to be the **hardness depth of the camshaft.** The optimal or target hardness depth for a camshaft is 4.5 mm. In addition, specifications state that, in order for the camshaft to wear properly, the hardness depth of a camshaft must be between 3.0 mm and 6.0 mm.

The automobile manufacturer was having serious problems with the process used to harden the camshaft. This problem was resulting in 12 percent rework and 9 percent scrap, or a total of 21 percent out-of-specification camshafts. The hardening process was automated. However, adjustments could be made to the electrical coil employed in the process. To begin study of the process, a problem-solving team selected 30 daily subgroups of $n = 5$ hardened camshafts and measured the hardness depth of each camshaft. For each subgroup, the team calculated the mean $\bar{x}$ and range R of the $n = 5$ hardness depth readings. The 30 subgroups are given in Table 17.9. The subgroup means and ranges are plotted in Figure 17.32. These means and ranges seem to exhibit substantial variability, which suggests that the hardening process was not in statistical control; we will compute control limits shortly.

FIGURE 17.32   **Graphs of Performance ($\bar{x}$ and R) for Hardness Depth Data (Using Coil #1)**

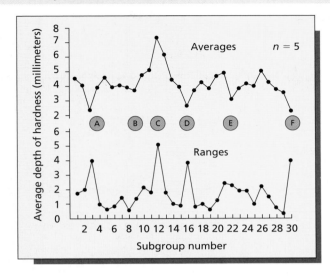

Although control limits had not yet been established, the problem-solving team took several actions to try to stabilize the process while the 30 subgroups were being collected:

1   At point A, which corresponds to a low average and a high range, the power on the coil was increased from 8.2 to 9.2.

2   At point B the problem-solving team found a bent coil. The coil was straightened, although at point B the subgroup mean and range do not suggest that any problem exists.

3   At point C, which corresponds to a high average and a high range, the power on the coil was decreased to 8.8.

4   At point D, which corresponds to a low average and a high range, the coil shorted out. The coil was straightened, and the team designed a gauge that could be used to check the coil spacing to the camshaft.

5   At point E, which corresponds to a low average, the spacing between the coil and the camshaft was decreased.

6   At point F, which corresponds to a low average and a high range, the first coil (Coil #1) was replaced. Its replacement (Coil #2) was a coil of the same type.

17.40   Using the data in Table 17.9:   **DS** Camshaft
    a   Calculate $\bar{\bar{x}}$ and $\bar{R}$ and then find the center lines and control limits for $\bar{x}$ and R charts for the camshaft hardness depths.
    b   Set up the $\bar{x}$ and R charts for the camshaft hardness depth data.
    c   Are the $\bar{x}$ and R charts in statistical control? Explain.

Examining the actions taken at points A through E (in Figure 17.32), the problem-solving team learned that the power on the coil should be roughly 8.8 and that it is important to monitor the spacing between the camshaft and the coil. It also learned that it may be important to check for bent coils. The problem-solving team then (after replacing Coil #1 with Coil #2) attempted to control the hardening process by using this knowledge. Thirty new daily subgroups of $n = 5$ hardness depths were collected. The $\bar{x}$ and R charts for these subgroups are given in Figure 17.33 on the next page.

17.41   Using the values of $\bar{\bar{x}}$ and $\bar{R}$ in Figure 17.33:   **DS** Camshaft
    a   Calculate the control limits for the $\bar{x}$ chart in Figure 17.33.
    b   Calculate the upper control limit for the R chart in Figure 17.33.
    c   Are the $\bar{x}$ and R charts for the 30 new subgroups using Coil #2 (which we recall was of the same type as Coil #1) in statistical control? Explain.

17.42   Consider the $\bar{x}$ and R charts in Figure 17.33.   **DS** Camshaft
    a   Calculate the natural tolerance limits for the improved process.
    b   Recalling that specifications state that the hardness depth of each camshaft must be between 3.0 mm. and 6.0 mm., is the improved process capable of meeting these specifications? Explain.
    c   Use $\bar{\bar{x}}$ and $\bar{R}$ to estimate the fraction of hardness depths that are out of specification for the improved process.

FIGURE 17.33   x̄ and R Charts for Hardness Depth Data Using Coil #2 (Same Type as Coil #1)

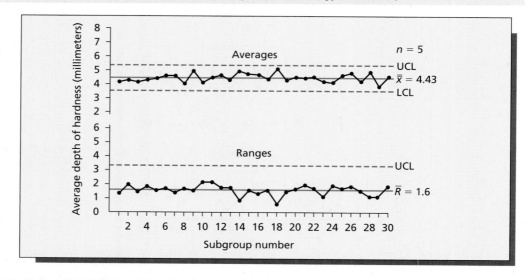

FIGURE 17.34   x̄ and R Charts for Hardness Depth Data Using a Redesigned Coil

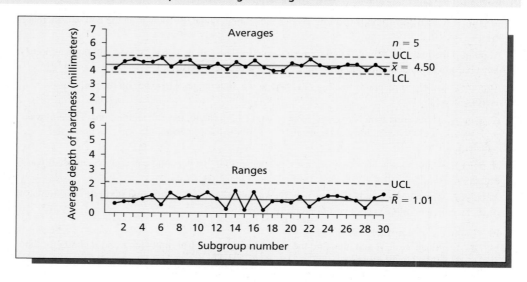

Because the hardening process shown in Figure 17.33 was not capable, the problem-solving team redesigned the coil to reduce the common cause variability of the process. Thirty new daily subgroups of $n = 5$ hardness depths were collected using the redesigned coil, and the resulting x̄ and R charts are given in Figure 17.34.

17.43   Using the values of $\bar{\bar{x}}$ and $\bar{R}$ given in Figure 17.34:   **DS** Camshaft
    a   Calculate the control limits for the x̄ and R charts in Figure 17.34.
    b   Is the process (using the redesigned coil) in statistical control? Explain.
    c   Calculate the natural tolerance limits for the process (using the redesigned coil).
    d   **(1)** Is the process (using the redesigned coil) capable of meeting specifications of 3.0 mm. to 6.0 mm.? Explain. **(2)** Find and interpret the sigma level capability.

17.44   A bank officer wishes to study how many credit cardholders attempt to exceed their established credit limits. To accomplish this, the officer randomly selects a weekly sample of 100 of the cardholders who have been issued credit cards by the bank, and the number of cardholders who have attempted to exceed their credit limit during the week is recorded. The numbers of cardholders who exceeded their credit limit in 20 consecutive weekly samples of 100 cardholders are, respectively, 1, 4, 9, 0, 4, 6, 0, 3, 8, 5, 3, 5, 2, 9, 4, 4, 3, 6, 4, and 0. **(1)** Construct a control chart for the data and determine if the data are in statistical control. **(2)** If 12 cardholders in next week's sample of 100 cardholders attempt to exceed their credit limit, should the bank regard this as unusual variation in the process?   **DS** CredLim

Appendix 17.1 ■ Control Charts Using MegaStat

X-bar and *R* charts in Figure 17.15 on page 704 (data file: HotChoc.xlsx):

- In cells A1, A2, and A3, enter the column labels Temp1, Temp2, and Temp3.

- In columns A, B, and C, enter the hot chocolate temperature data as 24 rows of 3 measurements, as laid out in the columns headed 1, 2, and 3 in Table 17.5 on page 704. When entered in this way, each row is a subgroup (sample) of three temperatures. Calculated means and ranges (as in Table 17.1 on page 689) need not be entered—only the raw data are needed.

- Select **Add-Ins : MegaStat : Quality Control Process Charts.**

- In the "Quality Control Process Charts" dialog box, click on "Variables (Xbar and R)."

- Use the AutoExpand feature to select the range A1 : C25 into the Input Range window. Here each row in the selected range is a subgroup (sample) of measurements.

- Click OK in the "Quality Control Process Charts" dialog box.

- The requested control charts are placed in an output file and may be edited using standard Excel editing features. See Appendix 1.1 (page 18) for additional information about editing Excel graphics.

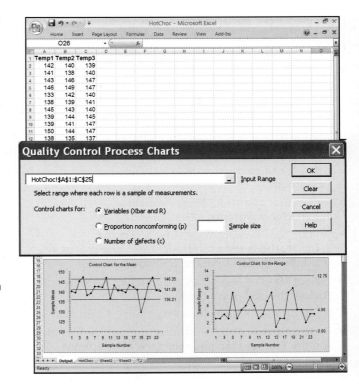

p control chart in Figure 17.23 on page 717 (data file: Invoice.xlsx):

- Enter the 30 weekly error counts from Table 17.7 (page 717) into Column A with the label Invoice in cell A1.

- Select **Add-Ins : MegaStat : Quality Control Process Charts.**

- In the "Quality Control Process Charts" dialog box, select "Proportion nonconforming (p)."

- Use the AutoExpand feature to enter the range A1 : A31 into the Input Range window.

- Enter the subgroup (sample) size (here equal to 100) into the Sample size box.

- Click OK in the "Quality Control Process Charts" dialog box.

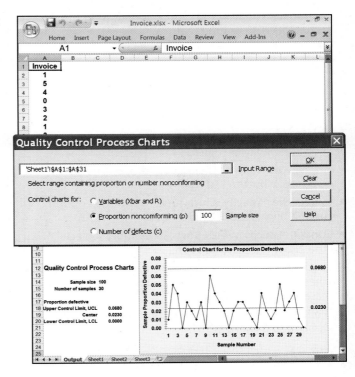

Appendix 17.2 ■ Control Charts Using MINITAB

Combined *X*-bar and *R* control charts for the hole location data in Figure 17.4 on page 695 (data file: HoleLoc.MTW):

- In the Data window, enter the hole location measurements from Figure 17.1 (page 689) into columns C1 through C5 as shown in the screen with the measurements for each subgroup in a single row of columns C1 through C5—columns C1 through C5 have variable names Meas1, Meas2, Meas3, Meas4, and Meas5, which correspond to the five measurements in a single subgroup.

- Select **Stat : Control Charts : Variables Charts for Subgroups : Xbar-R.**

- In the Xbar-R Chart dialog box, select the "Observations for a subgroup are in one row of columns" option from the pull-down menu.

- Select Meas1–Meas5 into the variables window below the pull-down menu.

- Click on the "Xbar-R Chart—Options..." button.

- In the "Xbar-R Chart—Options" dialog box, click on the Estimate tab and select the Rbar option for "Method for estimating standard deviation."

- Click OK in the "Xbar-R Chart—Options" dialog box.

- Click OK in the Xbar-R Chart dialog box.

- The combined *X*-bar and *R* charts are displayed in a graphics window and can be edited using the usual MINITAB editing features.

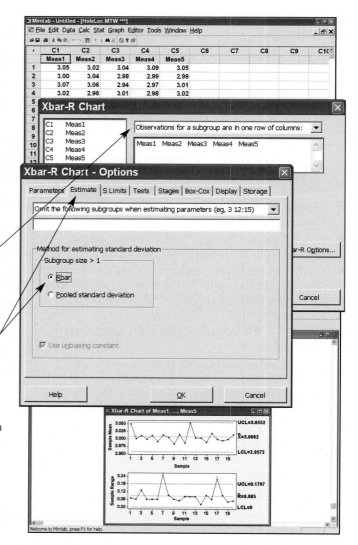

To delete subgroups of data from the control chart (as in Figure 17.7 on page 697):

- In the Xbar-R Chart dialog box, click on the Data Options... button.

- Select the "Specify which rows to exclude" option under "Include or Exclude."

- Under "Specify Which Rows To Exclude," select the "Row numbers" option.

- In the Row numbers window, enter the subgroups that are to be deleted—subgroups 7 and 17 in the case of Figure 17.7.

- Follow the previously given steps to construct the *X*-bar and *R* charts.

p **control chart** similar to Figure 17.23 on page 717 (data file: Invoice.MTW):

- In the Data window, enter the 30 weekly error counts from Table 17.7 (page 717) into column C1 with variable name Invoice.
- Select **Stat : Control Charts : Attributes Charts : p.**
- In the P Chart dialog box, enter Invoice into the Variables window.
- Enter 100 in the "Subgroup sizes" window to indicate that each error count is based on a sample of 100 invoices.
- Click OK in the P Chart dialog box.
- The *p* control chart will be displayed in a graphics window.

CHAPTER 18

Nonparametric Methods

Learning Objectives

After mastering the material in this chapter, you will be able to:

LO18-1 Use the sign test to test a hypothesis about a population median.

LO18-2 Compare the locations of two distributions using a rank sum test for independent samples.

LO18-3 Compare the locations of two distributions using a signed ranks test for paired samples.

LO18-4 Compare the locations of three or more distributions using a Kruskal–Wallis test for independent samples.

LO18-5 Measure and test the association between two variables by using Spearman's rank correlation coefficient.

Chapter Outline

Recall from Chapter 3 that the manufacturer of a DVD recorder has randomly selected a sample of 20 purchasers who have owned the recorder for one year. Each purchaser in the sample is asked to rank his or her satisfaction with the recorder along the following 10-point scale:

1	2	3	4	5	6	7	8	9	10
Not satisfied				Fairly satisfied					Extremely satisfied

The stem-and-leaf display below gives the 20 ratings obtained.

```
 1   0
 2
 3   0
 4
 5   00
 6
 7   0
 8   000000
 9   00000
10   0000
```

Let μ denote the mean rating that would be given by all purchasers who have owned the DVD recorder for one year, and suppose we wish to show that μ exceeds 7. To do this, we will test $H_0: \mu \leq 7$ versus $H_a: \mu > 7$. The mean and the standard deviation of the sample of 20 ratings are $\bar{x} = 7.7$ and $s = 2.4301$, and the test statistic t is

$$t = \frac{\bar{x} - 7}{s/\sqrt{n}} = \frac{7.7 - 7}{2.4301/\sqrt{20}} = 1.2882$$

Because $t = 1.2882$ is less than $t_{.10} = 1.328$ (based on 19 degrees of freedom), we cannot reject $H_0: \mu \leq 7$ by setting α equal to .10. That is, the t test does not provide even mildly strong evidence that μ exceeds 7. But how appropriate is the t test in this situation? The t test is, in fact, not appropriate for two reasons:

1 The t test assumes that, when the sample size n is small (less than 30), the sampled population is normally distributed (or, at least, mound-shaped and not highly skewed to the right or left). The stem-and-leaf display of the ratings indicates the population of all DVD recorder ratings might be highly skewed to the left.

2 The ratings of 1 and 3 in the stem-and-leaf display are **outliers** (see Figure 3.17 on page 123). These outliers affect both the sample mean and the sample standard deviation. First, the sample mean of 7.7 is "pulled down" by the low ratings and thus is smaller than the sample median, which is 8. Although there is not much difference here between the mean and the median, the outlier and overall skewness indicate that the median might be a better measure of central tendency. More important, however, is the fact that the low ratings inflate the sample standard deviation s. As a result, although the sample mean of 7.7 is

greater than 7, the inflated s of 2.4301 makes the denominator of the t statistic large enough to cause us to not reject $H_0: \mu \leq 7$. Intuitively, therefore, even if the population mean DVD recorder rating really does exceed 7, the t test is not **powerful enough** to tell us that this is true.

In addition, some statisticians would consider the t test to be inappropriate for a third reason. The variable DVD recorder rating is an *ordinal variable*. Recall from Section 1.3 that an **ordinal variable** is a **qualitative variable** with a meaningful **ordering, or ranking,** of the categories. In general, when the measurements of an ordinal variable are numerical, statisticians debate whether the ordinal variable is "somewhat quantitative." Statisticians who argue that DVD recorder rating is not somewhat quantitative would reason, for instance, that the difference between 10 ("extremely satisfied") and 6 ("fairly satisfied") may not be the same as the difference between 5 ("fairly satisfied") and 1 ("not satisfied"). In other words, although each difference is four rating points, the two differences may not be the same qualitatively. Other statisticians would argue that as soon as respondents see equally spaced numbers (even though the numbers are described by words), their responses are influenced enough to make the ordinal variable somewhat quantitative. In general, the choice of words associated with the numbers probably substantially affects whether an ordinal variable may be considered somewhat quantitative. However, in practice, numerical ordinal ratings are often analyzed as though they are quantitative. For example, although a teacher's effectiveness rating given by a student and a student's course grade are both ordinal variables with the possible measurements 4 ("excellent"), 3 ("good"), 2 ("average"), 1 ("poor"), and 0 ("unsatisfactory"), a teacher's effectiveness **average** and a student's grade point **average** are calculated. Furthermore, some statisticians would argue that when there are "fairly many" numerical ordinal ratings (for example, the 10 ratings in the DVD recorder example), it is even more reasonable to consider the ratings somewhat quantitative and thus to analyze means and variances. However, for statisticians who feel that numerical ordinal ratings should never be considered quantitative, analyzing the means and standard deviations of these ratings—and thus performing t tests—would always be considered inappropriate.

In general, consider the one-sample t test (see Section 9.3 on page 357), the two independent sample t tests (see Section 10.1 on page 381), the paired difference t test (see Section 10.2 on page 391), and the one-way analysis of variance F-test (see Section 12.2 on page 432). All of these procedures assume that the sampled populations are normally distributed (or mound-shaped and not highly skewed to the right or left). When this assumption is not satisfied, we can use techniques that do not require assumptions about the shapes of the probability distributions of the sampled populations. These techniques are often called **nonparametric methods,** and we discuss several of these methods in this chapter. Specifically, we consider four nonparametric tests that can be used in place of the previously mentioned *t* and *F*-tests. These four nonparametric tests are the **sign test,** the **Wilcoxon rank sum test,** the **Wilcoxon signed rank test,** and the **Kruskal–Wallis *H* test.** These tests require no assumptions about the probability distributions of the sampled populations. In addition, these nonparametric tests are usually better than the *t* and *F*-tests at correctly finding statistically significant differences in the presence of outliers and extreme skewness. Therefore, we say that the nonparametric tests can be **more powerful** than the *t* and *F* tests. For example, we will find in Section 18.1 that, although the *t* test does not allow us to conclude that the population **mean** DVD recorder rating exceeds 7, the nonparametric sign test does allow us to conclude that the population **median** DVD recorder rating exceeds 7.

Each nonparametric test discussed in this chapter assumes that each sampled population under consideration is described by a continuous probability distribution. However, in most situations, each nonparametric technique is slightly **statistically conservative** if the sampled population is described

by a discrete probability distribution. This means, for example, that a nonparametric hypothesis test has a slightly smaller chance of falsely rejecting the null hypothesis than the specified α value would seem to indicate, if the sampled population is described by a discrete probability distribution. Furthermore, because each nonparametric technique is based essentially on **ranking** the observed sample values, and not on the exact sizes of the sample values, each nonparametric technique can be used to analyze any type of data that can be ranked. This includes ordinal data (for example, teaching effectiveness ratings and DVD recorder ratings) in addition to quantitative data.

To conclude this introduction, we note that *t* and *F*-tests are more powerful (better at correctly finding statistically significant differences) than nonparametric tests when the sampled populations are normally distributed (or mound-shaped and not highly skewed to the right or left). In addition, nonparametric tests are largely limited to simple settings. For example, there is a nonparametric measure of correlation between two variables— **Spearman's rank correlation coefficient**—which is discussed at the end of this chapter. However, nonparametric tests do not extend easily to multiple regression and complex experimental designs. This is one reason why we have stressed *t* and *F* procedures in this book. These procedures can be extended to more advanced statistical methods.

LO18-1 Use the sign test to test a hypothesis about a population median.

18.1 The Sign Test: A Hypothesis Test about the Median ● ● ●

If a population is highly skewed to the right or left, then the population median might be a better measure of central tendency than the population mean. Furthermore, if the sample size is small and the population is highly skewed or clearly non–mound-shaped, then the *t* test for the population mean that we have presented in Section 9.3 (page 357) might not be valid. For these reasons, when we have taken a small sample and when we believe that the sampled population might be far from being normally distributed, it is sometimes useful to use a hypothesis test about the population median. This test, called the **sign test,** is valid for any sample size and population shape. To illustrate the sign test, we consider the following example.

EXAMPLE 18.1 The CD Player Case: Testing a Product Lifetime

The leading compact disc player is advertised to have a median lifetime (or time to failure) of 6,000 hours of continuous play. The developer of a new compact disc player wishes to show that the median lifetime of the new player exceeds 6,000 hours of continuous play. To this end, the developer randomly selects 20 new players and tests them in continuous play until each fails. Figure 18.1(a) presents the 20 lifetimes obtained (expressed in hours and arranged in increasing order), and Figure 18.1(b) shows a stem-and-leaf display of these lifetimes. The stem-and-leaf display and the three low lifetimes of 5, 947, and 2,142 suggest that the population of all lifetimes might be highly skewed to the left. In addition, the sample size is small. Therefore, it might be reasonable to use the sign test.

FIGURE 18.1	The Compact Disc Player Lifetime Data and Associated Statistical Analyses

(a) The compact disc player lifetime data ⊙ CompDisc

5	947	2,142	4,867	5,840	6,085	6,238	6,411	6,507	6,687
6,827	6,985	7,082	7,176	7,285	7,410	7,563	7,668	7,724	7,846

(c) MINITAB output of the sign test of H_0: $M_d = 6,000$ versus H_a: $M_d > 6,000$

```
Sign test of median = 6000 versus > 6000
              N    Below   Equal   Above        P      Median
LifeTime     20        5       0      15   0.0207        6757
```

(d) Excel add-in (MegaStat) output of the sign test of H_0: $M_d = 6,000$ versus H_a: $M_d > 6,000$

Sign Test

6000 hypothesized value	5 below	binomial
6757 median Life Time	0 equal	.0207 p-value (one-tailed, upper)
20 n	15 above	

(b) A stem-and-leaf display

```
0   005
0   947
1
1
2   142
2
3
3
4
4   867
5
5   840
6   085 238 411
6   507 687 827 985
7   082 176 285 410
7   563 668 724 846
```

In order to show that the population median lifetime, M_d, of the new compact disc player exceeds 6,000 (hours), recall that this median divides the population of ordered lifetimes into two equal parts. It follows that, if more than half of the individual population lifetimes exceed 6,000, then the population median, M_d, exceeds 6,000. Let p denote the proportion of the individual population lifetimes that exceed 6,000. Then, we can reject H_0: $M_d = 6,000$ in favor of H_a: $M_d > 6,000$ if we can reject H_0: $p = .5$ in favor of H_a: $p > .5$. Let x denote the total number of lifetimes that exceed 6,000 in a random sample of 20 lifetimes. If H_0: $p = .5$ is true, then x is a binomial random variable where $n = 20$ and $p = .5$. This says that if H_0: $p = .5$ is true, then we would expect $\mu_x = np = 20(.5) = 10$ of the 20 lifetimes to exceed 6,000. Considering the 20 lifetimes we have actually observed, we note that 15 of these 20 lifetimes exceed 6,000. The p-value for testing H_0: $p = .5$ versus H_a: $p > .5$ is the probability, computed assuming that H_0: $p = .5$ is true, of observing a sample result that is at least as contradictory to H_0 as the sample result we have actually observed. Since any number of lifetimes out of 20 lifetimes that is greater than or equal to 15 is at least this contradictory, we have

$$p\text{-value} = P(x \geq 15) = \sum_{x=15}^{20} \frac{20!}{x!(20-x)!}(.5)^x(.5)^{20-x}$$

Using the binomial distribution table in Table A.1 (pages 783–787), we find that

$$p\text{-value} = P(x \geq 15)$$
$$= P(x = 15) + P(x = 16) + P(x = 17) + P(x = 18)$$
$$+ P(x = 19) + P(x = 20)$$
$$= .0148 + .0046 + .0011 + .0002 + .0000 + .0000$$
$$= .0207$$

This says that if H_0: $p = .5$ is true, then the probability that at least 15 out of 20 lifetimes would exceed 6,000 is only .0207. Because it is difficult to believe that such a small chance would occur, we have strong evidence against H_0: $p = .5$ and in favor of H_a: $p > .5$. That is, we have strong evidence that H_0: $M_d = 6,000$ is false and H_a: $M_d > 6,000$ is true. This implies that it is reasonable to conclude that the median lifetime of the new compact disc player exceeds the advertised median lifetime of the market's leading compact disc player. Figure 18.1(c) and (d) present the MINITAB and Excel add-in (MegaStat) outputs of the sign test of H_0: $M_d = 6,000$ versus H_a: $M_d > 6,000$. In addition, the outputs tell us that a point estimate of the population median lifetime is the sample median of 6,757 hours.

BI

We summarize how to carry out the sign test in the following box:

The Sign Test for a Population Median

Suppose we have randomly selected a sample of size n from a population, and suppose we wish to test the null hypothesis $H_0: M_d = M_0$ versus one of $H_a: M_d < M_0$, $H_a: M_d > M_0$, or $H_a: M_d \neq M_0$ where M_d denotes the population median. Define the test statistic S as follows:

If the alternative is $H_a: M_d < M_0$, then $S =$ the number of sample measurements less than M_0.

If the alternative is $H_a: M_d > M_0$, then $S =$ the number of sample measurements greater than M_0.

If the alternative is $H_a: M_d \neq M_0$, then $S =$ the larger of S_1 and S_2

where $S_1 =$ the number of sample measurements less than M_0, and

$S_2 =$ the number of sample measurements greater than M_0.

Furthermore, define x to be a binomial variable with parameters n and $p = .5$. Then, we can test $H_0: M_d = M_0$ versus a particular alternative hypothesis at level of significance α by using the appropriate p-value.

Alternative Hypothesis	p-Value (reject H_0 if p-value $< \alpha$)
$H_a: M_d > M_0$	The probability that x is greater than or equal to S
$H_a: M_d < M_0$	The probability that x is greater than or equal to S
$H_a: M_d \neq M_0$	Twice the probability that x is greater than or equal to S

Here we can use Table A.1 (pages 783–787) to find the p-value.

When we take a large sample, we can use the normal approximation to the binomial distribution to implement the sign test. Here, when the null hypothesis $H_0: M_d = M_0$ (or $H_0: p = .5$) is true, the binomial variable x is approximately normally distributed with mean $np = n(.5) = .5n$ and standard deviation $\sqrt{np(1-p)} = \sqrt{n(.5)(1-.5)} = .5\sqrt{n}$. The test is based on the test statistic

$$z = \frac{(S - .5) - .5n}{.5\sqrt{n}}$$

where S is as defined in the previous box and where we subtract .5 from S as a correction for continuity. This motivates the following test:

The Large Sample Sign Test for a Population Median

Suppose we have taken a large sample (for this test, $n \geq 10$ will suffice). Define S as in the previous box, and define the test statistic

$$z = \frac{(S - .5) - .5n}{.5\sqrt{n}}$$

We can test $H_0: M_d = M_0$ versus a particular alternative hypothesis at level of significance α by using the appropriate critical value rule, or, equivalently, the corresponding p-value.

Alternative Hypothesis	Critical Value Rule: Reject H_0 if	p-Value (reject H_0 if p-value $< \alpha$)
$H_a: M_d > M_0$	$z > z_\alpha$	The area under the standard normal curve to the right of z
$H_a: M_d < M_0$	$z > z_\alpha$	The area under the standard normal curve to the right of z
$H_a: M_d \neq M_0$	$z > z_{\alpha/2}$	Twice the area under the standard normal curve to the right of z

EXAMPLE 18.2 The CD Player Case: Testing a Product Lifetime

Consider Example 18.1. Because the sample size $n = 20$ is greater than 10, we can use the large sample sign test to test $H_0: M_d = 6,000$ versus $H_a: M_d > 6,000$. Because $S = 15$ is the number of compact disc player lifetimes that exceed $M_0 = 6,000$, the test statistic z is

$$z = \frac{(S - .5) - .5n}{.5\sqrt{n}} = \frac{(15 - .5) - .5(20)}{.5\sqrt{20}} = 2.01$$

The p-value for the test is the area under the standard normal curve to the right of $z = 2.01$, which is $1 - .9778 = .0222$. Because this p-value is less than .05, we have strong evidence that $H_a: M_d > 6,000$ is true. Also, note that the large sample, approximate p-value of .0222 given by the normal distribution is fairly close to the exact p-value of .0207 given by the binomial distribution [see Figure 18.1(c) on page 735].

To conclude this section, we consider the DVD recorder rating example discussed in the chapter introduction, and we let M_d denote the median rating that would be given by all purchasers who have owned the DVD recorder for one year. Below we present the MINITAB output of the sign test of $H_0: M_d = 7.5$ versus $H_a: M_d > 7.5$:

```
Sign test of median = 7.500 versus > 7.500
               N   Below   Equal   Above        P   Median
DVD Rating    20       5       0      15   0.0207    8.000
```

Because the p-value of .0207 is less than .05, we have strong evidence that the population median rating exceeds 7.5. Furthermore, note that the sign test has reached this conclusion by showing that **more than 50 percent** of all DVD recorder ratings exceed 7.5. It follows, because a rating exceeding 7.5 is the same as a rating being at least 8 (because of the discrete nature of the ratings), that we have strong evidence that the population median rating is at least 8.

Exercises for Section 18.1

CONCEPTS

connect

18.1 What is a nonparametric test? Why would such a test be particularly useful when we must take a small sample?

18.2 When we perform the sign test, we use the sample data to compute a p-value. What probability distribution is used to compute the p-value? Explain why.

METHODS AND APPLICATIONS

18.3 Consider the following sample of five chemical yields: DS ChemYield

801   814   784   836   820

    a   Use this sample to test $H_0: M_d = 800$ versus $H_a: M_d \neq 800$ by setting $\alpha = .01$.
    b   Use this sample to test $H_0: M_d = 750$ versus $H_a: M_d > 750$ by setting $\alpha = .05$.

18.4 Consider the following sample of seven bad debt ratios: DS BadDebt

7%   4%   6%   7%   5%   4%   9%

Use this sample and the following MINITAB output to test the null hypothesis that the median bad debt ratio equals 3.5 percent versus the alternative hypothesis that the median bad debt ratio exceeds 3.5 percent by setting α equal to .05.

```
Sign test of median = 3.500 versus > 3.500
           N   Below   Equal   Above        P   Median
Ratio      7       0       0       7   0.0078    6.000
```

18.5 A local newspaper randomly selects 20 patrons of the Springwood Restaurant on a given Saturday night and has each patron rate the quality of his or her meal as 5 (excellent), 4 (good), 3 (average), 2 (poor), or 1 (unsatisfactory). When the results are summarized, it is found that there are 16 ratings of 5, 3 ratings of 4, and 1 rating of 3. Let M_d denote the population median rating that would be given by all possible patrons of the restaurant on the Saturday night.
    a   Test $H_0: M_d = 4.5$ versus $H_a: M_d > 4.5$ by setting $\alpha = .05$.
    b   Reason that your conclusion in part a implies that we have very strong evidence that the median rating that would be given by all possible patrons is 5.

18.6 Suppose that a particular type of plant has a median growing height of 20 inches in a specified time period when the best plant food currently on the market is used as directed. A developer of a new plant food wishes to show that the new plant food increases the median growing height. If a stem-and-leaf display indicates that the population of all growing heights using the new plant food is markedly nonnormal, it would be appropriate to use the sign test to test $H_0: M_d = 20$ versus $H_a: M_d > 20$. Here M_d denotes the population median growing height when the new plant food is

TABLE 18.1 Results of a Taste Test of Coke versus Pepsi ⊙S CokePep

Customer	Preference (Coke or Pepsi)	Value (Sign)
1	Coke	+1
2	Pepsi	−1
3	Pepsi	−1
4	Coke	+1
5	Coke	+1
6	Pepsi	−1
7	Coke	+1
8	Coke	+1
9	Pepsi	−1

Sign Test	0 hypothesized value	4 below	binomial
9 n	1 median Value (sign)	0 equal	1.0000 p-value (two-tailed)
		5 above	

used. Suppose that 13 out of 15 sample plants grown using the new plant food reach a height of more than 20 inches. Test H_0: $M_d = 20$ versus H_a: $M_d > 20$ by using the large sample sign test.

18.7 A common application of the sign test deals with analyzing consumer preferences. For instance, suppose that a blind taste test is administered to nine randomly selected convenience store customers. Each participant is asked to express a preference for either Coke or Pepsi after tasting unidentified samples of each soft drink. The sample results are expressed by recording a +1 for each consumer who prefers Coke and a −1 for each consumer who prefers Pepsi. Note that sometimes, rather than recording either a +1 or a −1, we simply record the sign + or −, hence the name "sign test." A zero is recorded if a consumer is unable to rank the two brands, and these observations are eliminated from the analysis.

The null hypothesis in this application says that there is no difference in preferences for Coke and Pepsi. If this null hypothesis is true, then the number of +1 values in the population of all preferences should equal the number of −1 values, which implies that the median preference $M_d = 0$ (and that the proportion p of +1 values equals .5). The alternative hypothesis says that there is a significant difference in preferences (or that there is a significant difference in the number of +1 values and −1 values in the population of all preferences). This implies that the median preference does not equal 0 (and that the proportion p of +1 values does not equal .5). ⊙S CokePep

a Table 18.1 gives the results of the taste test administered to the nine randomly selected consumers. If we consider testing H_0: $M_d = 0$ versus H_a: $M_d \neq 0$ where M_d is the median of the (+1 and −1) preference rankings, determine the values of S_1, S_2, and S for the sign test needed to test H_0 versus H_a. Identify the value of S on the Excel add-in (MegaStat) output.

b Use the value of S to find the p-value for testing H_0: $M_d = 0$ versus H_a: $M_d \neq 0$. Then use the p-value to test H_0 versus H_a by setting α equal to .10, .05, .01, and .001. How much evidence is there of a difference in the preferences for Coke and Pepsi? What do you conclude?

LO18-2 Compare the locations of two distributions using a rank sum test for independent samples.

18.2 The Wilcoxon Rank Sum Test ● ● ●

Recall that in Section 10.1 (page 381) we presented t tests for comparing two population means in an independent samples experiment. If the sampled populations are far from normally distributed and the sample sizes are small, these tests are not valid. In such a case, a nonparametric method should be used to compare the populations.

We have seen that the mean of a population measures the **central tendency,** or **location,** of the probability distribution describing the population. Thus, for instance, if a t test provides strong evidence that μ_1 is greater than μ_2, we might conclude that the probability distribution of population 1 is *shifted to the right* of the probability distribution of population 2. The nonparametric test for comparing the locations of two populations is not (necessarily) a test about the difference between population means. Rather, it is a more general test to detect whether the probability distribution of population 1 is shifted to the right (or left) of the probability distribution of population 2.[1] Furthermore, **the nonparametric test is valid for any shapes that might describe the sampled populations.**

---

[1]To be precise, we say that the probability distribution of population 1 is shifted to the right (left) of the probability distribution of population 2 if there is more than a 50 percent chance that a randomly selected observation from population 1 will be greater than (less than) a randomly selected observation from population 2.

In this section we present the **Wilcoxon rank sum test** (also called the **Mann–Whitney test**), which is used to compare the locations of two populations when **independent samples** are selected. To perform this test, we first combine all of the observations in both samples into a single set, and we rank these observations from smallest to largest, with the smallest observation receiving rank 1, the next smallest observation receiving rank 2, and so forth. The sum of the ranks of the observations in each sample is then calculated. If the probability distributions of the two populations are identical, we would expect the sum of the ranks for sample 1 to roughly equal the sum of the ranks for sample 2. However, if, for example, the sum of the ranks for sample 1 is substantially larger than the sum of the ranks for sample 2, this would suggest that the probability distribution of population 1 is shifted to the right of the probability distribution of population 2. We explain how to carry out the Wilcoxon rank sum test in the following box:

The Wilcoxon Rank Sum Test

et D_1 and D_2 denote the probability distributions of populations 1 and 2, and assume that we randomly select independent samples of sizes n_1 and n_2 from populations 1 and 2. Rank the $n_1 + n_2$ observations in the two samples from the smallest (rank 1) to the largest (rank $n_1 + n_2$). Here, if two or more observations are equal, we assign to each "tied" observation a rank equal to the average of the consecutive ranks that would otherwise be assigned to the tied observations. Let T_1 denote the sum of the ranks of the observations in sample 1, and let T_2 denote the sum of the ranks of the observations in sample 2. Furthermore, define the **test statistic T** to be T_1 if $n_1 \leq n_2$ and to be T_2 if $n_1 > n_2$. Then, we can test

$$H_0: D_1 \text{ and } D_2 \text{ are identical probability distributions}$$

versus a particular alternative hypothesis at level of significance α by using the appropriate critical value rule.

Alternative Hypothesis	Critical Value Rule: Reject H_0 if	
H_a: D_1 is shifted to the right of D_2	$T \geq T_U$	if $n_1 \leq n_2$
	$T \leq T_L$	if $n_1 > n_2$
H_a: D_1 is shifted to the left of D_2	$T \leq T_L$	if $n_1 \leq n_2$
	$T \geq T_U$	if $n_1 > n_2$
H_a: D_1 is shifted to the right or left of D_2	$T \leq T_L$ or $T \geq T_U$	

The first two alternative hypotheses above are **one-sided,** while the third alternative hypothesis is **two-sided.** The critical values T_U and T_L are given in Table A.15 (page 803) for values of n_1 and n_2 from 3 to 10.

Table 18.2 repeats a portion of Table A.15. This table gives the critical value (T_U or T_L) for testing a one-sided alternative hypothesis at level of significance $\alpha = .05$ and also gives the critical values (T_U and T_L) for testing a two-sided alternative hypothesis at level of significance $\alpha = .10$. The critical values are tabulated according to n_1 and n_2, the sizes of the samples taken from populations 1 and 2, respectively. For instance, as shown in Table 18.2, if we have taken a sample of size $n_1 = 10$ from population 1, and if we have taken a sample of size $n_2 = 7$ from

TABLE 18.2 **A Portion of the Wilcoxon Rank Sum Table: Critical Values for $\alpha = .05$ (One-Sided); $\alpha = .10$ (Two-Sided)**

n_2 \ n_1	3 T_L	3 T_U	4 T_L	4 T_U	5 T_L	5 T_U	6 T_L	6 T_U	7 T_L	7 T_U	8 T_L	8 T_U	9 T_L	9 T_U	10 T_L	10 T_U
3	6	15	7	17	7	20	8	22	9	24	9	27	10	29	11	31
4	7	17	12	24	13	27	14	30	15	33	16	36	17	39	18	42
5	7	20	13	27	19	36	20	40	22	43	24	46	25	50	26	54
6	8	22	14	30	20	40	28	50	30	54	32	58	33	63	35	67
7	9	24	15	33	22	43	30	54	39	66	41	71	43	76	46	80
8	9	27	16	36	24	46	32	58	41	71	52	84	54	90	57	95
9	10	29	17	39	25	50	33	63	43	76	54	90	66	105	69	111
10	11	31	18	42	26	54	35	67	46	80	57	95	69	111	83	127

$\alpha = .05$ one-sided; $\alpha = .10$ two-sided

population 2, then for a one-sided test with $\alpha = .05$, we use $T_U = 80$ or $T_L = 46$. Similarly, if $n_1 = 10$ and $n_2 = 7$, we use $T_U = 80$ and $T_L = 46$ for a two-sided test with $\alpha = .10$.

EXAMPLE 18.3 Studying Circuit Court Litigation Times

The State Court Administrator for the State of Oregon commissioned a study of two circuit court jurisdictions within the state to examine the effect of administrative rule differences on litigation processing time. The two jurisdictions of interest are Coos County and Lane County. Samples of 10 cases were selected at random from each jurisdiction. However, records for three of the cases selected from Lane County were incomplete, and the cases had to be discarded from the analysis, leaving $n_1 = 10$ cases for Coos County and $n_2 = 7$ cases for Lane County. Each selected case was examined to determine the total elapsed time (in days) required for processing the case, from filing to completion. The processing times are given in Figure 18.2(a). Because the corresponding box plots indicate that the population of all possible processing times for each county might be skewed to the right, we will perform the Wilcoxon rank sum test. It was theorized before the samples were taken that the administrative rules in Lane County were somewhat inefficient. Therefore, we will test

> H_0: the probability distributions of all possible processing times for Coos County and Lane County are identical

versus

> H_a: the probability distribution of all possible processing times for Coos County is shifted to the left of the probability distribution of all possible processing times for Lane County (note that this alternative hypothesis intuitively implies that the Coos County processing times are "systematically less than" the Lane County processing times)

To perform the test, we rank the $n_1 + n_2 = 10 + 7 = 17$ processing times in the two samples as shown in Figure 18.2(a). Note that, because there are two processing times of 145 that are tied as the sixth and seventh smallest processing times, we assign each of these an average rank of 6.5. The sum of the ranks of the processing times in sample 1 (Coos County) is $T_1 = 72.5$, and the sum of the ranks of the processing times in sample 2 (Lane County) is $T_2 = 80.5$. Because $n_1 = 10$ is greater

---

FIGURE 18.2   Analysis of the Coos County and Lane County Litigation Processing Times

(a) The Coos County and Lane County litigation processing times   DS Court

Coos County		Lane County		
Time	**Rank**	**Time**	**Rank**	
48	1	109	4	
97	2	145	6.5	
103	3	196	10	
117	5	273	13	
145	6.5	289	14	
151	8	417	16	
179	9	505	17	
220	11		$T_2 = 80.5$	
257	12			
294	15			
	$T_1 = 72.5$			

Box Plots of Coos and Lane

(b) MINITAB output of the Wilcoxon rank sum test for the litigation processing times

```
Coos     N = 10    Median = 148.0
Lane     N =  7    Median = 273.0
Point estimate for ETA1-ETA2 is -98.0
95.5 Percent CI for ETA1-ETA2 is (-248.0,7.9)
W = 72.5
Test of ETA1 = ETA2 vs ETA1 < ETA2 is significant at 0.0486
The test is significant at 0.0485 (adjusted for ties)
```

than $n_2 = 7$, the summary box tells us that the test statistic T is $T_2 = 80.5$. Because we are testing a "shifted left" alternative hypothesis, and because n_1 is greater than n_2, the summary box also tells us that we can reject H_0 in favor of H_a at the .05 level of significance if T is greater than or equal to T_U. Because $T = 80.5$ is greater than $T_U = 80$ (see Table 18.2), we conclude at the .05 level of significance that the Coos County processing times are shifted to the left of, and thus are "systematically less than," the Lane County processing times. This supports the theory that the Lane County administrative rules are somewhat inefficient.

Figure 18.2(b) presents the MINITAB output of the Wilcoxon rank sum test for the litigation processing times. In general, MINITAB gives T_1, the sum of the ranks of the observations in sample 1, as the test statistic, which MINITAB denotes as W. If, as in the present example, n_1 is greater than n_2 and thus the correct test statistic is T_2, **we can obtain T_2 by subtracting T_1 from $(n_1 + n_2)(n_1 + n_2 + 1)/2$.** This last quantity can be proven to equal the sum of the ranks of the $(n_1 + n_2)$ observations in both samples. In the present example, this quantity equals $(10 + 7)(10 + 7 + 1)/2 = (17)(18)/2$, or 153. Therefore, because the MINITAB output tells us that $T_1 = 72.5$, the correct test statistic T_2 is $(153 - 72.5) = 80.5$. In addition to giving T_1, MINITAB gives two p-values related to the hypothesis test. The first p-value—.0486—is calculated assuming that there are no ties. Because there is a tie, the second p-value—.0485—is adjusted accordingly and is more correct (although there is little difference in this situation).

In general, the Wilcoxon rank sum test tests the equality of the population medians if the distributions of the sampled populations have the same shapes and equal variances. MINITAB tells us that under these assumptions a point estimate of the difference in the population medians is -98.0 (days), and a 95.5 percent confidence interval for the difference in the population medians is $[-248.0, 7.9]$. Note that the point estimate of the difference in the population medians, which is -98.0, is not equal to the difference in the sample medians, which is $148.0 - 273.0 = -125.0$. In the present example, the box plots in Figure 18.2 indicate that the variances of the two populations are not equal. In fact, in most situations it is a bit too much to ask that the sampled populations have exactly the same shapes and equal variances (although we will see in Exercise 18.12 that this might be approximately true in some situations).

As another example, suppose that on a given Saturday night a local newspaper randomly selects 20 patrons from each of two restaurants and has each patron rate the quality of his or her meal as 5 (excellent), 4 (good), 3 (average), 2 (poor), or 1 (unsatisfactory). The following results are obtained:

Rating	Restaurant 1 Patrons	Restaurant 2 Patrons	Total Patrons	Ranks Involved	Average Rank	Restaurant 1 Rank Sum	Restaurant 2 Rank Sum
5	15	5	20	21–40	30.5	(15)(30.5) = 457.5	(5)(30.5) = 152.5
4	4	11	15	6–20	13	(4)(13) = 52	(11)(13) = 143
3	1	2	3	3, 4, 5	4	(1)(4) = 4	(2)(4) = 8
2	0	1	1	2	2	(0)(2) = 0	(1)(2) = 2
1	0	1	1	1	1	(0)(1) = 0	(1)(1) = 1
						$T_1 = 513.5$	$T_2 = 306.5$

Suppose that we wish to test

> H_0: The probability distributions of all possible Saturday night meal ratings
>   for restaurants 1 and 2 are identical

versus

> H_a: The probability distribution of all possible Saturday night meal ratings for
>   restaurant 1 is shifted to the right or left of the probability distribution of
>   all possible Saturday night meal ratings for restaurant 2.

Because there are only five numerical ordinal ratings, there are many ties. The above table shows how we determine the sum of the ranks for each sample. Because $n_1 = 20$ and $n_2 = 20$, we cannot obtain critical values by using Table A.15 (which gives critical values for sample sizes up to $n_1 = 10$ and $n_2 = 10$). However, we can use a large sample, normal approximation, which is valid if both n_1 and n_2 are at least 10. The normal approximation involves making two modifications. First, we replace the test statistic T in the previously given summary box by a standardized value of the test statistic. This standardized value, denoted z, is calculated by subtracting the mean

$\mu_T = n_i(n_1 + n_2 + 1)/2$ from the test statistic T and by then dividing the resulting difference by the standard deviation $\sigma_T = \sqrt{n_1 n_2(n_1 + n_2 + 1)/12}$. Here n_i in the expression for μ_T equals n_1 if the test statistic T is T_1 and equals n_2 if T is T_2. Second, when testing a one-sided alternative hypothesis, we replace the critical values T_U and T_L by the normal points z_α and $-z_\alpha$. When testing a two-sided alternative hypothesis, we replace T_U and T_L by $z_{\alpha/2}$ and $-z_{\alpha/2}$. For the current example, $n_1 = n_2$, and thus the test statistic T is $T_1 = 513.5$. Furthermore,

$$\mu_T = \frac{n_1(n_1 + n_2 + 1)}{2} = \frac{20(20 + 20 + 1)}{2} = 410$$

$$\sigma_T = \sqrt{\frac{n_1 n_2(n_1 + n_2 + 1)}{12}} = \sqrt{\frac{20(20)(41)}{12}} = 36.968455$$

and

$$z = \frac{T - \mu_T}{\sigma_T} = \frac{513.5 - 410}{36.968455} = 2.7997$$

Because we are testing a "shifted right or left" (that is, a two-sided) alternative hypothesis, the summary box tells us that we reject the null hypothesis if $T \leq T_L$ or $T \geq T_U$. Stated in terms of standardized values, we reject the null hypothesis if $z < -z_{\alpha/2}$ or $z > z_{\alpha/2}$ (here we use strict inequalities to be consistent with other normal distribution critical value conditions). If we set $\alpha = .01$, we use the critical values $-z_{.005} = -2.575$ and $z_{.005} = 2.575$. Because $z = 2.7997$ is greater than $z_{.005} = 2.575$, we reject the null hypothesis at the .01 level of significance. Therefore, we have very strong evidence that there is a systematic difference between the Saturday night meal ratings at restaurants 1 and 2. Looking at the original data, we would estimate that Saturday night meal ratings are higher at restaurant 1.

BI

To conclude this section, we make two comments. First, when there are ties, there is an adjusted formula for σ_T that takes the ties into account.[2] If (as in the restaurant example) we ignore the formula, the results we obtain are statistically conservative. Therefore, if we reject the null hypothesis by using the unadjusted formula, we would reject the null hypothesis by using the adjusted formula. Second, the Excel add-in (MegaStat) calculates p-values by using the large sample, normal approximation (and a *continuity correction*), even if the sample sizes n_1 and n_2 are small (less than 10). This will be illustrated in Exercise 18.12.

Exercises for Section 18.2

CONCEPTS

connect™

18.8   Explain the circumstances in which we use the Wilcoxon rank sum test.

18.9   Identify the parametric test corresponding to the Wilcoxon rank sum test. What assumption is needed for the validity of this parametric test (and not needed for the Wilcoxon rank sum test)?

METHODS AND APPLICATIONS

18.10   A loan officer at a bank wishes to compare the new car loan rates charged at banks in Ohio with the new car loan rates of Ohio credit unions. Two independent random samples of bank rates and credit union rates in Ohio are obtained with the following results (all rates are fixed rates):

Bank Rates:	4.25	3.50	3.25	4.00	4.10	3.75	3.50	4.25
Credit Union Rates:	3.25	2.25	2.75	3.00	2.50	3.00	2.40	2.50

Because both samples are small, the bank officer is uncertain about the shape of the distributions of bank and credit union new car loan rates. Therefore, the Wilcoxon rank sum test will be used to compare the two types of loan rates.   **DS** CarLoan

a   Let D_1 be the distribution of bank rates and let D_2 be the distribution of credit union rates. Carry out the Wilcoxon rank sum test to determine whether D_1 and D_2 are identical versus the alternative that D_1 is shifted to the right or left of D_2. Use $\alpha = .05$.

b   Carry out the Wilcoxon rank sum test to determine whether D_1 is shifted to the right of D_2. Use $\alpha = .025$. What do you conclude?

---
[2]The adjusted formula is quite complicated and will not be given here.

18.11 A company collected employee absenteeism data (in hours per year) at two of its manufacturing plants. The data were obtained by randomly selecting a sample from all of the employees at the first plant, and by randomly selecting another independent sample from all of the employees at the second plant. For each randomly selected employee, absenteeism records were used to determine the exact number of hours the employee has been absent during the past year. The following results were obtained: **DS** Absent

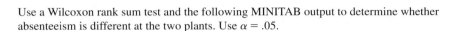

Plant 1:	10	131	53	37	59	29	45	26	39	36
Plant 2:	21	46	33	31	49	33	39	19	12	35

Use a Wilcoxon rank sum test and the following MINITAB output to determine whether absenteeism is different at the two plants. Use $\alpha = .05$.

```
            N   Median
Plant 1    10    38.00
Plant 2    10    33.00
Point estimate for ETA1-ETA2 is 7.00
95.5 Percent CI for ETA1-ETA2 is (-6.99,24.01)
W = 120.5
Test of ETA1 = ETA2 vs ETA1 not = ETA2 is significant at 0.2568
The test is significant at 0.2565 (adjusted for ties)
```

18.12 **THE CATALYST COMPARISON CASE**

The following table presents samples of hourly yields for catalysts XA-100 and ZB-200. We analyzed these data using a two independent sample t test in Example 10.2 (page 385).
DS Catalyst

Catalyst XA-100	Catalyst ZB-200
801	752
814	718
784	776
836	742
820	763

Box Plots of Yield by Catalyst

Wilcoxon-Mann/Whitney Test

n	sum of ranks			
5	40	**XA-100**	27.50 expected value	2.51 z
5	15	**ZB-200**	4.79 standard deviation	.0122 p-value (two-tailed)
10	55	**total**		

a Use a Wilcoxon rank sum test and the Excel add-in (MegaStat) output to test for systematic differences in the yields of the two catalysts. Use $\alpha = .05$.

b The p-value on the MegaStat output has been calculated by finding twice the area under the standard normal curve to the right of

$$z = \frac{39.5 - \mu_T}{\sigma_T} = \frac{39.5 - 27.5}{4.79} = 2.51$$

Here we have used a continuity correction and changed $T_1 = 40$ to 39.5. Verify the calculations of μ_T, σ_T, and the p-value.

c Assume that the second yield for catalyst ZB-200 in the above table is invalid. Use the remaining data to determine if we can conclude that the XA-100 yields are systematically higher than the ZB-200 yields. Set $\alpha = .05$.

18.13 Moore (2000) reports on a study by Boo (1997), who asked 303 randomly selected people at fairs:

How often do you think people become sick because of food they consume prepared at outdoor fairs and festivals?

The possible responses were 5 (always), 4 (often), 3 (more often than not), 2 (once in a while), and 1 (very rarely). The following data were obtained:

Response	Females	Males	Total
5	2	1	3
4	23	5	28
3	50	22	72
2	108	57	165
1	13	22	35

Gender	N	Sum of Scores
Female	196	31996.5
Male	107	14059.5

$T = 14059.5$ $z = -3.33353$
Test significant at 0.0009

Source: H. C. Boo, "Consumers' Perceptions and Concerns about Safety and Healthfulness of Food Served at Fairs and Festivals," M.S. thesis, Purdue University, 1997.

The computer output at the right of the data presents the results of a Wilcoxon rank sum test that attempts to determine if men and women systematically differ in their responses. Here the normal approximation has been used to calculate the p-value of .0009. What do you conclude?

LO18-3 Compare the locations of two distributions using a signed ranks test for paired samples.

18.3 The Wilcoxon Signed Ranks Test ◐ ● ●

In Section 10.2 (page 391) we presented a t test for comparing two population means in a paired difference experiment. If the sample size is small and the population of paired differences is far from normally distributed, this test is not valid and we should use a nonparametric test. In this section we present the **Wilcoxon signed ranks test,** which is a nonparametric test for comparing two populations when a **paired difference experiment** has been carried out.

The Wilcoxon Signed Ranks Test

Let D_1 and D_2 denote the probability distributions of populations 1 and 2, and assume that we have randomly selected n matched pairs of observations from populations 1 and 2. Calculate the paired differences of the n matched pairs by subtracting each paired population 2 observation from the corresponding population 1 observation, and rank the absolute values of the n paired differences from the smallest (rank 1) to the largest (rank n). Here paired differences equal to 0 are eliminated, and the number n of paired differences is reduced accordingly. Furthermore, if two or more absolute paired differences are equal, we assign to each "tied" absolute paired difference a rank equal to the average of the consecutive ranks that would otherwise be assigned to the tied absolute paired differences. Let

$T^- =$ the sum of the ranks associated with the negative paired differences

and

$T^+ =$ the sum of the ranks associated with the positive paired differences

We can test

$H_0: D_1$ and D_2 are identical probability distributions

versus a particular alternative hypothesis at level of significance α by using the appropriate test statistic and the corresponding critical value rule.

Alternative Hypothesis	Test Statistic	Critical Value Rule: Reject H_0 if
$H_a: D_1$ is shifted to the right of D_2	T^-	$T^- \leq T_0$
$H_a: D_1$ is shifted to the left of D_2	T^+	$T^+ \leq T_0$
$H_a: D_1$ is shifted to the right or left of D_2	$T =$ the smaller of T^- and T^+	$T \leq T_0$

The first two alternative hypotheses above are **one-sided,** while the third alternative hypothesis is **two-sided.** Values of T_0 are given in Table A.16 (page 804) for values of n from 5 to 50.

Table 18.3 repeats a portion of Table A.16. This table gives the critical value T_0 for testing one-sided and two-sided alternative hypotheses at several different values of α. The critical values are tabulated according to n, the number of paired differences. For instance, Table 18.3 shows that, if we are analyzing 10 paired differences, then the critical value for testing a one-sided alternative

TABLE 18.3   A Portion of the Wilcoxon Signed Ranks Table

One-Sided	Two-Sided	$n = 5$	$n = 6$	$n = 7$	$n = 8$	$n = 9$	$n = 10$
$\alpha = .05$	$\alpha = .10$	1	2	4	6	8	11
$\alpha = .025$	$\alpha = .05$		1	2	4	6	8
$\alpha = .01$	$\alpha = .02$			0	2	3	5
$\alpha = .005$	$\alpha = .01$				0	2	3
		$n = 11$	$n = 12$	$n = 13$	$n = 14$	$n = 15$	$n = 16$
$\alpha = .05$	$\alpha = .10$	14	17	21	26	30	36
$\alpha = .025$	$\alpha = .05$	11	14	17	21	25	30
$\alpha = .01$	$\alpha = .02$	7	10	13	16	20	24
$\alpha = .005$	$\alpha = .01$	5	7	10	13	16	19

hypothesis at the .01 level of significance is equal to $T_0 = 5$. This table also shows that we would use the critical value $T_0 = 5$ for testing a two-sided alternative hypothesis at level of significance $\alpha = .02$.

EXAMPLE 18.4 The Auto Insurance Case: Comparing Mean Repair Costs   C

Again consider the automobile repair cost data, which are given in Figure 18.3(a). We analyzed these data using a paired sample *t* test in Example 10.3 (pages 391 and 392). If we fear that the population of all possible paired differences of repair cost estimates at garages 1 and 2 may be far from normally distributed, we can perform the Wilcoxon signed ranks test. Here we test

> H_0: the probability distributions of the populations of all possible repair cost estimates at garages 1 and 2 are identical

versus

> H_a: the probability distribution of repair cost estimates at garage 1 is shifted to the left of the probability distribution of repair cost estimates at garage 2

To perform this test, we find the absolute value of each paired difference, and we assign ranks to the absolute differences [see Figure 18.3(a)]. Because of the form of the alternative hypothesis (see the preceding summary box), we use the test statistic

> T^+ = the sum of the ranks associated with the positive paired differences

FIGURE 18.3   Analysis of the Repair Cost Estimates at Two Garages

(a) Sample of $n = 7$ Paired Differences of the Repair Cost Estimates at Garages 1 and 2   DS Repair
**   (Cost Estimates in Hundreds of Dollars)**

Sample of $n = 7$ Damaged Cars	Repair Cost Estimates at Garage 1	Repair Cost Estimates at Garage 2	Sample of $n = 7$ Paired Differences	Absolute Paired Differences	Ranks
Car 1	$ 7.1	$ 7.9	$d_1 = -.8$	.8	4
Car 2	9.0	10.1	$d_2 = -1.1$	1.1	5
Car 3	11.0	12.2	$d_3 = -1.2$	1.2	6
Car 4	8.9	8.8	$d_4 = .1$	.1	1
Car 5	9.9	10.4	$d_5 = -.5$	.5	2
Car 6	9.1	9.8	$d_6 = -.7$	.7	3
Car 7	10.3	11.7	$d_7 = -1.4$	1.4	7

(b) MINITAB output of the Wilcoxon signed ranks test

```
Test of median = 0.0 versus median < 0.0
                N for    Wilcoxon                Estimated
          N     Test    Statistic       P          Median
G1 - G2   7      7           1.0     0.017         -0.8250
```

Because .1 is the only positive paired difference, and because the rank associated with this difference equals 1, we find that $T^+ = 1$. The alternative hypothesis is one-sided, and we are analyzing $n = 7$ paired differences. Therefore, Table 18.3 on the previous page tells us that we can test H_0 versus H_a at the .05, .025, and .01 levels of significance by setting the critical value T_0 equal to 4, 2, and 0, respectively. The critical value condition is $T^+ \leq T_0$. It follows that, because $T^+ = 1$ is less than or equal to 4 and 2, but is not less than or equal to 0, we can reject H_0 in favor of H_a at the .05 and .025 levels of significance, but not at the .01 level of significance. Therefore, we have strong evidence that the probability distribution of repair cost estimates at garage 1 is shifted to the left of the probability distribution of repair cost estimates at garage 2. That is, the repair cost estimates at garage 1 seem to be systematically lower than the repair cost estimates at garage 2. Figure 18.3(b) presents the MINITAB output of the Wilcoxon signed ranks test for this repair cost comparison. In general, MINITAB gives T^+ as the "Wilcoxon statistic," even if T^- is the appropriate test statistic. It can be shown that T^- **can be obtained by subtracting T^+ from** $n(n + 1)/2$, where n is the total number of paired differences being analyzed.

Notice that in Example 18.4 the nonparametric Wilcoxon signed ranks test would not allow us to reject H_0 in favor of H_a at the .01 level of significance. On the other hand, the *parametric* paired difference t test performed in Example 10.5 (page 394) did allow us to reject H_0: $\mu_1 - \mu_2 = 0$ in favor of H_a: $\mu_1 - \mu_2 < 0$ at the .01 level of significance. In general, **a parametric test is often** *more powerful* than the analogous nonparametric test. That is, the parametric test often allows us to reject H_0 at smaller values of α. Therefore, if the assumptions for the parametric test are satisfied—for example, if, when we are using small samples, the sampled populations are approximately normally distributed—it is preferable to use the parametric test. **The advantage of nonparametric tests is that they can be used without assuming that the sampled populations have the shapes of any particular probability distributions.** As an example, this can be important when reporting statistical conclusions to U.S. federal agencies. Federal guidelines specify that, when reporting statistical conclusions, the validity of the assumptions behind the statistical methods used must be fully justified. If, for instance, there are insufficient data to justify the assumption that the sampled populations are approximately normally distributed, then we must use a nonparametric method to make conclusions.

Finally, if the sample size n is at least 25, we can use a large sample approximation of the Wilcoxon signed ranks test. This is done by making two modifications. First, we replace the test statistic (T^- or T^+) by a standardized value of the test statistic. This standardized value is calculated by subtracting the mean $n(n + 1)/4$ from the test statistic (T^- or T^+) and then dividing the resulting difference by the standard deviation $\sqrt{n(n + 1)(2n + 1)/24}$. Second, when testing a one-sided alternative hypothesis, we replace the critical value T_0 by the normal point $-z_\alpha$. When testing a two-sided alternative hypothesis, we replace T_0 by $-z_{\alpha/2}$.

Exercises for Section 18.3

CONCEPTS

18.14 Explain the circumstances in which we use the Wilcoxon signed ranks test.

18.15 Identify the parametric test corresponding to the Wilcoxon signed ranks test. What assumption is needed for the validity of the parametric test (and not needed for the Wilcoxon signed ranks test)?

METHODS AND APPLICATIONS

18.16 Table 18.4 shows 30-year and 15-year fixed rate mortgage loans for a number of Oregon lending institutions. Use the Wilcoxon signed ranks test and the following MINITAB output to determine whether, for Oregon lending institutions, the distribution of 30-year rates is shifted to the right or left of the distribution of 15-year rates. Use $\alpha = .01$. Hint: As discussed in Example 18.4, MINITAB gives T^+ as the Wilcoxon statistic. Find T^- by subtracting T^+ from $n(n + 1)/2$, where $n = 9$.   DS MortDiff

```
Test of median = 0.0 versus median not = 0.0
                    N for    Wilcoxon              Estimated
              N     Test     Statistic      P       Median
30Yr - 15Yr   9      9         45.0       0.009     0.2355
```

TABLE 18.4   **Mortgage Loan Interest Rates for Nine Randomly Selected Oregon Lending Institutions**   ⒹⓈ MortDiff

Lending Institution	Annual Percentage Rate 30-Year	Annual Percentage Rate 15-Year	Difference
1	4.715	4.599	0.116
2	4.648	4.367	0.281
3	4.740	4.550	0.190
4	4.597	4.362	0.235
5	4.425	4.162	0.263
6	4.880	4.583	0.297
7	4.900	4.800	0.100
8	4.675	4.394	0.281
9	4.790	4.540	0.250

TABLE 18.5   **Pretest and Posttest Leadership Scores**   ⒹⓈ Leader

Manager	Pretest Score	Posttest Score	Difference
1	35	54	−19
2	27	43	−16
3	51	53	−2
4	38	50	−12
5	32	42	−10
6	44	58	−14
7	33	35	−2
8	26	39	−13
9	40	47	−7
10	50	48	2
11	36	41	−5
12	31	37	−6

18.17   A consumer advocacy group is concerned about the ability of tax preparation firms to correctly prepare complex returns. To test the performance of tax preparers in two different tax preparation firms—Quick Tax and Discount Tax—the group designed ten tax cases for families with gross annual incomes between $100,000 and $200,000. In a "tax-off" competition, the advocacy group randomly assigned pairs of preparers from the two firms to the ten cases and asked each preparer to compute the tax liability for his or her assigned case. The preparers' returns were collected, and the group computed the difference between each preparer's computed tax and the actual tax that should have been computed. The data below consist of the resulting two sets of tax computation errors, one for preparers from Quick Tax and the other for preparers from Discount Tax. Fully interpret the following MINITAB output of a Wilcoxon signed ranks test analysis of these data.   ⒹⓈ TaxErr

Tax Case	Quick Tax Errors	Discount Tax Errors	Difference
1	857	156	701
2	920	200	720
3	1,090	202	888
4	1,594	390	1,204
5	1,820	526	1,294
6	1,943	749	1,194
7	1,987	911	1,076
8	2,008	920	1,088
9	2,083	2,145	−62
10	2,439	2,602	−163

```
Test of median = 0.0 versus median not = 0.0
        N   N for Test   Wilcoxon Statistic     P   Estimated Median
Q-D 10          10              52.0         0.014           898.0
```

18.18   A human resources director wishes to assess the benefits of sending a company's managers to an innovative management course. Twelve of the company's managers are randomly selected to attend the course, and a psychologist interviews each participating manager before and after taking the course. Based on these interviews, the psychologist rates the manager's leadership ability on a 1-to-100 scale. The pretest and posttest leadership scores for each of the 12 managers are given in Table 18.5.   ⒹⓈ Leader

   a   Let D_1 be the distribution of leadership scores before taking the course, and let D_2 be the distribution of leadership scores after taking the course. Carry out the Wilcoxon signed ranks test to test whether D_1 and D_2 are identical (that is, the course has no effect on leadership scores) versus the alternative that D_2 is shifted to the right or left of D_1 (that is, the course affects leadership scores). Use $\alpha = .05$.

   b   Carry out the Wilcoxon signed ranks test to determine whether D_2 is shifted to the right of D_1. Use $\alpha = .05$. What do you conclude?

18.19   Recall that in Exercise 10.18 (page 396) we compared preexposure and postexposure attitude scores for an advertising study by using a paired difference t test. The data obtained and related Excel add-in (MegaStat) output are shown in Table 18.6 on the next page. Use the Wilcoxon signed ranks test and the MegaStat output to determine whether the distributions of preexposure and postexposure attitude scores are different. Use $\alpha = .05$.   ⒹⓈ AdStudy

TABLE 18.6 **Preexposure and Postexposure Attitude Scores for an Advertising Study**
 DS AdStudy

Subject	Preexposure Attitudes (A_1)	Postexposure Attitudes (A_2)	Attitude Change (d_i)	Wilcoxon Signed Rank Test
1	50	53	−3	variables: Pre. Attitudes(A1) - Post. Attitudes(A2)
2	25	27	−2	0 sum of positive ranks
3	30	38	−8	45 sum of negative ranks
4	50	55	−5	
5	60	61	−1	
6	80	85	−5	
7	45	45	0	9 n
8	30	31	−1	22.50 expected value
9	65	72	−7	7.89 standard deviation
10	70	78	−8	−2.85 z, corrected for ties
				.0043 p-value (two-tailed)

Source: Attitude Scores from W.R. Dillon, et al., *Essentials of Marketing Research*, p. 435. Copyright © 1993. Reprinted by permission of McGraw-Hill Companies, Inc.

LO18-4 Compare the locations of three or more distributions using a Kruskal–Wallis test for independent samples.

18.4 Comparing Several Populations Using the Kruskal–Wallis *H* Test ● ● ●

In this section we present the Kruskal–Wallis *H* test, a nonparametric technique for comparing the locations of three or more populations. This test requires no assumptions about the population probability distributions and assumes we use independent samples chosen randomly.

In general, suppose we wish to use the Kruskal–Wallis *H* test to compare the locations of *p* populations by using *p* independent samples of observations randomly selected from these populations. We first rank all of the observations in the *p* samples from smallest to largest. If n_i denotes the number of observations in the *i*th sample, we are ranking a total of $n = (n_1 + n_2 + \cdots + n_p)$ observations. Furthermore, we assign tied observations the average of the consecutive ranks that would otherwise be assigned to the tied observations. Next, we calculate the sum of the ranks of the observations in each sample. Letting T_i denote the rank sum for the *i*th sample, we obtain the rank sums $T_1, T_2, \ldots, T_p$. For example, consider the gasoline mileage case in Chapter 12, and suppose that North American Oil wishes to use the $p = 3$ independent samples of gasoline mileages to compare the locations of the populations of all gasoline mileages that could be obtained by using gasoline types *A*, *B*, and *C*. The gasoline mileage data are repeated in Table 18.7, along with the ranking (given in parentheses) of each observation in each sample. If we sum the ranks in each sample, we find that $T_1 = 37.5$, $T_2 = 63$, and $T_3 = 19.5$. Note that, although the box plots in Table 18.7 do not indicate any serious violations of the normality or equal variances assumptions, the samples are quite small, and thus we cannot be sure that these assumptions approximately hold. Therefore, it is reasonable to compare gasoline types *A*, *B*, and *C* by using the Kruskal–Wallis *H* test.

The Kruskal–Wallis *H* Test

Consider testing the null hypothesis H_0 that the *p* populations under consideration are identical versus the alternative hypothesis H_a that at least two populations differ in location (that is, are shifted either to the left or to the right of one another). We can reject H_0 in favor of H_a at level of significance α if the **Kruskal–Wallis *H* statistic**

is greater than the χ_α^2 point based on $p - 1$ degrees of freedom. Here, for this test to be valid, there should be five or more observations in each sample. Furthermore, the number of ties should be small relative to the total number of observations. Values of χ_α^2 are given in Table A.5 (page 794).

$$H = \frac{12}{n(n + 1)} \sum_{i=1}^{p} \frac{T_i^2}{n_i} - 3(n + 1)$$

TABLE 18.7   **The Gasoline Mileage Samples and Rank Sums**   Ⓓ GasMile2

Gasoline Type A	Gasoline Type B	Gasoline Type C
34.0 (3.5)	35.3 (9)	33.3 (2)
35.0 (8)	36.5 (13)	34.0 (3.5)
34.3 (5)	36.4 (12)	34.7 (6)
35.5 (10)	37.0 (14)	33.0 (1)
35.8 (11)	37.6 (15)	34.9 (7)
$T_1 = 37.5$	$T_2 = 63$	$T_3 = 19.5$

FIGURE 18.4   **MINITAB Output of the Kruskal–Wallis H Test in the Gasoline Mileage Case**

```
Kruskal-Wallis Test on Mileage
Type        N      Median    Ave Rank         Z
A           5       35.00         7.5     -0.31
B           5       36.50        12.6      2.82
C           5       34.00         3.9     -2.51
Overall    15                     8.0

H = 9.56    DF = 2    P = 0.008
H = 9.57    DF = 2    P = 0.008    (adjusted for ties)
```

In the gasoline mileage case, $\chi^2_{.05}$ based on $p - 1 = 2$ degrees of freedom is 5.99147 (see Table A.5). Furthermore, because $n = n_1 + n_2 + n_3 = 15$, the Kruskal–Wallis H statistic is

$$H = \frac{12}{15(15 + 1)}\left[\frac{(37.5)^2}{5} + \frac{(63)^2}{5} + \frac{(19.5)^2}{5}\right] - 3(15 + 1)$$

$$= \frac{12}{240}\left[\frac{1,406.25}{5} + \frac{3,969}{5} + \frac{380.25}{5}\right] - 48 = 9.555$$

Because $H = 9.555 > \chi^2_{.05} = 5.99147$, we can reject H_0 at the .05 level of significance. Therefore, we have strong evidence that at least two of the three populations of gasoline mileages differ in location. Figure 18.4 presents the MINITAB output of the Kruskal–Wallis H test in this gasoline mileage case.

To conclude this section, we note that, if the Kruskal–Wallis H test leads us to conclude that the p populations differ in location, there are various procedures for comparing pairs of populations. A simple procedure is to use the Wilcoxon rank sum test to compare pairs of populations. For example, if we use this test to make separate, **two-sided** comparisons of (1) gasoline types A and B, (2) gasoline types A and C, and (3) gasoline types B and C, and if we set α equal to .05 for each comparison, we find that the mileages given by gasoline type B differ systematically from the mileages given by gasoline types A and C. Examining the mileages in Table 18.7, we would estimate that gasoline type B gives the highest mileages. One problem, however, with using the Wilcoxon rank sum test to make pairwise comparisons is that it is difficult to know how to set α for each comparison. Therefore, some practitioners prefer to make **simultaneous** pairwise comparisons (such as given by the Tukey simultaneous confidence intervals discussed in Chapter 12). Gibbons (1985) discusses a nonparametric approach for making simultaneous pairwise comparisons.

Exercises for Section 18.4

CONCEPTS

18.20   Explain the circumstances in which we use the Kruskal–Wallis H test.

18.21   Identify the parametric test corresponding to the Kruskal–Wallis H test.

18.22   What are the assumptions needed for the validity of the parametric test identified in Exercise 18.21 that are not needed for the Kruskal–Wallis H test?

connect

| TABLE 18.8 | Display Panel Study Data (Time, in Seconds, Required to Stabilize Air Traffic Emergency Condition) DS Display3 |

Display Panel		
A	B	C
21	24	40
27	21	36
24	18	35
26	19	32
25	20	37

| TABLE 18.9 | Bottle Design Study Data (Sales during a 24-Hour Period) DS BottleDes |

Bottle Design		
A	B	C
16	33	23
18	31	27
19	37	21
17	29	28
13	34	25

| TABLE 18.10 | Bakery Sales Study Data (Sales in Cases) DS BakeSale |

Shelf Display Height		
Bottom (B)	Middle (M)	Top (T)
58.2	73.0	52.4
53.7	78.1	49.7
55.8	75.4	50.9
55.7	76.2	54.0
52.5	78.4	52.1
58.9	82.1	49.9

FIGURE 18.5   MINITAB Output of the Kruskal–Wallis H Test for the Bakery Sales Data

```
Kruskal-Wallis Test on Bakery Sales

Display   N    Median   Ave Rank      Z
Bottom    6    55.75        9.2    -0.19
Middle    6    77.15       15.5     3.37
Top       6    51.50        3.8    -3.18
Overall  18                 9.5
H = 14.36     DF = 2     P = 0.001
```

TABLE 18.11   Golf Ball Durability Test Results   DS GolfBall

Brand				Kruskal–Wallis Test				
Alpha	Best	Century	Divot	Median	n	Avg. Rank		13.834 H
281	270	218	364	251.00	5	6.80	Alpha	3 d.f.
220	334	244	302	307.00	5	13.40	Best	.0031 p-value
274	307	225	325	244.00	5	4.80	Century	
242	290	273	337	337.00	5	17.00	Divot	
251	331	249	355	277.50	20		Total	

METHODS AND APPLICATIONS

In each of Exercises 18.23 through 18.26, use the given independent samples to perform the Kruskal–Wallis H test of the null hypothesis H_0 that the corresponding populations are identical versus the alternative hypothesis H_a that at least two populations differ in location. Note that we analyzed each of these data sets using the one-way ANOVA F-test in the exercises of Chapter 12.

18.23   Use the Kruskal–Wallis H test to compare display panels A, B, and C using the data in Table 18.8. Use $\alpha = .05$.   DS Display3

18.24   Use the Kruskal–Wallis H test to compare bottle designs A, B, and C using the data in Table 18.9. Use $\alpha = .01$.   DS BottleDes

18.25   Use the Kruskal–Wallis H test and the MINITAB output in Figure 18.5 to compare the bottom (B), middle (M), and top (T) display heights using the data in Table 18.10. Use $\alpha = .05$. Then, repeat the analysis if the first sales value for the middle display height is found to be incorrect and must be removed from the data set.   DS BakeSale

18.26   Use the Kruskal–Wallis H test to compare golf ball brands Alpha, Best, Century, and Divot using the data in Table 18.11. Use $\alpha = .01$ and the Excel add-in (MegaStat) output on the right side of Table 18.11.   DS GolfBall

LO18-5 Measure and test the association between two variables by using Spearman's rank correlation coefficient.

18.5 Spearman's Rank Correlation Coefficient ● ● ●

In Section 14.6 (page 521) we showed how to test the significance of a population correlation coefficient. This test is based on the assumption that the population of all possible combinations of values of x and y has a bivariate normal probability distribution. If we fear that this assumption

TABLE 18.12   **Electronics World Sales Volume Data and Ranks for 15 Stores**
                   Ⓓⓢ Electronics

Store	Number of Households, x	Sales Volume, y	x-Rank	y-Rank	Difference, d	d^2
1	161	157.27	6	7	−1	1
2	99	93.28	1	1	0	0
3	135	136.81	5	5	0	0
4	120	123.79	4	3	1	1
5	164	153.51	7	6	1	1
6	221	241.74	13	14	−1	1
7	179	201.54	8	10	−2	4
8	204	206.71	9	11	−2	4
9	214	229.78	12	13	−1	1
10	101	135.22	2	4	−2	4
11	231	224.71	14	12	2	4
12	206	195.29	11	8	3	9
13	248	242.16	15	15	0	0
14	107	115.21	3	2	1	1
15	205	197.82	10	9	1	1

$\Sigma d_i^2 = 32$

is badly violated, we can use a nonparametric approach. One such approach is **Spearman's rank correlation coefficient,** which is denoted r_s.

To illustrate, suppose that Electronics World, a chain of stores that sells audio and video equipment, has gathered the data in Table 18.12. The company wishes to study the relationship between store sales volume in July of last year (y, measured in thousands of dollars) and the number of households in the store's area (x, measured in thousands). Spearman's rank correlation coefficient is found by first ranking the values of x and y separately (ties are treated by averaging the tied ranks). To calculate r_s, we use the formula given in Section 14.5 (page 520) for r and replace the x and y values in that formula by their ranks. If there are no ties in the ranks, this formula can be calculated by the simple equation

$$r_s = 1 - \frac{6\Sigma d_i^2}{n(n^2 - 1)}$$

where d_i is the difference between the x-rank and the y-rank for the ith observation (if there are few ties in the ranks, this formula is approximately valid). For example, Table 18.12 gives the ranks of x and y, the difference between the ranks, and the squared difference for each of the $n = 15$ stores in the Electronics World example. Because the sum of the squared differences is 32, we calculate r_s to be

$$r_s = 1 - \frac{6(32)}{15(225 - 1)} = .9429$$

Equivalently, if we have MINITAB (1) find the ranks of the x (household) values (which we call the *HRanks*) and the ranks of the y (sales) values (which we call the *SRanks*) and (2) use the formula given in Section 14.5 (page 520) for r to calculate the correlation coefficient between the *HRanks* and *SRanks,* we obtain the following output:

```
Pearson correlation of HRank and SRank = 0.943
```

This large positive value of r_s says that there is a strong positive rank correlation between the numbers of households and sales volumes in the sample.

In general, let ρ_s denote the **population rank correlation coefficient**—the rank correlation coefficient for the population of all possible (x, y) values. We can test the significance of ρ_s by using **Spearman's rank correlation test.**

Spearman's Rank Correlation Test

et r_s denote Spearman's rank correlation coefficient. Then, we can test H_0: $\rho_s = 0$ versus a particular alternative hypothesis at level of significance α by using the appropriate critical value rule.

Alternative Hypothesis	Critical Value Rule: Reject H_0 if
H_a: $\rho_s > 0$	$r_s > r_\alpha$
H_a: $\rho_s < 0$	$r_s < -r_\alpha$
H_a: $\rho_s \neq 0$	$\lvert r_s \rvert > r_{\alpha/2}$

Table A.17 (page 805) gives the critical values r_α, $-r_\alpha$, and $r_{\alpha/2}$ for sample sizes from 5 to 30. Note that for this test to be valid the number of ties encountered in ranking the observations should be small relative to the number of observations.

A portion of Table A.17 is reproduced here as Table 18.13. To illustrate using this table, suppose in the Electronics World example that we wish to test H_0: $\rho_s = 0$ versus H_a: $\rho_s > 0$ by setting $\alpha = .05$. Because there are $n = 15$ stores, Table 18.13 tells us that we use the critical value $r_{.05} = .441$. Because $r_s = .9429$ is greater than this critical value, we can reject H_0: $\rho_s = 0$ in favor of H_a: $\rho_s > 0$ by setting $\alpha = .05$. Therefore, we have strong evidence that in July of last year the sales volume of an Electronics World store was positively correlated with the number of households in the store's area.

To illustrate testing a two-sided alternative hypothesis, consider Table 18.14. This table presents the rankings of $n = 12$ midsize cars given by two automobile magazines. Here each magazine has ranked the cars from 1 (best) to 12 (worst) on the basis of overall ride. Because the two magazines sometimes have differing views, we cannot theorize about whether their rankings would be positively or negatively correlated. Therefore, we will test H_0: $\rho_s = 0$ versus H_a: $\rho_s \neq 0$. The summary box tells us that to perform this test at level of significance α, we use the critical value $r_{\alpha/2}$. To look up $r_{\alpha/2}$ in Table A.17 (or Table 18.13), we replace the table column head α by $\alpha/2$. For example, consider setting $\alpha = .05$. Then, because $\alpha/2 = .025$, we look in Table 18.13 for the value .025. Because there are $n = 12$ cars, we find that $r_{.025} = .591$. Spearman's rank correlation coefficient for the car ranking data can be calculated to be .8951. Because $r_s = .8951$ is greater than $r_{.025} = .591$, we reject H_0 at the .05 level of significance. Therefore, we conclude that the midsize car ride rankings given by the two magazines are correlated. Furthermore, because $r_s = .8951$, we estimate that these rankings are positively correlated.

To conclude this section, we make two comments. First, the car ranking example illustrates that Spearman's rank correlation coefficient and test can be used when the raw measurements of the x and/or y variables are themselves **ranks.** Ranks are measurements of an ordinal variable,

TABLE 18.13	Critical Values for Spearman's Rank Correlation Coefficient		
n	$\alpha = .05$	$\alpha = .025$	$\alpha = .01$	$\alpha = .005$
10	.564	.648	.745	.794
11	.523	.623	.736	.818
12	.497	.591	.703	.780
13	.475	.566	.673	.745
14	.457	.545	.646	.716
15	.441	.525	.623	.689
16	.425	.507	.601	.666
17	.412	.490	.582	.645
18	.399	.476	.564	.625
19	.388	.462	.549	.608
20	.377	.450	.534	.591

TABLE 18.14	Rankings of 12 Midsize Cars by Two Automobile Magazines
	DS CarRank

Car	Magazine 1 Ranking	Magazine 2 Ranking
1	5	7
2	1	1
3	4	5
4	7	4
5	6	6
6	8	10
7	9	8
8	12	11
9	2	3
10	3	2
11	10	12
12	11	9

and Spearman's nonparametric approach applies to ordinal variables. Second, it can be shown that if the sample size n is at least 10, then we can carry out an approximation to Spearman's rank correlation test by replacing r_s by the t statistic

$$t = \frac{r_s\sqrt{n-2}}{\sqrt{1-r_s^2}}$$

and by replacing the critical values r_α, $-r_\alpha$, and $r_{\alpha/2}$ by the t points t_α, $-t_\alpha$, and $t_{\alpha/2}$ (with $n-2$ degrees of freedom). Because Table A.17 (page 805) gives r_α points for sample sizes up to $n = 30$, this approximate procedure is particularly useful if the sample size exceeds 30. In this case, we can use the z points z_α, $-z_\alpha$, and $z_{\alpha/2}$ in place of the corresponding t points.

Exercises for Section 18.5

CONCEPTS

18.27 Explain the circumstances in which we use Spearman's rank correlation coefficient.

18.28 Write the formula that we use to compute Spearman's rank correlation coefficient when
  a There are no (or few) ties in the ranks of the x and y values.
  b There are many ties in the ranks of the x and y values.

METHODS AND APPLICATIONS

18.29 A sales manager ranks 10 people at the end of their training on the basis of their sales potential. A year later, the number of units sold by each person is determined. The following data and Excel add-in (MegaStat) output are obtained. Note that the manager's ranking of 1 is "best."
  DS SalesRank

Person	1	2	3	4	5	6	7	8	9	10
Manager's Ranking, x	7	4	2	6	1	10	3	5	9	8
Units Sold, y	770	630	820	580	720	440	690	810	560	470

	MgrRank, x	UnitSold, y
MgrRank, x	1.000	
UnitSold, y	−.721	1.000

$\pm.632$ critical value .05 (two-tail)
$\pm.765$ critical value .01 (two-tail)

10 sample size

  a Find r_s on the Excel add-in (MegaStat) output and use Table 18.13 to find the critical value for testing H_0: $\rho_s = 0$ versus H_a: $\rho_s \neq 0$ at the .05 level of significance. Do we reject H_0?
  b The MegaStat output gives approximate critical values for $\alpha = .05$ and $\alpha = .01$. Do these approximate critical values, which are based on the t distribution, differ by much from the exact critical values in Table 18.13 (recall that $n = 10$)?

18.30 Use the following MINITAB output to find r_s, and then test H_0: $\rho_s = 0$ versus H_a: $\rho_s > 0$ for the service time data below. **DS** CopyServ

Copiers Serviced, x	4	2	5	7	1	3	4	5	2	4	6
Minutes Required, y	109	58	138	189	37	82	103	134	68	112	154

Pearson correlation of CRank and MRank = 0.986

18.31 Compute r_s and test H_0: $\rho_s = 0$ versus H_a: $\rho_s > 0$ for the direct labor cost data below. **DS** DirLab

Batch Size, x	5	62	35	12	83	14	46	52	23	100	41	75
Direct Labor Cost, y	71	663	381	138	861	145	493	548	251	1,024	435	772

Chapter Summary

The validity of many of the inference procedures presented in this book requires that various assumptions be met. Often, for instance, a normality assumption is required. In this chapter we have learned that, when the needed assumptions are not met, we must employ a **nonparametric method.** Such a method does not require any assumptions about the shape(s) of the distribution(s) of the sampled population(s).

We first presented the **sign test,** which is a hypothesis test about a population median. This test is useful when we have taken a sample from a population that may not be normally distributed. We next presented two nonparametric tests for comparing the locations of two populations. The first such test, the **Wilcoxon rank sum test,** is appropriate when an **independent samples experiment** has been carried out. The second, the **Wilcoxon signed** ranks test, is appropriate when a **paired difference experiment** has been carried out. Both of these tests can be used without assuming that the sampled populations have the shapes of any particular probability distributions. We then discussed the **Kruskal–Wallis *H* test,** which is a nonparametric test for comparing the locations of several populations by using independent samples. This test, which employs the Chi-square distribution, can be used when the assumptions for one-way analysis of variance do not hold. Finally, we presented a nonparametric approach for testing the significance of a population correlation coefficient. Here we saw how to compute **Spearman's rank correlation coefficient,** and we discussed how to use this quantity to test the significance of the population correlation coefficient.

Glossary of Terms

Kruskal–Wallis *H* test: A nonparametric test for comparing the locations of three or more populations by using independent random samples. (page 748)

nonparametric test: A hypothesis test that requires no assumptions about the distribution(s) of the sampled population(s). (page 734)

sign test: A hypothesis test about a population median that requires no assumptions about the sampled population. (page 734)

Spearman's rank correlation coefficient: A correlation coefficient computed using the ranks of the observed values of two variables *x* and *y*. (page 751)

Wilcoxon rank sum test: A nonparametric test for comparing the locations of two populations when an independent samples experiment has been carried out. (page 739)

Wilcoxon signed ranks test: A nonparametric test for comparing the locations of two populations when a paired difference experiment has been carried out. (page 744)

Important Formulas and Tests

Sign test for a population median: page 736

Large sample sign test: page 736

Wilcoxon rank sum test: page 739

Wilcoxon rank sum test (large sample approximation): pages 741–742

Wilcoxon signed ranks test: page 744

Wilcoxon signed ranks test (large sample approximation): page 746

Kruskal–Wallis *H* test: page 748

Kruskal–Wallis *H* statistic: page 748

Spearman's rank correlation coefficient: page 751

Spearman's rank correlation test: page 752

Supplementary Exercises

connect

18.32 Again consider the price comparison situation in which weekly expenses were compared at two chains—Miller's and Albert's. Recall that independent random samples at the two chains yielded the following weekly expenses: **DS** ShopExp

Miller's

$119.25	$121.32	$122.34	$120.14	$122.19
$123.71	$121.72	$122.42	$123.63	$122.44

Albert's

$111.99	$114.88	$115.11	$117.02	$116.89
$116.62	$115.38	$114.40	$113.91	$111.87

Because the sample sizes are small, there might be reason to doubt that the populations of expenses at the two chains are normally distributed. Therefore, use a Wilcoxon rank sum test to determine whether expenses at Miller's and at Albert's differ. Use $\alpha = .05$.

18.33 A drug company wishes to compare the effects of three different drugs (*X*, *Y*, and *Z*) that are being developed to reduce cholesterol levels. Each drug is administered to six patients at the recommended dosage for six months. At the end of this period the reduction in cholesterol level is recorded for each patient. The results are given in Table 18.15. Assuming that the three samples are independent, use a nonparametric test to see whether the effects of the three drugs differ. Use $\alpha = .05$. **DS** CholRed

18.34 Table 18.16 gives the median 2009 and 2010 prices for used homes (in thousands of dollars) for six randomly selected U.S. housing markets. Use a nonparametric test to attempt to show that housing prices decreased from 2009 to 2010. Use $\alpha = .05$ and explain your conclusion. **DS** HomePrice

TABLE 18.15	Reduction of Cholesterol Levels Using Three Drugs DS CholRed		
	Drug		
X	**Y**		**Z**
22	40		15
31	35		9
19	47		14
27	41		11
25	39		21
18	33		5

TABLE 18.16	2009 and 2010 Median Prices for Used Homes (in Thousands of Dollars) for Six Randomly Selected Housing Markets DS HomePrice	
Housing Market	**2009 Median Price**	**2010 Median Price**
1	$243	$234
2	115	112
3	200	190
4	154	153
5	380	372
6	190	169

TABLE 18.17 Average Account Ages in 2010 and 2011 for 10 Randomly Selected Accounts DS AcctAge

Account	Average Age of Account in 2010 (Days)	Average Age of Account in 2011 (Days)
1	35	27
2	24	19
3	47	40
4	28	30
5	41	33
6	33	25
7	35	31
8	51	29
9	18	15
10	28	21

18.35 During 2011 a company implemented a number of policies aimed at reducing the ages of its customers' accounts. In order to assess the effectiveness of these measures, the company randomly selects 10 customer accounts. The average age of each account is determined for each of the years 2010 and 2011. These data are given in Table 18.17. Use a nonparametric technique to attempt to show that average account ages have decreased from 2010 to 2011. Use $\alpha = .05$. DS AcctAge

18.36 The following data concern the divorce rate (y) per 1,000 women and the percentage of the female population in the labor force (x): DS Divorce

Year	1890	1900	1910	1920	1930	1940	1950	1960	1970
Divorce Rate, y	3.0	4.1	4.7	8.0	7.5	8.8	10.3	9.2	14.9
% of Females in Labor Force, $x*$	18.9	20.6	25.4	23.7	24.8	27.4	31.4	34.8	42.6

*15 years old and over 1890–1930; 14 and over 1940–1960; 16 and over thereafter.
Source: U.S. Department of Commerce, Bureau of the Census, *Bicentennial Statistics,* Washington, D.C., 1976.

Use a nonparametric technique to attempt to show that x and y are positively correlated. Use $\alpha = .05$.

18.37 A loan officer wishes to compare the interest rates being charged for 48-month fixed-rate auto loans and 48-month variable-rate auto loans. Two independent, random samples of auto loan rates are selected. A sample of eight *48-month fixed-rate* auto loans had the following loan rates: DS AutoLoan

4.29%   3.75%   3.50%   3.99%   3.75%   3.99%   5.40%   4.00%

while a sample of five *48-month variable-rate* auto loans had loan rates as follows:

3.59%   2.75%   2.99%   2.50%   3.00%

Perform a nonparametric test to determine whether loan rates for 48-month fixed-rate auto loans differ from loan rates for 48-month variable-rate auto loans. Use $\alpha = .05$. Explain your conclusion.

18.38   A large bank wishes to limit the median debt-to-equity ratio for its portfolio of commercial loans to 1.5. The bank randomly selects 15 of its commercial loan accounts. Audits result in the following debt-to-equity ratios: **DS** DebtEq

1.31	1.05	1.45	1.21	1.19
1.78	1.37	1.41	1.22	1.11
1.46	1.33	1.29	1.32	1.65

Can it be concluded that the median debt-to-equity ratio is less than 1.5 at the .05 level of significance? Explain.

18.39   **Internet Exercise**   **DS** LaborFrc

Did labor force participation rates (LFPR) for women increase between 1968 and 1972? The Data and Story Library (DASL) contains LFPR figures for 1968 and 1972, for each of 19 cities. Go to the DASL website (http://lib.stat.cmu.edu/DASL/) and retrieve the Women in the Labor Force data set (http://lib.stat.cmu.edu/DASL/Datafiles/LaborForce.html). Produce appropriate graphical (histogram, stem-and-leaf, box plot) and numerical summaries of the LFPR data and conduct the following nonparametric statistical analyses (data sets: LaborFrc.xlsx, LaborFrc.mtw):

a   Do the data provide sufficient evidence to conclude that the LFPR for women *increased* between 1968 and 1972? Conduct a nonparametric, two-sample,

independent samples Wilcoxon rank sum test at the 0.01 level of significance. Clearly state the hypotheses and your conclusion. Report the *p*-value for your test.

b   Consider, as an alternative to the foregoing independent sample analysis, a paired sample procedure, the nonparametric Wilcoxon signed ranks test. Test once more the hypothesis of part *a*, this time using the Wilcoxon signed ranks test applied to the differences in LFPRs [1972−1968]. Again, clearly state your conclusion and *p*-value.

c   Between the two tests of parts *a* and *b*, which is the more appropriate for the current data situation? Why?

Appendix 18.1 ■ Nonparametric Methods Using MegaStat

Sign test for the median in Figure 18.1(d) on page 735 (data file: CompDisc.xlsx):

- Enter the compact disc data from Figure 18.1(a) on page 735 into column A with the label LifeTime in cell A1.

- Select **Add-Ins : MegaStat : Nonparametric Tests : Sign Test.**

- In the Sign Test dialog box, use the AutoExpand feature to enter the range A1: A21 into the "Input range" window.

- Enter the hypothesized median (here equal to 6000) into the "Hypothesized value" window.

- Select the desired alternative (in this case "greater than") from the drop-down menu in the Alternative box.

- Click OK in the Sign Test dialog box.

Wilcoxon (also known as Mann–Whitney) rank sum test for independent samples in Exercise 18.12 on page 743 (data file: Catalyst.xlsx):

- Enter the catalyst comparison data in Exercise 18.12 on page 743 as follows. Enter the data for Catalyst XA-100 into column A with label XA-100 in cell A1, and enter the data for Catalyst ZB-200 into column B with label ZB-200 in cell B1.

- Select **Add-Ins : MegaStat : Nonparametric Tests : Wilcoxon–Mann/Whitney Test.**

- In the "Wilcoxon–Mann/Whitney Test" dialog box, click in the Group 1 window to make it active and use the AutoExpand feature to enter the range A1:A6 into the Group 1 window.

- Click in the Group 2 window to make it active, and use the AutoExpand feature to enter the range B1:B6 into the Group 2 window.

- Select the desired alternative (in this case "not equal") from the drop-down menu in the Alternative box.

- Place a checkmark in the "Correct for ties" checkbox.

- Click OK in the "Wilcoxon–Mann/Whitney Test" dialog box.

Wilcoxon signed ranks test for paired differences in Table 18.6 on page 748 (data file: AdStudy.xlsx):

- Enter the advertising study data in Table 18.6 as follows. Enter the preexposure scores in column A with label PreAttitude, and enter the postexposure scores in column B with label PostAttitude.

- Select **Add-Ins : MegaStat : Nonparametric Tests : Wilcoxon Signed-Rank Test.**

- In the "Wilcoxon Signed Ranks Test" dialog box, click in the Group 1 window to make it active, and use the AutoExpand feature to enter the range A1:A11 into the Group 1 window.

- Click in the Group 2 window to make it active, and use the AutoExpand feature to enter the range B1:B11 into the Group 2 window.

- Select the desired alternative (in this case "not equal") from the drop-down menu in the Alternative box.

- Place a checkmark in the "Correct for ties" checkbox.

- Click OK in the "Wilcoxon Signed Ranks Test" dialog box.

Kruskal–Wallis *H* test for comparing several populations in Table 18.11 on page 750 (data file: GolfBall.xlsx):

- Enter the golf ball durability data in Table 18.11 into columns A, B, C, and D as shown in the screen with labels Alpha, Best, Century, and Divot.

- Select **Add-Ins : MegaStat : Nonparametric Tests : Kruskal Wallis Test.**

- In the "Kruskal–Wallis Test" dialog box, enter (by dragging with the mouse) the range A1:D6 into the "Input range" window. Each column in the selected range will be considered by MegaStat to be a group to be compared to the other groups.

- Place a checkmark in the "Correct for ties" checkbox.

- Click OK in the "Kruskal–Wallis Test" dialog box.

Spearman's rank correlation coefficient in Exercise 18.29 on page 753 (data file: SalesRank.xlsx):

- Enter the sales data in Exercise 18.29 into columns A and B. Enter the manager's rankings into column A with label "MgrRank, x" in cell A1, and enter the units sold into column B with label "UnitsSold, y" in cell B1.

- Select **Add-Ins : MegaStat : Nonparametric Tests : Spearman Coefficient of Rank Correlation.**

- In the "Spearman Coefficient of Rank Correlation" dialog box, enter (by dragging with the mouse) the range A1:B11 into the "Input range" window. Here, each column in the selected range will be considered by MegaStat to be a separate variable.

- Place a checkmark in the "Correct for ties" checkbox.

- Click OK in the "Spearman Coefficient of Rank Correlation" dialog box.

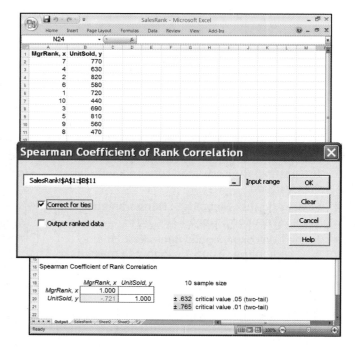

Appendix 18.2 ■ Nonparametric Methods Using MINITAB

Sign test for the median in Figure 18.1(c) on page 735 (data file: CompDisc.MTW):

- Enter the compact disc data from Figure 18.1(a) on page 735 into column C1 with variable name LifeTime.

- Select **Stat : Nonparametrics : 1-Sample Sign.**

- In the 1-Sample Sign dialog box, enter LifeTime into the Variables window.

- Select "Test median," and enter the number 6000 into the Test median window.

- Click on the "Alternative" arrow button, and select "greater than" from the pull-down menu.

- Click OK in the 1-Sample Sign dialog box to obtain the sign test results in the Session window.

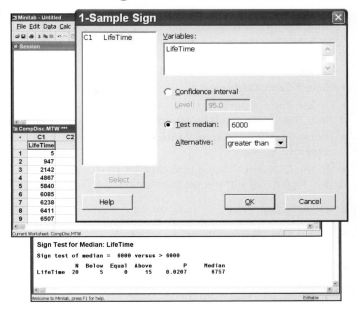

Wilcoxon (also known as Mann–Whitney) rank sum test for two independent samples in Figure 18.2(b) on page 740 (data file: Court.MTW):

- Enter the litigation data from Figure 18.2(a) on page 740 into two columns—Coos County data in column C1 with variable name Coos and Lane County data in column C2 with variable name Lane.

- Select **Stat : Nonparametrics : Mann–Whitney.**

- In the Mann–Whitney dialog box, enter Coos into the First Sample window and enter Lane into the Second Sample window.

- Type 95 in the Confidence level window.

- Click on the "Alternative" arrow button and select "less than" from the pull-down menu.

- Click OK in the Mann–Whitney dialog box to obtain test results in the Session window.

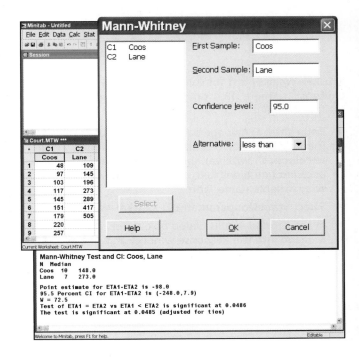

Wilcoxon signed ranks test for paired differences in Figure 18.3(b) on page 745 (data file: Repair.MTW):

- Enter the garage repair data from Figure 18.3(a) on page 745 into two columns—garage 1 cost estimates in column C1 with variable name Garage1 and garage 2 cost estimates in column C2 with variable name Garage2.

- Select **Calc : Calculator.**

- In the Calculator dialog box, enter G1 − G2 into the "Store result in variable" window.

- Enter Garage1 − Garage2 into the Expression window.

- In the Calculator dialog box, click OK to store the repair cost differences in column G1 − G2.

- Select **Stat : Nonparametrics : 1-Sample Wilcoxon.**

- In the 1-Sample Wilcoxon dialog box, enter 'G1 − G2' into the Variables window by selecting G1 − G2 from the variables list.

- In the 1-Sample Wilcoxon dialog box, select "Test median" and enter the number 0.0 into the Test median window.

- Click on the "Alternative" arrow button, and select "less than" from the pull-down menu.

- Click OK in the 1-Sample Wilcoxon dialog box to obtain the test results in the Session window.

Kruskal–Wallis *H* test for comparing several populations in Figure 18.4 on page 749 (data file: GasMile2.MTW):

- Enter the gas mileage data from Table 18.7 (page 749) into two columns—gas mileages in column C1 with variable name Mileage and gasoline type (A, B, or C) in column C2 with variable name Type.

- Select **Stat : Nonparametrics : Kruskal–Wallis.**

- In the Kruskal–Wallis dialog box, enter Mileage into the Response window and enter Type into the Factor window.

- Click OK in the Kruskal–Wallis dialog box to obtain test results in the Session window.

Spearman's rank correlation coefficient in Section 18.5 on page 751 (data file: Electronics.MTW):

- Enter the electronics sales data from Table 18.12 (page 751) into two columns—number of households in column C1 with variable name Households and sales volumes in column C2 with variable name Sales.

- Select **Data : Rank.**

- In the Rank dialog box, enter Households into the "Rank data in" window and enter HRank into the "Store ranks in" window.

- Click OK in the Rank dialog box to obtain column C3 with variable name HRank containing ranks for the Households observations.

- Select **Data : Rank.**

- In the Rank dialog box, enter Sales into the "Rank data in" window and enter SRank into the "Store ranks in" window.

- Click OK in the Rank dialog box to obtain column C4 with variable name SRank containing ranks for the Sales observations.

- Select **Stat : Basic Statistics : Correlation.**

- In the Correlation dialog box, enter HRank and SRank into the Variables window.

- Click on "Display *p*-values" to uncheck this option (or leave it checked, if desired).

- Click OK in the Correlation dialog box to obtain the rank correlation coefficient in the Session window.

CHAPTER 19

Decision Theory

Learning Objectives

After mastering the material in this chapter, you will be able to:

LO19-1 Make decisions under uncertainty and under risk and assess the value of perfect information.

LO19-2 Make decisions using posterior analysis and assess the value of sample information.

LO19-3 Make decisions using utility theory.

Chapter Outline

Every day businesses and the people who run them face a myriad of decisions. For instance, a manufacturer might need to decide where to locate a new factory and might also need to decide how large the new facility should be. Or, an investor might decide where to invest money from among several possible investment choices. In this chapter we study some probabilistic methods that can help a decision maker to make intelligent decisions. In Section 19.1 we introduce **decision theory.** We discuss the elements of a decision problem, and we present strategies for making decisions when we face various levels of uncertainty.

We also show how to construct a **decision tree,** which is a diagram that can help us analyze a decision problem, and we show how the concept of **expected value** can help us make decisions. In Section 19.2 we show how to use **sample information** to help make decisions, and we demonstrate how to assess the worth of sample information in order to decide whether the sample information should be obtained. We conclude this chapter with Section 19.3, which introduces using **utility theory** to help make decisions.

Many of this chapter's concepts are presented in the context of:

(C)

The Oil Company Case: An oil company uses decision theory to help decide whether to drill for oil on a particular site. The company can perform a seismic experiment at the site to obtain information about the site's potential, and

the company uses decision theory to decide whether to drill based on the various possible survey results. In addition, decision theory is employed to determine whether the seismic experiment should be carried out.

19.1 Introduction to Decision Theory ● ● ●

LO19-1 Make decisions under uncertainty and under risk and assess the value of perfect information.

Suppose that a real estate developer is proposing the development of a condominium complex on an exclusive parcel of lakefront property. The developer wishes to choose between three possible options—building a large complex, building a medium-sized complex, and building a small complex. The profitability of each option depends on the level of demand for condominium units after the complex has been built. For simplicity, the developer considers only two possible levels of demand—high or low; the developer must choose whether to build a large, medium, or small complex based on her beliefs about whether demand for condominium units will be high or low.

The real estate developer's situation requires a decision. **Decision theory** is a general approach that helps decision makers make intelligent choices. A decision theory problem typically involves the following elements:

1 **States of nature:** a set of potential future conditions that affects the results of the decision. For instance, the level of demand (high or low) for condominium units will affect profits after the developer chooses to build a large, medium, or small complex. Thus, we have two states of nature—high demand and low demand.

2 **Alternatives:** several alternative actions for the decision maker to choose from. For example, the real estate developer can choose between building a large, medium, or small condominium complex. Therefore, the developer has three alternatives—large, medium, and small.

3 **Payoffs:** a payoff for each alternative under each potential state of nature. The payoffs are often summarized in a **payoff table.** For instance, Table 19.1 gives a payoff table for the condominium complex situation. This table gives the profit[1] for each alternative under the different states of nature. For example, the payoff table tells us that, if the developer builds

---

TABLE 19.1 **A Payoff Table for the Condominium Complex Situation** (DS) Condo

Alternatives	States of Nature	
	Low Demand	High Demand
Small complex	$8 million	$8 million
Medium complex	$5 million	$15 million
Large complex	−$11 million	$22 million

---

[1]Here profits are really present values representing current dollar values of expected future income minus costs.

a large complex and if demand for units turns out to be high, a profit of $22 million will be realized. However, if the developer builds a large complex and if demand for units turns out to be low, a loss of $11 million will be suffered.

Once the states of nature have been identified, the alternatives have been listed, and the payoffs have been determined, we evaluate the alternatives by using a **decision criterion.** How this is done depends on the **degree of uncertainty** associated with the states of nature. Here we consider three possibilities:

1 **Certainty:** we know for certain which state of nature will actually occur.
2 **Uncertainty:** we have no information about the likelihoods of the various states of nature.
3 **Risk:** the likelihood (probability) of each state of nature can be estimated.

Decision making under certainty In the unlikely event that we know for certain which state of nature will actually occur, we simply choose the alternative that gives the best payoff for that state of nature. For instance, in the condominium complex situation, if we know that demand for units will be high, then the payoff table (see Table 19.1) tells us that the best alternative is to build a large complex and that this choice will yield a profit of $22 million. On the other hand, if we know that demand for units will be low, then the payoff table tells us that the best alternative is to build a small complex and that this choice will yield a profit of $8 million.

Of course, we rarely (if ever) know for certain which state of nature will actually occur. However, analyzing the payoff table in this way often provides insight into the nature of the problem. For instance, examining the payoff table tells us that, if we know that demand for units will be low, then building either a small complex or a medium complex will be far superior to building a large complex (which would yield an $11 million loss).

Decision making under uncertainty This is the exact opposite of certainty. Here we have no information about how likely the different states of nature are. That is, we have no idea how to assign probabilities to the different states of nature.

In such a case, several approaches are possible; we will discuss two commonly used methods. The first is called the **maximin criterion.**

Maximin: Find the worst possible payoff for each alternative, and then choose the alternative that yields the maximum worst possible payoff.

For instance, to apply the maximin criterion to the condominium complex situation, we proceed as follows (see Table 19.1):

1 If a small complex is built, the worst possible payoff is $8 million.
2 If a medium complex is built, the worst possible payoff is $5 million.
3 If a large complex is built, the worst possible payoff is −$11 million.

Because the maximum of these worst possible payoffs is $8 million, the developer should choose to build a small complex.

The maximin criterion is a *pessimistic approach* because it considers the worst possible payoff for each alternative. When an alternative is chosen using the maximin criterion, the actual payoff obtained may be higher than the maximum worst possible payoff. However, using the maximin criterion assures a "guaranteed minimum" payoff.

A second approach is called the **maximax criterion.**

Maximax: Find the best possible payoff for each alternative, and then choose the alternative that yields the maximum best possible payoff.

To apply the maximax criterion to the condominium complex situation, we proceed as follows (see Table 19.1):

1 If a small complex is built, the best possible payoff is $8 million.
2 If a medium complex is built, the best possible payoff is $15 million.
3 If a large complex is built, the best possible payoff is $22 million.

Because the maximum of these best possible payoffs is $22 million, the developer should choose to build a large complex.

The maximax criterion is an *optimistic approach* because we always choose the alternative that yields the highest possible payoff. This is a "go for broke" strategy, and the actual payoff obtained may be far less than the highest possible payoff. For example, in the condominium complex situation, if a large complex is built and demand for units turns out to be low, an $11 million loss will be suffered (instead of a $22 million profit).

Decision making under risk   In this case we can estimate the probability of occurrence for each state of nature. Thus, we have a situation in which we have more information about the states of nature than in the case of uncertainty and less information than in the case of certainty. Here a commonly used approach is to use the **expected monetary value criterion.** This involves computing the expected monetary payoff for each alternative and choosing the alternative with the largest expected payoff.

The expected value criterion can be employed by using *prior probabilities.* As an example, suppose that in the condominium complex situation the developer assigns prior probabilities of .7 and .3 to high and low demands, respectively, as shown in the **decision tree diagram** of Figure 19.1. We find the expected monetary value for each alternative by multiplying the probability of occurrence for each state of nature by the payoff associated with the state of nature and by summing these products. Referring to the payoff table in Table 19.1, the expected monetary values are as follows:

Small complex: Expected value = .3($8 million) + .7($8 million) = $8 million

Medium complex: Expected value = .3($5 million) + .7($15 million) = $12 million

Large complex: Expected value = .3(−$11 million) + .7($22 million) = $12.1 million

Choosing the alternative with the highest expected monetary value, the developer would choose to build a large complex.

Remember that the expected payoff is not necessarily equal to the actual payoff that will be realized. Rather, the expected payoff is the long-run average payoff that would be realized if many identical decisions were made. For instance, the expected monetary payoff of $12.1 million for a large complex is the average payoff that would be obtained if many large condominium complexes were built. Thus, the expected monetary value criterion is best used when many similar decisions will be made.

FIGURE 19.1   A Decision Tree for the Condominium Complex Situation

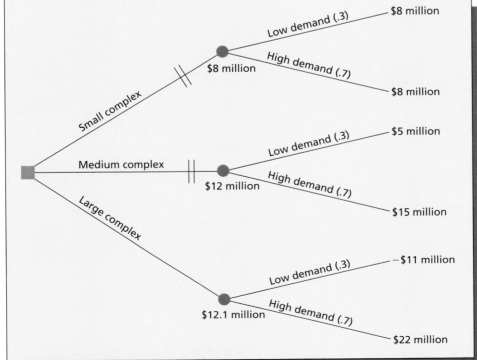

Using a decision tree   It is often convenient to depict the alternatives, states of nature, payoffs, and probabilities (in the case of risk) in the form of a **decision tree** or **tree diagram.** The diagram is made up of **nodes** and **branches.** We use square nodes to denote decision points and circular nodes to denote chance events. The branches emanating from a decision point represent alternatives, and the branches emanating from a circular node represent the possible states of nature. As we have seen, Figure 19.1 presents a decision tree for the condominium complex situation (in the case of risk as described previously). Notice that the payoffs are shown at the rightmost end of each branch and that the probabilities associated with the various states of nature are given in parentheses corresponding to each branch emanating from a chance node. The expected monetary values for the alternatives are shown below the chance nodes. The double slashes placed through the small complex and medium complex branches indicate that these alternatives would not be chosen (because of their lower expected payoffs) and that the large complex alternative would be selected.

A decision tree is particularly useful when a problem involves a sequence of decisions. For instance, in the condominium complex situation, if demand turns out to be low, it might be possible to improve payoffs by selling the condominiums at lower prices. Figure 19.2 shows a decision tree in which, after a decision to build a small, medium, or large condominium complex is made, the developer can choose to either keep the same prices or charge lower prices for condominium units. In order to analyze the decision tree, we start with the last (rightmost) decision to be made. For each decision we choose the alternative that gives the highest payoff. For instance, if the developer builds a large complex and demand turns out to be low, the developer should lower prices (as indicated by the double slash through the alternative of same prices). If decisions are followed by chance events, we choose the alternative that gives the highest expected monetary value. For example, again looking at Figure 19.2, we see that a medium complex should now be built because of its highest expected monetary value ($14.1 million). This is indicated by the double slashes drawn through the small and large complex alternatives. Looking at the entire decision tree in Figure 19.2, we see that the developer should build a medium complex and should sell condominium units at lower prices if demand turns out to be low.

FIGURE 19.2   A Decision Tree with Sequential Decisions

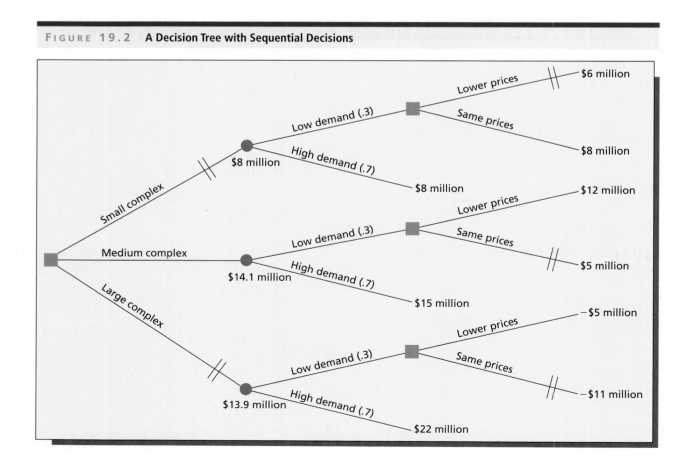

Sometimes it is possible to determine exactly which state of nature will occur in the future. For example, in the condominium complex situation, the level of demand for units might depend on whether a new resort casino is built in the area. While the developer may have prior probabilities concerning whether the casino will be built, it might be feasible to postpone a decision about the size of the condominium complex until a final decision about the resort casino has been made.

If we can find out exactly which state of nature will occur, we say we have obtained **perfect information.** There is usually a cost involved in obtaining this information (if it can be obtained at all). For instance, we might have to acquire an option on the lakefront property on which the condominium complex is to be built in order to postpone a decision about the size of the complex. Or perfect information might be acquired by conducting some sort of research that must be paid for. A question that arises here is whether it is worth the cost to obtain perfect information. We can answer this question by computing the **expected value of perfect information,** which we denote as the **EVPI.** The EVPI is defined as follows:

> EVPI = expected payoff under certainty − expected payoff under risk

For instance, if we consider the condominium complex situation depicted in the decision tree of Figure 19.1 on page 764, we found that the expected payoff under risk is $12.1 million (which is the expected payoff associated with building a large complex). To find the expected payoff under certainty, we find the highest payoff under each state of nature. Referring to Table 19.1, we see that if demand is low, the highest payoff is $8 million (when we build a small complex); we see that if demand is high, the highest payoff is $22 million (when we build a large complex). Because the prior probabilities of high and low demand are, respectively, .7 and .3, the expected payoff under certainty is .7($22 million) + .3($8 million) = $17.8 million. Therefore, the expected value of perfect information is $17.8 million − $12.1 million = $5.7 million. This is the maximum amount of money that the developer should be willing to pay to obtain perfect information. That is, the land option should be purchased if it costs $5.7 million or less. Then, if the casino is not built (and demand is low), a small condominium complex should be built; if the casino is built (and demand is high), a large condominium complex should be built. On the other hand, if the land option costs more than $5.7 million, the developer should choose the alternative having the highest expected payoff (which would mean building a large complex—see Figure 19.1).

Finally, another approach to dealing with risk involves assigning what we call **utilities** to monetary values. These utilities reflect the decision maker's attitude toward risk: that is, does the decision maker avoid risk or is he or she a risk taker? Here the decision maker chooses the alternative that **maximizes expected utility.** We will introduce this approach in Section 19.3.

Exercises for Section 19.1

CONCEPTS

connect

19.1 Explain the differences between (a) decision making under certainty, (b) decision making under uncertainty, and (c) decision making under risk.

19.2 Explain how to use the (a) maximin criterion, (b) maximax criterion, and (c) expected monetary value criterion.

19.3 Explain how to find the expected value of perfect information.

METHODS AND APPLICATIONS

Exercises 19.4 through 19.9 refer to an example in the book *Production/Operations Management* by William J. Stevenson. The example involves a capacity-planning problem in which a company must choose to build a small, medium, or large production facility. The payoff obtained will depend on whether future demand is low, moderate, or high, and the payoffs are as given in the following table: **DS** CapPlan

Alternatives	Possible Future Demand		
	Low	Moderate	High
Small facility	$10*	$10	$10
Medium facility	7	12	12
Large facility	−4	2	16

*Present value in $ millions.

Source: W. J. Stevenson, *Production/Operations Management,* 5th ed. (Burr Ridge, IL: Richard D. Irwin, 1996), p. 73.

19.4   Find the best alternative (and the resulting payoff) in the given payoff table if it is known with certainty that demand will be

    a Low.   **b** Medium.   **c** High.   **DS** CapPlan

19.5   Given the payoff table, find the alternative that would be chosen using the maximin criterion.
    DS CapPlan

19.6   Given the payoff table, find the alternative that would be chosen using the maximax criterion.
    DS CapPlan

19.7   Suppose that the company assigns prior probabilities of .3, .5, and .2 to low, moderate, and high demands, respectively.   **DS** CapPlan

    a   Find the expected monetary value for each alternative (small, medium, and large).

    b   What is the best alternative if we use the expected monetary value criterion?

19.8   Construct a decision tree for the information in the payoff table assuming that the prior probabilities of low, moderate, and high demands are, respectively, .3, .5, and .2.   **DS** CapPlan

FIGURE 19.3   **Decision Tree for Exercise 19.13**

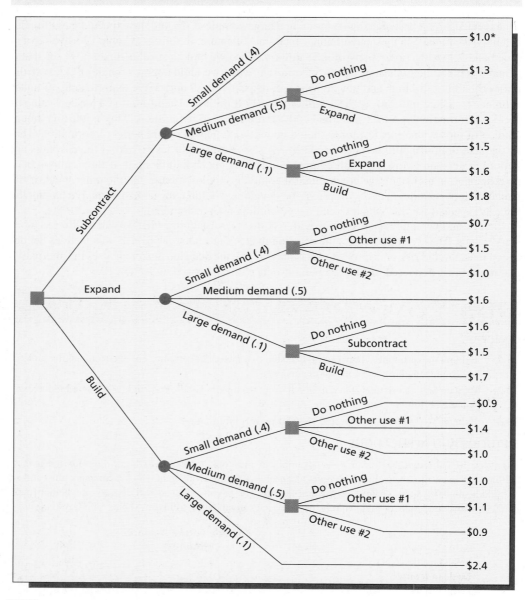

*Net present value in millions.

19.9   For the information in the payoff table find
  a   The expected payoff under certainty.
  b   The expected value of perfect information, EVPI.   ⑤ CapPlan

19.10   A firm wishes to choose the location for a new factory. Profits obtained will depend on whether a new railroad spur is constructed to serve the town in which the new factory will be located. The following payoff table summarizes the relevant information: ⑤ FactLoc

Alternatives	New Railroad Spur Built	No New Railroad Spur
Location *A*	$1*	$14
Location *B*	2	10
Location *C*	4	6

*Profits in $ millions.

Determine the location that should be chosen if the firm uses
  a   The maximin criterion.
  b   The maximax criterion.

19.11   Refer to the information given in Exercise 19.10. Using the probabilities of .60 for a new railroad spur and .40 for no new railroad spur   ⑤ FactLoc
  a   Compute the expected monetary value for each location.
  b   Find the location that should be selected using the expected monetary value criterion.
  c   Compute the EVPI, expected value of perfect information.

19.12   Construct a decision tree for the information given in Exercises 19.10 and 19.11.   ⑤ FactLoc

19.13   Figure 19.3 on the previous page gives a decision tree presented in the book *Production/ Operations Management* by William J. Stevenson. Use this tree diagram to do the following:
  a   Find the expected monetary value for each of the alternatives (subcontract, expand, and build).
  b   Determine the alternative that should be selected in order to maximize the expected monetary value.

19.2 Decision Making Using Posterior Probabilities ● ● ●

LO19-2 Make decisions using posterior analysis and assess the value of sample information.

We have seen that the *expected monetary value criterion* tells us to choose the alternative having the highest expected payoff. In Section 19.1 we computed expected payoffs by using *prior probabilities.* When we use the expected monetary value criterion to choose the best alternative based on expected values computed using prior probabilities, we call this **prior decision analysis.** Often, however, sample information can be obtained to help us make decisions. In such a case, we compute expected values by using *posterior probabilities,* and we call the analysis **posterior decision analysis.** In the following example we demonstrate how to carry out posterior analysis.

EXAMPLE 19.1 The Oil Company Case: Deciding Whether to Drill for Oil

Recall from Example 4.14 (pages 177–178) that an oil company wishes to decide whether to drill for oil on a particular site, and recall that the company has assigned prior probabilities .7, .2, and .1 to the states of nature $S_1 \equiv$ no oil, $S_2 \equiv$ some oil, and $S_3 \equiv$ much oil, respectively. Figure 19.4 on the next page gives a decision tree and payoff table for a *prior analysis* of the oil drilling situation. Here, using the prior probabilities, the expected monetary value associated with drilling is

$$.7(-\$700{,}000) + .2(\$500{,}000) + .1(\$2{,}000{,}000) = -\$190{,}000$$

while the expected monetary value associated with not drilling is

$$.7(0) + .2(0) + .1(0) = 0$$

Therefore, *prior analysis* tells us that the oil company should not drill.

   Next, remember that the oil company can obtain more information about the drilling site by performing a seismic experiment with three possible readings—low, medium, and high. The accuracy of the seismic experiment is expressed by the conditional probabilities in part (a) of Figure 19.5 on page 771. For instance, as explained in Example 4.14, $P(\text{high}\,|\,\text{none}) = .04$, $P(\text{high}\,|\,\text{some}) = .02$, and $P(\text{high}\,|\,\text{much}) = .96$. Also, recall that we can revise the prior

FIGURE 19.4　A Decision Tree and Payoff Table for a Prior Analysis of the Oil Company Case

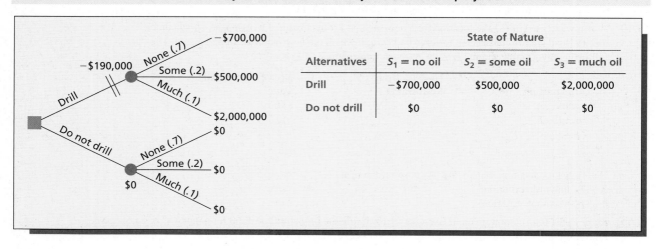

	State of Nature		
Alternatives	$S_1 \equiv$ no oil	$S_2 \equiv$ some oil	$S_3 \equiv$ much oil
Drill	−$700,000	$500,000	$2,000,000
Do not drill	$0	$0	$0

probabilities $P(\text{none}) = .7$, $P(\text{some}) = .2$, and $P(\text{much}) = .1$ to posterior probabilities by using Bayes' Theorem. For example, in Example 4.14 we calculated

$$P(\text{high}) = P(\text{none} \cap \text{high}) + P(\text{some} \cap \text{high}) + P(\text{much} \cap \text{high})$$
$$= P(\text{none})P(\text{high} \mid \text{none}) + P(\text{some})P(\text{high} \mid \text{some}) + P(\text{much})P(\text{high} \mid \text{much})$$
$$= (.7)(.04) + (.2)(.02) + (.1)(.96) = .128$$

Then Bayes' theorem says that

$$P(\text{none} \mid \text{high}) = \frac{P(\text{none} \cap \text{high})}{P(\text{high})} = \frac{P(\text{none})P(\text{high} \mid \text{none})}{P(\text{high})} = \frac{.7(.04)}{.128} = .21875$$

Similarly, we can compute $P(\text{some} \mid \text{high})$ and $P(\text{much} \mid \text{high})$ as follows.

$$P(\text{some} \mid \text{high}) = \frac{P(\text{some} \cap \text{high})}{P(\text{high})} = \frac{P(\text{some})P(\text{high} \mid \text{some})}{P(\text{high})} = \frac{.2(.02)}{.128} = .03125$$

$$P(\text{much} \mid \text{high}) = \frac{P(\text{much} \cap \text{high})}{P(\text{high})} = \frac{P(\text{much})P(\text{high} \mid \text{much})}{P(\text{high})} = \frac{.1(.96)}{.128} = .75$$

These calculations are summarized in the **probability revision table** in Figure 19.5(b). This table also shows that

$$P(\text{high}) = P(\text{none} \cap \text{high}) + P(\text{some} \cap \text{high}) + P(\text{much} \cap \text{high})$$
$$= .028 + .004 + .096 = .128$$

Part (c) of Figure 19.5 gives a probability revision table for calculating the probability of a medium reading and the posterior probabilities of no oil, some oil, and much oil given a medium reading, while part (d) of Figure 19.5 gives a probability revision table for calculating the probability of a low reading and the posterior probabilities of no oil, some oil, and much oil given a low reading. We find that $P(\text{medium}) = .226$ and that $P(\text{low}) = .646$.

Figure 19.6 on page 772 presents a decision tree for a *posterior analysis* of the oil drilling problem. The leftmost decision node represents the decision of whether to conduct the seismic experiment. The upper branch (no seismic survey) contains a second decision node representing the alternatives in our decision problem (that is, drill or do not drill). At the ends of the "drill" and "do not drill" branches, we have chance nodes that branch into the three states of nature—no oil (none), some oil (some), and much oil (much). The appropriate payoff is placed at the rightmost end of each branch, and because this uppermost branch corresponds to "no seismic survey," the probabilities in parentheses for the states of nature are the prior probabilities. The expected payoff associated with drilling (which we found to be −$190,000) is shown at the chance node for the "drill" branch, and the expected payoff associated with not drilling (which we found to be $0) is shown at the chance node for the "do not drill" branch.

FIGURE 19.5   A Tree Diagram and Probability Revision Tables for Bayes' Theorem in the Oil Company Case

(a) A tree diagram illustrating the prior and conditional probabilities

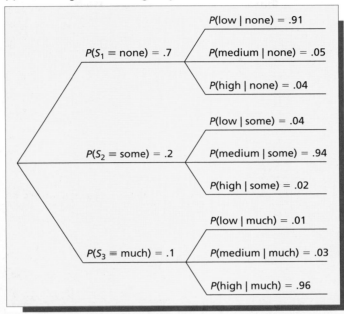

(b) A probability revision table for calculating the probability of a high reading and the posterior probabilities of no oil (S_1), some oil (S_2), and much oil (S_3) given a high reading

S_j	$P(S_j)$	$P(\text{high} \mid S_j)$	$P(S_j \cap \text{high}) = P(S_j)P(\text{high} \mid S_j)$	$P(S_j \mid \text{high}) = P(S_j \cap \text{high})/P(\text{high})$
$S_1 \equiv$ none	$P(\text{none}) = .7$	$P(\text{high} \mid \text{none}) = .04$	$P(\text{none} \cap \text{high}) = .7(.04) = .028$	$P(\text{none} \mid \text{high}) = .028/.128 = .21875$
$S_2 \equiv$ some	$P(\text{some}) = .2$	$P(\text{high} \mid \text{some}) = .02$	$P(\text{some} \cap \text{high}) = .2(.02) = .004$	$P(\text{some} \mid \text{high}) = .004/.128 = .03125$
$S_3 \equiv$ much	$P(\text{much}) = .1$	$P(\text{high} \mid \text{much}) = .96$	$P(\text{much} \cap \text{high}) = .1(.96) = .096$	$P(\text{much} \mid \text{high}) = .096/.128 = .75$
Total	1		$P(\text{high}) = .028 + .004 + .096 = .128$	1

(c) A probability revision table for calculating the probability of a medium reading and the posterior probabilities of no oil (S_1), some oil (S_2), and much oil (S_3) given a medium reading

S_j	$P(S_j)$	$P(\text{medium} \mid S_j)$	$P(S_j \cap \text{medium}) = P(S_j)P(\text{medium} \mid S_j)$	$P(S_j \mid \text{medium}) = P(S_j \cap \text{medium})/P(\text{medium})$
$S_1 \equiv$ none	$P(\text{none}) = .7$	$P(\text{medium} \mid \text{none}) = .05$	$P(\text{none} \cap \text{medium}) = .7(.05) = .035$	$P(\text{none} \mid \text{medium}) = .035/.226 = .15487$
$S_2 \equiv$ some	$P(\text{some}) = .2$	$P(\text{medium} \mid \text{some}) = .94$	$P(\text{some} \cap \text{medium}) = .2(.94) = .188$	$P(\text{some} \mid \text{medium}) = .188/.226 = .83186$
$S_3 \equiv$ much	$P(\text{much}) = .1$	$P(\text{medium} \mid \text{much}) = .03$	$P(\text{much} \cap \text{medium}) = .1(.03) = .003$	$P(\text{much} \mid \text{medium}) = .003/.226 = .01327$
Total	1		$P(\text{medium}) = .035 + .188 + .003 = .226$	1

(d) A probability revision table for calculating the probability of a low reading and the posterior probabilities of no oil (S_1), some oil (S_2) and much oil (S_3) given a low reading

S_j	$P(S_j)$	$P(\text{low} \mid S_j)$	$P(S_j \cap \text{low}) = P(S_j)P(\text{low} \mid S_j)$	$P(S_j \mid \text{low}) = P(S_j \cap \text{low})/P(\text{low})$
$S_1 \equiv$ none	$P(\text{none}) = .7$	$P(\text{low} \mid \text{none}) = .91$	$P(\text{none} \cap \text{low}) = .7(.91) = .637$	$P(\text{none} \mid \text{low}) = .637/.646 = .98607$
$S_2 \equiv$ some	$P(\text{some}) = .2$	$P(\text{low} \mid \text{some}) = .04$	$P(\text{some} \cap \text{low}) = .2(.04) = .008$	$P(\text{some} \mid \text{low}) = .008/.646 = .01238$
$S_3 \equiv$ much	$P(\text{much}) = .1$	$P(\text{low} \mid \text{much}) = .01$	$P(\text{much} \cap \text{low}) = .1(.01) = .001$	$P(\text{much} \mid \text{low}) = .001/.646 = .00155$
Total	1		$P(\text{low}) = .637 + .008 + .001 = .646$	1

The lower branch of the decision tree (seismic survey) has an extra chance node that branches into the three possible outcomes of the seismic experiment—low, medium, and high. The probabilities of these outcomes are shown on their respective branches. From the low, medium, and high branches, the tree branches into alternatives (drill and do not drill) and from alternatives into states of nature (none, some, and much). However, the probabilities in parentheses written beside the none, some, and much branches are the posterior probabilities that we computed in the probability revision tables in Figure 19.5. This is because advancing

FIGURE 19.6   A Decision Tree for a Posterior Analysis of the Oil Company Case

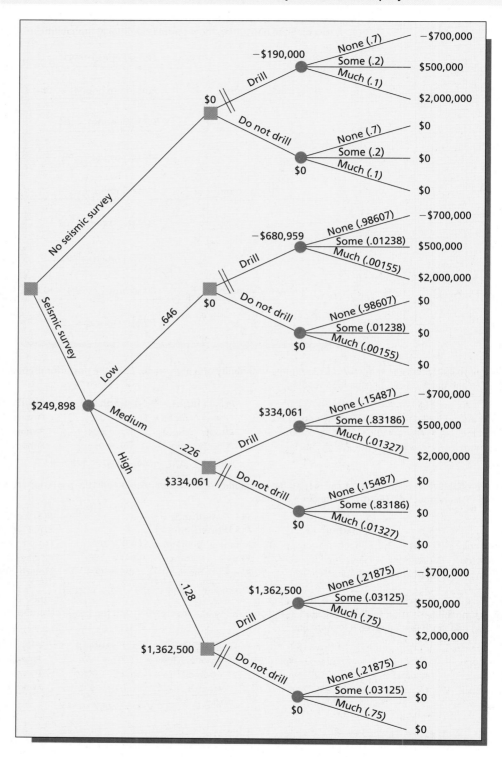

to the end of a particular branch in the lower part of the decision tree is conditional; that is, it depends on obtaining a particular experimental result (low, medium, or high).

We can now use the decision tree to determine the alternative (drill or do not drill) that should be selected given that the seismic experiment has been performed and has resulted in a particular outcome. First, suppose that the seismic experiment results in a high reading. Looking at the branch of the decision tree corresponding to a high reading, the expected monetary values associated with the "drill" and "do not drill" alternatives are

Drill: $.21875(-\$700,000) + .03125(\$500,000) + .75(\$2,000,000) = \$1,362,500$

Do not drill: $.21875(0) + .03125(0) + .75(0) = \$0$

These expected monetary values are placed on the decision tree corresponding to the "drill" and "do not drill" alternatives. They tell us that, if the seismic experiment results in a high reading, then the company should drill and the expected payoff will be $1,362,500. The double slash placed through the "do not drill" branch (at the very bottom of the decision tree) blocks off that branch and indicates that the company should drill if a high reading is obtained.

Next, suppose that the seismic experiment results in a medium reading. Looking at the branch corresponding to a medium reading, the expected monetary values are

Drill: $.15487(-\$700,000) + .83186(\$500,000) + .01327(\$2,000,000) = \$334,061$

Do not drill: $.15487(\$0) + .83186(\$0) + .01327(\$0) = \$0$

Therefore, if the seismic experiment results in a medium reading, the oil company should drill, and the expected payoff will be $334,061.

Finally, suppose that the seismic experiment results in a low reading. Looking at the branch corresponding to a low reading, the expected monetary values are

Drill: $.98607(-\$700,000) + .01238(\$500,000) + .00155(\$2,000,000) = -\$680,959$

Do not drill: $.98607(\$0) + .01238(\$0) + .00155(\$0) = \$0$

Therefore, if the seismic experiment results in a low reading, the oil company should not drill on the site.

We can summarize the results of our posterior analysis as follows:

Outcome of Seismic Experiment	Probability of Outcome	Decision	Expected Payoff
High	.128	Drill	$1,362,500
Medium	.226	Drill	$334,061
Low	.646	Do not drill	$0

If we carry out the seismic experiment, we now know what action should be taken for each possible outcome (low, medium, or high). However, there is a cost involved when we conduct the seismic experiment. If, for instance, it costs $100,000 to perform the seismic experiment, we need to investigate whether it is worth it to perform the experiment. This will depend on the expected worth of the information provided by the experiment. Naturally, we must decide whether the experiment is worth it *before* our posterior analysis is actually done. Therefore, when we assess the worth of the sample information, we say that we are performing a **preposterior analysis.**

In order to assess the worth of the sample information, we compute the **expected payoff of sampling.** To calculate this result, we find the expected payoff and the probability of each sample outcome (that is, at each possible outcome of the seismic experiment). Looking at the decision tree in Figure 19.6, we find the following:

Experimental Outcome	Expected Payoff	Probability
Low	$0	.646
Medium	$334,061	.226
High	$1,362,500	.128

Therefore, the **expected payoff of sampling,** which is denoted **EPS,** is

$$\text{EPS} = .646(\$0) + .226(\$334,061) + .128(\$1,362,500) = \$249,898$$

To find the worth of the sample information, we compare the expected payoff of sampling to the **expected payoff of no sampling,** which is denoted **EPNS.** The EPNS is the expected payoff of the alternative that we would choose by using the expected monetary value criterion with the prior probabilities. Recalling that we summarized our prior analysis in the tree diagram of Figure 19.4, we found that (based on the prior probabilities) we should choose not to drill and that the expected payoff of this action is $0. Therefore, EPNS = $0.

We compare the EPS and the EPNS by computing the **expected value of sample information,** which is denoted **EVSI** and is defined to be the expected payoff of sampling minus the expected payoff of no sampling. Therefore,

$$\text{EVSI} = \text{EPS} - \text{EPNS} = \$249,898 - \$0 = \$249,898$$

The EVSI is the expected gain from conducting the seismic experiment, and the oil company should pay no more than this amount to carry out the seismic experiment. If the experiment costs $100,000, then it is worth the expense to conduct the experiment. Moreover, the difference between the EVSI and the cost of sampling is called the **expected net gain of sampling,** which is denoted **ENGS.** Here

$$\text{ENGS} = \text{EVSI} - \$100,000 = \$249,898 - \$100,000 = \$149,898$$

As long as the ENGS is greater than $0, it is worthwhile to carry out the seismic experiment. That is, the oil company should carry out the seismic experiment before it chooses whether or not to drill. Then, as discussed earlier, our posterior analysis says that if the experiment gives a medium or high reading, the oil company should drill, and if the experiment gives a low reading, the oil company should not drill.

Exercises for Section 19.2

CONCEPTS

connect

19.14 Explain what is meant by each of the following and describe the purpose of each:
a Prior analysis.   b Posterior analysis.   c Preposterior analysis.

19.15 Define and interpret each of the following:
a Expected payoff of sampling, EPS.   c Expected value of sample information, EVSI.
b Expected payoff of no sampling, EPNS.   d Expected net gain of sampling, ENGS.

METHODS AND APPLICATIONS

Exercises 19.16 through 19.21 refer to the following situation.

In the book *Making Hard Decisions: An Introduction to Decision Analysis* (2nd ed.), Robert T. Clemen presents an example in which an investor wishes to choose between investing money in (1) a high-risk stock, (2) a low-risk stock, or (3) a savings account. The payoffs received from the two stocks will depend on the behavior of the stock market—that is, whether the market goes up, stays the same, or goes down over the investment period. In addition, in order to obtain more information about the market behavior that might be anticipated during the investment period, the investor can hire an economist as a consultant who will predict the future market behavior. The results of the consultation will be one of the following three possibilities: (1) "economist says up," (2) "economist says flat" (the same), or (3) "economist says down." The conditional probabilities that express the ability of the economist to accurately forecast market behavior are given in the following table: DS InvDec

Economist's Prediction	True Market State		
	Up	Flat	Down
"Economist says up"	.80	.15	.20
"Economist says flat"	.10	.70	.20
"Economist says down"	.10	.15	.60

For instance, using this table we see that $P(\text{"economist says up"} \mid \text{market up}) = .80$. Figure 19.7 gives an incomplete decision tree for the investor's situation. Notice that this decision tree gives all relevant payoffs and also gives the prior probabilities of up, flat, and down, which are, respectively, 0.5, 0.3, and 0.2. Using the information provided here, and any needed information on the decision tree of Figure 19.7, do the following:

FIGURE 19.7   **An Incomplete Decision Tree for the Investor's Decision Problem of Exercises 19.16 through 19.21**

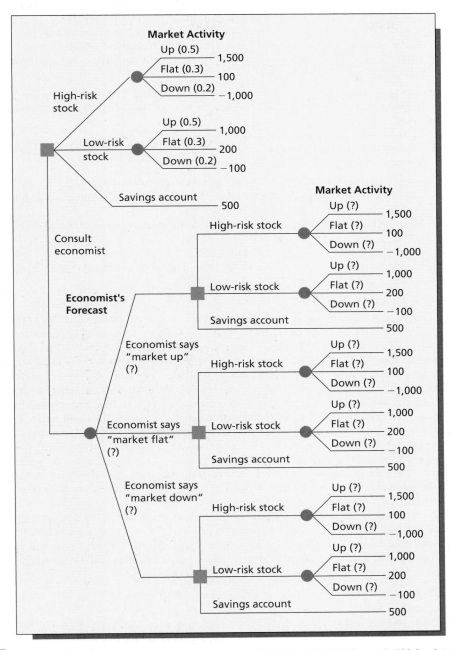

Source: From *Making Hard Decisions: An Introduction to Decision Analysis,* 2nd ed., by R. T. Clemen, © 1996. Reprinted with permission of Brooks/Cole, an imprint of the Wadsworth Group, a division of Thomson Learning. Fax 800-730-2215. P. 443

19.16   Identify and list each of the following for the investor's decision problem: ⊃Ⓢ InvDec
    a The investor's alternative actions.
    b The states of nature.
    c The possible results of sampling (that is, of information gathering).

19.17   Write out the payoff table for the investor's decision problem.   ⊃Ⓢ InvDec

19.18   Carry out a prior analysis of the investor's decision problem. That is, determine the invest-
    ment choice that should be made and find the expected monetary value of that choice
    assuming that the investor does not consult the economist about future stock market
    behavior.   ⊃Ⓢ InvDec

19.19   Set up probability revision tables to   🔵 InvDec
   a   Find the probability that the "economist says up" and find the posterior probabilities of market up, market flat, and market down given that the "economist says up."
   b   Find the probability that the "economist says flat," and find the posterior probabilities of market up, market flat, and market down given that the "economist says flat."
   c   Find the probability that the "economist says down," and find the posterior probabilities of market up, market flat, and market down given that the "economist says down."
   d   Reproduce the decision tree of Figure 19.7 and insert the probabilities you found in parts *a*, *b*, and *c* in their appropriate locations.

19.20   Carry out a posterior analysis of the investor's decision problem. That is, determine the investment choice that should be made and find the expected monetary value of that choice assuming   🔵 InvDec
   a   The economist says "market up."
   b   The economist says "market flat."
   c   The economist says "market down."

19.21   Carry out a preposterior analysis of the investor's decision problem by finding   🔵 InvDec
   a   The expected monetary value associated with consulting the economist; that is, find the EPS.
   b   The expected monetary value associated with not consulting the economist; that is, find the EPNS.
   c   The expected value of sample information, EVSI.
   d   The maximum amount the investor should be willing to pay for the economist's consulting advice.

Exercises 19.22 through 19.28 refer to the following situation.

A firm designs and manufactures automatic electronic control devices that are installed at customers' plant sites. The control devices are shipped by truck to customers' sites; while in transit, the devices sometimes get out of alignment. More specifically, a device has a prior probability of .10 of getting out of alignment during shipment. When a control device is delivered to the customer's plant site, the customer can install the device. If the customer installs the device, and if the device is in alignment, the manufacturer of the control device will realize a profit of $15,000. If the customer installs the device, and if the device is out of alignment, the manufacturer must dismantle, realign, and reinstall the device for the customer. This procedure costs $3,000, and therefore the manufacturer will realize a profit of $12,000. As an alternative to customer installation, the manufacturer can send two engineers to the customer's plant site to check the alignment of the control device, to realign the device if necessary before installation, and to supervise the installation. Because it is less costly to realign the device before it is installed, sending the engineers costs $500. Therefore, if the engineers are sent to assist with the installation, the manufacturer realizes a profit of $14,500 (this is true whether or not the engineers must realign the device at the site).

Before a control device is installed, a piece of test equipment can be used by the customer to check the device's alignment. The test equipment has two readings, "in" or "out" of alignment. Given that the control device is in alignment, there is a .8 probability that the test equipment will read "in." Given that the control device is out of alignment, there is a .9 probability that the test equipment will read "out."

19.22   Identify and list each of the following for the control device situation:
   a   The firm's alternative actions.
   b   The states of nature.
   c   The possible results of sampling (that is, of information gathering).

19.23   Write out the payoff table for the control device situation.

19.24   Construct a decision tree for a prior analysis of the control device situation. Then determine whether the engineers should be sent, assuming that the piece of test equipment is not employed to check the device's alignment. Also find the expected monetary value associated with the best alternative action.

19.25   Set up probability revision tables to
   a   Find the probability that the test equipment "reads in," and find the posterior probabilities of in alignment and out of alignment given that the test equipment "reads in."
   b   Find the probability that the test equipment "reads out," and find the posterior probabilities of in alignment and out of alignment given that the test equipment "reads out."

19.26   Construct a decision tree for a posterior and preposterior analysis of the control device situation.

19.27   Carry out a posterior analysis of the control device problem. That is, decide whether the engineers should be sent, and find the expected monetary value associated with either sending or not sending (depending on which is best) the engineers assuming
  a The test equipment "reads in."
  b The test equipment "reads out."

19.28   Carry out a preposterior analysis of the control device problem by finding
  a The expected monetary value associated with using the test equipment; that is, find the EPS.
  b The expected monetary value associated with not using the test equipment; that is, find the EPNS.
  c The expected value of sample information, EVSI.
  d The maximum amount that should be paid for using the test equipment.

19.3 Introduction to Utility Theory ● ● ●

LO19-3 Make decisions using utility theory.

Suppose that a decision maker is trying to decide whether to invest in one of two opportunities—Investment 1 or Investment 2—or not to invest in either of these opportunities. As shown in Table 19.2(a), (b), and (c) on the next page, the expected profits associated with Investment 1, Investment 2, and no investment are $32,000, $28,000, and $0. Thus, if the decision maker uses expected profit as a decision criterion, and decides to choose no more than one investment, the decision maker should choose Investment 1. However, as discussed earlier, the expected profit for an investment is the long-run average profit that would be realized if many identical investments could be made. If the decision maker will make only a limited number of investments (perhaps because of limited capital), he or she will not realize the expected profit. For example, a single undertaking of Investment 1 will result in either a profit of $50,000, a profit of $10,000, or a loss of $20,000. Some decision makers might prefer a single undertaking of Investment 2, because the potential loss is only $10,000. Other decision makers might be unwilling to risk $10,000 and would choose no investment.

There is a way to combine the various profits, probabilities, and the decision maker's individual attitude toward risk to make a decision that is best for the decision maker. The method is based on a theory of utility discussed by J. Von Neumann and O. Morgenstern in *Theory of Games and Economic Behavior* (Princeton University Press, Princeton, N.J., 1st ed., 1944; 2nd ed., 1947). This theory says that if a decision maker agrees with certain assumptions about rational behavior (we will not discuss the assumptions here), then the decision maker should replace the profits in the various investments by **utilities** and choose the investment that gives the **highest expected utility.** To find the utility of a particular profit, we first arrange the profits from largest to smallest. The utility of the largest profit is 1 and the utility of the smallest profit is 0. The utility of any particular intermediate profit is the probability, call it u, such that the decision maker is **indifferent** between (1) getting the particular intermediate profit with certainty and (2) playing a lottery (or game) in which the probability is u of getting the highest profit and the probability is $1 - u$ of getting the smallest profit. Table 19.2(d) arranges the profits in Table 19.2(a), (b), and (c) in increasing order and gives a specific decision maker's utility for each profit. The utility of .95 for $40,000 means that the decision maker is indifferent between (1) getting $40,000 with certainty and (2) playing a lottery in which the probability is .95 of getting $50,000 and the probability is .05 of losing $20,000. The utilities for the other profits are interpreted similarly. Table 19.2(f), (g), and (h) show the investments with profits replaced by utilities. Because Investment 2 has the highest expected utility, the decision maker should choose Investment 2.

Table 19.2(e) shows a plot of the specific decision maker's utilities versus the profits. The curve connecting the plot points is the **utility curve** for the decision maker. This curve is an example of a **risk averter's curve.** In general, a risk averter's curve portrays a rapid increase in utility for initial amounts of money followed by a gradual leveling off for larger amounts of money. This curve is appropriate for many individuals or businesses because the marginal value of each additional dollar is not as great once a large amount of money has been earned. A risk averter's curve is shown on the page margin, as are a **risk seeker's curve** and a **risk neutral's curve.** The risk seeker's curve represents an individual who is willing to take large risks to have the opportunity to make large profits. The risk neutral curve represents an individual for whom each additional dollar has the same value. It can be shown that this individual should choose the investment having the highest expected profit.

A risk averter's curve:

Utility

Dollar amount

A risk seeker's curve:

Utility

Dollar amount

A risk neutral's curve:

Utility

Dollar amount

TABLE 19.2 Three Possible Investments and Their Expected Utilities

(a) Investment 1 Profits

Profit	Probability
$50,000	.7
$10,000	.1
−$20,000	.2

Expected profit = 50,000(.7) + 10,000(.1) + (−20,000)(.2) = 32,000

(b) Investment 2 Profits

Profit	Probability
$40,000	.6
$30,000	.2
−$10,000	.2

Expected profit = 40,000(.6) + 30,000(.2) + (−10,000)(.2) = 28,000

(c) No Investment Profit

Profit	Probability
$0	1

Expected profit = 0(1) = 0

(d) Utilities

Profit	Utility
$50,000	1.00
$40,000	.95
$30,000	.90
$10,000	.75
$0	.60
−$10,000	.45
−$20,000	0.00

(e) A Utility Curve

Utility

Profit (in units of $1,000)

(f) Investment 1 Utilities

Utility	Probability
1.00	.7
.75	.1
0.00	.2

Expected utility = 1(.7) + .75(.1) + 0(.2) = .775

(g) Investment 2 Utilities

Utility	Probability
.95	.6
.90	.2
.45	.2

Expected utility = .95(.6) + .90(.2) + .45(.2) = .84

(h) No Investment Utility

Utility	Probability
.60	1

Expected utility = .60(1) = .60

Exercises for Section 19.3

connect

CONCEPTS

19.29 What is a utility?

19.30 What is a risk averter? A risk seeker? A risk neutral?

METHODS AND APPLICATIONS

19.31 Suppose that a decision maker has the opportunity to invest in an oil well drilling operation that has a .3 chance of yielding a profit of $1,000,000, a .4 chance of yielding a profit of $400,000, and a .3 chance of yielding a profit of −$100,000. Also, suppose that the decision maker's utilities for $400,000 and $0 are .9 and .7. Explain the meanings of these utilities.

19.32 Consider Exercise 19.31. Find the expected utility of the oil well drilling operation. Find the expected utility of not investing. What should the decision maker do if he/she wishes to maximize expected utility?

Chapter Summary

In Section 19.1 we presented an introduction to decision theory. We saw that a decision problem involves **states of nature, alternatives, payoffs,** and **decision criteria,** and we considered three degrees of uncertainty—**certainty, uncertainty,** and **risk.** In the case of *certainty,* we know which state of nature will actually occur. Here we simply choose the alternative that gives the best payoff. In the case of *uncertainty,* we have no information about the likelihood of the different states of nature. Here we discussed two commonly used decision criteria—the **maximin criterion** and the **maximax criterion.** In the case of *risk,* we are able to estimate the probability of occurrence for each state of nature. In this case we learned how to use the **expected monetary value criterion.** We also learned how to construct a **decision tree** in

Section 19.1, and we saw how to use such a tree to analyze a decision problem. In Section 19.2 we learned how to make decisions by using posterior probabilities. We explained how to perform a **posterior analysis** to determine the best alternative for each of several sampling results. Then we showed how to carry out a **pre-posterior analysis,** which allows us to assess the worth of sample information. In particular, we saw how to obtain the **expected value of sample information.** This quantity is the expected gain from sampling, which tells us the maximum amount we should be willing to pay for sample information. We concluded this chapter with Section 19.3, which introduced using **utility theory** to help make decisions.

Glossary of Terms

alternatives: Several alternative actions for a decision maker to choose from. (page 763)

certainty: When we know for certain which state of nature will actually occur. (page 764)

decision criterion: A rule used to make a decision. (page 764)

decision theory: An approach that helps decision makers to make intelligent choices. (page 763)

decision tree: A diagram consisting of nodes and branches that depicts the information for a decision problem. (pages 765, 766)

expected monetary value criterion: A decision criterion in which one computes the expected monetary payoff for each alternative and then chooses the alternative yielding the largest expected payoff. (page 765)

expected net gain of sampling: The difference between the expected value of sample information and the cost of sampling. If this quantity is positive, it is worth it to perform sampling. (page 774)

expected value of perfect information: The difference between the expected payoff under certainty and the expected payoff under risk. (page 767)

expected value of sample information: The difference between the expected payoff of sampling and the expected payoff of no sampling. This measures the expected gain from sampling. (page 774)

maximax criterion: A decision criterion in which one finds the best possible payoff for each alternative and then chooses the alternative that yields the maximum best possible payoff. (page 764)

maximin criterion: A decision criterion in which one finds the worst possible payoff for each alternative and then chooses the alternative that yields the maximum worst possible payoff. (page 764)

payoff table: A tabular summary of the payoffs in a decision problem. (page 763)

perfect information: Information that tells us exactly which state of nature will occur. (page 767)

posterior decision analysis: Using a decision criterion based on posterior probabilities to choose the best alternative in a decision problem. (page 769)

preposterior analysis: When we assess the worth of sample information before performing a posterior decision analysis. (page 773)

prior decision analysis: Using a decision criterion based on prior probabilities to choose the best alternative in a decision problem. (page 769)

risk: When the likelihood (probability) of each state of nature can be estimated. (page 764)

states of nature: A set of potential future conditions that will affect the results of a decision. (page 763)

uncertainty: When we have no information about the likelihoods of the various states of nature. (page 764)

utility: A measure of monetary value based on an individual's attitude toward risk. (page 777)

Important Formulas

Maximin criterion: page 764

Maximax criterion: page 764

Expected monetary value criterion: page 765

Decision tree diagram: pages 765, 766

Expected value of perfect information: page 767

Probability revision table: page 770

Expected payoff of sampling: page 773

Expected payoff of no sampling: page 773

Expected value of sample information: page 774

Expected net gain of sampling: page 774

Expected utility: page 777

Supplementary Exercises

19.33 In the book *Making Hard Decisions: An Introduction to Decision Analysis,* Robert T. Clemen presents a decision tree for a research and development decision (note that payoffs are given in millions of dollars, which is denoted by M). Based on this decision tree (shown in Figure 19.8 on the next page), answer the following:

   a Should development of the research project be continued or stopped? Justify your answer by using relevant calculations, and explain your reasoning.

   b If development is continued and if a patent is awarded, should the new technology be licensed, or should the company develop production and marketing to sell the product directly? Justify your answer by using relevant calculations and explain your reasoning.

19.34 In the book *Production/Operations Management,* William J. Stevenson presents a decision tree concerning a firm's decision about the size of a production facility. This decision tree is given in Figure 19.9 on the next page (payoffs are given in millions of dollars). Use the decision tree to determine which alternative (build small or build large) should be chosen in order to maximize the expected monetary payoff. What is the expected monetary payoff associated with the best alternative?

FIGURE 19.8   A Decision Tree for a Research and Development Decision for Exercise 19.33

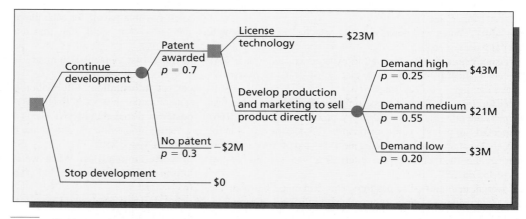

Source: A decision tree from R.T. Clemen, *Making Hard Decisions: An Introduction to Decision Analysis,* 2nd ed., p. 77, © 1996. Reprinted with permission of Brooks/Cole, a division of Thomson Learning. Fax 800-730-2215. P. 77

FIGURE 19.9   A Decision Tree for a Production Facility Decision for Exercises 19.34 and 19.35

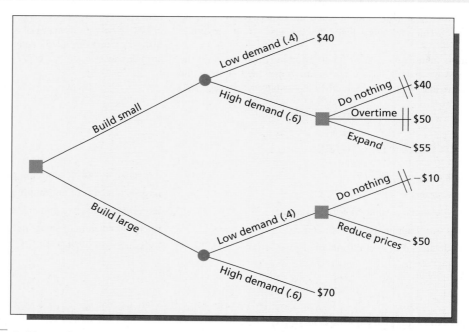

Source: Decision tree from W. J. Stevenson, *Production/Operations Management,* 6/e, p. 70, © 1999 McGraw-Hill Companies, Inc.

19.35 Consider the decision tree in Figure 19.9 and the situation described in Exercise 19.34. Suppose that a marketing research study can be done to obtain more information about whether demand will be high or low. The marketing research study will result in one of two outcomes: "favorable" (indicating that demand will be high) or "unfavorable" (indicating that demand will be low). The accuracy of marketing research studies like the one to be carried out can be expressed by the conditional probabilities in the following table:

Study Outcome	True Demand	
	High	Low
Favorable	.9	.2
Unfavorable	.1	.8

For instance, $P(\text{favorable} \mid \text{high}) = .9$ and $P(\text{unfavorable} \mid \text{low}) = .8$. Given the prior probabilities and payoffs in Figure 19.9, do the following:

a Carry out a posterior analysis. Find the best alternative (build small or build large) for each possible study result (favorable or unfavorable), and find the associated expected payoffs.

b Carry out a preposterior analysis. Determine the maximum amount that should be paid for the marketing research study.

19.36 THE OIL COMPANY CASE DS DrillTst

Again consider the oil company case that was described in Example 19.1. Recall that the oil company wishes to decide whether to drill and that the prior probabilities of no oil, some oil, and much oil are $P(\text{none}) = .7$, $P(\text{some}) = .2$, and $P(\text{much}) = .1$. Suppose that, instead of performing the seismic survey to obtain more information about the site, the oil company can perform a cheaper magnetic experiment having two possible results: a high reading and a low reading. The past performance of the magnetic experiment can be summarized as follows:

Magnetic Experiment Result	State of Nature		
	None	Some	Much
Low reading	.8	.4	.1
High reading	.2	.6	.9

Here, for example, $P(\text{low} \mid \text{none}) = .8$ and $P(\text{high} \mid \text{some}) = .6$. Recalling that the payoffs associated with no oil, some oil, and much oil are $-\$700,000$, $\$500,000$, and $\$2,000,000$, respectively, do the following:

a Draw a decision tree for this decision problem.

b Carry out a posterior analysis. Find the best alternative (drill or do not drill) for each possible result of the magnetic experiment (low or high), and find the associated expected payoffs.

c Carry out a preposterior analysis. Determine the maximum amount that should be paid for the magnetic experiment.

19.37 In an exercise in the book *Production/Operations Management*, 5th ed. (1996), William DS ThmPark
J. Stevenson considers a theme park whose lease is about to expire. The theme park's management wishes to decide whether to renew its lease for another 10 years or relocate near the site of a new motel complex. The town planning board is debating whether to approve the motel complex. A consultant estimates the payoffs of the theme park's alternatives under each state of nature as shown in the following payoff table:

Theme Park Options	Motel Approved	Motel Rejected
Renew lease	$500,000	$4,000,000
Relocate	$5,000,000	$100,000

a What alternative should the theme park choose if it uses the maximax criterion? What is the resulting payoff of this choice?

b What alternative should the theme park choose if it uses the maximin criterion? What is the resulting payoff of this choice?

19.38 Again consider the situation described in Exercise 19.37, and suppose that management believes there is a .35 probability that the motel complex will be approved.

a Draw a decision tree for the theme park's decision problem.

b Which alternative should be chosen if the theme park uses the maximum expected monetary value criterion? What is the expected monetary payoff for this choice?

c Suppose that management is offered the option of a temporary lease while the planning board decides whether to approve the motel complex. If the lease costs $100,000, should the theme park's management sign the lease? Justify your answer.

Appendix **A**

Statistical Tables

TABLE A.1   A Binomial Probability Table:
Binomial Probabilities (*n* between 2 and 6)

n = 2

$x\downarrow$	.05	.10	.15	.20	.25	.30	.35	.40	.45	.50	
0	.9025	.8100	.7225	.6400	.5625	.4900	.4225	.3600	.3025	.2500	2
1	.0950	.1800	.2550	.3200	.3750	.4200	.4550	.4800	.4950	.5000	1
2	.0025	.0100	.0225	.0400	.0625	.0900	.1225	.1600	.2025	.2500	0
	.95	.90	.85	.80	.75	.70	.65	.60	.55	.50	$x\uparrow$

n = 3

$x\downarrow$	.05	.10	.15	.20	.25	.30	.35	.40	.45	.50	
0	.8574	.7290	.6141	.5120	.4219	.3430	.2746	.2160	.1664	.1250	3
1	.1354	.2430	.3251	.3840	.4219	.4410	.4436	.4320	.4084	.3750	2
2	.0071	.0270	.0574	.0960	.1406	.1890	.2389	.2880	.3341	.3750	1
3	.0001	.0010	.0034	.0080	.0156	.0270	.0429	.0640	.0911	.1250	0
	.95	.90	.85	.80	.75	.70	.65	.60	.55	.50	$x\uparrow$

n = 4

$x\downarrow$	.05	.10	.15	.20	.25	.30	.35	.40	.45	.50	
0	.8145	.6561	.5220	.4096	.3164	.2401	.1785	.1296	.0915	.0625	4
1	.1715	.2916	.3685	.4096	.4219	.4116	.3845	.3456	.2995	.2500	3
2	.0135	.0486	.0975	.1536	.2109	.2646	.3105	.3456	.3675	.3750	2
3	.0005	.0036	.0115	.0256	.0469	.0756	.1115	.1536	.2005	.2500	1
4	.0000	.0001	.0005	.0016	.0039	.0081	.0150	.0256	.0410	.0625	0
	.95	.90	.85	.80	.75	.70	.65	.60	.55	.50	$x\uparrow$

n = 5

$x\downarrow$	.05	.10	.15	.20	.25	.30	.35	.40	.45	.50	
0	.7738	.5905	.4437	.3277	.2373	.1681	.1160	.0778	.0503	.0313	5
1	.2036	.3281	.3915	.4096	.3955	.3602	.3124	.2592	.2059	.1563	4
2	.0214	.0729	.1382	.2048	.2637	.3087	.3364	.3456	.3369	.3125	3
3	.0011	.0081	.0244	.0512	.0879	.1323	.1811	.2304	.2757	.3125	2
4	.0000	.0005	.0022	.0064	.0146	.0284	.0488	.0768	.1128	.1563	1
5	.0000	.0000	.0001	.0003	.0010	.0024	.0053	.0102	.0185	.0313	0
	.95	.90	.85	.80	.75	.70	.65	.60	.55	.50	$x\uparrow$

n = 6

$x\downarrow$	.05	.10	.15	.20	.25	.30	.35	.40	.45	.50	
0	.7351	.5314	.3771	.2621	.1780	.1176	.0754	.0467	.0277	.0156	6
1	.2321	.3543	.3993	.3932	.3560	.3025	.2437	.1866	.1359	.0938	5
2	.0305	.0984	.1762	.2458	.2966	.3241	.3280	.3110	.2780	.2344	4
3	.0021	.0146	.0415	.0819	.1318	.1852	.2355	.2765	.3032	.3125	3
4	.0001	.0012	.0055	.0154	.0330	.0595	.0951	.1382	.1861	.2344	2
5	.0000	.0001	.0004	.0015	.0044	.0102	.0205	.0369	.0609	.0938	1
6	.0000	.0000	.0000	.0001	.0002	.0007	.0018	.0041	.0083	.0156	0
	.95	.90	.85	.80	.75	.70	.65	.60	.55	.50	$x\uparrow$

(table continued)

TABLE A.1 (continued)
Binomial Probabilities (n between 7 and 10)

n = 7   p

x↓	.05	.10	.15	.20	.25	.30	.35	.40	.45	.50	
0	.6983	.4783	.3206	.2097	.1335	.0824	.0490	.0280	.0152	.0078	7
1	.2573	.3720	.3960	.3670	.3115	.2471	.1848	.1306	.0872	.0547	6
2	.0406	.1240	.2097	.2753	.3115	.3177	.2985	.2613	.2140	.1641	5
3	.0036	.0230	.0617	.1147	.1730	.2269	.2679	.2903	.2918	.2734	4
4	.0002	.0026	.0109	.0287	.0577	.0972	.1442	.1935	.2388	.2734	3
5	.0000	.0002	.0012	.0043	.0115	.0250	.0466	.0774	.1172	.1641	2
6	.0000	.0000	.0001	.0004	.0013	.0036	.0084	.0172	.0320	.0547	1
7	.0000	.0000	.0000	.0000	.0001	.0002	.0006	.0016	.0037	.0078	0
	.95	.90	.85	.80	.75	.70	.65	.60	.55	.50	x↑

n = 8   p

x↓	.05	.10	.15	.20	.25	.30	.35	.40	.45	.50	
0	.6634	.4305	.2725	.1678	.1001	.0576	.0319	.0168	.0084	.0039	8
1	.2793	.3826	.3847	.3355	.2670	.1977	.1373	.0896	.0548	.0313	7
2	.0515	.1488	.2376	.2936	.3115	.2965	.2587	.2090	.1569	.1094	6
3	.0054	.0331	.0839	.1468	.2076	.2541	.2786	.2787	.2568	.2188	5
4	.0004	.0046	.0185	.0459	.0865	.1361	.1875	.2322	.2627	.2734	4
5	.0000	.0004	.0026	.0092	.0231	.0467	.0808	.1239	.1719	.2188	3
6	.0000	.0000	.0002	.0011	.0038	.0100	.0217	.0413	.0703	.1094	2
7	.0000	.0000	.0000	.0001	.0004	.0012	.0033	.0079	.0164	.0313	1
8	.0000	.0000	.0000	.0000	.0000	.0001	.0002	.0007	.0017	.0039	0
	.95	.90	.85	.80	.75	.70	.65	.60	.55	.50	x↑

n = 9   p

x↓	.05	.10	.15	.20	.25	.30	.35	.40	.45	.50	
0	.6302	.3874	.2316	.1342	.0751	.0404	.0207	.0101	.0046	.0020	9
1	.2985	.3874	.3679	.3020	.2253	.1556	.1004	.0605	.0339	.0176	8
2	.0629	.1722	.2597	.3020	.3003	.2668	.2162	.1612	.1110	.0703	7
3	.0077	.0446	.1069	.1762	.2336	.2668	.2716	.2508	.2119	.1641	6
4	.0006	.0074	.0283	.0661	.1168	.1715	.2194	.2508	.2600	.2461	5
5	.0000	.0008	.0050	.0165	.0389	.0735	.1181	.1672	.2128	.2461	4
6	.0000	.0001	.0006	.0028	.0087	.0210	.0424	.0743	.1160	.1641	3
7	.0000	.0000	.0000	.0003	.0012	.0039	.0098	.0212	.0407	.0703	2
8	.0000	.0000	.0000	.0000	.0001	.0004	.0013	.0035	.0083	.0176	1
9	.0000	.0000	.0000	.0000	.0000	.0000	.0001	.0003	.0008	.0020	0
	.95	.90	.85	.80	.75	.70	.65	.60	.55	.50	x↑

n = 10   p

x↓	.05	.10	.15	.20	.25	.30	.35	.40	.45	.50	
0	.5987	.3487	.1969	.1074	.0563	.0282	.0135	.0060	.0025	.0010	10
1	.3151	.3874	.3474	.2684	.1877	.1211	.0725	.0403	.0207	.0098	9
2	.0746	.1937	.2759	.3020	.2816	.2335	.1757	.1209	.0763	.0439	8
3	.0105	.0574	.1298	.2013	.2503	.2668	.2522	.2150	.1665	.1172	7
4	.0010	.0112	.0401	.0881	.1460	.2001	.2377	.2508	.2384	.2051	6
5	.0001	.0015	.0085	.0264	.0584	.1029	.1536	.2007	.2340	.2461	5
6	.0000	.0001	.0012	.0055	.0162	.0368	.0689	.1115	.1596	.2051	4
7	.0000	.0000	.0001	.0008	.0031	.0090	.0212	.0425	.0746	.1172	3
8	.0000	.0000	.0000	.0001	.0004	.0014	.0043	.0106	.0229	.0439	2
9	.0000	.0000	.0000	.0000	.0000	.0001	.0005	.0016	.0042	.0098	1
10	.0000	.0000	.0000	.0000	.0000	.0000	.0000	.0001	.0003	.0010	0
	.95	.90	.85	.80	.75	.70	.65	.60	.55	.50	x↑

TABLE A.1 *(continued)*
Binomial Probabilities (*n* equal to 12, 14, and 15)

n = 12   *p*

x↓	.05	.10	.15	.20	.25	.30	.35	.40	.45	.50	
0	.5404	.2824	.1422	.0687	.0317	.0138	.0057	.0022	.0008	.0002	12
1	.3413	.3766	.3012	.2062	.1267	.0712	.0368	.0174	.0075	.0029	11
2	.0988	.2301	.2924	.2835	.2323	.1678	.1088	.0639	.0339	.0161	10
3	.0173	.0852	.1720	.2362	.2581	.2397	.1954	.1419	.0923	.0537	9
4	.0021	.0213	.0683	.1329	.1936	.2311	.2367	.2128	.1700	.1208	8
5	.0002	.0038	.0193	.0532	.1032	.1585	.2039	.2270	.2225	.1934	7
6	.0000	.0005	.0040	.0155	.0401	.0792	.1281	.1766	.2124	.2256	6
7	.0000	.0000	.0006	.0033	.0115	.0291	.0591	.1009	.1489	.1934	5
8	.0000	.0000	.0001	.0005	.0024	.0078	.0199	.0420	.0762	.1208	4
9	.0000	.0000	.0000	.0001	.0004	.0015	.0048	.0125	.0277	.0537	3
10	.0000	.0000	.0000	.0000	.0000	.0002	.0008	.0025	.0068	.0161	2
11	.0000	.0000	.0000	.0000	.0000	.0000	.0001	.0003	.0010	.0029	1
12	.0000	.0000	.0000	.0000	.0000	.0000	.0000	.0000	.0001	.0002	0
	.95	.90	.85	.80	.75	.70	.65	.60	.55	.50	x↑

n = 14   *p*

x↓	.05	.10	.15	.20	.25	.30	.35	.40	.45	.50	
0	.4877	.2288	.1028	.0440	.0178	.0068	.0024	.0008	.0002	.0001	14
1	.3593	.3559	.2539	.1539	.0832	.0407	.0181	.0073	.0027	.0009	13
2	.1229	.2570	.2912	.2501	.1802	.1134	.0634	.0317	.0141	.0056	12
3	.0259	.1142	.2056	.2501	.2402	.1943	.1366	.0845	.0462	.0222	11
4	.0037	.0349	.0998	.1720	.2202	.2290	.2022	.1549	.1040	.0611	10
5	.0004	.0078	.0352	.0860	.1468	.1963	.2178	.2066	.1701	.1222	9
6	.0000	.0013	.0093	.0322	.0734	.1262	.1759	.2066	.2088	.1833	8
7	.0000	.0002	.0019	.0092	.0280	.0618	.1082	.1574	.1952	.2095	7
8	.0000	.0000	.0003	.0020	.0082	.0232	.0510	.0918	.1398	.1833	6
9	.0000	.0000	.0000	.0003	.0018	.0066	.0183	.0408	.0762	.1222	5
10	.0000	.0000	.0000	.0000	.0003	.0014	.0049	.0136	.0312	.0611	4
11	.0000	.0000	.0000	.0000	.0000	.0002	.0010	.0033	.0093	.0222	3
12	.0000	.0000	.0000	.0000	.0000	.0000	.0001	.0005	.0019	.0056	2
13	.0000	.0000	.0000	.0000	.0000	.0000	.0000	.0001	.0002	.0009	1
14	.0000	.0000	.0000	.0000	.0000	.0000	.0000	.0000	.0000	.0001	0
	.95	.90	.85	.80	.75	.70	.65	.60	.55	.50	x↑

n = 15   *p*

x↓	.05	.10	.15	.20	.25	.30	.35	.40	.45	.50	
0	.4633	.2059	.0874	.0352	.0134	.0047	.0016	.0005	.0001	.0000	15
1	.3658	.3432	.2312	.1319	.0668	.0305	.0126	.0047	.0016	.0005	14
2	.1348	.2669	.2856	.2309	.1559	.0916	.0476	.0219	.0090	.0032	13
3	.0307	.1285	.2184	.2501	.2252	.1700	.1110	.0634	.0318	.0139	12
4	.0049	.0428	.1156	.1876	.2252	.2186	.1792	.1268	.0780	.0417	11
5	.0006	.0105	.0449	.1032	.1651	.2061	.2123	.1859	.1404	.0916	10
6	.0000	.0019	.0132	.0430	.0917	.1472	.1906	.2066	.1914	.1527	9
7	.0000	.0003	.0030	.0138	.0393	.0811	.1319	.1771	.2013	.1964	8
8	.0000	.0000	.0005	.0035	.0131	.0348	.0710	.1181	.1647	.1964	7
9	.0000	.0000	.0001	.0007	.0034	.0116	.0298	.0612	.1048	.1527	6
10	.0000	.0000	.0000	.0001	.0007	.0030	.0096	.0245	.0515	.0916	5
11	.0000	.0000	.0000	.0000	.0001	.0006	.0024	.0074	.0191	.0417	4
12	.0000	.0000	.0000	.0000	.0000	.0001	.0004	.0016	.0052	.0139	3
13	.0000	.0000	.0000	.0000	.0000	.0000	.0001	.0003	.0010	.0032	2
14	.0000	.0000	.0000	.0000	.0000	.0000	.0000	.0000	.0001	.0005	1
15	.0000	.0000	.0000	.0000	.0000	.0000	.0000	.0000	.0000	.0000	0
	.95	.90	.85	.80	.75	.70	.65	.60	.55	.50	x↑

(table continued)

TABLE A.1   *(continued)*
Binomial Probabilities (*n* equal to 16 and 18)

n = 16   *p*

x↓	.05	.10	.15	.20	.25	.30	.35	.40	.45	.50	
0	.4401	.1853	.0743	.0281	.0100	.0033	.0010	.0003	.0001	.0000	16
1	.3706	.3294	.2097	.1126	.0535	.0228	.0087	.0030	.0009	.0002	15
2	.1463	.2745	.2775	.2111	.1336	.0732	.0353	.0150	.0056	.0018	14
3	.0359	.1423	.2285	.2463	.2079	.1465	.0888	.0468	.0215	.0085	13
4	.0061	.0514	.1311	.2001	.2252	.2040	.1553	.1014	.0572	.0278	12
5	.0008	.0137	.0555	.1201	.1802	.2099	.2008	.1623	.1123	.0667	11
6	.0001	.0028	.0180	.0550	.1101	.1649	.1982	.1983	.1684	.1222	10
7	.0000	.0004	.0045	.0197	.0524	.1010	.1524	.1889	.1969	.1746	9
8	.0000	.0001	.0009	.0055	.0197	.0487	.0923	.1417	.1812	.1964	8
9	.0000	.0000	.0001	.0012	.0058	.0185	.0442	.0840	.1318	.1746	7
10	.0000	.0000	.0000	.0002	.0014	.0056	.0167	.0392	.0755	.1222	6
11	.0000	.0000	.0000	.0000	.0002	.0013	.0049	.0142	.0337	.0667	5
12	.0000	.0000	.0000	.0000	.0000	.0002	.0011	.0040	.0115	.0278	4
13	.0000	.0000	.0000	.0000	.0000	.0000	.0002	.0008	.0029	.0085	3
14	.0000	.0000	.0000	.0000	.0000	.0000	.0000	.0001	.0005	.0018	2
15	.0000	.0000	.0000	.0000	.0000	.0000	.0000	.0000	.0001	.0002	1
	.95	.90	.85	.80	.75	.70	.65	.60	.55	.50	x↑

n = 18   *p*

x↓	.05	.10	.15	.20	.25	.30	.35	.40	.45	.50	
0	.3972	.1501	.0536	.0180	.0056	.0016	.0004	.0001	.0000	.0000	18
1	.3763	.3002	.1704	.0811	.0338	.0126	.0042	.0012	.0003	.0001	17
2	.1683	.2835	.2556	.1723	.0958	.0458	.0190	.0069	.0022	.0006	16
3	.0473	.1680	.2406	.2297	.1704	.1046	.0547	.0246	.0095	.0031	15
4	.0093	.0700	.1592	.2153	.2130	.1681	.1104	.0614	.0291	.0117	14
5	.0014	.0218	.0787	.1507	.1988	.2017	.1664	.1146	.0666	.0327	13
6	.0002	.0052	.0301	.0816	.1436	.1873	.1941	.1655	.1181	.0708	12
7	.0000	.0010	.0091	.0350	.0820	.1376	.1792	.1892	.1657	.1214	11
8	.0000	.0002	.0022	.0120	.0376	.0811	.1327	.1734	.1864	.1669	10
9	.0000	.0000	.0004	.0033	.0139	.0386	.0794	.1284	.1694	.1855	9
10	.0000	.0000	.0001	.0008	.0042	.0149	.0385	.0771	.1248	.1669	8
11	.0000	.0000	.0000	.0001	.0010	.0046	.0151	.0374	.0742	.1214	7
12	.0000	.0000	.0000	.0000	.0002	.0012	.0047	.0145	.0354	.0708	6
13	.0000	.0000	.0000	.0000	.0000	.0002	.0012	.0045	.0134	.0327	5
14	.0000	.0000	.0000	.0000	.0000	.0000	.0002	.0011	.0039	.0117	4
15	.0000	.0000	.0000	.0000	.0000	.0000	.0000	.0002	.0009	.0031	3
16	.0000	.0000	.0000	.0000	.0000	.0000	.0000	.0000	.0001	.0006	2
17	.0000	.0000	.0000	.0000	.0000	.0000	.0000	.0000	.0000	.0001	1
	.95	.90	.85	.80	.75	.70	.65	.60	.55	.50	x↑

TABLE A.1   *(concluded)*
Binomial Probabilities (*n* equal to 20)

n = 20   **p**

x↓	.05	.10	.15	.20	.25	.30	.35	.40	.45	.50	
0	.3585	.1216	.0388	.0115	.0032	.0008	.0002	.0000	.0000	.0000	20
1	.3774	.2702	.1368	.0576	.0211	.0068	.0020	.0005	.0001	.0000	19
2	.1887	.2852	.2293	.1369	.0669	.0278	.0100	.0031	.0008	.0002	18
3	.0596	.1901	.2428	.2054	.1339	.0716	.0323	.0123	.0040	.0011	17
4	.0133	.0898	.1821	.2182	.1897	.1304	.0738	.0350	.0139	.0046	16
5	.0022	.0319	.1028	.1746	.2023	.1789	.1272	.0746	.0365	.0148	15
6	.0003	.0089	.0454	.1091	.1686	.1916	.1712	.1244	.0746	.0370	14
7	.0000	.0020	.0160	.0545	.1124	.1643	.1844	.1659	.1221	.0739	13
8	.0000	.0004	.0046	.0222	.0609	.1144	.1614	.1797	.1623	.1201	12
9	.0000	.0001	.0011	.0074	.0271	.0654	.1158	.1597	.1771	.1602	11
10	.0000	.0000	.0002	.0020	.0099	.0308	.0686	.1171	.1593	.1762	10
11	.0000	.0000	.0000	.0005	.0030	.0120	.0336	.0710	.1185	.1602	9
12	.0000	.0000	.0000	.0001	.0008	.0039	.0136	.0355	.0727	.1201	8
13	.0000	.0000	.0000	.0000	.0002	.0010	.0045	.0146	.0366	.0739	7
14	.0000	.0000	.0000	.0000	.0000	.0002	.0012	.0049	.0150	.0370	6
15	.0000	.0000	.0000	.0000	.0000	.0000	.0003	.0013	.0049	.0148	5
16	.0000	.0000	.0000	.0000	.0000	.0000	.0000	.0003	.0013	.0046	4
17	.0000	.0000	.0000	.0000	.0000	.0000	.0000	.0000	.0002	.0011	3
18	.0000	.0000	.0000	.0000	.0000	.0000	.0000	.0000	.0000	.0002	2
	.95	.90	.85	.80	.75	.70	.65	.60	.55	.50	x↑

Source: Binomial Probability Table from *Statistical Thinking for Managers,* 3rd Edition by D. K. Hildebrand & L. Ott, © 1991. Reprinted with permission of South-Western, a division of Thomson Learning, www.thomsonrights.com. Fax 800 730-2215.

TABLE A.2   **A Poisson Probability Table**
Poisson Probabilities (μ between .1 and 2.0)

μ

x	.1	.2	.3	.4	.5	.6	.7	.8	.9	1.0
0	.9048	.8187	.7408	.6703	.6065	.5488	.4966	.4493	.4066	.3679
1	.0905	.1637	.2222	.2681	.3033	.3293	.3476	.3595	.3659	.3679
2	.0045	.0164	.0333	.0536	.0758	.0988	.1217	.1438	.1647	.1839
3	.0002	.0011	.0033	.0072	.0126	.0198	.0284	.0383	.0494	.0613
4	.0000	.0001	.0003	.0007	.0016	.0030	.0050	.0077	.0111	.0153
5	.0000	.0000	.0000	.0001	.0002	.0004	.0007	.0012	.0020	.0031
6	.0000	.0000	.0000	.0000	.0000	.0000	.0001	.0002	.0003	.0005

μ

x	1.1	1.2	1.3	1.4	1.5	1.6	1.7	1.8	1.9	2.0
0	.3329	.3012	.2725	.2466	.2231	.2019	.1827	.1653	.1496	.1353
1	.3662	.3614	.3543	.3452	.3347	.3230	.3106	.2975	.2842	.2707
2	.2014	.2169	.2303	.2417	.2510	.2584	.2640	.2678	.2700	.2707
3	.0738	.0867	.0998	.1128	.1255	.1378	.1496	.1607	.1710	.1804
4	.0203	.0260	.0324	.0395	.0471	.0551	.0636	.0723	.0812	.0902
5	.0045	.0062	.0084	.0111	.0141	.0176	.0216	.0260	.0309	.0361
6	.0008	.0012	.0018	.0026	.0035	.0047	.0061	.0078	.0098	.0120
7	.0001	.0002	.0003	.0005	.0008	.0011	.0015	.0020	.0027	.0034
8	.0000	.0000	.0001	.0001	.0001	.0002	.0003	.0005	.0006	.0009

(table continued)

TABLE A.2   *(continued)*
Poisson Probabilities (μ between 2.1 and 5.0)

μ

x	2.1	2.2	2.3	2.4	2.5	2.6	2.7	2.8	2.9	3.0
0	.1225	.1108	.1003	.0907	.0821	.0743	.0672	.0608	.0550	.0498
1	.2572	.2438	.2306	.2177	.2052	.1931	.1815	.1703	.1596	.1494
2	.2700	.2681	.2652	.2613	.2565	.2510	.2450	.2384	.2314	.2240
3	.1890	.1966	.2033	.2090	.2138	.2176	.2205	.2225	.2237	.2240
4	.0992	.1082	.1169	.1254	.1336	.1414	.1488	.1557	.1622	.1680
5	.0417	.0476	.0538	.0602	.0668	.0735	.0804	.0872	.0940	.1008
6	.0146	.0174	.0206	.0241	.0278	.0319	.0362	.0407	.0455	.0504
7	.0044	.0055	.0068	.0083	.0099	.0118	.0139	.0163	.0188	.0216
8	.0011	.0015	.0019	.0025	.0031	.0038	.0047	.0057	.0068	.0081
9	.0003	.0004	.0005	.0007	.0009	.0011	.0014	.0018	.0022	.0027
10	.0001	.0001	.0001	.0002	.0002	.0003	.0004	.0005	.0006	.0008
11	.0000	.0000	.0000	.0000	.0000	.0001	.0001	.0001	.0002	.0002

μ

x	3.1	3.2	3.3	3.4	3.5	3.6	3.7	3.8	3.9	4.0
0	.0450	.0408	.0369	.0334	.0302	.0273	.0247	.0224	.0202	.0183
1	.1397	.1304	.1217	.1135	.1057	.0984	.0915	.0850	.0789	.0733
2	.2165	.2087	.2008	.1929	.1850	.1771	.1692	.1615	.1539	.1465
3	.2237	.2226	.2209	.2186	.2158	.2125	.2087	.2046	.2001	.1954
4	.1733	.1781	.1823	.1858	.1888	.1912	.1931	.1944	.1951	.1954
5	.1075	.1140	.1203	.1264	.1322	.1377	.1429	.1477	.1522	.1563
6	.0555	.0608	.0662	.0716	.0771	.0826	.0881	.0936	.0989	.1042
7	.0246	.0278	.0312	.0348	.0385	.0425	.0466	.0508	.0551	.0595
8	.0095	.0111	.0129	.0148	.0169	.0191	.0215	.0241	.0269	.0298
9	.0033	.0040	.0047	.0056	.0066	.0076	.0089	.0102	.0116	.0132
10	.0010	.0013	.0016	.0019	.0023	.0028	.0033	.0039	.0045	.0053
11	.0003	.0004	.0005	.0006	.0007	.0009	.0011	.0013	.0016	.0019
12	.0001	.0001	.0001	.0002	.0002	.0003	.0003	.0004	.0005	.0006
13	.0000	.0000	.0000	.0000	.0001	.0001	.0001	.0001	.0002	.0002

μ

x	4.1	4.2	4.3	4.4	4.5	4.6	4.7	4.8	4.9	5.0
0	.0166	.0150	.0136	.0123	.0111	.0101	.0091	.0082	.0074	.0067
1	.0679	.0630	.0583	.0540	.0500	.0462	.0427	.0395	.0365	.0337
2	.1393	.1323	.1254	.1188	.1125	.1063	.1005	.0948	.0894	.0842
3	.1904	.1852	.1798	.1743	.1687	.1631	.1574	.1517	.1460	.1404
4	.1951	.1944	.1933	.1917	.1898	.1875	.1849	.1820	.1789	.1755
5	.1600	.1633	.1662	.1687	.1708	.1725	.1738	.1747	.1753	.1755
6	.1093	.1143	.1191	.1237	.1281	.1323	.1362	.1398	.1432	.1462
7	.0640	.0686	.0732	.0778	.0824	.0869	.0914	.0959	.1002	.1044
8	.0328	.0360	.0393	.0428	.0463	.0500	.0537	.0575	.0614	.0653
9	.0150	.0168	.0188	.0209	.0232	.0255	.0281	.0307	.0334	.0363
10	.0061	.0071	.0081	.0092	.0104	.0118	.0132	.0147	.0164	.0181
11	.0023	.0027	.0032	.0037	.0043	.0049	.0056	.0064	.0073	.0082
12	.0008	.0009	.0011	.0013	.0016	.0019	.0022	.0026	.0030	.0034
13	.0002	.0003	.0004	.0005	.0006	.0007	.0008	.0009	.0011	.0013
14	.0001	.0001	.0001	.0001	.0002	.0002	.0003	.0003	.0004	.0005
15	.0000	.0000	.0000	.0000	.0001	.0001	.0001	.0001	.0001	.0002

TABLE A.2   *(concluded)*
Poisson Probabilities (μ between 5.5 and 20.0)

					μ					
x	5.5	6.0	6.5	7.0	7.5	8.0	8.5	9.0	9.5	10.0
0	.0041	.0025	.0015	.0009	.0006	.0003	.0002	.0001	.0001	.0000
1	.0225	.0149	.0098	.0064	.0041	.0027	.0017	.0011	.0007	.0005
2	.0618	.0446	.0318	.0223	.0156	.0107	.0074	.0050	.0034	.0023
3	.1133	.0892	.0688	.0521	.0389	.0286	.0208	.0150	.0107	.0076
4	.1558	.1339	.1118	.0912	.0729	.0573	.0443	.0337	.0254	.0189
5	.1714	.1606	.1454	.1277	.1094	.0916	.0752	.0607	.0483	.0378
6	.1571	.1606	.1575	.1490	.1367	.1221	.1066	.0911	.0764	.0631
7	.1234	.1377	.1462	.1490	.1465	.1396	.1294	.1171	.1037	.0901
8	.0849	.1033	.1188	.1304	.1373	.1396	.1375	.1318	.1232	.1126
9	.0519	.0688	.0858	.1014	.1144	.1241	.1299	.1318	.1300	.1251
10	.0285	.0413	.0558	.0710	.0858	.0993	.1104	.1186	.1235	.1251
11	.0143	.0225	.0330	.0452	.0585	.0722	.0853	.0970	.1067	.1137
12	.0065	.0113	.0179	.0263	.0366	.0481	.0604	.0728	.0844	.0948
13	.0028	.0052	.0089	.0142	.0211	.0296	.0395	.0504	.0617	.0729
14	.0011	.0022	.0041	.0071	.0113	.0169	.0240	.0324	.0419	.0521
15	.0004	.0009	.0018	.0033	.0057	.0090	.0136	.0194	.0265	.0347
16	.0001	.0003	.0007	.0014	.0026	.0045	.0072	.0109	.0157	.0217
17	.0000	.0001	.0003	.0006	.0012	.0021	.0036	.0058	.0088	.0128
18	.0000	.0000	.0001	.0002	.0005	.0009	.0017	.0029	.0046	.0071
19	.0000	.0000	.0000	.0001	.0002	.0004	.0008	.0014	.0023	.0037
20	.0000	.0000	.0000	.0000	.0001	.0002	.0003	.0006	.0011	.0019
21	.0000	.0000	.0000	.0000	.0000	.0001	.0001	.0003	.0005	.0009
22	.0000	.0000	.0000	.0000	.0000	.0000	.0001	.0001	.0002	.0004
23	.0000	.0000	.0000	.0000	.0000	.0000	.0000	.0000	.0001	.0002

					μ					
x	11.0	12.0	13.0	14.0	15.0	16.0	17.0	18.0	19.0	20.0
0	.0000	.0000	.0000	.0000	.0000	.0000	.0000	.0000	.0000	.0000
1	.0002	.0001	.0000	.0000	.0000	.0000	.0000	.0000	.0000	.0000
2	.0010	.0004	.0002	.0001	.0000	.0000	.0000	.0000	.0000	.0000
3	.0037	.0018	.0008	.0004	.0002	.0001	.0000	.0000	.0000	.0000
4	.0102	.0053	.0027	.0013	.0006	.0003	.0001	.0001	.0000	.0000
5	.0224	.0127	.0070	.0037	.0019	.0010	.0005	.0002	.0001	.0001
6	.0411	.0255	.0152	.0087	.0048	.0026	.0014	.0007	.0004	.0002
7	.0646	.0437	.0281	.0174	.0104	.0060	.0034	.0019	.0010	.0005
8	.0888	.0655	.0457	.0304	.0194	.0120	.0072	.0042	.0024	.0013
9	.1085	.0874	.0661	.0473	.0324	.0213	.0135	.0083	.0050	.0029
10	.1194	.1048	.0859	.0663	.0486	.0341	.0230	.0150	.0095	.0058
11	.1194	.1144	.1015	.0844	.0663	.0496	.0355	.0245	.0164	.0106
12	.1094	.1144	.1099	.0984	.0829	.0661	.0504	.0368	.0259	.0176
13	.0926	.1056	.1099	.1060	.0956	.0814	.0658	.0509	.0378	.0271
14	.0728	.0905	.1021	.1060	.1024	.0930	.0800	.0655	.0514	.0387
15	.0534	.0724	.0885	.0989	.1024	.0992	.0906	.0786	.0650	.0516
16	.0367	.0543	.0719	.0866	.0960	.0992	.0963	.0884	.0772	.0646
17	.0237	.0383	.0550	.0713	.0847	.0934	.0963	.0936	.0863	.0760
18	.0145	.0255	.0397	.0554	.0706	.0830	.0909	.0936	.0911	.0844
19	.0084	.0161	.0272	.0409	.0557	.0699	.0814	.0887	.0911	.0888
20	.0046	.0097	.0177	.0286	.0418	.0559	.0692	.0798	.0866	.0888
21	.0024	.0055	.0109	.0191	.0299	.0426	.0560	.0684	.0783	.0846
22	.0012	.0030	.0065	.0121	.0204	.0310	.0433	.0560	.0676	.0769
23	.0006	.0016	.0037	.0074	.0133	.0216	.0320	.0438	.0559	.0669
24	.0003	.0008	.0020	.0043	.0083	.0144	.0226	.0328	.0442	.0557
25	.0001	.0004	.0010	.0024	.0050	.0092	.0154	.0237	.0336	.0446
26	.0000	.0002	.0005	.0013	.0029	.0057	.0101	.0164	.0246	.0343
27	.0000	.0001	.0002	.0007	.0016	.0034	.0063	.0109	.0173	.0254
28	.0000	.0000	.0001	.0003	.0009	.0019	.0038	.0070	.0117	.0181
29	.0000	.0000	.0001	.0002	.0004	.0011	.0023	.0044	.0077	.0125
30	.0000	.0000	.0000	.0001	.0002	.0006	.0013	.0026	.0049	.0083
31	.0000	.0000	.0000	.0000	.0001	.0003	.0007	.0015	.0030	.0054
32	.0000	.0000	.0000	.0000	.0001	.0001	.0004	.0009	.0018	.0034
33	.0000	.0000	.0000	.0000	.0000	.0001	.0002	.0005	.0010	.0020

Source: Computed by D. K. Hildebrand. Found in D. K. Hildebrand and L. Ott, *Statistical Thinking for Managers,* 3rd ed. (Boston, MA: PWS-KENT Publishing Company, 1991).

TABLE A.3   Cumulative Areas under the Standard Normal Curve

z	0.00	0.01	0.02	0.03	0.04	0.05	0.06	0.07	0.08	0.09
−3.9	0.00005	0.00005	0.00004	0.00004	0.00004	0.00004	0.00004	0.00004	0.00003	0.00003
−3.8	0.00007	0.00007	0.00007	0.00006	0.00006	0.00006	0.00006	0.00005	0.00005	0.00005
−3.7	0.00011	0.00010	0.00010	0.00010	0.00009	0.00009	0.00008	0.00008	0.00008	0.00008
−3.6	0.00016	0.00015	0.00015	0.00014	0.00014	0.00013	0.00013	0.00012	0.00012	0.00011
−3.5	0.00023	0.00022	0.00022	0.00021	0.00020	0.00019	0.00019	0.00018	0.00017	0.00017
−3.4	0.00034	0.00032	0.00031	0.00030	0.00029	0.00028	0.00027	0.00026	0.00025	0.00024
−3.3	0.00048	0.00047	0.00045	0.00043	0.00042	0.00040	0.00039	0.00038	0.00036	0.00035
−3.2	0.00069	0.00066	0.00064	0.00062	0.00060	0.00058	0.00056	0.00054	0.00052	0.00050
−3.1	0.00097	0.00094	0.00090	0.00087	0.00084	0.00082	0.00079	0.00076	0.00074	0.00071
−3.0	0.00135	0.00131	0.00126	0.00122	0.00118	0.00114	0.00111	0.00107	0.00103	0.00100
−2.9	0.0019	0.0018	0.0018	0.0017	0.0016	0.0016	0.0015	0.0015	0.0014	0.0014
−2.8	0.0026	0.0025	0.0024	0.0023	0.0023	0.0022	0.0021	0.0021	0.0020	0.0019
−2.7	0.0035	0.0034	0.0033	0.0032	0.0031	0.0030	0.0029	0.0028	0.0027	0.0026
−2.6	0.0047	0.0045	0.0044	0.0043	0.0041	0.0040	0.0039	0.0038	0.0037	0.0036
−2.5	0.0062	0.0060	0.0059	0.0057	0.0055	0.0054	0.0052	0.0051	0.0049	0.0048
−2.4	0.0082	0.0080	0.0078	0.0075	0.0073	0.0071	0.0069	0.0068	0.0066	0.0064
−2.3	0.0107	0.0104	0.0102	0.0099	0.0096	0.0094	0.0091	0.0089	0.0087	0.0084
−2.2	0.0139	0.0136	0.0132	0.0129	0.0125	0.0122	0.0119	0.0116	0.0113	0.0110
−2.1	0.0179	0.0174	0.0170	0.0166	0.0162	0.0158	0.0154	0.0150	0.0146	0.0143
−2.0	0.0228	0.0222	0.0217	0.0212	0.0207	0.0202	0.0197	0.0192	0.0188	0.0183
−1.9	0.0287	0.0281	0.0274	0.0268	0.0262	0.0256	0.0250	0.0244	0.0239	0.0233
−1.8	0.0359	0.0351	0.0344	0.0336	0.0329	0.0322	0.0314	0.0307	0.0301	0.0294
−1.7	0.0446	0.0436	0.0427	0.0418	0.0409	0.0401	0.0392	0.0384	0.0375	0.0367
−1.6	0.0548	0.0537	0.0526	0.0516	0.0505	0.0495	0.0485	0.0475	0.0465	0.0455
−1.5	0.0668	0.0655	0.0643	0.0630	0.0618	0.0606	0.0594	0.0582	0.0571	0.0559
−1.4	0.0808	0.0793	0.0778	0.0764	0.0749	0.0735	0.0721	0.0708	0.0694	0.0681
−1.3	0.0968	0.0951	0.0934	0.0918	0.0901	0.0885	0.0869	0.0853	0.0838	0.0823
−1.2	0.1151	0.1131	0.1112	0.1093	0.1075	0.1056	0.1038	0.1020	0.1003	0.0985
−1.1	0.1357	0.1335	0.1314	0.1292	0.1271	0.1251	0.1230	0.1210	0.1190	0.1170
−1.0	0.1587	0.1562	0.1539	0.1515	0.1492	0.1469	0.1446	0.1423	0.1401	0.1379
−0.9	0.1841	0.1814	0.1788	0.1762	0.1736	0.1711	0.1685	0.1660	0.1635	0.1611
−0.8	0.2119	0.2090	0.2061	0.2033	0.2005	0.1977	0.1949	0.1922	0.1894	0.1867
−0.7	0.2420	0.2389	0.2358	0.2327	0.2296	0.2266	0.2236	0.2206	0.2177	0.2148
−0.6	0.2743	0.2709	0.2676	0.2643	0.2611	0.2578	0.2546	0.2514	0.2482	0.2451
−0.5	0.3085	0.3050	0.3015	0.2981	0.2946	0.2912	0.2877	0.2843	0.2810	0.2776
−0.4	0.3446	0.3409	0.3372	0.3336	0.3300	0.3264	0.3228	0.3192	0.3156	0.3121
−0.3	0.3821	0.3783	0.3745	0.3707	0.3669	0.3632	0.3594	0.3557	0.3520	0.3483
−0.2	0.4207	0.4168	0.4129	0.4090	0.4052	0.4013	0.3974	0.3936	0.3897	0.3859
−0.1	0.4602	0.4562	0.4522	0.4483	0.4443	0.4404	0.4364	0.4325	0.4286	0.4247
−0.0	0.5000	0.4960	0.4920	0.4880	0.4840	0.4801	0.4761	0.4721	0.4681	0.4641

TABLE A.3   Cumulative Areas under the Standard Normal Curve (*concluded*)

z	0.00	0.01	0.02	0.03	0.04	0.05	0.06	0.07	0.08	0.09
0.0	0.5000	0.5040	0.5080	0.5120	0.5160	0.5199	0.5239	0.5279	0.5319	0.5359
0.1	0.5398	0.5438	0.5478	0.5517	0.5557	0.5596	0.5636	0.5675	0.5714	0.5753
0.2	0.5793	0.5832	0.5871	0.5910	0.5948	0.5987	0.6026	0.6064	0.6103	0.6141
0.3	0.6179	0.6217	0.6255	0.6293	0.6331	0.6368	0.6406	0.6443	0.6480	0.6517
0.4	0.6554	0.6591	0.6628	0.6664	0.6700	0.6736	0.6772	0.6808	0.6844	0.6879
0.5	0.6915	0.6950	0.6985	0.7019	0.7054	0.7088	0.7123	0.7157	0.7190	0.7224
0.6	0.7257	0.7291	0.7324	0.7357	0.7389	0.7422	0.7454	0.7486	0.7518	0.7549
0.7	0.7580	0.7611	0.7642	0.7673	0.7704	0.7734	0.7764	0.7794	0.7823	0.7852
0.8	0.7881	0.7910	0.7939	0.7967	0.7995	0.8023	0.8051	0.8078	0.8106	0.8133
0.9	0.8159	0.8186	0.8212	0.8238	0.8264	0.8289	0.8315	0.8340	0.8365	0.8389
1.0	0.8413	0.8438	0.8461	0.8485	0.8508	0.8531	0.8554	0.8577	0.8599	0.8621
1.1	0.8643	0.8665	0.8686	0.8708	0.8729	0.8749	0.8770	0.8790	0.8810	0.8830
1.2	0.8849	0.8869	0.8888	0.8907	0.8925	0.8944	0.8962	0.8980	0.8997	0.9015
1.3	0.9032	0.9049	0.9066	0.9082	0.9099	0.9115	0.9131	0.9147	0.9162	0.9177
1.4	0.9192	0.9207	0.9222	0.9236	0.9251	0.9265	0.9279	0.9292	0.9306	0.9319
1.5	0.9332	0.9345	0.9357	0.9370	0.9382	0.9394	0.9406	0.9418	0.9429	0.9441
1.6	0.9452	0.9463	0.9474	0.9484	0.9495	0.9505	0.9515	0.9525	0.9535	0.9545
1.7	0.9554	0.9564	0.9573	0.9582	0.9591	0.9599	0.9608	0.9616	0.9625	0.9633
1.8	0.9641	0.9649	0.9656	0.9664	0.9671	0.9678	0.9686	0.9693	0.9699	0.9706
1.9	0.9713	0.9719	0.9726	0.9732	0.9738	0.9744	0.9750	0.9756	0.9761	0.9767
2.0	0.9772	0.9778	0.9783	0.9788	0.9793	0.9798	0.9803	0.9808	0.9812	0.9817
2.1	0.9821	0.9826	0.9830	0.9834	0.9838	0.9842	0.9846	0.9850	0.9854	0.9857
2.2	0.9861	0.9864	0.9868	0.9871	0.9875	0.9878	0.9881	0.9884	0.9887	0.9890
2.3	0.9893	0.9896	0.9898	0.9901	0.9904	0.9906	0.9909	0.9911	0.9913	0.9916
2.4	0.9918	0.9920	0.9922	0.9925	0.9927	0.9929	0.9931	0.9932	0.9934	0.9936
2.5	0.9938	0.9940	0.9941	0.9943	0.9945	0.9946	0.9948	0.9949	0.9951	0.9952
2.6	0.9953	0.9955	0.9956	0.9957	0.9959	0.9960	0.9961	0.9962	0.9963	0.9964
2.7	0.9965	0.9966	0.9967	0.9968	0.9969	0.9970	0.9971	0.9972	0.9973	0.9974
2.8	0.9974	0.9975	0.9976	0.9977	0.9977	0.9978	0.9979	0.9979	0.9980	0.9981
2.9	0.9981	0.9982	0.9982	0.9983	0.9984	0.9984	0.9985	0.9985	0.9986	0.9986
3.0	0.99865	0.99869	0.99874	0.99878	0.99882	0.99886	0.99889	0.99893	0.99897	0.99900
3.1	0.99903	0.99906	0.99910	0.99913	0.99916	0.99918	0.99921	0.99924	0.99926	0.99929
3.2	0.99931	0.99934	0.99936	0.99938	0.99940	0.99942	0.99944	0.99946	0.99948	0.99950
3.3	0.99952	0.99953	0.99955	0.99957	0.99958	0.99960	0.99961	0.99962	0.99964	0.99965
3.4	0.99966	0.99968	0.99969	0.99970	0.99971	0.99972	0.99973	0.99974	0.99975	0.99976
3.5	0.99977	0.99978	0.99978	0.99979	0.99980	0.99981	0.99981	0.99982	0.99983	0.99983
3.6	0.99984	0.99985	0.99985	0.99986	0.99986	0.99987	0.99987	0.99988	0.99988	0.99989
3.7	0.99989	0.99990	0.99990	0.99990	0.99991	0.99991	0.99992	0.99992	0.99992	0.99992
3.8	0.99993	0.99993	0.99993	0.99994	0.99994	0.99994	0.99994	0.99995	0.99995	0.99995
3.9	0.99995	0.99995	0.99996	0.99996	0.99996	0.99996	0.99996	0.99996	0.99997	0.99997

TABLE A.4   A t Table: Values of t_α for df = 1 through 48

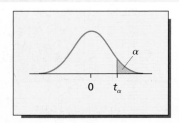

df	$t_{.100}$	$t_{.05}$	$t_{.025}$	$t_{.01}$	$t_{.005}$	$t_{.001}$	$t_{.0005}$
1	3.078	6.314	12.706	31.821	63.657	318.309	636.619
2	1.886	2.920	4.303	6.965	9.925	22.327	31.599
3	1.638	2.353	3.182	4.541	5.841	10.215	12.924
4	1.533	2.132	2.776	3.747	4.604	7.173	8.610
5	1.476	2.015	2.571	3.365	4.032	5.893	6.869
6	1.440	1.943	2.447	3.143	3.707	5.208	5.959
7	1.415	1.895	2.365	2.998	3.499	4.785	5.408
8	1.397	1.860	2.306	2.896	3.355	4.501	5.041
9	1.383	1.833	2.262	2.821	3.250	4.297	4.781
10	1.372	1.812	2.228	2.764	3.169	4.144	4.587
11	1.363	1.796	2.201	2.718	3.106	4.025	4.437
12	1.356	1.782	2.179	2.681	3.055	3.930	4.318
13	1.350	1.771	2.160	2.650	3.012	3.852	4.221
14	1.345	1.761	2.145	2.624	2.977	3.787	4.140
15	1.341	1.753	2.131	2.602	2.947	3.733	4.073
16	1.337	1.746	2.120	2.583	2.921	3.686	4.015
17	1.333	1.740	2.110	2.567	2.898	3.646	3.965
18	1.330	1.734	2.101	2.552	2.878	3.610	3.922
19	1.328	1.729	2.093	2.539	2.861	3.579	3.883
20	1.325	1.725	2.086	2.528	2.845	3.552	3.850
21	1.323	1.721	2.080	2.518	2.831	3.527	3.819
22	1.321	1.717	2.074	2.508	2.819	3.505	3.792
23	1.319	1.714	2.069	2.500	2.807	3.485	3.768
24	1.318	1.711	2.064	2.492	2.797	3.467	3.745
25	1.316	1.708	2.060	2.485	2.787	3.450	3.725
26	1.315	1.706	2.056	2.479	2.779	3.435	3.707
27	1.314	1.703	2.052	2.473	2.771	3.421	3.690
28	1.313	1.701	2.048	2.467	2.763	3.408	3.674
29	1.311	1.699	2.045	2.462	2.756	3.396	3.659
30	1.310	1.697	2.042	2.457	2.750	3.385	3.646
31	1.309	1.696	2.040	2.453	2.744	3.375	3.633
32	1.309	1.694	2.037	2.449	2.738	3.365	3.622
33	1.308	1.692	2.035	2.445	2.733	3.356	3.611
34	1.307	1.691	2.032	2.441	2.728	3.348	3.601
35	1.306	1.690	2.030	2.438	2.724	3.340	3.591
36	1.306	1.688	2.028	2.434	2.719	3.333	3.582
37	1.305	1.687	2.026	2.431	2.715	3.326	3.574
38	1.304	1.686	2.024	2.429	2.712	3.319	3.566
39	1.304	1.685	2.023	2.426	2.708	3.313	3.558
40	1.303	1.684	2.021	2.423	2.704	3.307	3.551
41	1.303	1.683	2.020	2.421	2.701	3.301	3.544
42	1.302	1.682	2.018	2.418	2.698	3.296	3.538
43	1.302	1.681	2.017	2.416	2.695	3.291	3.532
44	1.301	1.680	2.015	2.414	2.692	3.286	3.526
45	1.301	1.679	2.014	2.412	2.690	3.281	3.520
46	1.300	1.679	2.013	2.410	2.687	3.277	3.515
47	1.300	1.678	2.012	2.408	2.685	3.273	3.510
48	1.299	1.677	2.011	2.407	2.682	3.269	3.505

TABLE A.4   *(concluded)*
A *t* Table: Values of t_α for *df* = 49 through 100, 120, and ∞

df	$t_{.100}$	$t_{.05}$	$t_{.025}$	$t_{.01}$	$t_{.005}$	$t_{.001}$	$t_{.0005}$
49	1.299	1.677	2.010	2.405	2.680	3.265	3.500
50	1.299	1.676	2.009	2.403	2.678	3.261	3.496
51	1.298	1.675	2.008	2.402	2.676	3.258	3.492
52	1.298	1.675	2.007	2.400	2.674	3.255	3.488
53	1.298	1.674	2.006	2.399	2.672	3.251	3.484
54	1.297	1.674	2.005	2.397	2.670	3.248	3.480
55	1.297	1.673	2.004	2.396	2.668	3.245	3.476
56	1.297	1.673	2.003	2.395	2.667	3.242	3.473
57	1.297	1.672	2.002	2.394	2.665	3.239	3.470
58	1.296	1.672	2.002	2.392	2.663	3.237	3.466
59	1.296	1.671	2.001	2.391	2.662	3.234	3.463
60	1.296	1.671	2.000	2.390	2.660	3.232	3.460
61	1.296	1.670	2.000	2.389	2.659	3.229	3.457
62	1.295	1.670	1.999	2.388	2.657	3.227	3.454
63	1.295	1.669	1.998	2.387	2.656	3.225	3.452
64	1.295	1.669	1.998	2.386	2.655	3.223	3.449
65	1.295	1.669	1.997	2.385	2.654	3.220	3.447
66	1.295	1.668	1.997	2.384	2.652	3.218	3.444
67	1.294	1.668	1.996	2.383	2.651	3.216	3.442
68	1.294	1.668	1.995	2.382	2.650	3.214	3.439
69	1.294	1.667	1.995	2.382	2.649	3.213	3.437
70	1.294	1.667	1.994	2.381	2.648	3.211	3.435
71	1.294	1.667	1.994	2.380	2.647	3.209	3.433
72	1.293	1.666	1.993	2.379	2.646	3.207	3.431
73	1.293	1.666	1.993	2.379	2.645	3.206	3.429
74	1.293	1.666	1.993	2.378	2.644	3.204	3.427
75	1.293	1.665	1.992	2.377	2.643	3.202	3.425
76	1.293	1.665	1.992	2.376	2.642	3.201	3.423
77	1.293	1.665	1.991	2.376	2.641	3.199	3.421
78	1.292	1.665	1.991	2.375	2.640	3.198	3.420
79	1.292	1.664	1.990	2.374	2.640	3.197	3.418
80	1.292	1.664	1.990	2.374	2.639	3.195	3.416
81	1.292	1.664	1.990	2.373	2.638	3.194	3.415
82	1.292	1.664	1.989	2.373	2.637	3.193	3.413
83	1.292	1.663	1.989	2.372	2.636	3.191	3.412
84	1.292	1.663	1.989	2.372	2.636	3.190	3.410
85	1.292	1.663	1.988	2.371	2.635	3.189	3.409
86	1.291	1.663	1.988	2.370	2.634	3.188	3.407
87	1.291	1.663	1.988	2.370	2.634	3.187	3.406
88	1.291	1.662	1.987	2.369	2.633	3.185	3.405
89	1.291	1.662	1.987	2.369	2.632	3.184	3.403
90	1.291	1.662	1.987	2.368	2.632	3.183	3.402
91	1.291	1.662	1.986	2.368	2.631	3.182	3.401
92	1.291	1.662	1.986	2.368	2.630	3.181	3.399
93	1.291	1.661	1.986	2.367	2.630	3.180	3.398
94	1.291	1.661	1.986	2.367	2.629	3.179	3.397
95	1.291	1.661	1.985	2.366	2.629	3.178	3.396
96	1.290	1.661	1.985	2.366	2.628	3.177	3.395
97	1.290	1.661	1.985	2.365	2.627	3.176	3.394
98	1.290	1.661	1.984	2.365	2.627	3.175	3.393
99	1.290	1.660	1.984	2.365	2.626	3.175	3.392
100	1.290	1.660	1.984	2.364	2.626	3.174	3.390
120	1.289	1.658	1.980	2.358	2.617	3.160	3.373
∞	1.282	1.645	1.960	2.326	2.576	3.090	3.291

Source: Provided by J. B. Orris using Excel.

TABLE A.5 A Chi-Square Table: Values of χ^2_α

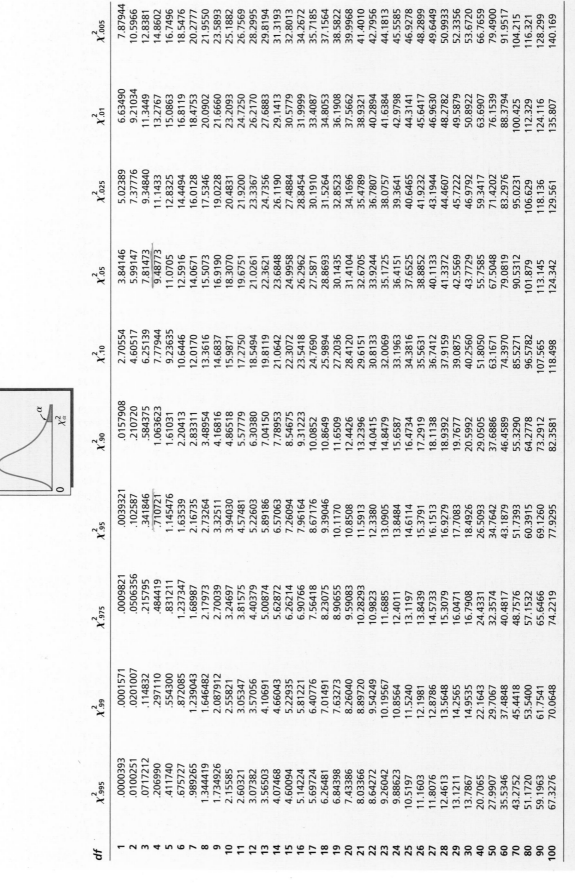

df	$\chi^2_{.995}$	$\chi^2_{.99}$	$\chi^2_{.975}$	$\chi^2_{.95}$	$\chi^2_{.90}$	$\chi^2_{.10}$	$\chi^2_{.05}$	$\chi^2_{.025}$	$\chi^2_{.01}$	$\chi^2_{.005}$
1	.0000393	.0001571	.0009821	.0039321	.0157908	2.70554	3.84146	5.02389	6.63490	7.87944
2	.0100251	.0201007	.0506356	.102587	.210720	4.60517	5.99147	7.37776	9.21034	10.5966
3	.0717212	.114832	.215795	.341846	.584375	6.25139	7.81473	9.34840	11.3449	12.8381
4	.206990	.297110	.484419	.710721	1.063623	7.77944	9.48773	11.1433	13.2767	14.8602
5	.411740	.554300	.831211	1.145476	1.61031	9.23635	11.0705	12.8325	15.0863	16.7496
6	.675727	.872085	1.237347	1.63539	2.20413	10.6446	12.5916	14.4494	16.8119	18.5476
7	.989265	1.239043	1.68987	2.16735	2.83311	12.0170	14.0671	16.0128	18.4753	20.2777
8	1.344419	1.646482	2.17973	2.73264	3.48954	13.3616	15.5073	17.5346	20.0902	21.9550
9	1.734926	2.087912	2.70039	3.32511	4.16816	14.6837	16.9190	19.0228	21.6660	23.5893
10	2.15585	2.55821	3.24697	3.94030	4.86518	15.9871	18.3070	20.4831	23.2093	25.1882
11	2.60321	3.05347	3.81575	4.57481	5.57779	17.2750	19.6751	21.9200	24.7250	26.7569
12	3.07382	3.57056	4.40379	5.22603	6.30380	18.5494	21.0261	23.3367	26.2170	28.2995
13	3.56503	4.10691	5.00874	5.89186	7.04150	19.8119	22.3621	24.7356	27.6883	29.8194
14	4.07468	4.66043	5.62872	6.57063	7.78953	21.0642	23.6848	26.1190	29.1413	31.3193
15	4.60094	5.22935	6.26214	7.26094	8.54675	22.3072	24.9958	27.4884	30.5779	32.8013
16	5.14224	5.81221	6.90766	7.96164	9.31223	23.5418	26.2962	28.8454	31.9999	34.2672
17	5.69724	6.40776	7.56418	8.67176	10.0852	24.7690	27.5871	30.1910	33.4087	35.7185
18	6.26481	7.01491	8.23075	9.39046	10.8649	25.9894	28.8693	31.5264	34.8053	37.1564
19	6.84398	7.63273	8.90655	10.1170	11.6509	27.2036	30.1435	32.8523	36.1908	38.5822
20	7.43386	8.26040	9.59083	10.8508	12.4426	28.4120	31.4104	34.1696	37.5662	39.9968
21	8.03366	8.89720	10.28293	11.5913	13.2396	29.6151	32.6705	35.4789	38.9321	41.4010
22	8.64272	9.54249	10.9823	12.3380	14.0415	30.8133	33.9244	36.7807	40.2894	42.7956
23	9.26042	10.19567	11.6885	13.0905	14.8479	32.0069	35.1725	38.0757	41.6384	44.1813
24	9.88623	10.8564	12.4011	13.8484	15.6587	33.1963	36.4151	39.3641	42.9798	45.5585
25	10.5197	11.5240	13.1197	14.6114	16.4734	34.3816	37.6525	40.6465	44.3141	46.9278
26	11.1603	12.1981	13.8439	15.3791	17.2919	35.5631	38.8852	41.9232	45.6417	48.2899
27	11.8076	12.8786	14.5733	16.1513	18.1138	36.7412	40.1133	43.1944	46.9630	49.6449
28	12.4613	13.5648	15.3079	16.9279	18.9392	37.9159	41.3372	44.4607	48.2782	50.9933
29	13.1211	14.2565	16.0471	17.7083	19.7677	39.0875	42.5569	45.7222	49.5879	52.3356
30	13.7867	14.9535	16.7908	18.4926	20.5992	40.2560	43.7729	46.9792	50.8922	53.6720
40	20.7065	22.1643	24.4331	26.5093	29.0505	51.8050	55.7585	59.3417	63.6907	66.7659
50	27.9907	29.7067	32.3574	34.7642	37.6886	63.1671	67.5048	71.4202	76.1539	79.4900
60	35.5346	37.4848	40.4817	43.1879	46.4589	74.3970	79.0819	83.2976	88.3794	91.9517
70	43.2752	45.4418	48.7576	51.7393	55.3290	85.5271	90.5312	95.0231	100.425	104.215
80	51.1720	53.5400	57.1532	60.3915	64.2778	96.5782	101.879	106.629	112.329	116.321
90	59.1963	61.7541	65.6466	69.1260	73.2912	107.565	113.145	118.136	124.116	128.299
100	67.3276	70.0648	74.2219	77.9295	82.3581	118.498	124.342	129.561	135.807	140.169

Source: C. M. Thompson, "Tables of the Percentage Points of the χ^2 Distribution," Biometrika 32 (1941), pp. 188–89. Reproduced by permission of the Biometrika Trustees.

TABLE A.6   An F Table: Values of $F_{.10}$

Numerator Degrees of Freedom (df_1)

df_2 \ df_1	1	2	3	4	5	6	7	8	9	10	12	15	20	24	30	40	60	120	∞
1	39.86	49.50	53.59	55.83	57.24	58.20	58.91	59.44	59.86	60.19	60.71	61.22	61.74	62.00	62.26	62.53	62.79	63.06	63.33
2	8.53	9.00	9.16	9.24	9.29	9.33	9.35	9.37	9.38	9.39	9.41	9.42	9.44	9.45	9.46	9.47	9.47	9.48	9.49
3	5.54	5.46	5.39	5.34	5.31	5.28	5.27	5.25	5.24	5.23	5.22	5.20	5.18	5.18	5.17	5.16	5.15	5.14	5.13
4	4.54	4.32	4.19	4.11	4.05	4.01	3.98	3.95	3.94	3.92	3.90	3.87	3.84	3.83	3.82	3.80	3.79	3.78	3.76
5	4.06	3.78	3.62	3.52	3.45	3.40	3.37	3.34	3.32	3.30	3.27	3.24	3.21	3.19	3.17	3.16	3.14	3.12	3.10
6	3.78	3.46	3.29	3.18	3.11	3.05	3.01	2.98	2.96	2.94	2.90	2.87	2.84	2.82	2.80	2.78	2.76	2.74	2.72
7	3.59	3.26	3.07	2.96	2.88	2.83	2.78	2.75	2.72	2.70	2.67	2.63	2.59	2.58	2.56	2.54	2.51	2.49	2.47
8	3.46	3.11	2.92	2.81	2.73	2.67	2.62	2.59	2.56	2.54	2.50	2.46	2.42	2.40	2.38	2.36	2.34	2.32	2.29
9	3.36	3.01	2.81	2.69	2.61	2.55	2.51	2.47	2.44	2.42	2.38	2.34	2.30	2.28	2.25	2.23	2.21	2.18	2.16
10	3.29	2.92	2.73	2.61	2.52	2.46	2.41	2.38	2.35	2.32	2.28	2.24	2.20	2.18	2.16	2.13	2.11	2.08	2.06
11	3.23	2.86	2.66	2.54	2.45	2.39	2.34	2.30	2.27	2.25	2.21	2.17	2.12	2.10	2.08	2.05	2.03	2.00	1.97
12	3.18	2.81	2.61	2.48	2.39	2.33	2.28	2.24	2.21	2.19	2.15	2.10	2.06	2.04	2.01	1.99	1.96	1.93	1.90
13	3.14	2.76	2.56	2.43	2.35	2.28	2.23	2.20	2.16	2.14	2.10	2.05	2.01	1.98	1.96	1.93	1.90	1.88	1.85
14	3.10	2.73	2.52	2.39	2.31	2.24	2.19	2.15	2.12	2.10	2.05	2.01	1.96	1.94	1.91	1.89	1.86	1.83	1.80
15	3.07	2.70	2.49	2.36	2.27	2.21	2.16	2.12	2.09	2.06	2.02	1.97	1.92	1.90	1.87	1.85	1.82	1.79	1.76
16	3.05	2.67	2.46	2.33	2.24	2.18	2.13	2.09	2.06	2.03	1.99	1.94	1.89	1.87	1.84	1.81	1.78	1.75	1.72
17	3.03	2.64	2.44	2.31	2.22	2.15	2.10	2.06	2.03	2.00	1.96	1.91	1.86	1.84	1.81	1.78	1.75	1.72	1.69
18	3.01	2.62	2.42	2.29	2.20	2.13	2.08	2.04	2.00	1.98	1.93	1.89	1.84	1.81	1.78	1.75	1.72	1.69	1.66
19	2.99	2.61	2.40	2.27	2.18	2.11	2.06	2.02	1.98	1.96	1.91	1.86	1.81	1.79	1.76	1.73	1.70	1.67	1.63
20	2.97	2.59	2.38	2.25	2.16	2.09	2.04	2.00	1.96	1.94	1.89	1.84	1.79	1.77	1.74	1.71	1.68	1.64	1.61
21	2.96	2.57	2.36	2.23	2.14	2.08	2.02	1.98	1.95	1.92	1.87	1.83	1.78	1.75	1.72	1.69	1.66	1.62	1.59
22	2.95	2.56	2.35	2.22	2.13	2.06	2.01	1.97	1.93	1.90	1.86	1.81	1.76	1.73	1.70	1.67	1.64	1.60	1.57
23	2.94	2.55	2.34	2.21	2.11	2.05	1.99	1.95	1.92	1.89	1.84	1.80	1.74	1.72	1.69	1.66	1.62	1.59	1.55
24	2.93	2.54	2.33	2.19	2.10	2.04	1.98	1.94	1.91	1.88	1.83	1.78	1.73	1.70	1.67	1.64	1.61	1.57	1.53
25	2.92	2.53	2.32	2.18	2.09	2.02	1.97	1.93	1.89	1.87	1.82	1.77	1.72	1.69	1.66	1.63	1.59	1.56	1.52
26	2.91	2.52	2.31	2.17	2.08	2.01	1.96	1.92	1.88	1.86	1.81	1.76	1.71	1.68	1.65	1.61	1.58	1.54	1.50
27	2.90	2.51	2.30	2.17	2.07	2.00	1.95	1.91	1.87	1.85	1.80	1.75	1.70	1.67	1.64	1.60	1.57	1.53	1.49
28	2.89	2.50	2.29	2.16	2.06	2.00	1.94	1.90	1.87	1.84	1.79	1.74	1.69	1.66	1.63	1.59	1.56	1.52	1.48
29	2.89	2.50	2.28	2.15	2.06	1.99	1.93	1.89	1.86	1.83	1.78	1.73	1.68	1.65	1.62	1.58	1.55	1.51	1.47
30	2.88	2.49	2.28	2.14	2.05	1.98	1.93	1.88	1.85	1.82	1.77	1.72	1.67	1.64	1.61	1.57	1.54	1.50	1.46
40	2.84	2.44	2.23	2.09	2.00	1.93	1.87	1.83	1.79	1.76	1.71	1.66	1.61	1.57	1.54	1.51	1.47	1.42	1.38
60	2.79	2.39	2.18	2.04	1.95	1.87	1.82	1.77	1.74	1.71	1.66	1.60	1.54	1.51	1.48	1.44	1.40	1.35	1.29
120	2.75	2.35	2.13	1.99	1.90	1.82	1.77	1.72	1.68	1.65	1.60	1.55	1.48	1.45	1.41	1.37	1.32	1.26	1.19
∞	2.71	2.30	2.08	1.94	1.85	1.77	1.72	1.67	1.63	1.60	1.55	1.49	1.42	1.38	1.34	1.30	1.24	1.17	1.00

Denominator Degrees of Freedom (df_2)

Source: M. Merrington and C. M. Thompson, "Tables of Percentage Points of the Inverted Beta (F)-Distribution," Biometrika 33 (1943), pp. 73–88. Reproduced by permission of the Biometrika Trustees.

TABLE A.7   An *F* Table: Values of $F_{.05}$

Numerator Degrees of Freedom (df_1)

df_2	1	2	3	4	5	6	7	8	9	10	12	15	20	24	30	40	60	120	∞
1	161.4	199.5	215.7	224.6	230.2	234.0	236.8	238.9	240.5	241.9	243.9	245.9	248.0	249.1	250.1	251.1	252.2	253.3	254.3
2	18.51	19.00	19.16	19.25	19.30	19.33	19.35	19.37	19.38	19.40	19.41	19.43	19.45	19.45	19.46	19.47	19.48	19.49	19.50
3	10.13	9.55	9.28	9.12	9.01	8.94	8.89	8.85	8.81	8.79	8.74	8.70	8.66	8.64	8.62	8.59	8.57	8.55	8.53
4	7.71	6.94	6.59	6.39	6.26	6.16	6.09	6.04	6.00	5.96	5.91	5.86	5.80	5.77	5.75	5.72	5.69	5.66	5.63
5	6.61	5.79	5.41	5.19	5.05	4.95	4.88	4.82	4.77	4.74	4.68	4.62	4.56	4.53	4.50	4.46	4.43	4.40	4.36
6	5.99	5.14	4.76	4.53	4.39	4.28	4.21	4.15	4.10	4.06	4.00	3.94	3.87	3.84	3.81	3.77	3.74	3.70	3.67
7	5.59	4.74	4.35	4.12	3.97	3.87	3.79	3.73	3.68	3.64	3.57	3.51	3.44	3.41	3.38	3.34	3.30	3.27	3.23
8	5.32	4.46	4.07	3.84	3.69	3.58	3.50	3.44	3.39	3.35	3.28	3.22	3.15	3.12	3.08	3.04	3.01	2.97	2.93
9	5.12	4.26	3.86	3.63	3.48	3.37	3.29	3.23	3.18	3.14	3.07	3.01	2.94	2.90	2.86	2.83	2.79	2.75	2.71
10	4.96	4.10	3.71	3.48	3.33	3.22	3.14	3.07	3.02	2.98	2.91	2.85	2.77	2.74	2.70	2.66	2.62	2.58	2.54
11	4.84	3.98	3.59	3.36	3.20	3.09	3.01	2.95	2.90	2.85	2.79	2.72	2.65	2.61	2.57	2.53	2.49	2.45	2.40
12	4.75	3.89	3.49	3.26	3.11	3.00	2.91	2.85	2.80	2.75	2.69	2.62	2.54	2.51	2.47	2.43	2.38	2.34	2.30
13	4.67	3.81	3.41	3.18	3.03	2.92	2.83	2.77	2.71	2.67	2.60	2.53	2.46	2.42	2.38	2.34	2.30	2.25	2.21
14	4.60	3.74	3.34	3.11	2.96	2.85	2.76	2.70	2.65	2.60	2.53	2.46	2.39	2.35	2.31	2.27	2.22	2.18	2.13
15	4.54	3.68	3.29	3.06	2.90	2.79	2.71	2.64	2.59	2.54	2.48	2.40	2.33	2.29	2.25	2.20	2.16	2.11	2.07
16	4.49	3.63	3.24	3.01	2.85	2.74	2.66	2.59	2.54	2.49	2.42	2.35	2.28	2.24	2.19	2.15	2.11	2.06	2.01
17	4.45	3.59	3.20	2.96	2.81	2.70	2.61	2.55	2.49	2.45	2.38	2.31	2.23	2.19	2.15	2.10	2.06	2.01	1.96
18	4.41	3.55	3.16	2.93	2.77	2.66	2.58	2.51	2.46	2.41	2.34	2.27	2.19	2.15	2.11	2.06	2.02	1.97	1.92
19	4.38	3.52	3.13	2.90	2.74	2.63	2.54	2.48	2.42	2.38	2.31	2.23	2.16	2.11	2.07	2.03	1.98	1.93	1.88
20	4.35	3.49	3.10	2.87	2.71	2.60	2.51	2.45	2.39	2.35	2.28	2.20	2.12	2.08	2.04	1.99	1.95	1.90	1.84
21	4.32	3.47	3.07	2.84	2.68	2.57	2.49	2.42	2.37	2.32	2.25	2.18	2.10	2.05	2.01	1.96	1.92	1.87	1.81
22	4.30	3.44	3.05	2.82	2.66	2.55	2.46	2.40	2.34	2.30	2.23	2.15	2.07	2.03	1.98	1.94	1.89	1.84	1.78
23	4.28	3.42	3.03	2.80	2.64	2.53	2.44	2.37	2.32	2.27	2.20	2.13	2.05	2.01	1.96	1.91	1.86	1.81	1.76
24	4.26	3.40	3.01	2.78	2.62	2.51	2.42	2.36	2.30	2.25	2.18	2.11	2.03	1.98	1.94	1.89	1.84	1.79	1.73
25	4.24	3.39	2.99	2.76	2.60	2.49	2.40	2.34	2.28	2.24	2.16	2.09	2.01	1.96	1.92	1.87	1.82	1.77	1.71
26	4.23	3.37	2.98	2.74	2.59	2.47	2.39	2.32	2.27	2.22	2.15	2.07	1.99	1.95	1.90	1.85	1.80	1.75	1.69
27	4.21	3.35	2.96	2.73	2.57	2.46	2.37	2.31	2.25	2.20	2.13	2.06	1.97	1.93	1.88	1.84	1.79	1.73	1.67
28	4.20	3.34	2.95	2.71	2.56	2.45	2.36	2.29	2.24	2.19	2.12	2.04	1.96	1.91	1.87	1.82	1.77	1.71	1.65
29	4.18	3.33	2.93	2.70	2.55	2.43	2.35	2.28	2.22	2.18	2.10	2.03	1.94	1.90	1.85	1.81	1.75	1.70	1.64
30	4.17	3.32	2.92	2.69	2.53	2.42	2.33	2.27	2.21	2.16	2.09	2.01	1.93	1.89	1.84	1.79	1.74	1.68	1.62
40	4.08	3.23	2.84	2.61	2.45	2.34	2.25	2.18	2.12	2.08	2.00	1.92	1.84	1.79	1.74	1.69	1.64	1.58	1.51
60	4.00	3.15	2.76	2.53	2.37	2.25	2.17	2.10	2.04	1.99	1.92	1.84	1.75	1.70	1.65	1.59	1.53	1.47	1.39
120	3.92	3.07	2.68	2.45	2.29	2.17	2.09	2.02	1.96	1.91	1.83	1.75	1.66	1.61	1.55	1.50	1.43	1.35	1.25
∞	3.84	3.00	2.60	2.37	2.21	2.10	2.01	1.94	1.88	1.83	1.75	1.67	1.57	1.52	1.46	1.39	1.32	1.22	1.00

Denominator Degrees of Freedom (df_2)

Source: M. Merrington and C. M. Thompson, "Tables of Percentage Points of the Inverted Beta (*F*)-Distribution," *Biometrika* 33 (1943), pp. 73–88. Reproduced by permission of the Biometrika Trustees.

TABLE A.8   An F Table: Values of $F_{.025}$

df_2 \ df_1	1	2	3	4	5	6	7	8	9	10	12	15	20	24	30	40	60	120	∞
1	647.8	799.5	864.2	899.6	921.8	937.1	948.2	956.7	963.3	968.6	976.7	984.9	993.1	997.2	1,001	1,006	1,010	1,014	1,018
2	38.51	39.00	39.17	39.25	39.30	39.33	39.36	39.37	39.39	39.40	39.41	39.43	39.45	39.46	39.46	39.47	39.48	39.49	39.50
3	17.44	16.04	15.44	15.10	14.88	14.73	14.62	14.54	14.47	14.42	14.34	14.25	14.17	14.12	14.08	14.04	13.99	13.95	13.90
4	12.22	10.65	9.98	9.60	9.36	9.20	9.07	8.98	8.90	8.84	8.75	8.66	8.56	8.51	8.46	8.41	8.36	8.31	8.26
5	10.01	8.43	7.76	7.39	7.15	6.98	6.85	6.76	6.68	6.62	6.52	6.43	6.33	6.28	6.23	6.18	6.12	6.07	6.02
6	8.81	7.26	6.60	6.23	5.99	5.82	5.70	5.60	5.52	5.46	5.37	5.27	5.17	5.12	5.07	5.01	4.96	4.90	4.85
7	8.07	6.54	5.89	5.52	5.29	5.12	4.99	4.90	4.82	4.76	4.67	4.57	4.47	4.42	4.36	4.31	4.25	4.20	4.14
8	7.57	6.06	5.42	5.05	4.82	4.65	4.53	4.43	4.36	4.30	4.20	4.10	4.00	3.95	3.89	3.84	3.78	3.73	3.67
9	7.21	5.71	5.08	4.72	4.48	4.32	4.20	4.10	4.03	3.96	3.87	3.77	3.67	3.61	3.56	3.51	3.45	3.39	3.33
10	6.94	5.46	4.83	4.47	4.24	4.07	3.95	3.85	3.78	3.72	3.62	3.52	3.42	3.37	3.31	3.26	3.20	3.14	3.08
11	6.72	5.26	4.63	4.28	4.04	3.88	3.76	3.66	3.59	3.53	3.43	3.33	3.23	3.17	3.12	3.06	3.00	2.94	2.88
12	6.55	5.10	4.47	4.12	3.89	3.73	3.61	3.51	3.44	3.37	3.28	3.18	3.07	3.02	2.96	2.91	2.85	2.79	2.72
13	6.41	4.97	4.35	4.00	3.77	3.60	3.48	3.39	3.31	3.25	3.15	3.05	2.95	2.89	2.84	2.78	2.72	2.66	2.60
14	6.30	4.86	4.24	3.89	3.66	3.50	3.38	3.29	3.21	3.15	3.05	2.95	2.84	2.79	2.73	2.67	2.61	2.55	2.49
15	6.20	4.77	4.15	3.80	3.58	3.41	3.29	3.20	3.12	3.06	2.96	2.86	2.76	2.70	2.64	2.59	2.52	2.46	2.40
16	6.12	4.69	4.08	3.73	3.50	3.34	3.22	3.12	3.05	2.99	2.89	2.79	2.68	2.63	2.57	2.51	2.45	2.38	2.32
17	6.04	4.62	4.01	3.66	3.44	3.28	3.16	3.06	2.98	2.92	2.82	2.72	2.62	2.56	2.50	2.44	2.38	2.32	2.25
18	5.98	4.56	3.95	3.61	3.38	3.22	3.10	3.01	2.93	2.87	2.77	2.67	2.56	2.50	2.44	2.38	2.32	2.26	2.19
19	5.92	4.51	3.90	3.56	3.33	3.17	3.05	2.96	2.88	2.82	2.72	2.62	2.51	2.45	2.39	2.33	2.27	2.20	2.13
20	5.87	4.46	3.86	3.51	3.29	3.13	3.01	2.91	2.84	2.77	2.68	2.57	2.46	2.41	2.35	2.29	2.22	2.16	2.09
21	5.83	4.42	3.82	3.48	3.25	3.09	2.97	2.87	2.80	2.73	2.64	2.53	2.42	2.37	2.31	2.25	2.18	2.11	2.04
22	5.79	4.38	3.78	3.44	3.22	3.05	2.93	2.84	2.76	2.70	2.60	2.50	2.39	2.33	2.27	2.21	2.14	2.08	2.00
23	5.75	4.35	3.75	3.41	3.18	3.02	2.90	2.81	2.73	2.67	2.57	2.47	2.36	2.30	2.24	2.18	2.11	2.04	1.97
24	5.72	4.32	3.72	3.38	3.15	2.99	2.87	2.78	2.70	2.64	2.54	2.44	2.33	2.27	2.21	2.15	2.08	2.01	1.94
25	5.69	4.29	3.69	3.35	3.13	2.97	2.85	2.75	2.68	2.61	2.51	2.41	2.30	2.24	2.18	2.12	2.05	1.98	1.91
26	5.66	4.27	3.67	3.33	3.10	2.94	2.82	2.73	2.65	2.59	2.49	2.39	2.28	2.22	2.16	2.09	2.03	1.95	1.88
27	5.63	4.24	3.65	3.31	3.08	2.92	2.80	2.71	2.63	2.57	2.47	2.36	2.25	2.19	2.13	2.07	2.00	1.93	1.85
28	5.61	4.22	3.63	3.29	3.06	2.90	2.78	2.69	2.61	2.55	2.45	2.34	2.23	2.17	2.11	2.05	1.98	1.91	1.83
29	5.59	4.20	3.61	3.27	3.04	2.88	2.76	2.67	2.59	2.53	2.43	2.32	2.21	2.15	2.09	2.03	1.96	1.89	1.81
30	5.57	4.18	3.59	3.25	3.03	2.87	2.75	2.65	2.57	2.51	2.41	2.31	2.20	2.14	2.07	2.01	1.94	1.87	1.79
40	5.42	4.05	3.46	3.13	2.90	2.74	2.62	2.53	2.45	2.39	2.29	2.18	2.07	2.01	1.94	1.88	1.80	1.72	1.64
60	5.29	3.93	3.34	3.01	2.79	2.63	2.51	2.41	2.33	2.27	2.17	2.06	1.94	1.88	1.82	1.74	1.67	1.58	1.48
120	5.15	3.80	3.23	2.89	2.67	2.52	2.39	2.30	2.22	2.16	2.05	1.94	1.82	1.76	1.69	1.61	1.53	1.43	1.31
∞	5.02	3.69	3.12	2.79	2.57	2.41	2.29	2.19	2.11	2.05	1.94	1.83	1.71	1.64	1.57	1.48	1.39	1.27	1.00

Numerator Degrees of Freedom (df_1)

Denominator Degrees of Freedom (df_2)

Source: M. Merrington and C. M. Thompson, "Tables of Percentage Points of the Inverted Beta (F)-Distribution," Biometrika 33 (1943), pp. 73–88. Reproduced by permission of the Biometrika Trustees.

TABLE A.9　An F Table: Values of $F_{.01}$

df_2 \ df_1	1	2	3	4	5	6	7	8	9	10	12	15	20	24	30	40	60	120	∞
1	4,052	4,999.5	5,403	5,625	5,764	5,859	5,928	5,982	6,022	6,056	6,106	6,157	6,209	6,235	6,261	6,287	6,313	6,339	6,366
2	98.50	99.00	99.17	99.25	99.30	99.33	99.36	99.37	99.39	99.40	99.42	99.43	99.45	99.46	99.47	99.47	99.48	99.49	99.50
3	34.12	30.82	29.46	28.71	28.24	27.91	27.67	27.49	27.35	27.23	27.05	26.87	26.69	26.60	26.50	26.41	26.32	26.22	26.13
4	21.20	18.00	16.69	15.98	15.52	15.21	14.98	14.80	14.66	14.55	14.37	14.20	14.02	13.93	13.84	13.75	13.65	13.56	13.46
5	16.26	13.27	12.06	11.39	10.97	10.67	10.46	10.29	10.16	10.05	9.89	9.72	9.55	9.47	9.38	9.29	9.20	9.11	9.02
6	13.75	10.92	9.78	9.15	8.75	8.47	8.26	8.10	7.98	7.87	7.72	7.56	7.40	7.31	7.23	7.14	7.06	6.97	6.88
7	12.25	9.55	8.45	7.85	7.46	7.19	6.99	6.84	6.72	6.62	6.47	6.31	6.16	6.07	5.99	5.91	5.82	5.74	5.65
8	11.26	8.65	7.59	7.01	6.63	6.37	6.18	6.03	5.91	5.81	5.67	5.52	5.36	5.28	5.20	5.12	5.03	4.95	4.86
9	10.56	8.02	6.99	6.42	6.06	5.80	5.61	5.47	5.35	5.26	5.11	4.96	4.81	4.73	4.65	4.57	4.48	4.40	4.31
10	10.04	7.56	6.55	5.99	5.64	5.39	5.20	5.06	4.94	4.85	4.71	4.56	4.41	4.33	4.25	4.17	4.08	4.00	3.91
11	9.65	7.21	6.22	5.67	5.32	5.07	4.89	4.74	4.63	4.54	4.40	4.25	4.10	4.02	3.94	3.86	3.78	3.69	3.60
12	9.33	6.93	5.95	5.41	5.06	4.82	4.64	4.50	4.39	4.30	4.16	4.01	3.86	3.78	3.70	3.62	3.54	3.45	3.36
13	9.07	6.70	5.74	5.21	4.86	4.62	4.44	4.30	4.19	4.10	3.96	3.82	3.66	3.59	3.51	3.43	3.34	3.25	3.17
14	8.86	6.51	5.56	5.04	4.69	4.46	4.28	4.14	4.03	3.94	3.80	3.66	3.51	3.43	3.35	3.27	3.18	3.09	3.00
15	8.68	6.36	5.42	4.89	4.56	4.32	4.14	4.00	3.89	3.80	3.67	3.52	3.37	3.29	3.21	3.13	3.05	2.96	2.87
16	8.53	6.23	5.29	4.77	4.44	4.20	4.03	3.89	3.78	3.69	3.55	3.41	3.26	3.18	3.10	3.02	2.93	2.84	2.75
17	8.40	6.11	5.18	4.67	4.34	4.10	3.93	3.79	3.68	3.59	3.46	3.31	3.16	3.08	3.00	2.92	2.83	2.75	2.65
18	8.29	6.01	5.09	4.58	4.25	4.01	3.84	3.71	3.60	3.51	3.37	3.23	3.08	3.00	2.92	2.84	2.75	2.66	2.57
19	8.18	5.93	5.01	4.50	4.17	3.94	3.77	3.63	3.52	3.43	3.30	3.15	3.00	2.92	2.84	2.76	2.67	2.58	2.49
20	8.10	5.85	4.94	4.43	4.10	3.87	3.70	3.56	3.46	3.37	3.23	3.09	2.94	2.86	2.78	2.69	2.61	2.52	2.42
21	8.02	5.78	4.87	4.37	4.04	3.81	3.64	3.51	3.40	3.31	3.17	3.03	2.88	2.80	2.72	2.64	2.55	2.46	2.36
22	7.95	5.72	4.82	4.31	3.99	3.76	3.59	3.45	3.35	3.26	3.12	2.98	2.83	2.75	2.67	2.58	2.50	2.40	2.31
23	7.88	5.66	4.76	4.26	3.94	3.71	3.54	3.41	3.30	3.21	3.07	2.93	2.78	2.70	2.62	2.54	2.45	2.35	2.26
24	7.82	5.61	4.72	4.22	3.90	3.67	3.50	3.36	3.26	3.17	3.03	2.89	2.74	2.66	2.58	2.49	2.40	2.31	2.21
25	7.77	5.57	4.68	4.18	3.85	3.63	3.46	3.32	3.22	3.13	2.99	2.85	2.70	2.62	2.54	2.45	2.36	2.27	2.17
26	7.72	5.53	4.64	4.14	3.82	3.59	3.42	3.29	3.18	3.09	2.96	2.81	2.66	2.58	2.50	2.42	2.33	2.23	2.13
27	7.68	5.49	4.60	4.11	3.78	3.56	3.39	3.26	3.15	3.06	2.93	2.78	2.63	2.55	2.47	2.38	2.29	2.20	2.10
28	7.64	5.45	4.57	4.07	3.75	3.53	3.36	3.23	3.12	3.03	2.90	2.75	2.60	2.52	2.44	2.35	2.26	2.17	2.06
29	7.60	5.42	4.54	4.04	3.73	3.50	3.33	3.20	3.09	3.00	2.87	2.73	2.57	2.49	2.41	2.33	2.23	2.14	2.03
30	7.56	5.39	4.51	4.02	3.70	3.47	3.30	3.17	3.07	2.98	2.84	2.70	2.55	2.47	2.39	2.30	2.21	2.11	2.01
40	7.31	5.18	4.31	3.83	3.51	3.29	3.12	2.99	2.89	2.80	2.66	2.52	2.37	2.29	2.20	2.11	2.02	1.92	1.80
60	7.08	4.98	4.13	3.65	3.34	3.12	2.95	2.82	2.72	2.63	2.50	2.35	2.20	2.12	2.03	1.94	1.84	1.73	1.60
120	6.85	4.79	3.95	3.48	3.17	2.96	2.79	2.66	2.56	2.47	2.34	2.19	2.03	1.95	1.86	1.76	1.66	1.53	1.38
∞	6.63	4.61	3.78	3.32	3.02	2.80	2.64	2.51	2.41	2.32	2.18	2.04	1.88	1.79	1.70	1.59	1.47	1.32	1.00

Numerator Degrees of Freedom (df_1)

Denominator Degrees of Freedom (df_2)

Source: M. Merrington and C. M. Thompson, "Tables of Percentage Points of the Inverted Beta (F)-Distribution," Biometrika 33 (1943), pp. 73–88. Reproduced by permission of the Biometrika Trustees.

TABLE A.10   Percentage Points of the Studentized Range

(Note: r is the "first value" and v is the "second value" referred to in Chapter 12.)

Entry is $q_{.05}$

v	r																		
	2	3	4	5	6	7	8	9	10	11	12	13	14	15	16	17	18	19	20
1	18.0	27.0	32.8	37.1	40.4	43.1	45.4	47.4	49.1	50.6	52.0	53.2	54.3	55.4	56.3	57.2	58.0	58.8	59.6
2	6.08	8.33	9.80	10.9	11.7	12.4	13.0	13.5	14.0	14.4	14.7	15.1	15.4	15.7	15.9	16.1	16.4	16.6	16.8
3	4.50	5.91	6.82	7.50	8.04	8.48	8.85	9.18	9.46	9.72	9.95	10.2	10.3	10.5	10.7	10.8	11.0	11.1	11.2
4	3.93	5.04	5.76	6.29	6.71	7.05	7.35	7.60	7.83	8.03	8.21	8.37	8.52	8.66	8.79	8.91	9.03	9.13	9.23
5	3.64	4.60	5.22	5.67	6.03	6.33	6.58	6.80	6.99	7.17	7.32	7.47	7.60	7.72	7.83	7.93	8.03	8.12	8.21
6	3.46	4.34	4.90	5.30	5.63	5.90	6.12	6.32	6.49	6.65	6.79	6.92	7.03	7.14	7.24	7.34	7.43	7.51	7.59
7	3.34	4.16	4.68	5.06	5.36	5.61	5.82	6.00	6.16	6.30	6.43	6.55	6.66	6.76	6.85	6.94	7.02	7.10	7.17
8	3.26	4.04	4.53	4.89	5.17	5.40	5.60	5.77	5.92	6.05	6.18	6.29	6.39	6.48	6.57	6.65	6.73	6.80	6.87
9	3.20	3.95	4.41	4.76	5.02	5.24	5.43	5.59	5.74	5.87	5.98	6.09	6.19	6.28	6.36	6.44	6.51	6.58	6.64
10	3.15	3.88	4.33	4.65	4.91	5.12	5.30	5.46	5.60	5.72	5.83	5.93	6.03	6.11	6.19	6.27	6.34	6.40	6.47
11	3.11	3.82	4.26	4.57	4.82	5.03	5.20	5.35	5.49	5.61	5.71	5.81	5.90	5.98	6.06	6.13	6.20	6.27	6.33
12	3.08	3.77	4.20	4.51	4.75	4.95	5.12	5.27	5.39	5.51	5.61	5.71	5.80	5.88	5.95	6.02	6.09	6.15	6.21
13	3.06	3.73	4.15	4.45	4.69	4.88	5.05	5.19	5.32	5.43	5.53	5.63	5.71	5.79	5.86	5.93	5.99	6.05	6.11
14	3.03	3.70	4.11	4.41	4.64	4.83	4.99	5.13	5.25	5.36	5.46	5.55	5.64	5.71	5.79	5.85	5.91	5.97	6.03
15	3.01	3.67	4.08	4.37	4.59	4.78	4.94	5.08	5.20	5.31	5.40	5.49	5.57	5.65	5.72	5.78	5.85	5.90	5.96
16	3.00	3.65	4.05	4.33	4.56	4.74	4.90	5.03	5.15	5.26	5.35	5.44	5.52	5.59	5.66	5.73	5.79	5.84	5.90
17	2.98	3.63	4.02	4.30	4.52	4.70	4.86	4.99	5.11	5.21	5.31	5.39	5.47	5.54	5.61	5.67	5.73	5.79	5.84
18	2.97	3.61	4.00	4.28	4.49	4.67	4.82	4.96	5.07	5.17	5.27	5.35	5.43	5.50	5.57	5.63	5.69	5.74	5.79
19	2.96	3.59	3.98	4.25	4.47	4.65	4.79	4.92	5.04	5.14	5.23	5.31	5.39	5.46	5.53	5.59	5.65	5.70	5.75
20	2.95	3.58	3.96	4.23	4.45	4.62	4.77	4.90	5.01	5.11	5.20	5.28	5.36	5.43	5.49	5.55	5.61	5.66	5.71
24	2.92	3.53	3.90	4.17	4.37	4.54	4.68	4.81	4.92	5.01	5.10	5.18	5.25	5.32	5.38	5.44	5.49	5.55	5.59
30	2.89	3.49	3.85	4.10	4.30	4.46	4.60	4.72	4.82	4.92	5.00	5.08	5.15	5.21	5.27	5.33	5.38	5.43	5.47
40	2.86	3.44	3.79	4.04	4.23	4.39	4.52	4.63	4.73	4.82	4.90	4.98	5.04	5.11	5.16	5.22	5.27	5.31	5.36
60	2.83	3.40	3.74	3.98	4.16	4.31	4.44	4.55	4.65	4.73	4.81	4.88	4.94	5.00	5.06	5.11	5.15	5.20	5.24
120	2.80	3.36	3.68	3.92	4.10	4.24	4.36	4.47	4.56	4.64	4.71	4.78	4.84	4.90	4.95	5.00	5.04	5.09	5.13
∞	2.77	3.31	3.63	3.86	4.03	4.17	4.29	4.39	4.47	4.55	4.62	4.68	4.74	4.80	4.85	4.89	4.93	4.97	5.01

(table continued)

TABLE A.10 (concluded)

Entry is $q_{.01}$

v	2	3	4	5	6	7	8	9	10	11	12	13	14	15	16	17	18	19	20
1	90.0	135	164	186	202	216	227	237	246	253	260	266	272	277	282	286	290	294	298
2	14.0	19.0	22.3	24.7	26.6	28.2	29.5	30.7	31.7	32.6	33.4	34.1	34.8	35.4	36.0	36.5	37.0	37.5	37.9
3	8.26	10.6	12.2	13.3	14.2	15.0	15.6	16.2	16.7	17.1	17.5	17.9	18.2	18.5	18.8	19.1	19.3	19.5	19.8
4	6.51	8.12	9.17	9.96	10.6	11.1	11.5	11.9	12.3	12.6	12.8	13.1	13.3	13.5	13.7	13.9	14.1	14.2	14.4
5	5.70	6.97	7.80	8.42	8.91	9.32	9.67	9.97	10.2	10.5	10.7	10.9	11.1	11.2	11.4	11.6	11.7	11.8	11.9
6	5.24	6.33	7.03	7.56	7.97	8.32	8.61	8.87	9.10	9.30	9.49	9.65	9.81	9.95	10.1	10.2	10.3	10.4	10.5
7	4.95	5.92	6.54	7.01	7.37	7.68	7.94	8.17	8.37	8.55	8.71	8.86	9.00	9.12	9.24	9.35	9.46	9.55	9.65
8	4.74	5.63	6.20	6.63	6.96	7.24	7.47	7.68	7.87	8.03	8.18	8.31	8.44	8.55	8.66	8.76	8.85	8.94	9.03
9	4.60	5.43	5.96	6.35	6.66	6.91	7.13	7.32	7.49	7.65	7.78	7.91	8.03	8.13	8.23	8.32	8.41	8.49	8.57
10	4.48	5.27	5.77	6.14	6.43	6.67	6.87	7.05	7.21	7.36	7.48	7.60	7.71	7.81	7.91	7.99	8.07	8.15	8.22
11	4.39	5.14	5.62	5.97	6.25	6.48	6.67	6.84	6.99	7.13	7.25	7.36	7.46	7.56	7.65	7.73	7.81	7.88	7.95
12	4.32	5.04	5.50	5.84	6.10	6.32	6.51	6.67	6.81	6.94	7.06	7.17	7.26	7.36	7.44	7.52	7.59	7.66	7.73
13	4.26	4.96	5.40	5.73	5.98	6.19	6.37	6.53	6.67	6.79	6.90	7.01	7.10	7.19	7.27	7.34	7.42	7.48	7.55
14	4.21	4.89	5.32	5.63	5.88	6.08	6.26	6.41	6.54	6.66	6.77	6.87	6.96	7.05	7.12	7.20	7.27	7.33	7.39
15	4.17	4.83	5.25	5.56	5.80	5.99	6.16	6.31	6.44	6.55	6.66	6.76	6.84	6.93	7.00	7.07	7.14	7.20	7.26
16	4.13	4.78	5.19	5.49	5.72	5.92	6.08	6.22	6.35	6.46	6.56	6.66	6.74	6.82	6.90	6.97	7.03	7.09	7.15
17	4.10	4.74	5.14	5.43	5.66	5.85	6.01	6.15	6.27	6.38	6.48	6.57	6.66	6.73	6.80	6.87	6.94	7.00	7.05
18	4.07	4.70	5.09	5.38	5.60	5.79	5.94	6.08	6.20	6.31	6.41	6.50	6.58	6.65	6.72	6.79	6.85	6.91	6.96
19	4.05	4.67	5.05	5.33	5.55	5.73	5.89	6.02	6.14	6.25	6.34	6.43	6.51	6.58	6.65	6.72	6.78	6.84	6.89
20	4.02	4.64	5.02	5.29	5.51	5.69	5.84	5.97	6.09	6.19	6.29	6.37	6.45	6.52	6.59	6.65	6.71	6.76	6.82
24	3.96	4.54	4.91	5.17	5.37	5.54	5.69	5.81	5.92	6.02	6.11	6.19	6.26	6.33	6.39	6.45	6.51	6.56	6.61
30	3.89	4.45	4.80	5.05	5.24	5.40	5.54	5.65	5.76	5.85	5.93	6.01	6.08	6.14	6.20	6.26	6.31	6.36	6.41
40	3.82	4.37	4.70	4.93	5.11	5.27	5.39	5.50	5.60	5.69	5.77	5.84	5.90	5.96	6.02	6.07	6.12	6.17	6.21
60	3.76	4.28	4.60	4.82	4.99	5.13	5.25	5.36	5.45	5.53	5.60	5.67	5.73	5.79	5.84	5.89	5.93	5.98	6.02
120	3.70	4.20	4.50	4.71	4.87	5.01	5.12	5.21	5.30	5.38	5.44	5.51	5.56	5.61	5.66	5.71	5.75	5.79	5.83
∞	3.64	4.12	4.40	4.60	4.76	4.88	4.99	5.08	5.16	5.23	5.29	5.35	5.40	5.45	5.49	5.54	5.57	5.61	5.65

r

Source: Henry Scheffe, The Analysis of Variance, pp. 414–16, ©1959 by John Wiley & Sons, Inc. Reprinted by permission of John Wiley & Sons, Inc.

TABLE A.12 Critical Values for the Durbin–Watson d Statistic ($\alpha = .025$)

	$k=1$		$k=2$		$k=3$		$k=4$		$k=5$	
n	$d_{L,.025}$	$d_{U,.025}$	$d_{L,.025}$	$d_{U,.025}$	$d_{L,.025}$	$d_{U,.025}$	$d_{L,.025}$	$d_{U,.025}$	$d_{L,.025}$	$d_{U,.025}$
15	0.95	1.23	0.83	1.40	0.71	1.61	0.59	1.84	0.48	2.09
16	0.98	1.24	0.86	1.40	0.75	1.59	0.64	1.80	0.53	2.03
17	1.01	1.25	0.90	1.40	0.79	1.58	0.68	1.77	0.57	1.98
18	1.03	1.26	0.93	1.40	0.82	1.56	0.72	1.74	0.62	1.93
19	1.06	1.28	0.96	1.41	0.86	1.55	0.76	1.72	0.66	1.90
20	1.08	1.28	0.99	1.41	0.89	1.55	0.79	1.70	0.70	1.87
21	1.10	1.30	1.01	1.41	0.92	1.54	0.83	1.69	0.73	1.84
22	1.12	1.31	1.04	1.42	0.95	1.54	0.86	1.68	0.77	1.82
23	1.14	1.32	1.06	1.42	0.97	1.54	0.89	1.67	0.80	1.80
24	1.16	1.33	1.08	1.43	1.00	1.54	0.91	1.66	0.83	1.79
25	1.18	1.34	1.10	1.43	1.02	1.54	0.94	1.65	0.86	1.77
26	1.19	1.35	1.12	1.44	1.04	1.54	0.96	1.65	0.88	1.76
27	1.21	1.36	1.13	1.44	1.06	1.54	0.99	1.64	0.91	1.75
28	1.22	1.37	1.15	1.45	1.08	1.54	1.01	1.64	0.93	1.74
29	1.24	1.38	1.17	1.45	1.10	1.54	1.03	1.63	0.96	1.73
30	1.25	1.38	1.18	1.46	1.12	1.54	1.05	1.63	0.98	1.73
31	1.26	1.39	1.20	1.47	1.13	1.55	1.07	1.63	1.00	1.72
32	1.27	1.40	1.21	1.47	1.15	1.55	1.08	1.63	1.02	1.71
33	1.28	1.41	1.22	1.48	1.16	1.55	1.10	1.63	1.04	1.71
34	1.29	1.41	1.24	1.48	1.17	1.55	1.12	1.63	1.06	1.70
35	1.30	1.42	1.25	1.48	1.19	1.55	1.13	1.63	1.07	1.70
36	1.31	1.43	1.26	1.49	1.20	1.56	1.15	1.63	1.09	1.70
37	1.32	1.43	1.27	1.49	1.21	1.56	1.16	1.62	1.10	1.70
38	1.33	1.44	1.28	1.50	1.23	1.56	1.17	1.62	1.12	1.70
39	1.34	1.44	1.29	1.50	1.24	1.56	1.19	1.63	1.13	1.69
40	1.35	1.45	1.30	1.51	1.25	1.57	1.20	1.63	1.15	1.69
45	1.39	1.48	1.34	1.53	1.30	1.58	1.25	1.63	1.21	1.69
50	1.42	1.50	1.38	1.54	1.34	1.59	1.30	1.64	1.26	1.69
55	1.45	1.52	1.41	1.56	1.37	1.60	1.33	1.64	1.30	1.69
60	1.47	1.54	1.44	1.57	1.40	1.61	1.37	1.65	1.33	1.69
65	1.49	1.55	1.46	1.59	1.43	1.62	1.40	1.66	1.36	1.69
70	1.51	1.57	1.48	1.60	1.45	1.63	1.42	1.66	1.39	1.70
75	1.53	1.58	1.50	1.61	1.47	1.64	1.45	1.67	1.42	1.70
80	1.54	1.59	1.52	1.62	1.49	1.65	1.47	1.67	1.44	1.70
85	1.56	1.60	1.53	1.63	1.51	1.65	1.49	1.68	1.46	1.71
90	1.57	1.61	1.55	1.64	1.53	1.66	1.50	1.69	1.48	1.71
95	1.58	1.62	1.56	1.65	1.54	1.67	1.52	1.69	1.50	1.71
100	1.59	1.63	1.57	1.65	1.55	1.67	1.53	1.70	1.51	1.72

TABLE A.11 Critical Values for the Durbin–Watson d Statistic ($\alpha = .05$)

	$k=1$		$k=2$		$k=3$		$k=4$		$k=5$	
n	$d_{L,.05}$	$d_{U,.05}$	$d_{L,.05}$	$d_{U,.05}$	$d_{L,.05}$	$d_{U,.05}$	$d_{L,.05}$	$d_{U,.05}$	$d_{L,.05}$	$d_{U,.05}$
15	1.08	1.36	0.95	1.54	0.82	1.75	0.69	1.97	0.56	2.21
16	1.10	1.37	0.98	1.54	0.86	1.73	0.74	1.93	0.62	2.15
17	1.13	1.38	1.02	1.54	0.90	1.71	0.78	1.90	0.67	2.10
18	1.16	1.39	1.05	1.53	0.93	1.69	0.82	1.87	0.71	2.06
19	1.18	1.40	1.08	1.53	0.97	1.68	0.86	1.85	0.75	2.02
20	1.20	1.41	1.10	1.54	1.00	1.68	0.90	1.83	0.79	1.99
21	1.22	1.42	1.13	1.54	1.03	1.67	0.93	1.81	0.83	1.96
22	1.24	1.43	1.15	1.54	1.05	1.66	0.96	1.80	0.86	1.94
23	1.26	1.44	1.17	1.54	1.08	1.66	0.99	1.79	0.90	1.92
24	1.27	1.45	1.19	1.55	1.10	1.66	1.01	1.78	0.93	1.90
25	1.29	1.45	1.21	1.55	1.12	1.66	1.04	1.77	0.95	1.89
26	1.30	1.46	1.22	1.55	1.14	1.65	1.06	1.76	0.98	1.88
27	1.32	1.47	1.24	1.56	1.16	1.65	1.08	1.76	1.01	1.86
28	1.33	1.48	1.26	1.56	1.18	1.65	1.10	1.75	1.03	1.85
29	1.34	1.48	1.27	1.56	1.20	1.65	1.12	1.74	1.05	1.84
30	1.35	1.49	1.28	1.57	1.21	1.65	1.14	1.74	1.07	1.83
31	1.36	1.50	1.30	1.57	1.23	1.65	1.16	1.74	1.09	1.83
32	1.37	1.50	1.31	1.57	1.24	1.65	1.18	1.73	1.11	1.82
33	1.38	1.51	1.32	1.58	1.26	1.65	1.19	1.73	1.13	1.81
34	1.39	1.51	1.33	1.58	1.27	1.65	1.21	1.73	1.15	1.81
35	1.40	1.52	1.34	1.58	1.28	1.65	1.22	1.73	1.16	1.80
36	1.41	1.52	1.35	1.59	1.29	1.65	1.24	1.73	1.18	1.80
37	1.42	1.53	1.36	1.59	1.31	1.66	1.25	1.72	1.19	1.80
38	1.43	1.54	1.37	1.59	1.32	1.66	1.26	1.72	1.21	1.79
39	1.43	1.54	1.38	1.60	1.33	1.66	1.27	1.72	1.22	1.79
40	1.44	1.54	1.39	1.60	1.34	1.66	1.29	1.72	1.23	1.79
45	1.48	1.57	1.43	1.62	1.38	1.67	1.34	1.72	1.29	1.78
50	1.50	1.59	1.46	1.63	1.42	1.67	1.38	1.72	1.34	1.77
55	1.53	1.60	1.49	1.64	1.45	1.68	1.41	1.72	1.38	1.77
60	1.55	1.62	1.51	1.65	1.48	1.69	1.44	1.73	1.41	1.77
65	1.57	1.63	1.54	1.66	1.50	1.70	1.47	1.73	1.44	1.77
70	1.58	1.64	1.55	1.67	1.52	1.70	1.49	1.74	1.46	1.77
75	1.60	1.65	1.57	1.68	1.54	1.71	1.51	1.74	1.49	1.77
80	1.61	1.66	1.59	1.69	1.56	1.72	1.53	1.74	1.51	1.77
85	1.62	1.67	1.60	1.70	1.57	1.72	1.55	1.75	1.52	1.77
90	1.63	1.68	1.61	1.70	1.59	1.73	1.57	1.75	1.54	1.78
95	1.64	1.69	1.62	1.71	1.60	1.73	1.58	1.75	1.56	1.78
100	1.65	1.69	1.63	1.72	1.61	1.74	1.59	1.76	1.57	1.78

TABLE A.14 Control Chart Constants for x̄ and R Charts

Subgroup Size, n	Chart for Averages (X̄) Factor for Control Limits, A_2	Chart for Ranges (R) Divisor for Estimate of Standard Deviation, d_2	D_3	Factors for Control Limits D_4
2	1.880	1.128	—	3.267
3	1.023	1.693	—	2.574
4	0.729	2.059	—	2.282
5	0.577	2.326	—	2.114
6	0.483	2.534	—	2.004
7	0.419	2.704	0.076	1.924
8	0.373	2.847	0.136	1.864
9	0.337	2.970	0.184	1.816
10	0.308	3.078	0.223	1.777
11	0.285	3.173	0.256	1.744
12	0.266	3.258	0.283	1.717
13	0.249	3.336	0.307	1.693
14	0.235	3.407	0.328	1.672
15	0.223	3.472	0.347	1.653
16	0.212	3.532	0.363	1.637
17	0.203	3.588	0.378	1.622
18	0.194	3.640	0.391	1.608
19	0.187	3.689	0.403	1.597
20	0.180	3.735	0.415	1.585
21	0.173	3.778	0.425	1.575
22	0.167	3.819	0.434	1.566
23	0.162	3.858	0.443	1.557
24	0.157	3.895	0.451	1.548
25	0.153	3.931	0.459	1.541

TABLE A.13 Critical Values for the Durbin–Watson d Statistic ($\alpha = .01$)

n	k = 1 $d_{L,.01}$	$d_{U,.01}$	k = 2 $d_{L,.01}$	$d_{U,.01}$	k = 3 $d_{L,.01}$	$d_{U,.01}$	k = 4 $d_{L,.01}$	$d_{U,.01}$	k = 5 $d_{L,.01}$	$d_{U,.01}$
15	0.81	1.07	0.70	1.25	0.59	1.46	0.49	1.70	0.39	1.96
16	0.84	1.09	0.74	1.25	0.63	1.44	0.53	1.66	0.44	1.90
17	0.87	1.10	0.77	1.25	0.67	1.43	0.57	1.63	0.48	1.85
18	0.90	1.12	0.80	1.26	0.71	1.42	0.61	1.60	0.52	1.80
19	0.93	1.13	0.83	1.26	0.74	1.41	0.65	1.58	0.56	1.77
20	0.95	1.15	0.86	1.27	0.77	1.41	0.68	1.57	0.60	1.74
21	0.97	1.16	0.89	1.27	0.80	1.41	0.72	1.55	0.63	1.71
22	1.00	1.17	0.91	1.28	0.83	1.40	0.75	1.54	0.66	1.69
23	1.02	1.19	0.94	1.29	0.86	1.40	0.77	1.53	0.70	1.67
24	1.04	1.20	0.96	1.30	0.88	1.41	0.80	1.53	0.72	1.66
25	1.05	1.21	0.98	1.30	0.90	1.41	0.83	1.52	0.75	1.65
26	1.07	1.22	1.00	1.31	0.93	1.41	0.85	1.52	0.78	1.64
27	1.09	1.23	1.02	1.32	0.95	1.41	0.88	1.51	0.81	1.63
28	1.10	1.24	1.04	1.32	0.97	1.41	0.90	1.51	0.83	1.62
29	1.12	1.25	1.05	1.33	0.99	1.42	0.92	1.51	0.85	1.61
30	1.13	1.26	1.07	1.34	1.01	1.42	0.94	1.51	0.88	1.61
31	1.15	1.27	1.08	1.34	1.02	1.42	0.96	1.51	0.90	1.60
32	1.16	1.28	1.10	1.35	1.04	1.43	0.98	1.51	0.92	1.60
33	1.17	1.29	1.11	1.36	1.05	1.43	1.00	1.51	0.94	1.59
34	1.18	1.30	1.13	1.36	1.07	1.43	1.01	1.51	0.95	1.59
35	1.19	1.31	1.14	1.37	1.08	1.44	1.03	1.51	0.97	1.59
36	1.21	1.32	1.15	1.38	1.10	1.44	1.04	1.51	0.99	1.59
37	1.22	1.32	1.16	1.38	1.11	1.45	1.06	1.51	1.00	1.59
38	1.23	1.33	1.18	1.39	1.12	1.45	1.07	1.52	1.02	1.58
39	1.24	1.34	1.19	1.39	1.14	1.45	1.09	1.52	1.03	1.58
40	1.25	1.34	1.20	1.40	1.15	1.46	1.10	1.52	1.05	1.58
45	1.29	1.38	1.24	1.42	1.20	1.48	1.16	1.53	1.11	1.58
50	1.32	1.40	1.28	1.45	1.24	1.49	1.20	1.54	1.16	1.59
55	1.36	1.43	1.32	1.47	1.28	1.51	1.25	1.55	1.21	1.59
60	1.38	1.45	1.35	1.48	1.32	1.52	1.28	1.56	1.25	1.60
65	1.41	1.47	1.38	1.50	1.35	1.53	1.31	1.57	1.28	1.61
70	1.43	1.49	1.40	1.52	1.37	1.55	1.34	1.58	1.31	1.61
75	1.45	1.50	1.42	1.53	1.39	1.56	1.37	1.59	1.34	1.62
80	1.47	1.52	1.44	1.54	1.42	1.57	1.39	1.60	1.36	1.62
85	1.48	1.53	1.46	1.55	1.43	1.58	1.41	1.60	1.39	1.63
90	1.50	1.54	1.47	1.56	1.45	1.59	1.43	1.61	1.41	1.64
95	1.51	1.55	1.49	1.57	1.47	1.60	1.45	1.62	1.42	1.64
100	1.52	1.56	1.50	1.58	1.48	1.60	1.46	1.63	1.44	1.65

Source: J. Durbin and G. S. Watson, "Testing for Serial Correlation in Least Squares Regression, II," *Biometrika* 30 (1951), pp. 159–78. Reproduced by permission of the Biometrika Trustees.

TABLE A.15   A Wilcoxon Rank Sum Table: Values of T_L and T_U

(a) $\alpha = .025$ One-Sided; $\alpha = .05$ Two-Sided

n_2 \ n_1	3		4		5		6		7		8		9		10	
	T_L	T_U	T_L	T_U	T_L	T_U	T_L	T_U	T_L	T_U	T_L	T_U	T_L	T_U	T_L	T_U
3	5	16	6	18	6	21	7	23	7	26	8	28	8	31	9	33
4	6	18	11	25	12	28	12	32	13	35	14	38	15	41	16	44
5	6	21	12	28	18	37	19	41	20	45	21	49	22	53	24	56
6	7	23	12	32	19	41	26	52	28	56	29	61	31	65	32	70
7	7	26	13	35	20	45	28	56	37	68	39	73	41	78	43	83
8	8	28	14	38	21	49	29	61	39	73	49	87	51	93	54	98
9	8	31	15	41	22	53	31	65	41	78	51	93	63	108	66	114
10	9	33	16	44	24	56	32	70	43	83	54	98	66	114	79	131

(b) $\alpha = .05$ One-Sided; $\alpha = .10$ Two-Sided

n_2 \ n_1	3		4		5		6		7		8		9		10	
	T_L	T_U	T_L	T_U	T_L	T_U	T_L	T_U	T_L	T_U	T_L	T_U	T_L	T_U	T_L	T_U
3	6	15	7	17	7	20	8	22	9	24	9	27	10	29	11	31
4	7	17	12	24	13	27	14	30	15	33	16	36	17	39	18	42
5	7	20	13	27	19	36	20	40	22	43	24	46	25	50	26	54
6	8	22	14	30	20	40	28	50	30	54	32	58	33	63	35	67
7	9	24	15	33	22	43	30	54	39	66	41	71	43	76	46	80
8	9	27	16	36	24	46	32	58	41	71	52	84	54	90	57	95
9	10	29	17	39	25	50	33	63	43	76	54	90	66	105	69	111
10	11	31	18	42	26	54	35	67	46	80	57	95	69	111	83	127

Source: F. Wilcoxon and R. A. Wilcox, "Some Rapid Approximate Statistical Procedures" (New York: American Cyanamid Company, 1964), pp. 20–23. Reproduced with the permission of American Cyanamid Company.

TABLE A.16　A Wilcoxon Signed Ranks Table: Values of T_0

One-Sided	Two-Sided	n = 5	n = 6	n = 7	n = 8	n = 9	n = 10
$\alpha = .05$	$\alpha = .10$	1	2	4	6	8	11
$\alpha = .025$	$\alpha = .05$		1	2	4	6	8
$\alpha = .01$	$\alpha = .02$			0	2	3	5
$\alpha = .005$	$\alpha = .01$				0	2	3

		n = 11	n = 12	n = 13	n = 14	n = 15	n = 16
$\alpha = .05$	$\alpha = .10$	14	17	21	26	30	36
$\alpha = .025$	$\alpha = .05$	11	14	17	21	25	30
$\alpha = .01$	$\alpha = .02$	7	10	13	16	20	24
$\alpha = .005$	$\alpha = .01$	5	7	10	13	16	19

		n = 17	n = 18	n = 19	n = 20	n = 21	n = 22
$\alpha = .05$	$\alpha = .10$	41	47	54	60	68	75
$\alpha = .025$	$\alpha = .05$	35	40	46	52	59	66
$\alpha = .01$	$\alpha = .02$	28	33	38	43	49	56
$\alpha = .005$	$\alpha = .01$	23	28	32	37	43	49

		n = 23	n = 24	n = 25	n = 26	n = 27	n = 28
$\alpha = .05$	$\alpha = .10$	83	92	101	110	120	130
$\alpha = .025$	$\alpha = .05$	73	81	90	98	107	117
$\alpha = .01$	$\alpha = .02$	62	69	77	85	93	102
$\alpha = .005$	$\alpha = .01$	55	61	68	76	84	92

		n = 29	n = 30	n = 31	n = 32	n = 33	n = 34
$\alpha = .05$	$\alpha = .10$	141	152	163	175	188	201
$\alpha = .025$	$\alpha = .05$	127	137	148	159	171	183
$\alpha = .01$	$\alpha = .02$	111	120	130	141	151	162
$\alpha = .005$	$\alpha = .01$	100	109	118	128	138	149

		n = 35	n = 36	n = 37	n = 38	n = 39	
$\alpha = .05$	$\alpha = .10$	214	228	242	256	271	
$\alpha = .025$	$\alpha = .05$	195	208	222	235	250	
$\alpha = .01$	$\alpha = .02$	174	186	198	211	224	
$\alpha = .005$	$\alpha = .01$	160	171	183	195	208	

		n = 40	n = 41	n = 42	n = 43	n = 44	n = 45
$\alpha = .05$	$\alpha = .10$	287	303	319	336	353	371
$\alpha = .025$	$\alpha = .05$	264	279	295	311	327	344
$\alpha = .01$	$\alpha = .02$	238	252	267	281	297	313
$\alpha = .005$	$\alpha = .01$	221	234	248	262	277	292

		n = 46	n = 47	n = 48	n = 49	n = 50	
$\alpha = .05$	$\alpha = .10$	389	408	427	446	466	
$\alpha = .025$	$\alpha = .05$	361	379	397	415	434	
$\alpha = .01$	$\alpha = .02$	329	345	362	380	398	
$\alpha = .005$	$\alpha = .01$	307	323	339	356	373	

Source: F. Wilcoxon and R. A. Wilcox, "Some Rapid Approximate Statistical Procedures" (New York: American Cyanamid Company, 1964), p. 28. Reproduced with the permission of American Cyanamid Company.

TABLE A.17   Critical Values for Spearman's Rank Correlation Coefficient

n	$\alpha = .05$	$\alpha = .025$	$\alpha = .01$	$\alpha = .005$	n	$\alpha = .05$	$\alpha = .025$	$\alpha = .01$	$\alpha = .005$
5	.900	—	—	—	18	.399	.476	.564	.625
6	.829	.886	.943	—	19	.388	.462	.549	.608
7	.714	.786	.893	—	20	.377	.450	.534	.591
8	.643	.738	.833	.881	21	.368	.438	.521	.576
9	.600	.683	.783	.833	22	.359	.428	.508	.562
10	.564	.648	.745	.794	23	.351	.418	.496	.549
11	.523	.623	.736	.818	24	.343	.409	.485	.537
12	.497	.591	.703	.780	25	.336	.400	.475	.526
13	.475	.566	.673	.745	26	.329	.392	.465	.515
14	.457	.545	.646	.716	27	.323	.385	.456	.505
15	.441	.525	.623	.689	28	.317	.377	.448	.496
16	.425	.507	.601	.666	29	.311	.370	.440	.487
17	.412	.490	.582	.645	30	.305	.364	.432	.478

Source: E. G. Olds, "Distribution of Sums of Squares of Rank Differences for Small Samples," *Annals of Mathematical Statistics,*
1938, 9. Reproduced with the permission of the editor, *Annals of Mathematical Statistics.*

TABLE A.18   A Table of Areas under the Standard Normal Curve

z	.00	.01	.02	.03	.04	.05	.06	.07	.08	.09
0.0	.0000	.0040	.0080	.0120	.0160	.0199	.0239	.0279	.0319	.0359
0.1	.0398	.0438	.0478	.0517	.0557	.0596	.0636	.0675	.0714	.0753
0.2	.0793	.0832	.0871	.0910	.0948	.0987	.1026	.1064	.1103	.1141
0.3	.1179	.1217	.1255	.1293	.1331	.1368	.1406	.1443	.1480	.1517
0.4	.1554	.1591	.1628	.1664	.1700	.1736	.1772	.1808	.1844	.1879
0.5	.1915	.1950	.1985	.2019	.2054	.2088	.2123	.2157	.2190	.2224
0.6	.2257	.2291	.2324	.2357	.2389	.2422	.2454	.2486	.2517	.2549
0.7	.2580	.2611	.2642	.2673	.2704	.2734	.2764	.2794	.2823	.2852
0.8	.2881	.2910	.2939	.2967	.2995	.3023	.3051	.3078	.3106	.3133
0.9	.3159	.3186	.3212	.3238	.3264	.3289	.3315	.3340	.3365	.3389
1.0	.3413	.3438	.3461	.3485	.3508	.3531	.3554	.3577	.3599	.3621
1.1	.3643	.3665	.3686	.3708	.3729	.3749	.3770	.3790	.3810	.3830
1.2	.3849	.3869	.3888	.3907	.3925	.3944	.3962	.3980	.3997	.4015
1.3	.4032	.4049	.4066	.4082	.4099	.4115	.4131	.4147	.4162	.4177
1.4	.4192	.4207	.4222	.4236	.4251	.4265	.4279	.4292	.4306	.4319
1.5	.4332	.4345	.4357	.4370	.4382	.4394	.4406	.4418	.4429	.4441
1.6	.4452	.4463	.4474	.4484	.4495	.4505	.4515	.4525	.4535	.4545
1.7	.4554	.4564	.4573	.4582	.4591	.4599	.4608	.4616	.4625	.4633
1.8	.4641	.4649	.4656	.4664	.4671	.4678	.4686	.4693	.4699	.4706
1.9	.4713	.4719	.4726	.4732	.4738	.4744	.4750	.4756	.4761	.4767
2.0	.4772	.4778	.4783	.4788	.4793	.4798	.4803	.4808	.4812	.4817
2.1	.4821	.4826	.4830	.4834	.4838	.4842	.4846	.4850	.4854	.4857
2.2	.4861	.4864	.4868	.4871	.4875	.4878	.4881	.4884	.4887	.4890
2.3	.4893	.4896	.4898	.4901	.4904	.4906	.4909	.4911	.4913	.4916
2.4	.4918	.4920	.4922	.4925	.4927	.4929	.4931	.4932	.4934	.4936
2.5	.4938	.4940	.4941	.4943	.4945	.4946	.4948	.4949	.4951	.4952
2.6	.4953	.4955	.4956	.4957	.4959	.4960	.4961	.4962	.4963	.4964
2.7	.4965	.4966	.4967	.4968	.4969	.4970	.4971	.4972	.4973	.4974
2.8	.4974	.4975	.4976	.4977	.4977	.4978	.4979	.4979	.4980	.4981
2.9	.4981	.4982	.4982	.4983	.4984	.4984	.4985	.4985	.4986	.4986
3.0	.4987	.4987	.4987	.4988	.4988	.4989	.4989	.4989	.4990	.4990

Source: A. Hald, *Statistical Tables and Formulas* (New York: Wiley, 1952), abridged from Table 1. Reproduced by permission
of the publisher.

Answers to Most Odd-Numbered Exercises

Chapter 1

1.3 Cross-sectional; time series
1.5 $398,000
1.7 Calculator sales tend to increase over time
1.13 Between .4 and 11.6 minutes; 60%
1.17 Ordinal; nominative; ordinal; nominative; ordinal; nominative
1.19 Between 146° and 173°

Chapter 2

2.5 a. 144
  b. 36

2.7 a.

Rating	Frequency	Relative Frequency
Average	1	.03
Good	5	.17
Very Good	10	.33
Outstanding	14	.47
	30	1.00

2.21 a. Between 40 and 46.
  b. Slightly skewed with a tail to the left.
2.23 a. Between 48 and 53.
  b. Symmetrical
2.29 Although most growth rates are ≤71%, 4 of the companies have growth rates of 87% or higher.
2.37 Payment times are right skewed, while ratings are left skewed.
2.39 That was a highly unusual year for Maris.
2.41 b. Slightly skewed with tail to left.
  c. No. 19 of 65 customers (29.2%) had scores below 42.
2.45 a. 17
  b. 14
  c. Those who prefer Rola seem to have purchased it, while those who prefer Koka have not tended to purchase Rola.
2.47 a. 22
  b. 4
  c. Those who prefer Rola appear to consume more Cola.
2.49 b. 1st row: 79.7%, 20.3%, 100%
  2nd row: 65.8%, 34.2%, 100%

c. 1st column: 50.2%, 49.8%, 100%
  2nd column: 33.0%, 67.0%, 100%
d. Viewers concerned with violence are more likely to say quality has declined.

2.51 The more generous a person is, the less likely they are to leave without tipping.
2.57 There is a positive linear relationship between home size and price.
2.59 Initially, cable rates dropped in response to satellite TV. As satellite rates increased, cable could too and still remain competitive.
2.61 Consumers tend to give better taste ratings to the restaurants they prefer.
2.65 a. No.
  b. Yes, strong trend.
  c. The line graph is better because it makes the growth apparent, but it exaggerates the trend.
  d. No.
2.67 The most frequent mechanical quality rating is average (23 out of 33). Only Lexus and Mercedes-Benz received a best rating.
2.69 For all three regions, average was the most frequent rating. US ratings were most consistently average (10 of 11). Better than average ratings went only to Europe and the Pacific Rim, but they each had more than one in the below average category.
2.71 See answer to 2.69.
2.73 In all regions, a majority received average design ratings. The US had the most below average ratings (3 of 11) and the Pacific Rim the most above average design ratings (4 of 13).
2.75 c. Skewed with a tail to the left.
2.77 26%. Probably.
2.79 (1) Private support is right skewed.
  (2) Total revenue is right skewed.
  (3) Fundraising efficiency is left skewed.
2.81 a. Heights: 12, 4.8, 3.8, 4.4, .84
2.83 The vertical scale has been broken, exaggerating the Chevy advantage.

Chapter 3

3.3 a. 9.6, 10, 10
  b. 103.33, 100, 90
3.5 a. Yes, $\bar{x} = 42.954 > 42$
  b. $\bar{x} <$ median $= 43$. There is a slight skewness to the left.
3.7 a. Yes, $\bar{x} = 50.575 > 50$.
  b. median $= 50.650$. They are close because the distribution is nearly symmetric.
3.9 Revenues are right skewed.
3.11 Player expenses are slightly right skewed.
3.13 Skewed to right.
3.15 a. They would argue the owners can afford current arrangement since the mean team income is $6.09 million.
  b. 13 teams made money while 17 lost money.
  c. Owners can argue that a majority of teams lost money and the median income was −$2.3 million.
3.19 range $= 10$; $\sigma^2 = 11.6$; $\sigma = 3.4059$
3.21 a. 2.47, 1.01, 0.25, 0.18, −0.42, −0.48, −0.54, −0.70, −0.88, −0.91
  b. 2.30, 1.33, 0.02, 0.10, −0.29, −0.55, −0.82, −0.79, −0.24, −1.08
3.23 a. The rule is appropriate.
  b. [48.9312, 52.2188];
    [47.2875, 53.8626];
    [45.6436, 55.5064]
  c. Yes
  d. 67.5%, 95%, 100%
    Yes
3.25 a. Somewhat reasonable
  b. [40.3076, 45.5924];
    [37.6652, 48.2348];
    [35.0228, 50.8772]
  c. Yes
  d. 63%, 98.46%, 100%; Yes
3.27 a. [−72.99, 94.85], [−5.72, 31.72], [−47.87, 116.77]
  c. 383.9; 72; 119.5.
    Fund 1 is most risky;
    Fund 2 is least risky.

3.31 a. 192   c. 141   e. 132
     b. 152   d. 171   f. 30
3.33 a. 10, 15, 17, 21, 29
     b. 20, 29, 31, 33, 35
     c. Payment times are right skewed with
        no outliers; design ratings left
        skewed with 2 low outliers.
3.35 30 year rates higher; variability similar;
     mean of differences is .444.
3.39 a. Strong positive linear association
        between x and y.
     b. $\hat{y} = 134.4751$
3.43 Weighted mean = 2.10
3.45 a. 4.6 lb.
     b. 3.8289
3.47 a. 51.5; 81.61; 9.0338
3.51 .4142
3.53 a. $-.0027$
     b. $9,864
3.57 a. Revenues are skewed right with two
        high outliers
     b. Numbers of employees skewed right
        with three high outliers

Chapter 4
4.3 b1. AA
    b2. AA, BB, CC
    b3. AB, AC, BA, BC, CA, CB
    b4. AA, AB, AC, BA, CA
    b5. AA, AB, BA, BB
    c. 1/9, 1/3, 2/3, 5/9, 4/9
4.5 b1. $PPPN, PPNP, PNPP, NPPP$
    b2. Outcomes with ≤ 2 P's (11)
    b3. Outcomes with ≥ 1 P (15)
    b4. $PPPP, NNNN$
    c. 1/4, 11/16, 15/16, 1/8
4.7 .15
4.11 a1. .25
     a2. .40
     a3. .10
     b1. .55
     b2. .45
     b3. .45
4.13 a. 5/8
     b. 21/40
     c. 19/40
     d. 3/8
     e. 31/40
4.15 .343
4.19 a. .6
     b. .4
     c. Dependent
4.21 .55
4.23 .1692
4.25 .31
4.27 b. .40
     c. Yes, $P(FRAUD|FIRE) = P(FRAUD)$
4.29 a. .874
     b. .996
     c. .004
4.31 .999946
4.33 a. .0295
     b. .9705
     c. Probably not
4.37 .0976; .6098; .2927
4.39 a. .0892
     b. No. Too many paying customers
        would lose credit.
4.41 .1549, .8318, .0133
4.43 .2466, .6164, .1370
4.51 .001

4.53 1/56
4.55 1/9; 1/9; 4/9
4.57 .04; .56; .26; .32
4.59 .9029
4.61 .9436
4.63 .721
4.65 .362
4.67 .502
4.69 Slight dependence
4.71 a. .2075
     b. .25
     c. .105
     d. .42
     e. Yes since $P(\text{bonus}) <$
        $P(\text{bonus}|\text{training})$
4.73 a. .1860
     b. It helps the case since $.186 > .015$
     c. .625
     d. It helps since $.625 > .10$
     e. .833. Fairly strong.

Chapter 5
5.3 a. Discrete
    b. Discrete
    c. Continuous
    d. Discrete
    e. Discrete
    f. Continuous
    g. Continuous
5.5 $p(x) \geq 0$, each x
$$\sum_{all\,x} p(x) = 1$$
5.9 $\mu_x = 2.1, \sigma_x^2 = 1.49,$
    $\sigma_x = 1.22$
5.11 b. $500
5.13 a.

x	$p(x)$
$400	.995
$-$49,600	.005

     b. $150
     c. $1,250
5.15 $-$4.20
5.17 3.86
5.21 a. $p(x) =$
$$\frac{5!}{x!\,(5-x)!}(.3)^x(.7)^{5-x}$$
     $x = 0, 1, 2, 3, 4, 5$
     c. .1323
     d. .9692
     e. .8369
     f. .0308
     g. .1631
     h. $\mu_x = 1.5, \sigma_x^2 = 1.05,$
        $\sigma_x = 1.024695$
     i. $[-.54939, 3.54939]$, .9692
5.23 a. $p(x) =$
$$\frac{15!}{x!\,(15-x)!}(.9)^x(.1)^{15-x}$$
     b1. .4509
     b2. .9873
     b3. .5491
     b4. .1837
     b5. .0022
     c. No, $P(x \leq 9)$ is very small
5.25 a1. .0625
     a2. .3125
     b1. .4119
     b2. .2517
     b3. .0059
     c. No, $P(x < 5)$ is very small

5.27 a. .9996, .0004
     b. .4845, .5155
     c. $p = 1/35$
     d. .000040019
5.31 a. $\mu_x = 2, \sigma_x^2 = 2, \sigma_x = 1.414$
     b. $[-.828, 4.828]$, .9473
        $[-2.242, 6.242]$, .9955
5.33 a. .7852
     b. .2148
     c. .1912
     d. .0087
5.35 a. Approximately zero
     b. Rate of comas unusually high.
5.39 a. 0
     b. .0714
     c. .4286
     d. .4286
     e. .0714
     f. .9286
     g. .5
     h. .9286
5.41 a. .1273
     b. .8727
5.43 $\dfrac{\binom{160}{6}\binom{40}{1}}{\binom{200}{7}} + \dfrac{\binom{160}{7}\binom{40}{0}}{\binom{200}{7}} \approx .5767$
5.47 a. $\mu_x = 10, \sigma_x = 1.077,$
        $\mu_y = 10, \sigma_y = 1.095, \sigma_{xy}^2 = .6$
     b. $\sigma_p^2 = .89, \sigma_p = .943$
5.49 b. 87,000
     c. 75%
     d. [46,454, 127,546]; 95%
5.51 a. .7373
     b1. .01733
     b2. .42067
     b3. .61291
     b4. .02361
     c. No. The probability is very small.
5.53 a. .2231
     b. .9344
     c. .9913
     d. .0025
5.55 .0025. Claim is probably not true.
5.57 .0037. Business failures are probably
     increasing.
5.59 .3328. The claim seems reasonable.

Chapter 6
6.7 $h = 1/125$
6.9 a. 3, 3, 1.73205
    b. $[1.268, 4.732]$, .57733
6.11 a. $f(x) = 1/20$ for $120 \leq x \leq 140$
     c. .5
     d. .25
6.13 $c = 1/6$
6.15 1.0
6.23 a. -1, one σ below μ
     b. -3, three σ below μ
     c. 0, equals μ
     d. 2, two σ above μ
     e. 4, four σ above μ
6.25 a. 2.33   d. -2.33
     b. 1.645 e. -1.645
     c. 2.05   f. -1.28
6.27 a. 696   f. 335.5
     b. 664.5 g. 696
     c. 304   h. 700
     d. 283   i. 300
     e. 717

6.29 a1. .9830
   a2. .0033
   a3. .0456
   b.   947
6.31 a. .0013
   b. Claim probably not true
6.33 .0424
6.35 a. 10%, 90%, −13.968
   b. −1.402, 26.202
6.37 a. $[\mu \pm 2.33\sigma]$
   b. [46.745, 54.405]
6.39 a. A: .3085
   B: .4013
   B is investigated more often
   b. A: .8413
   B: .6915
   A is investigated more often
   c. B
   d. Investigate if cost variance
   exceeds $5,000;
   .5987
6.41 $\mu = 700, \sigma = 100$
6.43 Both np and $n(1 - p) \geq 5$
6.45 a. $np = 80$ and $n(1 - p) = 120$
   both ≥ 5
   b1. .0558
   b2. .9875
   b3. .0125
   b4. .0025
   b5. .0015
6.47 a1. $np = 200$ and $n(1 - p) = 800$
   both ≥ 5
   a2. 200, 12.6491
   a3. Less than .001
   b. No
6.49 a. Less than .001
   b. No
6.55 a. $3e^{-3x}$ for $x \geq 0$
   c. .9502
   d. .4226
   e. .0025
   f. 1/3, 1/9, 1/3
   g. .9502
6.57 a. $(2/3)e^{-(2/3)x}$ for $x \geq 0$
   c1. .8647
   c2. .2498
   c3. .0695
   c4. .2835
6.59 a1. .1353
   a2. .2325
   a3. .2212
   b.   Probably not, probability is .2212
6.61 That the data come from a normal
   population.
6.65 .0062
6.67 a. .8944
   b. 73
6.69 a. .8944
   b. .7967
   c. .6911
6.71 298
6.73 .9306
6.77 2/3
6.79 a. .0062
   b. .6915
   c. 3.3275%
6.81 .7745

Chapter 7
7.3 Coca-Cola; Coca-Cola Enterprises;
   Reynolds American; Pepsi Bottling
   Group; Sara Lee

7.5 5:47
7.9 a. 10, .16, .4
   b. 500, .0025, .05
   c. 3, .0025, .05
   d. 100, .000625, .025
7.11 a. Normally distributed
   No, sample size is large (≥ 30)
   b. $\mu_{\bar{x}} = 20, \sigma_{\bar{x}} = .5$
   c. .0228
   d. .1093
7.13 30, 40, 50, 50, 60, 70
7.15 2/3
7.17 a. Normal distribution because $n \geq 30$
   b. 6, .247
   c. .0143
   d. 1.43%, conclude $\mu < 6$
7.19 a. .2206
   b. .0027
   c. Yes
7.25 a. .5, .001, .0316
   b. .1, .0009, .03
   c. .8, .0004, .02
   d. .98, .0000196, .004427
7.27 a. Approximately normal
   b. .9, .03
7.29 a. .0089
   b. Yes
7.31 a. .0122
   b. Yes.
7.33 No; yes.
7.35 a. .0294
   b. Yes.
7.43 selection bias, errors of observation,
   recording error (among others).
7.45 a. [49.151, 52.049]
   b. [50.088, 51.112]
   c. 40
7.47 a. .0049
   b. Yes.
7.49 a. .9544
   b. .0062

Chapter 8
8.5 It becomes shorter.
8.7 a. [50.064, 51.086]; [49.967, 51.183].
   b. Yes. All values in the interval
   exceed 50.
   c. No. Some values in the interval are
   below 50.
8.9 a. [42.31, 43.59]; [42.19, 43.71]
   b. Yes. All values in the interval exceed
   42.
   c. Yes. All values exceed 42.
8.11 a. [76.132, 89.068]
   b. [85.748, 100.252]
   c. Mean audit delay for public
   owner-controlled companies
   appears to be shorter.
8.15 1.363, 2.201, 4.025
   1.440, 2.447, 5.208
8.17 a. [3.442, 8.558]
8.19 a. [6.832, 7.968]
   b. Yes, 95% interval is below 8.
8.21 a. [786.609, 835.391]
   b. Yes, 95% interval is above 750
8.23 [4.969, 5.951]; Yes
8.29 a. $n = 262$
   b. $n = 452$
8.31 a. $n = 47$
   b. $n = 328$
8.33 $n = 54$

8.35 a. $p = .5$
   b. $p = .3$
   c. $p = .8$
8.37 Part a. [.304, .496],
   [.286, .514],
   [.274, .526]
   Part b. [.066, .134],
   [.060, .140],
   [.055, .145]
   Part c. [.841, .959],
   [.830, .970],
   [.823, .977]
   Part d. [.464, .736],
   [.439, .761],
   [.422, .778]
8.39 a. [.570, .630]
   b. Yes, the interval is above 0.5.
8.43 a. [.611, .729]
   b. Yes, interval above .6
8.45 [.264, .344]
   Yes, 95% interval exceeds .20.
8.47 $n = 1426$
8.51 a. [$514.399, $549.601]
   b. $5,559,932
   [$5,375,983.95, $5,743,880.05]
   c. Claim is very doubtful
8.53 a. $\hat{p} = .31$, [.2224, .3976]
   b. 410.13, [294.24, 526.02]
   c. $2942.40; these minimum savings
   for 12 months would pay for the new
   design.
8.55 a. $\hat{\tau} = $7,721,150$;
   [$7,110,966, $8,331,332]
   $\hat{\mu} = 298.16; [$274.60, $321.72]
   b. $\hat{\tau} = 12371.9$; [11001.99, 13741.82]
   $\hat{p} = .4778$; [.424, .530]
8.57 a. [63.59, 72.49]
   b. [52.29, 61.19]
   c. Yes. The interval for financial firms
   is below the one for industrial firms.
8.59 a. [56.47, 59.13]. Yes, the interval is
   below 60.
   b. $n = 144$
8.61 a. [25.1562, 27.2838]
   b. Yes, not much more than 25
8.63 $\hat{\tau} = 2,358.812$; [1656.92, 3060.70]

Chapter 9
9.3 a. $H_0: \mu \leq 42$ versus $H_a: \mu > 42$
   b. Type I: decide $\mu > 42$ when it isn't.
   Type II: decide $\mu \leq 42$ when it isn't.
9.5 a. $H_0: \mu = 3''$ versus $H_a: \mu \neq 3''$
   b. Type I: decide $\mu \neq 3''$ when it is $3''$.
   Type II: decide $\mu = 3''$ when it
   doesn't
9.7 a. $H_0: \mu \leq 60°$ versus $H_a: \mu > 60°$
   b. Type I: shut down unnecessarily
   Type II: fail to shut down when
   water is too warm.
   c. .05 to reduce β and avoid severe
   penalties occurring with Type II errors.
9.11 a. −2.0
   b. Fail to reject H_0
   c. .023
   d. Can reject H_0 at $\alpha = .10$ and .05; fail
   to reject H_0 at $\alpha = .01$ and .001.
   e. Strong
9.13 a. $H_0: \mu \leq 42$ versus $H_a: \mu > 42$
   b. $z = 2.91$. Since this exceeds the
   critical values 1.28, 1.645, and 2.33,
   can reject H_0 at $\alpha = .1, .05,$ and .01.
   Fail to reject H_0 at $\alpha = .001$

c. p-value $= .002$. Same conclusion as part (b)

d. Very strong

9.15 a. $H_0: \mu \le 60$ versus $H_a: \mu > 60$

b. $z = 2.41$; p-value $= .008$. Since $z > 1.645$ and p-value $< .05$, reject H_0 and shut down

9.17 $z = 3.09$ and p-value $= .001$. Since $z > 1.645$ and p-value $< .05$, shut down the plant.

9.19 a. $H_0: \mu = 16$ versus $H_a: \mu \ne 16$

b. $\bar{x} = 16.05$: (1) $z = 3.00$;
 (2) p-value $= .003$;
 (3) critical values ± 2.575;
 (4) [16.007, 16.093]; reject H_0 and decide to readjust.

 $\bar{x} = 15.96$: (1) $z = -2.40$;
 (2) p-value $= .016$;
 (3) critical values ± 2.575;
 (4) [15.917, 16.003]; fail to reject H_0 so don't readjust.

 $\bar{x} = 16.02$: (1) $z = 1.20$;
 (2) p-value $= .230$;
 (3) critical values ± 2.575;
 (4) [15.977, 16.063]; fail to reject H_0 so don't readjust.

 $\bar{x} = 15.94$: (1) $z = -3.60$;
 (2) p-value $= .000$;
 (3) critical values ± 2.575;
 (4) [15.897, 15.983]; reject H_0 and decide to readjust.

9.23 $t = -4.30$; reject H_0 at .10, .05, and .01 but not at .001.

9.25 (1) $t = 2.212 > 1.685$. Reject H_0 and decide the mean breaking strength exceeds 50.
 (2) The p-value provides strong evidence for $\mu > 50$.

9.27 a. (1) $H_0: \mu \le 3.5$ versus $H_a: \mu > 3.5$
 (2) Type I: decide Ohio mean higher when it isn't. Type II: decide Ohio mean isn't higher when it is.

b. (1) $t = 3.62 > 3.143$; reject H_0
 (2) The p-value provides very strong evidence for $\mu > 3.5$.

9.29 a. $H_0: \mu \le 42$ versus $H_a: \mu > 42$

b. (1) $t = 2.899 > 2.386$; reject H_0.
 (2) The p-value provides very strong evidence for $\mu > 42$.

9.31 a. $H_0: \mu = 750$ versus $H_a: \mu \ne 750$

b. (1) $t = 6.94 > 4.604$; reject H_0.
 (2) The p-value provides very strong evidence for $\mu \ne 750$.

9.33 Since $t = -4.97$ and p-value $= .000$, there is extremely strong evidence that $\mu < 18.8$

9.37 a. $H_0: p \le .5$ versus $H_a: p > .5$

b. $z = 1.19$. Do not reject H_0 at any α. There is little evidence.

9.39 a. $H_0: p \le .18$ versus $H_a: p > .18$

b. (1) p-value $= .0329$.
 (2) Reject H_0 at $\alpha = .10$ and .05 but not at .01 or .001.
 (3) There is strong evidence.

c. Possibly.

9.41 (1) $H_0: p = .73$ versus $H_a: p \ne .73$
 (2) $z = -.80$ and p-value $= .4238$ provide insufficient evidence to reject H_0 at any α.

9.47 a. .9279; .8315; .6772; .4840; .2946; .1492; .0618; .0207; .0055; .00118

b. No. Must increase n.

c. The power increases.

9.49 a. 246 b. 275

9.51 a. $H_0: \mu \ge 25$ versus $H_a: \mu < 25$

b. $t = -2.63$; reject H_0 at all α's except .001.

c. Very strong evidence.

d. Yes, if you believe the standard should be met.

9.53 a. $t = 2.50$. Reject H_0 at $\alpha = .10, .05, .01$ but not .001; very strong.

b. $t = 1.11$. Do not reject H_0 at any α.

9.55 a. Reject H_0 at $\alpha = .10$ and .05 but not at .01 or .001.

b. Strong evidence

9.57 $z = 2.44$; p-value $= .0073$
There is very strong evidence supporting the spokesman's claim.

9.59 There is some evidence.

9.61 a. $t = 4.92$. Reject H_0 at every α. There is extremely strong evidence the current mean is higher.

b. Yes. Extra expenses erode fundholders' account values.

Chapter 10

10.5 $t = 3.39$; reject H_0 at all α's except .001. There is very strong evidence that $\mu_1 - \mu_2 > 20$.

10.7 95% CI: [23.50, 36.50]. Yes, the entire interval is above 20.
Upper tail test: $t = 3.39$ ($df = 11$)
Reject H_0 at all α's except .001. Very strong evidence that $\mu_1 - \mu_2 > 20$.
Two tail test: $t = 3.39$. Reject H_0 at all α's except .001. There is very strong evidence that $\mu_1 - \mu_2 \ne 20$.

10.9 a. $H_0: \mu_1 - \mu_2 \le 0$ versus $H_a: \mu_1 - \mu_2 > 0$

b. $t = 1.97$. Reject H_0 at $\alpha = .10$ and .05 but not .01 or .001. Strong evidence.

c. $[-12.01, 412.01]$. A's mean could be anywhere from $12.01 lower to $412.01 higher than B's.

10.11 a. $H_0: \mu_1 - \mu_2 = 0$ versus $H_a: \mu_1 - \mu_2 \ne 0$

b. Reject H_0 at $\alpha = .10$, .05 but not .01 or .001; strong evidence

c. [$1.10, $100.90]

10.17 a. [100.141, 106.859]; yes. [98.723, 108.277]; no

b. $t = 2.32$; reject H_0 at $\alpha = .05$ but not .01; strong

c. $t = -4.31$; reject H_0 at $\alpha = .05, .01$; extremely strong.

10.19 a. $t = 6.18$; decide there is a difference.

b. A 95% confidence interval is [2.01, 4.49], so we can estimate the minimum to be 2.01 and the maximum to be 4.49.

10.21 a. $H_0: \mu_d = 0$ versus $H_a: \mu_d \ne 0$

b. $t = 3.89$;
reject H_0 at all α except .001; yes

c. p-value $= .006$; reject H_0 at all α except .001; very strong evidence

10.25 $z = -10.14$; reject H_0 at each value of α; extremely strong evidence

10.27 a. $H_0: p_1 - p_2 = 0$ versus $H_a: p_1 - p_2 \ne 0$

b. $z = 3.63$; reject H_0 at each value of α

c. $H_0: p_1 - p_2 \le .05$ versus $H_a: p_1 - p_2 > .05$
$z = 1.99$ and
p-value $= .0233$; strong evidence

d. [.0509, .1711]; yes

10.29 p-value $= .004$; very strong evidence [$-.057, -.011$]; $-.011$

10.31 a. $H_0: \mu_T - \mu_B = 0$ versus $H_a: \mu_T - \mu_B \ne 0$
$t = 1.54$; cannot reject H_0 at any value of α; little to no evidence.

b. $[-.09, .73]$

10.33 a. $H_0: \mu_d \le 0$ versus $H_a: \mu_d > 0$

b. $t = 10.00$; reject H_0 at all levels of α

c. p-value $= .000$; reject H_0 at all levels of α; extremely strong evidence

10.35 a. $t = 8.251$; reject $H_0: \mu_O - \mu_{JVC} = 0$ at $\alpha = .001$

b. [$32.69, $55.31]; probably

c. $t = 2.627$; reject $H_0: \mu_O - \mu_{JVC} \le 30$ at $\alpha = .05$

Chapter 11

11.3 a. $\chi^2_{.025} = 17.5346$; $\chi^2_{.01} = 20.0902$; $\chi^2_{.005} = 21.9550$

b. $\chi^2_{.99} = 5.81221$; $\chi^2_{.975} = 6.90766$; $\chi^2_{.10} = 23.5418$; $\chi^2_{.005} = 34.2672$

11.5 a. [12.31138, 69.40406]

b. $\chi^2 = 13.57$. Cannot reject H_0.

11.7 $\chi^2 = 11.62 < 17.7083$. Reject H_0.

11.9 (1) $\chi^2 = 6.72 < 13.8484$. Reject H_0.
(2) [.000085357, .000270944]; [.009239, .016460].
(3) Yes since $3(.016460) < .05$.

11.11 $\chi^2 = 16.0286$. Cannot reject H_0 at either .05 or .01.

11.15 a. 2.96

b. 4.68

c. 3.16

d. 8.81

11.17 $F = 2.47 > 2.40$. Reject H_0 at $\alpha = .05$.

11.19 $F = 1.727 < 4.03$. Cannot claim $\sigma_1 \ne \sigma_2$. Yes. The assumption of equal variances is reasonable.

11.21 $\chi^2 = 6.14 > 2.16735$. Cannot claim $\sigma^2 < 150$.

11.23 $F = .849 < F_{.05} \approx 1.93$. Cannot claim the new PP presentations have reduced variability.

Chapter 12 (Answers to several Even-Numbered Exercises also given)

12.1 Factor = independent variables in a designed experiment.
treatments = values of a factor (or combination of factors).
experimental units = entities to which treatments are assigned.
response variable = the dependent variable (or variable of interest).

12.3 Between-treatment variability measures differences in sample means, while within-treatment variability measures differences of measurements in the same samples.

12.5 a. $F = 184.57$, p-value = .000; reject H_0 and decide shelf height affects sales.
b. Point estimate of $\mu_M - \mu_B$ is 21.4; [17.681, 25.119], $\mu_T - \mu_B$: -4.3; [$-8.019, -.581$], $\mu_T - \mu_M$: -25.7; [$-29.419, -21.981$].
c. $\mu_M - \mu_B$: [18.35, 24.45]
d. μ_B: [53.65, 57.96]
μ_M: [75.04, 79.36]
μ_T: [49.34, 53.66]

12.7 a. $F = 43.36$, p-value = .000; reject H_0; designs affect sales
b. B $-$ A: [11.56, 20.84]
C $-$ A: [3.56, 12.84]
C $-$ B: [$-12.64, -3.36$]
Design B.
c. μ_A: [13.92, 19.28]
μ_B: [30.12, 35.48]
μ_C: [22.12, 27.48]

12.8 $F = 16.42$; p-value < .001; reject H_0; brands differ

12.9 (1) Divot $-$ Alpha: [38.41, 127.59]
Divot $-$ Century: [50.21, 139.39]
Divot $-$ Best: [$-14.39, 74.79$]
Century $-$ Alpha: [$-56.39, 32.79$]
Century $-$ Best: [$-109.19, -20.01$]
Best $-$ Alpha: [8.29, 97.39]
(2) Divot $-$ Alpha: $t = 5.33$
Divot $-$ Century: $t = 6.09$
Divot $-$ Best: $t = 1.94$
Best $-$ Century: $t = 4.15$
Best $-$ Alpha: $t = 3.39$
Alpha $-$ Century: $t = 0.76$
Divot and Best appear to be the most durable.
Divot: [313.26, 359.94]
Best: [283.06, 329.74]
Alpha: [230.26, 276.94]
Century: [218.46, 265.14]

12.10 When differences between experimental units may be concealing any true differences between the treatments.

12.13 a. $F = 36.23$; p-value = .000; reject H_0; sales methods differ
b. $F = 12.87$; p-value = .007; reject H_0; salesman effects differ
c. Method 1 $-$ Method 2: [$-2.30, 2.96$]
Method 1 $-$ Method 3: [2.37, 7.63]
Method 1 $-$ Method 4: [3.70, 8.96]
Method 2 $-$ Method 3: [2.04, 7.30]
Method 2 $-$ Method 4: [3.37, 8.63]
Method 3 $-$ Method 4: [$-1.30, 3.96$]
Methods 1 and 2

12.15 a. $F = 441.75$ and p-value = .000; reject H_0; keyboard brand effects differ.
b. $F = 107.69$ and p-value = .000; reject H_0; specialist effects differ.
c. A $-$ B: [8.55, 11.45]
A $-$ C: [12.05, 14.95]
B $-$ C: [2.05, 4.95]
Keyboard A

12.16 a. $F = 5.78$; p-value = .0115; reject H_0; soft drink brands affect sales.

b. Coke Classic $-$ New Coke: [7.98, 68.02]
Coke Classic $-$ Pepsi: [$-.22, 59.82$]
New Coke $-$ Pepsi: [$-38.22, 21.82$]
c. Yes, mean sales of Coke Classic were significantly higher than those of New Coke.

12.17 A combination of a level of factor 1 and a level of factor 2.

12.18 See figure at middle of page 446 in the text.

12.19 a. Plot suggests little interaction. $F = .66$ and p-value = .681; do not reject H_0. Conclude no interaction.
b. $F = 26.49$ and p-value = .000; reject H_0; display panel effects differ.
c. $F = 100.80$ and p-value = .000; reject H_0; emergency condition effects differ.
d. A $-$ B: [.49, 5.91]
A $-$ C: [$-6.81, -1.39$]
B $-$ C: [$-10.01, -4.59$]
e. 1 $-$ 2: [$-10.43, -4.17$]
1 $-$ 3: [$-18.13, -11.87$]
1 $-$ 4: [.77, 7.03]
2 $-$ 3: [$-10.83, -4.57$]
2 $-$ 4: [8.07, 14.33]
3 $-$ 4: [15.77, 22.03]
f. Panel B. No, there is no interaction.
g. [6.37, 12.63]

12.21 a. Plot suggests little interaction.
b. $F = .2195$ and p-value = .6519. Conclude no interaction.
c. $F = 26.5610$ and p-value = .0009. Conclude sales pressure affects sales.
d. $F = .6098$ and p-value = .4574. Cannot claim sales pitch affects sales.

12.23 Yes, the plot and the p-value both indicate interaction exists. CI when foreman 1 builds design C: [17.72, 19.88]

Chapter 13

13.7 a. Each $E_i \geq 5$
b. $\chi^2 = 300.605$; reject H_0

13.9 a. $\chi^2 = 137.14$; reject H_0
b. Differences between brand preferences

13.11 a1. [$-\infty, 10.185$]
a2. [10.185, 14.147]
a3. [14.147, 18.108]
a4. [18.108, 22.069]
a5. [22.069, 26.030]
a6. [26.030, ∞]
b. 1.5, 9, 22, 22, 9, 1.5
c. Can use χ^2 test
e. 1, 9, 30, 15, 8, 2
$\chi^2 = 5.581$
f. Fail to reject; normal

13.13 Fail to reject H_0; normal

13.17 a.

	40%
	60%
20%	80%

b.

16%	24%
40%	60%
80%	30%
4%	56%
6.67%	93.33%
20%	70%

c. $\chi^2 = 16.667$; reject H_0
d. Yes

13.19 a.

	24.24%
	22.73%
	53.03%
51.515%	48.485%

b. For Heavy/Yes cell: cell: 18.18%; row: 75%; column: 35.29%
c. $\chi^2 = 6.86$; fail to reject H_0
d. Possibly; can reject H_0 at $\alpha = .05$

13.21 a. $\chi^2 = 16.384$; reject H_0
b. [$-.216, -.072$]

13.23 1. $\chi^2 = 65.91$; reject H_0:
2. [.270, .376]

13.25 b. $\chi^2 = 20.941$; reject H_0
c. First time buyers prefer Japanese styling while repeat buyers prefer European.

13.27 $\chi^2 = 71.476$; reject H_0

Chapter 14

14.3 a. $b_0 = 15.84$; $b_1 = -.1279$
b_0 is the estimated mean gas consumption when the temperature is $0°$ F. b_1 is the estimated change in mean gas consumption corresponding to a $1°$ increase in temperature.
c. 10.724 MMcF in each case.

14.5 a. $b_0 = 11.4641$; $b_1 = 24.6022$
b_0 is the estimated mean length of a service call when 0 copiers are serviced (not practical!) while b_1 is the estimated change in mean length of a call when 1 more copier must be serviced.
b. 109.87 minutes in each case

14.7 b. b_0 is the estimated mean direct labor cost when the batch size is 0 (not practical!) while b_1 is the estimated mean change in labor cost when the batch size increases by one unit.
c. $\hat{y} = 18.488 + 10.146x$
d. 627.248 or $62,724.80 in each case.

14.11 $s^2 = .428$; $s = .654$

14.13 21.3002; 4.6152

14.15 74.6762; 8.6415

14.17 27.8530; 5.2776

14.21 a. $b_0 = 14.816$; $b_1 = 5.7066$
b. SSE = 1.438; $s = .5363$
c. $s_{b_1} = .3953$; $t = 14.44$
d. $t > 2.571$; reject H_0. Yes, there is strong evidence that $\beta_1 \neq 0$.
e. $t > 4.032$; reject H_0. Yes, there is very strong evidence that $\beta_1 \neq 0$.
f. p-value = .000. Can reject H_0 at all α's. Extremely strong evidence that $\beta_1 \neq 0$.
g. [4.6903, 6.7229]
h. [4.1128, 7.3004]
i. $s_{b_0} = 1.235$; $t = 12.00$
j. p-value = .000. Can reject H_0 at all α's. There is extremely strong evidence that $\beta_0 \neq 0$.
k. $SS_{xx} = 1.84069$;
$s_{b_0} = 1.235$,
$s_{b_1} = .3953$

14.23 a. $b_0 = 7.81409$; $b_1 = 2.6652$
b. SSE = 2.806; $s = .316561$
c. $s_{b_1} = .2585$; $t = 10.31$
d. $t > 2.048$; reject H_0. Yes, there is strong evidence that $\beta_1 \neq 0$.

e. $t > 2.763$; reject H_0. Yes, there is very strong evidence that $\beta_1 \neq 0$

f. p-value $= .000$. Can reject H_0 at all α's. There is extremely strong evidence that $\beta_1 \neq 0$.

g. [2.1358, 3.1946]

h. [1.9510, 3.3794]

i. $s_{b_0} = .07988$; $t = 97.82$

j. p-value $= .000$. Can reject H_0 at all α's. There is extremely strong evidence that $\beta_0 \neq 0$.

k. $SS_{xx} = 1.49967$; $s_{b_0} = .07988$; $s_{b_1} = .2585$

14.25 a. $b_0 = 48.02$; $b_1 = 5.7003$

b. $SSE = 896.8$; $s = 10.5880$

c. $s_{b_1} = .7457$; $t = 7.64$

d. $t > 2.306$; reject H_0. Yes, there is strong evidence that $\beta_1 \neq 0$.

e. $t > 3.355$; reject H_0. Yes, there is very strong evidence that $\beta_1 \neq 0$.

f. p-value $= .000$. Can reject H_0 at all α's. There is extremely strong evidence that $\beta_1 \neq 0$.

g. [3.9807, 7.4199]

h. [3.1985, 8.2021]

i. $s_{b_0} = 14.41$; $t = 3.33$

j. p-value $= .010$. Can reject H_0 at $\alpha = .10, .05$ but not at .01 or .001. There is strong evidence that $\beta_0 \neq 0$

k. $SS_{xx} = 201.6$; $s_{b_0} = 14.41$; $s_{b_1} = .7457$

14.27 a. $b_1 = 1.2731$. We estimate that for every increase of one unit in mean taste, mean preference will increase by 1.2731

b. [.9885, 1.5577]. We are 95% confident β_1 is in this interval.

14.31 a. 33.362; [32.813, 33.911]

b. 33.362; [31.878, 34.846]

c. .15773

14.33 a. 8.0806; [7.9479, 8.2133]

b. 8.0806; [7.4187, 8.7425]

c. .041902

d. [7.9016, 8.2596]; [7.1878, 8.9734]

e. (i) 8.4804; [8.3604, 8.6004]
(ii) 8.4804; [7.8209, 9.1398]
(iii) .034267
(iv) [8.3185, 8.6423]; [7.5909, 9.3699]

14.35 a. 162.03; [154.04, 170.02]

b. 162.03; [136.34, 187.72]

c. The second.

14.39 Explained variation $= 59.942$; $r^2 = .977$; $r = .988$

14.41 Explained variation $= 10.653$; $r^2 = .792$; $r = .890$

14.43 Explained variation $= 6550.7$; $r^2 = .880$; $r = .938$

14.47 Reject H_0: $\rho = 0$ at all four values of α

14.49 t test for significance of β_1

14.51 a. $F = 208.39$

b. $F > 6.61$. Reject H_0 and conclude there is a significant relationship at $\alpha = .05$

c. $F > 16.26$. Reject H_0 and conclude significant relationship at $\alpha = .01$

d. p-value $= .000$. Can reject H_0 at all levels of α. There is extremely strong evidence of a regression relationship.

14.53 a. $F = 106.30$

b. $F > 4.20$. Reject H_0: significant relationship at $\alpha = .05$

c. $F > 7.64$. Reject H_0: significant relationship at $\alpha = .01$

d. p-value $= .000$. Can reject H_0 at all levels of α. There is extremely strong evidence of a regression relationship.

14.55 a. $F = 58.43$

b. $F > 5.32$. Reject H_0: significant relationship at $\alpha = .05$.

c. $F > 11.26$. Reject H_0: significant relationship at $\alpha = .01$

d. p-value $= .000$. Can reject H_0 at all levels of α. There is extremely strong evidence of a regression relationship.

14.59 Approximate horizontal band appearance. No violations indicated.

14.61 (1) Cyclical plot. (2) $d = .473 < 1.27$; conclude errors are positively correlated.

14.63 The constant variance assumption seems reasonable because the plot is a horizontal band.

14.65 b. 483.089; [401.216, 581.668]

c. 1.2928

d. The chain is growing approximately 29% annually.

14.67 a. $b_1 = -6.4424$. For each unit increase in width difference, we estimate the mean accident rate will fall by 6.44.

b. p-value $= .000$. There is extremely strong evidence that $\beta_1 \neq 0$.

c. $r^2 = .984$. 98.4% of the variability in the accident rate is explained by width difference.

14.69 Aggressive: $b_1^* = .0163$; [.0075, .0251]. Defensive: $b_1^* = -.0046$; [$-.0066$, $-.0026$]. Neutral: $b_1^* = .0087$; [.0051, .0123]. Estimates of β_1 increase as return length increases for aggressive and neutral but decrease for defensive stocks.

14.71 a. $t = 4.5967$ and $F = 21.1299$ have p-values of .0002. There is extremely strong evidence of a relationship.

b. $b_1 = 35.2877$; [19.2204, 51.3550]

Chapter 15

15.3 a. $b_1 = -.0900$; $b_2 = .0825$

b. 10.334 in each case.

15.5 a. $b_1 = -2.3577$; $b_2 = 1.6122$; $b_3 = .5012$

b. $\hat{y} = 8.4111$

15.7 σ^2, σ

15.11 1. $SSE = 73.6$; $s^2 = 10.5$; $s = 3.24164$

2. Total variation $= 7447.5$; $SSE = 73.6$; Explained variation $= 7374.0$

3. $R^2 = 99.0\%$; $\overline{R}^2 = 98.7\%$

4. $F(\text{model}) = 350.87$

5. $350.87 > F_{.05} = 4.74$. Decide at least one of β_1, β_2 is not 0.

6. $350.87 > F_{.01} = 9.55$

7. p-value $= .000$. The model is significant at each level of α.

15.13 1. $SSE = 1{,}798{,}712.2$; $s^2 = 149{,}892.7$; $s = 387.1598$

2. Total variation $= 464{,}126{,}601.6$; $SSE = 1{,}798{,}712.2$; Explained variation $= 462{,}327{,}889.4$

3. $R^2 = 99.61\%$; $\overline{R}^2 = 99.52\%$

4. $F(\text{model}) = 1028.1309$

5. $1028.1309 > F_{.05} = 3.49$. Decide at least one of β_1, β_2, β_3 is not 0.

6. $1028.1309 > F_{.01} = 5.95$

7. p-value $= .000$. The model is significant at each level of α.

15.17 1. $b_0 = 29.347$, $s_{b_0} = 4.891$, $t = 6.00$; $b_1 = 5.6128$, $s_{b_1} = .2285$, $t = 24.56$; $b_2 = 3.8344$, $s_{b_2} = .4332$, $t = 8.85$

2. β_0: $t = 6.00 > 2.365$. Reject H_0 and conclude $\beta_0 \neq 0$ at $\alpha = .05$
β_1: $t = 24.56 > 2.365$; Reject H_0 and conclude $\beta_1 \neq 0$ at $\alpha = .05$
β_2: $t = 8.85 > 2.365$. Reject H_0 and conclude $\beta_2 \neq 0$ at $\alpha = .05$
Both x_1 and x_2 are significantly related to y at $\alpha = .05$.

3. As in part 2, all 3 t statistics exceed the critical value 3.499, so conclude β_0, β_1, and β_2 all differ from 0 at $\alpha = .01$. Both x_1 and x_2 are significantly related to y.

4. β_0: p-value $= .001$. Can reject H_0 at every α except .001.
β_1: p-value $= .000$. Can reject H_0 at every α.
β_2: p-value $= .000$. Can reject H_0 at every α.
There is extremely strong evidence that x_1 and x_2 are related to y.

5. β_0: [17.780, 40.914]
β_1: [5.072, 6.153]
β_2: [2.810, 4.860]

6. β_0: [12.233, 46.461]
β_1: [4.813, 6.412]
β_2: [2.319, 5.350]

15.19 1. $b_0 = 1946.8020$, $s_{b_0} = 504.1819$, $t = 3.8613$;
$b_1 = .0386$, $s_{b_1} = .0130$, $t = 2.9579$;
$b_2 = 1.0394$, $s_{b_2} = .0676$, $t = 15.3857$;
$b_3 = -413.7578$, $s_{b_3} = 98.5983$, $t = -4.1964$

2. β_0: $t = 3.8613 > 2.179$. Reject H_0 at $\alpha = .05$
β_1: $t = 2.9579 > 2.179$. Reject H_0 at $\alpha = .05$
β_2: $t = 15.3857 > 2.179$. Reject H_0 at $\alpha = .05$
β_3: $t = -4.1964 < -2.179$. Reject H_0 at $\alpha = .05$
x_1, x_2, and x_3 are significantly related to y at $\alpha = .05$.

3. β_0: $t = 3.8613 > 3.055$. Reject H_0 at $\alpha = .01$.
β_1: $t = 2.9579 < 3.055$. Cannot reject H_0 at $\alpha = .01$
β_2: $t = 15.3857 > 3.055$. Reject H_0 at $\alpha = .01$
β_3: $t = -4.1964 < -3.055$. Reject H_0 at $\alpha = .01$
x_2 and x_3 are significantly related to y at $\alpha = .01$.

4. β_0: p-value $= .0023$. Can reject H_0 at every α except .001
β_1: p-value $= .0120$. Can reject H_0 at $\alpha = .10$ and .05 but not at .01 or .001.
β_2: p-value $= .000$. Can reject H_0 at every α.
β_3: p-value $= .0012$. Can reject H_0 at every α except .001.
Evidence is extremely strong for x_2, very strong for x_3 and strong for x_1.

5. β_0: [848.1896, 3045.4144]
   β_1: [.0103, .0669]
   β_2: [.8921, 1.1867]
   β_3: [−628.6035, −198.9121]
6. β_0: [406.5263, 3487.0777]
   β_1: [−.0011, .0783]
   β_2: [.8329, 1.2459]
   β_3: [−714.9756, −112.5400]
15.23 a. 172.28; [168.56, 175.99]
   b. 172.28; [163.76, 180.80]
   c. [166.79, 177.77]; [159.68, 184.88]
15.25 [14,906.24, 16,886.26] Unusually high
15.29 a. Parallel linear plots with different
      intercepts.
   b. β_2 = mean difference between
      adoption times of stock and mutual
      companies of the same size.
   c. (1) $|t|$ = 5.5208; p-value < .001.
      Reject H_0 at both α's
      (2) Company types differ
      significantly.
      (3) [4.9770, 11.1339]
   d. Slopes equal; no interaction.
15.31 b. F = 184.57; p-value < .001; reject
      H_0. Display heights affect sales.
   c. $\mu_M − \mu_B$: (2) 21.4; (3) [18.35, 24.45];
      $|t|$ = 14.93. Middle and bottom
      heights yield different mean sales.
      $\mu_T − \mu_B$: (2) −4.3; (3) [−7.35,
      −1.25]; $|t|$ = 3.00. Top and bottom
      heights yield different mean sales.
      $\mu_M − \mu_T$: (2) 25.7.
   d. (1) 77.2; (2) [75.04, 79.36]
      (3) [71.486, 82.914].
   e. [22.65, 28.75]; $|t|$ = 17.94.
      Conclude $\mu_M − \mu_T \neq 0$. Middle
      and top heights yield different
      mean sales.
15.33 No interaction between expenditure and
   campaign type.
15.35 We include their product as an
   independent variable.
15.37 b. For houses with higher niceness
      ratings, price increases more quickly
      with size.
15.41 F(partial) = 2.095 < 3.97
   Do not reject the hypothesis that all
   5 coefficients are 0. Consider using the
   simpler model.
15.45 1. Since |SDR1| and |SDR2| < $t_{.005}$ =
      3.106 for all cases, no outlying
      values under either option.
   2. Hospital 14 is not inefficient when
      we take its size into account.
   3. Although one can argue for either
      option, Option 2 yields a narrower PI
      and its residual plot has more of a
      horizontal band appearance than
      Option 1.
   4. The questionable hospital is
      inefficient.
15.49 1. $\hat{p}(93)$ = .8977.
   2. 1.63
   3. With each extra point on test 1,
      we estimate the odds of success
      increase by 63%.
15.51 The positive coefficient on rooms and
   the negative coefficient on bedrooms
   imply that for a house of a fixed size,
   the expected price increases with extra
   rooms that are not bedrooms.

15.53 F = 19.60 > $F_{.05}$ = 3.42. Reject H_0
   and decide at least 2 campaigns have
   different effects.
15.55 Residuals fall in a horizontal band and
   the normal probability plot looks linear.
   The model assumptions seem
   appropriate.
15.57 In a model containing square feet and
   age: bathrooms, bedrooms, and rooms
   are not significant.
   $\hat{y}$ = 10.31302 + .0530(sqfeet) − .36(age)

Chapter 16
16.1 See pages 632–633 in text.
16.3 Data show no trend.
16.5 a. Plot shows linear growth.
   b. $\hat{y}$ = 290.089 + 8.667(21) = 472.1
16.7 1. ln $\hat{y}_{133}$ = 4.69618 + .0103075(133) +
      .01903(1) = 6.0861
   2. $\hat{y}_{133}$ = 439.703; [389.915,
      495.848]
16.9 See pages 642–643 in text.
16.11 See pages 644–645 in text.
16.13 linear trend.
16.15 666.6, 881.6, 482.1, 299.9.
16.17 a. 15.01, 40.54, 56.82, 22.02
   b. [12.21, 17.81]; [37.69, 43.39];
      [53.90, 59.74]; [19.04, 25.00]
16.21 S_{26} = 356.115
16.23 When the level and trend of the time
   series are changing slowly over time.
16.25 l_2 = .2(211) + .8(204.283 + 7.7102)
      = 211.795
   b_2 = .2(211.794 − 204.283) +
      .8(7.7102) = 7.6704
   $\hat{y}_{27}$ = l_{24} + 3b_{24} = 393.670 +
      3(7.5447) = 416.304
16.27 $\hat{y}_{21}$ = 475.916; [427.380, 524.453]
16.29 Differencing is used to transform a
   nonstationary time series into a
   stationary one.
16.31 1. The model is adequate.
   2. y^*_{169} = δ + y^*_{157} + $\phi_1(y^*_{168} − y^*_{156})$+
      $\phi_2(y^*_{167} − y^*_{155})$ + $\phi_3(y^*_{166} − y^*_{154})$ −
      $\theta_{12}\varepsilon_{157}$ + ε_{169}
   3. $\hat{y}^*_{169}$ = .038056 + 5.33648
      + .2392 (.10212) + .1322(.07934)
      − .2642 (−.00628)
      − .5271(.057297) + 0 = 5.38091
16.35 Method A: MAD = 3; MSD = 9;
   MAPE = 4.72%
   Method B: MAD = 2.67;
   MSD = 12.67; MAPE = 4.06%
16.39 The goods and services cost 123.47%
   more in March 2011 than in the base
   period; they cost 70% less in October
   1963 than in the base period.
16.41 a.

Year	1990	2000	2011
Index	100	124.50	232.89

   b.

Year	1990	2000	2011
Index	100	124.12	216.67

   c.

Year	1990	2000	2011
Index	100	116.36	180.18

16.43 $\hat{y}_t$ = 15.8899; [13.9132, 17.86671]

Chapter 17
17.9 b. Yes. No subgroup range is above
      12.76.

c. No. $\bar{x}$ is above 146.35 for subgroups
   4, 10, 22 and below 136.21 for
   subgroup 19.
d. Yes. All values are within limits.
17.11 a. $CL_{\bar{x}}$ = 841.45,
   $UCL_{\bar{x}}$ = 845.2116,
   $LCL_{\bar{x}}$ = 837.6884,
   CL_R = 5.16,
   UCL_R = 11.78, no LCL_R
   yes, both charts out of control
   c. $CL_{\bar{x}}$ = 841.40,
   $UCL_{\bar{x}}$ = 844.96,
   $LCL_{\bar{x}}$ = 837.84,
   CL_R = 4.88,
   UCL_R = 11.14,
   no LCL_R
   d. R chart in control; yes, can use $\bar{x}$ chart
   e. No, $\bar{x}$ chart out of control;
   process mean is changing
   f. $CL_{\bar{x}}$ = 840.46,
   $UCL_{\bar{x}}$ = 844.29,
   $LCL_{\bar{x}}$ = 836.63,
   CL_R = 5.25,
   UCL_R = 11.98,
   no LCL_R
   g. Yes, all within control limits
17.13 a. Run down; 9 points in B or beyond;
   3 points in A; run up.
   b. Alternating pattern.
17.19 a. [132.31, 149.15]
   b. min = 132.31; max = 149.15
   c. Yes. The tolerance limits are inside
   the specification limits.
   d. 3.30
17.21 a. [.6518, 1.0416]
   b. 1.0416 lb.
   c. No; weights might be as low as
   .6518 lb.
   d. .0681 or 6.81%
17.23 a. [50.9189, 54.2561]
   b. Can be reduced by .4189 lb.;
   .4189(1,000,000)($2) = $837,800
17.25 .8736
17.29 UCL = .19, LCL = .01
17.31 a. UCL = .6217,
   LCL = .4323
   b. In control, no
   assignable causes
17.33 a. UCL = .0853,
   LCL = .0187
   b. UCL = .057,
   LCL = .005; yes
17.41 a. $UCL_{\bar{x}}$ = 5.35,
   $LCL_{\bar{x}}$ = 3.51
   b. UCL_R = 3.38
   c. In control
17.43 a. $UCL_{\bar{x}}$ = 5.08,
   $LCL_{\bar{x}}$ = 3.92
   UCL_R = 2.135
   b. Yes, in control
   c. [3.20, 5.80]
   d. Yes, capable. Sigma level = 3.45

Chapter 18
18.3 a. S = 4; p-value = .375;
   do not reject H_0
   b. S = 5; p-value = .031;
   reject H_0
18.5 a. p-value = .0059; reject H_0

18.7 a. $S_1 = 4, S_2 = 5, S = 5$
b. p-value $= 1.0$; do not reject H_0 at any α; conclude no difference

18.11 $T_1 = 120.5$; do not reject H_0; no difference

18.13 Differences exist

18.17 $T^- = 3$; reject H_0 at $\alpha = .02$

18.19 $T = 0$; reject H_0; conclude scores differ

18.23 Reject H_0; panels differ

18.25 $H = 14.36$; reject H_0; display heights differ. After removing the value, $H = 13.35$. Conclusion remains the same.

18.29 a. $r_s = -.721$
.648; yes
b. No

18.31 $r_s = 1.0$; reject H_0

18.33 $H = 14.36$
p-value $= .001$
Drugs differ

18.35 $T^+ = 1.0$
p-value $= .004$; decreased

18.37 $T_1 = 75$
p-value $= .0066$
Loan rates differ

Chapter 19

19.5 Small facility

19.7 a. $10 million,
$10.5 million, $3 million
b. Medium facility

19.9 a. $12.2 million
b. $1.7 million

19.11 a. A: 6.2, B: 5.2, C: 4.8
b. Location A
c. $1.8 million

19.13 a. Subcontract: $1.23
Expand: $1.57
Build: $1.35
b. Expand

19.19 a. .485, .8247, .0928, .0825
b. .300, .1667, .700, .1333
c. .215, .2325, .2093, .5581

19.21 a. 822
b. 580
c. 242
d. 242

19.25 a. .73, .9863, .0137
b. .27, .6667, .3333

19.27 a. Do not send, $14,958.90
b. Send, $14,500

19.33 a. Should be continued since EMV (continue) = $15.5
b. Should be licensed since EMV (develop) = $22.9 < $23.

19.35 a. $P(F) = .62, P(H|F) = .871,$
$P(L|F) = .129; P(U) = .38,$
$P(H|U) = .158, P(L|U) = .842$
If favorable, build large.
If unfavorable, also build large.
b. EVSI = 0. Don't pay for advice.

19.37 a. Relocate; $5,000,000
b. Renew lease; $500,000

References

Abraham, B., and J. Ledolter. *Statistical Methods for Forecasting.* New York, NY: John Wiley & Sons, 1983.

Akaah, Ishmael P., and Edward A. Riordan. "Judgments of Marketing Professionals about Ethical Issues in Marketing Research: A Replication and Extension." *Journal of Marketing Research,* February 1989, pp. 112–20.

Ashton, Robert H., John J. Willingham, and Robert K. Elliott. "An Empirical Analysis of Audit Delay." *Journal of Accounting Research* 25, no. 2 (Autumn 1987), pp. 275–92.

Axcel, Amir. *Complete Business Statistics.* 3rd ed. Burr Ridge, IL: Irwin/McGraw-Hill, 1996.

Bayus, Barry L. "The Consumer and Durable Replacement Buyer." *Journal of Marketing* 55 (January 1991), pp. 42–51.

Beattie, Vivien, and Michael John Jones. "The Use and Abuse of Graphs in Annual Reports: Theoretical Framework and Empirical Study." *Accounting and Business Research* 22, no. 88 (Autumn 1992), pp. 291–303.

Blauw, Jan Nico, and Willem E. During. "Total Quality Control in Dutch Industry." *Quality Progress* (February 1990), pp. 50–51.

Blodgett, Jeffrey G., Donald H. Granbois, and Rockney G. Walters. "The Effects of Perceived Justice on Complainants' Negative Word-of-Mouth Behavior and Repatronage Intentions." *Journal of Retailing* 69, no. 4 (Winter 1993), pp. 399–428.

Bowerman, Bruce L., and Richard T. O'Connell. *Forecasting and Time Series: An Applied Approach.* 3rd ed. Belmont, CA: Duxbury Press, 1993.

Bowerman, Bruce L., and Richard T. O'Connell. *Linear Statistical Models: An Applied Approach.* 2nd ed. Boston, MA: PWS-KENT Publishing Company, 1990, pp. 457, 460–64, 729–974.

Bowerman, Bruce L., Richard T. O'Connell, and Emily S. Murphree, *Business Statistics in Practice.* 5th ed. Burr Ridge, IL: McGraw-Hill, Irwin, 2009.

Box, G. E. P., and G. M. Jenkins. *Time Series Analysis: Forecasting and Control.* 2nd ed. San Francisco, CA: Holden-Day, 1976.

Boyd, Thomas C., and Timothy C. Krehbiel. "The Effect of Promotion Timing on Major League Baseball Attendance." *Sport Marketing Quarterly* 8, no. 4 (1999), pp. 23–34.

Brown, R. G. *Smoothing, Forecasting and Prediction of Discrete Time Series.* Englewood Cliffs, NJ: Prentice Hall, 1962.

Carey, John, Robert Neff, and Lois Therrien. "The Prize and the Passion." *BusinessWeek* (Special 1991 bonus issue: The Quality Imperative), January 15, 1991, pp. 58–59.

Carslaw, Charles A. P. N., and Steven E. Kaplan. "An Examination of Audit Delay: Further Evidence from New Zealand." *Accounting and Business Research* 22, no. 85 (1991), pp. 21–32.

Cateora, Philip R. *International Marketing.* 9th ed. Homewood, IL: Irwin/McGraw-Hill, 1993, p. 262.

Clemen, Robert T. *Making Hard Decisions: An Introduction to Decision Analysis.* 2nd ed. Belmont, CA: Duxbury Press, 1996, p. 443.

Conlon, Edward J., and Thomas H. Stone. "Absence Schema and Managerial Judgment." *Journal of Management* 18, no. 3 (1992), pp. 435–54.

Cooper, Donald R., and C. William Emory. *Business Research Methods.* 5th ed. Homewood, IL: Richard D. Irwin, 1995, pp. 434–38, 450–51, 458–68.

Cuprisin, Tim. "Inside TV & Radio." *The Milwaukee Journal Sentinel,* April 26, 1995.

Dawson, Scott. "Consumer Responses to Electronic Article Surveillance Alarms." *Journal of Retailing* 69, no. 3 (Fall 1993), pp. 353–62.

Deming, W. Edwards. *Out of the Crisis.* Cambridge, MA: Massachusetts Institute of Technology Center for Advanced Engineering Study, 1986, pp. 18–96, 312–14.

Dielman, Terry. *Applied Regression Analysis for Business and Economics.* Belmont, CA: Duxbury Press, 1996.

Dillon, William R., Thomas J. Madden, and Neil H. Firtle. *Essentials of Marketing Research.* Homewood, IL: Richard D. Irwin Inc., 1993, pp. 382–84, 416–17, 419–20, 432–33, 445, 462–64, 524–27.

Dondero, Cort. "SPC Hits the Road." *Quality Progress,* January 1991, pp. 43–44.

Draper, N., and H. Smith. *Applied Regression Analysis.* 2nd ed. New York, NY: John Wiley & Sons, 1981.

Farnum, Nicholas R. *Modern Statistical Quality Control and Improvement.* Belmont, CA: Duxbury Press, 1994, p. 55.

Fitzgerald, Neil. "Relations Overcast by Cloudy Conditions." *CA Magazine,* April 1993, pp. 28–35.

Garvin, David A. *Managing Quality.* New York, NY: Free Press/Macmillan, 1988.

Gibbons, J. D. *Nonparametric Statistical Inference.* 2nd ed. New York, NY: McGraw-Hill, 1985.

Gitlow, Howard, Shelly Gitlow, Alan Oppenheim, and Rosa Oppenheim. *Tools and Methods for the Improvement of Quality.* Homewood, IL: Richard D. Irwin, 1989, pp. 14–25, 533–53.

Guthrie, James P., Curtis M. Grimm, and Ken G. Smith. "Environmental Change and Management Staffing: A Reply." *Journal of Management* 19, no. 4 (1993), pp. 889–96.

Kuhn, Susan E. "A Closer Look at Mutual Funds: Which Ones Really Deliver?" *Fortune,* October 7, 1991, pp. 29–30.

Kumar, V., Roger A. Kerin, and Arun Pereira. "An Empirical Assessment of Merger and Acquisition Activity in Retailing." *Journal of Retailing* 67, no. 3 (Fall 1991), pp. 321–38.

Magee, Robert P. *Advanced Managerial Accounting.* New York, NY: Harper & Row, 1986, p. 223.

Mahmood, Mo Adam, and Gary J. Mann. "Measuring the Organizational Impact of Information Technology Investment: An Exploratory Study." *Journal of Management Information Systems* 10, no. 1 (Summer 1993), pp. 97–122.

Martocchio, Joseph J. "The Financial Cost of Absence Decisions." *Journal of Management* 18, no. 1 (1992), pp. 133–52.

Mendenhall, W., and J. Reinmuth. *Statistics for Management Economics.* 4th ed. Boston, MA: PWS-KENT Publishing Company, 1982.

The Miami University Report. Miami University, Oxford, OH, vol. 8, no. 26, 1989.

Moore, David S. *The Basic Practice of Statistics.* 2nd ed. New York: W. H. Freeman and Company, 2000.

Moore, David S., and George P. McCabe. *Introduction to the Practice of Statistics.* 2nd ed. New York: W. H. Freeman, 1993.

Morris, Michael H., Ramon A. Avila, and Jeffrey Allen. "Individualism and the Modern Corporation: Implications for Innovation and Entrepreneurship." *Journal of Management* 19, no. 3 (1993), pp. 595–612.

Neter, J., M. Kutner, C. Nachtsheim, and W. Wasserman. *Applied Linear Statistical Models.* 4th ed. Homewood, IL: Irwin/McGraw-Hill, 1996.

Neter, J., W. Wasserman, and M. H. Kutner. *Applied Linear Statistical Models.* 2nd ed. Homewood, IL: Richard D. Irwin, 1985.

Nunnally, Bennie H., Jr., and D. Anthony Plath. *Cases in Finance.* Burr Ridge, IL: Richard D. Irwin, 1995, pp. 12-1–12-7.

Olmsted, Dan, and Gigi Anders. "Turned Off." *USA Weekend,* June 2–4, 1995.

Ott, Lyman. *An Introduction to Statistical Methods and Data Analysis.* 2nd ed. Boston, MA: PWS-Kent, 1987.

Schaeffer, R. L., William Mendenhall, and Lyman Ott. *Elementary Survey Sampling.* 3rd ed. Boston, MA: Duxbury Press, 1986.

Scherkenbach, William. *The Deming Route to Quality and Productivity: Road Maps and Roadblocks.* Washington, DC.: CEEPress Books, 1986.

Seigel, James C. "Managing with Statistical Models." SAE Technical Paper 820520. Warrendale, PA: Society for Automotive Engineers, Inc., 1982.

Sichelman, Lew. "Random Checks Find Loan Application Fibs." *The Journal-News* (Hamilton, Ohio), Sept. 26, 1992 (originally published in *The Washington Post*).

Siegel, Andrew F. *Practical Business Statistics.* 2nd ed. Homewood, IL: Richard D. Irwin, 1990, p. 588.

Silk, Alvin J., and Ernst R. Berndt. "Scale and Scope Effects on Advertising Agency Costs." *Marketing Science* 12, no. 1 (Winter 1993), pp. 53–72.

Stevenson, William J. *Production/Operations Management.* 6th ed. Homewood, IL: Irwin/McGraw-Hill, 1999, p. 228.

Thomas, Anisya S., and Kannan Ramaswamy. "Environmental Change and Management Staffing: A Comment." *Journal of Management* 19, no. 4 (1993), pp. 877–87.

Von Neumann, J., and O. Morgenstern. *Theory of Games and Economic Behavior.* 2nd ed. Princeton, NJ: Princeton University Press, 1947.

Walton, Mary. *The Deming Management Method.* New York, NY: Dodd, Mead & Company, 1986.

Weinberger, Marc G., and Harlan E. Spotts. "Humor in U.S. versus U.K. TV Commercials: A Comparison." *Journal of Advertising* 18, no. 2 (1989), pp. 39–44.

Wright, Thomas A., and Douglas G. Bonett. "Role of Employee Coping and Performance in Voluntary Employee Withdrawal: A Research Refinement and Elaboration." *Journal of Management* 19, no. 1 (1993) pp. 147–61.

Photo Credits

Index

Case Index

A *t* Table

df	$t_{.100}$	$t_{.050}$	$t_{.025}$	$t_{.01}$	$t_{.005}$	$t_{.001}$	$t_{.0005}$
1	3.078	6.314	12.706	31.821	63.657	318.31	636.62
2	1.886	2.920	4.303	6.965	9.925	22.326	31.598
3	1.638	2.353	3.182	4.541	5.841	10.213	12.924
4	1.533	2.132	2.776	3.747	4.604	7.173	8.610
5	1.476	2.015	2.571	3.365	4.032	5.893	6.869
6	1.440	1.943	2.447	3.143	3.707	5.208	5.959
7	1.415	1.895	2.365	2.998	3.499	4.785	5.408
8	1.397	1.860	2.306	2.896	3.355	4.501	5.041
9	1.383	1.833	2.262	2.821	3.250	4.297	4.781
10	1.372	1.812	2.228	2.764	3.169	4.144	4.587
11	1.363	1.796	2.201	2.718	3.106	4.025	4.437
12	1.356	1.782	2.179	2.681	3.055	3.930	4.318
13	1.350	1.771	2.160	2.650	3.012	3.852	4.221
14	1.345	1.761	2.145	2.624	2.977	3.787	4.140
15	1.341	1.753	2.131	2.602	2.947	3.733	4.073
16	1.337	1.746	2.120	2.583	2.921	3.686	4.015
17	1.333	1.740	2.110	2.567	2.898	3.646	3.965
18	1.330	1.734	2.101	2.552	2.878	3.610	3.922
19	1.328	1.729	2.093	2.539	2.861	3.579	3.883
20	1.325	1.725	2.086	2.528	2.845	3.552	3.850
21	1.323	1.721	2.080	2.518	2.831	3.527	3.819
22	1.321	1.717	2.074	2.508	2.819	3.505	3.792
23	1.319	1.714	2.069	2.500	2.807	3.485	3.767
24	1.318	1.711	2.064	2.492	2.797	3.467	3.745
25	1.316	1.708	2.060	2.485	2.787	3.450	3.725
26	1.315	1.706	2.056	2.479	2.779	3.435	3.707
27	1.314	1.703	2.052	2.473	2.771	3.421	3.690
28	1.313	1.701	2.048	2.467	2.763	3.408	3.674
29	1.311	1.699	2.045	2.462	2.756	3.396	3.659
30	1.310	1.697	2.042	2.457	2.750	3.385	3.646
40	1.303	1.684	2.021	2.423	2.704	3.307	3.551
60	1.296	1.671	2.000	2.390	2.660	3.232	3.460
120	1.289	1.658	1.980	2.358	2.617	3.160	3.373
∞	1.282	1.645	1.960	2.326	2.576	3.090	3.291

Cumulative Areas under the Standard Normal Curve

z	0.00	0.01	0.02	0.03	0.04	0.05	0.06	0.07	0.08	0.09
−3.9	0.00005	0.00005	0.00004	0.00004	0.00004	0.00004	0.00004	0.00004	0.00003	0.00003
−3.8	0.00007	0.00007	0.00007	0.00006	0.00006	0.00006	0.00006	0.00005	0.00005	0.00005
−3.7	0.00011	0.00010	0.00010	0.00010	0.00009	0.00009	0.00008	0.00008	0.00008	0.00008
−3.6	0.00016	0.00015	0.00015	0.00014	0.00014	0.00013	0.00013	0.00012	0.00012	0.00011
−3.5	0.00023	0.00022	0.00022	0.00021	0.00020	0.00019	0.00019	0.00018	0.00017	0.00017
−3.4	0.00034	0.00032	0.00031	0.00030	0.00029	0.00028	0.00027	0.00026	0.00025	0.00024
−3.3	0.00048	0.00047	0.00045	0.00043	0.00042	0.00040	0.00039	0.00038	0.00036	0.00035
−3.2	0.00069	0.00066	0.00064	0.00062	0.00060	0.00058	0.00056	0.00054	0.00052	0.00050
−3.1	0.00097	0.00094	0.00090	0.00087	0.00084	0.00082	0.00079	0.00076	0.00074	0.00071
−3.0	0.00135	0.00131	0.00126	0.00122	0.00118	0.00114	0.00111	0.00107	0.00103	0.00100
−2.9	0.0019	0.0018	0.0018	0.0017	0.0016	0.0016	0.0015	0.0015	0.0014	0.0014
−2.8	0.0026	0.0025	0.0024	0.0023	0.0023	0.0022	0.0021	0.0021	0.0020	0.0019
−2.7	0.0035	0.0034	0.0033	0.0032	0.0031	0.0030	0.0029	0.0028	0.0027	0.0026
−2.6	0.0047	0.0045	0.0044	0.0043	0.0041	0.0040	0.0039	0.0038	0.0037	0.0036
−2.5	0.0062	0.0060	0.0059	0.0057	0.0055	0.0054	0.0052	0.0051	0.0049	0.0048
−2.4	0.0082	0.0080	0.0078	0.0075	0.0073	0.0071	0.0069	0.0068	0.0066	0.0064
−2.3	0.0107	0.0104	0.0102	0.0099	0.0096	0.0094	0.0091	0.0089	0.0087	0.0084
−2.2	0.0139	0.0136	0.0132	0.0129	0.0125	0.0122	0.0119	0.0116	0.0113	0.0110
−2.1	0.0179	0.0174	0.0170	0.0166	0.0162	0.0158	0.0154	0.0150	0.0146	0.0143
−2.0	0.0228	0.0222	0.0217	0.0212	0.0207	0.0202	0.0197	0.0192	0.0188	0.0183
−1.9	0.0287	0.0281	0.0274	0.0268	0.0262	0.0256	0.0250	0.0244	0.0239	0.0233
−1.8	0.0359	0.0351	0.0344	0.0336	0.0329	0.0322	0.0314	0.0307	0.0301	0.0294
−1.7	0.0446	0.0436	0.0427	0.0418	0.0409	0.0401	0.0392	0.0384	0.0375	0.0367
−1.6	0.0548	0.0537	0.0526	0.0516	0.0505	0.0495	0.0485	0.0475	0.0465	0.0455
−1.5	0.0668	0.0655	0.0643	0.0630	0.0618	0.0606	0.0594	0.0582	0.0571	0.0559
−1.4	0.0808	0.0793	0.0778	0.0764	0.0749	0.0735	0.0721	0.0708	0.0694	0.0681
−1.3	0.0968	0.0951	0.0934	0.0918	0.0901	0.0885	0.0869	0.0853	0.0838	0.0823
−1.2	0.1151	0.1131	0.1112	0.1093	0.1075	0.1056	0.1038	0.1020	0.1003	0.0985
−1.1	0.1357	0.1335	0.1314	0.1292	0.1271	0.1251	0.1230	0.1210	0.1190	0.1170
−1.0	0.1587	0.1562	0.1539	0.1515	0.1492	0.1469	0.1446	0.1423	0.1401	0.1379
−0.9	0.1841	0.1814	0.1788	0.1762	0.1736	0.1711	0.1685	0.1660	0.1635	0.1611
−0.8	0.2119	0.2090	0.2061	0.2033	0.2005	0.1977	0.1949	0.1922	0.1894	0.1867
−0.7	0.2420	0.2389	0.2358	0.2327	0.2296	0.2266	0.2236	0.2206	0.2177	0.2148
−0.6	0.2743	0.2709	0.2676	0.2643	0.2611	0.2578	0.2546	0.2514	0.2482	0.2451
−0.5	0.3085	0.3050	0.3015	0.2981	0.2946	0.2912	0.2877	0.2843	0.2810	0.2776
−0.4	0.3446	0.3409	0.3372	0.3336	0.3300	0.3264	0.3228	0.3192	0.3156	0.3121
−0.3	0.3821	0.3783	0.3745	0.3707	0.3669	0.3632	0.3594	0.3557	0.3520	0.3483
−0.2	0.4207	0.4168	0.4129	0.4090	0.4052	0.4013	0.3974	0.3936	0.3897	0.3859
−0.1	0.4602	0.4562	0.4522	0.4483	0.4443	0.4404	0.4364	0.4325	0.4286	0.4247
−0.0	0.5000	0.4960	0.4920	0.4880	0.4840	0.4801	0.4761	0.4721	0.4681	0.4641